COMPLEX LITIGATION

CASES AND MATERIALS ON ADVANCED CIVIL PROCEDURE

Seventh Edition

■ ■ ■

Richard L. Marcus

Horace O. Coil ('57) Chair in Litigation, University of California
Hastings College of Law

Edward F. Sherman

David Boies Distinguished Chair in Law and
Moise S. Steeg, Jr., Professor of Law Emeritus
Tulane Law School

Howard M. Erichson

Professor of Law
Fordham University

Andrew D. Bradt

Professor of Law
University of California, Berkeley School of Law

AMERICAN CASEBOOK SERIES®

WEST
ACADEMIC
PUBLISHING

American Casebook Series is a trademark registered in the U.S. Patent and Trademark Office.

COPYRIGHT © 1985, 1992 WEST PUBLISHING CO.
© West, a Thomson business, 1998, 2004
© 2010 Thomson Reuters
© 2015 LEG, Inc. d/b/a West Academic
© 2021 LEG, Inc. d/b/a West Academic
      444 Cedar Street, Suite 700
      St. Paul, MN 55101
      1-877-888-1330

West, West Academic Publishing, and West Academic are trademarks of West Publishing Corporation, used under license.

Printed in the United States of America

ISBN: 978-1-64708-151-5

PREFACE

Since the first edition of this book appeared in 1985, complex litigation has changed a great deal. Indeed, a comparison of the Table of Contents of the first edition with the Table of Contents of this edition shows that the great majority of the material in the current edition consists of things that had not yet happened when the first edition appeared. Concerns over e-discovery did not exist in 1985. Nor did clashes over arbitration clauses that forbid classwide proceedings. Multidistrict litigation was a little-known backwater.

But some things have not changed: complex disputes emerge; parties litigate over those disputes; lawyers and judges find creative ways to resolve those disputes; and complex litigation remains a fruitful area of study. Indeed, its importance has only grown. By some counts, nearly half of pending civil cases in the federal court system are subject to an MDL order. When we began this casebook, we were attempting to fill a void in teaching materials for complex litigation or advanced civil procedure. There is no longer a void. Courses on complex litigation, class actions, and advanced civil procedure have become standard offerings in law schools, reflecting the reality that complex litigation is a pervasive part of the legal landscape. Students who wish to become complex litigation practitioners—or who simply wish to understand how complex disputes are resolved—appreciate that they need an advanced understanding of procedure.

As in past editions, we have embraced new developments while maintaining the book's core structure and key themes. The class actions material includes treatment of the Supreme Court's recent decisions as well as the 2018 amendments to Rule 23. Our treatment of multidistrict litigation has grown into a full chapter, in recognition of MDL's increasing prominence as a vehicle for resolving dispersed litigation. And our treatment of electronic discovery takes account of changes in practice and revisions to the Federal Rules of Civil Procedure, including the 2015 amendment on preservation of electronically stored information.

Our focus has remained broad-gauged. Unlike other books that emphasize particular categories of litigation, we include coverage pertinent to all major types of complex litigation. Users of this book should be able to emphasize mass tort litigation, social impact litigation, commercial litigation such as securities fraud, antitrust suits, or patent cases, or a variety of other complex cases. Alternatively, one could, like the authors, combine coverage of diverse types of complex litigation in a course examining the overlapping as well as the divergent procedural features of modern American litigation.

With this edition, Ed Sherman is no longer taking an active role in the development of new material, and we welcome our new co-author, Professor Andrew Bradt of UC Berkeley, who brings his unparalleled knowledge of MDL litigation to bear in this edition.

We have edited cases to improve their readability. Ellipses are used when any portion of text is deleted, but not when citations are omitted. We have taken out footnotes unless they add something significant, and left in the original number of the ones that remain. We continue to focus largely, though not entirely, on litigation in the federal courts. As a general matter, we have included developments through January, 2021.

We are indebted to many people. Over the years, many teachers have shared with us their thoughts on the book and on legal developments. We are grateful to colleagues who have offered background, insights, and suggestions. We are also indebted to our students, who have over the years challenged us, taught us, and inspired us. We are particularly indebted to our research assistants, Samantha Looker of Hastings, Sami Helgason of Fordham, and Natasha Geiling of UC Berkeley. Finally, we want to thank our spouses, (the late) Andrea Saltzman, Alice Sherman, Sara Ann Erichson and Lara Bradt, for their advice, help, and patience.

We are also grateful to the copyright holders identified in the footnote[1] for permission to reprint excerpts from copyrighted materials, in addition to the copyright holders on the cartoons in the book, which are identified where the cartoons appear. Except for granting us permission to reprint in this book the copyright holders have retained all rights.

RICHARD L. MARCUS
EDWARD F. SHERMAN
HOWARD M. ERICHSON
ANDREW D. BRADT

January, 2021

---

[1] The reprinted works are, in the order they appear in the book, as follows:

Chayes, The Role of the Judge in Public Law Litigation, 89 Harv. L. Rev. 1143 (1976), copyright © 1976, by Abram Chayes.

RAND Institute for Civil Justice, Class Action Dilemmas: Pursuing Public Goals for Private Gain, copyright © 2000, RAND Corp.

Heyburn, A View From the Panel: Part of the Solution, 82 Tulane L. Rev. 2225 (2008), copyright © 2008, the Hon. John Heyburn.

Weigel, The Judicial Panel on Multidistrict Litigation, Transferor Courts and Transferee Courts, 78 F.R.D. 575 (1978), copyright © 1978, West Publishing Co.

Sherman, The MDL Model for Resolving Complex Litigation if a Class Action is Not Possible, 82 Tulane L. Rev. 2205 (2008), copyright © 2008, Edward F. Sherman.

Fiss, Against Settlement, 93 Yale L.J. 1073 (1984), copyright © 1984, Yale Law Journal Co.

Issacharoff & Klonoff, The Public Value of Settlement, 78 Fordham L. Rev. 1177 (2009), copyright © 2009, the Fordham Law Review Association.

SUMMARY OF CONTENTS

TABLE OF CONTENTS

TABLE OF CASES

The principal cases are in bold type.

TABLE OF AUTHORITIES

COMPLEX LITIGATION

CASES AND MATERIALS ON ADVANCED CIVIL PROCEDURE

Seventh Edition

CHAPTER 1

THE NATURE OF COMPLEX LITIGATION

■ ■ ■

Like many other things, litigation has become more complex. In our world of unprecedented interconnectedness and information growth, it should be no surprise that disputes have become more complex, and that litigation has also. Many law firms specialize in complex litigation, and many others have departments dedicated to it. Some observers see complex litigation as essential to enforcing the law and righting widespread wrongs. But others see complex cases as wasteful, inefficient and unnecessary, perhaps even as symptoms of a widespread pathology in American civil litigation, gobbling up resources without providing any accompanying social advantage. In our last chapter, we will see that in recent decades many American companies have sought to avoid this form of litigation by insisting on arbitration of disputes.

Nobody has devised a litmus test to determine whether a given case is properly labeled complex. The various editions of the federal judiciary's Manual for Complex Litigation have not offered a firm definition. As a starting point, it may be said that three characteristics serve, individually or together, to distinguish complex cases. First, they may involve difficult legal and factual issues (often technical or scientific). Second, the sheer number of parties involved may make litigation complex where it would not be in a one-on-one litigation format. Third, the amount of money or the stakes involved may prompt litigation efforts of such dimension that a case that would otherwise not be complex becomes complex. In the view of an experienced judge, these are cases in which the ordinary rules "won't work," in part because 'complexity encourages the pursuit of outlier issues," and the parties "have a powerful resistance to reaching the merits too early." Curtis Karnow, Complexity in Litigation: A Differential Analysis, 18 U. Pa. J. Bus. Law 1 (2015).

Whatever the definition, complex litigation deserves study as a discrete area of dispute resolution. That is the purpose of this book, but it should be emphasized at the outset that this study provides insights that often apply to the judicial handling of all kinds of civil litigation. At the same time, a prime concern is to understand the ways in which lawyers and judges treat complex litigation differently from other litigation, and to think about whether different treatment is justified. To set the scene, this chapter provides a brief overview of issues that will be with us throughout the book.

A. THE METAMORPHOSIS OF LITIGATION

ABRAM CHAYES, THE ROLE OF THE JUDGE IN PUBLIC LAW LITIGATION
89 Harv. L. Rev. 1281, 1282–84 (1976).

We are witnessing the emergence of a new model of civil litigation and, I believe, our traditional conception of adjudication and the assumptions upon which it is based provide an increasingly unhelpful, indeed misleading, framework for assessing either the workability or the legitimacy of the roles of judge and court within this model.

In our received tradition, the lawsuit is a vehicle for settling disputes between private parties about private rights. The defining features of this conception of civil adjudication are:

    (1) The lawsuit is *bipolar.* Litigation is organized as a contest between two individuals or at least two unitary interests, diametrically opposed, to be decided on a winner-takes-all basis.

    (2) Litigation is *retrospective.* The controversy is about an identified set of completed events: whether they occurred, and if so, with what consequences for the legal relations of the parties.

    (3) *Right and remedy are interdependent.* The scope of the relief is derived more or less logically from the substantive violation under the general theory that the plaintiff will get compensation measured by the harm caused by the defendant's breach of duty—in contract by giving plaintiff the money he would have had absent the breach; in tort by paying the value of the damage caused.

    (4) The lawsuit is a *self-contained* episode. The impact of the judgment is confined to the parties. If plaintiff prevails there is a simple compensatory transfer, usually of money, but occasionally the return of a thing or the performance of a definite act. If defendant prevails, a loss lies where it has fallen. In either case, entry of judgment ends the court's involvement.

    (5) The process is *party-initiated* and *party-controlled.* The case is organized and the issues defined by exchanges between the parties. Responsibility for fact development is theirs. The trial judge is a neutral arbiter of their interactions who decides questions of law only if they are put in issue by an appropriate move of a party.

This capsule description of what I have called the traditional conception of adjudication is no doubt overdrawn. It was not often, if ever, expressed so severely; indeed, because it was so thoroughly taken for granted, there was little occasion to do so. Although I do not contend that the traditional conception ever conformed fully to what judges were doing in fact, I believe it has been central to our understanding and our analysis of the legal system.

Whatever its historical validity, the traditional model is clearly invalid as a description of much current civil litigation in the federal district courts. Perhaps the dominating characteristic of modern federal litigation is that lawsuits do not arise out of disputes between private parties about private rights. Instead, the object of litigation is the vindication of constitutional or statutory policies. The shift in the legal basis of the lawsuit explains many, but not all, facets of what is going on "in fact" in federal trial courts. For this reason, although the label is not wholly satisfactory, I shall call the emerging model "public law litigation."

The characteristic features of the public law model are very different from those of the traditional model. The party structure is sprawling and amorphous, subject to change over the course of the litigation. The traditional adversary relationship is suffused and intermixed with negotiating and mediating processes at every point. The judge is the dominant figure in organizing and guiding the case, and he draws for support not only on the parties and their counsel, but on a wide range of outsiders—masters, experts, and oversight personnel. Most important, the trial judge has increasingly become the creator and manager of complex forms of ongoing relief, which have widespread effects on persons not before the court and require the judge's continuing involvement in administration and implementation. School desegregation, employment discrimination, and prisoners' or inmates' rights cases come readily to mind as avatars of this new form of litigation. But it would be mistaken to suppose that it is confined to these areas. Antitrust, securities fraud and other aspects of the conduct of corporate business, bankruptcy and reorganizations, union governance, consumer fraud, housing discrimination, electoral reapportionment, environmental management—cases in all these fields display in varying degrees the features of public law litigation.

NOTES AND QUESTIONS

1. When the Federal Rules of Civil Procedure were adopted in 1938, it appeared (at least in hindsight) to be an era of "simple" litigation, and that is the "received tradition" that Prof. Chayes contrasted with the emerging reality he was describing. Whether things were really so "simple" before can be debated. See Theodore Eisenberg & Stephen Yeazell, The Ordinary and the Extraordinary in Institutional Litigation, 93 Harv. L. Rev. 465 (1980) (arguing that parallels to the sort of litigation Chayes described had existed long before).

Certainly some kinds of cases presented new challenges soon after the Federal Rules came into effect. The first version of complex litigation was initially called "protracted" litigation, involving large-scale actions between the government and large companies, or (rarely) between big companies themselves. By 1949, the Judicial Conference of the U.S. felt this emergent problem called for action, and a committee headed by Judge E. Barrett Prettyman produced a report on how to handle such cases in 1951. Procedure in Anti-Trust and Other Protracted Cases, 13 F.R.D. 62 (1951). This report led to publication of a "handbook" for such cases in 1960, and then a Manual for Complex Litigation in 1969. The 4th edition of the Manual was published in 2004.

Large-scale litigation of this sort continues today. One 21st century example is patent litigation, which can pit major companies against one another. During the 1980s, corporations, which had previously avoided litigating against one another, began using litigation as a weapon in competitive struggles. See Bryant Garth, From Civil Litigation to Private Justice: Legal Practice at War with the Profession and Its Values, 59 Brook. L. Rev. 931, 942 (1993) (describing rise of business litigation); Bryant Garth, Two Worlds of Civil Discovery: From Studies of Cost and Delay to the Markets in Legal Services and Legal Reform, 39 Bos. Col. L. Rev. 597, 605 (1998) (describing tendency of discovery costs to rise in high-stakes corporate litigation).

2.   The sort of complex litigation Professor Chayes emphasized, such as school desegregation or prisoners' rights cases, has been described as the "heroic model" of litigation enabled by the Federal Rules. See Richard Marcus, "Looking Backward" to 1938, 162 U. Pa. L. Rev. 1691, 1695–98 (2014). That sort of litigation continues to occur. See, e.g., Brown v. Plata, 563 U.S. 493 (2011) (class action leading to order for reduction in crowding in California prisons); Samuel Issacharoff, Class Actions and State Authority, 44 Loyola U. Chi. L.J. 369, 375 (2012) (labelling Brown v. Plata "the most significant class action litigation of the past decade").

But other kinds of litigation assumed center stage: "By the later 1990s, * * * Professor Chayes's model itself was outdated. Chayes may have succeeded in addressing the civil rights class actions of the 1960s and 1970s, but he failed to anticipate and 'capture the dynamics of modern mass tort litigation,' which came to dominate the litigation landscape in the 1980s and 1990s." Jonathan Molot, An Old Judicial Role for a New Litigation Era, 113 Yale L.J. 27, 29 (2003). This sort of litigation resulted partly from the concentration of production of goods and services in a smaller number of firms; quality and safety problems would likely affect many, either by causing them injuries or by reducing the value of the products they had bought. Mass injury claims involving such products as Vioxx (examined in detail in Chapter 7) and consumer class actions (examined in Chapter 5) reflect this development.

3.   In the 21st century, one response to these changes in the nature and stakes of litigation has been to encourage increased effort by the judge to control the litigation. See generally Richard Marcus, The New Role of American Judges: Reining in the American Litigator, 27 Hast. Int'l & Compar. L.Rev. 3 (2003). These developments will be examined in detail in Chapter 6, and also (with regard to judicial review of proposed settlements) in Chapter 7. They also bear on judicial decisions whether to combine separate cases

(examined in Chapters 3 and 4) and decisions about joinder of parties (Chapter 2).

4.   Much of the impact of 21st century complex litigation depends on "aggregation," the power of various procedural tools to combine cases into a single package of "mass" litigation. One starting point for aggregation was the revision of Rule 23, the class-action rule, in 1966. Another was the adoption in 1968 of the Multidistrict Litigation Act, which empowered a judicial panel to combine civil cases from across the federal judicial system before a single judge, confecting proceedings some judges have called "quasi-class actions." A third development has been the emergence in some cases of mass joinder, the so called "mass actions," that may assert claims on behalf of hundreds, or even thousands, of claimants. These developments could create litigation "magnets." Multidistrict (MDL) litigation (examined in Chapter 4) has been characterized as a "Field of Dreams" engine ("If you build it, they will come."). See Robert Klonoff, The Judicial Panel of Multidistrict Litigation: The Virtues of Unfettered Discretion, 89 UMKC L. Rev. ___ (forthcoming 2021) ("the entire success or failure of an entire category of litigation may turn on whether the cases are centralized in an MDL").

These aggregation maneuvers have become more widespread. In 2002, it was reported that "the class action device has changed from the more or less rare case fought out by titans of the bar in the top financial centers of the nation to the veritable bread and butter of firms of all shapes and sizes across the country." Benjamine Reid & Chris Coutroulis, Checkmate in Class Actions: Defensive Strategy in the Initial Moves, 28 Litigation Mag. 21, 21 (Winter 2002). In 2005, Congress passed the Class Action Fairness Act, with provisions to treat "mass actions" the same way as class actions. Meanwhile, a 2014 report reckoned that "[t]oday, fully one-third of all federal cases are MDL matters." Jaime Dodge, Facilitative Judging: Organizational Design in Mass Multidistrict Litigation, 64 Emory L.J. 329, 331 (2014). That proportion has increased, and MDL litigation (addressed in Chapter 4) has been characterized as a "rising behemoth." Douglas Smith, The Rising Behemoth: Multidistrict and Mass Tort Litigation in the United States (2020). This outcome may have been foreseen by the framers of the MDL statute in the 1960s. See Andrew Bradt, "A Radical Proposal": The Multidistrict Litigation Act of 1968, 165 U. Pa. L. Rev. 831 (2017).

In large measure, one's reaction to these developments likely depends on one's enthusiasm for using private civil litigation as a method for enforcing public law, a connection explored in the next section.

B. THE ROLE OF PROCEDURE IN THE PRIVATE ENFORCEMENT DEBATE

RAND INSTITUTE FOR CIVIL JUSTICE, CLASS ACTION DILEMMAS: PURSUING PUBLIC GOALS FOR PRIVATE GAIN
9, 49–51 (2000).

Whether and when to enable large numbers of individuals to bring claims collectively against a single or a few defendants has long been a subject of debate in the civil law. The language of the debate is the language of civil procedure: the formal rules that govern when and how plaintiffs may bring suits against defendants; how those defendants may contest the plaintiffs' claims; and how the adversaries may bring to bear the facts and law that are relevant to their dispute, so as to ultimately reach a resolution of the case. But underlying disagreements about procedural rules rests the sometimes unspoken but widely shared understanding that procedural rules have important effects on litigation outcomes. Nowhere in the law is this truth more evident than in the battle over the class action rule, which empowers plaintiffs to bring cases that otherwise either would not be possible or would only be possible in a very different form. At times, the protagonists in the class action debate have focused on "big questions," such as securing civil rights and protecting consumers, and at times they have focused on narrow technical issues, such as when the decision to permit a class action can be challenged. But the larger social and political conflicts of the day always echo in the rooms in which the proper uses of class actions are debated.

* * *

After more than 30 years of controversy, the U.S. legal system seems to have reached an uneasy accommodation with class actions seeking affirmation of rights—of children, taxpayers, prisoners, and other groups in society. There is political disagreement about which and whose rights we should honor, and Congress has enacted legislation forbidding the federally funded Legal Services Corporation to assist in bringing rights-based (or any other) class actions. But these actions reflect fundamental arguments about individual and group rights more than disagreement about the appropriateness of providing a vehicle, such as the class action, for collective litigation of these issues.

The history of the debate over Rule 23 shows that we have not reached a similar consensus on the appropriate uses of Rule 23(b)(3) damage class actions. Is the Rule 23(b)(3) class action primarily an administrative efficiency mechanism, a means for courts and parties to manage a large number of similar legal claims, without requiring each litigant to come forward and have his or her claim considered individually? Or is it primarily a means of enabling litigation that could not be brought on an individual basis, in pursuit of larger social goals such as enforcing government regulations and deterring unsafe or unfair business practices? As we have seen, clashing views on the objective of Rule 23(b)(3) are at the heart of past and present controversy over revising the class action rule.

But the distinction in the public debate between the *efficiency* and *enabling* goals of class actions for money damages is illusory. In practice, any change in court processes that provides more efficient means of litigating is likely to enable more litigation. Greater efficiency can lower the costs of bringing lawsuits, making it more attractive for litigants to sue and for lawyers to take their cases. Moreover, because Rule 23(b)(3) requires telling people that they may have a claim of which they were previously unaware, but does not require them to take any initial action to join in the litigation, virtually every damage class action has the potential to expand the pool of litigants beyond what it would have been without class litigation. In other words, whatever efficiencies it may achieve, Rule 23 is inherently an enabling mechanism.

When we take a closer look at the controversy over damage class actions, we can see that it is, in fact, a dispute about what kinds of lawsuits and what kinds of resolutions of lawsuits *the legal system should enable.*

Business representatives from diverse sectors of the economy argue that Rule 23(b)(3), in practice, enables large numbers of lawsuits about trivial or nonexistent violations of statutes and regulations that govern advertising, marketing, pricing and other business practices, and about trivial losses to individual consumers. They claim that such suits, in reality, are vehicles for enriching plaintiff class action attorneys, not mechanisms for ensuring that important legal rules are enforced or for compensating consumers. In the end, they say, consumers pay for this litigation in the form of increased product and service costs without receiving commensurate benefits.

Manufacturers argue, as well, that Rule 23(b)(3) enables massive product defect suits that rest on dubious scientific and technical evidence. Because of the huge financial exposure associated with these mega-lawsuits, manufacturers say they feel forced to settle damage class actions, rather than contest them. The end result, they claim, is to drive good products from the market and to deter investment in developing other beneficial products.

Consumer advocates counter that a prime purpose of Rule 23(b)(3) is to enable just the kind of regulatory enforcement suits—sometimes termed "private attorneys general suits"—that businesses complain about. They say that the public cannot rely on regulatory agencies to adequately enforce consumer protection statutes, because these agencies are often underfunded and sometimes subject to influence by the businesses that they regulate. They also believe that consumers ought to have a vehicle for obtaining compensation for losses that result from corporate wrong-doing, even when these losses are small. In addition, they support mass product defect litigation, which they believe provides a powerful incentive for businesses to invest in designing safer products.

But some consumer advocates and other public interest lawyers worry that, in practice, Rule 23(b)(3) enables otherwise good cases to produce bad *outcomes*—settlements that they say serve plaintiff class action attorneys and business defendants better than they serve consumers and the general public. As a result, these advocates argue, injured consumers get less compensation than they deserve and corporations do not pay enough in damages to deter future misconduct.

All these arguments revolve around questions of what injuries ought to be compensated and what behaviors ought to be deterred. A different argument about the enabling effects of Rule 23(b)(3) concerns the right of individualized consideration of one's legal claims. When class members' claims involve such small losses that they could not realistically be pursued through individual litigation, few people worry that class actions abrogate class members' rights to individual treatment of those claims. But legal scholars and some personal injury lawyers believe that creating a single product liability class action, by combining individual cases claiming significant damages, results in lawyers and courts running roughshod over individual litigants' rights.

NOTES AND QUESTIONS

1. Class actions originated as the litigation manifestation of groups that existed in society. Thus, the villagers of the Village of *X* might sue their landlord collectively. For a chronicle of that history of collective litigation, see Stephen Yeazell, From Medieval Group Litigation to the Modern Class Action (1987). The modern class action may sometimes reflect that sort of collectivity; perhaps the "heroic era" suit against school discrimination fit that model.

As the above excerpt emphasizes, however, many modern class actions reflect a law-enforcement goal that does not depend on a pre-existing (or other) relationship between the class members. For example, in a proposed class action claiming that credit-card charges were usurious, Chief Justice Warren Burger explained in 1980:

> The aggregation of individual claims in the context of a classwide suit is an evolutionary response to the existence of injuries unremedied by the regulatory action of government. Where it is not economically reasonable to obtain relief within the traditional framework of small individual suits for damages, aggrieved persons may be without any effective redress unless they may employ the class-action device.

Deposit Guaranty Nat. Bank v. Roper, 445 U.S. 326, 339 (1980). Chief Justice Burger also recognized that such litigation often depended on contingent fee arrangements that were "a natural outgrowth of the increasing reliance on the 'private attorney general' for the vindication of legal rights; obviously this development has been facilitated by Rule 23." Id. at 338.

2.   There can be no doubt that private enforcement has flowered since the 1970s:

> The vast increase in private enforcement actions under federal law that started in the late 1960s reflected in large part the congruence of three developments: (1) the enactment of many new federal statutes specifically authorizing (or interpreted to authorize) private rights of action, (2) the proliferation of means to finance private enforcement litigation, including Legal Services programs funded by the government, the growth of privately funded nonprofit advocacy organizations subvened through favorable tax treatment, particularly in the civil rights and environmental fields, damages provisions sufficient to attract lawyers relying on contingent fee agreements, statutory attorneys' fee-shifting provision favorable to prevailing plaintiffs, and the modern class action, and (3) changes in the legal profession, attracted by these new opportunities to do well, sometimes by doing good, and freed of some of the most seriously anti-competitive aspects of self-regulation (i.e., the ban on advertising).

Stephen Burbank, Sean Farhang & Herbert Kritzer, Private Enforcement, 17 Lewis & Clark L. Rev. 637, 647 (2013); see also William Rubenstein, On What a "Private Attorney General" Is—And Why It Matters, 57 Vand. L. Rev. 2129 (2004).

3.   The extent to which procedures should be adapted to enable private enforcement is an undercurrent running throughout many of the topics in this book. There is a "vast literature" on the choice between private and public enforcement. Margaret Lemos, Special Incentives to Sue, 95 Minn. L. Rev. 782, 782 n. 1 (2011). Much as the private enforcers of the "heroic" era described by Prof. Chayes may appear to be shining knights, profit-driven lawyers trying to exploit arguably minor failures to comply with detailed regulation sometimes seem less noble.

Professors Burbank, Farhang, and Kritzer summarize the arguments for enabling private enforcement: "On the positive side of the ledger, relative to administrative implementation, private enforcement regimes can: (1) multiply resources devoted to prosecuting enforcement actions; (2) shift the costs of regulation off of governmental budgets and onto the private sector; (3) take advantage of private information to detect violations; (4) encourage legal and policy innovation; (5) emit a clear and consistent signal that violations will be prosecuted, providing insurance against the risk that a system of administrative implementation will be subverted; (6) limit the need for direct and visible intervention by the bureaucracy in the economy and society; and (7) facilitate participatory and democratic governance." Burbank, et al., *supra*, 17 Lewis & Clark L. Rev. at 662.

These effects can be furthered or limited by decisions to permit joinder in individual litigation (Chapter 2), to consolidate multiple lawsuits (Chapters 3 and 4), to approve class-action status (Chapter 5), and to approve class-action or other group-wide settlements (Chapter 7). They also can be affected by the court's appointment of lead counsel, liaison counsel, and class counsel and determination of attorney fees for lawyers involved in such cases (Chapter 6).

4.   There is another side to the aggregation/private enforcement coin, however, and Professors Burbank, Farhang, and Kritzer recognize arguments against private enforcement: "[P]rivate enforcement regimes (1) empower judges, who lack policy expertise, to make policy; (2) tend to produce inconsistent and contradictory doctrine from courts; (3) weaken the administrative state's capacity to articulate a coherent regulatory scheme by preempting administrative rulemaking; (4) usurp prosecutorial discretion; (5) discourage cooperation with regulators and voluntary compliance; (6) weaken oversight of policy implementation by the legislative and executive branches; and (7) lack democratic legitimacy and accountability." Burbank, et al, *supra*, 17 Lewis & Clark L. Rev. at 667.

5.   As you consider the issues explored in this book, consider the ways in which the public-enforcement debate should bear on them. For example, the ongoing debate about confidentiality of material exchanged in discovery (see Chapter 5) includes arguments about providing this information to public enforcers. Similarly, the question of constraining electronic discovery and preservation of electronically stored information (also addressed in Chapter 5) raises issues introduced in the 1990s by Judge Patrick Higginbotham:

> Over the years access to the powerful federal engine of discovery has become central to a wide array of social policies. Congress has elected to use the private suit, private attorneys-general as an enforcing mechanism for the anti-trust laws, the securities laws, environmental laws, civil rights and more. In the main, the plaintiff in these suits must discover his evidence from the defendant. Calibration of discovery is calibration of the level of enforcement of the social policy set by Congress.

Patrick Higginbotham, Foreword, 49 Ala. L. Rev. 1, 4–5 (1997).

6.   At least for some, current procedural rules do not provide sufficient guidance on whether to enable private enforcement: "[C]lass action (or other representative litigation) mechanisms should not be designed or deployed [to enable private enforcement] on a general (trans-substantive) basis, an approach that necessarily neglects the different regulatory policies and goals of different bodies of substantive law." Burbank, et al., *supra*, 17 Lewis & Clark L. Rev. at 640–41. But Congress is deemed to legislate against the background of the Federal Rules, Califano v. Yamasaki, 442 U.S. 682, 700–01 (1979), so calibration depending on substantive claims depends significantly on the criteria established by those rules. Thus, a significant undercurrent, particularly with regard to class actions (see Chapter 5) is the extent to which class-action treatment depends on the issues raised by the underlying substantive law. The Supreme Court has focused on the ways in which those issues bear on the criteria for class certification under Rule 23. See, e.g., Wal-

Mart v. Dukes, *infra* p. 200. But it has seemed indifferent to whether the law that creates the claim also authorizes class actions on the claim. See Shady Grove Orthopedic Assoc., P.C. v. Allstate Ins. Co., 559 U.S. 393 (2010) (refusing to apply New York limitation on class actions to proposed class action asserting claims under New York law in federal court); see also Stephen Burbank & Tobias Wolff, Redeeming the Missed Opportunities of Shady Grove, 159 U. Pa. L. Rev. 17 (2010). Similar concerns can arise in relation to MDL consolidation (see Chapter 4), and some on the defense side argue that MDL practices hobble their ability to defend against unsupported claims included among the mass.

7. Given the enforcement potential of aggregation, some who fear class actions may try to ward them off by contract. One prominent effort to do so has been with arbitration clauses that require individual arbitration rather than litigation in the event of a dispute, and forbid assertion of claims in arbitration on a classwide basis. In 2013, the Supreme Court faced a challenge to such an arbitration clause by a plaintiff seeking to assert a federal antitrust claim in court. Plaintiff argued that the cost of hiring expert witnesses would make individual arbitration rather than classwide litigation unaffordable, but the Supreme Court (by a 5–4 vote) held that the clause was nonetheless enforceable, reasoning:

> [T]he antitrust laws do not guarantee an affordable procedural path to the vindication of every claim. Congress has taken some measures to facilitate the litigation of antitrust claims—for example, it enacted a multiplied-damages remedy. In enacting such measures, Congress has told us that it is willing to go, in certain respects, beyond the normal limits of law in advancing its goals of deterring and remedying unlawful trade practice.

American Express Co. v. Italian Colors Restaurant, 570 U.S. 228, 233 (2013). The use of arbitration clauses is explored at length in Chapter 10, but a more general question throughout the book is how courts should approach the "normal limits" of procedure when confronting aggregation designed to enforce public law.

8. Similar issues can arise with regard to preclusion. One concern is whether, by settling a class action, defendants can "purchase" preclusion protection against later claims by class members "represented" in the class suit. These issues are addressed in Chapter 7 on judicial review of class-action settlements. A related concern is that some class-action settlements may actually insulate defendants from legal action for conduct in the future. See James Grimmelmann, Future Conduct and the Limits of Class-Action Settlements, 91 N.C.L.Rev. 387 (2013). And private suits might prevent later enforcement actions by public entities. See, e.g., California v. IntelliGender, LLC, 771 F.3d 1169 (9th Cir. 2014), in which defendant argued that its prior settlement of a class action brought on behalf of purchasers of its product precluded an enforcement action by the State of California based on its consumer protection laws. The court held that the State's monetary claims for "restitution" were barred by the class-action settlement because the State was "in privity" with the private class-action plaintiffs. But because the State

sought to vindicate broader governmental interests than the private class action it could seek injunctive relief and civil penalties despite the class-action judgment. See Chapter 9 regarding the "privity" concept and the binding effects of class-action judgments.

C. THE AGGREGATION DEBATE

Aggregation of related cases for unitary pretrial preparation and trial (whether accomplished by joinder, consolidation, or class action) has therefore become one of the central issues in complex litigation. Indeed, it has even been endorsed for criminal cases. See Brandon Garrett, Aggregation in Criminal Law, 95 Calif. L. Rev. 383 (2007). For a thorough review of the various policies involved, see Edward Sherman, Aggregate Disposition of Related Cases: The Policy Issues, 10 Rev. Litig. 231 (1991); see also Richard Marcus, Still Confronting the Consolidation Conundrum, 88 Notre Dame L. Rev. 557 (2012).

As noted above, the legal rules governing combination leave judges considerable latitude to craft the dimensions of individual complex cases. Regularly the rules refer to whether the claims involve "common questions" or emerge from the "same transaction," and both of those terms are subject to considerable interpretation. Some argue that the rules themselves should be tightened up. See Robin Effron, The Shadow Rules of Joinder, 100 Geo. L.J. 759 (2012) (arguing that the current rules permit too much uncertainty about when aggregation should be required).

In 2010, the American Law Institute adopted Principles of Aggregate Litigation endorsing the following goals for aggregation: "(a) enforcing substantive rights and responsibilities; (b) promoting the efficient use of litigation resources; (c) facilitating binding resolutions of civil disputes; and (d) facilitating accurate and just resolutions of civil disputes by trial and settlement." ALI, Principles of Aggregate Litigation § 1.03. The application of these principles includes considerations addressed in the previous section.

The ALI Principles also identified the "internal objectives"—that is, the goals that should be pursued by lawyers who represent large groups of claimants—of aggregate proceedings. These issues emerge in part from our system's reliance on private enforcement and on the private bar to pursue that enforcement. The nonexclusive list of objectives identified by § 1.04(b) of the Principles is:

(1) maximizing the net value of the group of claims;

(2) compensating each claimant appropriately;

(3) obtaining a judicial resolution of the legality of challenged conduct and stopping unlawful conduct from continuing;

(4) obtaining the broadest possible nondivisible remedies for past misconduct; and

(5) enabling claimants to voice their concerns and facilitating the rendition of further relief that protects the rights of affected persons as defined by substantive law.

The frequent reality is that these objectives may be in tension with each other. For example, objective (3) may seem to conflict with objective (1), particularly if a settlement will produce a monetary benefit to the plaintiffs but not forbid continuation of the conduct involved. Similarly, obtaining the broadest possible injunctive relief (objective (4)) may not correspond to obtaining maximum monetary relief for the initiating plaintiffs (objective (1)). And enabling the claimants to voice their concerns, as at trial (objective (5)) may seem inconsistent with accepting what appears to be a favorable monetary settlement (objection (1)). Moreover, Objective (2) may point up divergences between claimants that could produce intra-group competition.

Section 1.04(a) directs that a lawyer representing such a grouping "should seek to advance the common objectives of those claimants." As just noted, there may be ways in which the objectives are not entirely "common." And the lawyer's interests may not be identical with those of the claimants. Recall that contingent fee arrangements may typify a considerable portion of modern complex litigation, and reflect on whether the lawyers' and claimants' interests may diverge when the lawyers want to maximize objective (1) and the claimants place greater value on objective (5), and in particular their interest in presenting their claims at trial. Consider the caution in Howard Erichson, Aggregation as Disempowerment: Red Flags in Class Action Settlements, 92 Notre Dame L. Rev. 859, 860 (2016):

Aggregation still holds out the promise of empowerment, but, in too many instances, collective litigation has become a tool for disempowering claimants. The very thing that makes aggregation empowering—the separation of ownership and control that consolidates power in claimants' lawyers—allows defendants to strike deals that benefit themselves and benefit claimants' counsel while disadvantaging claimants.

NOTES AND QUESTIONS

1. Many of the measures courts can use to address this set of issues are examined in this book. The basic decision whether to direct combined litigation is addressed in Chapter 2 (joinder of claims), Chapter 3 (consolidation of separate lawsuits), and Chapter 5 (class certification, focusing in part on adequacy of representation and typicality of class representatives). In addition, we will see that the court has the responsibility in class actions to appoint class counsel whose duty is defined in Rule 23(g)(4): "Class counsel must fairly and

adequately represent the interests of the class." In a variety of suits, courts must also decide how much the lawyers for the aggregate should be paid for their efforts. See Chapter 6 for discussion of judicial appointment and payment of counsel. In approving proposed class settlements, the court must attend to whether the attorney fees are warranted by the real relief for the class. See Chapter 6. Are American judges well equipped to make these decisions on a case-by-case basis?

2.   As the Aggregate Litigation principles demonstrate, "[t]he net value of a group of claims for monetary relief is the portion of any payment remaining after litigation costs, including attorneys' fees, are paid. Maximizing this value is a central objective of aggregate litigation primarily because it is a matter claimants normally care about greatly when litigating." Aggregate Litigation Principles § 1.04, comment e. In making this assessment, the Principles advise that the court should "rule out the objective of benefitting solely or primarily persons outside the aggregation, such as the general public or claimants' attorneys." Id., comment d. This admonition obviously bears on attorney fees, but also on interests in public enforcement. It may also bear on the use of "cy pres" remedies in class-action settlements. See Chapter 7.

3.   Regarding intra-group competition, the Principles advise that group compensation should serve interests in "horizontal equity" (paying similarly situated claimants similarly) and "vertical equity" (ensuring that "more deserving" claimants are paid more). Id., comment f. But these ideas may not be achievable (id.):

> Rough justice is normal in aggregate proceedings. In these cases, settlements usually involve an element of "damages averaging," which occurs when an allocation plan ignores some features of claims that might reasonably be expected to influence claimants' expected recoveries at trial. For example, a mass-tort settlement might pay smokers and nonsmokers the same amounts, even though smokers have shorter life expectancies.

Keep these issues in mind when you consider the use of "damage grids" in class-action personal injury settlements. In Amchem Products, Inc. v. Windsor, *infra* p. 311, the Court noted that plaintiffs in California tended to recover high verdicts; should that entitle them to a larger payout than plaintiffs from other states? Such issues are a feature of complex litigation.

4.   Consider also the trade-off between monetary and nonmonetary relief. In the absence of a fee-shifting statute entitling her to require the defendant to pay her fee, should claimants' counsel be expected to be entirely indifferent to going unpaid if it appears that a remedy emphasizing nonmonetary relief better serves the claimants' interests?

5.   In some circumstances, particularly consolidated cases, the court may appoint one attorney as lead or liaison counsel and direct that other retained counsel contribute part of their fees to a fund to pay this lawyer for her work for the "common benefit." How much authority should the court have to modify the agreements claimants have made with their lawyers? We will

return to this point in Chapter 7, regarding "quasi class actions," and in Chapter 6, regarding "taxation" of plaintiff counsel to generate a fund for "common benefit attorneys."

6.   It should be apparent that American aggregate litigation has become quite distinctive; the remainder of this book will examine many of those distinctive features. The rest of the world generally views this litigation with great suspicion, as illustrated by the following introduction by a Canadian professor at an international conference:

> U.S.-style class actions have become a flashpoint for debate over group litigation and the collective redress regimes emerging around the world. Everyone wants to develop better ways for consumers and others who suffer loss from mass harms to receive compensation for claims that are too small to litigate individually. Everyone wants to improve the means for encouraging responsible conduct on the party of those who might cause such harms. But everyone, at least outside the United States, seems also agree that they do not want to adopt U.S.-style class actions in their systems.

Janet Walker, "General Report," in Civil Procedure in Cross-Cultural Dialogue: Eurasia Context 413 (Dmitry Maleshin ed. 2012). As you proceed though the topics in this book, consider whether the rest of the world should take a more charitable view of our procedures.

7.   More recently, the rest of the world has begun to regard collective litigation as an attractive goal, particularly for situations involving widespread harms that are individually small but collectively large. Though governmental enforcers might more frequently address those problems in other countries than in the U.S., nations in the E.U. have increasingly recognized the need for aggregate litigation as a method of private enforcement. See Astrid Stadler, Emmanuel Jeuland & Vincent Smith, Collective and Mass Litigation in Europe: Model Rules for Effective Dispute Resolution (2020). In the U.S., meanwhile, a leading conservative academic has added his voice in support of aggregate litigation as a preferred private enforcement tool outside the control of governmental actors. See Brian Fitzpatrick, The Conservative Case for Class Actions (2019).

CHAPTER 2

JOINDER IN A UNITARY FORUM

■ ■ ■

A. PERMISSIVE PARTY JOINDER

MOSLEY V. GENERAL MOTORS CORP.

United States Court of Appeals, Eighth Circuit, 1974.
497 F.2d 1330.

Before ROSS and STEPHENSON, CIRCUIT JUDGES, and VAN PELT, SENIOR DISTRICT JUDGE.

ROSS, CIRCUIT JUDGE.

Nathaniel Mosley and nine other persons joined in bringing this action individually and as class representatives alleging that their rights guaranteed under 42 U.S.C. § 2000e et seq. and 42 U.S.C. § 1981 were denied by General Motors and Local 25, United Automobile, Aerospace and Agriculture Implement Workers of America [Union] by reason of their color and race. Each of the ten named plaintiffs had, prior to the filing of the complaint, filed a charge with the Equal Employment Opportunity Commission [EEOC] asserting the facts underlying these claims. Pursuant thereto, the EEOC made a reasonable cause finding that General Motors, Fisher Body Division and Chevrolet Division, and the Union had engaged in unlawful employment practices in violation of Title VII of the Civil Rights Act of 1964. Accordingly, the charging parties were notified by EEOC of their right to institute a civil action in the appropriate federal district court, pursuant to § 706(e) of Title VII, 42 U.S.C. § 2000e–5(e).

In each of the first eight counts of the twelve-count complaint, eight of the ten plaintiffs alleged that General Motors, Chevrolet Division, had engaged in unlawful employment practices by: "discriminating against Negroes as regards promotions, terms and conditions of employment"; "retaliating against Negro employees who protested actions made unlawful by Title VII of the Act and by discharging some because they protested said unlawful acts"; "failing to hire Negro employees as a class on the basis of race"; "failing to hire females as a class on the basis of sex"; "discharging Negro employees on the basis of race"; and "discriminating against Negroes and females in the granting of relief time." Each additionally charged that the defendant Union had engaged in unlawful employment practices "with respect to the granting of relief time to Negro and female employees" and "by failing to pursue 6a grievances." The remaining two plaintiffs made similar allegations against General Motors, Fisher Body Division. All of the individual plaintiffs requested injunctive relief, back pay, attorney's fees and costs. Counts XI and XII of the complaint were class action counts against the two individual divisions of General Motors. They also sought declaratory and injunctive relief, back pay, attorney's fees and costs.

General Motors moved to strike portions of each count of the twelve-count complaint, to dismiss Counts XI and XII, to make portions of Counts I through XII more definite, to determine the propriety of Counts XI and XII as class actions, to limit the scope of the class purportedly represented, and to determine under which section of Rule 23 Counts XI and XII were maintainable as class actions. The district court ordered that "insofar as the first ten counts are concerned, those ten counts shall be severed into ten separate causes of action," and each plaintiff was directed to bring a separate action based upon his complaint, duly and separately filed. The court also ordered that the class action would not be dismissed, but rather would be left open "to each of the plaintiffs herein, individually or collectively . . . to allege a separate cause of action on behalf of any class of persons which such plaintiff or plaintiffs may separately or individually represent."

In reaching this conclusion on joinder, the district court followed the reasoning of Smith v. North American Rockwell Corp., 50 F.R.D. 515 (N.D.Okla. 1970), which, in a somewhat analogous situation, found there was no right to relief arising out of the same transaction, occurrence or series of transactions or occurrences, and that there was no question of law or fact common to all plaintiffs sufficient to sustain joinder under Federal Rule of Civil Procedure 20(a). Similarly, the district court here felt that the plaintiffs' joint actions against General Motors and the Union presented a variety of issues having little relationship to one another; that they had only one common problem, i.e. the defendant; and that as pleaded the joint actions were completely unmanageable. Upon entering the order, and upon application of the plaintiffs, the district court found that its decision involved a controlling question of law as to which there is a substantial ground for difference of opinion and that any of the parties might make application for appeal under 28 U.S.C. § 1292(b). We granted the application to permit this interlocutory appeal and for the following reasons we affirm in part and reverse in part.

Rule 20(a) of the Federal Rules of Civil Procedure provides:

> All persons may join in one action as plaintiffs if they assert any right to relief jointly, severally, or in the alternative in respect of or arising out of the same transaction, occurrence, or series of transactions or occurrences and if any question of law or fact common to all these persons will arise in the action. . . .

Additionally, Rule 20(b) and Rule 42(b) vest in the district court the discretion to order separate trials or make such other orders as will prevent delay or prejudice. In this manner, the scope of the civil action is made a matter for the discretion of the district court, and a determination on the question of joinder of parties will be reversed on appeal only upon a showing of abuse of that discretion. To determine whether the district court's order was proper herein, we must look to the policy and law that have developed around the operation of Rule 20.

The purpose of the rule is to promote trial convenience and expedite the final determination of disputes, thereby preventing multiple lawsuits. Single trials generally tend to lessen the delay, expense and inconvenience to all concerned. Reflecting this policy, the Supreme Court has said:

> Under the Rules, the impulse is toward entertaining the broadest possible scope of action consistent with fairness to the parties; joinder of claims, parties and remedies is strongly encouraged.

United Mine Workers of America v. Gibbs, 383 U.S. 715, 724 (1966).

Permissive joinder is not, however, applicable in all cases. The rule imposes two specific requisites to the joinder of parties: (1) a right to relief must be asserted by, or against, each plaintiff or defendant relating to or arising out of the same *transaction or occurrence, or series of transactions or occurrences;* and (2) some *question of law or fact common* to all the parties must arise in the action.

In ascertaining whether a particular factual situation constitutes a single transaction or occurrence for purposes of Rule 20, a case by case approach is generally pursued. No hard and fast rules have been established under the rule. However, construction of the terms "transaction or occurrence" as used in the context of Rule 13(a) counterclaims offers some guide to the application of this test. For the purposes of the latter rule,

> "Transaction" is a word of flexible meaning. It may comprehend a series of many occurrences, depending not so much upon the immediateness of their connection as upon their logical relationship.

Moore v. New York Cotton Exchange, 270 U.S. 593 (1926). Accordingly, all "logically related" events entitling a person to institute a legal action against another generally are regarded as comprising a transaction or occurrence. The analogous interpretation of the terms as used in Rule 20 would permit all reasonably related claims for relief by or against different parties to be tried in a single proceeding. Absolute identity of all events is unnecessary.

This construction accords with the result reached in United States v. Mississippi, 380 U.S. 128 (1965), a suit brought by the United States against the State of Mississippi, the election commissioners, and six voting registrars of the State, charging them with engaging in acts and practices hampering and destroying the right of black citizens of Mississippi to vote. The district court concluded that the complaint improperly attempted to hold the six county registrars jointly liable for what amounted to nothing more than individual torts committed by them separately against separate applicants. In reversing, the Supreme Court said:

> But the complaint charged that the registrars had acted and were continuing to act as part of a state-wide system designed to enforce the registration laws in a way that would inevitably deprive colored people of the right to vote solely because of their color. On such an allegation the joinder of all the registrars as defendants in a single suit is authorized by Rule 20(a) of the Federal Rules of Civil Procedure. . . . These registrars were alleged to be carrying on activities which were part of a series of transactions or occurrences the validity of which depended to a large extent upon "question[s] of law or fact common to all of them."

Here too, then, the plaintiffs have asserted a right to relief arising out of the same transactions or occurrences. Each of the ten plaintiffs alleged that he had been injured by the same general policy of discrimination on the part of General Motors and the Union. Since a "state-wide system designed to enforce the registration laws in a way that would inevitably deprive colored people of the right to vote" was determined to arise out of the same series of transactions or occurrences, we conclude that a company-wide policy purportedly designed to discriminate against blacks in employment similarly arises out of the same series of transactions or occurrences. Thus the plaintiffs meet the first requisite for joinder under Rule 20(a).

The second requisite necessary to sustain a permissive joinder under the rule is that a question of law or fact common to all the parties will arise in the action. The rule does not require that all questions of law and fact raised by the dispute be common. Yet, neither does it establish any qualitative or quantitative test of commonality. For this reason, cases construing the parallel requirement under Federal Rule of Civil Procedure 23(a) provide a helpful framework for construction of the commonality required by Rule 20. In general, those cases that have focused on Rule 23(a)(2) have given it a permissive application so that common questions have been found to exist in a wide range of contexts. Specifically, with respect to employment discrimination cases under Title VII, courts have found that the discriminatory character of a defendant's conduct is basic to the class, and the fact that the individual class members may have suffered different effects from the alleged discrimination is immaterial for the purposes of the prerequisite. In this vein, one court has said:

> [A]lthough the actual effects of a discriminatory policy may thus vary throughout the class, the existence of the discriminatory

policy threatens the entire class. And whether the Damoclean threat of a racially discriminatory policy hangs over the racial class is a question of fact common to all the members of the class.

Hall v. Werthan Bag Corp., 251 F.Supp. 184, 186 (M.D.Tenn. 1966).

The right to relief here depends on the ability to demonstrate that each of the plaintiffs was wronged by racially discriminatory policies on the part of the defendants General Motors and the Union. The discriminatory character of the defendants' conduct is thus basic to each plaintiff's recovery. The fact that each plaintiff may have suffered different effects from the alleged discrimination is immaterial for the purposes of determining the common question of law or fact. Thus, we conclude that the second requisite for joinder under Rule 20(a) is also met by the complaint.

For the reasons set forth above, we conclude that the district court abused its discretion in severing the joined actions. The difficulties in ultimately adjudicating damages to the various plaintiffs are not so overwhelming as to require such severance. If appropriate, separate trials may be granted as to any particular issue after the determination of common questions.

NOTES AND QUESTIONS

1.   *Mosley* has been described as "possibly the leading case on joinder of Title VII plaintiffs." Miller v. Hygrade Food Products Corp., 202 F.R.D. 142, 144 n. 3 (E.D.Pa. 2001). It provides an example of joinder in a single suit of both multiple claims (arising under Title VII of the 1964 Civil Rights Act and § 1981) and multiple parties (ten people who had filed charges of discrimination with the Equal Employment Opportunity Commission). Joinder of multiple claims is permitted by Rule 18(a). Although Title VII and § 1981 have different elements in their statutory causes of action, a central issue in both is that the plaintiff was subjected to race discrimination. Are there occasions when joinder of claims against a single party should not be permitted because the claims are too dissimilar? See Committee Note to Amended Rule 18(a) (1966): "It is emphasized that amended Rule 18(a) deals only with pleading. As already indicated, a claim properly joined as a matter of pleading need not be proceeded with together with the other claims if fairness or convenience justifies separate treatment."

2.   It appears, in *Mosley,* that the claim of each of the ten plaintiffs is based on different events by which that plaintiff was allegedly discriminated against as to promotion, conditions of employment, failure to hire, etc. It also seems likely that different G.M. employees were responsible for the alleged acts of discrimination against each plaintiff. How then, can the right to relief which each plaintiff asserts be considered to arise out of "the same transaction, occurrence, or series of transactions or occurrences"? In Duke v. Uniroyal Inc., 928 F.2d 1413 (4th Cir. 1991), plaintiffs alleged age discrimination in

connection with the company's reduction in force program. The appellate court affirmed the trial court's refusal to sever their cases for trial:

> Both Duke and Fox were terminated on August 15, 1985, as part of the same reduction in force which was implemented by Uniroyal under a uniform policy adopted for selecting employees for discharge. The reduction was implemented by direction of Uniroyal's national sales manager in consultation with its manager of employee relations. Moreover, the decisions with respect to both Duke and Fox were the product of coordinated efforts in the selection of persons for discharge and in making transfers necessitated by restructuring of regions and departments. Plaintiffs' claims arise out of the same transaction, a single reduction in force, raising common questions of law and fact.

> While there was a broad variation of circumstances relating to the merits of the individual performances of each of the plaintiffs, this evidence could be easily distinguished by the jury.

Id. at 1420–21.

In Puricelli v. CNA Ins. Co., 185 F.R.D. 139 (N.D.N.Y. 1999), the court was willing to overlook "differences in the factual underpinnings" of the claims of two employees who alleged age discrimination, finding a common course of conduct reflecting a "new and aggressive management style" that made excessive demands on older employees. Is it relevant to a finding of the "same transaction" that evidence likely to be offered to prove the claim of discrimination would be applicable to all the joined parties? See Alexander v. Fulton County, 207 F.3d 1303 (11th Cir. 2000) (upholding joinder of 18 white employees of the sheriff's department alleging race discrimination by the new sheriff, noting that "each of the Plaintiffs' claims and the evidence of discrimination undoubtedly [is] relevant to every other plaintiff's core allegations of systemic discrimination").

3.   Differences in time, location, and persons involved can prevent joinder of discrimination claims. See Grayson v. K-Mart Corp., 849 F.Supp. 785 (N.D.Ga. 1994), in which eleven plaintiffs who had been fired as managers of K-Mart stores in different parts of the country sued claiming that the firings resulted from age discrimination. Defendant moved to sever. Citing *Mosley*, the court said that it was a "somewhat close question" whether joinder was proper under Rule 20, but found joinder improper since the employment decisions were made by different managers. "The decision to demote each plaintiff originated with his district manager and was derived within the context of the business circumstances of each plaintiff's store. Three different regional managers participated in the eleven demotion decisions at issue in these cases." Id. at 789. In Randleel v. Pizza Hut of America, Inc., 182 F.R.D. 542 (N.D.Ill. 1998), African-American customers claimed they were discriminated against in service at Pizza Hut restaurants in two different cities. The circumstances were somewhat different: denial of service, in one case, for not having an advance reservation, and, in another, after the dining

room closed. The court denied joinder on the basis that "[t]hese are factually discrete and unrelated incidents which occurred two months apart at restaurants in different states, and which involved different management teams and workers." We will see similar issues in Wal-Mart Stores, Inc. v. Dukes, *infra* p. 200 (refusing class action treatment in employment discrimination case).

4.   Similarity of conduct to which plaintiffs are subjected will not always insure joinder. Baughman v. Lee County, Mississippi, 554 F.Supp.2d 652 (N.D. Miss. 2008) was a § 1983 suit by 27 plaintiffs, each alleging that (s)he was unnecessarily strip-searched at the Lee County Jail in violation of constitutional rights. The district court ordered the claims severed:

> In analyzing the joinder issues in this case, the court finds persuasive the reasoning * * * in McFarland v. State Farm Fire & Cas. Co., 2006 WL 2577852 (S.D. Miss. 2006), a Hurricane Katrina case in which hundreds of plaintiffs sought to join together to assert insurance fraud and other claims against State Farm. This case, like *McFarland,* involves plaintiffs who assert what are superficially similar claims but which will require different fact witnesses and individualized proof regarding damages. This lawsuit does not arise from a single incident in which large numbers of inmates were strip-searched at the same time. To the contrary, the complaint alleges a series of allegedly unlawful strip searches which took place between 2005 and 2007, and each incident will require individualized proof regarding the circumstances and nature of the strip search in question. Moreover, each plaintiff alleges that he or she suffered emotional distress damages as a result of being strip searched, and federal law requires that, to recover emotional distress damages, a § 1983 plaintiff must demonstrate a "specific discernable injury to [his] emotional state" resulting from a constitutional violation, proven with evidence regarding the "nature and extent" of the harm. Patterson v. P.H.P. Healthcare Corp., 90 F.3d 927, 938–40 (5th Cir. 1996).

How is this distinguishable from *Mosley*?

5.   Modern communications technology has enabled companies to provide services to large numbers of persons through long-distance connections. It has also spawned intercepting of cable TV and internet services without permission. The interceptors act individually, but often with the same kind of interception device or method. Tele-Media Co. v. Antidormi, 179 F.R.D. 75, 77 (D. Conn. 1998) denied joinder in a single suit against 104 individuals, alleging that each had used an altered converter to obtain programming without paying. The court said: "Though the balance of pragmatic considerations may arguably point toward permitting the action to proceed as is, at least until the eve of trial, the same transaction test of Rule 20 stands in the way. Unless that requirement is to be ignored, the advantages of a single action must be achieved, to the extent they can be, through consolidation or other means." See also PPV Connection, Inc. v. Nieves-Sosa, 268 F.R.D. 42

(D.P.R. 2010), in which plaintiff sued "many defendants" under the federal Communications Act of 1934 for intercepting TV programming in violation of plaintiff's exclusive right to broadcast the programming. Most of the defendants operated bars or restaurants. One of the defendants challenged joinder under Rule 20. Although the court was persuaded that there was a common question because "the cases concern the same federal anti-piracy laws," it found that the "same transaction" requirement was not satisfied because there was no claim the defendants acted in concert. Plaintiff emphasized that it was suing all of them for pirating the same program, but the court found that insufficient (id. at 44):

> The Court does not find that intercepting the same live television program alone satisfied the sort of "connection" needed to establish [transactional connectedness]. * * * In his motion, defendant Rodriguez-Lespier stresses that there are significant differences between his venue, a restaurant, and the co-defendants' bars and pubs, which usually broadcast these types of television programs and charge entrance fees. The only evidence that is certain to be similar from the facts alleged is the timing of the broadcasting because the television program at issue was a live event. Thus, from the facts alleged and from what the Court can reasonably infer from the facts, it is likely that the defendants in this case will employ distinct defenses and encounter different evidence.

6.   In Barber v. America's Wholesale Lender, 289 F.R.D. 364 (M.D. Fla. 2013), 18 borrowers sued 9 different lenders, asserting claims arising out of 15 separate mortgages entered into with 10 different lenders. Plaintiffs claimed that they were duped into thinking they were getting traditional borrower/lender relationships with their particular lenders when, in reality, their loans were sold to third-party investors as part of a securitization process. The court held that Rule 20 was not satisfied: "Plaintiffs' claims involve conduct by different Defendants, different loan documents, different dates, and different operative factual scenarios. In addition, resolution of each claim would require individualized attention and likely require separate trials." Id. at 367.

7.   *Copyright infringement cases.* Copyright holders might seek to sue a number of defendants for violating their copyright by, for example, suing all distributors and bookstores for selling the same copyrighted book. If the defendants are unrelated, such joinder has generally been rejected. File sharing of music can raise a different twist. For example, BitTorrent peer-to-peer file sharing breaks a large file into pieces while tagging each piece with a common identifier, and users join forces to simultaneously download and upload pieces of the file from and to each other. This reduces the bottleneck of Internet traffic that normally occurs at the server where the entire file is located and allows for faster download speeds for users. This interconnected web of information flowing between users, or peers, is called a swarm. The argument for joining in one suit all BitTorrent users who download the same file because they are part of the same "swarm" is that they have all participated

in the same series of transactions, and "the individuals might well be actively sharing a file with one another, uploading and downloading pieces of the copyrighted work from the other members of the swarm." LCC v. Does 1–1058, 752 F.3d 990, 998 (D.C.Cir. 2014).

In *LCC v. Does 1–1058,* the copyright holder sued 1058 Does who allegedly downloaded a pornographic film called *Popular Demand* over a five-month period. The D.C. Circuit said there was no reason to think that the Doe defendants were participating in the same swarm at the same time (id. at 999):

> Two individuals who downloaded the same file five months apart are exceedingly unlikely to have had any interaction with one another whatsoever. Their only relationship is that they used the same protocol to access the same work. To paraphrase an analogy offered by amicus counsel at oral argument, two BitTorrent users who download the same file months apart are like two individuals who play at the same blackjack table at different times. They may have won the same amount of money, employed the same strategy, and perhaps even played with the same dealer, but they have still engaged in entirely separate transactions. And "[s]imply committing the same type of violation in the same way does not link defendants together for the purposes of joinder."

The courts are split on the Rule 20 issue in the file sharing situation. Some emphasize the coercive aspects. See, e.g., Patrick Collins, Inc. v. Doe 1, 288 F.R.D. 233, 237 (E.D.N.Y. 2012), quoting other judges in that district who decry "what is essentially an extortion scheme," "abusive litigation practices," and "unscrupulous tactics used by certain plaintiffs, particularly in the adult films industry, to shake down the owners of specific IP addresses from which copyrighted adult films were allegedly downloaded." Other courts, sometimes in the same district, permit joinder. See, e.g., Malibu Cinema LLC v. John Does 1–5, 285 F.R.D. 273 (S.D.N.Y. 2012) (upholding joinder of defendants who used file-sharing). See also Note, The Case Against Combating BitTorrent Piracy Through Mass John Doe Copyright Infringement Lawsuits, 111 Mich. L. Rev. 283 (2012) (arguing that judges should not allow discovery of the identity of alleged infringers without first ensuring that the court has jurisdiction over these defendants and that they were properly joined).

8.   The "same transaction or occurrence" test is used in several federal rules, and its exact meaning varies with the context. For example, when used in Rule 13(a) to require the filing of a counterclaim which "arises out of the transaction or occurrence that is the subject matter of the opposing party's claim," it has been interpreted as reflecting a policy of judicial economy; the test is satisfied if the "same evidence" will support the claim and counterclaim. Williams v. Robinson, 1 F.R.D. 211 (D.D.C. 1940). When used in Rule 15(c) to allow an amended pleading to relate back to the date of the original filing if it arose out of the "conduct, transaction, or occurrence set forth" in the original pleading, the test is said to reflect a liberal amendment policy so long as there was adequate notice at time of filing to satisfy the objectives of the statute of limitations. Tiller v. Atlantic Coast Line R. Co., 323 U.S. 574, 581 (1945).

Would it be reasonable to read the test in Rule 20(a) as aimed at allowing claims to be tried together when they make a just and efficient trial package? Or is that the purpose of the "common question of law or fact" requirement and thus "same transaction or occurrence" must mean something more?

IN RE STAND 'N SEAL PRODUCTS LIABILITY LITIGATION
United States District Court for Northern District of Georgia, 2009.
2009 WL 2224185.

THRASH, DISTRICT JUDGE.

* * *

This is one of the personal injury cases involving the Stand 'n Seal "Spray-On" Grout Sealer. Stand 'n Seal was a consumer product used to seal ceramic tile grout in kitchens, bathrooms, and similar areas. The purported advantage of Stand 'n Seal was that users could easily stand and spray the sealant onto the grout without the strain of using a brush and manually applying the sealant. The Plaintiffs say that the problems with Stand 'n Seal began when the manufacturer changed its chemical components.* * * The Plaintiffs say that users of Stand 'n Seal immediately began experiencing respiratory problems, such as chemical pneumonitis, from exposure to Stand 'n Seal. By August 31, 2005, Stand 'n Seal with Flexipel was recalled.

In this case, the Plaintiffs are seven individuals who purchased and used Stand 'n Seal. They all purchased the product in Georgia. The Plaintiffs assert claims for strict products liability, breach of warranty, and negligence against each of the companies involved in the manufacture, distribution, and sale of Stand 'n Seal with Flexipel. The Defendants now move to sever the claims of each Plaintiff, or in the alternative, order separate trials for each Plaintiff.

* * *

"Plainly, the central purpose of Rule 20 is to promote trial convenience and expedite the resolution of disputes, thereby eliminating unnecessary lawsuits." Alexander v. Fulton County, 207 F.3d 1303, 1323 (11th Cir. 2000). Therefore, courts liberally interpret Rule 20. "It may comprehend a series of many occurrences, depending not so much upon the immediateness of their connection as upon their logical relationship." If joinder is improper, then "the court may at any time, on just terms, add or drop a party. The court may also sever any claim against a party." Fed.R.Civ.P. 21. And, even if joinder is proper, "[f]or convenience, to avoid prejudice, or to expedite and economize, the court may order a separate trial of one or more separate issues, claims, crossclaims, counterclaims, or third-party claims." Fed.R.Civ.P. 42(b).

The Plaintiffs are properly joined under Rule 20 and separate trials are not necessary. The Plaintiffs each assert a right to relief arising out of the manufacture, distribution, and sale of Stand 'n Seal with Flexipel. Although the Plaintiffs purchased Stand 'n Seal at different times and suffered different injuries, their claims rely on the same core allegation: aerosolized Flexipel is hazardous. This core allegation satisfies the requirement of a series of logically related transactions or occurrences and the requirement of a question of law or fact common to all plaintiffs. *See* Abraham v. Volkswagen of Am., Inc., 795 F.2d 238, 251 (2d Cir. 1986) (allowing joinder where plaintiffs all alleged "the faulty valve stem seal as a single defect"); Poleon v. General Motors Corp., 1999 WL 1289473, at *3 (D.V.I. 1999) (allowing joinder where plaintiffs all alleged the "malfunctioning of the brake system and the failure of the air bag system to deploy" as the defect). This core allegation also distinguishes this case from the cases cited by the Defendants. See Saval v. BL Ltd., 710 F.2d 1027, 1031 (4th Cir. 1983) (denying joinder where plaintiffs "had not demonstrated that any of the alleged similar problems resulted from a common defect"); Coughlin v. Rogers, 130 F.3d 1348, 1350 (9th Cir. 1997) (denying joinder where the plaintiffs "do not allege that their claims arise out of a systematic pattern of events").

The Defendants say that, even if joinder is proper, the Court should order separate trials for each Plaintiff. Because the Plaintiffs' claims rely on the same core allegation that aerosolized Flexipel is hazardous, separate trials would require redundant testimony that is not in the interest of judicial economy. There is some risk of jury confusion and prejudice, but that risk is minimized by the straightforward nature of the Plaintiffs' claims and the appropriate use of jury instructions. *See* Alexander, 207 F.3d at 1325 ("[T]he potential for prejudice was minimized because of the core similarities in [p]laintiffs' claims."); Hanley v. First Investors Corp., 151 F.R.D. 76, 80 (E.D.Tex. 1993) ("[The jury] will be instructed to keep each plaintiff's claim separate, and to force each plaintiff to prove his or her claim and damages separately."). In addition, a single trial will serve more effectively as a bellwether trial in this multidistrict litigation.

NOTES AND QUESTIONS

1.   Although, as seen in *Mosley*, a common course of conduct may be grounds for upholding joinder in discrimination cases, should the same be true in product liability cases? *Stand 'n Seal* says that despite the fact that the plaintiffs purchased the product at different times and suffered different injuries, their claims rely on the "same core allegations"—that the chemical component is hazardous. It cites the Second Circuit opinion in *Abraham* which permitted joinder of the breach of warranty claims of 75 plaintiffs based on a faulty valve stem seal that caused it to harden and break over time in their VW Rabbit automobiles. *Abraham* overturned the lower court's contrary finding that because some of the defects alleged did not occur on all cars and

the mileage at which repairs were required varied greatly, the plaintiffs had not satisfied the same transaction or occurrence requirement. The court in *Stand 'n Seal* similarly cites *Poleon*, which allowed joinder of the claims of five police officers who were injured in three different accidents involving police vehicles in which the Antilocking Brake System and air bags malfunctioned. The court found it sufficient that the complaint alleged that all the vehicles were manufactured by GM in the same year and were of the same make and model and that each of the accidents was caused by the same defects in the brakes and air bags. "The controlling consideration," it said, "is the extent of any product defects, and absolute identity of all events is not necessary." If the *Poleon* defendant had responded that the accidents were not caused by the product defect, and therefore the individual circumstances of each accident would have to be considered, would joinder still have been appropriate? Likewise, in *Stand 'n Seal* if the defendant denied causation or alleged that the individual plaintiffs had failed to follow the directions for applying the product, would joinder be proper?

2.   Consider the "common issue" aspects of Dunavant v. Ford Motor Co., Civ. Ac. No. H–80–1159 (S.D. Tex. 1980): Forty-seven plaintiffs with personal injury and property damage claims, arising out of thirty separate accidents involving the alleged malfunction of the gear shift and transmission on their Ford automobiles, sued Ford in a federal district court in Houston, Texas. The accidents occurred in fourteen different states, over a period of four years. There was no relationship between any of the plaintiffs or any of the accidents other than the common claim that a similar product defect was to blame.

One might ask why a case would be structured in this way. Why didn't each of the plaintiffs file in his or her own state? The answer is often that in such areas as product liability, where considerable expertise, specialized experience, and capital is required of a plaintiff's attorney, cases may be referred by local attorneys to specialists who seek to reduce overall costs (and perhaps to improve their bargaining leverage) by joining a number of cases alleging similar product defects. But this also means that cases involving dissimilar factual situations, and perhaps dissimilar law, may be joined in one suit.

Ford stated in support of its motion for severance: "These vehicles were manufactured over a thirteen-year period and were equipped with a variety of combinations of various transmission types and transmission control systems. * * * Because the accident date and date of manufacture differ for each vehicle, the evidence which is admissible concerning the failure to warn and adequacy of warning issues and concerning post-accident or post-manufacture design modifications and changes to the language of the owner's manuals will differ from case to case. In addition, several states have enacted product liability statutes which affect the materiality of evidence concerning remedial measures, state-of-the-art, presumptions which favor a party, and defensive issues relating to the plaintiff's contributory negligence, comparative fault and use or misuse of the product." Should joinder have been permitted?

3. In re Rezulin Products Liability Litigation, 168 F.Supp.2d 136 (S.D.N.Y. 2001), involved the claims of eight diabetes patients against the manufacturer and various providers/distributors for personal injuries resulting from ingesting the drug Rezulin. The federal district judge to whom the cases had been transferred by the Multidistrict Litigation Panel (see Chapter 4) ordered the cases severed due to misjoinder. He cited the following authority:

> In the *Diet Drugs* litigation, Judge Bechtle found that plaintiffs alleging claims against drug manufacturers almost identical to those alleged here were misjoined because "the claims of plaintiffs who have not purchased or received diet drugs from an identical source, such as a physician, hospital or diet center, did not satisfy the transaction or occurrence requirement." In re Diet Drugs, 1999 WL 554584, at *4 (E.D.Pa. 1999). Similarly, in Simmons v. Wyeth Laboratories, Inc., 1996 WL 617492 (E.D.Pa. 1996), the court found that plaintiffs alleging similar claims against drug manufacturers were misjoined because "plaintiffs do not allege the exact nature of their injuries or damages, other than averring that plaintiffs experience one or more of numerous injuries and side effects." In short, plaintiffs' allegations could not "be said to have arisen from the same basic set of facts." The same reasoning applied in the *Bone Screws* litigation, where Judge Bechtle framed the relevant question as whether "the central facts of each plaintiff's claim arise on a somewhat individualized basis out of the same set of circumstances" and found that "joinder based on the belief that the same occurrence or transaction is satisfied by the fact that claimants have the same or similar device of a defendant manufacturer implanted in or about their spine is . . . not a proper joinder." In re Orthopedic Bone Screw Prods. Liab. Litig., 1995 WL 428683, at *1–2 (E.D.Pa. 1995).

The court rejected the plaintiffs' reliance on Abraham v. Volkswagen of America, Inc., 795 F.2d 238 (2d Cir. 1986):

> Unlike cases involving a pure product defect, toxic tort cases raise more complicated issues of causation and exposure. This is not, as was *Abraham,* a situation with an identical product defect allegedly causing identical results—breakage of the valve stem seal—which in turn caused different injuries depending on the circumstances of the particular accident. The plaintiffs * * * allege a defect (or defects) the precise contours of which are unknown and which may have caused different results—not merely different injuries—in patients depending on such variables as exposure to the drug, the patient's physical state at the time of taking the drug, and a host of other known and unknown factors that must be considered at trial with respect to each individual plaintiff. They do not allege that they received Rezulin from the same source or that they were exposed to Rezulin for similar periods of time. As in *Simmons,* they do not allege injuries specific to each of them so as to allow the Court

to determine how many plaintiffs, if any, share injuries in common. Joinder "of several plaintiffs who have no connection to each other in no way promotes trial convenience or expedites the adjudication of asserted claims." In re Diet Drugs, 1999 WL 554584, at *3. See also Kenvin v. Newburger, Loeb & Co., 37 F.R.D. 473 (S.D.N.Y. 1965) (misjoinder of defendant stockholders where, although "wrongdoing of each defendant was identical, the loans and securities involved and the dates on which the transactions were entered into differed * * * [P]laintiffs had alleged unrelated acts which happened to involve violations of the same . . . duty"). For these reasons, plaintiffs are misjoined.

Contrast Burton v. American Cyanamid, 128. F. Supp. 3d 1095 (E.D. Wis. 2015), in which 160 plaintiffs filed actions against the defendant arising out of lead-paint poisoning that occurred when they were children. The plaintiffs, however, were scattered across many states and ingested different types of lead paint at different times. To boot, their claims ran the gamut, including negligent manufacture and design, failure to warn, and negligent promotion and sale. The court denied the defendant's motion to sever, noting that "Plaintiffs' claims are sufficiently connected to allow the case to proceed in its present form. * * * [J]oinder is convenient to the parties, promotes efficient resolution of the case, and does not prejudice defendants." Id. at 1103–1104. Timeliness, however, was not the only issue. By its count, if severance had occurred earlier in the litigation, "the result would have been 835 separate motions before at least 4 different judges. I recognize that individual discovery and separate trials will likely be required. However, these things can be accomplished without the disadvantages attendant to dismissal or severance." Id. at 1104.

4. Proof of causation is often a problem in cases of exposure to potentially dangerous products, such as asbestos, tobacco, or pharmaceutical drugs. Since many people are often exposed, joinder or some form of aggregation can offer attractions in terms of judicial economy, efficiency, and uniformity, but the precise language of Rule 20 may dictate otherwise. In Insolia v. Philip Morris, 186 F.R.D. 547 (E.D.Wis. 1999), three individuals suffering from cancer sued five tobacco companies and two industry trade associations alleging a conspiracy to suppress adverse health reports and hide the dangers of smoking. The court first denied plaintiffs' motion for class action status and then severed the cases for improper joinder, stating:

> Rule 20 demands more than the bare allegation that all plaintiffs are victims of a fraudulent scheme perpetrated by one or more defendants; there must be some indication that each plaintiff has been induced to act by the same misrepresentation. * * *

Misrepresentation and conspiracy are not the only issues difficult to fit into the transaction requirement of Rule 20. Although there are few cases that address the problems associated with joining multiple plaintiffs in a single products liability action, for obvious reasons, these issues are of crucial importance to plaintiffs. As illustrated by In the Matter of Asbestos II Consolidated Pretrial, No. 86–C–1739, 1989 WL 56181 (N.D.Ill. May 10, 1989), medical and legal causation present formidable obstacles under Rule 20. *Asbestos II* involved a group of over 100 former pipefitters who brought a products liability action against several companies responsible for manufacturing asbestos. The district court concluded that these claims did not arise reasonably and logically out of the same series of transactions. Although all of the plaintiffs had contracted pleural asbestosis, the duration and magnitude of this disease varied from plaintiff to plaintiff. Even though all of the plaintiffs had belonged to the same union and had been exposed to asbestos products while working at common sites, exposure did not happen "at the same time [or] at the same place." Given that each claim turned on unique facts, the specter of jury confusion outweighed any benefit that might accrue to the parties and the court system by avoiding multiple lawsuits.

* * * I conclude that plaintiffs' claims do not arise from the same transaction or series of transactions, as they must in order to satisfy Rule 20. On the abstract level, dissimilarities in the claims brought by plaintiffs suggest that these claims are not related logically to one another. Plaintiffs began smoking at different ages; they brought different brands throughout their years as smokers; and they quit for different reasons and under different circumstances. * * * [P]laintiff Vincent Insolia began smoking almost two decades before the industry hatched its scheme and has not smoked for more than a quarter of a century. By contrast, plaintiffs Billy Mays and Maureen Lovejoy took up the habit in the early '50s and continued to smoke well into the '90s. Even if the conspiracy charged held together, serious questions exist regarding medical causation.

Is there no way to avoid trying separately every case of exposure to a product like asbestos or tobacco? We will return to this question in Chapter 5 on class actions.

5.   Assume that a railroad, having determined that fifty different persons have separately engaged in acts of vandalism against its property, sues all fifty in the same suit. Is joinder permissible? In Bridgeport Music, Inc. v. 11C Music, 202 F.R.D. 229 (M.D.Tenn. 2001), plaintiff companies that publish, record, and distribute music sued 770 publishing companies, copyright administrators, record labels, and entertainment companies for copyright infringement by "sampling" their music without paying royalties. Defendants challenged joinder, arguing that each infringing song represents a separate transaction requiring a unique set of proof. Plaintiffs argued that the claims were intricately interrelated, that the defendants inflicted the same harm against them, and that a small number of the defendants repeatedly infringed their copyrights and were involved in most of the infringing songs. How should the court rule?

6.   Should Rule 20(a) be broadly interpreted as a device for serving the interests of judicial efficiency? Would it be reasonable to read the test in Rule 20(a) as aimed at allowing claims to be tried together when they make a just and efficient trial package? Or is that the purpose of the "common question of law or fact" requirement, and thus "same transaction or occurrence" must mean something more? In requiring severance of the claims of 27 plaintiffs for unconstitutional strip-searching, the court gave short shrift to the argument that it would be costly in time and money to try the suits individually: "[I]t is not a goal of the federal judiciary to implement justice on the cheap by compromising the basic integrity of the judicial process." Baughman v. Lee County, *supra* p. 23, note 4. Should efficiency be a central factor?

HALL V. E.I. DU PONT DE NEMOURS & CO., INC.; CHANCE V. E.I. DU PONT DE NEMOURS & CO., INC.

United States District Court, Eastern District of New York, 1972.
345 F.Supp. 353.

WEINSTEIN, DISTRICT JUDGE.

These two cases arise out of eighteen separate accidents scattered across the nation in which children were injured by blasting caps. Damages are sought from manufacturers and their trade association, the Institute of Makers of Explosives (I.M.E.). The basic allegation is that the practice of the explosives industry during the 1950's—continuing until 1965—of not placing any warning upon individual blasting caps and of failing to take other safety measures created an unreasonable risk of harm resulting in plaintiffs' injuries.

* * *

I.   THE CHANCE CASE

Thirteen children were allegedly injured by blasting caps in twelve unrelated accidents between 1955 and 1959. The injuries occurred in the states of Alabama, California, Maryland, Montana, Nevada, North Carolina, Tennessee, Texas, Washington and West Virginia. Plaintiffs are citizens of the states in which their injuries occurred. They are now claiming damages against six manufacturers of blasting caps and the I.M.E. on the grounds of negligence, common law conspiracy, assault, and strict liability in tort. In addition, two parents sue for medical expenses. Federal jurisdiction is based on diversity of citizenship. 28 U.S.C. § 1332.

[None of the *Chance* plaintiffs could identify the manufacturer of the cap that caused his injury, but each alleged that the cap was manufactured jointly and severally by the 6 corporate defendants and I.M.E. The complaint alleged an industry practice of not placing a warning on the caps resulting from a conscious agreement between defendants who also lobbied against labeling legislation.

Defendants moved to dismiss for failure to state a claim, or for severance due to improper joinder. The court reserved ruling on "what choice-of-law principles are to be applied in a case such as this one where planning, design, manufacture, and sale of a product occurred in different states, and injury in yet others." It assumed a national body of state tort law as "a growing consensus on the substantive law in this country permits such a gross first approach to the preliminary motions before us."]

The central question raised by defendants' motion is whether the defendants can be held responsible as a group under any theory of joint liability for injuries arising out of their individual manufacture of blasting caps. Joint tort liability is not limited to a narrow set of relationships and circumstances. It has been imposed in a wide range of situations, requiring varying standards of care, in which defendants cooperate in various degrees, enter into business and property relationships, and undertake to supply goods for public consumption. Developments in negligence and strict tort liability have imposed extensive duties on manufacturers to guard against a broad spectrum of risks with regard to the general population. The reasoning underlying current policy justifies the extension of established doctrines of joint tort liability to the area of industry-wide cooperation in product manufacture and design.

[The court denied the motion to dismiss for failure to state a claim. Surveying modern tort law, Judge Weinstein identified several possibly applicable grounds for joint liability.

First, *concert of action* in creating a dangerous circumstance could support joint liability for resulting harms based either on an explicit agreement or an inference of tacit cooperation based on defendants' parallel behavior. Alternatively, adherence to an industry-wide standard or custom might support such a finding.

Second, *enterprise liability* might apply, given allegations that the entire blasting cap industry could be the logical locus for taking precautions. The judge cautioned, however, that this theory had "special applicability to industries composed of a small number of units."

Third, plaintiffs might avoid the burden of proving that a specific manufacturer produced the harmful cap by *alternative liability* as set forth in § 433B of the Restatement of Torts (Second):

(2) Where the tortious conduct of two or more actors has combined to bring about harm to the plaintiff, and one or more of the actors seeks to limit his liability on the ground that the harm is capable of apportionment among them, the burden of proof as to the apportionment is upon each such actor.

(3) Where the conduct of two or more actors is tortious, and it is proved that harm has been caused to the plaintiff by only one of them, but there is uncertainty as to which one has caused it, the

burden is upon each such actor to prove that he has not caused the harm.

In particular, as in the famous case of Summers v. Tice, 199 P.2d 1 (Cal. 1948) (two hunters negligently shot in the direction of plaintiff, who was hit by one bullet), plaintiffs might be able to show that all defendants owed a duty of care to them. In addition, each plaintiff would have to prove causation by showing by a preponderance of the evidence that the cap that caused the injury was produced by one of the named defendants rather than someone else.]

To justify permissive joinder of parties plaintiffs must show both a "common question of law or fact" and a right to relief "arising out of the same transaction or occurrence or series of transactions or occurrences." Fed.R.Civ.P. 20(a). Defendants move for severance of plaintiffs on the ground that the complaint fails to satisfy either requirement, and for dismissal or transfer of the claims thus severed. 28 U.S.C. § 1404(a). They assert that the substantive law of the ten states will govern liability, and hence the claims present no common question of law.

The question of which state's law will govern which aspects of this case cannot be settled by assertion. In diversity cases, a federal court is bound to apply the choice-of-law principles of the state in which it sits. Klaxon v. Stentor Electric Mfg. Co., 313 U.S. 487 (1941). Under New York law, the choice of applicable law in personal injury cases is not determined by the traditional "place of injury" test, but by "the flexible principle that the law to be applied to resolve a particular issue is 'the law of the jurisdiction which, because of its relationship or contact with the occurrence or the parties, has the greatest concern' with the matter in issue and 'the strongest interest' in its resolution."

The locus of defendants' joint activity was allegedly at least in part in New York, the location of the I.M.E. Whether proof of this connection would be sufficient to support the application of New York law to some or all of the claims is a complex question involving consideration of New York choice-of-law principles and federal constitutional law. The parties are directed to supply briefs on this issue and on the general question of the law applicable to the different aspects of this case. Prior to a full consideration of the choice-of-law question, this court cannot rule on whether the plaintiffs' claims contain a common question of law. It should be noted, however, that Rule 20(a) requires only "*any* common question of law or fact." Thus the presence of questions of law not common to all the plaintiffs will not, in itself, defeat joinder.

Plaintiffs' claims do contain, moreover, common questions of fact—for example, whether the defendants exercised joint control over the labeling of blasting caps and operated, for purposes of tort liability, as a joint enterprise with respect to such labeling. The presence of these questions satisfies the requirement of Rule 20(a) that "any question of law *or* fact common to all these persons" arise in the action.

Defendants also contend that because the accidents occurred at different times and places, plaintiffs' rights to relief do not arise out of the same transaction or occurrence, or series of transactions or occurrences. There is no rigid rule as to what constitutes "the same transaction or occurrence" for purposes of joinder under Rule 20(a). "[T]he approach must be the general one of whether there are enough ultimate factual concurrences that it would be fair to the parties to require them to defend jointly" against the several claims. Application of this flexible standard presents a certain challenge in this case. It would be neither fair nor convenient to any of the parties nor to the court to determine in this court all the relevant issues of fact involved in each accident. At the same time it would be unfair and burdensome to require each plaintiff to prove the alleged joint activities in ten separate and (to that extent) repetitive actions.

The solution does not lie in wholesale severance, and the cases cited by defendants do not support that result. * * * Rather, fairness to the parties may be maximized by permitting plaintiffs to litigate the issues of joint activity in this court, and then transferring the questions which turn on the particular facts of each accident to the federal districts in which the accidents occurred. *See* 28 U.S.C. § 1404(a), Rules 20(b) and 42(a) and (b), Federal Rules of Civil Procedure. Whether this procedure would entail full separate trials of different issues, or special findings of fact in this court, or other possible procedures, will be decided after consideration of the choice-of-law problem and in consultation with the parties.

II. THE HALL CASE

[In this case, three families, one each from New York, Ohio and North Dakota, sued two manufacturers of blasting caps, Du Pont and Hercules. Two families claimed that the offending cap in their cases were from Hercules, and the third asserted that it was from Du Pont. They nevertheless sought to join together in a single suit against the two manufacturers.

The court held that plaintiffs did not properly present a joint liability claim. Although noting that "[a] plaintiff is not required to implead all joint tortfeasors as indispensable parties" and that "the courts will normally honor plaintiff's choice of theory," Judge Weinstein concluded that "there are limits on the plaintiff's choice. One consideration is that some remedies and theories pose substantially more difficult problems of administration than others." Finding that "the redundant naming of an additional manufacturer results from the happenstance of joinder of claims by unrelated plaintiffs," the judge dismissed each family's claims against the manufacturer not accused of producing the cap that injured that child.]

With each plaintiff now having claims only against the manufacturer of the injury-causing cap, defendants' motion for severance under Rule 20(a) of the Federal Rules of Civil Procedure must be granted. While evidence of joint action or responsibility may well be relevant in the claims against each manufacturer, proof of such responsibility will not be necessary for recovery on each plaintiff's claims. Recovery in each case will turn on the legal-factual questions of negligence and strict liability, and on evidence about the circumstances of the separate accidents. The claims by the three groups of plaintiffs present sufficiently diverse questions of law and fact to require severance. [Pursuant to 28 U.S.C. § 1404(a), the court transferred the North Dakota and Ohio families' suits to their home jurisdictions, where the incidents in suit occurred.]

NOTES AND QUESTIONS

1.   Compare Judge Weinstein's treatment of the joinder questions in *Chance* and *Hall*. In *Hall*, he refused to allow a joint liability theory and did not even allow the two families suing Hercules to join together. Yet in *Chance* he not only upheld the joint liability theory but also allowed all 13 families, from ten states, to join. Is this a consistent application of Rule 20? Although upholding the joinder in *Chance*, Judge Weinstein did indicate that only "the issues of joint activity" would be tried together and then "the questions which turn on the particular facts of each accident" would be transferred "to the federal districts in which the accidents occurred." How would this be accomplished since individual suits were not filed in the districts where the accidents occurred? And what is to be gained if each case has to be tried individually? Judge Weinstein leaves open the question whether this "would entail full separate trials of different issues, or special findings of fact in this court." How would the latter procedure work?

2.   *Choice of law*: Differences in applicable law have presented obstacles to combined treatment of cases through consolidation and also to certifying class actions. Although the law of products liability may have become more uniform under the influence of the Restatement of Torts (Second), there is still considerable diversity in state product liability laws, going to such matters as, for example, standards of liability, burden of proof, availability and scope of defenses, evidentiary requirements, instructions to the jury, and damages. Judge Weinstein's treatment of the problem in the above decision reflects an aggressive view of similarities.

Judge Weinstein deferred a final ruling on whether the Rule 20(a) requirement of a "common question of law" was met until briefs were received on the conflict of laws issue. After considering the issue, he determined that, under the *Erie* doctrine, New York choice-of-law would apply. New York has abandoned the traditional rule requiring that the law of the place of injury be applied; it applies a more flexible rule focusing on the selection of the law most intimately concerned with the outcome of each particular issue. Judge Weinstein determined that in each of these cases New York would apply the substantive law of the state where the accident occurred. For a more detailed discussion of the application of choice of law rules in the class action context to determine whether the forum state can apply its own law, rather than the laws of the states where injury occurred, contracts were breached, etc., see *infra* pp. 392–404.

Should the application of the law of different states automatically prevent joinder? The answer depends, in part, on how different the various state laws are. Minor differences might be dealt with in a joint trial by such techniques as admission of evidence for limited purposes, instructions to the jury clarifying the differences between the various claims and use of special issues. But as major differences in the laws increase, and more state laws are involved, the possibility of a fair and efficient joint trial wanes. See 371 F.Supp. 439 (S.D.N.Y. 1974) for Judge Weinstein's determination and reasoning.

These choice of law problems might be removed if state law were displaced by creation of a federal common law standard, but the federal courts have felt that they lacked authority to do so. See Georgene Vairo, Multi-Tort Cases: Cause for More Darkness on the Subject, or a New Role for Federal Common Law?, 54 Fordham L. Rev. 167 (1985) (arguing that "the best of Swift v. Tyson be resurrected" and that federal courts prescribe common law rules). Compare Jackson v. Johns-Manville Sales Corp., 750 F.2d 1314 (5th Cir. 1985) (refusing to adopt federal common law for asbestos cases).

Another solution would be federal legislation. Proposals for federal legislation on products liability have been made but not adopted. It has also been suggested that in transferred cases federal courts be authorized to select a single rule of law to facilitate combined treatment of the cases. See American Law Institute, Complex Litigation: Statutory Recommendations and Analysis § 6.01 (1994); Thomas Rowe & Kenneth Sibley, Beyond Diversity, Federal Multiparty, Multiforum Jurisdiction, 135 U. Pa. L. Rev. 7 (1986).

3.   *The causation problem*: The above cases illustrate recurrent problems in modern tort cases concerning proof of causation. In *Chance*, the plaintiffs cannot identify the specific maker of an allegedly injurious product. Besides the theories outlined by Judge Weinstein, the California Supreme Court, in Sindell v. Abbott Laboratories, 607 P.2d 924 (Cal. 1980), cert. denied 449 U.S. 912 (1982), adopted a *market share liability* theory as a variant of the alternative liability theory of Summers v. Tice. The case involved DES, a drug marketed by some 200 companies from the 1940s through the 1960s and often used by patients who did not know the identity of the manufacturer of their product. Absent proof of the identity of the manufacturer, plaintiff could sue defendants who had together manufactured a "substantial share" of the total DES, and the burden of proof would then shift to the defendants to exonerate themselves. If they failed, it later held, they would shoulder liability to the extent of their percentage share of the market. Brown v. Superior Court, 751 P.2d 470 (Cal. 1988); compare Rutherford v. Owens-Illinois, Inc., 941 P.2d 1203 (Cal. 1997) (refusing to apply *Sindell* in asbestos cases).

Consider the implications of use of this theory for joinder under Rule 20. It could provide a basis for satisfying the Rule 20(a) "same transaction or occurrence" requirement in order to join a number of defendants whose activities (such as manufacturing) have been independent of those of other defendants. It also allows a suit to be filed without joining all the possible defendants who might be responsible for the plaintiff's injuries. Note also that the requirement that manufacturers who together hold a "substantial share" of the market be joined operates as something like a substantive compulsory joinder provision.

4.   The *Sindell* majority also did not provide a definition of the relevant market from which the various defendants' market shares would be determined. Is the market national, regional, state, or local? This factor would significantly affect which defendants must be joined in order to represent a "substantial share."

5.   Is the traditional individualized tort process unsuited for resolving mass exposure cases? See David Rosenberg, The Causal Connection in Mass Exposure Cases: A "Public Law" Vision of the Tort System, 97 Harv. L. Rev. 851 (1984), proposing a "public law" adjudication model. This model applies a "proportionality rule" whereby liability would be imposed "in proportion to the probability of causation assigned to the excess disease risk in the exposed population" despite the absence of individualized proof of the causal connection. A "market share" standard might often satisfy this rule, although "when market share and risk contribution diverge, apportionment should accord with the firm's contribution to risk." Thus a manufacturer's share could be reduced if it took greater care to avoid the risk than did other manufacturers. Is this a workable approach? Should it make class actions mandatory as a prerequisite for use of this liability theory?

B. COMPULSORY PARTY JOINDER

ELDREDGE V. CARPENTERS 46 NORTHERN CALIFORNIA COUNTIES JATC

United States Court of Appeals, Ninth Circuit, 1981.
662 F.2d 534, *cert. denied*, 459 U.S. 917 (1982).

Before FLETCHER and NELSON, CIRCUIT JUDGES, and KEEP, DISTRICT JUDGE.

FLETCHER, CIRCUIT JUDGE.

Plaintiffs Eldredge and Mazur brought suit under Title VII, 42 U.S.C. § 2000e–2, against the Carpenters 46 Northern California Counties Joint Apprenticeship and Training Committee (JATC), alleging sex discrimination in the operation of JATC's apprenticeship program. Plaintiffs brought the suit as a class action, but the district court has not yet considered the question of class certification.

Defendant JATC is a joint labor-management committee established under an agreement that provides for a trust fund contributed to by the parties to the master collective bargaining agreements in the Northern

California construction industry. JATC is composed of equal numbers of labor and management representatives, and acts as a board of trustees for the administration of the Carpenters Apprenticeship and Training Trust Fund for Northern California. It is responsible for establishing, supporting, and maintaining programs to educate and train journeymen and apprentices in all classifications covered by any collective bargaining agreement that requires employer contributions to the trust fund.

Plaintiffs allege that the process by which JATC selects applicants to its apprenticeship training program discriminates against women. Although JATC has employed other selection procedures in the past, it presently relies on what is known as the "unrestricted hunting license" system. Under this system, an individual must first convince an employer to hire him or her as a beginning apprentice. JATC then places the individual's name on its applicant register. The applicant enters into an apprenticeship agreement with JATC and is dispatched through the union hiring hall. An individual needs no prior training to become an apprentice; all that is required is that he or she be 17 years of age and have a high school diploma or its equivalent.

The master collective bargaining agreements under which JATC operates require employers to hire one apprentice for every five journeymen employed. The apprenticeship is a four-year program. Employers are under no obligation to hire beginning as opposed to experienced apprentices. In May of 1976, only thirteen of JATC's 3220 registered apprentices were women.

The essence of plaintiffs' complaint is that, by relying on the unrestricted hunting license system to recruit apprentices, JATC has adopted an entrance requirement for its program which is known to have a discriminatory effect on women. Plaintiffs argue that JATC knows that individual employers do not hire women under the unrestricted hunting license system, and that JATC's use of this system is therefore illegal under Title VII. The district court assumed for the purposes of its rule 19 analysis that plaintiffs had stated a claim on which relief could be granted.

The district court held that the 4500 employers and 60 union locals covered by the master labor agreement, or adequate representatives of their interests, were indispensable to the litigation under the standards imposed by rule 19(b). It ordered them joined within 60 days. Plaintiffs were granted extensions of time in which to explore the possibilities for joinder, but joinder of all 4500 employers proved impossible. The plaintiffs then sought to join the Northern California Homebuilders' Conference (NCHBC) to represent the absent employers' interests.[3] The court held this inadequate and dismissed the case. We conclude that the employers are not

---

[3] The NCHBC is a large employers' organization which negotiated the master labor agreement under which JATC operates. Not all of the employers who subscribe to the master agreement belong to the NCHBC.

necessary parties under rule 19(a) and thus cannot be indispensable parties under rule 19(b). We reverse.

Rule 19 requires two separate inquiries. First, are there persons who should be joined, either because their own interests or the interests of the parties might be harmed by their absence? Such persons, referred to as "necessary parties," must be joined if feasible. Fed.R.Civ.P. 19(a). Second, if parties determined to be necessary under rule 19(a) cannot be joined, should the action in "equity and good conscience" be dismissed? Only if the court determines that the action should be dismissed is the absent party labeled "indispensable." Fed.R.Civ.P. 19(b).

The nature of the rule 19 inquiry is described at some length in *Provident Tradesmens Bank & Trust Co. v. Patterson*, 390 U.S. 102 (1968). The inquiry should focus on the practical effects of joinder and nonjoinder. Rule 19 was revised in 1966 to emphasize its practical focus and to avoid the inflexible approach taken by many courts under the prior version of the rule.

Rule 19(a) describes two categories of persons who should be joined if feasible. If the absent employers fall into either of these two categories, they are "necessary parties."

The first category comprises those persons in whose absence "complete relief cannot be accorded among those already parties." Fed.R.Civ.P. 19(a)(1). This portion of the rule is concerned only with "relief as between the persons already parties, not as between a party and the absent person whose joinder is sought." The district court concluded that the absent employers could frustrate any relief granted against JATC, and that complete relief would therefore not be possible unless the employers were made parties. The court reasoned that the employers could defeat any order against JATC by refusing to hire any apprentices, by hiring only unregistered, nonunion apprentices, or by rejecting all female apprentices dispatched to them. We believe that the district court misapprehended the legal inquiry required by rule 19(a)(1).

If JATC's activities violate Title VII, a question not yet decided, then the court has both the power and the duty to enjoin those activities. The possibility that such an injunction may induce employers to avoid JATC's services, or ultimately to disband the training and referral system altogether, should not defeat the present action against JATC. JATC may not avoid its own liability for practices illegal under Title VII by relying on the employers' possible future conduct that might frustrate the remedial purposes of any court-ordered changes in the apprenticeship program. See, e.g., United States v. Sheet Metal Workers, Local 36, 416 F.2d 123, 132 & n. 16 (8th Cir. 1969) (enjoining union from continuing discriminatory referral practices, even though those practices were required by collective bargaining agreement with absent employers).

The district court appears to assume that the employers would discriminate against women because of their sex, and that they would refuse to hire women training in the apprentice program. There is no evidence to this effect in the record. On the contrary, the employers have previously participated, apparently successfully, in a state-mandated affirmative action program designed to increase the number of minority apprentices.

While it might be desirable to join all 4500 employers in order to eradicate sex discrimination in the industry, we conclude that relief on plaintiffs' claims against JATC as an entity could be afforded by an injunction against JATC alone. Both sides agree that JATC has the power under the trust fund agreement to structure its apprenticeship program in any way it sees fit. It is quite possible that a court-ordered restructuring of the program could effectively increase the participation of women in the apprenticeship program.

The second inquiry required by rule 19(a) concerns prejudice, either to the absent persons or to those already parties. Rule 19(a)[(1)(B)] provides that a person should be joined if he claims an interest relating to the subject of the action, and the disposition of the action may "as a practical matter impair or impede [the person's] ability to protect that interest."

The district court held that the employers should be joined since they have a right to select their own employees, a substantial interest that they have a right to protect. We disagree. The trust fund agreement grants full authority to JATC to structure the apprenticeship program and to select the apprentices. We conclude that the employers have by contract ceded to JATC whatever legally protectable interest they may have had in selecting apprentices to be trained. On the other hand, without the joinder of the employers, any court order that may be entered to enjoin JATC to institute programs cannot go beyond the authority granted JATC under the trust fund agreement. The absent employers are thus assured that an injunction against JATC will not trench on any rights reserved to the employers under the agreement. We must conclude that the employers' ability to protect whatever interest in employee selection they retain will not be "impaired or impeded" if they are not made parties. They are therefore not necessary parties under rule 19(a)[(1)(B)].

The district court was understandably concerned that the absent employers might have interests that would be unrepresented in the present suit. Although we have concluded that their interests are not the sort that would make the employers necessary under rule 19, on remand it is possible that some employers, or the NCHBC, may move to intervene. The district court may then consider whether to permit intervention under Fed.R.Civ.P. 24.

NOTES AND QUESTIONS

1.   The lower court in *Eldredge* relied heavily on the fact that the individual employers could frustrate the relief ordered against the JATC by refusing to hire women who were referred to them. It thus concluded that "the relief obtained in this lawsuit would serve only to swell the ranks of unemployed apprentices. This surely cannot be the 'complete relief' contemplated by Rule 19(a)." 440 F.Supp. at 520. Is this a proper consideration under Rule 19(a)? Who should be entitled to determine whether the relief available where certain persons are not made parties is satisfactory—the plaintiff or the judge?

Ten years after this decision, things had not changed much for the better. Although federal and state officials had set goals of 20% women in the construction trades in 1978, in 1991 it was reported that women constituted only 2% of the work force, and that the figure had remained virtually unchanged since 1983. Apprenticeship programs, in particular, were criticized as inadequate. See Katherine Bishop, Scant Success for California Efforts to Put Women in Construction Trades, N.Y. Times, Feb. 14, 1991 at A16 col. 1. Thereafter, women slipped below even the 2% figure. See Hard Times for Women in Construction, N.Y. Times, Sept. 27, 1992, at B2.

2.   Consider Justice Rehnquist's opinion, dissenting from the Supreme Court's denial of certiorari in *Eldredge,* 459 U.S. at 921–22:

> Although the Court of Appeals thought there was "no evidence" that "employers would refuse to hire women admitted to the apprentice program pursuant to any judgment that may be entered against JATC," the substance of respondents' complaint is that *employers* discriminate against women. The District Court correctly perceived the dilemma it and respondents faced. If it ordered relief against the JATC alone, it could not affect the alleged discriminatory practices. Rule 19(a)(1). If it ordered relief against the employers, it would almost certainly affect their right to select apprentices without affording them an opportunity to rebut the charge that they discriminate. Rule 19(a)(2)(i).
>
> The Court of Appeals sought to avoid the force of this argument by claiming that because the agreement that created JATC grants it "full authority to structure the apprenticeship program and to select the apprentices; the employers have by contract ceded to JATC whatever legally protectable interest they may have had in selecting apprentices to be trained." This is simply not correct. The agreement gives JATC authority only to select persons to refer to employers; an applicant does not become an apprentice and begin the training program until and unless an employer hires him. And, as noted above, employers have bargained to retain their right to reject any applicant for any reason. Yet the Court of Appeals rather cavalierly found, in a proceeding to which the employers were not parties, that the employers have ceded these rights.

The impropriety of the Court of Appeals' ruling is demonstrated by General Building Contractors Association, Inc. v. Pennsylvania, 458 U.S. 375 (1982), in which we considered a similar apprenticeship system. We held that a district court cannot issue an injunction against employers in an employment discrimination case under 42 U.S.C.A. § 1981 when the employers are not guilty of intentional discrimination. In that case there apparently was no hunting license system, and the discrimination was caused by the JATC and the union, but the bar to an injunction was the same as the bar that will face the District Court on remand in this case: it is improper for a court to act against a person who has not been found to have violated the law.

The Court of Appeals, as if recognizing the unsatisfactory posture of the litigation for providing meaningful adjudication and relief, commented that "on remand it is possible that some employers may move to intervene." But to secure full participation only by torturing the meaning of Rule 19 to avoid dismissal, in the hopes that the absent parties will then take it upon themselves to protect their interests, is not an appealing basis for the result reached by the Court of Appeals. It is respondents who have sought to affect the hiring practices of some 4500 employers; it is respondents, and not the absent employers, who should shoulder the responsibility of joining the necessarily affected employers or suffering dismissal of their lawsuit.

* * * Since courts will not, I am confident, begin issuing injunctions against non-parties, the approach of the Court of Appeals will tend to reduce the district courts to issuers of " 'paper' decrees which neither adjudicate nor, in the end, protect rights."

3. Is the central problem in *Eldredge* substantive or procedural? On remand in *Eldredge,* the trial court certified a plaintiff class of women applicants. Then, on cross motions for summary judgment, it entered judgment for defendant on the ground that plaintiffs were trying to hold it liable for discriminatory acts of third parties. The appellate court reversed in Eldredge v. Carpenters 46 Northern California Counties JATC, 833 F.2d 1334 (9th Cir. 1987), cert. denied 487 U.S. 1210 (1988), and directed entry of summary judgment for plaintiffs. It reasoned that, as a matter of substantive anti-discrimination law, a showing that a practice excluded a protected class in disproportionate numbers shifted the burden to the defendant to justify the practice. "The JATC does not contend that some factor other than the 'hunting license' system accounts for women's lower admission rate into its program. It cannot avoid liability for the effects of its own admission procedures by pointing to the discriminatory practices of those to whom it has delegated the power to select apprentices."

The district court had reasoned that the JATC stood in the same position as an employment agency, but the appellate court rejected that argument (id. at 1337):

The JATC, however, does not stand in the same position as an employment agency. It is not simply an intermediary between applicant and employer. Rather, it is the JATC that possesses the full authority to select the carpentry apprentices for Northern California. The district court failed to recognize that the employers were merely delegates of the JATC's power to determine which applicants will be admitted into the program. Because the JATC may, under the trust agreement, select apprentices in any way it deems appropriate, it violates Title VII if it used procedures that unjustifiably discriminate against a class of people protected under Title VII.

On further remand, the district court accepted the JATC's proposal to retain the first-job requirement and the hunting license for men and allow women admission to the program's educational aspects without satisfying the first-job requirement. The Court of Appeals reversed again, noting that the JATC had "waged a relentless battle to preserve the status quo" of the hunting license. Eldredge v. Carpenters 46 Northern California Counties JATC, 94 F.3d 1366, 1371 (9th Cir. 1996). The appellate court ordered the district judge to adopt a remedy eliminating the hunting license system and requiring that all job applicants be hired from a numerical referral list maintained by the JATC. In addition, it directed that the remedy include a 20% affirmative action program and that the court appoint a monitor of the JATC's compliance. It also directed the district court to consider the plaintiffs' request that all apprentices be instructed regarding workplace harassment. Reconsider the employment discrimination issues after reading Wal-Mart Stores, Inc. v. Dukes, *infra* p. 200.

4.   Contrast Shimkus v. Gersten Companies, 816 F.2d 1318 (9th Cir. 1987). Plaintiffs there demonstrated that defendant, which operated apartment houses, had discriminated against African Americans. The district court ordered that blacks receive preference in allocation of apartments in the future. The court of appeals held that this order was an abuse of discretion because the trial court did not order joinder of non-black minorities against whom the property management firm also discriminated (id. at 1332):

> Under Rule 19(a)[(1)(B)], these non-black minorities clearly have an interest related to the subject of this action: remedying housing discrimination in Gersten apartments. The disposition of this action without their joinder clearly impairs and impedes their ability to protect that interest. The *Shimkus* decree not only imposes an unfair burden on those minority persons but would require them to bring another federal action seeking [a] consent decree to avoid those burdens. * * * It would be ironic if a decree to remedy discrimination effectively pitted one minority group against another.

Similar issues may arise in employment discrimination litigation. For example, would a change in apprenticeship patterns have a practical impact on the interests of prospective male apprentices? See Martin v. Wilks, *infra* p. 69, suggesting that white males are necessary parties in employment discrimination litigation that results in an affirmative action decree which reduces their chances for promotion. How can a court fashion a remedy without raising at least some risk that it will pit one minority group against another? Are necessary party rules the way to address this problem? See Comment, Compulsory Joinder of Classes, 58 U.Chi.L.Rev. 1453 (1991) (arguing that classes be considered necessary parties).

5.   A nonparty is necessary if it has an interest relating to the subject of the action and disposition of the action in its absence may "as a practical matter impair or impede the person's ability to protect that interest." The term "as a practical matter" is used to indicate that even if a person would not be bound by a judgment in the case under claim preclusion (res judicata), it may still be a necessary party if its ability to protect its interest is impaired. See discussion in Chapter 9 regarding the requirement that, to be bound by a judgment, one must be a party or in privity with a party. In some instances, an equitable decree can have a practical impact on a nonparty because it changes the status quo. For example, in Ford Motor Co. v. Bisanz Brothers, Inc., 249 F.2d 22 (8th Cir. 1957), Ford, a nonparty, was found to be affected as a practical matter by a suit brought by adjoining property owners to enjoin the defendant railroad from using a spur line to the Ford plant since judgment for the plaintiffs could have resulted in Ford's loss of the railroad's services.

The "as a practical matter" standard is also applied to intervention of right under Rule 24(a) ("the applicant is so situated that the disposition of the action may as a practical matter impair or impede the applicant's ability to protect that interest"). Determining the practical effect of a potential judgment is a problem that can arise in environmental cases. In Conner v. Burford, 836 F.2d 1521 (9th Cir. 1988), a public interest organization sued the U.S. Forest Service and Fish and Wildlife Service alleging that defendants had issued oil and gas leases on national forest lands without an impact statement as required by the Endangered Species Act and National Environmental Policy Act. Some of the 700 lessees attempted to intervene and filed motions to vacate the lower court's judgment on the ground that they were indispensable parties. The court of appeals found them not to be indispensable because the lower court only enjoined government actions in approving surface-disturbing activity. It reasoned that the lessees were free to assert whatever claims they might have against the government, and if the government complied with the acts, their leases could take effect. Isn't this a classic example of a situation where the missing parties' interests are, as a practical matter, impeded or impaired?

One explanation for indifference to such problems is that the courts take a less-demanding attitude toward compliance with Rule 19 requirements in cases involving "public" rights seemingly on the theory that a "public interest litigant" must have a forum in which to contest governmental activity and vindicate public rights even though some nonparties might be affected as a result. For an argument that there should be no absolute exception to Rule 19 for cases involving "public" rights, and that some mechanism such as participation by representatives of nonparties should be used, see Carl Tobias, Rule 19 and the Public Rights Exception to Party Joinder, 65 N.C.L.Rev. 745 (1987).

6. Rule 20 is designed in part to foster efficiency in litigation by permitting joinder of all interested parties in a single case. Should Rule 19(a) similarly be read broadly to promote combined resolution of related claims? Professor Freer has argued that the rule should be revised to pressure plaintiffs to join all parties in one proceeding: "A plaintiff is entitled to due process, but has no right to sole possession of center stage; we need to tell the prima donna of the legal world that she must work with some co-stars. This can be done by expanding the federal court's power to order joinder for the express purpose of avoiding duplicative litigation." Richard Freer, Avoiding Duplicative Litigation: Rethinking Plaintiff Autonomy and the Court's Role in Defining the Litigative Unit, 50 U. Pitt. L. Rev. 809, 813 (1989).

In Temple v. Synthes Corp., Ltd., 498 U.S. 5 (1990) (per curiam), plaintiff filed a federal court products liability action against the manufacturer of a medical device that had been inserted into his spine. Because he was simultaneously pursuing state-court claims for malpractice against the doctor and hospital involved in the insertion of the device, defendant moved to dismiss for failure to join them in the federal court action, and the district court dismissed in the interest of judicial economy because the doctor and hospital could not be joined without destroying diversity of citizenship.

The Supreme Court reversed because "it is not necessary for all joint tortfeasors to be named as defendants in a single lawsuit." Its earlier decision in Provident Tradesmens Bank & Trust Co. v. Patterson, 390 U.S. 102 (1968), did mention that one focus of Rule 19 was "the interest of the courts and the public in complete, consistent, and efficient settlement of controversies," The Court explained that this consideration only came into play under Rule 19(b), dealing with the court's decision whether to dismiss when necessary parties could not be joined, and that the consideration had no bearing on whether nonparties were necessary within the meaning of Rule 19(a). Is this a sensible result in light of the fact that plaintiff had initiated parallel state-court proceedings against the hospital and doctor? Keep these issues in mind when we turn to duplicative litigation in Chapter 3.

The Rule 19(b) Determination

Rule 19(a) provides an analysis for determining whether an absentee is a person to be joined "if feasible." Courts and lawyers sometimes still use the old term "necessary party" (from the pre-1966 rule) to describe such a person although the current rule does not use that term. Under Rule 19(a), as restyled in 2007, "a person who is subject to service of process and whose joinder will not deprive the court of subject-matter jurisdiction must be joined" if the criteria set out there are met. Joinder is not always possible, as when the absentee comes from the same state as an opposing party and its joinder would destroy diversity jurisdiction, the absentee has insufficient contacts with the forum to permit personal jurisdiction, or venue would be improper. If the absentee cannot be joined, then Rule 19(b) requires an analysis of four factors to determine whether "in equity and good conscience, the action should proceed among the existing parties or should be dismissed." Before the 2007 restyling of the rule, it was said that if the dismissal was mandated, the absentee would be regarded as "indispensable."

Although the overall "equity and good conscience" orientation of Rule 19(b) is more flexible than Rule 19(a), the rule also provides four factors for making this determination, in part calling for scrutiny of matters very similar to those raised in Rule 19(a). The court is to assess the extent of the threatened prejudice should the case proceed and, rather than indulging theoretical possibilities, to determine whether actual prejudicial consequences are likely to befall either present or absent parties. In considering the adequacy of the judgment that would result, the Supreme Court has said that the court should refer to "the public stake in settling disputes by whole, whenever possible." Provident Tradesmens Bank & Trust Co. v. Patterson, 390 U.S. 102 (1968). Finally, the court is not to dismiss without reflecting on whether plaintiff would have an adequate remedy in the event of dismissal.

The first factor—"the extent to which the judgment rendered in the person's absence might be prejudicial to the person or those already parties"—overlaps with the analysis already made in Rule 19(a). However, while Rule 19(a) analysis asked whether the prejudice could arise from the person's absence, the Rule 19(b) analysis focuses on the extent of the prejudice that will occur now that joinder is not possible. Insufficient prejudice may be found if the absentee's interests are in fact represented by a party. Heckman v. United States, 224 U.S. 413 (1912). Where the interests of the absentee and a party are mutually exclusive (for example, rival claimants to a trust), prejudice is likely unless it can be shown to be mitigated under the circumstances. The absentee's ability to intervene may be considered in assessing the extent of prejudice to it. Burger King v. American Nat'l Bank & Trust Co., 119 F.R.D. 672, 678 (N.D.Ill. 1988).

The second factor—"the extent to which, by protective provisions in the judgment, by the shaping of relief, or other measures, the prejudice can be lessened or avoided"—requires a creative look at whether the judgment can be tailored to limit the prejudicial effect on a party. In Provident Tradesmens Bank & Trust Co. v. Patterson, 390 U.S. 102 (1968), the Supreme Court, in reversing a finding of indispensability, noted that payment to parties might have been withheld pending other suits and that the plaintiffs might have been willing to limit the amount of their claims. Prejudice might be reduced by "granting damages but not injunctive relief, delaying relief until litigation elsewhere runs its course, writing a narrowly drawn opinion that makes clear what issues are not being decided, inviting absent parties to intervene, and joining parties likely to protect the interest of the absent party." Fleming James, Geoffrey Hazard & John Leubsdorf, Civil Procedure 619 (5th ed. 2001).

The third factor—"whether a judgment rendered in the person's absence will be adequate"—requires an inquiry into whether a truncated suit without the absentee can be adequate for the existing parties. This factor overlaps with the "complete relief" criterion in Rule 19(a). The existing parties are likely to claim that a judgment is adequate since they structured the suit in that way (possibly because joinder of the absentee would have been fatal to the suit jurisdictionally). But it is for the court to decide whether piecemeal justice is adequate enough to warrant the expenditure of both party and judicial resources. See, e.g., Andreasen v. Progressive Express Ins. Co., 276 F. Supp. 3d 1317 (S.D.Fla. 2017) (denying motion to join additional defendant who would destroy complete diversity even though plaintiff might incur costs from suing that party in a separate lawsuit).

The last factor—"whether the plaintiff will have an adequate remedy if the action is dismissed"—requires an examination of whether there are other courts in which the suit can be brought with all the parties joined. In cases in which plaintiffs can proceed against all interested parties in state court, there are strong arguments for dismissing after review of the Rule 19(b) factors even though plaintiff would prefer to be in federal court. See, e.g., Pulitzer-Polster v. Pulitzer, 784 F.2d 1305 (5th Cir. 1986) (dismissing federal court suit where plaintiff already had suit against same defendant pending in state court even though plaintiff objected to delays in state-court suit). Because the availability of an adequate remedy in another court can often obviate the prejudice (although the plaintiff may thereby be denied its preferred choice of forum), this factor is sometimes said to be the most influential of the four if there is no alternative forum.

NOTES AND QUESTIONS

1.   The Rule 19(b) factors require a case-by-case determination of indispensability. Under the pre-1966 rule analysis, courts sometimes said that certain categories of absentees were not indispensable. The labels should not be determinative under the current Rule 19(b) analysis, but some courts still proclaim that, for example, joint tortfeasors, co-obligors, or potential indemnitors are not indispensable. Consider other categories of absent parties: seller of a product in a suit against the manufacturer, Spiller v. Tennessee Trailers, Inc., 97 F.R.D. 347 (N.D.Ga. 1982); limited partners, Schmidt v. E.N. Maisel & Associates, 105 F.R.D. 157 (N.D.Ill. 1985); nonparty to a commercial contract, Northrop Corp. v. McDonnell Douglas Corp., 705 F.2d 1030 (9th Cir. 1983).

2.   How should the Rule 19(b) analysis have been done in *Eldredge* had it been concluded that the employers or unions were necessary parties to be joined under Rule 19(a)? To begin with, since there would be no jurisdictional obstacle to joining them could the court still decline to insist on their joinder? The district court in *Eldredge* analyzed the problem as follows:

Although there is no procedural bar to joinder of the absent parties, the affected employers number 4500, and more than 60 local unions appear to be involved. Plaintiffs have represented that joinder is feasible without explaining how they intend to proceed in light of these numbers. The only alternatives appear to be certification of defendant classes or joinder of contractor associations in lieu of individual employer members, and District Councils, the Carpenters 46 Northern Counties Conference Board, or the International itself in lieu of union locals. That either of these alternatives can provide a feasible and adequate solution to the problems [that justify treating the nonparties as necessary under Rule 19(a)] is open to serious question. The former would raise a host of questions under Rule 23, while the latter would raise further questions under Rule 19 as to whether individual employers and union locals remain indispensable parties despite the joinder of their representatives. * * *

If joinder cannot be accomplished, the [factors that make the nonparties necessary under Rule 19(a)] will require that the action be dismissed pursuant to Rule 19(b). Any relief directed to the JATC alone would create a substantial possibility of prejudice to both employers and unions, as well as to the JATC itself. No form of decree or protective provisions sufficient to avoid or reduce this prejudice has been suggested, and the Court is aware of none. Most significantly, there is no evidence that a judgment rendered in the absence of these parties would have any significant effect on the evil complained of in this action. Plaintiffs' alternative remedy is, unfortunately, burdensome and expensive: to pursue in individual lawsuits those employers alleged to have discriminated. However, the Court cannot on this ground alone countenance any further expenditure of judicial resources in an action so unlikely to lead to effective relief.

440 F.Supp. at 526–27. Justice Rehnquist expressed agreement with this Rule 19(b) analysis. See 459 U.S. at 922.

3.   In Republic of Philippines v. Pimentel, 553 U.S. 851 (2008), the Court dealt with the application of Rule 19(b). The case arose out of the tangled litigation morass following the presidency of Ferdinand Marcos in the Philippines. The immediate action was an interpleader suit brought by Merrill Lynch to determine ownership of a Merrill Lynch account worth $35 million that was opened by a company created by Marcos. The interpleader action was filed at the urging of the district judge who had been presiding over a class action brought by victims of Marcos against the Marcos estate, which resulted in a judgment for nearly $2 billion against the estate. The class plaintiffs wanted to execute against the Merrill Lynch account, and the judge prodded Merrill Lynch into filing the interpleader action to determine whether it could do so.

The problem was that the Republic of the Philippines and a Commission it had established after Marcos fled the country to reclaim looted assets both asserted that the Merrill Lynch account assets were looted property of the Republic that, under Philippine law, belonged to it. These claims had been the subject of proceedings in a court in the Philippines since 1991. So the Republic and the Commission were—as all conceded—Rule 19(a) required parties. But they could not be joined over their objections because they were protected by sovereign immunity. Hence the question presented was whether dismissal was warranted under Rule 19(b). The Ninth Circuit ruled that dismissal was not required because the nonparties' claims—although not frivolous—would almost certainly be barred under the New York statute of limitations, and therefore constituted unimportant considerations in comparison to the interests of the class action plaintiffs in enforcing their judgment.

The Supreme Court held that this was wrong, placing great emphasis on Rule 19(b)(1) and the nature and importance of sovereign immunity protections. It observed that the restyled rule avoids the term "indispensable" party because it had "an unforgiving connotation that did not fit easily with a system that permits actions to proceed even when some persons who otherwise should be parties to the action cannot be joined." It also noted that "the considerations set forth in subdivision (b) are nonexclusive," emphasizing further that the rule is "based on equitable considerations." Applying Rule 19(b)(1) to this case, however, required that the interpleader action be dismissed. The lower courts' discounting of the absent parties' claims implicated the very concerns that the sovereign immunity doctrine was designed to protect against—the determination of the validity of claims by or against such entities in our courts. The Court recognized that "Rule 19 cannot be applied in a vacuum, and it may require some preliminary assessment of the merits of certain claims." Thus, if those claims are frivolous, the court could disregard them. But in this instance the absent parties' claims were not frivolous, and the lower courts failed to "accord proper weight to the compelling claim of sovereign immunity." "Dismissal under Rule 19(b) will mean, in some instances, that plaintiffs will be left without a forum for definitive resolution of their claims. But that result is contemplated under the doctrine of foreign sovereign immunity."

4.   The last factor—whether the plaintiff will have an adequate remedy if the action is dismissed—often requires a determination of whether the action could be brought in another American court where the missing party can be joined in compliance with subject matter jurisdiction, personal jurisdiction, and venue requirements. When the only other adequate forum would be in a foreign country, considerations akin to dismissal for *forum non conveniens* come into play. See Piper Aircraft Co. v. Reyno, 454 U.S. 235 (1981) (Scotland found to be an adequate forum, even though it did not recognize strict liability). In performing the adequacy calculus under *forum non conveniens,* "the defendant faces a rather low bar for establishing that the alternative forum is adequate. Courts have concluded, for example, that an alternative forum is adequate so long as the plaintiff will not be deprived of all remedies or subjected to unfair treatment there. A mere decrease in the amount potentially recoverable, or the lack of contingent fee arrangements or of a right to jury trial, or the loss of various other procedural advantages—such as the

alternative forum's restrictions on the scope or nature of discovery or other aggregation procedures—normally will not prevent dismissal. Likewise, general accusations of corruption, delay, or other problems with the alternative forum's judicial system normally will not suffice, because federal courts appear reluctant to look closely at the quality of justice or competence of judicial personnel in the alternative forum." 14D Charles Alan Wright, Arthur R. Miller & Edward H. Cooper, Federal Practice & Procedure § 3828.3 at (4th ed. 2020).

C. INTERVENTION

Intervention provides a means for an outsider who has an interest in a lawsuit to voluntarily join the suit as a party. Joinder of required parties under Rule 19, as has been discussed, provides one means of bringing in parties who have sufficient interest in the suit. A class action under Rule 23, as will be discussed in Chapter 5, provides another means of ensuring representation of persons who are not named parties and yet who have interests in the suit. Rule 24 intervention provides a third means of making someone with an interest a party, and it is the principal means for an excluded person or entity to force its way into the suit. In recent years, intervention has especially become a means by which organizations or groups with particular interests in a piece of litigation seek to participate directly as parties.

ANIMAL PROTECTION INSTITUTE V. MERRIAM
United States District Court, District of Minnesota, 2006.
242 F.R.D. 524.

ERICKSON, CHIEF UNITED STATES MAGISTRATE JUDGE.

This action arises from a Complaint, which was filed by the Animal Protection Institute ("API"), against Gene Merriam ("Merriam"), in his official capacity as the Commissioner of the Minnesota Department of Natural Resources ("DNR"), over the DNR's alleged violation of Section 9 of the Endangered Species Act, Title 16 U.S.C. § 1538 ("ESA"). The Plaintiff alleges that the DNR's authorization of certain trapping, and snaring activities, has caused the illegal taking of federally-protected Canada Lynx, Bald Eagles, and Gray Wolves, and therefore, the Plaintiff seeks declaratory and injunctive relief.

The Defendant consents to the Trappers Association's Motion to Intervene in this action, while the API opposes intervention, although it does not object to the participation of the Trappers Association as Amici Curiae.

Although Rule 24(a) does not address standing, our Court of Appeals has held that a party must have Article III standing in order to intervene as a matter of right. The test for standing requires that the litigant have suffered an injury in fact, be able to establish a causal relationship between the contested conduct and the alleged injury, and show that the injury would be redressed by a favorable decision. The law recognizes economic, non-economic, and indirect economic injuries, for standing purposes. In its pleadings, the Trappers Association has alleged direct and indirect economic injuries, in the form of decreased income from trapping for its members, and the additional expense of replacing traps and snares that are barred by injunction, as well as non-economic injuries in the form of decreased recreational trapping opportunities. We find these interests, both economic and non-economic, to establish the Trappers Association's standing to seek intervention.

The Parties do not dispute that the Motion to Intervene was timely, but disagree about the Trappers Association's other qualifications to intervene as a matter of right. A proposed intervenor must show that it has a significant protected interest in the subject matter of the litigation, which has been interpreted to be an interest that is "direct, substantial, and legally protectable." The interest test should be construed broadly, so as to include as many parties as practicable and, although the intervenor cannot rely on an interest that is "wholly remote and speculative," the interest may be contingent on the outcome of litigation. A party seeking to intervene need not establish that its interests will actually be impaired, but only that its ability to protect its interest will be impaired if it is denied permission to intervene.

The API contends that the sole issue at stake is the government's compliance with the ESA, and that, therefore, the Trappers Association, as a private entity, does not have a recognized interest in this litigation. We find that the ESA cases, which have been cited by the API, and in which intervention has been denied, are distinguishable. In Silver v. Babbitt, 166 F.R.D. 418, 426 (D.Ariz. 1994), the underlying issue was the failure of a Federal agency to comply with a statutory duty to designate critical habitat, and the Motion of the would-be intervenors, whose land could be affected by the agency's future designation, was found to be premature. Similarly, in Southwest Center for Biological Diversity v. United States Forest Service, 82 F.Supp.2d 1070, 1074 (D.Ariz. 2000), intervention was found to be inappropriate where the heart of the action was whether the United States Forest Service had complied with its duty in issuing certain grazing permits, and no entity, other than the government, had "a stronger incentive or greater informational ability to challenge th[at] claim."

In contrast, Courts in this Circuit have found that a party has satisfied its minimal burden of demonstrating a significant interest, when it has a long-standing stake in the subject of litigation, or when the party can show general recreational or aesthetic interests. A significant interest can also be shown when the outcome of the case has a potential impact on the intervenor's commercial or financial well-being. See South Dakota v.

Ubbelohde, 330 F.3d 1014, 1025 (8th Cir. 2003) (finding downstream parties had substantial interest in outcome of litigation that could result in decreased river water flows); but cf., Eischeid v. Dover Construction, Inc., 217 F.R.D. 448, 468 (N.D. Iowa 2003) (proposed intervenor "must show more than a mere economic interest"). Here, success by the API could immediately and significantly impair the established and substantial commercial, financial, and recreational interests, that the members of the Trappers Association hold in trapping and snaring non-protected wildlife in Minnesota, and therefore, the Association has shown a substantial interest in this litigation.

The second element of the Rule 24(a) test is closely related to the first, and requires a determination that the Trappers Association's interest could be impaired by the disposition of this case. The remedy sought by the API includes an injunction compelling the State of Minnesota to prohibit trapping, or to modify trapping regulations, in order to prevent the unintentional "taking" of the protected species in question. If the API prevails, then changes in regulations could substantially impair the ability of the Trappers Association members to trap and snare non-protected game, and resultantly, this element has also been satisfied.

Typically, a party seeking intervention faces only a "minimal burden" of showing the third element for intervention of right—namely, that its interests are not adequately represented by the parties. The adequacy of representation is determined by comparing the interests of the proposed intervenor with interests of the current parties to the action, and intervention is appropriate if the interests are disparate, even if they share the same legal goal.

The exception to this minimal burden standard is if the State, or an officer charged by law with representing the interest of the proposed intervenor, is a party in the case, which raises a rebuttable presumption of adequate representation. Our Court of Appeals has addressed this *parens patriae* doctrine, in assessing the final element of the Rule 24(a) test, and has determined that it does not apply in cases in which the government is a party, but a proposed intervenor's concern is not a matter of "sovereign interest," such as when the would-be intervenor's interests are more narrowly defined than are those of the State. See Mausolf v. Babbitt, 85 F.3d 1295, 1303 (8th Cir. 1996).

Here, the DNR's interest, in regulating trapping in Minnesota, is considerably broader than the interest of the Trappers Association, who simply seek to participate in currently lawful practices for trapping and snaring non-protected wildlife. The State has no particular interest in preserving the rights of trappers to continue in those practices, or to ensure that the equipment, which is now lawfully employed by the Association's members, will remain available in the future. In addition, as the Trappers Association argued at the Hearing, the Defendant is under no obligation to refrain from agreeing to a settlement, or to the imposition of injunctive relief, that would satisfy the API, but would severely prejudice the interests of the Association's membership. To insure that its interests are represented and protected in this action, we find that the Trappers Association should be allowed to intervene as a matter of right.

We note that we do not agree with API's argument that, if we allow the Trappers Association to intervene, its participation should be limited to the remedial stage. Although limited intervention is one option that a Court can consider when weighing a Rule 24(a) Motion, that is an appropriate solution only when the rights that the proposed intervenors seek to protect are not affected by the litigation portion of the Trial. The substantial interest that the Trappers Association alleges is the ability to continue to trap and snare non-protected species in Minnesota, and one possible outcome of the liability stage of this action could result in the Defendant agreeing to impose limitations on those activities, or ban them outright. To permit the Trappers Association to participate in this action only at the remedial stage could prejudicially deprive it of an opportunity to address the need for any changes in trapping or snaring.

Moreover, because many members of the Trappers Association engage in trapping and snaring for their livelihood, the Association is in a unique position to contribute factually to this action, which would not be possible if its participation as an intervenor were limited to the remedial stage. The information they propose to offer could well lead to a more informed appraisal of all competing interests.

Lastly, we note that, although we have found the Trappers Association is entitled to intervene as a matter of right, in the alternative, we also conclude that they are entitled to permissive intervention, see, Rule 24(a)(2), Federal Rules of Civil Procedure, as there appears to be little prospect that their participation would give rise to undue delay, or would prejudice the adjudication of the parties' rights, see South Dakota v. United States Department of Interior, 317 F.3d 783, 787 (8th Cir. 2003) (grant of permissive intervention is discretionary). Furthermore, failing to allow the Trappers Association to intervene, either as of right or permissively, would significantly increase the difficulty the Association would have in seeking an appeal of a decision that might satisfy both of the named Parties, but be detrimental to the Trappers Association's interests. See Stringfellow v. Concerned Neighbors in Action, 480 U.S. 370, 375–76 (1987) ("An intervenor, whether by right or permission, normally has the right to appeal an adverse final judgment by a trial court."). Accordingly, we grant the Association's Motion to Intervene.

NOTES AND QUESTIONS

1. *Comparison of Rule 24 intervention with required party practice under Rule 19.* Rule 24(a)(2) and Rule 19(a)(1)(B) speak in very similar terms

of the nonparty's interest, suggesting that they should be applied in the same way. Would that make sense? Consider whether a court may forgo addition of required parties on the ground that they are adequately represented by current parties to the case. In Smuck v. Hobson, 408 F.2d 175 (D.C.Cir. 1969), the court noted this similarity between the two rules and observed that "the fact that the two rules are entwined does not imply that an 'interest' for the purpose of one is precisely the same as for the other. The occasions upon which a petitioner should be allowed to intervene under Rule 24 are not necessarily limited to those situations when the trial court should compel him to become a party under Rule 19." Id. at 178. We will examine the "interest" requirement of Rule 24(a) in note 3 below.

2. *Standing for intervention.* To intervene "of right," one might be required to demonstrate standing, an inquiry that has been subject to considerable development with regard to whether plaintiffs may pursue claims they assert in court. You probably have encountered it in other classes. The standing requirement is designed to satisfy the Article III limitation of judicial power to "cases and controversies," and courts have asked whether plaintiffs suffered an "injury in fact" and whether the legal rule invoked was designed to protect the interest they asserted. The Supreme Court has not fully resolved this question. In Diamond v. Charles, 476 U.S. 54 (1986), it held that an anti-abortion intervenor lacked standing to appeal a Court of Appeals ruling that the state's abortion restrictions were unconstitutional after the state decided not to appeal further. In Hollingsworth v. Perry, 570 U.S. 693 (2013), the proponents of an initiative petition in California were allowed to intervene in a suit by same-sex couples against state officials challenging the constitutionality of a law banning same-sex marriages adopted pursuant to the initiative. The intervenors sought to appeal the district court's finding that the law was unconstitutional after state officials refused to do so. Stating that standing is required for those seeking appellate review, the Supreme Court held that the intervenors had no standing to appeal. Their only interest was to vindicate the constitutional validity of a generally applicable California law, and such a "generalized grievance" is insufficient to confer standing.

With respect to the district courts, the Supreme Court held, in Town of Chester v. Laroe Estates, 137 S.Ct. 1645 (2017), that an intervenor on the plaintiff's side must have Article III standing if it seeks relief different from that sought by the original plaintiff, "includ[ing] cases in which both the plaintiff and the intervenor seek separate money judgments in their own names." Id. at 1651. *Laroe* involved a failed real-estate development in the Town of Chester, which had refused to approve the project. The original owner of the property, Sherman, sued the Town on a variety of claims, and Laroe, which had entered into various agreements with Sherman sought to intervene under Rule 24(a)(2) to protect its interest in the property under the agreements. It wasn't clear, however, whether Laroe sought only an interest in the money judgment Sherman sought, or additional damages in its own name, so the Supreme Court remanded the case.

But *Laroe* dodged the more difficult questions: if the intervenor seeks the same relief as the plaintiff, must the intervenor have Article III standing? Or what if the intervenor seeks to come in on the defendants' side, as in *Animal Protection*?

Animal Protection tells us that at least in the Eighth Circuit, an intervenor must have standing, but in general this question has long proved difficult for the courts to resolve. For discussion, see Carl Tobias, Standing to Intervene, 1991 Wis.L.Rev. 415. In Mausolf v. Babbitt, 85 F.3d 1295 (8th Cir. 1996), the court held that a construction group could not intervene in a suit by snowmobilers to enjoin limitations on that activity, reasoning that "Congress could no more use Rule 24 to abrogate the Article III standing requirements than it could expand the Supreme Court's original jurisdiction by statute." For an example of an intervenor with standing, consider National Parks Conservation Assoc. v. U.S. Environmental Protection Agency, 759 F.3d 969 (8th Cir. 2014), in which environmental groups sought a court order that the EPA impose emission-control requirements on a power company. But complying with such requirements would cost the company millions of dollars, and the court found that it could intervene because it "has adequately alleged a concrete, particularized, and imminent injury to a legally protected interest."

But arguably there need not be any requirement to demonstrate standing at all if there is already an Article III case between the original parties? See Chiles v. Thornburgh, 865 F.2d 1197, 1212–13 (11th Cir. 1989): "[A] party seeking to intervene need not demonstrate that he has standing in addition to meeting the requirements of Rule 24 so long as there exists a justiciable case and controversy between the parties already in the lawsuit." See also San Juan County v. U.S., 503 F.3d 1163 (10th Cir. 2007), in which the court ruled that independent standing is not required, finding that the 2d, 5th, 6th, 9th and 11th circuits had ruled the same way, but that the 7th, 8th, and D.C. circuits require standing to intervene of right.

3.   *The Rule 24(a) interest requirement.* When the intervenor must demonstrate standing, the Rule 24(a) interest requirement should be satisfied. But in jurisdictions in which the intervenor does not have to demonstrate standing, the court must determine whether the applicant has raised an interest that satisfies the rule. In Donaldson v. United States, 400 U.S. 517 (1971), the Supreme Court said an intervenor's interest must be a "significant protectable interest." The intervenor there was a taxpayer who sought to intervene in a proceeding to enforce a subpoena IRS served on his employer to obtain information about his wages. The Court held that the taxpayer did not have such an interest in his employer's records.

A leading treatise opines that " 'significantly protectable interest' has not been a term of art in the law and there is sufficient room for disagreement about what it means so that this gloss on the rule is not likely to provide any more guidance than does the bare term 'interest' in Rule 24 itself." 7C Charles Wright, Arthur Miller & Mary Kay Kane, Federal Practice & Procedure § 1908.1 at 307–08 (3d ed. 2007). What was the "significant protectable interest" in *Animal Protection*? Some other examples may illuminate the issue.

In New Orleans Public Service, Inc. (NOPSI) v. United Gas Line Co., 732 F.2d 452 (5th Cir. 1984), the City of New Orleans sought to intervene on behalf of its rate payers in a suit by the local gas utility against its gas supplier for refunds of alleged overcharges in violation of the supply contract. Since the rate payers were not parties to this contract, the court found that they had no legal rights to enforce. Although they had a financial interest in the outcome of the case because the utility's costs would affect the rates charged, the court held that this was not sufficient for intervention of right. Thus, a financial or economic interest alone may not justify intervention. Otherwise, a company could intervene in any suit where a precedent might be established in which a similar company or industry was a party and might lose under similar circumstances.

But a "pocket-book interest" is often said to be required in order to differentiate an interest based solely on social, political, or moral concerns. For example, in Planned Parenthood v. Citizens for Community Action, 558 F.2d 861 (8th Cir. 1977), a citizens group opposed to abortion sought to intervene in a suit by a family planning clinic challenging a city ordinance imposing a moratorium on construction of abortion facilities. The court held that the intervenor had a significantly protectable interest in protecting property values because some of its members lived in the vicinity of the plaintiff's proposed clinic, and a real estate expert opined that presence of an abortion clinic would lower their property values.

Could anti-abortion views alone suffice? Contrast *Planned Parenthood* with Keith v. Daley, 764 F.2d 1265 (7th Cir. 1985), in which the court upheld the denial of an application for intervention by the Illinois Pro-Life Coalition (IPC) in an action brought by several doctors to enjoin the enforcement of the Illinois Abortion Law. The court found that IPC had no interest that would justify intervention due to its opposition to abortion:

> In an America whose freedom is secured by its ever vigilant guard on the openness of its "marketplace of ideas," IPC is encouraged to thrive, and to speak, lobby, promote, and persuade, so that its principles may become, if it is the will of the majority, the law of the land. Such a priceless right to free expression, however, does not also suggest that IPC has a right to intervene in every lawsuit involving abortion rights, or to forever defend statutes it helped to enact. Rule 24(a) precludes a conception of lawsuits, even "public law" suits, as necessary forums for such public policy debates.

Contrast Floyd v. City of New York, 770 F.3d 1051 (2d Cir. 2014), a long-running class action challenge to the stop-and-frisk practices of the New York Police Department. After a new mayor was elected and decided not to appeal a decree entered by the district court limiting stop-and-frisk practices, police unions sought to intervene to appeal, asserting that their members' reputations and collective bargaining rights were threatened by the decree. The court emphasized that the interests supporting intervention must be "direct, substantial, and legally protectable." Although the decree did mention certain police officers by name, plaintiffs had withdrawn their claims against individual police officers, and the case was limited to seeking a decree against the city's police practices. So the reputational effect would be too remote to justify intervention. And the police practices regulated by the order "fall squarely within the 'management rights' provision of the New York Administrative Code," and therefore within the city's discretion, so that the unions' collective bargaining rights were not infringed.

4. *Adequate protection by existing parties.* Assuming the intervenor invokes an appropriate interest, intervention may still be denied if that interest is adequately protected by existing parties to the litigation. Note that there is no similar ground under Rule 19(a) for declining to join "required parties." Consider how this requirement should be applied in the cases described in note 3 above.

Animal Protection cites the rule that when a State or an officer charged by law with representing the interest of the proposed intervenor is a party, there is a rebuttable presumption of adequate representation. Without this presumption, it is conceivable that a public interest or special interest group might be able to intervene in any case in which it believes it can bring additional legal resources and stronger resolve to the government's case. Why was that presumption found to be rebutted in *Animal Protection*? Was it shown that the Minnesota Department of Natural Resources (DNR) was incapable or unwilling to uphold its own orders allowing certain trapping activities? If, as the opinion says, "the State has no particular interest in preserving the rights of trappers to continue these practices," wouldn't that apply in most regulatory situations, thus overriding the presumption against intervention?

Contrast *Stuart v. Huff*, 706 F.3d 345 (4th Cir. 2013), in which various plaintiffs challenged the constitutionality of a North Carolina statute requiring that women seeking an abortion be provided with a "real-time ultrasound display of the fetus." Although the state defended the constitutionality of the statute, several pro-life groups sought to intervene on the ground that they considered the state's defense of the statute strategically deficient. The district court denied the motion to intervene, and the Fourth Circuit affirmed, holding that the intervenors had not overcome the presumption of adequate representation by the state. In so holding, the court noted: "There will often be differences of opinion among lawyers on the best way to approach a case. * * * To have such unremarkable divergences of view sow the seeds for intervention as of right risks generating endless squabbles at every juncture over how to proceed." Id. at 354. See also Planned Parenthood v. Kaul, 942 F.3d 793 (7th Cir. 2019) (denying state legislature's motion to intervene in suit challenging new state law limiting abortion on the ground that the state was adequately represented by its attorney general).

In finding that the intervenors' interests are not adequately represented, *Animal Protection* noted that the defendant is "under no obligation to refrain from agreeing to a settlement, or to the imposition of injunctive relief" that would prejudice the intervenor's interests. Planned Parenthood v. Citizens for Community Action, 558 F.2d 861 (8th Cir. 1977), in granting intervention, also cited the threat that the city and city council members who were sued over its ordinance imposing a moratorium on abortion clinics, would settle on less favorable terms than the intervenors wanted. That court found that "their respective interests, while not adverse, are disparate," that their litigation strategies might be different, and that the council members "are seeking to avoid personal liability." Likewise, in National Parks Conservation Association v. U.S. Environmental Protection Agency, 759 F. 3d 969 (8th Cir. 2014), the intervenor power company's interest in not being required to install costly emission-control technology was found to "diverge from the EPA's general interests in assuring that the proper regulatory procedures are followed." Contrast Bush v. Viterna, 740 F.2d 350 (5th Cir. 1984) ("the mere possibility that a party may at some future time enter into a settlement cannot alone show inadequate representation"); United States v. Carpenter, 298 F.3d 1122 (9th Cir. 2002) (denying intervention to environmental groups that objected to a proposed confidential settlement in a suit by the government, since the settlement did not necessarily indicate inadequate representation, and the ability of the government to settle cases would be "impaired if every party that the government represents could intervene" because settlement negotiations were confidential).

What happens if a party settles contrary to the wishes of an intervenor on its side? May intervenors continue their action? In holding that standing is required to intervene, the Seventh Circuit has emphasized that "a party cannot be forced to settle a case." An intervenor acquires the rights of a party, and, as a consequence, "intervention can impose substantial costs on the parties and the judiciary, not only by making the litigation more cumbersome but also (and more important) by blocking settlement." Solid Waste Agency v. U.S. Army Corps of Engineers, 101 F.3d 503, 507–08 (7th Cir. 1996). But recall the question of "standing to intervene" (note 2 above); an intervenor who seeks to pursue the litigation at this point would have to demonstrate standing in all courts.

5.   *Intervention for a limited purpose.* A distinctive set of issues exists when an intervenor seeks to participate in the litigation only in regard to a somewhat tangential matter. A recurrent example occurs when the intervenor seeks access to discovery material that is subject to a protective order entered in the case. For instance, League of Women Voters v. Newby, 963 F.3d 130 (D.C. Cir. 2020), involved a challenge to Kansas's ability to add a question to mail-in voter-registration form to require documentary proof of U.S. citizenship. Eagle Forum, a nonprofit group that advocates in favor of such a requirement, sought to intervene under Rule 24(b) for the purpose of gaining access to briefs and accompanying exhibits that had been filed under seal. Two years after Eagle Forum sought to intervene, the district court denied the motion on the grounds that its interests were adequately represented and that the documents did not qualify as judicial records to which the intervenor could attempt to gain access. The court of appeals reversed on both justifications— the parties, who were seeking to keep the documents from public view could not represent the intervenor's interest, and the briefs and accompanying exhibits did qualify as judicial records that the intervenor could seek to unseal. See also Chicago Tribune Co. v. Bridgestone/Firestone, Inc., *infra* p. 510 (media

outlets seek access to discovery documents produced by tire manufacturer in suit arising out of roll-over accident).

6. *Timeliness.* An application to intervene must be "timely." (When you reach Martin v. Wilks, *infra* p. 69, reflect on whether there is a similar requirement for protection of the nonparty's rights under Rule 19(a).) MasterCard Int'l, Inc. v. Visa Int'l Serv. Ass'n, Inc., 471 F.3d 377, 390 (2d Cir. 2006), explained that this factor is "flexible," and that the court should consider the following factors: "(a) the length of time the applicant knew or should have known of its interest before making the motion; (b) prejudice to existing parties resulting from the applicant's delay; (c) prejudice to the applicant if the motion is denied; and (d) the presence of unusual circumstances militating for or against a finding of timeliness."

Floyd v. City of New York, 770 F.3d 1051 (2d Cir. 2014), again provides an example. The underlying class action challenged the New York Police Department "stop and frisk" practices. It lasted for years and was vigorously resisted by the administration of Mayor Bloomberg but led, after trial, to entry of a decree finding constitutional violations and requiring changes in police practices. Then Mayor de Blasio was elected, partly on a platform of reforming police practices, and the new administration reached a settlement that largely accepted the district court decree. Police unions then sought to intervene, asserting the reputational interests of officers named in the proceedings and the union's alleged collective bargaining rights. The district court denied intervention partly on grounds of timeliness. See also Illinois v. City of Chicago, 912 F.3d 979 (7th Cir. 2019) (police union waited too long to seek to intervene in suit challenging city's police practices; the duty to intervene runs from "when the applicant has reason to know its interests *might* be adversely affected, not from when it knows for certain that they will be").

The court of appeals affirmed, noting that there was much publicity about the suit for years, and that "[i]t was widely understood that the views of the incumbent municipal administration [Mayor Bloomberg] were not shared by their likely successors [Mayor de Blasio]." Moreover, there was no showing that the City "was *ever* protecting the union members' reputations, much less their collective bargaining rights," so the "inherent conflict" of interests between employer and employees should have been apparent to the unions.

Contrast U.S. v. City of Detroit, 712 F.3d 925, 931 (6th Cir. 2013), a 30-year-old case in which the government asserted that the city had not complied with the Clean Water Act. In 2011, having lost patience with the city's failure to comply, the district judge abrogated some provisions of its collective bargaining agreements. The unions then sought to intervene, but the district judge denied intervention on timeliness grounds. The court of appeal reversed, reasoning that "[t]he mere passage of time—even 30 years—is not particularly important to the progressing-suit factor." It found the suit "has essentially been in a remedial, non-adversary posture from the start, and despite significant progress, cannot be expected to end any time soon."

7. *Permissive intervention.* Rule 24(b) allows permissive intervention without requiring a legally recognized "interest" in the property or transaction. Essentially, permissive intervention enables a judge to determine that a non-party can be useful in the action, such as providing factual or legal expertise, insight into the potential impact of its ruling, or obtaining a "buy-in" by that non-party that will assist in compliance with the judgment.

United States v. Reserve Mining Co., 56 F.R.D. 408 (1972), is a famous example. The U.S. sued to prevent discharges from the defendant's mining operations into Lake Superior alleged to constitute a public health hazard. Intervention was sought, as plaintiffs by adjoining states and environmental groups, and as defendants by local governments, individuals (the company had 11,000 employees in the area), businesses, and chambers of commerce. The judge granted intervention, relying in part on a provision of the relevant federal statute (Federal Water Pollution Control Act) that said a court must hear such evidence "as it deems necessary to a complete review of the standards and to a determination of all other issues." His attitude seemed to flow from his view that the case "transcends ordinary civil litigation and makes a reviewing court more of an administrative tribunal than a court in an ordinary adversary civil case," and that it is "imperative for the Court to obtain the fullest possible factual understanding of the conditions in northeastern Minnesota before rendering any judgment." Compare U.S. v. Wheeling-Pittsburgh Steel Corp., 866 F.2d 57 (3d Cir. 1988) (refusing intervention by state legislators urging that defendant steel company should be afforded more leeway to comply with air quality requirements on the ground that the Clean Air Act did not support such dispensation).

8. *Limitations on role of intervenors.* In *Reserve Mining*, the judge's intervention order imposed limits on the intervenors: the intervenors on both defense and plaintiff side must name a spokesman; for purposes of discovery, each side must work in unison; all motions which the parties agree should be brought must be a uniform presentation; witnesses and evidence must be agreed upon by the parties; and the U.S. Government and attorneys for Reserve Mining would act as liaison counsel and outline basic strategy and presentation of arguments and evidence. Does that mean that the intervenors will function as full parties? What if there is a disagreement between a party and its intervenors?

This sort of treatment is easier to justify when permissive intervention is granted than when intervention is of right. In J.B. Stringfellow v. Concerned Neighbors in Action, 480 U.S. 370 (1987), the trial court, in granting permissive intervention in a toxic cleanup case, said the intervenors could not assert a claim that was not already raised nor file motions or seek discovery without first conferring with all the litigants and obtaining permission from at least one. The Supreme Court upheld the restrictions, and Justice Brennan, concurring, said that "restrictions on participation may also be placed on an intervenor of right and on an original party."

Other courts, however, have eschewed limitations on intervenors' role for concern that, as parties bound by the judgment, their ability to protect their interests will be undermined. For example, in Columbus-America Discovery Group v. Atlantic Mut. Ins. Co., 974 F.2d 450 (4th Cir. 1992), even though the intervenors had delayed in seeking intervention until just before trial, the judge allowed them to intervene but denied them any discovery, insisting that the trial go forward as scheduled. After plaintiff defeated their claims, a divided court of appeals held that it was improper to impose conditions on intervenors of right and questioned the Advisory Committee Note to Rule 24 that authorized conditions on intervenors of right. A dissenting judge emphasized that the intervenors had no excuse for waiting so long to join the case, and that the district judge had allowed them some discovery while the trial was underway. See also 7C Charles Wright, Arthur Miller & Mary Kay Kane, Federal Practice & Procedure § 1922 (3d ed. 2007) (questioning propriety of limitations on intervenors of right). But note, as explored in Chapter 6, that in multiparty cases courts often appoint lead and liaison counsel and impose limitations on the litigation latitude afforded litigants as a matter of case management.

D. JURISDICTIONAL ISSUES WITH JOINING PARTIES

As we have thus far seen, modern procedure provides myriad opportunities to join multiple parties into a single suit, whether at the outset in the pleadings, or as the suit progresses and outsiders are brought into the litigation. But the joinder rules are not all-powerful. Although the philosophy of the Federal Rules of Civil Procedure and their modern state analogues tend toward maximal joinder of parties and claims to facilitate efficient resolution of controversies, those Rules cannot avoid constitutional and statutory limitations on jurisdiction. Federal Rule 82 states that the Federal Rules "do not extend or limit the jurisdiction of the district courts." As a result, restrictions on jurisdiction, both subject matter and personal, can present significant obstacles to joinder of parties in a single suit, even when such joinder would be efficient and practical.

Subject Matter Jurisdiction

Subject matter jurisdiction presents little difficulty in state court cases that are brought in courts of "general" subject matter jurisdiction. But, as you undoubtedly remember from your first-year course in Civil Procedure, the federal courts are courts of *limited* subject matter jurisdiction.

As a refresher, recall that federal court subject matter jurisdiction is restricted to those jurisdictional categories set out in Article III of the Constitution and in specific authorizing statutes. In cases based on federal question jurisdiction, under 28 U.S.C. § 1331, the claims stated in a well-pleaded complaint must arise under the Constitution, laws, or treaties of the United States. There is no automatic federal court jurisdiction over state-law claims between existing parties or over state-law claims against an additional party sought to be joined. In cases where jurisdiction is based on diversity of citizenship (other than mass and class actions, which will be covered in Chapter 5), the joinder of an additional party will sometimes destroy diversity. The diversity statute, 28 U.S.C. § 1332, imposes both an amount-in-controversy requirement of $75,000, and, since Strawbridge v. Curtiss, 7 U.S. (3 Cranch) 267 (1806), complete diversity. Thus, an additional party will destroy diversity if it is a citizen of the same state as one of the opposing parties.

In federal court, then, the question arises whether some form of jurisdiction can be devised to allow new parties to be joined or issues to be raised as to which there would not be federal court jurisdiction. If the jurisdictional requirements were strictly applied, litigation in federal courts would be inflexible in not allowing related parties and issues to be brought into a lawsuit. Over a number of decades, however, the Supreme Court carved out two forms of expanded jurisdiction.

Ancillary jurisdiction permitted the joinder of claims and parties over which a federal court does not have subject matter jurisdiction as an incident to disposition of the entire case before the court. It was particularly useful when procedural devices in the Federal Rules would otherwise be frustrated, for example, as to compulsory counterclaims (Rule 13(a)) (the landmark case is Moore v. New York Cotton Exchange, 270 U.S. 593 (1926) which allowed defendant to file a state law counterclaim to a federal antitrust claim); cross-claims (Rule 13(g)); impleader of third-party defendants (Rule 14); interpleader (Rule 22); and intervention as of right (Rule 24(a)). But the Supreme Court refused to extend ancillary jurisdiction when it would undercut the intent of the particular jurisdictional statute involved, as with the requirement of complete diversity. See Owen Equipment & Erection Co. v. Kroger, 437 U.S. 365 (1978) (plaintiff would not be allowed to assert a claim against a nondiverse third party defendant properly joined pursuant to Rule 14 because doing so would undercut the complete diversity requirement).

Pendent jurisdiction, like ancillary jurisdiction, developed out of considerations of "judicial economy, convenience and fairness to the litigants." In United Mine Workers v. Gibbs, 383 U.S. 715 (1966), for example, it was invoked to allow a federal court to entertain a state-law claim of conspiracy to interfere with contract rights which was closely related (i.e., derived from "a common nucleus of operative fact") to a federal claim based on violation of the Taft-Hartley Act. Some courts extended the doctrine from "claims" to "parties," as when a federal claim against an existing party is closely enough related to a state claim against another party even though there would be no independent basis of federal jurisdiction. See Charles Wright & Mary Kay Kane, Law of Federal Courts p. 109 (8th ed. 2016). However, the Supreme Court struck down such applications where it found them contrary to the congressional intent reflected in the particular federal jurisdictional statute. See Aldinger v. Howard, 427 U.S. 1 (1976) (plaintiff who had claim under 42 U.S.C. § 1983 against various county employees could not add claim against county based on state law because it was thought that county was immune to suit under § 1983).

§ 1367 Supplemental jurisdiction: In 28 U.S.C. § 1367, Congress extended supplemental jurisdiction to the full limits of the Constitution in federal question cases. However, in recognition of the statutory requirement for "complete diversity" in cases based on diversity jurisdiction, it denied supplemental jurisdiction "over claims by plaintiffs against persons made parties under Rule 14, 19, 20 or 24" when "inconsistent" with the jurisdictional requirements of diversity jurisdiction.

Subsection (a) authorizes the district courts to exercise jurisdiction over a supplemental claim whenever it forms "part of the same constitutional case or controversy under Article III" as the claim or claims that provide the basis for the district court's original jurisdiction. It explicitly authorizes exercise of jurisdiction over claims that involve the joinder or intervention of additional parties, thus approving the old "pendent party" jurisdiction. The same case or controversy has been viewed as including all claims arising out of a common nucleus of operate facts, though some courts have been willing to read the statute even more broadly. See Jones v. Ford Motor Credit Co., 358 F.3d 205 (2d Cir. 2004); Channell v. Citicorp Nat'l Servs., 89 F.3d 379 (7th Cir. 1996). For discussion of the potential scope of § 1367(a), see William Fletcher, "Common Nucleus of Operative Fact" and Defensive Set-Off: Beyond the *Gibbs* Test, 74 Ind. L.J. 171 (1998).

Subsection (b) prohibits supplemental jurisdiction when it would encourage plaintiffs to evade the complete diversity requirement of § 1332. It thus denies supplemental jurisdiction over "claims by *plaintiffs* against persons made parties under Rule 14, 19, 20, or 24," or over "claims by persons proposed to be joined as *plaintiffs* under Rule 19," or "seeking to intervene as *plaintiffs* under Rule 24" "when exercising supplemental jurisdiction over such claims would be inconsistent with the jurisdictional requirements of § 1332." Notice that subsection (b) denies supplemental jurisdiction over "claims by plaintiffs," or by necessary party plaintiffs joined under Rule 19, or by intervening plaintiffs under Rule 24, but not over claims of additional nondiverse plaintiffs that are joined pursuant to Rule 20. Plaintiff-intervenors would be excluded to the same extent as those sought to be joined as plaintiffs under Rule 19, a change from the prior law regarding intervenors of right.

Owen Equipment & Erection Co. v. Kroger, 437 U.S. 365 (1978), is a paradigm for a case in which supplemental jurisdiction would be "inconsistent with the jurisdictional requirements of § 1332" (i.e., a claim by a plaintiff against a nondiverse third-party defendant made a party under Rule 14, which would undermine the complete diversity requirement). See also TIG Ins. Co. v. Reliable Research Co., 334 F.3d 630 (7th Cir. 2003) (in suit by insurer, there was no supplemental jurisdiction over intervention on the plaintiff side by a title insurance company that had the same citizenship as defendant. Because subsection (b) applies only when federal-court jurisdiction is based solely on grounds of diversity, there are no similar obstacles to using supplemental jurisdiction for the addition of parties in cases relying on federal question jurisdiction, such as *Eldredge, supra* p. 38.

There was uncertainty after its passage as to whether § 1367 supplemental jurisdiction would apply to allow the claims of plaintiffs joined under Rule 20, or of class members under Rule 23, who individually could not meet the $75,000 amount in controversy requirement. After conflicting lower court opinions, the Supreme Court held that, under § 1367, supplemental jurisdiction would extend to these situations. In two cases consolidated for appeal, the Supreme Court held that § 1367 by its plain text authorized supplemental jurisdiction over all claims by diverse parties arising out of the same case or controversy. Rosario-Ortega v. Star-Kist Foods, Inc., 545 U.S. 546 (2005), involved a claim of more than $75,000 by a girl who was severely cut when opening a can of tuna, joined with the claims of her family for emotional distress arising out of the same can-opening incident. The Court held that where the other elements of jurisdiction are satisfied and at least one named plaintiff in the action satisfies § 1332(a)'s amount-in-controversy requirement, § 1367 authorizes supplemental jurisdiction over the claims of other plaintiffs in the same Article III case or controversy, even if those claims are for less than the requisite amount. But notwithstanding the ruling that one plaintiff can tag along with another plaintiff who satisfies the amount-in-controversy requirement, in dictum the Court said that § 1367 cannot be used to circumvent the complete diversity requirement. The companion case, Exxon Mobil Corp. v. Allapattah Services, Inc., 545 U.S. 546 (2005), was a class action by Exxon dealers for breach of their sales agreements, where the class representative, but not all class members, satisfied the amount in controversy. The Court held that supplemental jurisdiction extended to the claims of all class members. See further discussion of the class action context, see *infra* p. 363.

Personal Jurisdiction

Until recently, the biggest jurisdictional obstacle to joinder of parties in complex litigation tended to be subject matter jurisdiction in the federal courts. But in recent decades, the Supreme Court has decided a series of cases that have tightened restrictions on states' personal jurisdiction, and, by extension, the personal jurisdiction of federal district courts in most cases under Federal Rule 4(k)(1)(A). Prior to the Court's decision in

Goodyear Dunlop Tires Operations, S.A. v. Brown, 564 U.S. 915 (2011), many large corporate defendants were thought be subject to "general," or "all-purpose," jurisdiction in a state on the basis of "doing business" in that state. But in Goodyear, the Court held that general jurisdiction is justified only when the defendants' affiliations with the forum state "render them essentially at home in the forum state." Id. at 919. The Court explained that a natural person would typically be considered at home in the state of his domicile, and a corporation would typically be at home in the states in which it is incorporated and has its principal place of business.

The Court has left open the possibility that a corporation's contacts might be sufficient to subject to general jurisdiction in another state, but the Court's post-Goodyear general jurisdiction decisions have demonstrated that any such possibility is exceedingly slim. See BNSF Ry. Co. v. Tyrrell, 137 S.Ct. 1549 (2017) (holding that over 2,000 employees and 2,000 miles of track in the forum state did not justify general jurisdiction over a railroad company); Daimler AG v. Bauman, 571 U.S. 117 (2014) (holding that German automobile corporation was not subject to general jurisdiction in California despite substantial sales and operations in the state).

A plaintiff, of course, need not base personal jurisdiction on a theory of general jurisdiction. If his claims arise out of or relate to the defendant's contacts with the forum state, then the plaintiff may rely on a theory of *specific* jurisdiction. But specific jurisdiction is not always easy to establish, even when the plaintiff has been injured in the forum state. To illustrate, in World-Wide Volkswagen Corp. v. Woodson, 444 U.S. 286 (1980), plaintiffs were severely burned in an accident in Oklahoma due to an alleged defect in their car. They sued in Oklahoma state court, asserting claims against the German manufacturer of the car and also the New York dealership where they bought the car and World-Wide, which distributed these cars in New York, New Jersey, and Connecticut. The Court ruled that the dealer and the three-state distributor were not subject to suit in Oklahoma because their intentional contacts with the forum state were insufficient to warrant jurisdiction there. (Note that the German manufacturer did not object to jurisdiction in Oklahoma, likely because it would then have been a forgone conclusion that it would be subject to general jurisdiction due to its substantial sales and operations in Oklahoma; if this suit were to arise today, post-Goodyear, the claim against the German manufacturer would have to be based on specific jurisdiction.)

Perhaps the best illustration of how the limitations on general and specific jurisdiction can stymie joinder of parties in a single lawsuit is the Supreme Court's recent decision in Bristol-Myers Squibb v. Superior Court of California, San Francisco County, 137 S.Ct. 1773 (2017). In Bristol-Myers, 678 plaintiffs sued Bristol-Myers in California state court claiming that they suffered health problems due to taking the defendant's drug

Plavix. The plaintiffs had originally joined together in eight separate lawsuits, but the cases were assigned to a single judge under California's aggregation procedures. Of the 678 plaintiffs, 86 were from California, and the others were from 33 other states.

Bristol-Myers conceded that it was subject to jurisdiction in California with respect to the claims by the California plaintiffs, who had purchased Plavix in California and were injured there, but it challenged jurisdiction with respect to the claims by the non-California plaintiffs. Initially, the plaintiffs asserted jurisdiction on a theory of general jurisdiction based on Bristol-Myers's extensive contacts with California. Indeed, Bristol-Myers had extensive contacts with California: some 250 sales representatives, five research facilities, a small state-government advisory office, and, to boot, some $900 million worth of sales of Plavix from 2006 to 2012. For decades, such contacts would clearly have subjected Bristol-Myers to general jurisdiction in California, but after Goodyear and Daimler, such a theory was no longer sustainable—now, Bristol-Myers is probably subject to general jurisdiction only in Delaware, its state of incorporation, and New York, the state of its principal place of business.

Consequently, the plaintiffs changed tack and asserted that Bristol-Myers was subject to *specific* jurisdiction in California, because Bristol-Myers' Plavix-related activities in California were identical to its activities in other states. Moreover, since Bristol-Myers would already have to litigate against the California plaintiffs in San Francisco, it would be difficult to argue that jurisdiction would be unreasonable. (Indeed, Bristol-Myers conceded that litigating in California would not be unreasonably burdensome.) Nevertheless, in an 8–1 decision, the Supreme Court held that there was no jurisdiction over Bristol-Myers with respect to the non-Californians' claims. The Court's short opinion was straightforwardly doctrinal: because "all of the conduct giving rise to the nonresidents' claims occurred elsewhere," California did not have jurisdiction over Bristol-Myers with respect to those claims. 137 S.Ct. at 1783.

In dissent, Justice Sotomayor contended that the Court's decision would present serious obstacles to joinder in a unitary forum, *id.* at 1788–89:

> I fear the consequences of the majority's decision today will be substantial. Even absent a rigid requirement that a defendant's in-state conduct must actually cause a plaintiff's claim, the upshot of today's opinion is that plaintiffs cannot join their claims together and sue a defendant in a State in which only some of them have been injured. That rule is likely to have consequences far beyond this case.
>
> First, and most prominently, the Court's opinion in this case will make it profoundly difficult for plaintiffs who are injured in different States by a defendant's nationwide course of conduct to

sue that defendant in a single, consolidated action. The holding of today's opinion is that such an action cannot be brought in a State in which only some plaintiffs were injured. Not to worry, says the majority: The plaintiffs here could have sued Bristol-Myers in New York or Delaware; could "probably" have subdivided their separate claims into 34 lawsuits in the States in which they were injured; and might have been able to bring a single suit in federal court (an "open . . . question"). Even setting aside the majority's caveats, what is the purpose of such limitations? What interests are served by preventing the consolidation of claims and limiting the forums in which they can be consolidated? The effect of the Court's opinion today is to eliminate nationwide mass actions in any State other than those in which a defendant is "'essentially at home.'" See Daimler, 134 S.Ct. at 754. Such a rule hands one more tool to corporate defendants determined to prevent the aggregation of individual claims, and forces injured plaintiffs to bear the burden of bringing suit in what will often be far flung jurisdictions.

Second, the Court's opinion today may make it impossible to bring certain mass actions at all. After this case, it is difficult to imagine where it might be possible to bring a nationwide mass action against two or more defendants headquartered and incorporated in different States. There will be no State where both defendants are "at home," and so no State in which the suit can proceed. What about a nationwide mass action brought against a defendant not headquartered or incorporated in the United States? Such a defendant is not "at home" in any State. * * *

It "does not offend 'traditional notions of fair play and substantial justice'" to permit plaintiffs to aggregate claims arising out of a single nationwide course of conduct in a single suit in a single State where some, but not all, were injured. But that is exactly what the Court holds today is barred by the Due Process Clause.

As this edition was going to press, the Court decided two more cases that further clarify what it means for a case to "arise out of or relate to" the defendant's contacts with the forum state, which is significant to how broadly *Bristol-Myers* will constrict aggregation. Ford Motor Co. v. Mont. Eighth Jud. Dist., 141 S.Ct. 1017 (2021). One of the cases, Ford v. Bandemer, is illustrative. Bandemer was a passenger in a Ford Crown Victoria and was injured in an accident when the passenger-side airbag did not deploy. Bandemer was domiciled in Minnesota, which was also the state where the accident occurred. Understandably, he sued Ford and the driver, also a Minnesota domiciliary, together in Minnesota state court. Ford objected to the court's personal jurisdiction on the ground that the car was not originally sold in Minnesota; rather, it was originally sold in North

Dakota, and only came to be owned by the driver through the secondary market. In Ford's view, there should be jurisdiction only in the states where it is subject to general jurisdiction (Delaware and Michigan) or where its contacts bear a causal relation to the claim (North Dakota, where the car was originally sold; Michigan, where it was designed; or Ontario, Canada, where it was manufactured). The Supreme Court disagreed, holding that Bandemer's claim "relate[d] to" Ford's Minnesota activities. To what degree this case affects aggregation will surely be developed in the lower courts.

Ultimately, however, these limitations on personal jurisdiction present challenges to plaintiffs seeking to join their claims in a single lawsuit in a single court. As you study more complex mechanisms for aggregate litigation, such as Multidistrict Litigation (in Chapter 4) and Class Actions (in Chapter 5), consider the degree to which personal jurisdiction affects in which courts these cases may go forward. For analyses of these questions, see Andrew Bradt & D. Theodore Rave, Aggregation on Defendants' Terms: Bristol-Myers Squibb and the Federalization of Mass-Tort Litigation, 59 Bos. Col. L. Rev. 1251 (2018); Scott Dodson, Jurisdiction and Aggregation, 113 Nw. U. L. Rev. 1 (2018).

E. CONSEQUENCES OF FAILURE TO JOIN

MARTIN V. WILKS
Supreme Court of the United States, 1989.
490 U.S. 755.

CHIEF JUSTICE REHNQUIST delivered the opinion of the Court.

A group of white firefighters sued the City of Birmingham, Alabama (City) and the Jefferson County Personnel Board (Board) alleging that they were being denied promotions in favor of less qualified black firefighters. They claimed that the City and the Board were making promotion decisions on the basis of race in reliance on certain consent decrees, and that these decisions constituted impermissible racial discrimination in violation of the Constitution and federal statute. The District Court held that the white firefighters were precluded from challenging employment decisions taken pursuant to the decrees, even though these firefighters had not been parties to the proceedings in which the decrees were entered. We think this holding contravenes the general rule that a person cannot be deprived of his legal rights in a proceeding to which he is not a party.

The litigation in which the consent decrees were entered began in 1974, when the Ensley Branch of the NAACP and seven black individuals filed separate class-action complaints against the City and the Board. They alleged that both had engaged in racially discriminatory hiring and promotion practices in various public service jobs in violation of Title VII of the Civil Rights Act of 1964, 42 U.S.C. § 2000e *et seq.,* and other federal law. After a bench trial on some issues, but before judgment, the parties entered into two consent decrees, one between the black individuals and the City and the other between them and the Board. These proposed decrees set forth an extensive remedial scheme, including long-term and interim annual goals for the hiring of blacks as firefighters. The decrees also provided for goals for promotion of blacks within the department.

The District Court entered an order provisionally approving the decrees and directing publication of notice of the upcoming fairness hearings. Notice of the hearings, with a reference to the general nature of the decrees, was published in two local newspapers. At that hearing, the Birmingham Firefighters Association (BFA) appeared and filed objections as *amicus curiae*. After the hearing, but before final approval of the decrees, the BFA and two of its members also moved to intervene on the ground that the decrees would adversely affect their rights. The District Court denied the motions as untimely and approved the decrees. Seven white firefighters, all members of the BFA, then filed a complaint against the City and the Board seeking injunctive relief against enforcement of the decrees. The seven argued that the decrees would operate to illegally discriminate against them; the District Court denied relief.

Both the denial of intervention and the denial of injunctive relief were affirmed on appeal. The District Court had not abused its discretion in refusing to let the BFA intervene, thought the Eleventh Circuit, in part because the firefighters could "institut[e] an independent Title VII suit, asserting specific violations of their rights." And, for the same reason, petitioners had not adequately shown the potential for irreparable harm from the operation of the decrees necessary to obtain injunctive relief.

A new group of white firefighters, the *Wilks* respondents, then brought suit against the City and the Board in district court. They too alleged that, because of their race, they were being denied promotions in favor of less qualified blacks in violation of federal law. The Board and the City admitted to making race conscious employment decisions, but argued the decisions were unassailable because they were made pursuant to the consent decrees. A group of black individuals, the *Martin* petitioners, were allowed to intervene in their individual capacities to defend the decrees.

The defendants moved to dismiss the reverse discrimination cases as impermissible collateral attacks on the consent decrees. The District Court denied the motions, ruling that the decrees would provide a defense to claims of discrimination for employment decisions "mandated" by the decrees, leaving the principal issue for trial whether the challenged promotions were indeed required by the decrees. After trial the District Court granted the motion to dismiss. The court concluded that "if in fact the City was required to [make promotions of blacks] by the consent decree, then they would not be guilty of [illegal] racial discrimination" and that the defendants had "establish[ed] that the promotions of the black individuals were in fact required by the terms of the consent decree."

On appeal, the Eleventh Circuit reversed. It held that "[b]ecause . . . [the *Wilks* respondents] were neither parties nor privies to the consent decrees, . . . their independent claims of unlawful discrimination are not precluded." *In re Birmingham Reverse Discrimination Employment Litigation,* 833 F.2d 1492, 1498 (1987). The court explicitly rejected the doctrine of "impermissible collateral attack" espoused by other courts of appeals to immunize parties to a consent decree from charges of discrimination by nonparties for actions taken pursuant to the decree. Although it recognized a "strong public policy in favor of voluntary affirmative action plans," the panel acknowledged that this interest "must yield to the policy against requiring third parties to submit to bargains in which their interests were either ignored or sacrificed." The court remanded the case for trial of the discrimination claims, suggesting that the operative law for judging the consent decrees was that governing voluntary affirmative-action plans.

We granted certiorari, and now affirm the Eleventh Circuit's judgment. All agree that "[i]t is a principle of general application in Anglo-American jurisprudence that one is not bound by a judgment *in personam* in a litigation in which he is not designated as a party or to which he has not been made a party by service of process." *Hansberry v. Lee,* 311 U.S. 32, 40 (1940). This rule is part of our "deep-rooted historic tradition that everyone should have his own day in court." 18 Charles Wright, Arthur Miller & Edward Cooper, Federal Practice and Procedure § 4449, p. 417 (1981). A judgment or decree among parties to a lawsuit resolves issues as among them, but it does not conclude the rights of strangers to those proceedings.[2]

Petitioners argue that, because respondents failed to timely intervene in the initial proceedings, their current challenge to actions taken under the consent decree constitutes an impermissible "collateral attack." They argue that respondents were aware that the underlying suit might affect them and if they chose to pass up an opportunity to intervene, they should not be permitted to later litigate the issues in a new action. The position has sufficient appeal to have commanded the approval of the great majority of the federal courts of appeals, but we agree with the contrary view expressed by the Court of Appeals for the Eleventh Circuit in this case.

---

[2] We have recognized an exception to the general rule when, in certain limited circumstances, a person, although not a party, has his interests adequately represented by someone with the same interests who is a party. See *Hansberry v. Lee,* 311 U.S. 32, 41–42 (1940) ("class" or "representative" suits); Fed.Rule Civ.Proc. 23 (same); *Montana v. United States,* 440 U.S. 147, 154–155 (1979) (control of litigation on behalf of one of the parties in the litigation). Additionally, where a special remedial scheme exists expressly foreclosing successive litigation by nonlitigants, as for example in bankruptcy or probate, legal proceedings may terminate preexisting rights if the scheme is otherwise consistent with due process. See *NLRB v. Bildisco & Bildisco,* 465 U.S. 513, 529–530, n. 10 (1984) ("proof of claim must be presented to the Bankruptcy Court . . . or be lost"); Tulsa Professional Collection Services, Inc. v. Pope, 485 U.S. 478 (1988) (nonclaim statute terminating unsubmitted claims against the estate). Neither of these exceptions applies, however, in this case.

We begin with the words of Justice Brandeis in *Chase National Bank v. Norwalk,* 291 U.S. 431 (1934):

> "The law does not impose upon any person absolutely entitled to a hearing the burden of voluntary intervention in a suit to which he is a stranger. . . . Unless duly summoned to appear in a legal proceeding, a person not a privy may rest assured that a judgment recovered therein will not affect his legal rights."

While these words were written before the adoption of the Federal Rules of Civil Procedure, we think the Rules incorporate the same principle; a party seeking a judgment binding on another cannot obligate that person to intervene; he must be joined. Against the background of permissive intervention set forth in *Chase National Bank,* the drafters cast Rule 24, governing intervention, in permissive terms. See Fed. Rule Civ.Proc. 24(a) (intervention as of right) ("[u]pon timely application anyone shall be permitted to intervene"); Fed.Rule Civ.Proc. 24(b) (permissive intervention) ("[u]pon timely application anyone may be permitted to intervene"). They determined that the concern for finality and completeness of judgments would be "better [served] by mandatory joinder procedures." Accordingly, Rule 19(a) provides for mandatory joinder in circumstances where a judgment rendered in the absence of a person may "leave . . . persons already parties subject to a substantial risk of incurring . . . inconsistent obligations. . . ." Rule 19(b) sets forth the factors to be considered by a court in deciding whether to allow an action to proceed in the absence of an interested party.

Joinder as a party, rather than knowledge of a lawsuit and an opportunity to intervene, is the method by which potential parties are subjected to the jurisdiction of the court and bound by a judgment or decree.[6] The parties to a lawsuit presumably know better than anyone else the nature and scope of relief sought in the action, and at whose expense such relief might be granted. It makes sense, therefore, to place on them a burden of bringing in additional parties where such a step is indicated, rather than placing on potential additional parties a duty to intervene when they acquire knowledge of the lawsuit. The linchpin of the "impermissible collateral attack" doctrine—the attribution of preclusive effect to a failure to intervene—is therefore quite inconsistent with Rule 19 and Rule 24.

---

[6]   The dissent argues on the one hand that respondents have not been "bound" by the decree but rather, that they are only suffering practical adverse effects from the consent decree. On the other hand, the dissent characterizes respondents' suit not as an assertion of their own independent rights, but as a collateral attack on the consent decree which, it is said, can only proceed on very limited grounds. Respondents in their suit have alleged that they are being racially discriminated against by their employer in violation of Title VII: either the fact that the disputed employment decisions are being made pursuant to a consent decree is a defense to respondents' Title VII claims or it is not. If it is a defense to challenges to employment practices which would otherwise violate Title VII, it is very difficult to see why respondents are not being "bound" by the decree.

* * *

Petitioners also rely on our decision in *Provident Bank* [*v. Patterson*, 390 U.S. 102 (1968)], as authority for the view which they espouse. In that case we discussed Rule 19 shortly after parts of it had been substantially revised, but we expressly left open the question of whether preclusive effect might be attributed to a failure to intervene.

Petitioners contend that a different result should be reached because the need to join affected parties will be burdensome and ultimately discouraging to civil rights litigation. Potential adverse claimants may be numerous and difficult to identify; if they are not joined, the possibility for inconsistent judgments exists. Judicial resources will be needlessly consumed in relitigation of the same question.

Even if we were wholly persuaded by these arguments as a matter of policy, acceptance of them would require a rewriting rather than an interpretation of the relevant Rules. But we are not persuaded that their acceptance would lead to a more satisfactory method of handling cases like this one. It must be remembered that the alternatives are a duty to intervene based on knowledge, on the one hand, and some form of joinder, as the Rules presently provide, on the other. No one can seriously contend that an employer might successfully defend against a Title VII claim by one group of employees on the ground that its actions were required by an earlier decree entered in a suit brought against it by another, if the later group did not have adequate notice or knowledge of the earlier suit.

The difficulties petitioners foresee in identifying those who could be adversely affected by a decree granting broad remedial relief are undoubtedly present, but they arise from the nature of the relief sought and not because of any choice between mandatory intervention and joinder. Rule 19's provisions for joining interested parties are designed to accommodate the sort of complexities that may arise from a decree affecting numerous people in various ways. We doubt that a mandatory intervention rule would be any less awkward. As mentioned, plaintiffs who seek the aid of the courts to alter existing employment policies, or the employer who might be subject to conflicting decrees, are best able to bear the burden of designating those who would be adversely affected if plaintiffs prevail; these parties will generally have a better understanding of the scope of likely relief than employees who are not named but might be affected. Petitioners' alternative does not eliminate the need for, or difficulty of, identifying persons who, because of their interests, should be included in a lawsuit. It merely shifts that responsibility to less able shoulders.

Nor do we think that the system of joinder called for by the Rules is likely to produce more relitigation of issues than the converse rule. The breadth of a lawsuit and concomitant relief may be at least partially shaped in advance through Rule 19 to avoid needless clashes with future litigation. And even under a regime of mandatory intervention, parties who did not have adequate knowledge of the suit would relitigate issues. Additional questions about the adequacy and timeliness of knowledge would inevitably crop up. We think that the system of joinder presently contemplated by the Rules best serves the many interests involved in the run of litigated cases, including cases like the present one.

Petitioners also urge that the congressional policy favoring voluntary settlement of employment discrimination claims, referred to in cases such as *Carson v. American Brands, Inc.*, 450 U.S. 79 (1981), also supports the "impermissible collateral attack" doctrine. But once again it is essential to note just what is meant by "voluntary settlement." A voluntary settlement in the form of a consent decree between one group of employees and their employer cannot possibly "settle," voluntarily or otherwise, the conflicting claims of another group of employees who do not join in the agreement. This is true even if the second group of employees is a party to the litigation:

> "[P]arties who choose to resolve litigation through settlement may not dispose of the claims of a third party . . . without that party's agreement. A court's approval of a consent decree between some of the parties therefore cannot dispose of the valid claims of nonconsenting intervenors." *Firefighters v. Cleveland*, 478 U.S. 501 (1986).

Insofar as the argument is bottomed on the idea that it may be easier to settle claims among a disparate group of affected persons if they are all before the Court, joinder bids fair to accomplish that result as well as a regime of mandatory intervention.

For the foregoing reasons we affirm the decision of the Court of Appeals for the Eleventh Circuit. That court remanded the case for trial of the reverse discrimination claims. *Birmingham Reverse Discrimination*, 833 F.2d, at 1500–1502. Petitioners point to language in the District Court's findings of fact and conclusions of law which suggests that respondents will not prevail on the merits. We agree with the view of the Court of Appeals, however, that the proceedings in the District Court may have been affected by the mistaken view that respondents' claims on the merits were barred to the extent they were inconsistent with the consent decree.

Affirmed.

JUSTICE STEVENS, with whom JUSTICE BRENNAN, JUSTICE MARSHALL, and JUSTICE BLACKMUN join, dissenting.

As a matter of law there is a vast difference between persons who are actual parties to litigation and persons who merely have the kind of interest that may as a practical matter be impaired by the outcome of a case. Persons in the first category have a right to participate in a trial and to appeal from an adverse judgment; depending on whether they win or lose, their legal rights may be enhanced or impaired. Persons in the latter category have a right to intervene in the action in a timely fashion, or they may be joined as parties against their will. But if they remain on the sidelines, they may be harmed as a practical matter even though their legal rights are unaffected. One of the disadvantages of sideline-sitting is that the bystander has no right to appeal from a judgment no matter how harmful it may be.

In this case the Court quite rightly concludes that the white firefighters who brought the second series of Title VII cases could not be deprived of their legal rights in the first series of cases because they had neither intervened nor been joined as parties. See *Parklane Hosiery Co. v. Shore*, 439 U.S. 322, 327, n. 7 (1979). The consent decrees obviously could not deprive them of any contractual rights, such as seniority or accrued vacation pay, or of any other legal rights, such as the right to have their employer comply with federal statutes like Title VII.[4] There is no reason, however, why the consent decrees might not produce changes in conditions at the white firefighters' place of employment that, as a practical matter, may have a serious effect on their opportunities for employment or promotion even though they are not bound by the decrees in any legal sense. The fact that one of the effects of a decree is to curtail the job opportunities of nonparties does not mean that the nonparties have been deprived of legal rights or that they have standing to appeal from that decree without becoming parties.

Persons who have no right to appeal from a final judgment—either because the time to appeal has elapsed or because they never became parties to the case—may nevertheless collaterally attack a judgment on certain narrow grounds. If the court had no jurisdiction over the subject matter, or if the judgment is the product of corruption, duress, fraud, collusion, or mistake, under limited circumstances it may be set aside in

---

[4]   As Chief Justice Rehnquist has observed:

"Suppose, for example, that the Government sues a private corporation for alleged violations of the antitrust laws and then enters a consent decree. Surely, the existence of that decree does not preclude a future suit by another corporation alleging that the defendant company's conduct, even if authorized by the decree, constitutes an antitrust violation. The nonparty has an independent right to bring his own private antitrust action for treble damages or for injunctive relief. See 2 P. Areeda & D. Turner, Antitrust Law ¶ 330, p. 143 (1978). Similarly, if an action alleging unconstitutional prison conditions results in a consent decree, a prisoner subsequently harmed by prison conditions is not precluded from bringing suit on the mere plea that the conditions are in accordance with the consent decree. Such compliance might be relevant to a defense of good-faith immunity, but it would not suffice to block the suit altogether." *Ashley v. City of Jackson*, 464 U.S. 900, 902 (1983) (opinion dissenting from denial of certiorari).

In suggesting that compliance with a consent decree might be relevant to a defense of good-faith immunity, this passage recognizes that neither due process nor the Rules of Civil Procedure foreclose judicial recognition of a judgment that may have a practical effect on the interests of a nonparty.

an appropriate collateral proceeding. See Restatement (Second) of Judgments §§ 69–72 (1982); *Griffith v. Bank of New York,* 147 F.2d 899, 901 (CA2) (Clark, J.), cert. denied, 325 U.S. 874 (1945). This rule not only applies to parties to the original action, but also allows interested third parties collaterally to attack judgments. In both civil and criminal cases, however, the grounds that may be invoked to support a collateral attack are much more limited than those that may be asserted as error on direct appeal. Thus, a person who can foresee that a lawsuit is likely to have a practical impact on his interests may pay a heavy price if he elects to sit on the sidelines instead of intervening and taking the risk that his legal rights will be impaired.

In this case there is no dispute about the fact that the respondents are not parties to the consent decrees. It follows as a matter of course that they are not bound by those decrees. Those judgments could not, and did not, deprive them of any legal rights. The judgments did, however, have a practical impact on respondents' opportunities for advancement in their profession. For that reason, respondents had standing to challenge the validity of the decrees, but the grounds that they may advance in support of a collateral challenge are much more limited than would be allowed if they were parties prosecuting a direct appeal.[8]

The District Court's rulings in this case have been described incorrectly by both the Court of Appeals and this Court. The Court of Appeals repeatedly stated that the District Court had "in effect" held that the white firefighters were "bound" by a decree to which they were not parties. And this Court's opinion seems to assume that the District Court had interpreted its consent decrees in the earlier litigation as holding "that the white firefighters were precluded from challenging employment decisions taken pursuant to the decrees." It is important, therefore, to make clear exactly what the District Court did hold and why its judgment should be affirmed.

---

[8] The Eleventh Circuit, in a decision involving a previous attempt by white firefighters to set aside the consent decrees at issue in this litigation, itself observed: "There are . . . limitations on the extent to which a nonparty can undermine a prior judgment. A nonparty may not reopen the case and relitigate the merits anew; neither may he destroy the validity of the judgment between the parties." *United States v. Jefferson County,* 720 F.2d 1511, 1518 (1983).

Professors James and Hazard describe the rule as follows:

"Ordinarily, a nonparty has no legal interest in a judgment in an action between others. Such a judgment does not determine the nonparty's rights and obligations under the rules of res judicata and he may so assert if the judgment is relied upon against him. But in some situations one's interests, particularly in one's own personal legal status or claims to property, may be placed in practical jeopardy by a judgment between others. In such circumstances one may seek the aid of a court of equity, but *the grounds upon which one may rely are severely limited.* The general rule is that one must show either that the judgment was void for lack of jurisdiction of the subject matter or that it was the product of fraud directed at the petitioner." James & Hazard, Civil Procedure § 12.15, p. 681 (emphasis supplied).

I

[Justice Stevens described the prior proceedings, which addressed claims of discrimination in the police and fire departments. The proceedings included two trials and the fairness hearing on the consent decrees. Notice was given to interested persons and "a group of white firefighters—represented in part by the Birmingham Firefighters Association (BFA)—opposed any race-conscious relief." He cited findings in the lower court that "the record provided 'more than ample reason' to conclude that the City would eventually be held liable for discrimination against blacks at high-level positions in the fire and police departments." Evidence showed that Black officers comprised 79 of 480 police officers, but only 3 of 131 sergeants, and zero of the 40 lieutenants and captains. In the fire department, 42 of 453 firefighters were Black, and zero of the lieutenants, captains and battalion chiefs. When, several months after the decrees were entered, a group of white firefighters sued, the lower court, after an evidentiary hearing, found "without merit" their claims that promotions of blacks were contrary to the decrees and that the decrees were illegal and void. While an appeal was pending, the Wilks plaintiffs filed another suit alleging violations of Title VII. After a five-day trial, the lower court ruled orally that "a valid consent decree appropriately limited can be the basis for a defense against a charge of discrimination, even in the situation in which it is clear that the defendant in the litigation did act in a racially conscious manner." The district judge also found that the city had not promoted black officers who were unqualified or were demonstrably less qualified than whites who were not promoted, and concluded that the city had carried its burden of showing that "the promotions of the black individuals in this case were in fact required by the terms of the consent decrees."]

The written conclusions of law that he adopted are less clear than his oral opinion. He began by unequivocally stating: "The City Decree is lawful." He explained that "under all the relevant case law of the Eleventh Circuit and the Supreme Court, it is a proper remedial device, designed to overcome the effects of prior, illegal discrimination by the City of Birmingham." In that same conclusion, however, he did state that "plaintiffs cannot collaterally attack the Decree's validity." Yet, when read in context—and particularly in light of the court's finding that the decree was lawful under Eleventh Circuit and Supreme Court precedent—it is readily apparent that, at the extreme, this was intended as an alternative holding. More likely, it was an overstatement of the rule that collateral review is narrower in scope than appellate review. In any event, and regardless of one's reading of this lone sentence, it is absolutely clear that the court did not hold that respondents were bound by the decree. Nowhere in the District Court's lengthy findings of fact and conclusions of law is there a single word suggesting that respondents were bound by the consent decree or that the court intended to treat them as though they had been actual parties to that litigation and not merely as persons whose interests, as a practical matter, had been affected. Indeed, respondents, the Court of Appeals, and the majority opinion all fail to draw attention to any point in this case's long history at which the judge may have given the impression that any nonparty was legally bound by the consent decree.[20]

II

Regardless of whether the white firefighters were parties to the decrees granting relief to their black co-workers, it would be quite wrong to assume that they could never collaterally attack such a decree. If a litigant has standing, he or she can always collaterally attack a judgment for certain narrowly defined defects. On the other hand, a district court is not required to retry a case—or to sit in review of another court's judgment—every time an interested nonparty asserts that *some* error that might have been raised on direct appeal was committed. Such a broad allowance of collateral review would destroy the integrity of litigated judgments, would lead to an abundance of vexatious litigation, and would subvert the interest in comity between courts. Here, respondents have offered no circumstance that might justify reopening the District Court's settled judgment.

The implementation of a consent decree affecting the interests of a multitude of nonparties, and the reliance on that decree as a defense to a charge of discrimination in hiring and promotion decisions, raise a legitimate concern of collusion. No such allegation, however, has been raised. Moreover, there is compelling evidence that the decree was not collusive. In its decision approving the consent decree over the objection of the BFA and individual white firefighters, the District Court observed that there had been "no contention or suggestion" that the decrees were fraudulent or collusive. The record of the fairness hearing was made part of the record of this litigation and this finding was not contradicted. More significantly, the consent decrees were not negotiated until after the 1976 trial and the court's finding that the City had discriminated against black candidates for jobs as police officers and firefighters, and until after the 1979 trial, at which substantial evidence was presented suggesting that the City also discriminated against black candidates for promotion in the fire department. Like the record of the 1981 fairness hearing, the records of both of these prior proceedings were made part of the record in this case. Given this history, the lack of any indication of collusion, and the District

---

[20] In Provident Tradesmens Bank & Trust Co. v. Patterson, 390 U.S., at 114, we expressly did not decide whether a litigant might "be bound by [a] previous decision because, although technically a nonparty, he had purposely bypassed an adequate opportunity to intervene." Today, the Court answers this question, at least in the limited context of the instant dispute, holding that "[j]oinder as a party [under Fed.Rule Civ.Proc. 19], rather than knowledge of a lawsuit and an opportunity to intervene [under Fed.Rule Civ.Proc. 24], is the method by which potential parties are subjected to the jurisdiction of the court and bound by a judgment or decree." Because I conclude that the District Court did not hold that respondents were bound by the consent decrees, I do not reach this issue.

Court's finding that "there is more than ample reason for . . . the City of Birmingham to be concerned that [it] would be in time held liable for discrimination against blacks at higher level positions in the police and fire departments," it is evident that the decree was a product of genuine arm's-length negotiations.

Nor can it be maintained that the consent judgment is subject to reopening and further litigation because the relief it afforded was so out of line with settled legal doctrine that it "was transparently invalid or had only a frivolous pretense to validity." *Walker v. Birmingham,* 388 U.S. 307, 315 (1967) (suggesting that a contemnor might be allowed to challenge contempt citation on ground that underlying court order was "transparently invalid"). To the contrary, the type of race-conscious relief ordered in the consent decree is entirely consistent with this Court's approach to affirmative action. Given a sufficient predicate of racial discrimination, neither the Equal Protection Clause of the Fourteenth Amendment nor Title VII of the Civil Rights Act of 1964 erects a bar to affirmative action plans that benefit nonvictims and have some adverse effect on non-wrongdoers. * * *

Hence, there is no basis for collaterally attacking the judgment as collusive, fraudulent, or transparently invalid. Moreover, respondents do not claim—nor has there been any showing of—mistake, duress, or lack of jurisdiction. Instead, respondents are left to argue that somewhat different relief would have been more appropriate than the relief that was actually granted. Although this sort of issue may provide the basis for a direct appeal, it cannot, and should not, serve to open the door to relitigation of a settled judgment.

III

The facts that respondents are not bound by the decree and that they have no basis for a collateral attack, moreover, do not compel the conclusion that the District Court should have treated the decree as nonexistent for purposes of respondents' discrimination suit. That the decree may not directly interfere with any of the respondents' legal rights does not mean that it may not affect the factual setting in a way that negates respondents' claim. The fact that a criminal suspect is not a party to the issuance of a search warrant does not imply that the presence of a facially valid warrant may not be taken as evidence that the police acted in good faith. Similarly, the fact that an employer is acting under court compulsion may be evidence that the employer is acting in good faith and without discriminatory intent. Indeed, the threat of a contempt citation provides as good a reason to act as most, if not all, other business justifications.

After reviewing the evidence, the District Court found that the City had in fact acted under compulsion of the consent decree. Based on this finding, the court concluded that the City carried its burden of coming forward with a legitimate business reason for its promotion policy, and, accordingly, held that the promotion decisions were "not taken with the requisite discriminatory intent" necessary to make out a claim of disparate treatment under Title VII or the Equal Protection Clause. For this reason, and not because it thought that respondents were legally bound by the consent decree, the court entered an order in favor of the City and defendant-intervenors.

Of course, in some contexts a plaintiff might be able to demonstrate that reference to a consent decree is pretextual. For example, a plaintiff might be able to show that the consent decree was collusive and that the defendants simply obtained the court's rubber stamp on a private agreement that was in no way related to the eradication of pervasive racial discrimination. The plaintiff, alternatively, might be able to show that the defendants were not bound to obey the consent decree because the court that entered it was without jurisdiction. See *United States v. Mine Workers*, 330 U.S. 258, 291–294 (1947). Similarly, although more tenuous, a plaintiff might argue that the parties to the consent judgment were not bound because the order was "transparently invalid" and thus unenforceable. If the defendants were as a result not bound to implement the affirmative-action program, then the plaintiff might be able to show that the racial preference was not a product of the court order.

In a case such as this, however, in which there has been no showing that the decree was collusive, fraudulent, transparently invalid, or entered without jurisdiction, it would be "unconscionable" to conclude that obedience to an order remedying a Title VII violation could subject a defendant to additional liability. Rather, all of the reasons that support the Court's view that a police officer should not generally be held liable when he carries out the commands in a facially valid warrant apply with added force to city officials, or indeed to private employers, who obey the commands contained in a decree entered by a federal court. In fact, Equal Employment Opportunity Commission regulations concur in this assessment. They assert, "[t]he Commission interprets Title VII to mean that actions taken pursuant to the direction of a Court Order cannot give rise to liability under Title VII." 29 CFR § 1608.8 (1989).[30] Assuming that the District Court's findings of fact were not clearly erroneous—which of course is a matter that is not before us—it seems perfectly clear that its judgment should have been affirmed. Any other conclusion would subject large employers who seek to comply with the law by remedying past discrimination to a never-ending stream of litigation and potential liability. It is unfathomable that either Title VII or the Equal Protection Clause demands such a counter-productive result.

---

[30] Section 1608.8 does not differentiate between orders "entered by consent or after contested litigation." 29 CFR § 1608.8 (1989). Indeed, the reasoning in the Court's opinion today would seem equally applicable to litigated orders and consent decrees.

IV

The predecessor to this litigation was brought to change a pattern of hiring and promotion practices that had discriminated against black citizens in Birmingham for decades. The white respondents in this case are not responsible for that history of discrimination, but they are nevertheless beneficiaries of the discriminatory practices that the litigation was designed to correct. Any remedy that seeks to create employment conditions that would have obtained if there had been no violations of law will necessarily have an adverse impact on whites, who must now share their job and promotion opportunities with blacks.[31] Just as white employees in the past were innocent beneficiaries of illegal discriminatory practices, so is it inevitable that some of the same white employees will be innocent victims who must share some of the burdens resulting from the redress of the past wrongs.

There is nothing unusual about the fact that litigation between adverse parties may, as a practical matter, seriously impair the interests of third persons who elect to sit on the sidelines. Indeed, in complex litigation this Court has squarely held that a sideline-sitter may be bound as firmly as an actual party if he had adequate notice and a fair opportunity to intervene and if the judicial interest in finality is sufficiently strong. See *Penn-Central Merger and N & W Inclusion Cases,* 389 U.S. 486, 505–506 (1968).

There is no need, however, to go that far in order to agree with the District Court's eminently sensible view that compliance with the terms of a valid decree remedying violations of Title VII cannot itself violate that statute or the Equal Protection Clause.[32] The City of Birmingham, in entering into and complying with this decree, has made a substantial step toward the eradication of the long history of pervasive racial discrimination that has plagued its fire department. The District Court, after conducting a trial and carefully considering respondents' arguments, concluded that this effort is lawful and should go forward. Because respondents have thus already had their day in court and have failed to carry their burden, I would

---

[31] It is inevitable that nonminority employees or applicants will be less well off under an affirmative action plan than without it, no matter what form it takes. For example, even when an employer simply agrees to recruit minority job applicants more actively, white applicants suffer the "nebulous" harm of facing increased competition and the diminished likelihood of eventually being hired.

[32] In professing difficulty in understanding why respondents are not "bound" by a decree that provides a defense to employment practices that would otherwise violate Title VII, see [majority opinion] n. 6, the Court uses the word "bound" in a sense that is different from that used earlier in its opinion. A judgment against an employer requiring it to institute a seniority system may provide the employer with a defense to employment practices that would otherwise violate Title VII. In the sense in which the word "bound" is used in the cases cited by the Court [earlier in its opinion], only the parties to the litigation would be "bound" by the judgment. But employees who first worked for the company 180 days after the litigation ended would be "bound" by the judgment in the sense that the Court uses when it responds to my argument. The cases on which the Court relies are entirely consistent with my position. Its facile use of the word "bound" should not be allowed to conceal the obvious flaws in its analysis.

vacate the judgment of the Court of Appeals and remand for further proceedings consistent with this opinion.

NOTES AND QUESTIONS

1.   *Epilogue on Martin v. Wilks*: Litigation concerning Birmingham's affirmative action plans continued after the above decision by the Supreme Court. On remand in Martin v. Wilks, the district judge rejected plaintiffs' challenges, but the appellate court ruled for the white males on key points in their challenges to actions taken pursuant to the consent decree. In re Birmingham Reverse Discrimination Employment Litig., 20 F.3d 1525 (11th Cir. 1994). In particular, the appellate court criticized the provision setting the objective that 50% of promotions be to blacks, even though there were very few black firefighters, as an "arbitrary fixed quota. * * * Because non-black firefighters bear the entire burden of the race-based fire lieutenant promotion remedy in the decree, and because of the immediate and future ramifications of that burden, it is imperative that the remedy be related in some reasonable manner to the representation of blacks among firefighters." Id. at 1542–43.

Meanwhile, litigation in the original suit also continued when the district judge allowed plaintiffs in Martin v. Wilks to intervene for the limited purpose of arguing for modification of the decree. After the district court made some modifications, but rejected the more aggressive arguments for dismantling the decree, a different panel of the court of appeals found several aspects of the decree's preferential treatment of blacks and women in city employment unconstitutional. Ensley Branch, N.A.A.C.P. v. Seibels, 20 F.3d 1489 (11th Cir. 1994). The court of appeals found changed circumstances due to a "falling constitutional ceiling" on such provisions since 1981, when the decree was originally entered. Id. at 1504. It concluded that no showing of a compelling governmental interest justifying affirmative action had been made with regard to any city jobs except those in the fire and police departments. This opinion was later withdrawn, and a decision requiring reconsideration of race-based remedies outside the police and fire departments substituted. Ensley Branch, N.A.A.C.P. v. Seibels, 31 F.3d 1548 (11th Cir. 1994).

2.   Martin v. Wilks was one of a number of controversial employment discrimination decisions during the Court's 1988 Term that caused a significant public controversy. Reflect on the impact of the decision on issues you have considered elsewhere in this chapter. For example, does the decision indicate that in Eldredge v. Carpenters 46 Northern California Counties JATC (*supra* p. 38) the male apprentices should have been treated as necessary parties?

3.   In 1991 Congress passed, and the President signed, the Civil Rights Act of 1991. Among the provisions of that Act was an amendment to Title VII, now codified at 42 U.S.C. § 2000e–2(n)(1), to provide that "an employment practice that implements and is within the scope of a litigated or consent judgment or order that resolves a claim of employment discrimination under the Constitution or Federal civil rights laws may not be challenged * * * in a claim under the Constitution or Federal civil rights laws":

(i) by a person who, prior to the entry of the judgment or order * * * had—

> (I) actual notice of the proposed judgment or order sufficient to apprise such person that such judgment or order might adversely affect the interests and legal rights of such person and that an opportunity was available to present objections to such judgment or order by a future date certain; and

> (II) a reasonable opportunity to present objections to such judgment or order; or

(ii) by a person whose interests were adequately represented by another person who had previously challenged the judgment or order on the same legal grounds and with a similar factual situation, unless there has been an intervening change in law or fact.

What impact would this provision have had on the issues raised in Martin v. Wilks and on the application of Rules 19 and 24 in employment discrimination suits brought in the future? Does the statute create the equivalent of "mandatory intervention"? For discussion of the statute, see Andrea Catania & Charles Sullivan, Judging Judgments: The 1991 Civil Rights Act and the Lingering Ghost of Martin v. Wilks, 57 Brooklyn L. Rev. 995 (1992). Note that the act only applies to consent decrees arising in an employment discrimination case. See Wilson v. Minor, 220 F.3d 1297 (11th Cir. 2000) (voters who had not sought intervention could file an independent action challenging an injunction issued to remedy a Voting Rights Act violation).

4. The 1991 Act does not alter the standards for intervention under Rule 24. Edwards v. City of Houston, 78 F.3d 983 (5th Cir. 1996), involved a situation similar to that in Martin v. Wilks: African-American and Hispanic-American police officers sued the city, challenging promotional examinations as having a disproportional effect on their racial groups. Groups representing white, female, and Asian-American police officers moved to intervene to contest a proposed consent decree. The court denied intervention as untimely but permitted the groups to participate in the fairness hearing on the proposed decree. The Fifth Circuit reversed, finding the motion to intervene timely. It pointed out that the 1991 Act had no application as it only dealt with the situation where a nonparty files a subsequent suit collaterally attacking a decree. Here the nonparties simply appealed the denial of intervention. Six dissenting judges would have found the motion to intervene untimely as it came long after all officers had been notified of the suit and three months after the intervenors had received a copy of the proposed settlement. Is the standard for "actual notice" in the Act the same as the standard for timeliness under Rule 24?

5. In Martin v. Wilks the Court rejects the idea that parties can be required to intervene in order to protect their rights. Does the dissent disagree? Could a party who intervenes be worse off as a result? Consider whether the Martin v. Wilks respondents would have been allowed to make the claims they made in the second suit had they been allowed to intervene in the first action.

The United States, which was a party plaintiff in the first suit, joined the plaintiff white firefighters in the second suit. It was held to be collaterally estopped from attacking the consent decree. In re Birmingham Reverse Discrimination Employment Litigation, 833 F.2d 1492, 1501 (11th Cir. 1987).

In Independent Federation of Flight Attendants v. Zipes, 491 U.S. 754 (1989), the Court removed one impediment to intervention in Title VII cases by holding that intervenors who unsuccessfully oppose affirmative action decrees sought by Title VII plaintiffs may not be held liable to plaintiffs for the fees they incur resisting intervenors' arguments. The majority emphasized that "[a]n intervenor of the sort before us here is particularly welcome, since we have stressed the necessity of protecting, in Title VII litigation, 'the legitimate expectations of . . . employees innocent of any wrongdoing.' " The Court went on to reason that imposing fee liability on intervenors would "foster piecemeal litigation of complex civil rights controversies—a result that is strongly disfavored." Although unwilling to require intervention, the Court does appear to favor it.

6.   In EEOC v. Pipefitters' Local 120, 235 F.3d 244 (6th Cir. 2000), a consent decree was entered in a suit against a union involving alleged racial discrimination in work assignments. When contempt sanctions were sought years later against the union, the court ordered the contractors who hired union members to be joined as defendants for the first time pursuant to Rule 19(a). They were ordered to make any requests for referral of employees through the union in writing and to file with the court a form reporting such information as rate of pay, hours worked, and fringe benefits for each pipe fitter employed through the union. Two of the contractors objected that subjecting them to the consent decree violated the rule of Martin v. Wilks that a person cannot be deprived of his legal rights in a proceeding to which he is not a party. The court disagreed:

> The district court joined these defendant contractors to ensure complete relief on a prospective basis regarding the record-keeping and reporting requirements of the consent decree. * * * Their joinder did not subject them to liability for past conduct. They are not being deprived of legal rights by a retroactive application of the terms of the consent decree. The impact of joining [the contractors] is *de minimis* and prospective. The district court joined these defendants to enforce the decree against the Union, not for the binding effect it would have on [them]. * * *
>
> Numerous contractors that utilized the Union's hiring hall were not parties to the original consent decree. Thus, the Union's compliance with the decree, especially in light of the individual claims [of black pipefitters] and lax reporting and record-keeping, was impossible to gauge when non-party contractors hired union workers. This consideration and the need to modify the decree as a result of the Union's alleged contempt justify the district court's concern that "complete relief" could not be attained without joining [the contractors].

7. Would a rule forbidding collateral attack on employment discrimination decrees be constitutional? One commentator has concluded that "an unstated premise of the majority's holding is that the due process rights of the white firefighters necessarily would be violated by giving binding effect to a judgment in a proceeding in which they had not been joined formally as parties either under Rule 19 or 24." George Strickler, Martin v. Wilks, 64 Tulane L.Rev. 1557 (1990); see also Samuel Issacharoff, When Substance Mandates Procedure—Martin v. Wilks and the Rights of Vested Incumbents in Consent Decrees, 77 Cornell L. Rev. 189 (1992) (emphasizing protected property interests of incumbent public employees). Professor Kramer has argued, however, that with meaningful notice and the sort of opportunity to intervene that Rule 24 affords, such a requirement could be constitutional. See Larry Kramer, Consent Decrees and the Rights of Third Parties, 87 Mich.L.Rev. 321, 338–52 (1988). Would it have been constitutional to foreclose challenge in Martin v. Wilks?

8. When white firefighters did seek to intervene in the first action in Martin v. Wilks their application was rejected by the district court as untimely. Was this proper? "In a title VII suit * * * the remedy can take many forms: damages for back pay, retroactive seniority rights, and even special consideration for future promotions. Because the precise mix of these measures remains unclear until the parties settle or the judge issues a final order, outsiders cannot assess the threat a suit poses to their interests until late in the proceedings." Note, The Supreme Court—Leading Cases, 103 Harv. L. Rev. 310, 314–15 (1989). How could the intervenors on the defense side in that case know whether the court's decree really threatened their interests without knowing the terms of the decree? In Martin v. Wilks, there may have been substantial grounds for uncertainty about the contours of any eventual decree. After prevailing in part on liability, plaintiffs in the original case had a substantial claim for back pay, estimated by some as high as $5 million, but they were more interested in affirmative action in the future than money for the past. The city administration had by then changed, and the consent decree was negotiated by the city's first black mayor. The decree required the city to pay only $300,000, and the mayor stated that it was "the best business deal we had ever struck." See Stuart Taylor, Second Class Citizens, American Lawyer, Sept. 1989, at 42. For an argument that consent decrees present inherent risks that the parties to the negotiation will make a deal to maximize their interests at the expense of third parties who are not participating, see Douglas Laycock, Consent Decrees Without Consent: The Rights of Nonconsenting Third Parties, 1987 U. Chi. Legal F. 103.

Consider State v. City of Chicago, 912 F.3d 979 (7th Cir. 2019), in which the state of Illinois sued the Chicago police department alleging a pattern of excessive use of force. Two days after the case was filed, the parties moved to stay proceedings while they negotiated a consent decree. Immediately after the suit was filed, the police union publicly announced its opposition to the decree on the ground that it would affect its collective-bargaining rights. But instead of moving to intervene the union met separately with the state to ensure that the decree would not infringe its rights. Nine months later, the union moved to intervene despite that the proposed decree provided that it was not intended to impair or conflict with the union's collective-bargaining rights. The district court denied the motion, and the Seventh Circuit affirmed. In so holding, the court of appeals emphasized that the duty to seek intervention arises "when the applicant has reason to know its interests *might* be affected, not from when it knows for certain that they will be." Id. at 985. The court rejected the union's arguments that it had reasonably relied on the state to protect its interests. Indeed, the union's earlier meetings with the state demonstrated that it knew its rights might be affected. Moreover, the court concluded that the prejudice to the city and state would be great, given the complexity of the negotiations and the publicity attending the development of the consent decree. Id. at 987. See also the cases discussed in Section C, note 6, *supra*.

9.   Note that in Martin v. Wilks the African American plaintiffs from the first action were allowed to intervene in the second action. Were they intervenors of right? What interest did they have in the suit alleging violation of the rights of white firefighters?

10.   The dissent emphasizes the difference between impairing the legal rights of third parties and the way in which the outcome of the first litigation might "as a practical matter, seriously impair the interests of third parties who elect to sit on the sidelines." Does the majority disagree with this reasoning? How does the dissent's view compare to the treatment of Rule 19 and Rule 24 proposed by the majority? Recall that both those rules speak in terms of practical effects on the interests of nonparties, not legal rights of nonparties.

11.   How important is the fact that the first litigation was resolved by a consent decree? There is real concern that in such a situation the parties to the litigation may sacrifice the interests of others who are not involved as the easiest way to compromise their own differences. See Douglas Laycock, Consent Decrees Without Consent: The Rights of Nonconsenting Third Parties, 1987 U. Chi. Legal. F. 103; Thomas Mengler, Consent Decree Paradigms: Models Without Meaning, 29 Bos. Col. L. Rev. 291 (1988). Do these concerns explain the majority's decision?

The dissent points out that in this case the district court had already found that the city had discriminated illegally in making hiring decisions and had held a trial on whether it had discriminated in promotion as well, indicating that it felt there was a likelihood plaintiffs would prevail on that as well. If there had been no settlement, would an identical decree entered after a finding of discrimination in promotions have altered the majority's reasoning in Martin v. Wilks? To put this question in context, note that "litigated" decrees often involve substantial negotiation between the parties prompted by the court. The reason for this situation is that the court needs detailed input and proposals from the parties to fashion a remedy where the relief that is appropriate does not flow inexorably from the finding of a violation but depends instead on myriad details about the operation of a fairly complicated institution. Does this situation provide support for a broad attitude toward intervention?

12. If plaintiffs in the first action had made the white firefighters parties, as the Court says Rule 19 mandated, should they have been added as defendants? What claim could plaintiffs have asserted against them? Cf. Davenport v. International Bhd. of Teamsters, 166 F.3d 356, 366 (D.C.Cir. 1999) ("[W]hile Rule 19 provides for joinder of necessary parties, it does not create a cause of action against them. It is not enough that plaintiffs 'need' an injunction against [their employer] in order to obtain full relief. They must also have a right to such an injunction, and Rule 19 cannot provide such a right").

CHAPTER 3

MULTIPLE RELATED LAWSUITS

■ ■ ■

Litigation may be called complex because of the joinder of multiple parties, the difficulty of the issues involved, or the volume of discovery and evidence necessitating substantial court administration. Sometimes, however, cases take on complexities by virtue of their relationship to other cases. Although filed separately, cases can be so clearly related that they should be looked at as part of the same piece of litigation. If such cases are handled separately without considering their relationship to one another, the objective of just and efficient resolution of disputes may be frustrated. Allowing separate cases between the same parties on the same or similar issues to proceed independently is not only wasteful but encourages parties to forum or judge shop and to try to obtain an advantage by multiple litigation of the same matters. Even when separate cases have only some of the same parties or issues, separate litigation can be wasteful and can result in inconsistent or conflicting determinations, leading to uncertainty as to what has been decided and as to the impact of judgments in other suits. Thus, the Manual for Complex Litigation (4th) § 20 (2004) observes that "[c]ontrol over the proliferation of cases and coordination of multiple claims is crucial to effective management of complex litigation."

Duplicative litigation is the simultaneous prosecution of two or more suits in which some of the parties or issues are so closely related that the judgment in one will necessarily have a res judicata effect on the other. See Note, Federal Court Stays and Dismissals in Deference to Parallel State Court Proceedings, 44 U.Chi.L.Rev. 641 (1977). Sometimes the terms "parallel proceedings" and "exercise of concurrent jurisdiction" are also used to describe this situation. Three basic types of duplicative litigation have been identified—(1) multiple suits on the same claim by the same plaintiff against the same defendant ("repetitive" suits), (2) a separate suit filed by a defendant to the first action against the plaintiff to the first action, seeking a declaratory judgment that it is not liable under the conditions of the first action or asserting an affirmative claim that arises out of the same transaction or occurrence as the subject matter of the first action ("reactive" suits, though the two suits described may be brought in reverse order—a suit seeking a declaratory judgment of non-liability followed by an affirmative claim), and (3) separate actions by class members on the same cause of action raised in the class action, seeking to represent the same or a similar class (this last category will be discussed in the Chapter 5 on class actions). See Allan Vestal, Reactive Litigation, 47

Iowa L.Rev. 11 (1961); Allan Vestal, Repetitive Litigation, 45 Iowa L.Rev. 525 (1960). Under the third category, there may also be "overlapping class actions," that is, class actions filed in a number of courts, either federal or state, against the same (or some of the same) defendants, concerning the same matter, on behalf of classes with some of the same class members. Problems arising in this situation are addressed in Chapter 5.

Apart from strictly duplicative litigation, there are also many situations in which separate suits involve similar parties or issues, but res judicata will not apply. Examples are separate suits by different plaintiffs against the same defendant arising out of the same or a similar cause of action; separate suits involving some of the same and some different parties, having some of the same or similar causes of action; and separate suits by different parties litigating claims to the same rights, property, or *res*. These cases—which we will refer to as *related litigation*—raise somewhat different considerations than duplicative litigation, although some of the same concerns as to efficiency and economy, consistency in outcome, effective judicial administration, and (where applicable) avoidance of friction between state and federal courts arise in both.

This chapter addresses several ways to handle multiple related lawsuits—consolidation, stays, injunctions, and transfer. Chapter 4 will address another important way to handle multiple related lawsuits—federal multidistrict litigation.

A. CONSOLIDATION

Rule 42(a) allows a federal district court, if actions before it involve "a common question of law or fact" to "join for hearing or trial any or all the matters at issue in the actions" or to "consolidate the actions." Consolidation was "[o]ne of the earliest examples of case management based on inherent authority," and was viewed as "an inseparable aspect of the powers possessed by common-law and equity courts." Daniel Meador, Inherent Judicial Authority in the Conduct of Civil Litigation, 73 Texas L. Rev. 1805, 1807 (1995). "[C]onsolidation is permitted as a matter of convenience and economy in administration, but does not merge the suits into a single cause, or change the rights of the parties, or make those who are parties in one suit parties in another." Johnson v. Manhattan Railway Co., 289 U.S. 479, 496–497 (1933).

Consolidation can take place only when the actions are pending in the same division of the same federal district court. However, 28 U.S.C. § 1404(b) provides: "Upon motion, consent or stipulation of all parties, any action, suit or proceeding of a civil nature or any motion or hearing thereof, may be transferred, in the discretion of the court, from the division in which pending to any other division in the same district." Local court rules should be looked to for guidance.

KATZ V. REALTY EQUITIES CORP. OF NEW YORK

United States Court of Appeals, Second Circuit, 1975.
521 F.2d 1354.

Before WATERMAN, FRIENDLY and GURFEIN, CIRCUIT JUDGES.

WATERMAN, CIRCUIT JUDGE.

This appeal concerns an order of a district judge requiring the filing and service of a single consolidated complaint for pretrial purposes upon defendants in a number of related securities cases. We affirm the order which, under the circumstances present, was a proper exercise of the trial judge's authority in the management of the preliminary stages of complex multiparty litigation.

On March 8, 1974 the Securities and Exchange Commission commenced an enforcement action in the United States District Court for the Southern District of New York against Republic National Life Insurance Company ("Republic"), seven of its officers and directors, its auditor Peat Marwick Mitchell & Co., Realty Equities Corporation of New York ("Realty"), two of its officials, its auditor Westheimer, Fine, Berger & Co., and two other individuals. The SEC complaint alleges that the defendants participated in a scheme to defraud the investing public by concealing the actual facts of Realty's financial condition. Republic, which had large investments in Realty, advanced large sums of money, the SEC complaint alleges, through a series of intricate transactions, to Realty or related companies, so that Realty could repay existing indebtedness to Republic.

Patterned on the SEC complaint, twelve private actions were filed in the Southern District of New York based on the Realty-Republic transactions. In addition, four actions were filed in the Northern District of Texas and one action in the Middle District of Tennessee; these five actions were transferred to the Southern District of New York for pretrial purposes by the Judicial Panel on Multidistrict Litigation by order of August 22, 1974, and on August 26, 1974 the district court ordered them consolidated with the pending actions in the Southern District of New York which had been ordered consolidated two months previously.

On June 12, 1974 the district court sua sponte held a hearing to determine whether the actions then pending before it should be consolidated. On June 24, 1974 the district court filed an order of consolidation which provided in part:

Ordered:

(1) The above designated actions (sometimes herein "constituent actions") are hereby consolidated for all pretrial purposes to be had during the pendency of these actions in this District in accordance with the following terms which the Court

in the exercise of discretion makes applicable to foster the efficient and proper conduct of the claims asserted in the individual complaints in the said actions.

(2) A single consolidated complaint, supplemented and amended, shall be prepared and served herein by liaison counsel which shall set forth the claims for relief asserted in the constituent actions, collated into separately stated counts by class and derivative categories as to each kind of securities holders and at the head of each count shall specifically designate by name or other convenient reference the defendants against whom such count is asserted.

* * *

(11) At the conclusion of the pretrial proceedings, the Court will give consideration to a consolidated trial of the issues herein.

The order of the district court provided for the appointment of lead and liaison counsel for all plaintiffs. The order also stated that the answer of each defendant to the consolidated complaint "shall be deemed" to have asserted cross-claims in the nature of contribution and indemnification against all other defendants.

At the June 12 hearing, the appellants Klein, Hinds & Finke ("KHF") and Alexander Grant & Company ("Grant"), favored the use of consolidated discovery proceedings, but they objected to proceeding under a single consolidated complaint. After the consolidation order was entered the appellants filed a timely notice of appeal which was limited to the portion of the order providing for the consolidation for all pretrial purposes and for the filing of a single consolidated complaint. The sole objection pressed on appeal is to the use of a consolidated complaint.

KHF and Grant had been named as defendants in two of the private complaints, the Herman complaint, a class action brought on behalf of the holders of common stock of Republic, and the Katz complaint, a class action brought on behalf of the holders of common stock in Realty. They had not been named as defendants in the SEC action. In nearly identical language the complaints allege that the appellants violated § 10(b) of the Securities Exchange Act of 1934, 15 U.S.C. § 78j(b), and Rule 10b–5 promulgated thereunder:

> Grant and KHF were the independent auditors for Realty during certain relevant portions of the periods above described. Each discovered and knew of certain and many ways of the material problems between Realty and Republic, all as hereinabove described. Grant and KHF informed Realty of the fact that the financial statements of Realty and of FNR [First National Realty & Construction Corp., a Realty affiliate] would not be unqualified and both firms were replaced as auditors for

Realty. Yet both firms failed of their obligations to the public and to the SEC and Amex to fully disclose such facts and to alert the responsible authorities thereto. Instead each firm withheld the facts thereof in order to benefit themselves by not involving themselves therein, directly or indirectly, and to prevent damage to themselves and to other defendants, despite the further damage resulting to plaintiff and the class.

Thus the claims against Grant and KHF are limited. There is no allegation that they participated in the complicated real estate and financial transactions between Republic and Realty which are at the core of the SEC complaint and the private complaints based upon the SEC allegations.

The amended consolidated complaint was served on all defendants including KHF and Grant on October 15, 1974. Under it twenty-one plaintiffs sue thirty-nine defendants. Five different classes of plaintiffs allege a total of thirty counts against defendants. The classes consist of: persons who purchased securities in Realty; persons who purchased securities in Republic; holders of shares of Pacific National Life Assurance Company; owners of certain debentures of Realty; and holders of common stock in Mercantile Security Life Insurance Company. Two counts involve derivative claims on behalf of Realty and Republic, and one count is brought individually. Grant and KHF are named in three counts of the consolidated complaint. Each of these counts contains the § 10(b) and Rule 10b–5 allegations of the Katz and Herman complaints and the several plaintiffs are the purchasers of Realty securities, the purchasers of Republic securities, and stockholders of Realty suing derivatively. The remaining bulk of the consolidated complaint concerns the manipulative transactions between Realty and Republic, transactions which allegedly began in September 1970, after Grant and KHF were unable to present unqualified financial statements and after Grant and KHF had been replaced as auditors for Realty.

* * *

Here, under the broad heading that the district court lacked the authority to order a consolidated complaint, the appellants advance various objections to the use of a consolidated complaint: that the order accomplishes an impermissible merger of claims; that the decision in *Garber v. Randell,* [477 F.2d 711 (2d Cir. 1973)], excluding the law firm there, is indistinguishable and controlling; that the order inflicts substantial prejudice on the appellants. We are convinced, however, that the trial judge properly exercised his authority when he fashioned this pretrial order, an order appropriate for this complex litigation, and we affirm the order. We are confident that if the claimed prejudice to the appellants, which is now a premature and speculative apprehension, should occur, the trial judge will act vigorously to remedy the situation.

It is axiomatic that consolidation is a procedural device designed to promote judicial economy and that consolidation cannot effect a physical merger of the actions or the defenses of the separate parties. *Johnson v. Manhattan Ry. Co.,* 289 U.S. 479, 496–497 (1933). There is here, however, no indication that the court below intended a physical merger of claims or that one was accomplished despite the court's intent. Rather, it is evident that the district court limited the use of the consolidated complaint to the controversies' pretrial stages in order to prevent unnecessary duplication and in order to reduce the potential for confusion. At the preliminary hearing on consolidation the trial judge stated:

> It seems to me that the use of a single consolidated complaint need not necessarily foreclose the use of individual complaints at a trial, and in the same way as consolidated discovery would be useful and efficient, a single consolidated complaint during the discovery and pretrial period would be useful and efficient and could be without prejudice to unfurling the separate flags at trial, if necessary, to protect any legitimate interests that may have to be dealt with separately.
>
>   * * *
>
> I think I am going to try it. I will order a single consolidated complaint for pretrial purposes without prejudice, as I say, to whether or not there will be a consolidated trial and without prejudice to the use of the individual complaints as they stand now at a consolidated trial, and certainly without prejudice to their use in individual trials if that should eventuate.[4]

Also, it is stated in the consolidation order that any decision on a trial consolidation would await the conclusion of the pretrial proceedings. The instructions contained in paragraph 2 of the district court order for the collation of the separately stated counts and for the specific designations of the defendants is a further indication that the trial court, while retaining the particular attributes of each of the several complaints, was attempting to incorporate all the complaints into a single document for convenient pretrial handling.

---

[4] At a subsequent hearing on September 12, 1974, the district judge stated:

    This is a draft, and it isn't even a penultimate draft. It is to coordinate all the claims, and there can be one filed tomorrow and one after that, the day after tomorrow.

    The whole purpose of this complaint is to get organized for the discovery and pretrial phase. The order that I entered specifically recites that the pleadings in each constituent action stand, and when you go back to trial, the constituent actions will determine what will be tried and how, unless when we get to the trial it is agreed that a consolidation of the constituent complaints can be made.

    But for present purposes you have got to start somewhere, and the amended consolidated complaint is intended to wrap up all the claims so that we can get on with the business of discovery.

The use of the consolidated complaint here has significant attractions in keeping the preliminary stages of these cases within reasonable bounds. There are seventeen actions pending against thirty-nine defendants; many of the defendants are sued in most of the actions, some in but a few. A separate answer from each defendant to each complaint in which that defendant is named would involve literally hundreds of answers. As noted previously, all the complaints in the private actions track the SEC complaint, and the answers to each complaint would be substantially the same. The benefits of collecting, for example, sixteen identical answers in each of sixteen cases from one defendant is not readily discernible. It is true that those defendants named in only a small number of complaints, for example Grant and KHF, would not be overly burdened, but, nevertheless, the overall economies in reducing the proliferation of duplicative papers warrant the trial judge's efforts in the present circumstances. Moreover, it is apparent that a consolidated complaint also aids the consolidated discovery process which all parties, including the appellants, favor. Directing discovery to one complaint, rather than to seventeen complaints, avoids the possible confusion and the possible problems stemming from the situation where each plaintiff pursues his individual complaint. While it is true that carefully supervised and coordinated discovery proceedings would reduce the potential for chaos, the use of a consolidated complaint promotes the desired objective.

It therefore appears clear that in the circumstances here present which involve complex and multifaceted actions with a number of similar complaints, the adoption of a consolidated complaint is a device well-suited to achieving economies of effort on the part of the parties and of the court. Limited presently to the pretrial stages, the consolidated complaint does not supersede the individual complaints and does not impermissibly merge the rights or defenses of the various parties.

Appellants contend that we are not considering this issue afresh and that the Second Circuit's decision in *Garber v. Randell, supra,* compels the result they urge. We disagree. In *Garber* three class actions were instituted against fifty-eight defendants in which the plaintiffs alleged violations of the federal securities laws. The principal thrust of the complaints alleged the artificial inflation of the shares of National Student Marketing Corp. during a four year period through the publication of false and misleading information. One of the complaints, the last filed, also asserted claims that a law firm, White and Case, as counsel for National Student Marketing Corp., had participated in a merger transaction in which it had failed to disclose to stockholders that an accountant's comfort letter did not conform to the terms of the merger; had issued opinions on the validity of the merger agreement; and had transmitted, on behalf of National Student Marketing Corp., a false Form 8K to the SEC. The complaint also alleged that the law firm had on two other occasions rendered opinions on transactions in which the National Student Marketing Corp. had backdated activities.

The district court, in *Garber v. Randell,* after a hearing, issued an order of consolidation [for pretrial purposes, requiring plaintiffs to file a consolidated complaint]. * * * The law firm appealed from this order, as well as from another order denying its motion for severance. The Second Circuit held that joinder of the limited claims against White and Case with the other unrelated claims in a consolidated complaint "would be fundamentally unfair and would violate the principles underlying our decision in *MacAlister v. Guterma,* [263 F.2d 65 (2d Cir. 1958)], and the unbroken line of authority going back to *Johnson v. Manhattan Railway Co., supra.*"

The court, however, noted in a footnote that in other circumstances the use of a consolidated complaint might be appropriate, thus recognizing the authority of the district court to so order. * * * The principal reason was the limited and unrelated nature of the alleged misconduct by White and Case which occurred largely on one day and totally within a two-and-a-half month period. In addition, other significant factors were present. Only one of fifteen named plaintiffs brought suit against White and Case, and several of the other plaintiffs had expressly disassociated themselves from these assertions. One Natale, the sole plaintiff alleging the White and Case wrongdoing, had not purchased National Student Marketing Corp. shares on the open market, and it appeared questionable whether he was a proper class representative. White and Case argued that this fact was highly prejudicial because it made it much more difficult, if not impossible, for it to isolate and attack the infirmities of the action by Natale, for not only had he not purchased shares but he also was the only plaintiff seeking to assert claims against White and Case. Also, the only persons who had acquired shares after the date of the alleged concealment by the law firm would be in a position to claim damages, and therefore it would be necessary at some point to separate the claims against White and Case from the claims against the others.

These latter factors, present in *Garber,* are absent here. Thus far there has been no claim that Herman and Katz are improper class representatives. Appellate counsel at oral argument informed the court that the motion for class designation is still pending in the district court. The other plaintiffs have not disassociated themselves from the claims advanced against the appellants; indeed they argue that their acquiescence in proceeding in accord with the order prescribing the consolidated complaint constitutes a de facto amendment of their constituent complaints. The actions of Grant and KHF occurred prior to the transactions which form the bulk of the actions rather than in the midst of the manipulative activity as in *Garber,* and it is plaintiffs' contention that had the auditors been forthright the subsequent alleged wrongs might not have occurred.

These distinctions, however, are not in themselves compelling. Grant and KHF argue forcefully that in the main their fact-situation is analogous to that of White and Case: actors on the periphery of the main activities who must defend against claims having but a remote relation to the principal issues. They also stress that in both cases the order of consolidation limited the consolidation to the pretrial stages of the litigation.

Nevertheless, we choose not to adopt and apply the specific conclusion of *Garber* to the present case. *Garber's* broad holding was that the validity of a consolidated order must be examined with reference to the special underlying facts prompting the order, and with close attention alike to the potential economies of the consolidation on the one hand, and the threatened prejudice to a party or parties, on the other hand. We are not convinced here that the appellants have been presently prejudiced by the consolidated complaint or that the district court will not be alert to the possibility of prejudice to them in the future. Without a firm conviction that prejudice will result, we are most reluctant to interfere, and perhaps disrupt, the efforts of the district court which, without sacrificing the rights of the various parties, seeks to expedite this complex litigation.

The appellants claim that they have been prejudiced in two ways: the expansion of the classes in the consolidated complaint; and the deeming of cross-claims amongst the defendants during the discovery process. As noted *supra,* the Katz and Herman complaints were brought on behalf of purchasers of common stock of Realty and Republic respectively, while the consolidated complaint alleges claims on behalf of "purchasers of securities" in the companies. This expansion of the classes, for which there is no authority in the district court order, would of course increase the potential liability of Grant and KHF in the event that the consolidated complaint was used at trial. This is not the physical merger of claims, which the caselaw forbids, but rather an expansion of classes, which is also troubling. However, the classes have not yet been defined by the district court, and the appropriate place for appellants to object to the proposed definition of the proposed classes is before the district court.

The appellants did not appeal from that portion of the district court order which deemed the answer of each defendant to assert cross-claims for indemnification and contribution against all other defendants.[7] The

---

[7]   The relevant portion of the district court order reads as follows:

(9)   The answer of each defendant to the consolidated complaint (or latest amended complaint) in each of the above-captioned actions shall be deemed to assert cross-claims against all the other defendants therein for such sharing of liability in the nature of contribution and indemnification as exists under the Securities Act of 1933 (15 U.S.C. § 77a *et seq.*) and the Securities Exchange Act of 1934 (15 U.S.C. § 78a *et seq.*) as well as by state statutory and common law, except insofar as any defendant shall in his answer decline to assert such claims against any other defendant; such claims to be deemed asserted in the following form:

only issue before us, therefore, is the prejudicial effect to appellants of this order in connection with the apparently distinct issue of the consolidation of complaints, the issue appealed. It appears from the record that the preservation of cross-claims was designed only to serve as an economical device to facilitate the discovery process and to avoid the proliferation of pleadings. Upon the completion of the discovery and upon a fuller comprehension of the facts, the parties and court can better evaluate the cross-claims worthy of perusal. Appellants do not detail in what manner prejudice will result from this effort to simplify matters, nor do they explain how this is in any way related to the issue they raised before the court, the propriety of the use of a consolidated complaint.

We accordingly find there is no clear showing that the appellants have been prejudiced as a result of the district court's order requiring the filing of a consolidated complaint for pretrial purposes. The appellants' fear, perhaps substantial, that because of their peripheral involvement in the principal transactions involved in the litigation they will suffer prejudice, does not result from the consolidation of the complaints. The Katz and Herman complaints, like the other constituent complaints, parallel the SEC complaint, and are broad in scope; in these complaints the appellants are also peripheral defendants. At the preliminary hearing the district court expressly invited Grant and KHF to move for dismissal of the complaint. In addition, the use of the consolidated complaint for pretrial purposes does not impair appellants' subsequent recourse to the timely motion for severance. At present appellants' fears of prejudice are wholly speculative: if the classes are defined along the present lines, if a motion to dismiss is denied, if a motion for severance is denied, and if the consolidated complaint is used at trial, then appellants' right to their separate defenses may be jeopardized. This possibility is too remote to justify appellate intervention into the pretrial stages of this litigation; and, although we have accepted jurisdiction, we point out that the appeal is

---

FIRST CROSS-CLAIM AGAINST ALL OTHER DEFENDANTS

If plaintiffs recover judgment against the cross-claiming defendant, the cross-claiming defendant is, or may be, entitled to contribution under the Securities Act of 1933 (15 U.S.C. § 77(a) [77a] *et seq.*) and the Securities Exchange Act of 1934 (15 U.S.C. § 78(a) [78a] *et seq.*) from some or all of the defendants other than the cross-claiming defendant.

SECOND CROSS-CLAIM AGAINST ALL OTHER DEFENDANTS

If plaintiffs herein recover judgment against the cross-claiming defendant by reason of any of the acts, transactions or omissions alleged in the amended complaint, such judgment will have been brought about and caused wholly or primarily by the acts, transactions, commissions or omissions of some or all of the defendants and not by, or only secondarily by, any acts, transactions or omissions of the cross-claiming defendant.

By reason of the foregoing, the cross-claiming defendant is, or may be, entitled to indemnification or contribution for all or part of any such judgment recovered by plaintiffs herein,

and each defendant against whom such cross-claims have been asserted shall be deemed to have interposed answers to said cross-claims controverting the allegations contained therein and denying any liability in the nature of contribution or indemnification.

All cross-claims asserting claims other than for shared liability as hereinbefore described remain unaffected by the foregoing provisions of this order.

taken from an interlocutory order and that an appeal so taken comes close to violating the long-standing and accepted rule statutorily incorporated in 28 U.S.C. § 1291, a rule which has well served the federal courts for years.

Order affirmed.

NOTES AND QUESTIONS

1. "Consolidation holds out a bland, somewhat technocratic, uncontroversial face to the world." Richard Marcus, Confronting the Consolidation Conundrum, 1995 BYU L. Rev. 879, 887. Is that appearance really justified? The standard for consolidation under Rule 42(a) (that the actions involve "a common question of law or fact") is close to the second requirement for permissive joinder under Rule 20(a) ("any question of law or fact common to all plaintiffs will arise in the action"). It is also close to the requirement for permissive intervention under Rule 24(b) ("when an applicant's claim or defense and the main action have a question of law or fact in common"). Should the "common question" language in these three rules be interpreted in the same way? Is this a less demanding standard than in the "same transaction or occurrence" requirement for party joinder in Rule 20(a)?

2. The counterweight to the benefits of consolidation is the prejudice that may result from it. Is the more significant prejudice at trial or before trial? What effect will pretrial consolidation have on "bystander" defendants who are named in only one of the consolidated cases and who must decide how to protect their interests during massive discovery of the consolidated actions?

Rule 42(a) leaves a court wide latitude in deciding how much should be consolidated; a consolidation order may apply only to pretrial discovery, or to other aspects of pretrial, or to disposition of particular issues, or may be extended through trial and final judgment. The court has the power to alter its consolidation order or to use Rule 42(b) to order separate trials of any claims or issues "in furtherance of convenience or to avoid prejudice, or when separate trials will be conducive to expedition and economy." Courts sometimes refer to such orders as a severance (Rule 21 provides: "Misjoinder of parties is not a ground for dismissing an action. On motion or on its own, a court may at any time, on just terms, add or drop a party. The court may also sever any claim against a party"), although Rule 42(b) is the appropriate vehicle for ordering separate trials when there has previously been some form of consolidation.

3. The rule of Johnson v. Manhattan Railway Co., 289 U.S. 479 (1933), was that consolidated cases are not merged into a single case, even though there may be a consolidated complaint applicable to all the cases. The Supreme Court reaffirmed this rule in Hall v. Hall, 138 S.Ct. 1118 (2018). In Hall, a family will dispute led to a suit by the decedent's son against her daughter and also a suit by the daughter against the son. The cases were consolidated and tried together. After the jury returned its verdict, the district court ordered a new trial of the claims presented in one of the cases, but it entered judgment in the other against the daughter. The daughter appealed that judgment, but the court of appeals dismissed the appeal on the ground that due to the overlap

with the case still pending in district court the judgment should not be considered final. The Supreme Court reversed and held that the consolidation did not delay entry of an appealable final judgment. Per Chief Justice Roberts: "From the outset, we understood consolidation not as completely merging the constituent cases into one, but instead as enabling more efficient case management while preserving the distinct identities of the cases and the rights of the separate parties in them." Id. at 1125.

This outcome is consistent with the Court's unanimous holding in Gelboim v. Bank of America Corp., 574 U.S. 405 (2015), that a final judgment of dismissal of one case in a multidistrict litigation is appealable even though pretrial proceedings in the other cases continue in the transferee district. But in *Gelboim*, Justice Ginsburg recognized that sometimes district courts handling multidistrict litigation direct the parties to draft a "master complaint" that will "supersede prior individual pleadings," with the result of "merging the discrete actions for the duration of the MDL pretrial proceedings." Id. at 413, n.3. The scope of authority under Rule 42(a) to "merge" separate actions may be uncertain, however.

Consider In re TMI Litigation, 193 F.3d 613 (3d Cir. 1999), which involved consolidated cases of 2,000 plaintiffs seeking recovery for personal injuries resulting from the release of radioactive discharge from the Three Mile Island nuclear reactor. The court directed a "bellwether" trial of ten "trial plaintiffs." Defendants then moved for summary judgment on the ground that plaintiffs' expert scientific evidence was not admissible. The district court granted summary judgment as to all 2,000 plaintiffs, and not just the ten trial plaintiffs. The appellate court reversed, noting that "consolidation is not intended to affect the substantive rights of the parties to the consolidated cases." The non-trial plaintiffs had not been given an opportunity to object to the motion for summary judgment and therefore should not have been included in the court's judgment. See also Cella v. Togum Constructeur Ensembleier en Industrie Alimentaire, 173 F.3d 909, 912 (3d Cir. 1999) ("while a consolidation order may result in a single unit of litigation, such an order does not create a single case for jurisdiction purposes"); compare Schnabel v. Lui, 302 F.3d 1023, 1035 (9th Cir. 2002) ("we do not resolve the issue of whether consolidated actions in general retain their separate character under *Johnson* and its progeny, or are merged for purposes of determining personal jurisdiction").

4.   Paul Rheingold, The MER/29 Story—An Instance of Successful Mass Disaster Litigation, 56 Calif. L. Rev. 116 (1968) discussed the considerations that led 1,500 plaintiffs who had filed individual product liability suits against the manufacturer of the drug MER/29 not to seek consolidation for trial. The author was one of the plaintiffs' lawyers. He explained that "the most basic decision" for both sides was whether to consolidate the cases, even for pretrial purposes. A primary consideration was the opposition of plaintiffs' lawyers because they did not want to lose control of their individual cases and had a "concern for one's identity as a trial lawyer," as well as "the potential economic consequences of group trial." The plaintiffs' lawyers formed the MER/29 Group, each contributing $300 (this was 1968, but even so, this would be a small

amount in comparison with what such *consortia* expect today). It provided information on common issues and the status of individual trials and even conducted an "MER/29 School" for plaintiff lawyers before their individual trials. A reported disadvantage for plaintiffs of this "free enterprise" approach was that it "returned the balance of power" to the defendant as to which cases would be settled and which tried and in what order. Likewise, "[t]he defendant could and did select the cases it wanted tried. Good cases approaching trial were settled."

In contrast, a judge has broad discretionary powers to treat a consolidated case much like a single entity. The judge can appoint (or require the parties on each side to select) lead counsel through whom the parties must file motions or otherwise deal with the court. See *infra* p. 506. The parties can be required to file uniform pleadings which could result in the loss of individual claims or defenses. For a recent illustration, see Malden Transportation, Inc. v. Uber Technologies, Inc., 323 F.R.D. 118 (D. Mass. 2017), in which the court rejected plaintiffs' proposed "coordination" of separate actions as insufficient, and insisted that "consolidation" should instead occur, including the appointment of liaison counsel with authority to handle the consolidated cases. In so holding, the court explained that "[t]his litigation requires a single attorney to be accountable to the court and to negotiate with defendant on administrative matters." Id. at 121.

5.   In *Katz*, the court reiterated the familiar adage that consolidation does not "effect a physical merger of the actions." In the same vein, the court assured the parties that the original pleadings would remain in the case after the filing of the consolidated complaint. How reassuring are these statements? Can the individual characteristics of different cases really be preserved? Won't discovery proceed along the lines outlined in the coordinated complaint, with questions of relevance measured by it? How would such questions of relevance be decided in the absence of a consolidated complaint? The trial court's procedure also deems each defendant to have asserted a cross claim against every other defendant. Would this sort of provision be consistent with Rule 11? If the cases later revert to original pleadings without such cross claims, will these claims then disappear? How much more would be required to violate the rule against "physical merger" of the cases?

6.   Consolidation can create an action that resembles a class action, but with a few differences. Consolidation is restricted to pending cases and cannot encompass "future" parties as can a class action, and parties cannot opt out of a consolidated case (as they can a (b)(3) class action). See Charles Silver, Comparing Class Actions and Consolidations, 10 Rev.Litig. 495, 499–512 (1991); Judith Resnik, From "Cases" to "Litigation," 54 Law & Contemp. Probs. 5 (Summer 1991). Consolidation has been invoked in tandem with the class action to accomplish aggregation of asbestos tort cases. See Cimino v. Raymark Indus., Inc., No. B–86–0456–Ca, Mem. and Order 2–3 (1989) ("This court finds that the fairest and most efficient way of processing these cases is to join these 3,031 cases together under Fed.R.Civ.P. 42(a) for a single trial on the issues of state of the art and punitive damages, and to certify a class action under Rule

23(b)(3) for the remaining issues of exposure and actual damages."). Such use raises questions as to whether the two devices should be applied consistently. The American Law Institute's Complex Litigation Project placed principal emphasis on consolidation as a method for aggregating litigations from various locations and handling them together. For an examination of this proposal, contrasting the limitations prescribed by the ALI with those that confine a class action under Rule 23(b)(3), see Richard Marcus, Confronting the Consolidation Conundrum, 1995 BYU L. Rev. 879.

7. *Consolidated trials.* In *Katz*, the judge defers consideration of holding a consolidated trial and suggests that the parties can revive their superseded pleadings for separate trials. As you will see in the discussion of multidistrict transfer in Chapter 4, the MDL statute does not authorize transfer for trial. Consider the additional difficulties that may attend a consolidated trial, as compared to consolidated pretrial preparation. These sorts of concerns have proved especially challenging in mass tort consolidations, which are discussed in Chapter 8. One experienced lawyer warned that "before a consolidated trial of mass tort claims can occur, courts must carefully scrutinize the effect that consolidation will have on the jury's ability to weigh the evidence fairly. Particularly when causation is a key issue or when the tort is otherwise not mature, consolidation may be an abuse of discretion that the appellate courts increasingly are going out of their way to correct." Russell Jackson, Consolidation Reversals, Nat.L.J., Oct. 11, 2014.

8. *Related cases.* The Manual for Complex Litigation (4th) § 20.11 (2004) suggests:

> All related civil cases pending in the same court should initially be assigned to a single judge to determine whether consolidation, or at least coordination of pretrial, is feasible and will reduce conflicts and duplication.

And indeed in many, if not all, districts, there is a practice or rule regarding "related cases" that directs lawyers to notify the judge or court clerk if a recently filed case involves issues already pending before another judge. In most districts, this is accomplished by simply noting on the civil cover sheet that the case is related to another case pending in the district. Whether the case will ultimately be deemed related is a matter for each district's local rules, pursuant to 28 U.S.C. § 137, which allows each district to determine its rules of case assignment. Although in most districts, practice tends to be rather informal, some districts observe complicated procedures to determine whether a case is related to an already-pending case. For instance, in the Northern District of California, a determination of whether cases are related requires motion practice and the determination by the judge to whom the cases will be assigned. See N.D. Cal. Local Rule 3–12.

Related case treatment obviously serves interests of efficiency and economy by placing complex controversies involving numerous cases before a single judge who can become expert in the complexities of the litigation and perhaps achieve a fair resolution. For a prominent example, consider the litigation involving the pollution of the water supply in Flint, Michigan, a controversy that spawned dozens of federal lawsuits, all of which were assigned to Judge Judith Levy. Judge Levy treated the cases similarly to a multidistrict litigation by appointing lead counsel, overseeing coordinated discovery and motion practice, and posting all relevant documents, transcripts, and orders to a court website freely accessible to the public. Judge Levy's case management orders throughout the litigation are posted on the U.S. District Court for the Eastern District of Michigan's website: https://www.mied.us courts.gov/index.cfm?pageFunction=CasesOfInterest. For another prominent example, see Malden Transp., Inc. v. Uber Tech., 323 F.R.D. 118 (D. Mass. 2017).

But related-case treatment can also cause concern because related cases may involve many cases within a single district, but the power to resolve them is invested in a single judge, based entirely on to which judge the first case of the bunch was assigned. A prominent example arose in connection with the cases challenging the stop-and-frisk practices of the New York Police Department. The judge who was assigned that case was assigned it as a related case to an earlier case she had handled involving the police shooting of an immigrant named Amadou Diallo, which resulted from a stop-and-frisk incident. After the judge ruled that the police practices were unconstitutional, challenges were made to her accepting the case as related to the suit about Diallo, and eventually the court of appeals ordered that the case be assigned to another judge. The district court also changed its local rule for related-case assignments by adding a requirement that the party claiming a case is related to a pending case must file a statement "stating clearly and succinctly the basis for the contention," and permitting the other parties to object. For discussion, see Benjamin Weisler & Joseph Goldstein, Federal Court Alters Rules on Judge Assignments, N.Y. Times, Dec. 23, 2013.

B. STAY AND INJUNCTION

WILLIAM GLUCKIN & CO. V. INTERNATIONAL PLAYTEX CORP.

United States Court of Appeals, Second Circuit, 1969.
407 F.2d 177.

Before MOORE, SMITH and HAYS, CIRCUIT JUDGES.

MOORE, CIRCUIT JUDGE.

International Playtex Corporation (Playtex) appeals from an order entered in the District Court for the Southern District of New York granting a preliminary injunction which restrains Playtex from further prosecuting a patent infringement suit pending in the United States District Court for the Northern District of Georgia until final disposition of the instant case. The underlying suit here in the Southern District of New York was brought by William Gluckin & Co. (Gluckin) against Playtex for a declaration of patent invalidity and/or non-infringement.

Involved here are two patent infringement suits and the question is which takes priority over the other. The first-commenced action was instituted by the patent holder against the customer of an allegedly infringing manufacturer in the Northern District of Georgia. The second action is a declaratory judgment suit against the patent holder in the Southern District of New York.

On April 25, 1968, Playtex brought a patent infringement action against F.W. Woolworth & Co. (Woolworth), alleging in its complaint that Woolworth was selling a brassiere which infringed a patent which it owned. The action was instituted in the Northern District of Georgia ostensibly because Woolworth was selling the allegedly infringing brassiere at its store in Gainesville, Georgia. Playtex, a Delaware corporation, has three of its five manufacturing plants located in Georgia. Its principal place of business is in New York. Woolworth is a New York corporation, with its principal place of business there, and operates retail stores throughout the nation.

The manufacturer of the challenged brassiere sold by Woolworth is Gluckin, a New York corporation with its principal place of business in New York City. It is not licensed to do business in Georgia and, apparently, not subject to suit there. On May 28, 1968, after Playtex had filed its Georgia action, Gluckin brought a declaratory judgment action for patent invalidity and non-infringement against Playtex in the Southern District of New York.

On July 2, 1968, a preliminary injunction was issued by Judge Motley restraining Playtex from further prosecuting the Georgia suit. Judge Motley held that since the first filed suit was against a customer rather than against Gluckin itself and since New York was the most convenient forum for resolving the questions of patent validity and infringement, special circumstances existed which justified giving priority to the second-filed suit.

The general rule in this Circuit is that, as a principle of sound judicial administration, the first suit should have priority, "absent the showing of balance of convenience in favor of the second action." Mattel, Inc. v. Louis Marx & Co., 353 F.2d 421, 423 (2d Cir. 1965), petition for cert. dismissed, 384 U.S. 948 (1966), or unless there are special circumstances which justify giving priority to the second. In deciding between competing jurisdictions, it has often been stated that the balancing of convenience should be left to the sound discretion of the district courts. Kerotest Mfg. Co. v. C-O-Two Fire Equipment Co., 342 U.S. 180 (1952).

In *Mattel, supra,* two situations were posed which are said to constitute special circumstances justifying a departure from the "first-filed" rule of priority. The first example is the so-called "customer action" where the first-filed suit is against a customer of the alleged infringer while the second suit involves the infringer himself.

The second example is where forum shopping alone motivated the choice of the situs for the first suit. This, however, is not applicable to the present case because Judge Motley made no specific finding of forum shopping, nor is one inferable and because the reasons Playtex asserts justifying the choice of a Georgia forum are not wholly frivolous.

Judge Motley, relying on the "customer suit" exception to the first-filed rule mentioned in the *Mattel* case, granted the preliminary injunction. Playtex insists, however, that there is no reason why the first suit should be enjoined simply because the defendant happens to be a customer rather than a manufacturer. Section 271 of Title 35 declares manufacturing, using or selling infringing products actionable. Each act is identified as an act of infringement and each is proscribed. 35 U.S.C. § 281. Since Woolworth allegedly has itself "sold thousands of dollars of the infringing merchandise" and is "an infringer of the patent in suit every bit as much as the manufacturer of the infringing article," Playtex argues that it has the statutory right as a patentee to sue an infringing seller.

Playtex asserts, therefore, that before the first-filed suit can be enjoined, there must be a finding of harassment, probable harassment or forum shopping. Moreover, to rely on a "natural theatre" test as the District Court did, is said to be making an application of *forum non conveniens* which is not sanctioned by the statute.

In response Gluckin argues that the manufacturer of allegedly infringing goods is the real party in interest in the event his customer is charged with infringement of patents and this principle lies at the basis of judicial restraint on customer actions. Under the direction of the Supreme Court in *Kerotest,* where it was stated:

> Wise judicial administration, giving regard to conservation of judicial resources and comprehensive disposition of litigation, does not counsel rigid mechanical solution of such problems. The factors relevant to wise administration here are equitable in nature. Necessarily, an ample degree of discretion, appropriate for disciplined and experienced judges, must be left to the lower courts,

lower courts have properly exercised a broad degree of discretion in implementing this basic doctrine.

An inflexible approach to suits of this type is certainly to be avoided. Although the so-called "customer suit" exception to the first-filed rule appears to be in conflict with a flexible approach, as Playtex contends, we nonetheless feel that the issuance of the preliminary injunction in this case was not an abuse of discretion.

This Court, in *Mattel,* stated:

> We believe it to be a sound rule that the issues should be tried in the district where suit is first brought unless there are other factors of substance which support the exercise of the court's discretion that *the balance of convenience* is in favor of proceeding first in another district.

Judge Motley found that there were factors of substance indicating that the balance of convenience supported priority for the second-filed suit. The Court noted that (1) since Woolworth is simply a customer of Gluckin and upon whom Woolworth must rely exclusively, the primary party is really Gluckin; (2) the Woolworth employee who has the most knowledge concerning the allegedly infringing item is the Woolworth buyer in New York City; (3) no one connected with Woolworth in Gainesville where the first suit was filed, has any knowledge concerning the patent in suit; (4) the allegedly infringing manufacturer Gluckin is a New York corporation with its main offices in New York City; (5) Gluckin is not licensed to do business in Georgia; (6) the package in which the article is sold by Woolworth is designed, made and supplied by Gluckin, as are all the promotional materials; (7) arrangements for the purchase of the article were negotiated in New York City; (8) Gluckin's manufacturing plants are located in Pennsylvania and its design facility in New York City; (9) it sells and distributes its products to customers nationwide; (10) Playtex, though a Delaware corporation, has its main office and principal place of business in New York City and its design centers in New Jersey; (11) its marketing and purchasing activities are located in New York; (12) the alleged inventor of the Playtex brassiere at issue resides in New Jersey; (13) Playtex's records relating to the invention are in New York City and Georgia; and (14) witnesses who have knowledge of the patent reside in and about New York City.

The reasons for which Playtex chose Gainesville, Georgia, as the place of suit are assertedly (1) because of the location of three of its five plants in that State, (2) because the alleged infringement took place there, and (3) because of the possibility of an earlier trial date in the Northern District of Georgia. It also claims that some of its employees in its Georgia plants will be important witnesses in the action there and that their unique knowledge of the manufacturing process is important to that infringement suit. Playtex contends further that it brought suit in Georgia because of the economic interest in defendant and its employees in Georgia in preserving the substantial volume of business of defendant's patented product.

Judge Motley found Playtex's reasons for bringing suit against Woolworth in Georgia "not very persuasive."

The "whole of the war and all the parties to it" are in the Southern District of New York. Woolworth, the defendant in the Georgia action, has consented to be made a party here and is amenable to process here as well.

All the litigants involved have offices and principal places of business in New York City. Most of the witnesses whose testimony is relevant reside in the New York City area. Woolworth must look to Gluckin to supply evidence in its defense in the Georgia action. All counsel are from New York and the convenience of the major witnesses would unquestionably be better served by a New York venue.

Balancing the convenience of the parties and witnesses and with due regard to the weight given to the initial forum, a judgment that the Georgia suit should be restrained in order that the New York suit may proceed does not appear to be at all unreasonable.

NOTES AND QUESTIONS

1.   Could Woolworth have made a Rule 19 objection in Georgia because Gluckin was not a party to that case? Consider the following reasoning from another context:

> At the root of the preference for a manufacturer's declaratory judgment action is the recognition that, in reality, the manufacturer is the true defendant in the customer suit. * * * [I]t is a simple fact of life that a manufacturer must protect its customers, either as a matter of contract, or good business, or in order to avoid the damaging impact of an adverse ruling against its products.

Codex Corp. v. Milgo Electronic Corp., 553 F.2d 735, 737–38 (1st Cir. 1977).

2.   Why should the first suit generally have priority? Usually such duplicative litigation is reactive—the defendant in the first suit is filing suit in another court after being sued. In such cases, isn't it reasonable to preserve the first plaintiff's victory in the race to the courthouse in the absence of countervailing considerations like those in *Gluckin*?

At least on occasion, courts decline to prefer the first-filed suit. In Certified Restoration Dry Cleaning Network, LLC v. Tenke Corp., 511 F.3d 535 (6th Cir. 2007), plaintiff sent a cease-and-desist letter to defendant claiming defendant was violating a noncompete provision in a franchise contract between plaintiff and defendant. Defendant responded by suing in Ohio (its home) for a declaration that it had not violated the noncompete provision. Plaintiff then sued in Michigan (its home), seeking a preliminary injunction against defendant's breach of the provision. The appellate court held that plaintiff was entitled to the injunction, and also held that the first-filed rule should not apply to the Ohio action because the contract had a choice-of-forum clause designating Michigan as the place to resolve any disputes:

> The Ohio action filed by Defendants was the very kind of anticipatory suit which should not have been given deference under the first-to-file rule. * * * [T]he forum selection clause in the franchise agreement clearly mandated that the parties' dispute be resolved in a Michigan, rather than an Ohio, forum. By filing in Ohio courts, Defendants were attempting to forum shop as well as preempt

resolution of the parties' dispute by the proper forum. Thus, the Ohio action was not entitled to any deference under the first-to-file rule.

Compare Koresko v. Nationwide Life Ins. Co., 403 F.Supp.2d 394 (E.D.Pa. 2005) in which the court applied the first-filed rule in favor of a declaratory relief action filed in response to a demand letter, noting that "the party at the receiving end of a financial ultimatum is not required to unilaterally disarm and allow the party asserting the demand to control the choice of forum."

3.   A preliminary injunction requiring or forbidding conduct is a forceful remedy that may effectively moot the rest of the lawsuit. Rule 65(a) thus provides that the court may consolidate the application for a preliminary injunction with the hearing on the merits. Whether or not the court does that, the party seeking the injunction normally must show that it is likely to prevail on the merits and that it will suffer irreparable injury unless granted the injunction. See generally John Leubsdorf, The Standard for Preliminary Injunctions, 91 Harv. L. Rev. 525 (1978). Rather than focus on such issues, in *Gluckin* the court invokes concepts of "wise judicial administration." With respect to injunctions against the pursuit of collateral litigation, do these concerns supplant the traditional standards for a preliminary injunction?

4.   Rather than seek an injunction, a party involved in duplicative litigation can seek relief from the court in which it does not want to litigate. Specifically, it can ask that court to stay proceedings or to transfer the case to the court in which the other suit is pending under 28 U.S.C. § 1404(a). On the transfer motion, it is likely to make arguments about forum shopping and convenience to the witnesses similar to those considered in *Gluckin*. Would transfer (discussed in greater detail *infra* p. 117) be preferable to a stay because it would allow both cases to go forward under coordinated judicial handling? If one court refuses to transfer, should that decision affect the other court's ruling on a motion to enjoin prosecution of the untransferred case?

In ACF Industries, Inc. v. Guinn, 384 F.2d 15 (5th Cir. 1967), like *Gluckin* a duplicative patent infringement case, one trial judge entered a stay, but, when the case was reassigned, the new judge vacated the stay and denied a transfer motion. The Court of Appeals granted a writ of mandamus, holding that the second judge had abused his discretion. It found the denial of the transfer motion unimportant since "[a] stay order has virtually the same effect, and is granted for practically the same reasons that motivate a court in granting a transfer motion."

5.   It is often difficult to determine exactly what has motivated a party to file a duplicative suit and, in the absence of a bad faith motive, one federal court may be hesitant to enjoin suit in another. For example, in Span-Eng Assocs. v. Weidner, 771 F.2d 464 (10th Cir. 1985), plaintiffs in a securities fraud case in the federal court in Utah filed a similar suit in the federal court in Arizona after the Utah judge had denied their motion to amend the Utah complaint to add additional defendants. Feeling that the plaintiffs were circumventing his order, the Utah judge enjoined prosecution of the Arizona suit. The Tenth Circuit reversed, stressing that "the right to proceed in court

should not be denied except under the most extreme circumstances." Id. at 468. It found that the Utah suit had not progressed to such a point as to warrant an injunction in the interests of judicial economy. It also rejected the Utah court's conclusion that the plaintiffs were forum shopping, observing that they had to file suit to toll the running of limitations with respect to the additional defendants.

STANDARD MICROSYSTEMS CORP. V. TEXAS INSTRUMENTS INC.

United States Court of Appeals, Second Circuit, 1990.
916 F.2d 58.

Before OAKES and PRATT, CIRCUIT JUDGES, and LEVAL, DISTRICT JUDGE.

LEVAL, DISTRICT JUDGE:

This appeal seeks to enforce the Anti-Injunction Act, 28 U.S.C. § 2283. In a patent-licensing dispute, the district judge enjoined the defendant-appellant from prosecuting a suit which it had instituted against plaintiff-appellee in the Texas state courts. Because we hold that this order violated the terms of the Act, the injunction is vacated.

The dispute arises out of a patent cross-licensing agreement between Standard Microsystems Corp. ("SMC"), the plaintiff-appellee, and Texas Instruments, Inc., ("TI"), the defendant-appellant, dated October 1, 1976 (the "Agreement"). The Agreement grants to each party the right to make royalty-free use of semiconductor technology owned by the other. It apparently also contains provisions requiring the parties to keep the agreement confidential, and prohibiting the assignment of rights under the Agreement.

TI has licensed certain Japanese and Korean companies to exploit TI's "Kilby patents," which are part of the cross-licensed technology. SMC now proposes to transfer its rights under the Agreement to make royalty-free use of the same TI technology. It proposes to offer these rights to Japanese and Korean entities. TI apparently advised SMC that it would consider such a sale, and disclosure by SMC in preparation for such a sale, as a violation of the Agreement.

On Friday, January 19, 1990, SMC filed this action against TI in the Eastern District of New York. The complaint alleges violations of federal antitrust and securities statutes and breach of contract, and further seeks declaratory relief that SMC's actions do not breach its Agreement. Simultaneously with the filing of the suit, SMC obtained a temporary restraining order signed by Judge Joseph McLaughlin. The order restrained TI from terminating its License Agreement dated October 1, 1976, with plaintiff or revoking any of plaintiff's rights under that Agreement.

Judge McLaughlin's order included an Order to Show Cause setting a hearing before Judge Leonard Wexler, the assigned judge, on SMC's application for a preliminary injunction to be held on Monday, January 22, 1990.

At 8:00 a.m. on Monday morning, January 22, TI filed suit in the Texas state court against SMC. The suit seeks to bar SMC from making disclosures in violation of the Agreement and to bar SMC from interfering with TI's license negotiations in Japan.

On January 22, Judge Wexler continued the TRO and adjourned the preliminary injunction hearing to Friday, January 26.

On January 26, counsel for SMC advised Judge Wexler that SMC "would like [the court] to enjoin TI along the same lines as the temporary restraining order, to begin with. We would also like, Your honor, . . . to enjoin TI from specifically proceeding in the [Texas] State Court action or any other action with respect to the same contract issues. . . ."

Judge Wexler proceeded to make the following order:

> Until there is a determination, Mr. Cooper [TI's counsel], I'm directing [that] you, your firm, your client, [and] anyone connected with you are stayed from doing anything in Texas or in relationship to that action that has previously been filed. Cease and desist immediately.

That is the order from which TI appeals.

TI contends that Judge Wexler's order violates the Anti-Injunction Act, 28 U.S.C. § 2283. The Act provides:

> A court of the United States may not grant an injunction to stay proceedings in a State court except as expressly authorized by Act of Congress, or where necessary in aid of its jurisdiction, or to protect or effectuate its judgments.

Its purpose is, *inter alia,* to avoid intergovernmental friction that may result from a federal injunction staying state court proceedings. The Supreme Court has construed the Act to forbid a federal court from enjoining a party from prosecuting a state court action unless one of the three exceptions stated in the statute obtains. The three excepted circumstances are (i) the express provisions of another act of Congress authorizing such an order; (ii) necessity in aid of the federal court's jurisdiction and (iii) the need to protect or effectuate the federal court's judgments. *Atlantic Coast Line R.R. Co. v. Brotherhood of Locomotive Engineers,* 398 U.S. 281, 287–88 (1970).

None of the three statutory exceptions is here pertinent. There is no contrary act of Congress. And the injunction is not necessary either in aid of the federal court's jurisdiction or to protect or effectuate its judgments.

A number of circumstances may justify a finding that the exceptions govern. Where the federal court's jurisdiction is *in rem* and the state court action may effectively deprive the federal court of the opportunity to adjudicate as to the *res,* the exception for necessity "in aid of jurisdiction" may be appropriate. *Compare Kline v. Burke Construction Co.,* 260 U.S. 226 (1922) (declining to uphold federal court injunction against state court proceedings where contract obligations were in dispute, rather than rights relating to a *res*); *Heyman v. Kline,* 456 F.2d 123 (2d Cir.), *cert. denied,* 409 U.S. 847 (1972) (Act bars federal court injunction issued in *in personam* proceeding involving employment contract); *Vernitron Corp. v. Benjamin,* 440 F.2d 105 (2d Cir.), *cert. denied,* 402 U.S. 987 (1971) (reversing issuance of injunction justified only by the possibility of collateral estoppel in parallel securities litigations); *with Penn General Casualty Co. v. Pennsylvania ex rel. Schnader,* 294 U.S. 189 (1935) (affirming injunction against state court proceedings to protect court's ability to control and dispose of property in liquidation proceeding). Analogous circumstances may be found where a federal court is on the verge of settling a complex matter, and state court proceedings may undermine its ability to achieve that objective, *see In re Baldwin-United Corp.,* 770 F.2d 328, 337 (2d Cir. 1985) (upholding injunction against state court actions to protect ability of federal court to manage and to settle multidistrict class action proceeding which was far advanced and in which court had extensive involvement). Or, where a federal court has made conclusive rulings and their effect may be undermined by threatened relitigation in state courts, the exception may be appropriate. *See, e.g., Necchi Sewing Machine Sales Corp. v. Carl,* 260 F.Supp. 665, 669 (S.D.N.Y. 1966) (enjoining state court from hearing claims when federal court had found those claims to be properly heard only before an arbitrator).

The suits at issue here are *in personam* actions, brought on successive business days in two different courts, disputing the interpretation of a contract. The existence of the state court action does not in any way impair the jurisdiction of the federal court or its ability to render justice. It is well-settled that such circumstances as these do not justify invocation of the exceptions of the Anti-Injunction Act. *See Vendo Co. v. Lektro-Vend Corp.,* 433 U.S. 623, 642 (1977) (reversing injunction of state court proceedings which, like federal court action, involved dispute arising out of covenant not to compete; "[w]e have never viewed parallel *in personam* actions as interfering with the jurisdiction of either court").

> Each court is free to proceed in its own way and in its own time, without reference to the proceedings in the other court. Whenever a judgment is rendered in one of the courts and pleaded in the

other, the effect of that judgment is to be determined by application of the principles of *res adjudicata*. . . .

Vendo Co., 433 U.S. at 642; *see also Atlantic Coast Line R.R.*, 398 U.S. at 295 ("the state and federal courts had concurrent jurisdiction in this [labor dispute] and neither court was free to prevent either party from simultaneously pursuing claims in both courts").

SMC argues that, nonetheless, Judge Wexler's injunction must be affirmed because it falls within two additional judicially created exceptions to the Act. First, the Act has been held inapplicable to federal injunctions issued prior to the institution of the state court action. *Dombrowski v. Pfister*, 380 U.S. 479 (1965); *In re Baldwin-United Corp.*, 770 F.2d 328, 335 (2d Cir. 1985). This exception is based both on policy and the explicit terms of the act. Where no state court proceeding exists, there is less danger that a federal court injunction barring the institution of such a proceeding will cause affront to state authority. Furthermore, the Act bars grant of "an injunction to stay *proceedings* in a State court," 28 U.S.C. § 2283 (emph. added), which seems to refer literally to existing proceedings, rather than contemplated proceedings.

SMC contends this case falls within the *Dombrowski* exception because Judge McLaughlin's TRO predated the institution of the Texas action. The contention is frivolous. Although it is true that the TRO predated the Texas action, the TRO did not forbid TI from starting a separate action. The TRO restrained TI only "from terminating [SMC's] License Agreement . . . or revoking . . . [SMC's] rights under that Agreement." There is no factual basis for SMC's argument that TI's Texas court action was instituted in violation of a federal injunction barring such suit. No order was issued against TI's maintenance of its state court action until January 26, four days after TI started the action.

Second, SMC contends that, notwithstanding the Act, a state court action may be enjoined if a motion to bar the state court action was made before the state court action was started. This argument depends on an exception to the Act created by judicial decision in the Seventh Circuit, *Barancik v. Investors Funding Corp.*, 489 F.2d 933 (7th Cir. 1973), and followed in the First and Eighth Circuits, *see National City Lines, Inc. v. LLC Corp.*, 687 F.2d 1122, 1127–28 (8th Cir. 1982) (following *Barancik*); *Hyde Park Partners, L.P. v. Connolly*, 839 F.2d 837 (1st Cir. 1988), but rejected in the Sixth, *see Roth v. Bank of the Commonwealth*, 583 F.2d 527 (6th Cir. 1978) (criticizing reasoning of *Barancik*), *cert. dismissed*, 442 U.S. 925 (1979). This circuit has never considered the issue.

In *Barancik*, defendants filed an action in state court while plaintiff's preliminary injunction motion was pending in federal court seeking to bar defendants from commencing a separate legal action. The federal district judge enjoined prosecution of the state court action. The Seventh Circuit affirmed, noting that if the federal judge had immediately decided the motion, the injunction would have preceded the filing of the state court action and therefore, under *Dombrowski,* would not have violated the Anti-Injunction Act. The court found anomalous the possibility that the federal court's authority to rule on a pending motion could be terminated by the action of one of the litigants and concluded that the Anti-Injunction Act did not prohibit a stay of state court proceedings if the state court proceeding was commenced *after* filing of a motion seeking to enjoin it.

We have considerable doubt whether the *Barancik* rule should be adopted in this circuit. We do not find its reasoning compelling. The *Barancik* court found it "unseemly" that a court's power to rule could be defeated by the quicker action of a litigant. But it is axiomatic that one is not disabled from acting merely because an adverse litigant has *applied* for an order to bar such action. A party that has not been enjoined is ordinarily free to act, notwithstanding the pendency of applications to enjoin the action. In many circumstances litigants may lawfully moot an application by acting before the court has ruled. To enjoin conduct requires a judge's order, not merely an application for a judge's order. Where speed is needed, the rules of procedure provide for temporary restraining orders, even without notice, to prevent irreparable harm. *See* Fed.R.Civ.P. 65. However anomalous it may seem that a party can moot an issue by acting more rapidly than the court, it is far more anomalous and dangerous that a mere application for injunctive relief be deemed equivalent to a court's order issuing an injunction.

The *Barancik* rule, furthermore, creates a still more serious anomaly. Under *Barancik,* merely by filing an application for relief, a party nullifies an Act of Congress. In passing the Anti-Injunction Act, Congress meant to avoid friction in the relationship between federal courts and state courts. The *Barancik* rule places the power in the hands of the plaintiff unilaterally to nullify the effectiveness of an Act of Congress and to create exactly the kind of federal-state conflict that Congress sought to prevent.

We need not decide whether the *Barancik* rule will be followed in this circuit because, in any event, it does not apply to these facts.

At the time of TI's commencement of the Texas action, there was no application before the federal court to bar it from doing so. The Order to Show Cause sought a preliminary injunction barring TI from

"a.   coercing SMC's compliance in TI's interpretation of the License Agreement;

b.   interfering with SMC's dealings . . .;

c.   attempting to monopolize . . . through the coercive acts alleged herein; and

d.   Terminating the License Agreement and . . . revoking any of SMC's rights thereunder."

SMC's counsel reaches beyond the limits of ingenuity to contrive an argument that the Order to Show Cause applied for an injunction to bar the filing of a parallel action. The argument is to the effect that the application to enjoin TI's "attempt[s] to monopolize . . . through the coercive acts alleged herein," especially when combined with the concluding prayer for such "other and different relief as [the court] deems proper and just," incorporates by reference the allegation in the complaint of threats of "sham litigation." Taking all this together, SMC contends its application should be construed as having sought an injunction barring institution of the "sham" Texas action. The argument is more convoluted than convincing. In fact, there was no application before the court to bar TI from starting a lawsuit. Thus, even if we were to adopt the reasoning of *Barancik,* it would not apply to this case.

NOTES AND QUESTIONS

1.   A statute prohibiting federal courts from issuing an injunction "to stay proceedings in any court of a state" was passed by Congress in 1793, 1 Stat. 334, and since that time some form of anti-injunction statute has always existed. The present statute, 28 U.S.C. § 2283, was adopted as part of the 1948 Judicial Code, with the intent of specifying clear exceptions in response to a narrow reading of the then-existing statute in Toucey v. New York Life Insurance Co., 314 U.S. 118 (1941). Section 2283 reads:

> A court of the United States may not grant an injunction to stay proceedings in a State court except as expressly authorized by Act of Congress, or where necessary in aid of its jurisdiction, or to protect or effectuate its judgments.

The first exception—"as expressly authorized by Act of Congress"—has been interpreted as not requiring specific reference to § 2283 in a statute. Mitchum v. Foster, 407 U.S. 225 (1972), which found an express exception in the § 1983 civil rights statute, described the test as "whether an Act of Congress, clearly creating a federal right or remedy enforceable in a federal court of equity, could be given its intended scope only by the stay of a state court proceeding."

The second exception—"where necessary in aid of its jurisdiction"—has traditionally been applied when the "federal court's jurisdiction is in rem and the state court action may effectively deprive the federal court of the opportunity to adjudicate as to the res." Standard Microsystems Corp. v. Texas Instruments Inc., 916 F.2d 58, 59 (2d Cir. 1990); Mitchum v. Foster, 407 U.S. 225, 235–37 (1972).

The third exception—"to protect or effectuate its judgments"—allows an injunction to prevent relitigation of a suit in which a judgment has been entered. Rule 54(a) defines "judgment" as "any order from which an appeal lies."

The effect of § 2283 cannot be avoided by simply enjoining a party from prosecuting his state suit, as opposed to having the federal court stay the state court proceedings. However, § 2283 does not prohibit an injunction against a state officer who is about to institute proceedings to enforce an unconstitutional statute nor against state proceedings in which the state court is not performing a judicial function. Charles Wright & Mary Kay Kane, *supra*, at 300–01; Dombrowski v. Pfister, 380 U.S. 479 (1965).

2.   Section 2283 eliminates discretion to enjoin state-court proceedings, even if an injunction would prevent duplicative litigation and promote the efficient resolution of disputes. In Atlantic Coast Line Railroad Co. v. Brotherhood of Locomotive Engineers, 398 U.S. 281 (1970), the Supreme Court emphasized that "any doubts as to the propriety of a federal injunction against state court proceedings should be resolved in favor of permitting the state courts to proceed in an orderly fashion to finally determine the controversy." In Vendo Co. v. Lektro-Vend Corp., 433 U.S. 623 (1977), the Court confirmed that "the Act is an absolute prohibition against any injunction of any state-court proceedings, unless the injunction falls within one of the three specifically defined exceptions in the Act. The Act's purpose is to forestall the inevitable friction between the state and federal courts that ensues from the injunction of state judicial proceedings by a federal court."

3.   In Standard Microsystems the appellate court rejects the argument that the January 19 temporary restraining order should be interpreted to forbid the January 22 filing of the Texas state-court suit. Had plaintiff tried to have defendant held in contempt for filing the Texas suit, this result would seem unavoidable because the order was not clear enough to support a contempt citation. Should the same attitude apply to the Anti-Injunction Act issue? Given Judge Wexler's order on January 26 that the Texas suit not be prosecuted, isn't it reasonable to conclude that Judge McLaughlin would have explicitly forbidden the filing of the suit on January 19 had that been suggested to him? Assuming that the defendant was represented at the January 19 hearing at which the TRO issued, was it under an obligation to disclose its plan to file suit in Texas the following Monday?

4.   Note that the court says that the Anti-Injunction Act is designed to avoid "intergovernmental friction." How does it accomplish this objective? So long as the federal court enters an injunction before an action is filed in state court, the Act does not apply even if the party enjoined is a state official acting on behalf of the state. Even where a federal court cannot enjoin state proceedings, it is possible to ask the state court to stay its action. Would such a stay have been appropriate in *Standard Microsystems* on principles of wise judicial administration?

5.   The exception to the Anti-Injunction Act for injunctions that will "protect or effectuate" a federal court's judgment (called the "relitigation exception") has been interpreted narrowly. In Chick Kam Choo v. Exxon Corp., 486 U.S. 140 (1988), the plaintiff seaman sued in federal court to recover for injuries received in Singapore, and the federal court dismissed on *forum non conveniens* grounds. Plaintiff then sued in state court in Texas, and the

defendant reacted by filing an action in federal court to enjoin prosecution of the suit in state court. The Supreme Court invalidated the resulting federal-court injunction against the state court suit. Although it conceded that the earlier federal action had decided that dismissal was proper under federal *forum non conveniens* law, and that in admiralty actions state courts might be required to apply federal *forum non conveniens* law, the Court held the injunction was invalid because that question had not been resolved in the earlier federal action. It reasoned that "an essential prerequisite for applying the relitigation exception is that the claims or issues which the federal injunction insulates from litigation in state proceedings actually have been decided by the federal court."

6. Should federal courts take a different attitude toward enjoining prosecution of litigation in other countries? The Anti-Injunction Act certainly poses no obstacle to such injunctions, but principles of comity usually make courts reluctant to issue such injunctions. See Gau Shan Co. v. Bankers Trust Co., 956 F.2d 1349 (6th Cir. 1992); China Trade & Dev. Corp. v. M.V. Choong Yong, 837 F.2d 33 (2d Cir. 1987); Laker Airways v. Sabena, 731 F.2d 909 (D.C.Cir. 1984); compare Kaepa, Inc. v. Achilles Corp., 76 F.3d 624, 627 (5th Cir. 1996) ("We decline, however, to require a district court to genuflect before a vague and omnipotent notion of comity every time that it must decide whether to enjoin a foreign action.").

7. The Rule 13(a) compulsory counterclaim rule has been found not to be an express exception to the Anti-Injunction Act. See Seattle Totems Hockey Club, Inc. v. National Hockey League, 652 F.2d 852 (9th Cir. 1981); 6 Charles Wright, Arthur Miller & Mary Kay Kane, Federal Practice & Procedure § 1418 at 148 (2d ed. 1990). But if the purpose of the rule is "to prevent multiplicity of actions and to achieve resolution in a single lawsuit of all disputes arising out of common matters," Southern Const. Co. v. Pickard, 371 U.S. 57 (1962), should that ruling be reconsidered? Cf. Semmes Motors, Inc. v. Ford Motor Co., *supra* p. 108 (federal court "seized" of claim that would be compulsory counterclaim).

8. Although a federal court's ability to enjoin duplicative state proceedings is circumscribed by the act, that does not mean that a federal court should ordinarily stay the case before it. Aside from some discretionary abstention doctrines reserved for specific circumstances (and which are best left for the course in Federal Courts), in general, the Supreme Court has held that the federal courts have a "virtually unflagging obligation . . . to exercise the jurisdiction given them." Colorado River Water Conservation Dist. v. United States, 424 U.S. 800, 817 (1976).

But under "exceptional circumstances" and with the "clearest of justifications," a district court may dismiss or stay an action based on considerations of '[w]ise judicial administration, giving regard to conservation of judicial resources and comprehensive disposition of litigation.'" Moses H. Cone Memorial Hosp. v. Mercury Constr. Corp., 460 U.S. 1, 25–26 (1983). One example is Allied Machinery Service, Inc. v. Caterpillar Inc., 841 F.Supp. 406 (S.D.Fla. 1993), in which plaintiff filed an antitrust suit in a Florida state court based on the Florida antitrust statute. Three months later it filed suit in the federal district court alleging the same violations, this time based on the federal antitrust statute. The federal court granted defendants' motion to abstain in the interests of wise judicial administration. It especially focused on the facts that the state court obtained jurisdiction first; that if the federal court did not abstain, there would be duplicate suits over the identical claims; and that plaintiff voluntarily chose state court and only later, after state court proceedings were developing, filed in federal court which appeared to be forum shopping.

9.   On occasion one party will file a declaratory judgment action in a federal court to determine the rights and obligations of the parties to a disputed matter, and the other party will then file a suit for full relief based on the same matter in a state court. In Wilton v. Seven Falls Co., 515 U.S. 277 (1995), the Supreme Court characterized the discretion vested by the Declaratory Judgment Act as "unique" and held that it would "justify a standard vesting district courts with greater discretion in declaratory judgment actions than that presented under the 'exceptional circumstances' test of Colorado River." The proper reference in declaratory judgment cases, the Court said, is to Brillhart v. Excess Insurance Co., 316 U.S. 491 (1942), which upheld a stay by the federal court in a declaratory judgment action. Brillhart said that "ordinarily it would be uneconomical as well as vexatious for a federal court to proceed in a declaratory judgment suit where another suit is pending in a state court presenting the same issues, not governed by federal law, between the same parties." The question for a district court, in exercising its discretion concerning a stay, is "whether the questions in controversy between the parties to the federal suit, and which are not foreclosed under the applicable substantive law, can better be settled in the proceeding pending in the state court." Thus a court should consider "whether the claims of all parties in interest can satisfactorily be adjudicated in that proceeding, whether necessary parties have been joined, whether such parties are amenable to process in that proceeding, etc."

C. TRANSFER TO A MORE CONVENIENT FORUM

In 1948, 28 U.S.C. § 1404(a) was passed by Congress in order to modify the strictness of the federal common law doctrine of forum non conveniens which, as applied in Gulf Oil Corp. v. Gilbert, 330 U.S. 501 (1947), allowed a federal court to dismiss a suit, although it had personal and subject-matter jurisdiction and venue was proper, if there were another more convenient forum. Section 1404(a) contains a deceptively simple, one-sentence standard: "For the convenience of the parties and witnesses, in the interest of justice, a district court may transfer any civil action to any other district or division where it might have been brought or to any district or division to which all parties have consented."

Section 1404(a) can play an important role in helping to accomplish the consolidation of duplicative or related litigation by transferring related cases to the same federal district and allowing consolidation to take place there. But before transfer can be accomplished, unless the parties consent, it must be established that the transferee district is one "where it might have been brought" and that such transfer is "for the convenience of the parties and witnesses" and "in the interest of justice."

GINSEY INDUSTRIES, INC. V. I.T.K. PLASTICS, INC.

United States District Court, Eastern District of Pennsylvania, 1982.
545 F.Supp. 78.

LOUIS H. POLLAK, DISTRICT JUDGE.

Plaintiff, Ginsey Industries, is a Pennsylvania corporation with its principal place of business in Bellmahr, New Jersey, and defendant, I.T.K. Plastics, is a Massachusetts corporation with its principal place of business in Salem, Massachusetts. In the fall of 1981, plaintiff purchased vinyl plastic sheeting manufactured by defendant. After receiving shipment of the plastic, Ginsey determined that the plastic was not, in its view, fit for the purpose for which it was sold. Ginsey then filed this action to recover the payment it made to I.T.K. as well as consequential damages. This matter is now before the court on defendant's motion to dismiss for lack of personal jurisdiction or, in the alternative, for transfer to the District of Massachusetts.

I.T.K. first contends that its limited contact with this forum is insufficient to bring it within the reach of Pennsylvania's long-arm statute, 42 Pa.C.S.A. § 5301 *et seq.*, or to satisfy the due process standards set forth in *International Shoe Co. v. Washington,* 326 U.S. 310, 316 (1945). Alternatively, I.T.K. argues that transfer to the District of Massachusetts is warranted since a civil action involving the same parties and the same plastic products is currently pending there. In response, plaintiff has not come forward with any specific evidence to support this court's exercise of *in personam* jurisdiction over I.T.K. but has instead urged that if transfer is considered appropriate this case should be transferred to the District of New Jersey rather than the District of Massachusetts.

On the basis of the record as it now stands, it seems clear that I.T.K.'s connection with Pennsylvania is so tenuous that this court lacks a proper basis to exercise *in personam* jurisdiction. Perhaps further discovery might reveal some basis for linking I.T.K. to that forum but plaintiff has not sought to pursue this possibility. However, rather than simply dismissing plaintiff's complaint at this point, the better approach, in my view, would be to transfer this matter to a more appropriate forum.[1]

---

[1]   In *Goldlawr, Inc. v. Heiman,* 369 U.S. 463 (1962), the Court, over Justice Harlan's dissent, construed 28 U.S.C. § 1406(a) to authorize a district court to transfer to a proper district a case filed in a district where venue is improper, notwithstanding that the transferor court lacks *in personam* jurisdiction. In *United States v. Berkowitz,* [328 F.2d 358 (3d Cir. 1964), *cert. denied,* 379 U.S. 821 (1964)], our Court of Appeals extended the *Goldlawr* rationale to § 1404(a).

In considering a motion to transfer, a court must first determine that the transferee district is a district where the action "might have been brought." 28 U.S.C. § 1404(a); *Hoffman v. Blaski*, 363 U.S. 335 (1960). This criterion, however, does not provide any clear guidance in determining which of the two proposed transferee districts—New Jersey or Massachusetts—is more appropriate since both appear to be districts where plaintiff's claim could have been brought. Both courts clearly have jurisdiction over the subject matter of this case under 28 U.S.C. § 1332 by virtue of the diversity of citizenship of the parties, and both courts may properly exercise *in personam* jurisdiction over I.T.K. because of I.T.K.'s contacts with New Jersey and its residence in Massachusetts. Venue would also be proper in both districts under 28 U.S.C. § 1391(a).

I turn therefore to the more difficult question whether the balance of convenience weighs decisively in favor of one of the proposed districts. It is well-settled that "unless the balance is strongly in favor of the defendant, the plaintiff's choice of forum should rarely be disturbed." *Gulf Oil Corp. v. Gilbert,* 330 U.S. 501, 508 (1947). Therefore, since the District of New Jersey is clearly plaintiff's preferred alternative forum, that preference must be accorded substantial weight.

On the opposing scale, as defendant properly suggests, must be placed the interest in efficient judicial administration which might be advanced by transfer to the District of Massachusetts where an action involving the same parties is pending. By permitting two related cases which are filed initially in different districts to be consolidated, transfer plainly helps avoid needless duplication of effort. For as Justice Black remarked in *Continental Grain Co. v. Barge FBL-585,* 364 U.S. 19, 26 (1960): "To permit a situation in which two cases involving precisely the same issues are simultaneously pending in different District Courts leads to the wastefulness of time, energy and money that § 1404(a) was designed to prevent." This consideration, of course, loses some of its force where the two pending actions do not stem from precisely the same transaction. A comparison of the complaints filed in Massachusetts and in this action reveals that the actions involve distinct, albeit related, transactions: the Massachusetts allegations speak of an August, 1981 purchase of vinyl plastic valued at $14,000 which Ginsey allegedly failed to pay for; whereas the Pennsylvania claims describe an October or November, 1981 transaction involving a $30,000 payment by Ginsey for vinyl plastic which was rejected as defective. Nevertheless, it would appear that significant economies of time and effort can be achieved if these actions were consolidated in a single district. The essential questions of liability in both actions concern the fitness of I.T.K.'s vinyl products for the commercial purposes Ginsey sought to pursue. The witnesses who will testify about I.T.K.'s product and about Ginsey's reasons for purchasing that product are likely to be the same in both cases. To be sure, consolidation of these actions in the District of Massachusetts imposes a burden on Ginsey. But transfer to that district would, in my judgment, promote efficient judicial administration to such an extent that plaintiff's preference for New Jersey is outweighed. And consolidation ultimately benefits both parties since it is clearly more convenient to conduct related litigation in a single district rather than in two separate forums.

Accordingly, I will order that this matter be transferred to the District of Massachusetts.

NOTES AND QUESTIONS

1.   The "where it might have been brought" requirement of § 1404(a) can present an obstacle to transfer to the moving party's preferred district because that district must both be a proper venue and have personal jurisdiction over the defendant. See Jurisdictional Issues With Joining Parties, *supra* p. 62. But what if the defendant might have a viable objection to jurisdiction or venue in the transferee district but the parties consent to the transfer? In Hoffman v. Blaski, 363 U.S. 335 (1960), the Court held that the statute precluded transfer to a district where defendant would not have been subject to personal jurisdiction even though defendant was willing to waive its objections to jurisdiction. The willingness of the defendant to waive jurisdictional limitations was irrelevant; section 1404(a) was interpreted to require that plaintiff has the right to sue in the transferee district independently of the wishes of defendant. However convenient the transferee forum may be, therefore, it must be a district in which jurisdiction and venue would have been proper had plaintiff sued there originally. In 2011, the statute was amended to authorize transfer to "any district or division to which all parties have consented," as well as one in which it might have been brought.

2.   A § 1404(a) motion may be made at any time, although delay is a factor weighing against granting. Once a motion has been granted, the transferor court loses jurisdiction, and the suit proceeds in the transferee court as if it had originally been filed there. In Van Dusen v. Barrack, 376 U.S. 612 (1964), the Supreme Court held that the transferee court must apply the state law that would have been applied in the transferor court. "Thus if the law is unclear in the state in which the action is commenced, this argues against transfer, since a district judge in that state is presumably better able to fathom its law than is a district judge in the transferee state. Also the fact that the substantive law will not be changed by a transfer may cast doubt on the feasibility of consolidating the transferred case with other cases that were commenced in the court to which transfer is proposed, and may have an effect on the witnesses that will be necessary." Charles Wright & Mary Kay Kane, Law of Federal Courts 282 (6th ed. 2002). The plaintiff's ability to shop for favorable law received a boost in Ferens v. John Deere Co., 494 U.S. 516 (1990), which held that *Van Dusen* applies to a § 1404(a) transfer even if it is requested by the plaintiff.

3.   Section 1406(a), which is mentioned in footnote 1 in *Ginsey Industries,* is closely related in its purpose to § 1404(a). § 1406(a) provides:

> The district court of a district in which is filed a case laying venue in the wrong division or district shall dismiss, or if it be in the interest of justice, transfer such case to any district or division in which it could have been brought.

Section 1404(a) applies when venue is proper but transfer would serve the convenience of the parties and witnesses, while § 1406(a) allows transfer in the interests of justice when venue was improper in the first place. The holdings of *Goldlawr* and *Berkowitz* [see *Ginsey Industries* footnote 1], that § 1404(a) and § 1406(a) authorize transfer *even in* cases where personal jurisdiction over the defendant is lacking, raise a question as to which section applies when personal jurisdiction is lacking. Some courts have viewed § 1406(a) as the appropriate mechanism "when there exists an obstacle—either incorrect venue, absence of personal jurisdiction, or both—to a prompt adjudication on the merits in the forum where originally brought." Dubin v. United States, 380 F.2d 813, 816 (5th Cir. 1967). Thus, in a case like *Ginsey Industries,* where the original forum lacked personal jurisdiction over the defendant, § 1406(a) would be the proper motion for transfer. Other courts have seen § 1404(a) as allowing transfer when venue is proper but the court lacks personal jurisdiction. Sargent v. Genesco, Inc., 492 F.2d 750, 759 (5th Cir. 1974).

4.   Which section is used should make little difference unless it affects the choice of law decision upon transfer. Some courts have been troubled by the possibility that *Van Dusen,* a case of transfer under § 1404(a), would require the transferor law to apply even though personal jurisdiction was lacking in the original forum. That would allow a plaintiff to forum shop for substantive law by filing in any forum, whether or not it could obtain personal jurisdiction over the defendant there and capture that forum's law. In order to avoid that result, some courts have relied on § 1406(a) to transfer whenever personal jurisdiction or venue is lacking, then applying the transferee's law to prevent unfair forum shopping. See, e.g., Wisland v. Admiral Bev. Corp., 119 F.3d 733, 735–36 (8th Cir. 1997); cf. Ellis v. Great Southwestern Corp., 646 F.2d 1099 (5th Cir. 1981) (even if court purports to transfer under § 1404(a), if it lacks personal jurisdiction transferee law applies)

5.   *Effect of forum selection clause.* In Atlantic Marine Const. Co. v. U.S. District Court, 571 U.S. 49 (2014), the Supreme Court held that if there is a valid forum selection clause in a contract that agreement is decisive about whether the private interests of the parties favor transfer. Public interest factors in retaining the case in the district where it was filed should prevent transfer only in "unusual cases." It also ruled that after transfer pursuant to a forum selection clause the transferee federal court should apply the choice-of-law rules of that state, thus creating an exception to the rule from *Van Dusen* and *Ferens.*

6.   In *Ginsey,* the fact that another case involving similar, but not identical, issues was pending in the forum to which the defendant sought

transfer was a factor in granting a § 1404(a) transfer. Is the existence of related suits in a foreign nation's courts also significant on a *forum non conveniens* motion to dismiss? Guidi v. Inter-Continental Hotels Corp., 203 F.3d 180 (2d Cir. 2000), was a suit by the widows of two Americans who were killed when a fanatic shot up a hotel in Egypt operated by the defendant (an American company). The suit was dismissed by the district court, which emphasized that suits by two other hotel guests who were killed in the incident were pending in Egypt. The appellate court reversed, finding that pendency of related litigation was relevant to § 1404(a), but not to a *forum non conveniens* motion. It found that the district judge had not given adequate weight to the plaintiffs' choice of forum, particularly since they were Americans suing an American company at its business headquarters.

CHAPTER 4

MULTIDISTRICT LITIGATION

∎ ∎ ∎

The rise of multidistrict litigation, or "MDL," under 28 U.S.C. § 1407, has been one of the most significant developments of the last half century in civil procedure. What the MDL statute does seems simple enough on its face: it provides that when civil actions involving one or more common questions of fact are pending in multiple federal districts, they may be transferred to a single district for coordinated or consolidated pretrial proceedings. The decisions to create such a multidistrict litigation and to which "MDL transferee judge" the cases will be transferred are made by a group of seven federal judges, appointed by the Chief Justice, called the Judicial Panel on Multidistrict Litigation, or the "JPML." While before the MDL transferee judge the cases proceed through unified pretrial proceedings, thus avoiding the costs of duplicative discovery and motion practice and inconsistent rulings on legal questions. In theory, once pretrial proceedings conclude, the JPML is to remand the cases to the districts in which they were originally filed for trial.

In reality, however, this relatively simple concept has spawned an extraordinarily complex area of specialized practice, and, indeed, much controversy—largely because of the significant power reposed in the MDL transferee judge, and the fact that most cases transferred to an MDL are resolved there before remand, whether through mass settlement or dispositive motion. This controversy has only grown as MDL has become more prominent. Although there is room for argument about the precise statistics, which indicate that MDL currently makes up about a third of the federal civil docket, there is no doubt that MDL has become the primary mechanism for managing mass torts in the federal system. Beyond the numbers, what is clear is that prominent national litigation controversies will likely wind up in MDL proceedings—current examples are as varied as the litigations arising from the opioids crisis, concussions in the NFL, the Volkswagen Clean Diesel scandal, and injuries allegedly caused by defective drugs and products or in mass disasters. In this chapter, we will examine the origins of MDL, the role of the JPML, and the powers of the MDL judge. Understanding MDL is thus not only critical to a basic understanding of complex litigation generally, but also as a comparison to, and combination with, other forms of aggregate litigation, most importantly the class action, addressed in the next chapter.

A. THE MULTIDISTRICT LITIGATION STATUTE AND ITS ORIGINS

In 1968, Congress approved the statute authorizing MDL by unanimous consent, and President Johnson signed it with virtually no fanfare—perhaps a surprise to those considering MDL's importance today. But the roots of the statute extend decades earlier, to the increasingly prominent managerial role of federal judges in "protracted litigation," or, more evocatively, "big cases." As discussed in Chapter 1, by the end of the 1940s, several large-scale and complex antitrust cases had come to the federal courts, leading several prominent judges to develop methods of managing cases from the bench, many of which we will study throughout upcoming chapters. These judges insisted that they could not play a passive role in complex litigation—rather, they needed to exercise "rigid control" from the outset of litigation to avoid massive delays, costs, and inaccurate results in cases more complicated than the run-of-the-mill dispute. See Judicial Conference of the U.S., Procedure in Anti-Trust and Other Protracted Cases, 13 F.R.D. 41 (1951). We will examine these techniques in detail in Chapter 6.

As these views gradually gained currency, and more complex cases arose, in 1961 the most complex and widespread litigation to date confronted the federal courts. Virtually every significant maker of electrical equipment in the United States (including giants General Electric and Westinghouse) was indicted for price fixing and other anticompetitive conduct under the Sherman Act. Although the criminal cases were resolved relatively rapidly by guilty pleas, a tidal wave of civil litigation followed. The plaintiffs were, essentially, every public utility in the United States that had purchased equipment at inflated prices. Eventually some 2,000 cases, including over 25,000 claims, were filed in 35 federal districts.

Because the suits were in different districts, Rule 42(a) consolidation was not possible. Moreover, § 1404(a) procedures for transfer to a more convenient forum were inadequate to ensure that all the cases could be transferred to a single court. The courts were therefore forced to cope with the burden on an *ad hoc* basis, giving impetus to the creation by Chief Justice Warren of a Coordinating Committee for Multiple Litigation of the U.S. District Courts, composed of nine federal judges, which supervised nationwide coordinated discovery, pretrial orders, and motion practice for all electrical equipment cases. Among the Coordinating Committee's innovations were numerous case-management techniques that remain in use today, including centralized document depositories, regular scheduling conferences and orders, steering committees of lawyers to lead efforts on both sides of the litigation, and placing cases on different "tracks" for resolution. Although defendants (and some judges) eventually chafed at the Coordinating Committee's vigorous (some might say heavy-handed) management of the litigation, and its push to generate a speedy resolution, its efforts were extraordinarily successful. The entire electrical-equipment litigation was settled by the end of 1966. No less a figure than Chief Justice Warren lauded the "monumental effort" of the Coordinating Committee, without which "the district court calendars throughout the country could well have broken down."

Meanwhile, during the pendency of the electrical-equipment cases, it became clear to the Coordinating Committee that a permanent statutory mechanism to ensure unified treatment of related cases pending in multiple districts would be necessary. The judges on the committee came to this conclusion because they believed that complicated nationwide litigations like electrical equipment would increasingly become the norm; indeed, District Judge William Becker, who spearheaded the effort to create the MDL statute believed that it would be necessary to cope with a coming "litigation explosion," as the American economy became more interconnected, and Congress and the states created ever more causes of action.

Initially, the judges considered a "radical *forum non conveniens* statute" that would transfer all related cases to a single judge for all purposes, but they eventually concluded that such a statute would face too much opposition from the corporate defense bar, and perhaps federal judges who would not appreciate cases being "taken" from them. Consequently, the Reporter for the Committee, Dean Phil Neal of the University of Chicago, invented a "radical proposal": limited transfer of cases pending in multiple districts to a single district for consolidated pretrial proceedings followed by remand for trial. The judge to whom the cases would be transferred for this "multidistrict litigation" would be able to employ all of the tools of case management that had been developed before and during electrical equipment, and perhaps experiment with some new ones. Coordinated pretrial proceedings could therefore avoid delays, prevent costs of duplicative discovery, and avoid inconsistent pretrial rulings on legal questions. The decisions about whether to create a multidistrict litigation, and to whom it would be transferred, would be made by a committee of federal judges, the Judicial Panel on Multidistrict Litigation, whose members would be appointed by the Chief Justice.

Ultimately, this proposal became the Multidistrict Litigation Act of 1968, 28 U.S.C. § 1407, which created the Judicial Panel on Multidistrict Litigation to transfer cases with "common questions of fact" to a single federal judge "for coordinated or consolidated pretrial proceedings." Judge Becker, the statute's most energetic backer, predicted that the MDL statute would become a centerpiece of the federal courts. Ensuing developments vindicated this prediction. For a review of these developments, see Richard Marcus, Cure-All for an Era of Dispersed Litigation? Toward a Maximalist Use of the Multidistrict Panel's Transfer Power, 82 Tulane L. Rev. 2245 (2008) (reviewing evolution of Panel);

Andrew Bradt, "A Radical Proposal": The Multidistrict Litigation Act of 1968, 165 U. Pa. L. Rev. 831 (2017) (reviewing the creation of the statute).

B. THE ROLE OF THE JUDICIAL PANEL ON MULTIDISTRICT LITIGATION

JOHN G. HEYBURN II,* A VIEW FROM THE PANEL: PART OF THE SOLUTION
82 Tulane Law Review 2225, 2227–31, 2231–32, 2233–35, 2236–42 (2008).

Under § 1407, Congress gave the Panel broad powers to transfer[12] groups of cases to a single district court for the purpose of conducting pretrial proceedings without consideration for personal jurisdiction over the parties and without having to meet the venue requirements of 28 U.S.C. § 1404. Since the early years of its operation, the legal grounds for the Panel's actions have, for the most part, remained constant and become well-established. The Panel considers only two issues in resolving transfer motions under § 1407 in new dockets. First, the Panel considers whether common questions of fact among several pending civil actions exist such that centralization of those actions in a single district will further the convenience of the parties and witnesses and promote the just and efficient conduct of the actions. Second, the Panel considers which federal district and judge are best situated to handle the transferred matters. In deciding those issues, the Panel exercises its considerable and largely unfettered discretion within the unique circumstances that each motion presents. In fact, appeal from a Panel ruling seldom occurs and is available only by petition for a writ of mandamus or prohibition.

More often than not, the proposed dockets meet the § 1407 criteria and the Panel orders centralization. This has been true throughout the Panel's existence. For example, between 1970 and 1980, the annual "grant" rate on § 1407 motions in new dockets ranged from 51% (in 1980) to over 85% (in

---

* Chief Judge, U.S. District Court for the Western District of Kentucky; Chair, Judicial Panel on Multidistrict Litigation (2007–present).

[12] The Panel uses the terms *transfer* and *centralize* somewhat interchangeably (and this Article does so as well), although there is a technical difference. In general, the term *centralize* is used to describe the process by which the Panel, having found that a group of cases filed in multiple districts meets the § 1407 criteria, creates a new MDL and orders one or more of the cases transferred to a single district for "coordinated or consolidated" pretrial proceedings with one or more cases already pending there. 28 U.S.C. § 1407(a). The term *transfer* technically refers only to those cases that come from the transferor court(s). The Author will leave to the bloggers the job of answering that eternal question: What is the difference between coordination and consolidation? The Panel has previously stated:

> Clearly the term "coordinated" and the term "consolidated" denote different judicial functions. And we are of the view that a judge deciding whether to consolidate actions for all purposes is necessarily performing a different judicial function than a transferee judge who is supervising coordinated or consolidated pretrial proceedings under Section 1407.

In re S. Cent. States Bakery Prods. Antitrust Litig., 433 F. Supp. 1127, 1130 (J.P.M.L. 1977); *see In re* Equity Funding Corp. of Am. Sec. Litig., 375 F. Supp. 1378, 1384 (J.P.M.L. 1974) (same).

1972). Since 2000, that rate has ranged between 67% and 87%. Only in one year—1981—did the rate fall below 50%, and then only to 47%. For the last five years, the grant rates have ranged between 72% in 2007 and 86% in 2006. One should not infer from these statistics, however, that the Panel is somehow predisposed in favor of centralization. The opposite may indeed be true. The Panel is mindful that centralization is a limited exception to the generally applied rules of venue and jurisdiction. More likely, the data merely reflects the clarity of the standards that the Panel has applied faithfully and consistently over the years. As a result, practitioners who have done their homework will generally refrain from bringing unfounded motions that do not satisfy the prerequisites of § 1407.

Since its creation, the Panel has considered motions for centralization in over 1950 dockets involving more than 250,000 cases and literally millions of claims therein. These dockets encompass litigation categories as diverse as single accidents, such as airplane crashes, train wrecks, and hotel fires; mass torts, such as those involving asbestos and hormone replacement therapy drugs; other types of products liability; patent validity and infringement; antitrust price fixing; securities fraud; and employment practices. More recently, the Panel has noticed some uptick in the number of new dockets involving alleged violations of the Fair and Accurate Credit Transactions Act, as well as patent dockets involving Hatch-Waxman Act issues.

Among some common misconceptions about MDLs are that most are "mega-cases" and that they linger in the transferee courts for many years. To be sure, some MDLs meet the "mega-case" definition. And others, for various reasons, do remain in the transferee courts for lengthy periods of times. However, most MDLs do not fit either of these descriptions. Only thirty-seven out of about 300 active MDLs comprise more than 100 constituent actions and only ten have more than 1000.[29] By contrast, about one-half of all open MDLs are comprised of ten or fewer actions. And, while it is true that a handful of open MDLs are quite old, there are not many, the number of their actions and claims is dwindling, and there are valid reasons for their continued existence.[30] The data, in fact, show that the transferee courts do their utmost to resolve cases as expeditiously as

---

[29] The three largest current MDLs are MDL No. 875, *In re Asbestos Products Liability Litigation (No. VI)* (over 42,000 actions remain pending out of the approximately 120,000 centralized in the litigation); MDL No. 1657, *In re Vioxx Marketing, Sales Practices and Products Liability Litigation* (over 9300 pending actions), in which Judge Eldon Fallon has recently approved a settlement; and MDL No. 1769, *In re Seroquel Products Liability Litigation*, (over 5600 pending actions).

[30] The oldest MDL is MDL No. 381, *In re "Agent Orange" Products Liability Litigation*, which began in 1979 and is still receiving new tag-along cases. The second-oldest presently active MDL, which is MDL No. 799, *In re Air Disaster at Lockerbie, Scotland, on December 21, 1988*, has been prolonged, in part, by the extraordinarily complicated nature of the litigation (which involves claims against the Libyan government), as well as a postcentralization amendment to the Foreign Sovereign Immunities Act that resulted in the filing of additional actions in the MDL. The third oldest is MDL No. 875, *In re Asbestos Products Liability Litigation (No. VI)*, and, like MDL No. 381, new tag-along actions are still being transferred to this docket on a regular basis.

possible. Thus, of the 301 MDLs created from 1990 through 1999, only sixteen (or less than 6%) are still open. Similarly, of the 317 new MDLs created from 2000 through 2006, only 192 remain open. In most instances, cases are resolved (through settlement or otherwise) in the transferee court. * * *

Between 2003 and 2006, the Panel received over seventy motions for centralization annually.[35] In 2007, that number reached almost 100, with the filing of ninety-eight motions. Correspondingly, the number of MDL dockets has grown steadily over the years. At the conclusion of the 1997 fiscal year, there were 161 open MDL dockets encompassing just over 54,000 actions. At the close of the 2007 fiscal year, there were 297 open MDL dockets encompassing over 76,000 pending actions. * * *

The Panel does more than rule upon motions to create new MDLs. The Panel manages its own docket by transferring new cases to existing MDLs and remanding old cases to the transferor court when the transferee court has finished its work. This work happens quite efficiently and quietly every day. The Panel transfers new cases from other districts to existing MDLs when these so-called "tag-along" actions are brought to its attention, typically either by the clerk's office of the court where the action was filed or by one of the parties.[41] When the Panel receives such a notification, it may issue a Conditional Transfer Order (CTO) transferring the action to the designated MDL transferee court. In about 90% of the cases, no affected party opposes the CTO within the time established by the Panel, and the Panel automatically transfers the case to the transferee court. If a party opposes transfer, however, the Panel considers the matter at its next hearing session. In this manner, the Panel efficiently processes and transfers literally thousands of tag-along actions (over 6000 in 2007 alone) each year from their respective transferor courts to the involved MDLs.

The remand procedure is the reverse of, but similar to, the tag-along transfer procedure. The transferee court ordinarily lacks authority to try actions transferred from other jurisdictions, and one of the Panel's final responsibilities, therefore, is to remand individual cases to the original transferor court.[48] Upon receiving a suggestion of remand from the transferee judge (or upon motion by one or more of the parties or at the Panel's own initiative), the Panel issues a Conditional Remand Order (CRO). About 35% of the time, someone will file a notice of opposition. Where the transferee judge has suggested remand, however, the party seeking to vacate the CRO faces an uphill battle, as the Panel "gives great deference to a transferee judge's suggestion that an action pending before

---

[35] Although the Panel has authority to centralize actions "upon its own initiative," 28 U.S.C. § 1407(c) (2000), it has invoked that authority sparingly.

[41] Panel Rule 1.1 defines *tag-along action* as "a civil action pending in a district court and involving common questions of fact with actions previously transferred under Section 1407."

[48] The authority to remand an action to the transferor court rests with the Panel and not with the transferee court. *See In re* Roberts, 178 F.3d 181, 183 (3d Cir. 1999).

[that judge] is ripe for remand." Since 2000, the Panel has remanded over 2100 actions. * * *

As a general rule, the Panel considers that eliminating duplicate discovery in similar cases, avoiding conflicting judicial rulings, and conserving valuable judicial resources are sound reasons for centralizing pretrial proceedings with respect to a given group of actions. Every transfer decision has the potential to prejudice a particular party or claim among the many. In difficult cases, the Panel will weigh the likely benefits of centralization against the possibility of such resulting unfairness. The Panel's purpose is to benefit the judicial system and the litigants as a whole, not any particular party. Thus, the following considerations are usually of great interest to the Panel.

The Panel focuses solely upon the potential for convenience, efficiencies, and fairness in pretrial proceedings centralized before a single court. In doing so, the Panel evaluates whether the parties' legitimate discovery needs are substantially similar in all of the proposed transferee actions. Thus, the Panel looks to whether similar facts are at issue with respect to the various claims in the different cases. The greater the factual commonality of the cases, the more likely it is that centralization will benefit the involved parties and the system as a whole. The more troublesome dockets to evaluate are those where the potential transferee cases may contain different groups of plaintiffs or defendants and may contain some differing legal claims, yet nevertheless may appear to require similar factual discovery.

The Panel considers only the underlying record on its face and does not attempt to make independent judgments about the state of the record or the reasons for, or the correctness of, a particular transferor court ruling. The Panel does not consider the legal or factual strength of a given case, nor does it consider the likely outcome of pending jurisdictional motions. Indeed, it is important to emphasize that until the Panel's transfer order is actually filed in the transferee court, the transferor court is free to resolve any pending issues, including challenges to its own jurisdiction. Although the Panel has the power to separate claims from a transferred action and remand them to the transferor court, it is more likely to transfer the action in toto, and thereby afford maximum discretion to the transferee judge. In the Panel's view, the transferee judge is typically in the best position to determine whether unique legal claims can be handled within the MDL (for example, through the use of such pretrial techniques as separate discovery and motion tracks), or whether those claims should be returned to the transferor court.

The relative stage of pretrial proceedings in the various actions is often important. Centralization works best when a group of actions are all in the initial phases of discovery and motion practice. Older cases may be less suitable for transfer because significant discovery may have already occurred, and, thus, centralization with other cases could delay the more advanced actions. Nevertheless, more recently filed actions could benefit from coordination with those that are further advanced, as could the parties in all actions taken as a whole.

The number of actions in a proposed new MDL can also be important in determining whether the parties could benefit from centralization. The greater the number of cases and the greater number of common parties, the more likely it is that centralization will create significant efficiencies. A smaller number of relatively straightforward cases may not justify centralization. On the other hand, even two or three cases pending in different districts, each seeking class certification under similar facts, may be appropriate for centralization.

Finding the best district for centralization and identifying the best district judge to serve as the transferee judge are closely related issues. This is often the most difficult decision the Panel faces. The difficulty can arise from an abundance of good options; the absence of them, or from tactical differences among the parties, even among parties ostensibly on the same side. In a given docket, the particular location of the transferee court can be of greater importance because of the nature of the discovery and the concentration of the witnesses. In other dockets, location may be less of an overriding consideration, particularly where the litigation lacks a singular geographical focal point.

Other criteria that the Panel has considered in making its transferee court decision include the location of related grand jury proceedings, the existence of a qui tam action predicated on the same facts as those at issue in the MDL, the possibility of coordination with related state court proceedings, the location of the first-filed action, and the location of a majority of the actions. What is important to remember is that any single factor can only be properly evaluated in the context of both the particular docket and the other factors that may be relevant.

The ideal transferee judge is one with some existing knowledge of one of the cases to be centralized and who may already have some experience with complex cases, if the new docket appears to require it. For instance, a judge already assigned many of the transferee cases would be a likely choice, unless he or she is unable to devote the time to the combined transferee cases. On the other hand, the Panel may opt for an available experienced judge even though he or she does not sit in a district where one or more of the constituent actions were originally brought.

The willingness and motivation of a particular judge to handle an MDL docket are ultimately the true keys to whether centralization will benefit the parties and the judicial system. This may have little to do with the number of cases on the judge's docket and more to do with the presence of a few complex and time-consuming actions. The Panel may only become aware of such a circumstance via a telephone conference with that judge.

Depending on the situation, considerable interplay, both direct and indirect, may take place between the Panel and the transferor and proposed transferee courts. The Panel may make informal contact with various transferor and transferee judges to clarify matters.

Ultimately, the Panel's goal is to pair an experienced, knowledgeable, motivated, and available judge in a convenient location with a particular group of cases. The Panel therefore attempts to apply those factors in a given docket in the manner that will most benefit the litigants and the judiciary. The Panel's sole purpose is to benefit the system as a whole rather than a particular party or a particular point of view within the litigation. Clearly, such decisions involve considerable discretion and intuition.

As a general rule, the Panel likes to accommodate the parties in selecting an appropriate transferee district. Consequently, if the parties or a group of them can make a joint recommendation, the Panel may be favorably impressed. The Panel is particularly alert, however, to parties who may venture to use the MDL process for some substantive or procedural advantage, and will act to avert or deflect attempts by a party or parties to "game" the system.

Although the Panel's purpose is to "promote the just and efficient conduct of such actions" throughout the multidistrict litigation process, the Panel also recognizes that the MDL process itself may have some undesirable yet entirely avoidable side effects, such as temporarily slowing progress in ongoing cases. While Panel Rule 1.5 expressly provides that the pendency of a motion, CTO, or CRO before the Panel "does not affect or suspend orders and pretrial proceedings" in the transferor court, some district courts nevertheless elect to stay constituent proceedings (typically on the motion of one or more of the parties) while awaiting the Panel's decision on centralization. In such situations, the time tolled by the stay between the filing of the § 1407 transfer motion and its resolution may amount to dead time that can delay the existing litigation. The Panel recognizes that such a delay or dead time is disruptive and perhaps detrimental to one party or another.

Centralizing a large number of actions before a single judge also can create a somewhat unwieldy new MDL (at least initially). More delays can occur after the Panel enters its transfer order while the transferee court organizes the new files and convenes the parties. Centralization of cases may also create conflict among lawyers and between parties that did not previously exist. In this regard, the Panel notes that it can only do so much to further the "just and efficient conduct" of the involved actions; the parties and their counsel have their parts to play as well.

NOTES AND QUESTIONS

1.   In a 2010 interview with the Third Branch, the newsletter of the federal courts, Judge Heyburn reported on the number of § 1407 motions filed with the JPML for MDL centralization since its formation. See Panel Promotes Just and Efficient Conduct of Litigation, The Third Branch, Feb. 2010, at 1. The number of motions was relatively stable for five-year periods from 1970 through 1999 (173 in the first half of the 1970s up to slightly over 220 for the second half of the 1990s). Then it rose to 339 for 2000–2004, and to 469 for 2005–09, meaning that for that five-year period there were more than twice as many motions to centralize as in any similar period before 1995. In recent years, however, motions to centralize have declined to around mid-1990s levels, and the JPML has denied motions to centralize more often. Even at those levels, though, MDL's footprint in the federal system is substantial. Currently, around a third of pending federal civil cases are within MDLs, and typically about 20% of new civil cases in the federal courts every year are included in MDLs. For a statistical analysis of the importance of MDL over its life span, see Margaret Williams, The Effect of Multidistrict Litigation on the Federal Judiciary Over the Past 50 Years, 53 Ga. L. Rev. 1245 (2019). As of early 2021, there are 178 pending MDLs, in 45 districts, including over 330,000 separate actions. For regularly updated statistics, visit the JPML's website, https://www.jpml.uscourts.gov/.

What are the reasons for MDL's prominence? There is no single explanation. As will be discussed shortly, however, MDL centralization is increasingly seen by some as the most satisfactory and efficient vehicle for dealing with a flood of cases in which large numbers of persons complain of the same or similar conduct by defendants.

2.   An interesting facet of the statistics described in note 1 above is what Judge Heyburn referred to as "evolving judicial views of class certification." For instance, many cases that would benefit from consolidated treatment might not qualify for class certification. MDL's lower standard for aggregation makes this possible. For a discussion of MDL's rise alongside the decline of class certification in mass tort cases, see Thomas Willging & Emery Lee, From Class Actions to Multidistrict Consolidations: Aggregate Mass-Tort Litigation After *Ortiz*, 58 U. Kan. L. Rev. 775 (2010).

3.   Although the number of cases subject to an MDL order has increased, and MDL treatment may sometimes be treated as an alternative to class action treatment, "[c]ases consolidated for MDL pretrial proceedings ordinarily retain their separate identities." Gelboim v. Bank of America Corp., 574 U.S. 405 (2015). Indeed, as the Third Circuit expounded in 2016:

> A mass tort MDL is not a class action. It is a collection of separate lawsuits that are coordinated for pretrial proceedings—and *only* pretrial proceedings—before being remanded to their respective transferor courts. Some purely legal issues may apply in every case. But merits questions that are predicated on the existence or nonexistence of historical facts unique to each Plaintiff * * * generally

are not amenable to across-the-board resolution. Each Plaintiff deserves the opportunity to develop those sort of facts separately, and the District Court's understandable desire to streamline proceedings cannot override the Plaintiffs' basic trial rights.

In re Fosamax Prods. Liab. Litig., 852 F.3d 268, 302 (3d Cir. 2016).

But the pretrial proceedings in MDL do nevertheless provide for a high degree of aggregation. As in other consolidated cases, consolidated pleadings may be employed. Recall Katz v. Realty Equities Corp. of New York, *supra* p. 91. If that is done, the Supreme Court has explained the possible consequences as follows (*Gelboim*, 574 U.S. at 413 n.3):

> Parties may elect to file a "master complaint" and a corresponding "consolidated answer," which supersede prior individual pleadings. In such a case, the transferee court may treat the master pleadings as merging the discrete actions for the duration of the MDL pretrial proceedings. No merger occurs, however, when "the master complaint is not meant to be a pleading with legal effect but only an administrative summary of the claims brought by all the plaintiffs."

IN RE SHOULDER PAIN PUMP-CHONDROLYSIS PRODUCTS LIABILITY LITIGATION

Judicial Panel on Multidistrict Litigation, 2008.
571 F.Supp.2d 1367.

Before JOHN G. HEYBURN II, CHAIRMAN, J. FREDERICK MOTZ, ROBERT L. MILLER, JR., KATHRYN H. VRATIL, and DAVID R. HANSEN, JUDGES OF THE PANEL.

JOHN G. HEYBURN II, CHAIRMAN.

Plaintiffs in two actions pending in the District of Oregon and one action pending in the District of Minnesota have moved, pursuant to 28 U.S.C. § 1407, to centralize this litigation in the District of Oregon. This litigation currently consists of thirteen actions: six pending in the District of Oregon and one each in the Northern District of Alabama, the District of Colorado, the Southern District of Indiana, the Eastern District of Kentucky, the District of Minnesota, the Eastern District of New York, and the District of Utah, as listed on Schedule A.

Supporting centralization in the District of Oregon are plaintiffs in two other District of Oregon actions, a Northern District of Alabama action, a District of Colorado action, a Southern District of Indiana action, an Eastern District of Kentucky action, an Eastern District of New York action, and a District of Utah action, as well as plaintiffs in four potential tag-along actions pending in the District of Colorado, the Northern District of Florida, the Eastern District of New York, and the Western District of Virginia, respectively. Plaintiffs in the actions pending in the Northern

District of Alabama, the Southern District of Indiana, the Eastern District of New York, and the District of Utah advocate selection of their respective districts as transferee district, in the alternative. Responding defendants all oppose centralization. To the extent that they express a preference, most of these defendants support selection of either the Eastern District of Kentucky or the Northern District of Illinois as transferee district, if the Panel orders centralization over their objections.

On the basis of the papers filed and hearing session held, we are not persuaded that Section 1407 centralization would serve the convenience of the parties and witnesses or further the just and efficient conduct of this litigation at the present time. Although these personal injury actions have some commonality as to whether shoulder pain pumps and/or the anesthetic drugs used in those pumps cause *glenohumeral chondrolysis*, an indeterminate number of different pain pumps made by different manufacturers are at issue, as are different anesthetic drugs made by different pharmaceutical companies. Moreover, not all of the thirteen constituent actions involve pharmaceutical company defendants, and many defendants are sued only in a minority of those actions. The proponents of centralization have not convinced us that the efficiencies that might be gained by centralization would not be overwhelmed by the multiple individualized issues (including ones of liability and causation) that these actions appear to present. The parties can avail themselves of alternatives to Section 1407 transfer to minimize whatever possibilities there might be of duplicative discovery and/or inconsistent pretrial rulings.

IT IS THEREFORE ORDERED that the motion, pursuant to 28 U.S.C. § 1407, for centralization of these thirteen actions is denied.

IN RE AVIATION PRODUCTS LIABILITY LITIGATION
Judicial Panel on Multidistrict Litigation, 1972.
347 F.Supp. 1401.

PER CURIAM.

The cases comprising this products liability litigation can be segregated into two broad categories. One category consists of actions by corporate plaintiffs asserting claims for damages allegedly caused by defects in the design, manufacture and installation of a gas turbine helicopter engine produced by the Allison Division of General Motors Corporation. The other category consists of actions asserting claims for personal injuries sustained when a helicopter powered by the same type engine crashed because of an alleged in-flight engine failure.

Plaintiffs in twelve actions pending in seven different districts moved the Panel to transfer these cases (hereinafter referred to as the Schedule A cases) to a single district for coordinated or consolidated pretrial proceedings. The Panel issued an order to show cause why eight apparently related cases (hereinafter referred to as the Schedule B cases) should not also be considered for transfer pursuant to 28 U.S.C. § 1407. On the basis of the papers filed and the hearing held, we find that all of the Schedule A cases and some of the Schedule B cases will clearly benefit from transfer to a single district for coordinated or consolidated pretrial proceedings.

I.   Schedule A Cases

A.   Background

Plaintiffs in the Schedule A cases are represented by the same lead counsel. Each plaintiff is a corporate owner or operator of a commercial helicopter powered by a gas turbine engine designed and manufactured by the Detroit Diesel Allison Division of General Motors Corporation (hereinafter Allison). Each action concerns the design, manufacture and installation of the helicopter engine, known as the Allison 250-C18. Allegations concerning the design and manufacture of the helicopter frame are common to some of the cases, as are charges of improper performance of overhaul, modification and repair service.[1]

The claims for damages in each of the cases are similar: (1) damages to helicopters and to plaintiff's business as a result of crashes or emergency landings caused by premature failures and malfunctions of the helicopter's engine during flight; (2) damages to plaintiff's business as a result of down time required to make engine modifications and repairs specified by the Federal Aviation Agency and Allison.

B.   Arguments of the Parties

Movants urge that the existence of common questions of fact makes transfer to a single district for coordinated or consolidated pretrial proceedings necessary in order to promote the just and efficient conduct of the litigation and to avoid duplicitous discovery and unnecessary inconvenience to the parties and witnesses. Movants contend that the issue of fact central to each lawsuit is the airworthiness of the Allison 250-C18 engine, including its design, development, manufacture and installation. It is asserted that although the specific defects alleged in each separate case may not be identical they are all interwoven so as to cover the engine's general condition and airworthiness. It is also asserted that discovery common to all cases will concern the extent to which Allison controlled and directed the installation of the engine by the helicopter manufacturers and each incident of engine overhaul modification and repair performed by its authorized distributors.

---

[1]   Textron, Inc. (a division of Bell Helicopter Company) and Fairchild-Hiller Corporation designed and manufactured the helicopters involved in these actions. Aviation Power Supply (Western United States), The Southwest Airmotive Company (Central United States) and Airwork Corporation (Eastern United States) are the authorized distributors of the Allison 250-C18 engine and component parts and are the authorized overhaul and repair facilities for the engines.

Allison agrees that consolidation of the Schedule A cases for coordinated pretrial proceedings is necessary, but urges that transfer of the Lametti action [pending in D.Minn.] be denied because discovery is near completion. Allison also points out that transfer of the Freeman action [pending in W.D.Wash.] is unnecessary because that case settled shortly after trial began.

All other defendants[4] oppose transfer of any of the cases in which they are named. Although these defendants generally admit that certain common issues of fact are alleged, they argue that these issues are outnumbered by separate and distinct factual issues peculiar to each case. They assert that since the helicopters were operated in different environments under varying atmospheric conditions, both of which affect the performance of the aircraft and the engine, a substantial amount of local discovery concerning each mishap is necessary and will not be common.

These defendants contend that transfer will restrict their efforts to complete local discovery and will require them to participate in discovery not useful to them. They also contend that an important factor weighing against the desirability of transfer under Section 1407 is the lack of a single district with jurisdiction over all defendants, which precludes any real possibility of a common trial on liability.

C.   The Question of Transfer

It is clear from the legislative history of Section 1407 that multidistrict products liability litigation was envisioned as susceptible to effective treatment under Section 1407. There is no dispute that two of the three statutory requirements to transfer exist in this litigation: these are civil actions involving one or more common questions of fact which are pending in more than one district. The opposition to transfer, however, strongly urges that the issues of fact are not so common that the convenience of the parties and witnesses and the just and efficient conduct of the litigation will be promoted by transfer under Section 1407. We do not agree.

Each action against Allison will require discovery concerning the design, manufacture and installation of the Allison 250-C18 engine. Even though different component parts are involved in different cases, discovery common to all cases will concern engineers responsible for the overall design and development of the engine. And plaintiffs may also be interested in deposing the company officials who relied on those engineers. Furthermore, if it is true, as plaintiffs assert, that Allison controlled the installation of the engines by the airframe manufacturers and dictated the specifications regarding overhaul, modification and repair to the authorized distributors, discovery on these issues will likely be common.

---

[4]   Textron, Inc. (a division of Bell Helicopter Company), Fairchild-Hiller Corporation, Aviation Power Supply and Airwork Corporation.

We are convinced that transfer of the Schedule A cases to a single district for coordinated or consolidated pretrial proceedings is necessary. For the convenience of the parties and witnesses it is highly desirable that witnesses relevant to the common issues be deposed but once. And only through a coordinated pretrial discovery program, tailored to fit the discovery needs of each party and supervised by a single judge, can overlapping and duplicitous discovery be avoided and the just and efficient conduct of the litigation assured.[6]

The Manual for Complex and Multidistrict Litigation specifically resolves defendants' concern that transfer will involve them in unwanted discovery:

> [E]xpenses of counsel in attending depositions on oral interrogatories can be avoided by entry of an order providing an opportunity for a delayed examination by parties who cannot afford to attend all depositions or believe the depositions will not affect their interests. . . .

> Under this order a party with limited means or who in good faith believes the deposition is of no interest to him may without risk, decide not to be represented by counsel at the deposition in question. He may read a copy of the transcript of the initial examination and then decide whether he wishes to request a delayed examination on the ground that his interests were inadequately protected at the initial examination. *Manual* Part I, § 2.31 (1970).

Furthermore, defendants' argument regarding the unavailability of a single district with jurisdiction over all parties is misdirected.[7] Transfer of civil actions pursuant to 28 U.S.C. § 1407 is for pretrial purposes only and the fact that all parties are not amenable to suit in a particular district does not prevent transfer to that district for pretrial proceedings where the prerequisites of Section 1407 are otherwise satisfied. Succinctly, venue is not a criterion in deciding the propriety of transfer under Section 1407.

D. *Choice of Transferee Forum*

The Southern District of Indiana is the most appropriate transferee forum. Allison is the one party involved in all of the transferred cases and the majority of the common discovery will focus on it. Its plant and offices are located in Indianapolis and all its documents and necessary witnesses are there. Also, the transferred cases are fairly well-scattered throughout the country and Indianapolis provides a convenient geographical center for the litigation.

---

[6] *Cf. In re Plumbing Fixtures Litigation* where the short-line defendants and the full-line defendants were given different discovery schedules.

[7] Defendants' argument is better aimed at the appropriateness of a particular transferee forum.

Judge Morell E. Sharp of the Western District of Washington has conducted a complete discovery program in the now-settled *Freeman* action. His familiarity with the issues and discovery involved in this litigation will enable him to expedite the consolidated pretrial proceedings. Pursuant to 28 U.S.C. § 292(c), Judge Sharp has been designated to sit as a district judge in the Southern District of Indiana and this litigation will be assigned to him for pretrial proceedings.

II.   Schedule B Cases

A.   Cases Transferred

With respect to each action included in the Panel's show cause order, we have examined the complaint, read the briefs filed and heard oral argument. On the basis of our reasoning concerning the Schedule A cases, we conclude that, for the convenience of all parties and witnesses and the just and efficient conduct of the litigation, the following Schedule B cases should be transferred to the Southern District of Indiana for coordinated or consolidated pretrial proceedings.

1.   Arizona Helicopters, Inc. v. General Motors Corp. et al., District of Arizona, Civil Action No. Civ.-70–323–PHX

The allegations of plaintiff's complaint closely parallel those made by plaintiffs in the Schedule A cases. Plaintiff, owner of a helicopter powered by an Allison 250-C18 engine, alleges that as a result of engine failures it suffered damage to the aircraft, a loss of revenue due to inability to use the aircraft and additional pecuniary losses. It is alleged that these in-flight failures were a result of defects in the design, material, construction or workmanship (or some combination thereof) regarding the engine and its component parts.

All parties to this action oppose transfer. They claim that discovery is substantially complete, except for a few depositions scheduled to be taken in Indianapolis. Although the case had been scheduled for trial on July 11, 1972, we are advised by counsel that the trial date has been continued for approximately six months. In light of this development and to avoid the possibility of duplicitous discovery and unnecessary inconvenience to the Indianapolis witnesses, we think it best to order this case transferred to the Southern District of Indiana for the completion of pretrial discovery. Certainly if this is the only remaining discovery needed, Judge Sharp can devise a program to accommodate these parties and the action may be considered for remand to the District of Arizona.

2.   Sabine Offshore Services, Inc. v. General Motors Corp., Eastern District of Texas, Civil Action No. 7647

Plaintiff claims that it is entitled to recover damages for two separate helicopter crashes caused by in-flight engine failures. Both the plaintiff and defendant oppose transfer on the ground that this action does not present questions of fact common to the other cases. We do not agree. Plaintiff alleges that the helicopter's engine, an Allison 250-C18, was defective either in "workmanship, design or material at the time the helicopter's engine manufactured by defendant was delivered to plaintiff." Thus, as far as plaintiff's discovery is concerned, there definitely are areas in which questions of fact exist common to the transferred cases. We believe that both parties will benefit from participation in the consolidated pretrial proceedings before Judge Sharp. Once the common discovery is completed, of course, the action may be considered for remand to the Eastern District of Texas.

3. *Ranger et al. v. General Motors Corp. et al., District of Arizona, Civil Action No. Civ.–72–42–PCT*

This action, originally filed in state court and subsequently removed to federal court, consists of two claims. The first is a wrongful death claim brought by the personal representative of the estate of a pilot fatally injured in a helicopter crash; the second claim is brought by the corporate owner of two helicopters that were involved in several crashes, one of which resulted in the fatality complained of in the first claim.

A comparison of the second claim with the complaint filed in Elling Halvorsen, Inc., et al. v. Textron, Inc., et al., District of Arizona, Civil Action No. Civ.–71–58–PHX (a Schedule A case), reveals that similar allegations are made in that action involving the same parties and concerning the same helicopters and mishaps. Furthermore, counsel representing the corporate plaintiffs in the second claim also serve as lead counsel for the Schedule A plaintiffs. It is therefore clear that the second claim of the Marvel Ranger action should be consolidated with the other cases for the coordinated pretrial proceedings in the Southern District of Indiana and it is so ordered.

Although plaintiffs in the first claim have no objection to transfer of the second claim for coordinated or consolidated pretrial proceedings, they argue that their claim does not present questions of fact sufficiently common to the other actions to warrant transfer at this time. We agree. Section 1407(a) authorizes the Panel to "separate any claim" from the transferred action and to remand that claim to the transferor district. We therefore remand the first claim of the Marvel Ranger action to the District of Arizona, but without prejudice to later application for transfer should the parties find that discovery will duplicate discovery in the transferee district.

B. *Cases Not Transferred*

We have considered each of the remaining Schedule B cases on its own merits and have concluded that none of them present sufficient common questions of fact to warrant transfer to the Southern District of Indiana at this time.

1.   *Richard W. Black v. Fairchild Industries, Inc., et al., District of New Jersey, Civil Action No. 63–72 and*

John W. Thumann et al. v. Fairchild Industries, Inc., et al., District of Maryland, Civil Action No. 72–433M

Both cases are personal injury actions arising out of the crash of a helicopter en route from Baltimore Friendship Airport to Washington National Airport. Although plaintiffs allege that the crash resulted from a failure of the helicopter's engine, an Allison 250-C18, the complaints do not set forth any specific engine defect and we cannot conclude that discovery will involve issues of fact common to the transferred cases. Transfer is therefore denied without prejudice to later application if it is found during the course of pretrial that discovery will duplicate discovery in the transferee forum.

2.   *Mrs. Doyle R. Avant, Jr., et al. v. Fairchild-Hiller Corp. et al., Southern District of Texas, Civil Action No. 70–V–1 and*

Barbara G. Hall et al. v. Fairchild-Hiller Corp. et al., Southern District of Texas, Civil Action No. 70–V–2

These cases are wrongful death actions arising from the crash of a helicopter near Goliad, Texas. Transfer is opposed on the ground that discovery is complete and that trial is set for August 14, 1972. It is asserted that any discovery that remains does not involve questions of fact common to the transferred litigation. Transfer of these actions is therefore denied without prejudice to the right of a party to seek reconsideration at a later time.

3.   *Petroleum Helicopters, Inc. v. The Southwest Airmotive Co. et al., Western District of Louisiana, Civil Action No. 16224*

Plaintiff asserts claims for damages allegedly caused by defendant's negligence in servicing plaintiff's helicopter. Discovery only involves the maintenance and service performed by the defendant and the circumstances surrounding the forced landings. Since it appears that no questions of fact exist common to the transferred cases, transfer is denied, but without prejudice to later application if the parties deem it necessary to expand their discovery to encompass the discovery in the consolidated actions.

NOTES AND QUESTIONS

1.   What was the principal factor that led the Panel not to transfer in *Shoulder Pain*? The order says that the cases involved some different pain pumps made by different manufacturers. If the plaintiffs in each case alleged that the particular pump involved was likely to cause the same condition, *glenohumeral chondrolysis*, wouldn't that suggest enough commonality that the cases would benefit from joint discovery and pretrial? In *Aviation Products*, unrelated crashes or malfunctions were involved and different kinds of injuries

were alleged. Why did that not prevent transfer? How important to the decision in *Shoulder Pain* was the Panel's comment that "not all of the thirteen constituent actions involve pharmaceutical company defendants, and many defendants are sued only in a minority of those actions"? Wasn't the same true in *Aviation Products*? For disagreement with the Panel's decision in *Shoulder Pain* from one of the plaintiff lawyers seeking centralization, see Leslie O'Leary, Out on Your Own, Trial, Nov. 2010, at 36 (objecting that "[p]ain pump litigation is a notable example of the Panel's new reluctance to transfer products liability cases," which leaves the plaintiff lawyer "out on your own"). Cf. Comment, The Judicial Panel on Multidistrict Litigation: Time for Rethinking, 140 U. Pa. L. Rev. 711 (1991) (asserting that Panel pays insufficient attention to party interests). Why would plaintiffs favor transfer?

2. Although many major nationwide controversies will typically become the subject of an MDL, that is not always the case. Indeed, the JPML is attuned to the possibility that an MDL may actually be *less* efficient than allowing cases to run their course in multiple forums. A salient example is the attempt by plaintiffs in 263 cases against more than 100 insurers to convince the JPML that there ought to be an MDL covering all federal cases against insurers for business interruption losses caused by the COVID-19 pandemic and associated government shutdown orders. In refusing the request to create an MDL the Panel opined:

> [T]he proposed MDL raises significant managerial and efficiency concerns. A transferee court would have to establish a pretrial structure to manage the hundreds of plaintiffs—many with disparate views of the litigation—and more than one hundred insurers. The court also would have to identify common policies with identical or sufficiently similar policy language and oversee discovery that likely will differ insurer-to-insurer. To say this litigation would result in a complicated MDL seems an understatement. Managing such a litigation would be an ambitious undertaking for any jurist, and implementing a pretrial structure that yields efficiencies will take time. As counsel emphasized during oral argument, however, time is of the essence in this litigation. Many plaintiffs are on the brink of bankruptcy as a result of business lost due to the COVID-19 pandemic and the government closure orders. An industry-wide MDL in this instance will not promote a quick resolution of these matters.

> Put simply, the MDL that movants request entails very few common questions of fact, which are outweighed by the substantial convenience and efficiency challenges posed by managing a litigation involving the entire insurance industry. The proponents' arguments that these problems can be overcome are not persuasive. We therefore deny the motions for centralization.

> * * * With respect to the actions in this litigation involving other insurers, centralization does not appear appropriate. There are alternatives to centralization available to minimize any duplication in pretrial proceedings, including informal cooperation and

coordination of the actions. The parties also may seek to relate actions against a common insurer in a given district before one judge. Such alternatives appear practicable as to these insurers, given the limited number of actions and districts involved as to each.

In re COVID-19 Business Interruption Protection Ins. Litig., 2020 WL 4670700, at *2–4 (J.P.M.L. Aug. 12, 2020).

3.   It should be apparent that the Panel will sometimes transfer cases over the objections of numerous parties. Why would parties oppose transfer? In *Aviation Products,* all defendants except Allison opposed transfer on the ground it would involve them in unwanted discovery. How satisfactory is the Panel's response to that concern? Are "bystander" parties in multidistrict cases entitled to more or less solicitude than in single-district consolidation situations?

Mark Herrmann, To MDL or Not to MDL? A Defense Perspective, 24 Litigation 43 (Summer 1998), examines the practical implications of MDL treatment. For example, a defendant facing an imminent outburst of litigation might inaugurate MDL proceedings simply because these take time and it can use the resulting breather to "organize a defense, negotiate a global settlement, or file a bankruptcy proceeding." Moreover, MDL proceedings in federal court can allow the state court cases (not subject to this delay) to proceed faster.

On the other hand, there are several reasons why a defendant might oppose transfer, as outlined by defense-side lawyers Lori McGroder & Iain Kennedy, in When Coordination Isn't Key: Why and How to Oppose MDL Centralization, Bloomberg BNA Class Action Litigation Report, June 8, 2016, summarized as follows:

(a)   The "Field of Dreams" problem ("If you build it, they will come."): The creation of an MDL may prompt a surge of new cases. An example is a pharmaceutical litigation in which only about 50 actions had been filed, but a year after MDL centralization more than 2,300 were on file.

(b)   Avoiding MDL may exert downward pressure on total settlement figures. As McGroder and Kennedy explain: "Fragmented cases may allow a defendant to better leverage its relative size and resources."

(c)   Having cases in many courts may allow the defendant more latitude to strategically select cases to push to trial, thus creating momentum in its favor, and to control the pace of discovery.

Also, the MDL transfer may benefit the "major players" on the defense side, but not the "small fish." Ruth Dowling & Florence Crisp, Sometimes the Small Fry Get Swept Up in the Net, Nat.L.J., Sept. 20, 2010, report on the difficulties that an "uncommon" defendant can confront because it is "exceedingly difficult for a single defendant to seek an early exit from an MDL." (Recall the plight of the less central defendants in the consolidated proceeding in *Katz, supra* p. 91.) While an "industry giant" lowers its litigation costs by MDL treatment, as compared to defending dozens or hundreds of cases around the country, the uncommon defendant (which might not even have been sued but for the MDL) sees its costs rise. It also faces pressures "not to diverge from the larger pack of defendants."

4.   Judge Heyburn, then the Chair of the Panel, told us (see *supra* p. 126) that the Panel does not have a predisposition in favor of centralization of litigation. How should the Panel approach its task? It could adopt a "minimalist" attitude, generally leaving the question of coordination to individual judges using stay or injunctive powers or other methods. The Panel, then, might limit its role to avoiding duplicative discovery when there is no alternative to its intervention. On the other hand, it could take a more "maximalist" approach, regarding its power to combine litigation as a method to further combined resolution. Note that Judge Heyburn also says that transferee judges "do their utmost to resolve cases as expeditiously as possible" and that the biggest task for the Panel is finding a transferee judge with the "willingness and motivation" to "handle the MDL docket." Consider which judges would likely seek appointment to the Panel or exhibit that enthusiasm for handling an MDL docket. Wouldn't they be more likely to be judges who favor centralized, combined resolution? For an argument that the Panel has moved toward a "maximalist" orientation, and sometimes actually has taken a role in overseeing the way transferred cases are handled after concentration, see Richard Marcus, Cure-All for an Era of Dispersed Litigation? Toward a Maximalist Use of the Multidistrict Litigation Panel's Transfer Power, 82 Tul. L. Rev. 2245 (2008).

One federal judge who had served on the JPML described its approach thusly: "When we grant an MDL, we look to whether a judge has particular experience; we are telling the judge this is a different kind of case because we are giving it to *you*. We are asking them to bring their experience to bear and figure out what remedy and procedure to use." Abbe Gluck, Unorthodox Civil Procedure: Modern Multidistrict Litigation's Place in the Textbook Understandings of Procedure, 165 U. Pa. L. Rev. 1669, 1695 (2017).

5.   One area where the Panel has used its authority to do more than avoid duplicative discovery is in class actions. Where possibly overlapping class actions have been filed, the Panel has recognized this fact as strongly favoring transfer. See In re High Sulfur Content Gasoline Products Liability Litig., 344 F.Supp.2d 755 (J.P.M.L. 2004), in which the Panel placed special emphasis on avoiding inconsistent rulings with respect to class certification as a ground for transfer. According to David Herr, Multidistrict Litigation Manual § 5.25 at 119 (2005), "if there are conflicting or potentially conflicting class claims in the litigation, transfer is likely regardless of the presence or absence of other factors that would otherwise favor or militate against transfer."

For a similar effort by the Panel, consider In re Westinghouse Electric Corp. Uranium Contracts Litigation, 405 F.Supp. 316 (J.P.M.L. 1975). Westinghouse found itself unable to perform its contractual obligation to deliver uranium products to a number of utilities and other customers.

Westinghouse notified these customers that it considered itself excused from performance due to commercial impracticability pursuant to § 2–615 of the Uniform Commercial Code, and that it had established an allocation program that would provide each customer with approximately 19% of the amount it should receive under its contract. All the customers sued to enforce their contracts. Although the suits involved different contracts negotiated by different people at different times, the Panel transferred them for combined treatment, noting that transfer would "eliminate the possibility of colliding pretrial rulings by courts of coordinate jurisdiction, and avoid potentially conflicting preliminary injunctive demands on Westinghouse with respect to its delivery of uranium." For another example of aggressive use of the Panel's power, consider In re Asbestos Products Litigation, *infra* p. 153, n. 3.

6.   If the Panel concludes that combined treatment is appropriate, should it, or the transferee judge, be empowered to enjoin prosecution of other suits even if they are in state court? Professors Wright and Kane suggest that such cases may fall within the exception to the Anti-Injunction Act (see *infra* p. 357) for injunctions in aid of the federal court's jurisdiction: "This principle would seem to apply to prevent conflicting state actions where many similar suits have been consolidated by the Judicial Panel on Multidistrict Litigation under 28 U.S.C. § 1407. The purpose of consolidation is to provide coordinated treatment of these complex cases, and, as in actions in rem and school desegregation cases, it is intolerable to have different orders coming from different courts." Charles Wright & Mary Kay Kane, Law of Federal Courts 306 n.51 (6th ed. 2002).

7.   Should the transfer decision be deferred until preliminary motions are decided in the transferor court? See In re Crown Life Ins. Co. Premium Litig., 178 F.Supp.2d 1365 (J.P.M.L. 2001) (transfer not deferred until decision of plaintiff's motion to remand to state court; the transferee judge can rule on that). For example, in In re Standard & Poor's Rating Agency Litig., 23 F.Supp.3d 378 (S.D.N.Y. 2014), state officials asserted state law claims in state court, alleging that defendants had manipulated the LIBOR rate for interbank lending. Defendants removed on purported federal-question grounds and got all the cases transferred by the Panel even though the state officials had promptly moved to remand. The transferee judge then ruled that there was no federal-question jurisdiction and remanded all the cases to state court. Was the benefit of a single ruling sufficient to justify the delay occasioned by the multidistrict proceedings?

8.   Despite its broad powers, the Panel ordinarily cannot reach cases in state court. Indeed, the drafters of the statute did not wish to expand federal subject matter jurisdiction for MDL. The American Law Institute's Complex Litigation Project (1994), however, proposed *transfer* from state and federal courts to a transferee court (federal or state) that would then *consolidate* the cases for aggregate disposition. Federal "intrasystem consolidation" would be enhanced by expanding MDL transfer under § 1407 through use of a Complex Litigation Panel and extending authority to the transferee court over trial as well as pretrial. Federal-state "inter-system consolidation" would be

accomplished by expanded removal to federal court and consolidation of actions pending in state courts arising out of the same basic transaction that is the basis of a pending federal-court action. See American Law Institute, Complex Litigation: Statutory Recommendations and Analysis § 5.01 (1994). In aid of this mechanism are provisions for supplemental jurisdiction, § 5.03, anti-suit injunctions, § 5.04, court-ordered notice of intervention and preclusion, § 5.05, and a federal choice of law standard, §§ 6.01–6.07. Despite, or perhaps because of, its broad and comprehensive attempt to deal with duplicative cases in both federal and state courts, the ALI Project's proposals have not been adopted by Congress.

Parallel proceedings in a federal MDL and state courts can create challenging issues that the MDL court cannot fully avoid. For instance, in Retirement Systems of Alabama v. J.P. Morgan Chase & Co., 386 F.3d 419 (2d Cir. 2004), a federal MDL judge certified a class action and set a date for the trial. She then entered an injunction ordering an Alabama state court to postpone the trial of a related case (brought by plaintiffs who had opted out of the federal class action, against many of the same defendants) until after the federal trial scheduled three months later was completed. The district judge was worried that the state-court trial could interfere with the federal-court trial schedule. The Second Circuit found the injunction did not satisfy the "in aid of jurisdiction" exception to the Anti-Injunction Act, noting that there was no imminent settlement in federal court, duplicative motions for injunctive relief, or exposure of defendants to the risk of inconsistent injunctions. It found the claim that the state trial might delay the federal trial and interfere with the time and attention of the parties unpersuasive: "Any time parallel state and federal actions are proceeding against the same defendant, it is conceivable that occurrences in the state action will cause delay in the federal action, by provoking motion practice in federal court regarding the effects of state-court rulings, or simply by diverting the attention of the defendant," but that would not rise to the level of threatening the federal court's jurisdiction.

In 2002, Congress did adopt the Multiparty, Multiforum Trial Jurisdiction Act of 2002, 116 Stat. 1826. This Act adds 28 U.S.C. § 1369, which gives district courts original jurisdiction so long as there is minimal diversity in litigation "that arises from a single accident, where at least 75 natural persons have died in the accident at a discrete location." § 1369(a). But if the "substantial majority of all plaintiffs" are citizens of a single state, and the claims will be governed primarily by the law of that state, the federal court should abstain from exercising this jurisdiction. § 1369(b). The district court before which the action is pending is to notify the MDL Panel. § 1369(d). Because accidents causing 75 deaths are relatively rare, this statute is not invoked often.

A number of states have now also adopted procedures for consolidating state-court cases across the jurisdictional lines of individual courts. See, *e.g.*, California Rules of Court Rule 3.500 *et seq.*; D. Theodore Rave & Zachary D. Clopton, Texas MDL, 24 Lewis & Clark L. Rev. 395 (2020).

9. Once the decision has been made to create an MDL, the question then becomes where consolidated proceedings should take place. As leading

plaintiff-side lawyer Elizabeth Cabraser has noted, however, "it is not a 'where' question, but a 'who' question." Indeed, the JPML considers its choice of transferee district to be geographically unlimited; that is, it considers its choice unhampered by the limitations on personal jurisdiction or venue that might otherwise apply.

Whether recent rulings like that in Bristol-Myers Squibb v. Superior Court of California, *supra* p. 382, could limit the authority of the JPML might be debated. Since the Court partly emphasized notions of sovereignty in its decision, it might be argued that the constitutional ruling on state-court personal jurisdiction has no bearing on federal judges handling cases transferred within the federal system. Perhaps there is a Fifth Amendment limit on the power of the federal courts to achieve litigation economy in this way, but the Necessary and Proper Clause might go a long way toward solving any such concerns. On the other hand, the Supreme Court's recent restrictions on personal jurisdiction—and their focus on the proportionality of defendants' contacts to its amenability to litigation in a particular court—seem to apply equally to MDL as to other kinds of cases. Moreover, perhaps there is a colorable argument that *plaintiffs* ought not to be subject to personal jurisdiction in a far-flung MDL transferee district to whose jurisdiction they have not consented, and in which they are arguably not adequately represented. For analysis of these issues, see Andrew Bradt, The Long Arm of Multidistrict Litigation, 59 Wm. & Mary L. Rev. 1165 (2018).

To say that the JPML does not consider itself limited by restrictions on personal jurisdiction and venue is not, however, to say that geography is *never* relevant to the choice of transferee judge. As *Shoulder Pain* and *Aviation Products* exemplify, the JPML issues written orders explaining its decisions, including the choice of transferee judge. What examination of these decisions reveals is that the Panel's choices are *ad hoc*. That is not to say that they are arbitrary, but that they are tailored to the particulars of the cases before it. The extent to which the physical location of the transferee district matters varies. Consider the following, based on a study of five years' worth of transfer orders (*id.* at 1215–16):

> What one can say about JPML transfer orders is that they seem to give decent, practical reasons for choosing the transferee court and judge. But it is also fair to say that those reasons vary considerably. For instance, sometimes the location of the defendant's headquarters matters a great deal, while in other cases it does not. And in some cases, the experience of the MDL judge is a critical factor, while in other cases the JPML embraces the opportunity to send the case to a judge who has never overseen an MDL. In some cases, the fact that the transferee judge is already presiding over some of the component cases is important, while in others the JPML assigns the MDL to a judge who is not hearing any pending cases. In some cases, it matters that the parties have agreed to an MDL district, while in others the JPML chooses a district that no party has proposed. And sometimes the JPML chooses the busiest federal districts, citing their significant

resources, while other times it chooses a less busy district whose favorable docket conditions give it the bandwidth to take on an MDL case. You get the picture.

A recent study shows, however, that when plaintiffs and defendants do agree on a transferee district, the JPML is very likely to go along. And when there is disagreement, the Panel sides with the plaintiffs and defendants with roughly equal frequency. Although this is evenhanded treatment by the Panel, it does represent a significant departure from the norm that the plaintiff selects the forum. Is such a departure justified by the purposes of the MDL statute? For discussion, see Zachary Clopton & Andrew Bradt, Party Preferences in Multidistrict Litigation, 107 Cal. L. Rev. 1713 (2019).

C. POWERS OF THE TRANSFEREE COURT

STANLEY A. WEIGEL, THE JUDICIAL PANEL ON MULTIDISTRICT LITIGATION, TRANSFEROR COURTS AND TRANSFEREE COURTS
78 F.R.D. 575 (1978).

A transfer under Section 1407 becomes effective upon the filing of the Panel's order of transfer with the clerk in the transferee district. Thereafter it is generally accepted that the jurisdiction of the transferor court ceases and the transferee court assumes complete pretrial jurisdiction. The mere pendency of a motion or of an order to show cause before the Panel in no way limits the jurisdiction of the court in which the action is pending. Nor does such pendency before the Panel "affect or suspend orders and pretrial proceedings" in that court. All discovery in progress and all orders of the transferor court remain in effect after transfer unless and until modified by the transferee judge who may modify, expand, or vacate prior orders of the transferor court.

There are no decisions dealing with the question as to whether a transferor judge may [after remand of a case] modify, expand or vacate prior orders of a transferee judge. Modifications or expansions to further the effectiveness of such orders would appear to be proper—perhaps necessary in some instances. However, it would be improper to permit a transferor judge to overturn orders of a transferee judge even though error in the latter might result in reversal of the final judgment of the transferor court. If transferor judges were permitted to upset rulings of transferee judges, the result would be an undermining of the purpose and usefulness of transfer under Section 1407 for coordinated or consolidated pretrial proceedings because those proceedings would then lack the finality (at the trial court level) requisite to the convenience of witnesses and parties and to efficient conduct of actions.

Since the transfer order does deprive the transferor court of jurisdiction, the Panel undertakes to avoid ordering transfer when important motions have been fully submitted and await decision by the prospective transferor court. The Panel often accomplishes that objective informally by a letter from the Chairman of the Panel informing each transferor judge of the prospective transfer. The letter also advises that, if requested, the Panel will defer transfer until the judge decides any matter fully submitted and ripe for decision. Occasionally, the Panel will enter an order deferring decision on the question of transfer until a matter so submitted is decided by the prospective transferor judge. Or the Panel may stay transfer pending such decision.

* * *

The transferee judge assigned to multidistrict litigation possesses all pretrial powers over the transferred actions exercisable by a district court under the Federal Rules of Civil Procedure. In other words, the transferee judge may make any pretrial order that the transferor court might have made in the absence of transfer.

It is the province of the transferee judge to determine the degree and manner in which pretrial proceedings are coordinated or consolidated. The Panel has neither the power nor the inclination to make any determinations regarding the actual conduct of the coordinated or consolidated pretrial proceedings.

The transferee judge has control over all aspects of discovery. The unique discovery interests of any party can be accommodated by him in a schedule providing for discovery on non-common issues to proceed concurrently with those which are common. Or the transferee judge may leave discovery on any unique issue for the supervision of the transferor court upon remand. The transferee judge can make results of completed discovery available to parties in related actions, and to parties in actions that are later filed in the transferee district or in "tag-along" actions, i.e., those transferred by the Panel to be joined with cases previously ordered to be transferred.

* * *

It is generally accepted that a transferee judge has authority to decide all pretrial motions, including motions that may be dispositive, such as motions for judgment approving a settlement, for dismissal, for judgment on the pleadings, for summary judgment, for involuntary dismissal under Rule 41(b), for striking an affirmative defense, for voluntary dismissal under Rule 41(a) and to quash service of process. In several instances, there has been appellate review of the rulings of a transferee court on such motions. In each instance, the authority of the transferee court has either been taken for granted, or expressly affirmed.

IN RE FACTOR VIII OR IX CONCENTRATE
BLOOD PRODUCTS LITIGATION

United States District Court, Northern District of Illinois, 1996.
169 F.R.D. 632.

GRADY, DISTRICT JUDGE.

The broad question addressed in this opinion is whether a transferee court in multidistrict litigation under 28 U.S.C.A. § 1407 has the authority to limit the number of common-issue expert witnesses at trials which will take place after remand to the transferor districts. If the answer to that question is in the affirmative, then the second question is what the limit should be in this particular litigation.

[Plaintiffs, who suffer from hemophilia, must use "factor concentrates," which contain protein derived from the plasma of blood donors, to deal with their condition. Defendants produce virtually all of the factor concentrates used in the United States. Plaintiffs allege that they have become infected with the Human Immunodeficiency Virus (which causes AIDS) due to use of improperly prepared factor concentrates produced by defendants. Although plaintiffs claim that methods existed to protect against such infection, defendants claim that the risk was unforeseeable during the time plaintiffs became infected and also that no effective means existed to guard against the risk.

The JPML transferred all such cases to Judge Grady, who ultimately had over 190 pending before him. Judge Grady adopted a discovery schedule including a deadline for designation of expert witnesses and providing for depositions of those persons. Defendants designated 137 such expert witnesses, although they conceded that they did not intend to call that many in any particular trial. Unable to depose all 137, and fearing that failure to depose a particular witness before remand of cases that had been transferred might preclude a later deposition, plaintiffs moved for an order requiring defendants to shorten their list of experts. Defendants responded by arguing that Judge Grady lacked authority under § 1407 to make such an order because the statute gives the transferee judge authority over "pretrial" matters only.]

Defendants fundamentally misconceive the nature of multidistrict litigation and "the role of an MDL court." The source of their confusion is their failure to understand, or at least to acknowledge, the relationship between the "pretrial proceedings" referred to in § 1407 and the trial itself. The pretrial and the trial are not, as defendants imply, two unrelated phases of the case. Rather, they are part of a continuum that results in resolution of the case, and the relationship between them is intimate. "Pretrial" proceedings are conducted to prepare for trial. A judge who has no power to impose limits as to what will happen at trial is obviously a judge who has little ability to manage pretrial proceedings in a meaningful way, since there would be no assurance that the judge's efforts are directed toward what is likely to happen at trial. That it is essential for the "pretrial" judge to have the authority to enter orders that will be binding as to the conduct of the trial is recognized by Rule 16(c)[(2)(D), (M), (N) and (O)] of the Federal Rules of Civil Procedure, which gives the judge conducting pretrial conferences authority to enter a variety of orders that will shape the conduct of the trial, including authority to limit the number of expert witnesses and to establish time limits for presenting evidence at trial. Rule 16 conferences are not necessarily conducted by the same district judge who will ultimately try the case; and some district judges routinely refer Rule 16 conferences to magistrate judges who, in the absence of consent by the parties, could not even be authorized to try the case.

* * * Unless the transferee judge has the authority to enter pretrial orders that will govern the conduct of the trial, there would be little prospect that the "coordinated or consolidated pretrial proceedings" contemplated by [§ 1407] would "promote the just and efficient conduct of such actions." If the transfer is to serve the legislative purpose of § 1407, the transferee judge must have the same authority that any pretrial judge has to enter orders that will ensure the relevance of the pretrial proceedings to the conduct of any trial that occurs after remand to the transferor court. Rule 16 applies to multidistrict proceedings the same as it applies to individual cases, and the transferee court may exercise the authority granted under Rule 16(c)[(2)(D)] to limit the number of expert witnesses to be called at trial.

* * *

It is true, of course, that no pretrial judge, one managing an individual case as well as one managing consolidated pretrial proceedings in a multidistrict litigation, can anticipate everything that might happen up to the point of trial. Obviously, pretrial orders containing limitations that are overtaken by events are subject to adjustment by the judge who will try the case. For instance, a designated expert witness whose deposition has been taken may die before trial, necessitating the designation of a substitute. But the need for such adjustments is exceptional, not routine. Normally, witness limitations work well. This is especially true in the case of expert witnesses, who often are highly paid and, short of death, likely to be available for trial. Pretrial proceedings have to be conducted on the assumption that the needs of the trial can be fairly anticipated by the pretrial judge. Any other approach would render pretrial proceedings pointless.

This is not to suggest that in the absence of unforeseen developments the transferor judges in this litigation are bound by what this court does. The extent to which any transferor judge might see fit to vary what we do here is a matter of his or her own good judgment. We would expect any error on our part to be corrected before the case went to trial. This is not a matter of trying to tie the hands of the trial judge. It is a matter of defining what this court's authority is to enter orders that will bind the parties at trial to the extent the trial judge sees fit to enforce them. (It is also a matter of determining whether the transferor court can, as a matter of law, safely adhere to the orders of the transferee judge should he or she find it otherwise appropriate to do so.) But it is obvious that the objectives of § 1407 can best be achieved when a departure from the transferee judge's pretrial orders is the exception rather than the rule, and it is this court's impression that such departures are in fact exceptional.[3]

[Drawing in part on his own experience in having presided at one of thirteen factor concentrate cases that went to trial before the MDL consolidation, Judge Grady directed the defendants to designate collectively up to 24 common-issue expert witnesses that they would call to testify in trial of an MDL case.]

NOTES AND QUESTIONS

1.   As Judge Weigel's article points out, the transferee judge has authority under § 1407(a) over all "pretrial proceedings." There was some sentiment in Congress for permitting the judge to handle only discovery matters, but that seemed unworkable since the scope of discovery could depend on disposition of other motions, such as motions to dismiss, class certification, or for summary judgment. The drafters of the statute believed strongly that the transferee judge should have the power to rule on legal questions in order to avoid inconsistent rulings. See In re African-American Slave Descendants Litigation, 471 F.3d 754 (7th Cir. 2006) (emphasizing the transferee court's authority to rule on "a host of motions" which "can shape the litigation decisively").

Perhaps even more importantly, though, is the effect rulings on pretrial motions may have on the ultimate resolution of the litigation. Occasionally, a district court may grant a defendant's dispositive motion on all of the transferred cases, effectively ending the MDL. See, e.g., In re Zoloft (Sertralinehydrochloride) Prods. Liab. Litig., 176 F.Supp.3d 483, 501–512 (E.D. Pa. 2016) (granting summary judgment on 333 transferred cases in a single opinion). Even when a dispositive motion is denied, though, the denial provides important information to the parties:

> Indeed, even where motion practice or other litigation procedures do not completely resolve the litigation, they can have a profound effect on any subsequent settlement values even where the court does not eliminate all or a significant portion of the claims through dispositive rulings. In fact, in many cases, before settlement is feasible it is necessary for the MDL court to provide guidance regarding the scope of potential liability by ruling on dispositive motions.

---

[3]   The writer happens to be a current member of the Judicial Panel on Multidistrict Litigation.

Douglas G. Smith, The Rising Behemoth: Multidistrict and Mass Tort Litigation in the United States (2020).

But it is also clear that the transferee judge cannot hold a trial of a transferred case, and the statute commands that transferred cases be remanded at the conclusion of the "pretrial proceedings." See notes 4–5 below. It may be that Congress assumed there would be a clear line of demarcation between pretrial proceedings and the trial, but that dividing line has become muddy since 1968 due to the development of judicial management of litigation. We will examine this phenomenon in Chapter 6; for the present it is sufficient to appreciate that judges have undertaken to superintend all aspects of pretrial preparation, a shift that is reflected in the extensive expansion of Rule 16. See Rules 16(b) and (c). Should the "pretrial proceedings" provision of § 1407 be interpreted differently against the background of this change in judicial behavior?

2. Should Judge Grady's expert witness order be considered "pretrial" within the meaning of § 1407? Would it matter whether he had reason to think that defendants were trying to take advantage of plaintiffs through the discovery process? In connection with the Bendectin litigation, Professor Green has noted that "Merrell [the defendant] designated every expert witness it might conceivably ask to testify, thereby overwhelming plaintiffs with the number that had to be deposed." Michael Green, Bendectin and Birth Defects 131 (1996).

Defendants sought a writ of mandate to overturn Judge Grady's order, but the court of appeals denied the petition. In the Matter of Rhone-Poulenc Rorer Pharmaceuticals, Inc., 138 F.3d 695 (7th Cir. 1998). Because this was a petition for a writ of mandate, the court did not have to decide whether the defendants' arguments were correct but only whether the judge's order was usurpative. It offered the following observations:

> A judge presiding over pretrial proceedings has the power to limit the number of witnesses, and Judge Grady's action in limiting the number of the defendants' common-expert witnesses * * * is not so unreasonable in the circumstances that it can be considered usurpative. And, as he pointed out, it is inevitable that pretrial proceedings will affect the conduct of the trial itself, a notable example being a final pretrial order issued under Fed.R.Civ.P.16—an order that a judge presiding over pretrial proceedings by reference from the Multidistrict Litigation Panel has * * * the power to issue. The order challenged here is of that character.

> And the harm to the defendants is not irreparable. They can ask the judges to whom the cases will be retransferred for trial to disregard it, and should the defendants go on to lose that case, they can appeal and challenge the order, just as they can challenge any other interlocutory ruling they think constituted reversible error.

There are limits to the transferee judge's powers, however. In In re Korean Air Lines Co., 642 F.3d 685 (9th Cir. 2011), the appellate court ruled that the transferee judge had abused its discretion in denying plaintiffs leave to amend to add new claims. It acknowledged that the judge had broad discretion to do many things, such as designation of lead counsel, and phasing, timing, and coordination of the cases. "But when it comes to motions that can spell the life or death of a case, such as motions for summary judgment, motions to dismiss claims, or, as here, a motion to amend pleadings, it is important for the district court to articulate and apply the traditional standards governing such motions. A total disregard for the normal standards of assessing these critical motions would improperly subject MDL cases to different and ad hoc substantive rules." Id. at 700.

More recently, using similar reasoning, the Sixth Circuit *granted* a writ of mandate reversing the judge's decision in the National Prescription Opiate MDL to *allow* plaintiffs to amend their complaints to add new claims after the deadline set in a case management order. Although a district judge may allow such amendments on a showing of good cause, the appellate court ruled that the standard had not been met. The MDL judge had relied on his expertise in the litigation to justify his decision to allow the amendments as a matter of management of the centralized cases. The Sixth Circuit rejected this justification, stating that "MDLs are not some kind of border country, where the rules are few and the law rarely makes an appearance. * * * The rule of law applies in multidistrict litigation under 28 U.S.C. § 1407 just as it does in any individual case." In re Nat'l Prescription Opiate Litig., 956 F.3d 838, 841–844 (6th Cir. 2020). In the appellate court's view, the fact that the cases were part of an MDL could not justify a different standard of good cause to amend a pleading because inclusion in an MDL does not change the meaning of the Federal Rules. But does this seemingly banal conclusion go too far? Does the existence of an MDL truly not change the context in which the more discretionary standards of the Federal Rules apply?

3.   *Asbestos Cases*. In re Asbestos Products Liability Litigation (No. VI), 771 F.Supp. 415 (J.P.M.L. 1991), initially transferred over 26,000 asbestos personal injury cases for combined treatment before a single federal district judge in Philadelphia. (Recall that Judge Heyburn reported that, over the ensuing course of this MDL proceeding, approximately 120,000 cases were centralized. See *supra* p. 127 n. 29). The Panel assured the parties (many of whom opposed transfer) that it would not "result in their actions entering some black hole, never to be seen again." Id. at 423 n. 10. More specifically, although it emphasized that "[t]he Panel has neither the power nor the disposition to direct the transferee court in the exercise of its powers and discretion in pretrial rulings." It offered a number of suggestions about how the cases might be streamlined, including (1) a single national class action trial or other types of consolidated trials on product defect, state of the art, or punitive damages; (2) a case deferral program for plaintiffs who are not critically ill (i.e., pleural registries); (3) limited fund class action determinations; and (4) exploration of a global settlement of all cases pending in federal court. It also left open the possibility of developing a "nationwide roster of senior district or other judges available to follow actions remanded back to heavily impacted districts" if that seemed desirable to the transferee judge. It expressed hope that uniform case

management "will, in fact, lead to sizeable reductions in transaction costs (and especially in attorneys' fees)." Id. The Panel concluded that "[w]e emphasize our intention to do everything within our power to provide such assistance in this docket." Id. at 423.

In fact, the asbestos transfer was followed by an attempt to use the class action device to settle all yet-unfiled claims against certain asbestos defendants, but the Supreme Court ruled in 1997 that this effort was unsatisfactory under Rule 23. See Amchem Products, Inc. v. Windsor, *infra* p. 311. As the Court noted in that case, "[i]t is basic to comprehension of this proceeding to notice that no transferred case is included in the settlement at issue, and no case covered by the settlement existed as a civil action at the time of the MDL Panel transfer." See *infra* p. 313, n. 3.

The transferee judge in the asbestos litigation was praised by one of Judge Heyburn's predecessors as chair of the Panel for having "been able to keep to a minimum the corporations involved from going into bankruptcy, while at the same time assuring the plaintiffs with the most serious cases a fair and speedy resolution of their case. * * * Judge Weiner has miraculously disposed of approximately 63,500 separate cases, which translates into over 5,000,000 separate claims." Interview, Panel's Long-Time Chair Steps Down, The Third Branch, Dec. 2000, at 10. Not everyone was overjoyed, however. For example, in In re Patenaude, 210 F.3d 135 (3d Cir. 2000), three groups of plaintiffs sought remand of their asbestos cases to their transferor courts on the ground that they had been mired in the MDL proceeding for seven years while the principal activity there was discussion of settlement. The appellate court held that the transferee court has discretion on when to remand, and that settlement was a proper aspect of pretrial. See also In re Collins, 233 F.3d 809 (3d Cir. 2000) (plaintiffs, whose claims for compensatory damages but not for punitive damages were returned for trial, objected that the transferee judge had undertaken "the substantive task of preserving the assets available to satisfy asbestos claims by refusing to remand the punitive damages issue").

The asbestos MDL came to be called by some plaintiffs' lawyers a "black hole" from which their cases never emerged. See Eduardo C. Robreno, The Federal Asbestos Product Liability Multidistrict Litigation (MDL-875): Black Hole or New Paradigm?, 23 Widener L.J. 97, 111 (2013). Judge Robreno, on being appointed MDL judge, "eschewed aggregate or global approaches" and "considerably reduced the federal MDL docket, applying strict schedules and weeding out many cases for insufficient proof of harm or exposure, thus reducing the bargaining power of plaintiffs' "high inventory cases" lawyers." Edward Sherman, When Remand is Appropriate in Multidistrict Litigation, 75 La. L. Rev. 455, 473 (2014). See also Georgene Vairo, Lessons Learned by the Reporter: Is Disaggregation the Answer to the Asbestos Mess?, 99 Tul.L.Rev. 1019 (2014) (describing the testimony presented in hearings of the ABA TIPS Task Force on Asbestos Litigation and particularly praising the approach of Judge Robreno).

4. *Remand Required by Lexecon.* The MDL statute indicates that the cases will be remanded for trial, but in fact they rarely get remanded at all.

What is the explanation for this? One answer is that most cases settle, including transferred ones, and that settlement promotion is among the activities judges have embraced in their management of litigation. (We will examine this facet of MDL treatment in Chapter 7. See *infra* pp. 612–624) Another is that judges can dispose of cases on the merits with pretrial rulings on summary judgment or by dismissing claims. As Judge Heyburn comments, transferee judges "do their utmost to resolve cases as expeditiously as possible."

Yet another explanation depended in the past on a broad reading of the authority of the transferee judge to grant pretrial motions. Within a decade of adoption of § 1407, transferee judges found that transfer "for the convenience of the parties and witnesses, in the interest of justice," under § 1404(a) could often be a method for transferring cases to themselves for trial. Of course, that was possible only if the judge sat in a district in which the cases could originally have been brought, but, if so, it became an accepted practice for transferee judges to use § 1404(a). The practice was even embodied in a rule adopted by the Panel.

Despite the broad acceptance of self-transfer pursuant to § 1404(a), the Supreme Court held that it was improper in Lexecon Inc. v. Milberg Weiss Bershad Hynes & Lerach, 523 U.S. 26 (1998), because the statute says that at the completion of pretrial proceedings the action "shall be remanded * * * unless it shall have been previously terminated." The transferee judge in that case had resolved all but one of the claims by summary judgment. Over plaintiff's objections, he transferred the case to himself for trial of that claim pursuant to § 1404(a). Defendant prevailed at trial. Even though plaintiff made no claim of error in the conduct of the trial, the Supreme Court reversed because the statute "obligates the Panel to remand any pending case to its originating court when, at the latest, those pretrial proceedings have run their course." It rejected defendant's argument that the granting of the § 1404(a) motion constituted a "termination" that obviated remand, and concluded that defendant "may or may not be correct that permitting transferee courts to make self-assignments would be more desirable than preserving a plaintiff's choice of venue (to the degree that § 1407(a) does so), but the proper venue for resolving that issue remains the floor of Congress."

5.   *Strategies to Avoid Lexecon*. Are there still ways for transferee judges to retain control of cases by doing something comparable to a § 1404(a) transfer? Judge Heyburn explained as follows (82 Tul. L. Rev. 2225, 2234 n. 47 (2008)):

> Transferee judges are nothing if not resourceful where necessity dictates, and several appropriate strategies are available by which the *Lexecon* conundrum may be avoided. For example, provided the plaintiff is amenable and venue lies in the transferee district, the action could be refiled there. *See* MANUAL FOR COMPLEX LITIGATION (FOURTH) § 20.132, at 224 (2004). The parties could also agree to waive objections to venue. *See In re* Carbon Dioxide Indus. Antitrust Litig., 229 F.3d 1321, 1325–26 (11th Cir. 2000). Alternatively, the

transferee court could try a "bellwether" case that was originally filed in the transferee district, the result of which may promote settlement of the transferred actions in the MDL. *See* MANUAL FOR COMPLEX LITIGATION (FOURTH), *supra*, § 20.132, at 224; *see also In re* Air Crash Near Cali, Colom. on Dec. 20, 1995, Case No. 1:96–MD–01125–KMM (S.D. Fla. Jan. 12, 2000) (noting that plaintiffs in certain transferred actions had agreed to be bound by the results of a consolidated liability trial in the transferee court). Another option, suggested in the *Lexecon* opinion itself, is for the transferor court to transfer the action back to the transferee court under § 1404(a). *Lexecon*, 523 U.S. at 39 n. 2; *see also* Kenwin Shops, Inc. v. Bank of La., No. 97 Civ. 907 (LLM), 1999 WL 294800, at *1 (S.D.N.Y. May 11, 1999) (transferring an action remanded under § 1407 to the transferee court under § 1404). Still another option would be for the transferee judge to follow the action to the transferor court after obtaining an intracircuit or intercircuit assignment. *See* MANUAL FOR COMPLEX LITIGATION (FOURTH), *supra*, § 20.132, at 224; *see also* Dippin' Dots, Inc. v. Mosey, 476 F.3d 1337, 1341–42 (Fed. Cir. 2007) (stating that an MDL judge from the United States District Court for the Northern District of Georgia, sitting by designation, presided over the trial of a remanded action in the United States District Court for the Northern District of Texas).

6.   Indeed, despite *Lexecon*, judges often try cases within the MDL as "bellwethers." The results of these trials are not binding on anyone other than the parties to them, but they are thought to provide useful "data" to the other parties in the MDL about the relative strengths and weaknesses of the claims or defenses in the litigation. Such data may help the parties come to a compromise embodied in a mass settlement. Bellwether trials have come to be very popular in large MDLs, but there is little agreement about the correct way to select the bellwethers because each side has an interest in trying its strongest cases—arguably skewing the "data." Typically, judges choose the cases with some degree of party involvement, perhaps with each side nominating several cases (often allowing the other side to veto some of them). Professor Lahav argues that this is not an effective way of getting a representative sample of cases in the MDL. See Alexandra Lahav, A Primer on Bellwether Trials, 37 Rev. Litig. 185 (2018).

Sometimes, trials of cases in mass tort MDLs illustrate the difficulties that can emerge from the MDL court's efforts to streamline massive litigations. For some time, the largest pending MDL involved injuries allegedly caused by defective vaginal-mesh implants, which at one point included nearly 60,000 cases before Judge Goodwin in the Southern District of West Virginia. Judge Goodwin consolidated four cases for trial against defendant Boston Scientific. Boston Scientific appealed, primarily contending that it was unfair to try the four cases together. Concluding that "separate trials would have been largely repetitive, the court of appeals found that the district judge had avoided unfair prejudice to the defendants:

> [T]he district court endeavored throughout the trial to limit any potential jury confusion or prejudice resulting from the consolidation. At the outset of trial, the district court instructed the jury that the trial concerned four separate claims and informed them that they must treat each as "as if each have been tried by itself." During the trial, BSC had the opportunity to address each plaintiff's claims independently, and in fact pursued a comparative negligence defense as to one plaintiff that it did not pursue as to the other plaintiffs. Following trial and prior to jury deliberations, the district court emphasized that the jurors were not to "even consider that more than one claim was brought" in weighing the evidence and that they must consider each case separately. To promote independent review of each case, the district court made use of special interrogatories on separate verdict forms for each plaintiff.

Campbell v. Boston Sci. Corp., 882 F.3d 70, 74–75 (4th Cir. 2018). One might as how many cases could be thus batched for trial. If four can be, why not forty? Representative trials will be examined further in Chapter 8.

7. Appeal of an MDL judge's orders is governed by the statutes otherwise apply. As a general matter, then, appeal from a final judgment in a case in an MDL is appealable. See Gelboim v. Bank of America, 574 U.S. 405 (2015) (holding that final judgment in one case in an MDL was immediately appealable even though many other closely related cases in the MDL remained open). Appeals of non-final orders in an MDL are governed by the interlocutory appeal statute, 28 U.S.C. § 1292, which requires both that the district judge certifies the appeal and that the court of appeals accept it. (When an MDL court makes a ruling on class certification, it is governed by Federal Rule 23(f).) As a result, interlocutory appeals are reasonably rare, though not unheard of—particularly when the issue involves a challenging legal question central to the MDL. See, e.g., In re General Motors Ignition Switch Litig., 427 F. Supp. 3d 374 (S.D.N.Y. 2019) (certifying issue of viability of economic loss claims for interlocutory appeal). Recently, defense-side lawyers have sought expanded interlocutory review under the Federal Rules by either requiring mandatory appellate review or removing the requirement of district court certification of the issue for appellate review. Proponents of increased appellate review contended that such review was necessary because of the widespread effect of the MDL judge's rulings on issues affecting many cases in the MDL. Plaintiff-side lawyers opposed this measure on the grounds that an increase in appellate review would cause significant delays. For their part, judges also opposed such a measure on the ground that existing avenues for appellate review are sufficient. For the time being, the Rules Committee has decided not to act. Agenda Book for Jan. 5, 2021 Meeting of Committee on Rules of Practice and Procedure at 313–320.

8. *When Remand is Appropriate.* The transferee judge has discretion as to the timing of remand of MDL cases, and these factors are often considered, when: 1) common-issue discovery is completed, 2) all the common pretrial preparation issues have been resolved so that the cases are ready for individual

disposition on remand, and 3) the transferee judge no longer believes that a global settlement is possible if remand is deferred. Edward Sherman, *supra*, note 3, 75 La. L. Rev. at 462–69 (2014).

Professor Elizabeth Chamblee Burch, Remanding Multidistrict Litigation, 75 La. L. Rev. 399 (2014), has urged that early remand become "the norm" so that adverse consequences of transferee judges holding on to cases are avoided. The adverse consequences are said to include errors in private, global settlement that are non-appealable; not having local judges familiar with state laws when state substantive laws are involved; aggregate settlements that include coercive terms designed to control stakeholders' interests at the expense of non-lead attorneys and plaintiffs; not having jury trials that bring a community's diverse perspectives and norms to bear on fact finding; global settlements that encourage plaintiffs' attorneys to file weak claims; giving defendants strategic benefits of centralization and global settlement; and allowing transferee judges to receive self-interested benefits. Id. 469. Many of these adverse consequences seem to be a criticism of case aggregation itself and of MDL judges' encouraging global settlements.

In an article in the same symposium, Professor Sherman, *supra* note 3, 75 La.L.Rev. at 470, questioned Professor Burch's assertion that "coaxing settlement strays furthest from a judge's adjudicative role." He said: "[E]ncouragement of settlement is a primary objective of MDL practice in the interests of reducing the costs in both time and money of full-bore individual litigation." He commented further (id. at 474):

> A movement in recent years has called for earlier remand and, in particular, that transferee judges not keep cases even if there is a possibility of resolution or settlement. The investigations of the ABA TIPS Task Force on Asbestos and the asbestos MDL "black hole" experience indicate that actions by transferee judges in setting tight schedules and requiring proof of such elements as exposure and harm can be effective, as opposed to early and routine remand. Success in achieving global settlements in such MDL cases as Vioxx provide support for continuing to give transferee judges broad discretion as to the timing or remand.

9. *Status of Transferee Court's Orders on Remand.* Judge Weigel's article also suggests that, if the case is remanded, the transferor judge cannot change orders entered by the transferee judge. Ordinarily, one judge is not bound by the prior rulings of another judge who previously presided over a case. For example, Amarel v. Connell, 102 F.3d 1494 (9th Cir. 1996), a case not involving a transfer to another district, presented a problem like the one confronting a transferor judge after Judge Grady's order. The case was shifted from one district judge to another in the same district. The first judge had sanctioned defendants by prohibiting them from offering any expert testimony at trial because they failed to answer plaintiff's expert witness interrogatories. At trial before the second judge, however, defendants called an expert as a rebuttal witness and the witness was allowed to testify. As the appellate court saw the problem:

> We are confronted here with the delicate problem of two district court judges exercising their "broad discretion" over evidentiary rulings in different phases of the same case and reaching contradictory results. [The first judge] exercised his discretion in sanctioning defendants' discovery violations by prohibiting defendants from introducing expert testimony. The propriety of that decision is uncontested here. [The second judge] exercised her discretion to allow rebuttal testimony by the excluded defense expert.

Id. at 1515. Given the latitude afforded the trial judge to modify pretrial orders, the court of appeals found no error. See also In re Ford Motor Co., 591 F.3d 406 (5th Cir. 2009) (in multidistrict litigation, transferor courts should use law of the case doctrine to determine whether to revisit transferee court's decision).

10. Under the doctrine of "law of the case," a judge customarily will not overturn the orders of a prior judge on the same case unless there are changed circumstances. How should this doctrine apply in multidistrict litigation? Note that Judge Weigel points out that on occasion the Panel will delay transfer to permit the transferor judge to make rulings, and the orders thus entered by the transferor remain in effect unless changed by the transferee. How should the transferee approach orders already entered by the transferor?

In In re Upjohn Co. Antibiotic Cleocin Products Liability Litigation, 664 F.2d 114 (6th Cir. 1981), protective orders had been entered in several of the cases before they were transferred, but the transferee judge vacated or modified them and provided instead that plaintiffs could share discovery results with litigants not parties to the multidistrict proceeding. As the appellate court explained, Upjohn claimed that this was improper:

> There is, at first blush at least, some arguable merit in the claim that it is really none of the transferee court's business that the transferor court has earlier prohibited access to the discovery information by parties outside the multidistrict litigation. After all, the Panel's interest in consolidating discovery is to assist the parties to the cases so transferred. * * * [T]he transferor court must ultimately be responsible for the final resolution of the dispute upon remand, and might seem to be better positioned to foresee and thus to avoid the possible abuse of the discovery by its dissemination to outsiders. It can also be said that there is something unseemly in allowing plaintiffs to relitigate an issue which has already been fairly and fully heard in another court.

Nevertheless, it noted that "[t]he presence of protective orders in some of the cases, while not in others, would inevitably create conflicts which the transferee court would have to resolve." Accordingly, it held that "the transferee judge must necessarily have the final word."

How does law of the case work in such circumstances? As one judge presiding over consolidated antitrust actions put it, "[t]his principle is particularly applicable to multidistrict litigation, in which the presence of a large number of diverse parties might otherwise result in constant relitigation of the same legal issue." Philadelphia Housing Authority v. American Radiator and Standard Sanitary Corp., 323 F.Supp. 381 (E.D.Pa. 1970). But doesn't this mean that the "law of the case" should be the rule adopted by the transferee judge for *all* the transferred cases? For a careful and thorough examination of the law of the case problems that arise in multidistrict litigation, see Steinman, Law of the Case: A Judicial Puzzle in Consolidated and Transferred Cases and in Multidistrict Litigation, 135 U. Pa. L. Rev. 595 (1987).

11. Even where other judges clearly may regulate matters, they may defer to the transferee judge. In In the Matter of Orthopedic Bone Screw Products Liability Litigation, 79 F.3d 46 (7th Cir. 1996), nonparty depositions were scheduled in Wisconsin in connection with MDL proceedings before a district judge in Philadelphia. When the nonparty deponents sought a protective order, three Wisconsin judges "transferred" the motions to the judge in Philadelphia. The appellate court was uncertain whether there was any power so to "transfer," but found the result consistent with the purposes of § 1407 because the Philadelphia judge "is much better situated than is any of the three district judges in Wisconsin to know whether the depositions plaintiffs seek to take, and the questions they propose to ask, are appropriate, cost-justified steps toward resolution of the litigation." Id. at 48. Rule 45(f) now authorizes transfer of subpoena-related motions in all cases, not just MDL proceedings.

12. *Circuit Conflicts and Multidistrict Transfers.* We have seen that, regarding issues of state law, a transfer within the federal court system normally does not change the choice-of-law rules to be applied. See *supra* p. 120 n. 2. But the various federal courts of appeals sometimes disagree about the correct interpretation of federal law. Such circuit conflicts are often a reason for the Supreme Court to take a case to resolve the conflict, but until they are resolved they might complicate cases transferred for MDL treatment. In an early decision, In re Plumbing Fixtures Litigation, 342 F.Supp. 756 (J.P.M.L. 1972), the Panel suggested that the transferee court should be obliged to discern and apply the interpretation of federal law adopted in the circuit in which the case was filed. For an argument that federal courts should apply interpretations of federal law they determine to be correct and not defer to decisions from elsewhere in the country, see Richard Marcus, Conflicts Among Circuits and Transfers Within the Federal Judicial System, 93 Yale L.J. 677 (1984). For an argument that the transferee court should apply transferor court law because the cases are supposed to be remanded, see Jeffrey Rensberger, The Metasplit: The Law Applied After Transfer in Federal Question Cases, 2018 Wis. L. Rev. 847.

In re Korean Air Lines Disaster of Sept. 1, 1983, 829 F.2d 1171 (D.C.Cir. 1987), a decision authored by then-Judge Ruth Bader Ginsburg, the court held that reference to the transferor court's interpretation of federal law is not required. This decision has generally been followed, although not universally. Compare Eckstein v. Balcor Film Investors, 8 F.3d 1121, 1128 (7th Cir. 1993) (asserting that when federal law is non-uniform, the transferee court should use the law of the transferor forum); In re MTBE Products Liability Litig., 241

F.R.D. 435 (S.D.N.Y. 2007) (holding that transferor standards for class certification should govern because the question "whether to certify a class is not merely a pretrial issue"). See also Austin Schwing, Comity v. Unitary Law: A Clash of Principles in Choice-of-Law Analysis for Class Certification Proceedings in Multidistrict Litigation, 33 Seattle U.L.Rev. 361 (2010).

Related choice-of-law problems may arise in MDL proceedings when plaintiffs whose cases would be tagalong actions if filed in their home district and subsequently transferred decide to take a more direct route and file in the MDL forum. With state-law claims, filing in the home state would assure that state's choice of law would apply even after transfer. Andrew Bradt, The Shortest Distance: Direct Filing and Choice of Law in Multidistrict Litigation, 88 Notre Dame L. Rev. 759 (2012), urges that those who skip the obligatory transfer be permitted to select the choice-of-law rules of a forum in which they could have filed even though they filed directly in the MDL district.

CHAPTER 5

CLASS ACTIONS

■ ■ ■

A. INTRODUCTION

As Judge Posner has observed: "The class action is an ingenious procedural innovation that enables persons who have suffered a wrongful injury, but are too numerous for joinder of their claims alleging the same wrong committed by the same defendant or defendants to be feasible, to obtain relief as a group, a class as it is called. The device is especially important when each claim is too small to justify the expense of a separate suit, so that without a class action there would be no relief, however meritorious the claims." Eubank v. Pella Corp., 753 F.3d 718, 719 (7th Cir. 2014). But this ingenious innovation can pose serious risks: "The modern class action may be appropriately analogized to the invention of fire. If used properly, it can significantly advance societal goals. If misused, however, it quickly degenerates into something that causes significant harm." Martin Redish & Megan Kiernan, Avoiding Death by a Thousand Cuts: The Relitigation of Class Certification and the Realities of the Modern Class Action, 99 Iowa L. Rev. 1659, 1659 (2014).

Initially, "group litigation" resulted significantly from the law's recognition of groups in the larger society, such as "the residents of the Village of *X*." See generally Stephen Yeazell, From Medieval Group Litigation to the Modern Class Action (1987). The courts of equity built on this foundation to develop the equitable class action. When the Federal Rules were adopted in 1938, the equitable class action device was extended to all actions under the new merger of law and equity. Under original Rule 23, class actions were divided into three classifications—*true, hybrid,* and *spurious*—based on the type of "jural relation" between the class members.

A "true" class action involved a right which was "joint, or common, or secondary in the sense that the owner of a primary right refuses to enforce that right and a member of the class thereby becomes entitled to enforce it." In a "hybrid" class action the right involved was several rather than joint, but the object of the action was the adjudication of claims which affected specific property involved in the action. In both of these kinds of cases, the decree was binding on all class members. The "spurious" class action—where the right involved was several but there was a common question of law or fact affecting the several rights and a common relief was sought—was the poor stepchild, treated with suspicion and, unlike the other two types, not accorded a binding effect on all class members.

A contemporary lawyer can find considerable relief in the fact that the 1966 amendments to Rule 23 did away with the three "jural relationship" classifications of class actions. The 1966 amendments replaced the three classifications with functional tests aimed at ensuring that the underlying policies are satisfied. Four rather general prerequisites for class certification are set out—now often referred to as "numerosity," "commonality," "typicality" and "adequacy of representation" (Rule 23(a)). There are still three kinds of class actions (Rule 23(b)(1), 23(b)(2), and 23(b)(3) classes), but they are not tightly defined and mutually exclusive categories as were the pre-1966 classifications. As to a Rule 23(b)(3) class, which bears a superficial resemblance to the old spurious class action, there are special requirements, such as that common questions predominate, that the class action be found superior to other available methods, and that there not be undue management difficulties. Unlike the old spurious class action, the 23(b)(3) class action is binding on all members of the class (as are also the 23(b)(1) and 23(b)(2) class actions). The "common questions" Rule 23(b)(3) class action was controversial from the start, exciting a pitched battle within the Civil Rules Advisory Committee that developed the 1966 revisions to the rule. See John Rabiej, The Making of Class Action Rule 23—What Were We Thinking?, 24 Miss. Col. L. Rev. 323, 334–36 (2005) (detailing the debates within the Committee).

The amendments initially resulted in a somewhat overconfident use of class actions: "Cases often were certified as class actions on the basis of rather conclusory assertions of compliance with rule 23(a) and (b). Settlements were sometimes approved without an in-depth analysis of the underlying merits of the claim, the economics of the litigation, or the feasibility of distributing the funds to class members. In addition, fee petitions were not scrutinized as carefully as experience now suggests they should have been. Enthusiasm for the class action fed upon itself, and the procedure fell victim to overuse by its champions and misuse by some who sought to exploit it for reasons external to the merits of the case. Mistakes, in most cases honest mistakes of faith, were made. By the end of this first phase, class action practice had been given a very black eye." Arthur Miller, Of Frankenstein Monsters and Shining Knights: Myth, Reality, and the "Class Action Problem," 92 Harv. L. Rev. 664, 678 (1979).

The reaction, in the late 1960s and early 1970s, took many forms—proposals for new amendments to the rules, trial court hostility to class actions and to awards of attorneys' fees in class actions, and Supreme Court decisions restricting the availability of class actions on jurisdictional and due process grounds. But at the same time, many of the most important and intractable issues brought before courts in civil cases began to be presented in the class action format. In some areas, such as securities fraud, class actions continued to be important. More significantly, mass tort class actions emerged in the 1990s as instruments of major importance. In testimony before Congress in 1997, the chair of the Civil

Rules Advisory Committee said that use of the class action is "transforming the litigation landscape," and that "[c]lass actions are being certified at unprecedented rates, and they are involving a substantial [proportion], if not a majority of American citizens." Senate Subcommittee Holds Hearing on Class Action Litigation Reform, 66 U.S.L.W. 2294 (Nov. 16, 1997). "[T]he class action device has changed from the more or less rare case fought out by titans of the bar in top financial centers of the nation to the veritable bread and butter of firms of all shapes and sizes across the country." Benjamine Reid & Chris Coutroulis, Checkmate in Class Actions: Defensive Strategy in the Initial Moves, 28 Litigation 21, 21 (Winter 2002).

Continued tumult produced further calls for change. In 1995, Congress altered some aspects of class actions in securities fraud litigation in the Private Securities Litigation Reform Act. In 1996, the Advisory Committee on Civil Rules circulated the first formal proposed amendments for Rule 23 since 1966. See Proposed Amendments to the Federal Rules, 167 F.R.D. 523, 559–60 (1996), but controversy about changing the standards for class certification prompted the Committee to shelve the proposals except for addition of a new Rule 23(f) authorizing interlocutory review of class certification decisions. In 2003, extensive amendments to Rules 23(c) and (e) were adopted, and new Rules 23(g) and (h) were added to deal with appointment of class counsel and awards of attorney fees. In 2005, Congress adopted the Class Action Fairness Act, which expanded federal-court jurisdiction over class actions based on state-law claims, and also fortified some measures for reviewing the fairness of class-action settlements. In part, this legislation was based on a reported upsurge in state-court certification of nationwide class actions governed by the law of the certifying state. In part, it was premised on the idea that unfair settlements could undermine the rights of class members while enriching the lawyers who brought the suits. In 2018, further amendments to Rule 23(e) on approval of classwide settlements were adopted. Those changes are addressed in Chapter 7. For discussion, see Richard Marcus, Revolution v. Evolution In Class Action Reform, 96 N. Car. L. Rev. 903 (2018).

Overall, class actions in the U.S. have faced headwinds in the 21st century. See Richard Marcus, Bending in the Breeze: American Class Actions in the Twenty-First Century, 65 DePaul L. Rev. 497 (2016). For an unconventional take on American developments, see Brian Fitzpatrick, The Conservative Case for Class Actions (2019). Meanwhile, aggregate litigation has become increasingly familiar outside the United States. For discussion of these developments, see Astrid Stadler, Emmanuel Jeuland & Vincent Smith, Collective and Mass Litigation in Europe (2020); Viktoria Harsagi & C.H. van Rhee, Multi-Party Redress Mechanisms in Europe: Squeaking Mice? (2014); Christopher Hodges & Astrid Stadler, Resolving Mass Disputes (2013); Antonio Gidi, Class Actions in Comparative Perspective (2010).

B. THE NATURE OF CLASS ACTION PRACTICE

J.D. Mark F. Bernstein for *The Recorder*

Copyright © 2003 Mark F. Bernstein. Reprinted by permission.

As Professor Chayes observed, "I think it unlikely that the class action will ever be taught to behave in accordance with the precepts of the traditional model of litigation." Abram Chayes, The Role of the Judge in Public Law Litigation, 89 Harv. L. Rev. 1281, 1291 (1976). We begin, therefore, by considering the nature of class action practice, which places distinctive pressures on attorneys and courts. These pressures arise from a number of features of class actions that are not true, or are less true, of other cases. The named plaintiff is obligated to represent the best interests of the class and yet, at the same time, has personal interests to pursue. The attorney, as the person who usually structures and guides the suit (indeed, who sometimes has conceived of the suit and found the named plaintiff to bring it), has obligations to both the named plaintiff and the class. And the class-action apparatus suspends or strains many familiar doctrines such as the statute of limitations in unique ways.

HANSBERRY V. LEE

Supreme Court of the United States, 1940.
311 U.S. 32.

JUSTICE STONE delivered the opinion of the Court.

The question is whether the Supreme Court of Illinois, by its adjudication that petitioners in this case are bound by a judgment rendered in an earlier litigation to which they were not parties, has deprived them of the due process of law guaranteed by the Fourteenth Amendment.

[The Hansberrys, who were African American, bought and moved into a home in Chicago in an area covered by a racially restrictive covenant. In reaction, owners of neighboring homes sued in an Illinois state court to void the sale to the Hansberrys. The Hansberrys defended on the ground that the covenant never became effective because it wasn't signed by 95% of the homeowners in the area (encompassing about 500 homes), as required by its terms. The trial court found that only 54% of the landowners had signed the agreement.

The trial court nevertheless voided the sale to the Hansberrys and ordered them to move out because it found that they were bound by a decision that the covenant was valid in Burke v. Kleiman, an earlier suit to enforce the covenant in an Illinois state court. That suit was filed at the instance of the Woodlawn Property Owners Association, a neighborhood association, against Kleiman, a white property owner who rented to an African-American, and Hall, his black tenant. It was brought "on behalf of" all landowners in the area and alleged that the covenant had been signed by the required 95% of the owners. Defendants in the *Burke* case stipulated that the requisite number of signatures had been obtained and defended on the ground that the covenant should no longer be enforceable due to changed conditions. The court in *Burke* rejected that defense and held the agreement enforceable.

In *Hansberry,* the trial court found that it could not reopen the issue because *Burke* had been a class action that was binding on the Hansberry's grantor, and it had decided that there were enough signatures. The Illinois Supreme Court, noting that "[i]t cannot be seriously contended that [the *Burke* case] was not properly a representative suit," affirmed. It concluded that the stipulation in *Burke* that 95% had signed the covenant, while factually inaccurate, had not been collusive or fraudulent.]

State courts are free to attach such descriptive labels to litigations before them as they may choose and to attribute to them such consequences as they think appropriate under state constitutions and laws, subject only to the requirements of the Constitution of the United States. But when the judgment of a state court, ascribing to the judgment of another court the binding force and effect of *res judicata,* is challenged for want of due process it becomes the duty of this Court to examine the course of procedure in both litigations to ascertain whether the litigant whose rights have thus been adjudicated has been afforded such notice and opportunity to be heard as are requisite to the due process which the Constitution prescribes.

It is a principle of general application in Anglo-American jurisprudence that one is not bound by a judgment *in personam* in a litigation in which he is not designated as a party or to which he has not been made a party by service of process. *Pennoyer v. Neff,* 95 U.S. 714. A judgment rendered in such circumstances is not entitled to the full faith and credit which the Constitution and statute of the United States prescribes, and judicial action enforcing it against the person or property of the absent party is not that due process which the Fifth and Fourteenth Amendments require.

To these general rules there is a recognized exception that, to an extent not precisely defined by judicial opinion, the judgment in a "class" or "representative" suit, to which some members of the class are parties, may bind members of the class or those represented who were not made parties to it.

* * *

It is familiar doctrine of the federal courts that members of a class not present as parties to the litigation may be bound by the judgment where they are in fact adequately represented by parties who are present, or where they actually participate in the conduct of the litigation in which members of the class are present as parties, or where the interest of the members of the class, some of whom are present as parties, is joint, or where for any other reason the relationship between the parties present and those who are absent is such as legally to entitle the former to stand in judgment for the latter.

In all such cases, so far as it can be said that the members of the class who are present are, by generally recognized rules of law, entitled to stand in judgment for those who are not, we may assume for present purposes that such procedure affords a protection to the parties who are represented, though absent, which would satisfy the requirements of due process and full faith and credit. * * * We decide only that the procedure and the course of litigation sustained here by the plea of *res judicata* do not satisfy these requirements.

The restrictive agreement did not purport to create a joint obligation or liability. If valid and effective its promises were the several obligations of the signers and those claiming under them. The promises ran severally to every other signer. It is plain that in such circumstances all those alleged to be bound by the agreement would not constitute a single class in any litigation brought to enforce it. Those who sought to secure its benefits by enforcing it could not be said to be in the same class with or represent those whose interest was in resisting performance, for the agreement by its terms imposes obligations and confers rights on the owner of each plot of land who signs it. If those who thus seek to secure the benefits of the agreement were rightly regarded by the state Supreme Court as constituting a class, it is evident that those signers or their successors who are interested in challenging the validity of the agreement and resisting its performance are not of the same class in the sense that their interests are identical so that any group who had elected to enforce rights conferred by the agreement could be said to be acting in the interest of any others who were free to deny its obligation.

Because of the dual and potentially conflicting interests of those who are putative parties to the agreement in compelling or resisting its performance, it is impossible to say, solely because they are parties to it, that any two of them are of the same class. Nor without more, and with the due regard for the protection of the rights of absent parties which due process exacts, can some be permitted to stand in judgment for all.

It is one thing to say that some members of a class may represent other members in a litigation where the sole and common interest of the class in the litigation, is either to assert a common right or to challenge an asserted obligation. It is quite another to hold that all those who are free alternatively either to assert rights or to challenge them are of a single class, so that any group, merely because it is of the class so constituted, may be deemed adequately to represent any others of the class in litigating their interests in either alternative. Such a selection of representatives for purposes of litigation, whose substantial interests are not necessarily or even probably the same as those whom they are deemed to represent, does not afford that protection to absent parties which due process requires.

KLINE V. COLDWELL, BANKER & CO.
United States Court of Appeals, Ninth Circuit, 1974.
508 F.2d 226, *cert. denied*, 421 U.S. 963 (1975).

Before DUNIWAY and TRASK, CIRCUIT JUDGES, and POWELL, DISTRICT JUDGE.

[A couple sued on behalf of a class of approximately 400,000 sellers of residential real property in Los Angeles County alleging a conspiracy by realtors to fix an artificially high commission rate for such transactions. The named defendants included the Los Angeles Realty Board and 32 named realtors, who were sued on behalf of a class of approximately 2,000 realtors in the county. The court of appeals reversed orders by the district court certifying both a plaintiffs' and a defendants' class on the ground that plaintiff's reliance on the distribution of a commission schedule by the Los Angeles Realty Board to its members was insufficient to establish a price-fixing conspiracy by generalized means of proof and that the problems of proving conspiracy and injury by individualized proof prevented the case from satisfying the requirements of Rule 23(b)(3) that common questions of fact predominate and that the action be manageable.]

DUNIWAY, CIRCUIT JUDGE (concurring).

I concur in the judgment, but for somewhat different reasons.

* * *

I cannot believe that Rule 23, as amended, was intended or should be construed to authorize the kind of judicial juggernaut that plaintiffs and their counsel seek to create here. The plaintiffs Kline have been designated as the representatives of an estimated 400,000 sellers of real property in Los Angeles County, sellers of residential dwellings containing up to twelve units. The Klines sold one residence, in 1970, for $42,500. They paid a commission to one broker, Lelah Pierson, of 6%, or $2,550. She is a named defendant. Their theory of damages is that, but for the charged conspiracy, the commission would have been less, but they do not tell us how much less. If we assume that the broker would have done her work for nothing, an obviously improper assumption, their maximum damages would be $2,550, which, trebled, would be $7,650. Realistically, this is a grossly exaggerated figure. Yet the plaintiffs seek to parlay their claim into a lawsuit on behalf of 400,000 sellers, not one of whom, so far as we are advised, except the Sherman plaintiffs, has indicated the slightest interest in suing anyone. The Shermans, too, made but one sale. They paid a 6% commission of $2,700, which was divided between two brokers, neither of whom is named as a defendant. The plaintiffs, by this device, seek to recover from Ms. Pierson, among 2,000 others, $750,000,000 in damages, plus attorneys' fees and costs.

The named defendants are 32 real estate brokers and five associations of real estate brokers. They have been designated as representatives of a class of 2,000 brokers. Only one of the "representative" defendants, Ms. Pierson, ever dealt with the "representative" plaintiffs Kline.

At oral argument, plaintiffs explained how easy it will be for them to identify the members of the respective classes. First, they propose, under the aegis of the court, to compel the defendant associations to furnish them with lists showing the name and address of every broker who was a member of any of them at any time during the four year period preceding the filing of this action. These brokers, estimated at 2,000, will be the class of represented defendants. Next, plaintiffs propose, under the aegis of the court, to compel each of these 2,000 brokers to search his files and supply the name and address of every person who, during the same period, paid the broker a commission on a sale of residential property containing twelve units or less. These persons, estimated at 400,000, will be the class of represented plaintiffs. Plaintiffs do not tell us at whose expense all this is to be done.

Next, notice will be sent to each of the 400,000 represented plaintiffs. I would expect that the Rule 23 notice to each "represented" plaintiff, as prepared by plaintiffs' counsel, would give him a brief description of the nature of the case, and then would tell him (Rule 23(c)(2)([(B)(v)])) that he can "opt out," but would also tell him that, if he does not opt out, he will incur no financial obligation, while, if the suit is won, he will share in the loot. I wonder if this is proper. Why shouldn't a "represented" plaintiff be told that if he elects to participate in the alleged bonanza, he may, by so electing, subject himself to liability for his share of the costs of suit if the bonanza is not forthcoming? Why should the court offer him a free ride in a case in which the defendants' costs, if they win, may be very large, and will probably not be collectible from the named plaintiffs? Why shouldn't what I have said also apply to plaintiffs' attorneys' fees, unless there is an ironclad agreement by the attorneys that they will collect no fees from anyone if the suit is lost? Rule 23(c)([3])(B) states that the notice shall advise each member of the class that "the judgment, whether favorable or not, will include all members who do not request exclusion." In most cases, one of the incidents of an adverse judgment is liability for costs. No doubt it will be said that the potential liability for costs might cause many represented plaintiffs to opt out. If so, what is so wrong about that? It may also be said that the potential liability is meaningless. How would defendants collect? However, there may be a possible alternative. The real bonanza in a case like this, if it is won, will go to counsel. Perhaps the class action order could be conditioned upon an agreement by counsel that they will pay all costs of all defendants if the suit is lost!

* * *

I venture to suggest that none of the class action features of this case was dreamed up by the named plaintiffs, but that all of them are the brain children of their attorneys. In California, barratry is a crime (Cal.Pen.C. § 158). The Rules of Professional Conduct of the State Bar, authorized by Cal.Bus. and Prof.Code § 6076, provide (Rule 2 § a): "a member of the State Bar shall not solicit professional employment by advertisement or otherwise." Does solicitation cease to be solicitation when done under the aegis of a judge? If so, what has become of the centuries old policy of the law against stirring up litigation? Did the Supreme Court, when it adopted Rule 23, as amended, intend to abrogate that policy for a case like this? I am loath to believe that it did. I also have grave doubt whether such a change in the law, if intended, can properly be called a matter of procedure. In other words, I doubt that the Supreme Court has power, by a procedural rule, to abrogate the policy to which I have referred, assuming that that is what the Court intended.

Perhaps more important is the practical effect of such a suit as this. The burden that it can impose on the court—discovery, pre-trial, notice to the classes, etc., and on a jury, if one is ever empanelled, is staggering. It is inconceivable to me that such a case can ever be tried, unless the court is willing to deprive each defendant of his undoubted right to have his claimed liability proved, not by presumptions or assumptions, but by facts, with the burden of proof upon the plaintiff or plaintiffs, and to offer evidence in his defense. The same applies, if he is found liable, to proof of the damage of each "plaintiff." I doubt that plaintiffs' counsel expect the immense and unmanageable case that they seek to create to be tried. What they seek to create will become (whether they intend this result or not) an overwhelmingly costly and potent engine for the compulsion of settlements, whether just or unjust. Most, though by no means all, real estate brokers are small business men. They cannot afford even to participate in such an action as this, much less to defend it effectively. I suspect, for example, that this is true of Ms. Pierson. It is almost inevitable, if the judge's order is permitted to stand, and even if all potential defendants opt out, that many of the named defendants will settle for whatever amount they can bargain for, and without regard as to whether they are really liable or not, with a good chunk of the money going to plaintiffs' lawyers.

I do not say that the Rule 23(b)(3) class action is always unethical and improperly coercive. Doubtless there are circumstances in which it is the only viable means of obtaining relief for classes of truly and actively aggrieved plaintiffs. But courts should not be in the business of encouraging the creation of lawsuits like this one.

NOTES AND QUESTIONS

1. As Professor Chayes observed, class actions may fail in important ways to conform to our assumptions about ordinary lawsuits. Both Hansberry v. Lee and Kline v. Coldwell Banker suggest risks that can arise from use of the class action device. Are they the same sort of risks?

2. One set of risks is to the members of the class; *Hansberry* represents one symptom of that sort of risk—the risk that those pursuing the earlier class action will not have the same interests as Hansberry himself had. But how could that be known in advance as to all the members of the proposed class? Consider Professor Yeazell's views on *Hansberry:*

> If, as the Court suggested, the validity of a class depends on the subjective desire of the individuals constituting it to assert their rights, classes could consist only of individuals who had, individually, indicated that they wished to assert the rights in question. Because all persons are always free either to assert their claims or not, classes could consist only of volunteers.

> Where such representative litigants encompass *both* possible sides of a dispute, one's concern about unrepresented interests may diminish somewhat: one side of the litigation is defending a decision taken by representatives of all the members, and the other side is attacking that decision on behalf of dissatisfied members. Such an alignment may not exhaust every possible position, but it gives some assurances, particularly if the conceived unrepresented interests seem implausible.

> The difficulty with *Hansberry* is that neither of these two conditions obtained. The defendants in [the earlier suit] had not been such representative litigants. In addition, at the time the case was decided it may have been difficult even to define the interests that should have been represented. The residential contiguity meant that the plaintiff and defendant classes had multiple relationships with each other. It was thus far harder to say what the class interest was. The problem posed had two levels. The first was the question of whether interests not usually thought to be economic were at odds with economic ones; did a noneconomic interest in an integrated (or a segregated) neighborhood outweigh the interest in property values? To the extent that the class action is based on easy, objective identification of class interests, a situation like that in *Hansberry,* which involved both material and nonmaterial roles and values, will be almost impossible to handle. One cannot identify a single class interest among the tensions created by multiple relationships, some

of which are affective rather than financial. The problem is too *many* interests.

Moreover, the problem of too many plausible interests repeated itself on the purely material level. Even if one assumes that the class characteristics of the group involved only financial advantage, the picture remains unclear. For one could not with any certainty say whether it would be to the advantage of the class to increase the available market for its property by opening it to the excluded group, or whether the postulated decline in desirability would offset the greater demand resulting from the larger number of potential buyers.

Stephen Yeazell, From Medieval Group Litigation to the Modern Class Action 234–35 (1987). Keep these issues in mind regarding class definition, discussed in the next section.

3.   Would there be such risks of intraclass conflicts of interest in Kline v. Coldwell Banker? Presumably all the class members would have an interest in a rebate of part of the commission they paid. Should it matter that, as Judge Duniway suggests, only two of the 400,000 class members indicated an interest in filing suit? One answer is that they will individually recover rather modest amounts compared to the cost of prosecuting an antitrust suit; this appears to be an example of what has come to be called a "negative value" suit—one in which the cost of pursuing a claim dwarfs the recovery if the plaintiff is successful. But another consideration might be that—like the "class members" in Hansberry v. Lee—they would be bound by the outcome whether or not they were satisfied with it. Class actions are usually settled, and while the court must review the proposed settlement for fairness and attend then to class members' objections, the class members have little control over the settlement terms.

Yet another concern in many class actions is that the fee for the lawyer's services turns out to dwarf the amounts paid to class members. Assuming the lawyer's right to be paid is contingent on the success of the suit, consider how that can cause the lawyer's interests and the class members' interests to diverge. For the class members, the suit may resemble a giant lottery that could yield a modest payoff. For the attorney, it is serious business. Having located a class representative, fronted the costs of litigation, and invested years of time, the lawyer is likely to be reluctant to risk all on a trial. Indeed, given the "lodestar" measure of attorneys' fees awards (discussed *infra* p. 444), which emphasizes hours spent on the case, the lawyer has little to gain and much to lose by going to trial. As a practical matter the lawyer will control the settlement negotiations, and the court is required to scrutinize any proposed settlement and approve it only after a hearing. (See discussion *infra* p. 545.)

These conflicts have led some to endorse reconsideration of the effective incentives that affect the behavior of the lawyer for the class. Large negative value class actions such as Kline v. Coldwell, Banker present particular problems. First, there are "agency cost" problems of relying on a plaintiff with small stakes to monitor the behavior of a lawyer who is in a position to shirk on preparation or sacrifice the interests of the class to the lawyer's own interest in a large and secure fee. Second are the asymmetric stakes that result because the lawyer is the main actor on the plaintiff's side, but may not benefit in a commensurate way from increasing the value of the class recovery. Third is a cost differential that results because plaintiffs' counsel can increase defense costs, and thereby persuade defendants to make substantial "nuisance" settlements (payable principally to the lawyer) to put an end to the litigation. The hourly billing method of calculating attorneys' fees has been blamed for many of the problems he identifies. See generally John Coffee, The Regulation of Entrepreneurial Litigation: Balancing Fairness and Efficiency in the Large Class Action, 54 U.Chi.L.Rev. 877 (1987).

4.   Recall that the origin of "group" litigation was the medieval suit on behalf of the residents of a village or other grouping existing in society for other purposes. Should a class be conceived in the same way? David Shapiro, Class Actions: The Class as Party and Client, 73 Notre Dame L. Rev. 913 (1998), endorsed an "entity model" of the class action, likening it to "a whole range of voluntary private associations—congregations, trade unions, joint stock companies, corporations," noting that membership in such "voluntary associations" was not entirely voluntary. Could the proposed class in Kline v. Coldwell, Banker be conceived in this manner? Would it be proper to view the class in Hansberry v. Lee this way? Recall that the earlier suit there was brought on behalf of a neighborhood association.

5.   It seems, however, that much of Judge Duniway's concern is about unfairness to defendants. Some courts have agreed. See In re Rhone-Poulenc Rorer, Inc., 51 F.3d 1293 (7th Cir.), cert. denied, 516 U.S. 867 (1995) (Posner, J.) (expressing concern that class certification would convert risky litigation into a bet-the-company suit that would create irresistible settlement pressure); contrast In re Visa Check/MasterMoney Antitrust Litigation, 280 F.3d 124 (2d Cir. 2001) (Sotomayor, J.) ("The effect of certification on parties' leverage in settlement negotiations is a fact of life for class action litigants. While the sheer size of the class in this case may enhance this effect, this alone cannot defeat an otherwise proper certification.").

6.   Recall the concept of a "negative value" suit mentioned by Judge Posner at the beginning of this chapter. At least in such situations, one might say, the class action serves an important value in deterring behavior that would not otherwise be deterred. For example, in Linder v. Thrifty Oil Co., 2 P.3d 27 (Cal. 2000), the California Supreme Court concluded that class actions produce "several salutary by-products, including a therapeutic effect upon those sellers who indulge in fraudulent practices, and to legitimate business enterprises by curtailing illegitimate competition, and avoidance of the judicial process of the burden of multiple litigation involving identical claims." Are there counterarguments? Consider Kenneth Dam, Class Actions: Efficiency, Compensation, Deterrence, and Conflict of Interest, 4 J. Legal Stud. 47, 61 (1975):

> Deterrence, however, is not synonymous with overall efficiency. First, the administrative efficiency of the court system is an element

of overall efficiency. Hence, in obtaining an overall efficient solution, any administrative efficiency issues stemming from the impact of class actions on the court system must be weighed against overall efficiency gains from more comprehensive enforcement.

Second, a penalty system that induced enforcers to invest resources up to the value of an optimal penalty would lead to inefficient overenforcement. This is the economic justification for limiting the role of private attorney general to those members of the citizenry who have actually been injured. To the extent the class action frees the lawyer from weighing the interests of injured class members, the result may be inefficient overenforcement. It seems unlikely, however, that such a consequence would arise often. Although the class action brought by the lawyer-entrepreneur would not be cost-justified if brought on behalf of an individual plaintiff, it is likely to be cost-justified taking into account all of the claims involved. Otherwise, there would be no judgment from which the lawyer could derive his fees.

For an example of seeming over-enforcement using a class action, see Golan v. Freeeats.com, Inc., 930 F.3d 950 (8th Cir. 2019), a class action for 3.2 million illegal robocalls brought under the Telephone Consumer Protection Act, which authorizes a recovery of $500 per illegal call. Plaintiffs sought $1.6 billion, at $500 per call, but the district judge awarded $10 per call—$32 million. The court of appeals affirmed, finding plaintiff's billion-dollar demand "wholly disproportionate to the offense and obviously unreasonable."

7.   One difference between *Hansberry* and *Kline* is that the Illinois state-court procedure at the time of the first case in *Hansberry* evidently did not require class certification in a formal way, with judicial scrutiny of the propriety of declaring the case a class action, in the earlier suit. Under Rule 23, of course, a case must be a certified as a class action before it is binding on anyone else. Indeed, the process of certification has become quite elaborate. See Litigating Class Certification, *infra* p. 333. We turn next to that class-certification process. One thing to keep in mind is the extent to which requiring detailed evaluation of these issues up front guards against problems later on.

8.   For background on the social and political context of *Hansberry,* see Allen Kamp, The History Behind Hansberry v. Lee, 20 U.C. Davis L. Rev. 481 (1987). Professor Kamp reports that, after the Supreme Court held racially restrictive covenants valid in 1926, the Chicago Real Estate Board embarked on a program to impose them on white neighborhoods. This proved to be a massive task, however, owing to the need to get a lot of forms signed by owners (hence the problem with getting 95% of the owners to sign in *Hansberry* itself). Nevertheless, the campaign continued and succeeded in confining African Americans to certain limited areas of the city. The influx of African Americans into Chicago during the Depression put great stress on these arrangements, as there were estimated to be more than 50,000 more African-American residents of Chicago than units to house them in the areas where they were allowed to live. At the same time, due to the Depression the white population in adjacent

areas was declining, and vacant homes in the restricted areas could not be sold or leased to whites at any price while they commanded high prices from blacks, who had nowhere else to go. Professor Kamp explains that one of the reasons the Hansberrys were able to buy their house is that they were the only people who wanted to buy it. For further information, see Jay Tidmarsh, The Story of Hansberry: The Foundation for Modern Class Actions, in Civil Procedure Stories (K. Clermont, 2d ed. 2008), at 233.

9. *Ramifications of class-action treatment for other issues*: Although class actions are generally governed by the same rules that apply in other litigation, they do present some distinctive issues that deserve mention at the outset:

(a) *Statute of limitations*: Ordinarily the only way to stop ("toll") the running of the statute of limitations for an individual litigant is to file suit. But if class members had to do that—or intervene in the class action—in order to guard against a limitations defense, that could "frustrate the principal function of a class suit," the Supreme Court ruled in American Pipe & Const. Co. v. Utah, 414 U.S. 538 (1974). Accordingly, it held that the filing of a class action should toll the running of limitations for all members of the proposed class until the judge decided whether to certify the case as a class action. But the Court has held that this tolling effect does not permit a "follow on class action" filed by another putative class member after denial of class certification, although class members are then free to sue individually during the remaining limitations period. China Agritech, Inc. v. Resh, 138 S.Ct. 1800 (2018). And with a "statute of repose," the Court has held that an individual action by a class members is barred without regard to the toll. California Public Employees' Retirement System v. ANZ Securities, Inc., 137 S.Ct. 2042 (2017). For discussion, see Stephen Burbank & Tobias Wolff, Class Actions, Statutes of Limitations and Repose, and Federal Common Law, 167 U. Pa. L. Rev. 1 (2018).

(b) *Mootness*: In an individual suit, mootness may often overtake the claim of the plaintiff before the case is decided. In class actions, that result is modified. For one thing, permitting defendant to "buy off" individual claims before class certification by offering to pay the amount of the named plaintiff's claim would undermine the class-action idea. See Deposit Guaranty Nat. Bank v. Roper, 445 U.S. 326 (1980); compare Genesis Healthcare Corp. v. Symczyk, 569 U.S. 66 (2013) (holding that a settlement offer of full compensation to the named plaintiff in a "collective action" under the Fair Labor Standards Act could moot the case). In Campbell-Ewald Co. v. Gomez, 577 U.S. 153 (2016), the Court rejected the idea that an unaccepted pre-certification Rule 68 offer of judgment to the named plaintiff would moot a proposed class action, observing that "a would-be class representative with a live claim of her own must be accorded a fair opportunity to show that certification is warranted."

(c) *Remedies*: The fact that the suit is a class action should not ordinarily alter the remedies available. Nonetheless, the challenge of individual measurement of remedy may prompt creativity in class actions that would not be necessary in individual lawsuits. A prime example is the "fluid recovery" approach, which attempts to measure the overall damages suffered by the plaintiff class rather than undertaking to measure each individual class member's damages. For example, the Hart-Scott-Rodino Antitrust Improvements Act of 1976 provided that state attorneys general could sue for "aggregate damages" sustained by citizens of their states, based on a "reasonable system of estimating aggregate damages," but this method was not authorized for private class actions. See Milton Handler, Antitrust—Myth and Reality in an Inflationary Era, 50 NYU L. Rev. 211, 255 (1975). Some courts have denounced use of this method in class actions. See McLaughlin v. American Tobacco Co., 522 F.3d 215 (2d Cir. 2008) (holding that fluid recovery would violate the Rules Enabling Act and due process). In In re Compact Disc Minimum Advertised Price Antitrust Litigation, 216 F.R.D. 197 (D.Me. 2003), on the other hand, the court upheld a settlement based on the estimated aggregate amount of overcharges for CDs.

(d) *Preclusion*: Under the doctrine of claim preclusion, formerly called res judicata, an individual litigant would be foreclosed from filing a second case asserting a claim arising out of the same transaction as an earlier suit that reached judgment. That same attitude would create problems in class actions because the requirements for class certification may be satisfied for some claims but not for others. For example, it may be that common questions "predominate" (see Rule 23(b)(3)) for some claims, but not for other related claims. Should claim preclusion nonetheless bar the later assertion of individual claims that could not be included in the class action?

C. PREREQUISITES TO CLASS CERTIFICATION

For an action to go forward as a class action, the court must *certify* the class. Rule 23(a) sets out the four prerequisites for class certification, widely known as numerosity, commonality, typicality, and adequacy of representation. A case that satisfies Rule 23(a) must also fit within at least one of the categories described in Rule 23(b). Finally—or to be more accurate, firstly—a class action may be certified only if the class is adequately *definable*, and Rule 23(c)(1)(B) directs that an order certifying a class action "must define the class and the class claims, issues, or defenses."

1. CLASS DEFINITION

SIMER V. RIOS
United States Court of Appeals, Seventh Circuit, 1981.
661 F.2d 655, *cert. denied*, 456 U.S. 917 (1982).

Before SWYGERT, SENIOR CIRCUIT JUDGE, and PELL and WOOD, CIRCUIT JUDGES.

HARLINGTON WOOD, JR., CIRCUIT JUDGE.

This case raises many issues concerning the legality and eventual vacating of a settlement agreement entered into by the plaintiffs and the Community Services Administration (CSA).

Suit was initiated on September 24, 1979 by eight individuals and Gray Panthers of Chicago, an unincorporated non-profit organization, as a class action. The complaint alleged several claims against CSA for its administration of the Crisis Intervention Program (CIP).

CIP was a program funded under the Emergency Energy Conservation Services Program (EECSP), 42 U.S.C. § 2809(a)(5), and was designed "to enable low income individuals and families, including the elderly . . . to participate in the energy conservation programs designed to lessen the impact of the high cost of energy . . . and to reduce . . . energy consumption."

One aspect of this program provided cash assistance for fuel and utility bills to qualified individuals. The pertinent regulations adopted by CSA conditioned the grant of assistance payments upon the production of a shut-off notice from a utility company. Plaintiffs' complaint alleged that this regulation violated EECSP which provided that "[e]ligibility for any of the programs authorized under this section shall not be based solely on delinquency in payment of fuel bills." 42 U.S.C. § 2809(a)(5).

* * *

Initially we note that our review of the district court's denial of class certification is limited. We can reverse this determination only if the district court's decision denying certification was an abuse of discretion.

The parties, as did the district court, focus on the concept of "manageability" of a class action and whether the issue of each individual plaintiff's state of mind makes the class action unmanageable.[24] We agree

---

[24] Although the district court did not attempt to categorize which category of Rule 23(b) this class action fell under, its reference to the concept of manageability implies a determination that this was a 23(b)(3) class action. Fed.R.Civ.P. 23(b)(3)(D) (court must consider "difficulties likely to be encountered in the management of a class action.") At one point plaintiffs contend that this is a 23(b)(2) class because their complaint was framed as requesting declaratory, mandamus, and injunctive relief; and that manageability is not a proper consideration in a (b)(2) class determination. For the following reasons we reject plaintiffs' contentions.

First, it is not at all clear that the problems in managing a class action are not relevant in certifying (b)(1) and (b)(2) class actions. Some of the problems which arise in all of the subdivisions of Rule 23(b) are common to all forms of class action—identifying a class, cost of notice of settlement, and administrative burdens on the court in managing the litigation. This is especially true because the purpose of Rule 23 is to allow an efficient mechanism for disposing of multiple claims. Developments in the Law of Class Actions, *supra*, [89 Harv. L. Rev.] at 1322.

Second, the record before us indicates that this case, if certifiable, would have to be certified under Rule 23(b)(3). While plaintiffs attempt to characterize their complaint as one for declaratory and injunctive relief, it is clear that the final form of the relief obtained would be monetary in nature. Class certification under (b)(2) is not appropriate where the relief requested (or in this case obtained) is monetary in nature. Furthermore, although plaintiffs' complaint did request injunctive and declaratory relief, as we note below, the declaration as to the invalidity of the regulation and a judgment awarding relief to members of the class are two completely separate

that the issue of "state of mind" does make this case difficult to manage as a class action. However, we also conclude that the class action fails for other reasons.

It is axiomatic that for a class action to be certified a "class" must exist. *DeBremaecker v. Short*, 433 F.2d 733, 734 (5th Cir. 1970). In the present case serious problems existed in defining and identifying the members of the class. As noted above, the complaint defined the class as those individuals eligible for CIP assistance but who were denied assistance or who were discouraged from applying because of the existence of the invalid regulation promulgated by CSA.

Cases have recognized the difficulty of identifying class members whose membership in the class depends on each individual's state of mind. *DeBremaecker*, 433 F.2d at 734; *Chaffee v. Johnson*, 229 F.Supp. 445, 448 (S.D.Miss. 1964), *aff'd on other grounds*, 352 F.2d 514 (5th Cir. 1965), *cert. denied*, 384 U.S. 956 (1966); *Capaci v. Katz & Besthoff, Inc.*, 72 F.R.D. 71, 78 (E.D.La. 1976). In *DeBremaecker* a class action was filed on behalf of all state residents active in the peace movement who had been harassed or intimidated as well as those who feared harassment or intimidation in the exercise of their constitutional rights. The court held that this did not satisfy the requirement of an adequately defined and clearly ascertainable class. First, the court noted the ambiguity inherent in the term "peace movement." Even aside from this ambiguity, however, the court went on to discuss another problem in identifying the class—the theory of the complaint was that state law chilled residents in the exercise of their first amendment rights. It could not be concluded that all state residents were "chilled" in such a manner and therefore there was no way to identify those individuals affected by defendant's policies. *See also Chaffee*, 229 F.Supp. at 448 (class described as all persons working to end race discrimination and encouraging blacks to exercise rights held too vague because depends on each individual's state of mind); *cf. Simon v. Merrill Lynch, Pierce, Fenner and Smith, Inc.*, 482 F.2d 880, 882 (5th Cir. 1973) (differences in misrepresentation alleged as well as degrees of reliance thereon made class suit inappropriate).

Problems similar to those in *DeBremaecker* exist in the present case. The first problem is to identify those individuals who qualify for CIP assistance. This by no means is an easy or inexpensive task. *Cf. Ihrke v. Northern States Power Company*, 459 F.2d 566, 572 (8th Cir.), *vacated as moot*, 409 U.S. 815 (1972) (deny class certification because of vagueness of class which included all persons who because of poverty are unable to pay for utility service). After completing this task, the court and parties would have to proceed with the Sisyphean task of identifying those individuals

---

legal issues. The latter depends on proof of whether the existence of the invalid regulation discouraged class members from applying for the assistance. Plaintiffs actually requested that the class members be compensated in some form for these lost benefits—specifically, through the consent decree or funding of programs.

who not only qualified for CIP assistance, but also knew of the existence of the regulation and were discouraged from applying for assistance because of the shut-off notice requirement. Such an attempt to identify those individuals who were "chilled" would be a burden on the court and require a large expenditure of valuable court time.[25]

Identification of the class serves at least two obvious purposes in the context of certification. First, it alerts the court and parties to the burdens that such a process might entail. In this way the court can decide whether the class device simply would be an inefficient way of trying the lawsuit—for the parties as well as for its own congested docket. Second, identifying the class insures that those actually harmed by defendants' wrongful conduct will be the recipients of the relief eventually provided.

The district court was well aware of problems in identifying the class. At the hearing on January 4, 1980 the district court stated:

> How are we going to find out which persons were chilled from applying because of knowledge of this shutoff notice requirement? How are we going to gather the facts on which persons, other than your named plaintiffs, were turned down on that account in the region? We could spend the 15 million dollars gathering the facts in this case. I say that facetiously, but by the time we gather them, it will be another year down the road and then we would be in the '81 program before we decided who was actually entitled to any money. Is it worth it?

* * *

---

[25] In *Developments, supra*, [89 Harv. L. Rev.] at 1478 n. 128 it is observed that the "state of mind" rubric has been applied too loosely to reject class action suits where the class members could be identified by some action or objective manifestation. The article then goes on to critique the holdings in *DeBremaecker* and *Chaffee* because the class in each case actually was defined in terms of actions and not the beliefs of the plaintiffs.

While such a distinction between actions and beliefs may be difficult to articulate in great detail, we believe that even if this distinction has any validity in general, it does not require a different result in the present case. Arguably, the putative class members' state of mind could be described as conduct—failure to apply—rather than their state of mind—discouraged from applying, and therefore the criticism of the article would apply to this case. The change of characterization of the issue in the case from one of state of mind to conduct should not serve as a talisman to decide the difficult issue of whether an identifiable class exists. At best, the general statement that state of mind issues are present serves as a shorthand method of alerting the court and the parties that there might be difficulty in identifying the class members. Also, the classification of an issue as "belief" or "conduct" does not resolve the issue, since many matters of "conduct" by putative class members may nonetheless make the class difficult to identify.

We believe that whether characterized as "state of mind" or "conduct" the putative members of this class would be difficult to identify. In reaching this conclusion we emphasize the cost and time of the court and parties which would have to be expended before the class could even possibly be identified. Finally, the presence of state of mind issues should not be an automatic reason for denying class certification, and the above article emphasizes this point. However, in exercising its discretion, the district court may focus on this factor, among others, in considering the viability of a class suit. In the circumstances of this case we observe that not only were there problems in identifying the class, but also with the other requirements of Rule 23.

These statements make it evident that the district court, as well as the parties, were aware of the problems attendant to identifying the members of the class. The district court believed that it would require a great deal of its own time as well as a large amount of money to accomplish this task. In light of these circumstances this certainly was a proper factor for the district court to consider in denying class certification.

[The court also found that the requirement in Rule 23(b)(3) that questions common to the class "predominate" over questions affecting only individual members was not satisfied. Whether the regulation was inconsistent with the statute is a common class issue. However, proof of each member's state of mind would be necessary to show he was discouraged from applying for assistance by the regulation. Each member's damage would also have to be separately proven. The court found that procedural devices, such as subclasses and fluid recovery, would not remedy this problem of lack of predominance of common issues.]

SWYGERT, CIRCUIT JUDGE, dissenting.

* * *

I believe that the putative class defined in the complaint, met all of the prerequisites for certification imposed by Rule 23(a) and (b)(2).[12] As defendants conceded both in the trial court and in their brief on this appeal, the requirements of Fed.R.Civ.P. 23(a) are met. * * * In addition, defendants stated that "the putative class [meets] the requirements of Rule 23(b)(2), because CSA applied its regulations to the putative class generally. If these regulations were invalid, CSA would have an obligation to the entire putative class to remedy its error."[13]

Policy considerations weigh heavily in favor of certification in the case at bar. If classwide relief is denied, it is highly unlikely that the persons injured by CSA's illegal regulation will receive any relief. Because each

---

[12] A class action under 23(b)(2) seeking injunctive or declaratory relief may also include an incidental claim for monetary damages. *Society for Individual Rights, Inc. v. Hampton,* 528 F.2d 905, 906 (9th Cir. 1975).

I disagree with the majority's holding, n. 24 *supra,* that this class suit must be considered a 23(b)(3) rather than a 23(b)(2) action because the relief obtained was monetary in nature. "[A] class action for injunctive relief and damages properly brought under Rule 23(a) and (b)(2) should not be dismissed merely because a subsequent change in policy by the defendant has eliminated the necessity for future injunctive relief, leaving only the question of past damages for determination by the Court." *Arkansas Education Ass'n v. Board of Education,* 446 F.2d 763, 768 (8th Cir. 1971).

In the instant case, plaintiffs requested in the complaint a declaration that the regulation at issue was invalid, an injunction prohibiting CSA from returning the unused funds to the Treasury, and an injunction requiring CSA to extend the deadline to apply for 1979 funds. As defendants conceded in the district court and on this appeal, the relief requested by the putative class made it properly a 23(b)(2) action. A different conclusion is not required by the fact that CSA agreed not to return the funds to the Treasury pending the outcome or by the fact that the settlement called for monetary relief.

[13] Because I would hold that the instant case is maintainable as a 23(b)(2) class action, there is no need to reach the questions of predominance of common issues of law and fact or manageability as discussed by the majority.

putative class member would be entitled to a maximum of only $250.00, individual suits by those persons would be impractical. Further, if the judgment vacating the consent decree is affirmed, the unspent funds from the 1979 CIP will be returned to the Treasury, thus exhausting the funds which would have been available to provide the relief necessitated by the invalid regulation.

The majority notes that there is an argument that the inclusion in the class of persons "discouraged [by the invalid regulation] from applying for assistance" renders the class too ill-defined for certification because identification of class members depends on each individual's state of mind, and cites a line of cases holding that a class including "chilled" applicants cannot be certified. There is, however, a second line of authority that supports the proposition that a class may include "chilled" plaintiffs. *Yaffe v. Powers*, 454 F.2d 1362, 1365–66 (1st Cir. 1972) (class maintainable under Rule 23(b)(2)); *Carpenter v. Davis*, 424 F.2d 257, 260 (5th Cir. 1970).

The majority lists several problems that it believes would be encountered by the district court in attempting to identify class members in the instant case. First, the majority notes that identifying those who qualify for CIP aid "by no means is an easy or inexpensive task." That is hardly an insurmountable obstacle, because CSA in administering the program had to identify applicants who qualified for aid.

The majority characterizes as "Sisyphean" the job of identifying those qualified persons who were discouraged from applying for assistance. Although I agree with the majority that such a procedure would be a burden on the court, I believe that in certain cases considerations of justice require courts to undertake those tasks; I would find this to be such a case.

NOTES AND QUESTIONS

1. Judge Wood's majority opinion speaks of "the Sisyphean task of identifying those individuals who not only qualified for CIP assistance, but also knew of the existence of the regulation and were discouraged from applying for assistance because of the shut-off notice requirement." What if notices were posted in places where low income families are likely to see them (for example, low income housing units, post offices, welfare department offices, employment offices, and churches) notifying them of the class action and requesting that they contact the court or class attorney? Would it be sufficient that this might reach a number of persons who qualified for CIP but not all of them? What additional method could be used to show that those persons who responded to such notice also knew of the regulation and were discouraged from applying by the shut-off notice requirement? Could this be done by affidavit? By having such persons examined by a special master? Would it be appropriate to shift the burden to the government to disprove knowledge and chilling effect if an individual so indicated in a sworn affidavit?

As Judge Swygert points out in dissent, other cases have looked more favorably on class definitions that depended on state of mind for inclusion in the class. For example, in Yaffe v. Powers, 454 F.2d 1362 (1st Cir. 1972), plaintiffs challenged allegedly harassing police practices during peace demonstrations on behalf of a class of persons "who wish to * * * engage, in the City of Fall River, in peaceful political discussion * * * without surveillance." The district court refused to certify a class or to allow discovery regarding police action involving anyone but the named plaintiffs. The First Circuit reversed, stressing the fact that plaintiffs sued only for injunctive relief and reasoning that "[a]lthough notice to and therefore precise definition of the members of the suggested class are important to certification of a subdivision (b)(3) class, notice to the members of a (b)(2) class is not required, and the actual membership of the class need not therefore be precisely determined. In fact, the conduct complained of is the benchmark for determining whether a subdivision (b)(2) class exists." Should there be less concern with class definition in an injunctive, as opposed to a damage, class action? How should the class have been defined in Hansberry v. Lee, *supra* p. 166?

Some may regard lax class definitions as a symptom of a bygone era of "public law litigation" of the sort described by Prof. Chayes in Chapter 1. For example, in a 2008 decision the Seventh Circuit refused to follow one of its 1977 cases that approached these issues like the First Circuit's Yaffe v. Powers decision, *supra*, concluding that the 1977 case was "a relic of a time when the federal judiciary thought that structural injunctions taking control of executive functions were sensible. That time is past." Rahman v. Chertoff, 530 F.3d 622, 626 (7th Cir. 2008).

2.   Sometimes a seemingly objective class definition may prove very difficult to apply. Consider Jamie S. v. Milwaukee Public Schools, 668 F.3d 481 (7th Cir. 2012), in which plaintiffs proposed a class definition of students in the Milwaukee Public Schools (MPS) who were eligible for special educational services due to disabilities. The court observed that "[t]he problem with a class of potentially eligible but unidentified students is not that their rights might not have been violated but that the relevant criteria for class membership are unknown. By what standard is class membership to be determined? How is the court to decide whether there was reason to believe *in 2000–2005* that a presently unidentified child was *potentially eligible* for special-education services from MPS?" Id. at 495. Compare a class action on behalf of the "homeless." See Joyce v. City and County of San Francisco, 1994 WL 443464 (N.D.Cal. 1994), a suit on behalf of the "homeless" in San Francisco challenging a new police measure known as the Matrix Program. The court certified a class consisting of "those persons present in the City and County of San Francisco who (1) are without shelter, (2) lack the financial resources or mental capacity necessary to provide for their own shelter, and (3) have been cited or arrested for a violation of any of the portions of the Matrix Program now challenged." Is this class definition better than the proposed definition in Jamie S. v. Milwaukee Public Schools? Compare Willis v. City of Seattle, 943 F.3d 882 (9th Cir. 2019) (action by "four individuals who live outside on public property and seek to represent a class of approximately 2,000 other people similarly

situated" to challenge an alleged city policy of "sweeps" of homeless encampments).

3. *The "fail safe" class problem.* Some may be tempted to define a class as consisting of those whose rights have been violated, but this sort of definition is likely to be rejected on the grounds that it creates a "fail safe" class. In Randleman v. Fidelity Nat. Title Ins. Co., 646 F.3d 347 (6th Cir. 2011), the court explained that "[t]he class the district court initially certified was flawed in that it only included those who are 'entitled to relief.' This is an improper fail-safe class that shields the putative class members from receiving an adverse judgment. Either the class members win or, by virtue of losing, they are not in the class and, therefore, not bound by the judgment." Id. at 352. Similarly, In re Rodriguez, 695 F.3d 360, 369–70 (5th Cir. 2012), offered the following definition of a fail-safe class: "A fail-safe class is a class whose membership can only be ascertained by a determination of the merits of the class because the class is defined in terms of the ultimate question of liability."

4. *The "ascertainability" problem.* Class definitions may be objected to on the ground that they include people who do not have a claim, and in that sense do not have "standing" to sue. In Messner v. Northshore University Healthsystem, 669 F.3d 802 (7th Cir. 2012), the court observed that "[t]he problem posed by class members whose claims may fail on the merits for individual reasons is the obverse of a different problem with class definition: the problem of the 'fail-safe' class. * * * Defining a class so as to avoid, on the one hand, being over-inclusive and, on the other hand, the fail-safe problem is more of an art than a science." Id. at 825. One answer is that, so long as one named class representative has standing, there is no constitutional requirement to demonstrate that all other class members also have standing. Neale v. Volvo Cars of North America, LLC, 794 F.3d 353 (3d Cir. 2015). Compare Ramirez v. TransUnion LLC, 951 F.3d 1008 (9th Cir. 2020), cert. granted, 2020 WL 7366280 (Dec. 16, 2020) (holding that each class member must demonstrate standing to receive a money judgment, but also that this requirement was satisfied in this case).

But the problem of providing a class definition remains. This problem can be particularly difficult in consumer class actions relating to low-value products. For example, in Oshana v. Coca-Cola Co., 472 F.3d 506 (7th Cir. 2006), plaintiff claimed that defendant violated the Illinois Consumer Fraud and Deceptive Practices Act by advertising that the only sweetener in Diet Coke is aspartame even though Diet Coke sold in soda fountains (as opposed to grocery stores) is partly sweetened by saccharin. One difficulty was identifying the people who actually bought Coca Cola at a soda fountain. But even if that could be solved, serious problems remained (Id. at 514):

> Membership in Oshana's proposed class required only the purchase of a fountain Diet Coke from March 12, 1999, forward. Such a class could include millions who were not deceived and thus have no grievance under the IFCA. Some people may have bought fountain Diet Coke *because* it contained saccharin, and some people may have bought fountain Diet Coke *even though* it had saccharin. Countless

members of Oshana's putative class could not show any damage, let alone damage proximately caused by Coke's alleged deception.

Carrera v. Bayer Corp., 727 F.3d 300 (3d Cir. 2013), was a proposed class action under Florida law claiming that defendant overstated the health benefits of a low-cost product sold over the counter (claiming that it was metabolism enhancing), inflating the price by using its health claims. The court required that plaintiff offer an "administratively feasible" method of identifying actual consumers who bought the product and rejected the argument that because defendant sold $14 million worth of the product in Florida an overall estimate of the amount of the overcharges could be made. Plaintiffs proposed two types of evidence that could be used to determine who is a class member. The first—records that would track customers who use CVS loyalty cards or purchase online—was rejected because no other retailer than CVS has such cards and there was no evidence that other retailers have records covering the relevant periods. The second—affidavits of class members—was rejected because making false claims would be too easy: "It does not address the core concern of ascertainability, that a defendant must be able to challenge class membership." Even the named plaintiffs said in deposition that they had difficulty identifying the product they bought.

In the view of one California district judge, "*Carrera* eviscerates low purchase price consumer class actions in the Third Circuit. It appears that pursuant to *Carrera* in any case where the consumer does not have a verifiable record of its purchase, such as a receipt, and the manufacturer or seller does not keep a record of buyers, *Carrera* prohibits certification of the class. While this may be the law of the Third Circuit, it is not currently the law of the Ninth Circuit." McCray v. The Elations Co., 2014 WL 1779243, at *8 (C.D. Cal., Jan. 13, 2014). Other courts of appeals have rejected the Third Circuit's "strong version" of ascertainability. See Mullins v. Direct Digital, LLC, 795 F.3d 654 (7th Cir. 2015); Rikos v. Proctor & Gamble Co., 799 F.3d 497 (6th Cir. 2015); Briseno v. ConAgra Foods, Inc., 844 F.3d 1121 (9th Cir. 2017); In re Petrobras Securities, 862 F.3d 250 (2d Cir. 2017); Cherry v. Dometic Corp., 986 F.3d 1296 (11th Cir. 2021). See also Noel v. Thrifty Payless, Inc., 445 P.3d 626 (Cal. S.Ct. 2019) (holding that a class is ascertainable if it is "defined in objective terms that make the eventual identification of class members possible," and adding that "self-identification" could suffice). On the question of proof, consider also Judge Posner's observations in Pearson v. NBTY, Inc., 772 F.3d 778, 783 (7th Cir. 2014): "One would have thought, given the low ceiling on the amount of money that a member of the class could claim, that a sworn statement would be sufficient documentation, without requiring receipts or other business records likely to have been discarded."

5.   Can a court certify a class including persons who cannot be identified at present? Consider Robertson v. National Basketball Association, 389 F.Supp. 867 (S.D.N.Y. 1975), an antitrust action on behalf of "all presently active players, those who were active at the time the action was originally commenced, and future players in the NBA." Citing an affidavit which stated that "[o]f the literally hundreds of thousands of varsity high school players in

the United States and of the thousands of varsity college players, each year fewer than fifty are good enough to join the NBA," defendants objected to inclusion of future players. The court rejected the argument: "The class is neither amorphous, nor imprecise; at the present time there are three hundred and sixty-five class members. The fact that fifty to a hundred more members may be joining the class does not make it unmanageable."

6.   Sometimes the personal desires or preferences of class members may make defining an acceptable class impossible, or very difficult, in a (b)(2) class action. What if some members of the class do not agree with the position proposed to be taken on their behalf? In Pratt v. Chicago Housing Authority, 155 F.R.D. 177 (N.D.Ill. 1994), a class action was brought on behalf of residents of the Chicago Housing Authority challenging the constitutionality of the CHA's practices regarding warrantless searches of apartments as violations of the Fourth Amendment. The CHA developed this policy as a response to incidents of violence or gunfire, but owing to logistical problems the "raid" would never occur sooner than two days after the event upon which it was based. The court initially certified a plaintiff class but de-certified it after Local Advisory Council presidents for 18 of the 19 CHA developments moved to intervene on the defense side and presented a petition signed by over 5,000 CHA residents applauding the CHA's efforts to respond to violence in the projects. Although the class plaintiffs argued that this opposition within the class was irrelevant, the court was persuaded that the "prominent and vigorous dissent within the class" justified decertification. Should class members' preferences matter to whether the court protects their Fourth Amendment rights? For discussion, see Derrick Bell, Serving Two Masters: Integration Ideals and Client Interests in School Desegregation Litigation, 85 Yale L.J. 470 (1976) (describing tension between goal of integration and parental desires to place more emphasis on educational quality); William Rubenstein, Divided We Litigate: Addressing Disputes Among Group Members and Lawyers in Civil Rights Campaigns, 106 Yale L.J. 1623 (1997) (discussing the tension between individualism and group interests).

2.   OVERVIEW OF THE RULE 23(a) REQUIREMENTS

OPLCHENSKI V. PARFUMS GIVENCHY, INC.
United States District Court, Northern District of Illinois, 2008.
254 F.R.D. 489.

JOHN W. DARRAH, DISTRICT JUDGE.

Plaintiffs, Luba Oplchenski and Aida Norey, have filed a Fifth Amended Complaint ("Complaint") in this multi-defendant putative class-action lawsuit, challenging Defendants' classification of "rotators"—and others who worked in the fragrance and cosmetics industry at department stores—as independent contractors rather than employees, thereby excluding them from participation in various employee benefits and benefit plans. Pending before the Court is Plaintiffs' Amended Motion for Class Certification. * * *

To receive class certification, the named representatives must satisfy, for each class they seek to represent, all of the requirements under Fed.R.Civ.P. 23. First, the proposed class action must satisfy the following four elements of Rule 23(a): (1) numerosity: the class must be "so numerous that joinder of all members is impracticable"; (2) commonality: "there are questions of law or fact common to the class"; (3) typicality: "the claims or defenses of the representative parties are typical of the claims or defenses of the class"; and (4) adequacy of representation: "the representative parties will fairly and adequately protect the interests of the class." Fed.R.Civ.P. 23(a). In addition, in order to be certified, an action must be maintainable under at least one of the three provisions of Rule 23(b). * * *

Plaintiff Oplchenski performed services for Defendant Parfums Givenchy, Inc. ("PGI") as a rotator (also sometimes called fragrance specialist or fragrance model) in Chicago from February 1999 to August 2002. She was paid $17 per hour in 1999, $18 per hour in 2000, $19 per hour in 2001, and $25 per hour in 2002. Oplchenski's rate of pay was set by PGI "account executives"; Oplchenski did not set her rate of pay. Oplchenski was not offered any employment benefits, such as insurance and paid vacation. She recorded the time she worked on time sheets and submitted them to PGI for payment. PGI paid Oplchenski what she expected to be paid. PGI did not withhold any money for taxes or insurance, and Oplchenski was aware of this. She understood that she did not have health insurance through PGI. At the time, Oplchenski had other health insurance. Oplchenski received IRS Form 1099 at the end of each year in which she performed services for PGI. She did not receive or expect to receive a W-2. The timesheets she turned in to PGI for payment stated: "This payment is for services performed as an independent contractor. As such I understand that I have total responsibility for the payment of income taxes on these earnings and I am not eligible for any company or unemployment benefits."

Oplchenski also worked for a few hours for Defendant Guerlain, an affiliate of PGI, in 2004. When she worked for Guerlain, she was paid $18 per hour. She did not turn in time sheets as she did for PGI; rather, she reported her time through a phone-in system. Oplchenski did not expect to receive any employee benefits from Guerlain.

Plaintiff Norey performed services as a fragrance specialist for PGI and its American Designer Fragrances Division from early 2001 until early 2003. When Norey was retained by PGI, she met with an account executive, who told her she would be paid $20 per hour. When Norey was hired as a fragrance specialist, there was no discussion as to whether she would be considered an employee or independent contractor, and there was no discussion about whether she would receive company benefits. Norey kept track of the hours she worked in a notebook and then submitted her time on signed invoices containing the same language set forth above that appeared on Oplchenski's invoices. No taxes were withheld from payments made to Norey for her services, and she received an IRS Form 1099 at the end of each year she worked. During the time she worked, Norey received health insurance coverage through her husband's employment.

Plaintiffs contend that Oplchenski was discharged by her account executive on August 22, 2002, and Norey was constructively discharged in early 2003 when PGI stopped scheduling her for work. Oplchenski's lawyer sent letters to PGI to determine what benefit plans existed that were subject to the Employee Retirement Income Security Act ("ERISA") and asserted claims on Oplchenski's behalf with the fiduciaries of the various plans. According to Plaintiffs, the "plan fiduciaries rejected Oplchenski's claims and then engaged in a series of efforts to conceal information about the company's well-documented history of misclassifying sales personnel as independent contractors." Plaintiffs contend that they—and tens of thousands of others—were common-law employees mischaracterized by Defendants as independent contractors and thus excluded from participation in various employee benefits and benefit plans.

Plaintiffs' Complaint alleges nine causes of action: a claim for a violation of Section 502(a)(1)(B) of ERISA, 29 U.S.C. § 1132(a)(1)(B), based on Defendants' alleged withholding of benefits to Plaintiffs under the terms of benefit plans subject to ERISA (first claim for relief); a claim for unpaid compensation under the Illinois Wage and Payment Collection Act ("IWPCA") (second claim for relief); a claim for overtime compensation under the Illinois Minimum Wage Law ("IMWL") (third claim for relief); a claim for breach of contract for improperly requiring Plaintiffs to work as common-law employees but denying them pay and benefits paid to other common-law employees (fourth claim for relief); claims for breach of fiduciary duty under ERISA (fifth and seventh claims for relief); a claim for benefits under exhaustion provisions of ERISA (sixth claim for relief); a claim for violation of Section 502(c) of ERISA based on the failure to provide Oplchenski with a copy of the administrative record (eighth claim for relief); and a claim for breach of implied contract (ninth claim for relief).

Plaintiffs now ask the Court to allow "this action to proceed as a class action on behalf of all common law employees (using the United States Supreme Court definition under [National Mut. Ins. Co. v. Darden, 503 U.S. 318 (1992)]) of one or more of the companies who are or were affiliates of [Defendant Parfums Givenchy, Inc. ("PGI")] and its predecessors, successors, affiliates, parent companies and any other company who was transferred any rights, duties or obligations of [PGI] . . . who were misclassified or mislabeled as independent contractors and excluded from participation in various known and unknown pay, plans, programs, reimbursements or any other arrangements . . . to which they are or were entitled on account of their employment by such entities." Specifically, Plaintiffs seek an order certifying the following classes and subclass:

Class A: All employees of the PG Inc. Affiliates who were classified or labeled as independent contractors and excluded from participation in various known and unknown pay, plans, programs, reimbursements or any other arrangements to which they were entitled on account of their employment by such entities from 1975 to the present ("Pay and Benefit Plans"), including but not limited to the database of persons identified by defendants that was filed with the court as Dkt. 237–2, 237–3 and 237–4.

Class A Subclass: All employees of PG Inc. Affiliates who were classified or labeled as independent contractors who worked part time (i.e. worked 50 percent of the time) at any time prior to December 31, 2000 and who did not receive 25 options under the OPAL[4] Shares For All program.

Class B: All employees of PG Inc. Affiliates who were excluded because of their classification as independent contractors from the Christian Dior Perfumes, Inc. Pension Plan (effective January 1, 1977), Retirement Plan for Employees of Guerlain, Inc. (effective September 1, 1945) [renamed the LVMH Affiliates Pension Plan effective January 1, 2001], the LVMH Affiliates Retirement Plan, Wines & Spirits (effective January 1, 1989) and the LVMH Affiliates Retirement Plan and all participants in the LVMH Affiliates Retirement Plan who had their future benefit accruals reduced by a December 2000 amendment.

Class C: All employees of PG Inc. Affiliates who were excluded from the LVMH & Affiliates Medical and Dental Benefit Plan because of their classification as independent contractors, and all employees of PG Inc. Affiliates who were excluded from the Plan because of an unwritten 30 hour workweek requirement and/or subject to any other unwritten requirement including but not limited to eligibility to receive retiree medical benefits.

Plaintiffs ask the Court to appoint Oplchenski "as Class Representative of the Pay and Benefit Plans of Class A that are subject to ERISA"; Norey and Oplchenski as the "Class Representatives of the Pay and Benefit Plans of Class A that are not subject to ERISA"; and Oplchenski as the "Class Representative of Class B and Class C."

Numerosity

Plaintiffs contend the numerosity requirement is met because Defendants have produced a database identifying 39,737 unique social

---

[4]   "OPAL" refers to PGI's Options For All World-wide stock option plan.

security numbers of potential class members. Plaintiffs thus argue that "regardless of the ultimate scope of the class definition, the class easily satisfies the numerosity requirement." Defendants dispute this position, maintaining that the fact that social security numbers appear in a common database is insufficient to "group people in a class and satisfy Rule 23's numerosity requirement." Defendants contend Plaintiffs have failed to demonstrate numerosity because Plaintiffs have failed to estimate how many of the individuals appearing in the database actually meet the requirements for, and would have participated in, the various plans referenced for each of the subclasses Plaintiffs seek to have certified.

Although a plaintiff cannot rely on conclusory allegations or speculation as to class size, numerosity problems can be resolved subsequent to class certification. Generally, where class members number at least 40, joinder is considered impracticable and numerosity is satisfied. Furthermore, a finding of numerosity can be based on common sense assumptions. Plaintiffs have pointed to a database identifying nearly forty thousand "rotators" and others classified as independent contractors across the nation. With a nationwide field of potential class members so large, common sense assumptions suggest that the requisite number for class certification for each of the proposed classes and the subclass will be satisfied; the numerosity requirement has been met.

Commonality

Commonality exists where a class possesses common questions of law or fact. Fed.R.Civ.P. 23(a)(2). "Absolute commonality" is not required; commonality is satisfied if the plaintiff can demonstrate that a "common nucleus of operative fact" exists among the proposed class members. As courts in this district have recognized, the commonality standard is "quite low." Generally, a plaintiff need only show that there is at least one question of law or fact common to the class.

Plaintiffs contend the central issue in the case is whether Plaintiffs and the class members were common-law employees of Defendants under the standard set forth by the Supreme Court in [National Mut. Ins. Co. v.] Darden, 503 U.S. 318. There, the Supreme Court held that the term "employee," as used in the ERISA statute, incorporates traditional agency law criteria. The Court held the following common-law standard applies for determining who qualifies as an "employee" within the meaning of the ERISA statute:

> In determining whether a hired party is an employee under the general common law of agency, we consider the hiring party's right to control the manner and means by which the product is accomplished. Among the other factors relevant to this inquiry are the skill required; the source of the instrumentalities and tools; the location of the work; the duration of the relationship between the parties; whether the hiring party has the right to assign

additional projects to the hired party; the extent of the hired party's discretion over when and how long to work; the method of payment; the hired party's role in hiring and paying assistants; whether the work is part of the regular business of the hiring party; whether the hiring party is in business; the provision of employee benefits; and the tax treatment of the hired party.

According to Plaintiffs, the issue of Defendants' control over rotators is common to all of the proposed classes. Plaintiffs contend Defendants systematically exerted a high degree of control over rotators under the *Darden* criteria, and the determination of Defendants' control over rotators can be determined on a class-wide basis, even if there are factual disputes concerning the level of control exercised. Plaintiffs identify the following as issues—all involving, or derivative of, a determination of the *Darden* test— as being common to the class: "(1) Whether independent contractors were misclassified because they were, in reality, employees; (2) whether misclassifying employees as independent contractors and excluding them from benefit plans subject to ERISA constituted a breach of fiduciary duty under ERISA; (3) whether defendants' misclassification of rotators was fraudulent; (4) whether failure to provide a compliant § 204(h) notice [under ERISA] rendered purported plan amendments invalid; (5) whether defendants breached their fiduciary duty to the Plaintiffs and the Class by failing to inform them (i) that their worker classification had been challenged and the subject of an audit inquiry over a considerable time span, (ii) that their employer had entered into an agreement to change their classification that was later reneged."

Relying on the Seventh Circuit's post-*Darden* decision Trombetta v. Cragin Federal Bank for Savings Employee Stock Ownership Plan, 102 F.3d 1435, 1440 (7th Cir. 1997), Defendants contend the issue of Defendants' control of rotators under the *Darden* test is not a common issue but is "wholly immaterial" because the benefit plans under which Plaintiffs claim wrongful exclusion here did not define an "employee" in the same way as the ERISA statute or the common law. In *Trombetta*, the Seventh Circuit held that an employer is not obligated to define an employee for purposes of its benefit plans in the same way an employee is defined in the ERISA statute but, rather, "is free to define the terms in its plan however it wishes." In *Trombetta*, the court upheld an employer's decision to exclude loan originators from participating in an employee stock ownership program under the arbitrary and capricious standard. In reaching that holding, the court found that the trustees of the plan had discretionary authority to construe the terms of the plan and found their decision that loan originators were independent contractors rather than employees for purposes of the plan was not arbitrary and capricious.

Plaintiffs, in their reply, do not contest Defendants' assertion that the employee plans here in question adopted different definitions of an employee than the ERISA statute. Therefore, based on *Trombetta*, the *Darden* criteria are not necessarily dispositive of Plaintiffs' claims.

However, the *Darden* factors present at least one common issue of law or fact for purposes of the low threshold commonality requirement of Fed.R.Civ.P. 23(a)(2) and is not "wholly immaterial" in the case as Defendants assert. The criteria for participation in the various plans and benefits have not yet been established, but the record shows that Defendants went through a *Darden*-type analysis when they considered and rejected Oplchenski's claim for benefits. This suggests that the *Darden* factors are at least relevant to how Defendants define an employee for purposes of eligibility of Oplchenski for a benefit plan. Furthermore, the *Trombetta* court stated that the *Darden* factors are relevant in determining who has standing to sue under ERISA. In addition, Plaintiffs have alleged a number of claims under Illinois law, and it has not been shown that the common-law standard for establishing an employee-employer relationship does not apply to these claims. For all these reasons, *Darden* presents at least one common issue of law or fact for purposes of the low threshold commonality requirement of Fed.R.Civ.P. 23(a)(2).

Typicality

"The question of typicality in Rule 23(a)(3) is closely related to the preceding question of commonality." This requirement "primarily directs the district court to focus on whether the named representatives' claims have the same essential characteristics as the claims of the class at large." "A plaintiff's claim is typical if it arises from the same event or practice or course of conduct that gives rise to the claims of other class members and his or her claims are based on the same legal theory."

Plaintiffs assert the typicality requirement is met because their claims "arise from defendants' uniform classification of rotators as independent contractors and turn on the same legal analysis under the Supreme Court's analysis in *Darden*." Defendants dispute Plaintiffs' analysis because "rotators had very different experiences with the Defendant Companies depending on when they provided services, for which company they provided services, and to which Account Executive they were assigned. Their potential claims also differ significantly depending on which version of a plan was in effect during their period of service." Defendants point out how Plaintiffs' work situations differed from other potential class members with respect to the various plans. In support of this position, they submit the expert report of Dr. Matthew Mercurio, who provides a statistical analysis of differences in the work experiences of Plaintiffs from the proposed class of rotators.[6]

---

[6]   Plaintiffs have moved to strike the Mercurio report, as well as the report of another expert, Kenneth Maginot, submitted by Defendants in opposition to class certification on the basis that these experts were not disclosed to Plaintiffs prior to Defendants' filing their brief in opposition to class certification and because their opinions go to the merits of the case. The Motion to Strike is

Despite factual differences in the situations of the potential class members (which may ultimately result in different findings as to the various class members' eligibility for benefits under the plans), typicality is nevertheless satisfied because the potential claims of the class members all involve the same alleged course of conduct by Defendants—an alleged systematic determination by Defendants that rotators and others working in the fragrance area were independent contractors not employees. Further, as discussed above, the issue of Defendants' control of rotators under *Darden* is at least relevant. Defendants' arguments as to typicality— as well as their arguments as to commonality—are essentially that Plaintiffs have not shown that all of the proposed class members are in fact eligible for benefits under the terms of the various different plans asserted in the proposed classes and subclass. Defendants' arguments pertain more to the requirements for certification under Fed.R.Civ.P. 23(b) (discussed below) and do not demonstrate a lack of threshold commonality or typicality for purposes of class certification. The commonality inquiry under Rule 23(a) is only whether common issues of law or fact exist, and for the reasons discussed above, they do. Further, because the common issues identified include the same alleged course of conduct by Defendants in classifying workers, sufficient typicality also exists for purposes of Rule 23(a).

Adequacy of Representation

The final requirement of Rule 23(a) is whether "the representative parties will fairly and adequately protect the interests of the class." Courts in this district have used the following three factors to show adequacy: (1) the representative does not have conflicting or antagonistic interests compared with the class as a whole; (2) the representative is sufficiently interested in the case outcome to ensure vigorous advocacy; and (3) class counsel is experienced, competent and qualified.

Defendants rely on Robinson v. Sheriff of Cook County, 167 F.3d 1155 (7th Cir. 1999) for the proposition that a weakness in the class representative's claim casts doubt on a finding of adequacy. Defendants argue that the named Plaintiffs' claims are not adequate class representatives because there are a number of deficiencies in Oplchenski's claims, including that her ERISA claims are time-barred; she does not have standing to assert ERISA and OPAL claims; her alleged injuries were not caused by Defendants' alleged conduct; the requested relief will not redress her injuries; and as a former rotator, she lacks standing to seek prospective injunctive relief on the ERISA and OPAL claims. Plaintiffs dispute that Oplchenski's claims are time-barred and otherwise contest Defendants' contentions that Olpchenski lacks standing. Plaintiffs contend Defendants'

---

denied. The opinions of the experts pertain to issues to be addressed regarding class certification, not the merits of the underlying claims, and Defendants did not violate any rule or court order in failing to produce them. Therefore, the opinions are properly considered.

arguments are akin to a Rule 12(b) motion to dismiss and constitute an improper effort by Defendants "to get an early merits determination on issues the Court has already ruled too early to determine."

Although the Court is allowed to "look beyond the pleadings to determine whether the requirements of Rule 23 have been satisfied," the "weakness" arguments raised by Defendants are more appropriately addressed on a motion to dismiss or for judgment on the merits. It is undisputed that Plaintiffs are former rotators classified by Defendants as independent contractors rather than employees for purposes of various benefits; therefore, their interests do not differ from those of the class as a whole. Further, nothing in the record suggests that the named plaintiffs will not vigorously pursue the litigation on behalf of the class or that class counsel is not experienced, competent and qualified. This is sufficient to demonstrate adequacy of representation.

[The court turned to Rule 23(b). Although plaintiffs conceded that their claims for money damages would have to be evaluated under Rule 23(b)(3), they contended that their claims not involving monetary relief could be certified under Rule 23(b)(1) or 23(b)(2). Defendants countered that, since plaintiffs' relationship with defendants ended years before suit was filed, the real goal was to recover money. Finding that plaintiff's case is "one seeking predominately monetary damages," the court found that Rule 23(b)(3) should be applied.

The court held that plaintiffs could not show that common issues would "predominate," as required for certification under Rule 23(b)(3). Defendants pointed out that there were multiple plans that would apply to different class members differently, in part because they had different eligibility requirements. Some required an "employee" to elect to participate. Even under the Supreme Court's *Darden* test, it would be necessary to examine the varying experience of individual rotators. Moreover, if the court were to entertain claims of common-law breach of contract it would need to examine the pertinent provisions of the law of each state in which rotators worked.]

In sum, although Plaintiffs allege Defendants uniformly characterized rotators as independent contractors to exclude them from receiving various benefits, Plaintiffs have not shown that liability turns predominately on the common issue of whether Defendants controlled the manner and means of the rotators' work. Rather, Defendants have shown that liability would turn on individual issues, including the terms of the individual plans and whether each proposed class member meets the eligibility criteria for each of the plans and would have opted for benefits.

NOTES AND QUESTIONS

1. *Oplchenski* is an example of an increasingly frequent variety of class-action litigation—suits challenging employers' classification of certain

"employees" as exempt from legal protections accorded employees. Oplchenski relies on ERISA, but more often employees rely on the Fair Labor Standards Act (FLSA) and similar state laws requiring that employees receive overtime pay and breaks. See Note, Collective Confusion: FLSA Collective Actions, Rule 23 Class Actions, and the Rules Enabling Act, 61 Hast.L.J. 275 (2009) ("The recent boom of wage and hour litigation is one of the most striking developments of modern legal history."). A prominent defense-side lawyer explains: "The FLSA was enacted in 1938, but there wasn't much litigation until about 15 years ago, after which the number of class action cases just exploded. In fact, 91 percent of today's labor and employment class action suits are wage and hour related, for a few reasons. The standard for class certification in an FLSA matter is much lower compared to other employment law issues, and the pool of potential class members is significantly larger. In harassment cases, for instance, the class is limited to employees who claim to have been harassed, generally by a particular supervisor. Wage and hour class actions challenge a broad pay practice and can include all employees subject to that practice." Wage and Hour Class Actions in the Healthcare Industry: Legal Challenges and E-Discovery Solutions, The Metropolitan Corporate Counsel, Nov. 2014, at 12.

2.   This case introduces the four stated criteria for certification under Rule 23(a), which are considered further in the remainder of this section. Note the precision with which plaintiffs in this case address class definition, which was also analyzed in Simer v. Rios, *supra* p. 177. Was it necessary for plaintiffs to define three primary classes and one subclass? Each such class is normally expected to be free-standing in the sense that all Rule 23 requirements must be satisfied for each separate class or subclass. "[T]he litigation as to each subclass is treated as a separate law suit. * * * Under the provisions of Rule 23(c)([5]), a class may be divided into subclasses and each subclass treated as a class with the provisions of the rule to be construed and applied accordingly to each class." Betts v. Reliable Collection Agency, Ltd., 659 F.2d 1000 (9th Cir. 1981).

3.   In addressing the requirements of Rule 23, the court in *Oplchenski* had considerable information about the case. The depositions of both proposed class representatives had been taken. Defendants had produced detailed information about rotators who worked for them. Consider how much effort will be involved in gathering such information to support a class certification decision. We will return to these issues in a later section on Litigating Class Certification, *infra* p. 333.

4.   *Numerosity*: Rule 23(a)(1) says that a court should not certify a class unless "the class is so numerous that joinder of all members is impracticable." The idea seems to be that class certification should be done as something of a last resort because the court has no other way of handling the case. How should this factor have been analyzed in Simer v. Rios, *supra* p. 177? In *Oplchenski*, plaintiffs presented information from defendants showing thousands of potential class members. As the court notes, the court can make common sense

assumptions about whether there are too many class members to permit joinder.

What is the minimum number that should suffice? "Numerosity is presumed for classes larger than forty members." Pennsylvania Public School Employees' Retirement System v. Morgan, Stanley & Co., 772 F.3d 111, 120 (2d Cir. 2014); see Anderson v. Weinert Enterprizes, Inc., 986 F.3d 773 (7th Cir. 2021) (class of 37 members not numerous enough; "a class of over 40 is not inevitably endowed with numerosity status"). Though this is a common benchmark, it is not a rule. See Trevizo v. Adams, 455 F.3d 1155 (10th Cir. 2006) (joinder was practicable in suit with 84 putative class members); compare In re Gap Stores Securities Litigation, 79 F.R.D. 283 (N.D.Cal. 1978) (individual joinder of 91 parties "would be to require that the litigation be conducted through committees, that is, to make joinder a fiction for class adjudication").

Should even smaller groupings sometimes suffice? In J.D. v. Nagin, 255 F.R.D. 406 (E.D.La. 2009), plaintiffs challenged conditions at a juvenile facility called the Youth Service Center (YSC) with a maximum capacity of 30 residents at a time and a rotating population of juvenile residents. The court ruled that "[t]he mere fact that the population of the YSC is constantly revolving during the pendency of litigation renders any joinder impractical." In Jackson v. Danberg, 240 F.R.D. 145 (D.Del. 2007), plaintiffs challenged the state's method of carrying out execution by lethal injection on behalf of a class of 16 residents of death row. Noting that "there is no rigid minimum number of class members necessary to warrant certification" and that "the numerosity requirement has been relaxed in cases like this where injunctive and declaratory relief is sought," the court certified the class. Some courts have noted that employees may be unwilling to sue their employer in concluding that small numbers should suffice. See, e.g., Mullen v. Treasure Chest Casino, LLC, 186 F.3d 620 (5th.Cir. 1999) ("potential class members still employed by [defendant] might be unwilling to sue individually or join a suit for fear of retaliation at their jobs"). Should this sort of consideration justify use of class actions? Should individual litigants unwilling to sue be provided judicial relief nonetheless?

Estimates often suffice. In Arreola v. Godinez, 546 F.3d 788 (7th Cir. 2008), plaintiffs challenged a "no crutches" policy at a jail facility, but the district court denied class certification for lack of numerosity. Although plaintiff had provided the names and addresses of only 14 other prisoners who, like him, had been denied use of needed crutches, the court of appeals held that there was a basis to find that the class was sufficiently large although 14 would not be enough because a doctor attested to seeing at least one such prisoner a week, which supported an estimate of at least 350 such prisoners. See also Arnold Chapman and Paldo Sign & Display Co. v. Wagener Equities, Inc., 747 F.3d 489, 492 (7th Cir. 2014): "[A] class can be certified without determination of its size, so long as it's reasonable to believe it large enough to make joinder impracticable and thus justify a class action suit."

But numerosity may raise issues like the "ascertainability" issue mentioned above (*supra* p. 184 n. 4). In Mielo v. Steak 'N Shake Operations, Inc., 897 F.3d 467 (3d Cir. 2018), two wheelchair users sought to represent a nationwide class of disabled individuals concerning access to over 400 of defendant's restaurants. Each plaintiff had encountered difficulties at one of defendant's facilities due to a steep grade in the parking area. An investigator hired by plaintiffs' attorney had found similar grading at six other facilities operated by defendant. The district court certified a class in an action for injunctive relief requiring defendant to adopt accessibility policies for its restaurants, but the court of appeals held that plaintiffs had not satisfied numerosity. Plaintiffs did offer evidence that some 15 to 20 million Americans have mobility disabilities, but no evidence showing how many of these people would encounter accessibility difficulties at defendant's restaurants, whether due to grading or other obstacles.

Compare Judge Posner's views in Parko v. Shell Oil Co., 739 F.3d 1083, 1084–85 (7th Cir. 2014):

> To require the district judge to determine whether each of the 150 members of the class has sustained an injury—on the theory that if 140 have not, and so lack standing, and should be dropped from the class, certification should be denied and the 10 remaining plaintiffs be forced to sue (whether jointly or individually)—would make the class certification process unworkable; the process would require, in this case, 150 trials before the class could be certified. The defendants are thus asking us to put the cart before the horse. How many (if any) of the class members have a valid claim is the issue to be determined *after* the class is certified.

5.   *Commonality*: Recall the treatment of the "common question" requirements for joinder of parties under Rule 20(a) and transfer pursuant to the multidistrict litigation statute. Should courts be more demanding when class certification is sought? Would it, for example, be sufficient to satisfy Rule 23(a)(2) that cases had been transferred for multidistrict treatment pursuant to 28 U.S.C. § 1407?

In *Oplchenski*, the court says that the commonality requirement is "quite low" and that Rule 23(a)(2) is satisfied when there is at least one common question of law or fact. It then treats as sufficient plaintiffs' contention that the Supreme Court's standard in *Darden* for who is an "employee," drawing on the common-law definition, would suffice. But consider the variety of factors invoked by the criteria cited by the Supreme Court in *Darden*. Wouldn't they apply differently to different rotators? And plaintiffs concede that the employee plans involved in the case use different definitions that are not necessarily the same as the common-law definition. Compare the Court's attitude toward Rule 23(a)(2) in Wal-Mart Stores, Inc. v. Dukes, *infra* p. 200.

In at least some situations, class actions seem to attempt to combine claims that might not be properly joined under Rule 20(a). For example, Wiener v. Dannon Co., 255 F.R.D. 658 (C.D.Cal. 2009), two plaintiffs sued the maker of Dannon dairy products. One of them had purchased Activia yogurt, which contained a patented probiotic strain of bacteria Dannon claimed in advertising would naturally regulate digestion. The other plaintiff had purchased DanActive, a Dannon drinkable dairy product containing a different probiotic bacterium that Dannon ads said would strengthen the immune system. Later the plaintiff who purchased DanActive dropped out of the case, and the remaining plaintiff sought class certification. Citing the "permissive" view of Rule 23(a)(2), the court found commonality satisfied. But it held that the plaintiff who purchased only Activia was not typical of class members who purchased DanActive. Would a class made up of purchasers of Activia and DanActive have been proper if the class representative who bought DanActive had not dropped out of the case? Should claims about different products that were supposedly marketed with false assertions of different health benefits be considered to arise from the same transactions or series of transactions within the meaning of Rule 20(a)? If not, could Dannon have had the claims regarding Activia and DanActive severed? Should the common question requirement of Rule 23(a)(2) permit a class action grouping class members who would not be allowed to join in individual suits under Rule 20?

6.   *Typicality*: As explained by the court in Deiter v. Microsoft Corp., 436 F.3d 461, 466–67 (4th Cir. 2006):

> The typicality requirement goes to the heart of a representative party's ability to represent a class, particularly as it tends to merge with the commonality and adequacy-of-representation requirements. The representative party's interest in prosecuting his own case must simultaneously tend to advance the interests of the absent class members. For that essential reason, plaintiff's claim cannot be so different from the claims of absent class members that their claims will not be advanced by plaintiff's proof of his own individual claim. That is not to say that typicality requires that the plaintiff's claim and the claims of class members must be perfectly identical or perfectly aligned. But when the variation in claims strikes at the heart of the respective causes of action, we have readily denied class certification.

See also In re Schering Plough Corp. ERISA Litig., 589 F.3d 585 (3d Cir. 2009) (typicality ensures that "the class representatives are sufficiently *similar* to the rest of the class—in terms of their legal claims, factual circumstances, and stake in the litigation—so that certifying those individuals to represent the class will be fair to the rest of the proposed class").

In *Oplchenski*, the court also says that the typicality requirement is closely related to commonality, as does the Supreme Court. See Wal-Mart Stores, Inc. v. Dukes, *infra* p. 202 fn. 5. But can't they be conceived as addressing separate topics? "While the first two Rule 23 prerequisites, numerosity and commonality, require an examination of the proposed class, the latter two, typicality and adequate representation, require an examination of the class representatives." Riedel v. XTO Energy, Inc., 257 F.R.D. 494, 509 (E.D.Ark. 2009). Put differently, don't numerosity and commonality ensure that it is appropriate to use the class action device to address a certain issue, while typicality and adequacy ensure that this particular class representative should be allowed employ that device? Not all class members are typical, and perhaps some are inadequate even if they are typical.

In some instances, courts find significant differences between commonality and typicality. In Newton v. Merrill Lynch, Pierce, Fenner & Smith, Inc., 259 F.3d 154 (3d Cir. 2001), the court rejected a securities fraud class action for lack of commonality, but found that typicality was not a problem: "[T]ypicality does not require similarity of individual questions concerning reliance or damages on the part of class representatives. In fact, whether the class representatives' claims prove the claims of the entire class highlights important issues of individual reliance and damages that are more properly considered relevant under the predominance and superiority analysis." Id. at 184.

How carefully should the court scrutinize the claims of the proposed representatives and putative class members in making the typicality determination? In *Oplchenski*, defendant presented a statistical analysis showing differences between the experiences of the two class representatives and others in their proposed class. The court rejected these challenges on the ground that the claims were based on "the same alleged course of conduct by Defendants." Does that mean that every class member is typical? Class A seemingly included everyone who worked as a rotator from 1975 forward. Would somebody who worked for defendants only in 1975 be typical of a class member (perhaps born in 1975) who began work in 2000?

7. *Adequacy*: Finally, Rule 23(a)(4) seeks to ensure that "the representative parties will fairly and adequately protect the interests of the class." The concern is that the self-nominated representative may not be sufficiently aggressive in asserting the interests of the class. Defendants in *Oplchenski* argued that the proposed representatives are not adequate because their claims are weaker than those of other class members. Shouldn't this concern relate more to typicality? As the court says there, defendants offered no specifics indicating a conflict of interest between the class representatives and the class. But shouldn't it be unnerving that each class representative seeks to represent more than one class? Presumably plaintiffs propose four classes because the four groups have divergent interests. How can one of them simultaneously represent the interests of different classes? But other courts have also allowed plaintiffs to represent more than one subclass. See Schwarm v. Craighead, 233 F.R.D. 655 (E.D.Cal. 2006); Abels v. JBC Legal Group, 227 F.R.D. 541 (N.D.Cal. 2005).

3. THE RULE 23(a)(2) COMMONALITY REQUIREMENT

WAL-MART STORES, INC. V. DUKES
Supreme Court of the United States, 2011.
564 U.S. 338.

JUSTICE SCALIA delivered the opinion of the Court.

We are presented with one of the most expansive class actions ever. The District Court and the Court of Appeals approved the certification of a class comprising about one and a half million plaintiffs, current and former female employees of petitioner Wal-Mart who allege that the discretion exercised by their local supervisors over pay and promotion matters violates Title VII by discriminating against women. In addition to injunctive and declaratory relief, the plaintiffs seek an award of backpay. We consider whether the certification of the plaintiff class was consistent with Federal Rules of Civil Procedure 23(a) and (b)(2).

I

Petitioner Wal-Mart is the Nation's largest private employer. It operates four types of retail stores throughout the country: Discount Stores, Supercenters, Neighborhood Markets, and Sam's Clubs. Those stores are divided into seven nationwide divisions, which in turn comprise 41 regions of 80 to 85 stores apiece. Each store has between 40 and 53 separate departments and 80 to 500 staff positions. In all, Wal-Mart operates approximately 3,400 stores and employs more than one million people.

Pay and promotion decisions at Wal-Mart are generally committed to local managers' broad discretion, which is exercised "in a largely subjective manner." 222 F.R.D. 137, 145 (N.D.Cal. 2004). Local store managers may increase the wages of hourly employees (within limits) with only limited corporate oversight. As for salaried employees, such as store managers and their deputies, higher corporate authorities have discretion to set their pay within preestablished ranges.

Promotions work in a similar fashion. Wal-Mart permits store managers to apply their own subjective criteria when selecting candidates as "support managers," which is the first step on the path to management. Admission to Wal-Mart's management training program, however, does require that a candidate meet certain objective criteria, including an above-average performance rating, at least one year's tenure in the applicant's current position, and a willingness to relocate. But except for those requirements, regional and district managers have discretion to use their own judgment when selecting candidates for management training. Promotion to higher office—e.g., assistant manager, co-manager, or store manager—is similarly at the discretion of the employee's superiors after prescribed objective factors are satisfied.

The named plaintiffs in this lawsuit, representing the 1.5 million members of the certified class, are three current or former Wal-Mart employees who allege that the company discriminated against them on the basis of their sex by denying them equal pay or promotions, in violation of Title VII of the Civil Rights Act of 1964, 78 Stat. 253, as amended, 42 U.S.C. § 2000e–1 et seq.

Betty Dukes began working at a Pittsburg, California, Wal-Mart in 1994. She started as a cashier, but later sought and received a promotion to customer service manager. After a series of disciplinary violations, however, Dukes was demoted back to cashier and then to greeter. Dukes concedes she violated company policy, but contends that the disciplinary actions were in fact retaliation for invoking internal complaint procedures and that male employees have not been disciplined for similar infractions. Dukes also claims two male greeters in the Pittsburgh store are paid more than she is.

Christine Kwapnoski has worked at Sam's Club stores in Missouri and California for most of her adult life. She has held a number of positions, including a supervisory position. She claims that a male manager yelled at her frequently and screamed at female employees, but not at men. The manager in question "told her to 'doll up,' to wear some makeup, and to dress a little better."

The final named plaintiff, Edith Arana, worked at a Wal-Mart store in Duarte, California, from 1995 to 2001. In 2000, she approached the store manager on more than one occasion about management training, but was brushed off. Arana concluded she was being denied opportunity for advancement because of her sex. She initiated internal complaint procedures, whereupon she was told to apply directly to the district manager if she thought her store manager was being unfair. Arana, however, decided against that and never applied for management training again. In 2001, she was fired for failure to comply with Wal-Mart's timekeeping policy.

These plaintiffs, respondents here, do not allege that Wal-Mart has any express corporate policy against the advancement of women. Rather, they claim that their local managers' discretion over pay and promotions is exercised disproportionately in favor of men, leading to an unlawful disparate impact on female employees. And, respondents say, because Wal-Mart is aware of this effect, its refusal to cabin its managers' authority amounts to disparate treatment. Their complaint seeks injunctive and declaratory relief, punitive damages, and backpay. It does not ask for compensatory damages.

Importantly for our purposes, respondents claim that the discrimination to which they have been subjected is common to *all* Wal-Mart's female employees. The basic theory of their case is that a strong and uniform "corporate culture" permits bias against women to infect, perhaps subconsciously, the discretionary decisionmaking of each one of Wal-Mart's thousands of managers—thereby making every woman at the company the victim of one common discriminatory practice. Respondents therefore wish to litigate the Title VII claims of all female employees at Wal-Mart's stores in a nationwide class action.

* * * [R]espondents moved the District Court to certify a plaintiff class consisting of " '[a]ll women employed at any Wal-Mart domestic retail store at any time since December 26, 1998, who have been or may be subjected to Wal-Mart's challenged pay and management track promotions policies and practices.' " As evidence that there were indeed "questions of law or fact common to" all the women of Wal-Mart, as Rule 23(a)(2) requires, respondents relied chiefly on three forms of proof: statistical evidence about pay and promotion disparities between men and women at the company, anecdotal reports of discrimination from about 120 of Wal-Mart's female employees, and the testimony of a sociologist, Dr. William Bielby, who conducted a "social framework analysis" of Wal-Mart's "culture" and personnel practices, and concluded that the company was "vulnerable" to gender discrimination.

Wal-Mart unsuccessfully moved to strike much of this evidence. It also offered its own countervailing statistical and other proof in an effort to defeat Rule 23(a)'s requirements of commonality, typicality, and adequate representation. * * * [T]he District Court granted respondents' motion and certified their proposed class.

A divided en banc Court of Appeals substantially affirmed the District Court's certification order. 603 F.3d 571. The majority concluded that respondents' evidence of commonality was sufficient to "raise the common question whether Wal-Mart's female employees nationwide were subjected to a single set of corporate policies (not merely a number of independent discriminatory acts) that may have worked to unlawfully discriminate against them in violation of Title VII." It also agreed with the District Court that the named plaintiffs' claims were sufficiently typical of the class as a whole to satisfy Rule 23(a)(3), and that they could serve as adequate class representatives, see Rule 23(a)(4). * * *

II

* * * The crux of this case is commonality—the rule requiring a plaintiff to show that "there are questions of law or fact common to the class." Rule 23(a)(2).[5] That language is easy to misread, since "[a]ny

---

[5] We have previously stated in this context that "[t]he commonality and typicality requirements of Rule 23(a) tend to merge. Both serve as guideposts for determining whether under the particular circumstances maintenance of a class action is economical and whether the named plaintiff's claim and the class claims are so interrelated that the interests of the class members will be fairly and adequately protected in their absence. Those requirements therefore also tend to merge with the adequacy-of-representation requirement, although the latter requirement also raises concerns about the competency of class counsel and conflicts of interest." General Telephone Co. of Southwest v. Falcon, 457 U.S. 147, 157–158, n. 13 (1982). In light of our disposition of the

competently crafted class complaint literally raises common 'questions.' " Nagareda, Class Certification in the Age of Aggregate Proof, 84 N.Y.U.L.Rev. 97, 131–132 (2009). For example: Do all of us plaintiffs indeed work for Wal-Mart? Do our managers have discretion over pay? Is that an unlawful employment practice? What remedies should we get? Reciting these questions is not sufficient to obtain class certification. Commonality requires the plaintiff to demonstrate that the class members "have suffered the same injury," [General Telephone of the Southwest v.] Falcon, *supra*, at 157. This does not mean merely that they have all suffered a violation of the same provision of law. Title VII, for example, can be violated in many ways—by intentional discrimination, or by hiring and promotion criteria that result in disparate impact, and by the use of these practices on the part of many different superiors in a single company. Quite obviously, the mere claim by employees of the same company that they have suffered a Title VII injury, or even a disparate-impact Title VII injury, gives no cause to believe that all their claims can productively be litigated at once. Their claims must depend upon a common contention—for example, the assertion of discriminatory bias on the part of the same supervisor. That common contention, moreover, must be of such a nature that it is capable of classwide resolution—which means that determination of its truth or falsity will resolve an issue that is central to the validity of each one of the claims in one stroke.

> "What matters to class certification . . . is not the raising of common 'questions'—even in droves—but, rather the capacity of a classwide proceeding to generate common answers apt to drive the resolution of the litigation. Dissimilarities within the proposed class are what have the potential to impede the generation of common answers." Nagareda, *supra*, at 132.

Rule 23 does not set forth a mere pleading standard. A party seeking class certification must affirmatively demonstrate his compliance with the Rule—that is, he must be prepared to prove that there are *in fact* sufficiently numerous parties, common questions of fact, etc. * * *

In this case, proof of commonality necessarily overlaps with respondents' merits contention that Wal-Mart engages in a *pattern or practice* of discrimination. That is so because, in resolving an individual's Title VII claim, the crux of the inquiry is "the reason for a particular employment decision," Here respondents wish to sue about literally millions of employment decisions at once. Without some glue holding the alleged reasons for all those decisions together, it will be impossible to say that examination of all the class members' claims for relief will produce a common answer to the crucial question *why was I disfavored*.

---

commonality question, however, it is unnecessary to resolve whether respondents have satisfied the typicality and adequate-representation requirements of Rule 23(a).

This Court's opinion in *Falcon* describes how the commonality issue must be approached. There an employee who claimed that he was deliberately denied a promotion on account of race obtained certification of a class comprising all employees wrongfully denied promotions and all applicants wrongfully denied jobs. We rejected that composite class for lack of commonality and typicality, explaining:

> "Conceptually, there is a wide gap between (a) an individual's claim that he has been denied a promotion [or higher pay] on discriminatory grounds, and his otherwise unsupported allegation that the company has a policy of discrimination, and (b) the existence of a class of persons who have suffered the same injury as that individual, such that the individual's claim and the class claim will share common questions of law or fact and that the individual's claim will be typical of the class claims."

Falcon suggested two ways in which that conceptual gap might be bridged. First, if the employer "used a biased testing procedure to evaluate both applicants for employment and incumbent employees, a class action on behalf of every applicant or employee who might have been prejudiced by the test clearly would satisfy the commonality and typicality requirements of Rule 23(a)." Second, "[s]ignificant proof that an employer operated under a general policy of discrimination conceivably could justify a class of both applicants and employees if the discrimination manifested itself in hiring and promotion practices in the same general fashion, such as through entirely subjective decisionmaking processes." We think that statement precisely describes respondents' burden in this case. The first manner of bridging the gap obviously has no application here; Wal-Mart has no testing procedure or other companywide evaluation method that can be charged with bias. The whole point of permitting discretionary decisionmaking is to avoid evaluating employees under a common standard.

The second manner of bridging the gap requires "significant proof" that Wal-Mart "operated under a general policy of discrimination." That is entirely absent here. Wal-Mart's announced policy forbids sex discrimination, and as the District Court recognized the company imposes penalties for denials of equal employment opportunity. The only evidence of a "general policy of discrimination" respondents produced was the testimony of Dr. William Bielby, their sociological expert. Relying on "social framework" analysis, Bielby testified that Wal-Mart has a "strong corporate culture," that makes it " 'vulnerable' " to "gender bias." He could not, however, "determine with any specificity how regularly stereotypes play a meaningful role in employment decisions at Wal-Mart. At his deposition . . . Dr. Bielby conceded that he could not calculate whether 0.5 percent or 95 percent of the employment decisions at Wal-Mart might be determined by stereotyped thinking." The parties dispute whether Bielby's testimony even met the standards for the admission of expert testimony under Federal Rule of Civil Procedure 702 and our *Daubert* case, see Daubert v. Merrell Dow Pharmaceuticals, Inc., 509 U.S. 579 (1993).[8] The District Court concluded that *Daubert* did not apply to expert testimony at the certification stage of class-action proceedings. We doubt that is so, but even if properly considered, Bielby's testimony does nothing to advance respondents' case. "[W]hether 0.5 percent or 95 percent of the employment decisions at Wal-Mart might be determined by stereotyped thinking" is the essential question on which respondents' theory of commonality depends. If Bielby admittedly has no answer to that question, we can safely disregard what he has to say. It is worlds away from "significant proof" that Wal-Mart "operated under a general policy of discrimination."

The only corporate policy that the plaintiffs' evidence convincingly establishes is Wal-Mart's "policy" of *allowing discretion* by local supervisors over employment matters. On its face, of course, that is just the opposite of a uniform employment practice that would provide the commonality needed for a class action; it is a policy against having uniform employment practices. It is also a very common and presumptively reasonable way of doing business—one that we have said "should itself raise no inference of discriminatory conduct," Watson v. Fort Worth Bank & Trust, 487 U.S. 977, 990 (1988).

To be sure, we have recognized that, "in appropriate cases," giving discretion to lower-level supervisors can be the basis of Title VII liability under a disparate-impact theory—since "an employer's undisciplined system of subjective decisionmaking [can have] precisely the same effects as a system pervaded by impermissible intentional discrimination." Id., at 990–991. But the recognition that this type of Title VII claim "can" exist does not lead to the conclusion that every employee in a company using a system of discretion has such a claim in common. To the contrary, left to their own devices most managers in any corporation—and surely most managers in a corporation that forbids sex discrimination—would select sex-neutral, performance-based criteria for hiring and promotion that produce no actionable disparity at all. Others may choose to reward various attributes that produce disparate impact—such as scores on general aptitude tests or educational achievements. And still other managers may

---

[8]   Bielby's conclusions in this case have elicited criticism from the very scholars on whose conclusions he relies for his social-framework analysis. See Monahan, Walker & Mitchell, Contextual Evidence of Gender Discrimination: The Ascendance of "Social Frameworks," 94 Va. L.Rev. 1715, 1747 (2008) ("[Bielby's] research into conditions and behavior at Wal-Mart did not meet the standards expected of social scientific research into stereotyping and discrimination"); id., at 1745, 1747 ("[A] social framework necessarily contains only general statements about reliable patterns of relations among variables . . . and goes no further. . . . Dr. Bielby claimed to present a social framework, but he testified about social facts specific to Wal-Mart"); id., at 1747–1748 ("Dr. Bielby's report provides no verifiable method for measuring and testing any of the variables that were crucial to his conclusions and reflects nothing more than Dr. Bielby's 'expert judgment' about how general stereotyping research applied to all managers across all of Wal-Mart's stores nationwide for the multi-year class period").

be guilty of intentional discrimination that produces a sex-based disparity. In such a company, demonstrating the invalidity of one manager's use of discretion will do nothing to demonstrate the invalidity of another's. A party seeking to certify a nationwide class will be unable to show that all the employees' Title VII claims will in fact depend on the answers to common questions.

Respondents have not identified a common mode of exercising discretion that pervades the entire company—aside from their reliance on Dr. Bielby's social frameworks analysis that we have rejected. In a company of Wal-Mart's size and geographical scope, it is quite unbelievable that all managers would exercise their discretion in a common way without some common direction. Respondents attempt to make that showing by means of statistical and anecdotal evidence, but their evidence falls well short.

The statistical evidence consists primarily of regression analyses performed by Dr. Richard Drogin, a statistician, and Dr. Marc Bendick, a labor economist. Drogin conducted his analysis region-by-region, comparing the number of women promoted into management positions with the percentage of women in the available pool of hourly workers. After considering regional and national data, Drogin concluded that "there are statistically significant disparities between men and women at Wal-Mart . . . [and] these disparities . . . can be explained only by gender discrimination." Bendick compared work-force data from Wal-Mart and competitive retailers and concluded that Wal-Mart "promotes a lower percentage of women than its competitors."

Even if they are taken at face value, these studies are insufficient to establish that respondents' theory can be proved on a classwide basis. In *Falcon*, we held that one named plaintiff's experience of discrimination was insufficient to infer that "discriminatory treatment is typical of [the employer's employment] practices." A similar failure of inference arises here. As Judge Ikuta observed in her dissent, "[i]nformation about disparities at the regional and national level does not establish the existence of disparities at individual stores, let alone raise the inference that a company-wide policy of discrimination is implemented by discretionary decisions at the store and district level." 603 F.3d, at 637. A regional pay disparity, for example, may be attributable to only a small set of Wal-Mart stores, and cannot by itself establish the uniform, store-by-store disparity upon which the plaintiffs' theory of commonality depends.

There is another, more fundamental, respect in which respondents' statistical proof fails. Even if it established (as it does not) a pay or promotion pattern that differs from the nationwide figures or the regional figures in *all* of Wal-Mart's 3,400 stores, that would still not demonstrate that commonality of issue exists. Some managers will claim that the availability of women, or qualified women, or interested women, in their stores' area does not mirror the national or regional statistics. And almost all of them will claim to have been applying some sex-neutral, performance-based criteria—whose nature and effects will differ from store to store. In the landmark case of ours which held that giving discretion to lower-level supervisors can be the basis of Title VII liability under a disparate-impact theory, the plurality opinion conditioned that holding on the corollary that merely proving that the discretionary system has produced a racial or sexual disparity is *not enough*. "[T]he plaintiff must begin by identifying the specific employment practice that is challenged." *Watson*, 487 U.S., at 994. That is all the more necessary when a class of plaintiffs is sought to be certified. Other than the bare existence of delegated discretion, respondents have identified no "specific employment practice"—much less one that ties all their 1.5 million claims together. Merely showing that Wal-Mart's policy of discretion has produced an overall sex-based disparity does not suffice.

Respondents' anecdotal evidence suffers from the same defects, and in addition is too weak to raise any inference that all the individual, discretionary personnel decisions are discriminatory. In Teamsters v. United States, 431 U.S. 324 (1977), in addition to substantial statistical evidence of company-wide discrimination, the Government (as plaintiff) produced about 40 specific accounts of racial discrimination from particular individuals. That number was significant because the company involved had only 6,472 employees, of whom 571 were minorities, and the class itself consisted of around 334 persons, The 40 anecdotes thus represented roughly one account for every eight members of the class. Moreover, the Court of Appeals noted that the anecdotes came from individuals "spread throughout" the company who "for the most part" worked at the company's operational centers that employed the largest numbers of the class members. Here, by contrast, respondents filed some 120 affidavits reporting experiences of discrimination—about 1 for every 12,500 class members—relating to only some 235 out of Wal-Mart's 3,400 stores. More than half of these reports are concentrated in only six States (Alabama, California, Florida, Missouri, Texas, and Wisconsin); half of all States have only one or two anecdotes; and 14 States have no anecdotes about Wal-Mart's operations at all. Even if every single one of these accounts is true, that would not demonstrate that the entire company "operate[s] under a general policy of discrimination," *Falcon, supra*, at 159, n. 15, which is what respondents must show to certify a companywide class.[9]

The dissent misunderstands the nature of the foregoing analysis. It criticizes our focus on the dissimilarities between the putative class

---

[9]   The dissent says that we have adopted "a rule that a discrimination claim, if accompanied by anecdotes, must supply them in numbers proportionate to the size of the class." That is not quite accurate. A discrimination claimant is free to supply as few anecdotes as he wishes. But when the claim is that a company operates under a general policy of discrimination, a few anecdotes selected from literally millions of employment decisions prove nothing at all.

members on the ground that we have "blend[ed]" Rule 23(a)(2)'s commonality requirement with Rule 23(b)(3)'s inquiry into whether common questions "predominate" over individual ones. That is not so. We quite agree that for purposes of Rule 23(a)(2) " '[e]ven a single [common] question' " will do, post, at 376 (quoting Nagareda, The Preexistence Principle and the Structure of the Class Action, 103 Colum. L. Rev. 149, 176, n. 110 (2003)). We consider dissimilarities not in order to determine (as Rule 23(b)(3) requires) whether common questions predominate, but in order to determine (as Rule 23(a)(2) requires) whether there is "[e]ven a single [common] question." And there is not here. Because respondents provide no convincing proof of a companywide discriminatory pay and promotion policy, we have concluded that they have not established the existence of any common question.[10]

In sum, we agree with Chief Judge Kozinski that the members of the class:

> "held a multitude of different jobs, at different levels of Wal-Mart's hierarchy, for variable lengths of time, in 3,400 stores, sprinkled across 50 states, with a kaleidoscope of supervisors (male and female), subject to a variety of regional policies that all differed. . . . Some thrived while others did poorly. They have little in common but their sex and this lawsuit." 603 F.3d, at 652 (dissenting opinion).

The judgment of the Court of Appeals is Reversed.

JUSTICE GINSBURG, with whom JUSTICE BREYER, JUSTICE SOTOMAYOR, and JUSTICE KAGAN join, concurring in part and dissenting in part.

The class in this case, I agree with the Court, should not have been certified under Federal Rule of Civil Procedure 23(b)(2). The plaintiffs, alleging discrimination in violation of Title VII, 42 U.S.C. § 2000e et seq., seek monetary relief that is not merely incidental to any injunctive or declaratory relief that might be available. A putative class of this type may be certifiable under Rule 23(b)(3), if the plaintiffs show that common class questions "predominate" over issues affecting individuals—e.g., qualification for, and the amount of, backpay or compensatory damages— and that a class action is "superior" to other modes of adjudication.

Whether the class the plaintiffs describe meets the specific requirements of Rule 23(b)(3) is not before the Court, and I would reserve

---

[10] For this reason, there is no force to the dissent's attempt to distinguish *Falcon* on the ground that in that case there were " 'no common questions of law or fact' between the claims of the lead plaintiff and the applicant class." Here also there is nothing to unite all of the plaintiffs' claims, since (contrary to the dissent's contention), the same employment practices do not "touch and concern all members of the class."

that matter for consideration and decision on remand.[1] The Court, however, disqualifies the class at the starting gate, holding that the plaintiffs cannot cross the "commonality" line set by Rule 23(a)(2). In so ruling, the Court imports into the Rule 23(a) determination concerns properly addressed in a Rule 23(b)(3) assessment.

I

Rule 23(a)(2) establishes a preliminary requirement for maintaining a class action: "[T]here are questions of law or fact common to the class." The Rule "does not require that all questions of law or fact raised in the litigation be common," 1 H. Newberg & A. Conte, Newberg on Class Actions § 3.10, pp. 3–48 to 3–49 (3d ed. 1992); indeed, "[e]ven a single question of law or fact common to the members of the class will satisfy the commonality requirement," Nagareda, The Preexistence Principle and the Structure of the Class Action, 103 Colum. L. Rev. 149, 176, n. 110 (2003).

A "question" is ordinarily understood to be "[a] subject or point open to controversy." Thus, a "question" "common to the class" must be a dispute, either of fact or of law, the resolution of which will advance the determination of the class members' claims.[3]

The District Court, recognizing that "one significant issue common to the class may be sufficient to warrant certification," found that the plaintiffs easily met that test. Absent an error of law or an abuse of discretion, an appellate tribunal has no warrant to upset the District Court's finding of commonality.

The District Court certified a class of "[a]ll women employed at any Wal-Mart domestic retail store at any time since December 26, 1998." The named plaintiffs, led by Betty Dukes, propose to litigate, on behalf of the class, allegations that Wal-Mart discriminates on the basis of gender in pay and promotions. They allege that the company "[r]eli[es] on gender stereotypes in making employment decisions such as . . . promotion[s][and] pay." Wal-Mart permits those prejudices to infect personnel decisions, the plaintiffs contend, by leaving pay and promotions in the hands of "a nearly all male managerial workforce" using "arbitrary and subjective criteria." Further alleged barriers to the advancement of female employees include the company's requirement, "as a condition of promotion to management jobs, that employees be willing to relocate." Absent instruction otherwise, there is a risk that managers will act on the familiar assumption that

---

[1]   The plaintiffs requested Rule 23(b)(3) certification as an alternative, should their request for (b)(2) certification fail.

[3]   The Court suggests Rule 23(a)(2) must mean more than it says. If the word "questions" were taken literally, the majority asserts, plaintiffs could pass the Rule 23(a)(2) bar by "[r]eciting . . . questions" like "Do all of us plaintiffs indeed work for Wal-Mart?" Sensibly read, however, the word "questions" means disputed issues, not any utterance crafted in the grammatical form of a question.

women, because of their services to husband and children, are less mobile than men.

Women fill 70 percent of the hourly jobs in the retailer's stores but make up only "33 percent of management employees." "[T]he higher one looks in the organization the lower the percentage of women." The plaintiffs' "largely uncontested descriptive statistics" also show that women working in the company's stores "are paid less than men in every region" and "that the salary gap widens over time even for men and women hired into the same jobs at the same time."

The District Court identified "systems for ... promoting in-store employees" that were "sufficiently similar across regions and stores" to conclude that "the manner in which these systems affect the class raises issues that are common to all class members." The selection of employees for promotion to in-store management "is fairly characterized as a 'tap on the shoulder' process," in which managers have discretion about whose shoulders to tap. Vacancies are not regularly posted; from among those employees satisfying minimum qualifications, managers choose whom to promote on the basis of their own subjective impressions.

Wal-Mart's compensation policies also operate uniformly across stores, the District Court found. The retailer leaves open a $2 band for every position's hourly pay rate. Wal-Mart provides no standards or criteria for setting wages within that band, and thus does nothing to counter unconscious bias on the part of supervisors.

Wal-Mart's supervisors do not make their discretionary decisions in a vacuum. The District Court reviewed means Wal-Mart used to maintain a "carefully constructed ... corporate culture," such as frequent meetings to reinforce the common way of thinking, regular transfers of managers between stores to ensure uniformity throughout the company, monitoring of stores "on a close and constant basis," and "Wal-Mart TV," "broadcas[t] ... into all stores."

The plaintiffs' evidence, including class members' tales of their own experiences,[4] suggests that gender bias suffused Wal-Mart's company culture. Among illustrations, senior management often refer to female associates as "little Janie Qs." One manager told an employee that "[m]en are here to make a career and women aren't." A committee of female Wal-Mart executives concluded that "[s]tereotypes limit the opportunities offered to women."

Finally, the plaintiffs presented an expert's appraisal to show that the pay and promotions disparities at Wal-Mart "can be explained only by

---

[4] The majority purports to derive from Teamsters v. United States, 431 U.S. 324 (1977), a rule that a discrimination claim, if accompanied by anecdotes, must supply them in numbers proportionate to the size of the class. Teamsters, the Court acknowledges, see ante, n. 9, instructs that statistical evidence alone may suffice; that decision can hardly be said to establish a numerical floor before anecdotal evidence can be taken into account.

gender discrimination and not by . . . neutral variables." Using regression analyses, their expert, Richard Drogin, controlled for factors including, inter alia, job performance, length of time with the company, and the store where an employee worked.[5] The results, the District Court found, were sufficient to raise an "inference of discrimination."

C

The District Court's identification of a common question, whether Wal-Mart's pay and promotions policies gave rise to unlawful discrimination, was hardly infirm. The practice of delegating to supervisors large discretion to make personnel decisions, uncontrolled by formal standards, has long been known to have the potential to produce disparate effects. Managers, like all humankind, may be prey to biases of which they are unaware.[6] The risk of discrimination is heightened when those managers are predominantly of one sex, and are steeped in a corporate culture that perpetuates gender stereotypes.

The plaintiffs' allegations resemble those in one of the prototypical cases in this area, Leisner v. New York Tel. Co., 358 F.Supp. 359, 364–365 (S.D.N.Y. 1973). In deciding on promotions, supervisors in that case were to start with objective measures; but ultimately, they were to "look at the individual as a total individual." The final question they were to ask and answer: "Is this person going to be successful in our business?" It is hardly surprising that for many managers, the ideal candidate was someone with characteristics similar to their own.

We have held that "discretionary employment practices" can give rise to Title VII claims, not only when such practices are motivated by discriminatory intent but also when they produce discriminatory results. See Watson v. Fort Worth Bank & Trust, 487 U.S. 977, 988, 991 (1988). But see [majority opinion] ante, at 243 ("[P]roving that [a] discretionary system has produced a . . . disparity is not enough."). In Watson, as here, an employer had given its managers large authority over promotions. An employee sued the bank under Title VII, alleging that the "discretionary promotion system" caused a discriminatory effect based on race. Four different supervisors had declined, on separate occasions, to promote the employee. Their reasons were subjective and unknown. The employer, we

---

[5] The Court asserts that Drogin showed only average differences at the "regional and national level" between male and female employees. In fact, his regression analyses showed there were disparities within stores. The majority's contention to the contrary reflects only an arcane disagreement about statistical method—which the District Court resolved in the plaintiffs' favor. Appellate review is no occasion to disturb a trial court's handling of factual disputes of this order.

[6] An example vividly illustrates how subjective decisionmaking can be a vehicle for discrimination. Performing in symphony orchestras was long a male preserve. Goldin and Rouse, Orchestrating Impartiality: The Impact of "Blind" Auditions on Female Musicians, 90 Am. Econ. Rev. 715, 715–716 (2000). In the 1970's orchestras began hiring musicians through auditions open to all comers. Reviewers were to judge applicants solely on their musical abilities, yet subconscious bias led some reviewers to disfavor women. Orchestras that permitted reviewers to see the applicants hired far fewer female musicians than orchestras that conducted blind auditions, in which candidates played behind opaque screens.

noted "had not developed precise and formal criteria for evaluating candidates"; "[i]t relied instead on the subjective judgment of supervisors."

Aware of "the problem of subconscious stereotypes and prejudices," we held that the employer's "undisciplined system of subjective decisionmaking" was an "employment practic[e]" that "may be analyzed under the disparate impact approach."

The plaintiffs' allegations state claims of gender discrimination in the form of biased decisionmaking in both pay and promotions. The evidence reviewed by the District Court adequately demonstrated that resolving those claims would necessitate examination of particular policies and practices alleged to affect, adversely and globally, women employed at Wal-Mart's stores. Rule 23(a)(2), setting a necessary but not a sufficient criterion for class-action certification, demands nothing further.

II

The Court gives no credence to the key dispute common to the class: whether Wal-Mart's discretionary pay and promotion policies are discriminatory. "What matters," the Court asserts, "is not the raising of common 'questions,'" but whether there are "[d]issimilarities within the proposed class" that "have the potential to impede the generation of common answers."

The Court blends Rule 23(a)(2)'s threshold criterion with the more demanding criteria of Rule 23(b)(3), and thereby elevates the (a)(2) inquiry so that it is no longer "easily satisfied."[7] Rule 23(b)(3) certification requires, in addition to the four 23(a) findings, determinations that "questions of law or fact common to class members predominate over any questions affecting only individual members" and that "a class action is superior to other available methods for . . . adjudicating the controversy."

The Court's emphasis on differences between class members mimics the Rule 23(b)(3) inquiry into whether common questions "predominate" over individual issues. And by asking whether the individual differences "impede" common adjudication, the Court duplicates 23(b)(3)'s question whether "a class action is superior" to other modes of adjudication. Indeed, Professor Nagareda, whose "dissimilarities" inquiry the Court endorses, developed his position in the context of Rule 23(b)(3). "The Rule 23(b)(3) predominance inquiry" is meant to "tes[t] whether proposed classes are

---

[7]   The Court places considerable weight on General Telephone Co. of Southwest v. Falcon, 457 U.S. 147 (1982). That case has little relevance to the question before the Court today. The lead plaintiff in *Falcon* alleged discrimination evidenced by the company's failure to promote him and other Mexican-American employees and failure to hire Mexican-American applicants. There were "no common questions of law or fact" between the claims of the lead plaintiff and the applicant class. The plaintiff-employee alleged that the defendant-employer had discriminated against him intentionally. The applicant class claims, by contrast, were "advanced under the 'adverse impact' theory," appropriate for facially neutral practices. "[T]he only commonality [wa]s that respondent is a Mexican-American and he seeks to represent a class of Mexican-Americans." Here the same practices touch and concern all members of the class.

sufficiently cohesive to warrant adjudication by representation." Amchem Products, Inc. v. Windsor, 521 U.S. 591, 623 (1997). If courts must conduct a "dissimilarities" analysis at the Rule 23(a)(2) stage, no mission remains for Rule 23(b)(3).

Because Rule 23(a) is also a prerequisite for Rule 23(b)(1) and Rule 23(b)(2) classes, the Court's "dissimilarities" position is far reaching. Individual differences should not bar a Rule 23(b)(1) or Rule 23(b)(2) class, so long as the Rule 23(a) threshold is met. For example, in Franks v. Bowman Transp. Co., 424 U.S. 747 (1976), a Rule 23(b)(2) class of African-American truckdrivers complained that the defendant had discriminatorily refused to hire black applicants. We recognized that the "qualification[s] and performance" of individual class members might vary. "Generalizations concerning such individually applicable evidence," we cautioned, "cannot serve as a justification for the denial of [injunctive] relief to the entire class."

The "dissimilarities" approach leads the Court to train its attention on what distinguishes individual class members, rather than on what unites them. Given the lack of standards for pay and promotions, the majority says, "demonstrating the invalidity of one manager's use of discretion will do nothing to demonstrate the invalidity of another's."

Wal-Mart's delegation of discretion over pay and promotions is a policy uniform throughout all stores. The very nature of discretion is that people will exercise it in various ways. A system of delegated discretion, *Watson* held, is a practice actionable under Title VII when it produces discriminatory outcomes. A finding that Wal-Mart's pay and promotions practices in fact violate the law would be the first step in the usual order of proof for plaintiffs seeking individual remedies for company-wide discrimination. That each individual employee's unique circumstances will ultimately determine whether she is entitled to backpay or damages, § 2000e–5(g)(2)(A) (barring backpay if a plaintiff "was refused . . . advancement . . . for any reason other than discrimination"), should not factor into the Rule 23(a)(2) determination.

* * *

The Court errs in importing a "dissimilarities" notion suited to Rule 23(b)(3) into the Rule 23(a) commonality inquiry. I therefore cannot join Part II of the Court's opinion.

NOTES AND QUESTIONS

1.   *Postscript:* After the Supreme Court's decision, there were five regional "mini-*Dukes*" class actions against Wal-Mart, but only one of those was successful in obtaining class certification. But because the statute of limitations was tolled during the pendency of the class action, individual plaintiffs began filing suit, and Wal-Mart found itself facing "a wave of

lawsuits." Paige Smith & Robert Iofalla, Wal-Mart Faces New Legal Battle From Old Pay Bias Claims, Bloomberg Law News, May 28, 2019.

2.   In General Telephone Co. of the Southwest v. Falcon, 457 U.S. 147 (1982), the Court reversed a class certified under the Fifth Circuit's then prevailing "across the board" class certification policy that, as the Court described it, meant that "any victim of racial discrimination in employment may maintain an 'across the board' attack on all unequal employment practices alleged to have been committed by the employer pursuant to a policy of racial discrimination." The Court held that this attitude did not satisfy Rule 23.

The class representative in *Falcon* was a Mexican-American employee who had been hired under an affirmative action program at the company, and twice promoted before he was denied a promotion he claimed went to a less-qualified white employee. He sued on behalf of a class of all present or future Mexican-American employees of defendant, claiming that the company discriminated in hiring and promotions. The Court ruled that he did not satisfy the typicality requirement of Rule 23(a)(3), although it also noted that "[t]he commonality and typicality requirements of Rule 23(a) tend to merge." In particular, it was problematical that plaintiff sued on behalf of a class of job applicants as well as job holders. In some circumstances, that might present conflict problems: "In employment discrimination litigation, conflicts might arise, for example, between employees and applicants who were denied employment and who will, if granted relief, compete with employees for fringe benefits or seniority. Under Rule 23, the same plaintiff could not represent these classes."

In *Falcon*, the post-certification evolution of the case confirmed the suspicion that the job applicant and promotion classes should not be combined. After trial, the district court found that defendant had not discriminated against Falcon in hiring, but that it did discriminate against him in its promotion practices. But regarding class claims, it found no class-wide discrimination in promotion practices but that the company had discriminated in its hiring practices. The Supreme Court emphasized this disparity as showing that the class action was not appropriate:

> The trial of this class action followed a predictable course. Instead of raising common questions of law or fact, respondent's evidentiary approaches to the individual and class claims were entirely different. He attempted to sustain his individual claim by proving intentional discrimination. He tried to prove his class claims through statistical evidence of disparate impact. Ironically, the District Court rejected the class claim of promotion discrimination, which conceptually might have borne a closer typicality and commonality relationship with respondent's individual claim, but sustained the class claim of hiring discrimination. As the District Court's bifurcated findings on liability demonstrate, the individual and class claims might as well have been tried separately.

Could the same be said of the proposed class claim in *Wal-Mart*?

In its footnote 15, cited by the Court in *Wal-Mart*, the Court in *Falcon* also offered the following contrast to the facts it had before it:

> If petitioner used a biased testing procedure to evaluate both applicants for employment and incumbent employees, a class action on behalf of every applicant or employee who might have been prejudiced by the test clearly would satisfy the commonality and typicality requirements of Rule 23(a). Significant proof that an employer operated under a general policy of discrimination conceivably could justify a class of both applicants and employees if the discrimination manifested itself in hiring and promotion practices in the same general fashion, such as through entirely subjective decisionmaking processes. In this regard it is noteworthy that Title VII prohibits discriminatory *practices*, not an abstract policy of discrimination. The mere fact that an aggrieved private plaintiff is a member of an identifiable class of persons of the same race or national origin is insufficient to establish his standing to litigate on their behalf all possible claims of discrimination against a common employer.

3.   Justice Ginsburg objects in dissent to the Court's reliance on Rule 23(a)(2) as the ground for decision. Ordinarily courts have treated this requirement as easy to satisfy. Recall Oplchenski v. Parfums Givenchy, Inc., *supra* p. 186, which reports that the Rule 23(a)(2) commonality standard is "quite low." Justice Scalia's opinion reflects a different attitude. Dean Klonoff contends that "*Dukes* cannot be squared with the text, structure, or history of Rule 23(a)(2)." Robert Klonoff, The Decline of Class Actions, 90 Wash. U. L. Rev. 729, 776 (2013). Instead, the Court "conflated commonality and predominance," and improperly relied on Prof. Nagareda's work, for he was trying to define predominance when he offered the analysis that Justice Scalia invokes for application of Rule 23(a)(2). Id. at 778.

Some lower courts seem to regard *Wal-Mart* as an extreme case: "In *Wal-Mart*, the only feature common to all promotion decisions was the policy of delegating those discretionary decisions to individual store managers. In essence, all they had in common was that each one (or, more precisely, each manager's decision) was different." In re Johnson, 760 F.3d 66, 73 (D.C.Cir. 2014). But others conclude that "*Wal-Mart* has heightened the standards for establishing commonality under Rule 23(a)(2). * * * After *Wal-Mart*, Rule 23(a)(2)'s commonality requirements demands more than the presentation of questions that are common to the class." M.D. ex rel. Stuckenberg v. Perry, 675 F.3d 832, 839–40 (5th Cir. 2012).

Could the Court instead have reached a similar result in *Wal-Mart* by relying on the requirement in Rule 23(b)(2) that in class actions under that provision the plaintiff must show that defendant "has acted or refused to act on grounds that apply generally to the class"? Would that requirement have been satisfied in *Wal-Mart*? If Rule 23(a)(2) is not satisfied by the common questions actually presented in *Wal-Mart*, would that mean that a similar case satisfying the requirements of Rule 23(b)(1) could not be certified because this prerequisite to class treatment could not be satisfied? Justice Ginsburg suggests that on remand plaintiffs could renew their effort to have this case certified under Rule 23(b)(3). How could they do that if Rule 23(a)(2) must be satisfied in every case? In fact, on remand Judge Charles Breyer (brother of Justice Stephen Breyer) held that plaintiffs could not justify certification of a California-wide class. Dukes v. Wal-Mart Stores, Inc., 964 F.Supp.2d 1115 (N.D.Cal. 2013).

Should the same sort of common-questions reasoning apply to Rule 20 joinder issues? For example, does *Wal-Mart* raise questions about the propriety of the Rule 20 joinder in Mosley v. General Motors Corp., *supra* p. 17?

4. Is the central problem in *Wal-Mart* a Rule 23 problem or a Title VII problem? Richard Nagareda, Class Certification in the Age of Aggregate Proof, 84 N.Y.U. L. Rev. 97 (2009), cited by both the majority and the dissent, points out that in the background there is a vigorous debate in at least academic circles about whether "structural discrimination"—unconscious discrimination that results from pervasive social arrangements that produce assumptions influencing employment decisions—should be actionable under Title VII. It may be that giving discretion to managers would facilitate decisions based on such unconscious factors, and one way of looking at plaintiffs' argument is that Title VII should be implemented to correct for such societal imperfections (id. at 134):

> At bottom, these class actions involve contested efforts to alter the meaning of discrimination under Title VII to accord with an emerging body of research that draws on statistical analysis informed by sociology. The crucial point is that the legal meaning of discrimination in a case like *Dukes* bears decisively on the existence of fatal dissimilarities within the class and, as such, is properly the focus of class certification inquiry.

Does this analysis shed light on the disagreement between Justices Scalia and Ginsburg? Prof. Nagareda concludes that "the notion of Title VII liability for enabling discrimination—not battles over duelling expert submissions—forms the crux of the class certification dispute in *Dukes* and similar pattern-or-practice cases today." Id. at 153. According to him, the "right approach" in that case would be "to recognize that the cohesiveness of the proposed class turns on the proper meaning of prohibited discrimination under Title VII, to resolve the meaning of the statute squarely and forthrightly, and then to turn to the specifics of compliance with Rule 23 requirements." Id. at 162.

5. After the Court decided the *Wal-Mart* case, the New York Times published a negative editorial which elicited a letter from a female executive of Wal-Mart (June 28, 2011 at A20):

> I'm amazed by the negative and false assumptions I've seen about Wal-Mart since the Supreme Court's decision in the class action lawsuit on June 20. The Wal-Mart I know has offered a world of opportunity to me and countless other women.

When I started at Wal-Mart in 1992 in California, I rose from an hourly trainee to salaried store manager in less than four years. Soon I was asked to manage a larger store, where at one time four of my six assistant managers were women. All of this happened at the same time as the accusations in this lawsuit.

Anyone who believes she has a claim deserves her day in court, and the three plaintiffs can now have their individual cases heard on their merits. But as the court ruled, the class should never have been certified because the experiences that individual women had working at Wal-Mart were too different. The way the case was filed, I would technically have been a plaintiff in the case.

My experience has been profoundly different from those of the plaintiffs, which is exactly why the court rejected their attempt to sue Wal-Mart on my behalf.

The Supreme Court made the right decision.

Do these points show that the Court made the right decision?

6.   Plaintiffs in *Wal-Mart* relied heavily on an expert who presented "social framework analysis" of the company. Use of that sort of analysis was based on John Monahan & Laurens Walker, Social Science in Law 355–555 (4th ed. 1998). They began with what had already been known as the concept of "legislative facts," under which background information of this sort could be used to fashion legal rules. A prime example of that sort of use of social science research was in Brown v. Board of Education, 347 U.S. 483 (1954), in which the Court cited published reports of social scientists in support of its conclusion that racial segregation in public schools produces a sense of inferiority that affects a student's motivation to learn. Perhaps a similar use would be to support interpreting Title VII to combat "structural discrimination."

A different use of this sort of social science research would be to inform factfinders who must evaluate the circumstances in a given case, such as by showing that people often have greater difficulty identifying people of a different race in a case that relies on eyewitness identification. In such a case, an expert could be called to describe generally for the factfinder the nature of the social-science results. But with particular reference to the work done by plaintiffs' expert in *Wal-Mart*, the authors of the work on which he relied offered a caution about this sort of use of this sort of research:

> Any attempt to link basic research findings to specific organizational settings and outcomes requires that many assessments be made about the presence and operation within the organization of variables that have been found to be important within the basic research settings. To make these assessments in a scientifically reliable way, the variables must be clearly defined, measured, and their relationships systematically tested, with the definitions, measurements, and tests reported in a transparent way so that another researchers could attempt to replicate the assessments. To qualify as scientific, a system of measurement or testing cannot be a

private system that only one researcher (or expert) can apply. * * * Unfortunately, courts have allowed experts to link social frameworks to the facts of particular cases despite the experts' failure to meet these scientific requirements. As [Professor] Faigman states, "[e]xperts's case-specific conclusions appear largely to be based on an admixture of an unknown combination of knowledge of the subject, experience over the years, commitment to the client or cause, intuition, and blind faith. Science it is not."

John Monahan, Laurens Walker & Gregory Mitchell, Contextual Evidence of Gender Discrimination: The Ascendence of "Social Frameworks," 94 Va. L. Rev. 1715, 1738–39 (2008).

7. Would a different sort of workplace suit raise different issues? Consider Jenson v. Eveleth Taconite Co., 139 F.R.D. 657 (D.Minn. 1991), in which plaintiffs were women employed in a mining operation. They claimed their employer and union had discriminated against women in terms of hiring and conditions of employment. They also asserted that the employer had allowed, and perhaps fostered, a hostile work environment. Plaintiffs' attorney took the case thinking it was "a natural class action because the environment of the mine was so clearly hostile to all the women who worked there." Clara Bingham & Laura Gansler, Class Action: The Landmark Case That Changed Sexual Harassment Law 181 (2002). The 2005 movie "North Country," starring Charlize Theron, Frances McDormand, Sissy Spacek, and Woody Harrelson, was largely based on this story. Despite defendants' argument that sexual harassment claims could not be made on a class-wide basis, the court certified a class, finding that plaintiffs had "bridged the gap" between their individual claims and putative class claims (139 F.R.D. at 662):

> Plaintiffs do not purport to raise individual claims of sexual harassment. Rather, plaintiffs advance the view that incidents of sexual harassment constitute but one facet of their discrimination claims. They argue that the systemic offenses were so pervasive as to create an "oppressive work environment." Moreover, plaintiffs do not seek damages based on individual incidents of harassment, but instead seek class-wide injunctive, declaratory, and financial relief.

Compare Elkins v. American Showa, Inc., 219 F.R.D. 414 (S.D. Ohio 2002) (variations in the frequency and severity of harassment of female employees precluded a finding of commonality).

In Harris v. Forklift Systems, Inc., 510 U.S. 17 (1993), the Court held that a "reasonable person" standard should be used to determine whether sexual harassment has occurred, rather than making liability turn on whether a specific plaintiff suffered serious psychological injury as a result. Should this standard facilitate or impede class action treatment of such claims? In Brown v. Nucor Corp., 576 F.3d 149 (4th Cir. 2009), the court relied on Harris v. Forklift Systems, Inc., to hold that the district judge erred in failing to certify a class of African-American employees, concluding that "despite the formal classification of the plant into six production departments, the racist acts had plant-wide repercussions and affected all black employees." Id. at 157.

8.   Should similar reasoning apply to discrimination actions outside the employment field? Cases involving Rule 23(b)(3)'s "predominance" standard provide insights. In Jackson v. Motel 6 Multipurpose, Inc., 130 F.3d 999 (11th Cir. 1997), plaintiffs claimed that they were denied accommodations in Motel 6 motels, or provided substandard accommodations, due to defendant's policy and practice of racial discrimination at its 750 motels across the country. They sought both money damages and injunctive relief. Concluding that this was a (b)(3) action, the court relied on *Falcon* for the proposition that the alleged common question whether Motel 6 has a practice or policy of discrimination would not outweigh the individual questions:

> The *Jackson* plaintiffs' claims will require distinctly case-specific inquiries into the facts surrounding each alleged incident of discrimination. The issues that must be addressed include not only whether a particular plaintiff was denied a room or was rented a substandard room, but also whether there were any rooms vacant when that plaintiff inquired; whether the plaintiff had reservations; whether unclean rooms were rented to the plaintiff for reasons having nothing to do with the plaintiff's race; whether the plaintiff, at the time that he requested a room, exhibited any non-racial characteristics legitimately counseling renting him a room; and so on. * * * Indeed, we expect that most, if not all, of the plaintiffs' claims will stand or fall, not on the answer to the question whether Motel 6 has a practice or policy of racial discrimination, but on the resolution of these highly case-specific factual issues.

Id. at 1006. Would no amount of anecdotal evidence warrant a conclusion that non-white customers were victims of discrimination? Would limiting the suit to a request for an injunction make a difference? See also Rutstein v. Avis Rent-A-Car Systems, Inc., 211 F.3d 1228 (11th Cir. 2000), in which the court found that common questions were not satisfied in a suit alleging that Avis discriminated against customers thought to be Jewish in handling corporate accounts: "[T]he legitimate reasons why Avis might have judged an individual plaintiff to be 'unqualified' for a corporate account are far more various and individualized than in the employment context."

Contrast Klay v. Humana, Inc., 382 F.3d 1241 (11th Cir. 2004), upholding class certification under Rule 23(b)(3) in a suit charging HMOs with conspiring to underpay doctors. As the court put it, this was "a case of almost all doctors versus almost all major health maintenance organizations." It had begun as separate cases against Humana and additional separate cases against other HMOs. But the Judicial Panel on Multidistrict Litigation consolidated the Humana cases for pretrial preparation, and then added the suits against the other HMOs to that consolidated proceeding. After that combination by the Panel, plaintiffs filed an amended complaint against all the defendants on behalf of a class of all medical doctors who had treated patients of any of them.

Plaintiffs claimed that the HMOs had collaborated in "a decades-long nefarious conspiracy to undermine the American health care system," which the court labelled "a shadowy, mysterious 'Managed Case Enterprise.'" Id. at 1253. In particular, their goal was to curtail payments to doctors in violation of their promises of fair treatment. Plaintiffs claimed defendants thereby rendered themselves liable to the doctors under the Racketeer Influenced Corrupt Organizations statute (RICO). There was considerable diversity in the arrangements between doctors and HMOs. Some had contracts that provided a fee for services performed on a piecework basis, and others had contracts that paid for covered patients with less emphasis on services actually performed. Despite the variety of issues presented, the court distinguished its earlier rejection of discrimination class actions in Jackson v. Motel 6 and Rutstein v. Avis:

> *Motel 6* and *Rutstein* were both cases in which individuals were seeking to litigate separate discrimination claims that arose from a variety of individual incidents together in the same class action simply because they alleged that the acts of discrimination occurred pursuant to corporate policies. In the instant case, however, the plaintiffs' RICO claims are not simply individual allegations of underpayments lumped together, and the allegation of an official corporate policy or conspiracy is not simply a piece of circumstantial evidence being used to support such individual underpayment claims. Instead, the very gravamen of the RICO claims is the "pattern of racketeering activities" and the existence of a national conspiracy to underpay doctors. These are not facts from which jurors will be asked to infer the commission of wrongful acts against individual plaintiffs; these very facts constitute essential elements of each plaintiff's RICO claims.

4. ADEQUACY OF REPRESENTATION

PEIL V. NATIONAL SEMICONDUCTOR CORP.

United States District Court, Eastern District of Pennsylvania, 1980.
86 F.R.D. 357.

HANNUM, DISTRICT JUDGE.

[Plaintiff in this securities fraud suit bought 500 shares of National Semiconductor Corp. stock for $35.75 per share on Oct. 1, 1976, and sold them on Feb. 3, 1977 for $19.50 per share, a loss of $16.25 per share. He alleged that defendants (including officers of the company) misrepresented the financial health of the company to inflate the stock value while they sold their stock. He sought to represent a class of all who purchased the company's stock between July 1, 1976, and March 1, 1977.]

Adequate Representation. The fourth enumerated requirement of F.R.Civ.P. 23(a) provides that the "representative parties will fairly and adequately protect the interests of the class." In an effort to define this somewhat vague standard for representation, the Third Circuit has adopted the following rule to which a plaintiff must demonstrate his compliance:

> (1) they have no interests which are antagonistic to other members of the class, and (2) their attorney is capable of prosecuting the instant claim with some degree of expertise.

Wetzel v. Liberty Mutual Insurance Co., 508 F.2d 239, 247 (3d Cir. 1975).

The defendants apparently recognize the applicability of the rule articulated in *Wetzel* but offer a third requirement for adoption; that the plaintiff have first-hand knowledge of the facts giving rise to the cause of action. Essentially, the defendants contend that the plaintiff's counsel, Richard D. Greenfield, Esquire, is the real party in interest but for his lack of standing because he has unearthed the facts and unraveled the complexities attendant to their application to the securities laws. Reliance for this advancement is upon the decision rendered in *In re Goldchip Funding Co.*, 61 F.R.D. 592, 594–95 (M.D.Pa. 1974):

> In my view, facts regarding the personal qualities of the representatives themselves are relevant, indeed necessary, in determining whether "the representative parties will fairly and adequately protect the interests of the class." ... A proper representative can offer more to the prosecution of a class action than mere fulfillment of the procedural requirements of Rule 23. He can, for example, offer his personal knowledge of the factual circumstances, and aid in rendering decisions on practical and nonlegal problems which arise during the course of litigation. An attorney who prosecutes a class action with unfettered discretion becomes, in fact, a representative of the class. This is an unacceptable situation because of the possible conflicts of interest involved.

The *Wetzel* rule, as it presently obtains, implicitly recognizes that a class representative need not be the best of all possible representatives but rather one that will pursue a resolution of the controversy with the requisite vigor and in the interest of the class. What is "requisite" is determined by considering the nature of the litigation and the factual and legal basis underlying it; necessarily a case-by-case analysis. To require a person unschooled in the realm of our complex and abstract securities laws to have first-hand knowledge of facts cloaked in an alleged conspiratorial silence and which present themselves as a wrongdoing that may be actionable would render the class action device an impotent tool. In order to responsibly allege and later adequately prove the accusations contained in the plaintiff's Complaint, the plaintiff's counsel must have engaged in and will engage in extensive investigation and discovery conducted with a working knowledge of the securities laws.

The Court is cognizant of the fact that by it not requiring the class representative to have the degree of first-hand knowledge of the factual basis of this litigation suggested by the defendants, counsel may proceed without various restraints. The Court in *In re Goldchip Funding Co., supra,* expressed a similar concern in its ruling to the effect that such unbridled discretion of counsel may render him a class representative rather than its counsel, thereby creating a conflict of interest. The Court is unmoved by this assertion. Aside from the normal degree of flexibility enjoyed by counsel when presenting a client's case, the Court may intervene, if appropriate, pursuant to its inherent power to protect the class members. Moreover, much influence and control is exercised by the Court by the fact that it controls the fee award to the plaintiff's counsel should the plaintiff prevail. In essence, the Court recognizes the existence of its inherent powers to control the actions of the plaintiff's counsel in the event that a conflict of interest appears. Otherwise, counsel for both parties may exercise the discretion they deserve and enjoy when presenting their respective clients' positions.

Ruling in accordance with the numerous cases that expressly reject the *In re Goldchip Funding Co., supra,* precedent and declining to adopt the defendant's proposed third requirements to the *Wetzel* rule, the Court turns to the two existing requirements: (1) the representative has no antagonistic interests and (2) his counsel has the requisite expertise to prosecute the action. It is not disputed that the plaintiff carries no interest that could conceivably be considered antagonistic to the common interests of the class he seeks to represent. Accordingly, the Court deems this requirement satisfied. In addition, the second requirement is not contested and is therefore deemed satisfied. The plaintiff's counsel's ability to prosecute similar actions with a sufficient degree of expertise has been noted on at least one prior occasion. The Court is of the opinion, and so rules, that the plaintiff is an adequate class representative pursuant to the requirements of F.R.Civ.P. 23(a)(4).

RODRIGUEZ V. WEST PUBLISHING CORP.

United States Court of Appeals, Ninth Circuit, 2009.
563 F.3d 948.

Before O'SCANNLAIN, RYMER and WARDLAW, CIRCUIT JUDGES.

RYMER, CIRCUIT JUDGE.

[Plaintiffs, recent law school graduates who each purchased a BAR/BRI bar-preparation course between 1997 and 2006, filed a class action claiming that West (which purchased BAR/BRI in 2001) and Kaplan, Inc., violated the antitrust laws by entering into an agreement in 1997 to limit competition in providing bar-preparation services. This alleged agreement initially led Kaplan not to enter the bar-preparation field, which West supposedly monopolized by acquiring BAR/BRI. Among the practices targeted was West's offering first-year students a non-refundable option for BAR/BRI's course, offering free access to Westlaw to students who enrolled in the course, and advertising BAR/BRI programs constantly on Westlaw. The suit initially sought up to $1,000 for each of the estimated 300,000 class members, plus injunctive relief.

The district court certified a class consisting of all who purchased a bar review course from BAR/BRI from August 1997 until the present, and class members were notified they could opt out of the class by August, 2006. Negotiations thereafter led to a settlement agreement under which West and Kaplan agreed to create a $49 million settlement fund from which class members could recover up to 30% of what they paid for BAR/BRI courses. Defendants also agreed to change the way they did business, including stating on the form used to enroll law students that the initial payment to enroll is not a commitment to full payment. The class members were given notice of the proposed settlement as required by Rule 23(e). The notice informed the class that class counsel intended to apply to the court for incentive awards of $25,000 to four of the class representatives, and of $75,000 for three others.

Only later was it revealed that the retainer agreements between five of these class representatives and class counsel had included commitments by class counsel to apply for incentive awards according to a schedule: If the amount of a settlement were $500,000 or greater, counsel would seek an award of $10,000; if it were $1.5 million or more, counsel would seek a $25,000 award, and if it were $10 million or more, counsel would seek $75,000. Even though the $49 million settlement entitled them to $75,000 awards, two of the five class representatives who had obtained such commitments agreed to lower their requests to $25,000. Two other class representatives had no advance agreement regarding incentive awards, but counsel requested $25,000 awards for them also. A number of class members objected to the settlement, and in particular to the incentive award agreements, and appealed when the district court approved the settlement.]

Incentive awards are fairly typical in class action cases. See Theodore Eisenberg & Geoffrey P. Miller, Incentive Awards to Class Action Plaintiffs: An Empirical Study, 53 U.C.L.A. L.Rev. 1303 (2006) (finding twenty-eight percent of settled class actions between 1993 and 2002 included an incentive award to class representatives). Such awards are discretionary, and are intended to compensate class representatives for work done on behalf of the class, to make up for financial or reputational risk undertaken in bringing the action, and, sometimes, to recognize their willingness to act as a private attorney general. Awards are generally sought after a settlement or verdict has been achieved.

The incentive agreements entered into as part of the initial retention of counsel in this case, however, are quite different. Although they only bound counsel to apply for an award, thus leaving the decision whether actually to make one to the district judge, these agreements tied the promised request to the ultimate recovery and in so doing, put class counsel and the contracting class representatives into a conflict position from day one.

The arrangement was not disclosed when it should have been and where it was plainly relevant, at the class certification stage. Had it been, the district court would certainly have considered its effect in determining whether the conflicted plaintiffs * * * could adequately represent the class. The conflict might have been waived, or otherwise contained, but the point is that uncovering conflicts of interest between the named parties and the class they seek to represent is a critical purpose of the adequacy inquiry. * * * An absence of material conflicts of interest between the named plaintiffs and their counsel with other class members is central to adequacy and, in turn, to due process for absent members of the class.

In fact, the incentive agreements came to the fore when Objectors pounced on them in opposing class counsel's motion for incentive awards to the class representatives. This happened after preliminary approval of the settlement. In that context the district court held that the agreements were inappropriate and contrary to public policy for a number of reasons: they obligate class counsel to request an arbitrary award not reflective of the amount of work done, or the risks undertaken, or the time spent on the litigation; they create at least the appearance of impropriety; they violate the California Rules of Professional Conduct prohibiting fee-sharing with clients and among lawyers; and they encourage figurehead cases and bounty payments by potential class counsel. The court found it particularly problematic that the incentive agreements correlated the incentive request solely to the settlement or litigated recovery, as the effect was to make the contracting class representatives' interests actually different from the class's interests in settling a case instead of trying it to verdict, seeking injunctive relief, and insisting on compensation greater than $10 million. It further observed that the parties' failure to disclose their agreement to the court, and to the class, violated the contracting representatives' fiduciary duties to the class and duty of candor to the court.

We agree. By tying their compensation—in advance—to a sliding scale based on the amount recovered, the incentive agreements disjoined the contingency financial interests of the contracting representatives from the class. As the district court observed, once the threshold cash settlement was met, the agreements created a disincentive to go to trial; going to trial would put their $75,000 at risk in return for only a marginal individual gain even if the verdict were significantly greater than the settlement. The agreements also gave the contracting representatives an interest in a monetary settlement, as distinguished from other remedies, that set them apart from other members of the class. Further, agreements of this sort infect the class action environment with the troubling appearance of shopping plaintiffships. If allowed, ex ante incentive agreements could tempt potential plaintiffs to sell their lawsuits to attorneys who are the highest bidders, and vice-versa. * * *

In sum, we disapprove of the incentive agreements entered into between the named plaintiffs and class counsel in this case. They created an unacceptable disconnect between the interests of the contracting representatives and class counsel, on the one hand, and members of the class on the other. We expect those interests to be congruent. They also gave rise to a disturbing appearance of impropriety. And failing to disclose the incentive arrangements in connection with class certification compounded these problems by depriving the court, and the class, of the safeguard of informed judicial consideration of the adequacy of class representation.

[The court nonetheless held that the fact two class representatives had no incentive agreement permitted affirmance of settlement approval because it is not necessary that all class representatives satisfy Rule 23(a)(4).]

NOTES AND QUESTIONS

1.   The court in *Peil* notes that under Rule 23(a)(4) the class representative "need not be the best of all possible representatives." Given the constitutional concerns identified in *Hansberry*, should the courts insist on selecting the best person? Is judicial control of the lawyer's fee a sufficient surrogate for oversight by a knowledgeable class representative? Despite this concern, *Peil* states the usual interpretation of Rule 23(a)(4).

2.   Should courts be concerned with the personal characteristics, such as education level and honesty exhibited by proposed class representatives? At least some blemishes have led courts to reject proposed representatives. See, e.g., In re Sonus Networks, Inc., Securities Litigation, 229 F.R.D. 339 (D.Mass. 2005) (sole class representative withdrew after it was revealed that he had been convicted of selling cocaine and resisting arrest). But personal characteristics cannot absolutely disqualify proposed class representatives in some cases. Thus, in a suit claiming overcharges for writing bad checks, defendants urged that the proposed class representative should be rejected for "lack of honesty" because she had written a bad check. Noting that only people who have written bad checks could be in the class, the judge found that "a class action would be impossible if the Court were to condemn class representatives on the basis that they wrote bad checks." del Campo v. American Corrective Counseling Serv., Inc., 254 F.R.D. 585, 594 (N.D.Cal. 2008). See also Mississippi Protection & Advocacy System, Inc. v. Cotten, 929 F.2d 1054 (5th Cir. 1991) (in suit on behalf of occupants of state institution for developmentally disabled, such disability was not a bar to serving a class representative; "as a result of the developmental disability which requires their treatment, no patient at the Center is likely to be capable of representing

himself in this or any court"); Streeter v. Sheriff of Cook County, 256 F.R.D. 609 (N.D.Ill. 2009) (in action challenging jail conditions, "if convicted felons could not serve as class representatives, there would be no such thing as a class action in the prison or jail context"); see also CE Design Ltd. v. King Architectural Metals, Inc., 647 F.3d 721, 728 (7th Cir. 2011) ("We don't want to be misunderstood, however, as extending an invitation to defendants to try to derail legitimate class actions by conjuring up trivial credibility problems").

3.   Would it make more sense to focus on the level of commitment the class representative has to supervising the lawyer? In Scott v. New York City Carpenters Pension Plan, 224 F.R.D. 353 (S.D.N.Y. 2004), the judge held that proposed class representatives were not adequate (id. at 356):

> Both Scott and Spillers' alarming lack of familiarity with the suit, as well as little or nonexistent knowledge of their role as class representatives is manifest. Scott at his deposition stated that he did not know what allegations were contained in the complaint. He had not seen the complaint prior to his deposition [seventeen months after suit was filed]. He did not know for sure whether this was a class action suit. He did [not] know what a class representative was (or even that he was one). He had "not the slightest idea" of how many people are in the class. He had personally met with counsel only once in the three years prior to the deposition. * * * So complete is Scott's abdication of his role to his attorney that Scott stated that he would leave every decision up to his attorney and never question his advice.

See also Unger v. Amedisys Inc., 401 F.3d 316, 321 (5th Cir. 2005) (asserting that "class representatives must satisfy the court that they, and not counsel, are directing the litigation").

Perhaps law school graduates like the class representatives in *Rodriguez* are competent to supervise counsel, but how many others would be? Courts do not expect class representatives to have attended law school. See In re Nature's Sunshine Product's Inc. Securities Litig., 251 F.R.D. 656 (D. Utah 2008), in which the court rejected arguments that foreign class representatives for whom English was not their first language were inadequate for that reason and also found the record sufficient to show that they were adequate:

> In his deposition, Plaintiff Loh states that: he had a lot of communication with his counsel concerning the preparation of the complaint; he reviewed a draft of the complaint; and he reviewed a draft of the complaint before it was filed. Plaintiff Loh has: reviewed documents given to counsel; provided documents to counsel; and met with counsel prior to his deposition. Loh communicates regularly with counsel and communicates with counsel much more now that the case is in its discovery stage. Plaintiff Loh also indicated that he conducted various research before deciding to invest in Nature. Additionally, Plaintiff Loh's deposition makes clear that he understands his duties as a class representative and he understands the underlying allegations.

On this score, recall what activities of the class representatives justify an incentive award, and why the Ninth Circuit in *Rodriguez* said that the initial agreements about such awards were improper there.

4. *The PSLRA and the "empowered plaintiff" model*: In Elliott Weiss & John Beckerman, Let the Money Do the Monitoring: How Institutional Investors Can Reduce Agency Costs in Securities Class Actions, 104 Yale L.J. 2053 (1995), the authors argued that the existing practices—particularly rewarding the lawyer who files suit first with an appointment as lead counsel—tended to promote participation of "figurehead plaintiffs" and deter involvement of institutional investors who might be more effective in monitoring counsel.

Congress found this argument persuasive, and the Private Securities Litigation Reform Act accordingly directs the initial plaintiff in securities fraud actions to provide detailed notice about the claims to other investors, inviting them to express an interest in serving as "lead plaintiff." Thereafter, the court is to appoint as lead plaintiff the person "most capable of adequately representing the interests of class members." 15 U.S.C. § 78u–4(a)(3)(B)(i). In evaluating contenders for this position, the court should presume that "the person or group of persons . . . that has the largest financial interest in the relief sought by the class" is best qualified, although this presumption can be rebutted. Id., § 78u–4(a)(3)(B)(iii). The lead plaintiff then chooses the class counsel, who can be somebody other than the lawyer who filed the suit. In essence, the legislation empowers the lead plaintiff to choose the lawyer, somewhat supplanting the court's authority to appoint class counsel (discussed in Chapter 6, *infra* p. 436 n.6), and putting the lead plaintiff in a stronger position vis-a-vis class counsel than the ordinary class representative.

Although the PSLRA does direct that such appointments be done under the standards of Rule 23, it has been held that the presumption that the one with the largest losses should be preferred did not permit the district judge to favor somebody else on the ground that the judge thought the other potential representative would do a better job. In re Cavanaugh, 306 F.3d 726, 732 (9th Cir. 2002): "So long as the plaintiff with the largest losses satisfies the typicality and adequacy requirements, he is entitled to lead plaintiff status, even if the district court is convinced that some other plaintiff would do a better job." This requirement can mean that the court must make close calls about who has the largest losses. See Atansio v. Tenaris, S.A., 331 F.R.D. 21 (E.D.N.Y. 2019) (although institutional investor had purchased more shares and spent more money for them, individual investor had incurred a loss that was almost 33% higher); In re Advanced Tissue Sciences Securities Litigation, 184 F.R.D. 346 (S.D.Cal. 1998) (holding that the nod should go to a group with losses of $3,281,173 rather than another group with losses of $3,096,682).

Should Rule 23(a)(4) be changed or interpreted to require selection of the "best" representative? How would courts identify that person? Professor Fisch has urged that something like the PSLRA approach could work outside the securities fraud area, but only when three criteria have been satisfied: (1) the class includes members with a sufficient financial stake to make the effort to do a careful job selecting and monitoring class counsel; (2) the lead plaintiffs must be representative of the interests of class members; and (3) the size of class members' interest must correlate with sophistication in selecting and monitoring class counsel (as with institutional investors in securities fraud suits). Jill Fisch, Lawyers on the Auction Block: Evaluating the Selection of Class Counsel by Auction, 102 Colum. L. Rev. 649, 722 (2002). She suggests that these conditions may exist in shareholder derivative actions, but not in consumer class actions or mass tort suits, because in those cases there may not be a sufficient financial stake, or having the largest potential recovery (as for personal injuries in a mass tort case) does not suggest sophistication in hiring and supervising counsel.

5.   Nonetheless, the class representative should not be too closely identified with the lawyer. See London v. Wal-Mart Stores, Inc., 340 F.3d 1246 (11th Cir. 2003), a Truth In Lending Act action in which the class representative was a lifelong friend and former stock broker of class counsel. The court held that the longstanding relationship, coupled with the possibility that counsel might again retain the proposed class representative as his stock broker, created an undue potential conflict of interest in this case to favor the lawyer's interests over those of the class. See also Malchman v. Davis, 706 F.2d 426, 432 (2d Cir. 1983) (class representative is sister of chauffeur of class counsel); Wexler v. AT&T Corp., 323 F.R.D. 128 (E.D.N.Y. 2018) (class representative's marriage to former class counsel made her an inadequate class representative).

6.   If there is reason for concern about class representatives who are lambs led to the slaughter, is there also a concern with wolves who seek to exploit their status as class representatives? One view of the agreements sought by the class representatives in *Rodriguez* is that they exhibited just the sort of independence of class counsel that one would want from an "empowered" class representative. Does it appear that the arrangement they reached impaired their activities on behalf of the class? If it is important that they would receive no greater increase in incentive award for any settlements above $10 million, should it matter that the eventual settlement was for $49 million? Presumably that increase did create the possibility they would recover more on their claims as ordinary class members, but that increase seems paltry compared to the $50,000 they would garner (over what they would get for a $1.5 million settlement) were the settlement to be over $10 million. Note also that defendants agreed in the settlement to change their practices in the future. By definition, that could not benefit these class representatives, who have already graduated from law school, and there was no provision in the agreement for their fees to increase depending on such nonmonetary relief. Compare Radcliffe v. Hernandez, 818 F.3d 537 (9th Cir. 2016) (provision in attorney-client agreements required class representatives to support a proposed settlement in order to obtain their incentive awards).

In Rodriguez v. Disner, 688 F.3d 645 (9th Cir. 2012), a later decision in the same case, the court upheld denial of any fee award to the law firm appointed class counsel because "its representation of conflicting interests constituted an ethical violation." Then, in Radcliffe v. Experian Information Solutions, Inc., 705 F.3d 1157 (9th Cir. 2013), a class action under the Fair Credit Reporting Act, the settlement provided payments to class members of up to $750 depending on the nature of the harm shown, but the class representatives got incentive awards of $5,000, providing that they supported the settlement proposal. The court found the "disproportionately large payments" to "corrupt this settlement by undermining the adequacy of class representatives and class counsel." If the maximum class member recovery is $750, how much is disproportionate? If it were shown that the class representatives devoted a large amount of time and talent to overseeing the case, should that matter? Is conditioning incentive payments on supporting the settlement the real problem, rather than the amount?

In Johnson v. NPAS Solutions, LLC, 975 F.3d 1244 (11th Cir. 2020), the majority of a court of appeals panel held that an incentive award for a class representative is akin to a salary or a bounty, and forbidden by 19th century Supreme Court precedents. A dissenting judge emphasized that many courts had "recognized that incentive awards serve the purposes of Rule 23." See also Somogyi v. Freedom Mortg. Corp., ___ F.Supp.3d ___, 2020 WL 6146875 (D.N.J. Oct. 20, 2020) ("Until and unless the Supreme Court or the Third Circuit bans incentive awards or payments to class plaintiffs, they will be approved by this Court if appropriate under the circumstances").

7.   Perhaps we should favor "professional" class representatives. See Murray v. GMAC Mortg. Corp., 434 F.3d 948 (7th Cir. 2006), overturning a district court denial of class certification because the named plaintiff, her husband, and their children were participants in more than fifty suits asserting technical violations of the Fair Credit Reporting Act. Judge Easterbrook found this an unpersuasive reason for denying certification: "What the district judge did not explain, though, is why 'professional' is a dirty word. It implies experience, if not expertise." Id. at 954. But in securities fraud cases, courts have looked with particular skepticism on "professional plaintiffs." See In re Gibson Greetings Securities Litigation, 159 F.R.D. 499, 501 (S.D.Ohio 1994) (plaintiff who had filed 182 class actions was a "professional class action plaintiff" who would not adequately represent the class). The Private Securities Litigation Reform Act implements this concern in securities fraud class actions by directing that ordinarily no person should be allowed to be class representative in more than five such class actions at once. 15 U.S.C. §§ 77z–1(a)(3)(B)(vi); 78u–4(a)(3)(B)(vi).

8.   Another measure might be to do away with class representatives altogether. See Jonathan Macey & Geoffrey Miller, The Plaintiffs' Attorney's Role in Class Action and Derivative Litigation: Economic Analysis and Recommendations for Reform, 58 U.Chi.L.Rev. 1, 93–94 (1991) ("Because the named plaintiff is a figurehead, the adequacy of representation would not be harmed if plaintiffs' attorneys could file 'Jane Doe' or 'Richard Roe' complaints on behalf of fictitious absent class member without supplying an actual carcass for grilling over the hot coals of a deposition."); Jean Burns, Decorative

Figureheads: Eliminating Class Representatives in Class Actions, 42 Hastings L.J. 165 (1990).

9.   Putting aside personal failings of the representative, there may be actual conflicts in interest between the representative and some or all of the members of the class. Courts must be careful about concluding too quickly that a real conflict exists. See Robertson v. National Basketball Association, 389 F.Supp. 867 (S.D.N.Y. 1975) ("Class action determination will not be denied, nor will the formulation of subclasses be required in the absence of a showing that the alleged potential conflicts are real probabilities and not mere imaginative speculation.").

10.   Defendants also like to focus on the ability of the class representative to finance the litigation. In general, the courts have limited the inquiry into such matters. See Note, Discovery of Plaintiff's Financial Situation in Federal Class Actions: Heading 'Em Off at the Passbook, 30 Hast.L.J. 449 (1978). In Rand v. Monsanto Co., 926 F.2d 596 (7th Cir. 1991), in which the named plaintiff testified in his deposition that, given his maximum potential recovery of $1,135, he would not agree to be liable for costs up to $25,000. The district court denied class certification on this ground, but the court of appeals reversed in an opinion by Judge Easterbrook: "A conscientious plaintiff is likely to be willing to make some financial commitment to the case. But no person need be willing to stake his entire fortune for the benefit of strangers. Class lawsuits can be frightfully expensive * * *. No (sane) person would pay the entire costs of a securities class action in exchange for a maximum benefit of $1,135. None would put up $25,000 or even $2,500 against a hope of recovering $1,135." Id. at 599.

11.   If the proposed class representative is found wanting, what should the court do if the case otherwise may be suitable for class-action treatment? Consider Johnson v. American Credit Co., 581 F.2d 526, 533 n. 13 (5th Cir. 1978):

> When faced with a situation when no named plaintiff can represent a subclass, a trial court should consider whether it is in the interests of justice and judicial economy to postpone dismissal as to the subclass for a specified period in which members of the subclass could become plaintiffs by amendment of the complaint and thereby save the subclass action.

See also Birmingham Steel Corp. v. Tennessee Valley Auth., 353 F.3d 1331 (11th Cir. 2003) (requiring the court to allow class counsel a reasonable time to locate a substitute class representative if the first one is found inadequate). But in In re Williams-Sonoma, Inc., 947 F.3d 535 (9th Cir. 2020), a divided panel of the court overturned an order permitting plaintiff counsel to use discovery to locate a new class representative.

D. TYPES OF CLASS ACTIONS MAINTAINABLE

Class actions that satisfy Rule 23(a) must also meet the requirements of one of the various kinds of class actions described in Rule 23(b)(1),

23(b)(2), and 23(b)(3). Even if Rule 23(a) is fully satisfied, a court should certify only if a case satisfies Rule 23(b). We turn to application of those standards now. This section considers those types of class actions, as well as "issue classes" under Rule 23(c)(4) and defendant classes.

1. RULE 23(b)(1) CLASS ACTIONS

Rule 23(b)(1) authorizes certification of a "mandatory" class action (no opting out permitted) in situations that resemble those covered by Rule 19, which was addressed in Chapter 2. Rule 23(b)(1) class actions have been approached either as "limited fund" situations, or in terms of the risk of "incompatible standards" for the party opposing the class. Since Rule 23 was amended in 1966, these class actions have not been as important as class actions brought pursuant to Rules 23(b)(2) or (b)(3).

"Limited Fund" Class Actions

Rule 23(b)(1)(B) addresses situations in which adjudication as to some class members, "as a practical matter, would be dispositive of the interest of other [class] members." One of the possible occasions for certification under this rule was identified in the Committee Note accompanying the 1966 amendment as involving "claims made by numerous persons against a fund insufficient to satisfy all claims."

In Ortiz v. Fibreboard Corp., 527 U.S. 815 (1999), the Supreme Court confronted Rule 23(b)(1) class certification of a settlement class in an action that resulted from what it called "the elephantine mass of asbestos cases." In this litigation, Fibreboard faced massive litigation by asbestos personal injury plaintiffs but had a limited net worth. It seemed that Fibreboard's primary asset to fund payments to claimants must come from liability insurance policies it had for the years 1957–59, which seemed to have no aggregate limits on the insurers' liability for covered events. The insurers denied coverage, but a California trial court in 1990 found for Fibreboard, raising the possibility the insurers would have to cover all claims based on exposure during the time the policies were in effect. The insurers appealed, and there were strong indications that they would succeed in getting the liability ruling reversed, which would make the insurers' coverage unavailable to all the claimants.

Settlement negotiations ensued as the date for the appellate hearing in the California courts drew near. The insurers insisted on "total peace," and the device to provide that was a mandatory Rule 23(b)(1)(B) class action on behalf of all potential claimants who had not yet sued, binding them to make claims only against a $1.535 billion fund that the insurers would create as part of the settlement. Fibreboard, meanwhile, had a net worth estimated at $235 million and would be obligated to contribute only $10 million to the fund, 95% of which would come from other insurance proceeds.

The district court certified the settlement class under Rule 23(b)(1), finding that the insurance coverage plus Fibreboard's other assets constituted a "limited fund" that could be depleted by separate litigation by class members, leaving some empty-handed. In Amchem Products, Inc. v. Windsor, *infra* p. 311 we will examine the special challenges of certification only for settlement; this section addresses the handling of "limited fund" certification.

The Supreme Court held that although the rule was "on its face open to a more lenient limited fund concept," the drafting history of the 1966 amendments showed that Rule 23(b)(1)(B) should be limited by cases analogous to the old cases that had formed the "pedigree of the limited fund class action." The Court held that this provision was "consciously retrospective," compared to the framers' consciously aggressive addition of Rule 23(b)(3). Accordingly, it announced the following standard for certification under Rule 23(b)(1)(B):

> The first and most distinctive characteristic is that the totals of the aggregated liquidated claims and the fund available for satisfying them, set definitely at their maximums, demonstrate the inadequacy of the fund to pay all the claims. The concept driving this type of suit was insufficiency, which alone justified the limit on an early feast to avoid a later famine. The equity of the limitation is its necessity.

> Second, the whole of the inadequate fund was to be devoted to the overwhelming claims. It went without saying that the defendant or estate or constructive trustee with the inadequate assets had no opportunity to benefit himself or claimants of lower priority by holding back on the amount distributed to the class. The limited fund cases thus ensured that the class as a whole was given the best deal; they did not give a defendant a better deal than seriatim litigation would have produced.

> Third, the claimants identified by a common theory of recovery were treated equitably among themselves. The cases assume that the class will comprise everyone who might state a claim on a single or repeated set of facts, invoking a common theory of recovery, to be satisfied from the limited fund as the source of payment. * * * Once all similar claims were brought directly or by representation before the court, these antecedents of the mandatory class action presented straightforward models of equitable treatment, with the simple equity of a pro rata distribution providing the required fairness.

The Court concluded that the case before it did not satisfy these criteria. The limits of the fund had been set by the parties' agreement, not an independent finding by the court. This criterion might have been satisfied if it were established that open-ended liability would render the insurers insolvent, but that was not shown. The fact that Fibreboard did not commit all its assets to the settlement fund further showed that the whole fund was not devoted to satisfying plaintiffs' claims. Indeed, after the settlement was approved by the district court Fibreboard was acquired for $515 million, plus assumption of $85 million of its debts, suggesting an actual value closer to $600 million than the $235 million presented to the district court. As the Court observed, "Fibreboard was allowed to retain virtually all its net worth." And the settlement excluded from the class a large number of other personal injury claimants who had settled with Fibreboard but reserved the right to sue it in the future under some circumstances; "there can be no question that such a mandatory settlement class will not qualify when . . . class counsel agree to exclude what may turn out to be as much as a third of the claimants."

Justice Breyer (joined by Justice Stevens) dissented:

> There is no doubt in this case that the settlement made far more money available to satisfy asbestos claims than was likely to occur in its absence. And the District Court found that administering the fund would involve transaction costs of only 15%. A comparison of that 15% figure with the 61% transaction costs figure applicable to asbestos cases in general suggests hundreds of millions of dollars in savings—an amount greater than Fibreboard's net worth. And, of course, not only is it better for the injured plaintiffs, it is far better for Fibreboard, its employees, its creditors, and the communities where it is located for Fibreboard to remain a working enterprise, rather than slowly forcing it into bankruptcy while most of its money is spent on asbestos lawyers and expert witnesses. I would consequently find substantial compliance with the majority's third condition.

NOTES AND QUESTIONS

1.   For an historical analysis of the binding effect of early analogues to modern class actions, see Geoffrey Hazard, John Gedid & Stephen Sowle, An Historical Analysis of the Binding Effect of Class Suits, 146 U. Pa. L. Rev. 1849 (1998), cited by the Court in *Ortiz*. For a challenge to using Rule 23(b)(1)(B) in mass tort class actions, consider Richard Marcus, They Can't Do That, Can They? Tort Reform Via Rule 23, 80 Cornell L. Rev. 858, 880–81 (1995) (also cited by the Court in *Ortiz*):

> Rule 23(b)(1)(B) simply does not prescribe any standards for resolving competing claims to the limited fund, if one is found to exist. One animating objective for the class certifications in mass tort cases has been to subordinate punitive damages claims to compensatory damages claims. In some circumstances, the Bankruptcy Act may authorize a court to do this, but Rule 23 provides no similar warrant for doing so. * * * Moreover, the Bankruptcy Act affords some protections for the claimants affected by the cram-down, protections

that may not be replicated in the judge-fashioned alternative confected under Rule 23. At both a substantive and procedural level, then, the contrast between the Bankruptcy Act and the class action authorization provided in Rule 23(b)(1)(B) suggests the impropriety of aggressive use of the class action rule.

2. After *Ortiz* was decided, the court in In re Telectronics Pacing Systems, Inc., 221 F.3d 870 (6th Cir. 2000), invalidated a limited fund settlement class action in a mass tort litigation. The district court had relied in part on the prospect that plaintiffs' claims might lose. The appellate court stressed that the ability to prevail on the merits is different from the ability of a defendant to pay a judgment. And one must be restrained in finding an inability to pay on the ground that the potential liability is large (id. at 880):

> Presumably *all* companies have limited funds at some point—there is always the possibility that a large mass tort action or other litigation will put a company into bankruptcy. Should that eventuality threaten, we have a comprehensive bankruptcy scheme in this country for just such an occurrence. Simply demonstrating that there is a possibility, even a likelihood, that bankruptcy might at some point occur cannot be the basis for finding that there is a "limited fund" in an ongoing corporate concern. The district court cannot discharge the debt in advance of the occurrence, thereby usurping the bankruptcy scheme through settlement, even if it believes such an avenue to be in the best interests of most of the plaintiffs.

3. Sometimes there is a legal limit on the amount recoverable, and that may be considered in determining the assets available. For example, the Price-Anderson Act, a 1954 statute, limits total damages for certain accidents involving nuclear energy to $560 million. See 42 U.S.C. § 2210. That is a large amount, but it could certainly happen that an American "Chernobyl" would produce claims exceeding it. Indeed, that prospect must lie behind the enactment of the statute. See also 49 U.S.C. § 28103 (limiting passenger recoveries for a rail accident to a total of $200 million); In re Black Farmers Discrimination Litigation, 856 F.Supp.2d 1 (D.D.C. 2011) (noting that federal government may define the extent of its liability and thereby establish a limited fund).

Contractual limitations may also place a cap on the amount recoverable. Cf. State Farm Fire & Cas. Co. v. Tashire, 386 U.S. 523 (1967) (automobile liability insurance policy limiting coverage to $20,000 per occurrence justified interpleader of all claimants when insured's car was involved in accident with Greyhound bus). Compare the insurance coverage dispute in *Ortiz*.

4. Another recurrent stimulus for Rule 23(b)(1)(B) arguments in mass tort litigation is the prospect of punitive damages. In 1967, Judge Friendly posited that state law must place some limit on repetitive punitive damage verdicts for the same behavior, but assuming there are such limits they

probably will vary from state to state, making consideration of this factor difficult in multistate class actions.

Federal constitutional limitations on punitive damages awards would be uniform, however, opening the possibility of a limited fund analysis. But in Philip Morris USA v. Williams, 549 U.S. 346 (2007), the Court held that "the Constitution's Due Process Clause forbids a State to use a punitive damages award to punish a defendant for injury that it inflicts upon nonparties or those whom they directly represent, i.e., injury that it inflicts upon those who are essentially strangers to the litigation." Earlier, in State Farm Mut. Auto Ins. Co. v. Campbell, 538 U.S. 408 (2003), the Court had insisted that due process forbids consideration of defendant's actions regarding others in assessing punitive damages for the plaintiff before the court. Given these limitations, it would be difficult to show that later plaintiffs would be foreclosed from seeking punitive damages on the ground that defendant had already been "punished" for what it did to them by a punitive damages award in an action brought by another plaintiff, a central feature of efforts to justify limited fund treatment in punitive damages cases. See In re Simon II Litigation, 407 F.3d 125 (2d Cir. 2005), in which the court overturned certification of a nationwide punitive damages class in tobacco litigation seeking a single punitive award for the defendants' campaign to conceal the hazards of smoking. There was no way, the court held, to find that the award in a given smoker's case would bear a sufficient nexus to the harm suffered by others to justify the conclusion such an award would preclude later punitive damages awards to other plaintiffs. For evaluation of the prospects for certification on punitive damages grounds, see Elizabeth Cabraser & Robert Nelson, Class Action Treatment of Punitive Damages After Philip Morris v. Williams: We Can Get There From Here, 2 Charleston L. Rev. 407 (2008).

5.   The bankruptcy system already exists to deal with problems of this sort. Does it provide advantages over Rule 23(b)(1)(B) in situations that might fit the "limited fund" scenario? A National Commission thought so. See National Bankruptcy Review Commission: The Next Twenty Years 318–19 (1997) (citing the assurance of equality in distribution for similar creditors and preserving the going value of the concern). Judge Edith Jones, a member of the Commission who dissented from its report, objected to the lack of due process afforded in authorizing bankruptcy courts to resolve such future claims. Edith Jones, Rough Justice in Mass Future Claims: Should Bankruptcy Courts Direct Tort Reform?, 76 Texas L. Rev. 1695 (1998).

Professor Gibson, an expert in both civil procedure and bankruptcy, made a detailed comparison of pre-*Ortiz* limited fund mass tort class actions and bankruptcy reorganizations involving mass tort claimants for the Federal Judicial Center, and concluded that, though it sometimes is very deliberate and expensive, the bankruptcy system provides better protections for claimants and more equitable outcomes. See Elizabeth Gibson, Case Studies of Mass Tort Limited Fund Settlements and Bankruptcy Reorganizations (2000).

"Incompatible Standards" Class Actions

Rule 23(b)(1)(A) allows a class to be certified when "prosecuting separate actions by or against individual members of the class would create a risk of inconsistent or varying adjudications with respect to individual class members that would establish incompatible standards of conduct for the party opposing the class." This test looks to the impact on the party opposing the class and whether separate actions would subject it to incompatible standards. Notice the similarity to the test in Rule 19(a)(1)(B)(ii) for a required party. Recall Eldredge v. Carpenters 46 Northern California Counties JATC, *supra* p. 38. Owing to concerns like those under Rule 19, such class actions are "mandatory" in the sense that individual class members are ordinarily not allowed to opt out and file separate suits.

Paradigm cases under Rule 23(b)(1)(A) are suits by taxpayers to invalidate municipal action or suits by shareholders to compel the declaration of a dividend. A typical case is Van Gemert v. Boeing Co., 259 F.Supp. 125 (S.D.N.Y. 1966), where a class action of debenture holders against the corporation was certified because it sought to determine their right of conversion into common stock. If the corporation had been faced with individual suits by each debenture holder, the outcomes could have been different and it would have been subjected to incompatible standards as to its future conduct.

Where money damages are central to a case, courts have often refused to certify an "incompatible standards" class. A good example of this position is found in Alexander Grant & Co. v. McAlister, 116 F.R.D. 583 (S.D.Ohio 1987), which refused to certify an "incompatible standards" class on behalf of some 300 partners of the plaintiff company for purposes of defendant Harris' counterclaim:

> Harris argues that certification under Rule 23(b)(1)(A) is appropriate because if each partner was sued separately, some could be found liable while others could not and this inconsistency is what Rule 23(b)(1)(A) seeks to avoid. [The named class representative] responds that this is all conjecture, as there is no guarantee that there will be inconsistent results, and if different results are reached it may not be due to inconsistency, but rather due to the fact that the Grant partners are situated differently as to tenure as partners and involvement with [the partnership].
>
> To satisfy the requirements of Rule 23(b)(1)(A), there must be more than the mere possibility that inconsistent judgments and resolutions of identical questions of law would result if numerous actions are held instead of one class action. What is required is well-described in Employers Insurance of Wausau v. FDIC, 112 F.R.D. 52, 54 (E.D.Tenn. 1986):

The advisory committee notes make it clear that the situation in which a party is faced with inconsistent results requiring it to pay some class members but not others is covered by Rule 23(b)(3) not Rule 23(b)(1). See Advisory Committee Note of 1966 to Rule 23(b)(3). The risk of "incompatible standards of conduct" which Rule 23(b)(1)(A) was designed to protect against involves situations where the non-class party does not know, because of inconsistent adjudications, whether or not it is legally permissible for it to pursue a certain course of conduct. Thus, Rule 23(b)(1)(A) is designed to protect against the nonclass party's being placed in a stalemated or conflicted position and is applicable only to actions in which there is not only a risk of inconsistent adjudications but also where the nonclass party could be sued for *different and incompatible affirmative relief.*

A reading of Harris' arguments made in support of Rule 23(b)(1)(A) certification leads to the conclusion that certification under this provision is not appropriate. Harris is claiming that if there were separate suits, she might win on some and lose on others, even though the legal and factual issues involved are identical. At no point does she argue that anything more might result, and in light of the above law, without more there can be no certification under this provision. This is not like the situation of the validity of a single bond issue, allegedly invalid because of improper authority to issue the bonds, the typical Rule 23(b)(1)(A) type class.

Suits seeking court orders establishing a medical monitoring program might satisfy Rule 23(b)(1)(A). In In re Telectronics Pacing Systems, Inc., 172 F.R.D. 271 (S.D. Ohio 1997), the court concluded that "[t]he medical monitoring claim here is an ideal candidate" for Rule 23(b)(1)(A) treatment because separate adjudications would impair defendant's ability to pursue a single uniform medical monitoring program. Id. at 284–85. In 1998, defendant recommended a monitoring program. A later California class action sought a court order creating a fund to pay for such monitoring activities, but the district court there refused to certify one. On appeal, the court emphasized that the suit was basically for money—funding of monitoring—and added that even if differing courts devised separate medical monitoring programs that would lead only to "administrative difficulty" for defendant that would not warrant mandatory class action treatment. Zinser v. Accufix Research Institute, Inc., 253 F.3d 1180, 1194–95 (9th Cir. 2001). A dissenting judge denounced the majority's conclusion about the risk of conflicting orders as "altogether speculative and without support." Id. at 1199. Should it be significant that in this case it was *plaintiff* who was invoking a ground for class certification that is essentially designed to protect *defendant*, who opposed certification?

2. INJUNCTIVE/DECLARATORY RELIEF CLASS ACTIONS (RULE 23(b)(2))

Rule 23(b)(2) allows for a class action when "the party opposing the class has acted or refused to act on grounds that apply generally to the class, so that final injunctive relief or corresponding declaratory relief is appropriate respecting the class as a whole." Compared to the complex provisions of Rule 23(b)(1), this language is relatively simple. Indeed, in a broad range of suits seeking injunctive relief (of which the school desegregation and institutional restructuring suits are paradigms), there has been little difficulty in certifying a class. There are, however, questions as to the breadth of this type of class when monetary relief is also sought.

PARSONS V. RYAN
United States Court of Appeals, Ninth Circuit, 2014.
754 F.3d 657.

Before REINHARDT, NOONAN and WATFORD, CIRCUIT JUDGES.

REINHARDT, CIRCUIT JUDGE.

The defendants, senior officials of the Arizona Department of Corrections ("ADC") appeal an order certifying a class and subclass of inmates in Arizona's prison system who claim that they are subject to systematic Eighth Amendment violations. The inmates alleged that numerous policies and practices of statewide application governing medical care, dental care, mental health care, and conditions of confinement in isolation cells expose them to a substantial risk of serious harm to which the defendants are deliberately indifferent. The inmates seek declaratory and injunctive relief from the alleged constitutional violations. After reviewing the substantial record compiled by the plaintiffs, which includes four expert reports, hundreds of internal ADC documents, depositions of ADC staff, and inmate declarations, the district court * * * certified a class of inmates challenging ADC health care policies and practices, and a subclass of inmates challenging ADC isolation unit policies and practices. We conclude that the district court did not abuse its discretion in certifying the class and subclass, and therefore affirm the order of the district court.

[Arizona has approximately 33,000 inmates in ten prison facilities, and state law requires defendant Director of the ADC to provide medical and health services for them. Plaintiffs challenged nearly a dozen specific ADC policies and practices, including inadequate staffing, outright denials of medical care, lack of emergency treatment, failure to provide critical medication, grossly substandard dental care, and failure to provide therapy and psychiatric medication for mentally ill inmates.

In support of their motion to certify the class, plaintiffs relied on their 74-page complaint. For each alleged policy or practice, the complaint contained several paragraphs or pages of particularized factual allegations, such as providing prisoners with expired medication, providing specialty care only after long delays, and an alleged statewide policy of not providing timely emergency care. The court of appeals concluded that "the lengthy and comprehensive complaint in this case alleges that there exist a number of statewide, uniform ADC policies and practices concerning health care and isolation units, and that these policies and practices expose all members to the proposed class and subclass to a substantial risk of serious harm." These allegations were supported by hundreds of documents obtained in discovery from defendants. Plaintiffs also offered reports from four experts in prison medical care who reviewed defendants' practices and pronounced them inadequate. The court of appeals said that defendants did not rebut these reports.

Defendants argued that under Wal-Mart Stores, Inc. v. Dukes, *infra* p. 242, plaintiffs could not satisfy Rule 23(a)(2), which the court found to be "a sweeping assertion that after *Wal-Mart*, Eighth Amendment claims can *never* be brought in the form of a class actions." The court of appeals rejected the argument: "What all members of the putative class and subclass have in common is their alleged exposure, as a result of specified statewide ADC policies and practices that govern the overall conditions of health care services and confinement, to a substantial risk of serious future harm to which the defendants are allegedly deliberately indifferent."]

IV

Rule 23(b)(2) requires that "the party opposing the class has acted or refused to act on grounds that apply generally to the class, so that final injunctive relief or corresponding declaratory relief is appropriate respecting the class as a whole." Although we have certified many different kinds of Rule 23(b)(2) classes, the primary role of this provision has always been the certification of civil rights class actions. See Amchem Products, Inc. v. Windsor, 521 U.S. 591, 614 (1997) ("Rule 23(b)(2) permits class actions for declaratory or injunctive relief where 'the party opposing the class has acted or refused to act on grounds generally applicable to the class.' Civil rights cases against parties charged with unlawful, class-based discrimination are prime examples."). As Wright and Miller have explained:

> [S]ubdivision (b)(2) was added to Rule 23 in 1966 in part to make it clear that civil-rights suits for injunctive or declaratory relief can be brought as class actions . . . [T]he class suit is a uniquely appropriate procedure in civil-rights cases, which generally involve an allegation of discrimination against a group as well as the violation of rights of particular individuals. By their very nature, civil-rights class actions almost invariably involve a plaintiff class, although they may also be brought against a defendant class . . .

Of course, we do not interpret Rule 23(b)(2) in a manner that would prevent certification of the kinds of civil rights class action suits that it was intended to authorize.

Thus, following Rule 23(b)(2)'s text and purpose, courts have repeatedly invoked it to certify classes of inmates seeking declaratory and injunctive relief for alleged widespread Eighth Amendment violations in prison systems:

> [I]t should be noted that a common use of Rule 23(b)(2) is in prisoner actions brought to challenge various practices or rules in the prisons on the ground that they violate the constitution. For example, Rule 23(b)(2) class actions have been utilized to challenge prison policies or procedures alleged to . . . violate the prisoners' Eighth Amendment rights to be free from cruel and unusual punishment.

Id. at § 1776.1.

Here, the plaintiffs seek declaratory and injunctive remedies. In their prayer for relief, the plaintiffs request that the defendants be ordered "to develop and implement, as soon as practical, a plan to eliminate the substantial risk of serious harm that prisoner Plaintiffs and members of the Plaintiff Class suffer due to Defendants' inadequate medical, mental health, and dental care, and due to Defendants' isolation policies." The plaintiffs then specify 10 separate issues that the defendants should be required to address in any court-enforced plan designed to satisfy their alleged remedial obligations. These issues include staffing, screening, chronic care, emergency response, and medication and supplies.[32] The plaintiffs' expert reports also include descriptions of the kinds of court-ordered changes in ADC policy and practice that could alleviate the alleged systemic Eighth Amendment violations, as well as affirmations by all four experts that, in their experience, court-ordered injunctive relief could effectively alleviate the deficiencies in ADC policies and practices identified in their reports.

The district court concluded that the plaintiffs' claims "for injunctive relief stemming from allegedly unconstitutional conditions of confinement are the quintessential type of claims that Rule 23(b)(2) was meant to address." It explained that "the claims of systemic deficiencies in ADC's health care system and unconstitutional conditions of confinement in isolation units apply to all proposed class members," and firmly rejected the defendants' contention that "any proposed injunction here would be crafted at a stratospheric level of abstraction." It added that "the remedy in this case would not lie in providing specific care to specific inmates," but

---

[32] Under "Staffing," for example, the plaintiffs request that the defendants be required to ensure that "Staffing shall be sufficient to provide prisoner Plaintiffs and the Plaintiff Class with timely access to qualified and competent clinicians who can provide routine, urgent, emergent, and specialty health care."

rather "the level of care and resources would be raised for all inmates." "Thus," it concluded, "if successful, a proposed injunction addressing those [policies and] practices would ... prescribe a standard of conduct applicable to all class members." In other words, "relief for some inmates would necessarily result in injunctive relief for all inmates."

The district court did not abuse its broad discretion in determining that the plaintiffs have satisfied Rule 23(b)(2). In Wal-Mart [Stores, Inc. v. Dukes, *infra* p. 242], the Supreme Court summarized Rule 23(b)(2)'s requirements as follows:

> The key to the (b)(2) class is "the indivisible nature of the injunctive or declaratory remedy warranted—the notion that the conduct is such that it can be enjoined or declared unlawful only as to all of the class members or as to none of them." In other words, Rule 23(b)(2) applies only when a single injunction or declaratory judgment would provide relief to each member of the class. It does not authorize class certification when each individual class member would be entitled to a different injunction or declaratory judgment against the defendant. . . .

These requirements are unquestionably satisfied when members of a putative class seek uniform injunctive or declaratory relief from policies or practices that are generally applicable to the class as a whole. That inquiry does not require an examination of the viability or bases of the class members' claims for relief, does not require that the issues common to the class satisfy a Rule 23(b)(3)-like predominance test, and does not require a finding that all members of the class have suffered identical injuries.[33] Rather, as the text of the rule makes clear, this inquiry asks only whether "the party opposing the class has acted or refused to act on grounds that apply generally to the class."

In this case, all members of the putative class and subclass are allegedly exposed to a substantial risk of serious harm by a specified set of centralized ADC policies and practices of uniform and statewide

---

[33] As Wright & Miller observe [Fed. Prac. & Proc. § 1775]:

The term 'generally applicable' has been said to signify that the party opposing the class does not have to act directly against each member of the class. The key is whether the party's actions would affect all persons similarly situated so that those acts apply generally to the whole class. . . .

[C]ourts have interpreted this requirement to mean that the party opposing the class either has acted in a consistent manner toward members of the class so that the opposing party's actions may be viewed as part of a pattern of activity, or has established or acted pursuant to a regulatory scheme common to all class members. This is consistent with the intention of the Advisory Committee, which stated in its Note to the 1966 amendment of Rule 23 that: "Action or inaction is directed to a class within the meaning of this subdivision even if it has taken effect or is threatened only as to one or a few members of the class, provided it is based on grounds which have general application to the class." All the class members need not be aggrieved by or desire to challenge defendant's conduct in order for some of them to seek relief under Rule 23(b)(2). What is necessary is that the challenged conduct or lack of conduct be premised on a ground that is applicable to the entire class.

application. While each of the certified ADC policies and practices may not affect every member of the proposed class and subclass in exactly the same way, they constitute shared grounds for all inmates in the proposed class and subclass. In sum, by allegedly establishing systemic policies and practices that place every inmate in ADC custody in peril, and by allegedly doing so with deliberate indifference to the resulting risk of serious harm to them, the defendants have acted on grounds that apply generally to the proposed class and subclass, rendering certification under Rule 23(b)(2) appropriate.

The relief requested by the plaintiffs also conforms with Rule 23(b)(2)'s requirement that "final injunctive relief or corresponding declaratory relief is appropriate respecting the class as a whole." See Wal-Mart, 131 S.Ct. at 2557 (stating that Rule 23(b)(2) "does not authorize class certification when each individual class member would be entitled to a different injunction or declaratory judgment against the defendant"). Contrary to the defendants' assertion that each inmate's alleged injury is amenable only to individualized remedy, every inmate in the proposed class is allegedly suffering the same (or at least a similar) injury and that injury can be alleviated for every class member by uniform changes in statewide ADC policy and practice. For example, every inmate in ADC custody is allegedly placed at risk of harm by ADC's policy and practice of failing to employ enough doctors—an injury that can be remedied on a class-wide basis by an injunction that requires ADC to hire more doctors, with the exact number of necessary additional hires to be determined by the district court if, after a trial, it ultimately concludes that the defendants engaged in unlawful conduct. Thus, considering the nature and contours of the relief sought by the plaintiffs, the district court did not abuse its discretion in concluding that a single injunction and declaratory judgment could provide relief to each member of the proposed class and subclass.

WAL-MART STORES, INC. v. DUKES
United States Supreme Court, 2011.
564 U.S. 338.

JUSTICE SCALIA delivered the opinion of the Court.

[In this Title VII case on behalf of all female Wal-Mart employees alleging that defendant Wal-Mart had violated Title VII by creating a "culture" that was "vulnerable" to gender discrimination, the Court held that plaintiffs did not satisfy the common question requirement of Rule 23(a)(2). See *supra* p. 200. Plaintiffs sought backpay awards, and the Court also addressed the inclusion of those claims in a Rule 23(b)(2) class action. With regard to punitive damages claims, the district court decided to afford class members notice and a right to opt out, but not as to backpay claims. The Ninth Circuit decided en banc that the backpay claims could proceed under Rule 23(b)(2).]

III

We also conclude that respondents' claims for backpay were improperly certified under Federal Rule of Civil Procedure 23(b)(2). Our opinion in Ticor Title Ins. Co. v. Brown, 511 U.S. 117, 121 (1994) (per curiam) expressed serious doubt about whether claims for monetary relief may be certified under that provision. We now hold that they may not, at least where (as here) the monetary relief is not incidental to the injunctive or declaratory relief.

A

Rule 23(b)(2) allows class treatment when "the party opposing the class has acted or refused to act on grounds that apply generally to the class, so that final injunctive relief or corresponding declaratory relief is appropriate respecting the class as a whole." One possible reading of this provision is that it applies *only* to requests for such injunctive or declaratory relief and does not authorize the class certification of monetary claims at all. We need not reach that broader question in this case, because we think that, at a minimum, claims for *individualized* relief (like the backpay at issue here) do not satisfy the Rule. The key to the (b)(2) class is "the indivisible nature of the injunctive or declaratory remedy warranted—the notion that the conduct is such that it can be enjoined or declared unlawful only as to all of the class members or as to none of them." Nagareda, [Class Certification in An Age of Aggregate Proof,] 84 N.Y.U.L.Rev., at 132. In other words, Rule 23(b)(2) applies only when a single injunction or declaratory judgment would provide relief to each member of the class. It does not authorize class certification when each individual class member would be entitled to a different injunction or declaratory judgment against the defendant. Similarly, it does not authorize class certification when each class member would be entitled to an individualized award of monetary damages.

That interpretation accords with the history of the Rule. Because Rule 23 "stems from equity practice" that predated its codification, Amchem Products, Inc. v. Windsor, 521 U.S. 591, 613 (1997), in determining its meaning we have previously looked to the historical models on which the Rule was based, Ortiz v. Fibreboard Corp., 527 U.S. 815, 841–845 (1999). As we observed in *Amchem*, "[c]ivil rights cases against parties charged with unlawful, class-based discrimination are prime examples" of what (b)(2) is meant to capture. In particular, the Rule reflects a series of decisions involving challenges to racial segregation—conduct that was remedied by a single classwide order. In none of the cases cited by the Advisory Committee as examples of (b)(2)'s antecedents did the plaintiffs combine any claim for individualized relief with their classwide injunction.

Permitting the combination of individualized and classwide relief in a (b)(2) class is also inconsistent with the structure of Rule 23(b). Classes certified under (b)(1) and (b)(2) share the most traditional justifications for class treatment—that individual adjudications would be impossible or unworkable, as in a (b)(1) class, or that the relief sought must perforce affect the entire class at once, as in a (b)(2) class. For that reason these are also mandatory classes: The Rule provides no opportunity for (b)(1) or (b)(2) class members to opt out, and does not even oblige the District Court to afford them notice of the action. Rule 23(b)(3), by contrast, is an "adventuresome innovation" of the 1966 amendments, *Amchem*, 521 U.S., at 614, framed for situations "in which 'class-action treatment is not as clearly called for'," id., at 615. It allows class certification in a much wider set of circumstances but with greater procedural protections. Its only prerequisites are that "the questions of law or fact common to class members predominate over any questions affecting only individual members, and that a class action is superior to other available methods for fairly and efficiently adjudicating the controversy." Rule 23(b)(3). And unlike (b)(1) and (b)(2) classes, the (b)(3) class is not mandatory; class members are entitled to receive "the best notice that is practicable under the circumstances" and to withdraw from the class at their option. See Rule 23(c)(2)(B).

Given that structure, we think it clear that individualized monetary claims belong in Rule 23(b)(3). The procedural protections attending the (b)(3) class—predominance, superiority, mandatory notice, and the right to opt out—are missing from (b)(2) not because the Rule considers them unnecessary, but because it considers them unnecessary *to a (b)(2) class.* When a class seeks an indivisible injunction benefitting all its members at once, there is no reason to undertake a case-specific inquiry into whether class issues predominate or whether class action is a superior method of adjudicating the dispute. Predominance and superiority are self-evident. But with respect to each class member's individualized claim for money, that is not so—which is precisely why (b)(3) requires the judge to make findings about predominance and superiority before allowing the class. Similarly, (b)(2) does not require that class members be given notice and opt-out rights, presumably because it is thought (rightly or wrongly) that notice has no purpose when the class is mandatory, and that depriving people of their right to sue in this manner complies with the Due Process Clause. In the context of a class action predominantly for money damages we have held that absence of notice and opt-out violates due process. See Phillips Petroleum Co. v. Shutts, 472 U.S. 797, 812 (1985). While we have never held that to be so where the monetary claims do not predominate, the serious possibility that it may be so provides an additional reason not to read Rule 23(b)(2) to include the monetary claims here.

B

Against that conclusion, respondents argue that their claims for backpay were appropriately certified as part of a class under Rule 23(b)(2) because those claims do not "predominate" over their requests for injunctive and declaratory relief. They rely upon the Advisory Committee's statement that Rule 23(b)(2) "does not extend to cases in which the appropriate final relief relates *exclusively* or *predominantly* to money damages." 39 F.R.D., at 102 (emphasis added). The negative implication, they argue, is that it does extend to cases in which the appropriate final relief relates only partially and nonpredominantly to money damages. Of course it is the Rule itself, not the Advisory Committee's description of it, that governs. And a mere negative inference does not in our view suffice to establish a disposition that has no basis in the Rule's text, and that does obvious violence to the Rule's structural features. The mere "predominance" of a proper (b)(2) injunctive claim does nothing to justify elimination of Rule 23(b)(3)'s procedural protections: It neither establishes the superiority of class adjudication over *individual* adjudication nor cures the notice and opt-out problems. We fail to see why the Rule should be read to nullify these protections whenever a plaintiff class, at its option, combines its monetary claims with a request—even a "predominating request"—for an injunction.

Respondents' predominance test, moreover, creates perverse incentives for class representatives to place at risk potentially valid claims for monetary relief. In this case, for example, the named plaintiffs declined to include employees' claims for compensatory damages in their complaint. That strategy of including only backpay claims made it more likely that monetary relief would not "predominate." But it also created the possibility (if the predominance test were correct) that individual class members' compensatory-damages claims would be *precluded* by litigation they had no power to hold themselves apart from. If it were determined, for example, that a particular class member is not entitled to backpay because her denial of increased pay or a promotion was not the product of discrimination, that employee might be collaterally estopped from independently seeking compensatory damages based on that same denial. That possibility underscores the need for plaintiffs with individual monetary claims to decide *for themselves* whether to tie their fates to the class representatives' or go it alone—a choice Rule 23(b)(2) does not ensure that they have.

The predominance test would also require the District Court to reevaluate the roster of class members continually. The Ninth Circuit recognized the necessity for this when it concluded that those plaintiffs no longer employed by Wal-Mart lack standing to seek injunctive or declaratory relief against its employment practices. The Court of Appeals' response to that difficulty, however, was not to eliminate *all* former employees from the certified class, but to eliminate only those who had left the company's employ by the date the complaint was filed. That solution has no logical connection to the problem, since those who have left their Wal-Mart jobs since the complaint was filed have no more need for prospective relief than those who left beforehand. As a consequence, even though the validity of a (b)(2) class depends on whether "final injunctive relief or corresponding declaratory relief is appropriate respecting the class *as a whole*," Rule 23(b)(2) (emphasis added), about half the members of the class approved by the Ninth Circuit have no claim for injunctive or declaratory relief at all. Of course, the alternative (and logical) solution of excising plaintiffs from the class as they leave their employment may have struck the Court of Appeals as wasteful of the District Court's time. Which indeed it is, since if a backpay action were properly certified for class treatment under (b)(3), the ability to litigate a plaintiff's backpay claim as part of the class would not turn on the irrelevant question whether she is still employed at Wal-Mart. What follows from this, however, is not that some arbitrary limitation on class membership should be imposed but that the backpay claims should not be certified under Rule 23(b)(2) at all.

Finally, respondents argue that their backpay claims are appropriate for a (b)(2) class action because a backpay award is equitable in nature. The latter may be true, but it is irrelevant. The Rule does not speak of "equitable" remedies generally but of injunctions and declaratory judgments. As Title VII itself makes pellucidly clear, backpay is neither. See 42 U.S.C. § 2000e–5(g)(2)(B)(i) and (ii) (distinguishing between declaratory and injunctive relief and the payment of "backpay," see § 2000e–5(g)(2)(A)).

C

In Allison v. Citgo Petroleum Corp., 151 F.3d 402, 415 (C.A.5 1998), the Fifth Circuit held that a (b)(2) class would permit the certification of monetary relief that is "incidental to requested injunctive or declaratory relief," which it defined as "damages that flow directly from liability to the class *as a whole* on the claims forming the basis of the injunctive or declaratory relief." In that court's view, such "incidental damage should not require additional hearings to resolve the disparate merits of each individual's case; it should neither introduce new substantial legal or factual issues, nor entail complex individualized determinations." We need not decide in this case whether there are any forms of "incidental" monetary relief that are consistent with the interpretation of Rule 23(b)(2) we have announced and that comply with the Due Process Clause. Respondents do not argue that they can satisfy this standard, and in any event they cannot.

Contrary to the Ninth Circuit's view, Wal-Mart is entitled to individualized determinations of each employee's eligibility for backpay. Title VII includes a detailed remedial scheme. If a plaintiff prevails in showing that an employer has discriminated against him in violation of the statute, the court "may enjoin the respondent from engaging in such unlawful employment practice, and order such affirmative action as may be appropriate, [including] reinstatement or hiring of employees, with or without backpay ... or any other equitable relief as the court deems appropriate." § 2000e–5(g)(1). But if the employer can show that it took an adverse employment action against an employee for any reason other than discrimination, the court cannot order the "hiring, reinstatement, or promotion of an individual as an employee, or the payment to him of any backpay." § 2000e–5(g)(2)(A).

We have established a procedure for trying pattern-or-practice cases that gives effect to these statutory requirements. When the plaintiff seeks individual relief such as reinstatement or backpay after establishing a pattern or practice of discrimination, "a district court must usually conduct additional proceedings . . . to determine the scope of individual relief." At this phase, the burden of proof will shift to the company, but it will have the right to raise any individual affirmative defenses it may have, and to "demonstrate that the individual applicant was denied an employment opportunity for lawful reasons." [The Court concluded that "Trial by Formula" could not be substituted, using a sample of class members, with the results of that determination applied to the remainder. For further discussion, see Trial of Sample Cases, *infra* p. 644.]

NOTES AND QUESTIONS

1.   Recall the "public law" cases described by Prof. Chayes in Chapter 1. Rule 23(b)(2) was designed as a vehicle for such cases. Perhaps the most prominent recent example was Brown v. Plata, 563 U.S. 493 (2011), involving a claim regarding overcrowding in the California prisons with many general similarities to the claims made regarding the Arizona prisons in Parsons v. Ryan. Brown v. Plata has been described as "the most significant class action of the past decade." Samuel Issacharoff, Class Actions and State Authority, 44 Loyola U. Chi. L.J. 369, 375 (2012).

How readily should courts accept claims that defendant has engaged in a pattern or practice that can be changed by declaratory or injunctive relief? Should prison cases like *Parsons* be treated differently from employment discrimination cases like *Wal-Mart*? What injunction would have been appropriate on behalf of the proposed class in *Wal-Mart*? How should these issues have been approached in the original employment discrimination action in Martin v. Wilks, *supra* p. 69, involving exclusion of African American applicants for jobs as police officers or firefighters in Birmingham, Ala.?

2.   Is there really any need for class certification when plaintiffs seek injunctive relief? Could the court in *Parsons* enjoin defendants to provide proper medical care for the 14 named plaintiffs but not other prisoners? How about those sentenced to prison after the court enters its decree? Wouldn't any injunctive decree, in effect, affect all? In Gaye v. Warden Monmouth County Correctional Institution, 838 F.3d 297, 310 (3d Cir. 2016), the court noted that "there may be circumstances where certification is not appropriate because in view of the declaratory or injunctive relief ordered on an individual basis, there would be no meaningful additional benefit to prospective relief. The circumstances in which classwide relief offers no further benefit will be rare,

and courts should exercise great caution before denying certification on that basis."

One answer to the question why plaintiffs seeking only injunctive relief would seek certification is to assure enforceability of the injunction if it is obtained. What if defendants say they will abide the court's ruling on the legality of their practices? Does that make a classwide injunction unnecessary? In Ollier v. Sweetwater Union High School Dist., 251 F.R.D. 564 (S.D. Cal. 2008), a suit based on Title IX challenging unequal athletic facilities and programs for female students, the court rejected defendant's argument that "need" for a classwide injunction is relevant to class certification. It cited such considerations as mootness, suspension of the statute of limitations, notice to class members, and the availability of evidentiary materials as pertinent to its conclusion. See also Note, There is Always a Need: The "Necessity Doctrine" and Class Certification Against Governmental Agencies, 103 Mich. L. Rev. 1018 (2005) (arguing that denial of certification under Rule 23(b)(2) is warranted only very rarely even when the defendant is a governmental agency due to the need for class certification to ensure fully effective relief).

Sometimes class certification is essential to obtaining classwide injunctive relief. In Meyer v. CUNA Mut. Ins. Soc., 648 F.3d 154 (3d Cir. 2011), plaintiffs claimed that defendant had mishandled disability claims. The district judge at first certified a class, but later decertified it. Before decertifying the class, however, the court issued an injunction specifying procedures for defendant to use in processing disability claims and reserving jurisdiction over whether defendant had complied with the injunction. The court of appeals held that the injunction was overbroad because it "amounted to class-wide relief and no class was certified." Id. at 171. See also 18 U.S.C. § 2636 (directing that relief in prison conditions cases "shall extend no further than necessary to correct the violation of the federal right to a particular plaintiff").

3. At the same time, there may be strategic advantages for plaintiffs to seek certification under Rule 23(b)(2) rather than (b)(3). "Class action lawyers like to sue under [(b)(2)] because it is less demanding, in a variety of ways, than Rule 23(b)(3) suits, which are the only available alternative." Randall v. Rolls-Royce Corp., 637 F.3d 818, 825 (7th Cir. 2011). In particular, "plaintiffs may attempt to shoehorn damages actions into the Rule 23(b)(2) framework, depriving class members of notice and opt-out protections. The incentives to do so are large. Plaintiffs' counsel effectively gathers clients—often thousands of clients—by a certification under (b)(2). Defendants attempting to purchase res judicata may prefer certification under (b)(2) over (b)(3)." Bolin v. Sears, Roebuck & Co., 231 F.3d 970, 976 (5th Cir. 2000). See also In re Subway Footlong Marketing and Sales Practices Litig., 869 F.3d 551 (7th Cir. 2017) (certification under (b)(3) was denied, but "[r]ather than drop the suit as meritless, class counsel refocused their efforts on certifying an injunction class under Rule 23(b)(2)").

Should it be easier to obtain (b)(2) certification than (b)(3) certification? It is said that a (b)(2) class must be "cohesive." Was the class in Parsons v. Ryan cohesive? Arizona has about 33,000 inmates in its prison system. For a variety of reasons, such as gang behavior, the prisoners may not regard themselves as a cohesive group. Should that matter to certification for maintaining a class action under (b)(2)? "The requirements of predominance and superiority under Rule 23(b)(3) for maintaining a class action are less stringent than the cohesiveness requirement of Rule 23(b)(2). But the two inquiries are similar." Gates v. Rohm and Haas Co., 655 F.3d 255, 269–70 (3d Cir. 2011).

4.   For many years, backpay was routinely thought to be properly included in Title VII (b)(2) actions. Note, Certifying Classes and Subclasses in Title VII Suits, 99 Harv. L. Rev. 619 (1986) (written by Justice Kagan when she was a law student) observed that "[i]n the context of title VII litigation, a finding that a proposed class meets the requirements of rule 23(a) is equivalent to a holding that class suit may proceed. As a technical matter, the judge must also find that the action falls within one of the categories of suits specified in rule 23(b). The rule 23(b) requirements, however, have posed no obstacle to the certification of title VII classes. * * * The customary willingness of judges to certify title VII classes under Rule 23(b)(2), rather than under rule 23(b)(3), is significant." Id. at 621 n. 23. She also noted that "plaintiffs will often disagree about what formula the court should use to compute back-pay awards. Different formulas will favor (and disfavor) different subsets of the class." Id. at 632–33.

But the Civil Rights Act of 1991 expanded the relief available under Title VII to include emotional distress damages and the Fifth Circuit ruled in Allison v. Citgo Petroleum Corp., cited by the Court in *Wal-Mart*, that this type of monetary relief could not be included in a (b)(2) class action under Title VII. Before *Wal-Mart*, the lower courts often focused on whether the injunctive relief of the monetary relief "predominated." This analysis made some sense; if plaintiffs would not sue only for ineffective or unnecessary injunctive relief, including a request for that should be insufficient to support monetary relief under (b)(2). But sometimes monetary claims were permitted due to their connection to viable injunctive claims. *Wal-Mart* says that backpay itself is individualized relief that cannot be included in a Rule 23(b)(2) class. Instead, only "incidental" relief not involving "individualized" determinations would be allowed. How broadly should this confine (b)(2) class actions? Consider some possible cases:

(a)   The Governor directs that welfare and Medicaid payments to all recipients be cut 25%, leading a legal aid organization to file a 23(b)(2) class action on behalf of a class of recipients for an injunction restoring payments to their former level on the ground that reducing the benefits violates federal law. Nine months later, plaintiffs win their suit and obtain the injunction. Can the court also order the State to make payments to recipients for the amounts withheld for nine months under the Governor's program? That would seemingly require some individualized calculation because the benefits of different people differ from one another. In Fowler v. Guerin, 899 F.3d 1112 (9th Cir. 2018), the court held that (b)(2) certification was proper in a class action challenging the method used to calculate interest due on accounts because plaintiffs sought "an injunction requiring [defendant] to apply a single formula to [defendant's] electronic records to correct the amount of interest credited to class members' accounts."

(b) A bank institutes a new fee for certain transactions that arguably violates its uniform customer account agreement. A customer sues on behalf of a class of all customers with that account agreement seeking an injunction against continued collection of the fee. Plaintiffs win class certification under (b)(2) and the injunction. Can the court also order the bank to restore the fees charged during the time they were in effect to the accounts of customers who were charged? That would seemingly require an individualized determination (using the bank's records) to determine which customers were charged, and how much. Would that nonetheless be "merely incidental to any injunctive or declaratory relief"? Compare Berry v. Schulman, 807 F.3d 600 (4th Cir. 2015) (statutory damages claims "are not the kind of individualized clams that threaten class cohesion and were prohibited by *Dukes*" because "every class member would be entitled to the same amount of statutory damages, by rote calculation").

(c) A company operating a large number of gas stations is sued for failure to provide required access for mobility impaired customers. Plaintiffs seek an injunction and also statutory damages for class members unable to access the stations. See Molski v. Gliech, 318 F.3d 937 (9th Cir. 2003) (holding that injunctive relief was the "predominant" form of relief even though claims were also made for statutory damages).

(d) An insurance company discriminated for years against African American customers, either providing lesser coverage or charging higher premiums compared to white customers. Plaintiffs sought an injunction against resumption of these practices (which defendant had stopped), reformation of past policies to equalize benefits, and restoration of past overcharges or underpayment of benefits. Because policy terms varied over time, any class member's monetary entitlement would be extremely difficult to calculate. See In re Monumental Life Ins. Co., 365 F.3d 408 (5th Cir. 2004) (finding monetary relief "incidental" and rejecting the idea that there is a "sweat-of-the-brow" exception to (b)(2) certification).

(e) On behalf of all cigarette smokers in a state that recognizes a claim for medical monitoring, plaintiffs seek creation and funding of a program of monitoring. Is this really a suit for monetary relief (funding the program), as compared with the claim in Parsons v. Ryan? See Barnes v. American Tobacco Co., 161 F.3d 127 (3d Cir. 1998) (upholding denial of certification on the ground that individual issues precluded certification of a classwide program).

6. In *Wal-Mart*, the Court notes that there is a risk that class members might improperly be precluded from filing a separate individual action for monetary relief if they were not granted a right to exclude themselves in a (b)(2) class action that included monetary relief. Is that a challenge to all "mandatory" class actions that don't afford a right to opt out, or only to those that involve "money damages"? Is the right to money damages more important than the right to injunctive relief? How should that apply to the class members

in *Parsons* if some of them have claims for past harm caused be defendants' challenged policies? After a (b)(2) classwide injunction was entered regarding conditions in the Texas prison system in the 1980s, the courts struggled with the proper handling of individual claims brought by prisoners. See Green v. McKaskle, 770 F.2d 445 (5th Cir. 1985) (requiring that "equitable" claims of individual prisoners be handled through the class action); Green v. McKaskle, 788 F.3d 1116 (5th Cir. 1986) (holding that individual damage suits should be unaffected by the class-action decree, even with regard to issue preclusion). See also Rice v. City of Philadelphia, 66 F.R.D. 17 (E.D.Pa. 1974) (permitting class members in a (b)(2) case involving police practices to seek damages separately).

3. COMMON QUESTION CLASS ACTIONS (RULE 23(b)(3))

In Ortiz v. Fibreboard Corp., *supra* p. 232, the Court noted that during the 1966 drafting of amendments to Rule 23 "the Committee was consciously retrospective with intent to codify pre-Rule categories under Rule 23(b)(1), not forward-looking as it was in anticipating innovations under Rule 23(b)(3)." Rule 23(b)(3) built on the "spurious" class action that was authorized under the original rule. That provision, however, did not make the decision binding on the unnamed class members. A judge in one case nonetheless allowed "one way intervention" by class members seeking to prove their damages after defendant had been held liable. See Union Carbide & Carbon v. Nisley, 300 F.2d 561 (10th Cir. 1962). One goal of the rule revision was therefore to require class members to decide whether to be bound before defendant's liability was determined, ultimately accomplished by Rule 23(c)(2)'s directive that members of a (b)(3) class be given notice of class certification and a right to opt out. The Advisory Committee view was that this provision made binding effect constitutional under Hansberry v. Lee, *supra* p. 166.

But the more basic debate was about whether to abolish the spurious class action altogether, pitting John Frank, a member of the Advisory Committee, against its Reporter, Benjamin Kaplan. As recounted in John Rabiej, The Making of Class Action Rule 23—What Were We Thinking?, 24 Miss. Col. L. Rev. 323, 335–36 (2005):

> John Frank opposed spurious class actions. He vehemently opposed their use in tort cases. He championed the principle that each person has a right to litigate his or her own case, that enforcing a judgment against an absent class member would be contrary to fundamental principles of fairness. Frank was particularly vexed with the insidious incentives that spurious class actions, whose judgments bound absent class members, presented to class counsel willing to settle an action on less than most favorable terms in exchange for an award of lucrative attorney fees. In his view, defendant companies would "sell" a

settlement to the lowest bidder willing to settle a class action. Unscrupulous lawyers would barter away absent class members' rights in exchange for substantial attorney fees, which would still be realized in such cases. He was unconvinced that Kaplan's defense by providing notice to class members would be sufficient safeguard against lawyers' misconduct. * * *

Reporter Kaplan was equally adamant in his defense of the spurious class action, albeit in a revised form. He pointed out that spurious class actions had been indispensable in resolving private antitrust and fraud cases. And, most significantly, spurious class actions often represented the sole remedy available to poor people, who would otherwise have no practical legal recourse. At the same time, Kaplan did not concede the exclusion of mass torts from Rule 23. He persistently advocated a rule that would not foreclose class-action treatment of, at least, some mass-tort cases.

Eventually, Rule 23(b)(3) was adopted, but with a cautious Committee Note regarding mass tort cases:

> A "mass accident" resulting in injuries to numerous persons is ordinarily not appropriate for a class action because of the likelihood that significant questions, not only of damages but also of liability and defenses to liability, would be present, affecting the individuals in different ways. In these circumstances an action conducted nominally as a class action would degenerate in practice into multiple lawsuits separately tried.

More generally, Rule 23(b)(3) required a court to find that two criteria were satisfied in addition to those specified in Rule 23(a).

Predominance: The rule permits common question class actions only if the common questions "predominate." Recall that, for purposes of Rule 23(a)(2), commonality requires only that common questions *exist*, not that they outweigh the individual questions. "Rule 23(b)(3)'s predominance requirement is far more demanding than Rule 23(a)(2)'s commonality requirement." Sellers v. Rushmore Loan Manag. Serv., Inc., 941 F.3d 1031 (11th Cir. 2019). In the following cases, we will examine the application of the predominance concept, which could be compared to the joinder requirements of Rule 20(a). Some, however, think that it is not a useful inquiry: See Allan Erbsen, From "Predominance" to "Resolvability": A New Approach to Regulating Class Actions, 58 Vand. L. Rev. 995 (2005) (objecting that the predominance requirement "requires elaborate efforts to answer a question that is not worth asking" and that it "conflates the similarity and dissimilarity inquiries into a single balancing test"). Instead, the author proposes, the courts should focus on "resolvability." Compare § 2.02(a)(1) of the proposed American Law Institute's Principles of the Law of Aggregate Litigation (2010), which instructs a court to determine whether resolution of a common issue would "materially advance the resolution of multiple civil claims by addressing the core of the dispute * * * so as to generate significant judicial efficiencies." Judge Posner has explained that "[p]redominence is a qualitative rather than a quantitative concept." Parko v. Shell Oil Co., 739 F.3d 1083, 1085 (7th Cir. 2014). He has added: "If there are no common questions or only common questions, the issue of predominance is automatically resolved. Any other case requires 'weighing' unweighted factors, which is the kind of subjective determination that usually—including the determination whether to certify a class—is left to the district court, subject to light appellate review." Butler v. Sears, Roebuck & Co., 702 F.3d 359 (7th Cir. 2012) (later vacated by the Supreme Court).

Superiority: If predominance is satisfied, the court is also to determine whether "a class action is superior to other available methods for fairly and efficiently adjudicating the controversy." One consideration is whether individual claims are sufficiently large to support individual litigation—the "negative value" situation. This standard appears to call for a comparison of the various means of adjudicating claims; if a class action is the only way, that may weigh in favor of certification, providing that common questions predominate. But the district court does not have an entirely free hand in making this determination. In In re Aqua Dots Products Liability Litigation, 654 F.3d 748 (7th Cir. 2011), the district judge decided that a class action was not a superior way of dealing with the problem involved (the allegedly hazardous condition of a toy marketed by defendant) because defendant had inaugurated a very successful recall program. Speaking through Judge Easterbrook, the court of appeals was unpersuaded that this was proper: "The [district] court recognized that recall is not a form of 'adjudication' but decided that what it called a 'policy approach' is superior to following the Rule's text." Id. at 754. Rule 23(b)(3) refers to the superiority of various methods of "adjudicating the controversy," and "[a] district court is no more entitled to depart form Rule 23 than it would be to depart from one of the Supreme Court's decisions after deeming the Court's doctrine counterproductive." Id.

But the practical utility of class certification surely can matter. For example, in In re Vivendi Universal, S.A., Securities Litig., 242 F.R.D. 76 (S.D.N.Y. 2007), the court refused class certification of a worldwide class in part because of a showing that a number of other countries (in particular Germany and Austria) would not enforce such a judgment. Although enforcing a judgment favorable to plaintiffs might not be hampered thereby, defendants who prevail might be denied preclusion in the courts of those countries. See also In re Alstom SA Securities Litig., 253 F.R.D. 266 (S.D.N.Y. 2008) (treating a showing that it is probable that foreign courts would recognize a class-action judgment as preclusive as pertinent to superiority analysis).

As we shall see, (b)(3) has come to be the most frequently used provision since 1966. John Rabiej, The Making of the Class Action Rule 23, *supra*, 24 Miss. Col. L. Rev. at 323, reports that "[i]ts evolution from a convenient joinder device to a tremendous procedural engine would have astonished its authors," adding (id. at 323 n. 4):

> While testifying before the committee in 1996, [John Frank, a member of the committee that drafted Rule 26(b)(3),] recalled that the committee's idea of a "big case with plaintiffs unified as to liability but disparate as to damages was the Grand Canyon airplane crash." Professor Arthur Miller, an assistant to the committee's reporter, Professor Benjamin Kaplan, was more direct. He testified at one of the committee's public hearings in 1996 on Rule 23 that the 1966 committee had nothing specific on its mind regarding class actions. "Nothing was going on. There were a few antitrust cases, a few securities cases. The civil rights legislation was then putative. . . . And the rule was not thought of as having the kind of implication it now has."

AMGEN, INC. v. CONNECTICUT RETIREMENT PLANS AND TRUST FUNDS

United States Supreme Court, 2013.
568 U.S. 455.

JUSTICE GINSBURG delivered the opinion of the Court.

This case involves a securities-fraud complaint filed by Connecticut Retirement Plans and Trust Funds (Connecticut Retirement) against biotechnology company Amgen Inc. and several of its officers (collectively, Amgen). Seeking class-action certification under Federal Rule of Civil Procedure 23, Connecticut Retirement invoked the "fraud-on-the-market" presumption endorsed by this Court in Basic Inc. v. Levinson, 485 U.S. 224 (1988) * * *. The fraud-on-the-market premise is that the price of a security traded in an efficient market will reflect all publicly available information about a company; accordingly, a buyer of the security may be presumed to have relied on that information in purchasing the security.

Amgen has conceded the efficiency of the market for the securities at issue and has not contested the public character of the allegedly fraudulent statements on which Connecticut Retirement's complaint is based. Nor does Amgen here dispute that Connecticut Retirement meets all of the class-action prerequisites stated in Rule 23(a): (1) the alleged class "is so numerous that joinder of all members is impracticable"; (2) "there are questions of law or fact common to the class"; (3) Connecticut Retirement's claims are "typical of the claims . . . of the class"; and (4) Connecticut Retirement will "fairly and adequately protect the interests of the class."

The issue presented concerns the requirement stated in Rule 23(b)(3) that "the questions of law or fact common to class members predominate over any questions affecting only individual members." Amgen contends that to meet the predominance requirement, Connecticut Retirement must do more than plausibly plead that Amgen's alleged misrepresentations and misleading omissions materially affected Amgen's stock price. According to Amgen, certification must be denied unless Connecticut Retirement proves materiality, for immaterial misrepresentations or omissions, by definition, would have no impact on Amgen's stock price in an efficient market.

While Connecticut Retirement certainly must prove materiality to prevail on the merits, we hold that such proof is not a prerequisite to class certification. Rule 23(b)(3) requires a showing that questions common to the class predominate, not that those questions will be answered, on the merits, in favor of the class. Because materiality is judged according to an objective standard, the materiality of Amgen's alleged misrepresentations and omissions is a question common to all members of the class Connecticut Retirement would represent. The alleged misrepresentations and omissions, whether material or immaterial, would be so equally for all investors composing the class. As vital, the plaintiff class's inability to prove materiality would not result in individual questions predominating. Instead, a failure of proof on the issue of materiality would end the case, given that materiality is an essential element of the class members' securities-fraud claims. As to materiality, therefore, the class is entirely cohesive: It will prevail or fail in unison. In no event will the individual circumstances of particular class members bear on the inquiry.

Essentially, Amgen, also the dissenters from today's decision, would have us put the cart before the horse. To gain certification under Rule 23(b)(3), Amgen and the dissenters urge, Connecticut Retirement must first establish that it will win the fray. But the office of a Rule 23(b)(3) certification ruling is not to adjudicate the case; rather, it is to select the "metho[d]" best suited to adjudication of the controversy "fairly and efficiently."

I

A

This case involves the interaction between federal securities-fraud laws and Rule 23's requirements for class certification. * * * To recover damages in a private securities-fraud action under § 10(b) of the Securities Exchange Act of 1934, 15 U.S.C. § 78j(b), and Securities and Exchange Commission Rule 10b–5, 17 CFR § 240.10b–5 (2011), a plaintiff must prove "(1) a material misrepresentation or omission by the defendant; (2) scienter; (3) a connection between the misrepresentation or omission and the purchase or sale of a security; (4) reliance upon the misrepresentation or omission; (5) economic loss; and (6) loss causation."

"Reliance," we have explained, "is an essential element of the § 10(b) private cause of action" because "proof of reliance ensures that there is a proper connection between a defendant's misrepresentation and a plaintiff's injury." "The traditional (and most direct) way" for a plaintiff to demonstrate reliance "is by showing that he was aware of a company's statement and engaged in a relevant transaction . . . based on that specific misrepresentation." We have recognized, however, that requiring proof of direct reliance "would place an unnecessarily unrealistic evidentiary burden on [a] plaintiff who has traded on an impersonal market." *Basic*, 485 U.S., at 245. Accordingly, in *Basic* the Court endorsed the "fraud-on-the-market" theory, which permits certain Rule 10b–5 plaintiffs to invoke a rebuttable presumption of reliance on material misrepresentations aired to the general public.[1]

The fraud-on-the-market theory rests on the premise that certain well developed markets are efficient processors of public information. In such markets, the "market price of shares" will "reflec[t] all publicly available information." Few investors in such markets, if any, can consistently achieve above-market returns by trading based on publicly available information alone, for if such above-market returns were readily attainable, it would mean that market prices were not efficiently incorporating the full supply of public information.

In *Basic*, we held that if a market is shown to be efficient, courts may presume that investors who traded securities in that market relied on public, material misrepresentations regarding those securities. This presumption springs from the very concept of market efficiency. If a market is generally efficient in incorporating publicly available information into a security's market price, it is reasonable to presume that a particular public, material misrepresentation will be reflected in the security's price. Furthermore, it is reasonable to presume that most investors—knowing that they have little hope of outperforming the market in the long run based solely on their analysis of publicly available information—will rely on the security's market price as an unbiased assessment of the security's value in light of all public information. Thus, courts may presume that investors trading in efficient markets indirectly rely on public, material misrepresentations through their "reliance on the integrity of the price set by the market." "[T]he presumption," however, is "just that, and [can] be rebutted by appropriate evidence."

Although fraud on the market is a substantive doctrine of federal securities-fraud law that can be invoked by any Rule 10b–5 plaintiff, see, e.g., Blackie v. Barrack, 524 F.2d 891, 908 (C.A.9 1975), the doctrine has particular significance in securities-fraud class actions. Absent the fraud-

---

[1] Part IV of Justice Blackmun's opinion in *Basic*—the part endorsing the fraud-on-the-market theory—was joined by Justices Brennan, Marshall, and Stevens. Together, these Justices composed a majority of the quorum of six Justices who participated in the case.

on-the-market theory, the requirement that Rule 10b–5 plaintiffs establish reliance would ordinarily preclude certification of a class action seeking money damages because individual reliance issues would overwhelm questions common to the class. The fraud-on-the-market theory, however, facilitates class certification by recognizing a rebuttable presumption of classwide reliance on public, material misrepresentations when shares are traded in an efficient market.

B

In its complaint, Connecticut Retirement alleges that Amgen violated § 10(b) and Rule 10b–5 through certain misrepresentations and misleading omissions regarding the safety, efficacy, and marketing of two of its flagship drugs. According to Connecticut Retirement, these misrepresentations and omissions artificially inflated the price of Amgen's stock at the time Connecticut Retirement and numerous other securities buyers purchased the stock. When the truth came to light, Connecticut Retirement asserts, Amgen's stock price declined, resulting in financial losses to those who purchased the stock at the inflated price. In its answer to Connecticut Retirement's complaint, Amgen conceded that "[a]t all relevant times, the market for [its] securities," which are traded on the NASDAQ stock exchange, "was an efficient market"; thus, "the market for Amgen's securities promptly digested current information regarding Amgen from all publicly available sources and reflected such information in Amgen's stock price."

The District Court granted Connecticut Retirement's motion to certify a class action under Rule 23(b)(3) on behalf of all investors who purchased Amgen stock between the date of the first alleged misrepresentation and the date of the last alleged corrective disclosure. [On appeal, the court of appeals rejected Amgen's argument that plaintiffs should have to prove that its alleged misrepresentations were material, and that the district judge wrongly refused to consider Amgen's evidence that the market was well aware of the true facts.]

We granted Amgen's petition for certiorari to resolve a conflict among the Courts of Appeals over whether district courts must require plaintiffs to prove, and must allow defendants to present evidence rebutting, the element of materiality before certifying a class action under § 10(b) and Rule 10b–5.

II

A

The only issue before us in this case is whether Connecticut Retirement has satisfied Rule 23(b)(3)'s requirement that "questions of law or fact common to class members predominate over any questions affecting only individual members." Although we have cautioned that a court's class-certification analysis must be "rigorous" and may "entail some overlap with the merits of the plaintiff's underlying claim," Wal-Mart Stores, Inc. v. Dukes, 564 U.S. ___, ___ (2011), Rule 23 grants courts no license to engage in free-ranging merits inquiries at the certification stage. Merits questions may be considered to the extent—but only to the extent—that they are relevant to determining whether the Rule 23 prerequisites for class certification are satisfied.

Bearing firmly in mind that the focus of Rule 23(b)(3) is on the predominance of common questions, we turn to Amgen's contention that the courts below erred by failing to require Connecticut Retirement to prove the materiality of Amgen's alleged misrepresentations and omissions before certifying Connecticut Retirement's proposed class. As Amgen notes, materiality is not only an element of the Rule 10b–5 cause of action; it is also an essential predicate of the fraud-on-the-market theory. Because immaterial information, by definition, does not affect market price, it cannot be relied upon indirectly by investors who, as the fraud-on-the-market theory presumes, rely on the market price's integrity. Therefore, the fraud-on-the-market theory cannot apply absent a material misrepresentation or omission. And without the fraud-on-the-market theory, the element of reliance cannot be proved on a classwide basis through evidence common to the class. It thus follows, Amgen contends, that materiality must be proved before a securities-fraud class action can be certified.

Contrary to Amgen's argument, the key question in this case is not whether materiality is an essential predicate of the fraud-on-the-market theory; indisputably it is. Instead, the pivotal inquiry is whether proof of materiality is needed to ensure that the questions of law or fact common to the class will "predominate over any questions affecting only individual members" as the litigation progresses. Fed. Rule Civ. Proc. 23(b)(3). For two reasons, the answer to this question is clearly "no."

First, because "[t]he question of materiality . . . is an objective one, involving the significance of an omitted or misrepresented fact to a reasonable investor," materiality can be proved through evidence common to the class. Consequently, materiality is a "common questio[n]" for purposes of Rule 23(b)(3).

Second, there is no risk whatever that a failure of proof on the common question of materiality will result in individual questions predominating. Because materiality is an essential element of a Rule 10b–5 claim, Connecticut Retirement's failure to present sufficient evidence of materiality to defeat a summary-judgment motion or to prevail at trial would not cause individual reliance questions to overwhelm the questions common to the class. Instead, the failure of proof on the element of materiality would end the case for one and for all; no claim would remain in which individual reliance issues could potentially predominate.

* * * A failure of proof on the common question of materiality ends the litigation and thus will never cause individual questions of reliance or anything else to overwhelm questions common to the class. Therefore, under the plain language of Rule 23(b)(3), plaintiffs are not required to prove materiality at the class-certification stage. In other words, they need not, at that threshold, prove that the predominating question will be answered in their favor.

* * *

Rule 23(b)(3) * * * does not require a plaintiff seeking class certification to prove [as Justice Thomas argues in dissent] that each "elemen[t] of [her] claim [is] susceptible to classwide proof." What the rule does require is that common questions *predominate* over any questions affecting only individual [class] members." * * * Absent proof of materiality, the claim of the Rule 10b–5 class will fail in its entirety; there will be no remaining individual questions to adjudicate.

Consequently, proof of materiality is not required to establish that a proposed class is "sufficiently cohesive to warrant adjudication by representation"—the focus of the predominance inquiry under Rule 23(b)(3). No doubt a clever mind could conjure up fantastic scenarios in which an individual investor might rely on immaterial information (think of the superstitious investor who sells her securities based on a CEO's statement that a black cat crossed the CEO's path that morning). But such objectively unreasonable reliance does not give rise to a Rule 10b–5 claim. Thus, "the individualized questions of reliance" that hypothetically might arise when a failure of proof on the issue of materiality dooms the fraud-on-the-market class are far more imaginative than real. Such "individualized questions" do not undermine class cohesion and thus cannot be said to "predominate" for purposes of Rule 23(b)(3).

Because the question of materiality is common to the class, and because a failure of proof on that issue would not result in questions "affecting only individual members" predominating, Fed. Rule Civ. Proc. 23(b)(3), Connecticut Retirement was not required to prove the materiality of Amgen's alleged misrepresentations and omissions at the class-certification stage. This is not a case in which the asserted problem—i.e., that the plaintiff class cannot prove materiality—"exhibits some fatal dissimilarity" among class members that would make use of the class-action device inefficient or unfair. Nagareda, Class Certification in the Age of Aggregate Proof, 84 N.Y.U.L. Rev. 97, 107 (2009). Instead, what Amgen alleges is "a fatal similarity—[an alleged] failure of proof as to an element of the plaintiffs' cause of action." Ibid. Such a contention is properly addressed at trial or in a ruling on a summary-judgment motion. The allegation should not be resolved in deciding whether to certify a proposed class. Ibid.

B

Insisting that materiality must be proved at the class-certification stage, Amgen relies chiefly on two arguments, neither of which we find persuasive.

[First, Amgen argued that because the fraud-on-the-market theory depended on pre-certification proof that the stock traded in an efficient market, that the representations were publicly known, and that the transactions took place before the time the representations were corrected, that proof of materiality should also be required for class certification. The Court disagreed.]

As Amgen notes, market efficiency, publicity, and materiality can all be proved on a classwide basis. Furthermore, they are all essential predicates of the fraud-on-the-market theory. Unless those predicates are established, there is no basis for presuming that the defendant's alleged misrepresentations were reflected in the security's market price, and hence no grounding for any contention that investors indirectly relied on those misrepresentations through their reliance on the integrity of the market price. But unlike materiality, market efficiency and publicity are not indispensable elements of a Rule 10b–5 claim. Thus, where the market for a security is inefficient or the defendant's alleged misrepresentations were not aired publicly, a plaintiff cannot invoke the fraud-on-the-market presumption. She can, however, attempt to establish reliance through the "traditional" mode of demonstrating that she was personally "aware of [the defendant's] statement and engaged in a relevant transaction . . . based on that specific misrepresentation." Individualized reliance issues would predominate in such a lawsuit. The litigation, therefore, could not be certified under Rule 23(b)(3) as a class action, but the initiating plaintiff's claim would remain live; it would not be "dead on arrival."

A failure of proof on the issue of materiality, in contrast, not only precludes a plaintiff from invoking the fraud-on-the-market presumption of classwide reliance; it also establishes as a matter of law that the plaintiff cannot prevail on the merits of her Rule 10b–5 claim. Materiality thus differs from the market-efficiency and publicity predicates in this critical respect: While the failure of common, classwide proof on the issues of market efficiency and publicity leaves open the prospect of individualized proof of reliance, the failure of common proof on the issue of materiality ends the case for the class and for all individuals alleged to compose the class. In short, there can be no actionable reliance, individually or collectively, on immaterial information. Because a failure of proof on the issue of materiality, unlike the issues of market efficiency and publicity, does not give rise to any prospect of individual questions overwhelming common ones, materiality need not be proved prior to Rule 23(b)(3) class certification.

[Second, Amgen raised "policy considerations" supporting pre-certification proof of materiality, mainly stressing that certification can "exert substantial pressure on a defendant 'to settle rather than incur the costs of defending a class action and run the risk of potentially ruinous liability.'" The Court rejected this set of arguments. It concluded that "materiality does not differ from other essential elements of a Rule 10b–5 claim," but it had treated those as common questions for purposes of certification. Moreover, Congress had addressed settlement pressures resulting from class certification when it enacted the Private Securities Litigation Reform Act of 1995, and although it imposed heightened pleading requirements and a discovery stay it resisted calls to modify the fraud-on-the-market standard. "Amgen's argument, if embraced, would necessitate a mini-trial on the issue of materiality at the class-certification stage. * * * And, if certification is denied for failure to prove materiality, nonnamed class members would not be bound by that determination."]

* * *

III

Amgen also argues that the District Court erred by refusing to consider the rebuttal evidence Amgen proffered in opposing Connecticut Retirement's class-certification motion. This evidence, Amgen contends, showed that "in light of all the information available to the market," its alleged misrepresentations and misleading omissions "could not be presumed to have altered the market price because they would not have 'significantly altered the total mix of information made available.'" * * *

The District Court did not err, we agree with the Court of Appeals, by disregarding Amgen's rebuttal evidence in deciding whether Connecticut Retirement's proposed class satisfied Rule 23(b)(3)'s predominance requirement. The Court of Appeals concluded, and Amgen does not contest, that Amgen's rebuttal evidence aimed to prove that the misrepresentations and omissions alleged in Connecticut Retirement's complaint were immaterial. As explained above, however, the potential immateriality of Amgen's alleged misrepresentations and omissions is no barrier to finding that common questions predominate. If the alleged misrepresentations and omissions are ultimately found immaterial, the fraud-on-the-market presumption of classwide reliance will collapse. But again, as earlier explained, individual reliance questions will not overwhelm questions common to the class, for the class members' claims will have failed on their merits, thus bringing the litigation to a close. Therefore, just as a plaintiff class's inability to prove materiality creates no risk that individual questions will predominate, so even a definitive rebuttal on the issue of materiality would not undermine the predominance of questions common to the class.

JUSTICE ALITO, concurring.

I join the opinion of the Court with the understanding that the petitioners did not ask us to revisit *Basic*'s fraud-on-the-market presumption. As the dissent observes, more recent evidence suggests that the presumption may rest on a faulty economic premise. See Langevoort, Basic at Twenty: Rethinking Fraud on the Market, 2009 Wis. L. Rev. 151, 175–176. In light of this development, reconsideration of the *Basic* presumption may be appropriate.

JUSTICE SCALIA, dissenting.

[Although he joined much of Justice Thomas's dissent, Justice Scalia argued that the fraud-on-the-market rule should require before certification that plaintiffs establish that the challenged representation was material, because otherwise mere allegations of materiality would suffice. He stressed that class certification usually leads to a substantial settlement due to the risks of litigation and without regard to the merits.]

JUSTICE THOMAS, with whom JUSTICE KENNEDY joins, and with whom JUSTICE SCALIA joins except for Part I-B, dissenting.

The Court today allows plaintiffs to obtain certification of securities-fraud class actions without proof that common questions predominate over individualized questions of reliance, in contravention of Federal Rule of Civil Procedure 23(b)(3). The Court does so by all but eliminating materiality as one of the predicates of the fraud-on-the-market theory, which serves as an alternative mode of establishing reliance. Without demonstrating materiality at certification, plaintiffs cannot establish *Basic*'s fraud-on-the-market presumption. Without proof of fraud on the market, plaintiffs cannot show that otherwise individualized questions of reliance will predominate, as required by Rule 23(b)(3). And without satisfying Rule 23(b)(3), class certification is improper. Fraud on the market is thus a condition precedent to class certification, without which individualized questions of reliance will defeat certification.

[In Part IA of his opinion, Justice Thomas argued that Basic, Inc. v. Levinson, 485 U.S. 224 (1988), recognized that materiality is a necessary component of the fraud-on-the-market theory; if it is not proved the theory does not apply. He also noted that the theory itself has been challenged, in part because the question of "market efficiency" is not "a binary, yes or no question." But because the Court was not asked to reconsider *Basic*, he did not pursue that point.

In Part IB, he began by recognizing that the rule in *Basic* "is highly significant because it makes securities-fraud class actions possible by converting the inherently individual reliance inquiry into a question common to the class." And the Court's decision recognizes that, to invoke the *Basic* presumption, plaintiffs must show that the market was efficient and that the alleged misstatement was public. But leaving the question of materiality unresolved, he argued, raises the risk that "we learn *ex post* that certification was inappropriate because reliance was not, in fact, a common question," and that failure to demonstrate that the representations are material is failure to demonstrate that common questions predominate. "[N]othing in logic or precedent justifies ignoring at certification whether reliance is susceptible to Rule 23(b)(3) classwide proof simply because one predictive of reliance—materiality—will be resolved, if at all, much later in the litigation on an independent merits element." Plaintiff should be required "to carry his burden of establishing that questions of individualized reliance will not predominate."

In Part II, Justice Thomas relied on the "seminal fraud on the market case," Blackie v. Barrack, 524 F.2d 891 (9th Cir. 1975), in which the undisclosed fact was a $90 million loss, and the financial statements involved showed operating profits. "The [Ninth Circuit] left no doubt that the materiality of the $90 million shortfall in Ampex's financial statements was central to its determination that reliance could be presumed." Even though the materiality question also goes to the merits, Justice Thomas argued that it had to be resolved to decide whether to certify the class.]

NOTES AND QUESTIONS

1.   The fraud-on-the-market approach to establishing causation has been called "the sine qua non for any securities class action." James Cox, Understanding Causation in Private Securities Lawsuits: Building on *Amgen*, 66 Vand.L.Rev. 1719 (2013). Yet Basic, Inc. v. Levinson, 485 U.S. 224 (1988), was a 4–2 decision by a plurality of the Supreme Court. Although the decision "was a boon to plaintiffs, leading to a rapid increase in the number of fraud-on-the-market suits after 1988," Donald Langevoort, *Basic* at Twenty: Rethinking Fraud on the Market, 2009 Wis.L.Rev. 151, 171, it was followed by much academic debate about whether its premises were justified by academic research. It was also arguably eclipsed by the increasing importance of institutional traders and index funds, which seek to mimic a broad sector of the market rather than concentrating on individual companies. See also Donald Langevoort, Judgment Day for Fraud-on-the-Market: Reflections on *Amgen* and the Second Coming of *Halliburton*, 57 Ariz.L.Rev. 37 (2015). Nonetheless, it is said that securities fraud class actions have been "the 800-pound gorilla that dominates and overshadows other forms of class actions." John Coffee, Reforming the Securities Class Action: An Essay on Deterrence and Its Implementation, 106 Colum. L. Rev. 1539 (2006). See also Note, Congress, The Supreme Court, and the Rise of Securities Fraud Class Actions, 132 Harv. L. Rev. 1067 (2019) ("These actions have become much more frequent over the last three decades").

As Justice Alito's concurring opinion in *Amgen* suggests, some on the Court were receptive to reconsidering *Basic*. In Halliburton Co. v. Erica P. John Fund, Inc., 573 U.S. 258 (2014), by a vote of 6–3, the Court declined to undo *Basic*. Chief Justice Roberts wrote the opinion, explaining that *Basic* was a "long settled-precedent" and that no "special justification" had been advanced to support undoing it. To the contrary, the "academic debate" after *Basic* did not show a "fundamental shift in economic theory" that would justify overturning a precedent. Neither did decisions such as Wal-Mart Stores, Inc. v. Dukes, *supra* p. 200, provide a reason for abandoning *Basic*. To the contrary, the proper avenue to implementing policy concerns about securities class actions would be action by Congress, which showed in the Private Securities Litigation Reform Act of 1995 that it could adopt measures to control securities fraud class actions.

At the same time, the Court did hold that defendants opposing class certification in securities fraud suits could submit evidence to prove that their alleged misstatements or nondisclosures had no impact on stock prices. Concurring with two other Justices, Justice Ginsburg said that she joined the opinion on the express understanding that "it is incumbent on the defendant to show the absence of price impact," and that the Court's injection of this issue "may broaden the scope of discovery available at certification."

In an earlier decision in the same case, Erica P. John Fund, Inc. v. Halliburton Co., 563 U.S. 804 (2011), the Court held that plaintiffs did not have to prove "loss causation"—that defendant's conduct caused their claimed economic loss—to obtain certification. Speaking for the Court, Chief Justice Roberts reasoned that "[s]uch a rule contravenes *Basic*'s fundamental premise—that an investor presumptively relies on a misrepresentation so long as it was reflected in the market price at the time of his transaction." There will likely be considerable litigation about the proper application of these decisions.

Some courts have been quite partial to class actions in securities cases: "Class actions are a particularly appropriate and desirable means to resolve claims based on the securities laws, 'since the effectiveness of the securities laws may depend in large measure on the application of the class action device. * * * [T]he interests of justice require that in a doubtful case ... any error, if there is to be one, be committed in favor of allowing a class action.'" Eisenberg v. Gagnon, 766 F.2d 770, 785 (3d Cir. 1985). See also In re First Alliance Mortg. Co., 471 F.3d 977, 990 (9th Cir. 2006) (asserting that "this court has followed an approach that favors class treatment of fraud claims stemming from a 'common course of conduct.'").

2.   In *Amgen*, Justice Ginsburg begins by listing the six items that a plaintiff suing for securities fraud must prove. Is it necessary that common proof predominate as to each of those six issues in order to grant class certification? If not, how is the court to decide whether to certify, if resolution of some issues turns on individual proof? Contrast the issues that bear on the fraud-on-the-market doctrine. The Court emphasizes that "the failure of common proof on the issue of materiality ends the case for the class and for all individuals alleged to compose the class," and that "individual reliance questions will not overwhelm questions common to the class, for the class members' claims will have failed on their merits." Market efficiency and publicity are not among the six issues. How should they be handled at the

class-certification stage? We will examine related issues regarding Litigating Class Certification, *infra* p. 333.

3.   Should securities fraud law be interpreted to facilitate class actions? In Blackie v. Barrack, 524 F.2d 891 (9th Cir. 1975), the case that invented the fraud-on-the-market doctrine, the defendants objected that the court's elimination of individual proof of subjective reliance altered or abridged their substantive rights in violation of the Rules Enabling Act, which says that procedure rules may not do so. The Ninth Circuit responded that it was not interpreting Rule 23. "[W]e could, in the exercise of our Article III jurisdiction, transform the 10b–5 suit from its present private compensatory mold by predicating liability to purchasers solely on the materiality of a misrepresentation, regardless of transactional causation." Id. at 908 n. 24. Would it be appropriate to revise securities fraud law with Rule 23 requirements in mind? In Blair v. Equifax Check Services, Inc., 181 F.3d 832, 834 (7th Cir. 1999), the court observed: "Class certification also may have induced some judges to remake some substantive doctrine to render the litigation manageable." In Halliburton Co. v. Erica P. John Fund, Inc., 573 U.S. 258, 274 (2014), the Court quoted *Amgen* for the proposition that the fraud-on-the-market presumption is "a substantive doctrine of federal securities law," adding that "it provides a way of satisfying the reliance element of the Rule 10b–5 cause of action."

4.   Consider the requirement that a securities fraud plaintiff prove a material and public representation. In Blackie v. Barrack, *supra*, plaintiffs claimed that the defendant company's actual financial condition was misstated in some 45 documents issued over a 27-month period, and that these various documents did different things, such as overstating earnings, overstating the value of various assets, concealing expenses and other costs incurred for research and development, failing to write off certain assets, and failing to account for the proposed discontinuation of certain product lines. Defendants argued that this multitude of objections to a large of array of statements did not present common questions. The court disagreed, reasoning that the question should be "whether a defendant's course of conduct is in its broad outlines actionable, which is not defeated by slight differences in class members' positions." That test "is more than satisfied when a series of financial reports uniformly misrepresent a particular item in the financial statement." Carefully examining the allegedly improper documents, the court found "specific strands of misrepresentation running throughout the financial statements of the class period." It added that "even when unrelated misrepresentations are alleged as part of a common scheme, class members may share common factual questions, and trial in the same forum avoids duplicative proof." Id. at 903 n. 19.

Compare Crasto v. Kaskel's Estate, 63 F.R.D. 18 (S.D.N.Y. 1974), a securities class action was brought on behalf of all the tenants of a cooperative apartment. Plaintiffs alleged they purchased shares in it on the basis of misrepresentations, but the court, in refusing to certify the class, stressed that a variety of different oral and written statements were involved:

Unlike the common securities fraud case, in which a series of documents repeat identical or similar misrepresentations, here, each group of purchasers was relying on a materially different set of documents. When we include the alleged press releases, selling materials and written announcements, which may or may not have reached all the members of the class, the picture becomes even more jumbled and varied. Thus, it seems clear that the alleged misrepresentations are not common to the class even as to the written materials issued by defendants.

Oral representations, by their very nature, differ from person to person, especially where, as here, they are made by and to different people. Thus, at trial, in order to prove that the representations were made, plaintiffs would be required to call each class member who was allegedly deceived by oral representations. We conclude, therefore, that the question of misrepresentation here is an individual, not a common question.

Contrast Gutierrrez v. Wells Fargo Bank, NA, 704 F.3d 712 (9th Cir. 2012), not a securities fraud case but one claiming consumer deception by the bank, which magnified overdraft fees by using a "high-to-low" posting practice (debiting for the largest transaction first), with the result that there were many more such fees collected (allegedly some $1.4 billion in fees during a two-year period). But the bank's marketing materials and website said that debit-card purchases were "immediately" or "automatically" deducted. The district court said that these various statements sufficed to make the deception a common question and certified a class. The court of appeals agreed (id. at 729):

> The pervasive nature of Wells Fargo's misleading marketing materials amply demonstrates that class members, like the named plaintiffs, were exposed to the materials and likely relied on them. * * * Wells Fargo's speculation—that "some class members would have engaged in the same conduct irrespective of the alleged misrepresentation"—does not meet its burden of demonstrating that individual reliance issues predominate.

Is this a de facto fraud-on-the-market approach? How various could the sources of representations be and still satisfy the predominance standard?

5. How about securities fraud damages? Won't determining those always present significant individual questions? Different class members bought stock in different quantities at different times and for different prices. Should that doom certification? In Blackie v. Barrack the court thought not: "The amount of damages is invariably an individual question and does not defeat class action treatment. Moreover, in this situation we are confident that should the class prevail the amount of price inflation during the period can be charged and the process of computing individual damages will be virtually a mechanical task." How should this reasoning bear on the predominance analysis?

Proof of damages in securities fraud suits often relies on expert evidence to establish what the price would have been but for the misrepresentations or omissions at issue. Such proof can provide a relatively mechanical method of determining what loss given traders have suffered. Should the effort involved in performing this analysis be regarded as predominating as compared to the central question of materiality? Are the two really that different? Might the question of materiality have considerable effect on the estimated price effect? In In re IKO Roofing Shingle Prod. Liabil. Litigation, 757 F.3d 599 (7th Cir. 2014), a class action alleging false representations about roofing shingles, plaintiffs proposed either to prove that all purchasers were injured in the same amount per tile, or that they were injured by the amount of actual replacement costs expended for faulty tiles. The district judge refused to certify the class on the ground that "commonality of damages is essential." The court of appeals reversed, noting that the first method "could be applied to every member of the class," and that if the second method were used it "would require confining any class certification to questions of liability." Id. at 603.

6.   Another sticking point for class certification in securities fraud cases is the question whether the market is sufficiently efficient to support the *Basic* presumption. Amgen conceded this point in its pleadings, but many defendants do not. In In re Polymedica Corp. Securities Litig., 432 F.3d 1 (1st Cir. 2005), the district court held that plaintiffs had adequately shown market efficiency by proving that market professionals generally considered most publicly announced material statements. The Court of Appeals held that this was insufficient: "For application of the fraud on the market theory, we conclude that an efficient market is one in which the market price of the stock *fully reflects all* publicly available information." Id. at 14. But this does not require proof that the market exhibits "fundamental value efficiency"—that the values it provides for stocks accurately reflect the values of the firms involved. "[W]e do not suggest that stock price must accurately reflect the fundamental value of the stock." Id. at 16. See also In re Initial Public Offering Securities Litig., 471 F.3d 24, 43 (2d Cir. 2006) (overturning class certification on the ground that "the Plaintiffs' own allegations as to how slow the market was to correct the alleged price inflation despite what they also allege was widespread knowledge of the scheme indicate the very antithesis of an efficient market."). Should these decisions be reconsidered under *Amgen*?

7.   Class certification may not be appropriate due to individualized defenses under the doctrine enunciated in Gary Plastic Packaging Corp. v. Merrill Lynch, Pierce, Fenner & Smith, 903 F.2d 176, 179–80 (2d Cir. 1990), cert. denied, 498 U.S. 1025 (1991) (certification denied because of "danger that absent class members will suffer if their representative is preoccupied with defenses unique to it"). See Hanon v. Dataproducts Corp., 976 F.2d 497, 506–07 (9th Cir. 1992) (named plaintiff who had previously bought shares of stock and then filed derivative suits may be subject to defenses not available against other class members); Kovaleff v. Piano, 142 F.R.D. 406, 408 (S.D.N.Y. 1992) (no typicality due to the fact that the increase in his holdings in the stock by the named plaintiff after some disclosure of the alleged fraud raised defenses that could adversely impact the interests of the class); Hoexter v. Simmons,

140 F.R.D. 416, 422–23 (D.Ariz. 1991) (no typicality where unique defenses could be raised against named plaintiffs); Rolex Employees Retirement Trust v. Mentor Graphics Corp., 136 F.R.D. 658, 664 (D.Or. 1991) ("The certification of a class is questionable where it is predictable that a major focus of the litigation will be on an arguable defense unique to the named plaintiff or to a subclass.")

8.   Other legal developments could affect the viability of securities fraud class actions. In ATP Tour v. Deutscher Tennis Bund, 91 A.3d 554 (Del. 2014), the Delaware Supreme Court rejected a challenge to a corporate by-law that would require shareholders to pay defendant's litigation costs, including attorneys' fees, in litigation against the company. This was followed by multiple efforts to add such provisions to bylaws or corporate charters, some of them imposing this liability unless the shareholder is "completely successful" in the litigation. For an examination of the possible impact of such provisions on securities fraud class actions, see John Coffee, "Loser Pays": Who Will Be the Biggest Loser?, New York L.J., Nov. 20, 2014.

BEATON V. SPEEDYPC SOFTWARE
United States Court of Appeals, Seventh Circuit, 2018.
907 F.3d 1018.

Before WOOD, CHIEF JUDGE, SYKES, and HAMILTON, CIRCUIT JUDGES.

WOOD, CHIEF JUDGE.

When Archie Beaton's laptop started misbehaving, he looked for an at-home fix. An internet search turned up a product from SpeedyPC Software ("Speedy") [a Canadian corporation] that offered both a diagnosis and a cure. Beaton took advantage of Speedy's free trial, which warned that his device was in bad shape and encouraged him to purchase its software solution: SpeedyPC Pro. He did. But he was disappointed with the outcome: despite Speedy's promises, the software failed to improve his laptop's performance.

Beaton became convinced that he was the victim of a scam. He filed a consumer class action against Speedy, raising both contract and tort theories. The district court certified a nationwide class and an Illinois subclass of software purchasers. Hoping to dodge the consumer class action, Speedy turned to this court for relief. Because we find no abuse of discretion in the district court's certification orders, we affirm.

I

The ad for SpeedyPC Pro that Beaton found in August 2012 promised that Speedy's software would fix common problems affecting computer speed and performance and unleash the device's "true potential." It also offered a free scan to detect any problems. Beaton decided to give it a try, and so he downloaded and ran the free trial. After assessing the laptop's health across five modules, the program told Beaton that his computer was in critical condition as a result of hundreds of serious errors.

The free trial prompted Beaton to buy the licensed version of the software, which (he was promised) would fix the identified problems. Beaton was sold. Using his personal business's credit card, he purchased SpeedyPC Pro and ran it on his laptop. It began by scanning his device, just as the free trial had done. The program then told Beaton to click on "Fix All." Beaton dutifully did so. Yet nothing happened. Beaton ran the software a few more times, to no avail.

Feeling ripped off, and suspecting that his experience was not unique, Beaton sued Speedy in 2013 on behalf of a class of consumers defined as "All individuals and entities in the United States who have purchased SpeedyPC Pro." Despite Speedy's lofty pledges, Beaton claimed, the software failed to perform as advertised. Instead, it indiscriminately and misleadingly warned *all* users that their devices were in critical condition, scared them into buying SpeedyPC Pro, and then ran a functionally worthless "fix." The district court had jurisdiction over this putative class action under the Class Action Fairness Act, 28 U.S.C. § 1332(d)(2). * * *

The district court certified Beaton's class claims for breaches of the implied warranties of fitness for a particular purpose and merchantability. On behalf of a subclass consisting only of Illinois residents, the court certified claims for fraudulent misrepresentation under the Illinois Consumer Fraud and Deceptive Business Practices Act (ICFA). It rejected the proposed subclass insofar as it included residents from other states, because Beaton failed to identify the relevant consumer-protection laws of those states.

The court had the benefit of dueling expert testimony before it at the time it made these certification decisions. Beaton's expert, Craig Snead, described how the free trial operated across devices. Speedy's expert, Monty Myers, disputed Snead's account. Although the court had not yet issued its ruling on the parties' cross-motions to exclude the testimony of each other's expert, it ultimately denied both motions (with minor exceptions) roughly two months later. See Fed. R. Evid. 702. In that order, the court noted that it had "considered the challenged expert testimony for purposes of class certification only to the extent consistent with the rulings stated."

At that point, Speedy filed and we granted a petition for interlocutory appeal of the class certification decisions. See Fed. R. Civ. P. 23(f). * * *

[The court upheld the district court's rejection of defendant's *forum non conveniens* argument, which was premised on the choice-of-law clause in the software End User License Agreement plaintiff and all purchasers had to accept, providing that the law of British Columbia—defendant's home jurisdiction—should apply to any disputes arising under the agreement.]

III

Now we turn to the main event: the district court's decision to certify the nationwide class and the Illinois subclass. To certify under Rule 23, a district court must rigorously analyze whether the plaintiff satisfies the rule's requirements. * * * In evaluating these factors, the court must go beyond the pleadings and, to the extent necessary, take evidence on disputed issues that are material to certification. At this early stage of the litigation, the merits are not on the table. Beaton bears the burden of showing that each requirement is met by a preponderance of the evidence. We review the district court's class certification orders deferentially, leaving considerable room for the exercise of judgment unless the factual determinations are clearly erroneous oar there are errors of law.

* * *

B

To satisfy the commonality requirement found in Rule 23(a)(2), there needs to be one or more common questions of law or fact that are capable of class-wide resolution and are central to the claims' validity. The district court identified several such issues:

- Can the customers avail themselves of any implied warranties, or is the Agreement's disclaimer valid?

- What functions did the marketing materials represent that the software would perform?

- Did the software perform those functions?

Speedy takes exception to some of these questions, but most are amendable to class-wide resolution. See *Nikka Traders, Inc. v. Gizella Pastery Ltd.* (2012), D.L.F. 4th 120 para. 65 (Can B.C. Sup. Ct.) (describing the elements of claim for the implied warranty for fitness for a particular purpose); *Dream Carpets Ltd. v. Sandhedral*, [2009] B.C.W.D. 5070 para. 68 (Can B.C. Prov. Ct.) (elements for implied warranty of merchantability); *Dubey v. Pub. Storage, Inc.*, 918 N.E.2d 265 (Ill.App. 2009) (same for ICFA). And we can see additional common questions, including whether a reasonable consumer would be deceived by the advertisements' representations. Commonality is easily satisfied.

C

Second, we consider typicality. This requires us to evaluate whether Beaton's claims arise from the same events or course of conduct that gives rise to the putative class members' claims. The individual claims may feature some factual variations as long as they "have the same essential characteristics."

The district court thought this requirement satisfied because Beaton "appears to have seen the same representations as the other users of Speedy's free software, and the software appears to operate in the same way on each computer." Unlike Speedy, we do not take exception with the court's use of the word "appears" to describe the match between Beaton's claim and that of the other class members. This semantic choice suggests only that the court's determinations are preliminary, as they should be.

On the merits, neither of the court's findings reflects an abuse of discretion. We begin with the finding that Beaton saw the same representations as other users. Speedy emphasizes that some customers bought the software through third-party platforms, which could advertise as they saw fit. Yet the advertisements in the record, drawn from various sites, feature almost identical language. The class members were thus exposed to the same message (and promises) from Speedy.

Next, we turn to the court's determination that the free trial operated the same way across devices. Based on a review of the free trial's source code, Beaton's expert, Snead, concluded that the software was programmed to operate uniformly on all PCs, independent of any differences among individual devices. He asserted that the software universally reported "problems" and "errors," mislabeled innocuous and routine features, and issued a low performance rating before any scan had begun. In his view, the scan failed to account for factors that do influence a device's performance, and it incorporated factors that have no impact. Speedy's senior director of technical operations confirmed that the scan identified as problems characteristics that might not affect performance.

Speedy asks us to reject this evidence because Snead examined only the source code for the free trial's scanning portion, as opposed to the scanning or repair portions of the licensed software. It is not clear how similar the two scanning programs are, but that does not matter for our purposes. The district court was entitled to credit the evidence indicating that the free trial scan software did not differentiate between devices before declaring them to be in "critical condition." This is sufficient to show that Beaton's claims are typical. He focuses on Speedy's uniform (alleged) misrepresentation of computer health to induce users to buy its product. Though Speedy issued 19 different versions of the software during the class period, Snead opined that "the primary features and functionality remained consistent" across versions. Speedy's expert, Myers, disagreed with Snead's conclusions, and the company pointed to positive survey responses and third-party reviews to argue that Beaton's experience was atypical. But that just indicates that there are merits issues to be resolved. For class certification purposes, the district court needed only to find by a preponderance of the evidence that the software scanned Beaton's device in the same way as it scanned other class members' computers. We see no reason to reject its conclusion.

But, Speedy argues, the district court did not say out loud that it weighed both expert reports and found Snead's conclusions more persuasive. In fact, the court did not mention Myers's report at all. Speedy sees this as a glaring omission because the court had yet to rule on the Rule 702 cross-motions. It points out that a district court should not certify a class, and thereby raise the stakes of the litigation, based on faulty opinion evidence. Instead, it "must conclusively rule on any challenge to the expert's qualifications or submissions prior to ruling on a class certification motion," if the "expert's report or testimony is critical to class certification." Speedy concludes that the court erred by not doing so.

If this was error (a point we need not resolve), it was harmless. In its Rule 702 ruling, the district court made clear that it had considered only the expert testimony it later deemed admissible. Speedy gives us no reason to doubt the district court's assurance. And it is also worth recalling that the district court permitted additional merits discovery after its certification decision. Had Speedy wished to pursue the expert qualifications issue further, it could have done so. We thus find no abuse of discretion in the court's ruling on typicality.

[The court rejected defendant's "scattershot" challenges to adequacy under Rule 23(a)(4). Defendant "makes much ado of Beaton's decades-old manslaughter conviction," but "wholly unrelated criminal history" is irrelevant. Similarly, his failure to mention a marijuana conviction when asked about his criminal history was a "minor" discrepancy. The fact that he initially claimed to have paid $39.94 for the software, but his credit card statement said that he paid $9.97, was not a ground for finding him inadequate as "Beaton's credibility was not *severely* undermined by this detail."]

IV

After clearing the hurdles posed by Rule 23(a), a person wishing to bring a class action must also demonstrate that the action fits under one of the three subsections of Rule 23(b). As we said, the only one that applies to Beaton is Rule 23(b)(3), the common-question variant. It requires the putative class representative to show that questions of law or fact common to the class members predominate, and that the class device is the superior method for adjudicating those claims.

A

The guiding principle behind predominance is whether the proposed class's claims arise from a common nucleus of operative facts and issues. This requires more than a tally of common questions; the district court must consider their relative importance. On the other hand, not every issue must be amenable to common resolution; individual inquiries may be required after the class phase.

Speedy identified 10 individual issues that allegedly defeated predominance. The district court was not persuaded. It found that some were best addressed on a class-wide basis, and they outweighed the remaining individualized inquiries.

The district court did not abuse its discretion in so concluding. For example, it will be easy to ascertain from whom the class members purchased the software. The court found that they all bought it through the portal at the end of the free trial that redirected customers to two payment platforms. Similarly, the court found that users saw the same representations about the software's capabilities, and so a common answer to the question whether a reasonable customer would be deceived is possible. And based on the court's preliminary determination that the software's diagnostic mechanisms operated uniformly across devices, the trier of fact could reach a single answer on the software's functionality and value. Speedy insists that the court needs to inquire individually about each customer's level of satisfaction with the product. But dissatisfaction is not an element of any of the certified claims. If the product truly serves none of its functions, its users' subjective satisfaction is likely evidence of misrepresentation, not that the users were not harmed. See *In re Aqua Dots Prods. Liab. Litig.*, 654 F.3d 748, 750–51 (7th Cir. 2011) (purchasers suffered financial loss by paying more for products than they would have had they known the products' true quality).

Admittedly, some individualized questions remain. For instance, what was the class member's purpose (business or personal?) in buying the software? Did the class member seek a refund? What are each customer's damages? Speedy reminds us that we have frowned upon class treatment as a poor fit for warranty and fraud claims because they can involve so many individualized issues. But these theories do not automatically fail the predominance test. See *Amchem Prods., Inc. v. Windsor*, 521 U.S. 591, 625 (1997) (certain consumer-fraud cases readily establish predominance); *Suchanek v. Sturm Foods, Inc.*, 764 F.3d 750, 759–60 (7th Cir. 2014) (the fact that "[e]very consumer fraud case involves individual elements" does not preclude class actions). Speedy misreads Supreme Court precedent in arguing that *liability* with regard to all class members must be resolved in a single stroke. See *Wal-Mart Stores, Inc. v. Dukes*, 564 U.S. 338, 350 (2011) (requiring resolution in "one stroke" of a "common contention" central to the common claim).

The district court recognized that individualized inquiries could be handled through "streamlined mechanisms" such as affidavits and proper auditing procedures. We agree. Defendants' due process rights are not harmed by such case-management tools. *Mullins v. Direct Dig., LLC*, 795 F.3d 654, 667–72 (7th Cir. 2015). Speedy's attempts to distinguish *Mullins* as merely about proving class membership, and not liability, are unavailing. The company makes the obvious point that it can neither cross-examine an affidavit nor depose every class member. But Speedy will still have the opportunity to challenge the class members' credibility. It can obtain the testimony of a representative sample of the class members and, if necessary, present evidence contradicting statements found in particular affidavits.

Speedy also contends that there is a fatal lack of uniformity in the purpose for which each person acquired its software. We do not see that as a barrier to class treatment, however. It is true that the law of British Columbia insists that a particular purpose be brought clearly to the seller's attention. Compare *Kobelt Mfg. Co. v. Pac. Rim Engineered Prods. (1987) Ltd.* (2011) 84 B.L.R 4th 189, para. 104 (Can. B.C. Sup. Ct.) (leaky brakes did not violate an implied warranty because no implied communication that purchasers intended to use the brakes on drawworks), with *Wharton v. Tom Harris Chevrolet Oldsmobile Cadillac Ltd.* (2002) 97 B.C.L.R. 3d 307, para. 59–60 (Can. B.C. App. Ct.) (buzzing sound system violated implied warranty where salesman knew purchasers wanted a luxury vehicle). But we do not see that flaw here. The people who used the free trial and then bought SpeedyPC Pro were all concerned about the health and performance of their computers. Why they owned a computer is beside the point. To the extent it is relevant, each user's specific reason for buying the software can be established through affidavits, subject to the defendant's right to challenge them with evidence.

B

Finally, the district court had several reasons for concluding that a class action was the superior way to resolve this dispute. All are well-supported. First, common questions of fact and law predominate. Speedy insists that we should categorically reject class treatment for implied warranty and consumer fraud claims because of the choice-of-law clause. But that makes no sense here, since all parties agree that British Columbia law controls for the nationwide class and Illinois law for the subclass. And there is no risk of inconsistent rules with respect to recognition of the contractual choice-of-law clause, because that follows the forum, Illinois.

Second, the amount of damages to which each plaintiff would be entitled is so small that no one would bring this suit without the option of a class. "Rule 23(b)(3) was designed for situations such as this, in which the potential recovery is too slight to support individual suits, but injury is substantial in the aggregate." The fact that others have not sued over this software is more likely because "only a lunatic or a fanatic sues for $30" than it is because the software is flawless. Consumer class actions are a crucial deterrent against the proliferation of bogus products whose sticker price is dwarfed even by a court filing fee (now $400 for a civil case in federal district court). Though punitive damages may also deter, few litigants would risk filing suit on the off-chance that punitive damages would be recovered after years of litigation. The district court did not abuse its discretion in finding the class-action device superior.

V

Defendants spend much time and money fighting Rule 23 certifications to the hilt. Yet "certification is largely independent of the merits . . . and a certified class can go down in flames on the merits." We say this not to imply that the merits in this case favor either party, but simply to remind defendants that the class-action glass is sometimes half full: dismissed claims of a certified class end litigation once and for all. That, after all, is why settlement classes are so popular.

NOTES AND QUESTIONS

1.   According to Amanda Bronstad, Consumer Class Actions Nearly Tripled in the Past Decade, Report Says, Nat. L.J., Oct. 23, 2019, consumer class actions have proliferated, particularly for data breaches. The court in *Beaton* suggested that consumer class actions should be favored because individual class members rarely have significant stakes in the outcome. Compare securities fraud class actions under the PSLRA, in which some class members may have substantial claims even though others have claims of modest size. See *supra* p. 227 note 4. Many courts agree: "Consumer class actions of this variety, designed to recover relatively small price premiums in comparison to the expense and burden of litigation, are clearly superior to the alternative of forcing consumers to litigate on principle." Goldemberg v. Johnson & Johnson Consumer Companies, Inc., 317 F.R.D. 374, 397 (S.D.N.Y. 2016).

Should this attitude always apply? What if the class asserts claims for statutory damages? Consider Smilow v. Southwestern Bell Mobile Systems, Inc., 323 F.3d 32 (1st Cir. 2003), involving a claim by a cell phone customer that defendant's form contract said customers paid only for outgoing calls, but that defendant was nevertheless charging for incoming calls. Defendant contended that the contract permitted it to charge for incoming calls, the principal issue presented on the merits. Plaintiff asserted a claim under a Massachusetts law that would permit a $25 recovery for each customer; with a proposed class of 275,000 customers that would lead to a recovery of $6,875,000. Sheila Scheuerman, Due Process Forgotten: The Problem of Statutory Damages and Class Actions, 74 Mo. L. Rev. 103, 104 (2009) objects: "When combined with the procedural device of the class actions, aggregated statutory damages claims can result in absurd liability exposure in the hundreds of millions—or even billions—of dollars on behalf of a class whose actual damages are often nonexistent." See also Brian Fitzpatrick, The Conservative Case for Class Actions 116–17 (2019) (citing the Telephone Consumer Protection Act, authorizing a recovery of $500 for every robocall to a consumer, and urging that "extracompensatory" damages authorized in individual suits by such statutes should not be allowed in class actions). Does this use of class actions invite overkill?

2.   One recurrent form of consumer class action involves allegations about false or misleading advertisements, particularly on labels for food products. How should courts approach challenges to claims like "all natural" or "part of a healthy diet" that may appear on the labels of grocery items? If the products allegedly include trace amounts of "unnatural" ingredients, should it be assumed that all purchasers relied on the label claims of purity in making their purchasing decisions? Such claims have become so common in the U.S. district court in San Francisco that some have taken to calling it "food court." See Tommy Tobin, Julie Hussey & Carrie Akinaka, Notable Ruling: No Jury for False Advertising and UCL Suits, California Supreme Court Rules, Perkins Coie Consumer Protection Review, May 12, 2020 ("So many matters are heard in the Northern District of California that it has gained a reputation as the 'Food Court.' ").

Determining whether label claims support class certification calls for some evaluation of the likely importance of such claims. Note that in *Beaton* the court emphasized that Canadian cases show that the standard for evaluating them is a "reasonable consumer" approach. Should individual preferences matter, or is this more like the "fraud on the market" standard that has applied in securities class actions? One approach to these issues is expert testimony about the consumer impact of label claims. Frequently plaintiffs offer such evidence to show that consumers will pay more for a product due to such claims.

Rikos v. Procter & Gamble Co., 799 F.3d 497 (6th Cir. 2015), illustrates the way that the common issue may be shaped to suit class action treatment. This suit alleged that defendant's probiotic nutritional supplement Align did not actually improve consumers' digestion, as it was claimed to do. The majority of the court of appeals upheld class certification, noting that "[p]laintiffs all purchased Align because it allegedly promoted digestive health. This is the only reason to buy Align." Id. at 511. And this product had a "premium price point," considerably higher than the price of similar products. Defendant countered that at least some purchasers, for example those suffering from irritable bowel syndrome, did derive benefits from the product, and emphasized that some customers kept buying it. As a dissenting judge urged, "[i]f Align works to varying degrees—or at all—depending on each member's unique physiology, then the question of Align's efficacy involves myriad individual inquiries." Id. at 529. The majority concluded that plaintiffs' argument that the product was "snake oil" and did not work for anyone, so that defendant's argument went "solely to the merits." Id. at 519. Invoking the Supreme Court's decision in *Amgen, supra* p. 254, it held that plaintiffs need not prove materiality at the class certification stage, but only to prevail on the merits. But if the product actually was beneficial to some purchasers, would a class action be possible?

Does *Beaton* present similar questions about consumer reliance and materiality?

3.   In a case filed in "food court," plaintiffs alleged that the claim "Made From Real Ginger" on the label of Canada Dry ginger ale violated California

consumer protection laws because the product actually used artificial flavoring. Fitzhenry-Russell v. Dr. Pepper Snapple Group, Inc., 326 F.R.D. 592 (N.D. Cal. 2018). Understanding California consumer protection law to call (like the Canadian law in *Beaton*) for a "reasonable consumer" standard, the court distinguished the claim on the Canada Dry label from "All Natural" or "100% Natural" claims found insufficient to support class actions in other cases. The court relied on a "price premium survey" that showed consumers favored defendant's product in part due to the challenged claim. Tellingly, "Dr. Pepper's internal documents show that Dr. Pepper thought the 'Made From Real Ginger' claim *was* material." Specifically, defendant's internal documents showed that it sought "to capitalize on the alleged health halo ginger products have to consumers" by saying that this soda "fits into your healthy lifestyle." Id. at 613. "[T]hrough its marketing, it orchestrated a change in consumer perceptions * * * to make people believe that Canada Dry offers the health benefits of real ginger." Id. at 614. How often will a manufacturer's own marketing studies provide such support for class certification? How can plaintiff attorneys know about those studies before filing suit?

4.   In the Canada Dry ginger ale case, there was no question that all consumers were exposed to the label on the soft drink cans. Compare Hadley v. Kellogg Sales Co., 324 F.Supp.3d 1084 (N.D.Cal. 2018), in which the statements made on packaging of Raisin Bran and Raisin Bran Crunch differed from time to time during the proposed class period. Plaintiffs' response was to define subclasses consisting only of those who bought during a period when particular statements were on the packaging. Defendant objected that this strategy would enable plaintiffs to "effectively evade a lack of uniform exposure by gerrymandering the class to encompass only those individuals who saw specific advertisements and labels over a years-long period while excluding those who did not." Id. at 1097. The court rejected this argument, pointing out that relevant authority called for defining the class "to include only members who were exposed to advertising that is alleged to be materially misleading." How easy will it be to process claims based on when purchasers bought their Kellogg Raisin Bran?

5.   In some cases, at least, there is little concern about whether reliance may be presumed. Consider an earlier decision also written by Judge Wood. In Suchanek v. Sturm Foods, Inc., 764 F.3d 750 (7th Cir. 2014), defendant produced coffee pods that could be used in a popular coffeemaker in place of the expensive pods produced (using a patented process) by the manufacturer of the coffeemaker. But while the manufacturer's pods contained ground coffee, the defendant's pods contained at least 95% instant coffee. Defendant concluded that consumers would not buy its pods if they knew they used instant coffee, so the label said they contained "soluble" coffee. Besides that, defendant's products were packaged to look like the manufacturer's pods. Plaintiffs' experts reported (based on consumer surveys) that few consumers understood the label to mean that the pods contained instant coffee. The public reception of defendants' pods was "awful," generating a "flood of complaints" and leading to multiple class-action suits under state consumer protection laws. Defendant argued that there was no way to define the class of purchasers

who were misled, and the district judge denied certification. The court of appeals found error: "If the court thought that no class can be certified until proof exists that every member has been harmed, it was wrong." Id. at 757. And commonality was also satisfied by the dominant issue of whether the product was misrepresented; "a rule requiring 100% commonality would eviscerate consumer-fraud class actions." Id. at 759. True, plaintiffs would have to prove that damages were susceptible to measurement across the entire class, but plaintiffs' experts proposed a way to determine the actual value of pods with instant coffee and pods containing ground coffee.

6. Predominance of common issues may become complicated in consumer cases in which the purchase choices made by potential class members can depend on a variety of considerations. One possibility (examined *infra* at p. 297) might be to limit certification to common issues, such as whether labeling is misleading, leaving individual issues for later determination in follow-on proceedings. For an example, see In re IKO Roofing Shingle Prod. Liabil. Litig., 757 F.3d 599 (7th Cir. 2014), in which the court ruled that the common issue whether the products were defective would be complex and costly to prove while individual issues would be "readily determined" in individualized follow-on proceedings. Should this approach also inform the predominance determination?

7. In *Beaton* the choice of law provision in the consumer contracts meant that Canadian law applied to all the claims asserted by the nationwide U.S. class. But the Illinois claims could be asserted only on behalf of Illinois purchasers. As illustrated by Castano v. The American Tobacco Co., *infra* p. 280, choice of law issues may present major obstacles to certification of a multistate class. We will address those issues on p. 388.

8. *Beaton* could be filed in federal court even though it involved no federal law claim due to the Class Action Fairness Act. We will address this jurisdictional legislation *infra* p. 363.

9. Should consumer deception class actions be certified under Rule 23(b)(2)? Perhaps declaratory or injunctive relief to change the misleading advertising would be superior to trying to determine and distribute damages. In Japan, for example, class actions must be brought by consumer organizations and may only seek declaratory or injunctive relief.

Mass Tort Class Actions

Recall that, when Rule 23 was amended in 1966, there was extensive debate about whether it should permit mass tort personal injury class actions, leading to inclusion of a warning about the problems they would generate in the Committee Note. See *supra* p. 252.

Consistent with the Advisory Committee's admonition, courts were initially cautious about certifying such cases as (b)(3) class actions. For example, in Mertens v. Abbott Laboratories, 99 F.R.D. 38 (D.N.H. 1983), twelve New Hampshire residents who had been exposed to the drug DES in utero and claimed to have suffered serious personal injuries as a result sought to sue on behalf of others so exposed in their state. Plaintiffs argued that "the prohibitive cost of individual lawsuits would make the assertion of a claim an economic impossibility for most plaintiffs." But although the court found sufficient common issues to satisfy Rule 23(a)(2), it held that the predominance requirement of Rule 23(b)(3) was not satisfied. Explaining that its task in applying the predominance requirement was to "predict the evidence likely to be introduced at trial," the court saw considerable disparities. Plaintiffs urged that the question whether DES was toxic constituted an issue of "global liability" that should be regarded as predominant, but the court felt that the "details" that would remain unresolved "clearly outweigh the single determination that DES causes injury." The court concluded additionally that a class action would not be superior to adjudication in a more traditional fashion:

> If thousands of claims are brought, they will be dealt with in the same fashion as any other litigation. Indeed, judicial resources applied to each claim on an individual basis would doubtless be more effective than a general pronouncement applied to all cases without any real effect. * * * Other than the possibility of seeking to commit the law of New Hampshire in a particular direction, it is unlikely that anything of real value could be determined that would aid in the resolution of the claims of any individual plaintiff. In addition, it is doubtful if any decision at this level could be as effective as an appellate determination of some of the sweeping and intriguing questions raised in this litigation. Though old fashioned, *stare decisis* is not yet out of fashion.

As mass tort litigation became more familiar to courts, however, views began to change. A leading example was Jenkins v. Raymark Indus., Inc., 782 F.2d 468 (5th Cir. 1986), upholding class certification by Judge Robert Parker (E.D.Tex.) of a class action on behalf of the plaintiffs in nearly 900 personal injury actions pending in his district for injuries allegedly suffered as a result of exposure to asbestos at their workplaces in the region. Plaintiffs had sought class certification to determine the "state of the art" defense, arguing that this issue "consumes substantial resources in every asbestos trial, and that the evidence in each case was either identical or virtually so." Judge Parker found that this issue predominated under Rule 26(b)(3), and that a class action was superior to individual trials.

The Fifth Circuit affirmed, emphasizing the pressures on the traditional litigation model: "The courts are now being forced to rethink the alternatives and priorities by the current volume of litigation and more frequent mass disasters. * * * Judge Parker's plan is clearly superior to the alternative of repeating, hundreds of times over, the litigation of the state of the art issues with, as that experienced judge says, "days of the same witnesses, exhibits and issues from trial to trial."

Note that Judge Parker's certification had built-in limitations to it, however. It was limited to cases on file—only those who had sued were included in the class, so the class was defined with great precision. Those plaintiffs favored class certification. All of the claims were governed by Texas law, and all involved exposure in a limited number of local workplaces. In addition, as the appellate court noted: "From our view it seems that the defendants enjoy all of the advantages, and the plaintiffs incur the disadvantages, of the class action—with one exception: the cases are to be brought to trial. That counsel for plaintiffs would urge the class action under these circumstances is significant support for the district judge's decision.

The court in Sterling v. Velsicol Chemical Corp., 855 F.2d 1188 (6th Cir. 1988), also exhibited flexibility about class certification. Plaintiffs in this action sued the operator of a landfill for leakage of toxic substances. Eventually 97 named plaintiffs, who claimed that they had suffered various types of personal injuries, joined the suit. On its own motion, the district court certified a class under Rule 23(b)(3) and directed plaintiffs to select five representative plaintiffs for initial trial to establish liability and damages for their individual cases and for liability to the entire class and punitive damages, if any. After a bench trial, the court found defendant liable to plaintiffs on theories of strict liability, common law negligence, trespass and nuisance. The appellate court upheld class certification:

> [T]he problem of individualization of issues often is cited as a justification for denying class action treatment in mass tort accidents. * * *. In mass tort accidents, the factual and legal issues of a defendant's liability do not differ dramatically from one plaintiff to the next. No matter how individualized the issue of damages may be, these issues may be reserved for individual treatment with the question of liability tried as a class action. Consequently, the mere fact that questions peculiar to each individual member of the class remain after the common question of the defendant's liability have been resolved does not dictate the conclusion that a class action is impermissible.

CASTANO V. THE AMERICAN TOBACCO CO.

United States Court of Appeals, Fifth Circuit, 1996.
84 F.3d 734.

Before SMITH, DUHÉ, and DEMOSS, CIRCUIT JUDGES.

JERRY E. SMITH, CIRCUIT JUDGE:

In what may be the largest class action ever attempted in federal court, the district court in this case embarked "on a road certainly less traveled, if ever taken at all," Castano v. American Tobacco Co., 160 F.R.D. 544, 560 (E.D.La. 1995) (citing Edward C. Latham, The Poetry of Robert Frost, "The

Road Not Taken" 105 (1969)), and entered a class certification order. The court defined the class as:

(a) All nicotine-dependent persons in the United States . . . who have purchased and smoked cigarettes manufactured by the defendants;

(b) the estates, representatives, and administrators of these nicotine-dependent cigarette smokers; and

(c) the spouses, children, relatives and "significant others" of these nicotine-dependent cigarette smokers as their heirs or survivors.

The plaintiffs limit the claims to years since 1943.[1]

This matter comes before us on interlocutory appeal, under 28 U.S.C. § 1292(b), of the class certification order. Concluding that the district court abused its discretion in certifying the class, we reverse.

I.

A. The Class Complaint

The plaintiffs filed this class complaint against the defendant tobacco companies and the Tobacco Institute, Inc., seeking compensation solely for the injury of nicotine addiction. The gravamen of their complaint is the novel and wholly untested theory that the defendants fraudulently failed to inform consumers that nicotine is addictive and manipulated the level of nicotine in cigarettes to sustain their addictive nature. The class complaint alleges nine causes of action: fraud and deceit, negligent misrepresentation, intentional infliction of emotional distress, negligence and negligent infliction of emotional distress, violation of state consumer protection statutes, breach of express warranty, breach of implied warranty, strict product liability, and redhibition pursuant to the Louisiana Civil Code.

The plaintiffs seek compensatory and punitive damages and attorneys' fees. In addition, the plaintiffs seek equitable relief for fraud and deceit, negligent misrepresentation, violation of consumer protection statutes, and breach of express and implied warranty. The equitable remedies include a declaration that defendants are financially responsible for notifying all class members of nicotine's addictive nature, a declaration that the defendants manipulated nicotine levels with the intent to sustain

---

[1] The court defined "nicotine-dependent" as:

(a) All cigarette smokers who have been diagnosed by a medical practitioner as nicotine-dependent; and/or

(b) All regular cigarette smokers who were or have been advised by a medical practitioner that smoking has had or will have adverse health consequences who thereafter do not or have not quit smoking.

Id. at 561. The definition is based upon the criteria for "dependence" set forth in American Psychiatric Association, Diagnostic and Statistical Manual of Mental Disorders (4th ed.).

the addiction of plaintiffs and the class members, an order that the defendants disgorge any profits made from the sale of cigarettes, restitution for sums paid for cigarettes, and the establishment of a medical monitoring fund.

The plaintiffs initially defined the class as "all nicotine dependent persons in the United States," including current, former and deceased smokers since 1943. Plaintiffs conceded that addiction would have to be proven by each class member; the defendants argued that proving class membership will require individual mini-trials to determine whether addiction actually exists.

In response to the district court's inquiry, the plaintiffs proposed a four-phase trial plan. In phase 1, a jury would determine common issues of "core liability." Phase 1 issues would include (1) issues of law and fact relating to defendants' course of conduct, fraud, and negligence liability (including duty, standard of care, misrepresentation and concealment, knowledge, intent); (2) issues of law and fact relating to defendants' alleged conspiracy and concert of action; (3) issues of fact relating to the addictive nature/dependency creating characteristics and properties of nicotine; (4) issues of fact relating to nicotine cigarettes as defective products; (5) issues of fact relating to whether defendants' wrongful conduct was intentional, reckless or negligent; (6) identifying which defendants specifically targeted their advertising and promotional efforts to particular groups (e.g. youths, minorities, etc.); (7) availability of a presumption of reliance; (8) whether defendants' misrepresentations/suppression of fact and/or of addictive properties of nicotine preclude availability of a "personal choice" defense; (9) defendants' liability for actual damages, and the categories of such damages; (10) defendants' liability for emotional distress damages; and (11) defendants' liability for punitive damages.

Phase 1 would be followed by notice of the trial verdict and claim forms to class members. In phase 2, the jury would determine compensatory damages in sample plaintiff cases. The jury then would establish a ratio of punitive damages to compensatory damages, which ratio thereafter would apply to each class member.

Phase 3 would entail a complicated procedure to determine compensatory damages for individual class members. The trial plan envisions determination of absent class members' compensatory economic and emotional distress damages on the basis of claim forms, "subject to verification techniques and assertion of defendants' affirmative defenses under grouping, sampling, or representative procedures to be determined by the Court."

The trial plan left open how jury trials on class members' personal injury/wrongful death claims would be handled, but the trial plan discussed the possibility of bifurcation. In phase 4, the court would apply the punitive damage ratio based on individual damage awards and would conduct a review of the reasonableness of the award.

B.   The Class Certification Order

Following extensive briefing, the district court granted, in part, plaintiffs' motion for class certification, concluding that the prerequisites of Fed.R.Civ.P. 23(a) had been met. The court rejected certification, under Fed.R.Civ.P. 23(b)(2), of the plaintiffs' claim for equitable relief, including the claim for medical monitoring. Appellees have not cross-appealed that portion of the order.

The court did grant the plaintiffs' motion to certify the class under Fed.R.Civ.P. 23(b)(3), organizing the class action issues into four categories: (1) core liability; (2) injury-in-fact, proximate cause, reliance and affirmative defenses; (3) compensatory damages; and (4) punitive damages. It then analyzed each category to determine whether it met the predominance and superiority requirements of rule 23(b)(3). Using its power to sever issues for certification under Fed.R.Civ.P. 23(c)(4), the court certified the class on core liability and punitive damages, and certified the class conditionally pursuant to Fed.R.Civ.P. 23(c)(1).

1.   Core Liability Issues

The court defined core liability issues as "common factual issues [of] whether defendants knew cigarette smoking was addictive, failed to inform cigarette smokers of such, and took actions to addict cigarette smokers. Common legal issues include fraud, negligence, breach of warranty (express or implied), strict liability, and violation of consumer protection statutes."

The court found that the predominance requirement of rule 23(b)(3) was satisfied for the core liability issues. Without any specific analysis regarding the multitude of issues that make up "core liability," the court found that under Jenkins v. Raymark Indus., 782 F.2d 468 (5th Cir. 1986), common issues predominate because resolution of core liability issues would significantly advance the individual cases. The court did not discuss why "core liability" issues would be a significant, rather than just common, part of each individual trial, nor why the individual issues in the remaining categories did not predominate over the common "core liability" issues.

The only specific analysis on predominance analysis was on the plaintiffs' fraud claim. The court determined that it would be premature to hold that individual reliance issues predominate over common issues. Relying on Eisen v. Carlisle & Jacquelin, 417 U.S. 156 (1974), the court stated that it could not inquire into the merits of the plaintiffs' claim to determine whether reliance would be an issue in individual trials. Moreover, the court recognized the possibility that under state law, reliance can be inferred when a fraud claim is based on an omission.

Accordingly, the court was convinced that it could certify the class and defer the consideration of how reliance would affect predominance.

The court also deferred substantial consideration of how variations in state law would affect predominance. Relying on two district court opinions, the court concluded that issues of fraud, breach of warranty, negligence, intentional tort, and strict liability do not vary so much from state to state as to cause individual issues to predominate. The court noted that any determination of how state law variations affect predominance was premature, as the court had yet to make a choice of law determination. As for the consumer protection claims, the court also deferred analysis of state law variations, because "there has been no showing that the consumer protection statutes differ so much as to make individual issues predominate."

The court also concluded that a class action is superior to other methods for adjudication of the core liability issues. Relying heavily on *Jenkins*, the court noted that having this common issue litigated in a class action was superior to repeated trials of the same evidence. Recognizing serious problems with manageability, it determined that such problems were outweighed by "the specter of thousands, if not millions, of similar trials of liability proceeding in thousands of courtrooms around the nation."

2. Injury-in-fact, Proximate Cause, Reliance, Affirmative Defenses, and Compensatory Damages

Using the same methodology as it did for the core liability issues, the district court refused to certify the issues of injury-in-fact, proximate cause, reliance, affirmative defenses, and compensatory damages, concluding that the "issues are so overwhelmingly replete with individual circumstances that they quickly outweigh predominance and superiority." Specifically, the court found that whether a person suffered emotional injury from addiction, whether his addiction was caused by the defendants' actions, whether he relied on the defendants' misrepresentations, and whether affirmative defenses unique to each class member precluded recovery were all individual issues. As to compensatory damages and the claim for medical monitoring, the court concluded that such claims were so intertwined with proximate cause and affirmative defenses that class certification would not materially advance the individual cases.

3. Punitive Damages

In certifying punitive damages for class treatment, the court adopted the plaintiffs' trial plan for punitive damages: The class jury would develop a ratio of punitive damages to actual damages, and the court would apply that ratio in individual cases. As it did with the core liability issues, the court determined that variations in state law, including differing burdens of proof, did not preclude certification. Rather than conduct an independent review of predominance or superiority, the court relied on *Jenkins* * * * for support of its certification order.

II.

A district court must conduct a rigorous analysis of the rule 23 prerequisites before certifying a class. The decision to certify is within the broad discretion of the court, but that discretion must be exercised within the framework of rule 23. The party seeking certification bears the burden of proof.

The district court erred in its analysis in two distinct ways. First, it failed to consider how variations in state law affect predominance and superiority. Second, its predominance inquiry did not include consideration of how a trial on the merits would be conducted.

Each of these defects mandates reversal. Moreover, at this time, while the tort is immature, the class complaint must be dismissed, as class certification cannot be found to be a superior method of adjudication.

A.   *Variations in State Law*

Although rule 23(c)(1) requires that a class should be certified "as soon as practicable" and allows a court to certify a conditional class, it does not follow that the rule's requirements are lessened when the class is conditional. * * *

In a multi-state class action, variations in state law may swamp any common issues and defeat predominance. Accordingly, a district court must consider how variations in state law affect predominance and superiority. * * * A district court's duty to determine whether the plaintiff has borne its burden on class certification requires that a court consider variations in state law when a class action involves multiple jurisdictions. "In order to make the findings required to certify a class action under Rule 23(b)(3) . . . one must initially identify the substantive law issues which will control the outcome of the litigation." Alabama v. Blue Bird Body Co., 573 F.2d 309, 316 (5th Cir. 1978).

A requirement that a court know which law will apply before making a predominance determination is especially important when there may be differences in state law. Given the plaintiffs' burden, a court cannot rely on assurances of counsel that any problems with predominance or superiority can be overcome.

The able opinion in [*In re*] *School Asbestos* [*Litigation*, 789 F.2d 996 (3d Cir. 1986),] demonstrates what is required from a district court when variations in state law exist. There, the court affirmed class certification, despite variations in state law, because:

> To meet the problem of diversity in applicable state law, class
> plaintiffs have undertaken an extensive analysis of the variances
> in products liability among the jurisdictions. That review

separates the law into four categories. Even assuming additional permutations and combinations, plaintiffs have made a creditable showing, which apparently satisfied the district court, that class certification does not present insuperable obstacles. Although we have some doubt on this score, the effort may nonetheless prove successful.

789 F.2d at 1010.

A thorough review of the record demonstrates that, in this case, the district court did not properly consider how variations in state law affect predominance. The court acknowledged as much in its order granting class certification, for, in declining to make a choice of law determination, it noted that "[t]he parties have only briefly addressed the conflict of laws issue in this matter." Similarly, the court stated that "there has been no showing that the consumer protection statutes differ so much as to make individual issues predominate."

The district court's review of state law variances can hardly be considered extensive; it conducted a cursory review of state law variations and gave short shrift to the defendants' arguments concerning variations. In response to the defendants' extensive analysis of how state law varied on fraud, products liability, affirmative defenses, negligent infliction of emotional distress, consumer protection statutes, and punitive damages,[15] the court examined a sample phase 1 jury interrogatory and verdict form, a survey of medical monitoring decisions, a survey of consumer fraud class actions, and a survey of punitive damages law in the defendants' home states. The court also relied on two district court opinions granting certification in multi-state class actions.

---

[15] We find it difficult to fathom how common issues could predominate in this case when variations in state law are thoroughly considered. * * *

The *Castano* class suffers from many of the difficulties that the *Georgine* court [Georgine v. Amchem Prods., 83 F.3d at 626 (3d Cir. 1996)] found dispositive. The class members were exposed to nicotine through different products, for different amounts of time, and over different time periods. Each class member's knowledge about the effects of smoking differs, and each plaintiff began smoking for different reasons. Each of these factual differences impacts the application of legal rules such as causation, reliance, comparative fault, and other affirmative defenses.

Variations in state law magnify the differences. In a fraud claim, some states require justifiable reliance on a misrepresentation, while others require reasonable reliance. States impose varying standards to determine when there is a duty to disclose facts.

Products liability law also differs among states. Some state do not recognize strict liability. Some have adopted Restatement (Second) of Torts § 402A. Among the states that have adopted the Restatement, there are variations.

Differences in affirmative defenses also exist. Assumption of risk is a complete defense to a products claim in some states. In others, it is a part of comparative fault analysis. Some states utilize "pure" comparative fault, others follow a "greater fault bar," and still others use an "equal fault bar."

Negligent infliction of emotional distress also involves wide variations. Some states do not recognize the cause of action at all. Some require a physical impact.

Despite these overwhelming individual issues, common issues might predominate. We are, however, left to speculate. The point of detailing the alleged differences is to demonstrate the inquiry the district court failed to make.

The district court's consideration of state law variations was inadequate. The surveys provided by the plaintiffs failed to discuss, in any meaningful way, how the court could deal with variations in state law. The consumer fraud survey simply quoted a few state courts that had certified state class actions. The survey of punitive damages was limited to the defendants' home states. Moreover, the two district court opinions on which the court relied did not support the proposition that variations in state law could be ignored. Nothing in the record demonstrates that the court critically analyzed how variations in state law would affect predominance.

The court also failed to perform its duty to determine whether the class action would be manageable in light of state law variations. The court's only discussion of manageability is a citation to *Jenkins* and the claim that "[w]hile manageability of the liability issues in this case may well prove to be difficult, the Court finds that any such difficulties pale in comparison to the specter of thousands, if not millions, of similar trials of liability proceeding in thousands of courtrooms around the nation."

The problem with this approach is that it substitutes case-specific analysis with a generalized reference to *Jenkins*. The *Jenkins* court, however, was not faced with managing a novel claim involving eight causes of action, multiple jurisdictions, millions of plaintiffs, eight defendants, and over fifty years of alleged wrongful conduct. Instead, *Jenkins* involved only 893 personal injury asbestos cases, the law of only one state, and the prospect of trial occurring in only one district. Accordingly, for purposes of the instant case, *Jenkins* is largely inapposite.

In summary, whether the specter of millions of cases outweighs any manageability problems in this class is uncertain when the scope of any manageability problems is unknown. Absent considered judgment on the manageability of the class, a comparison to millions of individual trials is meaningless.

B. *Predominance*

The district court's second error was that it failed to consider how the plaintiffs' addiction claims would be tried, individually or on a class basis. The district court, based on Eisen v. Carlisle & Jacquelin, 417 U.S. 156, 177–78 (1974), believed that it could not go past the pleadings for the certification decision. The result was an incomplete and inadequate predominance inquiry.

* * * Absent knowledge of how addiction-as-injury cases would actually be tried, however, it was impossible for the court to know whether the common issues would be a "significant" portion of the individual trials. The court just assumed that because the common issues would play a part in every trial, they must be significant.[18] The court's synthesis of *Jenkins*

---

[18] The district court's approach to predominance stands in stark contrast to the methodology the district court used in *Jenkins*. There, the district judge had a vast amount of experience with

and *Eisen* would write the predominance requirement out of the rule, and any common issue would predominate if it were common to all the individual trials.

The court's treatment of the fraud claim also demonstrates the error inherent in its approach. * * * [A] fraud class action cannot be certified when individual reliance will be an issue. The district court * * * refused to consider whether reliance would be an issue in individual trials.

The problem with the district court's approach is that after the class trial, it might have decided that reliance must be proven in individual trials. The court then would have been faced with the difficult choice of decertifying the class after phase 1 and wasting judicial resources, or continuing with a class action that would have failed the predominance requirement of rule 23(b)(3).[21]

III.

In addition to the reasons given above, regarding the district court's procedural errors, this class must be decertified because it independently fails the superiority requirement of rule 23(b)(3). In the context of mass tort class actions, certification dramatically affects the stakes for defendants. Class certification magnifies and strengthens the number of unmeritorious claims. Aggregation of claims also makes it more likely that a defendant will be found liable and results in significantly higher damage awards.

In addition to skewing trial outcomes, class certification creates insurmountable pressure on defendants to settle, whereas individual trials would not. The risk of facing an all-or-nothing verdict presents too high a risk, even when the probability of an adverse judgment is low. [In re] Rhone-Poulenc [Rorer, Inc.], 51 F.3d [1293,] 1298 [(7th Cir. 1995)]. These settlements have been referred to as judicial blackmail.

It is no surprise then, that historically, certification of mass tort litigation classes has been disfavored.[23] The traditional concern over the

---

asbestos cases. He certified the state of the art defense because it was the most significant contested issue in each case. To the contrary, however, the district court in the instant case did not, and could not, have determined that the common issues would be a significant part of each case. Unlike the judge in *Jenkins*, the district judge [in this case] had no experience with this type of case and did not even inquire into how a case would be tried to determine whether the defendants' conduct would be a significant portion of each case.

   [21] Severing the defendants' conduct from reliance under rule 23(c)(4) does not save the class action. A district court cannot manufacture predominance through the nimble use of subdivision (c)(4). The proper interpretation of the interaction between subdivisions (b)(3) and (c)(4) is that a cause of action, as a whole, must satisfy the predominance requirement of (b)(3), and that (c)(4) is a housekeeping rule that allows courts to sever he common issues for a class trial.

   [23] At the time rule 23 was drafted, mass tort litigation as we now know it did not exist. The term had been applied to single-event accidents. Even in those cases, the advisory committee cautioned against certification. As modern mass tort litigation has evolved, courts have been willing to certify simple single disaster mass torts, see Sterling v. Velsicol Chem. Corp., 855 F.2d 1188, 1197 (6th Cir. 1988), but have been hesitant to certify more complex mass torts.

rights of defendants in mass tort class actions is magnified in the instant case. Our specific concern is that a mass tort cannot be properly certified without a prior track record of trials from which the district court can draw the information necessary to make the predominance and superiority analysis required by rule 23. This is because certification of an immature tort results in a higher than normal risk that the class action may not be superior to individual adjudication.

We first address the district court's superiority analysis. The court acknowledged the extensive manageability problems with this class. Such problems include difficult choice of law determinations, subclassing of eight claims with variations in state law, *Erie* guesses, notice to millions of class members, further subclassing to take account of transient plaintiffs, and the difficult procedure for determining who is nicotine-dependent. Cases with far fewer manageability problems have given courts pause.

The district court's rationale for certification in spite of such problems—i.e., that a class trial would preserve judicial resources in the millions of inevitable individual trials—is based on pure speculation. Not every mass tort is asbestos, and not every mass tort will result in the same judicial crises.[24] The judicial crisis to which the district court referred is only theoretical.

What the district court failed to consider, and what no court can determine at this time, is the very real possibility that the judicial crisis may fail to materialize.[25] The plaintiffs' claims are based on a new theory of liability and the existence of new evidence. Until plaintiffs decide to file individual claims, a court cannot, from the existence of injury, presume that all or even any plaintiffs will pursue legal remedies. Nor can a court make a superiority determination based on such speculation.

---

[24] There is reason to believe that even a mass tort like asbestos could be managed, without class certification, in a way that avoids judicial meltdown. In a case such as this one, where causation is a key element, disaggregation of claims allows courts to dismiss weak and frivolous claims on summary judgment. Where novel theories of recovery are advanced (such as addiction as injury), courts can aggressively weed out untenable theories. Courts can use case management techniques to avoid discovery abuses. The parties can also turn to mediation and arbitration to settle individual or aggregated cases.

[25] The plaintiffs, in seemingly inconsistent positions, argue that the lack of a judicial crisis justifies certification; they assert that the reason why individual plaintiffs have not filed claims is that the tobacco industry makes individual trials far too expensive and plaintiffs are rarely successful. The fact that a party continuously loses at trial does not justify class certification, however. The plaintiffs' argument, if accepted, would justify class treatment whenever a defendant has better attorneys and resources at its disposal.

The plaintiffs' claim also overstates the defendants' ability to outspend plaintiffs. Assuming arguendo that the defendants pool resources and outspend plaintiffs in individual trials, there is no reason why plaintiffs still cannot prevail. The class is represented by a consortium of well-financed plaintiffs' lawyers who, over time, can develop the expertise and specialized knowledge sufficient to beat the tobacco companies at their own game. Courts can also overcome the defendant's alleged advantages through coordination or consolidation of cases for discovery and other pretrial matters.

Severe manageability problems and the lack of a judicial crisis are not the only reasons why superiority is lacking. The most compelling rationale for finding superiority in a class action—the existence of a negative value suit—is missing in this case.

As he stated in the record, plaintiffs' counsel in this case has promised to inundate the courts with individual claims if class certification is denied. Independently of the reliability of this self-serving promise, there is reason to believe that individual suits are feasible. First, individual damage claims are high, and punitive damages are available in most states. The expense of litigation does not necessarily turn this case into a negative value suit, in part because the prevailing party may recover attorneys' fees under many consumer protection statutes.

In a case such as this one, where each plaintiff may receive a large award, and fee shifting often is available, we find Chief Judge Posner's analysis of superiority to be persuasive:

> For this consensus or maturing of judgment the district judge proposes to substitute a single trial before a single jury. . . . One jury . . . will hold the fate of an industry in the palm of its hand. . . . That kind of thing can happen in our system of civil justice. . . . But it need not be tolerated when the alternative exists of submitting an issue to multiple juries constituting in the aggregate a much larger and more diverse sample of decision-makers. That would not be a feasible option if the stakes to each class member were too slight to repay the cost of suit. . . . But this is not the case. . . . Each plaintiff if successful is apt to receive a judgment in the millions. With the aggregate stakes in the tens or hundreds of millions of dollars, or even in the billions, it is not a waste of judicial resources to conduct more than one trial, before more than six jurors, to determine whether a major segment of the international pharmaceutical industry is to follow the asbestos manufacturers into Chapter 11.

Rhone-Poulenc, 51 F.3d at 1300. So too here, we cannot say that it would be a waste to allow individual trials to proceed, before a district court engages in the complicated predominance and superiority analysis necessary to certify a class. * * *

The remaining rationale for superiority—judicial efficiency—is also lacking. In the context of an immature tort, any savings in judicial resources is speculative, and any imagined savings would be overwhelmed by the procedural problems that certification of a sui generis cause of action brings with it.

Even assuming arguendo that the tort system will see many more addiction-as-injury claims, a conclusion that certification will save judicial resources is premature at this stage of the litigation. Take for example the district court's plan to divide core liability from other issues such as comparative negligence and reliance. The assumption is that after a class verdict, the common issues will not be a part of follow-up trials. The court has no basis for that assumption.

It may be that comparative negligence will be raised in the individual trials, and the evidence presented at the class trial will have to be repeated. The same may be true for reliance. The net result may be a waste, not a savings, in judicial resources. Only after the courts have more experience with this type of case can a court certify issues in a way that preserves judicial resources.

Even assuming that certification at this time would result in judicial efficiencies in individual trials, certification of an immature tort brings with it unique problems that may consume more judicial resources than certification will save. These problems are not speculative; the district court faced, and ignored, many of the problems that immature torts can cause.

* * *

The district court's predominance inquiry, or lack of it, squarely presents the problems associated with certification of immature torts. Determining whether the common issues are a "significant" part of each individual case has an abstract quality to it when no court in this country has ever tried an injury-as-addiction claim. As the plaintiffs admitted to the district court, "we don't have the learning [curve] that is necessary to say to Your Honor 'this is precisely how this case can be tried and that will not run afoul of the teachings of the 5th Circuit.' "

Yet, an accurate finding on predominance is necessary before the court can certify a class. It may turn out that the defendant's conduct, while common, is a minor part of each trial. Premature certification deprives the defendant of the opportunity to present that argument to any court and risks decertification after considerable resources have been expended.

The court's analysis of reliance also demonstrates the potential judicial inefficiencies in immature tort class actions. Individual trials will determine whether individual reliance will be an issue. Rather than guess that reliance may be inferred, a district court should base its determination that individual reliance does not predominate on the wisdom of such individual trials. The risk that a district court will make the wrong guess, that the parties will engage in years of litigation, and that the class ultimately will be decertified (because reliance predominates over common issues) prevents this class action from being a superior method of adjudication.

* * *

Another factor weighing heavily in favor of individual trials is the risk that in order to make this class action manageable, the court will be forced to bifurcate issues in violation of the Seventh Amendment. This class action is permeated with individual issues, such as proximate causation, comparative negligence, reliance, and compensatory damages. In order to manage so many individual issues, the district court proposed to empanel a class jury to adjudicate common issues. A second jury, or a number of "second" juries, will pass on the individual issues, either on a case-by-case basis or through group trials of individual plaintiffs.

The Seventh Amendment entitles parties to have fact issues decided by one jury, and prohibits a second jury from reexamining those facts and issues. Thus, Constitution allows bifurcation of issues that are so separable that the second jury will not be called upon to reconsider findings of fact by the first:

> [T]his Court has cautioned that separation of issues is not the usual course that should be followed, and that the issue to be tried must be so distinct and separable from the others that a trial of it alone may be had without injustice. This limitation on the use of bifurcation is a recognition of the fact that inherent in the Seventh Amendment guarantee of a trial by jury is the general right of a litigant to have only one jury pass on a common issue of fact. The Supreme Court recognized this principle in Gasoline Products [Co., Inc. v. Champlin Refining Co., 283 U.S. 494 (1931)]. . . . The Court explained . . . that a partial new trial may not be "properly resorted to unless it clearly appears that the issue to be retried is so distinct and separable from the others that a trial of it alone may be had without injustice." Such a rule is dictated for the very practical reason that if separate juries are allowed to pass on issues involving overlapping legal and factual questions the verdicts rendered by each jury could be inconsistent.

Alabama v. Blue Bird Body Co., 573 F.2d 309, 318 (5th Cir. 1978).

* * *

Severing a defendant's conduct from comparative negligence results in the type of risk that our court forbade in *Blue Bird*. Comparative negligence, by definition, requires a comparison between the defendant's and the plaintiff's conduct. At a bare minimum, a second jury will rehear evidence of the defendant's conduct. There is a risk that in apportioning fault, the second jury could reevaluate the defendant's fault, determine that the defendant was not at fault, and apportion 100% of the fault to the plaintiff. In such a situation, the second jury would be impermissibly reconsidering the findings of a first jury. The risk of such reevaluation is so great that class treatment can hardly be said to be superior to individual adjudication.

The plaintiffs' final retort is that individual trials are inadequate because time is running out for many of the plaintiffs. They point out that prior litigation against the tobacco companies has taken up to ten years to wind through the legal system. While a compelling rhetorical argument, it is ultimately inconsistent with the plaintiffs' own arguments and ignores the realities of the legal system. First, the plaintiffs' reliance on prior personal injury cases is unpersuasive, as they admit that they have new evidence and are pursuing a claim entirely different from that of past plaintiffs.

Second, the plaintiffs' claim that time is running out ignores the reality of the class action device. In a complicated case involving multiple jurisdictions, the conflict of law question itself could take decades to work its way through the courts. Once that issue has been resolved, discovery, subclassing, and ultimately the class trial would take place. Next would come the appellate process. After the class trial, the individual trials and appeals on comparative negligence and damages would have to take place. The net result could be that the class action device would lengthen, not shorten, the time it takes for the plaintiffs to reach final judgment.

IV.

The district court abused its discretion by ignoring variations in state law and how a trial on the alleged causes of action would be tried. Those errors cannot be corrected on remand because of the novelty of the plaintiffs' claims. Accordingly, class treatment is not superior to individual adjudication.

We have once before stated that "traditional ways of proceeding reflect far more than habit. They reflect the very culture of the jury trial. . . ." In re Fibreboard Corp., 893 F.2d 706, 711 (5th Cir. 1990). The collective wisdom of individual juries is necessary before this court commits the fate of an entire industry or, indeed, the fate of a class of millions, to a single jury. For the forgoing reasons, we REVERSE and REMAND with instructions that the district court dismiss the class complaint.

NOTES AND QUESTIONS

1. *Castano* can be viewed as part of a judicial reaction against what some considered excessive use of class actions for mass torts. Shortly before the Fifth Circuit's *Castano* decision, cases in the Sixth and Seventh Circuits also imposed stricter standards on mass tort class actions. No absolute bar to mass tort class actions emerged, however. In Valentino v. Carter-Wallace, Inc., 97 F.3d 1227 (9th Cir. 1996), the court rejected the argument that it had adopted a rule that certification is never appropriate for a multi-state personal injury class action. The district court had conditionally certified a nationwide product liability class action on behalf of users of an epilepsy drug, claiming the manufacturer had not warned of serious side effects. Because the case involved only one manufacturer, only one product, and a single marketing

program over a relatively short period of time, the case was likely to be more manageable than other product liability class actions. Accordingly, certification might become appropriate after further proceedings in the district court, but the court did vacate the brief certification order entered by the district judge.

State-court decisions are sometimes receptive to mass tort class actions, particularly under distinctive laws of the state. For example, in In re West Virginia Rezulin Litigation, 585 S.E.2d 52 (W.Va. 2003), the state supreme court reversed the trial court's refusal to certify a class in pharmaceutical product litigation. Plaintiffs sought to represent a class of approximately 5,000 West Virginians who took the anti-diabetes drug Rezulin in a suit alleging that it caused liver damage in some users and that defendant manufacturer had concealed this risk. Eschewing absolute reliance on federal class-action cases, which it characterized as a "Pavlovian response to federal decisional law," the state court held that plaintiffs were entitled to class certification under W.Va.R.Civ.P. 23 on a claim for a medical monitoring fund under state consumer protection law. Common issues existed regarding the dangers posed by Rezulin, and proof of a specific loss was not required to support a claim under state consumer law. All that had to be shown was that class members had "a significantly increased risk of contracting a particular disease relative to what would be the case in the absence of exposure." Moreover, the court found that plaintiffs sought relief that would justify certification under Rule 23(b)(2) as well as Rule 23(b)(3).

2.   The *Castano* opinion noted that "in a multi-state class action, variations in state law may swamp any common issues and defeat predominance" and found that the lower court's consideration of state law variations was inadequate. This has been read as "imposing stringent tests on potential class plaintiffs that district courts must apply: The plaintiff has the burden of satisfying the court that class treatment is appropriate, the trial court must conduct a rigorous de novo review of state law, and conditional certification cannot justify a court's overlooking problems with predominance or superiority. *Castano* reflects a new scrutiny that is apprehensive of claims about the social utility of class actions in the mass tort setting." In re Masonite Corp. Hardboard Siding Products Liability Lit., 170 F.R.D. 417, 423 (E.D.La. 1997). In that case, the judge refused to certify a nationwide class of persons and entities whose buildings had Masonite siding, finding the state laws as to such issues as negligence, comparative fault, strict liability, and state of the art defense varied substantially: "this court cannot imagine managing a trial under the law of the jurisdictions on the defectiveness of Masonite siding." Id. at 425.

Since *Castano*, motions to certify nationwide class actions have often been accompanied by a much more careful analysis of state laws. Typically plaintiffs argue either that under choice of law doctrines, the law of one state will apply or that the laws of all the states fall into a small number of categories, allowing a jury to apply the different standards by answering different interrogatories. This harks back to In re School Asbestos Lit., 789 F.2d 996, 1010 (3d Cir.), cert.

denied, 479 U.S. 852 (1986), which approved a multistate class action for economic harms to property where the state laws would fit into four basic categories. In re Prudential Ins. Co. of America Sales Practices, 962 F.Supp. 450 (D.N.J. 1997), approved a settlement class action on behalf of a nationwide class of purchasers of insurance policies based on alleged misrepresentations relating to premiums (the "vanishing premium") and improper inducement to replace policies. The court cited "a series of charts setting forth comprehensive analyses of the various states' laws potentially applicable to their common law claims for fraud, breach of contract, implied obligations of good faith and fair dealing, negligence, and negligent misrepresentation." Id. at 525. It found that the laws fell into "a limited number of predictable patterns" and "a manageable number of jury instructions could be fashioned to comport with the elements of the common law claims in the many jurisdictions."

Despite attempts to find that different states' laws are sufficiently similar so that they can be fitted into a small number of categories, courts have often agreed with *Castano* that there are too many differences in a nationwide class action to make categorization manageable. See, e.g., In re Bridgestone/ Firestone, Inc., *infra* p. 392 (stating that if claims have to be adjudicated under the laws of fifty states "a single nationwide class is not manageable"); Spence v. Glock, 227 F.3d 308, 311 (5th Cir. 2000) (stating that where the laws of many different states would apply, variations in the law "may swamp any common issues and defeat predominance"). Compare Mejdrech v. Met-Coil Systems Corp., 319 F.3d 910 (7th Cir. 2003), a case alleging contamination from a leaking storage tank, in which the court said it was not "a case in which, because class members are scattered around the country and proceeding under the laws of different states, determination of class-wide issues would require the judge to create a composite legal standard that is the positive law of no jurisdiction." As *Mejdriech* suggests, a choice of law rule that provides for application of only one state's law can solve these problems. We will examine these issues in detail. See pp. 388–404 *infra*.

3.   The *Castano* opinion criticizes the lower court for believing that "it could not go past the pleadings for the certification decision." It says "a court must understand the claims, defenses, relevant facts, and applicable substantive law in order to make a meaningful determination of the certification issues." Does this mean the lower court should have asked how the plaintiffs planned to prove their addiction-as-injury claims and, if persuaded that this would be done with individualized, as opposed to classwide, evidence, should not have certified the class? For further discussion, see Litigating Class Certification, *infra* p. 333.

4.   How important to the holding in *Castano* is the concern that "class certification creates insurmountable pressure on defendants to settle?" Judge Posner placed great weight on that point in *Rhone-Poulenc*, discussed in *Castano*. Other courts have been less receptive to the argument that class certification creates improper settlement pressure. As the then-Judge Sotomayor put it in an antitrust case in which newspaper reports suggested that class-action damages might amount to $39 billion, "[t]he effect of

certification on parties' leverage in settlement negotiations is a fact of life for class action litigants. While the sheer size of the class in this case may enhance this effect, this alone cannot defeat an otherwise proper certification." In re Visa Check/MasterMoney Antitrust Litigation, 280 F.3d 124 (2d Cir. 2001).

5.   Does the charge of "judicial blackmail" referred to in *Castano* take on added weight because of the lack of prior litigation on the novel issue of liability for nicotine addiction? The opinion notes that with such "immature torts" there is no learning curve. This would increase the likelihood of error (which could be of monumental proportions given class treatment). Consistent with *Castano*'s demand for a "track record of trials from which [to] draw the information necessary to make the predominance and superiority requirements," one court ordered a limited number of individual trials "to familiarize itself and the parties with the contours of this litigation." In re Norplant Contraceptive Prods. Liability Lit., MDL No. 1039, Order of May 17, 1996 (E.D. Tex.).

In 1996, the Advisory Committee on the Civil Rules circulated a tentative draft of possible amendments to Rule 23(b)(3) that would have directed a court to make findings including attention to the "maturity of any related litigation." See Proposed Amendments to the Federal Rules, 167 F.R.D. 523, 559 (1996). The draft Committee Note explained that the possible addition of a maturity factor "reflects the need to support class adjudication by experience gained in completed litigation of several individual claims. If the results of individual litigation begin to converge, class adjudication may seem appropriate. Class adjudication may be inappropriate, however, if individual litigation continues to yield inconsistent results, or if individual litigation demonstrates that knowledge has not yet advanced far enough to support confident decision on a class basis." Id. at 562–63. Should this maturity consideration matter in a securities fraud class action? Eventually, amendments to add a "maturity" factor were shelved.

6.   The appellate court in *Castano* faults the lower court for failing to consider "the very real possibility that the judicial crisis may fail to materialize." Must there be a flood of individual case filings before class treatment is justified? That is what happened in asbestos litigation, but why shouldn't a class action be available to resolve a problem that has not yet generated lots of individual cases? The opinion recognizes that "negative-value" cases (cases in which each class member's injury is of such a small dollar value as to make individual litigation economically unfeasible) may be accorded class treatment without a judicial crisis of case filings. Even then, should a court consider that the class members stand to benefit so little that the transaction costs of a class action are not justified? Does deterrence of a defendant's wrongful conduct that affects many people by only a small dollar amount justify all "negative-value" class actions?

7.   In *Castano*, the court also objects that a bifurcated trial might create a risk of violating the Seventh Amendment's prohibition of reexamination of a prior jury verdict. This concern, which is not limited to class actions, is considered further in Chapter 8. See *infra* p. 634 n.6.

8. *Postscript on tobacco class actions*: Following the failure of the nationwide class in *Castano*, plaintiffs' attorneys began filing class actions state-by-state in state court. In Florida, a statewide class had a phase I trial, resulting in findings for the class as to such questions as whether smoking causes health conditions and whether defendants concealed information of adverse health effects were approved. The Florida Supreme Court approved those findings, but on remand continued treatment as a class action was found not feasible and the class was decertified. Class members could, however, proceed individually, with the findings in the class action trial given preclusive effect. Engle v. Liggett Group, Inc., 945 So.2d 1246 (Fla. 2006); see R.J. Reynolds Tobacco Co. v. Martin, 53 So.3d 1060 (Fla.App. 2010) (upholding judgment for $3.3 million in compensatory and $25 million in punitive damages based on *Engle* findings); Philip Morris, Inc. v. Douglas, 110 So.3d 419 (Fla. 2013) (rejecting argument that giving preclusive effect to class-action findings violated defendants' due process rights).

In Louisiana, a statewide class was certified for medical monitoring and a class trial resulted in jury findings that required tobacco companies to undertake smoking "cessation" programs. Scott v. American Tobacco Co., 725 So.2d 10 (La.App. 1998). The defendant companies were ordered to pay about $250 million (after attorneys' fees) into a trust to fund the program, and the court appointed independent trustees to administer the program. See also Scott v. American Tobacco Co., 36 So.3d 1046 (La.App. 2010). In In re Tobacco II Cases, 207 P.3d 20 (Cal. 2009), the California Supreme Court ruled that a class action was proper to assert claims of deceptive advertising and misleading statements about the addictive nature of nicotine and the health effects of smoking. Individual suits have continued as well. For a more general review of the impact of tobacco litigation on procedure, see Richard Marcus, Reassessing the Magnetic Pull of Mega-cases on Procedure, 51 DePaul L.Rev. 457 (2001).

Issue Certification Under Rule 23(c)(4)

Rule 23(c)(4) provides: "When appropriate, an action may be brought or maintained as a class action with respect to particular issues." In *Castano, supra* p. 288 fn.21, the court asserted that a court "may not manufacture predominance through the nimble use of subdivision (c)(4)." Instead, it asserted, "[t]he proper interpretation of the interaction between subdivision (b)(3) and (c)(4) is that a cause of action, as a whole, must satisfy the predominance requirement of (b)(3), that (c)(4) is a housekeeping rule that allows courts to sever the common issues for a class trial." 84 F.3d at 745 n.21. The Committee Note to the 1966 amendment to the rule, when (c)(4) was added, observed that "in a fraud or similar case the action may retain its 'class' character only through the adjudication of liability to the class; the members of the class may thereafter be required to come in individually and prove the amounts of their respective claims." Of course, whether *Castano* fit the mold the framers had in mind for a "fraud or similar case" could certainly be debated. At least some felt that the *Castano* interpretation should be followed. Thus, the Class Action Fairness Act, passed by the House of Representatives in 2017, but not passed by the Senate, included the following provision:

> A federal court shall not issue an order granting certification of a class action with respect to particular issues pursuant to Rule 23(c)(4) of the Federal Rules of Civil Procedure unless the entirety of the cause of action from which the particular issues arise satisfies all the class certification prerequisites of Rule 23(a) and Rule 23(b)(1), Rule 23(b)(2), or Rule 23(b)(3).

For academic support of this approach to Rule 23(c)(4), see Laura Hines, Challenging the Issue Class End-Run, 52 Emory L.J. 758 (2003) (warning against permitting (c)(4) to "transmogrify" (b)(3) class actions). But in Jenkins v. Raymark Indus., 782 F.2d 468 (5th Cir. 1986) (cited in *Castano*), the same court had seemingly looked with favor on using class certification of common issues and later resolution of individual issues in asbestos litigation. As the following case shows, there has been increasing judicial receptivity to using Rule 23(c)(4) for certification where that is a superior method of resolving cases.

MARTIN V. BEHR DAYTON THERMAL PRODUCTS LLC

United States Court of Appeals, Sixth Circuit, 2018.
896 F.3d 405.

Before GILMAN, ROGERS and STRANCH, CIRCUIT JUDGES

JANE V. STRANCH, CIRCUIT JUDGE.

This toxic tort class action case arises from Defendants' alleged contamination of the groundwater in the McCook Field neighborhood of Dayton, Ohio. Plaintiffs own properties in McCook Field, which is a low-income area surrounding a Superfund site. They allege that Defendants [Behr Dayton Thermal Products, Chrysler Motors, and Aramark Uniform and Career Apparel] released volatile organic compounds and other hazardous substances into the groundwater underlying their properties and were deliberately indifferent to the resultant harm. The district court denied Plaintiffs' motion for class certification under Federal Rule of Civil Procedure 23(b)(3), but certified seven issues for class treatment under Rule 23(c)(4). Defendants filed a Rule 23(f) petition to appeal the district court's issue-class certification order, and this court granted review. For the following reasons, we AFFIRM the district court's certification decision.

[30 named plaintiffs filed this class action against three companies, claiming that they had released toxic chemicals into the environment during operation of automotive and dry cleaning facilities, and that the toxic chemicals had seeped into the groundwater. Plaintiffs asserted that defendants knew of the contamination from at least 2000 but did not remediate. The U.S. Environmental Protection Agency initiated an emergency removal action in 2007, and designated the area as a Superfund site in 2009, alleging that defendants released trichloroethene (TCE), and that contaminated groundwater migrated into the area underlying plaintiffs' properties. Although plaintiffs have a municipal source for drinking water, they face the risk of toxic vapor intrusion into their homes, which may cause plaintiffs to inhale carcinogens.

Plaintiffs sought Rule 23(b)(3) class certification as to liability only for their claims for private nuisance, negligence, negligence per se, strict liability, and unjust enrichment. The district court declined to certify under Rule 23(b)(3) because under Ohio law regarding injury-in-fact and causation plaintiffs could not satisfy Rule 23(b)(3) predominance. Nevertheless, it did certify the following issues under what it called the "broad view" of Rule 23(c)(4):]

> Issue 1: Each Defendant's role in creating the contamination within their respective Plumes, including their historical operations, disposal practices, and chemical usage;
>
> Issue 2: Whether or not it was foreseeable to Chrysler and Aramark that their improper handling and disposal of TCE and/or PCE could cause the Behr-DTP and Aramark Plumes, respectively, and subsequent injuries;
>
> Issue 3: Whether Chrysler, Behr, and/or Aramark engaged in abnormally dangerous activities for which they are strictly liable;
>
> Issue 4: Whether contamination from the Chrysler-Behr Facility underlies the Chrysler-Behr and Chrysler-Behr-Aramark Class Areas;
>
> Issue 5: Whether contamination from the Aramark Facility underlies the Chrysler-Behr-Aramark Class Area;
>
> Issue 6: Whether Chrysler and/or Aramark's contamination, and all three Defendants' inaction, caused class members to incur the potential for vapor intrusion; and
>
> Issue 7: Whether Defendants negligently failed to investigate and remediate the contamination at and flowing from their respective Facilities.

The district court concluded its class certification decision by stating that it would "establish procedures by which the remaining individualized issues concerning fact-of-injury, proximate causation, and extent of damages can be resolved" and noting that any such procedures would comply with the Reexamination Clause of the Seventh Amendment.

Defendants filed a timely Rule 23(f) petition. They argued that the district court reached the wrong conclusion on the interaction between Rules 23(b)(3) and 23(c)(4) and that, even under the broad view, the issue classes do not pass muster. Defendants also raised Seventh Amendment arguments, citing the district court's mention of a potential procedure involving the use of a Special Master to resolve remaining issues.

* * *

Rule 23(b)(3) and Rule 23(c)(4)

As the district court and the parties point out, other circuits have disagreed about how Rule 23(b)(3)'s requirements interact with Rule 23(c)(4). Rule 23(b)(3) permits class certification where "the court finds that the questions of law or fact common to class members predominate over any questions affecting only individual members, and that a class action is superior to other available methods for fairly and efficiently adjudicating the controversy." Rule 23(c)(4) provides that, "[w]hen appropriate, an action may be brought or maintained as a class action with respect to particular issues."

Under what is known as the broad view, courts apply the Rule 23(b)(3) predominance and superiority prongs after common issues have been identified for class treatment under Rule 23(c)(4). The broad view permits utilizing Rule 23(c)(4) even where predominance has not been satisfied for the cause of action as a whole. *See In re Nassau Cty. Strip Search Cases*, 461 F.3d 219, 227 (2d Cir. 2006) (permitting issue certification "regardless of whether the claim as a whole satisfies Rule 23(b)(3)'s predominance requirement"); *Valentino v. Carter-Wallace, Inc.*, 97 F.3d 1227, 1234 (9th Cir. 1996) ("Even if the common questions do not predominate over the individual questions so that class certification of the entire action is warranted, Rule 23 authorizes the district court in appropriate cases to isolate the common issues under Rule 23(c)(4) and proceed with class treatment of these particular issues."). In addition to the Second and Ninth Circuits, the Fourth and Seventh Circuits have supported this approach.

The Fifth Circuit explained in a footnote what is known as "the narrow view," which prohibits issue classing if predominance has not been satisfied for the cause of action as a whole. *Castano*'s issue-class footnote has not been adopted by any other circuit, and subsequent caselaw from within the Fifth Circuit itself indicates that any potency the narrow view once held there has dwindled.

Two circuit court decisions have relied on a functional, superiority-like analysis instead of adopting either the broad or the narrow view. *See Gates v. Rohm & Haas Co.*, 655 F.3d 255, 273 (3d Cir. 2011) (evaluating issue certification based on the factors set forth in Principles of the Law of Aggregate Litigation §§ 2.02–05 (2010)); *In re St. Jude Med., Inc.*, 522 F.3d 836, 841 (8th Cir. 2008) (declining to certify issue classes because they "would do little to increase the efficiency of the litigation").

Our Circuit has not yet squarely addressed the interplay between Rule 23(b)(3) and Rule 23(c)(4), but the case at hand requires us to grapple with the two provisions. An evaluation of the broad approach persuades us of its merits.

First, the broad approach respects each provision's contribution to class determinations by maintaining Rule 23(b)(3)'s rigor without rendering Rule 23(c)(4) superfluous. The broad approach retains the predominance factor, but instructs courts to engage in the predominance inquiry *after* identifying issues suitable for class treatment. Accordingly, the broad view does not risk undermining the predominance requirement. By contrast, the narrow view would virtually nullify Rule 23(c)(4).

Second, the broad view flows naturally from Rule 23's text, which provides for issue classing "[w]hen appropriate." A prior version of Rule 23 even instructed that, after selecting issues for class treatment, the remainder of Rule 23's provisions "shall then be construed and applied accordingly." Although the Rule no longer contains this sequencing directive, the Advisory Committee made clear that the changes to the Rule's language were "stylistic only." Fed. R. Civ. P. 23(c)(4) adv. comm. n. to 2007 amend. The Advisory Committee has also declined to alter the language of Rule 23(c)(4) to reflect the narrow view or otherwise limit the use of issue classes. [The court cited the Advisory Committee agenda material quoted in the Notes and Questions below.]

Third, the concomitant application of Rule 23(b)(3)'s superiority requirement ensures that courts will not rely on issue certification where there exist only minor or insignificant common questions, but instead where the common questions render issue certification the superior method of resolution. Superiority therefore functions as a backstop against inefficient use of Rule 23(c)(4). In this way, the broad view also partakes of the functional approach employed in *Gates*, 655 F.3d at 273, and *St. Jude*, 522 F.3d at 841.

In sum, Rule 23(c)(4) contemplates using issue certification to retain a case's class character where common questions predominate within certain issues and where class treatment of those issues is the superior method of resolution. A requirement that predominance must first be satisfied for the entire cause of action would undercut the purpose of Rule 23(c)(4) and nullify its intended benefits. The broad approach is the proper reading of Rule 23, in light of the goals of that rule.

Application

Although the district court adopted the broad approach, its analysis did not include a robust application of predominance and superiority to the issues it certified for class treatment. The record nevertheless confirms that the issue classes satisfy both requirements, and this court may affirm for any reason supported by the record.

Predominance

Rule 23(b)(3)'s predominance inquiry asks whether "the questions of law or fact common to class members predominate over any question affecting only individual members." To evaluate predominance, "[a] court must first *characterize* the issues as common or individual and then *weigh* which predominate." * * *

Here, the district court certified only issues capable of resolution with generalized, class-wide proof. All seven of these issues are questions that need only be answered once because the answers apply the same way to each property owner within the [toxic] plumes. Expert evidence will be central to resolving Issues 1, 4, and 5. Such evidence will bear on all of the property owners within each plume in the same way. In addition, Issues 1, 2, 3, 6, and 7 turn on each Defendant's knowledge and conduct, which need only be established once for each plume.

The district court's determination that individualized inquiries predominate over the elements of actual injury and causation does not mean that the same individualized inquiries taint the certified issues. To the contrary, the certified issues do not overlap with actual injury or causation. Issue 6, to be sure, includes the word "caused," but whether Defendants created the risk of vapor intrusion is distinct from the ultimate question of whether they caused an actual injury to property owners. * * *

Nor have Defendants identified any individualized inquiries that outweigh the common questions prevalent *within each issue.* * * *

The Eighth Circuit's decision in *Ebert v. General Mills, Inc.*, 823 F.3d 472 (8th Cir. 2016), on which Defendants rely, does not indicate otherwise. There, the court found that the district court's certification of a liability class was an abuse of discretion because "even on the certified issue of liability, there are determinations contained within that analysis that are not suitable for class-wide determination." Specifically, the Eighth Circuit stated:

> Adjudicating claims of liability will require an inquiry into the causal relationship between the actions of General Mills and the resulting alleged vapor contamination. This analysis will include many additional considerations beyond the limited inquiry into General Mills' liability. And, even on the certified issue of liability, there are determinations contained within that analysis that are not suitable for class-wide determination. To resolve liability there must be a determination as to whether vapor contamination, if any, threatens or exists on each individual property as a result of General Mills' actions, and, if so, whether that contamination is wholly, or actually, attributable to General Mills in each instance.

The district court noted that these same problems arise from Ohio's construction of causation and actual injury, and in fact relied on *Ebert* when denying Plaintiffs' request for certification of two liability-only classes under Rule 23(b)(3). But predominance problems within a liability-only class do not automatically translate into predominance problems within an issue class, and Defendants fail to explain why *Ebert* extends to issue-only classes. Accordingly, their invocation of *Ebert*'s broad cautionary language does not map onto the specific certification order at issue here.

Superiority

[Turning to superiority, the court acknowledged that resolution of the certified issues would not resolve defendants' liability to any class member, but concluded that "resolving the certified issues will go a long way toward doing so, and this is the most efficient way of resolving the seven issues that the district court has certified." It also noted that "the properties are in a low-income neighborhood, meaning that class members might not otherwise be able to pursue their claims" and that all of these issues would have to be resolved in individual suits. It cited its own prior view that "small awards weigh in favor of class suits."]

The Seventh Amendment

[Defendants also argued that the district court's approach, possibly involving a special master to resolve individualized issues, would run afoul of the Reexamination Clause of the Seventh Amendment. But the court of appeals concluded that this possibility remained hypothetical because no the district court had not adopted any procedure for this purpose.]

CONCLUSION

This case has dragged on for ten years, but the district court's use of Rule 23(c)(4) issue classing took a meaningful step toward resolving Plaintiffs' claims. Under the broad view, the certification decision did not constitute an abuse of discretion. Nor, at this time, are any Seventh Amendment problems presented. We therefore AFFIRM the district court's issue-class certification decision and return this case to the district court with the expectation that it be moved expeditiously toward resolution.

NOTES AND QUESTIONS

1.   Is there any reason why class counsel would prefer Rule 23(c)(4) certification if they could obtain Rule 23(b)(3) certification? Consider whether they could obtain an attorney fee award under Rule 23(h) by prevailing on the certified issues. We will examine attorney fee awards in Chapter 6, *infra* p. 440. Won't issue certification always be a second best fallback?

2.   The court in *Martin* favors a "functional approach" to the predominance and superiority factors in Rule 23(b)(3) in place of the attitude in *Castano* that "nimble use" of (c)(4) should not be employed to "manufacture predominance." It has been said that "issue classes are now experiencing a

renaissance." Elizabeth Chamblee Burch, Constructing Issue Classes, 101 Va.L.Rev. 1855 (2015). Even the Fifth Circuit has observed that "predominance may be ensured in a mass accident case * * * by means of multi-phase trials under Rule 23(c)(4)." In re Deepwater Horizon, 739 F.3d 790, 816 (5th Cir. 2014).

Section 2.02(a)(1) of the American Law Institute Principles of Aggregate Litigation (2009) supports "aggregate treatment of a common issue" if it would "materially advance the resolution of multiple civil claims by addressing the core of the dispute in a manner superior to other realistic procedural alternatives, so as to generate significant judicial efficiencies." Consider how the Rule 23(b)(3) criteria apply in such settings:

(a) *Predominance*: In *Martin*, the court noted that resolution of the certified issues would depend on expert evidence and would apply in the same way to each property owner. Compare Hostetler v. Johnson Controls, Inc., 2018 WL 3868848 (N.D.Ind. Aug. 15, 2018), brought by five people who lived near defendant's factory, alleging that contamination released by the factory had migrated to neighboring properties. They sought to sue on behalf of a class of all persons who had owned or occupied property in the area, and requested certification under Rule 23(c)(4) of seven specific issues. The court refused to certify, emphasizing "what issues the Plaintiffs concede *will not* be resolved in the class, and will have to be resolved in the second phase":

> The Plaintiffs do not seek to establish that Johnson Controls was negligent. Nor do the Plaintiffs seek to establish that any individual plaintiff was ever exposed to contamination or that any contamination ever entered any of the structures in the class area. They concede that the second phase will require a "property-by-property estimate of the dose and duration of vapor exposure," and that each class member will have to individually prove that a completed pathway existed for vapor to enter their home and that the dose and duration of their exposure to cause their alleged injuries.

It added that "each individual trial in the second phase will require the presentation of evidence of Johnson Controls' conduct, and of each individual plaintiff's exposure to contamination and the amount and duration of that exposure." Id. at *8.

How confident can the court be at the class certification stage that such individualized proof will not be necessary even after certified issues are resolved? Recall that in its 1983 refusal to certify a class in a pharmaceutical products action the court in Mertens v. Abbott Laboratories, *supra* p. 278–279, the judge said that the court should "predict the evidence likely to be introduced at trial," and also noted that "it is unlikely that anything of real value could be determined that would aid in the resolution of the claims of any individual plaintiff." Might certified issues be expressed at such a level of abstraction that their resolution would not ultimately prove helpful? Should that possibility be regarded as going to predominance or superiority?

(b) *Superiority*: In *Martin*, the court pointed out that the class was made up of low income persons who might be unable to pursue their claims without class certification. Contrast the discussion of "negative value" claims in *Castano*. One might urge that class certification of common issues is usually superior. Consider the following view in Scott Dodson, Personal Jurisdiction and Aggregation, 113 Nw.U.L.Rev. 1, 4 (2018):

> In contrast to the burdens, inefficiencies, and potential unfairness of individualized litigation, aggregation makes sense from all perspectives. Aggregation permits the common issues to be litigated once, with all interests presented and determined in a single adjudication. Both plaintiffs and defendants can pool their resources and share information to make their litigation efforts more efficient and effective. The lawsuits can be heard in a single court before a single judge and jury, saving the judicial system, the witnesses, and the parties millions of dollars and a great deal of time.

Contrast the concern of Judge Posner, quoted in *Castano*, that "one jury * * * will hold the fate of an industry in the palm of its hand." Many have spoken of the "bet the company" potential of class certification. There has, to date, not been a surge of support for issue certification among defense interests. To the contrary, part of the support for adoption of Rule 23(f), which provides a route to immediate appellate review of certification orders (see Interlocutory Appeal of Class-Certification Decisions, *infra* p. 346) was that class certification could compel a defendant to settle. As the Committee Note accompanying that 1998 amendment to the rule said: "An order granting certification * * * may force a defendant to settle rather than incur the costs of defending a class action and run the risk of potentially ruinous liability."

3.   Assuming there is a critical common issue that might justify certification under Rule 23(c)(4), would certification still be justified if the issue had become moot? In In re Nassau County Strip Search Cases, 461 F.3d 219 (2d Cir. 2006), cited by the court in *Martin*, plaintiffs sought to represent a class of misdemeanor detainees who had been strip searched under a policy at the jail. When plaintiffs sought certification of the issue whether the policy violated the constitutional rights of the class members, defendants conceded liability and the district denied the motion to certify, noting that it had earlier denied certification on the ground that plaintiffs' claims, taken as a whole, did not satisfy Rule 23(b)(3). The court of appeals rejected this argument: "Eliminating conceded issues from Rule 23(b)(3)'s predominance calculus would undermine the goal of efficiency by requiring plaintiffs who share a 'commonality of the violation and the harm,' nonetheless to pursue separate and potentially numerous actions because, ironically, liability is so clear." Contrast the view of Justice Ginsburg, dissenting in Wal-Mart Stores, Inc. v. Dukes, *supra* p. 209, 564 U.S. 338, 369 n.3: "Sensibly read * * * the word 'questions' means disputed issues."

4.   In *Martin*, defendants argued that the district judge's contemplated trial plan would violate the Seventh Amendment's Reexamination Clause by permitting a second jury to revisit matters initially decided by the jury in the

trial of the certified issues when presented with individual claims in follow-on proceedings. In general, it has long been recognized that separation of issues into sequential trials may only be done when the issue decided later "is so distinct and separable from the others that a trial of it alone may be had without injustice." Gasoline Products Co. v. Champlin Refining Co., 283 U.S. 494 (1931). As the Seventh Circuit has recognized, "these competing considerations can be reconciled in a 'mass tort' case by carving at the joints of the parties' dispute." Mejdrech v. Met-Coil Systems Corp., 319 F.3d 910, 911 (7th Cir. 2003). We will return to these issues in Chapter 8, *infra* p. 630. Consider that issue preclusion can be applied without violating the Seventh Amendment; as in Engle v. Liggett Group, Inc., *supra* p. 297 note 8.

5. What effect would differences in state law have on certification under Rule 23(c)(4)? In *Castano*, the court emphasized that the claim asserted there was an "immature tort," and also that state law on the subject would likely not be the same coast to coast. In *Martin*, the claims were limited to residents of one neighborhood. Compare Evans v. Walter Industries, Inc., 449 F.3d 1159 (11th Cir. 2006), *infra* p. 365, in which plaintiffs sued 18 defendants for alleged contamination in an Alabama city caused by defendants' manufacturing facilities there. Plaintiffs sought to sue on behalf of a proposed class of all persons who came into contact with toxic waste deposited by any of the defendants over a period of decades. In that case, the court ruled that, under the Class Action Fairness Act, plaintiffs did not show that at least two-thirds of those class members were citizens of Alabama, and therefore that the case should remain in federal court. Could the federal court have certified a class under Rule 23(c)(4), given that a significant number of class members may have been citizens of other states?

6. As noted in Chapter 4, MDL proceedings often include class actions. Could certification under Rule 23(c)(4) be a useful tool in managing such cases? In In re FCA US LLC Monostable Electronic Gearshift Litigation, 334 F.R.D. 96 (E.D.Mich. 2019), the transferee judge in an MDL proceeding faced a variety of claims that defendant Chrysler had equipped three models of its cars with a defective gear shift device. For the 2015 model year, Chrysler adopted a different design, and in 2016 it issued a voluntary recall of cars with the challenged shift device, but asserted that accidents involving it were due to "improper usage." The judge was confronted with claims under a federal act and under the consumer laws of 23 states. The court rejected plaintiffs' request for certification under Rule 23(b)(3), but also found that "there are a number of discrete issues apparent from the record that are suitable subjects for class-wide adjudication" pursuant to Rule 23(c)(4). Using the "broad view" of the rule articulated in *Martin*, the court granted conditional certification even though Chrysler emphasized "elements of various claims that are *not* subject to common proofs." It added (id. at 111):

> The defendant also identifies several instances where it believes it has proofs that will defeat the plaintiffs' claims on the merits, either by negating crucial elements or successfully establishing an affirmative defense to liability. But the prospect that the answer to a

common question may favor the defendant rather than the plaintiffs certainly does not mean that class litigation of the issue is barred. In fact, it weighs in favor of addressing the issue expeditiously in a single proceeding to avoid the needless expense of adjudicating the same question in thousands of individual cases that might be doomed founder on the same common shoal.

7.   In *Martin*, the court cited the Advisory Committee decision not to proceed with a possible amendment to Rule 23 to deal with the issue class possibility. The agenda book for the November 2015 meeting of the Advisory Committee (pp. 90–91) explains:

> Considerable discussion has been had of the possible tension between the predominance requirement of Rule 23(b)(3) and the invitation in Rule 23(c)(4) to certify a class with regard to particular issues. Included in this discussion was the possibility of recommending an amendment to Rule 23(f) to authorize discretionary immediate review of the district court's resolution of such issues. Eventually, the conclusion was reached that there is no significant need for such a rule amendment. The various circuits seem to be in accord about the propriety of such treatment "[w]hen appropriate," as Rule 23(c)(4) now says. And this treatment may sometimes be warranted in actions under Rule 23(b)(2), a practice that might be called into question under some of the amendment ideas the [Rule 23] Subcommittee has examined. On balance, these issues appear not to warrant amendment of the rules.

4.   DEFENDANT CLASS ACTIONS

Although they are not a different category under Rule 23, defendant class actions present issues somewhat different from plaintiff class actions. It has been said that they are "as rare as unicorns." John Coffee, Class Action Accountability: Reconciling Exit, Voice, and Loyalty in Representative Litigation, 100 Colum. L. Rev. 370, 388 (2000). In a study of class actions in four judicial districts, the Federal Judicial Center found that there were 192 certified plaintiff class actions and one certified defendant class action in those districts. See Thomas Willging, Laural Hooper & Robert Niemic, An Empirical Analysis of Rule 23 to Address the Rulemaking Challenges, 71 N.Y.U.L. Rev. 74, 120 (1996). A 2010 study of all settled class actions in the federal courts in 2006–07 found that 688 were plaintiff class actions and three were defendant classes. Brian Fitzpatrick, An Empirical Study of Class Action Settlements and Their Fee Awards, 7 J. Empir. Legal Stud. 811 (2010). See Bell v. Brockett, 922 F.3d 502 (4th Cir. 2019) (upholding judgment against defendant class, and observing: "This case involves one of the rarest types of complex litigation, the defendant class action.").

Certification of defendant class actions therefore does not warrant as much attention as certification of plaintiff class actions. But they may sometimes be important. A judge who had certified a defendant class offered the following thoughts: "Defendant classes have been employed with good results in several areas of the law. Patent infringement cases may be the most common use of the device because the crucial question of patent validity can be resolved by bringing the class of alleged infringers together. Another common use of defendant classes is challenges to the validity of state laws where the class comprises all state officials who enforce the law. * * * In certain areas, defendant classes provide a fine method of organizing the litigation." Spencer Williams, Some Defendants Have Class: Reflections on the GAP Securities Litigation, 89 F.R.D. 287, 289–90 (1980).

Comment, Defendant Class Actions and Patent Infringement Litigation, 58 UCLA L. Rev. 843 (2011), argues that defendant class actions should be encouraged to enforce patents, and that opting out should be forbidden in such cases. The reasoning is summarized as follows (id. at 845):

> [D]efendant class actions appear to be an appropriate method of adjudicating patent infringement claims. Patent litigation is particularly costly and complex. The average cost of litigating a patent case ranges from $650,000 for a low-valued patent to $4.5 million for a high-valued patent. The highly technical nature of patent cases, combined with an often unqualified trier of fact, may lead to inconsistent legal determinations. Finally, the issues most often raised in patent litigation—claim construction, validity, and enforceability—generally focus on the plaintiff's patent claims and conduct and are thus common across a class of alleged infringers.

See also Comment, BlackBerry Users Unite! Expanding the Consumer Class Action to Include a Class Defense, 116 Yale L.J. 217 (2006); Assaf Hamdani & Alon Klement, The Class Defense, 93 Calif. L. Rev. 685 (2005) (urging use of defendant class actions to protect classes of alleged copyright infringers to overcome the natural advantage of the "moneyed" copyright holder suing many alleged infringers, such as those who download music).

In terms of incentives, however, there may be significant differences between plaintiff and defendant class actions. Plaintiffs might be expected to adopt a strategy like "pick a patsy" in selecting a class representative for a defendant class. And that representative might not approach the prospect of being found adequate with the same enthusiasm usual among plaintiff class representatives. As the Second Circuit noted in Marcera v. Chinlund, 595 F.2d 1231 (2d Cir. 1979), vacated on other grounds, 442 U.S. 915 (1979):

> In contrast with representatives of plaintiff classes, named defendants almost never choose their role as class champion—it is a potentially onerous one thrust upon them by their opponents.

* * * But courts must not readily accede to the wishes of named defendants in this area, for to permit them to abdicate so easily would utterly vitiate the effectiveness of the defendant class action of correcting widespread illegality.

At least sometimes, these concerns can be overcome. For example, in Thillens v. Community Currency Exchange Assoc. of Illinois, 97 F.R.D. 668 (N.D.Ill. 1983), the association was named as representative of its members, who had chosen it to represent them in various settings. See also Note, Defendant Class Actions, 91 Harv. L. Rev. 630 (1978) (arguing that associational representatives often suffice).

NOTES AND QUESTIONS

1.   In Rule 23(b)(3) defendant class actions, will all the class members opt out as soon as they receive notice that the class has been certified? Would they call unwanted attention to themselves by opting out, thereby inviting an individual suit? Is there anything the court or the plaintiff can do to deter such opting out?

2.   Could Rule 23(b)(2) be used to certify a mandatory defendant class? The rule authorizes class certification only when "the party *opposing* the class has acted or refused to act on grounds generally applicable to the class." The Second Circuit concluded in Marcera v. Chinlund, 595 F.2d 1231 (2d Cir. 1979), that a defendant class is permitted under Rule 23(b)(2). But the virtually unanimous view of other courts, and of the commentators, has been that the rule's language does not permit defendant classes under (b)(2). See Tilley v. TJX Companies, Inc., 345 F.3d 34, 39–40 (1st Cir. 2003). As the court put it in Henson v. East Lincoln Township, 814 F.2d 410, 414 (7th Cir. 1987): "The ease and speed with which the Federal Rules of Civil Procedure can be amended by those whom Congress entrusted with the responsibility for doing so should make federal judges hesitate to create new forms judicial proceeding in the teeth of the existing rules." But in Brown v. Kelly, 609 F.3d 467 (2d Cir. 2010), the Second Circuit adhered to its position in Marcera v. Chinlund, *supra*, that (b)(2) did permit certification of a defendant class.

3.   Defendant classes can be certified under Rule 23(b)(1), and sometimes are. For example, in Wyandotte Nation v. City of Kansas City, 214 F.R.D. 656 (D.Kan. 2003), an Indian tribe sued to recover what it claimed was its land and sought certification of a defendant class of over 1,300 individuals and entities listed as current record owners of the land. One of the defendants was a county government, and it joined in the motion to certify. Citing three earlier cases involving Indian tribes' efforts to obtain recovery of land in which defendant classes had been certified, the court decided that Rule 23(b)(1)(B) authorized certification. It also concluded that a mandatory class would be desirable because "preserving the right of class members to opt out * * * would inhibit efforts to achieve a resolution of the liability issues." Id. at 664.

In In re Integra Realty Resources, Inc., 354 F.3d 1246 (10th Cir. 2004), a trustee in bankruptcy sought relief for allegedly fraudulent transfer and unlawful distribution of a dividend by the bankrupt corporation to its 6,000 shareholders. The bankruptcy court certified a class of defendant shareholder recipients of the dividend under Rule 23(b)(1)(B), and the court of appeals affirmed. It reasoned that, given the centrality of the issue whether the distribution was unlawful, the findings in the first of the trustee's suits "would almost inevitably prove dispositive" in later cases. Id. at 1264. In part, it relied on the fact that all proceedings would be in the same bankruptcy court, which "further increases the likelihood that the first case would prove dispositive." Id. Compare Tilley v. TJX Companies, Inc., 345 F.3d 34, 42 (1st Cir. 2003) (noting that "the vast majority of courts" have ruled that "certification of a class under Rule 23(b)(1)(B) cannot rest solely on an anticipated stare decisis effects").

4. *Bilateral class actions*: There have been cases involving a plaintiff class against a defendant class, but these cases present singular difficulties. One may be whether the class representatives really have claims against all members of the defendant class. For example, in Angel Music, Inc. v. ABC Sports, Inc., 112 F.R.D. 70 (S.D.N.Y. 1986), plaintiff, the holder of the copyright of music ABC used as background music in its broadcast of the 1984 Olympics, sued on behalf of a class of music publishers against a defendant class of television stations and production affiliates. Plaintiff alleged that the defendant class members had a common practice of using copyrighted music in synchronization with visual images without paying for a license to do so, but the court held that plaintiff lacked standing to sue anyone but ABC.

E. CERTIFICATION SOLELY FOR SETTLEMENT

The question of certifying a class action may be viewed somewhat differently if the case is certified only for purposes of possible settlement. The court might then be spared the need to make difficult class certification determinations while the settlement negotiations are underway. At the same time, the court has some supervisory role in connection with those negotiations if it designates the lawyer who may negotiate on behalf of the class. See Rule 23(g)(3) (authorizing appointment of "interim counsel" to act for the putative class before class certification is decided). Moreover, the class certification decision itself may be significantly eased because some of the manageability complications that would be presented by attempting to manage a trial might be less pressing. Finally, class members deciding whether to opt out should have a clearer idea of the value of staying in the class since the settlement deal will then be a known quantity. These concerns led courts presented with Rule 23(b)(3) cases to uphold tentative certification for purposes of settlement negotiation even though certification might not be proper if a trial were necessary.

There are, however, serious potential drawbacks to this practice. Defendants may be able to "shop" for a favorably-inclined plaintiffs' lawyer. See Ace Heating & Plumbing Co. v. Crane Co., 453 F.2d 30, 33 (3d Cir. 1971) ("a person who unofficially represents the class during settlement negotiations may be under strong pressure to conform to the defendant's wishes [because] a negotiating defendant may not like his 'attitude' and may try to reach settlement with another member of the class"). Recall the comments of John Frank opposing the 1966 adoption of the Rule 23(b)(3) class action, *supra* pp. 251–252. As the court observed in Koby v. ARS National Services, Inc., 846 F.3d 1071 (9th Cir. 2017): "When, as here, a class settlement is negotiated prior to formal class certification, there is an increased risk that the named plaintiffs and their class counsel will breach their fiduciary obligations they owe to the absent class members."

One approach might be to forbid pre-certification settlements. As amended in 2018, however, Rule 23(e) now explicitly contemplates "a class proposed to be certified for purposes of settlement." Nevertheless, at least one district judge (Hon. William Alsup, N.D.Cal.) adopted a case management order prohibiting negotiation of a classwide settlement before certification unless the court had appointed interim class counsel under Rule 23(g)(3) and authorized counsel to conduct settlement negotiations. A defendant that wanted to negotiate such a settlement with putative class counsel not so anointed sought a writ of mandamus to require the judge to permit that negotiation, but the court of appeals refused the writ, stressing the discretion Rule 23 affords to district judges in the handling of class actions. In re Logitech, Inc., 784 Fed.Appx. 514 (9th Cir. 2019).

AMCHEM PRODUCTS, INC. V. WINDSOR
Supreme Court of the United States, 1997.
521 U.S. 591.

JUSTICE GINSBURG delivered the opinion of the Court.

This case concerns the legitimacy under Rule 23 of the Federal Rules of Civil Procedure of a class-action certification sought to achieve global settlement of current and future asbestos-related claims. The class proposed for certification potentially encompasses hundreds of thousands, perhaps millions, of individuals tied together by this commonality: each was, or some day may be, adversely affected by past exposure to asbestos products manufactured by one or more of 20 companies. Those companies, defendants in the lower courts, are petitioners here.

The United States District Court for the Eastern District of Pennsylvania certified the class for settlement only, finding that the proposed settlement was fair and that representation and notice had been adequate. That court enjoined class members from separately pursuing asbestos-related personal-injury suits in any court, federal or state, pending the issuance of a final order. The Court of Appeals for the Third Circuit vacated the District Court's orders, holding that the class certification failed to satisfy Rule 23's requirements in several critical respects. We affirm the Court of Appeals' judgment.

I

A

The settlement-class certification we confront evolved in response to an asbestos-litigation crisis. * * *

[In 1991,] the MDL Panel transferred all asbestos cases then filed, but not yet on trial in federal courts to a single district, the United States District Court for the Eastern District of Pennsylvania; pursuant to the transfer order, the collected cases were consolidated for pretrial proceedings before Judge Weiner. See In re Asbestos Products Liability Litigation (No. VI), 771 F. Supp. 415, 422–424 (JPML 1991) [*supra* p. 153 n. 3]. The order aggregated pending cases only; no authority resides in the MDL Panel to license for consolidated proceedings claims not yet filed.

B

After the consolidation, attorneys for plaintiffs and defendants formed separate steering committees and began settlement negotiations. Ronald L. Motley and Gene Locks—later appointed, along with Motley's law partner Joseph F. Rice, to represent the plaintiff class in this action—co-chaired the Plaintiffs' Steering Committee. Counsel for the Center for Claims Resolution (CCR), the consortium of 20 former asbestos manufacturers now before us as petitioners, participated in the Defendants' Steering Committee. Although the MDL order collected, transferred, and consolidated only cases already commenced in federal courts, settlement negotiations included efforts to find a "means of resolving . . . future cases."

* * *

[Initially, negotiations with Plaintiffs' Steering Committee were unsuccessful. Thereafter, CCR counsel approached the lawyers who had headed the Plaintiffs' Steering Committee in the unsuccessful negotiations, and a new round of negotiations began; that round yielded the mass settlement agreement now in controversy. At the time, the former heads of the Plaintiffs' Steering Committee represented thousands of plaintiffs with then-pending asbestos-related claims—claimants the parties to this suit call "inventory" plaintiffs. CCR indicated in these discussions that it would resist settlement of inventory cases absent "some kind of protection for the future."]

Settlement talks thus concentrated on devising an administrative scheme for disposition of asbestos claims not yet in litigation. In these negotiations, counsel for masses of inventory plaintiffs endeavored to represent the interests of the anticipated future claimants, although those lawyers then had no attorney-client relationship with such claimants.

Once negotiations seemed likely to produce an agreement purporting to bind potential plaintiffs, CCR agreed to settle, through separate agreements, the claims of plaintiffs who had already filed asbestos-related lawsuits. In one such agreement, CCR defendants promised to pay more than $200 million to gain release of the claims of numerous inventory plaintiffs. After settling the inventory claims, CCR, together with the plaintiffs' lawyers CCR had approached, launched this case, exclusively involving persons outside the MDL Panel's province—plaintiffs without already pending lawsuits.[3]

C

The class action thus instituted was not intended to be litigated. Rather, within the space of a single day, January 15, 1993, the settling parties—CCR defendants and the representatives of the plaintiff class described below—presented to the District Court a complaint, an answer, a proposed settlement agreement, and a joint motion for conditional class certification.

The complaint identified nine lead plaintiffs, designating them and members of their families as representatives of a class comprising all persons who had not filed an asbestos-related lawsuit against a CCR defendant as of the date the class action commenced, but who (1) had been exposed—occupationally or through the occupational exposure of a spouse or household member—to asbestos or products containing asbestos attributable to a CCR defendant, or (2) whose spouse or family member had been so exposed. Untold numbers of individuals may fall within this description. All named plaintiffs alleged that they or a member of their family had been exposed to asbestos-containing products of CCR defendants. More than half of the named plaintiffs alleged that they or their family members had already suffered various physical injuries as a result of the exposure. The others alleged that they had not yet manifested any asbestos-related condition. The complaint delineated no subclasses; all named plaintiffs were designated as representatives of the class as a whole.

The complaint invoked the District Court's diversity jurisdiction and asserted various state-law claims for relief, including (1) negligent failure to warn, (2) strict liability, (3) breach of express and implied warranty, (4) negligent infliction of emotional distress, (5) enhanced risk of disease, (6) medical monitoring, and (7) civil conspiracy. Each plaintiff requested unspecified damages in excess of $100,000. CCR defendants' answer denied the principal allegations of the complaint and asserted 11 affirmative defenses.

A stipulation of settlement accompanied the pleadings; it proposed to settle, and to preclude nearly all class members from litigating against CCR companies, all claims not filed before January 15, 1993, involving compensation for present and future asbestos-related personal injury or

---

[3] It is basic to comprehension of this proceeding to notice that no transferred case is included in the settlement at issue, and no case covered by the settlement existed as a civil action at the time of the MDL Panel transfer.

death. An exhaustive document exceeding 100 pages, the stipulation presents in detail an administrative mechanism and a schedule of payments to compensate class members who meet defined asbestos-exposure and medical requirements. The stipulation describes four categories of compensable disease: mesothelioma; lung cancer; certain "other cancers" (colon-rectal, laryngeal, esophageal, and stomach cancer); and "non-malignant conditions" (asbestosis and bilateral pleural thickening). Persons with "exceptional" medical claims—claims that do not fall within the four described diagnostic categories—may in some instances qualify for compensation, but the settlement caps the number of "exceptional" claims CCR must cover.

For each qualifying disease category, the stipulation specifies the range of damages CCR will pay to qualifying claimants. Payments under the settlement are not adjustable for inflation. Mesothelioma claimants—the most highly compensated category—are scheduled to receive between $20,000 and $200,000. The stipulation provides that CCR is to propose the level of compensation within the prescribed ranges; it also establishes procedures to resolve disputes over medical diagnoses and levels of compensation.

Compensation above the fixed ranges may be obtained for "extraordinary" claims. But the settlement places both numerical caps and dollar limits on such claims.[6] The settlement also imposes "case flow maximums," which cap the number of claims payable for each disease in a given year.

Class members are to receive no compensation for certain kinds of claims, even if otherwise applicable state law recognizes such claims. Claims that garner no compensation under the settlement include claims by family members of asbestos-exposed individuals for loss of consortium, and claims by so-called "exposure-only" plaintiffs for increased risk of cancer, fear of future asbestos-related injury, and medical monitoring. "Pleural" claims, which might be asserted by persons with asbestos-related plaques on their lungs but no accompanying physical impairment, are also excluded. Although not entitled to present compensation, exposure-only claimants and pleural claimants may qualify for benefits when and if they develop a compensable disease and meet the relevant exposure and medical criteria. Defendants forgo defenses to liability, including statute of limitations pleas.

Class members, in the main, are bound by the settlement in perpetuity, while CCR defendants may choose to withdraw from the settlement after ten years. A small number of class members—only a few

---

[6] Only three percent of the qualified mesothelioma, lung cancer, and "other cancer" claims, and only one percent of the total number of qualified "non-malignant condition" claims can be designated "extraordinary." Average expenditures are specified for claims found "extraordinary"; mesothelioma victims with compensable extraordinary claims, for example, receive, on average, $300,000.

per year—may reject the settlement and pursue their claims in court. Those permitted to exercise this option, however, may not assert any punitive damages claim or any claim for increased risk of cancer. Aspects of the administration of the settlement are to be monitored by the AFL-CIO and class counsel. Class counsel are to receive attorneys' fees in an amount to be approved by the District Court.

D

On January 29, 1993, as requested by the settling parties, the District Court conditionally certified, under Federal Rule of Civil Procedure 23(b)(3), an encompassing opt-out class. The certified class included persons occupationally exposed to defendants' asbestos products, and members of their families, who had not filed suit as of January 15. Judge Weiner appointed Locks, Motley, and Rice as class counsel, noting that "[t]he Court may in the future appoint additional counsel if it is deemed necessary and advisable." At no stage of the proceedings, however, were additional counsel in fact appointed. Nor was the class ever divided into subclasses. In a separate order, Judge Weiner assigned to Judge Reed, also of the Eastern District of Pennsylvania, "the task of conducting fairness proceedings and of determining whether the proposed settlement is fair to the class." Various class members raised objections to the settlement stipulation, and Judge Weiner granted the objectors full rights to participate in the subsequent proceedings.

In preliminary rulings, Judge Reed held that the District Court had subject-matter jurisdiction, and he approved the settling parties' elaborate plan for giving notice to the class. The court-approved notice informed recipients that they could exclude themselves from the class, if they so chose, within a three-month opt-out period.

Objectors raised numerous challenges to the settlement. They urged that the settlement unfairly disadvantaged those without currently compensable conditions in that it failed to adjust for inflation or to account for changes, over time, in medical understanding. They maintained that compensation levels were intolerably low in comparison to awards available in tort litigation or payments received by the inventory plaintiffs. And they objected to the absence of any compensation for certain claims, for example, medical monitoring, compensable under the tort law of several States. Rejecting these and all other objections, Judge Reed concluded that the settlement terms were fair and had been negotiated without collusion. He also found that adequate notice had been given to class members, and that final class certification under Rule 23(b)(3) was appropriate.

As to the specific prerequisites to certification, the District Court observed that the class satisfied Rule 23(a)(1)'s numerosity requirement, a matter no one debates. The Rule 23(a)(2) and (b)(3) requirements of commonality and preponderance were also satisfied, the District Court held, in that "[t]he members of the class have all been exposed to asbestos products supplied by the defendants and all share an interest in receiving prompt and fair compensation for their claims, while minimizing the risks and transaction costs inherent in the asbestos litigation process as it occurs presently in the tort system. Whether the proposed settlement satisfies this interest and is otherwise a fair, reasonable and adequate compromise of the claims of the class is a predominant issue for purposes of Rule 23(b)(3)." The District Court held next that the claims of the class representatives were "typical" of the class as a whole, a requirement of Rule 23(a)(3), and that, as Rule 23(b)(3) demands, the class settlement was "superior" to other methods of adjudication.

Strenuous objections had been asserted regarding the adequacy of representation, a Rule 23(a)(4) requirement. * * *

[T]he District Court rejected these objections. Subclasses were unnecessary, the District Court held, bearing in mind the added cost and confusion they would entail and the ability of class members to exclude themselves from the class during the three-month opt-out period. Reasoning that the representative plaintiffs "have a strong interest that recovery for all of the medical categories be maximized because they may have claims in any, or several categories," the District Court found "no antagonism of interest between class members with various medical conditions, or between persons with and without currently manifest asbestos impairment." Declaring class certification appropriate and the settlement fair, the District Court preliminarily enjoined all class members from commencing any asbestos-related suit against the CCR defendants in any state or federal court.

The objectors appealed. The United States Court of Appeals for the Third Circuit vacated the certification, holding that the requirements of Rule 23 had not been satisfied.

E

The Court of Appeals, in a long, heavily detailed opinion by Judge Becker, first noted several challenges by objectors to justiciability, subject-matter jurisdiction, and adequacy of notice. These challenges, the court said, raised "serious concerns." However, the court observed, "the jurisdictional issues in this case would not exist but for the [class action] certification." Turning to the class-certification issues and finding them dispositive, the Third Circuit declined to decide other questions.

On class-action prerequisites, the Court of Appeals referred to an earlier Third Circuit decision, In re General Motors Corp. Pick-Up Truck Fuel Tank Products Liability Litigation, 55 F. 3d 768 (CA3), cert. denied, 516 U.S. 824 (1995) (hereinafter *GM Trucks*), which held that although a class action may be certified for settlement purposes only, Rule 23(a)'s requirements must be satisfied as if the case were going to be litigated. The same rule should apply, the Third Circuit said, to class certification under

Rule 23(b)(3). While stating that the requirements of Rule 23(a) and (b)(3) must be met "without taking into account the settlement," the Court of Appeals in fact closely considered the terms of the settlement as it examined aspects of the case under Rule 23 criteria.

* * *

In contrast to mass torts involving a single accident, class members in this case were exposed to different asbestos-containing products, in different ways, over different periods, and for different amounts of time; some suffered no physical injury, others suffered disabling or deadly diseases. "These factual differences," the Third Circuit explained, "translate[d] into significant legal differences." State law governed and varied widely on such critical issues as "viability of [exposure-only] claims [and] availability of causes of action for medical monitoring, increased risk of cancer, and fear of future injury."[14] "[T]he number of uncommon issues in this humongous class action," the Third Circuit concluded, barred a determination, under existing tort law, that common questions predominated.

The Court of Appeals next found that "serious intra-class conflicts preclude[d] th[e] class from meeting the adequacy of representation requirement" of Rule 23(a)(4). Adverting to, but not resolving charges of attorney conflict of interests, the Third Circuit addressed the question whether the named plaintiffs could adequately advance the interests of all class members. The Court of Appeals acknowledged that the District Court was certainly correct to this extent: " '[T]he members of the class are united in seeking the maximum possible recovery for their asbestos-related claims.' " "But the settlement does more than simply provide a general recovery fund," the Court of Appeals immediately added; "[r]ather, it makes important judgments on how recovery is to be allocated among different kinds of plaintiffs, decisions that necessarily favor some claimants over others."

In the Third Circuit's view, the "most salient" divergence of interests separated plaintiffs already afflicted with an asbestos-related disease from plaintiffs without manifest injury (exposure-only plaintiffs). The latter would rationally want protection against inflation for distant recoveries. They would also seek sturdy back-end opt-out rights and "causation provisions that can keep pace with changing science and medicine, rather than freezing in place the science of 1993." Already injured parties, in contrast, would care little about such provisions and would rationally trade them for higher current payouts. These and other adverse interests, the Court of Appeals carefully explained, strongly suggested that an undivided

---

[14] Recoveries under the laws of different States spanned a wide range. Objectors assert, for example, that 15% of current mesothelioma claims arise in California, where the statewide average recovery is $419,674—or more than 209% above the $200,000 maximum specified in the settlement for mesothelioma claims not typed "extraordinary."

set of representatives could not adequately protect the discrete interests of both currently afflicted and exposure-only claimants.

The Third Circuit next rejected the District Court's determination that the named plaintiffs were "typical" of the class, noting that this Rule 23(a)(3) inquiry overlaps the adequacy of representation question: "both look to the potential for conflicts in the class." Evident conflict problems, the court said, led it to hold that "no set of representatives can be 'typical' of this class."

The Court of Appeals similarly rejected the District Court's assessment of the superiority of the class action. * * * "A series of statewide or more narrowly defined adjudications, either through consolidation under Rule 42(a) or as class actions under Rule 23, would seem preferable," the Court of Appeals said.

* * *

We granted certiorari, and now affirm.

II

Objectors assert in this Court, as they did in the District Court and Court of Appeals, an array of jurisdictional barriers. Most fundamentally, they maintain that the settlement proceeding instituted by class counsel and CCR is not a justiciable case or controversy within the confines of Article III of the Federal Constitution. In the main, they say, the proceeding is a nonadversarial endeavor to impose on countless individuals without currently ripe claims an administrative compensation regime binding on those individuals if and when they manifest injuries.

Furthermore, objectors urge that exposure-only claimants lack standing to sue: Either they have not yet sustained any cognizable injury or, to the extent the complaint states claims and demands relief for emotional distress, enhanced risk of disease, and medical monitoring, the settlement provides no redress. Objectors also argue that exposure-only claimants did not meet the then-current amount-in-controversy requirement (in excess of $50,000) specified for federal-court jurisdiction based upon diversity of citizenship. See 28 U.S.C. § 1332(a).

As earlier recounted, the Third Circuit declined to reach these issues because they "would not exist but for the [class action] certification." We agree that "[t]he class certification issues are dispositive;" because their resolution here is logically antecedent to the existence of any Article III issues, it is appropriate to reach them first. We therefore follow the path taken by the Court of Appeals, mindful that Rule 23's requirements must be interpreted in keeping with Article III constraints, and with the Rules Enabling Act, which instructs that rules of procedure "shall not abridge, enlarge or modify any substantive right," 28 U.S.C. § 2072(b). See also Fed.

Rule Civ. Proc. 82 ("rules shall not be construed to extend . . . the [subject matter] jurisdiction of the United States district courts").

III

To place this controversy in context, we briefly describe the characteristics of class actions for which the Federal Rules provide. [Justice Ginsburg described the evolution of Rule 23, noting that Rule 23(b)(3) was "the most adventuresome" innovation in the 1966 amendments. She quoted the Advisory Committee Note that (b)(3) applied in situations in which "class-action treatment is not as clearly called for" as under (b)(1) and (b)(2). She also noted that the rulemakers intended for courts to look carefully at the individual interests involved before certifying classes under (b)(3), quoting the Third Circuit's observation that "[e]ach plaintiff [in any action involving claims for personal injury and death] has a significant interest in individually controlling the prosecution of [his case]," and that each "ha[s] a substantial stake in making individual decisions whether to settle."]

In the decades since the 1966 revision of Rule 23, class action practice has become ever more "adventuresome" as a means of coping with claims too numerous to secure their "just, speedy, and inexpensive determination" one by one. See Fed. Rule Civ. Proc. 1. The development reflects concerns about the efficient use of court resources and the conservation of funds to compensate claimants who do not line up early in a litigation queue.

Among current applications of Rule 23(b)(3), the "settlement only" class has become a stock device. Although all Federal Circuits recognize the utility of Rule 23(b)(3) settlement classes, courts have divided on the extent to which a proffered settlement affects court surveillance under Rule 23's certification criteria.

In *GM Trucks* and in the instant case, the Third Circuit held that a class cannot be certified for settlement when certification for trial would be unwarranted. Other courts have held that settlement obviates or reduces the need to measure a proposed class against the enumerated Rule 23 requirements.

* * *

IV

We granted review to decide the role settlement may play, under existing Rule 23, in determining the propriety of class certification. The Third Circuit's opinion stated that each of the requirements of Rule 23(a) and (b)(3) "must be satisfied without taking into account the settlement." That statement, petitioners urge, is incorrect.

We agree with petitioners to this limited extent: settlement is relevant to a class certification. The Third Circuit's opinion bears modification in that respect. But, as we earlier observed, the Court of Appeals in fact did not ignore the settlement; instead, that court homed in on settlement terms in explaining why it found the absentees' interests inadequately represented. The Third Circuit's close inspection of the settlement in that regard was altogether proper.

Confronted with a request for settlement-only class certification, a district court need not inquire whether the case, if tried, would present intractable management problems, see Fed. Rule Civ. Proc. 23(b)(3)(D), for the proposal is that there be no trial. But other specifications of the rule—those designed to protect absentees by blocking unwarranted or overbroad class definitions—demand undiluted, even heightened, attention in the settlement context. Such attention is of vital importance, for a court asked to certify a settlement class will lack the opportunity, present when a case is litigated, to adjust the class, informed by the proceedings as they unfold. See Fed. Rule Civ. Proc. 23(c), (d).

And, of overriding importance, courts must be mindful that the rule as now composed sets the requirements they are bound to enforce. Federal Rules take effect after an extensive deliberative process involving many reviewers: a Rules Advisory Committee, public commenters, the Judicial Conference, this Court, the Congress. See 28 U.S.C. §§ 2073, 2074. The text of a rule thus proposed and reviewed limits judicial inventiveness. Courts are not free to amend a rule outside the process Congress ordered, a process properly tuned to the instruction that rules of procedure "shall not abridge . . . any substantive right." § 2072(b).

Rule 23(e), on settlement of class actions, * * * was designed to function as an additional requirement, not a superseding direction, for the "class action" to which Rule 23(e) refers is one qualified for certification under Rule 23(a) and (b). Cf. Eisen [v. Carlisle & Jacquelin], 417 U.S., at 176–177 (adequate representation does not eliminate additional requirement to provide notice). Subdivisions (a) and (b) focus court attention on whether a proposed class has sufficient unity so that absent members can fairly be bound by decisions of class representatives. That dominant concern persists when settlement, rather than trial, is proposed.

The safeguards provided by the Rule 23(a) and (b) class-qualifying criteria, we emphasize, are not impractical impediments—checks shorn of utility—in the settlement class context. First, the standards set for the protection of absent class members serve to inhibit appraisals of the chancellor's foot kind—class certifications dependent upon the court's gestalt judgment or overarching impression of the settlement's fairness.

Second, if a fairness inquiry under Rule 23(e) controlled certification, eclipsing Rule 23(a) and (b), and permitting class designation despite the impossibility of litigation, both class counsel and court would be disarmed. Class counsel confined to settlement negotiations could not use the threat of litigation to press for a better offer, and the court would face a bargain proffered for its approval without benefit of adversarial investigation, see, e.g., Kamilewicz v. Bank of Boston Corp., 100 F. 3d 1348, 1352 (C.A.7 1996) (Easterbrook, J., dissenting from denial of rehearing en banc) (parties "may even put one over on the court, in a staged performance"), cert. denied, 520 U.S. 1204 (1997).

Federal courts, in any case, lack authority to substitute for Rule 23's certification criteria a standard never adopted—that if a settlement is "fair," then certification is proper. Applying to this case criteria the rulemakers set, we conclude that the Third Circuit's appraisal is essentially correct. Although that court should have acknowledged that settlement is a factor in the calculus, a remand is not warranted on that account. The Court of Appeals' opinion amply demonstrates why—with or without a settlement on the table—the sprawling class the District Court certified does not satisfy Rule 23's requirements.

A

We address first the requirement of Rule 23(b)(3) that "[common] questions of law or fact . . . predominate over any questions affecting only individual members." The District Court concluded that predominance was satisfied based on two factors: class members' shared experience of asbestos exposure and their common "interest in receiving prompt and fair compensation for their claims, while minimizing the risks and transaction costs inherent in the asbestos litigation process as it occurs presently in the tort system." The settling parties also contend that the settlement's fairness is a common question, predominating over disparate legal issues that might be pivotal in litigation but become irrelevant under the settlement.

The predominance requirement stated in Rule 23(b)(3), we hold, is not met by the factors on which the District Court relied. The benefits asbestos-exposed persons might gain from the establishment of a grand-scale compensation scheme is a matter fit for legislative consideration, but it is not pertinent to the predominance inquiry. That inquiry trains on the legal or factual questions that qualify each class member's case as a genuine controversy, questions that preexist any settlement.[18]

The Rule 23(b)(3) predominance inquiry tests whether proposed classes are sufficiently cohesive to warrant adjudication by representation. The inquiry appropriate under Rule 23(e), on the other hand, protects unnamed class members "from unjust or unfair settlements affecting their rights when the representatives become fainthearted before the action is adjudicated or are able to secure satisfaction of their individual claims by

---

[18] In this respect, the predominance requirement of Rule 23(b)(3) is similar to the requirement of Rule 23(a)(3) that "claims or defenses" of the named representatives must be "typical of the claims or defenses of the class." The words "claims or defenses" in this context—just as in the context of Rule 24(b)(2) governing permissive intervention—"manifestly refer to the kinds of claims or defenses that can be raised in courts of law as part of an actual or impending law suit." Diamond v. Charles, 476 U.S. 54, 76–77 (1986) (O'Connor, J., concurring in part and concurring in judgment).

a compromise." But it is not the mission of Rule 23(e) to assure the class cohesion that legitimizes representative action in the first place. If a common interest in a fair compromise could satisfy the predominance requirement of Rule 23(b)(3), that vital prescription would be stripped of any meaning in the settlement context.

The District Court also relied upon this commonality: "The members of the class have all been exposed to asbestos products supplied by the defendants. . . ." Even if Rule 23(a)'s commonality requirement may be satisfied by that shared experience, the predominance criterion is far more demanding. Given the greater number of questions peculiar to the several categories of class members, and to individuals within each category, and the significance of those uncommon questions, any overarching dispute about the health consequences of asbestos exposure cannot satisfy the Rule 23(b)(3) predominance standard.

The Third Circuit highlighted the disparate questions undermining class cohesion in this case:

> "Class members were exposed to different asbestos-containing products, for different amounts of time, in different ways, and over different periods. Some class members suffer no physical injury or have only asymptomatic pleural changes, while others suffer from lung cancer, disabling asbestosis, or from mesothelioma. . . . Each has a different history of cigarette smoking, a factor that complicates the causation inquiry.

> "The [exposure-only] plaintiffs especially share little in common, either with each other or with the presently injured class members. It is unclear whether they will contract asbestos-related disease and, if so, what disease each will suffer. They will also incur different medical expenses because their monitoring and treatment will depend on singular circumstances and individual medical histories."

Differences in state law, the Court of Appeals observed, compound these disparities.

No settlement class called to our attention is as sprawling as this one. Predominance is a test readily met in certain cases alleging consumer or securities fraud or violations of the antitrust laws. Even mass tort cases arising from a common cause or disaster may, depending upon the circumstances, satisfy the predominance requirement. The Advisory Committee for the 1966 revision of Rule 23, it is true, noted that "mass accident" cases are likely to present "significant questions, not only of damages but of liability and defenses of liability, . . . affecting the individuals in different ways." And the Committee advised that such cases are "ordinarily not appropriate" for class treatment. But the text of the rule does not categorically exclude mass tort cases from class certification, and district courts, since the late 1970s, have been certifying such cases in increasing number. The Committee's warning, however, continues to call for caution when individual stakes are high and disparities among class members great. As the Third Circuit's opinion makes plain, the certification in this case does not follow the counsel of caution. That certification cannot be upheld, for it rests on a conception of Rule 23(b)(3)'s predominance requirement irreconcilable with the rule's design.

B

Nor can the class approved by the District Court satisfy Rule 23(a)(4)'s requirement that the named parties "will fairly and adequately protect the interests of the class." The adequacy inquiry under Rule 23(a)(4) serves to uncover conflicts of interest between named parties and the class they seek to represent. "[A] class representative must be part of the class and 'possess the same interest and suffer the same injury' as the class members." East Tex. Motor Freight System, Inc. v. Rodriguez, 431 U.S. 395, 403 (1977).[20]

As the Third Circuit pointed out, named parties with diverse medical conditions sought to act on behalf of a single giant class rather than on behalf of discrete subclasses. In significant respects, the interests of those within the single class are not aligned. Most saliently, for the currently injured, the critical goal is generous immediate payments. That goal tugs against the interest of exposure-only plaintiffs in ensuring an ample, inflation-protected fund for the future. Cf. General Telephone Co. of Northwest v. EEOC, 446 U.S. 318, 331 (1980) ("In employment discrimination litigation, conflicts might arise, for example, between employees and applicants who were denied employment and who will, if granted relief, compete with employees for fringe benefits or seniority. Under Rule 23, the same plaintiff could not represent these classes.")

The disparity between the currently injured and exposure-only categories of plaintiffs, and the diversity within each category are not made insignificant by the District Court's finding that petitioners' assets suffice to pay claims under the settlement. Although this is not a "limited fund" case certified under Rule 23(b)(1)(B), the terms of the settlement reflect essential allocation decisions designed to confine compensation and to limit defendants' liability. For example, as earlier described, the settlement includes no adjustment for inflation; only a few claimants per year can opt

---

[20] The adequacy-of-representation requirement "tend[s] to merge" with the commonality and typicality criteria of Rule 23(a), which "serve as guideposts for determining whether ... maintenance of a class action is economical and whether the named plaintiff's claim and the class claims are so interrelated that the interests of the class members will be fairly and adequately protected in their absence." General Telephone Co. of Southwest v. Falcon, 457 U.S. 147, 157 n. 13 (1982). The adequacy heading also factors in competency and conflicts of class counsel. Like the Third Circuit, we decline to address adequacy-of-counsel issues discretely in light of our conclusions that common questions of law or fact do not predominate and that the named plaintiffs cannot adequately represent the interests of this enormous class.

out at the back end; and loss-of-consortium claims are extinguished with no compensation.

The settling parties, in sum, achieved a global compromise with no structural assurance of fair and adequate representation for the diverse groups and individuals affected. Although the named parties alleged a range of complaints, each served generally as representative for the whole, not for a separate constituency. In another asbestos class action, the Second Circuit spoke precisely to this point:

> "[W]here differences among members of a class are such that subclasses must be established, we know of no authority that permits a court to approve a settlement without creating subclasses on the basis of consents by members of a unitary class, some of whom happen to be members of the distinct subgroups. The class representatives may well have thought that the Settlement serves the aggregate interests of the entire class. But the adversity among subgroups requires that the members of each subgroup cannot be bound to a settlement except by consents given by those who understand that their role is to represent solely the members of their respective subgroups."

In re Joint Eastern and Southern Dist. Asbestos Litigation, 982 F. 2d 721, 742–743 (C.A.2 1992), modified on reh'g sub nom. In re Findley, 993 F.2d 7 (1993). The Third Circuit found no assurance here—either in the terms of the settlement or in the structure of the negotiations—that the named plaintiffs operated under a proper understanding of their representational responsibilities. That assessment, we conclude, is on the mark.

C

Impediments to the provision of adequate notice, the Third Circuit emphasized, rendered highly problematic any endeavor to tie to a settlement class persons with no perceptible asbestos-related disease at the time of the settlement. Many persons in the exposure-only category, the Court of Appeals stressed, may not even know of their exposure, or realize the extent of the harm they may incur. Even if they fully appreciate the significance of class notice, those without current afflictions may not have the information or foresight needed to decide, intelligently, whether to stay in or opt out.

Family members of asbestos-exposed individuals may themselves fall prey to disease or may ultimately have ripe claims for loss of consortium. Yet large numbers of people in this category—future spouses and children of asbestos victims—could not be alerted to their class membership. And current spouses and children of the occupationally exposed may know nothing of that exposure.

Because we have concluded that the class in this case cannot satisfy the requirements of common issue predominance and adequacy of representation, we need not rule, definitively, on the notice given here. In accord with the Third Circuit, however, we recognize the gravity of the question whether class action notice sufficient under the Constitution and Rule 23 could ever be given to legions so unselfconscious and amorphous.

V

The argument is sensibly made that a nationwide administrative claims processing regime would provide the most secure, fair, and efficient means of compensating victims of asbestos exposure. Congress, however, has not adopted such a solution. And Rule 23, which must be interpreted with fidelity to the Rules Enabling Act and applied with the interests of absent class members in close view, cannot carry the large load CCR, class counsel, and the District Court heaped upon it. As this case exemplifies, the rulemakers' prescriptions for class actions may be endangered by "those who embrace [Rule 23] too enthusiastically just as [they are by] those who approach [the rule] with distaste."

* * *

For the reasons stated, the judgment of the Court of Appeals for the Third Circuit is affirmed.

JUSTICE O'CONNOR took no part in the consideration or decision of this case.

JUSTICE BREYER, with whom JUSTICE STEVENS joins, concurring in part and dissenting in part.

Although I agree with the Court's basic holding that "settlement is relevant to a class certification," I find several problems in its approach that lead me to a different conclusion. First, I believe that the need for settlement in this mass tort case, with hundreds of thousands of lawsuits, is greater than the Court's opinion suggests. Second, I would give more weight than would the majority to settlement-related issues for purposes of determining whether common issues predominate. Third, I am uncertain about the Court's determination of adequacy of representation, and do not believe it appropriate for this Court to second-guess the District Court on the matter without first having the Court of Appeals consider it. Fourth, I am uncertain about the tenor of an opinion that seems to suggest the settlement is unfair.

* * *

I believe the majority understates the importance of settlement in this case. [Justice Breyer reviewed the evolution of asbestos litigation, emphasizing its high transaction costs and uneven compensation. He also emphasized the vigor and contentiousness of the negotiations that produced the agreement presented to the district court, and the district court's conclusion that the agreement improved class members' chances of compensation.]

[T]he majority, in reviewing the District Court's determination that common "issues of fact and law predominate," says that the predominance "inquiry trains on the legal or factual questions that qualify each class member's case as a genuine controversy, questions that preexist any settlement." I find it difficult to interpret this sentence in a way that could lead me to the majority's conclusion. If the majority means that these pre-settlement questions are what matters, then how does it reconcile its statement with its basic conclusion that "settlement is relevant" to class certification, or with the numerous lower court authority that says that settlement is not only relevant, but important?

Nor do I understand how one could decide whether common questions "predominate" in the abstract—without looking at what is likely to be at issue in the proceedings that will ensue, namely, the settlement.

* * *

[C]ertain details of the settlement that are not discussed in the majority opinion suggest that the settlement may be of greater benefit to future plaintiffs than the majority suggests. The District Court concluded that future plaintiffs receive a "significant value" from the settlement due to variety of its items that benefit future plaintiffs, such as: (1) tolling the statute of limitations so that class members "will no longer be forced to file premature lawsuits or risk their claims being time-barred"; (2) waiver of defenses to liability; (3) payment of claims, if and when members become sick, pursuant to the settlement's compensation standards, which avoids "the uncertainties, long delays and high transaction costs [including attorney's fees] of the tort system"; (4) "some assurance that there will be funds available if and when they get sick," based on the finding that each defendant "has shown an ability to fund the payment of all qualifying claims" under the settlement; and (5) the right to additional compensation if cancer develops (many settlements for plaintiffs with noncancerous conditions bar such additional claims). For these reasons, and others, the District Court found that the distinction between present and future plaintiffs was "illusory."

NOTES AND QUESTIONS

1. *Ortiz*: Two years after *Amchem*, the Court confronted another proposed class-action settlement of asbestos personal injury claims, this time employing a mandatory Rule 23(b)(1)(B) certification to achieve "global peace." Ortiz v. Fibreboard Corp., 527 U.S. 815 (1999). For discussion of the application of the "limited fund" concept, see *supra* p. 231. In that case, as in *Amchem*, those with pending claims would not be included in the settlement class, which was to be limited to those who had not sued. Class counsel stood to benefit in terms of attorney fees from a parallel "inventory" settlement on behalf of some 45,000 plaintiffs with pending claims. In the view of the Court, there was a risk that these "inventory" plaintiffs may have obtained better terms than the

members of the proposed mandatory class. Rather than accept a "unitary" class, the Court ruled, under *Amchem* it would be necessary to define "homogeneous subclasses." The proposed class was defective because it lumped together claimants whose claims differed in serious ways. For example, those exposed to Fibreboard asbestos products before the pertinent insurance policies expired in 1959 were in a different position from those exposed only after that time. But the Court also recognized that "at some point there must be an end to reclassification with separate counsel." Nevertheless, the proposed deal lacked the "structural protections" required by *Amchem*, which might exist if there had been a "natural class." Justice Breyer dissented. He was not troubled by the fact that class counsel also had "inventory" claims that were settled outside the class action, noting that *all* lawyers experienced in asbestos litigation would likely have numerous clients, while still being the best choices to negotiate a settlement precisely due to that experience. He noted also that the district court that approved the proposed settlement found that the schedule of payments for "inventory" settlements was used also for the members of the class.

2.   One thing is clear from the Court's opinion in *Amchem*—the Third Circuit rule that the terms of a settlement are irrelevant to class certification is wrong, or "bears modification," in the Court's gentle phrase. The Third Circuit had held that only cases certifiable for litigation could be settled as class actions. For a forceful argument that class settlements should be permitted only for classes that have been certified for litigation, see Howard Erichson, The Problem of Settlement Class Actions, 82 Geo. Wash. L. Rev. 951, 987–88 (2014):

> The standard critique of *Amchem* is that the Supreme Court was *too cautious* with regard to settlement class actions, placing unnecessary restrictions on the freedom of parties to resolve their disputes by negotiation. * * * This Article contends that, as a statement of the law governing settlement class actions, *Amchem* deserves criticism for exactly the opposite reason—the Supreme Court was *not cautious enough*. * * * By permitting settlement class actions without plenary class certification, the Court invited defendants to use the settlement class tool to resolve widespread liability through negotiation with deleveraged would-be class counsel.

> It is time to abandon the settlement class action. Notwithstanding the device's attractiveness to defendants, to plaintiffs' counsel, and to judges as a means of achieving comprehensive resolutions, it does not withstand scrutiny as a legitimate exercise of judicial authority. There is no sound basis on which a settlement class action, in the absence of litigation class certification, should bind class members. We need to be clear on what a settlement class action is, or more precisely, what it is *not*. It is not a contract, at least not in the sense of an agreement to which the class members are parties. It is not an adjudication on the merits. Rather,

it is an act of judicial power premised on a negotiated resolution. But the underlying negotiation has the odd characteristic that the negotiator for the claimants is a prospective agent who has neither been authorized to act on behalf of the claimants nor been granted the power to take their claims to trial. This feature creates an asymmetrical dynamic that negates any argument that the act of judicial power is justified by a presumption of fair valuation of claims. The problem is not one of collusion or bad faith, but rather a structural problem built into the very definition of a settlement class action.

3. Although the Court took a different view, did it explain clearly how settlement should bear on class certification in a case such as *Amchem*? On one hand, Justice Ginsburg says that "the district court need not inquire whether the case, if tried, would present intractable management problems." On the other hand, she emphasizes that a Rule 23(e) fairness inquiry is not a "superseding factor" that obviates application of the Rule 23(a) and (b) requirements. Indeed, in some instances the fact of settlement should incline the court to be more skeptical about certification. What exactly is the predominance provision of (b)(3) supposed to mean in the settlement context? Compare Justice Breyer's criticism of the Court's explanation of how predominance of common questions bears on settlement-class certification.

Lower courts have been sensitive to the risk of intraclass conflicts of interest. In In re Payment Card Interchange Fee and Merchant Discount Antitrust Litigation, 827 F.3d 223 (2d Cir. 2016), the court overturned approval of a $7.5 billion settlement largely because the "unitary" class included class members with divergent interests. The underlying antitrust claim was brought on behalf of a class of merchants who claimed that Visa and Mastercard had conspired to inflate the fees merchants had to pay for credit card transactions. After very vigorous litigation involving over 400 depositions and production of over 80 million pages of documents, the parties arrived at a settlement with two features—a Rule 23(b)(3) class of merchants who accepted Visa or Mastercard payments from 2004 to 2012, and a Rule 23(b)(2) class of merchants accepting Visa or Mastercard payment from 2012 forward. The Rule 23(b)(3) class members were eligible for payments, making their lawyers eligible for over $500 million in attorney fees. For the 23(b)(2) class, an injunction would require defendants to adhere to specified practices through mid 2021, and would then release any further antitrust claims against them for all time so long as their practices did not significantly deviate from the injunction's terms. The court of appeals ruled that, under *Amchem*, the Rule 23(b)(2) class was not adequately represented, even though it contained many of the members of the 23(b)(3) class. At least some who had used the credit card services in the past might have ended their businesses, and others began operating only after the expiration of the 23(b)(3) class period. The $500 million attorney fee amount, meanwhile, was based entirely on the monetary relief for the (b)(3) class, and members of that class could opt out while the members of the (b)(2) class could not.

Compare Sullivan v. DB Investments, Inc., 667 F.3d 273 (3d Cir. 2011), an antitrust action involving diamonds, a plaintiff class included "indirect purchasers" asserting state-law claims. But it was uncertain whether some states recognized such claims, and class members from all states nonetheless were included in the settlement class. Class members from states that recognized such claims objected to having to share their money with those in states that did not recognize the claims. Defendant was adamant, however, that it would settle only for "global peace," and the court of appeals ultimately affirmed the district judge's approval of the settlement. It reasoned that "concerns regarding variations in state law largely dissipate when a court is considering the certification of a settlement class," id. at 297, and added that "courts are more inclined to find the predominance test met [in the settlement context], even when there are differences in applicable state laws." Id. at 304 n. 29. Judge Scirica, a renowned authority on class actions, added a concurring opinion pointing out that the "nature of the predominance analysis" depends on the purpose of the inquiry; in the settlement context it is largely concerned with fairness and must be pragmatic. Measured in that way, the proposed settlement was fair to all class members. Id. at 336–38. Does this analysis respond to Justice Breyer's concerns in *Amchem*?

4.   In 1996 the Advisory Committee circulated a draft of a proposed amendment to Rule 23 adding a new subdivision (b)(4) authorizing certification when "the parties to a settlement request certification under subdivision (b)(3) for purposes of settlement, even though the requirements of subdivision (b)(3) might not be met for purposes of trial." See Proposed Amendments to the Federal Rules, 167 F.R.D. 523, 559 (1996). This change would have formally recognized in Rule 23 that certification for settlement is different from certification for trial. After the Court's decision in *Amchem*, the Advisory Committee decided to defer further action on a rule amendment. Could changing Rule 23 profitably clarify the requirements of *Amchem*? In connection with the 2018 amendments to the rule, the Advisory Committee considered another such proposed amendment but did not pursue it.

5.   Does the agreement reached through negotiation in *Amchem* seem unfair? If it appears to be a reasonable deal for class members in general, do you think that the promising features of the agreement should have mattered more to the Court, as Justice Breyer argues? One way of viewing *Amchem* is that it represented a contest between the advocates of substantive justice for claimants and those who insisted on fealty to procedural principles. See Samuel Issacharoff, "Shocked": Mass Torts and Aggregate Asbestos Litigation after Amchem and Ortiz, 80 Tex. L. Rev. 1926 (2002) (asserting that the proceduralists won hands down in the Court's decision). Some might argue that this is an example of Voltaire's maxim "The perfect is the enemy of the good."

Asbestos litigation did not vanish as a result of this decision. To the contrary, after *Amchem* and *Ortiz*, *supra* p. 232, the level of asbestos personal injury filings rose dramatically. The CCR disbanded, having paid out some $5 billion to approximately 350,000 claimants, and at least five members of the CCR filed petitions in bankruptcy. For details, see Deborah Hensler, As Time

Goes By: Asbestos Litigation After Amchem and Ortiz, 80 Tex. L. Rev. 1899 (2002). As Professor Hensler detailed, it was far from clear that asbestos claimants were better off than they would have been under the Amchem settlement. Most asbestos claims were resolved by inventory settlements, and individual claimants had virtually no role in setting the terms of those settlements. In general, the settlements employed some sort of grid based on the amounts paid to prior claimants, like the one in the settlement in Amchem. Claimants in bankruptcy proceedings, meanwhile, appeared not to fare very well. But it is, of course, impossible to say whether the bankruptcy filings would have occurred anyway had the Supreme Court reached a different result. For further examination of the implications of aggregate treatment outside the class action setting, see Howard Erichson, Beyond the Class Action: Lawyer Loyalty and Client Autonomy in Non-Class Collective Representation, 2003 U. Chi. Legal F. 519.

6.   What effect should Amchem have had on certification for settlement in cases not involving asbestos claims? Shortly after the case was decided, one district judge concluded that "Amchem decimated the notion of some circuits that Rule 23 requisites were relaxed in the settlement context." Walker v. Liggett Group, 175 F.R.D. 226 (S.D.W.Va. 1997). But an experienced class action lawyer saw things differently: "We should expect that the long-term impact of Amchem will be essentially favorable to those class actions that pit individuals of average means against modern corporations involving claims too small to litigate feasibly on a case-by-case basis." Elizabeth Cabraser, Life After Amchem: The Class Struggle Continues, 31 Loyola L.A. L. Rev. 373, 378 (1998).

A possible example is a case handled by Elizabeth Cabraser, the lawyer just quoted—Hanlon v. Chrysler Corp., 150 F.3d 1011 (9th Cir. 1998), a nationwide class action alleging that defendant's minivans had defective rear latches. After litigation skirmishing in several courts that led to settlement discussions, an agreement was reached by which various cases were consolidated in one nationwide class action on behalf of some 3.3 million minivan owners. Three days after this suit was filed, the parties submitted a class-action settlement agreement that excluded any personal injury or death claims from its coverage. The settlement obligated defendant to replace latches on minivans and engage in outreach to alert owners of their right to a replacement. It also obligated defendant to make the minivans safe. The district court approved the settlement.

Objecting class members appealed. The court of appeals affirmed (id. at 1021):

> Unlike the class in Amchem, this class of minivan owners does not present an allocation dilemma. Potential plaintiffs are not divided into conflicting discrete categories, such as those with present health problems and those who may develop symptoms in the future. Rather, each potential plaintiff has the same problem: an allegedly defective rear latchgate which requires repair or commensurate compensation. The differences in severity of personal injury present

in *Amchem* are avoided here by excluding personal injury and wrongful death claims. Similarly, there is no structural conflict of interest based on variations in state law, for the named representatives include individuals from each state, and the differences in state remedies are not sufficiently substantial so as to warrant the creation of subclasses. Representatives of other potential subclasses are included among the named representatives, including owners of every minivan model. However, even if the named representatives did not include a broad cross-section of claimants, the prospects for irreparable conflict of interest are minimal in this case because of the relatively small differences in damages and potential remedies.

7.   One idea mentioned by Justice Ginsburg is providing class members with "sturdy back-end opt-out rights." Would provision of such rights be a way of dealing with the problem of future claimants? See Richard Nagareda, Autonomy, Peace, and Put Options in the Mass Tort Class Action, 115 Harv. L. Rev. 747 (2002); Rhonda Wasserman, The Curious Complications With Back-End Opt-Outs, 49 Will. & Mary L.Rev. 373 (2007). Prof. Nagareda suggests that a class action settlement that exchanges the right to sue for punitive damages in return for the choice between a pre-set payment and the right to sue the manufacturer for damages if class members get sick is like a put option. He argues that this would preserve the claimants' autonomy and protect defendant against a serious problem in "over-mature" mass tort litigation, which is that plaintiff counsel will press forward with claims for those who are not impaired as well as for the injured. Prof. Wasserman explores the difficulties that may arise with enforcing limitations on what back-end opt-out plaintiffs do when they file suit. For example, it may be difficult for the federal court that approved and entered the settlement to enjoin pursuit of punitive damages even though that is forbidden under its judgment, because various sorts of jurisdictional obstacles can confound the federal court's efforts at enforcement.

8.   What is the significance of *Amchem* for cases already certified for litigation purposes? In In re Integra Realty Resources, Inc., 354 F.3d 1246 (10th Cir. 2004), objectors to a class-action settlement urged that there had to be heightened scrutiny of the settlement under *Amchem*. The court rejected the argument (id. at 1262):

> We reject appellant's argument that the heightened scrutiny dictated by Amchem Prods., Inc. v. Windsor for settlement-only certifications applies to this case since here, unlike in *Amchem*, the class was certified before settlement negotiations began and the designated class counsel acted as the negotiator for the class.

9.   The *negotiation class certification idea:* Some have urged that courts could certify a "negotiation class" to pursue a settlement when divergent views among class members might otherwise frustrate that effort. See Francis McGovern & William Rubenstein, The Negotiation Class: A Cooperative Approach to Class Actions Involving Large Stakeholders, 99 Tex. L. Rev. 73

(2020). In the Opioids MDL, the transferee judge certified such a class of all local governments in the country seeking compensation for costs associated with the epidemic of opioid abuse. The district court's certification order gave class members a period of time to opt out and provided further that if they did not opt out and a settlement was negotiated on their behalf, they would be bound by that settlement if a supermajority of class members approved it. Of the 34,458 putative class members, only 556 opted out. But 37 state attorneys general (who asserted that the municipalities could not act independently of them, since they were creatures of the state) appealed, along with other objectors. In In re National Prescription Opiate Litigation, 976 F.3d 664 (6th Cir. 2020), a 2–1 panel of the court of appeals held that this effort "to foster a settlement through a novel means of a class action that binds an unprecedented number of municipalities into a single bloc" could not stand. It rejected the analogy to settlement class certification, saying that Rule 23 "clearly indicate[s] that certification of a class for settlement purposes may occur only after a settlement has been proposed." Judge Moore (a former civil procedure professor) dissented. There was a petition for review *en banc*, but that was denied.

10. In *Amchem*, the Court does not address the Article III issue raised by objectors who argued that a class-action settlement that was agreed upon before suit was filed (as was true there) was not a genuine "case or controversy" within Article III of the Constitution. That is not true, of course, of most cases in which settlement and class certification are proposed simultaneously; usually the proposed settlement results from hard bargaining that follows after the suit is filed. Should settlement class actions that are filed pursuant to a pre-arranged agreement be handled differently? Consider Martin Redish & Andrianna Kastanek, Settlement Class Actions, the Case-or-Controversy Requirement, and the Nature of the Adjudicatory Process, 73 U. Chi. L. Rev. 545, 547 (2006): "[B]ecause by its nature it does not involve any live dispute between the parties that a federal court is being asked to resolve through litigation, and because from the outset of the proceeding the parties are in full accord as to how the claims should be disposed of, there is missing the adverseness between the parties that is a central element of Article III's case-or-controversy requirement. The settlement class action, in short, is inherently unconstitutional." Notwithstanding that strong conclusion, the authors also conclude that in *Amchem* "the Supreme Court implicitly approved the concept of the settlement class as an alternative form of dispute resolution." Id. at 556. More generally, the authors find that consent decrees in other kinds of cases are also constitutionally impermissible. See id. at 569–70.

F. LITIGATING CLASS CERTIFICATION

IN RE HYDROGEN PEROXIDE ANTITRUST LITIGATION
United States Court of Appeals, Third Circuit, 2008.
552 F.3d 305.

Before SCIRICA, CHIEF JUDGE, AMBRO and FISHER, CIRCUIT JUDGES.

SCIRICA, CHIEF JUDGE.

At issue in this antitrust action are the standards a district court applies when deciding whether to certify a class. We will vacate the order certifying the class in this case and remand for proceedings consistent with this opinion.

In deciding whether to certify a class under Fed.R.Civ.P. 23, the district court must make whatever factual and legal inquiries are necessary and must consider all relevant evidence and arguments presented by the parties. In this appeal, we clarify three key aspects of class certification procedure. First, the decision to certify a class calls for findings by the court, not merely a "threshold showing" by a party, that each requirement of Rule 23 is met. Factual determinations supporting Rule 23 findings must be made by a preponderance of the evidence. Second, the court must resolve all factual or legal disputes relevant to class certification, even if they overlap with the merits—including disputes touching on elements of the cause of action. Third, the court's obligation to consider all relevant evidence and arguments extends to expert testimony, whether offered by a party seeking class certification or by a party opposing it.

I.

[Hydrogen peroxide, an inorganic liquid used most prominently as a bleach in the pulp and paper industry, is available in solutions of different concentrations and grades depending on its intended use. Plaintiff purchasers of hydrogen peroxide sued more than a dozen producers of the product, alleging price fixing. Products containing different concentrations have different supply and demand characteristics; defendants contend they are not economic substitutes for each other, but plaintiffs disagree.

After the U.S. Department of Justice and the European Commission began investigating possible violations of antitrust laws in the hydrogen peroxide industry, several private class actions were filed, and all were transferred by the Judicial Panel on Multidistrict Litigation in the Eastern District of Pennsylvania, where they were consolidated. Following extensive discovery, during which defendants provided plaintiffs all available sales transactions and other market data relevant to how hydrogen peroxide was bought and sold during the class period, plaintiffs moved for class certification.]

II.

Class certification is proper only "if the trial court is satisfied, after a rigorous analysis, that the prerequisites" of Rule 23 are met. Gen. Tel. Co. of Sw. v. Falcon, 457 U.S. 147, 161 (1982). "A class certification decision requires a thorough examination of the factual and legal allegations."

The trial court, well-positioned to decide which facts and legal arguments are most important to each Rule 23 requirement, possesses broad discretion to control proceedings and frame issues for consideration under Rule 23. But proper discretion does not soften the rule: a class may not be certified without a finding that each Rule 23 requirement is met. Careful application of Rule 23 accords with the pivotal status of class certification in large-scale litigation, because

> denying or granting class certification is often the defining moment in class actions (for it may sound the "death knell" of the litigation on the part of plaintiffs, or create unwarranted pressure to settle nonmeritorious claims on the part of defendants). . . .

Newton [v. Merrill Lynch, Pierce, Fenner & Smith, Inc.], 259 F.3d [154,] 162 [(3d Cir. 2001)]; see id. at 167 ("Irrespective of the merits, certification decisions may have a decisive effect on litigation."); see also Coopers & Lybrand v. Livesay, 437 U.S. 463, 476 (1978). In some cases, class certification "may force a defendant to settle rather than incur the costs of defending a class action and run the risk of potentially ruinous liability." Fed.R.Civ.P. 23 advisory committee's note, 1998 Amendments. Accordingly, the potential for unwarranted settlement pressure "is a factor we weigh in our certification calculus." The Supreme Court recently cautioned that certain antitrust class actions may present prime opportunities for plaintiffs to exert pressure upon defendants to settle weak claims. See Bell Atl. Corp. v. Twombly, 550 U.S. 544 (2007).

III.

Here, the District Court found the Rule 23(a) requirements were met, a determination defendants do not now challenge. * * *

Only the predominance requirement is disputed in this appeal. Predominance "tests whether proposed classes are sufficiently cohesive to warrant adjudication by representation," Amchem [Products, Inc. v. Windsor], 521 U.S. at 623, a standard "far more demanding" than the commonality requirement of Rule 23(a), id. at 623–24, "requiring more than a common claim," Newton, 259 F.3d at 187. "Issues common to the class must predominate over individual issues. . . ." Because the "nature of the evidence that will suffice to resolve a question determines whether the question is common or individual," " 'a district court must formulate some prediction as to how specific issues will play out in order to determine whether common or individual issues predominate in a given case,' " "If proof of the essential elements of the cause of action requires individual treatment, then class certification is unsuitable." Accordingly, we examine the elements of plaintiffs' claim "through the prism" of Rule 23 to determine whether the District Court properly certified the class.

A.

The elements of plaintiffs' claim are (1) a violation of the antitrust laws—here, § 1 of the Sherman Act, (2) individual injury resulting from that violation, and (3) measurable damages. Importantly, individual injury (also known as antitrust impact) is an element of the cause of action; to prevail on the merits, every class member must prove at least some antitrust impact resulting from the alleged violation. *Newton*, 259 F.3d at 188 (In antitrust and securities fraud class actions, "[p]roof of injury (whether or not an injury occurred at all) must be distinguished from calculation of damages (which determines the actual value of the injury)").

In antitrust cases, impact often is critically important for the purpose of evaluating Rule 23(b)(3)'s predominance requirement because it is an element of the claim that may call for individual, as opposed to common, proof.

Plaintiffs' burden at the class certification stage is not to prove the element of antitrust impact, although in order to prevail on the merits each class member must do so. Instead, the task for plaintiffs at class certification is to demonstrate that the element of antitrust impact is capable of proof at trial through evidence that is common to the class rather than individual to its members. Deciding this issue calls for the district court's rigorous assessment of the available evidence and the method or methods by which plaintiffs propose to use the evidence to prove impact at trial.

Here, the District Court found the predominance requirement was met because plaintiffs would be able to use common, as opposed to individualized, evidence to prove antitrust impact at trial. On appeal, defendants contend the District Court erred in three principal respects in finding plaintiffs satisfied the predominance requirement: (1) by applying too lenient a standard of proof for class certification, (2) by failing meaningfully to consider the views of defendants' expert while crediting plaintiffs' expert, and (3) by erroneously applying presumption of antitrust impact. * * *

B.

We summarize briefly the evidence and arguments offered to the District Court. As noted, both plaintiffs and defendants presented the opinions of expert economists. [The opinions of the two expert economists were "irreconcilable." Beyer, plaintiff's expert, opined that a "market analysis" suggested that conditions in the hydrogen peroxide industry favored a conspiracy that would impact the entire plaintiff class. He emphasized his view that hydrogen peroxide products are fungible, so that producers compete on price rather than quality, that production is highly concentrated, and that there are high barriers to entry. He asserted that—consistent with his expectations—prices moved similarly over time and pointed to two potential approaches to estimating damages on a classwide basis, "benchmark analysis," which would compare actual prices during the alleged conspiracy with prices existing before the class period, and "regression analysis," which might provide an estimate of the relationship between the price of hydrogen peroxide and demand and supply variables.

Defendants' expert, Ordower, disputed plaintiffs' claim that the various hydrogen peroxide products involved are fungible, finding instead that they have different supply and demand characteristics. He further found that there was no tendency for prices charged individual customers to move together, noting in part that a number of contracts for this product were individually negotiated. He emphasized that some class members' prices declined while those paid by others rose during the class period. Defendants asserted that this factor "goes to the core of the predominance issue" and that plaintiffs' expert only "promised" to come up with a method to overcome the obstacle.

The district court nonetheless denied defendants' *Daubert* motion to exclude Beyer's opinions, observing that "because the evidence is here offered for the limited purpose of class certification, our inquiry is perhaps less exacting than it might be for evidence to be presented at trial." It held that plaintiffs' showing was adequate for class certification because their expert proposed reliable methods for proving impact and damages.]

IV.

A.

Defendants contend the District Court applied too lenient a standard of proof with respect to the Rule 23 requirements by (1) accepting only a "threshold showing" by plaintiffs rather than making its own determination, (2) requiring only that plaintiffs demonstrate their "intention" to prove impact on a class-wide basis, and (3) singling out antitrust actions as appropriate for class treatment even when compliance with Rule 23 is "in doubt."

Although it is clear that the party seeking certification must convince the district court that the requirements of Rule 23 are met, little guidance is available on the subject of the proper standard of "proof" for class certification. The Supreme Court has described the inquiry as a "rigorous analysis," *Falcon*, 457 U.S. at 161, and a "close look," *Amchem*, 521 U.S. at 615, but it has elaborated no further.

1.

The following principles guide a district court's class certification analysis. First, the requirements set out in Rule 23 are not mere pleading rules. The court may " 'delve beyond the pleadings to determine whether the requirements for class certification are satisfied.' "

An overlap between a class certification requirement and the merits of a claim is no reason to decline to resolve relevant disputes when necessary to determine whether a class certification requirement is met. Some uncertainty ensued when the Supreme Court declared in Eisen v. Carlisle & Jacquelin, 417 U.S. 156 (1974), that there is "nothing in either the language or history of Rule 23 that gives a court any authority to conduct a preliminary inquiry into the merits of a suit in order to determine whether it may be maintained as a class action." Only a few years later, in addressing whether a party may bring an interlocutory appeal when a district court denies class certification,[16] the Supreme Court pointed out that "the class determination generally involves considerations that are 'enmeshed in the factual and legal issues comprising the plaintiff's cause of action.' " [Coopers & Lybrand v.] Livesay, 437 U.S. at 469 [(1978)]. * * * *Eisen* is best understood to preclude only a merits inquiry that is not necessary to determine a Rule 23 requirement. Other courts of appeals have agreed. Because the decision whether to certify a class "requires a thorough examination of the factual and legal allegations," the court's rigorous analysis may include a "preliminary inquiry into the merits," and the court may "consider the substantive elements of the plaintiffs' case in order to envision the form that a trial on those issues would take." A contested requirement is not forfeited in favor of the party seeking certification merely because it is similar or even identical to one normally decided by a trier of fact. Although the district court's findings for the purpose of class certification are conclusive on that topic, they do not bind the fact-finder on the merits.[19]

The evidence and arguments a district court considers in the class certification decision call for rigorous analysis. A party's assurance to the court that it intends or plans to meet the requirements is insufficient.

Support for our analysis is drawn from amendments to Rule 23 that took effect in 2003. First, amended Rule 23(c)(1)(A) altered the timing requirement for the class certification decision. The amended rule calls for a decision on class certification "[a]t an early practicable time after a person sues or is sued as a class representative," while the prior version had required that decision be made "as soon as practicable after commencement of an action." We recognized in Weiss v. Regal Collections, 385 F.3d 337, 347 (3d Cir. 2004), that this change in language, though subtle, reflects the need for a thorough evaluation of the Rule 23 factors-for this reason the

---

[16] This case pre-dated Fed.R.Civ.P. 23(f), which provides for interlocutory appeals from class certification orders.

[19] "[T]he determination as to a Rule 23 requirement is made only for purposes of class certification and is not binding on the trier of facts, even if that trier is the class certification judge." [In re] IPO [Securities Litigation], 471 F.3d [24,] 41 [(2d Cir. 2006)].

rule does not "require or encourage premature certification determinations." We explained:

> Fed.R.Civ.P. 23 directs that certification decisions be made "at an early practicable time." Fed.R.Civ.P. 23(c)(1)(a). This recent amendment replaced the language of the old rule: The former " 'as soon as practicable' exaction neither reflect[ed] prevailing practice nor capture[ed] the many valid reasons that may justify deferring the initial certification decision." See Fed.R.Civ.P. 23(c)(1)(a) Advisory Committee Notes. . . .

> Allowing time for limited discovery supporting certification motions may . . . be necessary for sound judicial administration.[20]

Relatedly, in introducing the concept of a "trial plan," the Advisory Committee's 2003 note focuses attention on a rigorous evaluation of the likely shape of a trial on the issues:

> A critical need is to determine how the case will be tried. An increasing number of courts require a party requesting class certification to present a "trial plan" that describes the issues likely to be presented at trial and tests whether they are susceptible of class-wide proof.

Additionally, the 2003 amendments eliminated the language that had appeared in Rule 23(c)(1) providing that a class certification "may be conditional." The Advisory Committee's note explains: "A court that is not satisfied that the requirements of Rule 23 have been met should refuse certification until they have been met." * * *

While these amendments do not alter the substantive standards for class certification, they guide the trial court in its proper task—to consider carefully all relevant evidence and make a definitive determination that the requirements of Rule 23 have been met before certifying a class.

To summarize: because each requirement of Rule 23 must be met, a district court errs as a matter of law when it fails to resolve a genuine legal or factual dispute relevant to determining the requirements.

---

[20] The Advisory Committee's note [to the 2003 amendment to Rule 23(c)] explains:

Time may be needed to gather information necessary to make the certification decision. Although an evaluation of the probable outcome on the merits is not properly part of the certification decision, discovery in aid of the certification decision often includes information required to identify the nature of the issues that actually will be presented at trial. In this sense it is appropriate to conduct controlled discovery into the "merits," limited to those aspects relevant to making the certification decision on an informed basis. Active judicial supervision may be required to achieve the most effective balance that expedites an informed certification determination without forcing an artificial and ultimately wasteful division between "certification discovery" and "merits discovery."

2.

Class certification requires a finding that each of the requirements of Rule 23 has been met.[22] Factual determinations necessary to make Rule 23 findings must be made by a preponderance of the evidence. In other words, to certify a class the district court must find that the evidence more likely than not establishes each fact necessary to meet the requirements of Rule 23.

In reviewing a district court's judgment on class certification, we apply the abuse of discretion standard. A district court abuses its discretion in deciding whether to certify a class action if its "decision rests upon a clearly erroneous finding of fact, an errant conclusion of law or an improper application of law to fact." Under these Rule 23 standards, a district court exercising proper discretion in deciding whether to certify a class will resolve factual disputes by a preponderance of the evidence and make findings that each Rule 23 requirement is met or is not met, having considered all relevant evidence and arguments presented by the parties. The abuse of discretion standard requires the judge to exercise sound discretion—failing that, the judge's decision is not entitled to the deference attendant to discretionary rulings.

If a class is certified, "the text of the order or an incorporated opinion must include (1) a readily discernible, clear, and precise statement of the parameters defining the class or classes to be certified, and (2) a readily discernible, clear, and complete list of the claims, issues or defenses to be treated on a class basis."

B.

Although the District Court properly described the class certification decision as requiring "rigorous analysis," some statements in its opinion depart from the standards we have articulated. The District Court stated, "So long as plaintiffs demonstrate their intention to prove a significant portion of their case through factual evidence and legal arguments common to all class members, that will now suffice. It will not do here to make judgments about whether plaintiffs have adduced enough evidence or whether their evidence is more or less credible than defendants'." With respect to predominance, the District Court stated that "[p]laintiffs need only make a threshold showing that the element of impact will predominantly involve generalized issues of proof, rather than questions which are particular to each member of the plaintiff class." As we have explained, proper analysis under Rule 23 requires rigorous consideration

---

[22] As the Court of Appeals for the First Circuit has explained [*New Motor Vehicles*, 522 F.3d at 24],

> [Some] circuits' use of the term 'findings' in this context should not be confused with binding findings on the merits. The judge's consideration of merits issues at the class certification stage pertains only to that stage; the ultimate factfinder, whether judge or jury, must still reach its own determination on these issues.

of all the evidence and arguments offered by the parties. It is incorrect to state that a plaintiff need only demonstrate an "intention" to try the case in a manner that satisfies the predominance requirement. Similarly, invoking the phrase "threshold showing" risks misapplying Rule 23. A "threshold showing" could signify, incorrectly, that the burden on the party seeking certification is a lenient one (such as a prima facie showing or a burden of production) or that the party seeking certification receives deference or a presumption in its favor. So defined, "threshold showing" is an inadequate and improper standard. "[T]he requirements of Rule 23 must be met, not just supported by some evidence."

Citing Cumberland Farms, Inc. v. Browning-Ferris Industries, 120 F.R.D. 642, 645 (E.D.Pa. 1988), the District Court reasoned, "[i]t is well recognized that private enforcement of [antitrust] laws is a necessary supplement to government action. With that in mind, in an alleged horizontal price-fixing conspiracy case when a court is in doubt as to whether or not to certify a class action, the court should err in favor of allowing the class." See also Eisenberg v. Gagnon, 766 F.2d 770, 785 (3d Cir. 1985) (citing Kahan v. Rosenstiel, 424 F.2d 161, 169 (3d Cir. 1970)) (advising that in a "doubtful" case when presented with a putative securities class action, court should err, if at all, in favor of certification). These statements invite error. * * * *Eisenberg* predates the recent amendments to Rule 23 which, as noted, reject tentative decisions on certification and encourage development of a record sufficient for informed analysis. We recognize the Supreme Court has observed that "[p]redominance is a test readily met in certain cases alleging consumer or securities fraud or violations of the antitrust laws." *Amchem*, 521 U.S. at 625. But it does not follow that a court should relax its certification analysis, or presume a requirement for certification is met, merely because a plaintiff's claims fall within one of those substantive categories. "[A]ctual, not presumed, conformance" with the Rule 23 requirements remains necessary.

To the extent that the District Court's analysis reflects application of incorrect standards, remand is appropriate. We recognize that the able District Court did not have the benefit of the standards we have articulated. Faced with complex, fact-intensive disputes, trial courts have expended considerable effort to interpret and apply faithfully the requirements of Rule 23. One important reason for granting interlocutory appeals under Fed.R.Civ.P. 23(f) is to address "novel or unsettled questions of law" like those presented here.

C.

Defendants contend the District Court erred as a matter of law in failing to consider the expert testimony of defendants' expert, Ordover, instead deferring to the opinion of plaintiffs' expert, Beyer. Plaintiffs do not dispute that a district court may properly consider expert opinion with respect to Rule 23 requirements at the class certification stage, but maintain that in this case the District Court considered and rejected Ordover's opinion and defendants' arguments based on it.

In addressing defendants' *Daubert* motion to exclude Beyer's opinion, the court discussed whether it should consider Ordover's opinion in deciding whether Beyer's opinion was admissible. The court stated it would be improper to "weigh the relative credibility of the parties' experts"—in other words, to weigh Ordover's opinion against Beyer's—for the purpose of deciding whether to admit or exclude Beyer's opinion. Concluding Beyer's opinion was admissible, the court denied the *Daubert* motion. But in addressing the Rule 23 requirements, the court did not confront Ordover's analysis or his substantive rebuttal of Beyer's points. Nor did the court address Ordover's finding of substantial price disparities among similarly situated purchasers of hydrogen peroxide. The court appears to have assumed it was barred from weighing Ordover's opinion against Beyer's for the purpose of deciding whether the requirements of Rule 23 had been met. This was erroneous.

1.

Expert opinion with respect to class certification, like any matter relevant to a Rule 23 requirement, calls for rigorous analysis. It follows that opinion testimony should not be uncritically accepted as establishing a Rule 23 requirement merely because the court holds the testimony should not be excluded, under Daubert or for any other reason. See *IPO*, 471 F.3d at 42 (rejecting the view that "an expert's testimony may establish a component of a Rule 23 requirement simply by being not fatally flawed" and instructing that "[a] district judge is to assess all of the relevant evidence admitted at the class certification stage and determine whether each Rule 23 requirement has been met, just as the judge would resolve a dispute about any other threshold prerequisite for continuing a lawsuit"). Under Rule 23 the district court must be "satisfied," *Falcon*, 457 U.S. at 161 or "persuaded," *IPO*, 471 F.3d at 41, that each requirement is met before certifying a class. Like any evidence, admissible expert opinion may persuade its audience, or it may not. This point is especially important to bear in mind when a party opposing certification offers expert opinion. The district court may be persuaded by the testimony of either (or neither) party's expert with respect to whether a certification requirement is met. Weighing conflicting expert testimony at the certification stage is not only permissible; it may be integral to the rigorous analysis Rule 23 demands.

Resolving expert disputes in order to determine whether a class certification requirement has been met is always a task for the court—no matter whether a dispute might appear to implicate the "credibility" of one or more experts, a matter resembling those usually reserved for a trier of fact. Rigorous analysis need not be hampered by a concern for avoiding credibility issues; as noted, findings with respect to class certification do not bind the ultimate fact-finder on the merits. A court's determination that an expert's opinion is persuasive or unpersuasive on a Rule 23 requirement does not preclude a different view at the merits stage of the case.

That weighing expert opinions is proper does not make it necessary in every case or unlimited in scope. As the Court of Appeals for the Second Circuit instructed,

> To avoid the risk that a Rule 23 hearing will extend into a protracted mini-trial of substantial portions of the underlying litigation, a district judge must be accorded considerable discretion to limit both discovery and the extent of the hearing on Rule 23 requirements. But even with some limits on discovery and the extent of the hearing, the district judge must receive enough evidence, by affidavits, documents, or testimony, to be satisfied that each Rule 23 requirement has been met.

IPO, 471 F.3d at 41. In its sound discretion, a district court may find it unnecessary to consider certain expert opinion with respect to a certification requirement, but it may not decline to resolve a genuine legal or factual dispute because of concern for an overlap with the merits. Genuine disputes with respect to the Rule 23 requirements must be resolved, after considering all relevant evidence submitted by the parties.

2.

[The court distinguished an earlier antitrust case in which it had treated the analysis of Beyer, the same expert used by plaintiffs in this case, as sufficient to support class certification, using a similar methodology. That case did not involve a defense expert opinion disputing Beyer's conclusions, as was true in this case.]

We do not question plaintiffs' general proposition, which the District Court accepted, that a conspiracy to maintain prices could, in theory, impact the entire class despite a decrease in prices for some customers in parts of the class period, and despite some divergence in the prices different plaintiffs paid. But the question at class certification stage is whether, if such impact is plausible in theory, it is also susceptible to proof at trial through available evidence common to the class. When the latter issue is genuinely disputed, the district court must resolve it after considering all relevant evidence. Here, the District Court apparently believed it was barred from resolving disputes between the plaintiffs' and defendants' experts. Rule 23 calls for consideration of all relevant evidence and arguments, including relevant expert testimony of the parties. Accordingly, we will vacate the order certifying the class and remand for proceedings consistent with this opinion.

D.

[The court distinguished an earlier antitrust case in which it had said that proof of a nationwide conspiracy that raised prices could sometimes support a presumption of impact on all class members.] The record in this case is different. Although the price of hydrogen peroxide rose at some points during the lengthy class period, the price was lower, not higher, at the end of the class period than at the beginning. And the evidence, as interpreted by defendants' expert, shows that through much of the class period the production of hydrogen peroxide was increasing rather than decreasing. Moreover, there was an active dispute between the experts as to the "price structure in the industry" * * *. Defendants cited, for example, [defense expert] Ordover's empirical analysis showing substantial price disparities among similarly situated customers. Accordingly, defendants contended, it was far from "clear the violation result[ed] in harm to the entire class," It is not apparent that the District Court considered, or believed it had the authority to consider, all the evidence in the record with respect to this dispute.

* * * Applying a presumption of impact based solely on an unadorned allegation of price-fixing would appear to conflict with the 2003 amendments to Rule 23, which emphasize the need for a careful, fact-based approach, informed, if necessary, by discovery.

V.

For the foregoing reasons, we will vacate the class certification order and remand for proceedings consistent with this opinion.

NOTES AND QUESTIONS

1.   It was central to the 1966 amendments that the certification question should usually be resolved before the court decided the merits of the suit. In part, that was due to the introduction in 1966 of the (b)(3) class action, with the right to opt out. One goal was to avoid what was called "one-way intervention," which could occur if class members already knew whether the suit was successful before they made their opt-out decisions. Thus, the 1966 version of Rule 23(c) said that modifications in the certification order could only be made before "decision on the merits." Some judges even seemed to think that they could not entertain a defendant's motion to dismiss under Rule 12(b)(6) or for summary judgment until class certification had been resolved. With the passage of time, courts' insistence that no "merits" decisions could be made until class certification was resolved abated. For a review of these developments, see Richard Marcus, Scrutinizing the Merits on Class Certification, 79 Geo.Wash.L.Rev. 324 (2011). In In re Lamictal Direct Purchaser Antitrust Litigation, 957 F.3d 184, 191 (3d Cir. 2020), the Third Circuit adhered to "our long-standing rule announced in *Hydrogen Peroxide*."

The Supreme Court has supported this new attitude. In Wal-Mart Stores, Inc. v. Dukes, 564 U.S. 338 (2011), *supra* p. 200, the Court emphasized the need for "rigorous analysis" of the showing supporting certification, and recognized that "[f]requently, that 'rigorous analysis' will entail some overlap with the merits of plaintiff's underlying claim. That cannot be helped." Id. at 2551. But the Court has also cautioned that "Rule 23 grants courts no license to engage in free-ranging merits inquiries at the certification stage. Merits questions may be considered to the extent—but only to the extent—that they are relevant to determining whether the Rule 23 prerequisites for class certification are satisfied." Amgen, Inc. v. Connecticut Retirement Plans and Trust Funds, 568 U.S. 455 (2013), *supra* p. 258.

2. Does focusing on the merits at the certification stage permit a form of "one-way intervention"? In *Hydrogen Peroxide*, the court says that the district court must make a finding, by a preponderance of the evidence, about whether to accept the theories of plaintiffs' expert, at least for class certification, and make "findings" as well. It also says that these "findings" leave the issues open for trial, even if it is a nonjury trial to the court.

3. A recurrent concern is that class certification will compel defendants to settle. Is that more likely under the *Hydrogen Peroxide* regime? Should grant of certification imply that plaintiffs will win, and therefore suggest that a substantial settlement is warranted? As the Seventh Circuit conceded in In re Allstate Corp. Securities Litig., 966 F.3d 595, 603 (7th Cir. 2020): "We recognize the contradiction built into the standard. The judge must examine the evidence for its cohesiveness while studiously ignoring its bearing on the merits questions." The Third Circuit explained that "the analysis is not a merits determination. [Instead, it is] much like a court's preview of the merits of a case when imposing a preliminary injunction." Harnish v. Widener University School of Law, 833 F.3d 298, 305 (3d Cir. 2016). But one factor bearing on the preliminary injunction ruling is whether the plaintiff is likely to prevail on the merits. Perhaps courts *should* focus on the merits before certifying a class. For an argument that the judge should assess plaintiffs' likelihood of success and certify only if the claim seems viable, see Robert Bone & Davie Evans, Class Certification and the Substantive Merits, 51 Duke L.J. 1251 (2002).

4. As *Hydrogen Peroxide* illustrates, one recurrent issue is expert testimony. Perhaps judges should insist that such evidence satisfy the *Daubert* reliability standard before basing certification on it. For an argument that courts should only consider evidence in regard to certification that would be admissible at trial, see Linda Mullenix, Putting Proponents to Their Proof: Evidentiary Rules at Class Certification, 82 Geo.Wash.L.Rev. 606 (2014). See also Note, Form, Substance, and Rule 23: The Applicability of the Federal Rules of Evidence to Class Certification, 95 N.Y.U. L. Rev. 1561 (2020). In In re Blood Reagents Antitrust Litig., 783 F.3d 183 (3d Cir. 2015), the court said that it was improper to rely on expert testimony to support certification unless that testimony satisfied *Daubert*. "Expert testimony that is insufficiently reliable to satisfy the *Daubert* standard cannot 'prove' that Rule 23(a) prerequisites have been met 'in fact.'" Id. at 18

If the expert evidence satisfies *Daubert*, does that mean that certification should be granted? In Grodzitsky v. American Honda Motor Co., 957 F.3d 979 (9th Cir. 2020), the court implied that admissibility alone may suffice: "Plaintiffs do not need to demonstrate that they will prevail on the merits to satisfy commonality; they need only show that a classwide proceeding would 'generate common answers apt to drive the resolution of the litigation.' " Id. at 989. Consider the views of the court in In re Ethylene Propylene Diene Monomer Antitrust Litigation, 256 F.R.D. 82 (D. Conn. 2009), a case in which plaintiffs supported class certification with an opinion of the same expert used by plaintiffs in *Hydrogen Peroxide* (id. at 102 n. 11):

> In this case, Beyer has actually presented an econometric model that purports to show that antitrust impact is susceptible to common proof. Although the defense experts claim to dispute the feasibility of constructing an econometric model using proof common to the class, their reports are better characterized as disputing the results of the plaintiff's modeling. To resolve this dispute would be to place myself in the role of the ultimate factfinder by choosing which expert's econometric model or theory is "correct." Therefore, having presented a working econometric model that demonstrates class-wide impact and injury using proof common to the class, the plaintiffs here have gone further than the plaintiffs in *Hydrogen Peroxide* in establishing that the requirements of Rule 23 have been met.

Contrast In re Rail Freight Fuel Surcharge Antitrust Litig., 934 F.3d 619 (D.C.Cir. 2019), in which the district court concluded that the expert testimony on which plaintiffs relied was admissible under *Daubert*, but nevertheless also concluded that it did not justify certification. The court of appeals affirmed, finding that "reliability under rule 23 is a higher standard than reliability under *Daubert*."

5.   In *Hydrogen Peroxide*, plaintiffs submitted a trial plan in support of their motion to certify the class. Could they do that without complete discovery? Should plaintiffs submit such a plan in every case? In Vega v. T-Mobile USA, Inc., 564 F.3d 1256 (11th Cir. 2009), the court elaborated on the importance of a trial plan (id. at 1279 n. 20):

> We do not mean to say that submission of a trial plan by plaintiff is necessarily a prerequisite, as a matter of law, for a finding of superiority in every case. Nonetheless, a plaintiff seeking class certification bears the burden of establishing every element of Rule 23, which includes superiority in Rule 23(b)(3) cases, and courts must consider how a case will be tried as part of the superiority assessment. Accordingly, the proposal of a workable trial plan will often go a long way toward demonstrating that manageability concerns do not excessively undermine the superiority of the class action vehicle. Moreover, there is a direct correlation between the importance of a realistic, clear, detailed, and specific trial plan and the magnitude of the manageability problems that a putative class action presents. We therefore recommend that district courts make it

a usual practice to direct plaintiffs to present feasible trial plans, which should include proposed jury instructions, as early as practicable when seeking class certification.

6.   The timing of class certification decisions is obviously of great tactical importance. Should defendants be able to make "preemptive" motions to deny class certification? "Nothing in the plain language of Rule 23(c)(1)(A) either vests plaintiffs with the exclusive right to put the class certification issue before the district court or prohibits a defendant from seeking early resolution of the class certification question." Vinole v. Countrywide Home Loans, Inc., 571 F.3d 935, 939–40 (9th Cir. 2009). Compare Rosenberg v. LoanDepot.com LLC, 435 F.Supp.3d 308, 315 (D.Mass. 2020) (pre-discovery motions to strike class action allegations are disfavored).

7.   *Modifications of class definition or decertification*: Before class certification involved such rigorous efforts, there were occasions in which class definitions were substantially modified, or a certified class was decertified, a considerable time after initial class certification. In some instances, such decertification has been held to trigger the Rule 23(e) review required for dismissal of a certified class action. See Payne v. Travenol Laboratories, Inc., 673 F.2d 798 (5th Cir.), cert. denied, 459 U.S. 1038 (1982). Decertification after class notice has been sent may raise issues about notifying excluded former class members that they are no longer included. See Birmingham Steel Corp. v. Tennessee Valley Authority, 353 F.3d 1331 (11th Cir. 2003) ("once a district court has decertified a class, it must ensure that notification of this action be sent to the class members, in order that the latter can be alerted that the statute of limitations has begun to run again on their individual claims"). Expansion of the class definition after liability is determined, on the other hand, might subject defendant to a broader remedy than was originally involved. See Kilgo v. Bowman Transportation, Inc., 789 F.2d 859 (11th Cir. 1986) (upholding expansion where defendant could not assert it was prejudiced). Presumably the number of occasions for such action will decline as the class-certification decision itself is based on a fuller examination of the issues and the evidence.

Interlocutory Appeal of
Class-Certification Decisions

Hydrogen Peroxide involved interlocutory review of the district court's decision to certify the class pursuant to Rule 23(f). Until that provision was adopted in 1998, obtaining prompt review of a class-certification decision was extremely difficult because certification decisions are by definition interlocutory.

Blair v. Equifax Check Serv., Inc., 181 F.3d 832 (7th Cir. 1999), the leading case interpreting Rule 23(f), explored the criteria that bear on whether to accept an appeal, albeit eschewing a bright line approach. It suggested that, where class certification is denied, the "death knell" idea that denial of certification spelled death for the case might suffice, but cautioned that courts be "wary lest the mind hear a bell that is not tolling" in cases that will be pursued despite the denial of class certification. The obverse is in cases in which certification is granted if "the stakes are large and the risk of a settlement or other disposition that does not reflect the merits of the claim is substantial." In those situations, however, the appellant must demonstrate that the certification is questionable. Finally, allowing an appeal may facilitate in the development of the law, thereby making rule amendments unnecessary. If an appeal is allowed, "a stay would depend on a demonstration that the probability of error in the class certification decision is high enough that the costs of pressing ahead in the district court exceed the costs of waiting."

Should interlocutory review sometimes extend beyond class certification? The American Law Institute's Principles of Aggregate Litigation urge that when a court certifies a class action only with regard to certain issues (recall Martin v. Behr Dayton Thermal Products LLC, *supra* p. 298), an immediate review of the district court's resolution of those issues must be available. See ALI, Principles of the Law of Aggregate Litigation § 2.09 (2010); cf. 28 U.S.C. § 1441(e)(3) (providing for immediate appeal of federal court's decision regarding liability before remand to state court for determination of damages in action that could have been brought in federal court under 28 U.S.C. § 1369).

For general discussion, see Michael Solimine & Christine Hines, Deciding to Decide: Class Action Certification and Interlocutory Review by the United States Courts of Appeals Under Rule 23(f), 41 Will. & Mary L. Rev. 1531 (2000). Robert Klonoff, The Decline of Class Actions, 90 Wash. U. L. Rev. 729, 741 (2013), found that the availability of review under Rule 23(f) favored defendants more often than it favored plaintiffs:

> [I]n terms of sheer numbers, Rule 23(f) has served primarily as a device to protect defendants. [The Appendix to the article] reflects all Rule 23(f) appeals accepted from November 30, 1998, through May 31, 2012. Out of the 209 Rule 23(f) appeals accepted, 144 (or about 69 percent) were appeals by defendants after a grant of class certification, whereas only 65 (31 percent) were appeals by plaintiffs after a denial of class certification. Of the 144 appeals by defendants, defendants were successful in 101 cases (a 70 percent reversal rate). Of the 65 appeals by plaintiffs, plaintiffs prevailed in only 26 cases (or 30 percent of the time). Thus, even when plaintiffs convinced the appellate court to grant review, they lost in the majority of cases. In short, with respect to appellate court review pursuant to Rule 23(f), defendants have benefitted more from Rule 23(f) than have plaintiffs.

Does this show that Rule 23(f) was a bad idea? Alternatively, does it suggest that some district judges were too adventuresome in granting class certification? How much should a court of appeals' ruling confine what the district judge can do on remand? In Gene & Gene, LLC v. Biopay, LLC, 624 F.3d 698 (5th Cir. 2010), the appellate court ruled that the district judge incorrectly found that class-wide proof would suffice, and remanded "for further proceedings not inconsistent with this opinion." The district court then reopened discovery and re-certified the class based on new information, but the court of appeals rejected that because "the district court erred in considering 'new' evidence disclosed during the reopened discovery." Id. at 764.

It does appear that plaintiffs sometimes chafe at the limits the rule places on getting appellate review of denial of certification. In Microsoft Corp. v. Baker, 137 S.Ct. 1702 (2017), when the court of appeals denied their Rule 23(f) petition for review of denial of certification, plaintiffs voluntarily dismissed and sought to appeal the resulting judgment, challenging the denial of certification. But the Supreme Court held that this maneuver was not allowed because it would frustrate the discretion the rule gives the appellate court, and rejected the appeal. In Nutraceutical Corp. v. Lambert, 139 S.Ct. 710 (2019), the district court decertified the class it had originally certified. Plaintiffs moved for reconsideration in the district court rather than immediately seeking appellate review. When the district court refused reconsideration, they sought review under Rule 23(f). The Ninth Circuit granted review and reversed, but the Supreme Court held that the right to review had expired 14 days after the decertification order because the time limit in Rule 23(f) is "inflexible."

G. OVERLAPPING CLASS ACTIONS

IN RE DIET DRUGS

United States Court of Appeals, Third Circuit, 2002.
282 F.3d 220.

Before: SCIRICA, GREENBERG, COWEN, CIRCUIT JUDGES.

SCIRICA, CIRCUIT JUDGE.

In this matter involving competing mass tort class actions in federal and state courts, we address an interlocutory appeal in a complex multidistrict federal class action comprising six million members from an order enjoining a mass opt out of a state class. We will affirm.

I.

The underlying case involves two drugs, both appetite suppressants, fenfluramine—marketed as "Pondimin"—and dexfenfluramine—marketed as "Redux." Both drugs were in great demand. Between 1995 and 1997, four million people took Pondimin and two million people took Redux. In 1997, data came to light suggesting a link between the drugs' use and valvular heart disease. In July 1997, the United States Food and Drug Administration issued a public health advisory alert. On September 15,

1997, American Home Products removed both drugs from the market. Subsequent clinical studies support the view the drugs may cause valvular heart damage.

Following the FDA's issuance of the public health warning, several lawsuits were filed. The number of lawsuits increased exponentially after American Home Products withdrew the diet drugs from the market. Approximately eighteen thousand individual lawsuits and over one hundred putative class actions were filed in federal and state courts around the country. American Home Products removed many of the state cases to federal courts, increasing the number of federal cases. In December 1997, the Judicial Panel for Multidistrict Litigation transferred all the federal actions to Judge Louis Bechtle in the United States District Court for the Eastern District of Pennsylvania, creating Multidistrict Litigation 1203 ("MDL 1203").

In April 1999, American Home Products began "global" settlement talks with plaintiffs in the federal action together with several plaintiffs in similar state class actions. The parties reached a tentative settlement agreement for a nationwide class in November 1999. Known as the "*Brown* class," the proposed class included all persons in the United States, as well as their representatives and dependents, who had ingested either or both of the diet drugs. The global settlement contemplated different kinds of relief, including medical care, medical screening, payments for injury, and refunds of the drugs' purchase price.

The purchase-price-relief provisions were separated into two sections, one for those who had taken the drugs for sixty days or less, the other for those who had taken the drugs for more than sixty days. Short term users were to be paid $30 per month's use of Pondimin, and $60 per month's use of Redux. Long term users would receive the same amounts per month, subject to a $500 cap and the availability of sufficient money in an overall settlement fund. Unlike short term users, long term users were entitled to other benefits, such as medical screening.

The District Court entered an order on November 23, 1999, conditionally certifying a nationwide settlement class and, concurrently, preliminarily approving the settlement. To opt out, a class member was to "sign and submit written notice to the Claims Administrator[s] with a copy to American Home Products, clearly manifesting the Class Member's intent to opt out of the Settlement." The opt-out period extended until March 23, 2000. The court scheduled a fairness hearing for May 1, 2000 on class certification and final settlement approval. On August 28, 2000, the District Court entered a final order certifying the class and approving the settlement.

In July 1997—after the FDA warning, but before American Home Products withdrew the drugs from the market—appellants filed a putative class action in [Hidalgo County,] Texas state court, Gonzalez et al. v.

Medeva Pharmaceuticals, Inc., et al. The *Gonzalez* case was one of the first cases filed and preceded the creation of MDL 1203 by several months. The proposed *Gonzalez* class, including all Texas purchasers of the two diet drugs, was a subset of what would become the *Brown* class. The Gonzalez action was limited insofar as it sought actual purchase-price recovery only, together with treble damages under the Texas Deceptive Trade Practices Act-Consumer Protection Act, Tex. Bus. & Comm.Code, § 17.41 et seq.

[Although the *Gonzalez* complaint did not assert a federal claim, American Home Products removed in early 1998 on ground of diversity, contending that the nondiverse defendant had been fraudulently joined, and the case was transferred under MDL 1203 to Philadelphia. Plaintiffs moved to remand, assuring the federal judge that the nondiverse defendant was a proper defendant, and also claiming that the amount in controversy requirement was not satisfied because they did not seek an award of statutory attorney fees. Eventually, during the MDL 1203 opt-out period in early 2000, the federal judge in Philadelphia granted the motion to remand, finding the nondiverse defendant to be a proper defendant.

A month after remand, the *Gonzalez* plaintiffs filed an amended complaint dropping all claims against the nondiverse defendant and adding a claim for attorney fees. A week after that, the Hidalgo County court certified a class of all who purchased the drugs in Texas. On the same day it certified the class, the Texas court set a hearing for the following morning on plaintiffs' motion to opt all members of the *Gonzalez* class out of *Brown*. At that time, there were eight days remaining before the end of the opt-out period in *Brown*.

Slightly before noon on the following day, American Home Products obtained a TRO from the federal court in Philadelphia to prevent the application to the Texas court. But on the same morning the Texas court granted the order requested by the *Gonzalez* plaintiffs. The Texas court later issued an order "clarifying" that it had acted before the federal court had entered its order.

Shortly after that, American Home Products again removed *Gonzalez* on grounds of diversity. Along with class counsel in *Brown*, it also moved the federal court in Philadelphia for a permanent injunction, and the federal court entered PTO 1227.]

PTO 1227, entitled "Permanent Injunction and Declaration Regarding Purported Class-Wide Opt-Outs," contains two main parts. The first is an injunction directed primarily at counsel for the *Gonzalez* class:

> Counsel for the named plaintiffs in Gonzalez v. Medeva Pharmaceuticals, Inc., et al., originally filed in Hidalgo County, Texas . . . and removed to the United States District Court for the Southern District of Texas on March 28, 2000, and all those acting in concert with them, are hereby permanently enjoined from

taking any action to effect, secure, or issue notice of any purported class opt out, on behalf of the unnamed absent members of any class which may have been certified in *Gonzalez*, from the class action settlement which this Court has conditionally certified and preliminary [sic] approved. . . .

The second part is declaratory in nature. It states, "Insofar as the Hidalgo County order purports to affect or determine the opt out status of any member of the MDL 1203 class it is null and void and of no effect." The District Court also stated, "The Hidalgo County's order is also null and void and of no effect insofar as it purports to authorize or effect a partial opt-out on behalf of any member of the MDL 1203 class." This was because the Texas order "interfere[d] with [the District] Court's authority to determine the means and methods by which members of such class may elect to opt out of the MDL-1203 class."

[The *Gonzalez* plaintiffs thereafter moved to remand, but the federal judge in Texas referred the issue to the judge in Philadelphia. After the case was transferred to Philadelphia by the MDL Panel, plaintiffs made no further attempt to obtain a remand. But they did appeal PTO 1227. Thereafter, the district court approved the settlement in *Brown* and, in conjunction with that, issued a blanket injunction against commencement or prosecution of parallel actions in other courts by class members.]

* * *

This case illustrates the remarkable extent to which lawsuits can be turned into procedural entanglements. One view of this may be that the actions taken here represent nothing more than astute lawyering. Another is that the legal jockeying employed by both sides exhibits a proclivity to attempt to manipulate the rules for immediate tactical advantage—a use at odds with the purposes of these rules, and one dissonant with the equitable nature of class action proceedings.

Rather than enter this tenebrous world of procedural machinations, we think it preferable to address the *Gonzalez* plaintiffs' main arguments. As we discuss, the District Court's order was an appropriate exercise of its authority regardless of the status of the Texas opt-out order.

IV.

a. *Anti-Injunction Act/All Writs Act.*

The District Court issued PTO 1227 under the All Writs Act, which provides "all courts established by Act of Congress may issue all writs necessary or appropriate in aid of their respective jurisdictions and agreeable to the usages and principles of law." 28 U.S.C. § 1651. The power granted by the All Writs Act is limited by the Anti-Injunction Act, 28 U.S.C. § 2283, which prohibits, with certain specified exceptions, injunctions by federal courts that have the effect of staying a state court proceeding.

Appellants contend the District Court's order was prohibited by the Anti-Injunction Act. American Home Products and the *Brown* plaintiffs claim the injunction falls under one of the Act's exceptions. We hold the District Court's order was not barred by the Anti Injunction Act and was a valid exercise of its power under the All Writs Act.

[Because PTO 1227 had the effect of staying the Texas court's proceedings, it is subject to the Anti-Injunction Act, and the only possibly applicable exception to that Act is the "in aid of jurisdiction" exception. The court recognized that ordinarily in personam actions in state and federal court may proceed concurrently, with the effect of any judgment ultimately rendered determined by preclusion rules. But a federal injunction may issue "to prevent a state court from so interfering with a federal court's consideration or disposition of a case as to seriously impair the federal court's flexibility and authority to decide that case."]

Several factors are relevant to determine whether sufficient interference is threatened to justify an injunction otherwise prohibited by the Anti-Injunction Act. First, we look to the nature of the federal action to determine what kinds of state court interference would sufficiently impair the federal proceeding. Second, we assess the state court's actions, in order to determine whether they present a sufficient threat to the federal action. And finally, we consider principles of federalism and comity, for a primary aim of the Anti-Injunction Act is "to prevent needless friction between the state and federal courts."

We turn first to the nature of the federal action. While, as noted, the "necessary in aid of jurisdiction" exception does not ordinarily permit injunctions merely to prevent duplicative actions in personam, federal courts are permitted to stay later-initiated state court proceedings over the same res in actions in rem, because "the exercise by the state court of jurisdiction over the same res necessarily impairs, and may defeat, the jurisdiction of the federal court already attached." Federal courts may also issue such injunctions to protect exclusive federal jurisdiction of a case that has been removed from state court.

We have recognized another category of federal cases for which state court actions present a special threat to the jurisdiction of the federal court. Under an appropriate set of facts, a federal court entertaining complex litigation, especially when it involves a substantial class of persons from multiple states, or represents a consolidation of cases from multiple districts, may appropriately enjoin state court proceedings in order to protect its jurisdiction. Carlough v. Amchem Prods., Inc., 10 F.3d 189, 202–04 (3d Cir. 1993). *Carlough* involved a nationwide class of plaintiffs and several defendants—primarily manufacturers of asbestos-related products—and third-party defendants—primarily insurance providers. We found the complexity of the case to be a substantial factor in justifying the injunction imposed.

Implicit in *Carlough* is the recognition that maintaining "the federal court's flexibility and authority to decide" such complex nationwide cases makes special demands on the court that may justify an injunction otherwise prohibited by the Anti-Injunction Act. Several other courts have concurred.[12] See, e.g., Hanlon v. Chrysler Corp., 150 F.3d 1011 (9th Cir. 1998); Winkler [v. Eli Lilly & Co.], 101 F.3d at 1203 [(7th Cir. 1996)] ("[T]he Anti-Injunction Act does not bar courts with jurisdiction over complex multidistrict litigation from issuing injunctions to protect the integrity of their rulings."); In re Corrugated Container Antitrust Litig., 659 F.2d 1332, 1334–35 (5th Cir. Unit A 1981) (approving injunction in a "complicated antitrust action [that] has required a great deal of the district court's time and has necessitated that it maintain a flexible approach in resolving the various claims of the many parties.").

This is not to say that class actions are, by virtue of that categorization alone, exempt from the general rule that in personam cases must be permitted to proceed in parallel. Federal courts ordinarily refrain from enjoining a state action even where the state court is asked to approve a settlement substantially similar to one the federal court has already rejected. That a state court may resolve an issue first (which may operate as res judicata), is not by itself a sufficient threat to the federal court's jurisdiction that justifies an injunction, unless the proceedings in state courts threaten to "frustrate proceedings and disrupt the orderly resolution of the federal litigation." Still, while the potentially preclusive effects of the state action may not themselves justify an injunction, they might do so indirectly. If, for example, the possibility of an earlier state court judgment is disruptive to settlement negotiations in federal court, the existence of the state court action might sufficiently interfere with the federal court's flexibility to justify an injunction.

The threat to the federal court's jurisdiction posed by parallel state actions is particularly significant where there are conditional class certifications and impending settlements in federal actions. Many—though not all—of the cases permitting injunctions in complex litigation cases involve injunctions issued as the parties approached settlement. Complex cases in the later stages—where, for instance, settlement negotiations are underway—embody an enormous amount of time and expenditure of

---

[12] In several cases, courts have analogized complex litigation cases to actions in rem. As one court reasoned, "the district court had before it a class action proceeding so far advanced that it was the virtual equivalent of a res over which the district judge required full control." [In re] Baldwin-United, 770 F.2d at 337 [(2d Cir. 1985)]; see also Battle [v. Liberty Nat'l Life Ins. Co.] 877 F.2d at 882 [(11th Cir. 1987)] ("[I]t makes sense to consider this case, involving years of litigation and mountains of paperwork, as similar to a res to be administered."). The in rem analogy may help to bring into focus what makes these cases stand apart. In cases in rem, "the jurisdiction over the same res necessarily impairs, and may defeat, the jurisdiction of the federal court already attached." Similarly, where complex cases are sufficiently developed, mere exercise of parallel jurisdiction by the state court may present enough of a threat to the jurisdiction of the federal court to justify issuance of an injunction. See *Baldwin-United*, 770 F.2d at 337 (noting such cases, like cases in rem, are ones in which "it is intolerable to have conflicting orders from different courts").

resources. It is in the nature of complex litigation that the parties often seek complicated, comprehensive settlements to resolve as many claims as possible in one proceeding. These cases are especially vulnerable to parallel state actions that may "frustrate the district court's efforts to craft a settlement in the multi-district litigation before it," thereby destroying the ability to achieve the benefits of consolidation. In complex cases where certification or settlement has received conditional approval, or perhaps even where settlement is pending, the challenges facing the overseeing court are such that it is likely that almost any parallel litigation in other fora presents a genuine threat to the jurisdiction of the federal court.

This case amply highlights these concerns. MDL 1203 represented the consolidation of over two thousand cases that had been filed in or removed to federal court. The *Brown* class finally certified comprised six million members. The District Court entered well over one thousand orders in the case. This massive consolidation enabled the possibility of a global resolution that promised to minimize the various difficulties associated with duplicative and competing lawsuits. The central events in this dispute occurred after two years of exhaustive work by the parties and the District Court, and after a conditional class certification and preliminary settlement had been negotiated and approved by the District Court. There can be no doubt that keeping this enormously complicated settlement process on track required careful management by the District Court. Any state court action that might interfere with the District Court's oversight of the settlement at that time, given the careful balancing it embodied, was a serious threat to the District Court's ability to manage the final stages of this complex litigation.[13] Duplicative and competing actions were substantially more likely to "frustrate proceedings and disrupt the orderly resolution" of this dispute at the time PTO 1227 was issued than they would be in ordinary actions in personam. This is especially true where, as here, the litigants in state court have the ability to tailor their state actions to the terms of the pending federal settlement.

Determining the applicability of the *Carlough* rule also requires assessment of the character of the state court action, for we must assess the level of interference with the federal action actually threatened by the state court proceeding. In *Carlough*, our approval of the injunction was supported by the direct threat to the federal action the state court action represented. After the district court had provisionally certified the *Carlough* class, and after a preliminary settlement had been negotiated and presented to the court, a parallel action was filed in West Virginia. As here, the plaintiffs in that case—Gore v. Amchem Products, Inc.—sought

---

[13] Among other vulnerabilities, it is worth highlighting one example. The settlement agreement in this case expressly permitted American Home Products to terminate the settlement agreement, at its discretion, based on the number of opt outs. That provision was, of course, created with the complicated opt-out provisions crafted specifically for MDL 1203 in mind. External actions that would disturb that balance, by altering the number of opt outs through a different mechanism, clearly would substantially interfere with MDL 1203.

an order of the state court opting out the members of the West Virginia class from the federal class. They also sought a declaration that *Carlough* would not be binding on the members of the West Virginia class.

We viewed the filing of the West Virginia action as an intentional "preemptive strike" against the federal action. The purpose of the West Virginia filing was "to challenge the propriety of the federal class action." Id. We found "it difficult to imagine a more detrimental effect upon the district court's ability to effectuate the settlement of this complex and far-reaching matter then would occur if the West Virginia state court was permitted to make a determination regarding the validity of the federal settlement."

* * *

The interference that would have been caused by the Hidalgo County court's order implicates the same concerns that animated our decision in *Carlough*. The Texas court's order directly affected the identity of the parties to MDL 1203 and did so contrary to a previous District Court order. It sought to "declare what the federal court should and should not do with respect to the federal settlement." Furthermore, as in *Carlough*, the Texas order would have created confusion among those who were members of both the federal and the state classes. It would be difficult to discern which, if any, action one was a party to, especially since the Texas order was entered during, and shortly before the end of, the MDL 1203 opt-out period.

[The court rejected the argument that the order entered by the Texas suit presented a situation different from *Carlough* because *Gonzalez* had been filed before *Brown* was filed. The key act in *Gonzalez* was not the filing of the suit but the motion for a class-wide opt-out order, and that occurred after *Brown* was at an advanced stage.]

Because an injunction must be necessary in aid of jurisdiction to fall under this application to the Anti-Injunction Act, it is important to carefully tailor such injunctions to meet the needs of the case. Notably, the relief we approved in *Carlough* was substantially broader than the relief granted by the District Court here. The federal order in *Carlough* enjoined the West Virginia plaintiffs, as well as their attorneys and representatives, from pursuing the *Gore* action or initiating similar litigation in any other forum. The injunction in *Carlough* effectively stayed the entire parallel state action, not only the attempted opt out, or other portions directed squarely at the federal action. Here, by contrast, the District Court's order enjoined only the pursuit of the attempted mass opt out-the part of *Gonzalez* that unquestionably interfered with the management of MDL 1203. It did not prevent the *Gonzalez* plaintiffs from individually opting out. Furthermore, the injunction was not directed at a proceeding in which plaintiffs had merely requested relief that threatened to interfere with the federal action, it was directed at a proceeding in which the state court had actually granted such a request, making the interference substantially more manifest. Under these circumstances, we find the District Court's injunction to be well within its "sound discretion."

The propriety of an injunction directed at the Texas order is also consistent with considerations of federalism and comity. The Texas plaintiffs who wished to opt out of the *Brown* class were given an adequate opportunity to individually opt out of the federal action, a factor we found significant in *Carlough*. As such, Texas residents retained the option to commence lawsuits in the forum of their choice. Furthermore, the injunction only prevented application of a particular order that was directed squarely at the federal action. It did not so much interfere with the state court proceeding as prevent state court interference with the federal proceeding. Failing to act on the Hidalgo County order threatened to "create the very 'needless friction between state and federal courts' which the Anti Injunction Act was designed to prevent." "While the Anti-Injunction Act is designed to avoid disharmony between federal and state systems, the exception in § 2283 reflects congressional recognition that injunctions may sometimes be necessary in order to avoid that disharmony."

* * *

Our holding that PTO 1227 was necessary in aid of the District Court's jurisdiction for purposes of the Anti-Injunction Act necessarily implies it was authorized under the All Writs Act as well. For the All Writs Act grants federal courts the authority to issue all writs "necessary or appropriate in aid" of a court's jurisdiction. 28 U.S.C. § 1651(a). * * *

b.   Full Faith and Credit Act.

[The *Gonzalez* plaintiffs argued that the federal court was obligated to give full faith and credit to the Texas court's order. The court rejected this argument on the ground that Texas law does not extend preclusive effect to orders that are "collateral or incidental to the main suit," such as the order in question.]

c.   The Rooker-Feldman Doctrine.

[Appellants also claimed that PTO 1227 exceeded the district court's authority under the Rooker v. Fidelity Trust Co., 263 U.S. 413 (1923), and D.C. Court of Appeals v. Feldman, 460 U.S. 462 (1982), limiting the authority of federal courts to review decisions of state courts. The court rejected this argument on the ground that the doctrine did not defeat a district court's authority to manage its own litigation. "Appellants' approach would permit a state court to issue orders directed squarely at the inner working of federal cases, subject only to reversal by superior state courts and the United States Supreme Court. This approach would undermine the federalism values the doctrine seeks to protect." Since *Diet Drugs* was decided, the Supreme Court has ruled that the doctrine is inapplicable to parallel litigation in state and federal courts even if the state court enters judgment first, but only when "the losing party in state court filed suit in federal court after the state proceedings ended, complaining of an injury caused by the state-court judgment and seeking review and rejection of that judgment." Exxon Mobil Corp. v. Saudi Basic Industries Corp., 544 U.S. 280 (2005).]

NOTES AND QUESTIONS

1.   *The relitigation exception to the Anti-Injunction Act.* In Smith v. Bayer, 564 U.S. 299 (2011), the Supreme Court took a narrow view of the relitigation exception of the Anti-Injunction Act, which authorizes a federal court to enter an injunction "to protect or effectuate its judgments." Some lower courts had regarded this exception as sufficient to support a federal-court injunction against requests that a state court approve a class action after the federal court had ruled that class certification was not justified. See In re Bridgestone/Firestone, Inc., Tires Products Litigation, 333 F.3d 763 (7th Cir. 2003) (upholding federal-court injunction forbidding members of proposed nationwide class to request that any state court certify such a class because the Seventh Circuit had ruled that such certification was not proper, and allowing re-litigation of certification in state courts could eventually lead a maverick state court to grant certification).

In *Smith*, the overlapping class actions were both filed initially in a West Virginia state court, and both asserted claims on behalf of a putative class of West Virginia consumers, claiming that one of defendant's prescription drugs was hazardous. Neither plaintiff knew about the other plaintiff's suit. Only one of these cases could be removed to federal court, and after removal it was transferred to Minnesota pursuant to an existing MDL Panel order centralizing federal cases involving this drug. Some time later, plaintiffs in both cases moved for class certification. The Minnesota federal court concluded that West Virginia law required that each plaintiff prove "actual injury" from use of the drug, and that this requirement meant that individual issues would predominate. So it denied class certification, and also dismissed the plaintiff's individual claim because he could not prove physical injury due to use of the drug.

Defendant Bayer then asked the Minnesota federal court to enjoin Smith, the plaintiff making the claim in West Virginia state court, from seeking class certification in that court. Bayer served this motion on Smith's lawyers; that was the first they had heard of the other case. The district court granted the injunction, and the Eighth Circuit affirmed on the theory that the issue of class certification had been resolved by the decision in Minnesota.

The Supreme Court emphasized that it took a "narrow" interpretation of the exceptions to the Anti-Injunction Act, and reversed for two reasons. First, the class certification standards in the West Virginia court were not the same as the issues under Rule 23. Although the state class-action rule was very similar to Rule 23, state courts "can and do apply identically worded procedural provisions in widely varying ways." And the West Virginia Supreme Court had made decisions "declaring its independence from federal courts' interpretation of the Federal Rules—and particularly Rule 23." Indeed, it had disapproved the approach to predominance that the Minnesota federal court had embraced in denying certification. Accordingly, a state court proceeding under West Virginia law "would decide a different question than the one the federal court had earlier resolved."

Second, under Taylor v. Sturgell, 553 U.S. 880 (2008) (*infra* p. 660), there was no ground for binding the West Virginia plaintiff by the outcome of the Minnesota federal-court ruling even if it were under the same legal standard because the Minnesota court never appointed the plaintiff there to act as a class representative of Smith, the plaintiff in the West Virginia case, or anybody else.

Accordingly, federal courts that rule against class certification or refuse to approve proposed class-action settlements cannot seek to bind state courts by those results. See also In re General Motors Corp. Pick-Up Truck Fuel Tank Prods. Liabil. Litig., 134 F.3d 133 (3d Cir. 1998), in which the federal court refused to approve a proposed settlement and the plaintiffs lawyers who had unsuccessfully proposed that settlement in federal court "repaired to the 18th Judicial District for the Parish of Iberville, Louisiana, where a similar suit had been pending, restructured their deal, and submitted it to the Louisiana court, which ultimately approved it" as a nationwide class-action settlement. Dissident class members asked the federal court to enjoin the Louisiana proceedings, but there was no ground for doing so.

Diet Drugs itself illustrated the limits of the relitigation exception. The settlement agreement there permitted class members to opt out later if they developed certain conditions, and then to pursue relief for those conditions in state court, but provided further that they could not also seek punitive or other multiple damages after opting out. Several opt-out class members nonetheless sought to introduce evidence and make arguments in state-court proceedings that appeared to transgress these limitations. The federal judge then enjoined them from offering specific evidence or making specific arguments in their state-court trials. In In re Diet Drugs Products Liability Litigation, 369 F.3d 293 (3d Cir. 2004), the appellate court noted that the case involved "guerilla warfare from the opt-out lawyers," but held that this injunction could not be justified under the relitigation exception because the settlement did not settle the whole claims of these later opt-outs, but only limited the remedies they could seek. The injunction could be upheld, however, on the ground it was in aid of jurisdiction because "the punitive damages release is a central pillar of the settlement agreement." But it ruled that the district judge had unduly intruded into the conduct of the state-court cases with some specific portions of its injunction. For a careful analysis of the complications that may attend such settlement provisions, including jurisdictional issues, see Rhonda Wasserman, The Curious Complications With Back-end Opt-out Rights, 49 Will. & Mary L.Rev. 373 (2007).

2. *The Class Action Fairness Act.* In Smith v. Bayer, *supra* note 1, the Supreme Court noted that Congress had provided a remedy for the problem of overlapping class actions by expanding the grounds for federal-court jurisdiction in class actions making claims based on state law. "Once removal takes place, Federal Rule 23 governs certification. And federal courts may consolidate multiple overlapping suits against a single defendant in one court [as happened in this case]. Finally, we would expect federal courts to apply principles of comity to each other's class certification decisions when addressing a common dispute." 564 U.S. at 317. For discussion of CAFA, see the next section of this chapter and Richard Marcus, Assessing CAFA's Stated Jurisdictional Policy, 156 U. Pa. L. Rev. 1765 (2008).

3. Is it always true that state courts will be less careful or protective than federal courts? Consider Adkins v. Nestle Purina PetCare Co., 779 F.3d 481 (7th Cir. 2015), which involved overlapping class actions contending that defendant's dog food was harmful to dogs. One case was in federal court, and sought certification as a national class action. The other was a statewide class action in a Missouri state court, in which the Missouri court had already certified a class. The Missouri case was set for trial in May 2015, when a proposed settlement of the federal-court case was presented to the federal judge for initial review. After approving notice to the class with regard to that settlement, the federal court also entered an injunction against continued litigation of the Missouri case which "stopped it cold."

The Seventh Circuit stayed the injunction. The federal-court litigants argued that the injunction was necessary to protect the federal court's jurisdiction because allowing the Missouri case to go forward might "tank the entire settlement." The court of appeals found no ground for an injunction, reasoning that the collapse of the settlement would not cause irreparable injury to the federal-court litigants. And the Anti-Injunction Act precluded such an injunction before the federal court formally approved its settlement and entered a judgment in favor of the class. "[W]hy is preserving a particular settlement 'necessary' to federal jurisdiction? * * * Parallel state and federal litigation is common. * * * Yet the potential effect of one suit on the other does not justify an injunction." For another instance when the court of appeals vacated an injunction (issued by the same federal judge) against a state-court class action that was proceeding toward trial, see Reynolds v. Beneficial National Bank, 288 F.3d 277 (7th Cir. 2002), in which there were intimations that the federal-court settlement offered significantly less relief than the state-court case.

4. One alternative to dueling orders is cooperation. For discussion of examples of cooperation between federal judges and state-court judges, see William Schwarzer, Nancy Weiss & Alan Hirsch, Judicial Federalism in Action: Coordination of Litigation in State and Federal Courts, 78 Va.L.Rev. 1689 (1992); Manual for Complex Litigation (4th) §§ 20.3–20.31. Might this approach have been helpful in *Diet Drugs*? We will see an example of such cooperation in In re New Motor Vehicles Canadian Export Litigation, *infra* p. 414.

It is not always clear how courts that are cooperative should cooperate. For example, in Faught v. American Home Shield Corp., 661 F.3d 1040 (11th Cir. 2011), parallel class actions were proceeding in state court in California and federal court in Alabama. After the California state court rejected a proposed settlement on the ground that it offered too little, plaintiff lawyers in that case sought an injunction requiring that defendant alter its challenged practices. But before the California court ruled on that motion, a settlement was proposed in the federal case in Alabama, so the state court in California stayed its proceedings and the federal court approved the proposed settlement. Objectors in Alabama appealed approval of that settlement on the ground that the notice sent out by the Alabama court did not adequately inform class members that the settlement was similar to the one rejected by the California court. Finding at least five differences between the settlements in the two cases, the federal court of appeals held that the federal court did not abuse its discretion in approving the settlement.

5. Despite all these concerns, the court in *Diet Drugs* emphasizes some remarkable features of that litigation to justify the order there. There were over 2,000 cases consolidated before a single federal court that had before it a class of over six million and had already entered 1,000 orders in that case. How often would such circumstances be presented? One example was Carlough v. Amchem Prods., Inc., 10 F.3d 189 (3d Cir. 1993), involving an injunction entered by the federal district court in *Amchem, supra* p. 311, to prevent a dissident plaintiff lawyer from obtaining a state-court order that would result in the secession of all the West Virginians in that nationwide class action.

More generally, injunctive power has been upheld in the context of imminent settlement of actions consolidated by the MDL Panel. In re Baldwin-United Corp., 770 F.2d 328 (2d Cir. 1985); see also In re Joint E. & S. Dists. Asbestos Litig., 120 B.R. 648 (Bkrtcy., E. & S.D.N.Y. 1990), rev'd on other grounds, In re Johns-Manville Corp., 27 F.3d 48 (2d Cir. 1994). Note, however, that this argument does not work if the federal court refuses to approve the settlement.

6. In *Diet Drugs*, the federal court had certified a nationwide class action, while the Texas state court had certified an in-state class action. Under *Castano, supra* p. 280, which certification is easier to justify? Should federal courts defer to state-court statewide class actions? The Class Action Fairness Act seems to recognize the legitimacy of state courts entertaining some statewide class actions by excluding them from its removal provisions if the defendant is also local. The Act also limits the broad sweep of minimal diversity federal-court jurisdiction to larger class actions (those with more than $5 million in controversy and 100 class members) and to exclude even those class actions if state interests were paramount (e.g., those based on the forum's law and in which the primary defendant and two-thirds of the plaintiff class members were residents of the forum state). But that would mean, for example, that a class action in a Texas state court brought under Texas consumer protection, tort, or environmental laws against a national corporation that was incorporated in Delaware and whose principal place of business was in New

York that injured Texas residents by its activities in Texas could be removed to federal court. For further consideration of CAFA, see *infra* p. 363.

H. SUBJECT MATTER JURISDICTION

Class actions asserting federal claims can be in federal court on that ground, even if they also assert nonfederal claims. For class actions asserting only state-law claims, however, subject-matter jurisdiction can be a barrier to litigating the case in federal court. Lately, controversy has swirled around these issues, and it is useful to introduce the background.

Complete Diversity: The Supreme Court's requirement of complete diversity, see Strawbridge v. Curtiss, 7 U.S. 267 (1806); Owen Equipment & Erection Co. v. Kroger, 437 U.S. 365 (1978), would present substantial difficulties if it had to be satisfied as to all class members.

These difficulties were solved by Supreme Tribe of Ben-Hur v. Cauble, 255 U.S. 356 (1921), which held the diversity statute satisfied in a class action provided only that all the *named* plaintiffs were diverse to all the defendants. Plaintiff, a fraternal benefit association organized under the laws of Indiana, filed a bill in the federal district court to enjoin defendants, who were members of the association, from prosecuting actions against it in state court. The association's theory was that the defendants were bound by the result in an earlier federal-court case in which they were members of a class that made the same claims against the association. Since all the defendants were Indiana citizens, the district court held that they were not bound because including them in the earlier class action would have defeated federal jurisdiction.

The Supreme Court reversed, finding: "Diversity of citizenship gave the District Court jurisdiction. Indiana citizens were of the class represented. The intervention of the Indiana citizens in this suit would not have defeated the jurisdiction already acquired. Being thus represented, we think it must necessarily follow that their rights were concluded by the original decree." This suggestion of ancillary jurisdiction, however, would not serve to distinguish *Ben-Hur* from *Strawbridge,* and thus *Ben-Hur* can be viewed as weakening the "complete diversity" rule in class actions. It conveniently serves the exigencies of class actions by providing that only the citizenship of the named plaintiffs will be considered for purposes of satisfying diversity.

In Devlin v. Scardelletti, 536 U.S. 1 (2002), the Court explained that "[t]he rule that nonnamed class members cannot defeat complete diversity is * * * justified by the goals of class action litigation. Ease of administration of class actions would be compromised by having to consider the citizenship of all class members, many of whom may even be unknown, in determining jurisdiction."

Although the rule that only the citizenship of named class representatives need be considered permits plaintiffs to obtain access to federal court even though there is not complete diversity, sometimes plaintiffs may not want to be in federal court. Recall In re Diet Drugs, *supra* p. 348. Choosing a non-diverse class representative or adding a non-diverse defendant could then prevent removal.

Jurisdictional Amount: 28 U.S.C. § 1332 also requires that "the matter in controversy exceeds the sum or value of $75,000." This requirement became a substantial impediment to federal class actions involving state claims that are small or modest.

In Snyder v. Harris, 394 U.S. 332 (1969), none of the named plaintiffs seeking to represent a Rule 23(b)(3) class had an individual claim in excess of the jurisdictional minimum, although the aggregate of the claims on behalf of the class was well over the jurisdictional minimum. Plaintiffs argued that the 1966 amendments to Rule 23 authorized such aggregation for jurisdictional purposes. The Court disagreed, relying by analogy on joinder cases, and holding that aggregation is allowed *only* where "two or more plaintiffs unite to enforce a single title or right in which they have a common and undivided interest."

The Supreme Court took *Snyder* a step farther in Zahn v. International Paper Co., 414 U.S. 291 (1973). The named plaintiffs there had claims in excess of the jurisdictional minimum, but other members of the plaintiff class did not. Plaintiffs argued that there was ancillary jurisdiction over the claims of the class members, but the Court held that every member of the class must satisfy the jurisdictional minimum if the claims are not joint. The rule of *Zahn* is clear enough, but its result is difficult to reconcile with *Ben-Hur* unless one emphasizes differences between "joint" rights (which were involved in *Ben-Hur*) and "separate" rights. But in *Ben-Hur* the Court did not limit its holding to joint interests, and such a limitation makes no policy sense. As Professor Currie has written, "it is when interests are several that an out-of-state party is most likely to need the jurisdiction provided by *Ben-Hur* to protect him from bias in the local court; when interests are joint, a biased tribunal may be unable to injure the outsider without harming a local coparty as well." David Currie, Pendent Parties, 45 U.Chi.L.Rev. 753, 762–63 (1978). According to Professor Miller, the Supreme Court's "restrictive decisions" in *Snyder* and *Zahn* sent "shock waves." Arthur Miller, Of Frankenstein Monsters and Shining Knights: Myth, Reality, and the "Class Action Problem," 92 Harv. L. Rev. 664, 679–80 (1979).

The supplemental jurisdiction statute, 28 U.S.C. § 1367, appeared on its face to overrule *Zahn*. Section 1367(a) grants district courts that have original jurisdiction over the claim of one plaintiff supplemental jurisdiction over any other claims that form a part of the same case or controversy, which would include "pendent" claims of other class members.

This grant is limited in diversity cases by § 1367(b), but that limitation does not appear to apply in class actions. The legislative history nevertheless said that "[t]his section is not intended to affect the jurisdictional requirements of 28 U.S.C. § 1332 in diversity-only class actions, as those requirements were interpreted prior to Finley [v. United States, 490 U.S. 545 (1989)]." H.R.Rep. No. 734, 101st Cong., 2d Sess., 1990 U.S.Cong. & Admin.News 6860, 6875 (citing *Zahn* and *Ben-Hur*). In Exxon Mobil Corp. v. Allapattah Services, Inc., 545 U.S. 546 (2005), however, the Court held that the statute's clear terms did overrule *Zahn*; so long as the class representative has a claim that satisfies the amount-in-controversy requirements, there is supplemental jurisdiction over the claims of all unnamed class members without regard to their amount. That solution would not work if no plaintiff had a large enough claim, but the former need to demonstrate that every class member had a large enough claim disappeared.

The Class Action Fairness Act

Although these developments cleared the way for plaintiffs who wanted to file class actions in federal court to do so more often, plaintiffs often did not want to litigate in federal court. For a variety of reasons ranging from class-certification standards to standards for admissibility of expert evidence to a desire to avoid MDL centralization, some plaintiffs preferred to sue in state court. Indeed, there were assertions that some plaintiffs' attorneys wanted to file their nationwide class actions in a small number of "magnet" state courts in which they would receive favorable treatment on both class certification and the substantive law to be applied. The term "drive-by certification" was coined to describe this sort of activity. It may be that In re Diet Drugs, *supra* p. 348, involved elements of such an effort. Recall that the overlapping state-court class action there, Gonzalez v. Medeva Pharmaceuticals, Inc., was filed in Hidalgo County, Texas, and that the state-court judge certified the class and ordered a classwide "opt-out" from the federal class settlement with apparent alacrity.

These concerns led to introduction in succeeding Congresses of the Class Action Fairness Act (CAFA), finally adopted in 2005 after a long and heated debate. The Senate Report accompanying the compromise bill that was adopted explained it as follows (S.Rep. 109–14 at 4):

> [C]urrent law enables lawyers to "game" the procedural rules to keep nationwide or multi-state class actions in state courts whose judges have reputations for readily certifying classes and approving settlements without regard to class member interests. * * * Multiple class action cases purporting to assert the same claims on behalf of the same people often proceed simultaneously in different state courts, causing judicial inefficiencies and promoting collusive activity. Finally, many state courts freely

issue rulings in class action cases that have nationwide ramifications, sometimes overturning well-established laws and policies of other jurisdictions.

There were some examples of such untoward results. For example, until it was reversed, a decision of an Illinois state court granted nationwide relief for use of cheaper parts for repairs on damaged cars, even though that thrift was authorized (perhaps required) under the laws of some states. See Avery v. State Farm Mut. Auto. Ins. Co., 835 N.E.2d 801 (Ill. 2005) (noting that "the application of the uniquely restrictive Illinois law to the whole country * * * illustrates the potentially abusive power one remote county court could exercise"). But whether such results were frequent was debatable and debated. A Federal Judicial Center study found no significant difference between federal courts and state courts in class-certification or settlement-approval decisions. See Thomas Willging & Shannon Wheatman, An Empirical Examination of Attorneys' Choice of Forum in Class Action Litigation 34–36 (2005). Many—including members of Congress—fiercely resisted CAFA. Some predicted that it would spell the end of state-court class actions.

As eventually adopted (see 28 U.S.C. §§ 1332(d); 1453), CAFA changed both the diversity and amount-in-controversy prongs of federal subject-matter jurisdiction. It adopted a "minimal diversity" standard; so long as any member of the plaintiff class has a citizenship different from any defendant the case would be eligible for federal court. It adopted a $5 million amount-in-controversy standard, but abandoned *Snyder*; the standard is satisfied if the claims of the class, in the aggregate, exceed $5 million.

CAFA did not end strategic maneuvering. Five years after the Act went into effect, it was reported that "federal district courts in California have seen an explosion in consumer class actions. In 2004 (the year before CAFA's enactment) California federal courts issued about one-third more decisions in such cases than any other state. In 2007, however, California's share had increased to well over three times that of any other state." Archis Parasharami & Kevin Ranlett, The Class Action Fairness Act, Five Years Later, Nat.L.J., April 12, 2010. See also Emery Lee & Thomas Willging, The Impact of the Class Action Fairness Act on the Federal Courts: An Empirical Analysis of Filings and Removals, 156 U. Pa. L. Rev. 1723, 1759 Fig. 6 (2008) (showing that filings in the Ninth Circuit were more than six times as numerous as before CAFA, while filings in the Seventh Circuit were less than twice as numerous). Perhaps a new version of the former "magnet jurisdiction" phenomenon has emerged, but this time the magnets are circuits perceived as friendly to class actions.

To preserve some state-court jurisdiction for truly "local" class actions, CAFA authorized remand of class actions removed from state court or federal-court decline of jurisdiction in specified circumstances. But because

Congress was convinced that plaintiff lawyers would sometimes go to great lengths to avoid federal court, the grounds for remand are very narrow. We turn to application of the statutory standards.

EVANS V. WALTER INDUSTRIES, INC.
United States Court of Appeals, 11th Circuit, 2006.
449 F.3d 1159.

Before TJOFLAT, ANDERSON and DUBINA, CIRCUIT JUDGES.

ANDERSON, CIRCUIT JUDGE.

Appellants United Defense LP, MeadWestvaco Corporation, Scientific-Atlanta, Inc., and Huron Valley Steel Corporation challenge the district court's decision to remand this case to the Alabama state court. Appellants argue that this case belongs in federal court under the recently-enacted Class Action Fairness Act ("CAFA"), and because the plaintiffs fraudulently joined non-diverse defendants in order to evade federal jurisdiction. We hold that the federal district court has jurisdiction over this case under CAFA. We need not reach the issue of fraudulent misjoinder.

On April 8, 2005, plaintiffs filed this case in the Circuit Court of Calhoun County, Alabama, on behalf of a class of people who were allegedly injured by the actions of 18 named defendants and a number of fictitious defendants. The plaintiffs allege that the defendants operated manufacturing facilities in the Anniston, Alabama, area. Plaintiffs allege both property damage and personal injury that they attribute to defendants' release of various waste substances over an approximately 85-year period. Four of the defendants removed this case to federal court under CAFA, which expanded federal jurisdiction for class actions. Defendants' Notice of Removal also contained a footnote that stated that defendants believed that plaintiffs may have improperly joined non-diverse defendants.

Plaintiffs filed a motion to remand the case to state court. Plaintiffs' sole argument for remand was that the case fell within CAFA's "local controversy" exception to federal jurisdiction. Plaintiffs argued that their case was a local controversy because more than two-thirds of the plaintiff class were Alabama citizens and at least one Alabama defendant, U.S. Pipe, was a "significant" defendant within the meaning of CAFA. Plaintiffs proffered the affidavits of two of their attorneys to support their claim. The district court agreed that this case fell within CAFA's local controversy exception, and remanded the case to state court. The four removing defendants appeal the district court's ruling.

* * *

CAFA and the Local Controversy Exception

1. Legal Background

Congress enacted CAFA on February 18, 2005. Under CAFA, federal courts now have original jurisdiction over class actions in which the amount in controversy exceeds $5,000,000 and there is minimal diversity (at least one plaintiff and one defendant are from different states). 28 U.S.C. § 1332(d)(2). CAFA, however, does have an exception to federal jurisdiction for cases that are truly local in nature. 28 U.S.C. § 1332(d)(4)(A).

In this case, the parties do not dispute that the controversy exceeds $5,000,000 and that there is minimal diversity. The issue before us is whether this case falls within CAFA's local controversy exception to federal jurisdiction. CAFA's local controversy exception provides:

(4) A district court shall decline to exercise jurisdiction under paragraph (2)—

    (A)(i)   over a class action in which—

        (I) greater than two-thirds of the members of all proposed plaintiff classes in the aggregate are citizens of the State in which the action was originally filed;

        (II) at least 1 defendant is a defendant—

            (aa) from whom significant relief is sought by members of the plaintiff class;

            (bb) whose alleged conduct forms a significant basis for the claims asserted by the proposed plaintiff class; and

            (cc) who is a citizen of the State in which the action was originally filed; and

        (III) principal injuries resulting from the alleged conduct or any related conduct of each defendant were incurred in the State in which the action was originally filed; and

    (ii) during the 3-year period preceding the filing of that class action, no other class action has been filed asserting the same or similar factual allegations against any of the defendants on behalf of the same or other persons;

CAFA's language favors federal jurisdiction over class actions and CAFA's legislative history suggests that Congress intended the local controversy exception to be a narrow one, with all doubts resolved "in favor of exercising jurisdiction over the case." S.Rep. No. 109–14 at 42. The Senate Report on CAFA further states that the local controversy exception:

is a narrow exception that was carefully drafted to ensure that it does not become a jurisdictional loophole. Thus, the Committee wishes to stress that in assessing whether each of these criteria is satisfied by a particular case, a federal court should bear in mind that the purpose of each of these criteria is to identify a truly local controversy—a controversy that uniquely affects a particular locality to the exclusion of all others.

The language and structure of CAFA itself indicates that Congress contemplated broad federal court jurisdiction, with only narrow exceptions. These notions are fully confirmed in the legislative history.

2.   The Burden of Proof

The district court correctly determined that the plaintiffs bear the burden of establishing that they fall within CAFA's local controversy exception. CAFA allows for removal of class actions that meet certain minimal requirements. CAFA does not change the traditional rule that the party seeking to remove the case to federal court bears the burden of establishing federal jurisdiction. The parties do not dispute that the defendants have carried this burden and established that this action meets CAFA's basic requirements for removal to federal court—i.e., the controversy exceeds $5,000,000 and at least one plaintiff and one defendant are from different states (the minimal diversity requirement). However, when a party seeks to avail itself of an express statutory exception to federal jurisdiction granted under CAFA, as in this case, we hold that the party seeking remand bears the burden of proof with regard to that exception.[3]

[The court held that "the plaintiffs bear the burden of proving the local controversy exception to the jurisdiction otherwise established."]

We turn next to the merits of the local controversy exception as applied to this case. The parties dispute only two prongs of the local controversy exception: (1) whether more than two-thirds of the plaintiff class members are Alabama citizens; and (2) whether U.S. Pipe is a defendant from whom "significant relief" is sought and whose conduct forms a "significant basis" for the claims asserted by the plaintiffs. We conclude that plaintiffs have failed to prove either prong.

___

[3]   Moreover, placing the burden of proof on the plaintiff in this situation is not only consistent with the statutory design, we believe it places the burden on the party most capable of bearing it. The local controversy exception will require evidence about the composition of the plaintiff class. The plaintiffs have defined the class and have better access to information about the scope and composition of that class. With respect to the "significant defendant" prong, both plaintiffs and defendants have access to relevant information. Defendants have better access to information about conduct by the defendants, but plaintiffs have better access to information about which plaintiffs are injured and their relationship to various defendants.

3.   Citizenship of Plaintiff Class

To avail themselves of the local controversy exception, the plaintiffs must prove that greater than two-thirds of the proposed class members are Alabama citizens. In this case, the class includes:

> All property owners, lessees, licensees of properties on which the class defendants' [sic] deposited waste substances . . . and/or engaged in conduct or practices that allowed such substances and materials to migrate to and/or become located on the plaintiffs' property [and]

> All individuals who have come in contact . . . with any of the class defendants' deposited waste substances . . . who as a result of which has suffered personal injury or damages to their health, safety and welfare.

The complaint alleges harms from 18 defendants extending over a period of at least 85 years. The district court held that plaintiffs had adduced sufficient evidence that more than two-thirds of the plaintiff class are Alabama citizens. We disagree.

Plaintiffs have offered little proof that Alabama citizens comprise at least two-thirds of the plaintiff class. In order to prove that two-thirds of the plaintiff class are Alabama citizens, the plaintiffs submitted an affidavit by attorney Jennifer Smith.[5] Smith avers that she reviewed or interviewed 10,118 potential plaintiffs. Of these, Smith determined that 5200 are members of the class. Of the 5200 class members, 4876 (93.8%) are Alabama residents. The plaintiffs argue that if 93.8% of the known plaintiffs are Alabama residents, then surely two-thirds of the entire plaintiff class are Alabama citizens.

We are not persuaded by plaintiffs' argument. Smith's affidavit tells us nothing about how she selected the 10,118 people who were considered "potential plaintiffs." We do not know if these 10,118 people represent both the property damage and personal injury classes. We do not know if Smith's method favored people currently living in Anniston over people who have left the area.[6] In short, we know nothing about the percentage of the total class represented by the 10,118 people on which plaintiffs' evidence depends. Moreover, the class, as defined in the complaint, is extremely broad, extending over an 85-year period. We do not know if Smith made any effort to estimate the number of people with claims who no longer live in Alabama.

---

[5]   In light of our resolution of this case, we need not reach issues relating to the admissibility of the evidence contained in the affidavits of the several attorneys participating in this case.

[6]   At oral argument, plaintiffs' counsel suggested that most of the potential plaintiffs had contacted the attorneys after hearing about the case through "word of mouth." It seems likely that people in Anniston are most likely to have heard about the case and contacted the attorneys. Potential plaintiffs outside of Anniston would seem to be under-represented in such a pool.

In sum, plaintiffs have not carried their burden of demonstrating that more than two-thirds of the plaintiff class are Alabama citizens. We understand that evidence of class citizenship might be difficult to produce in this case. That difficulty, however, is to a considerable degree a function of the composition of the class designed by plaintiffs. The local controversy exception is designed to ensure that state courts hear cases of a truly local nature. We have no way of knowing what percentage of the plaintiff class are Alabama citizens. We conclude that the evidence adduced by the plaintiffs wholly fails to present a credible estimate of the percentage of the plaintiff class who are citizens of Alabama. Accordingly, we hold that Plaintiffs have failed to prove that more than two-thirds of the plaintiff class are Alabama citizens.

4. Significant Defendant Test

We also hold that plaintiffs have failed to prove the "significant defendant" prong of the local controversy exception. In order to avail themselves of the local controversy exception, pursuant to § 1332(d)(4)(A), the plaintiffs must prove that:

(II) at least 1 defendant is a defendant

    (aa) from whom significant relief is sought by members of the plaintiff class;

    (bb) whose alleged conduct forms a significant basis for the claims asserted by the proposed plaintiff class; and

    (cc) who is a citizen of the State in which the action was originally filed.

The district court held that U.S. Pipe, an Alabama corporation, was a significant defendant. We disagree and hold that plaintiffs have failed to prove that U.S. Pipe was a significant defendant as defined by CAFA.

Only a few courts have interpreted the local controversy exception to federal jurisdiction. At least two courts have held that a class seeks "significant relief" against a defendant when the relief sought against that defendant is a significant portion of the entire relief sought by the class. See Robinson v. Cheetah Transportation, No. 06–0005, 2006 WL 468820 (W.D.La. Feb.27, 2006). As the *Robinson* court stated:

whether a putative class seeks significant relief from an in-state defendant includes not only an assessment of how many members of the class were harmed by the defendant's actions, but also a comparison of the relief sought between all defendants and each defendant's ability to pay a potential judgment.

U.S. Pipe operated two metal casting facilities in Anniston during the relevant time period: a foundry located at 2101 W. 10th Street and another foundry at 1831 Front Street. The district court held that the plaintiffs sought significant relief from U.S. Pipe because: (1) the complaint accused all the defendants of contamination in the Anniston area; and (2) U.S. Pipe owned and operated two foundry facilities during a substantial portion of the relevant time period.

Plaintiffs rely on their complaint and an attorney affidavit to establish that U.S. Pipe is a significant defendant. These documents, however, do not provide any enlightenment at all with respect to the significance of the relief that is sought against U.S. Pipe, or its comparative significance relative to the relief sought from the other 17 named co-defendants. In short, there is simply no evidence that U.S. Pipe was "significant" with respect to liability.

With respect to whether the conduct of U.S. Pipe "forms a significant basis" for the plaintiffs' claims, plaintiffs' evidence offers no insight into whether U.S. Pipe played a significant role in the alleged contamination, as opposed to a lesser role, or even a minimal role. The evidence does not indicate that a significant number or percentage of putative class members may have claims against U.S. Pipe, or indeed that any plaintiff has such a claim.[7]

Moreover, the limited facts before this court give rise to an inference that U.S. Pipe is not a significant defendant. The plaintiffs charge that U.S. Pipe has operated two facilities in Anniston: one on West 10th Street and the property at 1831 Front Street. The evidence shows that U.S. Pipe sold the 10th Street location in 1951 and believes that operations ceased considerably before 1951. The number of plaintiffs injured by pre-1951 foundry operations is very unlikely to be significant when compared to the class as a whole. U.S. Pipe did operate the Front Street location from 1961–2003. However, that site appears to be somewhat south of the area occupied by most of the class members identified by plaintiffs. Numerous other defendants have operations much nearer the largest concentration of identified class members, suggesting that U.S. Pipe's liability might not be significant compared to other defendants, and that the conduct of U.S. Pipe might not form a significant basis for the claims of the class. Plaintiffs do allege in their complaint that the defendants gave out foundry sand as fill dirt to local residents but, again, we have no evidence about whether U.S. Pipe has significant liability for distributing fill dirt, or that its conduct in this regard forms a significant basis for the claims of the class.

---

[7] The parties dispute whether the complaint can fairly be read to allege joint and several liability on the part of the defendants. We need not resolve that dispute. Even if the complaint does, and even if that satisfied the plaintiffs' burden with respect to the significant relief prong, § 1332(d)(4)(a)(i)(II)(aa), plaintiffs nevertheless have failed to satisfy § 1332(d)(4)(a)(i)(II)(bb), which requires that the "alleged conduct [of a significant defendant] form[ ] a significant basis for the claims asserted by the proposed class." In other words, the mere fact that relief might be sought against U.S. Pipe for the conduct of others (via joint liability) does not convert the conduct of others into conduct of U.S. Pipe so as to also satisfy the "significant basis" requirement.

NOTES AND QUESTIONS

1.   CAFA has been called "the most significant change in class action practice" since the 1966 amendments to Rule 23. Edward Sherman, Class Action Fairness Act and the Federalization of Class Actions, 238 F.R.D. 504, 504 (2007). It certainly made it far easier to file a state-law class action in federal court or remove it to federal court. But it did not put an end to state-court class actions. In California, for example, the rate of class-action filings in state court fell in 2005 compared to 2004, but was still higher than in each year from 2000 to 2003. Findings of the Study of California Class Action Litigation, 2000–2006, at 3, Fig. 1 (First Interim Report, March 2009). One way of evaluating CAFA is to consider how it would have affected bringing the cases we have examined in federal court:

(a)   Could the earlier state-court suit in Hansberry v. Lee (*supra* p. 166) have been filed in federal court?

(b)   If Simer v. Rios (*supra* p. 177) had not involved a federal claim, could it have been filed in federal court?

(c)   In Martin v. Behr Dayton Thermal Products LLC (*supra* p. 298), could plaintiffs have filed their suit in federal court before CAFA?

(d)   In In re Diet Drugs (*supra* p. 348), could Gonzalez v. Medeva Pharmaceuticals, Inc., which was filed in state court in Hidalgo County, Texas, have been removed to federal court?

2.   As in most instances, a party invoking federal jurisdiction bears the burden of showing that it is justified. Thus, a defendant seeking to remove under CAFA, as in *Evans*, must show that the class consists of at least 100 persons, and that at least $5 million is in controversy. See Lowdermilk v. U.S. Bank NA, 479 F.3d 994 (9th Cir. 2007) (holding that when plaintiffs' prayer is for "in total, less than five million dollars," defendant must show that actually more is in issue); Abrego v. Dow Chem. Co., 443 F.3d 676 (9th Cir. 2006) (holding that CAFA does not change the requirement that a removing defendant must show that jurisdiction has been established). How readily can defendant make these showings?

Some plaintiffs' efforts to defeat removal do not work, however. In Standard Fire Ins. Co. v. Knowles, 568 U.S. 588 (2013), the Court rejected a strategy adopted by some plaintiffs to try to defeat removal—stipulating to limit the classwide recovery to less than $5 million. The Court held that such a stipulation does not limit the federal court's jurisdiction because "a plaintiff who files a proposed class action cannot legally bind members of the proposed class before the class is certified." Because jurisdiction depended on whether the case was removable as filed, therefore, the stipulation offered by plaintiff was irrelevant.

In Dart Cherokee Basin Operating Co. v. Owens, 574 U.S. 81 (2014), plaintiff claimed that the removal notice was defective because defendant did not include evidence supporting its assertions that CAFA was satisfied in its removal notice, but the Court held that 28 U.S.C. § 1446(a) requires only a "short and plain" statement of the grounds for removal, and that such a statement need not include evidence. The Court also rejected the notion that there should be a "presumption" against removal, noting that "no antiremoval presumption attends cases invoking CAFA, which Congress enacted to facilitate adjudication of certain class actions in federal court."

3. In Brill v. Countrywide Home Loans, 427 F.3d 446 (7th Cir. 2005), plaintiff received a fax advertisement from defendant and sued defendant under the Telephone Consumer Protection Act on behalf of a class of recipients of the faxed advertisement. Under the Act, the court may award $500 per fax improperly sent, an amount that could be trebled if defendant acted willfully or knowingly. Defendant removed the case to federal court under CAFA. In its removal petition, defendant asserted that it faxed at least 3,800 of the ads. The district court granted plaintiff's motion to remand on the ground that defendant had not conceded that it would be held liable for treble damages for acting willfully, and that therefore the $5 million figure was not satisfied.

The court of appeals reversed, reasoning that the removing party need show only a reasonable probability that the stakes exceed the minimum. "The demonstration [to support removal] concerns what the plaintiff is claiming (and thus the amount in controversy between the parties), not whether plaintiff is likely to win or be awarded everything he seeks. Countrywide did all that is necessary by admitting that one of its employees sent at least 3,800 fax ads. * * * Countrywide did not have to confess liability in order to show that the controversy exceeds the threshold." Id. at 449.

In Brill, Countrywide was in a position to determine how many faxed ads had been sent and the statutorily authorized recoveries for those faxes. Were defendants in a similar position in Evans? In Evans, the court says in footnote 3 that making plaintiffs show that two-thirds of the class is in-state to obtain a remand on the local controversy ground is a task the plaintiffs can shoulder easier than the defendants. Would that be true in a case like Countrywide? Even if defendant can state with confidence the number of class members, how readily can it state the aggregate amount of their claims? Recall that the ordinary amount-in-controversy requirement asks whether plaintiffs' prayer for damages in excess of the minimum amount is made in "good faith." When cases are filed in state court, no such prayer may be made at all, and defendants have to resort to sources outside the pleadings to demonstrate the dimensions of the relief sought. But at least they are dealing with plaintiffs who have made claims. With a class action, isn't the process a good deal more hypothetical? In the class action, one is often dealing with an uncertain number of class members who have not affirmatively made any claim for relief. How readily can a defendant show that those hypothetical claims, in the aggregate, exceed $5 million? This hypothetical inquiry about claims that have not been asserted yet resembles the inquiry formerly required under Zahn, when federal-court jurisdiction depended on showing that each class member's claim was for an amount exceeding the minimum.

4. The courts place the burden of justifying remand on the party seeking remand. In Evans, the court also asserts that plaintiff is well situated to

shoulder this burden. Would that have been true in Brill v. Countrywide Home Loans, Inc., discussed in the previous note? Was plaintiff well situated to show that two-thirds of the class members were in-state in *Evans*? If not, was that due to the class definition? Could plaintiffs improve their chances of remaining in state court by strategic definition of the class? How about a class defined as "all residents of the State of X who were exposed to defendant's product"? Would that sort of class definition have worked to defeat CAFA jurisdiction in Gonzalez v. Medeva Pharmaceuticals, Inc., the Texas state-court class action in In re Diet Drugs, *supra* p. 348, had CAFA then been in force? Note that 28 U.S.C. § 1332(d)(4)(A)(II) says that the federal court shall decline to exercise jurisdiction only if "during the 3-year period preceding the filing of that class action, no other class action has been filed asserting the same or similar factual allegations against any of the defendants on behalf of the same or other persons."

There can be very close calls even in cases that seem clearly local, as illustrated by two cases resulting from Hurricane Katrina. In Preston v. Tenet Healthsystem Memorial Medical Center, Inc., 485 F.3d 804 (5th Cir. 2007), plaintiffs sued in state court a month after the hurricane on behalf of a class of patients in a New Orleans hospital and their next of kin, asserting that the hospital failed to have proper emergency procedures at the time the hurricane struck. A list of the 256 patients in the hospital showed that only 2.83% gave an out-of-state address. The district court granted a remand under the discretionary remand provisions of 28 U.S.C. § 1332(d)(3), which require a showing only that one-third of the class members are local. Contrast the companion case Weems v. Touro Infirmary, 485 F.3d 793 (5th Cir. 2007), a class action filed in state court on behalf of patients at another New Orleans medical facility. In this case, the district court remanded on the ground that remand was mandatory under the provision applicable when two-thirds of the class members are local. Although it recognized "the undeniably local character of this class action lawsuit," the appellate court reversed. This case was filed nearly a year after the hurricane. As in the other case, the medical records indicated that the great majority of patients were Louisiana residents at the time of the storm, but given the post-Katrina diaspora of residents of the New Orleans area, the court found that it could not presume that they were still Louisiana residents when the suit was filed on that ground alone. Plaintiffs would have to come up with post-Katrina proof of residence. "Despite the logistical challenges of offering reliable evidence at this preliminary jurisdictional stage, CAFA does not permit the courts to make a citizenship determination based on a record bare of any evidence showing class members' intent to be domiciled in Louisiana." Id. at 802. See also In re Sprint Nextel Corp., 593 F.3d 669 (7th Cir. 2010) (plaintiffs failed to submit evidence showing that two thirds of class limited to those who had a Kansas cell phone number and received their billing at a Kansas address were Kansas citizens).

5. It is difficult to imagine many class actions more local in basic character than *Evans* or the Hurricane Katrina cases discussed in note 4 above. The fact that these cases can be removed to federal court under CAFA suggests that it far exceeded its aim of providing a national forum for truly

multistate cases. Was this overreaching justified? Consider Richard Marcus, Assessing CAFA's Jurisdictional Policy, 156 U. Pa. L. Rev. 1765, 1807 (2008):

> [T]here was a considerable reason to believe that plaintiffs' lawyers would strive mightily to avoid federal courts and would exploit any opportunity to do so if they could configure their cases to evade the newly created jurisdiction. In light of that experience, it may have been justified as a matter of jurisdictional policy to define the exceptions to federal-court jurisdiction very narrowly so as to ensure that the new jurisdiction reaches all cases that are truly multistate. Overbreadth, then, would be a result of the desire to guarantee that lawyers could not evade the new jurisdiction in any case of the sort Congress sought to afford a federal forum. And the statute has a safety valve. It gives the district judge authority to decline to exercise the new jurisdiction in a number of instances when it initially does apply, and the considerations include a focus on whether there was an effort to evade federal-court jurisdiction [citing 28 U.S.C. § 1332(d)(3)].

6. Recall the heightened need for discovery introduced in connection with Litigating Class Certification, *supra* p. 333. If plaintiffs want to invoke the local controversy exceptions to CAFA jurisdiction, can they have discovery to obtain information about the number and residence of class members? The legislative history takes a dim view of such discovery (S. Rep. 109–14 (109th Cong., 1st Sess.) at 44):

> The Committee understands that in assessing the various criteria established in all these new jurisdictional provisions, a federal court may have to engage in some fact-finding, not unlike what is necessitated by the existing jurisdictional statutes. However, the Committee cautions that these jurisdictional determinations should be made largely on the basis of readily available information. Allowing substantial, burdensome discovery on jurisdictional issues would be contrary to the intent of these provisions to encourage the exercise of federal jurisdiction over class actions.

But defense lawyers considering the same point anticipated that they would confront discovery about these topics:

> These determinations would appear to require significant discovery from defendants early in the litigation. If defendants are forced to reveal considerable information about the size and location of plaintiff-customers and the injuries they have sustained, that would seem to encourage early settlement because it would give plaintiffs' counsel more information about their claims and potential damages earlier than they might otherwise obtain it.

William Sullivan & James Fazio, Changing the Game, S.F. Recorder, June 8, 2007, at 4, 5; see also Evon Ben-Yehuda, Class-Action Law Could Spark Growth of Jurisdiction Experts, S.F. Daily J., Aug. 26, 2005, at 1 (suggesting that there might be a need for expert testimony on whether two-thirds of the class members are citizens of one state).

7.　In *Evans*, the court mentions but does not discuss defendants' contention that a local defendant was "fraudulently joined." The idea is that plaintiffs' counsel seeks to prevent removal by joining a local defendant to prevent complete diversity but without any real expectation of obtaining significant relief from these local defendants. One of the witnesses who testified in support of CAFA before Congress was the widow of a Mississippi pharmacist, who said that her husband had been driven to an early grave in part by being named as a defendant in a large number of individual-plaintiff pharmaceutical products suits. He had filled prescriptions for the drugs involved, and plaintiffs had sued him in addition to the pharmaceutical companies in order to prevent removal. See Hearing on H.R. 2341, 107th Cong. 34–36 (2002) (testimony of Hilda Bankston). CAFA's minimal diversity provision overcomes this strategy in terms of initial removability. But note the court's analysis of defendant U.S. Pipe in *Evans*. The "significant defendant" provision discussed there is an additional way of dealing with tactics like fraudulent joinder. How easily can the courts apply this provision? Does it look to what plaintiffs have in mind?

8.　One reason for opposition to CAFA was that it would hobble states' ability to provide protection for their citizens. Citing the broad definition of "class action" under 28 U.S.C. § 1332(d)(1)(B), some urged that removal should even be available in enforcement actions brought by state attorneys general, if they sought to recover money for injuries suffered by citizens of the state. In Mississippi ex rel. Hood v. AU Optronics Corp., 571 U.S. 161 (2014), the Court rejected this argument. But a federal class action can affect the remedies an attorney general can seek. See California v. IntelliGender, LLC, 771 F.3d 1169 (9th Cir. 2014) (due to settlement of private class action in federal court due to CAFA, state attorney general could not seek restitution for state residents, but could seek civil penalties and an injunction). See also Canela v. Costco Wholesale Corp., 965 F.3d 694 (9th Cir. 2020) ("class action" under California Private Attorney Generals Act (PAGA) for violation of state labor law was not filed under a "similar state statute" because PAGA did not require numerosity, commonality, or typicality. As a consequence, the action was not removable under CAFA.)

In Home Depot U.S.A. v. Jackson, 139 S.Ct. 1743 (2019), a state court defendant filed a counterclaim and third-party class action, and the third-party counterclaim defendant sought to remove. The Court held that CAFA limited removals to the "defendant," which did not include the plaintiff and third-party class action defendant. See also Saskatchewan Mut. Ins. Co. v. CE Design, Ltd., 865 F.3d 537 (7th Cir. 2017) (CAFA removal available only for a plaintiff class; the statute refers to "defendants" only as class opponents, not as class representatives).

9.　CAFA jurisdiction may end if plaintiff drops class-action claims. In Gale & Kowalyshyn, LLC v. Chicago Title Ins. Co., 929 F.3d 74 (2d Cir. 2019), plaintiffs originally filed a class action in federal court, invoking CAFA jurisdiction. After more than a decade of litigation, they filed a fourth amendment complaint, dropping their class action claims. The district court dismissed for lack of jurisdiction and the court of appeals affirmed. Note that, had plaintiffs filed their original class action complaint in state court and had defendants then removed under CAFA, the district court could have remanded to state court. But because the case was originally filed in federal court that was not possible.

I. PERSONAL JURISDICTION

As CAFA illustrates (see Section H above), jurisdiction is an important consideration in regard to class actions. But until recently, the chief focus had been on subject matter jurisdiction. As noted in section H, the amount-in-controversy requirement was (pre CAFA) applied separately to each class member. But the question whether there was diversity of citizenship depended only on the citizenship of the named class representatives.

When class members were from many states, complicated questions of personal jurisdiction could arise. But for some time the most prominent sort of multistate class action was brought against a large business. For a long time, the courts found that in such cases there would be "general jurisdiction" to entertain claims against such defendants, so long as the claims were relatively pertinent to the activity of the defendant in the forum state. Of course, that would normally be essential to certification of a multistate class action. If the claims did not turn on similar factual issues, common questions would not predominate. Indeed, even if the claims did turn on similar fact issues, a class action might not be proper if the claims of different class members were governed by differing state law. We will return to this problem in In re Bridgestone/Firestone, Inc., *infra* p. 392.

Personal jurisdiction questions now can prove more challenging than in the past. In significant measure, that is because in Goodyear Dunlop Tires Operations, S.A. v. Brown, 564 U.S. 915 (2011), the Court held that general jurisdiction is only justified when defendants' affiliations with the forum state "are so 'continuous and systematic' as to render them essentially at home in the forum state." Particularly for large commercial enterprises (like manufacturers of products) that would be true in only the state in which they were incorporated and (if different) the state in which the company's headquarters were located. For a non-U.S. company, then, it would be possible that no U.S. state could exercise general personal jurisdiction. This doctrinal change was "a radical departure from decades of case law holding that general jurisdiction was appropriate where a company was doing business in the forum—in the sense of having continuous and systematic general business contacts with the forum." Tanya Monestier, Where is Home Depot "At Home"?: *Daimler v. Bauman* and the End of Doing Business Jurisdiction, 66 Hast. L.J. 233, 236 (2014).

But plaintiffs do not always have to rely on general jurisdiction. Indeed, its principal function was often to support jurisdiction when plaintiff's claims had nothing to do with the defendant's activities in the forum state. When the claim related to the defendant's local activities, that could support "specific jurisdiction," which was established for the current case only and did not imply that everyone wanting to sue the defendant could sue in the forum just because the current plaintiff could sue there.

The question when specific jurisdiction was proper accordingly became critical in numerous cases, particularly those involving products. To illustrate, in World-Wide Volkswagen Corp. v. Woodson, 444 U.S. 286 (1980), plaintiffs were severely burned in an accident in Oklahoma due to an alleged defect in their car. They sued in an Oklahoma state court, asserting claims against the German manufacturer of the car and also the New York dealership where they bought the car and World-Wide, which distributed these cars in New York, New Jersey, and Connecticut. The Court ruled that the dealer and the three-state distributor were not subject to suit in Oklahoma.

The German manufacturer sold lots of cars just like the plaintiffs' car in Oklahoma, but that might not mean that specific jurisdiction would be available there for this suit since the plaintiffs' purchase was not made in the state. On the other hand, the German company clearly did seek to serve the Oklahoma market. The Supreme Court did not address jurisdiction over the German company in *World-Wide*. As Justice Ginsburg later observed, however, "the foreign manufacturer of the Audi in *World-Wide Volkswagen* did not object to the jurisdiction of the Oklahoma courts. * * * [T]he Court's opinion indicates that an objection to jurisdiction by the manufacturer * * * would have been unavailing." J. McIntyre Machinery, Ltd. v. Nicastro, 564 U.S. 873, 906 (2011). In Ford Motor Co. v. Montana Eighth Judicial District, 141 S.Ct. 1017 (2021), the Court upheld jurisdiction in a suit against the manufacturer resulting from a crash in the forum involving a Ford originally sold in another state.

Other decisions address the question of personal jurisdiction in aggregate litigation.

Jurisdiction Over Claims of Absent Class Members—Phillips Petroleum v. Shutts

In Phillips Petroleum Co. v. Shutts, 472 U.S. 797 (1985). the Court rebuffed a challenge to personal jurisdiction "over" the claims of class members. The underlying claims related to interest payments to lessors of natural gas on land in 11 states that Phillips Petroleum had leased from many landowners. Plaintiffs, Kansas residents, filed a class action in a Kansas state court on behalf of all 33,000 lessors even though fewer than 1,000 of the lessors were Kansas residents and less than one percent of the gas leases were on Kansas land. Plaintiffs nonetheless asked that the interest payments be calculated at the rate set by Kansas law, which appeared to be considerably more favorable to lessors than the interest rate that would apply under the law of the states where most of the leases were located and in which most of the lessors resided.

As with Rule 23, Kansas class action practice relied on an opt-out system; class members were entitled to notice of class certification, but included in the class unless they excluded themselves. Phillips Petroleum objected to the Kansas court asserting personal jurisdiction over non-Kansas class members, arguing that the decision could compromise the class members' rights. The Supreme Court held that, even though it was the defendant, Phillips could raise this objection because it risked being denied full faith and credit to any judgment in the class action if it won the case but out-of-state class members could argue that the judgment did not bind them because the Kansas court could not assert jurisdiction over their claims.

But the Court rejected Phillips' personal jurisdiction argument:

> The burdens placed by a State upon an absent class-action plaintiff are not of the same order or magnitude as those it places upon an absent defendant. An out-of-state defendant summoned by a plaintiff is faced with the full powers of the forum State to render judgment *against* it. The defendant must generally hire counsel and travel to the forum to defend itself from the plaintiff's claim, or suffer a default judgment. The defendant may be forced to participate in extended and often costly discovery, and will be forced to respond in damages or to comply with some other form of remedy imposed by the court should it lose the suit. The defendant may also face liability for court costs and attorney's fees. These burdens are substantial, and the minimum contacts requirement of the Due Process Clause prevents the forum State from unfairly imposing them upon the defendant.

> A class-action plaintiff, however, is in quite a different posture. The Court noted this difference in *Hansberry v. Lee,* 311 U.S. 32, 40–41 (1940), which explained that a "class" or "representative" suit was an exception to the rule that one could not be bound by judgment *in personam* unless one was made fully a party in the traditional sense. *Ibid.,* citing *Pennoyer v. Neff,* 95 U.S. (5 Otto) 714 (1878). As the Court pointed out in *Hansberry,* the class action was an invention of equity to enable it to proceed to a decree in suits where the number of those interested in the litigation was too great to permit joinder. The absent parties would be bound by the decree so long as the named parties adequately represented the absent class and the prosecution of the litigation was within the common interest.

Modern plaintiff class actions follow the same goals, permitting litigation of a suit involving common questions when there are too many plaintiffs for proper joinder. Class actions also may permit the plaintiffs to pool claims which would be uneconomical to litigate individually. For example, this lawsuit involves claims averaging about $100 per plaintiff; most of the plaintiffs would have no realistic day in court if a class action were not available.

In sharp contrast to the predicament of a defendant haled into an out-of-state forum, the plaintiffs in this suit were not haled anywhere to defend themselves upon pain of a default judgment. As commentators have noted, from the plaintiffs' point of view a class action resembles a "quasi-administrative proceeding, conducted by the judge."

A plaintiff class in Kansas and numerous other jurisdictions cannot first be certified unless the judge, with the aid of the named plaintiffs and defendant, conducts an inquiry into the common nature of the named plaintiffs' and the absent plaintiffs' claims, the adequacy of representation, the jurisdiction possessed over the class, and any other matters that will bear upon proper representation of the absent plaintiffs' interest. See, *e.g.,* Kan.Stat.Ann. § 60–223 (1983); Fed.Rule Civ.Proc. 23. Unlike a defendant in a civil suit, a class-action plaintiff is not required to fend for himself. See Kan.Stat.Ann. § 60–223(d) (1983). The court and named plaintiffs protect his interests. Indeed, the class-action defendant itself has a great interest in ensuring that the absent plaintiff's claims are properly before the forum. In this case, for example, the defendant sought to avoid class certification by alleging that the absent plaintiffs would not be adequately represented and were not amenable to jurisdiction.

The concern of the typical class-action rules for the absent plaintiffs is manifested in other ways. Most jurisdictions, including Kansas, require that a class action, once certified, may not be dismissed or compromised without the approval of the court. In many jurisdictions such as Kansas the court may amend the pleadings to ensure that all sections of the class are represented adequately. Kan.Stat.Ann. § 60–223(d) (1983); see also, *e.g.,* Fed.Rule Civ.Proc. 23(d).

Besides this continuing solicitude for their rights, absent plaintiff class members are not subject to other burdens imposed upon defendants. They need not hire counsel or appear. They are almost never subject to counterclaims or cross-claims, or liability for fees or costs. Absent plaintiff class members are not subject to coercive or punitive remedies. Nor will an adverse judgment typically bind an absent plaintiff for any damages, although a valid adverse judgment may extinguish any of the plaintiff's claims which were litigated.

Unlike a defendant in a normal civil suit, an absent class-action plaintiff is not required to do anything. He may sit back and allow the litigation to run its course, content in knowing that there are safe-guards provided for his protection. In most class actions an absent plaintiff is provided at least with an opportunity to "opt out" of the class, and if he takes advantage of that opportunity he is removed from the litigation entirely. This was true of the Kansas proceedings in this case. The Kansas procedure provided for the mailing of a notice to each class member by first-class mail. The notice, as we have previously indicated, described the action and informed the class member that he could appear in person or by counsel, in default of which he would be represented by the named plaintiffs and their attorneys. The notice further stated that class members would be included in the class and bound by the judgment unless they "opted out" by executing and returning a "request for exclusion" that was included in the notice.

Petitioner contends, however, that the "opt out" procedure provided by Kansas is not good enough, and that an "opt in" procedure is required to satisfy the Due Process Clause of the Fourteenth Amendment. Insofar as plaintiffs who have no minimum contacts with the forum State are concerned, an "opt in" provision would require that each class member affirmatively consent to his inclusion within the class.

Because States place fewer burdens upon absent class plaintiffs than they do upon absent defendants in nonclass suits, the Due Process Clause need not and does not afford the former as much protection from state-court jurisdiction as it does the latter. The Fourteenth Amendment does protect "persons," not "defendants," however, so absent plaintiffs as well as absent defendants are entitled to some protection from the jurisdiction of a forum State which seeks to adjudicate their claims. In this case we hold that a forum State may exercise jurisdiction over the claim of an absent class-action plaintiff, even though that plaintiff may not possess the minimum contacts with the forum which would support personal jurisdiction over a defendant. If the forum State wishes to bind an absent plaintiff concerning a claim for money damages or similar relief at law,[3] it must provide minimal

---

[3] Our holding today is limited to those class actions which seek to bind known plaintiffs concerning claims wholly or predominately for money judgments. We intimate no view concerning other types of class actions, such as those seeking equitable relief. Nor, of course, does our

procedural due process protection. The plaintiff must receive notice plus an opportunity to be heard and participate in the litigation, whether in person or through counsel. The notice must be the best practicable, "reasonably calculated, under all the circumstances, to apprise interested parties of the pendency of the action and afford them an opportunity to present their objections." *Mullane,* 339 U.S., at 314–315; cf. *Eisen v. Carlisle & Jacquelin,* 417 U.S. 156, 174–175 (1974). The notice should describe the action and the plaintiffs' rights in it. Additionally, we hold that due process requires at a minimum that an absent plaintiff be provided with an opportunity to remove himself from the class by executing and returning an "opt out" or "request for exclusion" form to the court. Finally, the Due Process Clause of course requires that the named plaintiff at all times adequately represent the interests of the absent class members. *Hansberry,* 311 U.S., at 42–43, 45.

NOTES AND QUESTIONS

1.   The Court says that the due process rights of absent members of a class are satisfied by the right to opt out. Is the right to opt out constitutionally required in every class action, even if there is no issue of personal jurisdiction? Assume a state court class action by citizens of the state against a defendant that is also a citizen of the state. Does due process require a right to opt out whether or not it is provided by the class action procedure of the state in question?

2.   Should there be a right to opt out in (b)(1) or (b)(2) class actions? In a footnote, the Court says that its holding is only about class actions seeking to bind known plaintiffs concerning claims for money. Recall what the Court said in Wal-Mart Stores, Inc v. Dukes (*supra* pp. 243–244):

> Classes certified under (b)(1) and (b)(2) share the most traditional justifications for class treatment—that individual adjudications would be impossible or unworkable, as in a (b)(1) class, or that the relief sought must perforce affect the entire class at once, as in a (b)(2) class. For that reason these are also mandatory classes. The Rule provides no opportunity for (b)(1) or (b)(2) class members to opt out, and does not even oblige the District Court to afford them notice of the action.

3.   *Choice of law*: Though the Court upheld Kansas jurisdiction over the claims of absent class members, as explained below it did not permit Kansas to apply its law to decide the claims of those absent class members unless the claims had some connection to Kansas. Those issues are addressed *infra* p. 388.

---

discussion of personal jurisdiction address class actions where the jurisdiction is asserted against a *defendant* class.

4.   After *Phillips Petroleum*, there were rarely problems with personal jurisdiction over the claims of unnamed plaintiff class members. But a recent decision has raised doubts about jurisdiction over defendants. We turn to those issues now.

Jurisdiction over Defendant—Bristol-Myers Squibb v. Superior Court

The Court's decision in Bristol-Myers Squibb Co. v. Superior Court, 137 S.Ct. 1773 (2017), has raised questions about whether personal jurisdiction over defendant will present serious difficulties in aggregate litigation, including class actions. That case was not a class action. Instead, it resulted from what looked like a strategic effort to obtain a California state court forum for many non-California plaintiffs. Recall that CAFA includes "mass action" provisions that apply when more than 100 plaintiffs seek a joint trial of state law claims and there is minimum diversity, providing that the aggregate claims of the plaintiffs exceed $5 million. It seemed that the litigation aggregated by a California procedure like MDL practice in San Francisco Superior Court was tailored to avoid removal under CAFA.

There were some 592 plaintiffs in total, 86 of them from California and others from 33 other states. They all claimed to have suffered serious health problems due to taking defendant's drug Plavix. The 592 plaintiffs filed a total of eight separate suits, none with as many as 100 plaintiffs and each including a number of California plaintiffs. All plaintiffs sought to assert claims under California law.

Defendant Bristol Myers had a sizable presence in California. It employed about 250 sales representatives in the state, and had sold more than $900 million worth of Plavix in the state between 2006 and 2012. It also had five research facilities in California, employing about 160 researchers, and a small state-government advisory office in Sacramento, the state capitol. Under prevailing standards for general jurisdiction of a few decades ago, that level of activity would almost certainly have supported California jurisdiction. Defendant was the sort of major corporation that for years had been found subject to general jurisdiction in California due to its longstanding and extensive activities there, but it was not "at home" in that state. It was incorporated in Delaware, and had its headquarters in New York. Over 50% of its work force worked in New York and New Jersey, where Plavix was designed, the regulatory approval process was managed, and the marketing program for the drug was developed.

So plaintiffs had to rely on specific jurisdiction. Bristol Myers did not challenge specific jurisdiction with regard to the claims of the California plaintiffs, but argued that there could not be jurisdiction over the claims of the other plaintiffs. In a 4–3 decision, the Supreme Court of California rejected this argument, using a "sliding scale" approach to specific jurisdiction that "the more wide-ranging the defendant's forum contacts, the more readily is shown a connection between the forum contacts and the claim." Since the overlap between the claims[of the Californians and the non-Californians was sufficient to support joinder, it was also sufficient to justify specific jurisdiction.

The Supreme Court rejected this argument as a "loose and spurious form of general jurisdiction" in an 8–1 decision. Instead: "What is needed—and what is missing here—is a connection between the forum and the specific claims at issue."

But since the suits would continue with regard to the California plaintiffs, it was difficult to say that the litigation burden on the defendant of adding the non-Californians' claims was significant. That was not critical to the Court (137 S.Ct. at 1780–81):

> Assessing this burden obviously requires a court to consider the practical problems resulting from litigation in the forum, but it also encompasses the more abstract matter of submitting to the coercive power of a State that may have little legitimate interest in the claims in question. As we have put it, restrictions on personal jurisdiction "are more than a guarantee of immunity from inconvenient or distant litigation. They are a consequence of territorial limitations on the power of the respective States." Hanson v. Denckla, 357 U.S. 235, 251 (1958). * * * "The sovereignty of each state ... implie[s] a limitation on the sovereignty of all its sister States." World-Wide Volkswagen v. Woodson, 444 U.S. [286] 293 [(1980).] And at times, this federalism interest may be decisive.

The federalism interest defeated jurisdiction over the nonresidents' claims in *Bristol Myers* because "all the conduct giving rise to the nonresidents' claims occurred elsewhere." Id. at 1782.

Plaintiffs in *Bristol-Myers* relied on the Court's decision in Phillips Petroleum Co. v. Shutts, *supra*, to support jurisdiction in their case, arguing that finding jurisdiction absent in their case would mean that it should have been found missing over Phillips Petroleum in the earlier case. The Court rejected the argument in *Bristol-Myers*, noting that Phillips may have thought general jurisdiction would defeat any objection it made under 1970s views of that form of jurisdiction. In any event, "the fact remains the Phillips did not assert that Kansas improperly exercised personal jurisdiction over it," and the Court's decision in the earlier case distinguished the authority of a state court to exercise jurisdiction over nonresident members of a plaintiff class from its authority to exercise jurisdiction over an out-of-state defendant. Id. at 1783. *Bristol Myers* raised that question with regard to jurisdiction over defendant to entertain the claims of the non-California plaintiffs.

As explored below, the impact of *Bristol-Myers* is now being debated. Here is one forecast:

> Plaintiffs who have similar claims stemming from a defendant's nationwide course of conduct (like a nationally marketed defective product) and wish to sue together will now face a more limited set of options. * * * [A]fter *Bristol-Myers*, mass-tort plaintiffs can either (1) assemble a nationwide group to sue together in state court in the defendant's home state or potentially a state where it directed nationwide conduct; (2) sue individually or in smaller groups in their home states' courts if they can find a way to avoid removal; or (3) sue in, or allow removal to, federal court (either in their home state or the defendant's) where their cases will be aggregated for pretrial proceedings in an MDL. In short, if the plaintiffs want to aggregate after *Bristol-Myers*, they will have to do so on the defendant's terms—either on the defendant's home turf or in an MDL.

Andrew Bradt & Theodore Rave, Aggregation on Defendants' Terms: *Bristol-Myers Squibb* and the Federalization of Mass-Tort Litigation, 59 Bos. Col. L. Rev. 1251, 1256–57 (2018).

NOTES AND QUESTIONS

1. Could Phillips Petroleum have defeated the Kansas suit by objecting to inclusion in the class of non-Kansas class members? Recall that only about 3% of the class members there were from Kansas, and fewer than 1% of the leases involved were in Kansas? In *Bristol-Myers*, plaintiffs argued that it would be "absurd" to believe the *Phillips Petroleum* Court would have reached an opposite result had Phillips objected on the grounds raised by Bristol-Myers. After the Court's decision in *Phillips Petroleum*, Congress adopted CAFA, partly to respond to the perceived threat of nationwide class actions in state court. Had Phillips successfully raised the *Bristol Myers* argument, would CAFA have been necessary? Would CAFA have allowed removal in *Phillips Petroleum*?

2. *Applicable to class actions?* Justice Sotomayor was the lone dissenter in *Bristol-Myers*, arguing that it would "eliminate nationwide mass actions in any State other than those in which the defendant is 'essentially at home.'" Id. at 1789. At least some lower courts have so concluded: "The Court believes that it is more likely than not based on the Supreme Court's comments about federalism that the courts will apply *Bristol-Myers Squibb* to outlaw nationwide class actions in a forum, such as in this case, where there is no general jurisdiction over the Defendants." DeBernardis v. NBTY, Inc., 2018 WL 461228 (N.D. Ill, Jan. 18, 2018). Compare Al Haj v. Pfizer, Inc., 338 F.Supp.3d 815 (N.D. Ill. 2018) (concluding that *Bristol Myers* did not produce an "extraordinary sea change in class action practice").

In Mussat v. IQVIA, Inc., 953 F.3d 441 (7th Cir. 2020), a three-judge panel held that it was error to strike class action allegations in a proposed nationwide class action brought by an Illinois plaintiff under the federal Telephone Consumer Protection Act. It reasoned that class actions "are different from many other types of aggregation." Id. at 446. Unnamed class members are not formal parties in the same sense that the named plaintiffs from outside California were parties in *Bristol-Myers Squibb*. Class certification does provide a basis for making the class-action judgment binding on all the members of the class, but that is because "the lead plaintiffs earn the right to represent the interests of absent class members by satisfying all four criteria of Rule 23(a) and one branch of Rule 23(b)." Id. at 447. Finally, the Supreme Court explicitly recognized in *Bristol-Myers Squibb* that it did not reach the question whether the ruling applied to suits in federal court and, as Justice Sotomayor pointed out in dissent, the opinion did not reach the question whether the holding would apply to class actions.

In Molock v. Whole Foods Market Group, Inc., 952 F.3d 293 (D.C. Cir. 2020), the court held that defendant's pre-certification motion to dismiss the claims of out-of-state putative class members was premature. The case involved a proposed multistate class of defendant's employees under the federal Fair Labor Standards Act and under parallel state laws. The majority reasoned that "putative class members—at issue in this case—are *always* treated as nonparties." Id. at 297. "Motions to dismiss nonparties for lack of personal jurisdiction are thus premature." Id. at 298. A dissenting judge thought the motion to dismiss was not premature, and that *Bristol-Myers Squibb* applied (id. at 306):

> Although the Supreme Court avoided opining on whether its reasoning in the mass action context would apply also to class actions, it seems to me that logic says that it does. After all, like the mass action in *Bristol-Myers*, a class action is just a species of joinder, which "merely enables a federal court to adjudicate claims of multiple parties at once, instead of in separate suits." And since the requirements of personal jurisdiction must be satisfied independently for "the specific claims at issue," I think that personal jurisdiction over claims asserted on behalf of absent class members must be analyzed on a claim-by-claim basis.

Thus, the lower courts continue to debate this subject.

3. *Applicable to Multidistrict Litigation?* Recall that the Judicial Panel on Multidistrict Litigation has routinely transferred class actions presenting the risk of certification of overlapping classes for centralized pretrial treatment. Meanwhile, the existence of state court class actions overlapping with federal court class actions has produced difficulties on occasion. Recall In re Diet Drugs, *supra* p. 348. Would *Bristol-Myers* eliminate or reduce the risk of such overlap between federal and state court class actions? Reportedly, Bristol Myers urged the Court not to interfere with MDL centralization. See

Bradt & Rave, *supra*, 59 Bos.Col.L. Rev. at 1254 ("Bristol-Myers enthusiastically endorsed the MDL process.").

In In re Chinese-Manufactured Drywall Products Liability Litigation, 2017 WL 5971622 (E.D. La., Nov. 30, 2017), the court stressed that the personal-jurisdiction issues before it depended on whether there was jurisdiction in the transferor courts:

> [T]his Court, as a transferee court, has the same pre-trial jurisdiction as the transferor courts where the cases were initially filed. Congress passed the MDL statute and enabled class actions because Congress recognizes the need for efficiency—for plaintiffs and defendants as well as the judicial system—in managing such mass filings. Class action promotes "efficiency and economy of litigation."

4. *Applicable in federal court?* In *Bristol-Myers*, the Court confronted individual claims pending in a state court. The Court's opinion explicitly noted that "we leave open the question whether the Fifth Amendment imposes the same restrictions on the exercise of personal jurisdiction by a federal court." 137 S.Ct. at 1784.

At least in federal suits asserting federal claims, it might seem odd for a federal court's jurisdiction to be confined by concerns about federalism. In Sloan v. General Motors LLC, 287 F.Supp.3d 840 (N.D. Cal. 2018), the court denied a motion to dismiss based on *Bristol-Myers* in a suit on behalf of a national class asserting claims partly based on federal consumer protection laws (id. at 858–59):

> In contrast to *Bristol-Myers*, the due process right does not obtain here in the same manner because all federal courts, regardless of where they sit, represent the same federal sovereign, not the sovereignty of a foreign state government. There is no risk of a state court exceeding the bounds of its state's sovereignty and subjecting residents of another state to the coercing power of its courts. Therefore, where a federal court presides over litigation involving a federal question, the due process analysis does not incorporate the interstate sovereignty concerns that animated *Bristol-Myers*.

The court went on to rule that it also could entertain state law claims arising out of the same course of conduct under the doctrine of pendent personal jurisdiction. Id. at 859–61; see Action Embroidery Corp. v. Atlantic Embroidery, Inc., 368 F.3d 1174 (9th Cir. 2004) (upholding federal court's pendent personal jurisdiction over state-law antitrust claims contained in the same complaint as federal claims).

As noted above, it seems that CAFA assumed that nationwide class actions based on state law could go forward, but authorized filing in, or removal to, federal court. Should this expectation bear on the application of *Bristol-Myers*? The court in In re Chinese-Manufactured Drywall Products Liability Litigation thought so (2017 WL 5971622 at *18):

Defendants argue that CAFA is irrelevant because it involves subject matter jurisdiction and not personal jurisdiction. Nevertheless, CAFA illustrates that personal jurisdiction in federal court is permissible even when there are nonresident plaintiffs or class members whose claims arise from conduct outside of the forum state. These are the claims over which CAFA grants subject matter jurisdiction.

5. *Undermining aggregation?* Will *Bristol Myers* undermine the efficiency goals sought by aggregation? See Scott Dodson, Personal Jurisdiction and Aggregation, 113 Nw.U.L.Rev. 1 (2018) (stressing the efficiencies for all parties of aggregate litigation). Dissenting Justice Sotomayor warned that the decision would "make it impossible to bring a nationwide mass action in state court against defendants who are 'at home' in different states." 137 S.Ct. at 1784.

6. *The problem of non-U.S. companies*: In *Bristol-Myers*, the Court observed that its decision "does not prevent the California and out-of-state plaintiffs from joining together in a consolidated action the States that have general jurisdiction over BMS." 137 S.Ct. at 1783. But that would not be true of non-U.S. companies. They would not be "at home" in any American state. For an argument that national contacts should justify suit in any American state against such entities, see William Dodge & Scott Dodson, Personal Jurisdiction and Aliens, 116 Mich.L. Rev. 1205 (2018).

7. *Effect on class definition*: In *Bristol-Myers*, the Court noted a lot of possible connections with California that plaintiffs did not allege: "the nonresidents were not prescribed Plavix in California, did not ingest Plavix in California, and were not injured by Plavix in California." 137 S.Ct. at 1781. In a proposed class action on behalf of users of Plavix, could jurisdictional difficulties be overcome by a class definition? Would those solutions create problems of ascertainability? Recall p. 184 n.4 *supra*. Under the Seventh Circuit and D.C. Circuit rulings described in note 2 above, indeed, a challenge to jurisdiction may be premature until class certification. Consider how that might affect certification only for purposes of settlement, given that defendants can waive objections to personal jurisdiction.

8. *Effect on (b)(2) class actions?* Recall that Rule 23(b)(2) permits a class action seeking a class-wide injunction. There has been much concern about "nationwide" injunctions. See Samuel Bray, Multiple Chancellors: Reforming the Nationwide Injunction, 131 Harv. L. Rev. 417 (2017); Amanda Frost, In Defense of Nationwide Injunctions, 93 NYU L. Rev. 1065 (2018). Could personal jurisdiction limitations confine injunctions in (b)(2) cases to citizens of the forum state?

9. *Relation to choice of law*: Plaintiffs in *Bristol-Myers* sought to rely on California product liability law. In distinguishing the case, the court in In re Chinese-Manufactured Drywall Product Liability Litigation emphasized that "in *BMS*, the individual non-resident plaintiffs desired to disregard their own states' laws and instead apply California's consumer protection laws before a

California jury. The Supreme Court rightly halted this form of forum shopping." 2017 WL 5971622 at 16. We turn to choice of law now.

J. CHOICE OF LAW

PHILLIPS PETROLEUM CO. v. SHUTTS
United States Supreme Court, 1985.
472 U.S. 797.

JUSTICE REHNQUIST delivered the opinion of the Court.

[A class action in a Kansas state court asserted that Phillips Petroleum had underpaid interest to the 33,000 members of a class of lessors of natural gas installations. The Court addressed the question whether Kansas law on interest payments—singularly favorable to the plaintiffs—should be applied.]

The Kansas courts applied Kansas contract and Kansas equity law to every claim in this case, notwithstanding that over 99% of the gas leases and some 97% of the plaintiffs in the case had no apparent connection to the State of Kansas except for this lawsuit. Petitioner protested that the Kansas courts should apply the laws of the States where the leases were located, or at least apply Texas and Oklahoma law because so many of the leases came from those States. The Kansas courts disregarded this contention and found petitioner liable for interest on the suspended royalties as a matter of Kansas law, and set the interest rates under Kansas equity principles.

Petitioner contends that total application of Kansas substantive law violated the constitutional limitations on choice of law mandated by the Due Process Clause of the Fourteenth Amendment and the Full Faith and Credit Clause of Article IV, § 1. We must first determine whether Kansas law conflicts in any material way with any other law which could apply. There can be no injury in applying Kansas law if it is not in conflict with that of any other jurisdiction connected to this suit.

Petitioner claims that Kansas law conflicts with that of a number of States connected to this litigation, especially Texas and Oklahoma. These putative conflicts range from the direct to the tangential, and may be addressed by the Supreme Court of Kansas on remand under the correct constitutional standard. For example, there is no recorded Oklahoma decision dealing with interest liability for suspended royalties: whether Oklahoma is likely to impose liability would require a survey of Oklahoma oil and gas law. Even if Oklahoma found such liability, petitioner shows that Oklahoma would most likely apply its constitutional and statutory 6% interest rate rather than the much higher Kansas rates applied in this litigation.

Additionally, petitioner points to an Oklahoma statute which excuses liability for interest if a creditor accepts payment of the full principal without a claim for interest, Okla.Stat., Tit. 23, § 8 (1951). Petitioner contends that by ignoring this statute the Kansas courts created liability that does not exist in Oklahoma.

Petitioner also points out several conflicts between Kansas and Texas law. Although Texas recognizes interest liability for suspended royalties, Texas has never awarded any such interest at a rate greater than 6%, which corresponds with the Texas constitutional and statutory rate. Moreover, at least one court interpreting Texas law appears to have held that Texas excuses interest liability once the gas company offers to take an indemnity from the royalty owner and pay him the suspended royalty while the price increase is still tentative. Such a rule is contrary to Kansas law as applied below, but if applied to the Texas plaintiffs or leases in this case, would vastly reduce petitioner's liability.

The conflicts on the applicable interest rates, alone—which we do not think can be labeled "false conflicts" without a more thoroughgoing treatment than was accorded them by the Supreme Court of Kansas— certainly amounted to millions of dollars in liability. We think that the Supreme Court of Kansas erred in deciding on the basis that it did that the application of its laws to all claims would be constitutional.

Four Terms ago we addressed a similar situation in *Allstate Ins. Co. v. Hague,* 449 U.S. 302 (1981). In that case we were confronted with two conflicting rules of state insurance law. Minnesota permitted the "stacking" of separate uninsured motorist policies while Wisconsin did not. Although the decedent lived in Wisconsin, took out insurance policies and was killed there, he was employed in Minnesota, and after his death his widow moved to Minnesota for reasons unrelated to the litigation, and was appointed personal representative of his estate. She filed suit in Minnesota courts, which applied the Minnesota stacking rule.

The plurality in *Allstate* noted that a particular set of facts giving rise to litigation could justify, constitutionally, the application of more than one jurisdiction's laws. The plurality recognized, however, that the Due Process Clause and the Full Faith and Credit Clause provided modest restrictions on the application of forum law. These restrictions required "that for a State's substantive law to be selected in a constitutionally permissible manner, that State must have a significant contact or significant aggregation of contacts, creating state interests, such that choice of its law is neither arbitrary nor fundamentally unfair." The dissenting Justices were in substantial agreement with this principle. *Id.* at 332 (opinion of Powell, J., joined by Burger, C.J., and Rehnquist, J.). The dissent stressed that the Due Process Clause prohibited the application of law which was only casually or slightly related to the litigation, while the Full Faith and Credit Clause required the forum to respect the laws and judgments of other States, subject to the forum's own interests in furthering its public policy.

The plurality in *Allstate* affirmed the application of Minnesota law because of the forum's significant contacts to the litigation which supported the State's interest in applying its law. Kansas' contacts to this litigation, as explained by the Kansas Supreme Court, can be gleaned from the opinion below.

Petitioner owns property and conducts substantial business in the State, so Kansas certainly has an interest in regulating petitioner's conduct in Kansas. Moreover, oil and gas extraction is an important business to Kansas, and although only a few leases in issue are located in Kansas, hundreds of Kansas plaintiffs were affected by petitioner's suspension of royalties; thus the court held that the State has a real interest in protecting "the rights of these royalty owners both as individual residents of [Kansas] and as members of this particular class of plaintiffs." The Kansas Supreme Court pointed out that Kansas courts are quite familiar with this type of lawsuit, and "[t]he plaintiff class members have indicated their desire to have this action determined under the laws of Kansas." Finally, the Kansas court buttressed its use of Kansas law by stating that this lawsuit was analogous to a suit against a "common fund" located in Kansas.

We do not lightly discount this description of Kansas' contacts with this litigation and its interest in applying its law. There is, however, no "common fund" located in Kansas that would require or support the application of only Kansas law to all these claims. As the Kansas court noted, petitioner commingled the suspended royalties with its general corporate accounts. There is no specific identifiable res in Kansas, nor is there any limited amount which may be depleted before every plaintiff is compensated. Only by somehow aggregating all the separate claims in this case could a "common fund" in any sense be created, and the term becomes all but meaningless when used in such an expansive sense.

We also give little credence to the idea that Kansas law should apply to all claims because the plaintiffs, by failing to opt out, evinced their desire to be bound by Kansas law. Even if one could say that the plaintiffs "consented" to the application of Kansas law by not opting out, plaintiff's desire for forum law is rarely, if ever controlling. In most cases the plaintiff shows his obvious wish for forum law by filing there. "If a plaintiff could choose the substantive rules to be applied to an action . . . the invitation to forum shopping would be irresistible." *Allstate, supra,* 449 U.S., at 337 (opinion of Powell, J.). Even if a plaintiff evidences his desire for forum law by moving to the forum, we have generally accorded such a move little or no significance. In *Allstate* the plaintiff's move to the forum was only relevant because it was unrelated and prior to the litigation. Thus the plaintiffs' desire for Kansas law, manifested by their participation in this Kansas lawsuit, bears little relevance.

The Supreme Court of Kansas in its opinion in this case expressed the view that by reason of the fact that it was adjudicating a nationwide class action, it had much greater latitude in applying its own law to the transactions in question than might otherwise be the case:

> "The general rule is that the law of the forum applies unless it is expressly shown that a different law governs, and in case of doubt, the law of the forum is preferred. . . . Where a state court determines it has jurisdiction over a nationwide class action and procedural due process guarantees of notice and adequate representation are present, we believe the law of the forum should be applied unless compelling reasons exist for applying a different law. . . . Compelling reasons do not exist to require this court to look to other state laws to determine the rights of the parties involved in this lawsuit."

We think that this is something of a "bootstrap" argument. The Kansas class-action statute, like those of most other jurisdictions, requires that there be "common issues of law or fact." But while a State may, for the reasons we have previously stated, assume jurisdiction over the claims of plaintiffs whose principal contacts are with other States, it may not use this assumption of jurisdiction as an added weight in the scale when considering the permissible constitutional limits on choice of substantive law. It may not take a transaction with little or no relationship to the forum and apply the law of the forum in order to satisfy the procedural requirement that there be a "common question of law." The issue of personal jurisdiction over plaintiffs in a class action is entirely distinct from the question of the constitutional limitations on choice of law; the latter calculus is not altered by the fact that it may be more difficult or more burdensome to comply with the constitutional limitations because of the large number of transactions which the State proposes to adjudicate and which have little connection with the forum.

Kansas must have a "significant contact or significant aggregation of contacts" to the claims asserted by each member of the plaintiff class, contacts "creating state interests," in order to ensure that the choice of Kansas law is not arbitrary or unfair. *Allstate,* 449 U.S., at 312–313. Given Kansas' lack of "interest" in claims unrelated to that State, and the substantive conflict with jurisdictions such as Texas, we conclude that application of Kansas law to every claim in this case is sufficiently arbitrary and unfair as to exceed constitutional limits.

When considering fairness in this context, an important element is the expectation of the parties. See *Allstate, supra,* 449 U.S., at 333 (opinion of Powell, J.). There is no indication that when the leases involving land and royalty owners outside of Kansas were executed, the parties had any idea that Kansas law would control. Neither the Due Process Clause nor the Full Faith and Credit Clause requires Kansas "to substitute for its own

[laws], applicable to persons and events within it, the conflicting statute of another state," *Pacific Employers Ins. Co. v. Industrial Accident Comm'n,* 306 U.S. 493, 502 (1939), but Kansas "may not abrogate the rights of parties beyond its borders having no relation to anything done or to be done within them." *Home Ins. Co. v. Dick,* 281 U.S., at 410.

Here the Supreme Court of Kansas took the view that in a nationwide class action where procedural due process guarantees of notice and adequate representation were met, "the law of the forum should be applied unless compelling reasons exist for applying a different law." Whatever practical reasons may have commended this rule to the Supreme Court of Kansas, for the reasons already stated we do not believe that it is consistent with the decisions of this Court. We make no effort to determine for ourselves which law must apply to the various transactions involved in this lawsuit, and we reaffirm our observation in *Allstate* that in many situations a state court may be free to apply one of several choices of law. But the constitutional limitations laid down in cases such as *Allstate* and *Home Ins. Co. v. Dick, supra,* must be respected even in a nationwide class action.

We therefore affirm the judgment of the Supreme Court of Kansas insofar as it upheld the jurisdiction of the Kansas courts over the plaintiff class members in this case, and reverse its judgment insofar as it held that Kansas law was applicable to all of the transactions which it sought to adjudicate. We remand the case to that court for further proceedings not inconsistent with this opinion.

IN RE BRIDGESTONE/FIRESTONE, INC.

United States Court of Appeals, Seventh Circuit, 2002.
288 F.3d 1012, *cert. denied,* 537 U.S. 1105 (2003).

Before EASTERBROOK, MANION and KANNE, CIRCUIT JUDGES.

EASTERBROOK, CIRCUIT JUDGE.

Firestone tires on Ford Explorer SUVs experienced an abnormally high failure rate during the late 1990s. In August 2000, while the National Highway Transportation Safety Administration was investigating, Firestone recalled and replaced some of those tires. Ford and Firestone replaced additional tires during 2001. Many suits have been filed as a result of injuries and deaths related to the tire failures. Other suits were filed by persons who own (or owned) Ford Explorers or Firestone tires that have so far performed properly; these persons seek compensation for the *risk* of failure, which may be reflected in diminished resale value of the vehicles and perhaps in mental stress. The Judicial Panel on Multidistrict Litigation transferred suits filed in, or removed to, federal court to the Southern District of Indiana for consolidated pretrial proceedings under 28 U.S.C. § 1407(a). Once these have been completed, the cases must be

returned to the originating districts for decision on the merits. In an effort
to prevent retransfer, counsel representing many of the plaintiffs filed a
new consolidated suit in Indianapolis and asked the judge to certify it as a
nationwide class action, which would make all other suits redundant. The
district court obliged and certified two nationwide classes: the first includes
everyone who owns, owned, leases, or leased a Ford Explorer of model year
1991 through 2001 anytime before the first recall, and the second includes
all owners and lessees from 1990 until today of Firestone ATX, ATX II,
Firehawk ATX, ATX 23 Degree, Widetrack Radial Baja, or Wilderness tire
models, or any other Firestone tire "substantially similar" to them. More
than 60 million tires and 3 million vehicles fit these definitions.

No class action is proper unless all litigants are governed by the same
legal rules. Otherwise the class cannot satisfy the commonality and
superiority requirements of Fed.R.Civ.P. 23(a), (b)(3). Yet state laws about
theories such as those presented by our plaintiffs differ, and such
differences have led us to hold that other warranty, fraud, or products-
liability suits may not proceed as nationwide classes. The district judge,
well aware of this principle, recognized that uniform law would be essential
to class certification. Because plaintiffs' claims rest on state law, the choice-
of-law rules come from the state in which the federal court sits. See Klaxon
v. Stentor Electric Manufacturing Co., 313 U.S. 487 (1941). The district
judge concluded that Indiana law points to the headquarters of the
defendants, because that is where the products are designed and the
important decisions about disclosures and sales are made. Ford and
Firestone engaged in conduct that was uniform across the nation, which
the district court took to imply the appropriateness of uniform law. This
ruling means that all claims by the Explorer class will be resolved under
Michigan law and all claims by the tire class will be resolved under
Tennessee law. According to the district court, other obstacles (such as the
fact that the six named tire models represent 67 designs for different sizes
and performance criteria, and that half of all 1996 and 1997 model
Explorers came with Goodyear tires) are worth overcoming in light of the
efficiency of class treatment. Nor did the district court deem it important
that Firestone's tires were designed in Ohio, and many were manufactured
outside Tennessee, as many of Ford's vehicles are manufactured outside
Michigan.

[The court explained that it decided to review the decision under Rule
23(f) because the stakes were so large that settlement became "almost
inevitable" after class certification.]

Indiana is a *lex loci delicti* state: in all but exceptional cases it applies
the law of the place where harm occurred. See Hubbard Manufacturing Co.
v. Greeson, 515 N.E.2d 1071 (Ind. 1987). Those class members who suffered
injury or death as a result of defects were harmed in the states where the
tires failed. As a practical matter, these class members can be ignored; they

are sure to opt out and litigate independently. These classes therefore effectively include only those consumers whose loss (if any) is financial rather than physical: it is the class of persons whose tires did *not* fail, whose vehicles did *not* roll over. Many class members face no future threat of failure either, because about 30 million tires were recalled and replaced, while other tires have been used up and discarded. Financial loss (if any, a qualification we will not repeat) was suffered in the places where the vehicles and tires were purchased at excessive prices or resold at depressed prices. Those injuries occurred in all 50 states, the District of Columbia, Puerto Rico, and U.S. territories such as Guam. The *lex loci delicti* principle points to the places of these injuries, not the defendants' corporate headquarters, as the source of law.

Plaintiffs concede that until 1987 this would have been Indiana's approach. They contend, however, that *Hubbard* changed everything by holding that when the place of the injury "bears little connection to the legal action" a court may consider other factors, such as the place of the conduct causing the injury and the residence of the parties. It is conceivable, we suppose, that Indiana might think that a financial (or physical) injury to one of its residents, occurring within the state's borders, "bears little connection to the legal action", but the proof of that pudding is in the eating. Has Indiana since 1987 applied the law of a state where a product was designed, or promotional materials drafted, to a suit arising out of an injury in Indiana? As far as we can tell, the answer is no—not even once, and the state has had plenty of opportunities. Yet since 1987 both Indiana and this court have routinely applied Indiana law when injury caused by a defective product occurred in Indiana to Indiana residents. Neither Indiana nor any other state has applied a uniform place-of-the-defendant's-headquarters rule to products-liability cases. It is not hard to devise an argument that such a uniform rule would be good on many dimensions, but that argument has not carried the day with state judges, and it is state law rather than a quest for efficiency in litigation (or in product design decisions) that controls.

"Ah, but this is not a products-liability case!" So plaintiffs respond to the conspicuous lack of support from state decisions. And indeed it is not a products-liability suit, since all who suffered physical injury are bound to opt out. No injury, no tort, is an ingredient of every state's law. Plaintiffs describe the injury as financial rather than physical and seek to move the suit out of the tort domain and into that of contract (the vehicle was not the flawless one described and thus is not merchantable, a warranty theory) and consumer fraud (on the theory that selling products with undisclosed attributes, and thus worth less than represented, is fraudulent). It is not clear that this maneuver actually moves the locus from tort to contract. If tort law fully compensates those who are physically injured, then any recoveries by those whose products function properly mean excess compensation. As a result, most states would not entertain the sort of theory that plaintiffs press. [The court cited cases from a number of states.]

Obviously plaintiffs believe that Michigan and Tennessee are in the favorable minority; we need not decide. If recovery for breach of warranty or consumer fraud is possible, the injury is decidedly where the *consumer* is located, rather than where the seller maintains its headquarters. A contract for the sale of a car in Indiana is governed by Indiana law unless it contains a choice-of-law clause, and plaintiffs do not want to enforce any choice-of-law clause. Plaintiffs have not cited, and we could not find, any Indiana case applying any law other than Indiana's to warranty or fraud claims arising from consumer products designed (or contract terms written) out of state, unless a choice-of-law clause was involved. State consumer-protection laws vary considerably, and courts must respect these differences rather than apply one state's law to sales in other states with different rules. See BMW of North America, Inc. v. Gore, 517 U.S. 559, 568–73 (1996). We do not for a second suppose that Indiana would apply Michigan law to an auto sale if Michigan permitted auto companies to conceal defects from customers; nor do we think it likely that Indiana would apply Korean law (no matter *what* Korean law on the subject may provide) to claims of deceit in the sale of Hyundai automobiles, in Indiana, to residents of Indiana, or French law to the sale of cars equipped with Michelin tires. Indiana has consistently said that sales of products in Indiana must conform to Indiana's consumer-protection laws and its rules of contract law. It follows that Indiana's choice-of-law rule selects the 50 states and multiple territories where the buyers live, and not the place of the sellers' headquarters, for these suits.

Against all of this plaintiffs set a single decision: KPMG Peat Marwick v. Asher, 689 N.E.2d 1283 (Ind.App. 1997). This decision holds that the adequacy of services rendered by an accountant in Missouri to a business whose headquarters were in Missouri is governed by Missouri law, even when a suit is filed by unpaid lenders who live in Indiana. This is a straightforward application of *lex loci delicti*. The injury, if any, was suffered by the business, which hired and paid the accountant for professional services rendered directly to the client; those who dealt with the audited firm, such as the plaintiffs in *KPMG Peat Marwick*, suffer a derivative injury. Similarly a malpractice claim against a firm's lawyer is determined by the law of the state where the services are performed, for that state's law supplies the standard of performance and that is where the client normally would suffer injury. Investors may be able to step into a corporation's shoes and assert a derivative claim, and in some states * * * investors may have a direct claim too; but because the firm remains the lawyer's or accountant's client one body of law must apply to this single transaction. Sales of a consumer product in 50 states do not lead to derivative claims, and each sale is a separate transaction in the place of the sale. *KPMG Peat Marwick* accordingly has no bearing on consumers' suits against manufacturers of allegedly defective products.

Because these claims must be adjudicated under the law of so many jurisdictions, a single nationwide class is not manageable. Lest we soon see a Rule 23(f) petition to review the certification of 50 state classes, we add that this litigation is not manageable as a class action even on a statewide basis. About 20% of the Ford Explorers were shipped without Firestone tires. The Firestone tires supplied with the majority of the vehicles were recalled at different times; they may well have differed in their propensity to fail, and this would require sub-subclassing among those owners of Ford Explorers with Firestone tires. Some of the vehicles were resold and others have not been; the resales may have reflected different discounts that could require vehicle-specific litigation. Plaintiffs contend that many of the failures occurred because Ford and Firestone advised the owners to underinflate their tires, leading them to overheat. Other factors also affect heating; the failure rate (and hence the discount) may have been higher in Arizona than in Alaska. Of those vehicles that have not yet been resold, some will be resold in the future (by which time the tire replacements may have alleviated or eliminated any discount) and some never will be resold. Owners who wring the last possible mile out of their vehicles receive everything they paid for and have claims that differ from owners who sold their Explorers to the second-hand market during the height of the publicity in 2000. Some owners drove their SUVs off the road over rugged terrain, while others never used the "sport" or "utility" features; these differences also affect resale prices.

Firestone's tires likewise exhibit variability; that's why fewer than half of those included in the tire class were recalled. The tire class includes many buyers who used Firestone tires on vehicles other than Ford Explorers, and who therefore were not advised to underinflate their tires. (Note that this description does not reflect any view of the merits; we are repeating rather than endorsing plaintiffs' contention that Ford counseled "underinflation.") The six trade names listed in the class certification order comprise 67 master tire specifications: "Firehawk ATX" tires, for example, come in multiple diameters, widths, and tread designs; their safety features and failure modes differ accordingly. Plaintiffs say that all 67 specifications had three particular shortcomings that led to excess failures. But whether a particular feature is required for safe operation depends on *other* attributes of the tires, and as these other attributes varied across the 67 master specifications it would not be possible to make a once-and-for-all decision about whether all 60 million tires were defective, even if the law were uniform. There are other differences too, but the ones we have mentioned preclude any finding "that the questions of law or fact common to the members of the class predominate over any questions affecting only individual members, and that a class action is superior to other available methods for the fair and efficient adjudication of the controversy."

Fed.R.Civ.P. 23(b)(3). Regulation by the NHTSA, coupled with tort litigation by persons suffering physical injury, is far superior to a suit by millions of *uninjured* buyers for dealing with consumer products that are said to be failure-prone.

The district judge did not doubt that differences within the class would lead to difficulties in managing the litigation. But the judge thought it better to cope with these differences than to scatter the suits to the winds and require hundreds of judges to resolve thousands of claims under 50 or more bodies of law. Efficiency is a vital goal in any legal system—but the vision of "efficiency" underlying this class certification is the model of the central planner. Plaintiffs share the premise of the ALI's Complex Litigation Project (1993), which devotes more than 700 pages to an analysis of means to consolidate litigation as quickly as possible, by which the authors mean, before multiple trials break out. The authors take as given the benefits of that step. Yet the benefits are elusive. The central planning model—one case, one court, one set of rules, one settlement price for all involved—suppresses information that is vital to accurate resolution. What *is* the law of Michigan, or Arkansas, or Guam, as applied to this problem? Judges and lawyers will have to guess, because the central planning model keeps the litigation far away from state courts. (Ford asked us to certify legal questions to the Supreme Court of Michigan, to ensure that genuine state law was applied if Michigan's law were to govern the whole country; the plaintiffs stoutly resisted that proposal.) And if the law were clear, how would the facts (and thus the damages per plaintiff) be ascertained? One suit is an all-or-none affair, with high risk even if the parties supply all the information at their disposal. Getting things right the first time would be an accident. * * * When courts think of efficiency, they should think of market models rather than central-planning models.

Our decision in [In re] Rhone-Poulenc Rorer, [51 F.3d 1293 (7th Cir. 1995)], made this point, and it is worth reiterating: only "a decentralized process of multiple trials, involving different juries, and different standards of liability, in different jurisdictions" (51 F.3d at 1299) will yield the information needed for accurate evaluation of mass tort claims. Once a series of decisions or settlements has produced an accurate evaluation of a subset of the claims (say, 1995 Explorers in Arizona equipped with a particular tire specification) the others in that subset can be settled or resolved at an established price.

No matter what one makes of the decentralized approach as an original matter, it is hard to adopt the central-planner model without violence not only to Rule 23 but also to principles of federalism. Differences across states may be costly for courts and litigants alike, but they are a fundamental aspect of our federal republic and must not be overridden in a quest to clear the queue in court. See BMW v. Gore, 517 U.S. at 568–73. Tempting as it is to alter doctrine in order to facilitate class treatment, judges must resist so that all parties' legal rights may be respected. Amchem Products, Inc. v. Windsor, 521 U.S. 591, 613 (1997).

NOTES AND QUESTIONS

1.   As demonstrated by Castano v. The American Tobacco Co., *supra* p. 280, differences in state law may pose a powerful obstacle to class certification. *Shutts* (*supra* p. 388) places constitutional limits on efforts by states to solve those problems by applying one set of legal rules to all class members. On remand, the Kansas Supreme Court determined that, on the question whether prejudgment interest was due, the law of Kansas was not different from that of the other five states whose law was briefed by Phillips, and that the prejudgment interest rate applied by all would be the same. Shutts v. Phillips Petroleum Co., 732 P.2d 1286 (Kan. 1987), cert. denied, 487 U.S. 1223 (1988). As to post-judgment interest, however, there were disparities in the rates of the different states. On that issue, the court directed that the interest be determined by the law of the state in which the lease was located without explaining how it decided on that standard. See 732 P.2d at 1314. Should the court instead have tried to determine which law, within the range allowed by due process, would best further the interests of plaintiffs or defendants, or give claimants a choice between the law of their state of residence and the law of the state in which the lease was located where those differed?

2.   Should courts approach choice of law in class actions in the same way they do in individual suits? For example, Ysbrand v. DaimlerChrysler Corp., 81 P.3d 618 (Okla. 2003), was a suit alleging defective installation of air bags in minivans. The court held that, under the "most significant relationship" test, the law of Michigan, defendant's principal place of business, would apply to breach of warranty claims. This conclusion was based on Michigan's interest "in having its regulatory scheme applied to the conduct of a Michigan manufacturer." But the court found that the law of the states in which the class members were domiciled should be applied to fraud claims, making a class action on those claims unmanageable. In Farmers Ins. Exch. v. Leonard & Sawyer, 125 S.W.3d 55 (Tex.App. 2003), a contract-claim class action by agents against their company for failure to pay bonuses as promised, the court applied the law of California to the claims of all class members because the insurance group had its principal place of business in California, and administered the bonus contracts from there. These factors outweighed the interests of the states in which the agents performed their duties.

Shutts' emphasis on the need to examine each claim to assess the constitutional limits on choice of law strengthens the argument that the class action should be viewed that way. But in consolidated cases courts have seemed to strain to find a single set of legal rules applicable. For example, In re Air Crash Disaster Near Chicago, Illinois, on May 25, 1979, 644 F.2d 633 (7th Cir. 1981), involved cases gathered pursuant to a multidistrict transfer. Presented with the question whether plaintiffs could seek punitive damages, the court surveyed the choice-of-law doctrines of many states and ended up concluding, rather remarkably, that all of these states would choose to apply

Illinois law. Cf. Boardman Petroleum, Inc. v. Federated Mut. Ins. Co., 135 F.3d 750 (11th Cir. 1998) (in transferred consolidated cases, court uses "balancing of interests" test because "of necessity only one state's law may be applied").

In Mazza v. American Honda Motor Co., 666 F.3d 581 (9th Cir. 2012), the court applied California choice-of-law principles to reject arguments that a California federal court should apply that state's distinctive Unfair Business Practices law to all claims in a nationwide class even though defendant's American headquarters were located in California. Defense-side lawyers predicted that this decision would spell the end of nationwide class actions under California law. See Blaine Evanson & Andrew Pappas, An End to Nationwide Consumer Class Actions?, S.F. Daily Journal, Jan. 20, 2014, at 4. For an argument that states indulging in a "presumption of similarity" to apply forum law to all class members is improper, see Michael Green, Horizontal *Erie* and the Presumption of Forum Law, 109 Mich.L.Rev. 1237 (2011).

3.   In *Bridgestone/Firestone*, the court notes and rejects the "central planning" attitude of the ALI Complex Litigation Project. That Project proposed that where otherwise-applicable laws conflict in consolidated proceedings for transactionally related cases under proposed expanded transfer and removal provisions, the transferee judge be directed to choose a single controlling law for all cases, and it proposed choice of law guidelines that could be used for the purpose. See American Law Institute, Complex Litigation: Statutory Recommendations and Analysis §§ 6.01 (mass torts); 6.02–6.03 (mass contracts); 6.04 (statutes of limitation); 6.05 (monetary relief generally); 6.06 (punitive damages) (1994). Note that, as the court recognizes, the conduct of defendants in *Bridgestone/Firestone* was uniform and directed from a single place. Do those circumstances support efforts to find a single set of rules to measure the legality of that conduct? Consider the view of the Third Circuit when approving a nationwide settlement in In re Prudential Ins. Co. of America Sales Practices Litig., 148 F.3d 283, 290 (3d Cir. 1998):

> It may be argued that problems national in scope deserve the attention of the national courts when there is appropriate federal jurisdiction. * * * [F]airness counsels that plaintiffs similarly injured by the same course of deceptive conduct receive similar results with respect to liability and damages.

Reconsider the choice-of-law decision found improper in *Shutts*. Except for constitutional limitations, was that improper? Would a federal court entertaining the same case do things differently? Patrick Woolley, Choice of Law and the Protection of Class Members in Class Suits Certified Under Federal Rules of Civil Procedure 23(b)(3), 2004 Mich.St.L.Rev. 799, argues that a state-law presumption that forum law should govern in a class action should, under Klaxon Co. v. Stentor Elec. Mfg. Co., 313 U.S. 487 (1941), be applied by the federal court as well.

4.   Does *Shutts* hold that due process requires a separate choice of law analysis for every class member? In In re St. Jude Medical, Inc., 425 F.3d 1116 (8th Cir. 2005), the court reversed certification of a nationwide class asserting

claims under the Minnesota consumer protection statutes for alleged defects in heart valve implants. Reversal was required, the court concluded, "because the district court did not conduct a thorough conflicts-of-law analysis with respect to each plaintiff class member before applying Minnesota law." Id. at 1120. Compare General Motors Corp. v. Bryant, 285 S.W.3d 634 (Ark. 2008) (rejecting a requirement that the court conduct a rigorous choice of law analysis before determining whether common questions predominate).

5.   Looking to the law of the home state of every class member (not to mention other countries) can be difficult. For example, in Zinser v. Accufix Research Institute, Inc., 253 F.3d 1180 (9th Cir. 2001), plaintiffs proposed that Colorado law be applied to the claims of all class members in a proposed nationwide products liability class action. Because the case was in a California federal court, the pertinent choice of law rules were the California version of the "governmental interest" analysis, which looks to which state's interests would be "more impaired" were its law not applied. As applied to this proposed nationwide class action, this analysis led to a byzantine choice of law determination (id. at 1188):

> As the district court explained, "the three-part California choice of law inquiry requires comparison of each non-forum state's law and interest with California's law and interest *separately*." As required by California law, Zinser thus must apply California's three-part conflict test to *each* non-forum state with an interest in the application of its law. Also, because Zinser seeks certification of three separate claims—negligence, products liability, and medical monitoring—this conflicts test must be applied to *each* claim upon which certification is sought.

The reality is that choice of law is hard to do. Thus, a district judge trying to navigate this thicket complained that "[t]he law on 'choice of law' in the various states and in the federal courts is a veritable jungle, which, if the law can be found out, leads not to a 'rule of action' but a reign of chaos dominated in each case by the judge's 'informed guess' as to what some other state than the one in which he sits would hold its law to be." In re Paris Air Crash of March 3, 1974, 399 F.Supp. 732, 739 (C.D.Cal. 1975). This situation has not improved dramatically since. For a more recent illustration, see Senne v. Kansas City Royals Baseball Corp., 934 F.3d 918 (9th Cir. 2019), in which the majority spent ten pages working through California's multi-step choice of law standards, and Judge Ikuta vigorously contested the majority's choice of law analysis in her dissent.

6.   Besides state choice-of-law doctrine, as *Shutts* suggests, due process limits a state's desire to apply its own law. In BMW of North America v. Gore, 517 U.S. 559 (1996), cited by the court in *Bridgestone/Firestone*, plaintiff in an individual suit received a large punitive damages award that the state court recognized was premised in large measure on proof that defendant had treated other customers in other states the same way it treated him. But there was no showing that the conduct in question was unlawful in the states where these customers resided, and the Court concluded that "Alabama does not have the

power * * * to punish BMW for conduct that was lawful where it occurred and had no impact on Alabama or its residents." Id. at 572–73. In State Farm Mut. Auto. Ins. Co. v. Campbell, 538 U.S. 408 (2003), it reiterated that "[a] state cannot punish a defendant for conduct that may have been lawful where it occurred."

The same constraints would seem to matter in class actions. Urging that choice of law should be understood as an integral part of substantive law, Professor Kramer has argued that impulses toward class-action choice of law practices that facilitate aggregate treatment should be resisted:

> Because choice of law is part of the process of defining the parties' rights, it should not change simply because, as a matter of administrative convenience and efficiency, we have combined many claims in one proceeding; whatever choice-of-law rules we use to define substantive rights should be the same for ordinary and complex cases.

Larry Kramer, Choice of Law in Complex Litigation, 71 N.Y.U.L. Rev. 547, 549 (1996).

7.   In *Bridgestone/Firestone*, the court says that "[n]o class action is proper unless all litigants are governed by the same legal rules." In Washington Mutual Bank v. Superior Court, 15 P.3d 1071 (Cal. 2001), the California Supreme Court insisted on a careful analysis of these questions at the outset in state-court class actions:

> [W]e hold that a class action proponent must credibly demonstrate, through a thorough analysis of the applicable state laws, that state law variations will not swamp common issues and defeat predominance. Additionally, the proponent's presentation must be sufficient to permit the trial court, at the time of certification, to make a detailed assessment of how any state law differences could be managed fairly and efficiently at trial, for example, through the creation of a manageable number of subclasses.

Professor Kramer does not think that the problem is necessarily insurmountable (Kramer, *supra*, 71 N.Y.U.L.Rev. at 584):

> [C]omplex litigation could really become unmanageable if, once the various substantive laws were compiled and organized, the judge still had to perform hundreds or thousands of individualized choice-of-law analyses. But because variation in the legal rules is not great, once the state-by-state survey is completed, judges will find a relatively small number of conflicts and an equally small number of approaches to choice of law. At that point, claims can be grouped and the task of resolving the conflicts completed in a fairly efficient manner. It may not be fun, but it is far from impossible.

Courts have sometimes been receptive to this approach have also cautioned: "The burden of showing uniformity or the existence of only a small number of applicable standards (that is, 'groupability') among the laws of the fifth states rests squarely with the plaintiffs." Klay v. Humana, Inc., 382 F.3d 1241, 1262 (11th Cir. 2004). When plaintiffs do a cursory job, the court need not do their work for them, as the Third Circuit explained in Gradalski v. Quest Diagnostics, Inc., 767 F.3d 175 (3d Cir. 2014):

> We agree with the District Court [which denied certification] and conclude that while grouping, in general, may be a permissible approach to nationwide class action litigation, in this case Appellants did not provide enough information or analysis of the classes they proposed. For example, in In re Prudential [Ins. Co. Sales Practices Litig., 148 F.3d 283 (3d Cir. 1998)], we noted that the grouping proposal there consisted of a "series of charts setting forth comprehensive analyses of the various states' laws potentially applicable to their common law claims." Such in-depth treatment justified the District Court's decision to group state laws in that case, but is lacking here.

Should the court be equally demanding about the showing supporting grouping when certification is sought only for purposes of settlement? In Sullivan v. DB Investments, Inc., 667 F.3d 273, 303–04 (3d Cir. 2011), the court said no: "Because we are presented with a settlement class certification, we are not as concerned with formulating some prediction as to how [variations in state law] would play out at trial, for the proposal is that there be no trial. As such, we simply need not inquire whether the varying state treatments * * * would present the type of 'insuperable obstacles' or 'intractable management problems' pertinent to certification of a litigation class." Accord, In re Hyundai and Kia Fuel Economy Litig., 926 F.3d 539 (9th Cir. 2019) (en banc).

8.   Is state law likely to be more uniform on some subjects than others? Recall that there are Restatements and Uniform Laws that have many adherents. But even on those topics, uniformity may prove elusive. Consider the views of a leading treatise: "The Uniform Commercial Code is not uniform." James White & Robert Summers, Uniform Commercial Code 7 (2d ed. 1980); see Powers v. Lycoming Engines, 272 F.R.D. 414 (E.D.Pa. 2011) (finding that all states but one had adopted UCC § 2–314, but that their interpretations different significantly). How is the court to determine whether there is a real conflict in the laws of the various states? What if the jury instructions in the various states are virtually identical? Should appellate decisions that appear divergent be considered as well? If the jury is to be instructed in the same way in all the affected states, can't a trial be handled without difficulty despite any supposed differences in applicable law?

9.   Differences in applicable law could defeat certification of even a mandatory class. In Casa Orlando Apartments, Ltd. v. Federal Nat. Mortg. Ass'n, 624 F.3d 185 (5th Cir. 2010), the court rejected certification under Rule 23(b)(1)(A) even though the suit challenged allegedly nationwide practices involving the federal agency Fannie Mae (id. at 198):

> [W]e find that various state laws apply to different class members. Therefore, varying judgments with respect to Plaintiffs' injunctive

requests would not be "incompatible" but rather would reflect diverse state fiduciary law. As the Supreme Court has advised, Rule 23(b)(1)(A) encompasses cases in which the defendant is obliged to treat members of the class alike. Here, various state laws may result in some class members having a fiduciary relationship with Fannie Mae while others do not. Under Rule 23(b)(1)(A), dissimilar outcomes that result from differing state laws are insufficient to justify class certification.

10. *Effect of preemption*: Preemption has been important in litigation arising in a number of areas in which there is federal regulation, including banking, environmental law, business practices, pension and insurance benefits, and product liability (particularly as to pharmaceuticals and medical devices). In general, it has been raised by defendants seeking to defeat state-law tort claims on the ground that federal regulations preempt state law, and that only federal requirements apply. See, e.g., Wyeth v. Levine, 555 U.S. 555 (2009) (holding that state-law failure-to-warn claims could proceed despite defendant's argument that they were preempted because the warning label had been approved by the federal Food & Drug Administration); Mary Davis, The Battle Over Implied Preemption: Products Liability and the FDA, 48 Bos.Coll.L.Rev. 1089 (2007). Where preemption applies, the requirements of state law no longer matter. Although preemption has been regarded as assisting defense interests, might it not also serve the interests of plaintiffs seeking nationwide certification? Samuel Issacharoff & Catherine Sharkey, Backdoor Federalism, 53 UCLA L. Rev. 1353, 1365–98 (2006), examines preemption from this perspective and reasons that the existence of a national market should support the application of a single law in class actions, as explored in the next note regarding CAFA. To the extent nationwide legal provisions define the obligations of national manufacturers, would that not solve the choice of law problem for class actions?

11. Should CAFA affect choice of law issues in class actions in cases subject to its jurisdictional provisions? Consider Issacharoff & Sharkey, *supra*, 53 UCLA L. Rev. at 1419–20:

> Although CAFA declared its intent to leave Erie [Railroad Co. v. Tompkins, 304 U.S. 64 (1938)] untouched, once national-market cases are jurisdictionally isolated in federal courts, the need to develop incremental decisional law to address the particular concerns of these cases will be inescapable. * * * The likely effect of CAFA will then be to allow a body of national law to develop that corresponds to the demands of an undifferentiated market in which products are manufactured and sent to consumers across a distributional chain of ever-expanding geographic reach.

See also Samuel Issacharoff, Settled Expectations in a World of Unsettled Law: Choice of Law After the Class Action Fairness Act, 106 Colum. L. Rev. 1839 (2006); Samuel Issacharoff, Getting Beyond Kansas, 74 UMKC L. Rev. 613 (2006). But the legislative history of CAFA denies any such intention, and many cases subject to federal jurisdiction under CAFA certainly do not implicate national interests. See Evans v. Walter Indus., Inc., *supra* p. 365. For a critique of this argument that CAFA supports development of nationwide legal principles, see Richard Marcus, Assessing CAFA's Stated Jurisdictional Policy, 156 U. Pa. L. Rev. 1765, 1808–20 (2008).

K. NOTICE, OPT OUT, AND COMMUNICATIONS WITH CLASS MEMBERS

Notice and Right to Opt Out

Rule 23(c)(2)(B) says that in (b)(3) class actions "the court must direct to class members the best notice that is practicable under the circumstances, including individual notice to all members who can be identified through reasonable effort," and that this notice must provide them a right to opt out. For (b)(1) and (b)(2) class actions, Rule 23(c)(2)(A) says that "the court may direct appropriate notice to the class," although in such cases Rule 23(e)(1) requires "notice in a reasonable manner to all class members who would be bound" by a proposed settlement. Though class members may then object to the proposed settlement, there is no rule provision requiring a right to opt out in (b)(1) or (b)(2) class actions.

Individual notice is required in Rule 23(b)(3) class actions partly to address due process concerns. For decades, it was assumed that the "gold standard" for notice was first class mail. But U.S. mail no longer occupies the central place it held for Americans through the 20th century, and in 2018 Rule 23(c)(2)(B) was amended to call for notice "by one or more of the following: United States mail, electronic means, or other appropriate means." The Committee Note accompanying the amendment explained that the rule does not prefer any means of notice; instead, it "relies on courts and counsel to focus on the means or combination of means most likely to be effective in the case before the court." For a pre-amendment example of notice issues, consider Roes, 1–2 v. SFBSC Manag. LLC, 944 F.3d 1035 (9th Cir. 2019), a class action on behalf of exotic dancers who are "transient" and hard to reach by U.S. mail. Objectors pointed out that email would probably work better, but defendants said they did not have email addresses. The court was unmoved: "[E]ven if, as defendants suggest, email notice was infeasible, information about the settlement could have been electronically disseminated through social media or postings on any relevant online message boards." Id. At 1047.

NOTES AND QUESTIONS

1. What is the purpose of notice? Two general possibilities exist. First, class members can *monitor* the conduct of the class action and apply to the court for relief if they think it is being mis-handled. Should notice to millions of class members be required for that purpose. Cf. Mullane v. Central Hanover Bank & Trust Co., 339 U.S. 306 (1950) (notice reasonably calculated to reach

most of those affected should safeguard the interests of all because those notified can raise objections on behalf of all). Second, each class member can, where permitted, make a personal *decision whether to opt out*. For this purpose, it would not seem that notice to any class member is a substitute for notice to another.

Do these considerations matter less in (b)(1) and (b)(2) class actions than in (b)(3) class actions? See Larionoff v. United States, 533 F.2d 1167 (D.C.Cir. 1975) (stating that "members of a Rule 23(b)(1) class are likely to be more unified in the sense that there will probably be little interest on the part of individual members in controlling and directing their own separate litigation"). But for an argument that lack of notice in (b)(2) class actions violates due process, see Mark Weber, Preclusion and Procedural Due Process in Rule 23(b)(2) Class Actions, 21 U.Mich.J.Law Reform 347 (1988).

2. How much is notice really worth to class members? In 1972, Prof. Miller found that many who received notice in one antitrust class action clearly did not understand the notices they received. See Arthur Miller, Problems in Giving Notice in Class Actions, 58 F.R.D. 313, 321–22 (1972) (quoting letters back to the clerk of court from class members). Rule 23(c)(2)(B) now says that in (b)(3) cases the notice must be clear and concise and be in "plain, easily understood language." The Manual for Complex Litigation (4th) points out that question-and-answer formats can make information easier for many readers to absorb, and also makes suggestions for increasing comprehension.

3. Should the cost of notice ever matter? In Larson v. AT & T Mobility LLC, 687 F.3d 109 (3d Cir. 2012), defendant agreed to search certain of records to identify class members eligible for benefits under a settlement, and the district court decided to approve its search without including additional searches that would take a month or two and cost about $100,000 more. The court of appeals held this was inadequate, rejecting the idea that "costs are the primary driver in the judgment on notice." Id. at 128.

Contrast Hughes v. Kore of Indiana Enter., Inc., 731 F.3d 672 (7th Cir. 2013), a class action based on defendant's failure to post notices about charges for using its ATMs. After concluding that the possible payout would be only $4 per transaction, the district court decertified the case. But the court of appeals ruled that extensive and expensive efforts to identify class members were not required, and that posting a sticker on ATMs and printing the users' names in a local paper would suffice, given that there was no indication that any individual class members wanted to sue for this small recovery. Allowing the class action to go forward in this manner could be a "wake up" call for defendants.

4. Ordinarily plaintiff cannot use discovery to get a list of class members even if it can be obtained from defendant's records. Oppenheimer Fund, Inc. v. Sanders, 437 U.S. 340 (1978) (compilation of the list was not relevant to any substantive issue in the case). Note that discovery about numerosity might resemble this kind of discovery, but it is different because it bears on an issue the court must decide. Sometimes the effort involved to identify class members

can be very costly. See In re Domestic Air Transportation Antitrust Litigation, 141 F.R.D. 534 (N.D.Ga. 1992) (estimate of 1.2 million hours necessary to identify United Airlines customers in the class).

5.   Using electronic means to give notice may be a small part of the potential for internet-based communications to improve governance and oversight in class actions. For an examination of those possibilities, see Elizabeth Cabraser & Samuel Issacharoff, The Participatory Class Action, 92 N.Y.U.L.Rev. 846 (2017). In 2019, the Federal Trade Commission released a report on its study of class notice practices, also highlighting new methods. For discussion, see Perry Cooper, Class Settlement Portal, Other Innovations Could Improve Payouts, Bloomberg Law News, Oct. 31, 2019; Perry Cooper, FTC Looking for Ways to Improve Consumer Responses to Class Deals, Bloomberg Law News, Sept. 11, 2019.

Communications with Unnamed Class Members

Notice is a formal communication in the name of the court with class members. There may be many other communications with them about the case, and courts may be called upon to regulate those communications. For some time, courts routinely ordered that class counsel have no communications before certification with unnamed class members. In Gulf Oil Co. v. Bernard, 452 U.S. 89 (1981), the Court held that such orders could only be entered on a showing that counsel had engaged or were about to engage in some impropriety. In particular, the Court noted that counsel may need to communicate with class members to prepare a class-certification motion or for other matters of case preparation.

Communications between the class opponent and class members can be more problematical. Such communications may be necessary in some instances, such as a suit by a class of employees against the employer. Assuming the employment relationship continues, the parties must continue to communicate with each other about work assignments, etc. But the potential for coercive activity is obviously present as well. For example, in Wang v. Chinese Daily News, Inc., 623 F.3d 743 (9th Cir. 2010), an action under the Fair Labor Standards Act and California labor laws, defendant supposedly launched a campaign to persuade class members to opt out that included what the district court found were coercive tactics. Current employees opted out at a 90% rate, and former employees at a 25% rate. The district court nullified the opt outs and directed that there be a second opt-out period after the trial on the merits. The court of appeals approved. So district courts can regulate the time, place and manner of contacts by the class opponent with class members if there are indicates of improprieties. See Note, Limiting Coercive Speech in Class Actions, 114 Yale L.J. 1953 (2005) (arguing that there should be prophylactic limitations on communications between defendant and class members when there is a "structurally coercive relationship" between them).

NOTES AND QUESTIONS

1.   Before class certification, it is difficult to say that a normal attorney-client relationship exists between unnamed class members and the proposed class counsel. Professional responsibility rules generally require counsel for a party not to communicate with an opposing party represented by counsel. How should that affect the behavior of the defendant's lawyer in a class action? Are unnamed class members "parties" at that point? Should they be regarded as represented by class counsel even though the court has not yet appointed counsel to represent the class?

2.   If there are no limitations on communications with class members, what should the court do if they execute releases, perhaps for consideration, of the claims asserted on their behalf in the class action? Settlements with individual class members can be viewed as akin to opting out of the case. But Rule 23(e) is meant to give the court supervisory power and responsibility regarding the fairness of classwide settlements. See *infra* p. 545 for discussion of the court's performance of that duty. Most courts find they have authority after certification to regulate contacts between the defendant and plaintiff class members to avoid overreaching.

3.   The rules change once a court has determined that the action can be maintained as a class action. Before certification it may be said that the class members are not "represented by" class counsel for purposes of A.B.A. Model Rule of Professional Conduct 4.2, which forbids communication by an attorney with an opposing party represented by counsel. Once the class has been certified and class counsel appointed, however, the rules governing communications apply as though each class member is the client of class counsel. Manual for Complex Litigation (4th) § 21.33 (2004). See Dodona I, LLC v. Goldman, Sachs & Co., 300 F.R.D. 182 (S.D.N.Y. 2014) (court would not restrict defendant's communications with class members, but noted that the rules of professional conduct called for defense counsel to limit their communications to class counsel); compare Camp v. Alexander, 300 F.R.D. 617 (N.D.Cal. 2014) (employer's letters to potential class members accusing named plaintiff of greed and attacking plaintiff counsel were improper).

The relationship between class counsel and class members after class certification is not exactly the same as the relationship between a lawyer and an individual client. For example, in Wyly v. Milberg Weiss Bershad & Schulman, 850 N.Y.S.2d 14 (N.Y.App.Div. 2007), aff'd, 908 N.E.2d 888 (N.Y. 2009), the court held that such a class member did not have an absolute right to obtain all counsel's files in relation to a settled class action. Although a class member had some of the benefits of the attorney-client relationship, such as the right to privileged communications with counsel and prohibition against attempts by defense counsel to communicate with him, he did not have other rights, such as the right to fire class counsel or an absolute right of access to counsel's files.

Attorneys' use of the Internet can also complicate the attorney-client relationship. In Barton v. United States District Court, 410 F.3d 1104 (9th Cir.

2005), a law firm interested in asserted claims for users of Paxil posted a questionnaire on the Internet seeking information from "potential class members." But to submit the form, it was necessary to click a "yes" box that acknowledged that the questionnaire "does not constitute a request for legal advice and that I am not forming an attorney client relationship by submitting this information." The four plaintiffs involved in the litigation filled out and submitted these forms, as did thousands of other people. Eventually, the district court did not certify a class, and these four people filed suit as individual clients of the law firm. As their cases were approaching trial, defendant demanded production of their answers to the questionnaire. The court of appeals held that under California law (see Fed. R. Evid. 501) the disclaimer—necessary to protect against malpractice liability—did not prevent the prospective clients from relying on confidentiality even though there was no existing attorney-client relationship.

4. The defendant is not the only potential source of efforts to subvert the class action. In Georgine v. Amchem Products, Inc., 160 F.R.D. 478 (E.D.Pa. 1995), the judge invalidated the opt-outs of class members on the ground that many of them had been misled about the terms of the settlement by objecting plaintiff lawyers. Some 235,000 class members had sent in opt-out forms, but more than 95% of these opt-outs had evidently been on forms provided by the objectors rather than the court. The judge found that over 62,500 misleading letters had been sent out by objectors, and that at least 667,550 people had been misled by these letters or by advertisements the objectors placed in newspapers. He therefore ordered that those who opted out be noticed again and given another opportunity to decide whether to opt out. Thereafter, the Supreme Court upheld objectors' arguments that the class had been certified improperly. See Amchem Products, Inc. v. Windsor, *supra* p. 311. For a more recent example, see Kathleen Dailey, CVS Wage Deal Opponents Blocked from "Soliciting" Class Opt-Outs, Bloomberg Law News, Nov. 3, 2020 (describing emergency injunction against online efforts by proposed intervenors in class action who set up a website with opt-out forms and instructions).

5. *Discovery from unnamed class members.* For a defendant sued by a large class, one inviting tactic would be to send interrogatories to be answered separately by each class member on pain of dismissal of the class member's claim. The conventional response of courts is that discovery from unnamed class members will be allowed only in unusual circumstances. For a thoughtful examination of the issues, see Fishon v. Peloton Interactive, Inc., 336 F.R.D. 67 (S.D.N.Y. 2020), a proposed class action on behalf of purchasers of defendant's fitness products, asserting that defendant had falsely claimed its products were worth more than they were actually worth. Defendant contended that discovery would show that many or most purchasers paid little or no attention to the challenged representations, and sought to take depositions of 21 potential class members in an effort to show that individual issues would predominate. Assured that the discovery was not "sought to harass or deter membership in the class," and that it was "necessary for purposes of the class certification determination," the court authorized ten depositions. See also In re Porsche Automobil Holding SE, 985 F.3d 115, 121

(1st Cir. 2021) ("courts should be attentive to the possibility of abuse when discovery is targeted directly or indirectly at passive class members"). Keep these issues in mind when we turn to screening claims in MDL proceedings, *infra* p. 451.

CHAPTER 6

MANAGING COMPLEX LITIGATION

∎ ∎ ∎

A. INTRODUCTION

This chapter focuses on a variety of techniques and issues related to the central role of the judge in modern complex litigation, and in other modern litigation. Until relatively recently, the American judge was ordinarily a "hands off" background figure who only got involved when a party filed a motion or the case was ready for trial. Beginning in the 1960s, however, many metropolitan federal courts adopted the "single assignment" system under which cases were assigned to the same judge for all purposes, and those judges began attending more carefully to supervision of those cases. In addition, the adoption of the MDL statute in 1968 (addressed in Chapter 4) meant that MDL transferee judges had a responsibility to manage the pretrial development of those cases.

As summarized in 1981 by Chief Judge Robert Peckham (N.D.Cal.), a leader in the judicial management movement, a judge using this approach would summon counsel for a conference early in the litigation, and use the occasion to establish a plan for the development of the case, and in particular the discovery that needed to be done, an activity that also "helps to illuminate possible grounds for motions to dismiss and for summary judgment." As the same time, the judge could "be alert to the particularly combative attorney who, if the case is not actively managed during pretrial, might succeed in turning a trial that should be a molehill into a mountain. * * * The meeting itself warns the attorneys that they have a vigilant judge, and it may therefore prod attorneys who might otherwise be less than diligent into transferring the case to their 'active' files. The conference can also give the judge a 'feel' for the case and the attorneys; he may pick up early signals that an attorney tends to be careless or to procrastinate, perhaps warranting a fairly rigid timetable and a warning that it will be strictly enforced. * * * He may glean that one or both attorneys are confused about important legal or other issues in the action, so that the later, formal pretrial conference and order should be comprehensive." Robert Peckham, The Federal Judge as Case Manager: The New Role in Guiding a Case From Filing to Disposition, 69 Calif. L. Rev. 770, 781–82 (1981). By this means, Judge Peckham urged, courts could achieve significant gains in efficiency.

This departure from the customary passive role of judges excited some opposition. Some see political overtones. See Sandra Gavin, Managerial

Justice in a Post-*Daubert* World: A Reliability Paradigm, 234 F.R.D. 196 (2006) (arguing that the array of management tools used by federal judges represents a "shift to the right"). Lest it seem that judicial management intrinsically favors defendants, consider Adam Slater, Streamlining MDLs, Trial Magazine, July 2016, at 60. Slater represented plaintiffs in an MDL involving claimed injuries due to use of a pharmaceutical product. "This MDL's process has been an exemplar of current trends in mass tort discovery, offering solutions to the inevitable defense-orchestrated roadblocks in most mass tort cases." Those tactics were overcome: "The court's aggressive oversight changed the litigation's entire dynamic, and it has produced swift decisions and relentless progress."

Professor Resnik has raised serious questions about this judicial activity, noting that "[m]anagement is a new form of 'judicial activism,' a behavior that usually attracts substantial criticism." Judith Resnik, Managerial Judges, 96 Harv. L. Rev. 374, 374 (1982). "Judicial management has its own techniques, goals, and values, which appear to elevate speed over deliberation, impartiality, and fairness." Id. at 380. District judges performing these tasks would have vast new powers not subject to effective review by appellate courts. She worried that, under this new arrangement there would be threats to judicial impartiality. In their managerial role, judges would receive extensive information and develop intense feelings about the lawyers with whom they interact. "[L]itigants who incur a judge's displeasure may suffer judicial hostility or even vengeance with little hope of relief." Id. at 425. At the same time, she cautioned, claims of actual improvements in efficiency could not be proved; it may be that the duration of cases and rate of disposition would be the same without this extensive judicial involvement. Some judges also resisted the shift to judicial management. See Patrick Higginbotham, Bureaucratizing the Courts? Finding MDL's Place in the Traditional Legal Culture, 99 Judicature 44 (2015).

Judge Peckham responded to Professor Resnik's critique by arguing that "[a] judge's duty has never been purely adjudication. Judges have long engaged in some form of case and calendar management as well as court administration, mediation, regulation of the bar, and other professional activities." Robert Peckham, A Judicial Response to the Cost of Litigation: Case Management, Two-Stage Discovery Planning and Alternative Dispute Resolution, 37 Rutgers L. Rev. 253, 253 (1985). He emphasized that judges develop the ability to "compartmentalize the relevant from the irrelevant and to detach one's emotional from one's rational faculties." Id. at 262. Although appellate review is unlikely to curtail this activity, "a settlement which results from one party's collapse in the face of the other party's unsupervised dilatory tactics is a far more probable example of an unfair and unreviewable termination of the action." Id. at 264. Finally, he argued, Professor Resnik "wishes to preserve the laissez-faire character of the adversarial system. I contend, however, that our adversarial system has run amok and that the movement toward judicial oversight represents an effort to preserve the best qualities of the system." Id. at 265.

The debate between Judge Peckham and Professor Resnik in the 1980s provides the backdrop for consideration of judicial management in the 21st century. In complex cases, at least, active judicial management has become a strongly encouraged norm. Indeed, the opening line of the Manual for Complex Litigation urges judges to consider themselves not only as adjudicators, but also as active supervisors and planners: "Fair and efficient resolution of complex litigation requires at least that * * * the court exercise early and effective supervision (and, where necessary control) [and that] the judge and counsel collaborate to develop and carry out a comprehensive plan for the conduct of pretrial and trial proceedings." Manual for Complex Litigation (4th) § 10.1 (2004).

Certainly the trend of the rules has been to foster the activity Judge Peckham endorsed. Beginning in 1983, Rule 16(b) directed judges to enter scheduling orders in most cases. As amended in 1993, Rule 26(d) provides that the parties should not commence formal discovery until they confer pursuant to Rule 26(f) to develop a discovery plan. That discovery plan must then be submitted to the court for consideration in connection with a scheduling order under Rule 16(b), which should be entered only after the judge interacts with the lawyers, and which must set deadlines for adding parties, filing motions, and completing discovery. The Rule 16(b) order may also deal with a wide variety of other things.

Case management is not limited to the U.S. federal courts. To the contrary, it has been likened to the more active control that judges in Continental judicial systems exert over private litigation, and has emerged in other common law systems as well:

The California Experience: Dealing with somewhat similar concerns about delay and cost of litigation, California took a different course in the 1980s with its Trial Court Delay Reduction Act, which was added to its Government Code, not its Code of Civil Procedure. See Richard Marcus, Malaise of the Litigation Superpower, in Civil Justice in Crisis (A. Zuckerman, ed., 1999), at 71, 103–04. This legislation commanded prompter handling of litigation and led to computer-generated deadlines that prompted strong objections from lawyers. See id. at 106–07. In light of these concerns, the Legislature modified the Act in 1990 to introduce more flexibility. Despite that injection of flexibility, concerns about rigidity remained and the implementing rules were amended to ensure that continuances would be flexibly granted and that multiple factors were considered in setting litigation schedules. See Cal. Rules of Court 3.750–3.771 (dealing with management of complex cases and class actions).

Case Management in England: Based on a comprehensive study of English civil litigation in the mid-1990s, England adopted new Civil Procedure Rules in 1998 that "transformed English civil procedure" and represent "a radical departure from past practice." Adrian Zuckerman, Civil Procedure 1 (2003). One "cornerstone" of this new regime is case management. Neil Andrews, English Civil Procedure 337 (2003). Case management in England is handled differently from the U.S. federal courts because England does not use a single assignment system. Instead, it emphasizes reliance on management teams of "procedural judges" and tracking according to case type to assign cases to one of three tracks. Within each track, there are firm timetables and limitations on the amount of litigation activity the parties may undertake without authorization by the judge. Although this regime has curtailed attorney latitude, it is said not to have eroded the basically adversarial nature of English litigation. For discussion, see Zuckerman, *supra*, chs. 10 and 11, and Andrews, *supra*, chs. 2 and 13.

As we turn to the specific activities that occupy judges, then, it is important to keep the background debate in mind. Have judges intruded too much into litigation before them? Should they become even more active?

B. SCHEDULING ORDERS

IN RE NEW MOTOR VEHICLES CANADIAN EXPORT ANTITRUST LITIGATION

United States District Court, District of Maine, 2005.
229 F.R.D. 35.

HORNBY, DISTRICT JUDGE.

The issue here is whether to entertain now, in the midst of an otherwise carefully planned schedule for managing this case, a defendant's summary judgment motion whose timing caught everyone by surprise. I conclude that the correct answer is "No." I Grant the plaintiffs' motion to stay action on the motion. To explain why, I begin with a description of previous proceedings, to give a flavor of their complexity and the need for judicial management.

Previous Proceedings

On June 26 and August 12, 2003, the Judicial Panel on Multidistrict Litigation transferred 26 cases to this Court from around the country. The cases involve federal and state antitrust claims, state consumer protection claims, and claims for unjust enrichment, all growing out of allegations that car manufacturers, dealers and trade associations improperly restrict the entry of Canadian cars into the American market. Currently there are 23 defendants, 57 plaintiffs (seeking class status), and the service list includes 68 lawyers. By a procedural order dated July 31, 2003, all discovery was immediately stayed until an initial pretrial conference could be held. I made clear that I would follow the procedures of the Manual for Complex Litigation (Third) (now Fourth).

The first conference was held September 26, 2003. At that time, the defendants' lawyer spoke of the cases as a "monster" and told me that with over seventy pending lawsuits, coordination with state courts was imperative so that the state cases not "get out ahead of whatever schedule we adopt here." The defendants' lawyers expressed their strong interest in having the case move forward in planned stages.

On October 1, 2003, the plaintiffs filed a Consolidated Amended Complaint. On October 3, 2003, I entered a Stipulated Protective Order to protect such matters as the defendants' confidential competitive and financial information. On October 7, 2003, I appointed liaison counsel for the plaintiffs and liaison counsel for the defendants.

Substantial discussion ensued on how to coordinate these consolidated federal multidistrict proceedings with a variety of parallel state court proceedings. The discussions went forward in lawyer correspondence and telephone calls among themselves and with the Court, conferences of counsel with the Court, status reports, and correspondence by me with state judges and telephone calls and a visit with one of them.

In the meantime, motion practice was proceeding in the form of motions to dismiss on a variety of grounds. On November 17, 2003, I expressed in a written order my concern over the repetitiveness of the defendants' filings in connection with a motion to dismiss.

Oral argument on the motions to dismiss occurred on January 5, 2004. On March 4, 2004, I granted three defendants' motion to dismiss for lack of personal jurisdiction, deferred action as to one defendant pending some discovery, and denied the motion as to two other defendants. I granted in part and denied in part a separate motion to dismiss for failure to state a claim upon which relief can be granted. The 44 pages it took to rule on the motions are some indication of their difficulty. On April 21, 2004, on the defendants' request I entered a limited certificate for interlocutory appellate review as to the two defendants whose motion to dismiss for lack of personal jurisdiction I had denied. (The court of appeals declined the interlocutory appeal.)

On April 23, 2004, the plaintiffs filed a Second Amended Complaint in response to my ruling on the motion to dismiss for failure to state a claim upon which relief can be granted.

On April 28, 2004, I entered a Joint Coordination Order designed for use in both this federal multidistrict proceeding and in the parallel state court proceedings around the country. It reflected the input of the lawyers and my conferences with Judge Richard Kramer of the California Superior Court. It has subsequently been entered in a number of the state court proceedings as well.

On June 10, 2004, all defendants filed a motion to dismiss some of the claims in the Second Amended Complaint. On that date, certain defendants also filed a motion to decline supplemental jurisdiction over the state law claims and to dismiss the state law claims against the Canadian defendants for lack of personal jurisdiction.

On June 14, 2004, the lawyers for all parties filed a joint proposed schedule for future events, including discovery, that would carry the litigation up through a proposed class certification schedule. A conference of counsel then occurred in court on June 16, 2004. Although it was obvious to everyone that there would be motions for summary judgment at the end of discovery, no one ever suggested that the schedule or the state of the record would permit a summary judgment motion sooner. Having already ruled on two very complex motions to dismiss and with two more such motions, even more complex, pending before me, I certainly would have wanted to discuss the timing of any such additional motions if they had been in anyone's contemplation.[1] But there was no hint of any such motions. On June 16, 2004, I entered a Scheduling Order accordingly, that scheduled events up through the time of setting a class certification schedule. I also notified all the state judges with parallel actions, certainly with no suggestion that summary judgment motions were imminent.

On August 11, 2004, I entered a Master Protective Order. On August 25, 2004, I held oral argument on the second round of motions to dismiss. On September 7, 2004, I denied the motion to dismiss for lack of personal jurisdiction and the motion to decline supplemental jurisdiction. On December 8, 2004, I denied a motion by certain Tennessee state court plaintiffs to intervene solely to participate in discovery. On December 8, I also granted in part and denied in part the defendants' motion to dismiss certain state law claims. That 90-page ruling required me to review the antitrust laws of 11 states, the consumer protection laws of 29 states and the District of Columbia, and the common law of unjust enrichment as applied to the state antitrust and consumer protection claims.

On January 26, 2005, Magistrate Judge Kravchuk held a telephone conference of counsel. She permitted the plaintiffs to file a Third Amended Complaint in light of my December 8 ruling, but only upon assurance by the defendants' lawyer that permitting the amendment would not occasion any new substantive motions.

On January 27, 2005, the parties asked me to resolve their disagreement over how to structure the class certification debate. On February 11, 2005, I denied a motion for reconsideration of my December 8 ruling on the motion to dismiss, saying that if the motion arguments

---

[1] I did express my concern over the new motion practice following my previous rulings on motions to dismiss, but determined that it was appropriate in light of dramatic changes in the amended complaint. I also made clear my concern that the litigation as a whole move forward in an orderly and strategic fashion.

"have any merit, they can be presented at the stage of summary judgment motion practice." I hardly had in mind that we had almost reached that stage.

On February 15, 2005, I held another conference of counsel. General Motors' lawyer spoke extensively on class certification issues, but made no mention of any summary judgment motions in the offing. All the indications were that the lawyers for all parties were cooperating on discovery and schedule issues. I made clear that I did "not want the schedule strung out. We have been at this for quite a while now."

On February 25, 2005, I entered a procedural order requiring the parties to clarify their positions on whether these cases would remain in Maine after pretrial proceedings. On March 7, 2005, I denied another motion for limited intervention by certain Tennessee state court plaintiffs and denied an attempt by outside counsel to dismiss the Tennessee claims already existing in this case.

On March 11, 2005, the parties filed a stipulation that all these cases would remain in the District of Maine and not be subject to transfer back to their originating districts.

On March 15, 2005, I entered a procedural order permitting the parties to proceed with class certification by designating exemplar classes for the state damages claims. In that order I also scheduled the class certification proceedings up through a December 6, 2005, hearing on the class-certification motion. This schedule was in response to the parties' proposals. I understood that the schedule that they proposed and I adopted was the quickest the parties could move, devoting their full energies to these issues. Under this schedule: both parties were to complete document production by May 13, 2005 and class-certification-related depositions by July 1, 2005; the plaintiffs must disclose their class-certification experts and file their class-certification brief and expert reports by July 29, 2005; the defendants must complete depositions of the plaintiffs' class-certification experts by August 30, 2005, and disclose their class certification experts and file their opposition brief and expert reports by September 30, 2005; and the plaintiffs must complete depositions of the defendants' experts by October 28, 2005, and file their reply brief and any expert rebuttal report by November 18, 2005. I expected that everyone's attention would be focused on these issues. If I had thought there were time for other matters, I would have shortened the proposed schedule. On March 15, 2005, I also updated all the state judges, again with no reference to contemplated summary judgment practice in the offing.

So it is an understatement to say that I was surprised to receive an electronic notice on June 10, 2005, that General Motors had just filed its motion for summary judgment. There is not yet a discovery deadline. Under the schedule contained in the procedural order of March 15, 2005, class-related discovery is not scheduled to end until October 28, 2005. I had thought that with all the previous motion practice, appointment of liaison counsel, conferences among lawyers and with the judge and magistrate judge, and coordination with state judges, all parties were on the same page on the orderly progress of this complex multidistrict litigation, and that all were now focused on the class certification issue, with summary judgment practice to come later. In some consternation I asked Magistrate Judge Kravchuk to convene an immediate conference of counsel to find out what was going on. After a telephone conference, she permitted the plaintiffs to file a motion to stay their response to General Motors' summary judgment motion. General Motors has now responded to the plaintiffs' motion to stay, as have defendants Nissan North America and Ford Motor Company.

Analysis

General Motors says that it has the right to file a motion for summary judgment at any time and without the Court's permission.[3] Perhaps. Perhaps I also have the "right" arbitrarily to deny such a motion. (Denial of summary judgment is an unappealable interlocutory order, except in special cases such as qualified immunity defenses). But neither is good practice. My goal as a trial judge is to move cases along to an orderly conclusion with only unavoidable expense and delays, and to treat all substantive issues fairly. In return, I expect the lawyers to behave with candor and, when we discuss scheduling, to inform me or the magistrate judge what lies ahead, not keep certain cards up their sleeves. That is true in the ordinary case; it is even more important in a multidistrict case, where there are a multitude of parties and lawyers, the issues are complex, the expenses are high, and the Court will likely be called upon to approve an attorney's fee request at the end of the case.

In fact, I do not believe that General Motors has the right to file its motion when and how it chooses in the context of this litigation. Federal Rule of Civil Procedure 16 gives a trial judge extensive power over management issues. I can call a conference to "discourag[e] wasteful pretrial activities"[4] and to "establish[ ] early and continuing control so that the case will not be protracted because of lack of management."

---

[3] As Magistrate Judge Kravchuk reported following her June 17, 2005, conference of counsel:

> General Motors takes the position that it is entitled to file a Rule 56 motion at any stage of the proceeding, notwithstanding the court's scheduling order entered after consultation with the parties at the commencement of this proceeding. Its stated position is that plaintiffs should be able to file a substantive response without any additional discovery, as Fed.R.Civ.P. 11(b)(3) requires the plaintiffs to have the necessary information to withstand this motion in their possession at the time they filed their complaint. (General Motors does not explain why it waited more than one year to file this particular motion.)

There has been no objection to Magistrate Judge Kravchuk's report. In its response to the motion to stay, General Motors says that is "is entitled to move for summary judgment 'at any time,' and, if its motion is well-founded, to have judgment in its favor 'rendered forthwith,' " quoting Federal Rule of Civil Procedure 56(b) and (c).

[4] According to the Manual for Complex Litigation, "Motion practice can be a source of substantial cost and delay." Manual for Complex Litigation (Fourth) § 11.32 (2004).

Fed.R.Civ.P. 16(a). That was one of the important purposes of the various conferences that I have held in this litigation. At such a conference, I can "take appropriate action, with respect to . . . the need for adopting special procedures for managing potentially difficult or protracted actions that may involve complex issues, multiple parties, difficult legal questions, or unusual proof problems." Id. 16(c)[(2)(L)]. That was certainly the situation here. I am also empowered to take action with respect to "the appropriateness and timing of summary adjudication under Rule 56." Id. 16(c)[(2)(E)].[5] The specificity of that authority limits the parties' power over timing that might otherwise exist under Rule 56. See Julian v. Equifax Check Servs., Inc., 178 F.R.D. 10, 14 (D.Conn. 1998) (because "[s]ummary judgment motions are often the most significant pretrial matters and are typically the most time-consuming motions[,] . . . [i]mposing reasonable limits on when they may be filed . . . is critical for the scheduling of trial in individual cases and the management of the entire docket").

Implicitly the parties and I dealt with that timing issue in a schedule that did not contemplate summary judgment motions until later.[6] Such a schedule "shall not be modified except upon a showing of good cause and by leave of the district judge or, when authorized by local rule, by a magistrate judge," Fed.R.Civ.P. 16(b), and the "order shall control the subsequent course of the action unless modified by a subsequent order," id. 16(e). General Motors did not make any request to deviate from the schedule proposed and entered. Indeed, other defendants were unaware that summary judgment motions could be filed now and have stated that if General Motors gets to have its motion heard, they want to file such motions as well. (So much for the scheduling order and the Court's attempt to manage the litigation.) Moreover, had I been alerted that there were legitimate summary judgment motions that needed to be heard before the close of discovery, I would have wanted discussion of delaying the class certification schedule. One of the issues at stake is always which should come first, dispositive motions or class certification, given the different collateral consequences. I would have wanted discussion of the basis for the motion, whether discovery should be focused or limited to deal with its issues first, and its effect on the rest of the schedule. See Manual for Complex Litigation (Fourth) § 11.34. None of that occurred. Instead, I received a stealth motion.

---

[5] Rule 16(b)[(3)(A)] also authorizes a scheduling order "that limits the time . . . to file motions."

[6] Although summary judgment practice is not limited to the close of discovery under Rule 56, that is generally when it is most useful. By then the plaintiffs have whatever information there is to resist the motion and do not need to request a Rule 56(f) delay. General Motors suggests that it would be agreeable to some delay while discovery focuses on the issues raised by its motion. That might have been a useful proposal at a conference of counsel when we were establishing the schedule for class certification; now it would simply be disruptive.

As should be apparent, I am granting the motion to stay because it is not time for summary judgment practice under the scheduling order, not because of the plaintiffs' inability to respond to the summary judgment motion. There is thus no need for a Rule 56([d]) delay.

In short, General Motors should not have filed its motion. Alternatively, it should have alerted the Court and the other parties at earlier opportunities that a summary judgment motion would be in order before class certification. Alternatively still, if the idea dawned late upon it, General Motors should have requested permission to introduce this addition into the schedule.[7] I therefore Grant the plaintiffs' motion to stay action on General Motors' summary judgment motion.[8]

Let there be no mistake. This litigation is difficult and complex enough without surprises. I expect no more.

NOTES AND QUESTIONS

1. The judge in *New Motor Vehicles* expressed his "concern that the litigation as a whole move forward in an orderly and strategic fashion." What would have happened if the judge had not taken the initiative to engage in the scheduling and other management activities described in the decision? Would the parties have been tempted to play off judges against one another? Judge Hornby notes that he conferred with Judge Richard Kramer of San Francisco Superior Court. Judge Kramer was the designated Complex Litigation Judge of that court, authorized to maintain control over cases deemed complex there. Is coordination among judges like Judge Hornby and Judge Kramer superior to independent action by judges? Recall the discussion in Ch. 3 of stays and injunctions with regard to parallel litigation in other courts. For a general discussion, see William Schwarzer, Nancy Weiss & Alan Hirsch, Judicial Federalism in Action: Coordination of Litigation in State and Federal Courts, 78 Va.L.Rev. 1689 (1992). Does such judicial cooperation provide additional reasons for curtailing parties' opportunities to act unilaterally?

2. Note the other actions taken by Judge Hornby that deal with matters we will shortly address or have already addressed:

(a) Scheduling discovery and briefing for class certification. See Litigating Class Certification, *supra* p. 333.

(b) Appointing liaison counsel. See Judicial Selection of Counsel, *infra* p. 425.

(c) Entering a stipulated protective order. See Protective Orders and Discovery Confidentiality, *infra* p. 507.

3. Ordinarily the burdens of preparing and presenting a full class-certification motion are quite considerable. Indeed, Judge Hornby says that "I expected that everyone's attention would be focused on these issues." If

---

[7] I would entertain imposing sanctions against General Motors under Rule 16(f), but for the fact that the scheduling order fails to state expressly that "No summary judgment motions shall be filed until. . . ."

[8] I recognize that if I denied the summary judgment motion there would be nothing to appeal. By granting the stay, I open myself to possible mandamus. If General Motors truly believes that it has the right to determine the schedule in this case, it can seek mandamus relief in the court of appeals. Otherwise, the scheduling of such motions will be on the agenda after the class certification is resolved.

General Motors really has a motion for summary judgment that can put an end to its involvement in the litigation or significantly pare it down, should it not be permitted to bring that up before the class-certification effort?

4.   Judge Hornby stresses cooperation among the lawyers as important to orderly management of the case. Judge Peckham (*supra* pp. 411–413) emphasized that pretrial conferences enable the judge to determine whether lawyers are unduly combative. How vigorously should judges insist that opposing lawyers cooperate? Is that consistent with the general precepts of our adversary system? A 2015 amendment to Fed. R. Civ. P. 1 added a directive that the rules be "employed by the court and the parties" to secure the just, speedy, and inexpensive determination of every action. The Committee Note observed that "[m]ost lawyers and parties cooperate to achieve these ends." Should the rule command cooperation? How would that command be enforced? In 2011, the Sedona Conference, a private organization, issued its "Cooperation Proclamation," and a large number of judges have signed that proclamation.

5.   It should be apparent that, despite their innocuous title, scheduling orders are serious things. Should they be applied as vigorously in litigation that is less complicated than a "monster" case like *New Motor Vehicles*? One suspects that General Motors, due to its size, was a major defendant from the outset. Should the court allow more latitude for peripheral defendants, perhaps those added to the case after it was initially filed (and possibly after the scheduling order was entered)?

Scheduling orders can put litigants in difficult positions. For example, in Otero v. Buslee, 695 F.2d 1244 (10th Cir. 1982), defendants delayed discovery past the cutoff date while awaiting the court's ruling on cross motions for summary judgment. As the cutoff date approached, defendants moved for an extension, but the court did not rule on either motion for summary judgment or the motion to extend the time for discovery until after the cutoff date, and then denied both summary-judgment motions and the motion to extend the discovery cutoff. After judgment was entered against defendants, they appealed on the ground they had been treated unfairly. The appellate court upheld the denial of leave to conduct discovery after the cutoff date. Should defendants have been required to embark on (possibly expensive) discovery while potentially dispositive motions were pending? The appellate court reasoned as follows (id. at 1248 n. 1):

> The defendants' desire to avoid needless discovery is laudable. However, they filed their motion to extend the discovery period on April 16, two weeks before the deadline. By then, they doubted that the court would decide the summary judgment motions before the end of the discovery period. By not taking the depositions in the ensuing two weeks—which was feasible given the relative lack of complexity of the case—the defendants gambled that the court would grant their extension. To allow them to assume such an extension, and to grant it by overturning the trial court, would render discovery deadlines meaningless and would deprive the trial court of the discretion it needs to ensure fair and orderly discovery.

How should the court develop a schedule for cases before it? For a case like *New Motor Vehicles*, the schedule is likely to emerge from extended conferences with the court. But Rule 16(b) calls for a scheduling order in most cases. Couldn't the preparation of individualized schedules for ordinary cases become a burden? Would standard schedules be appropriate? Consider Stephen Subrin, Federal Rules, Local Rules, and State Rules: Uniformity, Divergence, and Emerging Procedural Patterns, 137 U. Pa. L. Rev. 1999, 2049 (1989): "Case-by-case management developed because the transaction costs of procedural rules with broad attorney latitude were too high. As a result of federal local rules and state experimentation, the judiciary has already demonstrated that it thinks the transaction costs of ad hoc case-by-case management are also too high. Judges are already turning to formal limitations and definitions in order to reduce transaction costs."

6. Professor Resnik was concerned that judges would not be able to disregard information they learned in managing cases before them, or overcome emotional reactions resulting from their close involvement in the management of those cases. In Adam Wistrich, Chris Guthrie & Jeffrey Rachlinski, Can Judges Ignore Inadmissible Information? The Difficulty of Deliberately Disregarding, 153 U. Pa. L. Rev. 1251 (2005), the authors find based on experiments focusing on criminal cases that judges display a surprising ability to ignore such information in some circumstances, but that they are generally unable to avoid being influenced by relevant but inadmissible information in other circumstances. Thus, judges were able to disregard evidence seized in violation of constitutional rights when determining whether probable cause existed. But they had difficulty disregarding demands disclosed during a settlement conference, conversations protected by the attorney-client privilege, prior sexual histories of alleged rape victims, prior convictions of a plaintiff, and information the government promised not to rely upon in sentencing.

7. Is there a realistic alternative to judicial management? Before the adoption of the Federal Rules of Civil Procedure in 1938, pretrial litigation was not nearly as important as it became afterwards. In part that was due to the strictness of pleading requirements, and in part due to the absence of discovery on the scale permitted under the 1938 rules. Given those developments, is case management a necessary response? Consider Richard Marcus, Slouching Toward Discretion, 78 Notre Dame L. Rev. 1561, 1589–90 (2003):

> Without case management, the growing centrality of the pretrial phase meant that the lawyers would be free of substantial constraint from anyone in their use of very substantial powers—most notably in discovery—that modern American procedure conferred on them. * * * Viewed in this light, case management might be seen not just as an increase in judicial discretion, but also as a consequence of the increased lawyer discretion provided under the new rules. Of necessity case management escaped frequent oversight by appellate courts, but a laissez-faire attitude toward lawyer latitude hardly seems preferable.

8.   Notice that Judge Hornby says that he is granting the motion for a stay rather than denying the motion for summary judgment in part to permit General Motors to seek a writ of mandamus from the court of appeals. Should appellate courts attempt to supervise case management activities like those undertaken by Judge Hornby? Recall that Professor Resnik expressed concern that the managerial activities of judges are effectively immune to review by appellate courts. Does *New Motor Vehicles* bear her out?

Arguments have been made for a rule change to expand the opportunity for interlocutory appellate review in MDL litigation. Perhaps courts of appeals should take a more aggressive approach to complex litigation than to other cases. A possible example of a more aggressive attitude is In re National Prescription Opiate Litigation, 956 F.3d 838 (6th Cir. 2020). In that massive MDL litigation, the district court's scheduling order set a deadline for amending the pleadings in the cases against pharmacy companies that were on "Track One" slated for an early trial. One group of defendants moved for summary judgment after "massive discovery," and plaintiffs sought in response to amend their complaint to assert additional claims that they had "expressly disavowed 18 months before." The district court refused to rule on defendants' summary judgment motions, granted plaintiffs leave to amend, refused to permit defendants to make Rule 12(b)(6) motions directed to the amended complaint, and ordered the pharmacy companies to produce data on every prescription for opioids filled by any of these defendants for more than a decade.

The court of appeals granted a writ of mandamus overturning the order permitting the amendment of the complaint more than 18 months after the deadline for amendment in the scheduling order. "Not a circuit court in the country, as far as we can tell, would allow a district court to amend its scheduling order under these circumstances." Id. at 843–44. Consider whether leave to amend would, in an ordinary case, support mandamus. Cf. Rule 15(b) (authorizing amendments during and after trial). Should appellate courts be more interventionist or more deferential to district court management in complex litigation.

9.   *Sanctions.* Judge Hornby mentions that he might have imposed sanctions on General Motors for filing its "stealth" summary-judgment motion had his scheduling order been clearer. What sort of sanction might he use? In complex litigation, sanctions can be seen as a symptom of a failure of judicial management. Consider the admonition in § 10.151 of the Manual for Complex Litigation (4th) (2004):

> [A] resort to sanctions may reflect a breakdown of case management. Close judicial oversight and a clear, specific, and reasonable management program, developed with the participation of counsel, will reduce the potential for sanctionable conduct because the parties will know what the judge expects of them.

One possibility would be for the court to react to disobedience of its management orders by deciding the case against the disobedient party. In Link

v. Wabash R.R. Co., 370 U.S. 626 (1962), the district court dismissed a suit when plaintiff's lawyer failed to appear for a pretrial conference. It observed that "[w]e need not decide whether unexplained absence from a pretrial conference *alone* would justify a dismissal with prejudice if the record showed no other evidence of dilatoriness," and rejected plaintiff's argument that he should not be deprived of his claim due to his lawyer's mistake in failing to appear for the conference because "each party is deemed bound by the acts of his lawyer." Should these sorts of sanctions be favored to enforce case management orders? In general the lower courts have not ordinarily pursued the most aggressive use of sanctions that the Supreme Court decisions might seem to authorize.

Could Judge Hornby have justified merits sanctions against General Motors in *New Motor Vehicles*? Would monetary sanctions be better? At least they don't directly affect the outcome of a case, and for a variety of sorts of misconduct monetary sanctions may be imposed. Sometimes the cost of certain activities is required to be imposed on a litigant. See, e.g., Rule 16(f) (cost of noncompliance with Rule 16 orders); Rule 37(a)(5) (cost of discovery motion imposed on losing party unless its position was substantially justified); Rule 37(c)(2) (cost of proving point that should have been admitted under Rule 36 imposed on party that failed to admit). In *New Motor Vehicles*, Judge Hornby probably had this sort of sanction in mind, but he was concerned that his earlier orders had not been clear enough to warrant them. How clear must a judge be in managing a case to justify this sort of sanctions on parties the judge concludes are disobedient? Recall Prof. Resnik's concerns (*supra* p. 413) about the risk that judges might develop intense feelings about the behavior of lawyers or parties before them. Would that risk be a reason to favor limiting sanctions to situations in which it was crystal clear what the judge wanted done? Another possibility would be to hold the offending lawyers or parties in contempt of court. How would such sanctions affect the ability of the parties and the court to cooperate thereafter?

10. *Magistrate Judge involvement in case management:* Note the involvement of a Magistrate Judge had a prominent role in the management of the *New Motor Vehicles* litigation. These judicial officers are appointed by the district court for eight-year terms, and often bear heavy responsibilities in regard to a variety of important matters, including discovery and scheduling. Any "nondispositive" matters they decide may be reviewed by the district judge, but these orders may be set aside only when "clearly erroneous or contrary to law." See Rule 72(a).

Another role for magistrate judges is possible under Rule 73, if the parties consent to the magistrate judge exercising full jurisdiction to decide the case. That can include a court or jury trial, and may be a way to reach trial sooner than would be possible before the district judge, who must give priority to criminal cases. During pretrial conferences, the district judge may "remind the parties of the magistrate judge's availability," but must also advise them that "they are free to withhold consent without adverse substantive consequences."

C. JUDICIAL SELECTION OF COUNSEL

In complex litigation, judges may, in effect, be called upon to hire lawyers through designation of lead counsel, liaison counsel, or class counsel. In *New Motor Vehicles, supra* p. 414, one of the judge's earliest acts was to appoint liaison counsel for both plaintiffs and defendants. As we shall see, courts have long understood that, in a variety of circumstances, they have not only authority, but a responsibility, to designate lawyers to act on behalf of litigants who did not directly hire these lawyers. The situations in which such appointments must be made have increased in frequency and importance. For example, since 2003 Rule 23(g) has directed the court to appoint class counsel when certifying a class action, and authorized the appointment of "interim counsel" before that. Discharging such appointment responsibilities involves assessments that differ some from traditional judicial duties. The Manual for Complex Litigation (4th) § 10.224 (2004) observes:

> Few decisions by the court in complex litigation are as difficult and sensitive as the appointment of designated counsel. There is often intense competition for appointment by the court as designated counsel, an appointment that may implicitly promise large fees and a prominent role in the litigation. Side agreements among lawyers may also have a significant effect on positions taken in the proceedings. At the same time, because appointment of designated counsel will alter the usual dynamics of client representation in important ways, attorneys will have legitimate concerns that their clients' interests be adequately represented.

> For these reasons, the judge is advised to take an active part in the decision on the appointment of counsel. Deferring to proposals by counsel without independent examination, even those that seem to have the concurrence of a majority of those affected, invites problems down the road if designated counsel turn out to be unwilling or unable to discharge their responsibilities satisfactorily or if they incur excessive costs.

Judges are aware of the demands of this responsibility: "Appointment of class counsel is an extraordinary practice with respect to dictating and limiting class members' control over the attorney-client relationship and thus requires a heightened level of scrutiny to ensure that the interests of the class members are adequately represented and protected." In re JP Morgan Chase Cash Balance Litigation, 242 F.R.D. 265, 277 (S.D.N.Y. 2007).

Actually, judges have long had this responsibility. For example, in MacAlister v. Guterma, 263 F.2d 65 (2d Cir. 1958), the court of appeals vacated the district court's order declining to appoint lead counsel to handle three consolidated stockholders' derivative actions. It reasoned that "the appointment of general counsel" can be necessary to avoid "overlapping duplication in motion practices and pre-trial procedures occasioned by competing counsel." It warned against indulging "misapplied notions concerning interference with a party's right to his own counsel," and quoted an 1899 New York state court that said: "[T]here can be but one master of a litigation on the side of the plaintiffs. It is also plain that it would be as easy to drive a span of horses pulling in diverging directions, as to conduct a litigation by separate, independent action of various plaintiffs, acting without concert, and with possible discord."

In re Cardinal Health, Inc. ERISA Litigation
United States District Court, Southern District of Ohio, 2005.
225 F.R.D. 552.

Marbley, District Judge.

I.   Introduction

This matter comes before the Court on five Plaintiffs' motions to appoint Lead Counsel and Liaison Counsel for this Consolidated ERISA Action.[1] The ERISA Plaintiffs are suing Cardinal Health, Inc. ("Cardinal Health") on behalf of the Cardinal Health Profit Sharing, Retirement and Savings Plan ("Cardinal Plan") and the Syncor International Corporation. Employees' Savings and Stock Ownership Plan ("Syncor Plan"). Five of the Plaintiffs have moved to appoint Lead Counsel and Liaison Counsel. The Court GRANTS the McKeehan Plaintiffs' Motion to Appoint Co-Lead Plaintiffs, Co-Lead Counsel, and Liaison Counsel; DENIES the DeCarlo and Heitholt Plaintiffs' Motion to Appoint Lead Plaintiffs, Co-Lead Counsel and Liaison Counsel; DENIES the Salinas and Jones Plaintiffs' Motion to Appoint Co-Lead ERISA Plaintiffs, Co-Lead ERISA Counsel, and Liaison ERISA Counsel; DENIES in part and GRANTS in part Plaintiff Daniel Kelly's Motion to Consolidate the ERISA cases and to Appoint Co-Lead Counsel and Liaison Counsel; and DENIES in part and GRANTS in part Plaintiff Harry Anderson's Motion to Consolidate the ERISA cases and to Appoint Co-Lead Counsel and Liaison Counsel.

[The court provided a chart identifying the five competing groups of proposed lead and liaison counsel, as identified further in the court's discussion of the competing applicants below.]

II.   Analysis

A.   Overview of the Court's Role in Appointing Lead Counsel

Because of the large number of parties in this ERISA action, efficient management of the action mandates the selection of lead counsel and liaison counsel. Selection of lead counsel is a duty often left to the court if

---

[1] On December 15, 2004, the Court consolidated fourteen ERISA actions into one Consolidated ERISA Action.

the parties cannot decide amongst themselves. Courts should consider the following factors when appointing lead counsel: experience; prior success record; the number, size, and extent of involvement of represented litigants; the advanced stage of proceedings in a particular suit; and the nature of the causes of action alleged.

Federal Rule of Civil Procedure 23(g), which outlines the requirements for class counsel, requires, above all, that the chosen counsel "fairly and adequately represent the interests of the class." Fed.R.Civ.P. 23(g)[(4)]. Although the case sub judice involves only a putative class, Rule 23(g)[(1)] will apply if the class is certified.

Rule 23(g) enumerates the following factors a court must consider when choosing lead counsel:

- work counsel has done in identifying or investigating potential claims in the action;

- counsel's experience in handling class actions, other complex litigation, and claims of the type asserted in the action;

- counsel's knowledge of the applicable law; and

- the resources counsel will commit to representing the class.[3]

Complex litigation often involves numerous parties with similar interests, such that traditional procedures in which all papers are filed with every counsel becomes unduly cumbersome. Manual for Complex Litigation (4th ed. 2004) ("MCL") § 10.22. Courts can effectively help manage such litigation by appointing lead and liaison counsel. Id. Before appointing lead counsel, courts should engage in an "independent review" of attorneys' submissions regarding lead counsel and "ensure that counsel appointed to leading roles are qualified and responsible, that they will fairly and adequately represent all of the parties on their side, and that their charges will be reasonable." Id. at § 10.221. Additionally, the court should be confident that any counsel appointed will fulfill its obligation "to act fairly, efficiently, and economically in the interest of all parties and parties' counsel." Id.

B. Applicants for Lead Counsel

i. McKeehan Plaintiffs Proposed Counsel: Schatz & Nobel and Stull, Stull & Brody

Each firm has an impressive resume and is qualified to be lead counsel, but the Court finds the McKeehan Plaintiffs' proposed counsel, Schatz & Nobel and Stull, Stull & Brody, will best be able to represent fairly and adequately the class because of their extensive experience in ERISA litigation. In re Terazosin Hydrochloride, 220 F.R.D. 672, 702 (S.D.Fla.

---

[3] The rule also provides that a court "may consider any other matter pertinent to counsel's ability to fairly and adequately represent the interests of the class."

2004) (finding the proposed counsel's "experience in, and knowledge of, the applicable law in this field" the "most persuasive" factor when choosing lead counsel).

Schatz & Nobel and Stull, Stull & Brody have been appointed lead or co-lead counsel in several major ERISA litigations and have an established relationship with one another. [The court cited two 2003 cases in which these two firms were appointed co-lead counsel and another one from 2002.] The doubts expressed by other Plaintiffs, namely the Heitholt Plaintiffs, regarding the competency of Schatz & Nobel are undermined by the fact that the Heitholt Plaintiffs' proposed co-counsel, Schiffrin & Barroway, asked Schatz & Nobel to be its co-lead counsel in the case sub judice.[4] Schiffrin & Barroway paired with another firm when Schatz & Nobel declined the invitation.

Likewise, the Court also finds the proposed co-liaison counsel, Clark, Perdue, Roberts & Scott, LPA, competent and able to carry out the duties required of liaison counsel.

Schatz & Nobel and Stull, Stull & Brody have also demonstrated a commitment to identifying and investigating potential claims in the action. See Fed.R.Civ.P. 23(g)(1)([A])(i) (explaining that courts should consider the work counsel has done in identifying or investigating potential claims in the action). The Court finds that the McKeehan Plaintiffs' complaint, while not as detailed or lengthy as some Plaintiffs' complaints, adequately meets the requirements of Federal Rule of Civil Procedure 8, which requires only a short and plain statement of claims. Here, the McKeehan Complaint contains the grounds for jurisdiction and outlines the two counts on which the Plaintiffs believe relief should be granted, and identifies the relief requested.

Additionally, the McKeehan Plaintiffs have demonstrated their consistent commitment to this case by filing several well-argued briefs with the Court on a range of issues, including consolidation versus coordination and various aspects of Lead Counsel appointments.

The Court also finds that Schatz & Nobel and Stull, Stull & Brody will be able to commit adequate resources. See Manual for Complex Litigation § 10.221 (instructing courts to ensure the designated counsel is able to represent adequately all of the parties on their side). Although the Heitholt Plaintiffs allege that this case's demands will overwhelm Schatz & Nobel and Stull, Stull & Brody, the Court surmises that if these firms managed the workload in similarly large ERISA suits on prior occasions, they can handle this litigation, too.

---

[4] According to the McKeehan Plaintiffs, Joseph Meltzer, from Schiffrin & Barroway, asked Robert Izard, from Schatz & Nobel, to prosecute the Cardinal Health litigation as co-lead counsel. Robert Izard declined due to Schiffrin & Barroway's involvement in the Brown v. Syncor International Corp., Case No. CACV03–6503 (N.D.Cal.) (complaint filed on Sept. 11, 2003) ("Syncor Action").

In sum, the Court finds that Schatz & Nobel and Stull, Stull & Brody have a high level of ERISA expertise and are willing to commit each firm's resources to this case such that they fairly and adequately represent all parties on their side. The Court also finds that, should the putative class be certified, these firms have the experience and resources to represent adequately the certified class. The Court hereby GRANTS the McKeehan Plaintiffs' Motion to Appoint Lead Counsel and Liaison Counsel.

ii.   Heitholt Plaintiffs: Keller Rohrback and Schiffrin & Barroway

Schiffrin & Barroway and Keller Rohrback have impressive ERISA backgrounds and have been appointed by several courts to be lead counsel in major ERISA litigation, but the Court finds that the Plaintiffs' interests will be better served by the McKeehan Plaintiffs' proposed counsel for two reasons.

First, several Plaintiffs argue that Schiffrin & Barroway's representation of the ERISA class in Brown v. Syncor International Corp., Case No. CACV03–6503 (N.D.Cal.) ("Syncor Action") (complaint filed on Sept. 11, 2003), will create a conflict of interest because the defendant, Syncor International Corp. ("Syncor"), merged with Cardinal Health in June 2002. Plaintiffs argue that Cardinal Health will be liable for any judgments or settlement costs imposed on Syncor, thus reducing the settlement funds available in the case sub judice and creating an irreconcilable conflict of interest for Schiffrin & Barroway. Plaintiffs also assert that Schiffrin & Barroway's representation of the Syncor Plan participants both against Syncor and against Cardinal Health will create a situation in which one group of plaintiffs is inevitably favored.

The Heitholt Plaintiffs, however, insist that no conflict of interest exists because Syncor, now renamed Cardinal Health 414, Inc. ("Cardinal 414"), and Cardinal Health have a parent/subsidiary relationship and assert that a subsidiary's liability does not extend to the parent corporation. The Heitholt Plaintiffs also point to the Merger Agreement, which states that "Syncor shall continue its existence under the laws of the State of Delaware as a wholly owned subsidiary of Cardinal."[6]

Counsel cannot represent different classes of plaintiffs with conflicting claims who are seeking recovery from a common pool of assets. See Kuper v. Quantum Chem Corp., 145 F.R.D. 80, 83 (S.D.Ohio 1992); see also ABA Code of Professional Responsibility, DR 5–105 and EC 5014 (prohibiting counsel from representing different plaintiffs with conflicting claims against the same defendant because it creates "the appearance of divided loyalties of counsel"). If the amount sought by each proposed class could exceed the total assets of the Defendants, then "competing claims may

---

[6]   The Merger Agreement also provided that Syncor would maintain its own ERISA plan, but that Cardinal Health shares would be substituted as the Syncor Plan's stock investment alternative.

impair counsel's ability to vigorously pursue the interest of both classes." *Kuper* at 83; see also Dietrich v. Bauer, 192 F.R.D. 119, 126 (S.D.N.Y. 2000) (finding counsel can represent two overlapping classes of plaintiffs as long as the class actions are waged against different defendants). Thus, if Cardinal Health and Syncor are now the same company, Schiffrin & Barroway does have a conflict of interest.

Here, Cardinal Health and Cardinal 414 appear to have a parent/subsidiary relationship. The Heitholt Plaintiffs are correct in asserting that subsidiary liability does not extend to a parent unless the subsidiary is "so dominated and controlled" by the parent "that it has no more than a paper existence." The Heitholt Plaintiffs have proffered evidence to demonstrate that Cardinal 414 is a truly separate entity, e.g., the Merger Agreement's characterization of Syncor as a "surviving corporation" and a Certificate of Good Standing from the Ohio Secretary of State certifying Cardinal 414 as a foreign corporation properly registered in Ohio. The Court, however, is not entirely convinced that Cardinal 414 is truly separate in nature. Without additional evidence establishing Cardinal 414 as a legitimate subsidiary, the possibility exists that Schiffrin & Barroway would end up representing two classes of plaintiffs against, in essence, the same defendant.

Second, with some reluctance, the Court turns to Schiffrin & Barroway's apparent transgressions in Moore v. Halliburton, Co., No. 3:02–CV–1152–M, 2004 WL 2092019, at *1 (N.D.Tex. Sept. 9, 2004). There, the court refused to approve a settlement agreement, in part, because of Schiffrin & Barroway's questionable tactics. The court explained that from February through April 2003, Schiffrin & Barroway commenced settlement negotiations with the defendant, Halliburton, without informing the lead plaintiff, the Archdiocese of Milwaukee Supporting Fund ("AMSF") that settlement discussions were ongoing. When AMSF challenged the fairness, reasonableness, and adequacy of the proposed settlement, the court held a fairness hearing and found the settlement's benefit to the plaintiffs wanting. The court found that Schiffrin & Barroway, by taking one of the lead plaintiffs out of the "decision-making loop[,] deprived the class of the benefits of multiple Lead Plaintiffs." The court continued as follows:

The Court is dismayed that Lead Counsel here felt at liberty to exclude any of the Lead Plaintiffs from significant involvement in material activities in the case, which settlement surely is. No one can know how active involvement of AMSF in the negotiations might have affected the outcome of the negotiations.

Moreover, the court expressed concern about the "vigor of Lead Counsel's settlement advocacy," noting that lead counsel supported a release that would have extinguished claims completely unrelated to the suit. The court also expressed suspicion because the $6 million proposed settlement, which was negotiated by Schiffrin & Barroway, would have guaranteed Schiffrin & Barroway approximately $1,500,000 in attorneys fees, leaving a net recovery of $3,000,000 for a class of 800,000 potential claimants.[8]

Although Schiffrin & Barroway explained that the matter stemmed from a disagreement about which firm was actually appointed lead counsel, the Court is not confident that the Heitholt Plaintiffs' proposed counsel will best be able to represent fairly and adequately the interests of all parties on their side.[9]

Accordingly, because of the possibility of an appearance of divided loyalties if Schiffrin & Barroway represented two classes of plaintiffs against Cardinal Health and Cardinal 414 and due to the difficulties the firm encountered in Moore v. Halliburton, Co., the Court DENIES the Heitholt Plaintiffs' motion to appoint Lead Counsel.

iii.   The Kelly Group Plaintiffs: Squitieri & Fearon and Wechsler Harwood

Proposed counsel for the Kelly Group, Squitieri & Fearon and Wechsler Harwood, do not appear as experienced in ERISA litigation as Schatz & Nobel and Stull, Stull & Brody. Although the Kelly Group's Proposed Counsel are extremely experienced in large litigation, particularly in securities, each firm's ERISA experience has been more limited than that found in the McKeehan Plaintiffs' proposed counsel's resumes. Additionally, the McKeehan Plaintiffs' proposed counsel have an established relationship.

The Kelly Group's formation of the Cardinal Health ERISA Litigation Steering Committee ("CHELSC"), a group aimed at ensuring Plaintiffs have a substantial role in the litigation, is impressive, but the Court finds the ERISA background of each candidate to be a more persuasive factor than the formation of a steering group.[10] Accordingly, the Court DENIES Daniel Kelly's Motion (on behalf of the Kelly Group) to Appoint Co-Lead Counsel and Liaison Counsel.

iv.   Salinas Plaintiffs: Barrett Johnston & Parsley and Whatley & Drake

The Salinas Plaintiffs' counsel have extremely impressive resumes. Barrett Johnston & Parsley has extensive securities class action experience

---

[8]   The court further noted that if all 800,000 claimants submitted claims, an investor with 100 shares would recover approximately 62 cents. Id. at *5; see also Gretchen Morgenson, Judge Rejects Proposed Halliburton Settlement, N.Y. Times, Sept. 11, 2004, at C2.

[9]   The Heitholt Plaintiffs argue that Moore v. Halliburton, Corp. was a securities action and, thus, inapposite to this ERISA action. When designating Lead Counsel, this Court is obligated to "consider any other matter pertinent to counsel's ability to fairly and adequately represent the interests of the [putative] class." Fed.R.Civ.P. 23(g)(1)[(B)]. Regardless of the legal theory underlying Halliburton, the Court finds the case pertinent to the matter at hand.

[10]   The Court also notes the hastiness with which the CHELSC Agreement appears to have been prepared. The Agreement was not dated, and Daniel Kelly was the only Plaintiff to sign it even though it purports to represent all six members of the Kelly Group.

and substantial labor union based ERISA experience. Whatley & Drake also has formidable complex litigation experience, including some major ERISA litigation. The McKeehan Plaintiffs' proposed counsel, however, maintain an edge because they have more experience litigating ERISA cases similar to the one sub judice. Thus, the Court DENIES Salinas and Jones Plaintiffs' Motion for Appointment of Co-Lead ERISA Plaintiffs, Co-Lead ERISA Counsel, and Liaison ERISA Counsel.

v.   Anderson Plaintiffs: Emerson Poynter

With regard to Emerson Poynter, the proposed counsel for Plaintiff Harry Anderson, the firm's securities litigation experience is substantial; however, the Court finds that other Lead Counsel candidates have superior ERISA experience. The Court DENIES Plaintiff Harry B. Anderson's Motion to appoint Lead Counsel.

III. Duties of Counsel

The Court hereby designates Schatz and Nobel and Stull, Stull & Brody as Co-Lead counsel and Clark, Perdue, Roberts & Scott as Liaison Counsel.

The designated Co-Lead Counsel shall have the following responsibilities:

- Sign any consolidated complaint, motions, briefs, discovery requests, objections, stipulations, or notices on behalf of the Plaintiffs for any matters arising during pretrial proceedings;

- Co-lead Counsel shall designate other firms of attorneys as necessary to serve as members of Plaintiffs' Steering Committee. Members of the Steering Committee shall be available for conferences with Co-lead Counsel to consult and advise on strategy and, at the option of Co-lead Counsel, to participate in settlement negotiations.

- Chair and participate in meetings of the Steering Committee;

- Conduct all pretrial proceedings on behalf of Plaintiffs;

- Brief and argue motions;

- Initiate and conduct discovery consistent with the requirements of Fed.R.Civ.P. 26(b)(1), 26(2), and 26(g);

- Employ and consult with experts;

- Accept service on behalf of all Plaintiffs;

- Conduct settlement negotiations on behalf of Plaintiffs, but not enter binding agreements except to the extent expressly authorized;

- Call meetings on behalf of Plaintiffs' counsel;

- Distribute to all Plaintiffs' counsel copies of all notices, orders, and decisions of the Court; maintain an up-to-date list of counsel available to all Plaintiffs' counsel on request; keep a complete file of all papers and discovery materials filed or generated in the Consolidated ERISA Action, which shall be available to all Plaintiffs' counsel at reasonable hours.

- Perform such other duties as may be incidental to proper coordination of Plaintiffs' pretrial activities or authorized by further order of the court.

All counsel in the Cardinal Health ERISA litigation shall keep contemporaneous time records and shall periodically submit summaries or other records of time and expenses to Lead Counsel as requested.

NOTES AND QUESTIONS

1.   Although Rule 23(g) provides a specific analysis for appointment of class counsel, it is important to appreciate that the practice originated in—and is equally important in—consolidated litigation outside the class action context. Whether in class actions or other consolidated litigation, appointment of lead counsel often leads to orders like the one above in In re Cardinal Health ERISA Litigation. See also the sample order in the Manual for Complex Litigation (4th) (2004) § 40.22, with similar proposed provisions. How effectively will such an order limit the actions of lead counsel and preserve the autonomy of individual plaintiffs to pursue their own cases as they desire? If such discord appears, what effect will that have on plaintiffs' chances of success? How is one to decide whether a single position need be taken by all plaintiffs? The Manual for Complex Litigation's form order ends with the following directive for other counsel:

> Counsel for plaintiffs who disagree with lead counsel (or those acting on behalf of lead counsel) or who have individual or divergent positions may present written and oral arguments, conduct examinations of deponents, or otherwise act separately on behalf of their clients as appropriate, provided that in doing so they do not repeat arguments, questions, or actions of lead counsel.

2.   Can the economies sought by the court be achieved without inappropriately inhibiting the freedom of the lawyers? Some sacrifice of individual freedom of action is essential to achieve overall fairness. Even in the absence of action by the court, the parties may voluntarily decide to act in a coordinated fashion. Dando Cellini, An Overview of Antitrust Class Actions, 49 Antitrust L.J. 1501, 1504 (1980), summarized the situation in 1980 regarding antitrust class actions as follows:

> Even where the court does not formally appoint liaison counsel or lead counsel, everything in an antitrust class action is handled by committee, anyway. Those of you who have participated in meetings of counsel in such cases know that your experience in the courtroom

does you precious little good; what you would need, ideally, is experience in a state legislature. In fact, it is often the best trial lawyers who have the hardest time adapting to what have become the accepted procedures for handling antitrust class actions. A good trial lawyer's tenacious pursuit of his own theory of the case and his unwillingness to compromise his own client's interests in the slightest respect for the good of the majority are almost immediately taken as signs of pigheadedness on the part of his fellow counsel. The result is that he is quickly ostracized from the decision-making inner circle of lawyers on his side of the case, thereby further diminishing his ability to influence the course of the proceedings.

3.   What effect should the log-rolling process described in note 2 have on the court's choices in designating lead counsel? The Manual for Complex Litigation urges judges not to defer to proposals by counsel. But even under Rule 23(g), courts may treat alliances among counsel as important in selecting class counsel. In In re Air Cargo Shipping Serv. Antitrust Litigation, 240 F.R.D. 56 (E.D.N.Y. 2006), one team of applicants reported that 48 firms involved in the litigation supported their appointment, while another said 29 firms supported them. Although it recognized that Rule 23(g) says nothing about the number of attorneys supporting a given applicant, the court observed: "Nevertheless, that large numbers of experienced counsel are satisfied to be represented by these two competing applicants is some measure of the respect they command and the confidence of their peers that they will server well in the role."

Should this factor matter at all? Consider John Coffee, The Regulation of Entrepreneurial Litigation: Balancing Fairness and Efficiency in the Large Class Action, 54 U.Chi.L.Rev. 877, 907–08 (1987):

> Until recently, the Manual for Complex Litigation instructed the trial court to let the plaintiffs' attorneys elect their own lead counsel. The result was the legal equivalent of an unsupervised political convention without procedural rules or even a credentials committee. Rival slates would form. Competing groups would invite other attorneys into the action in order to secure their vote for lead counsel. Eventually, a political compromise would emerge. The price of such a compromise was often both overstaffing and an acceptance of the free-riding or marginally competent attorney whose vote gave him leverage his ability did not.

In at least some instances, unstructured lobbying by lawyers seemed to have produced excesses. A very famous example is In re Fine Paper Antitrust Litigation, 98 F.R.D. 48 (E.D.Pa. 1983), a set of antitrust class actions, the court appointed lead counsel who had the support of many other lawyers. At an organizational meeting of the *Fine Paper* lawyers, voting was "one firm one vote," with the result that Campbell Office Supply Co. had five law firms representing it and therefore got five votes, but the State of California had only one vote. A California deputy attorney general objected that "we have a group of private attorneys here without substantial clients. * * * [Y]ou have three or four of the most prominent antitrust attorneys in this country representing a mom and pop greeting card store. * * * Their clients have nothing at stake. The defendants could buy all their clients for less than probably a month's attorneys' fees. What is really at stake here is attorneys' fees." Eventually, the judge concluded that "the polestar of plaintiff's organizational structure in this case was patronage, not efficiency." See also Mike Leonard, Pension Fund Loses Allergan Class Status as Judge Rips Lawyers, Bloomberg Law News, Sept. 30, 2020 (judge removes lead plaintiff in securities fraud class action because lead counsel entered into an "utterly disingenuous" fee-splitting agreement to share fees 55/45 with another firm the judge had refused to appoint as co-lead counsel). Compare Flanagan, Lieberman, Hoffman & Swaim v. Ohio Public Employees Retirement Sys., 814 F.3d 652 (2d Cir. 2015) (overturning district court order forbidding class counsel from sharing a portion of their fees with lawyers not appointed by the court).

4.   For the judge to take a more active role in selecting counsel, however, means that the judge must also scrutinize prospective lawyers from the perspective of a client and evaluate matters that ordinarily would not be within judicial business. In *Cardinal Health*, for example, the judge was obliged to evaluate arguments that the selected counsel had conflicts of interest, including having to review and evaluate a merger agreement involving the Cardinal Health ERISA plan. It also found itself critiquing the performance of another applicant in an earlier case, and finding that conflict-of-interest problems afflicted that firm. One might characterize some of the arguments made on these subjects as "mudslinging." Finally, the court was called upon to evaluate the facility of various law firms in handling ERISA cases. Is this an appropriate activity for judges? If not, how are clients supposed to do the same sort of thing in hiring lawyers?

However capable judges may be in making these kinds of determinations, they may reach different conclusions. In Nowak v. Ford Motor Co., 240 F.R.D. 355 (E.D.Mich. 2006), another ERISA action, the judge found that Keller Rohrback and Schiffrin & Barroway—the firms found to have a conflict in *Cardinal Health* and to be tainted with possible deficiencies in an earlier litigation—were the superior choice. Another contender for the position in that case relied on *Cardinal Health* to show that Keller Rohrback and Schiffrin & Barroway should not be selected, but this judge was not persuaded (id. at 366–67):

> The reasoning of the *Cardinal Health* opinion seems incomplete and overly cautious. The court never made any finding that Cardinal Health would be liable for the debts of its subsidiary, Syncor. Nor did it find that the assets of Cardinal Health did not exceed the full amount of both the plaintiff groups' claims against Cardinal Health and Syncor, which is an essential element needed to demonstrate a conflict of interest in such a situation. At the hearing on this motion, counsel arguing for Schiffrin & Barroway and Keller Rohrback also indicated that Cardinal Health in that litigation had a fiduciary insurance policy to provide another source of funding of any judgment

or settlement against it. The *Cardinal Health* opinion also cites DR 5–105 and EC 5–14, which prohibited joint representation where there was an "appearance of divided loyalties of counsel." Having taught a course in legal ethics for many years, it was my understanding that decades ago when Ohio and nearly all states abandoned the ABA Code of Professional Responsibility and its Disciplinary Rule and adopted versions of the ABA Model Rules of Professional Conduct, the new rules abandoned this "appearance of divided loyalty" standard and drafted more precise conflict guidelines. For various reasons, while recognizing the importance of the conflict issues raised in *Cardinal Health*, that opinion does not demonstrate a sufficient factual basis to find that Schiffrin & Barroway was acting inappropriately.

Should involvement in parallel litigation sometimes be a plus? In Allen v. Stewart Title Guar. Co., 246 F.R.D. 218 (E.D.Pa. 2007), the court found the fact one law firm represented a class in a parallel state-court action not to suggest any problems of conflict of interest. To the contrary, it noted that this firm's "role in the state proceeding would guard against any potential 'reverse auction' problems."

5.   *Adequacy*: At a minimum, Rule 23(g)(2) says that the court may not appoint a lawyer class counsel unless the lawyer is "adequate." (If there are competing applicants, the court must appoint the candidate "best able to represent the interests of the class.") How adequate does a sole applicant have to be? In Creative Montessori Learning Centers v. Ashford Gear LLC, 662 F.3d 913 (7th Cir. 2011), the district court certified the class even though the lawyers who filed the case had deceptively obtained the information on which they based the suit. On appeal, Judge Posner noted that "[t]his is a difficult role for a court to play—accustomed as judges in our system are to playing the role of arbiter of an adversary proceeding rather than imitating a Continental-style investigating magistrate," but "[w]hen class counsel have demonstrated a lack of integrity, a court can have no confidence that they will act as conscientious fiduciaries of the class." Id. at 917–18. Accordingly, the district judge was wrong to say that only the "most egregious misconduct" could ever justify denial of class status. "Misconduct that creates a serious doubt that counsel will represent the class loyally requires denial of class certification." Id. at 918.

6.   *The Private Securities Litigation Reform Act (PSLRA) Approach*: The PSLRA refashions the securities fraud class action to place primary responsibility on the lead plaintiff, who should be the class member "most capable of adequately representing the class members." 15 U.S.C. § 78u–4(a)(3)(B)(i). The Act adds that the applicant for the position with the greatest financial stake in the outcome of the case is presumed to be the most capable unless that presumption is rebutted. Id., § 78u–4(a)(3)(B)(iii). What role does the court have under the PSLRA? The judge is to determine whether the proposed lead plaintiff satisfies the requirements of Rule 23, such as adequacy

of representation. See *supra* p. 220 for discussion of adequacy of representation.

In In re Cavanaugh, 306 F.3d 726 (9th Cir. 2002), the district judge concluded that the group with the largest stake in the recovery would not be an adequate representative because this group had hired Milberg Weiss, an extremely prominent law firm, on terms that the judge thought were too generous to the firm, and therefore disadvantageous for the class. The judge accordingly appointed another lead plaintiff, who had a different arrangement with a smaller firm. The Ninth Circuit held that this appointment went beyond the judge's authority under the PSLRA. "So long as the plaintiff with the largest losses satisfies the typicality and adequacy requirements, he is entitled to lead plaintiff status, even if the district court is convinced the some other plaintiff would do a better job." Id. at 732. Choice of counsel is not a ground for preferring one lead plaintiff over another, for that is customarily left to the client. "Selecting a lawyer in whom a litigant has confidence is an important client prerogative and we will not lightly infer Congress meant to take away this prerogative from securities plaintiffs." Id. at 734. Ultimately, the court will have to pass on the reasonableness of the fee award, but that will not occur until the end of the case, and only if the case is won. Moreover, "[a] plaintiff facing large losses and a tough case may rationally conclude that he will be better off by hiring the more expensive, and more formidable, advocate, who may intimidate defendants into a prompt settlement on favorable terms." Id. at 735. In Cohen v. U.S. District Court, 586 F.3d 703 (9th Cir. 2009), the court explained further: "In the event that the district court determines the lead plaintiff has not made a reasonable choice of counsel, the court should articulate its reasons for disapproving plaintiff's choice and provide an opportunity for lead plaintiff to select acceptable counsel." In most instances, however, there is no opportunity for the court to defer to a designated "client" to make the choice of counsel. For discussion of the difficulty of expanding the PSLRA's "empowered plaintiff" model, see *supra* p. 227 n. 4.

7. What else should courts emphasize in choosing lawyers? For example, should diversity be a criterion? A federal judge in San Francisco declined to appoint two prominent firms as interim co-lead counsel due to "a lack of diversity in the proposed lead counsel." Ralph Chapoco, Calls For Diversity Spread to Complex Class Litigation, Bloomberg Law News, July 31, 2020. Is this appropriate? In Martin v. Blessing, 571 U.S. 1040 (2013), a denial of certiorari, Justice Alito raised questions about a judge who "insists that class counsel 'ensure that the lawyers staffed on the case fairly reflect the class composition in terms of relevant race and gender metrics.' " He said that this district judge used this criterion often, and concluded: "If the challenged appointment practice continues and is not addressed by the Court of Appeals, future review may be warranted."

But if the judge is to approach the appointment of leadership counsel from the perspective of clients, it is worth noting that several prominent clients emphasize diversity in their decisions to hire lawyers. See, e.g., Sara Randazzo, Law Firms' Clients Want Proof of Diversity, Wall St.J., Nov. 3, 2020; Ruiqi

Chen, HP Legal Chief Rivera: Demand Diversity, Law Firms Will Listen, Bloomberg Law News, Oct. 13, 2020; Ellen Rosen, Facebook Pushes Outside Law Firms to Become More Diverse, N.Y. Times, April 2, 2017. In MDL litigation in particular, growing emphasis is being placed on diversity. See Elizabeth Cabraser, Increasing Leadership Diversity in the Courtroom, Trial Magazine, June 2017, at 40. See also Howard Erichson, Beyond the Class Action: Lawyer Loyalty and Client Autonomy in Non-Class Collective Representation, 2003 U. Chi. Legal F. 519 (urging that the practices used for selecting class counsel be used also in other complex litigation).

At least in some situations, judges do seem to take account of diversity in selecting leadership counsel. For example, in In re Ethicon, Inc., Power Morcellator Prod. Liabil. Litig., MDL No. 2652 (involving a product used in hysterectomies), Judge Vratil (D.Kan.) appointed the first female-majority plaintiff steering committee. Diane Zhang, A Milestone in Gender Equality, Trial Magazine, July 2016, at 45, reported that one of the lawyers (a male) said:

> From the first telephone conference we had, Aimee [another plaintiff lawyer] and I decided that this was a long-overdue milestone, so it was entirely deliberate [that the PSC have a majority of women]. Throughout the process, Aimee and I emphasized the importance of this milestone for the bar.

8.   Could a court properly appoint a sole practitioner to represent a class? Might that also be regarded as a diversity consideration? In Waudby v. Verizon Wireless Services, LLC, 248 F.R.D. 173 (D.N.J. 2008), one applicant was a consortium of law firms known as Carella Byrne and the other was a sole practitioner. The court noted that "[w]hile Carella Byrne are proven, high-powered litigators involved in some of the most complex class-action lawsuits in the country, Scott A. Bursor, while experienced, is a sole practitioner. It would be untenable for the court to permit Mr. Bursor alone to represent the proposed class." When there is only one applicant, Rule 23(g)(2) directs the court to appoint that lawyer if "adequate." In LeBeau v. United States, 222 F.R.D. 613 (D.S.D. 2004), the court contacted and appointed an experienced lawyer known to the judge rather than the lawyer who brought the case because, although this lawyer was the sole applicant for class counsel, he "is not equipped to represent the class without associating other counsel":

> Mr. Grossberg has a sole practice apparently without any staff assistance and he does not explain how he will handle the workload of a class action. * * * There is no evidence in the record that Mr. Grossberg has handled other class actions, or that his office has any staff to, for example, prepare the class notice, mail the nearly 2,000 notices, field telephone calls from class members with questions and track the class members who opt out of the class.

9.   Public entities: Should courts regard state attorneys general or other public officials as preferable voices for the interests of the class because they are "above the fray"? Ordinarily, of course, governmental bodies are not class

members. But public officials could be deputized to sue to enforce citizens' rights; the doctrine of parens patriae is an example of that sort of thing. Private class actions, by way of contrast, are pursued by private actors. Edward Brunet, Class Action Objectors: Extortionist Free Riders or Fairness Guarantors, 2003 U. Chi. Legal F. 403, notes that "[p]articipation in class actions by states is increasingly common." Id. at 449. Although Professor Brunet examines the role of governmental agencies as objectors, might they be preferred as lead plaintiffs or class representatives where willing to serve, and relied upon to select appropriate counsel? Professor Brunet notes that "[g]overnment attorneys have different incentives than class action counsel. * * * Rather than aspire to monetary awards, the typical agency attorney seeks prominence generally, and peer group acceptance, particularly." Id. at 454. Would this orientation be preferable to the profit seeking of private counsel?

10. *Claims against class counsel*: In Bobbitt v. Milberg LLP, 801 F.3d 1066 (9th Cir. 2015), the prominent Milberg law firm obtained class certification for a securities fraud class action, with the firm as class counsel. But it then failed to meet the court's deadline for disclosure of expert evidence, resulting in the striking of plaintiffs' expert witness list, and decertification of the class. Milberg unsuccessfully appealed those rulings, but did not notify the members of the class. That led to a class action against the law firm on behalf of the members of the class certified in the securities fraud action. See also Janik v. Rudy, Exelrod & Zieff, 14 Cal.Rptr.3d 751 (Cal.Ct.App. 2004) (class counsel were sued by a class member for failure to assert a claim that plaintiff contended would have allowed a larger recovery in the class action).

11. *Relation to fee awards*: Note that the court in *Cardinal Health* ordered that all counsel involved in prosecuting the plaintiffs' claims keep contemporaneous time records and, upon request, submit them to lead counsel. Presumably, lead counsel has some responsibility to avoid wasteful duplication of activity. Consider how that responsibility may appear to the other lawyers to invite intrusion into their representational activity on behalf of their clients. Besides their role in monitoring, such time records are likely to be critical to any attorneys' fee award the court enters in this case. We turn to attorneys' fees awards next.

12. *Fees for non-leadership counsel:* In *Cardinal Health*, the court's order appointing leadership counsel specifies that only those lawyers may conduct the litigation—filing motions, initiating discovery, etc. As we will see below, courts often direct that a "common benefit fund" be created to compensate leadership for these activities, and often direct that a portion of the fees generated by any settlement or judgment in favor of a claimant, whether in a class action or an MDL proceeding, be deposited into this common benefit fund. Some non-leadership lawyers (sometimes called IRPAs—Individually Represented Plaintiffs' Attorneys) may regard this required contribution as a sort of "tax" on their fees, but judges may regard these lawyers as "free riders" benefitting from the work of leadership counsel and relieved of the need to prepare their cases themselves. Beyond "taxing" the fees for these non-leadership lawyers, some courts also "cap" the fees they may charge their

clients at percentages lower than the ones specified in their retention agreements. See, e.g., In re Vioxx Products Liability Litig., 574 F.Supp.2d 606 (E.D.La. 2008); In re Zyprexa Products Liability Litig., 424 F.Supp.2d 488 (E.D.N.Y. 2006). Consider the effect of these fee orders on non-leadership counsel, who are also prevented from actively litigating the cases on behalf of their clients. That is one way of appreciating the importance of appointment by the court to the lawyers involved.

D. COURT-AWARDED ATTORNEYS' FEES

In the 1980s, many noted that attorneys' fee awards had become a sort of cottage industry for the legal profession. Since then, it has become a genuine industry. Indeed, there are entire books devoted to the problems of attorneys' fee awards. See, e.g., Alan Hirsch, Diane Sheehey & Tom Willging, Awarding Attorneys' Fees and Managing Fee Litigation (FJC 3d ed. 2015); Mary Derfner & Arthur Wolf, Court-Awarded Attorney Fees (2007) ; Robert Rossi, Attorneys' Fees (3d ed. 2007) .

At first blush, awards of attorneys' fees may not seem to be tools of judicial control of litigation. In operation, however, they can serve that purpose. Recall Peil v. National Semiconductor Corp., *supra* p. 222 ("much influence and control is exercised by the Court by the fact that it controls the fee award to plaintiffs' counsel"). Particularly in complex litigation, the judge's authority to determine how much one set of lawyers will be paid exerts a considerable influence on the way those lawyers approach the litigation.

In class actions, this authority has increasingly been viewed as important to the healthy functioning of this procedural device. "In a class action, whether the attorneys' fees come from a common fund or are otherwise paid, the district court must exercise its inherent authority to assure that the amount and mode of payment of attorneys' fees are fair and proper." Zucker v. Occidental Petroleum Corp., 192 F.3d 1323, 1328 (9th Cir. 1999); see also RAND, Executive Summary, Class Action Dilemmas 33 (1999) ("The single most important action that judges can take to support the public goals of class action litigation is to reward class action attorneys only for lawsuits that actually accomplish something of value to class members and society."). Judges have undertaken similar tasks in multidistrict litigation. In both settings, this focus may begin as part of the judge's involvement in appointing counsel.

1. AUTHORITY TO AWARD ATTORNEYS' FEES

The United States adheres generally to the "American Rule" that each litigant must pay its own lawyer, so that some exception to that rule must be found to justify fee-shifting. Manual for Complex Litigation (4th) § 14.11 (2004) outlines many of the grounds for fee awards. The Supreme Court held in Alyeska Pipeline Serv. Co. v. Wilderness Society, 421 U.S. 240

(1975), that the federal courts did not have authority to create exceptions to the American Rule. But several exceptions merit mention:

Fee-Shifting Statutes: Perhaps the most common is a fee-shifting statute, by which a legislature often declares that enforcement of a law is a matter of such importance that a successful plaintiff must be awarded a "reasonable fee." In such cases, there may be a hot debate about whether the plaintiff is actually a prevailing party. At a minimum, that means that the plaintiff must obtain relief in court (or by settlement), and often the extent of that relief casts a large shadow over the fee-award process. In complex litigation, particularly the sorts of cases described by Prof. Chayes in Ch. 1, there are often claims that invoke a fee-shifting statute.

Common fund: Where the litigation activities of one person created a fund for a number of other persons or conferred a benefit on them, American courts early allowed the litigant to recover from the fund thus created an amount including the attorneys' fees incurred in creating the fund. The premise was a theory of unjust enrichment—the passive beneficiaries of litigation should shoulder their fair share of the cost of creating the fund if they were to receive it. In Boeing Co. v. Van Gemert, 444 U.S. 472 (1980), a shareholders' derivative action, the Court broadly endorsed application of the common fund approach to support deducting the attorneys' fee not only from the share of the resulting fund claimed by shareholders, but also from the share not claimed. It ruled that the right of these nonclaimants to "share the harvest of the lawsuit" must be recognized even if they didn't avail themselves of it. This principle can also apply to class members who object to proposed settlements during proceedings regarding court approval of class action settlements under Rule 23(e). See *infra* p. 586. If the objections produce improvements in the settlement, the objectors may be eligible for a fee award to compensate them for the efforts expended in improving the settlement.

This analysis may often apply to Rule 23(b)(3) class actions, but may not work in (b)(2) actions. For example, in Geier v. Sundquist, 372 F.3d 784 (6th Cir. 2004), a suit requiring the state of Tennessee to develop a unitary university system, the court ruled that the doctrine was not applicable "where litigants are vindicating a social grievance" and also noted also that "there simply is no fund."

Lead and liaison counsel: The common fund doctrine has been used to justify fee shifting in consolidated cases where lead counsel is appointed. As the Manual for Complex Litigation (4th) § 14.215 (2004) explains, "[l]ead and liaison counsel may have been appointed by the court to perform functions necessary for the management of the case but not properly charged to their clients." Accordingly, it advises, the court should make a determination early in the case of how these lawyers are to be compensated for this work, "including setting up a fund to which designated parties should contribute in specified proportions." This approach is more common with respect to fees for plaintiff's attorneys.

In re Vioxx Prod. Liabil. Litig., 760 F.Supp.2d 640 (E.D.La. 2010), provides a striking example of this method of attorney compensation. The transferee judge appointed "common benefit lawyers" to organize and implement a massive discovery effort. They conducted thousands of depositions and argued more than 1,000 discovery motions. Eventually, after six bellwether trials, the cases settled and some $4.3 billion in settlement funds was distributed to over 32,000 claimants in 31 months. The judge observed: "This efficiency is unprecedented in mass tort settlements of this size." This *Vioxx* decision is featured in the last section of Chapter 7, on settlement via MDL.

Invoking his "inherent managerial authority," the judge also invoked provisions of the settlement agreement to uphold his power to reallocate fees from individual lawyers to common benefit lawyers. This prospect produced what he called a "taffy pull" between the common benefit lawyers and the retained counsel for thousands of individual claimants. "The tension in this case is between the attorneys who have done common benefit work and the primary attorneys who have not." Eventually the judge directed that 6% of any settlement be paid into a fund and that common benefit attorneys be awarded fees from that fund, which included about 20% of the total attorney fee payments in Vioxx litigation. Similar disputes attended a request by the steering committee in litigation arising out of the Deepwater Horizon oil well explosion to direct that 6% of any settlement be deposited into such a fund. See John Schwartz, Plaintiffs' Lawyers in a Bitter Dispute Over Fees in Gulf Oil Spill Cases, N.Y. Times, Dec. 4, 2011.

These arrangements may be challenged and provoke considerable controversy. But for much litigation it may be that the model of a "purely private contest" has for some time seemed "a nostalgic luxury no longer available in the hard-pressed federal courts," as the court put it in In re Air Crash Disaster at Fla. Everglades on Dec. 29, 1972, 549 F.2d 1006 (5th Cir. 1977). Thus, in In re Three Additional Appeals Arising Out of the San Juan Dupont Plaza Hotel Fire Litigation, 93 F.3d 1 (1st Cir. 1996), the court rejected the arguments of insurers added as defendants late in the litigation that they should not have to contribute to a fund for defense common benefit costs, even though they said they would rather "go it alone." But see In re Showa Denko K.K. L-Tryptophan Prod. Liabil. Litig., 953 F.2d 162 (4th Cir. 1992) (holding that transferee court lacked power to require contributions from plaintiffs not before the court).

2. DETERMINING THE AMOUNT TO BE AWARDED

It would be pleasing to be able to report that the computation of fee awards has proved to be straightforward, but it has not. "Of all the tasks facing trial court judges in class action litigation, one of the most difficult is determining the appropriate fee." Theodore Eisenberg & Geoffrey Miller, Attorney Fees in Class Action Settlements: An Empirical Study, 1 J. Empir. Legal Stud. 27, 27 (2004). Setting the fee is, however, one means by which the judge can wield power over the lawyers, either at the outset of litigation or at the end.

In large measure, the challenge of fee litigation results from changes within the legal marketplace. In general terms, most lawyers tended not to be terribly "businesslike" about their fee arrangements and billing until the 1960s or 1970s. By the early 1970s, however, those concerned with law office economics had begun to urge lawyers to focus on the amount of time they spent on matters in determining the amount they charged for their services, and billing on the basis of hourly rates became widespread, along with such law firm management techniques as billable budgets setting the number of hours lawyers should bill in a year. Many young associates still live with those managerial techniques.

For a long time, however, many have expressed unhappiness with billing by the hour. For one thing, hourly rates for some lawyers have reached stratospheric levels. See Debra Cassens Weiss, Top Law Firms Boost Hourly Rates for Equity Partners by 3.9%, Leaving Mid-Tier Firms $400 behind, ABA Journal, June 8, 2016 (reporting that the average hourly billing rate for equity partners at the most profitable firms was $1,085); see also Shane Group, Inc. v. Blue Cross Blue Shield of Michigan, 825 F.3d 299, 310 (6th Cir. 2016) (saying of the requested billing rates: "These are Bentley rates, not Cadillac rates"). "Many clients grew accustomed to pushing back on price during the [2008] recession and continue to demand discounts." Jennifer Smith, On Sale: The $1,150-per-Hour Lawyer, Wall St.J., April 10, 2013. Reports of "alternative billing arrangements" are rife, but the prevalence of such methods is less certain. "Alternative fee arrangements are like teenage sex. There's a lot more people talking about it than doing it—and those that are doing it don't really know what they're doing." Tamara Loomis, GCs Say the Pressure's On to Get Rid of the Billable Hour, S.F. Recorder, Aug. 21, 2009, at 2 (quoting an "industry observer"). See also Sam Skolnick, Law Firm Sites Talk About Alternative Fees, But Use Appears Thin, Bloomberg Law News, June 19, 2019.

The challenge to hourly billing had, by 2010, become a matter of general interest. Curbing Those Long Lucrative Hours, The Economist, July 24, 2010, reported that "[t]he billable hour is not dead, but many people would like to kill it." The article quotes the general counsel of the Association of Corporate Counsel as saying that "value-based" billing is now reported to be the measure in 15% to 30% of corporate client work, compared to 3% a few years before.

It is universally recognized that courts' fee awards should "mimic the market." As a consequence, the problem of determining the amount to award has proved, like other problems of fee shifting, to be "surprisingly complex." Thomas Rowe, Predicting the Effects of Attorney Fee Shifting, 47 Law & Contemp. Probs. 139, 140 (Winter 1984). In this section, we will look at the two conventional approaches developed by the lower courts— called the "lodestar" and the "common fund" approach increasingly preferred to the lodestar for cases that generate considerable recoveries. As the extensive treatment in the literature of attorneys' fees awards suggests, we can only introduce the issues. But it is not difficult to appreciate why they are often hotly litigated, and why judges increasingly attend to these issues at the outset of litigation.

a. The Emergence of the Lodestar

The lodestar approach is the hourly billing method implemented in court beginning in the 1970s. For small-recovery cases involving statutory fee-shifting, the Supreme Court announced that the lodestar approach was "the guiding light of our fee-shifting jurisprudence." City of Burlington v. Dague, 505 U.S. 557 (1992). In a series of cases, it developed that jurisprudence.

Perhaps the leading case was Hensley v. Eckerhart, 461 U.S. 424 (1983), in which a legal services lawyer pursued a class action against a state-operated facility that housed patients deemed dangerous to themselves or others. After a three-week trial, the district court found constitutional violations in five of six main areas that plaintiffs raised. Relying on a fee-shifting statue, plaintiff counsel then requested a fee award for nearly 3,000 hours spent over the five-year course of the litigation. The Supreme Court declared that "[w]here a plaintiff has obtained excellent results, his attorney should recover a fully compensatory fee. Normally this will encompass all hours reasonably expended on the litigation, and indeed in some cases of exceptional success an enhanced award may be justified. * * * [T]he most critical factor is the degree of success obtained." But work on unsuccessful claims should not be compensated, and an attorney seeking a fee award, like an attorney in private practice, should use "billing judgment" in deciding how much work really proved beneficial and deserved compensation.

Writing for the Court, Justice Powell recognized that the district court had discretion to fashion an appropriate fee award, and exhorted: "A request for attorney's fees should not result in a second major litigation. Ideally, of course, litigants will settle the amount of the fee." That may have been unrealistic. Judge Easterbrook deemed it "an unattainable dream" because the stakes "ensure that the parties will pursue all available opportunities for litigation." Kirchoff v. Flynn, 786 F.2d 320, 325 (7th Cir. 1986). Surely there are many cases in which the parties do settle the amount of the fee. Indeed, as we shall see in Ch. 7, one concern in regard to settlement approval in class actions is that the defendant has readily agreed to a fat fee for class counsel in return for slim pickings for class members. But Judge Easterbrook's predication has proved accurate for a significant number of cases.

NOTES AND QUESTIONS

1.   *Prevailing party*: In order to claim a fee award, a party must "prevail." For plaintiffs, that means that they are entitled to a fee award under a fee-shifting statute if they succeed on "any significant issue in litigation which achieves some of the benefit the parties sought in bringing the suit." Texas State Teachers Ass'n v. Garland Indep. School Dist., 489 U.S. 782 (1989). But obviously they don't have to win on every claim, and (as noted again below) they are supposed to exclude work done on unsuccessful claims from their fee request.

2.   *Hours worked:* Under the lodestar method, this is a key factor. It is also the sort of thing that young law firm associates often learn matters a lot to their employers. Should all hours be considered equal? Sometimes lawyers put in a remarkable number of hours on a case. See Peter Lattman, Kirkland Files Big Tab for UAL Bankruptcy Work, Wall St.J., March 9, 2006, at A11 (reporting that one Kirkland & Ellis lawyer billed 10,231 hours during the 38 month restructuring, some 3230 hours per year, or nearly nine hours per day, 365 days a year). Could the lawyer have been working at peak efficiency during all those hours? One ground for refusing to pay for lawyer work is that it was wasteful or inefficient. How easily could a court make a determination that the lawyers wasted time?

3.   *Billing rate:* The basic problem in many fee award cases is that there is no market in the usual sense to assist in setting fees. See, e.g., Vizcaino v. Microsoft Corp., 290 F.3d 1043, 1049 (9th Cir. 2002) ("in employment class actions like this one, no ascertainable 'market' exists. The 'market' is simply counsel's expectation of court-awarded fees."). Even if some Wall Street lawyers do command $1,000 per hour, most lawyers do not. The most difficult problems are often presented by lawyers who only handle cases in which a fee recovery is possible, and agree with their clients that the award will be their sole payment. How can it be said that these lawyers have a regular hourly fee? Often they submit affidavits from lawyers who do bill by the hour to establish what their rates would be if they did that also. This may sometimes allow public interest lawyers to collect "silk stocking" rates. See New York State Ass'n for Retarded Children, Inc. v. Carey, 711 F.2d 1136 (2d Cir. 1983) (plaintiff's lawyers awarded fees based on a schedule used by Wall Street firm Cravath, Swain & Moore for associate time). See also Student Public Interest Res. Group v. AT & T Bell Laboratories, 842 F.2d 1436 (3d Cir. 1988) (public interest law firm that customarily charged its clients rates dramatically lower than those charged by commercial law firms could use those commercial rates for purposes of a fee award).

4.   *Quality multiplier:* Once the lodestar is determined, the court may alter it using what the lower courts have come to call "multipliers." One is for the high quality of the work done by the lawyers. (Maybe that should already appear in the hourly rate, but the idea here is to focus on the work done on this

specific case.) The Supreme Court has been very strict with quality multipliers. In Perdue v. Kenny A. ex rel. Winn, 559 U.S. 542 (2010), an action brought pro bono on behalf of children in the Georgia foster care system, the district judge awarded 175% of the lodestar on the ground plaintiffs' lawyers exhibited "a higher degree of skill, commitment, dedication and professionalism * * * than the Court has seen displayed by the attorneys in any other case during its 27 years on the bench." Nonetheless, the Supreme Court held that this increase was not proper, in part because "the District Court did not employ a methodology that permitted meaningful appellate review."

5. *"Billing judgment" and the degree of success*: Only prevailing plaintiffs may seek a fee award, but they may not recover a "full" fee (comparable to what a private lawyer would bill) unless they achieve substantial success. As noted above, time spent only on unsuccessful claims should be excluded. In addition, the lawyer should scale back the lodestar with an eye to the actual relief obtained.

In City of Riverside v. Rivera, 477 U.S. 561 (1986), plaintiffs sued a variety of police officers for illegal arrest and ultimately obtained judgments against some of them totaling $33,000. The district court then awarded $245,000 in attorneys' fees, characterizing the results obtained as "excellent." The district court also suggested that it would have granted an injunction had one been requested, and observed that the police misconduct "had to be stopped and * * * nothing short of having a lawsuit like this would have stopped it." Defendants appealed. Writing for a plurality of four, Justice Brennan upheld the award, stressing the public benefit advanced by civil rights litigation. Justice Rehnquist, joined by three other justices, dissented, urging that "billing judgment" required scaling back the award. Justice Powell cast a deciding vote for affirmance, on the ground that the district court's findings were not clearly erroneous, but cautioned that the fee seemed unreasonable on its face, and that in his view "[w]here recovery of private damages is the purpose of a civil rights litigation, a district court in fixing fees, is obligated to give primary consideration to the amount of damages awarded as compared to the amount sought."

In Millea v. Metro-North R.R., 658 F.3d 154 (2d Cir. 2011), a Family Medical Leave Act case in which plaintiff recovered $612.50, plaintiff sought an attorneys fee award of $144,792, but the district court awarded only $204 (one third of the damages award). The court of appeals reversed (id. at 168): "The $612.50 award was not de minimis; to the contrary, the award was more than 100% of the damages Millea sought on that claim. It was not a derisory or contemptuous rejection by the jury. * * * True, where the plaintiff manages to prevail on a technicality in a mostly frivolous lawsuit, a court should award no attorneys' fees to discourage such lawsuits. However, "[t]hat is not to say that all nominal damages awards are de minimis. Nominal relief does not necessarily a nominal victory make. FMLA claims are often small-ticket items, and small damages awards should be expected without raising the inference that the victory was technical or de minimis." What should the district judge do on remand? At what point is it unreasonable to spend nearly $150,000 in lawyer time pursuing a monetary claim for less than $1,000?

6. *Contingency multiplier:* For some time, lower courts regularly increased the lodestar to compensate lawyers for the risk that they would not be paid at all, often doubling the lodestar. See John Leubsdorf, The Contingency Factor in Attorney Fee Awards, 90 Yale L.J. 473 (1981). In City of Burlington v. Dague, 505 U.S. 557 (1992), the Court held that contingency enhancement is not allowed. Justice Scalia, writing for the Court, contended that there was a risk of encouraging non-meritorious litigation and that allowing enhancement for contingency causes double counting because the difficulty of establishing the merits will be reflected in the hourly rate (better lawyers are needed for tougher cases) and the amount of time spent on the case (lawyers take longer on tougher cases). In the process, the Court disregarded the argument that a lawyer with an ordinary billing rate presented with a choice between a contingent case and one in which payment was certain would always choose the latter if money were the only consideration. Compare Coleman v. Kaye, 87 F.3d 1491 (3d Cir. 1996) (New Jersey law rejects *Dague*, so the lodestar must be adjusted to reflect risk of nonrecovery because the fee award is based on New Jersey law); Chieftain Royalty Co. v. Everest Energy Inst. Fund, 861 F.3d 1182 (10th Cir. 2017) (state law determines the fee measurement when the claim is based on state law).

b. The Challenge to the Lodestar

The lodestar has been widely assailed. For example, in In re Activision Securities Litig., 723 F.Supp. 1373 (N.D.Cal. 1989), the judge presiding over a proposed fee award in a settled securities fraud class action complained that she was "abandoned by the adversary system" and confronted with "a mountain of computerized billing records" from which to apply the lodestar factors.

> The question this court is compelled to ask is, "Is this process necessary?" Under a cost-benefit analysis, the answer would be a resounding, "No!" Not only do the [lodestar] analyses consume an undue amount of court time with little resulting advantage to anyone, but, in fact, it may be to the detriment of the class members. They are forced to wait until the court has done a thorough, conscientious analysis of the attorneys' fee petition. Or, class members may suffer a further diminution of their fund when a special master is retained and paid from the fund. Most important, however, is the effect the process has on the litigation and the timing of settlement. Where attorneys must depend on a lodestar approach there is little incentive to arrive at an early settlement. The history of these cases demonstrates this as noted below in the discussion of typical percentage awards.

The judge decided that, in the future, she would use a percentage approach instead, awarding counsel a percentage of the amount recovered for the class. This judge was not alone in preferring a percentage approach for many common fund cases. Indeed, the Supreme Court had seemed to approve that in a case involving a statutory fee shifting statute, Blum v. Stenson, 465 U.S. 886, 900 n. 16 (1984). The Manual for Complex Litigation (4th) § 14.121 (2004) reports that "the vast majority of courts of appeals now permit or direct district courts to use the percentage method in common-fund cases." See also Laffitte v. Robert Half Int'l, Inc., 376 P.3d 672 (Cal. 2017) (California joins "the overwhelming majority of federal and state courts" in embracing the percentage fee measure). The Private Securities Litigation Reform Act of 1995 directed that in suits governed by that Act "[t]otal attorneys' fees * * * shall not exceed a reasonable percentage of the amount of any damages and prejudgment interest paid to the class." 15 U.S.C. § 77z–1(a)(6). Given the low recoveries in civil rights and like cases, no such movement has surfaced in ordinary civil rights cases and other low-value cases in which statutory fee awards are designed to provide an incentive for counsel to take the cases.

NOTES AND QUESTIONS

1.   *Valuing the settlement*: As we shall see in Ch. 7 when we examine the court's role in evaluating proposed class-action settlements, it is not always easy to determine the value of a settlement. Even in settlements only for money, there may be uncertainties. For example, a judge who favored using the lodestar dissented from the move to percentage fee awards: "What is 30% of *up to* $70 million payable over a period of years? * * * The point is that 'percentage' is a relational concept, Percentage *of what*? Fifty percent is neither a lot nor a little, until one knows what the underlying whole is. Half of one cookie isn't much. Half of a full cookie jar may be a lot." Matter of Superior Beverage/Glass Container Consolidated Pretrial, 133 F.R.D. 119 (N.D.Ill. 1990). See also Linneman v. Vita-Mix Corp., 970 F.3d 621 (6th Cir. 2020) (Class Action Fairness Act prohibits use of lodestar when there is a coupon settlement).

2.   *Setting the percentage*: Obviously, the percentage selected is important. But Professor Dawson, examining efforts earlier in the 20th century to determine the "nationwide average," criticized them because the cases cited "showed wild variations ranging up and down the scale from two and one-half to forty-nine percent." John Dawson, Lawyers and Involuntary Clients in Public Interest Litigation, 88 Harv. L. Rev. 849, 876 (1975). Given the magnitude of dollar difference that results from a change in the percentage, is there a way to derive a proper percentage?

Some courts have questioned the use of a "benchmark." See Goldberger v. Integrated Resources, Inc., 209 F.3d 43 (2d Cir. 2000) (insisting on a multifactor analysis because the court is "disturbed by the essential notion of a benchmark" since "we cannot know precisely what fees common fund plaintiffs in an efficient market for legal services would agree to"). The Seventh Circuit, on the other hand, directs district judges to try to estimate the terms of a contract that private plaintiffs would negotiate with their lawyers at the outset of the case, and concluded that "[t]he second circuit's consider-everything approach, by contrast, lacks a benchmark: a list of factors without a rule of decision is just chopped salad." In re Synthroid Marketing Litigation, 264 F.3d 712 (7th Cir. 2001).

In In re Synthroid Marketing Litigation, *supra*, the Seventh Circuit also endorsed making the percentage determination early in the case, and also rejected the district court's announcement that in "megafund" cases (over $75 million) she would not award more than 10% of the fund. "On remand, the district court must estimate the terms of the contract that private plaintiffs would have negotiated with their lawyers, had bargaining occurred at the outset of the case." Id. at 718. How readily can a court do this? Could it ever result in an "escalating" percentage, in which counsel get a larger percentage of amounts recovered over a baseline? Brian Fitzpatrick, Do Class Action Lawyers Make Too Little?, 158 U. Pa. L. Rev. 2043 (2010), suggests that the lawyers are not paid enough, given that his research shows that they got only 15% of the $16 billion paid in settlements, while the typical percentage of contingency-fee lawyers is much higher. Given the declining percentage ordinarily used as the amount goes up, one might say that divergence is the goal of the judges. Are they wrong?

3. Another goal of the fee measurement process is to avoid windfalls for the lawyer. Would there be a risk of such windfalls if a percentage method were adopted in large dollar cases? Consider John Dawson, Lawyers and Involuntary Clients in Public Interest Litigation, 88 Harv. L. Rev. 849, 922 (1975):

> It is in the massive class action that sharing-of-benefit formulas for measuring fees appear in the most lurid light. It is to be expected that the classes will grow large as the purposes to be served grow more ambitious, to prevent or redress injuries to broad sectors of the population or to scattered but very numerous individuals. These features of the modernized class action when combined with sharing-of-benefit formulas provide an advantage that is not even to be found in stockholders' suits. It enables lawyers, almost miraculously, to increase the importance and usefulness of their public service and, in the same proportion, to magnify their own income, usually without adding significantly to their own workload. For if such formulas control, multiplying the members in the class and thereby the recovery will automatically multiply fees.

In securities class actions, there may be particular problems in this regard. Professor Alexander found that settlements in securities class actions appear not to reflect the merits of the claims. Based on this conclusion, she cautioned against a percentage approach in Do the Merits Matter? A Study of Settlements in Securities Class Actions, 43 Stan. L. Rev. 497, 579 (1991):

> If outcomes do not reflect the merits, changing to a percentage of the recovery formula is exactly the wrong thing to do. At least the

lodestar method assures that discovery will be done and the lawyers will be exposed to the facts of the case. To guarantee a fee as a fixed percentage of any recovery, however, regardless of the amount of work done, would add one more incentive to ignore the merits. If the benchmark percentage applies to fees plus expenses, it would work even more strongly against taking account of the merits by giving plaintiffs' attorneys an incentive to minimize expenses, which generally are related to information-gathering (experts, depositions, and so on).

In In re Cendant PRIDES Litigation, 243 F.3d 722 (3d Cir. 2001), the class action settlement had a value of over $340 million. Noting that this settlement enabled participating class members to recover fully, the district judge concluded that "counsel should not be penalized by a slavish application of the lodestar," given counsel's "gifted execution of responsibilities." Id. at 734. It awarded a fee of $19 million, some 5.7% of the settlement. The appellate court noted that, even taking the highest billing rates and accepting all hours worked, this would involve a multiplier of seven beyond the lodestar. Moreover, "this case was neither legally nor factually complex and did not require significant motion practice or discovery by [counsel], and the entire duration of the case from the filing of the Amended Complaint to the submission of a Settlement Agreement to the District Court was only four months." Id. at 742–43. It compared the fee awards in more than a dozen other cases with large recoveries (id. at 737–38), and concluded that the award in the PRIDES case could not be justified on the record made.

4.   In 2004, Professors Eisenberg and Miller published a study of fee awards in hundreds of class actions settled during the period 1993 to 2002. Somewhat underscoring arguments in favor of the percentage approach, they found "an overwhelming correlation between class recovery and attorney fees." Theodore Eisenberg & Geoffrey Miller, Attorney Fees in Class Action Settlements: An Empirical Study, 1 J. Empir. Legal Stud. 27, 72 (2004). They summarize their results as follows (id. at 28):

> The relation between fees and recovery is remarkably linear on a log scale, and is similar between cases in which no fee-shifting statute applies and cases in which the plaintiff had a right to seek reimbursement under a fee-shifting statute. The presence of high risk is associated with a higher fee, as is the presence of the case in federal rather than state court. Contrary to popular belief, we found no robust evidence that either recoveries for plaintiffs or fees of their attorneys as a percentage of the class recovery increased during the time period studied. Nor does the presence or absence of objectors to settlement have a discernable effect on fees.

E. SCREENING CLAIMS

IN RE TAXOTERE (DOCETAXEL) PRODUCTS LIABILITY LITIGATION

United States Court of Appeals, Fifth Circuit, 2020.
966 F.3d 351.

Before CLEMENT, SOUTHWICK and HIGGINSON, CIRCUIT JUDGES.

STEPHEN A. HIGGINSON, CIRCUIT JUDGE.

Dorothy Kuykendall alleges that she used defendants' prescription chemotherapy drug from 2011 to 2012 and now suffers from permanent hair loss. As a plaintiff in this multidistrict litigation ("MDL"), she was required to serve defendants with a completed fact sheet disclosing details of her personal and medical history soon after filing her short form complaint. When she failed to do so, the district court dismissed her case with prejudice. For the following reasons, we AFFIRM.

I.

Defendants are manufacturers of Taxotere, a prescription chemotherapy drug commonly prescribed to patients diagnosed with breast cancer, and Docetaxel, the generic version of Taxotere. According to plaintiffs, defendants were aware that their drugs caused hair loss yet failed to warn potential users of this negative side effect. In 2016, the Judicial Panel on Multidistrict Litigation consolidated all cases with similar claims and transferred them to the Eastern District of Louisiana. As of December 2019, there were 11,971 individual actions pending in this MDL.

Soon after the cases were consolidated, the district court issued several pretrial orders intended to streamline the discovery process and ensure the efficient management of plaintiffs' claims. In Amended Pretrial Order No. 22, the court ordered each plaintiff to complete a Plaintiff Fact Sheet ("PFS") within seventy-five days of the date that her case was docketed in the MDL. The PFS required each plaintiff to answer detailed questions about her race, family, medical history, cancer diagnosis, and treatment regimen. In addition to the PFS, plaintiffs were required to provide defendants with authorizations for the release of medical records.

If a plaintiff failed to complete and serve the necessary disclosures by the deadline, defendants were directed to file a notice of deficiency on MDL Centrality, an electronic database. After receiving a notice of deficiency, plaintiffs had thirty days to submit a compliant PFS. If they failed to do so, defendants were permitted to serve a notice of non-compliance upon Plaintiffs' Liaison Counsel. Plaintiffs were then given an additional thirty days to cure the deficiencies. If a plaintiff still failed to provide the "complete and verified disclosures" by that deadline, defendants could add the plaintiff to the court's "call docket" for the next scheduled hearing. The district court's pretrial order explicitly warned plaintiffs that their cases could be dismissed if they failed to establish good cause during the hearing for their continued discovery deficiencies.

Dorothy Kuykendall filed a short form complaint on November 29, 2018. Accordingly, her PFS was due seventy-five days later, on February 12, 2019. After she failed to file the required form by the deadline, defendants served her with a notice of non-compliance on March 26, 2019. Under Pretrial Order No. 22A, the notice of non-compliance gave Kuykendall an additional thirty days, or until April 25, 2019, to serve defendants with the necessary information.

When Kuykendall again failed to cure the deficiencies, the defendants placed her name on the call docket for the next court hearing, scheduled for May 21, 2019. Next to Kuykendall's name, the defendants included a notation stating "No PFS submitted."

The court was unable to address Kuykendall's case during the May 21 conference, so it scheduled a follow-up conference for May 29, 2019. On May 21, Kuykendall uploaded a few documents to MDL Centrality, including a signed declaration and two photographs, but she did not file a PFS. Five days later, Kuykendall finally submitted a PFS, though the document was missing responses to several important questions, including spousal information, weight and height information, and information regarding her prescribing doctor.

At the May 29 hearing, the defendants acknowledged that Kuykendall had submitted a PFS after the original hearing date but before the rescheduled hearing. However, defense counsel informed the court that Kuykendall's PFS contained "a significant number of blanks," including "the date of cancer diagnosis, the cancer markers that go to staging, the dates of chemotherapy treatment, the name of the prescribing oncologist, prior medication history, and a list of other medical providers." Kuykendall's counsel acknowledged that her PFS was incomplete, but reported that it was his belief that "[a]ll of the appropriate boxes have been checked." He further explained that any remaining blanks were caused by the "difficulty" of obtaining information from clients, including "health insurance information [and] identifying each pharmacy drugstore."

The court gave Kuykendall an additional thirty days to cure the deficiencies identified by defendants during the hearing. On July 1, 2019, after the court's extension had expired and Kuykendall had not provided an updated PFS, the defendants sent Kuykendall a notice of deficiency that identified the continued omissions and deficiencies in her PFS. Two days later, on July 3, defendants included Kuykendall on a list of plaintiffs whose cases were subject to immediate dismissal. In a short order without analysis, the district court dismissed Kuykendall's case with prejudice on July 11, 2019.

That same day, Kuykendall filed a letter in which she claimed to be "blindsided" by the list of deficiencies alleged by the defendants during the May 29 hearing. The letter faulted the defendants for seeking immediate dismissal, rather than giving Kuykendall an additional thirty days to respond to the most recent notice of deficiency. Though the letter was dated July 9, it was not filed on the docket until July 11. Just a few days before filing the letter, but several days *after* the court's thirty-day extension had expired, Kuykendall submitted a first and second amended PFS on MDL Centrality. Those forms included some previously missing information, but they continued to omit certain information, including her children's addresses and her height.

Construing Kuykendall's letter as a motion for reconsideration, the court issued a decision supplementing its dismissal order. The court explained that Kuykendall's counsel was provided with ample notice of the deficiencies in her PFS, and concluded that Kuykendall's failure to upload new documents to MDL Centrality during the thirty-day extension period demonstrated that she "made no effort to comply with the Court's order." Kuykendall filed a timely notice of appeal on August 8, 2019.

II.

We review a district court's imposition of sanctions, including the dismissal of a case with prejudice, for an abuse of discretion. *See, e.g., Law Funder, L.L.C. v. Munoz*, 924 F.3d 753, 758 (5th Cir. 2019). "A trial court abuses its discretion when its ruling is based on an erroneous view of the law or a clearly erroneous assessment of the evidence." *In re Deepwater Horizon (Barrera)*, 907 F.3d 232, 234 (5th Cir. 2018).

III.

District courts are vested with the power to "manage their own affairs so as to achieve the orderly and expeditious disposition of cases." *Woodson v. Surgitek, Inc.*, 57 F.3d 1406, 1417 (5th Cir. 1995) (quoting *Link v. Wabash R.R. Co.*, 370 U.S. 626, 630–31, 82 S.Ct. 1386, 8 L.Ed.2d 734 (1962)). This power necessarily includes the "power . . . to control [the court's] docket by dismissing a case as a sanction for a party's failure to obey court orders." Because of the severity of such a sanction, however, we have "limited the district court's discretion in dismissing cases with prejudice." "[W]e have previously deemed dismissal with prejudice to be a 'draconian remedy' and a 'remedy of last resort.' "

Here, the parties have two primary disagreements: (1) which of two legal standards governs a district court's involuntary dismissal in the context of an MDL, and (2) whether the district court erred in applying the applicable legal standard to Kuykendall's case.

A.

Kuykendall argues that the district court's dismissal order can be affirmed only if it satisfies the fact-intensive six-factor test articulated in

Law Funder. Under *Law Funder*, a dismissal with prejudice will be affirmed if (1) it is "just"; (2) it is "related to the particular 'claim' which was at issue in the order"; (3) the violation was willful or in bad faith; (4) "the client, rather than counsel, is responsible for the violation"; (5) the violation caused substantial prejudice to the opposing party; and (6) "a lesser sanction would not 'substantially achieve the desired deterrent effect.'" In contrast, defendants argue that the district court's dismissal order need only meet the two-factor test articulated by this court in the context of the *Deepwater Horizon* MDL. *See, e.g., Barrera*, 907 F.3d at 235.

Our cases have used variable language to describe the appropriate test for evaluating a district court's order dismissing a case with prejudice. In one line of cases involving dismissals for discovery order violations, we have suggested that litigation-ending sanctions must meet a multi-factor, fact-intensive test. In another group of cases involving dismissals for "docket management" purposes, we have articulated a two-factor test, affirming dismissals with prejudice as long as (1) there is a "clear record of delay or contumacious conduct by the plaintiff," and (2) "lesser sanctions would not serve the best interests of justice." *See Price v. McGlathery*, 792 F.2d 472, 474 (5th Cir. 1986) (per curiam) (quoting *Rogers v. Kroger Co.*, 669 F.2d 317, 320 (5th Cir. 1982)). Even when evaluating these two factors, however, we have explained that other "aggravating" factors—such as "the extent to which the plaintiff, as distinguished from his counsel, was personally responsible for the delay, the degree of actual prejudice to the defendant, and whether the delay was the result of intentional conduct"— may also be relevant to the analysis. * * * While "aggravating factors must 'usually' be found" to support a dismissal with prejudice, "we have not said that they must 'always' be found."

We need not completely reconcile these competing standards here. Several of our recent decisions stemming from the *Deepwater Horizon* MDL have clarified that the two-factor test articulated in *Rogers* applies to a district court's dismissal with prejudice in the unique context of an MDL. In *Barrera*, we affirmed the district court's dismissal of several plaintiffs in the *Deepwater Horizon* MDL for failure to comply with a pretrial order mandating that each individual plaintiff file a "wet-ink signature." We upheld the district court's dismissal order after we observed that the plaintiffs had exhibited a "clear record of delay or contumacious conduct by the plaintiff" and that "lesser sanctions would not service the best interests of justice." * * *[W]e declined to consider any "aggravating factors," such as the willfulness of the violation or the party responsible for the violation.

Since *Barrera*, we have repeatedly applied this same two-factor test to evaluate dismissal orders that resulted from plaintiffs' failure to comply with the district court's discovery orders in the *Deepwater Horizon* MDL. We have explained that the complexity of managing an MDL necessitates a standard that gives district courts greater flexibility to dismiss a plaintiff for a discovery violation. *See Barrera*, 907 F.3d at 235 ("[T]here is a special deference required in the context of an MDL."); *see also In re Asbestos Prods. Liab. Litig. (No. VI)*, 718 F.3d 236, 248 (3d Cir. 2013) (observing that "the very purpose of the centralization before the transferee judge is the efficient progress of the cases in preparation for trial"); *In re Fannie Mae Sec. Litig.*, 552 F.3d 814, 822 (D.C. Cir. 2009) ("District judges must have authority to manage their dockets, especially during massive litigation such as [an MDL], and we owe deference to their decisions whether and how to enforce the deadlines they impose.").

Other circuits have echoed these principles in evaluating similar MDL dismissals in the context of missing Plaintiff Fact Sheets. The *Deepwater Horizon* two-factor test helps animate the goals of strict enforcement and efficient management by making it easier for district courts to dismiss non-complying plaintiffs in MDLs. We therefore apply this two-factor test to the district court's dismissal of Kuykendall's case.

B.

The district court was not required to make specific factual findings on each of the *Deepwater Horizon* prongs before dismissing Kuykendall's case. Our independent review of the record confirms that both prongs are satisfied, and, as a result, the district court did not abuse its discretion in dismissing Kuykendall with prejudice.

i.

First, there is "a clear record of delay or contumacious conduct by the plaintiff." Despite numerous extensions and grace periods, Kuykendall consistently failed to submit a complete PFS. Her initial PFS was due on February 12, 2019, but she failed to submit any version of the required PFS—even an incomplete one—by that deadline. Under the terms of Amended Pretrial Order 22, she had until April 25, 2019 to submit a complete PFS after the defendants filed a notice of non-compliance, but she missed that deadline as well. The next deadline was May 21, 2019—the date of the original call docket hearing—but she also failed to submit a PFS to MDL Centrality before that date. Although Kuykendall eventually submitted a PFS before the rescheduled May 29 hearing, that document was incomplete, missing "readily ascertainable information like her place of birth, her current weight and height, and whether she has certain health conditions such as low iron." Even when the district court gave her an additional thirty-day extension to cure those gaps, Kuykendall failed to submit a revised document before the new deadline expired.[6] Though she

---

[6] We are not persuaded by Kuykendall's argument that the district court erred when it deviated from the procedures set forth in its pretrial orders and imposed a thirty-day extension for Kuykendall's PFS, rather than requiring the defendants to first provide Kuykendall with a written deficiency notice. Kuykendall did not object to these procedures during the May 29 hearing, so we review her challenge for plain error only. "We review a district court's interpretation of its own orders with deference, particularly in the MDL context." It was not plainly erroneous for the district court to determine that the notice provided to Kuykendall during the May 29 hearing was

eventually submitted two amended PFSs soon *after* that deadline, those documents also were missing information, including her height and her children's addresses.

Altogether, Kuykendall failed to comply with the court's order to submit a complete PFS for nearly five months. This is similar to the plaintiffs' conduct in *Barrera*, where we held that there was a clear record of delay. As in *Barrera*, Kuykendall was given ample notice of the potential consequences of her failure to comply with the district court's orders. Pretrial Order No. 22A warned plaintiffs that failure to comply with the PFS requirements could lead to "possible dismissal with prejudice or other appropriate relief." Despite this warning, Kuykendall did not seek additional extensions or provide an explanation for her failure to submit a PFS. And hundreds of other plaintiffs complied with the court's orders, "demonstrating it was not logistically impossible" to do so within the timeline set forth in the court's pretrial orders.

Kuykendall argues that her delay was not nearly as long as the delay in many other cases where we have affirmed dismissal orders. Because this case involves an MDL, however, the district court was empowered to "establish [a] schedule[ ] with [a] *firm* cutoff date[ ]." Though a delay of five months might be "insignificant" in some contexts, "administering cases in multidistrict litigation is different from administering cases on a routine docket." As a result, Kuykendall exhibited a clear record of delay sufficient to meet the first prong in the *Deepwater Horizon* test.

ii

The record also demonstrates that lesser sanctions would not have "serve[d] the best interests of justice." * * * Kuykendall was given several extensions by the district court, but she continuously failed to file a complete PFS on MDL Centrality. "Providing plaintiff with a second or third chance" is *itself* "a lenient sanction, which, when met with further default, may justify imposition of the ultimate sanction of dismissal with prejudice." Though Kuykendall provided other forms of discovery and eventually submitted a partial PFS, she consistently failed to comply with the court's initial order—to provide a complete PFS by the required deadline. Given this record, it is "unclear what lesser sanctions could have been appropriate following the district court's warnings and second chances." Therefore, the record also supports a showing on the second prong of the *Deepwater Horizon* test.

---

sufficient to replace the notice typically provided in the form of a notice of deficiency. Furthermore, the procedures used by the district court here—specifically, addressing deficient cases during a monthly "call docket"—have been explicitly endorsed by the Federal Judicial Center. Margaret S. Williams et al., Plaintiff Fact Sheets in Multidistrict Litigation Proceedings, Federal Judicial Center and Judicial Panel on Multidistrict Litigation (2019).

NOTES AND QUESTIONS

1.   *Epilogue:* In In re Taxotere Products Liability Litigation, 462 F.Supp.3d 650 (E.D.La. 2020), the court granted summary judgment with regard to nearly 200 claims listed in the Appendix to its opinion on the ground that a label change in December 2015 defeated the failure-to-warn claims of all plaintiffs who began treatment on or after Dec. 15, 2015. The Appendix listed each claim individually, along with the date on which treatment began. Although the decision does not say so, it seems likely that this date came from these plaintiffs' PFS submissions.

2.   In Rogers v. Kroger Co., 669 F.2d 317 (5th Cir. 1982), the court held that the district judge had abused discretion by dismissing when plaintiff's newly hired substitute counsel reported for trial but declared herself unprepared to proceed, requesting a two-week continuance of the trial. Among other things, the district judge noted that this lawyer had been unprepared without cause in another case before him. Defendant opposed a continuance and proclaimed itself ready to proceed to trial, and the district court dismissed with prejudice under Rule 41(b). The appellate court concluded that the record did not show "egregious and sometimes outrageous delays" such that "plaintiff's conduct has threatened the integrity of the judicial process." Moreover, the record did not show that the district judge had considered less severe sanctions. Only when "three aggravating elements"—plaintiff culpability, prejudice to defendant, and intentional conduct by plaintiff or counsel—were shown by the record would dismissal as a sanction be affirmed.

Compare Link v. Wabash R.R. Co., 370 U.S. 626 (1962), upholding dismissal for failure to prosecute when plaintiff's counsel did not attend a pretrial conference, though he did call the judge's secretary on the morning of the scheduled conference and report that he would be unable to attend because he was preparing papers for filing in state court in another case. The district court *sua sponte* dismissed the case, and plaintiff argued on appeal that dismissal was improper, particularly in the absence of a motion by defendant. The Court upheld the dismissal, and rejected the argument that plaintiff should not suffer for his lawyer's failure to appear at the pretrial conference. Stressing that plaintiff had responded to discovery, Justice Black urged in dissent that "the plaintiff simply had no way of knowing that there was even the slightest danger that his potentially valuable lawsuit was going to be thrown out of court because of some default on the part of his lawyer."

3.   Would the delays in *Taxotere* satisfy the standard the court adopted in its *Rogers* decision? Did defendant suffer any significant prejudice due to the delayed submission of plaintiff's PFS? Should it matter whether her lawyer was a part of appointed leadership? Recall that lawyers not appointed to leadership positions (sometimes called IRPAs—Individually Represented Plaintiffs' Attorneys), may sometimes not be closely involved in the litigation of the MDL cases. Should leadership counsel have taken responsibility for ensuring that plaintiff responded to the PFS order in a timely fashion?

The court stresses that in MDL litigation appellate courts should be more flexible about dismissals of individual cases for failure to satisfy requirements like submitting a PFS. As introduced in Chapter 4, the number of cases in MDL proceedings—particularly mass tort proceedings like this one—has increased a great deal since the beginning of this century. Sometimes it appears that claims are submitted without the kind of scrutiny that would ordinarily precede the filing of an individual case. In In re Mentor Corp. Obtape Transobturator Sling Products Litigation, 2016 WL 4705827 (M.D.Ga. Sept. 7, 2016), the judge reported that after an MDL order was entered by the Judicial Panel on Multidistrict Litigation, the original 22 cases "exploded to more than 850 cases, which explosion appears to have been fueled, at least in part, by an onslaught of lawyer television solicitations." Some have characterized this sort of upsurge as the "Field of Dreams" phenomenon—"If you build it, they will come."

It appears that such lawyer outreach does occur on occasion. For example, Francesca Mari, The Lawyer Whose Clients Didn't Exist, Atlantic Magazine, May 2020, reported on a Texas lawyer who submitted many claims in the *Deepwater Horizon* litigation cited by the court in *Taxotere*. The lawyer engaged the services of a man "who made a living pitching potential mass torts to lawyers, as well as recruiting plaintiffs for the cases," and eventually invested $10 million to get 40,000 clients with claims in the MDL. That portfolio of cases landed the lawyer a place on the court-appointed plaintiff leadership but also led to a federal indictment against the lawyer for submitting fake claims in the MDL. See also Douglas Smith, The Rising Behemoth: Multidistrict and Mass Tort Litigation in the United States 13 (2020) (asserting that plaintiff law firms "are essentially able to purchase cases from companies that conduct mass advertising").

The eye-popping *Deepwater Horizon* story gained a great deal of attention, but it is not typical. Some assert, however, that unfounded claims in MDL mass tort litigations sometimes constitute 20% to 30% of the claims. See Submission 20–CV–AA to the Advisory Committee on Civil Rules (Sept. 9, 2020). In 2017 the House of Representatives passed legislation to add the following provision to the MDL statute, but the Senate did not act on the bill:

> In any coordinated or consolidated pretrial proceedings pursuant to subsection (b), counsel for a plaintiff asserting a claim seeking redress for personal injury whose civil actions is assigned to or directly filed in the proceedings shall make a submission sufficient to demonstrate that there is evidentiary support (including but not limited to medical records) for the factual contentions in plaintiff's complaint regarding the alleged injury, the exposure to the risk that alleged caused the injury, and the alleged cause of the injury. The submission must be made within the first 45 days after the civil action is transferred to or directly filed in the proceedings. That deadline shall not be extended. Within 90 days after the submission deadline, the judge or judges to whom the action is assigned shall enter an order determining whether the submission is sufficient and

shall dismiss an action without prejudice if the submission is found to be insufficient. If a plaintiff in an action dismissed without prejudice fails to tender a sufficient submission within the following 30 days, the action shall be dismissed with prejudice.

Is this regime more demanding than the PFS requirement involved in *Taxotere*? Would complying with this statutory directive have been difficult for the district judge in the *Mentor Corp.* MDL *supra,* who saw the original 22 cases "explode" to more than 850 cases?

4. *Plaintiff fact sheets:* The PFS practice involved in *Taxotere* is different from the provision adopted by the House. A Federal Judicial Center study of PFS practices in mass tort litigation in 2019 showed that they are employed in some 87% of MDL litigations with 1,000 or more claims, and that in about half the proceedings in which they are used there was evidence that plaintiffs that did not satisfy the PFS requirement faced motions to dismiss. The report also indicated that such PFS requirements usually sought claimants' health records, personal identifying information, and litigation history. Margaret Williams, Emery Lee III & Jason Cantone, Plaintiff Fact Sheets in Multidistrict Litigation: Products Liability Proceedings 2008–2018 (March 2019). A prominent plaintiff lawyer reported that using fact sheets that "replace formal interrogatories with supposedly less onerous, more fact-oriented formats is now a common practice in mass tort multidistrict litigation." Elizabeth Cabraser & Katherine Lehe, Uncovering Discovery, 12 Sedona Conf. J. 1, 8 n.40 (2011).

5. *The "census" alternative:* Fact sheets sometimes are quite long and burdensome, and they can require a great deal of negotiation. Recently MDL transferee judges have begun to experiment with a less demanding alternative called a "census" of claims. Like a fact sheet, it seeks some basic information about claimants' use of the product involved and development of the sort of condition at issue in the litigation after use of the product. One of the experiments is in the MDL in San Francisco involving JUUL products, presenting claims that the company improperly induced underage customers to use the product. The stated goal of the census process is to acquaint the court with the dimensions and nature of the claims pending in the MDL proceeding, which may affect management of the cases. Though not particularly designed to screen out groundless cases, it has led to dismissals of some 45 of more than a thousand cases pending in that case. See Martina Barash, JUUL Gets Smattering of Cases Dismissed from Litigation, for Now, Bloomberg Law News, Oct. 23, 2020. One plaintiff lawyer sought an extension for completing a PFS, explaining that the client "has been asked to provide intimate details through a PFS about matters teenagers generally prefer to keep private."

6. *Lone Pine orders:* Invented in Lore v. Lone Pine Corp., 1986 WL 637507 (N.J.Super.Ct. 1986), *Lone Pine* orders usually seek the same sort of information as fact sheets, but go beyond that information to require also that proof of causation, often depending on medical or other expert affidavits, be supplied before claims are allowed to proceed. See Avila v. Willits Environmental Remediation Trust, 633 F.3d 828 (9th Cir. 2011), involving

toxic contamination due to operation of a chrome plating facility in the town for 50 years. There were more than 1,000 named plaintiffs, present and former residents of the town, and the order also required those who moved to the town after the facility stopped operation to submit expert affidavits supporting their claims to have been injured due to the pollution. The court of appeals affirmed dismissal of claims by plaintiffs who failed for more than a year to submit affidavits, and rejected plaintiffs' argument that the order "impermissibly made discovery unilateral." See also Acuna v. Brown & Root, Inc, 200 F.3d 335 (5th Cir. 2000) (upholding dismissals when some 1,000 plaintiffs tried to satisfy such an order by submitting identical form affidavits all from the same expert).

Consider whether individual plaintiffs should be required at the outset to provide such expert affidavits. Nora Freeman Engstrom, The Lessons of *Lone Pine*, 129 Yale L.J. 2, 21–22 (2019) outlines four differences between a commonplace PFS and a *Lone Pine* order:

> First, *Lone Pine* orders typically inquire as to specific causation. They demand evidence that product or contaminant x actually caused plaintiff's injury or ailment y. Plaintiff fact sheets do not. Second, *Lone Pine* orders demand that plaintiffs supply information from qualified experts (sometimes from experts whose testimony would pass muster under *Daubert* and Rule of Evidence 702). Plaintiff fact sheets, by contrast, demand information from only the plaintiff and only information that is easily obtainable or already on the plaintiff's possession. Third, owing to their heavy reliance on notoriously pricey medical experts, *Lone Pine* orders are expensive; to enter a *Lone Pine* order is to impose a costly burden on plaintiffs. Fact sheets, by contrast "offer plaintiffs' counsel an easy and inexpensive opportunity to satisfy initial discovery obligations." A final key difference, which lurks below the surface, is that plaintiff facts sheets are relatively uncontroversial, whereas, particularly within the plaintiffs' bar, *Lone Pine* reception has been decidedly mixed.

7. One objection to each of these techniques for screening claims in mass tort litigation is that they make the playing field uneven, and in defendants' favor. Often plaintiffs are not able to get extensive discovery until they satisfy the PFS or *Lone Pine* requirements. Consider whether, for example, defendant in a class action could routinely compel class members to submit similar information on pain of dismissal of their claims. See *supra* p. 408 note 5. On the other hand, class members often have to submit detailed claims to get paid from settlement proceeds, as explained in Chapter 7. See *infra* p. 571. Some plaintiff lawyers, concerned perhaps about conduct like that of the Texas lawyer described in note 2 above, are receptive to measures that may weed out groundless claims. Such culling might be important in connection with selecting leadership counsel, and with apportioning settlement proceeds, and ensuring that only those with demonstrable claims are included in settlements. But on the defense side, there is still support for stronger measures. A letter from corporate general counsel asserted that "[a]n initial census rule could

solve the problem by requiring evidence of exposure to the alleged harm and evidence of injury to be produced within 60 days. This would strongly discourage meritless claims." Joint Statement From 45 Corporate General Counsel to the Advisory Committee on Civil Rules, no. 19–CV–AA (Oct. 3, 2019).

By way of contrast, courts are cautious about *Lone Pine* orders. Consider Adinolfe v. United Technologies Corp., 768 F.3d 1161, 1168 (11th Cir. 2014):

> As a general matter, we do not think that it is legally appropriate (or for that matter wise) for a district court to issue a *Lone Pine* order requiring factual support for the plaintiffs' claims before it has determined that those claims survive a motion to dismiss under *Twombly*. It is one thing to demand that plaintiffs come forward with some evidence supporting certain basic elements of their claims as a way of organizing (and maybe bifurcating) the discovery process once a case is at issue, and dealing with discrete issues or claims by way of partial summary judgment motions. It is quite another to begin compiling, analyzing, and addressing evidence (pro and con) concerning the plaintiffs' allegations without reciprocal discovery before those allegations have been determined to be legally sufficient under Rule 12(b)(6). * * *

> Whatever the general propriety and/or utility of *Lone Pine* orders * * * they should not be used as (or become) the platforms for pseudo-summary judgment motions at a time when the case is not at issue and the parties have not engaged in reciprocal discovery. * * * *Lone Pine* orders might become the practical equivalent of a heightened court-imposed quasi-pleading standard, something the Supreme court has frowned on.

As a comparison, consider when in an individual suit the plaintiff would have to submit expert reports. See Rule 26(a)(2)(B) (submission required 90 days before trial unless the scheduling order has set a different date). Should courts considering *Lone Pine* orders take that timing feature into account? Except for a *Lone Pine* order, could defendants usually require plaintiffs to submit expert support for their claims at the outset of the case?

8. *Sanctioning lawyers*: In In re Engle Cases, 283 F.Supp.3d 1174 (M.D.Fla. 2017), a joint order by four district judges imposed more than $9 million in sanctions on two lawyers who had filed some 1,250 groundless complaints in tobacco litigation in the district. The court found that the lawyers had violated their professional responsibility obligations, noting (in an 80-page order) their "refusal to aid the Court in purging these cases," id. at 1258, and repeatedly making false assertions to the court that there were good grounds for the suits. The court also referred the lawyers to the state bar for investigation of possible bar discipline for their behavior.

9. However much caution judges employ in deploying such measures, note the standard of review the appellate courts bring to supervision of this case management activity. Were the court to grant summary judgment, for

example, that ruling would be subject to de novo review upon appeal. But sanctions for failure to comply with a PFS order or a *Lone Pine* order are reviewed for abuse of discretion, and courts say they are particularly inclined to defer to the management decisions in MDL cases, given the enormous challenges those cases pose for the judges presiding over them. Balanced against that concern, however, is the risk that in a mass of claims groundless ones may be extremely hard to challenge.

F. MANAGING DISCOVERY

Copyright © 2001 Mark F. Bernstein. Reprinted by permission.

The court's role in managing discovery builds on the lawyer's role in managing it. The Federal Rules of Civil Procedure were intended to work a revolution in the nature of pretrial preparation, and they did. See Stephen Subrin, Fishing Expeditions Allowed: The Historical Background of the 1938 Federal Discovery Rules, 39 Bos.Coll.L.Rev. 691 (1998). Indeed, it is routinely said that discovery is the arena in which lawsuits are won and lost. The trial lawyer of the past has been replaced by the "litigator" of today. Since discovery often commands the bulk of the litigator's efforts, it deserves substantial attention. Students should have a good grasp of the basic concepts from introductory civil procedure; the coverage here builds on that base. Whether or not the original rulesmakers foresaw the Information Age, now that we live in that age we must deal with the discovery consequences.

For generations, technology has had a major effect on discovery. Consider the consequences of the introduction of the photocopier in the 1960s on the amount of material that could be obtained using Rule 34. For decades, lawyers have appreciated that the only way to deal with the volume of information that modern discovery can produce is by developing systems at the outset that cope with the information generated. See, e.g., James Halverson, Coping With the Fruits of Discovery in the Complex Case—The Systems Approach to Litigation Support, 44 Antitrust L.J. 39 (1975). Planning for such an effort is critical. In complex litigation involving dispersed suits, the need for managing information could provide an edge to the defense side. But beginning in the 1960s, plaintiff lawyers cooperated with each other in ways that counteracted that advantage. For an early description involving such litigation, see Paul Rheingold, The MER/29 Story—An Instance of Successful Mass Disaster Litigation, 56 Cal. L. Rev. 116, 124 (1968) (asserting that "unified action by the plaintiffs served to counteract the defendant's natural advantages").

Planning is obviously central to managing discovery information. The Federal Rules have directed that some of this planning is supposed to be collaborative, to happen early in the litigation, and to involve the judge. Thus, Rule 26(a)(1) calls for initial disclosure of certain information, and Rule 26(f) directs the lawyers to confer to devise a discovery plan for the case that should be submitted to the court before it enters a scheduling order. Meanwhile, Rule 26(d) interdicts formal discovery until the conference about a discovery plan has occurred and, as amended in 2015, Rule 1 now emphasizes cooperation among opposing counsel. Judicial oversight of discovery therefore lies at the heart of overall judicial management of litigation, and is likely to be the focus of early orders.

The transformation worked by the computer has had enormous implications for discovery practice. A 2011 report said that "[w]e generate over 1.8 zettabytes of digital information a year. By some estimates that's nearly 30 million times the amount of information contained in all the books ever published." Kari Krause, When Data Disappears, N.Y. Times, Aug. 7, 2011. The upsurge in use of social media, workplace technology, and electronic businesses since that time surely eclipses the 2011 figures. "More data has been created in the last two years than in the entire previous history of the human race, and the amount of data is expected to increase 10-fold by 2020." Gordon v. T.G.R. Logistics, Inc., 321 F.R.D. 401 (D.Wyo. 2017).

This section therefore introduces four core concerns of modern discovery, particularly in complex litigation. First, it examines the growing importance of E-Discovery, an activity that began to emerge around the year 2000 and has grown into a multi-billion dollar industry. It then turns to the related concerns of preservation of both electronically stored information and hard-copy material. Together, those two topics control the amount of information that is available for use in complex litigation. The next subject—preserving privilege protection—is one of key importance to young lawyers, who may be called upon to ensure that materials that can be held back are not turned over in discovery. Finally, the last topic is discovery confidentiality and protective orders, which can somewhat reduce the risks associated with large-scale discovery productions.

1. E-DISCOVERY

J.D. Mark F. Bernstein for *The Recorder*

THREE THINGS EVERY LAWYER SHOULD LEARN ABOUT E-DISCOVERY.

1. LEARN THE DETAILS OF THE AMENDED FEDERAL RULES.

Hmm... Rule 34(b) is new... Doo,

2. LEARN THE DIFFERENT FILE PRODUCTION FORMATS.

Native? Paper?

3. LEARN THE CORRECT WAY TO BURN A CD.

ALL FILES HAVE BEEN DELETED. NO!!

Copyright © 2006, Mark Bernstein. Reprinted by permission.

Since 2000, electronic discovery has surely been the hottest topic in discovery practice. "Perhaps no area of law is evolving faster than E-discovery." Michele Lange, E-Discovery Trends to Watch in 2017, Today's General Counsel, Feb/Mar 2017 at 26. Some urge that it be "considered a specialized substantive expertise in the same vein as, for example, patent law." Janet Kwuon & Karen Wan, High Stakes for Missteps in EDD, N.J.L.J., Dec. 31, 2007, at E2. In the words of one federal judge speaking at a conference in 2014, "E-Discovery is pervasive. It's like understanding civil procedure. You're not going to be a civil litigator without understanding the rules of civil procedure. Similarly, you're no longer going to be able to conduct litigation of any complexity without understanding E-Discovery." Joe Dysart, Learn or Lose, ABA Journal, April 2014, at 32 (quoting Magistrate Judge James C. Francis, S.D.N.Y.). As another judge put it, only half humorously, in City of Rockford v. Mallinckrodt ARD, Inc., 326 F.R.D. 489, 492 n.2 (N.D.Ill. 2018):

> The court pauses for a moment here to calm down litigators less familiar with ESI. (You know who you are.) In life, there are many things to be scared of, including, but not limited to, spiders, sharks, and clowns, definitely clowns. ESI is not something to be scared of. The same is true for all the terms and jargon related to ESI. Discovery of ESI is still discovery, governed by the same Federal Rules of Civil Procedure. So don't freak out.

The ABA has announced that appropriate understanding and use of technology is a fundamental aspect of lawyer competence. See ABA Model Rule 1.1 Comment 8 (stating that a lawyer should keep abreast of changes affecting "the benefits and risks associated with relevant technology"). A formal opinion of the State Bar of California, issued in 2011, said that "[a]ttorney competence related to litigation generally requires, at a minimum, a basic understanding of, and facility with, issues related to e-discovery * * *. On a case-by-case basis, the duty of competence may require a higher level of technical knowledge and ability, depending on the nature of the e-discovery issues involved in a given matter and the nature of the ESI involved." St. Bar of California Standing Committee on Professional Responsibility, Formal Opinion 11–0004. Probably today's law students—who grew up in a digital world—are better prepared to deal competently with these issues than many seasoned litigators.

In 2006, the Federal Rules of Civil Procedure were amended in several ways designed to deal with the demands of E-Discovery. In 2015, further amendments went into effect, including an important one regarding preservation of electronically stored information. One provision deserves emphasis at the outset: Rule 26(f)(3)(C) now directs that the parties address in their discovery plan (to be provided to the judge before the Rule 16(b) scheduling order is entered) any issues regarding discovery of electronically stored information. Judges therefore have a basis in the rules for insisting that the lawyers grapple with these issues at the outset. Many states have parallel rules for their state court. For a thorough treatment of e-discovery, see Shira Scheindlin & Daniel Capra, Electronic Discovery and Digital Evidence (3d ed. 2015).

The two cases below illustrate both the burdens and the privacy considerations that bear on e-discovery.

PENTEL V. SHEPARD

United States District Court, District of Minnesota, 2019.
2019 WL 3729770.

TONY N. LEUNG, UNITED STATES MAGISTRATE JUDGE.

[Plaintiffs sued Shepard, a former officer who had been suspended from the Mendota Heights city police force for improperly using a database for personal purposes. Plaintiffs claimed their data had been accessed by Shepard, and sought to pursue class claims for others whose data Shepard had accessed. They served a subpoena on the Minnesota Department of Public Safety (DPS) seeking to learn about others whose data was accessed by Shepard.]

II. BACKGROUND

This is a putative class action for alleged violations of the Driver's Privacy Protection Act ("DPPA"), 18 U.S.C. § 2721 *et seq.*, and the Minnesota Government Data Practices Act ("MGDPA"), Minn. Stat. § 13.01 *et seq.*, based on improper accesses of "private, personal and confidential drivers' license information" by Shepard, a police officer formerly employed by the City.

A. LEMS Database

In the performance of their duties, law enforcement officers have access to a number of different databases containing "license plate information and other private drivers' license information regarding

Minnesota drivers," such as "names, dates of birth, driver's license numbers, addresses, driver's license photos, weights, heights, [and] various health and disability information." These databases "may be accessed and queried by different means, including entering a person's name, license plate number, or driver's license number."

One of these databases is the Law Enforcement Message Switch ("LEMS") database. The LEMS database is managed by the Minnesota Bureau of Criminal Apprehension ("BCA"), a division of DPS. The LEMS database "was the original method of access" for this type of information "and was the only method of access for several decades." At the hearing, counsel for DPS stated that the LEMS database dates back to the 1980s. While there are other databases available, the "LEMS [database] is heavily used by law enforcement officers because it returns criminal history and other useful data that [other databases] do not."

1. Determining the Source of a LEMS Access

The "LEMS [database] is typically accessed through terminals in police stations and via devices in squad cars." Unlike other databases, use of the LEMS database is not tied to the identity of a particular user. Instead, use of the LEMS database is tied to the access device and the agency to which it is registered. When the LEMS database is accessed, the agency identifier, device identifier, date and time of the access, type of query, and information returned are logged. This means that audits for use of the LEMS database do not return information showing accesses by a particular law enforcement officer. Rather, audits show only that the information was accessed by a particular device registered to a particular agency.

Accordingly, determining whether a specific law enforcement officer, i.e., Shepard, performed any one access of the LEMS database reflected in these audit returns is a multistep process. Because use of the LEMS database is not tied to the identity of a particular user, the City must undergo a series of crosschecks to determine whether Shepard was in fact the officer querying the LEMS database for each access. First, the City must contact its IT provider to determine which of its officers "was signed into the device at the time of the query." Second, the City "check[s] the schedule to make sure the officer signed in was working on the date and time of the query." Third, the City "check[s] squad assignment sheets to ensure the device was located in the squad the officer was assigned to." This process is complicated by the fact that "[d]evices can be moved between squads [and], therefore, [the City] ... often ha[s] to find an additional verification source such as reports of citations written around the same time." For each access, the process can "take anywhere from a few minutes to an hour to verify this information."

2. LEMS Audit Returns

LEMS audit data is also less "user-friendly" than audit data from other databases. The "average LEMS audit return" for a single access/search is two to three pages, and the data returned is difficult to decipher.

In addition, some of the information in the LEMS database—for example, federal criminal history information—is protected from disclosure by federal law. *See, e.g.*, 28 C.F.R. § 20.33 (dissemination of criminal history record information). An excerpted LEMS audit return submitted to the Court states in no uncertain terms, and often multiple times per page, that "THIS RETURN IS OF FEDERAL DATA. THE FBI IMPOSES RESTRICTIONS ON THE RELEASE OF THIS DATA." This LEMS audit return also reflects that the "query [w]as . . . sent to . . . the FBI," and appears to show queries of the National Crime Information Center ("NCIC"). [Given the sensitivity of the information, redaction may often be necessary to maintain confidentiality.]

At the hearing [on plaintiffs' motion to compel enforcement of their subpoena], counsel for DPS explained that when LEMS data has been sought in the past, the BCA reviews the data and performs the necessary redactions. Counsel for DPS further explained that this is a labor-intensive process. The data is first assembled into a document, which then must be physically reviewed for protected information. In a prior case DPS's counsel was involved in, it took weeks for the BCA to review and redact a LEMS audit return that was between 600 and 800 pages long.

B. DPS Subpoena for LEMS Accesses

In mid-January 2019, Plaintiffs subpoenaed DPS for LEMS audit returns showing, in relevant part, individuals other than Plaintiffs that Shepard looked up by name or license plate number from May 25, 2014 to November 3, 2017. At the time Plaintiffs subpoenaed DPS, the City had agreed to assist Plaintiffs in sorting through the LEMS audit returns to determine which accesses were performed by Shepard.

1. Burden to DPS/BCA

DPS objected on grounds that the requested LEMS audit returns would be unduly burdensome because of the volume of responsive information and the amount of redaction required to remove "sensitive data" protected from disclosure under federal law. To estimate the volume of information responsive to Plaintiffs' subpoena, the BCA gathered LEMS audit returns for the City for one day. The audit returns for the sample day were approximately 200 pages long. Based on the BCA and counsel for DPS's experience, the sample audit returns were in line with expectations as "[a]n average LEMS audit return is 2–3 pages per search, and if the City . . . was running 70–100 searches a day, a number that seems reasonable, that would produce a volume of audit returns in the neighborhood of 211 pages."

Extrapolating the sample audit returns for a single day to the three-and-a-half-year period requested by Plaintiffs, the BCA estimated that Plaintiffs' subpoena would result in approximately 102,200 searches and 306,600 pages of LEMS audit returns, which would then have to be reviewed and redacted. The BCA estimated that "it would take hundreds, if not thousands, of hours to redact the restricted federal criminal data from these returns." At the hearing, counsel for DPS also explained that the BCA had not attempted to retrieve this much LEMS audit data before and there were logistical concerns over assembling the sheer volume of audit returns in a useful way.

2.   Burden to the City

After receiving the BCA's estimate about the volume of LEMS audit data potentially responsive to Plaintiffs' subpoena, the City withdrew its prior offer to sort through the LEMS audit returns to determine which accesses were performed by Shepard on grounds of undue burden. In light of the multistep process the City must undergo to determine whether any one particular access was performed by Shepard, the City estimates that "[e]ven if it took 2 minutes an access to determine whether Shepard made the access, it would take 20 months at 7 hours a day of uninterrupted work" to review the LEMS audit returns and "cost the City approximately $153,380–$190,952." The City notes that, as part of an internal investigation, it took approximately 3 months to review the data associated with roughly 270 accesses.

III. MOTION TO COMPEL

Plaintiffs seek to compel non-party DPS to provide the LEMS audit returns for an approximately three-and-a-half-year period to the City, to have the City then determine which accesses were made by Shepard, and then for the City to identify to Plaintiffs those accesses made by Shepard and the identity of the individuals accessed. Plaintiffs also request that the Court order the City to notify individuals who were the subjects of accesses included in a 2017 disciplinary action against Shepard under Minn. Stat. § 13.055, subd. 2(a).

[The court noted that Rule 45(d)(1) directs that courts should avoid imposing undue burdens on nonparties receiving subpoenas, which it found to invoke the proportionality factors in Rule 26(b)(1).]

Here, the LEMS audit returns Plaintiffs seek to compel would require an enormous amount resources to produce, creating a tremendous burden on both non-party DPS and the City. For DPS, there are questions of technical feasibility related to assembly and production as well as the substantial amount of time needed not only to amass the information but then physically to review and redact hundreds of thousands of pages of audit returns for more than three years. Then, for each of the thousands of accesses predicted, the City would need to perform a costly, time-consuming multistep process to determine whether the access was in fact made by Shepard.

Balanced against these heavy burdens is the highly speculative usefulness of this information to Plaintiffs' claims. Plaintiffs claim that the LEMS audit returns are "essential to a determination if Shepard obtained the driver's license data of enough individuals for an impermissible reason to satisfy Rule 23(a)(1)'s numerosity requirement." But, even if the City and DPS perform all of the work requested, the end result would simply be raw access information. Plaintiffs would merely know that Shepard accessed an individual's information in the LEMS database at a particular point. The LEMS audit returns will not speak to the purpose for Shepard's access—permissible or otherwise.

As DPS points out, "[P]laintiffs must show more than just driver's license searches by . . . Shepard" to sustain a claim under the DPPA. Thus, even if the Court were to grant Plaintiffs' motion, the LEMS audit returns requested "will shed little light on the question of how many people had their data *wrongfully* accessed by [Shepard]" because Plaintiffs will have difficulty differentiating wrongful accesses from lawful accesses. Again, the LEMS audit returns will merely reflect Shepard's accesses—both permissible and impermissible. In fact, Plaintiffs' counsel acknowledged as much prior to subpoenaing DPS. [The court noted that plaintiffs would need to "[d]etermine which accesses by Shepard were not for a permissible purpose, possibly through further written discovery and depositions of your clients, to establish individual claims and meet Rule 23 requirements."]

In the end [as defendants argue], the LEMS audit returns themselves "will . . . be of little use to determine the numerosity of [P]laintiffs' proposed class," *i.e.*, individuals whose data was accessed for an *impermissible* purpose. While "Plaintiffs are well-positioned to argue why Shepard's search of their own data was improper[, t]hey are not well-positioned to speculate as to why his search of other people['s] data may have been improper." Plaintiffs are essentially engaging in a costly fishing expedition, the fruits of which will require considerable extra time and expense to chase down Plaintiffs' suspicions. *See* Fed. R. Civ. P. 1, 26(b)(1).

Plaintiffs also assert that "[w]ithout the identities of these individuals, the federal rights of the class members would be lost." Plaintiffs do not explain this blanket assertion, but later state that the City is "running out the clock on those individuals." Plaintiffs cannot use personal information from state motor vehicle records to solicit participation in this lawsuit. Individuals may request audits of accesses to their driver's license information if they themselves suspect or are concerned that their information may have been accessed for an impermissible purpose. And, if Plaintiffs prevail on Count II of their Complaint [under the Minnesota statute], the City may well be required to inform individuals whose information was impermissibly accessed by Shepard of those accesses.

Further, individuals may also bring their own claims under the DPPA if they believe their information was accessed for an impermissible purpose. Plaintiffs have not persuasively articulated with any sort of specificity how the rights of other individuals rise and fall with the LEMS audit returns at issue.

Based on the foregoing, the Court concludes that the LEMS audit returns requested by Plaintiffs are not proportional to the needs of this case when taking into account the massive burden to non-party DPS and the City, the speculative probative value of the data in resolving the issues in this litigation, and the increased delay and expense that would result. These are the very types of considerations mandated by Rule 26(b)(1). Therefore, Plaintiffs' motion is denied with respect to the LEMS audit returns.

E.E.O.C. v. SIMPLY STORAGE MANAGEMENT, LLC

United States District Court, S.D. Ind., 2010.
270 F.R.D. 430.

DEBRA McVICKER LYNCH, MAGISTRATE JUDGE.

On September 29, 2009, the EEOC filed a complaint on behalf of two named claimants and similarly situated individuals who allege the defendant businesses (collectively referred to in this Order as "Simply Storage") are liable for sexual harassment by a supervisor. The EEOC amended its complaint in November 2009 to sue different defendants, but the EEOC did not change its substantive allegations or the named claimants.

On April 16, 2010, the EEOC requested a discovery conference because counsel for the parties disagree about the proper scope of discovery as it relates to the two issues identified above. These disputes affect both pending written discovery requests and the scope of upcoming depositions. The disputed requests for production of documents that seek SNS information are:

> *REQUEST NO. 1*: All photographs or videos posted by Joanie Zupan or anyone on her behalf on Facebook or MySpace from April 23, 2007 to the present.

> *REQUEST NO. 2*: Electronic copies of Joanie Zupan's complete profile on Facebook and MySpace (including all updates, changes, or modifications to Zupan's profile) and all status updates, messages, wall comments, causes joined, groups joined, activity streams, blog entries, details, blurbs, comments, and applications (including, but not limited to, "How well do you know me" and the "Naughty Application") for the period from April 23, 2007 to the present. To the extent electronic copies are not available, please provide the documents in hard copy form.

REQUEST NO. 3: All photographs or videos posted by Tara Strahl or anyone on her behalf on Facebook or MySpace from October 11, 2007 to November 26, 2008.

REQUEST NO. 4: Electronic copies of Tara Strahl's complete profile on Facebook and MySpace (including all updates, changes, or modifications to Strahl's profile) and all status updates, messages, wall comments, causes joined, groups joined, activity streams, blog entries, details, blurbs, comments, and applications (including, but not limited to, "How well do you know me" and the "Naughty Application") for the period from October 11, 2007 to November 26, 2008. To the extent electronic copies are not available, please provide these documents in hard copy form.

The EEOC objects to production of all SNS content (and to similar deposition questioning) on the grounds that the requests are overbroad, not relevant, unduly burdensome because they improperly infringe on claimants' privacy, and will harass and embarrass the claimants. Simply Storage claims that discovery of these matters is proper because certain EEOC supplemental discovery responses place the emotional health of particular claimants at issue beyond that typically encountered with "garden variety emotional distress claims." Simply Storage's Interrogatory No. 4 asked for details about the EEOC's damage calculation, and the EEOC responded in pertinent part:

[I]t is known that Bunny Baker, Marilou Burkett, and Ellen Martin sustained "garden variety" and non ongoing emotional distress in association with the sexual harassment they endured, which includes emotional pain and suffering, loss of enjoyment of life, anxiety, fear, bitterness, humiliation, embarrassment and inconvenience. They do not claim ongoing emotional harm. Defendants' sexually hostile workplace increased Tara Strahl's anxiety for which she sought medical treatment. As a result of the sexual harassment she experienced, Joanalle Zupan became depressed and suffers from post traumatic stress disorder.

Simply Storage's Interrogatory No. 8 requested information about any medical or psychological counseling or treatment the claimants had sought related to their employment with Simply Storage and the EEOC responded in pertinent part:

Discussion

[The court described the provisions of Rule 26(b)(1) on the scope of discovery and proportionality of discovery.]

Discovery of Two Claimants' Social Networking Sites

A. General Principles Applicable to Discovery of SNS

The EEOC does not argue that Facebook and MySpace profiles contain no relevant information. It insists, however, that production should be limited to content that directly addresses or comments on matters alleged in the complaint. Simply Storage contends that the nature of the injuries Ms. Zupan and Ms. Strahl have alleged implicates all their social communications (*i.e., all* their Facebook and MySpace content).

Discovery of SNS requires the application of basic discovery principles in a novel context. And despite the popularity of SNS and the frequency with which this issue might be expected to arise, remarkably few published decisions provide guidance on the issues presented here. At bottom, though, the main challenge in this case is not one unique to electronically stored information generally or to social networking sites in particular. Rather, the challenge is to define appropriately broad limits—but limits nevertheless—on the discoverability of social communications in light of a subject as amorphous as emotional and mental health, and to do so in a way that provides meaningful direction to the parties. The court will first outline the principles it will apply in confronting this challenge.

1. *SNS content is not shielded from discovery simply because it is "locked" or "private."*

Although privacy concerns may be germane to the question of whether requested discovery is burdensome or oppressive and whether it has been sought for a proper purpose in the litigation, a person's expectation and intent that her communications be maintained as private is not a legitimate basis for shielding those communications from discovery. Two decisions factually similar to this one have recognized this threshold point. As in other cases when privacy or confidentiality concerns have been raised, those interests can be addressed by an appropriate protective order, like the one already entered in this case.

2. *SNS content must be produced when it is relevant to a claim or defense in the case.*

Simply Storage argues that all the content of Ms. Zupan's and Ms. Strahl's social networking sites is relevant, must be produced, and can be the subject of questioning during their depositions. Although, as noted above, the contours of social communications relevant to a claimant's mental and emotional health are difficult to define, that does not mean that everything must be disclosed. * * *

Moreover, the simple fact that a claimant has *had* social communications is not necessarily probative of the particular mental and emotional health matters at issue in the case. Rather, it must be the substance of the communication that determines relevance. *See Rozell v.*

Ross-Holst, 2006 WL 163143 (S.D.N.Y. Jan.20, 2006). As the *Rozell* court put it,

> To be sure, anything that a person says or does might in some theoretical sense be reflective of her emotional state. But that is hardly justification for requiring the production of every thought she may have reduced to writing or, indeed, the deposition of everyone she may have talked to.

For example, if a claimant sent a message to a friend saying she always looks forward to going to work, the person to whom she sent the message and the substance of the message are what should be considered to determine whether the message is relevant. (And that message would be relevant in this case.) But the mere fact that the claimant has made a communication is not relevant because it is not probative of a claim or defense in this litigation. The *Rozell* decision also notes, however, that the defendant may argue the *absence* of relevant communications casts doubt on the plaintiff's claims.

3. *Allegations of depression, stress disorders, and like injuries do not automatically render all SNS communications relevant, but the scope of relevant communications is broader than that urged by the EEOC.*

In *Mackelprang [v. Fidelity Nat'l Title Agency of Nevada, Inc.],* 2007 WL 119149 [(D.Nev. 2007)], the defendants had obtained the plaintiff's public MySpace profile after she had alleged sexual harassment claims against them. The court held that the defendants could discover private messages exchanged with third parties that contain information regarding her sexual harassment allegations or her alleged emotional distress. The court expressly ruled, however, that emails consisting of sexually explicit communications between the plaintiff and third persons and that did not relate to her employment with the defendants were not discoverable.

A similar situation was presented in *Rozell,* 2006 WL 163143, at *3, where the court rejected the defendants' claim that the plaintiff who had alleged sexual harassment should produce all of her email communications. When the plaintiff had complained about the supervisor, the supervisor retaliated by hacking into her emails. The defendants had requested the disclosure of all emails in the plaintiff's account, but the court required production of only the intercepted emails. *Id.* The court reasoned the contents of those emails were relevant to assess plaintiff's claimed damages.

It is reasonable to expect severe emotional or mental injury to manifest itself in some SNS content, and an examination of that content might reveal whether onset occurred, when, and the degree of distress. Further, information that evidences other stressors that could have produced the alleged emotional distress is also relevant. Thus, the court determines that some SNS discovery is appropriate here. The next question is the permissible scope of that discovery.

The EEOC's view that the claimants should be required to produce only communications that directly reference the matters alleged in the complaint is too restrictive. This standard likely would not encompass clearly relevant communications and in fact would tend only to yield production of communications supportive of the claimants' allegations. It might not, for example, yield information inconsistent with the claimants' allegations of injury or about other potential causes of the injury. And although some employees may note occurrences of harassment on their profiles, not many employees would routinely note non-events on their profiles, such as, "My supervisor didn't sexually harass me today." A definition of relevant SNS content broader than that urged by the EEOC is therefore necessary.

B. The Scope of SNS Discovery to Be Permitted in this Case

1. *The Claimants' Verbal Communications*

With these considerations in mind, the court determines that the appropriate scope of relevance is any profiles, postings, or messages (including status updates, wall comments, causes joined, groups joined, activity streams, blog entries) and SNS applications for claimants Zupan and Strahl for the period from April 23, 2007, through the present that reveal, refer, or relate to any emotion, feeling, or mental state, as well as communications that reveal, refer, or relate to events that could reasonably be expected to produce a significant emotion, feeling, or mental state.

2. *Third-party Communications*

Third-party communications to Ms. Zupan and Ms. Strahl must be produced if they place these claimants' own communications in context.

3. *Photographs and Videos*

The parties have also raised the production of photographs depicting each of the claimants or the pictures posted on their profiles in which they do not appear as an issue distinct from the disclosure of communications. The same test set forth above can be used to determine whether particular pictures should be produced. For example, pictures of the claimant taken during the relevant time period and posted on a claimant's profile will generally be discoverable because the context of the picture and the claimant's appearance may reveal the claimant's emotional or mental status. On the other hand, a picture posted on a third party's profile in which a claimant is merely "tagged," is less likely to be relevant. In general, a picture or video depicting someone other than the claimant is unlikely to fall within the definition set out above. These are general guidelines provided for the parties' reference and not final determinations of what pictures must be produced consistent with the guidelines above.

C. Further Considerations

1. *Carrying Out this Order*

The court's determination of relevant material is crafted to capture all arguably relevant materials, in accord with the liberal discovery standard of Rule 26. In carrying out this Order, the EEOC should err in favor of production.

The court acknowledges that it has not drawn these lines with the precision litigants and their counsel typically seek. But the difficulty of drawing sharp lines of relevance is not a difficulty unique to the subject matter of this litigation or to social networking communications. Lawyers are frequently called upon to make judgment calls—in good faith and consistent with their obligations as officers of the court—about what information is responsive to another party's discovery requests. Discovery is intended to be a self-regulating process that depends on the reasonableness and cooperation of counsel. Fed.R.Civ.P. 37(a)(1). Here, in the first instance, the EEOC's counsel will make those determinations based on the guidelines the court has provided. As with discovery generally, Simply Storage can further inquire of counsel and the claimants (in their depositions) about what has and has not been produced and can challenge the production if it believes the production falls short of the requirements of this order. * * *

3. *Privacy Concerns*

The court agrees with the EEOC that broad discovery of the claimants' SNS could reveal private information that may embarrass them. Other courts have observed, however, that this is the inevitable result of alleging these sorts of injuries. Further, the court finds that this concern is outweighed by the fact that the production here would be of information that the claimants have already shared with at least one other person through private messages or a larger number of people through postings. As one judge observed, "Facebook is not used as a means by which account holders carry on monologues with themselves." The court has entered an agreed protective order that limits disclosure of certain discovery materials, and counsel should confer about whether that protection is appropriate here.

NOTES AND QUESTIONS

1. As noted at the outset, these two cases illustrate the variety of issues that e-discovery can present. The variations, however, are many. Consider the variety of ways in which Americans use social media nowadays. Consider also that much interaction that formerly was done in person or via telephone (and therefore not memorialized in a way that was discoverable) is now done by text or email or some other digital means of communication that (at least potentially) creates material subject to discovery. The problem of preserving

that potential discovery material is addressed in the next sub-section. The question in this sub-section is whether, assuming the material exists, it is subject to discovery.

2.   The burden issues may often be substantial with large organizations like the City and the governmental agency in *Pentel* and also with large businesses. It may seem to parties opposing large organizations that they should have ready access to information within their "possession, custody, or control," in the words of Rule 34. But the actual effort involved may be surprisingly large. Consider Nece v. Quicken Loans, Inc., 2018 WL 1072052 (M.D.Fla.Feb. 27, 2018), like *Pentel* a putative class action. Plaintiff had applied for a mortgage from defendant, and later filed a proposed class action under the Telephone Consumer Privacy Act claiming that defendant had made unauthorized robocalls to her number and continued doing so after she demanded that it stop because her number was on a do-not-call list. Before class certification was resolved, plaintiff requested that defendant produce what the court called "every shred of documentation in any form about every do-not-call request that Quicken received between September 2012 and June 2013." Noting that "the requests require collecting and reviewing at least three million e-mails, a review that might cost millions of dollars," the court refused to compel defendant to comply.

A major problem is to identify in a large cache of digital information which items are actually responsive to the discovery request. In *Simply Storage,* the court recognizes that tough calls may be necessary, but says that's the kind of "judgment call" lawyers must often make in response to discovery. Consider how much more difficult that sort of judgment call becomes when the supply of potentially responsive digital material is huge. The solution has increasingly been to use *technology-assisted review* (TAR), sometimes called "predictive coding," which relies on AI methods to cull digital materials responsive to a request. Some time ago, "keyword searches" were employed, but the problem of deducing what search terms would appear in relevant material sought but not (often) in other materials bred impatience with that method. Provision of such services has given birth to an e-discovery industry forecast to total $22 billion by 2022. E-Discovery Market Growth, Legaltech News, April 2016, at 2. A RAND Corporation study forecast in 2012 that only AI techniques could limit escalating e-discovery costs. See Nicholas Pace & Laura Zakaras, Where the Money Goes (RAND 2012). Corporate clients may insist that key review decisions be made in house, as explained in Monica Enand, Cloud Enables Law Department Control of E-Discovery, Today's General Counsel, April/May 2016, at 18:

> Corporate legal departments have long wanted to in-source e-discovery in order to improve control over processes and stem runaway costs. A 2015 Thomson Reuters study focusing on legal department in-sourcing and efficiency found that 94 percent of corporate counsel rate cost as a frustrating aspect of e-discovery. According to that same study, 79 percent say they're becoming less

reliant on outside resources and redirecting the work in-house, as they seek to regain control and save money.

One option courts may consider is to insist that the requesting party pay part of the cost of reviewing materials. In general, under the American Rule that each side must pay its own litigation expenses, that cost shifting is not available; allowing "requester pays" routinely might stifle needed discovery. But instances in which cost-shifting is ordered show how costly it can be. For example, a magistrate judge ordered a former chief executive suing his firm to pay nearly all of the defendant's expenses for TAR of about 322,000 documents at the former CEO's request—$750,000. See Jacklyn Wille, Spirit AeroSystems Forces Ex-CEO to Pay $750,000 for E-Discovery, Bloomberg Law News, Oct. 30, 2020. Consider the impact such an order would have on an ordinary individual litigant.

3.   On the other side of the ledger, the specifics preserved in digital communications may have great value in determining the facts behind a suit. Before digital communication became the norm, litigators were often left to try to "refresh" witnesses' memories using contemporary documents years after the events in question. To take a high-profile example of what is available now, consider the criminal case against Elizabeth Holmes, the founder and CEO of Theranos. The SEC obtained a "trove of texts" she exchanged with the president of the company that appeared to indicate that both of them were well aware of the difficulties the company was encountering in delivering on the promises it had put out to the investing community. For example, one "obscenity-laden 2014 message" to Holmes from the president described the company's laboratory as a "disaster zone." See Joel Rosenblatt, Holmes Texted She Was "Praying" for Theranos Regulatory Approval, Bloomberg Legal News, Nov. 23, 2020. Surely law students nowadays can imagine times when they have been similarly unguarded in digital communications.

The *Simply Storage* ruling focuses on social media. It is likely that almost all law students nowadays have experience with social media. How much importance should be attached to what litigants post? Are people always candid when choosing what to post? "Because social networking websites enable users to craft a desired image to display to others, social scientists have posited that outside observers can misinterpret that impression." Kathryn Brown, Why the Psychology of Social Networking Should Influence the Evidentiary Relevance of Facebook Photographs, 14 Vand.J.Ent. & Tech.L. 357 (2014). Putting aside efforts to paint a rosy picture, how often do digital communications include snide comments or "inside jokes" that may look odd or worse in court? Should these concerns bear on proportionality decisions regarding discovery of digital material?

Email and texting may have more evidentiary importance. The unguarded nature of digital communication has long been recognized by lawyers. "Employees say things in e-mail messages that would never be stated directly to a person or consciously memorialized in writing." James Pooley & David Shaw, Finding What's Out There: Technical and Legal Aspects of Discovery, 4 Tex. Intell. Prop. L.J. 57, 63 (1994); see also Thunderstruck, The Economist,

May 25, 2002, at 14 ("to put in a near-indestructible e-mail the sorts of comments you might vent round the water-cooler is to invite trouble."). Not surprisingly, "divorce lawyers have found a virtual treasure trove in sites like Facebook." Anna Scott, Lawyers Relish Mining Social Networking Sites for Gold, S.F. Daily Journal, Oct. 1, 2010. "Social networking platforms like Facebook and Twitter have increasingly become litigation resources, providing a wealth of statements and images used to contradict the claims and defenses of the opposing party." Paul Cowie & Marlene Nicholas, Employment in an Age of Social Media, S.F. Recorder, Nov. 4, 2013.

4. The court in *Simply Storage* notes that some digital media may involve substantial privacy interests. With regard to claims for emotional distress, a frequent reason for defendants to demand production of plaintiffs' social media postings, consider the views of the court in Gordon v. T.G.R. Logistics, Inc. 321 F.R.D. 401, 403 (D.Wyo. 2017):

> While it is conceivable that almost any post to social media will provide some relevant information concerning a person's physical and/or emotional health, it also has the potential to disclose much more information than has historically occurred in civil litigation. While we can debate the wisdom of individuals posting information which has historically been considered private, we must recognize that people are providing a great deal of personal information publicly to a very loosely defined group of "friends," or even the entire public internet.

In Henson v. Turn, Inc., 2018 WL 5281629 (N.D.Cal. Oct. 22, 2018), the court quoted an "academic study" as follows:

> Web browsing history is inextricably linked to personal information. The pages a user visits can reveal her location, interests, purchases, employment states, sexual orientation, financial challenges, medical conditions and more. * * * In mid-2011, we discovered that an advertising network, Epic Marketplace, had publicly exposed its interest segment data, offering a rare glimpse of what third-party trackers seek to learn about users. * * * [W]e found that the free online dating website OkCupid was sending to the data provider Lotame [information showing] how often a user drinks, smokes, and does drugs.

Beyond that, it may be that the ubiquitous smartphone creates a unique privacy concern. "Modern cell phones are not just another technological convenience. With all they contain and all they may reveal, they hold for many Americans 'the privacies of life.' " Riley v. California, 573 U.S. 373, 403 (2014). Recall that proportionality is an important consideration in ordering discovery. Some suggest that privacy concerns should be considered in making a proportionality determination. In wage and hour litigation involving employees who work off the employer's premises, it has become commonplace to demand access to the GPS information on the employees' phones. But courts do not always grant such discovery. See Williams v. United States, 331 F.R.D.

1 (D.D.C. 2019) (refusing discovery of location data on a smartphone because privacy interests outweighed relevance).

5.   Assuming one is inclined to limit discovery of social media to less than everything, how readily can a party or court describe what must be revealed? Consider the effort by the court in *Simply Storage* to define what must be turned over. In Mailhoit v. Home Depot U.S.A., Inc., 285 F.R.D. 566 (C.D.Cal. 2012), also a workplace harassment suit, plaintiff claimed PTSD stemming from her employment with defendant. Defendant made a Rule 34 request for all postings or messages from plaintiff that "reveal, refer, or relate to any emotion, feeling, or mental state of Plaintiff, as well as communications by or from Plaintiff that reveal, refer, or relate to events that could reasonably be expected to produce a significant emotion, feeling, or mental state." The court found that this request did not satisfy Rule 34(b)'s requirement that a request state what was sought with "reasonable particularity" (id. at 571):

> Plaintiff has placed her emotional state at issue in this action and it is conceivable that some SNS communications may support or undermine her claims of emotional distress. Nonetheless, the extremely broad description of the material sought by this category failed to put a "reasonable person of ordinary intelligence" on notice of which specific documents or information would be responsive to the request.

6.   *BYOD:* In *Pentel*, one complicating factor was that officers could use multiple devices to access the confidential database. But similar difficulties can be presented by the reality that many employers have adopted policies known by the acronym BYOD—bring your own device. For a variety of reasons, they have found that employees prefer to use their own electronic devices at work for both business and personal purposes. As the workplace has become a 24/7 experience for employees (sometimes generating wage and hour claims), it has also produced a much larger number of places where lawyers may have to look for responsive materials than was necessary in the old days of file rooms. Every employee may have and carry about a smart phone that retains more information than was stored on an old fashioned file room. Christopher Cox & John Stratford, Drafting BYOD Policies, Today's General Counsel, Fall 2017, at 16, observe that "allowing employees to use personal devices for business purposes leads to expanded discovery obligations. Employers may also be held responsible for failure to sufficiently preserve information where employee-owned devices containing business communications, including text messages, are lost or unavailable." We will deal with preservation in the next sub-section.

In addition, coupled with business use of social media, there may be disputes about who owns what. See, e.g., Lauren Weber, Leaving a Job? Better Watch Your Cellphone, Wall St.J., Jan. 22, 2014 (describing remote wiping of former employees' smart phones and observing that "[p]hone wiping is just another example of the complications that emerge when the distinctions between our work and personal lives collapse"); L.M. Sixel, Who Owns Employee's Online Rep?, S.F. Chronicle, Aug. 18, 2013 (describing disputes between former employees and their former employers about who owns the online presence developed by the employee while working for the employer). Working from home during the COVID pandemic may complicate this picture.

7. *Form of production*: For some time, parties found too often that the form in which digital information was produced did not work after it was produced. Anyone who has ever received an attachment to an e-mail message that wouldn't open can appreciate this concern. Cf. In re Seroquel Products Liability Litigation, 244 F.R.D. 650 (M.D.Fla. 2007) (defendant produced email and attachments in a 3.75 million page file with no page breaks). As amended in 2006, Rule 34(b)(1)(C) therefore permits the party making the request to specify the form or forms in which it wants to receive the information. If that is not done, Rule 34(b)(2)(E)(ii) requires the responding party to use a form in which it ordinarily maintains the information (sometimes called "native format") or a "reasonably usable" format. In any event, even if it objects to the form specified in the request, the responding party must specify the form it intends to use before making production. See Rule 34(b)(2)(D). It is not to be assumed that "native format" is best, and it is also uncertain whether "metadata" is useful. See Wyeth v. Impax Labs, Inc., 248 F.R.D. 169, 171 (D.Del. 2006) ("Most metadata is of limited evidentiary value, and reviewing it can waste litigation resources."). On the other hand, focusing on metadata may sometimes be crucial. See Mark Sadaka, What You Should Know About Metadata, Trial Magazine, January 2012, at 44.

8. *Discovery regarding the Internet of Things*. An article in Law Technology News in early 2015 predicted that the advent of many consumer products that have network connectivity indicated that "an inflection point for law, business, and technology is staring at us." Eric Post, The Internet of Things, Law Tech. News, Feb. 2015, at 52. "Today there are around 10 billion Internet-connected devices in the world. * * * [B]y 2020 there will be 75 billion." The author asks: "How would you respond to a discovery request to provide data from potentially relevant corporate IoT devices, such as the break room coffeemaker or refrigerator, the restroom hand dryer, a company supplied Fitbit fitness tracker, individual cubicle printers and smart office light bulbs?" He adds that such devices don't have substantial data storage capabilities. "Imagine trying to place a litigation hold on the log data for a specific floor section's smart light bulbs." Are these concerns realistic?

2. EVIDENCE PRESERVATION

FREIDIG V. TARGET CORP.

United States District Court, W.D. Wis., 2018.
329 F.R.D. 199.

JAMES D. PETERSON, DISTRICT JUDGE.

Plaintiff Carla Freidig slipped on a puddle and fell in a store owned by defendant Target Corporation. She says that the fall injured her wrist, and she sued Target under Wisconsin's common law of negligence and

Wisconsin's safe-place statute, Wis. Stat. § 101.11. Target moves for summary judgment on both claims. Freidig concedes that she cannot support a claim for negligence, so the court will grant Target's motion on that claim, which leaves only her safe-place claim.

Target contends that Freidig's claim under the safe-place statute fails [because] Target did not have notice of the puddle. The court will deny the motion for summary judgment on Freidig's safe-place claim. Target has security video of the fall itself, which is enough to allow a reasonable jury to find that the fall caused the injury to Freidig's wrist. So causation is a disputed fact that will have to be resolved at trial.

* * *

On July 2, 2016, Carla Freidig was walking through an empty checkout lane at a Target store. Freidig slipped on a puddle and fell on her knees. While falling, she reached out with her left hand and braced herself on the checkout counter.

After the fall, Target employees came to help Freidig. She had pain in both of her knees and in her left toes. She did not report any other pain at that time. Target employees gave Freidig ice for her knees and toes. An employee inspected the area where Freidig fell and found a puddle of clear liquid that was about the size of a basketball. Freidig filled out a guest incident report that said she hurt her knees and toes because she slipped on a puddle.

Target investigated the accident and took a formal, recorded statement from Sarah Raemisch, a Target employee. Raemisch said she had walked through that area 10 to 15 minutes prior to Freidig's fall. She did not notice any liquid on the floor, but she only "sometimes" looks for spills and hazards. She said that "to [her] knowledge," she was the last person to walk through the area before Freidig. She was facing away from the checkout lane at the time of Freidig's fall ("when I heard it, it was like a loud kind of like scream . . . I turned around and she was kneeling").

Freidig's slip and fall were captured on Target's security camera. Target has a policy to preserve video recording of accidents in its stores, including from 20 minutes before the accident to 20 minutes after. But for reasons unexplained by either side, Target preserved video beginning only six seconds before Freidig's accident. So the recording does not show Raemisch's walk through the area or show how the puddle was formed. Recording that is not preserved is overwritten after 30 days, so the recording of the lead-up to Freidig's fall is gone for good.

* * *

Target contends that Freidig cannot show that it had actual or constructive notice of the puddle. In response, Freidig filed a motion for relief under Rule 37(e), contending that Target failed to take reasonable steps to preserve video of the checkout lane. Freidig argues that if Target had preserved video of the lane prior to Freidig's fall, it would have shown whether the puddle was on the floor long enough to give Target constructive notice.

The court concludes that Freidig's ability to show actual or constructive notice is impaired by the loss of the video. The court also concludes that Target had a duty to preserve the video and will grant Freidig relief under Rule 37(e)(1). Based on the record, including the relief granted under Rule 37(e)(1), the court concludes that a reasonable juror could find that Target had constructive notice of the puddle.

1. Notice under the safe-place statute

The safe-place statute requires employers and owners of public buildings to "adopt and use methods and processes reasonably adequate" to maintain and repair their buildings and to "do every other thing reasonably necessary to protect the life, health, safety, and welfare of . . . employees and frequenters." Wis. Stat. § 101.11(1). The statute imposes a higher duty than ordinary care on employers and owners of places of employment and public buildings: "to construct, to repair, and to maintain a safe place of employment or public building." The statute does not make a defendant liable for every injury caused by an unsafe condition in its building. The duty to repair or maintain a building arises only when the defendant has actual or constructive notice of an unsafe condition.

There is no evidence that Target had actual notice of the puddle, but Freidig could prove that Target had constructive notice if she can show that the puddle "existed a long enough time for a reasonably vigilant owner to discover and repair it." The parties agree that if Freidig cannot adduce any evidence as to how long the puddle was on the floor, then she cannot show that Target had constructive notice. *See Kaufman v. State St. Ltd. Partnership*, 187 Wis.2d 54, 522 N.W.2d 249, 252 (Ct. App. 1994) ("Ordinarily, constructive notice cannot be found when there is no evidence as to the length of time the condition existed."); *Kochanski v. Speedway SuperAmerica, LLC*, 2014 WI 72, ¶ 36, 356 Wis.2d 1, 850 N.W.2d 160 ("Speculation as to how long the unsafe condition existed and what reasonable inspection would entail are insufficient to establish constructive notice.").

Freidig contends that the puddle was present at least 10 to 15 minutes prior to her fall, when Target's employee, Sarah Raemisch, walked through the area. Freidig construes Raemisch's statement to mean that she was the last person to walk through the area. Because the puddle could not have formed on its own, Freidig argues that it follows that the puddle was present for at least 10 to 15 minutes if no one else was in the area to cause the spill after Raemisch and before Freidig.

But Raemisch's statement does not unequivocally establish that no one was in the area after Raemisch walked through. Raemisch said that "[t]o her knowledge" she was the last person through the area before the fall. But Raemisch did not say that she was monitoring the area, or that she even remained in the area throughout those 10 to 15 minutes. And even though Raemisch was nearby when Freidig fell, Raemisch was facing a different direction and had to turn around to see what happened.

Target argues that Freidig has no evidence to corroborate Raemisch's equivocal statement, so she cannot establish that Target had constructive notice of the puddle. The court does not agree. Target is entitled to summary judgment only if it can establish that Freidig does not have evidence sufficient to support a reasonable verdict in her favor. Raemisch's statement is somewhat equivocal, and her credibility might be impeached based on her lack of definitive knowledge of what happened before the fall. But Freidig does not have to prove her case on summary judgment. A reasonable jury could find, based on Raemisch's statement that to her knowledge no one else walked through the area of the fall, that no one did walk through that area.

And there is another factor to consider: the missing video. Freidig contends that if Target had followed its video preservation policy and preserved the 20 minutes of video footage prior to Freidig's accident, then Freidig could have used that footage to show whether any other person walked through the area after Raemisch. So Freidig asks for relief under Rule 37(e) for Target's spoliation of the video.

2. Prerequisites for relief under Rule 37(e)

In 2015, Rule 37 was amended to create a standard procedure for handling issues regarding a party's failure to preserve electronically stored information (ESI). The amended rule states:

(e) Failure to Preserve Electronically Stored Information. If electronically stored information that should have been preserved in the anticipation or conduct of litigation is lost because a party failed to take reasonable steps to preserve it, and it cannot be restored or replaced through additional discovery, the court:

(1) upon finding prejudice to another party from loss of the information, may order measures no greater than necessary to cure the prejudice; or

(2) only upon finding that the party acted with the intent to deprive another party of the information's use in the litigation may:

(A) presume that the lost information was unfavorable to the party;

(B) instruct the jury that it may or must presume the information was unfavorable to the party; or

(C) dismiss the action or enter a default judgment.

The text of Rule 37(e) can be broken into several components. The introductory clause lists three prerequisites that the court must find before it may consider relief under subsections (1) or (2). First, the footage "should have been preserved in the anticipation or conduct of litigation." Second, the footage was lost because Target "failed to take reasonable steps to preserve it." Third, the footage "cannot be restored or replaced through additional discovery."

The court will consider each requirement.

a. The footage should have been preserved in anticipation of litigation

Rule 37(e) is based on the common-law duty "to preserve relevant information when litigation is reasonably foreseeable." Fed. R. Civ. P. 37(e) advisory committee's note to 2015 amendment.

When a party is aware of an accident that it knows is likely to cause litigation, it triggers the party's duty to preserve evidence. That is the case here. Freidig filled out a guest incident report that said she was injured after slipping on a puddle in a checkout lane. This report gave Target notice of potential litigation. Target was well aware that an accident similar to Freidig's could lead to litigation, as reflected in its video retention policies and its formal investigation. Indeed, multiple cases that have held that Target had a duty to preserve video footage under similar circumstances. [The court cited four other cases involving Target.]

Target also should have been aware that the lead-up to the fall itself was relevant to a potential suit from Freidig. Target has a policy to preserve 20 minutes of footage before and after an accident. Although this policy does not itself create a duty to preserve, it does show that Target is aware, as a general matter, that footage prior to an accident is commonly relevant to litigation. That is especially true in this case because Target's investigator took a statement from Raemisch that she had walked through that area 10 to 15 minutes prior to Freidig's fall and had not noticed a puddle. So even without the policy, a reasonable party in Target's position would have realized that footage of those 10 to 15 minutes was relevant to how the puddle was formed.

Target contends that it did not have a duty to preserve because Freidig's attorney did not send a letter notifying Target of litigation. It cites [a case involving] the destruction of video footage that was unrelated to the accident in question or its cause. *See Mahaffey v. Marriott Internat'l Inc.*, 898 F.Supp.2d 54, 59–60 (D.D.C. 2012) (defendant had duty to preserve evidence concerning plaintiff's injury in a hotel elevator, but defendant could not have reasonably known that video footage from a different part of the hotel was relevant to plaintiff's identification of witnesses). * * * The foreseeability of litigation is a fact-intensive question that must be assessed on a case-by-case basis. * * *

Target also says that even if it had a duty to preserve, it could not have reasonably known that a recording of more than the fall itself would be relevant to litigation. It argues that if it is required to preserve additional recording beyond the fall itself, then there is no limit to the amount of recording that a plaintiff could demand. But Target overstates the difficulty posed by its duty to preserve. Target does not have a duty to preserve any arbitrary amount of recording that a plaintiff requests. It has a duty to preserve the recording of relevant events. In this case, Target should have known from its internal investigation that, at a minimum, recording from the time of Raemisch's walkthrough to the time of Freidig's fall was relevant to possible litigation. Its own video retention policies would cover the period relevant to this case.

b. Target did not take reasonable steps to preserve the video

When Target preserved the video of Freidig's fall, it chose to preserve recording of only the fall itself. As a result, the other recording was automatically overwritten a month later. Target did not take any steps to preserve it, reasonable or otherwise.

On this issue, Target rehashes its previous arguments regarding the scope of the recording it was required to preserve. It argues that it took reasonable steps to preserve ESI, because it preserved the recording of the fall itself. But this only raises the question as to why Target chose not to also preserve video that demonstrated how the puddle was formed.

Target also says that the individual employee who preserved the video lacked legal training, and he or she may have reasonably believed that only recording of the fall itself should be preserved. But Target cannot dodge its responsibilities by claiming that its employee was ignorant; Target is responsible for its employees' actions.

c. The lost footage cannot be restored or replaced through additional discovery

No backups of the deleted recording exist, nor is there recording from another camera that captured Freidig's fall. Target says that Freidig did not depose Raemisch or other Target employees, and it argues that she could have obtained comparable evidence if she had. But that is not what Rule 37(e) means by "restore or replace." This provision is referring to digital backups and the likelihood that electronic documents have multiple versions. *See* Fed. R. Civ. P. 37(e) advisory committee's note to 2015 amendment (*"Because electronically stored information often exists in multiple locations*, loss from one source may often be harmless when substitute information can be found elsewhere.") (emphasis added). The availability of non-electronic evidence is a factor that speaks to prejudice, not whether the lost evidence can be restored.

It's true that Freidig could have engaged in more aggressive discovery, and if she had, she might have developed a stronger case. But it's more likely that she would not have discovered any evidence equivalent to the lost recording. As Target points out, Raemisch simply does not have the personal knowledge to say with certainty whether anyone else walked through the checkout lane. And she does not have any more knowledge now than she did when she gave her prior statement. Besides Raemisch, the nearest Target employee was working at a register two aisles away, and the preserved video recording shows that she was facing away from the lane with the puddle. So it's unlikely that her testimony would be any more useful.

The court concludes that Target did not take reasonable steps to preserve the recording of the lead-up to the fall and that the recording cannot be restored or replaced. The court next considers what remedy, if any, is appropriate under subsections (1) or (2).

3.   Relief under Rule 37(e)(1)

The court may order a remedy under Rule 37(e)(1) if it concludes that Freidig is prejudiced by the loss of the video. The rule does not place the burden to prove prejudice on either party. *See* Fed. R. Civ. P. 37(e) advisory committee's note to 2015 amendment. But case law suggests that Target has the burden to disprove prejudice because it violated its retention policy.

Even if Target has the burden, this does not mean that Freidig is automatically entitled to relief. The court must still determine the scope of the prejudice, and it cannot do so unless it has some idea about what the lost recording contained. Therefore, "the court must have some evidence regarding the particular nature of the missing ESI." Put another way, the loss of inconsequential ESI, or detrimental ESI, does not entitle the other party to relief. So if evidence suggests that the lost recording would have helped Freidig's claim, then Freidig suffered prejudice. But if the evidence suggests that the lost recording would have been detrimental or inconsequential to Freidig's claim, then she did not.

In this case, the only evidence of the content of the missing video is Raemisch's statement, and it suggests that the missing video would have helped Freidig's claim. Raemisch said that she did not notice the puddle, and that to her knowledge, no one else walked through the area after she did. Target has no evidence at all to suggest that, contrary to Raemisch's statement, someone else made the puddle after Raemisch walked through. So the available evidence suggests that the lost recording would have been helpful to Freidig.

Relief under Rule 37(e)(1) must be "no greater than necessary to cure the prejudice." For example, in *Barbera v. Pearson Educ., Inc.*, 906 F.3d

621, 627 (7th Cir. 2018), the defendant failed to preserve emails related to the plaintiff's discrimination claim, so an appropriate remedy was an order that the defendant could not contest the plaintiff's recollection of the emails. But the plaintiff was not entitled to a favorable ruling on the ultimate legal issue. Instead, the court adopted several of the plaintiff's proposed findings and then continued to analyze those findings within the larger context of the case. The court will follow that approach here.

Freidig is prejudiced because she cannot corroborate Raemisch's statement that no one walked through the area after Raemisch. So, for the purposes of summary judgment at least, the court will credit Raemisch's statement that she was the last person to walk through the area. Accordingly, the court concludes that Freidig has adduced sufficient evidence that the puddle was there for at least 10 or 15 minutes before Freidig's fall, and that the puddle was there when Raemisch walked through the area.

Under the safe-place statute, Target had constructive notice of the puddle if it existed "a long enough time for a reasonably vigilant owner to discover and repair it." This is typically a question of fact left to the jury, and it includes considerations of "the surrounding facts and circumstances, including the nature of the business and the nature of the defect." Wis. Stat. § 101.11(1). Target has not shown that 15 minutes is not long enough to meet this standard or that Target missed the puddle despite procedures that were reasonably vigilant. So drawing all inferences in the light most favorable to Freidig, a reasonable jury could conclude that Target had constructive notice of the puddle before Freidig's fall.

4. Relief under Rule 37(e)(2)

Freidig also requests sanctions under Rule 37(e)(2), specifically an instruction to the jury that it may presume that the deleted video was unfavorable to Target. Rule 37(e)(2) allows the court to grant this sanction only if it finds that Target deleted the footage with "the intent to deprive another party of the information's use in the litigation." This requires actual evidence of intent. An employee's destruction of evidence—even if in violation of company policy—is not necessarily a bad-faith act by the company.

Freidig does not adduce any evidence of Target's intent. Instead, she says that the court should require Target to produce the employee who preserved the video so that he or she can explain why Target's video preservation policy was not followed. But the moving party, here Freidig, has the burden of proving intent in a motion for sanctions based on spoliation of evidence. *See Martinez v. City of Chicago,* No. 14–CV–369, 2016 WL 3538823, at *23 (N.D. Ill. June 29, 2016) ("a violation of a records retention policy creates a rebuttable presumption that the missing evidence was unfavorable to the responsible party, but this does not eliminate the need to show bad faith in order to warrant the adverse inference instruction"). Because Freidig did not adduce any evidence of Target's intent, the court will deny her request for sanctions under Rule 37(e)(2).

NOTES AND QUESTIONS

1.   The 2015 amendment to Rule 37(e) responded to concerns that spoliation arguments were often raised in connection with electronically stored information. The Committee Note (frequently quoted by courts interpreting the rule and worth reading, as in *Freidig*) identifies issues it addresses. Among the points:

(a)   *Source of preservation obligation:* The rule focuses on "the common-law obligation to preserve in the anticipation of litigation" rather than create a new preservation obligation. Thus, pre-2015 cases remain instructive.

(b)   *Reasonable steps:* The rule does not require "perfection in preserving all relevant electronically stored information," because that may be impossible in light of "the ever-increasing volume of electronically stored information and the multitude of devices that generate such information." Though failure to take any steps is often unreasonable, proportionality matters. "The court should be sensitive to party resources * * * and parties (including governmental parties) may have limited staff and resources to devote to those efforts."

(c)   *Prejudice:* The court may enter a Rule 37(e) order only on finding prejudice, but the rule "does not place a burden of proving or disproving prejudice on one party or the other. * * * The rule leaves judges with discretion to determine how best to assess prejudice in particular cases."

(d)   *Measures to cure prejudice:* There is no "all purpose hierarchy" for the selection of the appropriate measure. Such measures may include forbidding the party that lost the information from putting on certain evidence, and permitting the parties to present the jury with evidence and argument about the loss of information. One possibility is "to exclude a specific item of evidence to offset prejudice caused by failure to preserve other evidence that might contradict the excluded item of evidence."

(e)   *Serious sanctions:* Rule 37(e)(2) sanctions may not be imposed for negligence in preservation, but only when a party lost the information to prevent its use in litigation. If the court finds that intent, it need not find prejudice to impose sanctions, but such a finding does not require use of any of the sanctions permitted under the rule.

For an examination of the impact of the 2015 amendment, see Thomas Allman, Dealing With Prejudice: How Amended Rule 37(e) Has Refocused ESI Spoliation Measures, 26 Rich. J. Law & Tech. 1 (2020).

2.   *Freidig* is not a complex case, but it illustrates the preservation issues that can emerge in MDL and other complex litigation involving allegedly dangerous conditions or products. Plaintiff concedes that she cannot prove negligence, but claims she can rely on the Wisconsin safe-place statute. Given

that she will testify that she slipped on a puddle, and Target employees evidently will confirm there was a puddle, is it clear that failure to preserve the full 20 minutes of video prejudiced her? How much more evidence did she need to defeat Target's summary-judgment motion? Did Target have to adopt a policy of preserving 20 minutes of video before a fall in a store? If not, why would failure to adhere to such a policy be important in the application of a rule that focuses on a common law preservation duty? How much assistance will plaintiff derive from the court's order at trial? Can plaintiff offer evidence at trial that Target failed to preserve 20 minutes worth of pre-accident video? Should permitting plaintiff to offer that evidence depend on a finding that Target failed to preserve the video to suppress its contents? Could the video have actually helped Target (for example, by showing that other customers had been in the area before plaintiff passed through)? If so, how could the court find that failure to preserve the full 20 minutes prejudiced plaintiff? If a Target employee claimed to have seen another customer in the area where plaintiff slipped and fell, could the court prevent that employee from testifying to "cure" the prejudice caused by loss of the video?

3. *Freidig* also presents a simple example of the *trigger* for preservation obligations. The filing of suit is not necessary, but appreciation that a suit is likely often is. For example, in Alabama Aircraft Indus., Inc. v. Boeing Co., 319 F.R.D. 730 (N.D. Ala. 2017), plaintiff claimed that Boeing had improperly purported to terminate a contract between the two companies, and that Boeing had made unauthorized use of its proprietary information. After negotiation between the general counsels of the two companies, Boeing agreed to set up a "firewall" between Boeing employees working on its ongoing project and those who worked with plaintiff, and also directed that the employees involved with plaintiff deliver their information to its general counsel. Notwithstanding that, two Boeing employees accessed the computer of a high-ranking Boeing employee and deleted his files related to dealings with plaintiff. In addition, an in-house counsel removed two computer disks that had been submitted to the Boeing legal department and then lost them. The court had no difficulty concluding that Boeing foresaw litigation, emphasizing that it "sought the legal advice of Jeana McFerron-Berron, in-house *litigation* counsel." Id. at 741.

Compare Carlucci v. Piper Aircraft Corp., 102 F.R.D. 472 (S.D.Fla. 1984), aff'd in part, rev'd in part, 775 F.2d 1440 (11th Cir. 1985), in which plaintiffs sued for wrongful death in connection with the crash of a plane manufactured by defendant. The court eventually entered default on the issue of liability, finding that defendant had continuously obstructed discovery. It also found persuasive the testimony of two former employees that Piper had embarked on an extensive document-destruction policy (102 F.R.D. at 481):

> The policy was initiated in the late 1960s or the early 1970's when [the employees] received the instruction from J. Myers, the flight test supervisor and their direct superior, to "purge" the department's files. The stated purpose of the destruction of records was the elimination of documents that might be detrimental to Piper in a law suit. Wrisley and Lister were delegated the discretion to determine which

documents were to be destroyed. The initial purging involved hundreds of flight test department documents. They were also directed to retrieve copies of the detrimental documents from other departments. Thereafter, the destruction of all potentially harmful documents was an ongoing process.

Should this have been sufficient, standing alone, to justify a default? Note that at the time these documents were destroyed there was evidently no pending litigation or claims regarding the products in question. Perhaps the answer is that this would now be handled under Rule 37(e)(2), but that does not fully address the trigger issue.

4.   Putting aside issues of trigger, the *Carlucci* case in the previous note seems a prime illustration of the sort of intent to obstruct on which Rule 37(e)(2) focuses. Could any such argument be made in *Freidig*? Some recent cases offer graphic illustrations of such wrongdoing. In CAT3, LLC v. Black Lineage, Inc., 164 F.Supp.3d 488 (S.D.N.Y. 2016), the court found "clear and convincing evidence" that plaintiffs altered critical emails "to gain an advantage in the litigation." Id. at 500. Similarly, in Paisley Park Ent., Inc. v. Boxill, 330 F.R.D. 226 (D.Minn. 2019), two of the prime actors not only failed to suspend the auto-erase function of their phones but also wiped and destroyed their phones after suit was filed and even after the court had ordered preservation. In Steves & Sons, Inc. v. Jeld-Wen, Inc., 327 F.R.D. 96 (E.D.Va. 2018), a former employee of defendant who had taken a job with plaintiff emailed his new bosses advising them of the risk defendant might make a claim for trade secret misappropriation and recommending that they delete all their relevant emails before a discovery order was entered. When plaintiff later filed an antitrust suit against defendant, defendant learned of the possible misappropriation claims during discovery and found the emails recommending deletion of incriminating material. But the court concluded it would not impose sanctions because defendant failed to show that the information could not be restored or recovered.

Not all cases are so clear, however. For example, in Moody v. CSX Transportation, Inc., 271 F.Supp.3d 410 (W.D.N.Y. 2017), after a train accident one of defendant's employees uploaded data from the train's event recorder to defendant's data vault, but selected the wrong file to upload from his laptop. And then defendant did not check to see that the correct file had been uploaded after plaintiff filed suit despite the Rule 26(a)(1) obligation to disclose any evidence on which it would rely. The court found that "defendant's repeated failure over a period of years to confirm that the data had been properly preserved * * * is so stunningly derelict as to evince intentionality." Id. at 432.

5.   Once the obligation to preserve arises, there are important questions about the scope of that obligation. No organization can keep everything forever; that explains the advent of "automatic discard" settings on various electronic information systems. On the general question of adhering to retention policies, consider Chris Sanchirico, Detection Avoidance, 81 NYU L. Rev. 1331, 1356 (2006), noting that "the chief expense is not in drafting the policy, but in enforcing it":

Presumably, few firms promote on the basis of how well an employee complies with its document policy; few bonuses reflect a job well done in this regard. More likely, routine instructions to comply with the firm's document retention policy sit long untended on employees' lists of low-priority things to do. * * *

Indeed, to the extent that employees would, without prodding, give document retention policies a first thought, this is likely to be immediately accompanied by second thoughts. Neglecting document cleanup might not seem like such a bad idea, given a modicum of foresight about the fact that, in future states of the world where such documents become important, the employee's interests may not always line up with those of the firm. Thus, while a midlevel supervisor may urge her subordinates to shred documents, she may decide to keep a choice collection in her own personal files, anticipating the possibility of later trading these for leniency with prosecutors and regulators.

Will preservation efforts be pursued more assiduously when lawyers become involved? The preservation obligation is not limited to defendants, or to corporations, or to materials owned by the party. Consider Silvestri v. General Motors Corp., 271 F.3d 583 (4th Cir. 2001). Plaintiff there was injured in an automobile collision, and claimed that his injuries were worsened because the air bag failed to deploy. The car belonged to the husband of plaintiff's landlord. While he was in the hospital recovering from his injuries in the crash, plaintiff's parents hired a lawyer who sent accident reconstruction experts to examine the crash scene and the car, but neither plaintiff nor his lawyer made efforts to have the car retained in its post-crash condition until GM inspected it. Instead, the owner (not the plaintiff) sold the car to a collision repair outfit that repaired it and sold it.

When plaintiff sued GM three years later, it located the car in Quebec, where the new owner lived, but due to the repairs it could not then test the airbag equipment that plaintiff claimed had malfunctioned. Applying "the federal law of spoliation," id. at 590, the court upheld dismissal of plaintiff's suit. Plaintiff clearly had access to the car, because his experts inspected it, but he made no effort to buy it, preserve it against change, or notify GM. Dismissal was appropriate because plaintiff's conduct was "so prejudicial that it substantially denied the defendant the ability to defend the claim." Id. at 593. If the plaintiff were impecunious, what should have been done?

6. When lawyers do become involved, they may bear a special responsibility. For example, in Zubulake v. UBS Warburg LLC, 229 F.R.D. 422 (S.D.N.H. 2004), Judge Scheindlin found the efforts of defendant's lawyers deficient even though they did announce a "litigation hold" in response to claims of gender bias:

[C]ounsel must become fully familiar with her client's document retention policies, as well as the client's data retention architecture. This will invariably involve speaking with information technology personnel, who can explain system-wide backup procedures and the actual (as opposed to theoretical) implementation of the firm's recycling policy. It will also involve communicating with "the key players" in the litigation, in order to understand how they stored information. In this case, for example, some UBS employees created separate computer files pertaining to Zubulake, while others printed out relevant e-mails and retained them in hard copy only. Unless counsel interviews each employee, it is impossible to determine whether all potential sources of information have been inspected.

And counsel must monitor compliance thereafter, but "[a] lawyer cannot be obliged to monitor her client like a parent watching a child. At some point, the client must bear responsibility for a failure to preserve." "At the end of the day, however, the duty to preserve and produce documents rests on the party. Once that duty is made clear to a party, either by court order or by instructions from counsel, that party is on notice of its obligations, and acts at its own peril." Recall that clients may increasingly be insisting on controlling E-Discovery to contain costs. How readily can counsel perform their responsibilities when the client does so?

7.   *Document retention policies*: The focus on the needs of document retention has spawned renewed attention to policies on what should be maintained. Some say that " 'document retention policy' is one of the great Orwellian misnomers of modern litigation practice. It invariably refers to a policy requiring the periodic destruction of documents." Charles Yablon, Stupid Lawyer Tricks: An Essay on Discovery Abuse, 96 Colum. L. Rev. 1618, 1632 n. 47 (1996). Yet having such a policy and following it can protect a party against an adverse consequence when documents have been discarded. See Stevenson v. Union Pacific R.R., 354 F.3d 739, 747 (8th Cir. 2004) ("Where a routine document retention policy has been followed in this context, * * * there must be some indication of an intent to destroy the evidence for the purpose of obstructing or suppressing the truth in order to sanction an adverse inference instruction."); Coates v. Johnson & Johnson, 756 F.2d 524, 551 (7th Cir. 1985) (because documents were destroyed under routine procedures, there is no ground for inferring that defendant's agents were conscious of a weak case when they destroyed them). No organization can keep all materials forever, and consistency about what should be retained is a sensible measure. Perhaps the Target policy involved in *Freidig* is such a policy; having one invites objections if it's not followed.

8.   *Document preservation orders:* Rule 37(e) does not require a court order to trigger the preservation obligation, but sometimes courts do enter such orders. In Paisley Park Ent., Inc. v. Boxill, 330 F.R.D. 226 (D.Minn. 2019), the court's scheduling order directed the parties to preserve "all electronic documents that bear on any claims, defenses, or the subject matter of this lawsuit," and warned that failure to comply would subject the non-complying party to "any and all appropriate remedies." Should courts routinely enter such broad orders?

The Manual for Complex Litigation recognizes that it may be appropriate to enter a preservation order early in the case, but its sample order emphasizes negotiation of terms between the parties. See Manual for Complex Litigation (4th) § 40.25 (2004). The Manual also notes that "[a] blanket preservation order may be prohibitively expensive and unduly burdensome for parties dependent on computer systems for their day-to-day operations. In addition, a preservation order will likely be ineffective if it is formulated without reliable information from the responding party regarding what data-management systems are already in place, the volume of data affected, and the costs and technical feasibility of implementation." Id., § 11.422.

9. *Additional consequences of failure to preserve*: In Micron Technology, Inc. v. Rambus, Inc., 645 F.3d 1311 (Fed.Cir. 2011), the court declared a patent unenforceable because the patent holder had directed its employees to hold a "shredding party" before it commenced a patent infringement suit. In New Jersey, a Rutgers University undergraduate who was charged with a hate crime for posting images of his roommate's romantic encounter with another man online was also charged with a cover-up for altering a Twitter post. See Lisa Foderaro, Roommate Faces Hate-Crime Charges in Rutgers Spying-Suicide Case, N.Y. Times, April 21, 2011. See also Clifford Krauss, Former BP Worker Is Found Guilty of Obstruction in Gulf Oil Spill Case, N.Y. Times, Dec. 19, 2013 (reporting that defendant, a BP engineer, was convicted of deleting more than 200 text messages despite notices from BP to retain information about the explosion of the Deepwater Horizon well in the Gulf of Mexico).

10. *Attitude abroad toward U.S. discovery and preservation*: In other countries, particularly those with some version of the "right to be forgotten," preserving information may be regarded as "processing" the information and subject to legal requirements that identifying information be removed. This dissonance may pose serious problems for litigants that engage in activities in other countries but find themselves parties to litigation in U.S. courts. For discussion of the general issues, see Paul Schwartz & Daniel Solove, Reconciling Personal Information in the United States and European Union, 102 Cal. L. Rev. 877 (2014).

3. PRESERVING PRIVILEGE PROTECTION

"The inadvertent production of a privileged document is a specter that haunts every document intensive case." F.D.I.C. v. Marine Midland Realty Credit Corp., 138 F.R.D. 479, 479–80 (E.D.Va. 1991). As a consequence, a large amount of lawyer time in complex litigation is spent asserting and preserving privilege claims. Privilege protection was long viewed suspiciously, and broad doctrines of waiver were employed to permit other parties to broach that protection. In particular, it was held that disclosure of one privileged document led to a *subject matter waiver*—the privilege was lost as to all document on the same subject. That was the haunting specter.

In 1993, Rule 26(b)(5)(A) was added, requiring that parties withholding material on claim of privilege give notice that they have done so, including details about the materials withheld—frequently called a "privilege log." In 2006, Rule 26(b)(5)(B) was added to specify the procedures to be used when allegedly privileged material is turned over. In 2008, Fed. R. Evid. 502 was added. Further amendments in 2015 to Rules 26(f) and 16(b) call attention to Rule 502 at the beginning of the case. We turn to these developments now. As you read the following case, consider whether we should feel sympathy for the associate tasked with screening for privileged material before production.

RHOADS INDUSTRIES, INC. V. BUILDING MATERIALS CORP.

United States District Court, Eastern District of Pennsylvania, 2008.
254 F.R.D. 216.

BAYLSON, DISTRICT JUDGE.

Recently enacted Federal Rule of Evidence 502 adopts a national standard that an inadvertent disclosure of privileged information does not waive the privilege if the holder of the privilege took reasonable steps to prevent disclosure and to rectify the error. A dispute in this case requires review of the procedure used by the Plaintiff, which resulted in the inadvertent disclosure of over eight hundred documents. Should this result in a waiver of the privilege? Judges have often grappled with this issue, adjudicating disputes as to whether the allegedly inadvertent production of privileged materials was truly inadvertent, or careless, or reflected a complete absence of control over the discovery process.

In this case, Plaintiff Rhoads Industries, Inc. ("Rhoads") admits that it produced to the Defendants over eight hundred electronic documents which were privileged and asserts that the production was inadvertent. In accordance with the provisions of Rule 26(b)(5)(B), Defendants, upon receiving notice of the inadvertent production, segregated the asserted privileged documents, provided them for in camera review by the Court, and then the parties agreed that the documents could be returned to Rhoads for logging on a privilege log and for further review.

Defendants in this case have filed a joint motion to deem certain of Plaintiff Rhoads Industries, Inc.'s ("Rhoads") privilege claims waived. The parties have engaged in extensive briefing on this issue. Rhoads has filed affidavits and supporting documents by individuals who were personally involved in its production of documents, and an evidentiary hearing was held on November 5, 2008. Further argument was held on November 13, 2008.

Defendants' motions are based on contentions that Rhoads' document production was careless, that Rhoads delayed too long in seeking return of the documents, that Rhoads failed to produce complete and accurate privilege logs, and that the Court should deny Rhoads' request that the documents be returned and conclude that Rhoads waived the privilege as to those documents.[2] Defendants' motions will be granted as to the privileged communications not logged as of June 30, 2008, but otherwise will be denied.

A. Factual Background of the Case

Rhoads specializes in building large-scale construction projects. It entered into a $5.584 million contract with Defendant Building Materials Corporation of America, also known as GAF, to construct a plant in Quakertown, Pennsylvania. Alleging breach of contract and other claims, Rhoads instituted this suit and also named as a Defendant R.W. Cooper & Associates, Inc., asserting against it a claim of negligent misrepresentation. [Extensive discovery ensued.] Summary Judgment Motions are pending and have been extensively briefed, but I determined that disposition of this privilege issue should precede consideration of the Summary Judgment Motions.

B. Rule 502 and Standards for Determining Waiver by Inadvertent Disclosure

In enacting Rule 502, Congress specified that it will apply in all proceedings commenced after the date of enactment, and "insofar as is just and practicable, in all proceedings pending" when enacted. I conclude that it would be just and practicable to apply Rule 502 in the present case because it sets a well defined standard, consistent with existing mainstream legal principles on the topic of inadvertent waiver.

This national standard, which the Committee Note states is a "middle ground" among the many precedents, provides as follows:

(b) Inadvertent disclosure. When made in a federal proceeding or to a federal office or agency, the disclosure does not operate as a waiver in a federal or state proceeding if:

(1) the disclosure is inadvertent;

---

[2] Defendants do not assert that Rhoads' conduct was purposeful or warrants finding a general waiver of the attorney-client privilege.

(2)　the holder of the privilege or protection took reasonable steps to prevent disclosure, and

(3)　the holder promptly took reasonable steps to rectify the error, including (if applicable) following Fed.R.Civ.P. 26(b)(5)(B). * * *

The Advisory Committee Note to Rule 502 summarizes the multi-factor test used by a majority of courts:

The stated factors (none of which are dispositive) are the reasonableness of precautions taken, the time taken to rectify the error, the scope of discovery, the extent of disclosure and the overriding issue of fairness. The rule does not explicitly codify that test, because it is really a set of non-determinative guidelines that vary from case to case. The rule is flexible enough to accommodate any of those listed factors.

* * *

C.　Mandatory Privilege Log

Under Federal Rule 26(b)(5), when a party withholds information otherwise discoverable by claiming attorney-client privilege in the information, that party must "describe the nature of the documents, communications, or tangible things not produced or disclosed . . . in a manner that . . . will enable other parties to assess the claim." Fed.R.Civ.P. 26(b)(5)(A)(ii). "[F]ailure to assert a privilege properly may amount to a waiver of that privilege." * * *

D.　Facts Re: Production of Privileged Documents and Logs

At the evidentiary hearing on the privilege issue, Rhoads called two witnesses—Kimberly Buchinsky, an associate of one of Rhoads' firms, Gowa Lincoln P.C., who was directly involved in the production of documents on behalf of Rhoads to the Defendants; and Salvatore Gramaglia, a specialist in information technology retained by Rhoads, who was assigned to work with Ms. Buchinsky in the production of documents to the Defendants and screening and elimination of privileged documents in this case. Based on the briefs submitted, the testimony of Mr. Gramaglia and Ms. Buchinsky, and representations by counsel, the following facts are relevant to the production of privileged documents and privilege logs.

In February 2007, Rhoads began preparing for this litigation and thereafter retained consulting experts. In June 2007, Rhoads realized that extensive electronic discovery would be involved in this case. For that purpose, it directed its IT consultant, Mr. Gramaglia, to research various software programs. After testing a trial version of the program, Mr. Gramaglia purchased a computer program called Discovery Attender (or "Sherpa") to perform the necessary electronic searches. Mr. Gramaglia and Ms. Buchinsky began identifying mailboxes and e-mail addresses of persons that would have relevant information to Rhoads's project with GAF. Gramaglia and Buchinsky reasonably believed that the computer program would screen out all privileged materials.

The fact that Rhoads retained a consultant who recommended and used a fairly sophisticated screening device shows that Rhoads substantially complied with the following Explanatory Note to Rule 502:

> A party that uses advanced analytical software applications and linguistic tools in screening for privilege and work product may be found to have taken "reasonable steps" to prevent inadvertent disclosure. The implementation of an efficient system of records management before litigation may also be relevant.

Rhoads pursued settlement efforts prior to instigating litigation, which were unsuccessful. Rhoads filed its Complaint on November 13, 2007. Discovery commenced shortly thereafter. In November and December, Mr. Warshawer—counsel brought in for the purposes of this litigation—held several meetings with Ms. Buchinsky and Mr. Gramaglia to discuss electronic discovery and observe the Sherpa program. Mr. Gowa—a partner with Gowa Lincoln, one of Rhoads's regular counsel—also was involved in discussions with Mr. Gramaglia and Ms. Buchinsky about the scope of electronic discovery and the search terms to be used in relevant searches.

During January and February 2008, using the search terms he received from Rhoads's attorneys, Mr. Gramaglia initially identified 210,635 unique e-mail messages as being responsive to Defendants' discovery requests. In order to filter out privileged e-mails, he ran the following searches in the address line of all emails: *rhoadsinc* and either *gowa*, *ballard*, or *cpmi*.[5] Through this search, Mr. Gramaglia designated 2,000 e-mails as privileged; these e-mails were removed from the folder ultimately produced to Defendants. However, these e-mails were not placed on a privilege log at that time. Mr. Gramaglia re-ran the above search to be certain that all e-mails meeting the designated criteria had been removed, verifying the accuracy of the search.

Due to the large number of e-mails remaining (208,635), Rhoads's counsel revised the keyword search to arrive at 78,000 e-mail messages it believed to be responsive and non-privileged as of February 26, 2008. Ms. Buchinksy then conducted a separate manual review of e-mails from specific e-mail mailboxes (but not all of the mailboxes subject to the keyword search described above) and removed certain documents as privileged, logging them on a privilege log. In addition to the e-mail messages, Rhoads counsel also reviewed twenty-two boxes of non-electronic documents for privilege. On May 13, 2008, Rhoads produced to Defendants

---

[5]   Gowa Lincoln is Rhoads's law firm representing it in this case and other non-litigation matters. Ballard is another law firm that represents Rhoads. CPMI was retained by Rhoads as a non-testifying expert in this case.

three hard drives containing the responsive electronic documents, including the 78,000 e-mails identified by the Sherpa search. On June 6, 2008, in response to [the court's] Order, Rhoads produced two separate privilege logs to Defendants: one detailing privileged electronic documents as a result of Ms. Buchinsky's manual review and one detailing privileged non-electronic documents.

On June 5, 2008, Defendant GAF's counsel notified Plaintiff's counsel via e-mail that certain documents that appeared to be privileged had been produced. Plaintiff responded immediately via e-mail stating that no privilege had been waived and this was likely a case of inadvertent production. Over the next two and a half weeks, Plaintiff conducted nine depositions and responded to R.W. Cooper's Motion to Dismiss before addressing the privilege issue. On or about June 23, 2008, Ms. Buchinsky began reviewing the 78,000 e-mails produced as a result of the Sherpa search and generated a new privilege log that identified 812 of these e-mails as privileged. Rhoads produced this new privilege log to Defendants on June 30, 2008, as an attachment to a letter invoking Rule 26(b)(5)(B) to have Defendants sequester the inadvertently produced documents.

On August 19, 2008, Defendant R.W. Cooper filed a Motion to Deem that Plaintiff had Waived the Privilege as to the approximately 800 inadvertently produced documents. Defendant GAF filed a Motion Joining Cooper's Motion on August 25, 2008. Defendants do not dispute that the production was inadvertent and that the software purchased by Rhoads was designed to ferret out privileged documents. Defendants do argue, and have substantial facts to support the conclusion, that Rhoads's technical consultant and counsel were not sufficiently careful to review the software screening and to take steps to prevent disclosure when it appeared obvious that privileged material had filtered through the screening procedure.

At the first hearing held on the waiver of privilege on November 5, 2008, the three separate logs described above were produced, and Mr. Gramaglia and Ms. Buchinsky testified, explaining how the logs were created and how they relate to each other. Also at the hearing Rhoads admitted that the 2,000 e-mails originally set aside as privileged as a result of the Sherpa search had not been identified on a privilege log. Ms. Buchinsky testified that she believed her manual review of e-mails contained in specific mailboxes would have captured these privileged e-mails and therefore would have appeared on her June 6th log of electronic documents. This Court ordered that any documents not on a privilege log as of the date of that hearing should be produced, absent exceptional circumstances.

After the hearing, Rhoads inspected the 2,000 e-mail documents set aside as a result of the Sherpa search and created a fourth privilege log produced to Defendants on November 12, 2008, and discussed at the hearing which took place on November 13, 2008. On the logs and in its attendant letter, Rhoads identified that, of the 2,000 e-mail documents, 941 documents were duplicative. Of the 1,059 unique documents, it identified 548 documents as non-responsive and 511 as responsive broken down as follows: 335 privileged documents and 176 non-privileged documents. In addition, of the responsive, privileged documents, 215 had been previously logged [on pre-hearing privilege logs]. Rhoads did not present any exceptional circumstances as to why these documents should not be produced but did agree to produce the 176 non-privileged documents that had not been previously produced. Defendants presented additional argument that has led this Court to question whether Rhoads may still be retaining privileged and un-logged documents.

Based on my statement at the November 5 hearing and for the reasons set forth below, I ordered, at the conclusion of the November 13 hearing, that any responsive, non-attorney-work-product documents not placed on a privilege log as of June 30, 2008 must be produced to Defendants, including those logged on [the fourth, post-hearing privilege log]. I took the issue of waiver of privilege as to the 812 documents listed on the June 30, 2008 privilege log under advisement and will now discuss this issue.

[The judge held that the party claiming privilege had the burden of proof regarding whether a privilege applied to a document, but that the party claiming waiver had the burden of proof to show waiver. The judge then carefully reviewed the evidence presented, distinguishing between factors that favored plaintiff and those that favored defendant.

Among the facts favoring plaintiff were the fact that it purchased a special software program that its technical consultant had tested and found satisfactory. Its use of only "Gowa" as a search term (rather than also using outside counsel's names) was reasonably based on its belief that Gowa would appear on all emails going to the client, and the fact it did not use "privileged" or "confidential" as search terms made sense because these words appeared a the bottom of every email. Ms. Buchinsky spent over 40 hours reviewing for privilege before production, and other attorneys spent significant hours on privilege review also. Only about 1% or 2% of the documents produced were privileged, "a small proportion" of the total production. Production was done under a tight discovery schedule, and Ms. Buchinsky was simultaneously helping prepare for nine depositions to be taken over twelve days when defendant gave notice by email that potentially privileged documents had been produced. Plaintiff invoked Rule 26(b)(5)(B) when it filed its privilege log three weeks after being notified of the problem. So plaintiffs had shown "general compliance with Rule 502," and that "loss of privilege would be highly prejudicial to the Plaintiff."

Favoring defendant was the fact plaintiff should have used additional search terms, and that "Ms. Buchinsky had no prior experience doing a privilege review and her supervising attorneys did not provide any detailed oversight." Relying exclusively on a keyword search to conduct a privilege review is "risky," and there was no testing of the quality of the keyword search that was used. More than 800 assertedly privileged documents produced is "still a large number of documents regardless of the percentage produced." Plaintiff had "abundant time to review its own documents" before filing suit, and the time crunch it later faced resulted from plaintiff "not providing adequate resources (e.g. attorneys or paralegals)" to address privilege review. Moreover, it took over three weeks for plaintiff produce a privilege log even after being notified of the problem.]

Conclusion

1.   Ruling on Privilege Log

Concerning the privileged documents produced by Rhoads which were not listed on any of the logs served by June 30, 2008, the obligation to log privileged documents is mandatory under the specific terms of Rule 26(b)(5). Despite Rhoads's attempts to justify, explain and minimize its failure to log all of its inadvertently privileged documents by June 30, 2008, the Court finds that the delay in doing so until November 12, 2008 [after the hearing], is too long and inexcusable. This conclusion does not entail any analysis of F.R.E. 502, because of the clear mandate of Federal Rule of Civil Procedure 26(b)(5).

2.   Ruling on Inadvertently Disclosed Documents on Privileged Logs as of June 30, 2008

In approaching a conclusion, and recognizing that Rule 502 is a recent addition to the law, I believe that the most appropriate approach is to first determine whether the producing party has at least minimally complied with the three factors stated in Rule 502, i.e., that the waiver was inadvertent, the party took reasonable steps to prevent disclosure, and attempted to rectify the error.

In this case, there is no dispute that the production of the privileged documents was inadvertent; the dispute is over whether the steps taken by Rhoads were "reasonable." Consistent with the Committee Note to Rule 502, I conclude that once the producing party has shown at least minimal compliance with the three factors in Rule 502, but "reasonableness" is in dispute. * * *

Although Rhoads took steps to prevent disclosure and to rectify the error, its efforts were, to some extent, not reasonable. * * * The most significant factor, after listening to the witnesses and arguments of counsel, is that Rhoads failed to prepare for the segregation and review of privileged documents sufficiently far in advance of the inevitable production of a large volume of documents. Once this lawsuit seeking millions of dollars in damages was filed, Rhoads was under an obligation to put adequate resources to the task of preparing the documents, which was completely within Rhoads's control. An understandable desire to minimize costs of litigation and to be frugal in spending a client's money cannot be an after-the-fact excuse for a failed screening of privileged documents, just as I refuse to use hindsight to criticize Rhoads for mistakes that were made but perhaps unforeseeable. Although hindsight is surely twenty-twenty, if it is not to be used, it cannot be used to favor one side to the prejudice of the other.

I find that * * * the interest of justice strongly favors Rhoads. Loss of the attorney-client privilege in a high-stakes, hard-fought litigation is a severe sanction and can lead to serious prejudice. Although I have little knowledge of the content of Rhoads's privileged documents, I assume they contain candid assessments of the facts and strategy in this case, as to which Rhoads understandably has a high degree of proprietary interest.

On the other hand, denying these documents to Defendants is not prejudicial to Defendants because, in the first place, they have no right or expectation to any of Rhoads's privileged communications, and further, because of my ruling on the privileged documents not logged by June 30, 2008, the Defendants will receive a significant number of privileged documents. Furthermore, there has been abundant discovery on the merits of this case, and expert depositions await completion.[8]

The other factor that I have considered in reaching this conclusion is that the Defendants, as the moving party challenging the assertion of privilege, have the burden of proof. Considering all of the factors, I find that the Defendants have not met that burden of proof as to the privileged documents logged by June 30, 2008.

This discussion need not be extended to extol in any detail the societal and historical value which the law attaches to privileged communications between attorney and client. Except for the privilege log issue, disturbance of these communications is not justified under all of the facts and circumstances of this case, as reviewed above.[9]

NOTES AND QUESTIONS

1. One court has observed that Fed. R. Evid. 502 "creates a new framework for managing disclosure issues in a cost-effective manner in an age of large electronic document productions." Coburn Group LLC v. Whitecap Advisors LLC, 640 F.Supp.2d 1032 (N.D.Ill. 2009); see also Judson Atkinson Candies, Inc. v. Latini-Hohberger Dhimantec, 529 F.3d 371, 388 (7th Cir. 2008) ("Where discovery is extensive, mistakes are inevitable and claims of

---

[8] There is a lingering issue as to whether any of Rhoads's privileged documents were disclosed to its testifying experts. Defense counsel may explore this in the expert depositions, if not before.

[9] Rhoads's production of privileged documents, notwithstanding that it was inadvertent, has led to extensive briefing and preparation for hearings and argument, and Defendants have incurred considerable costs because of this production. Although I believe it would be equitable for Rhoads to reimburse Defendants for some portion of their attorneys fees in dealing with this issue, Defendants have not made such a request, and the rules do not specifically provide for the award of expenses in this situation.

inadvertence are properly honored so long as appropriate precautions are taken.").

2.   Rule 502(a) makes an important modification to the traditional "subject matter" breadth of waiver, which meant that release of one privileged item produced a waiver also with regard to any other items on the same subject. Rule 502(a) limits waiver to situations in which the disclosure is intentional and the withheld and disclosed materials "ought in fairness to be considered together." Cf. Fed. R. Evid. 106 (directing that when a part of a writing is introduced into evidence, another party may insist that any other part that "ought in fairness be considered contemporaneously" be admitted in evidence at that time).

A prime example of litigation in which it may be argued that the subject matter breadth of waiver should still apply is patent infringement, for defendants may seek to avoid treble damages by stressing their reliance on advice of counsel. That reliance would normally be treated as intentional disclosure of attorney advice. When patent infringement defendants rely on advice of counsel, they usually must reveal all opinions of counsel regarding patent validity or infringement. Why? "If the rule were limited to only particular counsel, a party might get several viewpoints and assert reliance on only one, thus barring an inquiry as to the actuality or reasonableness of that reliance." Technitrol, Inc. v. Digital Equip. Corp., 181 U.S.P.Q. 731, 732 (N.D.Ill. 1974). In patent litigation, this limitation has been tempered to exclude opinions from litigation counsel retained to defend patent infringement litigation if these attorneys did not provide advice about the underlying conduct. In re Seagate Technology, LLC, 497 F.3d 1360 (Fed.Cir. 2007).

3.   *Rhoads Industries* also emphasizes the importance of timely and thorough preparation of a privilege log, and rules that the materials listed on the privilege log that was not delivered until after the evidentiary hearing must be turned over because they were listed too late. Consider the effort sometimes involved in preparing a log. For discussion, see John Facciola & Jonathan Redgrave, Asserting and Challenging Privilege Claims in Modern Litigation: The Facciola-Redgrave Framework, 4 Fed.Cts.L.Rev. 19 (2009) (noting that "[p]rivilege logs have emerged as a staple in litigation today," and offering suggestions about how to handle them). The idea is that a privilege log should include sufficient information for the opposing party and the court to determine whether materials claimed to be privileged actually are. How detailed should such logs be? Note that failure to compile a sufficient log can itself result in waiver of privilege protection. Is there a risk that compiling the log itself will prove a waste of time and money? At least one judge has found that software used to prepare privilege logs relies on generic description of the materials listed with the result of "the modern privilege log being as expensive as it is useless." Chevron Corp. v. Weinberg Group, 286 F.R.D. 95, 99 (D.D.C. 2012).

There can be considerable difficulties in determining how much detail should be included in the log. One recurrent problem results from the frequent use of email to interact in large organizations. That can mean that there are many nonidentical email strings. Must each of those be logged, and must each entry include a listing of every other communication included in the string? One concern might be that some of the messages were not privileged, but the fact they were forwarded to counsel could be privileged and would be revealed if the log for the message to counsel must reveal what was attached to it. See *Muro v. Target Corp.*, 243 F.R.D. 301 (N.D.Ill. 2007) (holding that only the communication to the lawyer need be identified, not all attached or forwarded additional communications in the string). In *Rhoads Indus. Inc. v. Building Materials Corp.*, 254 F.R.D. 238 (E.D.Pa. 2008), a subsequent decision in the case reproduced above, Judge Baylson held that it would suffice to identify only the message to the lawyer. He explained as follows (id. at 241 n.5):

> An email string may be analogous to a meeting that takes place in a conference room between attorney and client for the purpose of seeking legal advice. The facts discussed at the meeting must be disclosed in discovery, but the communications that take place at the meeting are privileged. As a result of the meeting if the client prepares a letter to the attorney summarizing those communications, both the discussions at the meeting and the letter itself are clearly privileged.

> In the world of electronic communications, a series of email messages, among people employed by the client but working in different locations, can replace the meeting and subsequent letter. Some of the communications may not include copies to the attorney, but after the exchange of email messages among the client's employees, all contained within one email string, the last and most recent email, attaching all the prior emails, is then sent to the attorney with a request for legal advice based on the underlying email messages.

4. Rule 502(b) clarifies some prior uncertainty about the proper standard regarding inadvertent production of privileged material. It focuses attention on three things:

(a) *Inadvertence*: In cases decided before Rule 502 was adopted, there was sometimes a fairly elaborate analysis of whether a given disclosure should be regarded as "inadvertent." It appears that Rule 502(b) is "much simpler, essentially asking whether the party intended a privileged or work product document to be produced or whether the production was a mistake." *Coburn Group, LLC v. Whitecap Advisors LLC*, 640 F.Supp.2d 1032 (N.D.Ill. 2009).

(b) *Reasonable steps to prevent disclosure*: The Chair of the Senate Judiciary Committee explained that Rule 502 was needed because "[b]illions of dollars are spent each year in litigation to protect against the inadvertent disclosure of privileged materials." S.Rep. 110–264, 110th Cong., 2d Sess., at 2. Would too exacting a standard for "reasonable steps" defeat the purpose of the rule, which was partly to reduce this financial burden? Consider the reliance on electronic searching of electronically stored information in *Rhoads*

Industries. Should that method generally be sufficient? Some producing parties clearly do not do enough. For example, in Infor Global Solutions, Inc. v. St. Paul Fire & Marine Ins. Co., 2009 WL 2390174 (N.D.Cal., Aug. 3, 2009), plaintiff produced a CD to defendant even though it had not been able to open the files on the CD, and found after production that the CD contained privileged material. The court ruled that plaintiff had not taken reasonable steps to prevent disclosure: "Under Rule 502 * * *, plaintiff Infor has not shown that it undertook any reasonable steps to prevent disclosure here. Rather, plaintiff Infor admits that it took a chance that privileged documents would not be on the compact disc it produced." See also Victor Stanley, Inc. v. Creative Pipe, Inc., 250 F.R.D. 251 (D.Md. 2008) (holding that defendants' use of a keyword search using seventy search terms was not adequate, and noting that "not all keyword searches are created equal").

In *Rhoads Industries*, the judge criticized plaintiff for failure "to put adequate resources to the task of preparing the documents," relying on an overworked associate though she had no prior experience with privilege review, and was not closely supervised by more experienced attorneys. Compare Heriot v. Byrne, 257 F.R.D. 645 (N.D.Ill. 2009) (finding reliance on a paralegal sufficient). But it must be realized that the review can sometimes be quite difficult. Consider the views of the court in Coburn Group LLC v. Whitecap Advisors LLC, 640 F.Supp.2d 1032, 1040 (N.D.Ill. 2009):

> Unquestionably, reviewing documents for work product can be challenging because sometimes there are subtleties to the determination. As [plaintiff] points out, whether a document is work product can rest on facts not apparent from the face of the document, as in this case. Here, although there are clues on the face of the e-mail, the fact that it was prepared to provide information to [counsel] is not apparent from the document itself. But the document review cannot be deemed unreasonable solely because a document slipped through which on close examination with additional information turns out to be privileged work product. If that were the standard, Rule 502(b) would have no purpose; the starting point of a Rule 502(b) analysis is that a privileged or protected document was, in fact, turned over.

(c) *Reasonable steps to rectify the error*: Rule 26(b)(5)(B) now provides a procedure for guarding against misuse of inadvertently produced privileged information. But it can only be employed once the producing party realizes the mistake was made. The Committee Note to Rule 502 says that "[t]he rule does not require the producing party to engage in a post-production review to determine whether any protected communication or information has been produced by mistake. But the rule does require the producing party to follow up on any obvious indications that a protected communication or information has been produced inadvertently." Nonetheless, the judge in *Rhoads Industries* criticized plaintiff for failing to catch the mistakes on its own.

This "reasonable steps" inquiry is likely to focus largely on time. See Jones v. Eagle-North Hills Shopping Centre, L.P., 239 F.R.D. 684 (E.D.Ok. 2007) (holding that no waiver occurred when plaintiff's counsel requested that defense counsel delete the privileged document eight minutes after mistakenly producing it), but also on what might be called reliance by the other party on being able to use the information. For example, in Bobbitt v. Academy of Court Reporting, 2008 WL 4056323 (W.D.Mich. 2008), plaintiff refused to return materials after defendants had demanded their return and, eight days after that refusal, filed a motion for class certification referring to the emails in question. Defendant nonetheless did not dispute their use until more than four months after that, and the court found this effort "a day late and a dollar short." Contrast Bensel v. Air Line Pilots Ass'n, 248 F.R.D. 177, 180 (D.N.J. 2008), in which the privilege holder waited almost a year before moving for a protective order against use of the privileged materials that were produced, but promptly submitted a privilege log listing these materials and made informal efforts to resolve the issue before seeking the assistance of the court.

5.   Rule 502(d) also permits the court to enter an order providing that production is not a waiver. The Committee Note to Rule 502(d) explains: "[T]he court order may provide for return of documents without waiver irrespective of the care taken by the disclosing party." Is there any reason *not* to agree to a Rule 502(d) order? In 2015 Rules 26(f) and 16(b) were amended to call the parties' and the court's attention to Rule 502 right at the beginning of the litigation. A prominent magistrate judge said "it is malpractice to not seek a 502(d) order from the court before you seek documents." Carol Young, ESI Confidential: The Best Ways to Protect Privileged Information, The Legal Intelligencer, Feb. 1, 2016 (quoting Judge Andrew Peck).

Other Privilege Waiver Issues

Besides inadvertent production, litigators must also keep in mind other ways privilege protection may be lost:

Disclosure to testifying experts: As noted in *Rhoads Industries*, disclosure of privileged material to testifying experts has often been a ground for compelled disclosure. Rule 26(a)(2)(B) requires a full report from specially retained testifying experts, including all "data or other information" considered by the expert in reaching the opinion to be offered at trial. That provision has often been held to include all attorney-expert communications, effectively abrogating any protections that would otherwise apply. A 2010 amendment added new provisions to Rule 26(b)(4) providing work product protection for many communications between attorneys and their expert witnesses, and also changed the disclosure requirements of Rule 26(a)(2)(B) so that it calls for disclosure of "facts or data" counsel provided to expert witnesses, rather than the prior requirement that the expert's report include all "data or other information" so disclosed.

Witness preparation: When the witness is not a testifying expert, Fed. R. Evid. 612 provides that any materials used by the witness to refresh recollection during testimony or before may be subject to discovery. Unless foreseen, this possibility may lead to waiver:

> [W]hile many good lawyers forget to do so, it is always worth asking the witness if she brought any documents to the deposition. This question often is so productive that seasoned practitioners routinely ask it. You are taking a big chance if you do not do so. It is simply astounding how many witnesses, sophisticated and unsophisticated, show up for depositions with a sheaf of documents in their briefcases. Often, their own attorneys have not even seen the documents. You have to remember to get them to open the briefcase. My practice is to bury this question in a series of routine background questions. I try to ask it when the witness has become comfortable with me and the opposing attorney does not appear to be paying too much attention. Almost every time, witnesses, especially non-parties, respond that, yes, they did bring documents. Some have even handed them to me before an opposing attorney could object. At least half the time, the question unearths a useful document that was not previously produced in discovery, such as a calendar, notebook or personal file.

Laurin Mills, Taking Chances at Depositions, Litigation, Fall 2001, at 30, 33. For an illustration, see Maldonado-Rodriguez v. Grupo Hima, 326 F.R.D. 367 (D.P.R. 2019) (plaintiff's expert handed draft report to defense counsel during deposition, but immediate invocation of work product by plaintiff counsel avoided a waiver).

Putting privileged material "in issue": As in patent cases (see note 2 on p. 502 *supra*), on other occasions advice of counsel may be relevant to an issue raised in a case. Some courts have taken a broad view of this ground for waiver. See, e.g., Pitney-Bowes, Inc. v. Mestre, 86 F.R.D. 444 (S.D.Fla. 1980) (holding that plaintiff seeking to reform a contract had to reveal advice of counsel about the meaning of the contract); United States v. Exxon Corp., 94 F.R.D. 246 (D.D.C. 1981) ("a party waives the protection of the attorney-client privilege when he voluntarily injects into the suit the question of his state of mind"). The predominant view, however, is as expressed in Rhone-Poulenc Rorer, Inc. v. Home Indemnity Co., 32 F.3d 851 (3d Cir. 1994): "Advice is not in issue merely because the attorney's advice might affect the client's state of mind in a relevant manner. The advice of counsel is placed in issue where the client asserts a claim or defense, and attempts to prove that claim or defense by disclosing or describing an attorney-client communication."

Sharing with others having common interests: In multi-party cases, it is essential that co-parties be able to discuss their mutual interests candidly. Therefore, even though disclosure of attorney-client privileged matters to others generally waives the privilege, disclosure to others with common litigation interests does not. See, e.g., California Oak Foundation

v. County of Tehama, 94 Cal.Rptr.3d 902 (Cal.Ct.App. 2009) (under California environmental statutes, required interaction about approving projects means that sharing of privileged information between a developer and a county is protected); Deborah Bartel, Reconceptualizing the Joint Defense Doctrine, 65 Ford. L. Rev. 871 (1996). Whether protection will endure is sometimes disputed. Compare Cheeves v. Southern Clays, Inc., 128 F.R.D. 128 (M.D.Ga. 1989) (common interests of corporate seller of assets and buyer not sufficient even though sale went through) with Hewlett-Packard Co. v. Bausch & Lomb, Inc., 115 F.R.D. 308 (N.D.Cal. 1987) (sharing of attorney letter about patent validity with prospective purchaser of a division of patent holder did not waive attorney-client privilege in unrelated patent infringement suit even though the purchase transaction ultimately did not go through).

4. PROTECTIVE ORDERS AND DISCOVERY CONFIDENTIALITY

Recall that in *New Motor Vehicles, supra* p. 414, one of the first things that the judge did in managing the case was to enter a stipulated protective order. That sort of arrangement is a commonplace feature of complex litigation. "Complex litigation will frequently involve information or documents that a party considers sensitive." Manual for Complex Litigation (4th) § 11.432 (2004). Beginning in the 1970s, courts entered protective orders to restrict dissemination of materials obtained through discovery with increasing frequency. A famous example is Zenith Radio Corp. v. Matsushita Elec. Indus. Co., 529 F.Supp. 866 (E.D.Pa. 1981), a massive antitrust litigation. As the judge explained, a reading of the complaints, "which spanned the law of anti-trust and focused on defendants' price behavior," showed that "large quantities of sensitive commercial data would be sought in discovery." Id. at 892.

One way of handling questions of confidentiality would be for the producing party to object to discovery, leading to a contested protective order proceeding, either on motion of the producing party or in response to a motion to compel discovery. In such a proceeding, the burden would be on the party seeking the court's protection to establish that the materials were eligible for that protection. To show "good cause" for a protective order under Rule 26(c), the moving party would have to make a specific showing (a) that the materials contained sensitive information that was kept secret, (b) that disclosure would likely cause a specific harm, and (c) that issuance of the order was supported by "good cause".

In *Zenith* (as in *New Motor Vehicles*), however, the parties took a different course. They stipulated to what is called an "umbrella" protective order, which permitted parties to designate materials they produced as confidential and limited dissemination of materials so designated. The judge observed that he was "unaware of any case in the past half-dozen

years of even a modicum of complexity where an umbrella protective order
* * * has not been agreed to by the parties and approved by the court.
Protective orders have been used so frequently that a degree of
standardization is appearing." Id. at 889. For an example of such an order,
see Manual for Complex Litigation (4th) § 40.27 (2004). See also Howard
Erichson, Court-Ordered Confidentiality in Discovery, 81 Chi.-Kent L. Rev.
357 (2006) (urging that courts not enter stipulated protective orders unless
supported by some showing of recognized need). When should courts enter
such orders? In In re Terrorist Attacks on September 11, 2001, 454
F.Supp.2d 220 (S.D.N.Y. 2006), the court treated "broad assertions of good
cause" as sufficient to justify such an order even though they might
ordinarily not suffice:

> [T]his multidistrict litigation amounts to one of the largest private
> lawsuits in United States history. Defendant-by-defendant good
> cause determinations for individual protective orders at this
> juncture in this case, much less document-by-document
> confidentiality determinations where no protective order has
> issued, would impose an enormous burden upon the Court and
> severely hinder its progress toward resolution of pretrial matters.

The designation process provided by an umbrella order relies on the
first instance on the party's lawyer. "[T]here is a danger here that counsel
will err on the side of caution by designating confidential any potentially
sensitive document," but "[t]he designation of a document as confidential
may be viewed as equivalent to a motion for protective order and subject to
the sanctions of Fed.R.Civ.P. 26(g)." Cipollone v. Liggett Group, Inc., 785
F.2d 1108, 1122 n. 17 (3d Cir. 1986), cert. denied, 484 U.S. 976 (1987). See
In re Ullico Inc. Litigation, 237 F.R.D. 314 (D.D.C. 2006) (finding that
defendant abused the authority to stamp documents confidential by
designating over 99% of the documents it produced that way). The sample
order in the Manual for Complex Litigation (4th) (2004) provides as follows
(§ 40.27(c)):

> Only documents containing trade secrets, special formulas,
> company security matters, customer lists, financial data,
> projected sales data, production data, matters relating to mergers
> and acquisitions, and data which touch upon the topic of price may
> be designated confidential. * * * [T]he information subject to a
> confidentiality designation may include the following: customer
> names; proprietary licensing, distribution, marketing, design,
> development, research, and manufacturing information—not
> publicly filed with any federal or state regulatory authority—
> regarding products and medicines, whether currently marketed or
> under development; clinical studies not publicly filed with any
> federal or state regulatory authority; information concerning
> competitors; production information; personnel records and

information; financial information not publicly filed with any federal or state regulatory authority.

In *Zenith, supra,* the parties produced some 35 million documents after entering into the protective order. One defendant stamped over 77,000 documents confidential, and plaintiff produced over 100,000 documents on paper preprinted with a confidentiality designation. As trial approached, the judge directed the parties to file pretrial statements in connection with summary judgment motions. Plaintiff's pretrial statement was 17,000 pages long and cross-referenced over 250,000 documents. After a five-week hearing to determine the admissibility of this material, the court granted defendants' motion for summary judgment. The Supreme Court later affirmed this summary-judgment ruling. Matsushita Elec. Indus. Co. v. Zenith Radio Corp., 475 U.S. 574 (1986).

After the district judge granted defendants' motion for summary judgment, plaintiff sought to have the confidentiality provisions lifted, seemingly in part so that it could supply copies of discovery materials to governmental authorities. Plaintiff made an across-the-board challenge to the restrictions on releasing the documents, claiming that defendants had overused the confidentiality stamp, and that continued protection had to be justified document-by-document. Defendants submitted affidavits concerning the ways in which the information could be used to their commercial disadvantage. One method would be to discern defendants' pricing strategies. "Of equal if not greater concern to defendants is the possible consequence of exposure of [details about their arrangements with retailers], in that customer relationships could be impaired if those retailers knew the terms on which a manufacturer sold to the retailer's competitors." In at least some instances, defendants had accorded more favorable treatment to some retailers than others.

Plaintiff urged that defendants had to make a detailed showing to justify continued protection. The judge acknowledged that "[i]n practical terms, it may well be that courts apply a less rigorous standard to consent [protective] orders, although we doubt that any judge would approve a consent order not demonstrably rooted in Rule 26(c), both as a matter of judicial authority and out of concern for potential public access rights." *Zenith,* 529 F.Supp. at 889 n. 40. The judge concluded that the defendants' showing was sufficient because it demonstrated with adequate specificity that defendants maintained the confidentiality of the information and risked competitive disadvantage should it be disclosed. A document-by-document showing was not necessary. Moreover, the judge rejected plaintiff's argument for wholesale declassification because it was not raised at the time of production of the documents, concluding that a party could not "sit on its hands while the mountain of discovery materials grows and then attempt to challenge the protection of such material with the same ease with which it could have raised an objection contemporaneously." Id. at 893–94. He added:

> In terms of complex case management, we also believe that wholesale declassification is a poor, inappropriate, and unfair tool, not only with respect to the interests of the litigants, but also with respect to the interests of third parties who are frequently drawn into the vortex. It is common that, in response to a subpoena to attend a deposition and produce related documents, and in reliance upon an umbrella confidential order, third parties divulge sensitive commercial information * * *.

It should be apparent that there are many efficiency considerations that can be furthered by entry of protective orders in complex litigation. In the 1970s, one objection to such protective orders was that they infringed the First Amendment rights of litigants by limiting their ability to speak about information they acquired through discovery. In In re Halkin, 598 F.2d 176 (D.C.Cir. 1979), the court ruled that a protective order was analogous to a "prior restraint" on speech, and therefore that it could only be justified in the very rare instances when a court may issue a prior restraint. What impact would this ruling have had on cases like *New Motor Vehicles* or *Zenith*? For criticism of this view, see Richard Marcus, Myth and Reality in Protective Order Litigation, 69 Cornell L.Rev. 1 (1983). In Seattle Times Co. v. Rhinehart, 467 U.S. 20 (1984), the Court held that in the "unique" setting of pretrial civil discovery, "good cause" under Rule 26(c) sufficed to uphold a protective order against First Amendment free-expression challenges. For analysis, see Robert Post, The Management of Speech, Discretion and Rights, 1984 Sup.Ct.Rev. 169. Although this constitutional issue receded, some favor returning it to the fore. See Dustin Benham, Dirty Secrets: The First Amendment in Protective-Order Litigation, 35 Cardozo L. Rev. 1781 (2014). In any event, other issues remain.

CHICAGO TRIBUNE CO. V. BRIDGESTONE/FIRESTONE, INC.

United States Court of Appeals, Eleventh Circuit, 2001.
263 F.3d 1304.

Before BLACK, RONEY and COX, CIRCUIT JUDGES.

PER CURIAM:

This is an appeal of the district court's order unsealing documents previously filed pursuant to a protective order entered by stipulation of the parties. See Fed.R.Civ.P. 26(c)[(1)(G)]. We vacate and remand with instructions for the district court to determine whether "good cause" exists for maintaining the documents under seal.

I.   Background

Daniel Van Etten, an eighteen-year old football player from West Virginia University, died as a result of injuries sustained in a roll-over automobile accident. In April of 1998, his parents filed suit in the Southern District of Georgia, claiming that Bridgestone/Firestone, Inc.'s negligent design and manufacture of the tires on Daniel's Ford Explorer were the proximate cause of his death. At the beginning of the litigation, in what has become commonplace in the federal courts, the parties stipulated to a protective order allowing each other to designate particular documents as confidential and subject to protection under Federal Rule of Civil Procedure 26(c)[(1)(G)]. This method replaces the need to litigate the claim to protection document by document, and postpones the necessary showing of "good cause" required for entry of a protective order until the confidential designation is challenged. As the district court noted, this allowed Bridgestone/Firestone, Inc. (Firestone) to temporarily enjoy the protection of Rule 26(c), making Firestone's documents presumptively confidential until challenged.[2]

Consistent with local rule, documents produced pursuant to discovery requests were not filed with the court. The protective order required the parties filing confidential material with the court in connection with a pleading or motion to place the documents in a sealed, marked envelope. The documents were to be used only for preparation and conduct of the action, and only counsel, their paralegals and technical consultants, as well as the court and its staff, were privy to the content of any confidential document. Of the nearly three hundred documents filed in the action, fifteen were placed under seal.

Following discovery, Firestone moved for summary judgment. The district court denied the motion, and shortly thereafter the parties settled. In accordance with the terms of the protective order, the confidential documents remained sealed.

In the months following settlement, media scrutiny of tire tread separation accidents intensified, and members of the media, now appellees[3] (collectively, "the Press"), sought leave to intervene for the purpose of unsealing Firestone's documents. Firestone agreed to unseal some of the material, but objected to disclosure of nine documents and ten pages excerpted from legal briefs, claiming that these particular items contain trade secrets. In support of this claim, Firestone appended a privilege log

---

[2]   See Manual for Complex Litigation (Third) § 21.432 (1995) (noting that "[u]mbrella orders provide that all assertedly confidential material disclosed . . . is presumptively protected unless challenged. The orders are made without a particularized showing to support the claim for protection, but such a showing must be made whenever a claim under an order is challenged.").

[3]   Appellees are: the Chicago Tribune Company; the Washington Post Company; CBS Broadcasting, Inc.; and Los Angeles Times Communications, L.L.C.

and the affidavit of John Goudie, the Senior Product Engineer in Firestone's Product Analysis Department.

The district court granted the Press's motion to intervene as well as its consolidated motion to unseal the remaining documents, determining that the Goudie affidavit was too general and conclusory to carry Firestone's burden of showing "that the closure of the records filed with this Court is necessitated by a compelling interest and that the closure is narrowly tailored to that compelling interest." Accordingly, the district court ordered the documents unsealed, but, granting in part Firestone's motion to stay disclosure pending appeal, delayed the unsealing. We granted Firestone's emergency motion for a stay pending Firestone's appeal.

* * *

IV. Discussion

Firestone's main contention is that the district court applied the wrong standard when it required Firestone to show that sealing the documents is necessitated by a compelling governmental interest and is narrowly tailored to that interest. Firestone argues for application of Rule 26's "good cause" standard, which balances the asserted right of access against the other party's interest in keeping the information confidential.

The Press argues that two sources supply a right of access to Firestone's documents, both requiring application of the standard used by the district court. The Press first relies on the common-law right to inspect and copy judicial records, a right grounded in the democratic process, as "[t]he operations of the courts and the judicial conduct of judges are matters of utmost public concern." Landmark Comm. v. Virginia, 435 U.S. 829, 839 (1978). The Press argues that in cases concerning health and safety or where there is a particularly strong public interest in court records, the common-law right of access is measured by the compelling interest standard.

Additionally, the Press contends that there is a First Amendment right of access to court records and documents in civil cases. The Press cites Newman v. Graddick, 696 F.2d 796 (11th Cir. 1983), for the proposition that the compelling interest standard applies to civil as well as criminal proceedings. Accordingly, the Press argues that whether the right of access is grounded in the common law or the Constitution, the compelling interest standard applies.

Because the parties' arguments concern three different bases for disclosure of the sealed documents, it is necessary for us to limn the bounds of the common-law right of access, the constitutional right of access, and Federal Rule of Civil Procedure 26(c). We consider first the constitutional right of access.

A. Constitutional Right of Access

The media and general public's First Amendment right of access to criminal trial proceedings [is] firmly established * * *. For a court to exclude the press and public from a criminal proceeding, "it must be shown that the denial is necessitated by a compelling governmental interest, and is narrowly tailored to serve that interest."

The constitutional right of access has a more limited application in the civil context than it does in the criminal. Nonetheless, this court has extended the scope of the constitutional right of access to include civil actions pertaining to the release or incarceration of prisoners and their confinement. [Newman v. Graddick, 696 F.2d 796 (11th Cir. 1983).] Materials merely gathered as a result of the civil discovery process, however, do not fall within the scope of the constitutional right of access's compelling interest standard.

Public disclosure of discovery material is subject to the discretion of the trial court and the federal rules that circumscribe that discretion. See Seattle Times Co. v. Rhinehart, 467 U.S. 20, 33 (1984). Where discovery materials are concerned, the constitutional right of access standard is identical to that of Rule 26(c) of the Federal Rules of Civil Procedure. Accordingly, where a third party seeks access to material disclosed during discovery and covered by a protective order, the constitutional right of access, like Rule 26, requires a showing of good cause by the party seeking protection.

The district court required Firestone to meet a compelling interest standard. To the extent this was predicated on a constitutional right of access, it was error. All of the documents were produced during the discovery phase of the litigation, and the protective order did not restrict the dissemination of information gained from other sources. As we later discuss more fully, the adequacy of Firestone's good cause showing remains to be determined upon remand; because the Rule 26 standard is identical, the resolution of that issue will necessarily decide the Press's constitutional right of access claim.

B. Common-Law Right of Access

The common-law right of access to judicial proceedings, an essential component of our system of justice, is instrumental in securing the integrity of the process. See Richmond Newspapers [v. Virginia], 448 U.S. at 564–74 (providing panegyric on the value of openness). Beyond establishing a general presumption that criminal and civil actions should be conducted publicly, the common-law right of access includes the right to inspect and copy public records and documents. Nixon v. Warner Comm., Inc., 435 U.S. 589, 597 (1978). The right to inspect and copy is not absolute, however, and a judge's exercise of discretion in deciding whether to release judicial records should be informed by a "sensitive appreciation of the circumstances that led to . . . [the] production [of the particular document in question]." Not unlike the Rule 26 standard, the common-law right of access requires a balancing of competing interests.

Although there is some disagreement about where precisely the line should be drawn, when applying the common-law right of access federal courts traditionally distinguish between those items which may properly be considered public or judicial records and those that may not; the media and public presumptively have access to the former, but not to the latter. An illustrative example is the treatment of discovery material, for which there is no common-law right of access, as these materials are neither public documents nor judicial records.

In certain narrow circumstances, the common-law right of access demands heightened scrutiny of a court's decision to conceal records from the public and the media. Where the trial court conceals the record of an entire case, making no distinction between those documents that are sensitive or privileged and those that are not, it must be shown that "the denial [of access] is necessitated by a compelling governmental interest, and is narrowly tailored to that interest." * * *

The common-law right of access standard as it applies to particular documents requires the court to balance the competing interests of the parties. We turn now to an examination of the documents at issue, and the context of the proceeding in which they were submitted to the court.

The Firestone documents were produced during discovery, but all of them were also filed with the court, under seal, in connection with pre-trial motions. Some of the documents were submitted to support motions to compel discovery; others were submitted to support summary judgment motions. Significantly, all the documents were submitted under seal, and all were submitted by the Van Ettens: Firestone did not submit the documents for judicial consideration.

The Press contends, and the district court agreed, that because the documents were filed with the court they are judicial records and therefore subject to the common-law right of access. Such an approach does not distinguish between material filed with discovery motions and material filed in connection with more substantive motions.[10] We think a more refined approach is called for, one that accounts both for the tradition favoring access, as well as the unique function discovery serves in modern proceedings. The better rule is that material filed with discovery motions is not subject to the common-law right of access, whereas discovery material filed in connection with pretrial motions that require judicial resolution of the merits is subject to the common-law right, and we so hold.

---

[10] We note that absent a contrary court order or local rule, the default rule under the Federal Rules of Civil Procedure is that discovery materials must be filed with the district court. See Fed.R.Civ.P. 5(d). The prospect of all discovery material being presumptively subject to the right of access would likely lead to an increased resistance to discovery requests.

This means that the Firestone documents filed in connection with motions to compel discovery are not subject to the common-law right of access.

Additionally, where a party has sought the protection of Rule 26, the fact that sealed material is subsequently submitted in connection with a substantive motion does not mean that the confidentiality imposed by Rule 26 is automatically foregone. Before disclosure is appropriate, a court must first conduct the common-law right of access balancing test. Because in this context the common-law right of access, like the constitutional right, requires the court to balance the respective interests of the parties, the Press's common-law right to the Firestone documents filed in connection with the motion for summary judgment may be resolved by the Rule 26 good cause balancing test. We turn next to a discussion of Rule 26.

C. Federal Rule of Civil Procedure 26(c)

Rule 26(c) permits a court upon motion of a party to make a protective order requiring "that a trade secret or other confidential research, development, or commercial information not be revealed or be revealed only in a designated way." Fed.R.Civ.P. 26(c)[(1)(G)]. The prerequisite is a showing of "good cause" made by the party seeking protection. Federal courts have superimposed a balancing of interests approach for Rule 26's good cause requirement. This standard requires the district court to balance the party's interest in obtaining access against the other party's interest in keeping the information confidential.

Since the confidential designation was not challenged until the Press intervened, Firestone's Response to Intervenors' Motion to Unseal is the document that must establish good cause for continued protection under Rule 26. Although the district court discusses the adequacy of Firestone's Response in the order unsealing Firestone's documents, we do not find a determination by the district court that the request for a protective order was not supported by good cause. Because this conclusion is necessary to a resolution of the matter, we must remand to the district court for a determination of whether good cause exists for a protective order under Rule 26.

The first question that must be addressed on remand is whether Firestone's presumptively confidential documents do in fact contain trade secrets. Firestone argues that the sealed documents meet all of the commonly accepted criteria that define this category. These criteria require that Firestone must have consistently treated the information as closely guarded secrets, that the information represents substantial value to Firestone, that it would be valuable to Firestone's competitors, and that it derives its value by virtue of the effort of its creation and lack of dissemination.[13] Firestone argues that the Goudie affidavit and privilege log established each of these criteria.

* * * Because trade secret status is the only basis Firestone provides for nondisclosure, should the district court conclude that Firestone's documents do not fall within this category, good cause does not support the protective order, and the documents may be unsealed.

Should the district court determine that these documents do in fact contain trade secrets, the district court must balance Firestone's interest in keeping the information confidential against the Press's contention that disclosure serves the public's legitimate interest in health and safety. In its order the district court stated that "[e]ven assuming that the sealed material could be classified as trade secrets, concerns of public health and safety trump any right to shield such material from public scrutiny." The district court made no factual findings, however, that support the conclusion that the public's health and safety are sufficiently impacted by the information contained in these specific documents to trump Firestone's interest in keeping trade secret information confidential.[15] See generally Ruckelshaus v. Monsanto Co., 467 U.S. 986 (1984) (discussing takings of proprietary trade secret information and attendant Fifth Amendment implications). Because whether good cause exists for a protective order is a factual matter to be decided by the nature and character of the information in question, this determination, supported by findings of fact, must be conducted upon remand.

BLACK, CIRCUIT JUDGE, specially concurring:

I concur fully in the Court's holding regarding the press's rights under the Constitution, the common law, and Fed.R.Civ.P. 26(c). I write

---

[13] See Ruckelshaus v. Monsanto Co., 467 U.S. 986, 1001 (1984) (noting that Restatement of Torts defines a trade secret as "any formula, pattern, device or compilation of information which is used in one's business, and which gives him an opportunity to obtain an advantage over competitors who do not know or use it"); Unif. Trade Secrets Act § 1(4), 14 U.L.A. 438 (1985) (defining "trade secret" as "information, including a formula, pattern, compilation, program, device, method, technique, or process, that: (i) derives independent economic value, actual or potential, from not being generally known to, and not being readily ascertainable by proper means by, other persons who can obtain economic value from its disclosure or use, and (ii) is the subject of efforts that are reasonable under the circumstances to maintain its secrecy").

[15] We also note that the district court did not discuss Firestone's reliance on the terms of the stipulated protective order. As we noted in United States v. Anderson, 799 F.2d 1438 (11th Cir. 1986), agreements to treat certain materials voluntarily produced during discovery as confidential facilitate the discovery process: "[l]itigants should not be discouraged from putting their discovery agreements in writing, and district judges should not be discouraged from facilitating voluntary discovery." This is particularly the case where the party filing the presumptively confidential discovery material with the court is not the party claiming confidentiality, but that party's adversary, as is the case here. As the District of Columbia Court of Appeals noted in Mokhiber v. Davis, 537 A.2d 1100 (D.C.App. 1988), "[b]y submitting pleadings and motions to the court for decision, one enters the public arena of courtroom proceedings and exposes oneself . . . to the risk . . . of public scrutiny." The assumption is that one voluntarily forgoes confidentiality when one submits material for dispute resolution in a judicial forum. There is no voluntariness, of course, where one's adversary submits the presumptively confidential material. On remand, the district court should consider the fact that Firestone has exhibited behavior consistent with its claim of reliance in connection with the good cause balancing test.

separately to express my concern about third parties—who have no cause of action before the court—using the discovery process as a means to unearth documents to which they otherwise would have no right to inspect and copy.

This Court has previously commented:

> Discovery, whether civil or criminal, is essentially a private process because the litigants and the courts assume that the *sole purpose* of discovery is to assist trial preparation. That is why parties regularly agree, and courts often order, that discovery information will remain private.
>
> If it were otherwise and discovery information and discovery orders were readily available to the public and the press, the consequences to the smooth functioning of the discovery process would be severe. Not only would voluntary discovery be chilled, but whatever discovery and court encouragement that would take place would be oral, which is undesirable to the extent that it creates misunderstanding and surprise for the litigants and the trial judge.

United States v. Anderson, 799 F.2d 1438, 1441 (11th Cir. 1986). Simply stated, the purpose of discovery is to resolve legal disputes between parties, not to provide newsworthy material.

To facilitate prompt discovery and the timely resolution of disputes, this Court has upheld the use of umbrella protective orders similar to the one used in this case. In these cases, we did not permit the media to challenge each and every document protected by the umbrella order. Instead, the media was permitted only to challenge the umbrella order as being too broad, based on a variety of factors. We have restricted the scope of the media's challenge because a document-by-document approach would not only burden the trial court, but, more importantly, it would interfere with the free flow of information during discovery.[3] Such interference by parties who have no interest in the underlying litigation could seriously impair an Article III court from carrying out its core function—resolving cases and controversies.

In light of the strong interest in having unimpeded discovery, third parties may be barred from accessing documents even when the documents are not protected by a privilege (like the trade-secret privilege), as long as the umbrella order itself meets the good cause requirement. Here, however, the Court concludes that "trade secret status is the only basis Firestone provides for nondisclosure...." Therefore, absent a showing that the

---

[3]   In this case, the litigation has ceased, and therefore the press is not disrupting an active discovery proceeding. Nonetheless, the free flow of information will cease if parties resist entering umbrella orders because they fear such orders could be subject to document-by-document, post-judgment attacks.

challenged documents are trade secrets, "good cause does not support the [umbrella] order, and the documents may be unsealed." In some future case, however, a party may argue that, although the individual documents fail to qualify as privileged material, they nonetheless should be sealed because the umbrella order is necessary to facilitate the free flow of information and thus satisfies the good cause requirement. Since the Court has concluded that Firestone has not adequately preserved this argument, I concur in its holding.

NOTES AND QUESTIONS

1. This case illustrates the most controversial current aspect of protective order litigation. Some states have embraced a public access approach to discovery to address concerns about public safety. The Florida "Sunshine in Litigation Act," Fla.Stats. § 69.081, strictly limits entry of protective orders that could "conceal" information about a "public hazard," which is defined as follows:

> (2) As used in this section, "public hazard" means an instrumentality, including but not limited to any device, instrument, person, procedure, product, or a condition of a device, instrument, person, procedure or product, that has caused or is likely to cause injury.

Similarly, Texas Rule of Civil Procedure 76a provides that "court records" are open to the general public, and treats unfiled discovery as a "court record" if it contains "matters that have a probable adverse effect upon the general public health or safety."

Congress has also considered legislation of this sort. For example, the proposed "Sunshine in Litigation Act of 2014," S. 2364, 113th Cong., 2nd Sess., proposed adding a new 28 U.S.C. § 1660(a)(1) as follows:

> [I]n any action in which the pleadings state facts that are relevant to the protection of public health or safety, a court shall not enter an order under rule 26(c) of the Federal Rules of Civil Procedure restricting the disclosure of information obtained through discovery, an order approving a settlement agreement that would restrict the disclosure of such information, or an order restricting access to court records in a civil case unless the court has made findings of fact that—
>
> > (A) such order would not restrict the disclosure of information which is relevant to the protection of public health or safety; or
> >
> > (B)(i) the public interest in the disclosure of potential health or safety hazards is outweighed by a specific and substantial interest in maintaining the confidentiality of the information or records in question; and
> >
> > (ii) the requested protective order is no broader than necessary to protect the privacy interest asserted.

What effect would adoption of such legislation have on the management of complex litigation? How should a court handling a case like *New Motor Vehicles, supra* p. 414, or *Zenith, supra* pp. 507–508, comply with the findings requirement of this proposed legislation? Note that the stipulated "umbrella" protective orders in those cases were entered before discovery began.

2.   Should litigation be viewed as a method to uncover risks? Can judges determine whether discovered information really indicates that there is a public risk involved in a case? Note the views of Judge Black in *Chicago Tribune* that discovery is essentially a private process. Should it be? For discussion of this point, see Alan Morrison, Protective Orders, Plaintiffs, Defendants and the Public Interest in Disclosure: Where Does the Balance Lie?, 24 U.Rich.L.Rev. 109 (1989) (arguing for judicial involvement in determining whether confidential information implicates public interest); Richard Marcus, The Discovery Confidentiality Controversy, 1991 U.Ill.L.Rev. 457 (criticizing broad public access approach); Arthur Miller, Confidentiality, Protective Orders, and Public Access to the Courts, 105 Harv. L. Rev. 427 (1991).

Contrast Newman v. Graddick, 696 F.2d 796 (11th Cir. 1983), a class action by inmates in the Alabama prisons challenging overcrowding. After a consent decree was entered but overcrowding worsened, the district court directed prison officials to submit lists of prisoners "least deserving of further incarceration," with an eye to possibly directing the release of specific prisoners to reduce crowding. Two newspapers sought to obtain copies of the lists, and the appellate court reversed the district judge's refusal to permit access. Should the issues involved in *Chicago Tribune* be considered comparable? Note that the litigation involved the operation of a public facility, and the materials were being considered by a judge in connection with a possible order to release specific prisoners before they had completed their sentences. See Richard Marcus, Myth and Reality in Protective Order Litigation, 69 Cornell L. Rev. 1, 50–52 (1983) (discussing the public interest in governmental acts).

3.   Compare the attitude toward unfiled discovery materials in note 1 above with the view of the common-law right of access in *Chicago Tribune Co.* In Seattle Times Co. v. Rhinehart, 467 U.S. 20 (1984), the Court said:

> [P]retrial depositions and interrogatories are not public components of a civil trial. Such proceedings were not open to the public at common law and, in general, they are conducted in private as a matter of modern practice. Much of the information that surfaces during pretrial discovery may be unrelated, or only tangentially related, to the underlying cause of action. Therefore, restraints placed on discovered, but not yet admitted, information are not a restriction on a traditionally public source of information.

As amended in 2000, Rule 5(d) says that discovery documents must not be filed in court unless they are "used in the proceeding." In S.E.C. v. TheStreet.com, 273 F.3d 222 (2d Cir. 2001), the court dealt with an argument that the Federal Rules create a "statutory right of access to discovery materials," and noted that "the recent amendment to [Rule 5(d)] provides no presumption of filing of all discovery materials, let alone public access to them. Indeed, the rule now *prohibits* the filing of certain discovery materials unless they are used in the proceeding or the court orders filing." Id. at 233 n. 11.

4.   Is the public interest in information exchanged in discovery comparable to interest in information used in the proceeding and filed in court? Some courts see unimpeded access as central to the Federal Rules: "It is well-established that the fruits of pre-trial discovery are, in the absence of a court order to the contrary, presumptively public. Rule 26(c) authorizes a district court to override this presumption when 'good cause' is shown." San Jose Mercury News, Inc. v. United States District Court, 187 F.3d 1096, 1103 (9th Cir. 1999). Is this view consistent with the purpose of discovery? Would Judge Black, who concurred in *Chicago Tribune*, agree with it? Compare Bond v. Utreras, 585 F.3d 1061, 1066 (7th Cir. 2009) (stating that "there is no constitutional or common-law right to public access to discovery materials exchanged by the parties but not filed with the court. Unfiled discovery is private, not public."). See also Richard Marcus, A Modest Proposal: Recognizing (At Last) That the Federal Rules Do Not Declare That Discovery Is Presumptively Public, 81 Chi.-Kent L.Rev. 331 (2006) (emphasizing the privacy issues in the background with regard to discovery, and the additional intrusiveness of E-Discovery). Consider the views of the court in Mokhiber v. Davis, 537 A.2d 1100, 1112 (D.C.App. 1988):

> [T]he public should enjoy the right to view new kinds of proceedings when they are like traditional ones in this significant respect: that access will serve the same values and policies which underlie the common law's recognition of the public right to view other parts of court procedure and which, indeed, are similar to those values and policies upon which asserted first amendment rights are justified.
> * * *
>
> The discovery process is clearly an important element of civil litigation. The manner in which it proceeds may prove decisive to the outcome of particular disputes, and the availability of mandatory discovery has greatly affected the way in which our courts do justice. Moreover, discovery procedures have become a continuing focus of controversy and reform within the judiciary and the legal community. This debate has arisen precisely because discovery is so important in trial practice. * * * We disagree with the view that "discovery proceedings are fundamentally different from proceedings to which the courts have recognized a public right of access."

Are these arguments persuasive? Consider the contrasting views of the court in Anderson v. Cryovac, Inc., 805 F.2d 1, 12 (1st Cir. 1986):

> Nor does public access to the discovery process play a significant role in the administration of justice. Indeed, if such access were to be mandated, the civil discovery process might actually be made more complicated and burdensome than it already is. * * * The public's

interest is in seeing that the process works and the parties are able to explore the issues without excessive waste or delay. But rather than facilitate an efficient and complete exploration of the facts and issues, a public right of access would unduly complicate the process.

5. *Access to filed materials*: Once items are filed in court, the rules may change. See Shane Group, Inc. v. Blue Cross Blue Shield of Michigan, 825 F.3d 299, 306 (6th Cir. 2019) (rejecting district court sealing of filed materials submitted in support of judicial approval of proposed class-action settlement— "These are protective order justifications, not sealing justifications."). There is a strong constitutional argument for public access to court files. Not every country has a similar view. See, e.g., Peter Murray & Rolf Stürner, German Civil Justice 182 (2004) ("Case records in civil cases in Germany are not open to the public either before or after judgment."). Should such access be afforded to permit the public to evaluate the behavior of its judges? Given that discovery materials are filed in court only when used in the action, when should there be a limit on access to them? See Apple, Inc. v. Samsung Elec. Corp., 727 F.3d 1214 (Fed.Cir. 2013) (holding that the district court's refusal to grant the parties' request that their financial information be filed under seal was an abuse of discretion).

In *Chicago Tribune Co.*, the documents in issue were filed under seal. When should that be allowed? Both constitutional and common law protections guarantee that trials be public. In a series of criminal cases, the Supreme Court has overturned the closure of the trial and certain pretrial events. In Globe Newspaper Co. v. Superior Court, 457 U.S. 596 (1982), the Court explained that this right was based both on the historical openness of courts and on certain functional considerations:

> [T]he right of access to criminal trials plays a particularly significant role in the functioning of the judicial process and the government as a whole. Public scrutiny of a criminal trial enhances the quality and safeguards the integrity of the factfinding process, with benefits to both the defendant and to society as a whole. Moreover, public access to the criminal trial fosters an appearance of fairness, thereby heightening public respect for the judicial process. And in the broadest terms, public access to criminal trials permits the public to participate in and serve as a check upon the judicial process—an essential component in our structure of self-government.

The same sort of right of access to trial is thought to apply to civil cases. How should this attitude apply to pretrial motions? In *Chicago Tribune Co.*, the court says that it does not apply to pretrial discovery motions. To some extent, that reaction is essential; otherwise an argument could be made that a court's in camera examination of documents to determine whether they were privileged would result in public access to the documents even if they were held to be privileged. But the materials submitted in relation to the summary judgment motion seem to stand on a different footing. That motion could result to a decision on the merits in lieu of trial. At least in many instances, access would seem necessary.

The success of the motion is not critical on the access point. In Alabama Dep't of Corrections v. Advance Local Media, LLC, 918 F.3d 1161 (11th Cir. 2019), a Death Row prisoner facing execution sought relief due to the condition of his veins, which he said would make use of the state's lethal injection method cruel and unusual punishment. The state moved for summary judgment and, under a protective order, presented a redacted version of its execution protocol for in camera review, with copies to plaintiff's lawyers. The district court denied defendant's motion and stayed the execution, but the court of appeals vacated the stay. The state then tried unsuccessfully to execute plaintiff, drawing intense media scrutiny. The media were granted leave to intervene to seek access to the protocol, and the district court unsealed the previously sealed transcript of its hearings and also unsealed the execution protocol. The court of appeals affirmed, while also noting that courts "should not permit public access to discovery materials that are not filed with substantive motions." Id. at 1167. See also Center for Auto Safety v. Chrysler Group, LLC, 809 F.3d 1092 (9th Cir. 2016) (plaintiffs filed some of the 86,000 documents produced under a protective order in support of their motion for a preliminary injunction, which was denied; the court of appeals held that preliminary-injunction materials may not be kept under seal).

6. *Access to evidence used at trial*: Although filed materials may receive fairly firm protection if filed under seal, that protection is likely to dissolve when trial begins. As an illustration, see Ramon Sherr, Apple's Secrets Revealed at Trial, Wall St.J., Aug. 4–5, 2012, at B1, which recounts the testimony of officers of Apple, "one of the world's most secretive companies," during the trial of its patent infringement suit against Samsung. According to the article, "each item was quickly disseminated and discussed in tweets and blog posts by people tracking the high-stakes case."

7. In *Chicago Tribune*, the court emphasizes that the only ground put forward for protection under Rule 26(c) was that the items in question were trade secrets. How readily can a court determine whether something is a genuine trade secret? Trade secret is "at best a nebulous concept which * * * is somewhat incapable of definition," Kodekey Elecs., Inc. v. Mechanex Corp., 486 F.2d 449, 453–54 n. 3 (10th Cir. 1973), and "[t]he subject matter that has been awarded trade secret protection can be extraordinarily broad." Ramon Klitzke, Trade Secrets: Important Quasi-Property Right, 41 Bus. Law. 555, 558 (1986). Compare the information involved in Zenith Radio Corp. v. Matsushita Elec. Indus. Co., *supra* pp. 507–508, which would reveal that defendants had made more favorable deals with some customers than with others. Assuming that is confidential and important information, should courts prevent parties from revealing it?

Note that Rule 26(c)(1)(G) goes beyond trade secrets and includes "other confidential research, development or commercial information." That is not the limit of the court's power to grant protective orders: "Although courts may be more likely to grant protective orders for the information listed in Rule 26(c)(1)(G), courts have consistently granted protective orders that prevent disclosure or many types of information." Phillips ex rel. Estate of Byrd v.

General Motors Corp., 307 F.3d 1206, 1212 (9th Cir. 2002). In *Phillips*, the appellate court vacated the district judge's decision not to provide protection for a confidential settlement agreement because the district judge seemed unaware that Rule 26(c) would permit that protection.

8.   Sometimes efforts to circumvent protective orders reach remarkable extremes. For example, in Hunt v. Enzo Biochem, Inc., 904 F.Supp.2d 337 (S.D.N.Y. 2012), a nonparty witness who had received material covered by a protective order arranged to pass it along in a rendezvous at a rest stop on the New Jersey Turnpike. When called to account, one of the participants claimed that the New York judge had no authority to impose sanctions on him because he was not subject to the court's jurisdiction, not having entered New York to obtain the materials. The judge ruled she did have jurisdiction because he knowingly violated her order. See also Eli Lilly & Co. v. Gottstein, 617 F.3d 186 (2d Cir. 2010) (upholding contempt sanctions for an elaborate plot by which an Alaska attorney obtained documents from an expert witness and passed them along to a New York Times reporter).

CHAPTER 7

SETTLING COMPLEX CASES

■ ■ ■

Most cases settle; complex cases are no exception. Indeed, the high stakes and multiple interests involved in complex litigation give settlement greater significance and, for some participants, added urgency. In mass disputes, the endgame is often some form of "global settlement"—a comprehensive negotiated resolution. Such settlements take various forms. Class settlements, settlement-only class actions, non-class aggregate settlements, and pre-packaged bankruptcies each carry their own set of opportunities and complications.

Whatever the form, settlements raise distinct issues in the context of complex litigation. While judges encourage settlement in all varieties of litigation, judicial promotion of settlement in complex cases is part of a larger story of enhanced judicial management. Class action settlements raise unique issues concerning judicial settlement approval, forms of relief, and the role of objectors. In non-class actions, settlements involving multiple parties present special concerns of conflicts of interest and informed consent.

A. PROMOTION OF SETTLEMENT

Settlements are "out-of-court" resolutions in the sense that they conclude a dispute by agreement rather than by adjudication. This does not mean, however, that they render judges irrelevant. Judges often play an active role in settlements, particularly in complex disputes. In class actions, the judge necessarily participates because class action settlements require judicial approval. Consent judgments, too, require judicial approval and certain remedies—especially in cases involving institutional reform—require ongoing judicial supervision. Even in cases where settlements require neither judicial approval nor ongoing judicial involvement, judges frequently take steps to promote settlement. Before we turn to *how* judges promote settlement, consider *whether* judges ought to think of settlement-promotion as part of their job. The first two excerpts offer competing views on this question.

1. THE VALUES OF ADJUDICATION AND SETTLEMENT

OWEN M. FISS, AGAINST SETTLEMENT
93 Yale L.J. 1073, 1085–87 (1984).

The dispute-resolution story makes settlement appear as a perfect substitute for judgment * * * by trivializing the remedial dimensions of a lawsuit, and also by reducing the social function of the lawsuit to one of resolving private disputes: In that story, settlement appears to achieve exactly the same purpose as judgment—peace between the parties—but at considerably less expense to society. The two quarreling neighbors turn to a court in order to resolve their dispute, and society makes courts available because it wants to aid in the achievement of their private ends or to secure the peace.

In my view, however, the purpose of adjudication should be understood in broader terms. Adjudication uses public resources, and employs not strangers chosen by the parties but public officials chosen by a process in which the public participates. These officials, like members of the legislative and executive branches, possess a power that has been defined and conferred by public law, not by private agreement. Their job is not to maximize the ends of private parties, nor simply to secure the peace, but to explicate and give force to the values embodied in authoritative texts such as the Constitution and statutes: to interpret those values and to bring reality into accord with them. This duty is not discharged when the parties settle.

In our political system, courts are reactive institutions. They do not search out interpretive occasions, but instead wait for others to bring matters to their attention. They also rely for the most part on others to investigate and present the law and facts. A settlement will thereby deprive a court of the occasion, and perhaps even the ability, to render an interpretation. A court cannot proceed (or not proceed very far) in the face of a settlement. To be against settlement is not to urge that parties be "forced" to litigate, since that would interfere with their autonomy and distort the adjudicative process; the parties will be inclined to make the court believe that their bargain is justice. To be against settlement is only to suggest that when the parties settle, society gets less than what appears, and for a price it does not know it is paying. Parties might settle while leaving justice undone. The settlement of a school suit might secure the peace, but not racial equality. Although the parties are prepared to live under the terms they bargained for, and although such peaceful coexistence may be a necessary precondition of justice, and itself a state of affairs to be valued, it is not justice itself. To settle for something means to accept less than some ideal.

I recognize that judges often announce settlements not with a sense of frustration or disappointment, as my account of adjudication might suggest, but with a sigh of relief. But this sigh should be seen for precisely what it is: It is not a recognition that a job is done, nor an acknowledgment that a job need not be done because justice has been secured. It is instead based on another sentiment altogether, namely, that another case has been "moved along," which is true whether or not justice has been done or even needs to be done. Or the sigh might be based on the fact that the agony of judgment has been avoided.

There is, of course, sometimes a value to avoidance, not just to the judge, who is thereby relieved of the need to make or enforce a hard decision, but also to society, which sometimes thrives by masking its basic contradictions. But will settlement result in avoidance when it is most appropriate? * * * Someone has to confront the betrayal of our deepest ideals and be prepared to turn the world upside down to bring those ideals to fruition.

SAMUEL ISSACHAROFF & ROBERT H. KLONOFF, THE PUBLIC VALUE OF SETTLEMENT
78 Fordham L. Rev. 1177, 1195–98 (2009).

Perhaps the biggest indictment of settlements is that they frequently achieve peace but not justice. According to Fiss, settlements frequently "deprive a court of the occasion, and perhaps even the ability, to render an interpretation." In his view, "[p]arties might settle while leaving justice undone."

Fiss is certainly correct that, in most settlements, defendants do not admit liability. And in some cases, such as certain types of civil rights cases cited by Fiss—there may well be no substitute for a formal judgment to articulate the critical underlying social and legal values. But the passage of time allows us to revisit Fiss's assertion and to ask whether the tradeoffs he advocates represent a significant part of what courts actually do. Even in the domain of class actions, the structural injunction is a dying breed. Available statistics suggest that the vast majority of class actions are damages actions under Federal Rule of Civil Procedure 23(b)(3) or a state counterpart. In recent years, civil rights class action lawsuits—which are normally brought under Rule 23(b)(2)—have been declining, both in absolute numbers and as a percentage of class claims.

In suits primarily or exclusively about damages, when a defendant agrees to a large payout but professes innocence on the charges alleged, most people assume—correctly—that the defendant would not have settled had it not believed there was at least some evidentiary basis for the claim. More fundamentally, in most damages actions, the claimants are concerned less about a court finding of wrongdoing than they are about recovering compensation for their injuries. Moreover, there is a strong societal interest in obtaining the deterrent effects that come from compensation in ex post facto settlements. The notion that claimants in suits seeking exclusively or primarily damages are disserved by not obtaining a formal court finding of wrongdoing does not comport with reality in many circumstances.

Consider an asbestos case, for example, where the class members are suffering significant injuries as a result of asbestos exposure. Fiss's premise is that the best outcome for the claimants and for the public is to forgo a settlement and litigate at trial. But with discovery and court delays, it could take many years for a trial, even on common issues. And follow-up proceedings would inevitably be necessary to adjudicate individual causation and damages questions for potentially thousands of claimants. Many of the class members might not even survive long enough to have their cases adjudicated. In this circumstance, most class members would no doubt prefer an early settlement to a long wait for a judicial finding of wrongdoing. * * * No one is served when plaintiffs' counsel insist on litigating a case that defendants would settle on financial terms favorable to the class. * * * Who can say that the trial route, as opposed to the settlement route, is the only "just" way to proceed?

NOTES AND QUESTIONS

1.   Is settlement a goal worth promoting? Proponents of settlement urge that negotiated resolutions not only offer efficiency benefits by reducing litigation costs, but also offer a superior way to resolve most disputes. To Fiss, on the other hand, "settlement is a capitulation to the conditions of mass society and should be neither encouraged nor praised." 93 Yale L.J. at 1075. The Fiss article spawned numerous responses from scholars, judges, and lawyers, most of whom object to Fiss's dim view of settlement. See, e.g., Andrew McThenia & Thomas Schaffer, For Reconciliation, 94 Yale L.J. 1660 (1985); Carrie Menkel-Meadow, Whose Dispute Is It Anyway? A Philosophical and Democratic Defense of Settlement (in Some Cases), 83 Geo. L.J. 2663 (1995); Symposium, Against Settlement: Twenty-Five Years Later, 78 Fordham L. Rev. 1117 (2009).

2.   In which type of litigation—simple or complex—is the argument against settlement most compelling? Recall Professor Chayes' distinction between traditional bipolar litigation and "public law litigation." Abram Chayes, The Role of the Judge in Public Law Litigation, supra p. 2. Is Fiss's argument in favor of adjudication aimed primarily at public law cases and other disputes with high stakes and multiple competing interests? Interestingly, courts often insist that public policy favors settlement especially in complex litigation. See, e.g., In re Syncor ERISA Litig., 516 F.3d 1095, 1101 (9th Cir. 2008) ("[T]here is a strong judicial policy that favors settlements, particularly where complex class action litigation is concerned."); Colella v. University of Pittsburgh, 569 F.Supp.2d 525, 530 (W.D. Pa. 2008) ("The strong public policy and high judicial favor for negotiated settlements of litigation is

particularly keen 'in class actions and other complex cases where substantial judicial resources can be conserved by avoiding formal litigation.' ").

3.   In Robinson v. Shelby Cty. Bd. of Educ., 566 F.3d 642 (6th Cir. 2009), a school desegregation class action, the district court rejected the parties' agreement to declare the district a unitary school system. The Sixth Circuit, reversing, emphasized the policy in favor of settlement:

> [I]t is also well-established that "[p]ublic policy strongly favors settlement of disputes without litigation. . . . Settlement agreements should therefore be upheld whenever equitable and policy considerations so permit." This policy applies equally to desegregation cases.

The voluntary settlement of school desegregation controversies is to be encouraged, even though such litigation implicates the important civil rights of the plaintiff class:

> [D]espite the importance of the substantive rights of the class members, settlement is an appropriate method of arriving at a school desegregation remedy. While courts should be extremely sensitive to the possibilities for abuse where a compromise of the civil rights of a class is proposed, a blanket prohibition of compromise could result, in many cases, in abandonment of the substantial benefits which can result from voluntary resolution of litigation, without a commensurate increase in the protection accorded the civil rights of the class. Indeed, it appears that school desegregation is one of the areas in which voluntary resolution is preferable to full litigation because the spirit of cooperation inherent in good faith settlement is essential to the true long-range success of any desegregation remedy. A remedial decree reached through agreement between the parties may, because of the community cooperation it inspires, more effectively implement the constitutional guarantee of equal protection than a seemingly more stringent court-ordered remedy which the community views as imposed upon it from the outside.

Id. at 648 (quoting Ford Motor Co. v. Mustangs Unlimited, Inc., 487 F.3d 465, 469 (6th Cir. 2007) and Armstrong v. Bd. of School Directors of City of Milwaukee, 616 F.2d 305, 317–18 (7th Cir. 1980)). Do you agree that settlement should be encouraged in school desegregation cases and other "public law" litigation?

4.   Rule 16 lists "facilitating settlement" as one of the purposes of a pretrial conference. Fed.R.Civ.P. 16(a)(5). The rule authorizes judges in pretrial conferences to "take appropriate action" on, among other things, "settling the case and using special procedures to assist in resolving the dispute when authorized by statute or local rule." Fed.R.Civ.P. 16(c)(2)(I). Some find this activity troubling:

The most controversial of all judicial management tools—the judicial settlement conference—is the one that strays the furthest from the judiciary's traditional adjudicative role. When a judge calls parties into his or her chambers to urge a settlement, his or her actions bear almost no resemblance to the traditional judicial role. Parties do not file motions to trigger, or prevent, judicial intervention. There are no legal standards to govern judicial conduct in settlement negotiations. And there generally is no appellate review either of the judge's tactics or the judge's views regarding the merits of the case.

Jonathan Molot, An Old Judicial Role for a New Litigation Era, 113 Yale L.J. 27, 43–44 (2003).

5.   Even if settlement is a goal worth promoting, should such promotion be handled by someone other than the judge charged with pretrial decisions and overseeing a trial? See Ellen Deason, Beyond "Managerial Judges": Appropriate Roles in Settlement, 78 Ohio St. L.J. 73 (2017) (questioning whether judges should play a "dual-neutral role" as both adjudicator and settlement facilitator). On the power a judge holds over the lawyers, consider Peter Schuck, The Role of Judges in Settling Complex Cases: The Agent Orange Example, 53 U.Chi.L.Rev. 337, 358 (1986):

The essential, unvarnished fact is this: The lawyers know—and the judge knows that the lawyers know—that the judge is in a position to make many decisions of vital concern to them and their clients in the future, both in this case and in subsequent cases in which they will appear before that judge. Many of these decisions entail the exercise of some judicial discretion. Some, like the pace and nature of discovery, the time of trial, and the admissibility of expert testimony, are almost wholly discretionary. Especially in a complex case, even those decisions that are in principle not discretionary are often not appealable as a legal or practical matter. Some of the most important decisions from the lawyers' selfish point of view—class certification, appointment of lead counsel, and the award of attorneys' fees and costs—may turn upon the judge's perception of a particular lawyer's ability and performance. Rightly or wrongly, lawyers believe that these decisions are more likely to be favorable, at least at the margin, if the judge regards the lawyers as reasonable and cooperative. It would be astonishing, under these circumstances, if lawyers did not seek to present themselves as conciliatory actors who are anxious to please the court.

Judges presiding over mass litigation often appoint various judicial adjuncts—including not only magistrate judges but also special masters and settlement administrators—to facilitate and administer settlements. These appointments, while solving the dual-neutral problem raised above, present their own set of questions regarding cost, transparency, and accountability. See Elizabeth Chamblee Burch & Margaret S. Williams, Judicial Adjuncts in Multidistrict Litigation, 120 Colum. L. Rev. 2129 (2020).

6.   In addition to participating in settlement discussions, the judge may become an enforcer of a settlement agreement if disputes arise about it. In Lynch, Inc. v. SamataMason Inc., 279 F.3d 487 (7th Cir. 2002), a magistrate judge concluded at the end of an off-the-record settlement conference that the parties had reached a settlement. When they later could not agree on one provision for the written settlement agreement, the magistrate judge directed both to submit proposed provisions so he could determine whether the issue had been settled and, if so, which version correctly reflected the settlement that had been reached. Thereafter, he determined that the defendant's version was the correct one and directed the parties to execute an agreement including that provision. When plaintiff refused, the magistrate judge dismissed with prejudice. The court of appeals affirmed, finding that under applicable Illinois law an oral settlement agreement could be binding unless barred by the statute of frauds, which plaintiff did not contend applied. Although it affirmed the enforcement of the off-the-record agreement, the court emphasized that putting the settlement terms into the record and getting the parties to agree on the record is not only the standard practice but the better practice. See also Doi v. Halekulani Corp., 276 F.3d 1131 (9th Cir. 2002) (plaintiff sanctioned for trying to renegotiate settlement agreement after saying she agreed to the settlement when pressed by the judge in open court).

7.   Is settlement a legitimate goal of the rules of civil procedure? When Rule 1 instructs that the Federal Rules of Civil Procedure should be construed, administered, and employed "to secure the just, speedy, and inexpensive determination of every action and proceeding," does *determination* solely mean adjudication or does it also include negotiated resolution? The language of multiple federal rules leaves no doubt that the rulemakers have embraced settlement as a significant objective of the litigation process. Not only does Rule 16 name settlement facilitation as one purpose of pretrial conferences, but Rule 26(f) instructs parties at discovery conferences to consider "the possibilities for promptly settling or resolving the case." Fed.R.Civ.P. 26(f)(2). Rule 68 on formal offers of judgment explicitly incentivizes settlement. More broadly, a settlement-oriented view of the litigation process might consider a wide variety of procedural rules—including those on pleading and discovery— as providing litigants with information about claims and defenses so that the parties can negotiate a reasonable resolution of the dispute.

2.   COMPELLING PARTICIPATION IN SETTLEMENT PROCESSES

While most judges treat settlement as a worthy goal and the law provides various tools for promoting settlement, judges vary widely in how aggressively they use those tools. The following case considers how far a judge can go in pushing parties toward settlement.

IN RE ATLANTIC PIPE CORP.

United States Court of Appeals, First Circuit, 2002.
304 F.3d 135.

Before BOUDIN, CHIEF JUDGE, SELYA, CIRCUIT JUDGE, and GREENBERG, SENIOR CIRCUIT JUDGE.

SELYA, CIRCUIT JUDGE.

This mandamus proceeding requires us to resolve an issue of importance to judges and practitioners alike: Does a district court possess the authority to compel an unwilling party to participate in, and share the costs of, non-binding mediation conducted by a private mediator? We hold that a court may order mandatory mediation pursuant to an explicit statutory provision or local rule. We further hold that where, as here, no such authorizing medium exists, a court nonetheless may order mandatory mediation through the use of its inherent powers as long as the case is an appropriate one and the order contains adequate safeguards. Because the mediation order here at issue lacks such safeguards (although it does not fall far short), we vacate it and remand the matter for further proceedings.

BACKGROUND

In January 1996, Thames-Dick Superaqueduct Partners (Thames-Dick) entered into a master agreement with the Puerto Rico Aqueduct and Sewer Authority (PRASA) to construct, operate, and maintain the North Coast Superaqueduct Project (the Project). Thames-Dick granted subcontracts for various portions of the work, including a subcontract for construction management to Dick Corp. of Puerto Rico (Dick-PR), a subcontract for the operation and maintenance of the Project to Thames Water International, Ltd. (Thames Water), and a subcontract for the fabrication of pipe to Atlantic Pipe Corp. (APC). After the Project had been built, a segment of the pipeline burst. Thames-Dick incurred significant costs in repairing the damage. Not surprisingly, it sought to recover those costs from other parties. In response, one of PRASA's insurers filed a declaratory judgment action in a local court to determine whether Thames-Dick's claims were covered under its policy. The litigation ballooned, soon involving a number of parties and a myriad of issues above and beyond insurance coverage.

On April 25, 2001, the hostilities spilled over into federal court. Two entities beneficially interested in the master agreement—CPA Group International and Chiang, Patel & Yerby, Inc. (collectively CPA)—sued Thames-Dick, Dick-PR, Thames Water, and various insurers in the United States District Court for the District of Puerto Rico, seeking remuneration for consulting services rendered in connection with repairs to the Project. A googol of claims, counterclaims, cross-claims, and third-party complaints followed. Some of these were brought against APC (the petitioner here). To complicate matters, one of the defendants moved to dismiss on grounds that, inter alia, (1) CPA had failed to join an indispensable party whose presence would destroy diversity jurisdiction, and (2) the existence of the parallel proceeding in the local court counseled in favor of abstention.

While this motion was pending before the district court, Thames-Dick asked that the case be referred to mediation and suggested Professor Eric Green as a suitable mediator. The district court granted the motion over APC's objection and ordered non-binding mediation to proceed before Professor Green. The court pronounced mediation likely to conserve judicial resources; directed all parties to undertake mediation in good faith; stayed discovery pending completion of the mediation; and declared that participation in the mediation would not prejudice the parties' positions vis-à-vis the pending motion or the litigation as a whole. The court also stated that if mediation failed to produce a global settlement, the case would proceed to trial.

After moving unsuccessfully for reconsideration of the mediation order, APC sought relief by way of mandamus. Its petition alleged that the district court did not have the authority to require mediation (especially in light of unresolved questions as to the court's subject-matter jurisdiction) and, in all events, could not force APC to pay a share of the expenses of the mediation. * * *

Prior to argument in this court, two notable developments occurred. First, the district court considered and rejected the challenges to its exercise of jurisdiction. Second, APC rejected an offer by Thames-Dick to pay its share of the mediator's fees.

JURISDICTION

[Respondents objected to the use of mandamus because APC would not suffer irreparable harm, but the court explained that irreparable harm need not be shown for "advisory mandamus." It held that "this case is fit for advisory mandamus because the extent of a trial court's power to order mandatory mediation presents a systemically important issue as to which this court has not yet spoken" and because "that issue is capable of significant repetition prior to effective review."]

THE MERITS

There are four potential sources of judicial authority for ordering mandatory non-binding mediation of pending cases, namely, (a) the court's local rules, (b) an applicable statute, (c) the Federal Rules of Civil Procedure, and (d) the court's inherent powers. Because the district court did not identify the basis of its assumed authority, we consider each of these sources.

A.   *The Local Rules.*

A district court's local rules may provide an appropriate source of authority for ordering parties to participate in mediation. [The District of

Puerto Rico's local rules described a plan to implement an alternative dispute resolution (ADR) program as directed by the Civil Justice Reform Act of 1990 (CJRA), 28 U.S.C. §§ 471–482. However, the district's ADR program had not yet been implemented, and therefore the local rules did not provide a sound basis for the court's authority to compel mediation in this case.]

B. *The ADR Act.*

There is only one potential source of statutory authority for ordering mandatory non-binding mediation here: the Alternative Dispute Resolution Act of 1998 (ADR Act), 28 U.S.C. §§ 651–658. Congress passed the ADR Act to promote the utilization of alternative dispute resolution methods in the federal courts and to set appropriate guidelines for their use. The Act lists mediation as an appropriate ADR process. *Id.* § 651(a). Moreover, it sanctions the participation of "professional neutrals from the private sector" as mediators. *Id.* § 653(b). Finally, the Act requires district courts to obtain litigants' consent only when they order arbitration, *id.* § 652(a), not when they order the use of other ADR mechanisms (such as non-binding mediation).

Despite the broad sweep of these provisions, the Act is quite clear that some form of the ADR procedures it endorses must be adopted in each judicial district by local rule. *See id.* § 651(b) (directing each district court to "devise and implement its own alternative dispute resolution program, by local rule adopted under [28 U.S.C.] section 2071(a), to encourage and promote the use of alternative dispute resolution in its district"). In the absence of such local rules, the ADR Act itself does not authorize any specific court to use a particular ADR mechanism. Because the District of Puerto Rico has not yet complied with the Act's mandate, the mediation order here at issue cannot be justified under the ADR Act. * * *

C. *The Civil Rules.*

The respondents next argue that the district court possessed the authority to require mediation by virtue of the Federal Rules of Civil Procedure. They concentrate their attention on Fed.R.Civ.P. 16, which states in pertinent part that "the court may take appropriate action[ ] with respect to . . . settlement and the use of special procedures to assist in resolving the dispute when authorized by statute or local rule. . . ." Fed.R.Civ.P. 16(c)[(2)(I)]. But the words "when authorized by statute or local rule" are a frank limitation on the district courts' authority to order mediation thereunder, and we must adhere to that circumscription. *See Schlagenhauf v. Holder,* 379 U.S. 104, 121 (1964) (explaining that the Civil Rules "should not be expanded by disregarding plainly expressed limitations"). Because there is no statute or local rule authorizing mandatory private mediation in the District of Puerto Rico, Rule 16(c)[(2)(I)] does not assist the respondents' cause.

D. *Inherent Powers.*

Even apart from positive law, district courts have substantial inherent power to manage and control their calendars. *See Link* [*v. Wabash R.R.*, 370 U.S. 626, 630–31 (1963)]. This inherent power takes many forms. By way of illustration, a district court may use its inherent power to compel represented clients to attend pretrial settlement conferences, even though such a practice is not specifically authorized in the Civil Rules.

Of course, a district court's inherent powers are not infinite. There are at least four limiting principles. First, inherent powers must be used in a way reasonably suited to the enhancement of the court's processes, including the orderly and expeditious disposition of pending cases. Second, inherent powers cannot be exercised in a manner that contradicts an applicable statute or rule. Third, the use of inherent powers must comport with procedural fairness. And, finally, inherent powers "must be exercised with restraint and discretion." [*Chambers v. NASCO*, 501 U.S. 32, 44 (1991).]

[The court noted concerns that other courts had raised about compelling participation in ADR processes, citing *Strandell v. Jackson County*, 838 F.2d 884 (7th Cir. 1987) and *In re NLO, Inc.*, 5 F.3d 154, 157–58 (6th Cir. 1993).] The concerns articulated by these two respected courts plainly apply to mandatory mediation orders. When mediation is forced upon unwilling litigants, it stands to reason that the likelihood of settlement is diminished. Requiring parties to invest substantial amounts of time and money in mediation under such circumstances may well be inefficient. *Cf.* Richard A. Posner, *The Summary Jury Trial and Other Methods of Alternative Dispute Resolution: Some Cautionary Observations*, 53 U.Chi.L.Rev. 366, 369–72 (1986) (offering a model to evaluate ADR techniques in terms of their capacity to encourage settlements).

The fact remains, however, that none of these considerations establishes that mandatory mediation is always inappropriate. There may well be specific cases in which such a protocol is likely to conserve judicial resources without significantly burdening the objectors' rights to a full, fair, and speedy trial. Much depends on the idiosyncrasies of the particular case and the details of the mediation order.

In some cases, a court may be warranted in believing that compulsory mediation could yield significant benefits even if one or more parties object. After all, a party may resist mediation simply out of unfamiliarity with the process or out of fear that a willingness to submit would be perceived as a lack of confidence in her legal position. In such an instance, the party's initial reservations are likely to evaporate as the mediation progresses, and negotiations could well produce a beneficial outcome, at reduced cost and greater speed, than would a trial. While the possibility that parties will fail to reach agreement remains ever present, the boon of settlement can be worth the risk.

This is particularly true in complex cases involving multiple claims and parties. The fair and expeditious resolution of such cases often is helped along by creative solutions—solutions that simply are not available in the binary framework of traditional adversarial litigation. Mediation with the assistance of a skilled facilitator gives parties an opportunity to explore a much wider range of options, including those that go beyond conventional zero-sum resolutions. Mindful of these potential advantages, we hold that it is within a district court's inherent power to order non-consensual mediation in those cases in which that step seems reasonably likely to serve the interests of justice.

E. *The Mediation Order.*

Our determination that the district courts have inherent power to refer cases to non-binding mediation is made with a recognition that any such order must be crafted in a manner that preserves procedural fairness and shields objecting parties from undue burdens. We thus turn to the specifics of the mediation order entered in this case. As with any exercise of a district court's inherent powers, we review the entry of that order for abuse of discretion.

As an initial matter, we agree with the lower court that the complexity of this case militates in favor of ordering mediation. At last count, the suit involves twelve parties, asserting a welter of claims, counterclaims, cross-claims, and third-party claims predicated on a wide variety of theories. The pendency of nearly parallel litigation in the Puerto Rican courts, which features a slightly different cast of characters and claims that are related to but not completely congruent with those asserted here, further complicates the matter. Untangling the intricate web of relationships among the parties, along with the difficult and fact-intensive arguments made by each, will be time-consuming and will impose significant costs on the parties and the court. Against this backdrop, mediation holds out the dual prospect of advantaging the litigants and conserving scarce judicial resources.

In an effort to parry this thrust, APC raises a series of objections. * * * APC posits that the appointment of a private mediator proposed by one of the parties is per se improper (and, thus, invalidates the order). We do not agree. The district court has inherent power to "appoint persons unconnected with the court to aid judges in the performance of specific judicial duties." *Ex parte Peterson*, 253 U.S. 300, 312 (1920). In the context of non-binding mediation, the mediator does not decide the merits of the case and has no authority to coerce settlement. Thus, in the absence of a contrary statute or rule, it is perfectly acceptable for the district court to appoint a qualified and neutral private party as a mediator. The mere fact that the mediator was proposed by one of the parties is insufficient to establish bias in favor of that party. *Cf. TechSearch, L.L.C. v. Intel Corp.*, 286 F.3d 1360, 1379 n. 3 (Fed.Cir. 2002) (noting that technical advisors typically would be selected from a list of candidates submitted by the parties).

We hasten to add that the litigants are free to challenge the qualifications or neutrality of any suggested mediator (whether or not nominated by a party to the case). APC, for example, had a full opportunity to present its views about the suggested mediator both in its opposition to the motion for mediation and in its motion for reconsideration of the mediation order. Despite these opportunities, APC offered no convincing reason to spark a belief that Professor Green, a nationally recognized mediator with significant experience in sprawling cases, is an unacceptable choice. When a court enters a mediation order, it necessarily makes an independent determination that the mediator it appoints is both qualified and neutral. Because the court made that implicit determination here in a manner that was procedurally fair (if not ideal), we find no abuse of discretion in its selection of Professor Green.[7]

APC also grouses that it should not be forced to share the costs of an unwanted mediation. We have held, however, that courts have the power under Fed.R.Civ.P. 26(f) to issue pretrial cost-sharing orders in complex litigation. *See In re San Juan Dupont Plaza Hotel Fire Litig.,* 994 F.2d 956, 965 (1st Cir. 1993). Given the difficulties facing trial courts in cases involving multiple parties and multiple claims, we are hesitant to limit that power to the traditional discovery context. This is especially true in complicated cases, where the potential value of mediation lies not only in promoting settlement but also in clarifying the issues remaining for trial.

The short of the matter is that, without default cost-sharing rules, the use of valuable ADR techniques (like mediation) becomes hostage to the parties' ability to agree on the concomitant financial arrangements. This means that the district court's inherent power to order private mediation in appropriate cases would be rendered nugatory absent the corollary power to order the sharing of reasonable mediation costs. To avoid this pitfall, we hold that the district court, in an appropriate case, is empowered to order the sharing of reasonable costs and expenses associated with mandatory non-binding mediation.

The remainder of APC's arguments are not so easily dispatched. Even when generically appropriate, a mediation order must contain procedural and substantive safeguards to ensure fairness to all parties involved. The mediation order in this case does not quite meet that test. In particular,

---

[7]   We say "not ideal" because, in an ideal world, it would be preferable for the district court, before naming a mediator, to solicit the names of potential nominees from all parties and to provide an opportunity for the parties to comment upon each others' proposed nominees.

the order does not set limits on the duration of the mediation or the expense associated therewith.[8]

We need not wax longiloquent. As entered, the order simply requires the parties to mediate; it does not set forth either a timetable for the mediation or a cap on the fees that the mediator may charge. The figures that have been bandied about in the briefs—$900 per hour or $9,000 per mediation day—are quite large and should not be left to the mediator's whim. Relatedly, because the mediator is to be paid an hourly rate, the court should have set an outside limit on the number of hours to be devoted to mediation. Equally as important, it is trite but often true that justice delayed is justice denied. An unsuccessful mediation will postpone the ultimate resolution of the case—indeed, the district court has stayed all discovery pending the completion of the mediation—and, thus, prolong the litigation. For these reasons, the district court should have set a definite time frame for the mediation.

The respondents suggest that the district court did not need to articulate any limitations in its mediation order because the mediation process will remain under the district court's ultimate supervision; the court retains the ability to curtail any excessive expenditures of time or money; and a dissatisfied party can easily return to the court at any time. While this might be enough of a safeguard in many instances, the instant litigation is sufficiently complicated and the mediation efforts are likely to be sufficiently expensive that, here, reasonable time limits and fee constraints, set in advance, are appropriate.

A court intent on ordering non-consensual mediation should take other precautions as well. For example, the court should make it clear (as did the able district court in this case) that participation in mediation will not be taken as a waiver of any litigation position. The important point is that the protections we have mentioned are not intended to comprise an exhaustive list, but, rather, to illustrate that when a district court orders a party to participate in mediation, it should take care to assuage legitimate concerns about the possible negative consequences of such an order.

To recapitulate, we rule that a mandatory mediation order issued under the district court's inherent power is valid in an appropriate case. We also rule that this is an appropriate case. We hold, however, that the district court's failure to set reasonable limits on the duration of the mediation and on the mediator's fees dooms the decree.

CONCLUSION

We admire the district court's pragmatic and innovative approach to this massive litigation. Our core holding—that ordering mandatory

---

[8]   We do not assign significant weight to Thames-Dick's belated offer to pay APC's share of the mediator's fee. There are other expenses involved, and there is too much of a risk that "free rider" status will itself breed problems.

mediation is a proper exercise of a district court's inherent power, subject, however, to a variety of terms and conditions—validates that approach. We are mindful that this holding is in tension with the opinions of the Sixth and Seventh Circuits in *NLO* and *Strandell*, respectively, but we believe it is justified by the important goal of promoting flexibility and creative problem-solving in the handling of complex litigation.

That said, the need of the district judge in this case to construct his own mediation regime ad hoc underscores the greater need of the district court as an institution to adopt an ADR program and memorialize it in its local rules. In the ADR Act, Congress directed that "[e]ach United States district court shall authorize, by local rule under section 2071(a), the use of alternative dispute resolution processes in all civil actions. . . ." 28 U.S.C. § 651(b). While Congress did not set a firm deadline for compliance with this directive, the statute was enacted four years ago. This omission having been noted, we are confident that the district court will move expediently to bring the District of Puerto Rico into compliance.

We need go no further. For the reasons set forth above, we vacate the district court's mediation order and remand for further proceedings consistent with this opinion. The district court is free to order mediation if it continues to believe that such a course is advisable or, in the alternative, to proceed with discovery and trial.

NOTES AND QUESTIONS

1. Should judges have the power to command participation in mediation? What if a party insists that it has no interest in settling and wants the court to adjudicate the dispute? Consider again Professor Fiss's view on the role of courts (*supra* p. 526), as well as the Issacharoff-Klonoff rejoinder about settlement as a means to achieving justice (*supra* p. 527).

2. In G. Heileman Brewing Co. v. Joseph Oat Corp., 871 F.2d 648 (7th Cir. 1989), the Seventh Circuit ruled that a federal district court has inherent power to order a party represented by an attorney to attend a pretrial settlement conference and that the court may impose sanctions for failure to comply. Although Rule 16(a) only provided that a court may order "the attorneys and any unrepresented parties" to attend a pretrial conference, the court found the trial judge had inherent judicial authority to order the defendant Oat Corporation to send a "corporate representative." (Rule 16(c)(1) now provides that "[i]f appropriate, the court may require that a party or its representative be present or reasonably available by other means to consider possible settlement," but this provision was not added until 1993.) The district court also ordered that the corporate representative come "with authority to settle." Oat sent a corporate counsel from its New Jersey headquarters, together with its outside lawyer from Philadelphia, to attend the conference in Madison, Wisconsin, where the court sat. The district court found Oat had violated its order to send a "corporate official with authority to settle" and

imposed a sanction of $5,860, representing the costs and attorneys' fees of the opposing parties to attend the conference.

The majority in *Heileman* conceded that circumstances could arise in which requiring a corporate representative to appear "would be so onerous, so clearly unproductive, or so expensive in relation to the size, value, and complexity of the case that it might be an abuse of discretion." However, it found no such situation here, where the claim was sizable ($4 million) and turned on complex factual and legal issues, where the trial was expected to be lengthy (one to three months), and where the corporation had sent an attorney from Philadelphia to speak for it, whose expenses would not have exceeded sending a corporate representative from Camden.

As for the order's requirement that the corporate representative have "authority to settle," the majority made it clear this did not mean "corporate representatives must come to court willing to settle on someone else's terms, but only that they come to court in order to consider the possibility of settlement." The corporate representative was only required "to hold a position within the corporate entity allowing him to speak definitively and to commit the corporation to a particular position in the litigation." If sanctions had been imposed "because the representative refused to make an offer to pay money— that is, refused to submit to settlement coercion," the court said, "we would be faced with a decidedly different issue—a situation we would not countenance."

Judge Posner, dissenting, expressed the concern "that in their zeal to settle cases judges may ignore the value of other people's time." Noting that Oat Corporation had stated its unwillingness to consider a monetary settlement, he wondered what purpose was served by the court's order: "Oat had made clear that it was not prepared to settle the case on any terms that required it to pay money. That was its prerogative, which once exercised made the magistrate's continued insistence on Oat's sending an executive to [the pretrial conference] arbitrary, unreasonable, willful, and indeed petulant."

Consider the majority's distinction between "settlement coercion" and requiring a party to send a representative "to consider the possibility of settlement." If the defendant sent a corporate representative who said only, "I have authority to settle for zero," would it have been in compliance with the order?

3.   Sending a person with settlement authority becomes more complicated when such authority resides in a body such as a city council or corporate board. See Nueces County v. De Pena, 953 S.W.2d 835 (Tex.App. 1997) (finding that a county judge lacked authority to settle a dispute on behalf of the commissioners court and therefore did not need to attend mediation); Schwartzman, Inc. v. ACF Industries, Inc., 167 F.R.D. 694, 698–699 (D.N.M. 1996) ("[G]ood faith participation of a qualified representative," even if not absolute settlement authority, is central to full, effective participation, *quoting* the 1993 Advisory Committee Notes to Rule 16(c) that "[p]articularly in litigation in which governmental agencies or large amounts of money are involved, there may be no one with on-the-spot settlement authority, and the

most that should be expected is access to a person who would have a major role in submitting a recommendation to the body or board with ultimate decision-making authority").

When the settlement authority for a large organization rests with one person, it is often unrealistic to expect him or her to attend ADR proceedings in all cases involving the organization. See U.S. v. Lake County Bd. of Comm'rs, 2007 WL 1202408 (N.D.Ind. Apr. 19, 2007) (denying motion to require presence of the Assistant Attorney General of the U.S. who had final settlement authority because he oversees a staff of 300 attorneys nationwide, and his attendance only can be practically accomplished telephonically); In re United States, 149 F.3d 332, 334 (5th Cir. 1998) ("the district court should consider alternatively ordering the Attorney General to have the person or persons identified as holding full settlement authority consider settlement in advance of the mediation and be fully prepared and available by telephone to discuss settlement at the time of mediation").

4. Ironically, sometimes the best way to promote settlement is to schedule a trial. The Manual for Complex Litigation explains, "Setting a firm trial date is generally the most effective means to motivate parties to settle." Manual for Complex Litigation (4th) § 13.13 (2004), echoing advice that judges have passed down for years. Thus, while cases like *Atlantic Pipe* and *G. Heileman* show that judges may promote settlement by requiring participation in mediation or pretrial conferences, most judges also understand the importance of keeping the case moving through discovery and pretrial and toward trial.

5. Trials may encourage settlement in another way. In mass litigation involving numerous individual actions, a small number of individual trials may yield information about outcomes and settlement values sufficient to enable the parties to negotiate a global settlement of thousands of other claims. Courts often refer to such individual trials as "bellwether trials." A judge overseeing mass litigation, such as an MDL transferee judge, may schedule a series of bellwether trials early in the litigation with the hope that the trial outcomes will assist both sides in reaching a broader resolution. Some courts permit counsel for both sides to select representative cases, while others use random sampling techniques. For further discussion of bellwether trials, see p. 649 *infra* as well as the discussion in Chapter 4 at p. 156 *supra*.

ADR Mechanisms to Facilitate Settlement

In *Atlantic Pipe*, the judge sent the parties to mediation. Mediation is one type of alternative dispute resolution (ADR) mechanism that judges and lawyers use to facilitate settlement. Here, we briefly describe several of these mechanisms. Keep in mind the difference between facilitative ADR mechanisms, discussed here, and binding arbitration, discussed in Chapter 10. Both involve the participation of a third-party neutral other than the judge, and both typically are included under the definitional umbrella of "alternative dispute resolution." That, however, is where the similarities end. Facilitative ADR mechanisms are intended to help the parties negotiate a settlement, but ultimately it remains the parties' decision whether to settle; if the parties fail to reach an agreement, their lawsuit proceeds. Binding arbitration, by contrast, results in a decision by the arbitrator that concludes the dispute. Arbitration ordinarily occurs when the parties have agreed contractually that they will be bound by an arbitrator's decision.

For the parties, the benefits of facilitative ADR may include quicker resolutions, lower litigation expenses, less intrusive discovery, greater confidentiality, and preservation of relationships between the parties. For the court system, ADR holds the potential to reduce costs and unclog dockets by resolving some disputes without trial and appeal. As you read about the various facilitative ADR mechanisms, think about what types of complex disputes might lend themselves to each approach.

a.   *Mediation*

A mediator is a neutral third party whose job is to assist the parties in negotiating a resolution of their dispute. Mediation is the quintessential *facilitative* ADR technique. Its purpose is not to render a decision, but rather to facilitate the parties' quest for a negotiated resolution. Depending on the case and the individual mediator, some of the techniques used in mediation may have an evaluative component, such as helping the parties see the strengths of the other side's case. Successful mediation sometimes depends upon helping the parties find outcomes that satisfy the interests of both sides.

Mediation can be either independent or court-annexed. Independent mediation is used when parties desire to reach a settlement but believe they will be better able to reach agreement with the help of a neutral third party. To engage in mediation that is not required by the court or other law, the parties must agree on the terms of the mediation, the identity of the mediator, and who will bear the costs. Attorneys and former judges often serve as mediators; several organizations maintain rosters of experienced mediators for hire. Occasionally, contracts include mediation clauses that require the parties to attempt to resolve their dispute through mediation before filing a lawsuit. See, e.g., Crandall v. Grbic, 138 P.3d 365 (Kan.App. 2006) (upholding summary judgment for defendant, in part because plaintiff filed lawsuit before going to mediation as required by contract).

Often, mediation is conducted under the auspices of the court. As we saw in In re Atlantic Pipe Corp., *supra* p. 532, courts have the power to compel parties to participate in mediation, and many courts have local rules that require mediation in certain types of cases before going to trial.

In federal multidistrict litigation, mediation is routinely used for helping parties move toward settlement. Complex multiparty litigation may be especially well suited to mediation, given the difficulty of coordinating multiple sets of competing interests. Bringing a mediator onboard early in the litigation helps parties focus on the possibility of settlement. Indeed, in a guide for MDL transferee judges published by the Judicial Panel on Multidistrict Litigation and the Federal Judicial Center, one of its ten recommendations is to "Encourage an Early Mediation Process":

> As soon as you are satisfied that plaintiffs' claims have at least some arguable merit, it may be a good idea to suggest that counsel establish a mediation structure, select a mediator, and begin settlement negotiations simultaneous with discovery and the briefing of preliminary motions. Although early negotiations may not bear immediate fruit, they do require all parties to keep the endgame in mind even in the initial phases of the litigation.

Judicial Panel on Multidistrict Litigation & Federal Judicial Center, Ten Steps to Better Case Management: A Guide for Multidistrict Litigation Transferee Judges 7 (2d ed. 2014). Note that the guide says that early negotiations help MDL parties "keep the endgame in mind." What endgame is it referring to? That a guide for judges assumes the endgame of MDL is settlement, rather than adjudication, reveals much about the realities of mass litigation and the important role of mediation.

b.   *Non-Binding Arbitration*

If mediation is the quintessential facilitative ADR technique, then arbitration is the quintessential *evaluative* ADR technique. An arbitrator is a third-party neutral who hears both sides of a dispute and whose job is to render a decision. Many contracts include arbitration clauses that require parties to submit their disputes to binding arbitration rather than litigation. Here, we consider *non-binding* arbitration as an ADR technique for encouraging parties to settle.

Non-binding arbitration ordinarily occurs as a court-annexed process. Court-annexed non-binding arbitration has been adopted by local rule in a number of federal district courts. It provides the parties and attorneys an opportunity to present their cases and obtain a non-binding decision. Court-annexed arbitration generally takes place early in the litigation before full discovery has been undertaken. This carries the obvious disadvantage of incomplete information, but the equally obvious advantage of possibly resolving the dispute before the largest litigation expenses have been incurred.

The Eastern District of New York, for example, adopted a local rule requiring arbitration in all lawsuits up to $150,000, excluding civil rights and certain other categories of cases. E.D.N.Y. Local Civil Rule 83.7. The arbitrations take place at the courthouse and are heard by one arbitrator or, on request, by a panel of three arbitrators. The Federal Rules of

Evidence serve as guidelines but are not rigidly enforced. The arbitrator's decision is non-binding; if any party requests a trial de novo, the case proceeds to trial as if it had not been arbitrated. However, if no party makes a demand for trial within thirty days after the entry of judgment on the arbitration award, then the arbitrator's decision becomes a final, non-appealable judgment of the court. In other words, the mandatory arbitration process results in a decision that becomes the default resolution of the dispute. After the arbitration, the parties may negotiate a settlement, they may demand a trial, or they may choose to accept the arbitrator's decision.

c. Early Neutral Evaluation

Some names are self-explanatory. Early Neutral Evaluation (ENE) offers parties a neutral, frank assessment of their cases early in the litigation process. The neutral third party who gives the evaluation is an experienced lawyer who knows the subject matter area. Settlement need not be the only, or even the primary, goal of ENE. By providing lawyers and litigants with a "reality check" concerning the various claims and defenses, ENE may help the parties focus on the key issues in dispute. This, in turn, may permit more streamlined discovery, resolution by dispositive motion, or a clearer path to trial.

The local rules of the Northern District of California, where ENE was pioneered, describe the process as follows: "In Early Neutral Evaluation (ENE) the parties and their counsel, in a confidential session, make compact presentations of their claims and defenses, including key evidence as developed at that juncture, and receive a non-binding evaluation by an experienced neutral lawyer with subject matter expertise. The evaluator also helps identify areas of agreement, offers case-planning suggestions and, if requested by the parties, settlement assistance." N.D. Cal. ADR Local Rule 5–1.

d. Summary Jury Trial

The summary jury trial is an abbreviated proceeding in which the lawyers present shortened versions of their cases to a jury assembled by the court. The jury is empaneled from the court's actual jury pool, pursuant to the court's power. The "trial" takes place in a courtroom with a judge presiding. After each party makes its short presentation, the jury renders a "verdict." Unlike a real trial, the verdict is not a binding result that determines the outcome. Rather, it is a non-binding statement of the jury's view based on the summary presentations, much like non-binding arbitration or ENE. Although the jury in a summary jury trial looks much like a jury in an actual civil trial, its function is more akin to that of a focus group.

B. CLASS ACTION SETTLEMENTS

Overwhelmingly, certified class actions settle. Because class actions magnify the all-or-nothing aspect of trial, they create pressure on both sides to reach a negotiated resolution. Indeed, the irony of class action trial plans in so-called "litigation class actions" is that at the class certification stage, lawyers present detailed trial plans as they argue about whether a class trial would be manageable, but both the lawyers and the judge recognize the unlikelihood of actually reaching trial. Meanwhile, because a case may be certified instead as a "settlement class action"—that is, a class action solely for purposes of settlement—some class settlements occur in cases that could not have been litigated as class actions.

This portion of the chapter explores some of the unique issues presented by class action settlements. First and most importantly, class settlements require judicial approval and thus raise questions about how judges should evaluate the fairness of a negotiated resolution. Second, class settlements often involve non-monetary relief such as institutional reform, cy pres remedies, and coupons. Third, while the settlement approval process is non-adversarial between class counsel and the defendant, objectors may come forward to argue against approval of the class settlement.

Two aspects of class action settlements are treated in other chapters. Chapter 5 addresses the certification of settlement class actions, *supra* p. 310. Chapter 9 addresses the binding effect of approved class settlements as a matter of claim preclusion and issue preclusion, *infra* p. 673.

1. JUDICIAL APPROVAL

Most settlements—outside of class actions—are simply contracts between the parties. In the typical litigation settlement, one party (the defendant) agrees to pay a sum of money, in exchange for which the other party (the plaintiff) agrees to release its claim and to dismiss the lawsuit. Class actions, however, cannot settle merely by agreement of the parties, because most of those who would be bound by the settlement—the class members—are not at the table. The class representatives and class counsel are charged with representing the interests of the entire class in negotiating a settlement, but the agreement does not bind the class unless the court enters judgment approving the settlement.

Rule 23(e), which was amended in 2018, governs class action settlements. It says that the claims of a certified class "may be settled, voluntarily dismissed, or compromised only with the court's approval." It goes on to instruct courts on how to handle the class settlement approval process. The court must direct reasonable notice of the proposed settlement to class members. Fed.R.Civ.P. 23(e)(1). The court must hold a hearing to evaluate the settlement, and the court may approve the settlement only if the court finds that it is "fair, reasonable, and adequate." Fed.R.Civ.P. 23(e)(2). The court must allow class members to present their objections to the settlement proposal. Fed.R.Civ.P. 23(e)(5).

Class settlement approval ordinarily involves a two-step process. *See* Fed.R.Civ.P. 23(e)(1); Manual for Complex Litigation (4th) § 21.632 (2004). First, the court does a preliminary review of the proposed settlement based on a presentation from its advocates. The reason for this preliminary review is to avoid the burden and expense of notice and a fairness hearing if it is clear that the proposed settlement does not pass muster. The 2018 amendments to Rule 23 spelled out the court's obligation to conduct this preliminary analysis before directing notice to the class, *see* Fed.R.Civ.P. 23(e)(1)(B), as well as the parties' obligation to provide the court with sufficient information to enable it to determine whether the settlement is likely to succeed and therefore that notice is warranted, *see* Fed.R.Civ.P. 23(e)(1)(A). The Advisory Committee emphasized the seriousness of this first step, including the parties' burden to "frontload" information:

> The decision to give notice of a proposed settlement to the class is an important event. It should be based on a solid record supporting the conclusion that the proposed settlement will likely earn final approval after notice and an opportunity to object. The parties must provide the court with information sufficient to determine whether notice should be sent. At the time they seek notice to the class, the proponents of the settlement should ordinarily provide the court with all available materials they intend to submit to support approval under Rule 23(e)(2) and that they intend to make available to class members.

Rule 23(e)(1) Advisory Committee Note (2018).

If this preliminary determination about the adequacy of the settlement suggests that giving notice to the class is worthwhile, the court must direct notice to the class under Rule 23(e)(1). It has been said that the court has "virtually complete discretion" in selecting the kind of notice. Franks v. Kroger Co., 649 F.2d 1216, 1222 (6th Cir. 1981). The 2003 Advisory Committee Note points out, however, that individual notice may be appropriate if there is a right to opt out or if class members must file claims to qualify for the benefits of the settlement. The notice should describe the terms of the settlement adequately to allow class members to decide whether to opt out (if allowed at that point) or to object. In addition, it may include information on the proposed attorney fee award to class counsel. Rule 23(h)(1) requires notice to the class of the motion for attorney fees; combining the two items in one notice saves effort.

The notice should afford class members a reasonable time to review the proposed settlement and inform them of the deadline for objecting to the settlement. If there are objectors, the court has the benefit of an adversary presentation in connection with its final review of the proposed settlement. As explained by the Manual for Complex Litigation (4th) § 21.62 (2004):

> Rule [23(e)(2)] establishes that the settlement must be fair, reasonable, and adequate. Fairness calls for a comparative analysis of the treatment of class members vis-à-vis each other and vis-à-vis similar individuals with similar claims who are not in the class. Reasonableness depends on an analysis of the class allegations and claims and the responsiveness of the settlement to those claims. Adequacy of the settlement involves a comparison of the relief granted relative to what class members might have obtained without using the class action process.

It is no easy task determining the fairness of a class settlement. Hearings on class settlements can be lengthy and detailed. In *Amchem*, *supra* p. 311, the fairness hearing lasted 18 days and the court entered 300 findings of fact and 103 conclusions of law based on that hearing. Moreover, as the following case demonstrates, courts sometimes deal with a complex cast of characters—class representatives, class counsel, and objectors—all of whom purport to represent the interests of the class.

PARKER V. ANDERSON
United States Court of Appeals, Fifth Circuit, 1982.
667 F.2d 1204, *cert. denied*, 459 U.S. 828 (1982).

Before THORNBERRY, REAVLEY and POLITZ, CIRCUIT JUDGES.

POLITZ, CIRCUIT JUDGE.

We review the district court's approval of a settlement of a class action suit against Bell Helicopter Company and its award of attorneys' fees. The court's approval was granted over the objection of all but one of the eleven named plaintiffs as well as over the objections of a number of class plaintiffs. Improprieties are claimed to have occurred in the settlement negotiations and the agreement is challenged as inadequate in its terms.

[Seven employment discrimination suits were brought by a total of eleven named plaintiffs against Bell Helicopter Co. After the suits were consolidated, the court conditionally certified a class under Rule 23(b)(2) and designated lead counsel. Shortly before trial was to commence, class counsel Howard Specter opened settlement discussions with counsel for defendant.]

* * *

During March 1980, class counsel met with the various named plaintiffs and discussed the tentative settlement proposal. Each of the eleven named plaintiffs authorized their counsel to note their approval of the class settlement, subject to Bell's acceptance of their individual demands which included a demand of $100,000 for one plaintiff, $84,000 for another, and guarantees of promotion to specific jobs for others. Bell countered with an offer of $1,500 each for ten of the named plaintiffs and $2,500 plus a future promotion for the eleventh.

On March 26, 1980, associate class counsel Barber met with all named plaintiffs to discuss the suit and proposed settlement. A discussion of the evidence, particularly the statistics plaintiffs were relying on, was planned. No serious discussion of the lawsuit was possible; plaintiffs were interested primarily in discussing their personal monetary demands. Apparently convinced that Bell's offer to them was too little, nine of the eleven plaintiffs expressed opposition to the settlement.[3]

On March 29, 1980, the attorneys for the parties approved a proposed Stipulation of Compromise and Agreement which embodied 18 of the 19 points contained in the tentative agreement confected on February 19, 1980. The proposal required Bell to deposit $1,250,000 in an interest bearing account to be distributed to the class members when and as directed by the court. Certain affirmative relief measures projected to cost Bell approximately $1,000,000 to implement and maintain, were included. The proposal was made applicable only to the members of the class; Bell agreed to sever the individual claims of the named plaintiffs. Those claims are still pending.

[All but one of the named plaintiffs fired class counsel and, through new counsel, attacked the adequacy of the settlement. The trial court nevertheless gave notice to the class, held a hearing, and approved the settlement over the objections of the ten original plaintiffs plus some objecting unnamed class members. The ten original plaintiffs, now objectors, appealed.]

* * *

Objectors contend that the attorneys did not represent the class fairly and adequately during negotiations. They contend that counsel failed to consult with them, withheld certain information, and misrepresented material matters. The record does not support any of these assertions.

This inquiry must be placed in proper perspective. Objectors' personal claims were not before the district court and are not before us; they were severed and are still pending. Rather, the objectors stand before us as representatives of the absentee class members. The question presented by this appeal is whether class counsel provided fair and adequate legal representation to the class as a whole. Necessarily, much of what counsel does for the class is by and through the class representatives, but that is

---

[3] The trial court capsulated the evidence about the meeting as follows:

Angry and offended at what seemed to them small counteroffers, and fortified with a case of beer, the plaintiffs were ill disposed to listen to any explanation of the deficiencies of the statistical case against Bell. Posturing and wild talk took the place of reasoned analysis. At the close of the meeting, the plaintiffs voted to "reject" the settlement.

neither the ultimate nor the key determinant. The compelling obligation of class counsel in class action litigation is to the group which makes up the class. Counsel must be aware of and motivated by that which is in the maximum best interests of the class considered as a unit.

The duty owed to the client sharply distinguishes litigation on behalf of one or more individuals and litigation on behalf of a class. Objectors emphasize the duty of counsel in non-class litigation. The prevailing principles in that situation cannot be imported wholesale into a class action setting. The fairness and adequacy of counsel's performance cannot be gauged in terms of the representation of the named plaintiffs. In addressing this point in our recent decision of *Kincade v. General Tire & Rubber Co.*, 635 F.2d 501, 508 (5th Cir. 1981), we stated:

> Appellants' argument that the settlement cannot be applied to them because they did not authorize their attorney . . . to settle the case or otherwise consent to the settlement is also easily disposed of. Because the "client" in a class action consists of numerous unnamed class members as well as the representatives, and because "[t]he class itself often speaks in several voices . . ., it may be impossible for the class attorney to do more than act in what he believes to be the best interests of the class as a whole. . . ." *Pettway v. American Cast Iron Pipe Co.*, 576 F.2d 1157, 1216 (5th Cir. 1978).

The courts have recognized that the duty owed by class counsel is to the entire class and is not dependent on the special desires of the named plaintiffs. It has been held that agreement of the named plaintiffs is not essential to approval of a settlement which the trial court finds to be fair and reasonable. "Because of the unique nature of the attorney-client relationship in a class action, the cases cited by appellants holding that an attorney cannot settle his individual client's case without the authorization of the client are simply inapplicable." *Kincade*, 635 F.2d at 508; *Flinn v. FMC Corp.*, 528 F.2d 1169, 1174 n. 19 (4th Cir. 1975), cert. denied, 424 U.S. 967 (1976) ("Appellants do not argue, nor may they under the authorities, that the assent of the class plaintiffs is essential to the settlement, provided the trial court finds it fair and reasonable."). The rationale implicit in these decisions is sound: the named plaintiffs should not be permitted to hold the absentee class hostage by refusing to assent to an otherwise fair and adequate settlement in order to secure their individual demands. The trial court was not impressed favorably by the motivation of the objectors, finding as a fact that: "Plaintiff-objectors opposed the settlement in bad faith, primarily to gain leverage in settling their individual claims against Bell at exorbitant figures."

We measure class counsel's performance of the duty to represent the class fairly and adequately as we gauge the fairness and adequacy of the settlement. It will follow generally that an attorney who secures and submits a fair and adequate settlement has represented the client class fairly and adequately. In this instance, we affirm the trial judge's findings as to the settlement and necessarily reject the contention that the attorneys' performance in confecting the settlement was inadequate.

* * *

We note over 30 contacts between a member of Specter's staff and the class representatives during that period. In addition, the record reflects substantial contacts between class counsel and the representatives during March and April of 1980. During that period, the class attorneys advised the representatives of the terms of the proposed settlement, evaluated the evidentiary bases for the case, held meetings to discuss the settlement, and attempted to negotiate a monetary increase for some of the individual representatives.[9] Objectors suggest that these contacts are immaterial, contending that the February 29 letter was, in effect, the final settlement agreement. This objection is not well taken. As appellees point out, the tentative agreement was conditional, incomplete, and subject to approval, including the ultimate approval of the court.

The trial court reached the following conclusions: "Counsel consulted regularly and frequently with the class representatives throughout the case"; during March "all named plaintiffs consulted their attorneys about the class action settlement and authorized them to convey binding offers to Bell and to approve class settlement on their behalf if accepted," and "lead counsel behaved appropriately in negotiating the tentative settlement as spokesman for the class, immediately advising the named plaintiffs and associate counsel of its terms by letter, and ascertaining the named plaintiffs' reaction to the settlement before presenting it to the court." We perceive no error in these findings.

NOTES AND QUESTIONS

1. Faced with a split between class counsel and most of the class representatives, the court in *Parker* had to decide whom to trust, or more to the point, whom to mistrust. Consider the incentives of the players in the settlement approval process. First, consider the class representatives. Do class representatives have interests that might lead them to object to a reasonable settlement? The *Parker* court clearly thought so.

---

[9] For example, in a letter to plaintiff Mackey, dated March 25, 1980, lead counsel devoted approximately four pages to a detailed evaluation of the strengths and weaknesses of the case. In summarizing his purpose for writing he stated: "I want you to have a clear understanding of the risks which you are running before you decide what course to take and whether to seek to settle or take your chances in court." A similar letter was sent to plaintiff Odom.

In addition, on at least two occasions, it was the named plaintiffs that refused to accept counseling and evaluations offered by class counsel. After the February 29 letter [between counsel regarding tentative settlement] but before the final settlement agreement, associate counsel Barber met with plaintiffs to discuss the case. Instead of rational discussion, he was confronted with hostility and anger. After the March 28 agreement, but before the settlement hearing, lead counsel offered to discuss settlement with plaintiffs individually. The invitation went begging.

Next, consider the incentives of class counsel, which the *Parker* court did not mention. Do lawyers for a plaintiff class have interests that might lead them to recommend an inadequate settlement? See John C. Coffee, Jr., Class Action Accountability: Reconciling Exit, Voice, and Loyalty in Representative Litigation, 100 Colum. L. Rev. 370, 391 (2000) (arguing that the reluctance of counsel to risk all on a litigated outcome is more likely to incline lawyers to accept "cheap settlements" than corrupt payoffs in which they get overpaid). Recall also the concerns about conflicts of interest in *Amchem*, *supra* p. 311, concerning the "inventory settlements" class counsel made for their own individual clients in conjunction with the class settlements.

Finally, consider the judge. Does a district judge have any incentives with regard to a proposed class settlement? Keep in mind that judges face institutional pressures to keep their dockets moving by concluding cases promptly, and that class actions impose particularly large burdens on courts.

2. In *Parker*, the court severed the claims of the class representatives, freeing them from the settlement they found objectionable and permitting them to proceed individually. Does this make things better or worse? On the one hand, it seems unfair to force plaintiffs to accept what they see as an unsatisfactory settlement. If they were suing individually, the decision to accept or reject the settlement would belong to them. Should they be worse off simply because they agreed to serve as class representatives? On the other hand, if other class members wished to decline the *Parker* settlement, would they be permitted to exclude themselves? In *Parker*, did Rule 23 provide class members a right to opt out of this class action? (Hint: What type of class action did the court certify?) Was the court giving a special advantage to the class representatives by severing their claims when all other class members would be bound by the settlement?

3. Did the class representatives in *Parker* adequately protect the class? When the court granted class certification in *Parker*, it necessarily found that the class representatives would "fairly and adequately protect the interests of the class." Fed.R.Civ.P. 23(a)(4). If the court later concluded that the representatives were withholding assent to a reasonable settlement in order to maximize personal gain, should it have reconsidered whether they were proper representatives? What are the court's options at that stage? Also, class certification meant that the court concluded that the class representatives had claims that were "typical" of the class. Fed.R.Civ.P. 23(a)(3). If so, and if the settlement was adequate for the other class members, why did the court allow the class representatives to exclude themselves?

4. Is it improper for the class representatives to want something extra from the case? In some instances the class representatives may be able to obtain bonus compensation for having undertaken the rigors of representing the class, but that amount should reflect the burden on them as representatives. The Private Securities Litigation Act directs that class representatives in securities fraud cases may be paid extra only upon a showing that they have incurred actual costs or losses of income as a result of their service as class representatives. 15 U.S.C. §§ 77z–1(a)(4); 78u–4(a)(4).

One Court of Appeals recently held that bonuses for class representatives are prohibited, see Johnson v. NPAS Solutions, LLC, 975 F.3d 1244 (11th Cir. 2020), but this view has not taken hold more broadly.

5.　In *Parker*, the class representatives commanded class counsel to reject the settlement, but counsel went ahead to present it to the court. In the lawyer-client relationship, aren't clients the principals and lawyers the agents? How does the lawyer's duty of loyalty in class actions differ from non-class representation? As amended in 2003, Rule 23 directs that class counsel "must fairly and adequately represent the interests of the class." Fed.R.Civ.P. 23(g)(4). In Lazy Oil Co. v. Witco Corp., 166 F.3d 581 (3d Cir. 1999), three of four class representatives objected to the proposed settlement and argued that class counsel ("their" lawyer) could not represent the class and oppose their objections. The appellate court adopted a balancing approach to the disqualification issue, comparing the interest of the class in continued representation by experienced counsel against the actual prejudice to the objectors due to being opposed by their former counsel. It explained (id. at 589):

> In many class actions, one or more class representatives will object to a settlement and become adverse parties to the remaining class representatives (and the rest of the class). If, by applying the usual rules on attorney-client relations, class counsel could easily be disqualified in these cases, not only would the objectors enjoy great "leverage," but many fair and reasonable settlements would be undermined by the need to find substitute counsel after months or even years of fruitful settlement negotiations.

Conversely, class counsel may decide to represent objectors rather than proponents of a settlement. In Eubank v. Pella, 753 F.3d 718, 722–23 (7th Cir. 2014), one of the class lawyers opposed the proposed settlement that his former partner had negotiated, and represented four former class representatives as objectors. The Seventh Circuit approved of the switch: "A lawyer's switching sides in the same lawsuit would normally be considered a fatal conflict of interest, but the courts are lenient when it is a class action lawyer. For often 'only the attorneys who have represented the class, rather than any of the class members themselves, have substantial familiarity with the prior proceedings, the fruits of discovery, the actual potential of the litigation.' "

IN RE PAYMENT CARD INTERCHANGE FEE AND MERCHANT DISCOUNT ANTITRUST LITIGATION

United States District Court, Eastern District of New York, 2019.
330 F.R.D. 11.

BRODIE, DISTRICT JUDGE.

A putative Rule 23(b)(3) class of over twelve million nationwide merchants brought an antitrust action under the Sherman Act, 15 U.S.C. §§ 1 and 2, and state antitrust laws, against Defendants Visa and Mastercard networks, as well as various issuing and acquiring banks. Plaintiffs are merchants that accept(ed) Visa- and Mastercard-branded cards, and have alleged that Defendants harmed competition and charged the merchants supracompetitive fees by creating unlawful contracts and rules and by engaging in various antitrust conspiracies.

Plaintiffs sought both injunctive and monetary relief, and after years of litigation, former District Judge John Gleeson approved a settlement for an injunctive relief class and a monetary damages relief class, which was vacated by the Second Circuit on June 30, 2016, and remanded to this Court. After additional extensive discovery and renegotiations, the named representatives of the damages class (the "Rule 23(b)(3) Class Plaintiffs) and Defendants reached a new and separate settlement agreement.

Currently before the Court is the Rule 23(b)(3) Class Plaintiffs' Motion for Class Settlement Preliminary Approval. The Rule 23(b)(3) Class Plaintiffs and Defendants move for preliminary approval of the settlement and preliminary certification of a settlement class under Rule 23(b)(3) of the Federal Rules of Civil Procedure. In support of the motion, interim class counsel for the Rule 23(b)(3) class ("Rule 23(b)(3) Class Counsel" or "Class Counsel") submitted a memorandum of law, a superseding Rule 23(b)(3) class settlement agreement—with amended escrow agreements, a proposed Notice Plan, proposed Class Notices, and a proposed Plan of Administration and Distribution, among other items—and the declarations of two mediators who facilitated settlement discussions.

For the reasons discussed below, on January 24, 2019, the Court granted the Motion for Class Settlement Preliminary Approval.

I. Background

[Interchange fees and merchant discount fees are amounts that merchants pay to financial companies for each credit card transaction. Merchants asserted claims that Visa, Mastercard, and others violated antitrust laws by conspiring to fix fees at artificially high levels. Multiple class actions, as well as individual lawsuits by large retailers, were consolidated before District Judge John Gleeson in 2005 for pretrial handling as multidistrict litigation.

In 2013, Judge Gleeson approved a pair of settlement class actions— both a non-opt-out Rule 23(b)(2) settlement for injunctive relief and an opt-out Rule 23(b)(3) settlement for damages. In re Payment Card Interchange Fee & Merch. Disc. Antitrust Litig., 986 F.Supp.2d 207 (E.D.N.Y. 2013) (*Interchange Fees I*), rev'd, 827 F.3d 223 (2d Cir. 2016) (*Interchange Fees II*). On appeal, the Second Circuit vacated the settlement on the ground that the class action should not have been certified. *Interchange Fees II*, 827 F.3d 223 (2d Cir. 2016). The Second Circuit reasoned that, because a single set of counsel represented both the (b)(2) and the (b)(3) classes, and a conflict of interest exists between class members seeking policies for the future and class members seeking compensation for past harm, the conflict precluded a finding of adequate representation under Rule 23(a)(4).

Despite its concerns about whether the (b)(2) class in particular had been adequately represented, the Second Circuit acknowledged the massive effort that had already been devoted to this litigation: Discovery included over 400 depositions, 17 expert reports, 32 days of expert deposition testimony, and production of over 80 million pages of documents; the parties fully briefed motions for class certification, a motion to dismiss, and cross-motions for summary judgment; and they participated in multiple lengthy mediation sessions.

On remand, Judge Margo Brodie appointed separate groups of interim class counsel to represent the (b)(2) class and the (b)(3) class. In June 2018, after renewed discovery and further mediation, the lawyers for the (b)(3) class reached an agreement with the defendants for a settlement class action. The Superseding Settlement Agreement provided for as much as $6.26 billion in relief before opt-out reductions and expense takedowns, which Counsel believed to be the largest cash settlement in antitrust class action history.]

II. Discussion

a. Preliminary approval of a proposed settlement

Rule 23(e) of the Federal Rules of Civil Procedure sets forth the standards and procedures that apply to class action settlements. Under Rule 23(e), a court may grant final approval of a proposed settlement "only after a hearing and only on finding that it is *fair, reasonable, and adequate.*" Fed. R. Civ. P. 23(e)(2) (emphasis added). A class action settlement approval procedure typically occurs in two stages: (1) preliminary approval—where "prior to notice to the class, a court makes a preliminary evaluation of fairness," and (2) final approval—where "notice of a hearing is given to the class members, [and] class members and settling parties are provided the opportunity to be heard on the question of final court approval." *In re LIBOR-Based Fin. Instruments Antitrust Litig.*, No. 11–CV–5450, 2016 WL 7625708, at *2 (S.D.N.Y. Dec. 21, 2016).

During the preliminary approval stage, a court "must review the proposed terms of settlement and make a preliminary determination on the fairness, reasonableness and adequacy of the settlement terms." *In re Initial Pub. Offering Sec. Litig.*, 243 F.R.D. [79,] 87 [(S.D.N.Y. 2007)]. The judicial role in reviewing a proposed settlement is demanding. *Zink v. First Niagara Bank, N.A.*, 155 F.Supp.3d 297, 308 (W.D.N.Y. 2016) (noting that such review "is demanding because the adversariness of litigation is often lost after the agreement to settle."). * * *

i. Preliminary approval standards

New amendments to Rule 23 took effect on December 1, 2018. These amendments alter the standards that guide a court's preliminary approval analysis.[20] Prior to the amendments, Rule 23 did not specify standards for courts to follow when deciding whether to grant preliminary approval * * *

Under the new Rule 23(e), in weighing a grant of preliminary approval, district courts must determine whether "giving notice is justified by the parties' showing that the court *will likely be able to*: (i) approve the proposal under Rule 23(e)(2); and (ii) certify the class for purposes of judgment on the proposal." Fed. R. Civ. P. 23(e)(1)(B)(i–ii). Because Rule 23(e)(2) sets forth the factors that a court must consider when weighing *final* approval, it appears that courts must assess at the preliminary approval stage whether the parties have shown that the court will likely find that the factors weigh in favor of final settlement approval. This standard appears to be more exacting than the prior requirement.

ii.   Preliminary approval factors

Prior to the December 1, 2018 amendments, Rule 23(e)(2) was silent on the factors that courts needed to assess when weighing final approval—the Rule only required that courts hold a final fairness hearing and find the proposed settlement to be "fair, reasonable, and adequate." District courts therefore looked to guidance from, and factors set forth in, circuit law and treatises in making the assessment. Courts in the Second Circuit have traditionally considered nine factors, known as the *Grinnell* factors, to assist in weighing final approval and determining whether a settlement is substantively "fair, reasonable, and adequate." These factors are:

> (1) the complexity, expense and likely duration of the litigation; (2) the reaction of the class to the settlement; (3) the stage of the proceedings and the amount of discovery completed; (4) the risks of establishing liability; (5) the risks of establishing damages; (6) the risks of maintaining the class through the trial; (7) the ability of the defendants to withstand a greater judgment; (8) the range of reasonableness of the settlement fund in light of the best possible recovery; and (9) the range of reasonableness of the settlement fund to a possible recovery in light of all the attendant risks of litigation.

In re Initial Pub. Offering Sec. Litig., 260 F.R.D. 81, 88 (S.D.N.Y. 2009) (citing City of Detroit v. Grinnell Corp., 495 F.2d 448, 463 (2d Cir. 1974)), abrogated on other grounds by Goldberger v. Integrated Res., 209 F.3d 43 (2d Cir. 2000).

The amended Rule 23(e)(2) requires courts to consider whether:

> (A) the class representatives and class counsel have adequately represented the class;

---

[20] Among other things, the new amendments set forth standards under Rule 23(e)(1)(B)(i–ii) that a district court must ensure are met prior to a grant of *preliminary approval* of a proposed settlement, and factors under Rule 23(e)(2) that a district court must now consider when evaluating whether to grant *final approval* of a proposed settlement. *See* Fed. R. Civ. P. 23(e).

(B) the proposal was negotiated at arm's length;

(C) the relief provided for the class is adequate, taking into account:

> (i)   the costs, risks, and delay of trial and appeal;
>
> (ii) the effectiveness of any proposed method of distributing relief to the class, including the method of processing class-member claims, if required;
>
> (iii) the terms of any proposed award of attorney's fees, including timing of payment; and
>
> (iv) any agreement required to be identified under Rule 23(e)(3); and

(D) the proposal treats class members equitably relative to each other.

Paragraphs (A) and (B) constitute the "procedural" analysis factors, and examine "the conduct of the litigation and of the negotiations leading up to the proposed settlement." Fed. R. Civ. P. 23 advisory committee's note to 2018 amendment. Paragraphs (C) and (D) constitute the "substantive" analysis factors, and examine "[t]he relief that the settlement is expected to provide to class members. . . ."

The Court understands the new Rule 23(e) factors to add to, rather than displace, the *Grinnell* factors. See id. ("The goal of this amendment is not to displace any factor, but rather to focus the court and the lawyers on the core concerns of procedure and substance that should guide the decision whether to approve the proposal."). * * * Accordingly, the Court considers both sets of factors below in its analysis of whether the Court will likely find that the proposed settlement is fair, reasonable, and adequate, and grant final approval.

iii. The Court Will Likely Approve the Proposed Settlement

The Court first considers the Rule 23(e)(2) factors, and then considers additional *Grinnell* factors not otherwise addressed by the Rule 23(e)(2) factors. * * * After consideration of all relevant factors in issuing the January 24, 2019 Order, the Court concluded for the following reasons that based on the record before it, it will likely grant final approval of the proposed settlement.

1. Adequate representation by class representatives and class counsel

* * * In its review of the prior settlement approval, the Second Circuit concluded "that class members of the (b)(2) class were inadequately represented in violation of both Rule 23(a)(4) and the Due Process Clause." *Interchange Fees II*, 827 F.3d at 231. The Second Circuit held that the "class representatives had interests antagonistic to those of some of the class

members they were representing," because the (b)(3) damages class "would want to maximize cash compensation for past harm," while the (b)(2) injunctive class "would want to maximize restraints on network rules to prevent harm in the future," and thus, "[t]he class counsel and class representatives who negotiated and entered into the Settlement Agreement were in the position to trade diminution of (b)(2) relief for increase of (b)(3) relief." *Id.* at 233–34. In addition, the Second Circuit held that the issue of unitary representation was exacerbated "because the members of the worse-off (b)(2) class could not opt out." *Id.* at 234.

The structural defect of unitary representation no longer exists—the (b)(2) and (b)(3) classes now have separate interim Class Counsel. The (b)(2) and (b)(3) classes also now have separate class representatives, i.e., Class Plaintiffs. The named Rule 23(b)(3) Class Plaintiffs seek to represent a finite class that desires and will receive the same type of relief—damages for past harm. Thus, all Rule 23(b)(3) Class Plaintiffs and members of the Rule 23(b)(3) class will have the same incentive to "maximize cash compensation for past harm." *Id.* at 233. Moreover, the Rule 23(b)(3) class will have "opt out" rights. See Fed.R.Civ.P. 23(c)(2)(B)(v).

For these and the following reasons, the Court finds that the bifurcation of the (b)(2) and (b)(3) classes and their Class Counsel sufficiently addresses the Second Circuit's concern and that this factor will likely weigh in favor of a grant of final approval.

[The court discussed the adequacy of the class representatives, the lack of conflicts of interest, and the adequacy of class counsel.]

2. Arms-length negotiations

"A 'presumption of fairness, adequacy, and reasonableness may attach to a class settlement reached in arm's-length negotiations between experienced, capable counsel after meaningful discovery.' " *Wal-Mart Stores, Inc. v. Visa U.S.A., Inc.,* 396 F.3d 96, 116 (2d Cir. 2005). * * *

As set forth above, the parties have engaged in protracted discovery for over a decade. In addition, two highly qualified mediators have assisted both sets of settlement negotiations in this action. * * * Since the separation of the (b)(2) and (b)(3) classes, both mediators have been involved "in the (b)(3) class action to restart mediation for the damage claims only." Over the course of more than a year, the parties have engaged in twelve "mediation sessions," including six day-long sessions. On June 2, 2018, the mediators issued a mediators' proposal to the parties, and on June 5, 2018, received "unanimous consent" from the parties to move forward. "The settlement negotiations were extended, extraordinarily complicated, and contentious. On several occasions the discussions were on the verge of collapsing." Both mediators state that Rule 23(b)(3) class counsel at all times emphasized the need to be independent from any Rule 23(b)(2) class claims resolution, and at no time were (b)(2) Class Counsel involved in the Rule 23(b)(3) class negotiations. Accordingly, the Court finds that this factor will likely weigh in favor of granting final approval.

3.   Adequate relief for the class

In assessing whether the settlement provides adequate relief for the putative class under Rule 23(e)(2)(C), the Court is directed to consider [the rule's four factors].

A.   Costs, risks, and delay of trial and appeal

Under this Rule 23(e)(2) factor, "courts may need to forecast the likely range of possible classwide recoveries and the likelihood of success in obtaining such results." Fed. R. Civ. P. 23 advisory committee's note to 2018 amendment. This assessment implicates several *Grinnell* factors, including: (i) the complexity, expense and likely duration of the litigation; (ii) the risks of establishing liability; (iii) the risks of establishing damages; and (iv) the risks of maintaining the class through the trial. The Court uses these *Grinnell* factors to guide its assessment of whether the Court will likely find that this Rule 23(e)(2) factor will weigh in favor of granting final approval.

(1)   The complexity, expense, and likely duration of the litigation

* * * This case is complex and costly. The present litigation has been active for over a decade, and has involved litigation in both district and appellate courts. The proposed class include millions of putative members, and encompasses alleged injuries from 2004, approximately fourteen years ago. The first phase of MDL discovery alone involved 370 depositions, and multiple expert reports, and according to Class Counsel, "Class Plaintiffs have reviewed and analyzed more than 65 million pages of documents." * * * Because of the complexity and difficulty of the issues in this case, it requires, and would continue to require, costly counsel and experts, and a wealth of time. This subfactor will likely weigh in favor of granting final approval.

(2)   The risks of establishing liability

"This factor does not require the Court to adjudicate the disputed issues or decide unsettled questions; rather, the Court need only assess the risks of litigation against the certainty of recovery under the proposed settlement." *In re Glob. Crossing Sec. & ERISA Litig.*, 225 F.R.D. at 459. * * *

Based on the fact that the parties have briefed motions to dismiss, *Daubert* motions, class certification motions, and motions for summary judgment, Class Counsel has had to consider the requirements for and risks of establishing liability in this case. If the case were to proceed to trial, many of these motions would have to be relitigated, and they present challenges to recovery. Indeed, "[t]hese motions would have to be briefed and argued again, given the significant legal and factual developments, and additional discovery since their original briefing and argument over six years ago." * * *

Further, since the prior motions were briefed and argued, several important legal and factual developments may increase the risk that Class Plaintiffs face in establishing liability. Of particular concern to Class Counsel is the Supreme Court's decision in *Ohio v. American Express Co.*, 138 S.Ct. 2274 (2018). [*American Express* analyzed a credit card network as a single two-sided market, not as two separate markets of cardholders and merchants.] Thus, Class Plaintiffs would need to prove harm in this new, two-sided market, consisting of both merchants and cardholders, and would perhaps face greater difficulty in proving that the procompetitive justifications of interchange fees outweigh their harm.

In addition to the Supreme Court's *American Express* decision, other developments in the payment card markets may increase Class Plaintiffs' legal uncertainty and affect whether Class Plaintiffs will be able to prove ongoing antitrust claims and injuries. * * * For these reasons, the Court finds that this subfactor will likely weigh in favor of granting final approval.

(3) The risks of establishing damages

"[T]he history of antitrust litigation is replete with cases in which antitrust plaintiffs succeeded at trial on liability, but recovered no damages, or only negligible damages, at trial, or on appeal." *Wal-Mart Stores*, 396 F.3d at 118.

As Judge Gleeson noted in his final approval decision, "[e]ven if liability is established, Class Plaintiffs would still face the problems and complexities inherent in proving damages to the jury. . . . These damages-related issues may not be insurmountable, but they are formidable." *Interchange Fees I*, 986 F.Supp.2d at 229. The parties previously submitted competing expert reports on damages, and at a trial, damages would likely be heavily contested. * * *

Based on the opinions of multiple experts, there will be risks associated with establishing damages in this case. The Court finds that this subfactor will likely weigh in favor of granting final approval.

(4) The risks of maintaining the class through the trial

* * * Class Plaintiffs previously moved for class certification over Defendants' objection, but the Court never ruled on the motion, instead approving the Original Settlement Agreement. * * * Although Class Counsel has provided enough information for the Court to determine that it will likely be able to certify the class at the final approval stage for settlement purposes, there is no guarantee that the class could be certified if the parties proceeded with the litigation, and Defendants have indicated

that they are only consenting to class certification for the purposes of settlement. For these reasons, the Court finds that this subfactor will likely weigh in favor of granting final approval.

B. Effectiveness of distributing relief to the class

This factor requires courts to look at "the method of processing class-member claims." Fed. R. Civ. P. 23(e)(2)(C)(ii). "A claims processing method should deter or defeat unjustified claims, but the court should be alert to whether the claims process is unduly demanding." Fed. R. Civ. P. 23 advisory committee's note to 2018 amendment. The method used in the present action is set forth primarily in the Plan of Administration and Distribution. * * *

Class Counsel, who are experienced and competent in complex class actions, prepared the Plan of Administration and Distribution. Under its terms, the Class Administrator will estimate the interchange fees paid by each claimant during the class period, and each claimant will receive a *pro rata* share of the settlement fund based on its interchange fees paid. Claimants will have the opportunity to "contest the accuracy of the statement or estimates" made by the Class Administrator. If the Court grants final approval, and once claims are estimated, the Class Administrator will disseminate a claim form. According to Class Counsel, the majority of the claim form can be "pre-populated" with data provided by Visa and potentially other Defendants. Once a claim form is received, the Class Administrator will commence its audit, and "[c]laimants whose claims are denied, or who disagree with the final calculation of their claims, may challenge such denials or final calculations in writing, together with supporting documentation, mailed or emailed to the Class Administrator within thirty days after receipt of the notice of the denial or final calculation. . . ." A website containing relevant documents and forms in multiple languages, and telephone support will be available to "obtain information and request documents related to the claims process."

The Court finds that, at this stage, the Plan of Administration and Distribution appears to be an effective form of relief distribution, and that this factor will likely weigh in favor of granting final approval.

C. The terms of any proposed award of attorneys' fees

Class Counsel "intend to apply for an Attorneys' Fee Award in a reasonable amount not to exceed ten percent (10%) of the Total Cash Consideration and for Expense Awards comprising all reasonable expenses and costs incurred not to exceed $40 million." * * *

In cases with large settlement awards, courts have noted that smaller percentage awards of attorneys' fees are reasonable. *See, e.g., Wal-Mart Stores*, 396 F.3d at 106 (upholding a district court's award of $220,290,160.44, which amounted to 6.5 percent of a $3.05 billion settlement fund, or a 3.5 multiplier of the lodestar amount, and noting that "the sheer size of the instant fund makes a smaller percentage appropriate").

The proposal by Class Counsel to seek up to ten percent of any settlement is comparable to the percentage of attorneys' fees previously awarded by Judge Gleeson in this action. The Court is aware that Rule 23(b)(3) Class Counsel have expended enormous time and effort in litigating this action and should be rewarded for those efforts.

Accordingly, the Court finds that this subfactor does not weigh against preliminary approval. The Court will engage in a full analysis at the final approval stage or thereafter, taking into consideration the "mega-case" nature of the suit, as well as the six *Goldberger* factors [for evaluating attorneys' fees].

D. Release from liability

"The law is well established in this Circuit and others that class action releases may include claims not presented and even those which could not have been presented as long as the released conduct arises out of the 'identical factual predicate' as the settled conduct." *Wal-Mart Stores*, 396 F.3d at 107 * * * Courts have denied preliminary approval where releases from liability are deemed to be overly broad.

In vacating the prior settlement approval, the Second Circuit expressed concern over the Original Settlement Agreement's broad release provisions, noting that Class Plaintiffs' authority to " 'release claims that were or could have been pled in exchange for settlement relief . . . 'is limited by the "identical factual predicate" and "adequacy of representation" doctrines.' " *Interchange Fees II*, 827 F.3d at 236–37. * * *

[The court proceeded to examine, in detail, the releases in the Original Settlement Agreement and the release in the Superseding Settlement Agreement.]

Having clarified the parties' intent with regard to the language in the Release Provision, the Court is satisfied that the terms of the release comport with the Second Circuit's standards. To ensure that putative class members understand what rights they are releasing, the parties have included language in the Class Notices to clarify the scope of the Release Provision and to clarify that it comports with the identical factual predicate test. [Therefore, the Court will likely find that the Superseding Settlement Agreement is fair, reasonable, and adequate at the final approval stage.]

4. Equitable treatment of class members relative to one another

Consideration under this Rule 23(e)(2) factor "could include whether the apportionment of relief among class members takes appropriate account of differences among their claims, and whether the scope of the release may affect class members in different ways that bear on the apportionment of relief." Fed. R. Civ. P. 23 advisory committee's note to 2018 amendment.

For the reasons set forth * * * the Court finds that the *pro rata* distribution scheme is sufficiently equitable. Further, the scope of the release applies uniformly to putative class members, and does not appear to affect the apportionment of the relief to class members, apart from securing the opportunity to participate in the (b)(2) action. Accordingly, the Court finds that this factor will likely weigh in favor of granting final approval.

> 5.   The ability of Defendants to withstand a greater judgment

Undoubtedly, Defendants can withstand a greater judgment. Defendants have agreed to pay a maximum settlement award of $6.26 billion. Although the agreed upon payment is objectively a large sum of money, it is less so when viewed in perspective. [The court noted the extraordinarily large amounts of money involved in interchange fees. Although the court found this factor weighed against approval, the court stated that "it does not necessarily preclude a finding that the settlement is fair."]

> 6.   The range of reasonableness of the settlement in light of the best possible recovery and all the attendant risks of litigation

* * * The monetary settlement award could be as much as $6.26 billion, but will be no less than approximately $5.56 billion after the opt-out reductions, which the parties represent is "the largest ever class settlement fund in an antitrust action." A large settlement figure, however, does not mandate a finding that the award falls within a range of reasonableness. * * *

The Court looks to information in the record to estimate what the best possible recovery might be in this case. Assuming Class Plaintiffs can establish liability and recover damages, based on the expert reports exchanged in 2009 and 2010, the parties presented competing figures for what the best possible recovery would be. From 2004 to 2008 alone, for example, Class Plaintiffs' claim that they can attribute over $100 billion in damages to Defendants' unlawful conduct. For the same period, Defendants contend that they would be responsible for no more than $661 million in damages. When analyzing the terms of the Original Settlement Agreement, Judge Gleeson found that the figure agreed to, $7.25 billion, "represent[ed] approximately 2.5% of total interchange fees paid by class members during the class period, and thus 2.5% of the largest possible estimate of actual damage to merchants." Interchange Fees I, 986 F.Supp.2d at 229. Despite the $7.25 billion figure, objectors argued that the amount represented "only a few months of interchange fee collections" when divided among the millions of merchants that could claim damages. The same is true of the settlement currently before the Court.

However, "the fact that a proposed settlement may only amount to a fraction of the potential recovery does not, in and of itself, mean that the proposed settlement is grossly inadequate and should be disapproved." Grinnell, 495 F.2d at 455. "There is no reason, at least in theory, why a satisfactory settlement could not amount to a hundredth or even a thousandth part of a single percent of the potential recovery." Id. at 455 n.2.

[Taking into account the size of the recovery, the risks of litigation, and the fact that the class members had already secured several changes to Visa's and Mastercard's policies, the court concluded that the $6.5 billion settlement figure fell within a range of reasonableness.]

In sum, for the foregoing reasons, the Court finds that under the Rule 23(e)(2) and the *Grinnell* factors, preliminary approval of the settlement is warranted because the Court will likely find the Superseding Settlement Agreement to be fair, reasonable, and adequate at the final approval stage.

b.   Certification of settlement class

In 2009, the parties submitted motions to the Court on the issue of class certification. On November 19, 2009, Judge Orenstein [the Magistrate Judge assigned to these matters] heard oral argument on the motions, but reserved making a recommendation at that time. After the parties informed the Court of their intent to settle the case, the Court deemed the class certification motions withdrawn without prejudice. * * *

"The ultimate decision to certify the class for purposes of settlement cannot be made until the hearing on final approval of the proposed settlement." Fed. R. Civ. P. 23 advisory committee's note to 2018 amendment. When deciding whether to grant preliminary approval, district courts must determine whether "giving notice is justified by the parties' showing that the court *will likely be able to* . . . certify the class for purposes of judgment on the proposal." Fed. R. Civ. P. 23(e)(1)(B)(ii) (emphasis added). The Court therefore looks to the factors for class certification to make this determination. [Based on the record, the court concluded that certification of the proposed class was likely at the final approval stage.]

c.   Appointment of Class Counsel

When a district court certifies a class, it must appoint class counsel. [The court found that Interim Class Counsel had fairly and adequately represented the class, and therefore appointed them as Class Counsel under Rule 23(g).]

d.   Notice Plan and Plan of Allocation and Distribution

Once a court has determined that "giving notice is justified by the parties' showing that the court will likely be able to" approve the proposed settlement and certify the class, the court "must direct notice in a reasonable manner to all class members who would be bound by the proposal. . . ." Fed. R. Civ. P. 23(e)(1)(B)(i–ii). "For any class certified under Rule 23(b)(3)—or upon ordering notice under Rule 23(e)(1) to a class proposed to be certified for purposes of settlement under Rule 23(b)(3)— the court must direct to class members the best notice that is practicable under the circumstances." Fed. R. Civ. P. 23(c)(2)(B). * * *

Both the Publication Notice and the Long Form Notice satisfy each of the Rule 23(c)(2)(B) requirements and adequately notify class members of the proposed settlement. The Publication Notice describes basic information in plain, clear terms, including the class claims, the class definition, potential attorneys' fees and expense awards, the date and location of the final approval fairness hearing, and merchant rights including opt-out and objection rights. The Long Form Notice includes frequently asked questions and the full text of the release. The Court therefore finds the Class Notices to be sufficient and reasonable.

The Court also finds reasonable the manner in which the notices will be provided. The "Long Form Notice will be sent via First Class mail," and "an Email Notice will also be sent" to available email addresses * * * For the foregoing reasons the Court found the Notice Plan and proposed Class Notices to be reasonable and constitute "the best notice that is practicable under the circumstances." *See* Fed. R. Civ. P. 23(c)(2)(B).

e.   Final approval procedure

The Court has set forth a schedule with deadlines for the mailing and publication of the Class Notices and the notice of exclusion, exclusion and opt out requests, submission of written statements of objection, submission of notices of intention to appear at the final approval hearing, submission of motions for class settlement final approval, filing of the Class Administrator report, submission of responses to objections, and the final approval hearing. * * *

III. Conclusion

For the foregoing reasons, on January 24, 2019, the Court preliminarily approved the Superseding Settlement Agreement and preliminarily granted class certification for the purposes of settlement, appointed Class Counsel and the Class Administrator, and approved the proposed Notice Plan, Class Notices, and Plan of Administration and Distribution.

NOTES AND QUESTIONS

1.   Ten months after the decision above in the *Interchange Fee* litigation, the court held a final fairness hearing. After hearing objectors' arguments, including objections that the compensation was inadequate and that the releases were too broad, the court certified the settlement class and approved the settlement. In approving the final settlement agreement, the court

reviewed an additional *Grinnell* factor—the reaction of the class to the settlement. The court received 675 exclusion requests and 176 objections— numbers that the court noted were dramatically fewer than were received in 2013 in response to the original settlement agreement. Although a number of prominent retailers such as Walmart and Target had opted out, the overall number of opt-outs and objections was small in light of the 16 million notices that were sent to merchants and the 12 million estimated class members.

2.   As the court notes, prior to the 2018 amendments to Rule 23, Courts of Appeals had developed their own lists of factors for evaluating class settlements. See, e.g., Girsh v. Jepson, 521 F.2d 153, 157 (3d Cir. 1975); City of Detroit v. Grinnell Corp., 495 F.2d 448, 463 (2d Cir. 1974). Courts within these circuits regularly reviewed settlements by running through "the *Girsh* factors," "the *Grinnell* factors," and so on. In *Interchange Fee*, the court lists the *Grinnell* factors as well as the Rule 23 factors. Of the *Grinnell* factors, how many are not already encompassed in the Rule 23 list of factors? Of those, how useful are they to the analysis? As you think about how courts ought to evaluate proposed class settlements, are there any important factors that are missing from both lists? Note that even as the *Interchange Fee* court applied the new factors under Rule 23(e), it considered a few of the old *Grinnell* factors as well. Old habits die hard, or perhaps judges continue to find value in the earlier lists of factors, even as they largely embrace the pared-down list in the revised rule.

3.   In terms of the court's role in scrutinizing settlements, a starting point is the attitude judges should take toward them. On the one hand, judges routinely tout the public policy in favor of settlement of complex disputes. See notes 2–3 on p. 528–529, *supra*. On the other hand, judges have become increasingly aware of the risk that class counsel and defendants may propose settlement terms that disserve class members. Consider this argument in favor of a relatively aggressive role for district judges in policing class settlements:

> The interests of defendants and of class action lawyers line up in important ways that do not match the interests of the class members. Both defendants and class counsel prefer to make settlements comprehensive— defendants in order to strengthen protection from liability, and class counsel in order to build fees. Class members, by contrast, might be better off retaining claims that are poorly compensated in the deal. Both defendants and class counsel prefer to settle promptly to reduce litigation costs. Fees may not fully reward class counsel for additional hours spent on litigation, and, more to the point, they do not sufficiently reward the risk plaintiffs' attorneys incur if they fail to take the bird in hand. Class members may benefit by holding out for a better deal, but the lawyers who control the negotiation do not fully internalize that benefit. Both a defendant and class counsel share an interest in making a settlement appear larger to the judge than its true value to class members or its true cost to the defendant, in order to secure judicial approval of the settlement and fee. Finally, class counsel may trade larger attorneys' fees for

smaller class recovery, permitting a defendant to lower its overall settlement cost. These aligned interests explain why some defendants negotiate fees with class counsel. They explain why some class settlements include stunningly broad releases even when large swaths of claimants get little or nothing of value. And they explain why some class settlements include otherwise inexplicable remedies—illusory injunctive relief, predictably unclaimed funds, non-transferable coupons, or off-point cy pres awards—to create the illusion of value for the class.

Defendants, in short, have coopted the power of plaintiff aggregation. They have learned how to buy res judicata on the cheap. Defendants and their lawyers understand that aggregation puts control in the hands of plaintiffs' lawyers rather than plaintiffs, and defendants and their lawyers know that they have something of value to offer these plaintiffs' lawyers in exchange for advantageous settlement terms. In settlement, aggregation disempowers claimants by empowering their lawyers.

Howard M. Erichson, Aggregation as Disempowerment: Red Flags in Class Action Settlements, 92 Notre Dame L. Rev. 859, 863–64 (2016). See also Pearson v. Target Corp., 893 F.3d 980, 982 (7th Cir. 2018) ("Inequitable settlements are an unfortunate recurring bug in our system of class litigation. . . . All too often, class counsel negotiate a settlement with substantial attorneys' fees but meager benefits for the class.").

4. One of the *Grinnell* factors the court weighed was the risk that the plaintiffs could not maintain the class action through trial. The fact that there was "no guarantee that the class could be certified if the parties proceeded with the litigation," the court reasoned, weighed in favor of approving the settlement. Is that right? If the class could not be certified for trial, doesn't that provide a reason to *disapprove* the settlement? Recall *Amchem*, *supra* p. 311, and its requirement that settlement class actions meet the cohesiveness requirements of Rule 23(a) and (b). If the class cannot be certified for trial, the class lacks bargaining leverage because it can only settle, not litigate. Shouldn't that make the court suspicious about whether class counsel have gotten full value for the class? See John C. Coffee, Jr., Class Wars: The Dilemma of the Mass Tort Class Action, 95 Colum. L. Rev. 1343, 1370–73 (1995) (describing the "reverse auction" that results when contending plaintiff counsel compete with each other to make a deal with defendant); Howard M. Erichson, The Problem of Settlement Class Actions, 82 Geo. Wash. L. Rev. 951, 957–61 (2014) (framing the settlement-class-action problem as "selling something that one does not have").

As a possible example of such a reverse auction, consider Reynolds v. Beneficial National Bank, 288 F.3d 277 (7th Cir. 2002), in which there were two class actions. One was a state-court class action in Texas, which was set for trial with a certified class against two defendants. The other was a proposed nationwide class action in federal court in Chicago, which had languished for some time when the lawyer for one of the defendants suggested to the lawyers who filed the federal case that his client might be willing to settle within a certain dollar range. Eventually, the lawyers for the Chicago class reached an agreement with both defendants for a figure in the range first suggested by one of them. The settlement provided class counsel a hefty fee but offered class members only a certificate for a discount on further services from defendants, even though the Texas case seemed likely to produce a large money judgment for the class there, and the federal judge in Chicago enjoined further pursuit of the Texas case as a means of enforcing the settlement. Reversing approval of the settlement, Judge Posner admonished that judges must use "the highest degree of vigilance in scrutinizing proposed settlements" to protect the class from "lawyers for the class who may * * * place their pecuniary self-interest ahead of that of the class." Id. at 279.

5.   Under the Rule 23(e)(2) factor of "equitable treatment of class members relative to one another," the *Interchange Fee* court mentioned that consideration "could include whether the apportionment of relief among class members takes appropriate account of differences among their claims." Differences among claims may include not only factual distinctions but also differences in applicable law. Recall that the *Interchange Fee* litigation included not only federal antitrust claims, but also claims under state law. How should a court evaluate a proposed class settlement if state-law differences are significant? Should a nationwide class settlement strive to treat all class members equally regardless of the law that would apply to their individual claims? Or, on the contrary, should class members receive different settlement amounts depending on the strength of the claims and defenses under state law applicable to each claim? One response is to create subclasses. If each state subclass or group subclass has separate representation, they can attempt to negotiate an overall settlement with varying compensation. The practical problem is that multiplying the parties at the bargaining table, and adding layers of complexity to the compensation scheme, decreases the chance of reaching any settlement.

In Sullivan v. DB Investments, Inc., 667 F.3d 273 (3d Cir. 2011) (en banc), the Third Circuit upheld a nationwide settlement class action despite objections that the deal failed to account for differences in state antitrust law. The suit charged the diamond company DeBeers with price-fixing, and included claims by direct purchasers and indirect purchasers. Under Supreme Court precedent, the indirect purchasers had no claims under federal antitrust law, but some states had adopted legislation permitting indirect purchasers to assert price-fixing claims under state law. The settlement class action provided $22.5 million for the direct purchasers and $272.5 million for the indirect purchasers. Some of the indirect purchasers objected that the settlement should have given more to class members in states that permitted such claims; the settlement's equal treatment of class members whose states denied them such claims, in effect, diluted the settlement recovery for class members whose states permitted the claims. A panel of the court found this argument persuasive, finding that the settlement "wrongly allowed the sovereignty of the states to be subordinated to DeBeers's desire to resolve all indirect purchaser claims simultaneously," 613 F.3d 134, 152, but the full court rejected it en banc, upholding the district court's ruling that variations in state law did not outweigh the commonalities or render the settlement unfair. Had the DeBeers antitrust class action gone to trial, could a court have ignored the difference between states that permitted indirect purchaser claims and those that did not? If a court could not have ignored this difference in adjudication, what is the argument for nonetheless approving the class settlement?

Similarly, the Ninth Circuit ruled in In re Hyundai and Kia Fuel Economy Litig., 926 F.3d 539 (9th Cir. 2019) (en banc), that differences in state law did not preclude certification for purposes of settlement. In doing so, it rejected an earlier panel decision in the same case that held that the district court improperly certified a class for purposes of settlement without first conducting a rigorous choice of law analysis.

6. The Class Action Fairness Act of 2005 includes a number of provisions designed to strengthen fairness review of proposed class settlements. First, 28 U.S.C. § 1712 controls the use of coupon settlements (see *infra* pp. 574–575). Second, 28 U.S.C. § 1713 prohibits settlements that require any class member "to pay sums to class counsel that would result in a net loss to the class member" unless the court makes a written finding that nonmonetary benefits substantially outweigh the monetary loss. This provision was probably prompted by a notorious case, Kamilewicz v. Bank of Boston Corp., 92 F.3d 506 (7th Cir. 1996), in which some class members found that their bank accounts were debited more to pay class counsel's fees than they were credited by the settlement. Third, 28 U.S.C. § 1714 prohibits class settlements that provide "greater sums to some class members than to others solely on the basis that the class members to whom the greater sums are to be paid are located in closer geographic proximity to the court." Finally, 28 U.S.C. § 1715 adds a notification requirement. It requires that certain federal and state government officials be notified of a proposed class settlement at least 90 days before it is approved.

7. When the judge has actively promoted settlement (see *supra* p. 530 note 5), that involvement complicates the settlement approval task. Consider Professor Schuck's comments about the class settlement in the Agent Orange litigation, which resulted in large measure from the active involvement of Judge Weinstein and his special settlement masters:

> The settlement, after all, was not an agreement that the lawyers had negotiated and drafted by themselves and brought to the court for its evaluation and approval. It was in fact Weinstein's own creation in every sense of the word. If he had not contrived the settlement, by all accounts it would not have occurred when and in the form it did; indeed, it might not have occurred at all. His hand (and those of his special masters) appeared in every provision, every detail, of the document. * * *

> Weinstein had also invested an enormous amount of the court's resources in the effort. * * * He had devoted a great deal of his own time and energy to the search for settlement and had placed his

considerable personal and judicial reputation on the line in extracting concessions and accommodations from both sides in the interests of securing an agreement. * * *

Given these firm commitments to a settlement almost entirely of his own construction, it was inconceivable that Judge Weinstein would fail to find the agreement "fair, reasonable, and adequate." In effect, he was acting as judge in what had come to be his own case insofar as the settlement was concerned. As to that issue, at least, he was plainly interested in the outcome. For this reason alone, he should have left the Rule 23(e) evaluation of the settlement to another, more detached judge.

Peter Schuck, Agent Orange on Trial 178–79 (1986).

8.   There are two ways in which a class action settlement may include a "settlement opt-out"—that is, an opportunity for class members to exclude themselves from the settlement. First, a class settlement may provide a second opt-out for class members who failed to opt out initially but do not wish to participate in the settlement. Second, in any Rule 23(b)(3) *settlement class action*, class members have the chance to opt out after the terms of the settlement are known because the class is certified solely for purposes of the settlement.

In a Rule 23(b)(3) class action that has been certified for litigation and then reaches a settlement, the parties may include in their settlement a provision permitting class members to opt out of the settlement. This second opt-out (remember that class members in a Rule 23(b)(3) class action would have had an initial opportunity to opt out when the class was certified) may result from the parties' negotiations or it may be driven by the court. Indeed, Rule 23 was amended in 2003 to provide that "the court may refuse to approve a settlement unless it affords a new opportunity to request exclusion to individual class members who had an earlier opportunity to request exclusion but did not do so." Fed.R.Civ.P. 23(e)(4). For an example of a court requiring a second opt-out, see Dare v. Knox County, 457 F.Supp.2d 52 (D.Me. 2006). In theory, the second opt-out appears to be an appealing way to move forward with a class settlement while providing a safety valve to permit exit by class members who feel the settlement treats them unfairly. In practice, however, courts and lawyers have not embraced the second opt-out and its use remains uncommon.

Much more commonly, class members may exclude themselves from settlement class actions. By definition, a settlement class action (discussed at p. 310 *supra*) is certified after a settlement has been negotiated and solely for purposes of that settlement. If it is certified under Rule 23(b)(3), then class members have the right to exclude themselves. By the very nature of a settlement class action, this opt-out right occurs after the settlement is known.

9.   What if a plaintiff files a lawsuit as a class action and reaches an individual settlement with the defendant before the court has decided whether to certify the class? Should judicial approval be required to settle a *putative*

class action? A settlement at that point would bind only the named plaintiff, not the absent class members. Thus, the standard reason for requiring judicial approval—that the settlement would bind absent class members—is missing. Nonetheless, why might it make sense to require judicial approval? Before 2003, it was regularly held that Rule 23(e) also required some court scrutiny of a proposed individual settlement with the class representative before certification had been decided. The 2003 amendments to Rule 23(e), however, made it clear that the requirement of judicial approval applies only to the settlement, voluntary dismissal, or compromise of the "claims, issues, or defenses of a certified class."

10. If defendants can settle with class representatives prior to class certification, does this mean that defendants can "pick off" named plaintiffs with individual settlements as a strategy for getting out of class actions? If all of the class representatives accept a defendant's individual settlement offers, then indeed the class action goes away, although of course it can reappear with a different named plaintiff. But suppose the class representatives do not wish to accept the defendant's offer. Can the defendant pick off the named plaintiffs anyway, by offering to pay the full value of their claims and thereby mooting their lawsuits?

The Supreme Court addressed a version of this question in Genesis Healthcare Corp. v. Symczyk, 569 U.S. 66 (2013). The federal Fair Labor Standards Act (FLSA), 29 U.S.C. § 216(b), authorizes employees to file "collective actions" on behalf of themselves and other employees similarly situated (essentially, opt-in class actions). Laura Symczyk filed such a collective action against Genesis, alleging that the company violated the FLSA by deducting pay for meal breaks even when employees worked during the breaks. Genesis made a Rule 68 offer of judgment—a formal settlement offer— of $7,500 to satisfy the full amount of Symczyk's individual claim for unpaid wages. When she did not accept the offer, Genesis moved to dismiss her lawsuit as moot. The Third Circuit accepted the plaintiff's argument that the defendant should not be permitted to short-circuit the collective action process by picking off named plaintiffs. 656 F.3d 189 (3d Cir. 2011). The Supreme Court reversed by a 5–4 vote. The Court declined to reach the issue of whether an unaccepted offer that would fully satisfy a plaintiff's claim renders the claim moot. Rather, the Court assumed based on the proceedings below that the offer had mooted Symczyk's individual claim, and analyzed whether the collective action could proceed. The Court concluded that "the mere presence of collective-action allegations in the complaint cannot save the suit from mootness once the individual claim is satisfied." 569 U.S. at 73.

Three years later, however, in Campbell-Ewald Co. v. Gomez, 577 U.S. 153 (2016), the Supreme Court held that a Rule 23 class action was not mooted by the defendant's unaccepted pre-class-certification Rule 68 offer of judgment to the putative class representative for the full amount of damages. While the Court left the door slightly ajar by declining to answer whether a defendant could moot a class action by placing full payment in escrow for the putative class representative, *Campbell-Ewald* largely seems to have foreclosed the pick-off strategy for Rule 23 class actions.

11. Settlements often depend on claims projections. What if those projections are wrong? In In re Diet Drugs Products Liability Litig., 385 F.3d 386 (3d Cir. 2004), widely known as the "fen-phen" litigation, the class settlement provided a schedule for payments to class members and obligated the defendant to fund payments up to $3.75 billion, an amount the court was assured would suffice. After the settlement was approved, the resulting trust was inundated with far more claims than the experts had anticipated. The parties negotiated an amendment to the class settlement agreement permitting class members whose claims were unpaid due to lack of funds to opt out and sue the defendant, but not to seek punitive damages. The amendment provided that the defendant could prevent opt-outs by choosing to pay the amounts specified in the settlement agreement even though the trust lacked sufficient funds to pay them. Objectors challenged the amendment on the ground that it took away the right to punitive damages while giving the class nothing in return. The court affirmed approval of the amended plan, rejecting arguments that the original settlement approval was flawed because of the mistake about adequacy of funding.

2. DISTRIBUTING SETTLEMENT FUNDS

Unlike settlements of non-class litigation in which distribution of settlement funds may be relatively straightforward, class settlements may involve considerable work after the settlement is approved and implemented. Class settlements involving individualized monetary relief often require a process for inviting and evaluating claims. The settlement should provide specifics on how distribution of funds will be achieved, since the court should ensure that the criteria and procedures are fair to class members. Although some proof may be required for claims, it need not be of the quality or quantity that might be required in a contested trial. For general discussion, see Manual for Complex Litigation (4th) § 21.66 (2004).

Ideally, settlement funds or benefits can be distributed to class members directly, without the need for recipients to jump over any hurdles. Defendants or others often possess information about their consumers, members, investors, or employees. If class members can be identified using information available to defendants or class counsel, and if settlement amounts need not vary individually based on presently unavailable information, then a settlement should employ a direct payment process rather than a claims-made process. See, e.g., In re Elec. Books Antitrust Litig., 2013 WL 7045299 (S.D.N.Y. Dec. 9, 2013) (credits for class members were added to their Amazon accounts without the need for recipients to file claims).

Often, however, a claims process is needed. In general, class members who do not satisfy claims procedures are barred from future litigation even though they do not share in the proceeds of the settlement. Kyriazi v. Western Electric Co., 647 F.2d 388 (3d Cir. 1981).

There may be disputes on the application of criteria for eligibility. For example, the settlement for litigation involving fen-phen (see In re Diet Drugs, *supra* p. 348) required medical certification of claims. The trust administering the settlement fund later sued a doctor, asserting that she had signed off on claims for people who did not qualify. The doctor had allegedly reviewed more than 10,000 echocardiograms at the behest of plaintiff law firms to determine whether claimants qualified for payment. Supposedly she found that some 40 to 70 percent of claimants had serious heart damage, and received several million dollars for her efforts. The judge overseeing the settlement described this doctor's process as "a mass production operation that would have been the envy of Henry Ford." Other doctors supposedly had fee arrangements under which they were paid a premium for cases in which they found heart disease. The judge ordered an audit of all claims submitted to the trust. See Reed Abelson & Jonathan Glater, Tough Questions are Raised on Fen-Phen Compensation, N.Y. Times, Oct. 7, 2003, at C1.

Claims rates in class actions are notoriously low. Perhaps this is inevitable in consumer class actions where individual recoveries are small. But what if a low claims rate is not merely an unavoidable incident of small-claim aggregation, but rather an intentional strategy to reduce the number of payouts? In Pearson v. NBTY, 772 F.3d 778 (7th Cir. 2014), the Seventh Circuit reversed a district court's approval of a settlement class action concerning false labeling of glucosamine pills. The district court had accepted the parties' valuation of the settlement at $20.2 million, but less than one percent of the class members actually filed claims, for a total payout to the class of $865,284. The Seventh Circuit, in a scathing opinion by Judge Posner, described the problems with the claims process (id. at 783):

> Another of the links is captioned "Claim Form," and if you clicked on that you'd see a "Glucosamine Settlement Claim Form." The form required the claimant to list cash register receipts or other documentation indicating the date and place at which he or she had bought the product. The form advised the claimant that "The Claims Administrator and the Parties have the right to audit all claims for completeness, waste, fraud, and abuse. Filing a false claim may violate certain criminal or civil laws." Further, the claimant was—in boldface—required to "certify under penalty of perjury that the foregoing is true and correct to the best of my knowledge."

> One would have thought, given the low ceiling on the amount of money that a member of the class could claim, that a sworn statement would be sufficient documentation, without requiring

receipts or other business records likely to have been discarded. The requirement of needlessly elaborate documentation, the threats of criminal prosecution, and the fact that a claimant might feel obliged to wade through the five other documents accessible from the opening screen of the website, help to explain why so few recipients of the postcard notice bothered to submit a claim. It's hard to resist the inference that Rexall was trying to minimize the number of claims that class members would file, in order to minimize the cost of the settlement to it. Class counsel also benefited from minimization of the claims, because the fewer the claims, the more money Rexall would be willing to give class counsel to induce settlement. Rexall has no reason to care about the allocation of its cost of settlement between class counsel and class members; all it cares about as a rational maximizer of its net worth is the bottom line—how much the settlement is likely to cost it. When the parties to a class action expect that the reasonableness of the attorneys' fees allowed to class counsel will be judged against the potential rather than actual or at least reasonably foreseeable benefits to the class, class counsel lack any incentive to push back against the defendant's creating a burdensome claims process in order to minimize the number of claims.

Judge Posner observed that class action notice was sent by postcard to 4.72 million consumers "whom Rexall knew (through pharmacy loyalty programs and the like) to have bought its glucosamine pills," and that instead of or in addition to the claims-form process, "Rexall could have mailed $3 checks to all 4.72 million postcard recipients." Id. at 784.

3. NON-MONETARY RELIEF IN CLASS SETTLEMENTS

Injunctive Relief

Many class actions are brought for the purpose of achieving institutional reform or other types of injunctive relief. We saw some of these cases in our exploration of Rule 23(b)(2) class actions, *supra* p. 237. When parties negotiate resolutions of injunctive relief class actions, the settlement may take the form of a consent decree in which a defendant agrees to do certain things or refrain from doing certain things, and the court retains power to enforce the decree. For example, the settlement of an employment discrimination class action might require the employer to alter certain hiring or promotion practices, and the settlement of a prison reform class action might require the department of corrections to change certain prison conditions or policies.

Coupon Settlements

Settling by providing coupons or credits that can be used to purchase more products or services may be considerably more attractive to defendants than paying out large sums of money. Coupon settlements, however, have attracted criticism and came to be seen as emblematic of broader problems with class action litigation. See Edward F. Sherman, Consumer Class Actions: Who are the Real Winners?, 56 Maine L. Rev. 223 (2004) (calling coupon settlements "[o]ne of the most criticized aspects of consumer class actions").

Responding to such criticism, Congress included a provision in the Class Action Fairness Act of 2005, 28 U.S.C. § 1712, to reduce the risk of collusive or inadequate coupon settlements in federal court. The section does not define "coupon settlement," which might apply to a variety of forms of nonmonetary compensation. Robert Klonoff and Mark Herrmann describe the problems that drove Congress to act:

> The legislative history reveals congressional concern about settlements in which class members merely receive coupons (e.g., good for ten dollars off the purchase of another product sold by the defendant) while class counsel receive enormous attorneys' fees. Examples of unfair coupon settlements identified in the legislative history include:
>
> > (1) Litigation in which Microsoft settled antitrust cases by agreeing to give consumers a $5 to $10 voucher good for future purchases of computer hardware or software. Consumers were required to follow onerous procedures to receive and redeem the vouchers.
> >
> > (2) A case in which Blockbuster was accused of charging excessive late fees. Class members received $1 discount coupons for future video rentals, while class counsel divided up $9.25 million in fees.
> >
> > (3) Cases involving faulty pipes, in which homeowners received 8% off their purchase of new plumbing, but class counsel in Alabama and Tennessee received $38.4 million and $45 million in fees, respectively.

Robert Klonoff & Mark Herrmann, The Class Action Fairness Act: An Ill-Conceived Approach to Class Settlements, 80 Tulane L. Rev. 1695, 1698–99 (2006) (citing S. Rep. No. 109–14 (2005), at 15–19).

Section 1712 regulates attorneys' fee awards in class actions with coupon settlements. If a settlement includes coupons, "the portion of any attorney's fee award to class counsel that is attributable to the award of the coupons shall be based on the value to class members of the coupons that are redeemed." 28 U.S.C. § 1712(a). There is an enormous difference between valuing a settlement based on the real value of coupons actually claimed and redeemed, as opposed to the face value of the coupon settlement. For example, suppose a proposed settlement would provide one million class members with coupons for a $100 discount off the defendant's products or services. The face value of the settlement is $100 million. For purposes of settlement approval and class counsel fees, the lawyers would like the court to see it as a $100 million settlement. But in all likelihood, only a small percent of the class members would claim their coupons, and of those, some would never actually use the coupons. Many of the class members may have no interest in purchasing more of the defendant's products or services. Thus, rather than one million coupons, the number of coupons actually redeemed may be fewer than fifty thousand. Moreover, the actual value of each coupon likely is much lower than $100, at least if the discount applies to the sticker price of the products or services, rather than to the lowest price actually available.

Section 1712 also addresses judicial scrutiny of coupon settlements. It provides that a court may approve a settlement including coupons only after a hearing and based on a written finding that the settlement is "fair, reasonable, and adequate for class members." 28 U.S.C. § 1712(e).

As with so many aspects of class settlements, the details matter. With settlements that offer a credit or discount for goods and services (regardless of whether the word *coupon* is used), worthwhile questions include whether the benefit can be transferred, whether it can be stacked on top of existing credits and discounts, and whether its use is restricted by date, purpose, or otherwise. See Howard M. Erichson, Aggregation as Disempowerment: Red Flags in Class Action Settlements, 92 Notre Dame L. Rev. 859, 878–79 (2016) ("At their best, coupons or credits present opportunities for non-zero-sum gains in settlement by providing value to class members greater than the cost to defendants. The best coupons or credits are transferable, stackable, and unrestricted. In practice, however, coupon settlements sometimes provide little benefit to class members.").

Creative approaches can enhance the real value of coupon settlements. If coupons can be transferred and aggregated, then a secondary market in coupons becomes possible. Not only does this increase the likelihood that coupons will be claimed and redeemed, it also has the potential to provide the court with information about the market value of the coupons. If class counsel fees are paid in coupons rather than cash, as some critics have suggested, then lawyers have a stronger incentive to ensure that the coupons have real value. See Christopher Leslie, A Market-Based Approach to Coupon Settlements, 49 UCLA L. Rev. 991 (2002). In an antitrust class action against Sotheby's and Christie's auction houses, class counsel agreed to receive fees that were 80 percent cash and 20 percent coupons, the same cash-coupons ratio as class members received in the settlement. In re Auction Houses Antitrust Litig., 2001 WL 170792 *17 (S.D.N.Y. Feb. 22, 2001).

The Cy Pres Doctrine and Fluid Recovery

Providing monetary compensation directly to class members is not always feasible. In some cases, class members cannot be individually identified or located. In others, the individual amounts are so small as to be dwarfed by the administrative expense of getting the money to each class member. In such situations, courts turn to the cy pres doctrine and fluid recovery.

A classic example of a class action fluid recovery is Daar v. Yellow Cab Co., 433 P.2d 732 (Cal. 1967). It was a class action brought by a taxicab customer against a taxicab company, claiming the company had overcharged customers for four years. Identifying and locating all the customers who had used that particular company's taxicabs, however, would have been impossible. After the California Supreme Court upheld the class action and the propriety of reaching a lump sum damages amount, the parties reached a settlement with a substantial cy pres component. Of the $1.4 million settlement, $950,000 was to be provided by requiring the company to lower its fares for a future period. See 4 Newberg on Class Actions § 11:20 n. 13 (4th ed. 2009). Obviously, the *Daar* settlement represented an imperfect remedy, both overinclusive and underinclusive. Some beneficiaries of the settlement were never in fact overcharged, and some victims of the overcharging would never receive the benefit of the settlement. But under the circumstances, wasn't it the best remedy that could be achieved?

What should happen with class action settlement funds that remain unclaimed? Consider the following case's treatment of this important application of the cy pres doctrine.

DENNIS V. KELLOGG CO.

United States Court of Appeals, Ninth Circuit, 2012.
697 F.3d 858.

Before TROTT and THOMAS, CIRCUIT JUDGES, and DUFFY, DISTRICT JUDGE sitting by designation.

TROTT, CIRCUIT JUDGE.

Most cases in our judicial system never make it to trial. Litigants often find it advantageous to secure a resolution more quickly by settling the case and negotiating a result the parties can tolerate, even though neither side can call it a total win. Normally, that is the end of the story, and the parties walk away—not entirely happy, but not entirely unhappy either.

In a class action, however, any settlement must be approved by the court to ensure that class counsel and the named plaintiffs do not place their own interests above those of the absent class members. In this false advertising case, we confront a class action settlement, negotiated prior to class certification, that includes *cy pres* distributions of money and food to unidentified charities. It also includes $2 million in attorneys' fees while offering class members a sum of (at most) $15.

After carefully reviewing the class settlement, we conclude that it must be set aside. The district court did not apply the correct legal standards governing *cy pres* distributions and thus abused its discretion in approving the settlement. The settlement neither identifies the ultimate recipients of the product and cash *cy pres* awards nor sets forth any limiting restriction on those recipients, other than characterizing them as charities that feed the indigent. To the extent that we can meaningfully review such distributions where the parties fail to identify the recipients, we hold that both *cy pres* portions of the settlement are not sufficiently related to the plaintiff class or to the class's underlying false advertising claims. Moreover, the $5.5 million valuation the parties attach to the product *cy pres* distribution is, at best, questionable. We therefore reverse the district court's approval of the settlement, vacate the judgment and the award of attorneys' fees, and remand for further proceedings consistent with this opinion.

I. BACKGROUND

[In January 2008, Kellogg Co. began a marketing campaign that claimed that its Frosted Mini-Wheats cereal was scientifically proven to improve children's cognitive functions for several hours after breakfast. Plaintiff Harry Dennis filed a class action in the Southern District of California, alleging that the marketing claims were false. Dennis's lawyer joined forces with a lawyer pursuing a similar claim in Ohio. After settlement discussions and mediation with Kellogg, the lawyers and Kellogg reached agreement in principle to settle the claims on a nationwide class action basis. The plaintiffs filed a joint amended class action complaint, asserting claims under California's Unfair Competition Law (UCL) and California's Consumer Legal Remedies Act (CLRA), claims under similar laws of other states, and unjust enrichment. The parties continued to work out settlement details and ultimately agreed to the following terms:]

- Kellogg agreed to establish a $2.75 million settlement fund for distribution to class members on a claims-made basis. Class members submitting claims would receive $5 per box of cereal purchased, up to a maximum of $15. Any remaining funds would not revert to Kellogg, but would instead be donated to unidentified "charities chosen by the parties and approved by the Court pursuant to the *cy pres* doctrine. . . . If the total amount of eligible claims exceeds the Settlement Fund, then each claim's award shall be proportionately reduced."

- Kellogg agreed to distribute, also pursuant to the cy pres doctrine, $5.5 million "worth" of specific Kellogg food items to charities that feed the indigent. The settlement does not specify the recipient charities, nor does it indicate how this

$5.5 million in food will be valued—at cost, wholesale, retail, or by some other measure.

- Kellogg agreed that for three years, it would "refrain from using in its advertising and on its labeling for the Product any assertion to the effect that 'eating a bowl of Kellogg's® Frosted Mini-Wheats cereal for breakfast is clinically shown to improve attentiveness by nearly 20%.' " Kellogg would still be allowed to claim that "[c]linical studies have shown that kids who eat a filling breakfast like Frosted Mini-Wheats have an 11% better attentiveness in school than kids who skip breakfast."

- Kellogg agreed to pay class counsel's attorneys' fees and costs "not to exceed a total of $2 million." Class counsel eventually requested the full $2 million in fees and costs.

- The Plaintiffs agreed to release all claims arising out of the challenged advertising. Together with notice and administrative costs approximated at $391,500, the parties value the settlement, or the constructive common fund, at $10,641,500.

The claims period has now closed. Although there is nothing in the record to indicate how many class members submitted claims, class counsel represented at oral argument that the claims submitted total approximately $800,000.

On the Plaintiffs' motion, the district court certified the class—defined as "[a]ll persons or entities in the United States who purchased the Product" during the settlement class period—granted preliminary approval of the settlement, and approved the proposed class notice. Because Kellogg sells its products to wholesalers, not directly to consumers, there was no way to identify each member of the class. Therefore, the class notice was published in *Parents* magazine and other "targeted sources based on market research about consumers who purchased the products," including 375 websites.

Two class members objected to the settlement: Stephanie Berg and Omar Rivero (Objectors). As relevant to this appeal, the Objectors argued that the settlement's use of *cy pres* relief was improper because "the only relationship between this lawsuit and feeding the indigent is that they both involve food in some way." They argued also that the *cy pres* distributions would benefit class counsel and Kellogg, but not the class members, because class members "have no idea how their funds might be used or in whose hands their monies will end up." Finally, the Objectors argued that the attorneys' fees—which represented approximately 19% of a common fund allegedly worth over $10.64 million—were excessive.

[The district court approved both the settlement and the requested attorneys' fees. The objectors appealed.]

II. STANDARD OF REVIEW

The settlement of a class action must be fair, adequate, and reasonable. Fed. R. Civ. P. 23(e)(2). "We review a district court's approval of a proposed class action settlement, including a proposed *cy pres* settlement distribution, for abuse of discretion. A court abuses its discretion when it fails to apply the correct legal standard or bases its decision on unreasonable findings of fact."

Appellate review of a settlement agreement is generally "extremely limited." But where, as here, class counsel negotiates a settlement agreement before the class is even certified, courts "must be particularly vigilant not only for explicit collusion, but also for more subtle signs that class counsel have allowed pursuit of their own self-interests and that of certain class members to infect the negotiations." In such a case, settlement approval "requires a higher standard of fairness" and "a more probing inquiry than may normally be required under Rule 23(e)." * * *

III. DISCUSSION

* * *

Cy pres is shorthand for the old equitable doctrine "cy *près comme possible*"—French for "as near as possible." Although the doctrine originated in the area of wills as a way to effectuate the testator's intent in making charitable gifts, federal courts now frequently apply it in the settlement of class actions " 'where the proof of individual claims would be burdensome or distribution of damages costly.' " Used in lieu of direct distribution of damages to silent class members, this alternative allows for "aggregate calculation of damages, the use of summary claim procedures, and distribution of unclaimed funds to indirectly benefit the entire class." To ensure that the settlement retains some connection to the plaintiff class and the underlying claims, however, a *cy pres* award must qualify as "the next best distribution" to giving the funds directly to class members.

Not just any worthy recipient can qualify as an appropriate *cy pres* beneficiary. To avoid the "many nascent dangers to the fairness of the distribution process," we require that there be "a driving nexus between the plaintiff class and the *cy pres* beneficiaries." A *cy pres* award must be "guided by (1) the objectives of the underlying statute(s) and (2) the interests of the silent class members," and must not benefit a group "too remote from the plaintiff class," Thus, in addition to asking "whether the *class settlement,* taken as a whole, is fair, reasonable, and adequate to all concerned," we must also determine "whether the *distribution* of the approved class settlement complies with our standards governing *cy pres* awards."

A review of our relevant precedent reveals that the settlement here fails to satisfy those standards. * * *

The *cy pres* awards in the settlement here are likewise divorced from the concerns embodied in consumer protection laws such as the UCL and the CLRA. As California courts have stated, "[t]he UCL is designed to preserve fair competition among business competitors and protect the public from nefarious and unscrupulous business practices," and the purpose of the CLRA is similarly "to protect consumers against unfair and deceptive business practices," Cal. Civ. Code § 1760. Although there is no way to identify either the product or the cash *cy pres* beneficiaries from this record, we do know that according to the settlement, any charity to receive a portion of the *cy pres* distributions will be one that feeds the indigent. This noble goal, however, has "little or nothing to do with the purposes of the underlying lawsuit or the class of plaintiffs involved."

At oral argument, Kellogg's counsel frequently asserted that donating food to charities who feed the indigent relates to the underlying class claims because this case is about "the nutritional value of food." With respect, that is simply not true, and saying it repeatedly does not make it so. The complaint nowhere alleged that the cereal was unhealthy or lacked nutritional value. And no law allows a consumer to sue a company for selling cereal that does not improve attentiveness. The gravamen of this lawsuit is that Kellogg *advertised* that its cereal *did* improve attentiveness. Those alleged misrepresentations are what provided the Plaintiffs with a cause of action under the UCL and the CLRA, not the nutritional value of Frosted Mini-Wheats. Thus, appropriate *cy pres* recipients are not charities that feed the needy, but organizations dedicated to protecting consumers from, or redressing injuries caused by, false advertising. On the face of the settlement's language, "charities that provide food for the indigent" may not serve a single person within the plaintiff class of purchasers of Frosted Mini-Wheats.

Our concerns are not placated by the settlement provision that the charities will be identified at a later date and approved by the court—a decision from which the Objectors might again appeal. Our standards of review governing precertification settlement agreements require that we carefully review the entire settlement, paying special attention to "terms of the agreement contain[ing] convincing indications that the incentives favoring pursuit of self-interest rather than the class's interests in fact influenced the outcome of the negotiations." *Cy pres* distributions present a particular danger in this regard. "When selection of *cy pres* beneficiaries is not tethered to the nature of the lawsuit and the interests of the silent class members, the selection process may answer to the whims and self interests of the parties, their counsel, or the court." This record leaves open the distinct possibility that the asserted $5.5 million value of the product *cy pres* award and the remaining cash *cy pres* award will only be of serendipitous value to the class purportedly protected by the settlement. The difficulty here is that, by failing to identify the *cy pres* recipients, the parties have restricted our ability to undertake the searching inquiry that our precedent requires. The *cy pres* problem presented in this case is of the parties' own making, and encouraging multiple costly appeals by punting down the line our review of the settlement agreement is no solution.

On remand, the parties are free to negotiate a new settlement or proceed with litigation. If they again decide to settle, they must correct the additional serious deficiencies we find in this settlement agreement. Not only does the settlement fail to identify the *cy pres* recipients of the unclaimed money and food, but it is unacceptably vague and possibly misleading in other areas as well.

The settlement states only that Kellogg will donate "$5.5 million *worth*" of food. (emphasis added). But the settlement document gives no hint as to how that $5.5 million will be valued. Is it valued at Kellogg's cost? At wholesale value? At retail? The exact answer to this question has important ramifications relating to the accurate valuation of the constructive common fund and thereby the reasonableness of attorneys' fees. Kellogg stated at oral argument and in its briefs to the district court that it will value the food donation at wholesale, but the only legally-enforceable document—the settlement—says nothing of the sort. Additionally, the settlement fails to include any restrictions on how Kellogg accounts for the *cy pres* distributions. Can Kellogg use the value of the distributions as tax deductions because they will go to charity? And given that Kellogg already donates both food and money to charities every year—which is unquestionably an admirable act—will the *cy pres* distributions be in addition to that which Kellogg has already obligated itself to donate, or can Kellogg use previously budgeted funds or surplus production to offset its settlement obligations? Again, the settlement is silent, and we have only Kellogg's statements as to its future intentions. All of this vagueness detracts from our ability to determine the true value of the constructive common fund.

Moreover, Plaintiffs' counsel tells us that settlements like this serve the purposes of "restitutionary disgorgement and deterrence." If the product *cy pres* distribution is form over substance and not worth nearly as much to Kellogg as the settlement claims, then these goals are not served. To the contrary, the settlement is a paper tiger.

This deficiency raises in turn serious issues about the alleged dollar value of the product *cy pres* award, an important number used to measure the appropriateness of attorneys' fees. For example, if the alleged $5.5 million value of the product *cy pres* distribution turns out on close examination to be an illusion and is subtracted from the alleged $10.64 million value of the common fund, the dollar value of the settlement fund plummets to $5.14 million, and the $2 million attorneys' fees award becomes 38.9% of the total, which is clearly excessive under our guidelines. This possibility gives us an additional reason to be vigilant regarding the particulars of this class action settlement: is it all that it appears to be? Are the assigned numbers real, or not? This issue is particularly critical with a *cy pres* product settlement that has a tenuous relationship to the class allegedly damaged by the conduct in question. The issue of the valuation of this aspect of a settlement must be examined with great care to eliminate the possibility that it serves only the "self-interests" of the attorneys and the parties, and not the class, by assigning a dollar number to the fund that is fictitious.

Neither class counsel nor Kellogg offers any credible reason for the mysteries in the current settlement. To approve this settlement despite its opacity would be to abdicate our responsibility to be "particularly vigilant" of pre-certification class action settlements.

For the foregoing reasons, we conclude that the district court did not apply the correct legal standards for *cy pres* distributions as set forth in [our precedents]. Therefore, the approval of the settlement was an abuse of discretion.

We do not have the authority to strike down only the *cy pres* portions of the settlement. "It is the settlement taken as a whole, rather than the individual component parts, that must be examined for overall fairness," and we cannot "delete, modify or substitute certain provisions. The settlement must stand or fall in its entirety." Thus, we reverse the district court's order approving the settlement and dismissing the case, vacate the judgment and award of attorneys' fees, and remand for further proceedings.

NOTES AND QUESTIONS

1. After the Ninth Circuit's decision, Kellogg negotiated a revised settlement. The new settlement increased the cash payment to class members and eliminated the charitable food distribution. It included a cy pres component, but instead of organizations that feed the indigent, the recipients were specified consumer advocacy groups. The district court approved the revised settlement. Dennis v. Kellogg Co., 2013 WL 6055326 (S.D. Cal. Nov. 14, 2013).

2. Why did the district court approve the initial settlement? Was it unreasonable to remedy Kellogg's alleged consumer fraud in part by distributing food to the needy? Does your answer depend on whether you think the purpose of false advertising laws is compensation, as opposed to disgorgement and deterrence?

3. The cy pres remedy in *Dennis* included two parts. One part addressed how to dispose of the remainder of the $2.75 million settlement fund after class members' claims had been paid. This reflects the predominant use of cy pres in class actions—disposal of remaining funds from monetary settlements.

Because claims rates in class actions generally are quite low, a pool of funds often remains after the submitted claims have been satisfied. What should be done with the remainder?

Consider the options for handling funds that remain after a claims process has concluded. The funds could revert to the defendant, on the theory that the defendant has finished compensating every class member who submitted a claim. But wouldn't reversion result in underdeterrence and underenforcement of the law? Courts have treated reversion clauses as red flags. See, e.g., Roes v. SFBSC Management, 944 F.3d 1035, 1059 (9th Cir. 2019) (reversing approval of a proposed class settlement in part because of "concerns regarding the perverse incentives and implicit collusion raised by the reversionary clause"). Alternatively, the funds could escheat to the state as a kind of unclaimed property. But don't the claims belong to the class members rather than the general public? The funds could be allocated in a second distribution to those class members who did submit claims. But wouldn't this give a windfall to certain class members? Finally, there is the cy pres option: the funds could be paid to a charitable organization that serves the same set of interests as those pursued by the class action. Giving the funds to an organization not only ensures that the defendant parts with the money to advance the goals of deterrence and disgorgement, but also—in theory—comes closest to compensating all of the members of the class. That is the general idea behind the use of cy pres for class settlement remainders, but as you see in *Dennis*, the devil is in the details.

The amounts of such remainders can be huge. In a class settlement with Toshiba Corporation involving claims of defective laptop computers, $350 million remained in the settlement fund after payments to class members and class counsel. The money was used to create a foundation to make computers available in low-income school districts. See Hells Angels, American Lawyer, June 2003, at 15.

In addition to using cy pres to address the residue problem, the *Dennis* settlement included an independent cy pres remedy of $5.5 million of food donations to the needy. Why did the parties insert this in a settlement of consumer claims? An optimistic answer might be charitable impulse; a more cynical answer would be that the lawyers bulked up the apparent size of the settlement to support a large fee request.

4. "Cy pres" and "fluid recovery" refer to related concepts in class actions. Professor Redish explains the difference:

> As the term has been most often used, cy pres refers to the designation of a portion of unclaimed damage or settlement funds to a charitable use that is in some way related to the subject of the suit. As employed here, fluid class recovery applies to an effort—either in a class settlement or as part of a class award—to approximate the injured class of consumers through the provision of relief to future consumers. The assumption is that the class of future users will likely substantially overlap with the injured class of past consumers.

Martin Redish et al., Cy Pres Relief and the Pathologies of the Modern Class Action: A Normative and Empirical Analysis, 62 Fla. L. Rev. 617 (2010). Fluid recovery has been used in cases involving antitrust price-fixing or consumer overpayments, such as Daar v. Yellow Cab (discussed *supra* p. 576). Could fluid recovery have been used in a case like *Dennis*?

5.   California Code Civ. Proc. § 384 contains explicit cy pres authority. It is designed "to ensure that the unpaid cash residue and unclaimed or abandoned funds in class action litigation are distributed, to the fullest extent possible, in a manner designed either to further the purposes of the underlying class action or causes of action, or to promote justice for all Californians." Accordingly, the court is to determine the total amount that would be paid to all class members and set a date for a report on how much was actually paid to the class members. On receiving that report, "the court shall amend the judgment to direct the defendant to pay the sum of the unpaid residue * * * to nonprofit organizations or foundations to support projects that will benefit the class or similarly situated persons, or that promote the law consistent with the objectives and purposes of the underlying cause of action, to child advocacy groups, or to nonprofit organizations providing civil legal services to the indigent."

6.   Courts have faced criticism over their use of the cy pres doctrine to distribute funds to charitable organizations. A New York Times article commented that "Judges all over the country have gotten into the business of doling out leftover class-action settlement money, sometimes to organizations only tangentially related to the subject of the lawsuit. Hospitals are popular, as are law schools and legal aid societies." Adam Liptak, Doling Out Other People's Money, N.Y. Times, Nov. 26, 2007. The article described a troubling phenomenon—charities lobbying judges to try to obtain money from class actions. It quoted a former federal judge who said, "It made me more than a little uncomfortable that groups would solicit me for consideration as recipients of cy pres awards," and that he knew that other judges felt similarly uneasy about the system.

7.   The ALI's Principles of the Law of Aggregate Litigation would not prohibit cy pres settlements, but they suggest a cautious approach. First, the ALI emphasizes that cy pres remedies are appropriate only if direct compensation to class members is not feasible: "If individual class members can be identified through reasonable effort, and the distributions are sufficiently large to make individual distributions economically viable, settlement proceeds should be distributed directly to individual class members." American Law Inst., Principles of the Law of Aggregate Litigation § 3.07(a) (2010). It takes a similar approach to cy pres distributions of funds that remain from monetary settlements: "If the settlement involves individual distributions to class members and funds remain after distributions (because some class members could not be identified or chose not to participate), the settlement should presumptively provide for further distributions to participating class members unless the amounts involved are too small to make individual distributions economically viable or other specific reasons

exist that would make such further distributions impossible or unfair." Id. at § 3.07(b). If individual distributions are not viable, either for the entire settlement or for the unclaimed funds, a cy pres approach may be used to provide the funds to "a recipient whose interests reasonably approximate those being pursued by the class." Id. § 3.07(c). Only if no such recipient can be identified may the court approve "a recipient that does not reasonably approximate the interests being pursued by the class." Id. Does the ALI approach strike the right balance?

8.   Because the cy pres doctrine means looking for a next-best remedy, it presumes the infeasibility of providing relief directly to the class. Thus, a settlement including a cy pres remedy requires a court to consider the adequacy of the claims process. In Pearson v. NBTY, 772 F.3d 778 (7th Cir. 2014) (discussed *supra* p. 572), the court rejected a settlement because, among other things, the deal included a cy pres component when it could have done a better job of compensating the class:

> [T]here is no validity to the $1.13 million cy pres award in this case. A cy pres award is supposed to be limited to money that can't feasibly be awarded to the intended beneficiaries, here consisting of the class members. * * * The [charitable recipient] seems perfectly reputable, but it is entitled to receive money intended to compensate victims of consumer fraud only if it's infeasible to provide that compensation to the victims—which has not been demonstrated.

Similarly, in Oetting v. Green Jacobson, P.C., 775 F.3d 1060 (8th Cir. 2015), the Eighth Circuit—embracing the ALI perspective—reversed a district court's approval of a cy pres distribution on the ground that further distribution to the class was feasible.

9.   In contrast to its disapproval of the cy pres remedy in Dennis v. Kellogg, the Ninth Circuit took a more permissive view of cy pres in Lane v. Facebook, Inc., 696 F.3d 811 (9th Cir. 2012). The suit involved a challenge to a Facebook program called Beacon, which broadcast information about Facebook members' non-Facebook Internet activities to others in the member's network, even if members did not affirmatively consent. Plaintiffs brought a class action alleging violations of their privacy rights. After mediation, the parties negotiated a settlement class action. Facebook agreed to terminate Beacon (but could reinstate it by a different name), and to pay $9.5 million, of which approximately $3 million would go to class counsel fees and costs. The remaining $6.5 million would be used to establish a new entity, the Digital Trust Foundation, to educate the public about online privacy. One of the organization's three directors would be Facebook's director of public policy. The district court approved the settlement, and a majority of the Ninth Circuit panel affirmed, stating that "[t]he district court's review of a class-action settlement that calls for a cy pres remedy is not substantively different from that of any other class-action settlement except that the court should not find the settlement fair, adequate, and reasonable unless the cy pres remedy 'account[s] for the nature of the plaintiffs' lawsuit, the objectives of the underlying statutes, and the interests of the silent class members.' " Id. at 819–

20. The fact that Facebook placed an employee on the new organization's board did not require disapproval, even though that director presumably will "ensure that the funds will not be used in a way that harms Facebook" because "defendants can certainly be expected to structure a settlement in a way that does the least harm to their interests." Id. at 821. One judge dissented, arguing that the deal gave nothing to the class while providing millions to the lawyers. The Supreme Court denied certiorari in the Facebook case, but Chief Justice Roberts issued a statement lambasting the deal and observing that "[i]n a suitable case, this Court may need to clarify the limits on the use of such remedies." Marek v. Lane, 571 U.S. 1003 (2013) (Statement of Roberts, C.J., concurring in the denial of certiorari).

10. The very possibility of cy pres relief may defeat arguments against class certification in the small-claims setting. In Hughes v. Kore of Indiana Enter., Inc., 731 F.3d 672 (7th Cir. 2013) (discussed at p. 405 *supra* on the issue of class notice), the Seventh Circuit reversed a district court's decertification of a class of ATM users. The district judge had decertified the class upon concluding that class members could get at most $3.57 per transaction, but the Seventh Circuit rejected this reasoning on the grounds that the class might obtain a cy pres judgment or settlement (id. at 675–76):

> The smaller the stakes to each victim of unlawful conduct, the greater the economies of class action treatment * * *. But in this case the amount of damages that each class member can expect to recover is probably too small even to warrant the bother, slight as it may be, of submitting a proof of claim in the class action proceeding.
>
> Since distribution of damages to the class members would provide no meaningful relief, the best solution may be what is called (with some imprecision) a "cy pres" decree. Such a decree awards to a charity the money that would otherwise go to the members of the class as damages, if distribution to the class members is infeasible. Payment of $10,000 to a charity whose mission coincided with, or at least overlapped, the interest of the class (such as a foundation concerned with consumer protection) would amplify the effect of the modest damages in protecting consumers. A foundation that receives $10,000 can use the money to do something to minimize violations of the Electronic Funds Transfer Act; as a practical matter, class members each given $3.57 cannot.

4. THE ROLE OF OBJECTORS

IN RE UNITEDHEALTH GROUP INC. PSLRA LITIGATION
United States District Court, District of Minnesota, 2009.
643 F.Supp.2d 1107.

ROSENBAUM, DISTRICT JUDGE.

The remoras are loose again. The Court has received a motion from attorneys Edward Siegel, Edward Cochran, Stuart Yoes, and Scott Browne (styling themselves "Objectors' Counsel"), seeking an award of fees. Their motion is emphatically denied.

Background

[The court preliminarily approved a proposed settlement and gave notice to the class. Objectors' Counsel filed a one-page document on the last date for objections, and two weeks later submitted an untimely document objecting to class counsel's request for attorneys' fees. The court ultimately approved the class action settlement.]

Analysis

Rule 23 allows a court to award "reasonable attorney's fees." Fed. R. Civ. P. 23(h). Such an award is committed to the court's sound discretion. Those objecting to a class action settlement are not entitled to a fee award unless they confer a benefit on the class. See In re Cardinal Health, Inc. Sec. Litig., 550 F.Supp.2d 751, 753 (S.D.Ohio 2008). Objectors may add value to the process by:

> (1) transforming the fairness hearing into a truly adversarial proceeding; (2) supplying the Court with both precedent and argument to gauge the reasonableness of the settlement and lead counsel's fee request; and (3) preventing collusion between lead plaintiff and defendants.

Id. These objectors have contributed nothing. Instead, in a pleading which may charitably be described as disingenuous, Objectors' Counsel argue they assisted the Court in finding class counsel's fee request unreasonable. They claim their efforts convinced the Court to reduce class counsel's fee from $110 million to $64.8 million. They have the temerity to suggest they are the ones who saved the class $45 million in attorney fees, entitling them to a six-figure fee of their own.[1]

Their suggestion is laughable. If the Court may be permitted an egregious paraphrase of Winston S. Churchill: Seldom in the field of securities litigation was so little owed by so many to so few. Objectors' Counsel make "outlandish fee requests in return for doing virtually nothing." *In re Cardinal Health*, 550 F. Supp. 2d at 753. And nothing is the quantity of assistance they have provided to the Court and the class. Their goal was, and is, to hijack as many dollars for themselves as they can wrest from a negotiated settlement. Objectors' eight-page-long, two-week-late pleading presented no facts, offered no law, and raised no argument upon which the Court relied in its deliberation or ruling concerning class counsel's motion for fees. Indeed, the Court expressly rejected the lion's share of objectors' arguments directed to the use of paralegals and contract attorneys. Objectors' request and their motion ill-befit attorneys admitted

---

[1] Objectors' Counsel maintain their "lodestar" is "approximately $74,500," and request a multiplier of 2.5. [Docket No. 846, at ¶ 8.] The Court considers it preposterous that any legitimate lawyer would charge $74,500 to prepare an eight-page submission, and submit it tardy to boot.

to the bar. Accordingly, the Court holds, as a matter of fact and law, objectors have conferred no benefit whatsoever on the class or on the Court. Objectors' Counsel are entitled to an award equal to their contribution . . . nothing.

IN RE FOREIGN EXCHANGE BENCHMARK RATES ANTITRUST LITIGATION
United States District Court, Southern District of New York, 2019.
334 F.R.D. 62.

SCHOFIELD, DISTRICT JUDGE.

Class Counsel, objector-appellant Keith Kornell and objector Keith Kornell d/b/a/ Crown and Kornell Corp ("Objector") seek an indicative ruling pursuant to Federal Rules of Civil Procedure 23(e)(5)(B)(i), 23(h) and 62.1, that the Court would approve their agreement of settlement ("the Agreement") if the Second Circuit remanded for that purpose. Pursuant to the Agreement, the Objector would dismiss with prejudice his appeal in the United States Court of Appeals for the Second Circuit, which is scheduled for imminent oral argument. In exchange for this dismissal, Class Counsel would pay the Objector's counsel $300,000 for his time objecting to the attorneys' fee award. The payment would be made from Class Counsel's fees and not from the Net Settlement Fund, and $5,000 of the payment would go to Keith Kornell as an incentive award. As explained below, the motion is denied, and the Court declines to issue an indicative ruling.

I.   STANDARD

Rule 23(e)(5) permits class members to object to proposed class action settlements and requires court approval of any payment in connection with "forgoing, dismissing, or abandoning an appeal from a judgment approving" a settlement. Fed. R. Civ. P. 23(e)(5)(A)–(B)(ii). If the parties do not obtain such approval "before an appeal has been docketed in the court of appeals, the procedure of Rule 62.1 applies while the appeal remains pending." Fed. R. Civ. P. 23(e)(5)(C). Rule 62.1 permits the court to make an indicative ruling when the court lacks authority to grant a motion because an appeal has been taken. Fed. R. Civ. P. 62.1(a).

II.   DISCUSSION

The Advisory Committee Notes to Rule 23(e)(5)(B) preface the discussion with the observation that "[g]ood-faith objections" can assist the court in evaluating a proposed class action settlement, and that it is "legitimate for an objector to seek payment for providing such assistance." Fed. R. Civ. P. 23(e)(5) Advisory Committee Note to 2018 Amendment. However, the note continues:

> But some objectors may be seeking only personal gain, and using objections to obtain benefits for themselves rather than assisting in the settlement-review process. At least in some instances, it

> seems that objectors—or their counsel—have sought to obtain
> consideration for withdrawing their objections or dismissing
> appeals from judgments approving class settlements. And class
> counsel sometimes may feel that avoiding the delay produced by
> an appeal justifies providing payment or other consideration to
> these objectors. Although the payment may advance class
> interests in a particular case, allowing payment perpetuates a
> system that can encourage objections advanced for improper
> purposes.

Id. The Agreement here seems to fit that description; the Agreement does little more than benefit Objector's counsel and "perpetuate[ ] a system that can encourage objections advanced for improper purposes." *Id.*

The Objector has appealed the settlement on the basis that the Class Counsel fee award was too great. However, the Objector is willing to withdraw his appeal and voluntarily dismiss it with prejudice, so long as Objector's counsel shares in the supposedly excessive funds awarded to Class Counsel. The only benefit to class members is to avoid further delay in the distribution of the settlement fund that the Objector already has caused by filing the appeal. This type of agreement is precisely what the court-approval provision in Rule 23(e)(5)(B) is meant to address.

Objector's counsel points to the Court's decision to award attorney's fees valued at 13% of the settlement fund—less than Class Counsel's proposed 16.5%—as evidence that the Court "in part" adopted the objection, thereby purportedly saving $80 million for the Class. As should be evident from the fee award decision, the amount of the award had nothing to do with the Objector's objection. That the Court's fee award minimally correlates with the premise of the objection should not be construed as helpful assistance from the Objector.

More important is the precedential concern associated with granting the instant motion. * * * While Class Counsel expressed its belief that the Agreement would be in the best interest of the Settlement Classes, that view is premised on the notion that resolving the appeal would "eliminate uncertainty", "make the fee award final" and allow for the second distribution from the Settlement Fund. Approving agreements in these circumstances would serve only to encourage objectors or their attorneys to extract this type of payment, and "make a living [as serial objectors] simply by filing frivolous appeals and thereby slowing down the execution of settlements." In re Polyurethane Foam Antitrust Litig., 178 F.Supp.3d 635, 639 (N.D.Ohio 2016). Granting the indicative ruling motion and approving the Agreement would make this Court complicit in a practice that undermines the integrity of class action procedure, and needlessly provide putative objectors with potentially dubious claims precedential support for a practice of fee extraction.

III. CONCLUSION

While the Court shares Class Counsel's concerns about further delays in the distribution of the settlement fund to class members, for the foregoing reasons, the parties' joint motion is DENIED.

NOTES AND QUESTIONS

1. In case you are wondering, a remora (see the first line of the *UnitedHealth* court's opinion) is a fish with a sucking disc on the top of its head by which it clings to larger fishes or passing ships. That pretty much sums up the *UnitedHealth* court's view of the objectors, doesn't it?

2. In *Foreign Exchange*, the court deployed Rule 23(e)(5) to reject a payoff to an objector. This subsection was adopted in 2003 and expanded in 2018 to ward off objectors who seek only to obtain a buyoff or gain individual leverage.

The Seventh Circuit considered the problem of rent-seeking objectors in *Pearson v. Target Corp.*, 968 F.3d 827, 829 (7th Cir. 2020), in which the relevant events predated the 2018 amendment to Rule 23(e)(5):

> We address here a recurring problem in class-action litigation known colloquially as "objector blackmail." The scenario is familiar to class-action litigators on both offense and defense. A plaintiff class and a defendant submit a proposed settlement for approval by the district court. A few class members object to the settlement but the court approves it as fair, reasonable, and adequate under Federal Rule of Civil Procedure 23(e)(2). The objectors then file appeals. As it turns out, though, they are willing to abandon their appeals in return for sizable side payments that do not benefit the plaintiff class: a figurative "blackmail" by selfish holdouts threatening to disrupt collective action unless they are paid off. See Brian T. Fitzpatrick, The End of Objector Blackmail?, 62 Vand. L. Rev. 1623, 1624 (2009).
>
> That's what happened here. Three objectors appealed the denial of their objections to a class action settlement and then dismissed their appeals in exchange for side payments. * * * The question before us now is whether, on motion of another class member, the district court had the equitable power to remedy the problem by ordering the settling objectors to disgorge for the benefit of the class the proceeds of their private settlements. The district court held that it did not, finding that the objectors had not intended or committed an illegal act nor taken money out of the common fund.
>
> We reverse. Falsely flying the class's colors, these three objectors extracted $130,000 in what economists would call rents from the litigation process simply by showing up and objecting to consummation of the settlement to slow things down until they were paid. We hold that settling an objection that asserts the class's rights

in return for a private payment to the objector is inequitable and that disgorgement is the most appropriate remedy.

To what extent do Rule 23(e)(5)'s requirements, as implemented by the *Foreign Exchange* court, render the *Pearson* disgorgement approach unnecessary?

3. The judges in *UnitedHealth*, *Foreign Exchange*, and *Pearson* take a dim view of objectors who seek only to enrich themselves, but judges also recognize that objectors can serve an important function in class actions. Without objectors, a court would receive no adversarial presentation on the fairness of a settlement. The court would hear only from class counsel and defense counsel, both of whom support the proposed deal. Recall the objectors in *Amchem Products v. Windsor*, *supra* p. 311, who successfully persuaded the appellate courts that the settlement class action did not treat all class members fairly and should not have been approved. And Stephanie Berg and Omar Rivero, who successfully objected to the cy pres remedy in *Dennis v. Kellogg*, *supra* p. 576.

In Shaw v. Toshiba America Information Systems, Inc., 91 F.Supp.2d 942 (E.D.Tex. 2000), the court denounced "professional objectors who seek out class actions to simply extract a fee by lodging generic, unhelpful protests," but also awarded $6 million in attorney fees to objectors who successfully got the redemption time for coupons doubled.

Professor Edward Brunet acknowledges that some objectors are free-riders or extortionists who seek fees or pay-offs without adding any useful input, and he concedes that "objectors may be the least popular litigation participants in the history of civil procedure," but he emphasizes that some objectors truly enhance the quality of judicial review of class settlements:

> Not all objectors, however, will have such nefarious intentions. In addition to focusing upon the typical monitor—an absent class member unhappy with a proposed settlement—this Article will focus on several other types of emerging monitors who have the potential to monitor the class more productively. One such party is the public interest group monitor. At present, several public interest groups routinely seek intervention to participate in critiquing allegedly unfair proposed class actions settlements. * * *

> The state is another potentially useful monitor of class action abuse. A federal agency or a state Attorney General's office has often provided input into the fairness of a proposed class action settlement or has even purported to represent the class itself. The impact of governmental bodies objecting into class suits should help produce a settlement consistent with the public interest. It seems intuitive that the state can monitor class action plaintiffs' attorneys and their opposing counsel. Administrative agency attorneys are specialists who should have the appropriate incentives to monitor effectively, and they lack the opportunism faced by private counsel representing objectors. * * *

My general thesis is that a closed, private procedure in which a trial judge assesses a proposed class action settlement with only input from class counsel and defense counsel is far less efficient or fair than a procedure in which input is received from one or more objectors.

Edward Brunet, Class Action Objectors: Extortionist Free Riders or Fairness Guarantors, 2003 U. Chi. Legal F. 403.

4.   In Eubank v. Pella, 753 F.3d 718, 720–21 (7th Cir. 2014), the Seventh Circuit noted its concern that class counsel might "sell out the class by agreeing with the defendant to recommend that the judge approve a settlement involving a meager recovery for the class but generous compensation for the lawyers," and hailed the objectors:

Fortunately the settlement, including the amount of attorneys' fees to award to class counsel, must be approved by the district judge presiding over the case; unfortunately American judges are accustomed to presiding over adversary proceedings. They expect the clash of the adversaries to generate the information that the judge needs to decide the case. And so when a judge is being urged by both adversaries to approve the class-action settlement that they've negotiated, he's at a disadvantage in evaluating the fairness of the settlement to the class.

Enter the objectors. Members of the class who smell a rat can object to approval of the settlement. * * * In this case, despite the presence of objectors, the district court approved a class action settlement that is inequitable—even scandalous. The case underscores the importance both of objectors (for they are the appellants in this case—without them there would have been no appellate challenge to the settlement) and of intense judicial scrutiny of proposed class action settlements.

5.   To what extent may objectors participate in the litigation without actually becoming parties? Class members may be permitted to intervene in a class action. Should such intervention be required for a class member who seeks to appeal the district court's approval of a settlement? In Devlin v. Scardelletti, 536 U.S. 1 (2002), the Supreme Court ruled that class members who object to a settlement may appeal without having been permitted to intervene. Otherwise, the district court could constrain their ability to delay or disrupt proceedings by denying leave to intervene on the ground that their objections were unwarranted. By contrast, in Hernandez v. Restoration Hardware, Inc., 409 P.2d 281 (Cal. 2018), the California Supreme Court rejected the *Devlin* approach and held that, under California law, unnamed class members may not appeal a class judgment, settlement, or fee award unless they intervene.

C. NON-CLASS AGGREGATE SETTLEMENTS

THE TAX AUTHORITY, INC. V. JACKSON HEWITT, INC.

Supreme Court of New Jersey, 2006.
898 A.2d 512.

JUSTICE WALLACE delivered the opinion of the Court.

The issue presented is whether our Rule of Professional Conduct (RPC) 1.8(g) prohibits an attorney who represents more than one client from entering into an aggregate settlement of the clients' claims without each client consenting to the settlement after its terms are known. In the present case, an attorney agreed to represent 154 individual franchisee-plaintiffs in their claims against franchisor-defendant Jackson Hewitt, Inc. Each plaintiff entered into an identical retainer agreement that provided for settlement of the matter if a weighted majority of plaintiffs approved the settlement. A Steering Committee of four plaintiffs was established to represent the interests of all 154 individual plaintiffs. After the Steering Committee negotiated a settlement in principle, a weighted majority of plaintiffs approved it, but eighteen others did not. Defendant sought to enforce the settlement against all plaintiffs, and the motion court granted that application. The Appellate Division held that the fee agreement violated RPC 1.8(g) because it required advance consent to abide by the majority's decision and reversed. We hold that RPC 1.8(g) forbids an attorney from obtaining advance consent from his clients to abide by the majority's decision about the merits of an aggregate settlement. However, for the reasons expressed in section IV of this opinion, we apply this decision prospectively. We reverse and remand.

I.

Defendant Jackson Hewitt is a nationwide tax preparation service with its principal place of business in Parsippany, New Jersey. It has franchises throughout the United States. Plaintiff The Tax Authority, Inc. is a franchisee of Jackson Hewitt with its principal place of business in Maple Shade, New Jersey.

As part of their business operation, franchisees make Refund Anticipation Loans (RAL) to individual taxpayers in anticipation of the taxpayers receiving refunds from the Internal Revenue Service. The loans are repaid when the refunds are received. Prior to the 2000 tax season, Jackson Hewitt distributed monetary rebates called "Performance Incentive Rebates" arising out of those loans to its eligible franchisees. Beginning in the 2000 tax season, Jackson Hewitt discontinued issuing those rebates.

The individual franchisees believed that Jackson Hewitt breached the franchise agreement by failing to issue rebates. Because the franchise agreement prohibited the franchisees from filing a class action lawsuit against Jackson Hewitt or its affiliates, the franchisees collectively retained attorney Eric H. Karp (Karp) of Witmer, Karp, Warner & Thuotte LLP in Boston to represent the group in a mass lawsuit. As part of that representation, each of the 154 plaintiffs entered into an identical attorney-client retainer agreement with Karp. Plaintiffs agreed that the matter would be pursued on a collective basis with fees being shared by each plaintiff on a per-RAL basis. Each retainer agreement provided that

> [t]he Client agrees that the Matter may be resolved by settlement as to any portion or all of the Matter upon a vote of a weighted majority of the Client and all of the Co-Plaintiffs. Each Plaintiff shall have one vote for each funded RAL for the 2002 Tax Season. The Client will be eligible to vote only if current in all payments required under this agreement. . . . A quorum for such vote shall be sixty percent (60%) of the votes eligible to be cast.

In addition to the majority-rules provision, the agreement provided that a four person Steering Committee would make the decisions regarding "all strategic and similar procedural matters other than the decision to settle the matter." The members of the Steering Committee were Robert Phillips, Robert Schiesel, George Alberici, and Kenneth Leese. Leese is the owner and president of the sole plaintiff herein, The Tax Authority.

The retainer agreement also specified that settlement proceeds would be apportioned according to each plaintiff's proportionate share of the RAL reserve. Specifically, the agreement provided that "[t]he Client will share in the net proceeds in the same ratio as its contribution to the RAL reserve for the 2002 Tax Season bears to the total contribution to the RAL reserve of all Co-Plaintiffs for the 2002 Tax Season." Formulas to calculate net proceeds, client contributions, and other necessary figures were also included. Prior to signing the retainer agreement, each plaintiff had an opportunity to consult with outside counsel.

* * *

In August 2002, Karp filed a single complaint against Jackson Hewitt, naming each of the 154 franchisees as individual plaintiffs. Thereafter, the parties agreed to mediate their dispute. During mediation, Jackson Hewitt and the three member Steering Committee represented by Karp negotiated a settlement in principle that was reduced to a two-page document titled "JAMS Settlement Agreement" (JAMS Settlement). Jackson Hewitt's representatives and the three members of the Steering Committee all signed the JAMS Settlement, which was conditioned on approval by plaintiffs and by Jackson Hewitt's Board of Directors.

Karp had previously established a password-protected website to inform plaintiffs of developments in the case. In response to questions from various plaintiffs regarding the JAMS Settlement, on July 15, 2003, Karp posted an eleven-page document on the website that included a spreadsheet showing the calculation of each plaintiff's estimated net participation in the cash portion of the settlement. Karp later certified that Leese assisted one of Karp's associates "in creating and finalizing" the spreadsheet.

Leese helped to arrange a telephone conference call among most of the plaintiffs for the next day. During the conference call, which lasted approximately three hours, Karp attempted to answer any questions plaintiffs had about the JAMS Settlement. On July 17, 2003, and July 22, 2003, Karp submitted settlement ballots to plaintiffs and established August 1, 2003, as the deadline for voting.

At some point, Leese began to challenge Karp concerning the settlement. Leese believed that the other two members of the Steering Committee were meeting secretly with Karp. Leese then resigned from the Steering Committee on August 7, 2003, and declined to participate in a conference call of the Steering Committee scheduled for that same day.

Ultimately, a weighted majority of plaintiffs approved the JAMS Settlement. Counsel prepared a more detailed, formal settlement agreement. On October 30, 2003, Karp posted to the website a copy of the formal settlement agreement and emailed a copy to each plaintiff. He requested that each plaintiff submit a signed duplicate copy of the agreement to him by November 12, 2003. That deadline was later extended to November 17, 2003. On November 21, 2003, Karp emailed every plaintiff and posted a notice to the website stating that any plaintiff who did not submit a response by December 1, 2003, would be presumed to have declined the settlement. That communication also indicated that Karp would ask the court for leave to withdraw as counsel for parties declining the agreement due to a conflict between those plaintiffs who had signed the settlement agreement and those who had not. On November 24, 2003, Karp reiterated the settlement deadline of December 1, 2003, and informed plaintiffs that on December 2, 2003, he would file a motion to withdraw as counsel for those plaintiffs who had not signed the agreement.

On December 2, 2003, Karp filed the promised motion, originally seeking relief from representation of twenty-six of the 154 plaintiffs. The following day, Jackson Hewitt filed a motion to enforce the settlement agreement against all plaintiffs.

Karp filed a certification and a supplemental certification in the matter. He certified that after the JAMS Settlement was signed, Leese had assisted his associate in creating and finalizing the spreadsheet that showed each plaintiff's estimated net share in the proceeds. Karp set forth his efforts to explain the settlement to plaintiffs and stated that as of December 17, 2003, he had received signed approval from all but twenty plaintiffs.

Three plaintiffs filed certifications in opposition to the settlement. Frederick Roberts claimed that Karp did not fully inform him of the "facts and circumstances of the proposed settlement" and that Karp failed to answer his questions regarding the settlement agreement. Susan McCumsey certified that after Robert Schiesel died in July 2002, she did not have proper representation on the Steering Committee. Leese certified that he had been a member of the Steering Committee and that initially, the entire Steering Committee had regular discussions with Karp. However, after the JAMS Settlement was signed on July 1, 2003, Leese claimed that his involvement with Karp and the Steering Committee changed. Leese stated in part:

> 7.   Once I began to challenge Mr. Karp, I learned that the remaining members of the steering committee were meeting with Mr. Karp without my knowledge.
>
> 8.   As a result, I believe that the plaintiff body did not have full representation once the steering committee began meeting without my knowledge or participation.
>
> 9.   When I learned of this development, I terminated my relationship with Mr. Karp and was no longer a member of the steering committee. By the time the trial court heard argument on the motions, only eighteen plaintiffs had not yet signed the settlement agreement. Fourteen of those eighteen plaintiffs were represented by counsel and four were not. They asserted that Karp violated RPC 1.8(g) by obtaining advance consent to abide by any settlement approved by a majority of plaintiffs, and that therefore, they should not be bound by the settlement.

The trial court granted both Karp's motion to withdraw as counsel for the non-signing plaintiffs and Jackson Hewitt's motion to enforce the settlement agreement. [Based on a difference between the former and current version of the aggregate settlement rule,] the court concluded that the weighted majority provision in the retainer agreement did not violate RPC 1.8(g) and that invalidating the settlement agreement would be "imminently unfair" to plaintiffs who favored the settlement and to defendant.

The Tax Authority was the sole plaintiff to appeal. The Appellate Division reversed, holding that an attorney-client agreement with a weighted majority provision for settlement of litigation was contrary to RPC 1.8(g) and unenforceable. In a thorough and well-reasoned opinion, Judge Weissbard found that "[t]he critical provision of the RPC is that the client consent to the final settlement." While recognizing that some commentators advance good reasons for simultaneous representation and majority-rules provisions in retainer agreements, the Appellate Division observed that any change in the current interpretation of RPC 1.8(g) should come from the Supreme Court.

We granted defendant's petition for certification. Defendant informed us at oral argument that except for The Tax Authority, the settlement has been executed and the appropriate monies disbursed to all other plaintiffs.

II.

Defendant's main argument is that the Appellate Division incorrectly interpreted RPC 1.8(g) to preclude parties from agreeing to settle in any manner other than by unanimous consent. It asserts that "the Appellate Division relied almost exclusively on non-New Jersey authority applying DR 5–106, rather than authority interpreting RPC 1.8(g), notwithstanding the textual differences" between the two rules. Defendant also contends that the judgment below undermines New Jersey's strong public policy in favor of settling disputes. Alternatively, defendant urges that this is an issue of first impression, so if this Court affirms the judgment, the ruling should be applied prospectively only.

In contrast, The Tax Authority contends that the Appellate Division properly interpreted RPC 1.8(g). It maintains that a majority-rules mechanism to govern settlement creates an inherent conflict of interest between the parties and their counsel. The Tax Authority further argues that RPC 1.8(g) is necessary to safeguard the individual interests of each client, and that because the safeguards of court oversight for class actions are not present, each client must individually consent to a settlement agreement after the terms of the settlement are made known.

III.

* * * [T]his Court has promulgated Rules of Professional Conduct that govern attorneys in New Jersey. Those rules "serve as a road map for the conduct of attorneys to guide them in their relationships with their clients, other attorneys, the courts, and the public." The "[a]greements between attorneys and clients concerning the client-lawyer relationship generally are enforceable, provided the agreements satisfy both the general requirements for contracts and the special requirements of professional ethics." * * * "A retainer agreement may not provide for unreasonable fees or for the unreasonable waiver of the clients' rights."

An agreement that violates the ethical rules governing the attorney-client relationship may be declared unenforceable.

* * * At the time the conduct in the present case took place, RPC 1.8(g) provided that

> [a] lawyer who represents two or more clients shall not participate in making an aggregate settlement of the claims of or against the clients, or in a criminal case an aggregated agreement as to guilty or no contest pleas, unless each client consents after consultation, including disclosure of the existence and nature of all the claims

or pleas involved and of the participation of each person in the settlement.

* * * That rule is commonly referred to as the "aggregate settlement" rule. See Lynn A. Baker & Charles Silver, The Aggregate Settlement Rule and Ideals of Client Service, 41 S. Tex. L. Rev. 227, 234 (1999).

The seminal case interpreting [DR 5–106, the prior version of the aggregate settlement rule,] is Hayes v. Eagle-Picher Industries, Inc., 513 F.2d 892 (10th Cir. 1975). There, the eighteen plaintiffs retained a single lawyer to file an action against the defendant. On the eve of trial, the parties reached a settlement agreement, which thirteen of the eighteen plaintiffs approved. The following day, in open court, the trial court inquired whether any of the plaintiffs were opposed to the settlement. After receiving no objections, the court entered a judgment of settlement. Thereafter, two members of the plaintiff group claimed they did not hear the court's question and challenged the settlement. After initially vacating the judgment, the trial court reconsidered and reinstated the settlement.

The Tenth Circuit reversed, finding that an agreement that authorized settlement of a case "contrary to the wishes of the client and without his approving the terms of the settlement is opposed to the basic fundamentals of the attorney-client relationship." The court was troubled by the majority-rules provision, stating that [i]t is difficult to see how this could be binding on non-consenting plaintiffs as of the time of the proposed settlement and in the light of the terms agreed on. In other words, it would seem that plaintiffs would have the right to agree or refuse to agree once the terms of the settlement were made known to them.

The court also found that the agreement posed an ethical problem for attorneys under [DR 5–106]. In the court's view, that rule "requires the attorney to refrain from participating in a settlement on behalf of two or more clients unless each of them consents to it." The court reasoned that "it was untenable for the lawyer to seek to represent both the clients who favored the settlement and those who opposed it." As a result, the court concluded that "in a non-class action case such as the present one," an arrangement that allows a majority to control the rights of the minority "is violative of the basic tenets of the attorney-client relationship in that it delegates to the attorney powers which allow him to act not only contrary to the wishes of his client, but to act in a manner disloyal to his client and to his client's interests." Id. at 894–95.

More than ten years later, the Appellate Court of Illinois reached a similar result. In Knisley v. City of Jacksonville, 497 N.E.2d 883 (Ill.App. 1986), also decided under DR 5–106, the court invalidated a settlement agreement that had been approved by a majority of the plaintiffs. There, the sixty-one plaintiffs sought to enjoin the City of Jacksonville from issuing certain building permits. After the plaintiffs' attorney entered into negotiations with the defendants, the attorney called a meeting of the plaintiffs to present a proposed settlement. The attorney testified that as a result of that meeting, he believed that he had authority to settle. When the defendants rejected the attorney's first settlement offer, a second settlement agreement was drafted. Thereafter, the attorney contacted a majority of the plaintiffs; a majority agreed to the settlement. After the attorney drafted documents to execute the settlement, one of the plaintiffs called the attorney to indicate her dissatisfaction with the settlement. The attorney then held a second meeting with the plaintiffs, in which a "controversy arose among the plaintiffs as to whether the case should be settled." As a result of that meeting, the attorney sought to withdraw as the plaintiffs' counsel. Subsequently, the defendants filed a petition to enforce the settlement, and the trial court granted the petition.

The appellate court reversed the trial court's enforcement of the settlement against those plaintiffs who opposed the settlement on appeal. The court, however, affirmed the judgment for the plaintiffs who either approved the settlement or did not participate in the appeal. In reaching its conclusion, the court first found that the record was "adequate to indicate that the plaintiffs never consented to be bound by the majority." Second, the court concluded that enforcing the settlement against the dissenting plaintiffs would be "completely at odds" with DR 5–106, observing that *Hayes* was "remarkabl[y] similar[ ] to the instant case." Id. at 886–87.

The court then discussed the "sharp distinction" between class action lawsuits and simple joinder actions. Id. at 887. The court noted that unlike class action lawsuits, which require a court to determine the reasonableness of a settlement, "[i]n a joinder action there is no judicial review of the settlement and a party should not be bound unless he has specifically agreed to it." The court found that "[f]undamental fairness is violated when a settlement is allowed to bind parties who object and no safeguards have been added to protect their interests." Id. at 888.

[New Jersey's RPC 1.8(g) was modified effective January 1, 2004, to include the term "informed consent." As modified, the rule provides:

> A lawyer who represents two or more clients shall not participate in making an aggregate settlement of the claims of or against the clients . . . unless each client gives informed consent after a consultation that shall include disclosure of the existence and nature of all the claims . . . and of the participation of each person in the settlement.

"Informed consent" is defined as "the agreement by a person to a proposed course of conduct after the lawyer has communicated adequate information and explanation about the material risks of and reasonably available alternatives to the proposed course of conduct." N.J. Court Rules, RPC 1.0(e).]

Most scholars and commentators agree that a majority-rules provision is forbidden under RPC 1.8(g). See, e.g., Howard M. Erichson, A Typology of Aggregate Settlements, 80 Notre Dame L.Rev. 1769, 1809 (2005) ("As currently understood, the rule does not allow clients to agree ex ante to be bound by majority rule on settlement offers, for example."); Nancy J. Moore, The Case Against Changing the Aggregate Settlement Rule in Mass Tort Lawsuits, 41 S. Tex. L. Rev. 149, 165 (1999) ("[T]he aggregate settlement rule forbids lawyers from entering settlement over the objection of any plaintiff, even when that plaintiff has agreed in advance to be bound by a vote of a majority or a supermajority."); Charles Silver & Lynn A. Baker, Mass Lawsuits and the Aggregate Settlement Rule, 32 Wake Forest L.Rev. 733, 763 (1997) ("The Rule clearly contemplates that a lawyer will confer with his or her clients before closing a deal whose details have already been hammered out.").

The underpinning of [the aggregate settlement rule] is that when a lawyer represents more than one client, each client has the right to accept or reject the settlement after the terms are known. Simply stated, RPC 1.8(g) imposes two requirements on lawyers representing multiple clients. The first is that the terms of the settlement must be disclosed to each client. The second is that after the terms of the settlement are known, each client must agree to the settlement.

We conclude that RPC 1.8(g) forbids an attorney from obtaining consent in advance from multiple clients that each will abide by a majority decision in respect of an aggregate settlement. Before a client may be bound by a settlement, he or she must have knowledge of the terms of the settlement and agree to them.

IV.

Before the Appellate Division, defendant asserted that even if The Tax Authority was not bound by the majority vote, principles of equitable estoppel require the court to enforce the agreement because of the circumstances at the time the settlement was reached. The Appellate Division rejected that argument. Defendant does not make that same argument here but asserts that even if the majority-rules provision is invalid, this Court "should determine that such decisions on issues of first impression should only apply prospectively and that [The Tax Authority] remains bound by the settlement agreement."

The general rule is that judicial decisions will be applied retroactively. Even so, "[o]ur tradition is to confine a decision to prospective application when fairness and justice require." * * *

Such is the case here. This is the first opportunity for this Court to interpret RPC 1.8(g). Plaintiffs' counsel represented plaintiffs that were from many different states and successfully sought to have all plaintiffs agree in advance to be bound by a weighted majority. That effort was a plausible, although incorrect, interpretation of RPC 1.8(g). In addition, defendant was led to believe that plaintiffs had agreed among themselves to be bound by a weighted majority vote and relied on that in reaching the settlement. The Tax Authority's president, Leese, was a member of the Steering Committee, assisted in reaching the JAMS Settlement, and signed it. Subsequently, he was actively involved in negotiating the voting mechanism for plaintiffs' approval of the settlement but ultimately rejected the final settlement. All of the other plaintiffs have consented to the settlement, and defendant has satisfied its terms with all other plaintiffs.

On balance, we conclude that prospective application of our holding, and thus enforcement of the settlement against The Tax Authority, is the appropriate and equitable disposition of this matter.

V.

Lastly, we recognize that some commentators have proposed that RPC 1.8(g) be changed to accommodate mass lawsuits. Professors Charles Silver and Lynn Baker suggest the rule should be amended to permit litigants to agree to abide by majority rule. Silver & Baker, *supra*, 32 Wake Forest L.Rev. at 769–70. They agree that "[b]ecause the stakes are so large and the issues so complex, settlement is both more urgent and more difficult in mass lawsuits than in other litigation, and the aggregate settlement rule is a complication that often gets in the way." Id. at 735–36. The complications they refer to include generating expense and delay, preventing defendants from obtaining finality, invading plaintiffs' privacy, and allowing a single claimant to hold out or block an entire settlement. Id. at 755–56.

In light of those and other concerns advanced in favor of permitting less than unanimous agreement in multi-plaintiff mass litigation, we refer this issue to the Commission on Ethics Reform for its review and recommendation to the Court.

NOTES AND QUESTIONS

1.   What was wrong with the settlement in *Tax Authority*? The 154 plaintiffs explicitly agreed that they would be represented jointly and that they would all be bound by a settlement based on a weighted majority vote. Was such joint representation and advance consent an irrational choice on the part of the plaintiffs? Joint representation provided the benefits of efficiency and solidarity, and the advance settlement consent provided settlement leverage because it gave the lawyer the ability to negotiate to deliver peace to the defendant. If rational clients could have chosen this approach to settlement, then why does the court hold that it was impermissible?

2.   Despite the court's holding about the impermissibility of the advance consent provision, note that the court chose to apply its ruling prospectively only. Thus, it enforced the settlement in this case. What are the advantages

and disadvantages of the court's declining to apply its holding about aggregate settlements to this case?

3. Model Rule of Professional Conduct 1.8(g), which has been adopted in some form in every state, requires informed consent from each client who is to be bound by an aggregate settlement. To some extent, this rule is a corollary of the principle that the decision whether to settle belongs to the client, not the lawyer. But it is also a rule about conflicts of interest. Every aggregate settlement involves conflicts of interest among the clients whose claims are resolved in the deal. Even if the settlement allocation is not strictly zero-sum (whatever one person gets, another loses), trade-offs among client interests are unavoidable. Like many other conflicts of interest, the conflicts involved in most aggregate settlements are permissible as long as each client gives informed consent. See Model Rule of Professional Conduct 1.7(b). A New York ethics opinion explains the relationship between the aggregate settlement rule, Rule 1.8(g), and conflicts of interest:

> As explained in the ABA's *Ethical Guidelines for Settlement Negotiations* (2002): "[e]ven when the lawyer's initial conclusion that multiple clients can be represented was well-founded ... consideration later of possible settlement options can generate circumstances where interests emerge as potentially divergent, if not actually conflicting. Conflicts can arise from differences among clients in the strength of their positions or the level of their interests in settlement, or from proposals to treat clients in different ways or to treat differently positioned clients in the same way." *Id.* § 3.5. A lawyer must discuss these risks and potential conflicts with each prospective client to obtain the informed consent required to proceed with the joint representation. Rules 1.7 and 1.8(g) thus work in tandem to ensure that clients are fully informed of the potential conflicts that could arise from joint representation, including the conflicts that could arise in connection with the negotiation and acceptance of aggregate settlements.

Association of the Bar of the City of New York, Formal Op. 2009–6.

4. What are the salient similarities and differences between class action settlements and non-class aggregate settlements? The *Tax Authority* case was not a class action, but rather involved the claims of 154 individually named plaintiffs. Thus, the procedural protections of Rule 23 or its state court equivalent—judicial review of the settlement, judicial control of fees, appointment of class counsel, class certification, and so on—did not apply. Instead of the *procedural* protections of the class action rule, the interests of clients in non-class aggregate settlements are protected primarily by the *ethical* protections of the aggregate settlement rule. Which rule offers superior protection for settling claimants?

5. The 154 plaintiffs in *Tax Authority* asserted their claims in a single lawsuit as a matter of permissive party joinder, pursuant to New Jersey's equivalent of Rule 20 of the Federal Rules of Civil Procedure. Did the aggregate

settlement issue in *Tax Authority* depend on whether the parties joined their claims in a single lawsuit? Did it depend on whether any lawsuit was filed at all?

6. We have seen non-class mass settlements before. Recall the discussion of "inventory settlements" in asbestos litigation, *supra* p. 232. In *Amchem*, the attorneys negotiated settlements of large numbers of individual claims alongside the class claims. Those inventory settlements were non-class aggregate settlements that required each client's consent.

7. The aggregate settlement rule requires that a lawyer obtain each client's informed consent to an aggregate settlement after disclosing the terms of the deal. How much disclosure should be required? Consider the following list from an ABA ethics opinion:

> In order to ensure a valid and informed consent to an aggregate settlement or aggregated agreement, Rule 1.8(g) requires a lawyer to disclose, at a minimum, the following information to the clients for whom or to whom the settlement or agreement proposal is made:
>
> - The total amount of the aggregate settlement or the result of the aggregated agreement.
>
> - The existence and nature of all of the claims, defenses, or pleas involved in the aggregate settlement or aggregated agreement.
>
> - The details of every other client's participation in the aggregate settlement or aggregated agreement, whether it be their settlement contributions, their settlement receipts, the resolution of their criminal charges, or any other contribution or receipt of something of value as a result of the aggregate resolution. For example, if one client is favored over the other(s) by receiving non-monetary remuneration, that fact must be disclosed to the other client(s).
>
> - The total fees and costs to be paid to the lawyer as a result of the aggregate settlement, if the lawyer's fees and/or costs will be paid, in whole or in part, from the proceeds of the settlement or by an opposing party or parties.
>
> - The method by which costs (including costs already paid by the lawyer as well as costs to be paid out of the settlement proceeds) are to be apportioned among them.

ABA Formal Op. 06–438 (2006). Should each of these disclosures be required for every aggregate settlement? The opinion says that "at a minimum" the lawyer must disclose "[t]he details of every other client's participation in the aggregate settlement." In a mass tort settlement involving thousands of individuals with various diseases or other injuries, must every client be informed of every other client's name, disease, personal risk factors, and individual settlement amount? Or should it suffice to inform each client of the overall terms of the deal, including the settlement matrix and the basis for allocation, without revealing individual names?

8.   Rule 1.8(g) does not define the term "aggregate settlement." Suppose a lawyer represents fifty clients with claims against a particular defendant. Consider whether Rule 1.8(g)'s requirement of disclosure and informed consent should apply to each of the following types of settlements:

- The defendant offers a lump sum to settle with all fifty claimants on an all-or-nothing basis.

- The settlement is not all-or-nothing, but it contains a "walkaway clause" giving the defendant the right to void the settlement unless at least 90 percent of the claimants accept it.

- The settlement permits each claimant independently to accept or reject the offer, but is a "matrix settlement" that assigns a settlement value to each of the fifty claimants based on age, injury, and other specified factors.

- The settlement offers a flat per capita dollar amount for each claimant.

- The defendant negotiates an individual settlement amount for each of the fifty claimants, and each claimant can accept or reject it individually, but the settlement negotiations occur during a single negotiating session between the defendant's lawyer and the claimants' lawyer.

On the various forms of multi-plaintiff settlements, see Howard Erichson, A Typology of Aggregate Settlements, 80 Notre Dame L. Rev. 1769 (2005).

The ABA ethics opinion on aggregate settlements offers this definition: "An aggregate settlement or aggregated agreement occurs when two or more clients who are represented by the same lawyer together resolve their claims or defenses or pleas." ABA Formal Op. 06–438 (2006). The ABA opinion's definition leaves open questions about which types of deals are subject to Rule 1.8(g). In the last example (individual amounts, independently considered), are the fifty claims "together resolve[d]"?

The ALI Principles of the Law of Aggregate Litigation offer a more satisfying definition. Section 3.16 suggests that an aggregate settlement is one in which the resolution of the claims of multiple claimants is "interdependent." It then defines interdependence in terms of collective conditions or collective allocation. American Law Inst., Principles of the Law of Aggregate Litigation § 3.16 (2010). In other words, a non-class settlement of the claims of multiple claimants is an "aggregate settlement" if it is contingent on acceptance by other claimants (i.e., a settlement with an all-or-nothing provision or walkaway clause), or if the allocation of settlement funds is determined collectively (i.e., matrix, per capita, or any other group approach, rather than individual negotiations). Of the examples above, which would qualify as aggregate settlements under the ALI definition?

9.   On the question of whether clients may consent to an aggregate settlement before the settlement terms are known, other authorities agree with the conclusion of the New Jersey Supreme Court in *Tax Authority* that such advance consent is impermissible under Rule 1.8(g). In addition to the cases cited in *Tax Authority*, see ABA Formal Op. 06–438 (2006); Assoc. of the Bar of the City of New York, Formal Op. 2009–6. The New York ethics opinion explains the prohibition in terms of the unavailability of information:

> [B]ecause of the dynamics of litigation and the settlement process, "informed consent" to an advance waiver is virtually a contradiction in terms. * * * In most cases, at the outset of an engagement, and indeed at any point prior to an actual settlement negotiation, it may be difficult, if not impossible, for a lawyer to possess, and therefore disclose, enough information to enable the client to understand the risks of waiving the right to approve a settlement following disclosure of all material facts and terms. The client therefore would be in no position to intelligently evaluate the waiver of the right.

10.   As the court mentions at the end of the *Tax Authority* opinion, some commentators have urged a rethinking of the aggregate settlement rule to permit advance consent. The ALI proposed a significant legal reform that would permit claimants in large-scale multi-claimant disputes to agree in advance to be bound by an aggregate settlement based on a supermajority vote: "In lieu of [informed consent after the terms of the settlement are known], individual claimants may, before the receipt of a proposed settlement offer, enter into an agreement in writing through shared counsel allowing each participating claimant to be bound by a substantial-majority vote of all claimants concerning an aggregate-settlement proposal. . . ." American Law Inst., Principles of the Law of Aggregate Litigation § 3.17(b) (2010). Whether the agreement is entered at the outset of the lawyer-client relationship or thereafter, it would be binding only if the claimants give "informed consent" to that agreement. Id. at § 3.17(b)(2). The lawyer must explain to claimants that if they do not wish to give advance settlement consent, they have the option of being represented by the lawyer on a traditional basis. Id. at § 3.17(b)(4). The enforceability of an advance consent agreement, under the ALI proposal, "should depend on whether, based on all facts and circumstances, the agreement is fair and reasonable from a procedural standpoint. Facts and circumstances to be considered include the timing of the agreement, the sophistication of the claimants, the information disclosed to the claimants, and whether the terms of the settlement were reviewed by a neutral or special master . . ., whether the claimants have some prior common relationship, and whether the claims of the claimants are similar." Id. at § 3.17(d). If a settlement is reached pursuant to the advance consent and voting process, its enforceability "should depend on whether . . . the settlement is substantively fair and reasonable." Id. at § 3.17(e). A claimant would be permitted "to challenge the fairness of the settlement" in court. Id. at § 3.18(b).

If the ALI proposal were adopted, how would it play out in a case like *Tax Authority*? Would it function differently in a mass tort such as asbestos? Think about differences in the sophistication of the claimants as well as in the uniformity of the claims. Does the proposal strike the right balance between respecting individual autonomy and facilitating the resolution of mass disputes?

Do you see the resemblance between settlements under the ALI proposal and class action settlements? One way to think about the proposal is that it would create a kind of settlement-only opt-in class action. Like a class settlement, a settlement under the ALI proposal would bind all group members as long as the settlement received the proper approval. The ALI proposal even includes a numerosity requirement and the possibility of judicial review. Because the proposal would bind claimants to a settlement as in a class action, it reintroduces some of the procedural protections of Rule 23. However, because the ALI proposal addresses only non-class settlements, it lacks any "class certification" process to determine whether the claims are sufficiently cohesive to warrant collective resolution. Does the Supreme Court's analysis in Amchem Products v. Windsor, *supra* p. 311, shed any light on the pros and cons of the ALI proposal for non-class aggregate settlements? For a critical analysis of the ALI proposal, see Howard Erichson & Benjamin Zipursky, Consent versus Closure, 96 Cornell L. Rev. 265 (2011).

11. In mass tort litigation, defendants frequently seek global settlements that resolve all or nearly all of the claims. Achieving a comprehensive resolution of personal injury or wrongful death claims, however, can be difficult. The class certification standard in mass torts makes it difficult to achieve a global resolution by using a settlement class action, as we saw in Amchem Products v. Windsor, *supra* p. 311 and Ortiz v. Fibreboard, *supra* p. 232. Unlike class actions, non-class settlements cannot bind unidentified claimants and thus cannot ordinarily provide as comprehensive a resolution of mass litigation. Even if all or most of the claimants can be identified, however, non-class aggregate settlements are a tough way for a defendant to get peace. The aggregate settlement rule requires each claimant's individual consent. Thus, if a settlement is conditioned upon acceptance by all of the claimants, a single claimant can hold up the deal. If a settlement is not conditioned upon acceptance by all claimants, then the defendant risks going forward with an incomplete settlement as some claimants continue to pursue their claims in court. By including a walkaway clause that conditions a non-class aggregate settlement on the participation of a specified percentage of the eligible claimants, a defendant may be assured of at least some level of finality while leaving enough of a safety valve for claimants to decline the settlement without spoiling the deal for everyone.

12. Some defendants have resorted to more creative, and more troubling, approaches to get claimants on board for non-class aggregate settlements. The Merck pharmaceutical company faced massive litigation over claims that its painkiller Vioxx caused heart attacks and strokes. In the early trials (see pp. 651–652 *infra* on the MDL judge's use of bellwether trials in the Vioxx litigation), most plaintiffs lost but several plaintiffs won significant verdicts. In 2007, Merck negotiated a $4.85 billion settlement with a number of the

leading plaintiffs' lawyers. The settlement offer was available to about 50,000 claimants who had filed Vioxx lawsuits against Merck or who had tolling agreements (agreements suspending the running of the statute of limitations and thereby postponing the need to file suit). To receive a payment, a claimant would have to pass through several "eligibility gates" by showing that the claimant had taken a certain amount of Vioxx and had suffered either a heart attack or stroke within a certain period of time. Individual settlement amounts would be determined by a point system and claims process, all of which was spelled out in detail in the settlement agreement, which Merck and the negotiating plaintiffs' lawyers made publicly available. Merck insisted that plaintiffs' lawyers should not be able to sign up some of their clients to participate in the settlement while pursuing other clients' claims in court. Therefore, the Vioxx settlement included terms intended to protect against such incomplete participation:

> § 1.2.8.1.   By submitting an Enrollment Form, the Enrolling Counsel affirms that he has recommended, or * * * will recommend by no later than the [deadline], to 100% of the Eligible Claimants represented by such Enrolling Counsel that such Eligible Claimants enroll in the Program.

> § 1.2.8.2. If any such Eligible Claimant disregards such recommendation, or for any other reason fails (or has failed) to submit a non-deficient and non-defective Enrollment Form on or before the [deadline], such Enrolling Counsel shall, * * * to the extent permitted by the equivalents to Rules 1.16 and 5.6 of the ABA Model Rules of Professional Conduct in the relevant jurisdiction(s), (i) take (or have taken, as the case may be) all necessary steps to disengage and withdraw from the representation of such Eligible Claimant and to forego any Interest in such Eligible Claimant and (ii) cause (or have caused, as the case may be) each other Enrolling Counsel, and each other counsel with an Interest in any Enrolled Program Claimant, which has an Interest in such Eligible Claimant to do the same.

Do you see how these terms made it likely that the settlement would get nearly universal participation by eligible claimants? Are these terms consistent with the aggregate settlement rule and other ethical constraints on lawyers?

13. *Settling multi-defendant litigation.* The *Tax Authority* case, the ALI proposal, and the Vioxx settlement largely concern the problems of settling multi-plaintiff litigation. Litigation involving numerous defendants raises a different set of settlement problems. Multi-defendant litigation becomes particularly intricate when settlements are reached with some but not other defendants. Sometimes plaintiffs engage in log-rolling to ratchet up settlement amounts and to provide a "litigation war chest" as the litigation evolves. See, e.g., In re Corrugated Container Antitrust Litigation, 643 F.2d 195 (5th Cir. 1981) (plaintiffs increased the settlement price for defendants as settlements were reached). Settlement agreements can include provisions going beyond price, such as agreements to provide discovery. They may even reduce the amount due from defendants who settle early if later settlements are cheaper.

For example, in Cintech Industrial Coatings, Inc. v. Bennett Indus., Inc., 85 F.3d 1198 (6th Cir. 1996), a settling defendant obtained a "most favored nation" clause that entitled it to better terms if plaintiffs later settled on such terms with another defendant. Then plaintiffs dismissed as to another defendant because they lacked evidence against it, and the settling defendant asked for all of its money back. The court held the clause inapplicable to this situation, which was not a "settlement" covered by the agreement. Finally, the possibility that the nonsettling defendants will seek contribution from those ready to settle may prevent settlement. See Franklin v. Kaypro Corp., 884 F.2d 1222 (9th Cir. 1989) (observing that a defendant that refuses to settle can force all to trial because of the risk of liability for contribution should the remaining defendant lose at trial). In some instances, however, the court can cut off that ability. See, e.g., Cal.Code Civ.Proc. § 877.6 (authorizing the court to cut off contribution claims on finding that the settlement has been made in good faith); Note, Multiple Defendant Settlement in 10b–5: Good Faith Contribution Bar, 40 Hast.L.J. 1253 (1989).

Note that these situations may involve efforts by plaintiffs to exploit conflicts of interest between settling and non-settling defendants. To counter the divide-and-conquer strategy, defendants' lawyers often coordinate their efforts, trying to present a united front. What are the ethical constraints on such coordination? Conflicts of interest make it difficult for one lawyer to represent multiple defendants unless their interests are strongly aligned. If aligned defendants are jointly represented, can they agree in advance to be bound by a settlement based on a majority vote? In other words, should the *Tax Authority* interpretation of Rule 1.8(g) apply to the reverse situation in which a settlement resolves claims against multiple defendants?

14. In connection with the settlement-by-vote process in *Tax Authority*, consider the "negotiation class action" concept that was proposed in the opioid litigation, which we briefly described *supra* p. 331 after *Amchem*. The number and complexity of claims and parties in the opioid litigation made any attempt at settlement daunting, so the leading plaintiffs' lawyers proposed a creative structure for attempting to achieve a settlement. Their proposed "negotiation class action" offered a hybrid between a settlement class action under Rule 23 and the sort of voting-based settlement process used in *Tax Authority* and proposed by the ALI. The negotiation class action was certified by Judge Dan Polster, the district judge overseeing the MDL, but reversed by the Sixth Circuit. In re Nat'l Prescription Opiate Litig., 332 F.R.D. 532 (N.D. Ohio 2019), rev'd, 976 F.3d 664 (6th Cir. 2020). The concept was proposed in a law review article by Professors Francis McGovern and William Rubenstein, The Negotiation Class: A Cooperative Approach to Class Actions Involving Large Stakeholders, 99 Tex. L. Rev. 73 (2020). Judge Polster described the concept as follows:

> The idea is to undertake the class certification and opt-out process prior to a settlement being reached, as is done in a normal class action geared toward trial. This will fix a class size and provide the Defendants a sense of the precise scope of the group with whom

they are negotiating. The class members' rights are protected in several critical ways. At the front end, before having to make the opt-out decision, the class members can calculate their share of any future settlement; here, groups of Plaintiffs and Plaintiffs' attorneys have worked together to establish a public health-based settlement allocation plan, the details of which are all made available to the Class and public at a case website, www.opioidsnegotiationclass.info. At the back end, each class member will be entitled to vote (yes or no) on whether a proposed settlement amount is sufficient, and no settlement will be deemed accepted unless it garners a supermajority (75%) of those voting; here, a proposal will need to secure approval from six separate supermajority vote counts, reflecting different slices of the class. Additionally, of course, the Court protects the absent class members: Rule 23 requires that the Court make specific determinations before permitting a class action to go forward, Fed. R. Civ. P. 23(a), (b)(3), (c), (g), and similarly requires that the Court—independent of the class's vote—approve any proposed settlement and attorney's fees, Fed. R. Civ. P. 23(e), (h).

As discussed more fully below, the Court is mindful of the fact that this is a novel procedure * * *. Regardless, there is nothing coercive about this process: no Defendant has to employ it. There is nothing exclusive about this process: it does not interfere with the States settling their own cases any way they want, and it does not stop parties in the MDL from settling in other ways. And there is nothing intrusive about this process: it does not stop any litigation from continuing and in no way interferes with the upcoming bellwether trials in this MDL. This process simply provides an option—and in the Court's opinion, it is a powerful, creative, and helpful one.

332 F.R.D. at 537. The Sixth Circuit, however, reversed on grounds that, even if the negotiation class action procedure might be useful for resolving the opioid litigation or other mass torts, the procedure is not authorized by Rule 23. In re Nat'l Prescription Opiate Litig., 976 F.3d 664 (6th Cir. 2020).

In what ways does the proposed negotiation class action resemble a settlement class action? In what ways does it resemble a non-class aggregate settlement with a supermajority voting procedure? Compared with each, does the negotiation class action hold out greater promise of achieving a comprehensive negotiated resolution in intractable cases? Compared with each, does the negotiation class action offer more or fewer safeguards against unfair settlements?

15. *Bankruptcy as a settlement mechanism.* Bankruptcy offers powerful tools for the aggregated handling of complex disputes, whether by litigation or settlement. First, the *automatic stay* provision of the Bankruptcy Code, 11 U.S.C. § 362(a), abruptly halts other litigation against the debtor. It stays the prosecution of lawsuits pending against the debtor in any court and bars new lawsuits on claims that arose before the bankruptcy petition. Second, the

district court where a bankruptcy proceeding is pending has *exclusive jurisdiction* over the property of the debtor and the estate. 28 U.S.C. § 1334(e). Anyone with a claim against the debtor must pursue it within the bankruptcy proceedings. Exclusive power thus functions as a consolidating mechanism.

Defendants facing overwhelming liability may find bankruptcy a more attractive way to negotiate a settlement than either a class action or a non-class aggregate settlement. By negotiating with claimants/creditors over the terms of a pre-packaged Chapter 11 bankruptcy reorganization, the defendant/debtor may try to resolve mass litigation. Professor Samuel Issacharoff (who later argued the negotiation class certification appeal in the opioids litigation) commented on the significance of such "pre-packs," especially in the context of the Bankruptcy Code's provision for resolving asbestos claims, 11 U.S.C. § 524(g):

> [I]t is noteworthy that the most important post-*Amchem* judicial developments on the proper considerations for the resolution of mass harms come not through the processes of litigation in Article III courts, but through a specific exception for asbestos bankruptcies under Section 524(g) of the Bankruptcy Code. Rather than the formalized processes of class actions, Section 524(g) places a premium on private work-outs of mass torts * * * and offers the finality of bankruptcy protection for properly consummated private settlements. A debtor seeking bankruptcy protection for asbestos liabilities may proceed through a "pre-packaged" bankruptcy (known in the trade as "pre-packs") by showing that the plan is supported by a majority of the affected claimants, representing two-thirds of the amounts claimed against the debtor. The real work is done by the requirement that the reorganization be supported by 75 percent of the debtor's asbestos claimants in order for the debtor to be able to get a "channeling injunction"—the bankruptcy procedure that forecloses any claim against the debtor not obtained ("channeled through") the bankruptcy court. The channeling injunction is critical because it provides protection against claims made not only by present claimants (including the minority who might oppose the reorganization), but by future claimants as well.

> To the untutored eye, the 524(g) workout looks strikingly similar to the efforts to obtain a judicial imprimatur for work-outs of present and future claims, as were struck down in *Amchem* and *Ortiz*. For good reason, as it appears that way to the tutored eye as well. The practical effect is that an agreement broadly supported by present claimants can be used to cram down the claims not only of dissenting plaintiffs, but of future claimants as well. The bankruptcy work-out includes a Future Claimants Representative who assumes a fiduciary responsibility. But the major difference is that the statutory scheme substitutes an Article I judge for an Article III judge, hardly a stirring form of enhanced protection for the due process interests that are at stake.

Because Section 524(g) provided a more welcoming port for judicially supervised and judicially enforced private settlement, the locus of asbestos work-outs shifted there following *Amchem* and *Ortiz*. Perhaps not surprisingly, the most significant mass tort "class action" case following *Amchem* and *Ortiz* emerges not from the overly formalized class action context but from the more flexible procedures of bankruptcy. In *In re Combustion Engineering*, [391 F.3d 190 (3d Cir. 2004),] Chief Judge Scirica of the Third Circuit had to apply to a complicated pre-pack what the *Amchem* Court defined as the "structural assurance of fair and adequate representation for the diverse groups and individuals affected." At immediate issue in *Combustion Engineering* was a multitiered payment scheme that created a private pre-petition trust for the bulk of the payout to present claimants and what was in effect a diminished corpus to serve as the bankruptcy estate for satisfying future claimants. The two were linked because the approval of the bankruptcy trust was the predicate for the realization of the pre-petition trust and, accordingly, present claimants had a strong incentive to vote for the plan in order to get the benefits of the second trust.

Examining the disputed reorganization as a bankruptcy case, Judge Scirica was able to recapture the essential equitable inquiry that was obscured by the procedural formalism of *Amchem* and *Ortiz*. As the Supreme Court has insisted, "[e]quality of distribution among creditors is a central policy of the Bankruptcy Code." The Court looked to the class action asbestos cases for the controlling principles of equity and concluded, "[t]hough *Ortiz* was decided under [Rule] 23(b)(1)(B), the Court's requirement of fair treatment for all claimants—a principle at the core of equity—also applies in the context of this case." As applied to the case, the proposed resolution failed, not because of any formal requirements of Rule 23 or any hypothesized need to return to the premise of the "day-in-court" ideal, but because the concerns of equity were sufficient to strike down a plan that gave preferential treatment to a group of voting claimants at the expense of those neither present nor voting.

Samuel Issacharoff, Private Claims, Aggregate Rights, 2008 Sup. Ct. Rev. 183, 209–11 (2009).

Compare the prepackaged bankruptcy that Issacharoff describes with the settlement class actions of *Amchem*, *supra* p. 311 and *Ortiz*, *supra* p. 232. All three involved companies facing massive asbestos liability. In all three, the companies negotiated global resolutions but needed a court's imprimatur to give binding effect to their negotiated resolutions. In each case, the resolution was ultimately rejected for failure to meet the relevant legal requirements, while each case also raised fundamental concerns about equitable treatment of claimants in mass resolutions. Despite these similarities, however, *Amchem*, *Ortiz*, and *Combustion Engineering* invoked three different legal regimes—

Rule 23(b)(3), Rule 23(b)(1)(B), and Chapter 11—each of which carries distinct requirements, draws on a different history, and implicates different policies.

A pre-packaged bankruptcy such as the one in *Combustion Engineering* involves a bankruptcy voting process in which a supermajority of claimants must approve the proposed reorganization plan. Compare bankruptcy, in this regard, with class actions, where class members have no power to vote down a proposed settlement. Class members assert objections to a proposed settlement and, in some case, may vote with their feet by opting out, but that is not the same as having the collective power to disapprove a proposed deal. By contrast, in *Tax Authority*, *supra* p. 593, the retainer agreements established a process (which the court found illegal) for the claimants to vote on a proposed non-class aggregate settlement. In its requirements for voting and for court approval, does the bankruptcy approach resemble a settlement class action, a non-class aggregate settlement based on a voting procedure, or both?

D. MULTIDISTRICT LITIGATION AS A SETTLEMENT PROCESS

As we saw in Chapter 4, the MDL statute authorizes consolidation only for pretrial purposes. In theory, MDL achieves aggregate *handling* of the litigation process, not an aggregate *resolution* of the dispute. Often, however, transferee judges treat MDL as an opportunity to achieve global resolutions of mass disputes. Although the transferee court lacks the power to adjudicate by trial all of the transferred cases, it is well situated to manage the litigation in a way that encourages global settlement.

Consider the relationship between class actions and MDL. Within MDL, leadership counsel may negotiate a settlement class action or class action settlement, along the lines explored in Part B *supra*, and the MDL transferee judge may achieve a comprehensive, binding resolution of the dispute by approving such a settlement. Alternatively, within MDL, leadership counsel may negotiate a comprehensive settlement on a non-class basis, along the lines explored in Part C *supra*.

We will examine two important questions about the use of MDL for resolution of mass disputes, building on the discussion of MDL in Chapter 4. First, how do transferee judges wield their pretrial power, as well as their limited power to try individual cases, to drive global settlements? The Sherman article considers a model of MDL resolution, focusing in particular on the Vioxx pharmaceutical litigation. Second, if MDL can be used for mass resolution through settlement, how does that affect the power and duties of the MDL judge? Turning again to the Vioxx MDL, we will see an example of a transferee judge asserting power to regulate the litigation as a "quasi-class action."

EDWARD F. SHERMAN, THE MDL MODEL FOR RESOLVING COMPLEX LITIGATION IF A CLASS ACTION IS NOT POSSIBLE

82 Tul.L.Rev. 2205 (2008).

* * *

Developments in recent years have made the MDL model more attractive as a central device for resolving complex litigation. A number of federal courts have applied increasingly stringent requirements for class certification, particularly for cases arising in multiple states. Thus, federal MDL litigation like *In re Vioxx Products Liability Litigation*, against a single pharmaceutical company on behalf of some 20,000 persons in all fifty states who alleged heart attacks and strokes from taking the medication, could likely not have been certified as a nationwide class action. Differences in state law standards, as well as individualized issues as to such matters as prior medical condition, length of time taking the drug, and injuries alleged, would demonstrate a lack of predominance of common issues, as well as problems with typicality and manageability.

The Class Action Fairness Act of 2005 (CAFA) [see p. 363 *supra*] was another blow to the centrality of the class action for resolving mass complex litigation. CAFA allows defendants to remove to federal court most multistate class actions. Given the aversion of many federal courts to class certification of multistate class actions, CAFA removal could often mean that a case would not be certified as a class action in the federal court. In order to avoid this, plaintiffs lawyers might file state-only class actions in state courts under the limited exceptions to CAFA or avoid class actions entirely by filing individual suits (usually in state courts that have been perceived in recent years as more sympathetic to plaintiffs than federal courts). However, this increases the likelihood of disparate litigation in multiple courts and overlapping class actions, making global settlement more difficult.

MDL transfer and consolidation can be an attractive procedural mechanism for dealing with this problem. An MDL transferee judge need not rely on the class action, with its demanding requirements, to achieve the benefits of aggregation and promote a global settlement. In fact, in most mass tort cases today (like Vioxx), class certification is unlikely. Furthermore, although a federal transferee judge does not have jurisdiction over related state cases, settlement negotiations as to the federal cases can be coordinated with the attorneys in the state cases, and the federal MDL can serve as a catalyst for a global settlement. As demonstrated in Vioxx, joint negotiations between lawyers in the state and federal actions, and the collaboration of state judges with the federal MDL judge, can bridge the jurisdictional divide to accomplish an aggregate settlement without resort to class actions.

Seeking Settlement

Although MDL transferee judges cannot try transferred cases unless they were filed in their district court, judges have a number of creative ways to try to accomplish settlement without the need for a transfer back. The Manual for Complex Litigation provides four examples. One of the most promising are bellwether trials of cases that are filed (or dismissed and refiled) in the transferee district, as was done in Vioxx. The information provided the attorneys regarding strengths and weaknesses across the spectrum of related cases helps them to assess the value of the consolidated litigation and makes possible a more reasoned decision as to an aggregate or global settlement. * * *

In contrast to the stringent rules that govern class actions, MDL is a looser and more flexible structure allowing for transfer and consolidation based on pragmatic considerations. The statute requires only "one or more common questions of fact" and that transfer will be for the "convenience of parties and witnesses and will promote the just and efficient conduct of [the] actions." 28 U.S.C. § 1407(a). Furthermore, the only appeal from the Panel's decision to transfer is for an extraordinary writ (and no appeal from an order denying transfer), in contrast to the availability of interlocutory appeal of class certification decisions. This enables the MDL transferee judge to begin the pretrial process immediately with little likelihood that the transfer will be overturned and to structure it for the broadest possible settlement.* * *

Perhaps the most critical decision the Panel has to make is the selection of the judge to whom an MDL case is transferred. The location of most of the witnesses and evidence is an important factor, but it is often availability and experience that leads to the transfer to a particular judge. The attorneys in the Vioxx litigation stressed the importance of the selection of the right transferee judge and the layers of responsibility among the various steering and liaison committees appointed by him. They viewed as critical to a successful MDL a "hands on" judge with experience with complex cases, tight supervision of discovery, coordination of counsel, and judicial promotion of settlement. Although a bias in favor of transferee judges who favor settlement has been raised, all federal judges today have a responsibility to actively promote settlement, and that should be especially true for MDL litigation. The MDL judge has to be proactive because she has a limited time to put the litigation into a posture for settlement in order to avoid the inefficiency and lack of uniformity of returning all cases to their originating courts. The powers of transferee judges are similar to those of any judge presiding over a consolidated piece of litigation. The lack of a right to try transferred cases filed in other districts is a significant limitation that could be viewed as diminishing management powers. On the other hand, this limitation gives MDL judges a limited time to prepare the case for trial or settlement and, like all time limits, can help to concentrate the parties' attention on settlement. The Vioxx MDL judge noted that his announcement at the end of the bellwether trials that he was considering remanding the cases helped to motivate the parties to actively negotiate for settlement. * * *

The Vioxx Litigation

Between 1999 and 2004, some 105 million prescriptions for Merck Inc.'s popular pain-killing drug Vioxx were written, and the drug was taken by some 20 million persons. It was removed from the market in 2004 after evidence surfaced that it increased the risk of heart attacks and strokes. Thousands of individual suits and numerous class actions were filed against Merck in state and federal courts throughout the country alleging product liability, tort, fraud, and warranty claims.

On February 16, 2005, the Panel on Multidistrict Litigation transferred suits representing the claims of over 4,000 plaintiffs that had been filed in federal courts against Merck (ultimately increased to some 20,000) to the U.S. Court for Eastern District of Louisiana. * * * The *Vioxx* transferee judge, Judge Eldon E. Fallon, set about bringing the Vioxx litigation to a stage where a settlement was possible, overseeing coordinated discovery and ordering "bellwether trials" of a handful of selected cases. Out of the hundreds of attorneys who had individual cases, a small number were appointed to serve in such positions as Lead Counsel, Plaintiff's Liaison Counsel, Plaintiffs' Steering Committee, and Negotiating Plaintiff Counsel. Plaintiffs' motion for a class action as to damage claims was denied by Judge Fallon on the ground that the condition and circumstances surrounding the taking of the drug by each person were so individualized and based on potentially differing state laws that the "predominance of common questions" requirement could not be met.

The Vioxx Global Settlement

At the court's encouragement, negotiations with the defendant Merck took place over an extended period. Settlement was complicated because an even larger number of Vioxx cases were pending in state courts (some 30,000), and the federal transferee court had no jurisdiction over them. However, representative counsel from the state cases were included in the negotiations, and on November 9, 2007, a global settlement was announced between Merck and the Executive Committee of the Plaintiffs' Steering Committee in the federal MDL and representatives of plaintiffs' counsel in the coordinated proceedings in the three state courts where most of the state cases were pending (New Jersey, California, and Texas). Merck agreed to pay $4.85 billion to be paid pursuant to a complex administrative and claims procedure. Judge Fallon, sitting with the coordinated proceedings judges from New Jersey and California, received the agreement in open court. The agreement settled the claims in all Vioxx cases then pending in federal and state courts, and established an administrative framework, with Judge Fallon as Chief Administrator, and Special Masters to be appointed by him, to oversee the settlement. The claims process was to be administered by a private claims consultant company.

This was a unique approach to resolving the problem of related cases pending in both federal and state courts. It could only have come about through coordination and collaboration between the representatives of the federal and state plaintiffs' counsel as well as between Judge Fallon and the state court judges. One reason for its success, in contrast to the asbestos global settlement which the U.S. Supreme Court had struck down in *Amchem Products, Inc. v. Windsor,* [*supra* p. 311] was its limited scope. It applied only to pending cases filed by persons who claimed to have suffered injuries from taking the drug. Unlike asbestos, a drug like Vioxx has a short latency period, and there was virtually no likelihood that, at the time of settlement, persons who took the drug had not yet manifested injury. Unlike a class action settlement, it was limited to pending cases and did not attempt to settle cases filed after the date of the settlement. Merck ran the risk of having to try or settle new cases filed after the date of settlement, but because of the short latency period and the passage of some three years since the drug was taken off the market, it was not expected that the number would be large. In order for Merck to have the security of settling most of the likely claims against it, the agreement required that 85% of the plaintiffs in pending cases would enroll in the settlement in order for it to take effect. This is a common provision in global settlements, and was not a problem here since more than 95% of plaintiffs ultimately enrolled in the settlement.

Plaintiffs' attorneys who wanted to participate in the settlement were required to submit the enrollment forms of 100% of their Vioxx clients. They were also required to recommend to each of their clients that he or she accept and enroll in the settlement and, if the client did not, to withdraw from representation of that client. This was obviously intended to prevent plaintiffs' attorneys with multiple Vioxx cases from "cherry picking," settling the weaker ones under the agreement but holding out the stronger ones, thus undercutting any assurance to Merck that most of the claims against it were covered by the settlement. [Questions were raised as to whether] this requirement was in conflict with the Model Rules of Professional Responsibility and similar state rules. The settlement did provide that if an attorney did not withdraw from any particular case, there could be review ultimately by the Chief Administrator (apparently including whether professional duties prevented withdrawal). A further clarification was added, which seems to have put to rest professional responsibility concerns of plaintiffs' attorneys, stating: "Each Enrolling Counsel is expected to exercise his or her independent judgment in the best interest of each client individually before determining whether to recommend enrollment in the Program." [Once the requisite percentage of

SEC. D MULTIDISTRICT LITIGATION AS A SETTLEMENT PROCESS   617

plaintiffs had enrolled and administration of the settlement began to go forward under Judge Fallon as Chief Administrator, he turned to the issue of the fees to be paid to the various plaintiffs' attorneys.]

IN RE VIOXX PRODUCTS LIABILITY LITIGATION

United States District Court, Eastern District of Louisiana, 2008.
574 F.Supp.2d 606.

ELDON E. FALLON, DISTRICT JUDGE.

With interim settlement payments scheduled to begin, the Court finds that it is appropriate at this time to address the issue of individual attorneys' fees. For the reasons listed below, the Court orders that individual attorneys' fees for all counsel representing claimants enrolled in the Vioxx Settlement Program will be capped at 32% plus reasonable costs. At a later date, after giving the parties due notice and an opportunity to be heard, the Court will determine the amount of fees and costs to be awarded to those attorneys who performed common benefit work. Pursuant to the terms of the Settlement Agreement, these latter amounts will be deducted from the individual plaintiffs' attorneys' fees.

* * *

The Federal Rules of Civil Procedure expressly provide that district courts may require reasonable fees in class actions. *See* Fed. R. Civ. P. 23(g)(1)(C)(iii); Fed. R. Civ. P. 23(h); *see also* Manual for Complex Litigation (Fourth) § 22.927 (2004). In the *Zyprexa* MDL, the court found that several factors counseled in favor of treating the case as a quasi-class action, subjecting the settlement program to review under the court's general equitable powers. *See In re Zyprexa Prods. Liab. Litig.*, 424 F.Supp.2d 488, 491 (E.D.N.Y. 2006). In particular, the court in *Zyprexa* noted as persuasive "[t]he large number of plaintiffs subject to the same settlement matrix approved by the court; the utilization of special masters appointed by the court to control discovery and to assist in reaching and administering a settlement; the court's order for a huge escrow fund; and other interventions by the court." As a result, the court found that the settlement was subject to the court's "imposition of fiduciary standards to ensure fair treatment to all parties and counsel regarding fees and expenses." *See id.*; *see also In re Guidant Corp. Implantable Defibrillators Prods. Liab. Litig.*, 2008 WL 682174, at *18 (D.Minn. Mar. 7, 2008) (characterizing a mass tort proceeding as a quasi-class action and subjecting the global settlement to the court's equitable authority). Turning to the instant case, the Court notes that there are substantial similarities between the global settlement currently before the Court and the global settlement at issue in *Zyprexa*. First, the court in *Zyprexa* found that the case could be treated as a quasi-class action in part because of "[t]he large number of plaintiffs subject to the same settlement matrix approved by the court." *In re Zyprexa*, 424 F.Supp.2d at 491. Similarly, there are approximately 50,000 eligible claimants currently enrolled in the Vioxx Settlement Program, all of whom are subject to the same settlement matrix for awarding points and valuating claims. Second, like the court in *Zyprexa*, which utilized special masters "to control discovery and to assist in reaching and administering a settlement," this Court has benefited from the efforts of special masters throughout the course of the MDL proceedings and the settlement administration. Moreover, the $4.85 billion settlement fund in the instant case is similar to the large settlement fund held in escrow in *Zyprexa*. In light of these factors, the Court finds that the Vioxx global settlement may properly be analyzed as occurring in a quasi-class action, giving the Court equitable authority to review contingent fee contracts for reasonableness.

[The court noted that in addition to its "equitable authority over the global settlement," it has a duty to exercise "ethical supervision over the parties."] With large corporations now seeking to achieve global peace by resolving mass tort litigations simultaneously in state and federal courts, settlement agreements such as the one currently before the Court will likely become more common. *See, e.g., In re Guidant*, 2008 WL 682174, at *3 (noting that the parties "contemplated a global settlement covering Plaintiffs from both the MDL and state cases, and included Plaintiffs whose cases had been filed or transferred to the MDL, Plaintiffs whose cases were filed outside the MDL in state court proceedings, and potential Plaintiffs who had not yet filed their cases"). As these global settlements occur more frequently, however, and as the public consciousness focuses more closely on the outcome of mass tort litigations, there will also be a growing need to protect the public's trust in the judicial process. *See In re Zyprexa*, 424 F.Supp.2d at 494 ("Public understanding of the fairness of the judicial process in handling mass torts—and particularly those involving pharmaceuticals with potential widespread health consequences—is a significant aspect of complex national litigations involving thousands of parties.").

The potential harm to the public's perception of the judicial process is especially acute in the instant case because of the large number of claimants participating in the settlement. The approximately 50,000 plaintiffs and the $4.85 billion settlement fund have captured the public's attention, resulting in a heightened degree of public scrutiny on the settlement proceedings and the judicial process in general. Disproportionate results and inconsistent standards threaten to damage the public's faith in the judicial resolution of mass tort litigation by creating an impression of inherent unfairness. *Id.* at 494 ("Litigations like the present one are an important tool for the protection of consumers in our modern corporate society, and they must be conducted so that they will not be viewed as abusive by the public; they are in fact highly beneficial to the public when adequately controlled."). "These considerations are enhanced where, as here, the Judicial Panel on Multidistrict Litigation has assembled all related federal cases for coordinated or consolidated pretrial proceedings . . . [to] *promote the just and efficient conduct of such actions.'* "

[In addition, because many Vioxx claimants were elderly and in poor health, the court noted that it has "an increased responsibility to ensure that the fees are both consistent and reasonable."]

The terms of the Settlement Agreement in this case provide further support for the Court's authority to examine the reasonableness of the contingent fee contracts. The Settlement Agreement expressly grants this Court the authority to oversee various aspects of the global settlement administration. [For example, the Agreement contemplates that the court appoint an Allocation Committee concerning fees and consider its recommendations in determining common benefit work and gives the court the express authority to modify any provision if it determines the provision "is prohibited or unenforceable."]

In light of this Court's equitable authority over the settlement, its inherent authority to exercise ethical supervision over the parties, and its express authority under the terms of the Settlement Agreement, the Court finds that it has the authority to examine the contingent fee contracts in the global settlement for reasonableness, regardless of whether the claimants filed their cases in state or federal courts. In the interest of fairness and uniformity, it is both necessary and desirable that a single court be able to set a reasonable limitation on contingent fees in this global settlement proceeding. Having overseen not only the course of the MDL proceedings but also the administration of the Vioxx Settlement Program, this Court is uniquely situated to examine the reasonableness of attorneys' fees for claimants enrolled in the global settlement.

[To determine a reasonable limitation on individual contingent fees in the context of the Vioxx settlement, the court looked at state statutes that limit contingent fees and decisions by other courts that capped fees in similar situations.] The instant case presents something of a matter of first impression, due in large part to the global nature of the settlement, the large number of plaintiffs participating in the settlement, and the considerable amount of money in the settlement fund. With little precedent bearing directly on the facts of the instant case, the Court finds guidance in the decisions of other district courts dealing with similar global settlements. For example, the MDL court in *Guidant* examined contingent fee arrangements in the context of a comparable global settlement resolving state and federal claims. *See In re Guidant*, 2008 WL 682174, at * 3 (noting that the global settlement covered "Plaintiffs from both the MDL and state cases, and included Plaintiffs whose cases had been filed or transferred to the MDL, Plaintiffs whose cases were filed outside the MDL in state court proceedings, and potential Plaintiffs who had not yet filed their cases"). The global settlement agreement in *Guidant* provided the district court with authority over the administration of the settlement proceedings, including the authority to decide the amount of fees for common benefit payment. In determining the amount of the common benefit payment fees, the court also addressed the reasonableness of contingent fee contracts, taking into consideration the economies of scale provided by the coordinated proceedings and the global settlement. Accordingly, the court capped all individual case contingency fees at 20%, reserving to the parties the right to petition to the special masters for an upward departure subject to certain limiting factors. Pursuant to the court's limitations, however, no counsel could recover more than 33% in contingent fees.

[Turning to the Vioxx litigation and settlement, the court considered the challenges of the litigation as well as economies of scale due to the global settlement.] Instead of pursuing individual discovery, filing individual motions, engaging in individual settlement negotiations, or preparing individual trial plans, attorneys for eligible claimants who wish to participate in the settlement need only enroll the claimants in the settlement and then carefully monitor their progress through the claims valuation process. These economies of scale must cut both ways. The attorneys have benefited from a uniform and highly efficient resolution procedure; the claimants should similarly benefit from fees reduced to reflect that uniformity and efficiency. Even though the unique facts of certain cases may have initially warranted disparate contingent fee arrangements, these individual characteristics no longer control the calculus for determining reasonable fees. *See In re Guidant*, 2008 WL 682174, at *18 ("Because of the mass nature of this MDL, the fact that several firms/attorneys benefited from economies of scale, and the fact that many did or should have benefited in different degrees from the coordinated discovery, motion practice, and/or global settlement negotiations, there is a high likelihood that the previously negotiated contingency fee contracts would result in excessive fees."); *In re Zyprexa*, 424 F.Supp.2d at 493 ("[T]hese firms all benefitted from the effectiveness of coordinated discovery carried out in conjunction with the plaintiffs' steering committee and from other economies of scale, suggesting a need for reconsideration of fee arrangements that may have been fair when the individual litigations were commenced.").

In consideration of the various state rules dealing with contingent fees and the decisions of other district courts faced with comparable situations, the Court finds that the individual contingent fee arrangements for attorneys representing claimants enrolled in the Vioxx global settlement should be capped at 32% plus reasonable costs. In reaching this determination, the Court acknowledges the complexity and risk involved in pursuing these cases as well as the fact that any award for common benefit work will later be deducted from this sum. Nevertheless, in light of the large number of plaintiffs, the global settlement, the considerable settlement fund, and the unique contours of this litigation, the Court finds that this is a fair and reasonable framework for apportioning fees. Although perhaps a reduction from the standard 33?% to 40% contingent fee applicable on a single-case basis, this reduction will not result in a paltry award for the attorneys. With a total settlement fund of $4.85 billion, limiting attorneys' fees to 32% of the net recovery means that the attorneys in this case will receive more than $1.55 billion.

NOTES AND QUESTIONS

1.   Dean Sherman and Judge Fallon both offer positive visions of the MDL judge's role in resolving complex disputes by making MDL a fertile ground for settlement negotiations. Others, however, emphasize concerns that the drive of MDL judges to achieve comprehensive resolutions—combined with the fee incentives for plaintiffs' lawyers, the desire of defendants for protection from liability, and cozy relationships among repeat-player lawyers in MDL leadership positions—creates pressure to settle in ways that may not reflect fair resolutions of the plaintiffs' claims. See, e.g., Elizabeth Chamblee Burch, Mass Tort Deals: Backroom Bargaining in Multidistrict Litigation (Cambridge U. Press 2019).

One transferor district judge, voicing frustration that a case had not been remanded to him for trial after being transferred to MDL, wrote that "it is almost a point of honor among transferee judges acting pursuant to Section 1407(a) that cases so transferred shall be settled rather than sent back to their home courts for trial. This, in turn, reinforces the unfortunate tendency to hang on to transferred cases to enhance the likelihood of settlement. Indeed, MDL practice actively encourages retention even of trial-ready cases in order to 'encourage' settlement." DeLaventura v. Columbia Acorn Tr., 417 F.Supp.2d 147, 152 (D. Mass. 2006).

Should MDL judges make it their primary objective to prepare cases for trial? Or, to the contrary, should MDL judges make it their primary objective to bring about comprehensive negotiated resolutions? In other words, does remand for trial represent a successful completion of the MDL process or a failure to achieve MDL's full promise? When the Judicial Panel on Multidistrict Litigation selects an experienced transferee judge for the next big MDL—something that many judges consider a plum role—should the Panel prefer judges who have successfully shepherded MDL cases to mass settlements? If so, consider the incentives and judicial culture created by such a preference. These remain hotly debated questions among judges, lawyers, and academics. See, e.g., Abbe R. Gluck, Unorthodox Civil Procedure: Modern Multidistrict Litigation's Place in the Textbook Understandings of Procedure, 165 U. Pa. L. Rev. 1669 (2017).

2.   If the goal of comprehensive settlements in MDL is a worthwhile objective, should Congress consider this objective when deciding which matters are suitable for federal court jurisdiction? Consider the views of Judge Weinstein in In re Zyprexa Products Liability Litig., 238 F.R.D. 539, 542 (E.D.N.Y. 2006):

It may be useful for Congress to consider expanding the Class Action Fairness Act from class actions to at least some national MDL, non-Rule 23, aggregate actions. As use of the class action device to aggregate claims has become more difficult, MDL consolidation has increased in importance as a means of achieving final, global resolution of mass national disputes.

Even without federal jurisdiction to embrace all related cases, MDL proceedings nevertheless provide a powerful focus for settlement promotion. In *Vioxx*, for example, Judge Fallon involved state-court judges with large dockets of Vioxx cases in settlement discussions. More generally, federal MDL judges may coordinate with state judges presiding over similar cases. For example, in In re New Motor Vehicles Canadian Export Antitrust Litigation, *supra* p. 414, the federal judge initiated early and regular contact with state-court judges handling related cases. An experienced defense-side lawyer observed that seeking MDL centralization may be an effective way of persuading state-court judges to follow the federal leader: "Without an MDL proceeding, there is no obvious leader among the federal judges handling federal cases. It can thus be very difficult to convince state court judges to follow the lead of any one particular federal judge." Mark Herrmann, To MDL or Not to MDL? A Defense Perspective, 24 Litigation 43, 46 (Summer 1998).

3.   Note the broad scope of Judge Fallon's order capping the attorneys' fees for claimants who enrolled in the Vioxx settlement. Is the order limited to cases that were pending in the MDL? Does it apply to claimants whose actions were pending in state court and thus not eligible for MDL transfer? What about claimants who had not even filed lawsuits? In thinking about the Vioxx order, consider two distinct questions: First, do contingent fee contracts fall within the realm of pretrial matters over which an MDL judge may exercise control? Second, even if an MDL court may control fees in the cases that are part of the MDL, may it assert the same power over cases that are not part of the MDL? As to both of these questions, consider whether the global settlement fundamentally altered the nature of the Vioxx litigation and whether anyone was better situated than Judge Fallon to exercise supervision. Is that enough?

4.   Judge Fallon used the phrase "quasi-class action" in invoking his power to review the Vioxx settlement and to control the fees that attorneys charged clients who participated in that settlement. Is the class action analogy valid? Judge Fallon denied class certification in the Vioxx litigation, but he turned to the class action analogy to support his authority over the settlement and fees. The objecting attorneys argued that this was not a class action, where a court must approve a settlement, and that the MDL statute has no comparable requirement: "Class action rules do not become applicable simply because a large number of cases settle. Individual differences remain, not only as to the characteristics of each individual claim, but also as to the relationship between each plaintiff and his attorney." Memorandum in Support of Motion for Reconsideration/Revision of Order Capping Contingent Fees, In re Vioxx Prods. Liabil. Litig. (E.D.La.), Dec. 10, 2008, at 7. The reasons for judicial control of fees in class actions, they argued, do not apply to MDL: "Unlike a

class action, there are no 'nonparty' or 'absentee' plaintiffs in this MDL. Each plaintiff is personally represented by the attorney of his choice." The imposition of a cap, they maintained, could lead to clients being unable to engage skilled attorneys to take on the risk of financing difficult litigation.

Other MDL judges have similarly used the "quasi-class action" analogy when asserting power over attorney's fees. They point out that policies supporting judicial control of fees in class actions also apply to MDL consolidations which have a large number of plaintiffs subject to one settlement matrix, use court-appointed special masters to help administer the settlement, create a large escrow fund, and involve other court interventions. The argument is that the MDL form of aggregate litigation has so altered the traditional single-party lawsuit through a high degree of court supervision and aggregate procedures that judicial supervision of attorneys' fees, as in class actions, is authorized. For a vigorous rejection of the quasi class doctrine, see Linda Mullenix, Dubious Doctrines: The Quasi Class Action, 80 U.Cin.L.Rev. 389 (2012).

5. The MDL statute itself provides some support for assertion of equitable powers for fee-capping by a transferee judge. It directs the MDL panel to centralize cases only when it is possible to strike a balance between efficiency and fairness. Since the Panel exerts no oversight once the cases are transferred, it is up to the transferee judge to use equitable authority to ensure that the aggregate procedures achieve the proper balance. The transferee court is encouraged to be innovative. Thus, the argument is that whatever the strength of the class action analogy, consolidated MDL cases warrant judicial supervision of attorney's fees to protect the interests of the claimants against undue erosion of their recoveries by excessive attorney's fees.

Professor Ratner has questioned the effort to find authority for this activity in the MDL statute. See Morris Ratner, Achieving Procedural Goals Through Indirection: The Use of Ethics Doctrine to Justify Contingency Caps in MDL Aggregate Settlements, 26 Geo.J.Legal Ethics 59, 72 (2013):

> The word "just" in the MDL statute may be sufficiently elastic to imply that plaintiffs should enjoy some or all of the scale economy advantage that MDL litigation produces for their attorneys; but the leap from just pretrial management to re-allocation of attorneys' fees is arguably a big one. It involves clearing the hurdle of a powerful tradition of honoring privately negotiated attorney fee contracts. * * * When imposing fee caps the courts imposed across-the-board fee caps. These caps impacted different MDL plaintiffs differently, not depending on the scale economy advantage each plaintiff enjoyed, but, rather, depending merely on the original contingency fee agreement. Plaintiffs who agreed to pay more at the outset benefitted more from the caps, even if they did not necessarily benefit from more common benefit work than did those plaintiffs whose original contingency fee agreements were closer to the cap.

6.   If the mix of inherent judicial powers, analogy to class actions, the MDL statute, and the altered status of the attorney-client relationship under MDL consolidation is enough to justify Judge Fallon's capping order, how far does that authority go? Is it present in all MDL consolidations (even though the statute does not specifically provide for it)? Is it present in all consolidated cases since they necessarily involve replacing the primary representation of the individual's attorney with an altered aggregate form of representation? Or is it present only in some MDL and ordinary consolidation cases in which there are special concerns over a conflict of interest between attorneys and clients or special needs for a more expansive form of case management? Is it limited to global settlements, or could an MDL judge assert similar authority over cases that are resolved by adjudication or by individual settlements?

7.   In *Vioxx*, settlement was accomplished in part by an agreement of all the plaintiff lawyers to urge their clients to accept the settlement, and an undertaking by the lawyers not to continue representing clients who did not accept the settlement. This sort of arrangement raises issues under rules of professional responsibility, as discussed in note 12 on p. 606, *supra*, in connection with The Tax Authority v. Jackson Hewitt and the ethics rules on aggregate settlements.

CHAPTER 8

TRYING COMPLEX CASES

■ ■ ■

In the mid-twentieth century, a thoughtful observer of the American litigation scene could declare that "[t]he heart of the judicial process is the trial in court. All that precedes the trial is but preparation. All that follows is but the correction of error, if error there be." Sidney Simpson, The Problem of Trial, in D.D. Field, Centenary Essays 141, 142 (1949). Into the 1980s, courts still declared that trial was "the centerpiece of the litigation." Walters v. Inexco Oil Co., 440 So.2d 268, 275 (Miss. 1983). But these declarations no longer ring true. One explanation is the rising cost of pretrial litigation, particularly in complex cases. Others may include the emergence of the case management movement profiled in Chapter 6 and judicial promotion of settlement, examined in Chapter 7.

Nevertheless, even complex cases must be tried if they are not settled or otherwise resolved before trial. And it may be that trials of complex cases are on an upswing. See Robert Klonoff, Class Actions in the Year 2026: A Prognosis, 65 Emory L.J. 729, 733 (2016) (asserting that "the scope and sheer number of class action trials constitutes an important new trend"). The case management movement examined in Chapter 6 largely focused on changing the court's pretrial role. Building on the pretrial conferences to manage pretrial activities, judges have come to rely increasingly on the final pretrial conference under Rule 16(e) as a method of resolving in advance issues that formerly would be addressed at trial. Rule 26(a)(3) requires the parties to disclose some information about their evidence at trial. Local rules often require pretrial statements for final pretrial conferences to include much more than Rule 26(a)(3).

The trial itself largely continues to follow the format that gradually developed in Anglo-American jurisprudence. The starting point is the Seventh Amendment's guarantee of a jury trial. That would not apply in some of the cases we've studied in this course because they did not involve claims for damages. For example, recall Parsons v. Ryan, *supra* p. 238, and the sort of litigation described by Professor Chayes in Chapter 1. Usually, however, there is a right to jury trial, in the traditional jury trial format. But that traditional format can be, and increasingly has been, modified in the trial of complex cases. As you consider the modifications explored in this chapter, reflect on the values that might be furthered by the traditional trial. At least where credibility determinations are important, in-court assessment of the demeanor of witnesses while testifying has been considered critical to accurate decision making. The opportunity to tell their story to the judge and/or jury could also be important to litigants anxious to have their "day in court." Nevertheless, "[l]itigants may be the only participants in the litigation process who actually like trials. * * * [T]he most frequently cited objective of lay litigants in adjudicatory proceedings was to 'tell my side of the story,' a function not generally provided by bargaining or court-mediated settlement processes." Deborah Hensler, Resolving Mass Toxic Torts: Myths and Realities, 1989 U.Ill.L.Rev. 89, 98–99.

The first section of this chapter sketches some relatively recent initiatives to streamline or improve the traditional trial format. The second deals with something introduced in relation to class certification as to certain issues under Rule 23(c)(4) (see *supra* p. 297)—separation of issues for sequential resolution. Finally, the third section addresses the possibility of "representative" trials, which might generate outcomes binding on other cases or (as with "bellwether" trials in MDL proceedings) provide guidance for settlement.

A. MODIFIED TRIAL METHODS

Whatever may be said in favor of the traditional jury trial, it is clear that it could fail to function well in complex cases. During the 1970s and 1980s, some argued that jury trials in complex cases violated litigants' due process rights because the issues were too difficult for jurors to resolve. The argument against using juries in complex cases has largely disappeared, but innovation in trial methods for such cases flowered beginning in the 1990s. Since then, the focus has been on methods to improve juror comprehension in complex cases, with the view that "courts should 'pull out all the stops' with respect to juror education and use all available devices to improve and assist jury decisionmaking in these cases." Matthew Reiber & Jill Weinberg, The Complexity of Complexity: An Empirical Study of Juror Competence in Civil Cases, 78 U.Cin.L.Rev. 929 (2010). We turn, therefore, to specific modifications in the traditional trial format that facilitate trial of complex cases.

Jury Empowerment. Empowerment is a term used in a variety of contexts where there is a desire to give people involved in a process a feeling of involvement and control. The traditional trial format did little to empower the jurors. Designed by lawyers and judges, the format required the jurors to remain passive and observe, without even the outlet of discussing the case among themselves until deliberations began. Many courts have broken with some of these traditions in a number of areas:

Particularly in complex cases, some grounding in the applicable legal principles can be helpful to the jurors in focusing on the important parts of the evidence. Judges may therefore begin the trial with preinstructions on the area of law that will be involved in the case. See Manual for Complex Litigation (4th) § 12.432 (2004) (providing suggestions about preliminary instructions). Likewise, judges have long made efforts to simplify instructions, particularly in complicated areas of the law, to assist the jury in understanding the law. "Most judges give jurors copies of the instructions to use during deliberations." Manual for Complex Litigation (4th) § 12.434 (2004). In lengthy trials, some courts will also allow the lawyers to make interim arguments during the presentation of evidence to explain how the pieces of evidence fit together or to emphasize their view about the importance or believability of given pieces of evidence.

Other innovations resemble measures used by students. Most law students take notes in class as an aid to recalling points made. Note-taking by jurors may also help to focus attention on key points because it involves selectivity, which in turn may prompt jurors to sift through evidence in choosing the items to record. Something like assigned reading may also be helpful: "A trial judge should encourage counsel in complex civil cases to include key documents, exhibits, and other appropriate materials in notebooks for use by jurors during trial to assist them in their duties." Cal. Rules of Ct. 2.1032. Perhaps being a juror in the trial of a complex case is like being a law student in a tough securities, antitrust, or toxic tort course.

As complex litigation—both in class actions and MDL proceedings—increasingly has national significance, perhaps there will come a time to rethink the traditionally local nature of the jury pool. It has been argued that "[i]n cases of national scope, the civil jury is in crisis," due in large measure to forum shopping for local juries thought to be favorably inclined, perhaps a feature of "magnet jurisdictions." "The problem stems from a disconnect between the scope of each controversy and the scope of the pool from which jurors are drawn to decide it. If the community affected by the litigation is national, then a local decisionmaker may not fairly represent the relevant constituency." Laura Dooley, National Juries for National Litigation, 83 NYU L.Rev. 411, 412 (2008).

Use of technology. As emphasized by our coverage of e-discovery, evidence preservation and privilege protection, *supra* pp. 464–505, technology has transformed pretrial litigation. Should technology also transform the trial itself? Some think so: "The use of electronic visuals is as significant as the introduction of cross-examination in the 1870s and formal discovery in the 1930s. This will be the greatest change in advocacy in the career of anybody alive or about to be conceived." Lisa Brennan, Pitching the Gen-X Jury: As Jurors Get Younger, Law Schools Are Thinking More like MTV, Nat.L.J., June 7, 2004 (quoting a law professor). For an argument in favor of "virtual trials," see Paul Carrington, Virtual Civil Litigation: A Visit to John Bunyan's Celestial City, 98 Colum. L. Rev. 1516 (1998).

Three decades ago, lawyers who relied on technology in a trial in Texas reported on creative use of technology then available: "What the jury saw was the creation of a production studio, and not merely the playback of a tape made in the deposition room." Michael Buxton & Michael Glover, Managing a Big Case Down to Size, 15 Litigation Mag. 22, 22–23 (Summer 1989). Is this a desirable direction? As one federal judge phrased the question, "In the final analysis, *should* trials have the look of the television evening news?" Nancy Gertner, Videoconferencing: Learning Through Screens, 12 Wm. & Mary L. Bill Rts. J. 769, 773 (2004).

The Federal Rules have not yet embraced the most aggressive possible use of technology during trials. To the contrary, Rule 43(a) adheres to the traditional trial format:

> At trial, the witnesses' testimony must be taken in open court unless a federal statute, the Federal Rules of Evidence, these rules, or other rules adopted by the Supreme Court provide otherwise. For good cause in compelling circumstances and with appropriate safeguards, the court may permit testimony in open court by contemporaneous transmission from a different location.

The Committee Note accompanying the adoption of the above provision opines that "[t]he very ceremony of trial and the presence of the factfinder may exert a powerful force for truthtelling."

Lawyers and judges are cautious about innovation, but the COVID pandemic, and the resulting lockdown of many courthouses, have prompted reliance on technology to take the place of events traditionally handled in person or in court. Depositions went virtual rather quickly, and some courts suggested that the "Zoom deposition" might become the "new normal." Faford v. Grand Trunk Western R.R., 335 F.R.D. 503, 505 (E.D.Mich. 2020); For discussion, see Stephanie Russell-Kraft, Depositions Go Virtual During Pandemic, May Remain That Way, Bloomberg Law News, May 22, 2020.

But trial is different. That is the focus of Rule 43(a), quoted above. At least during the pandemic, however, given the impossibility of in-court in-person trials, at least some courts attempted to rely on virtual testimony, at least in court trials. See Daniel McLane & Michael Pest, Avoid Losing Control of a Remote Witness: Some Suggestions, Bloomberg Law News, Nov. 20, 2020 (describing virtual bench trial in the W.D. Pa. and worrying that such trials "are more susceptible to improper witness and attorney interaction"). The Committee Note to present Rule 43(a) recommends that, if remote testimony is allowed, safeguards be adopted "that protect against influence by persons present with the witness."

As of this writing, then, it is not clear whether the COVID pandemic will stimulate a broad adoption of virtual trial methods. For a review of these issues, see Scott Dodson, Lee Rosenthal & Christopher Dodson, The Zooming of Federal Civil Litigation, 104 Judicature (no. 3) 7 (2020). Stay tuned to find out whether a "new normal" actually emerges.

Limiting the duration of trial or the amount of evidence permitted at trial. Decades ago, judges began responding to the challenges of trial in complex cases by establishing time limits for trial and limiting the amount of evidence the parties could offer. In part, that sort of effort flowed from the sense lawyers can't be trusted to limit the amount of evidence they offer on their own. See U.S. v. Reaves, 636 F.Supp. 1575, 1576–77 (E.D.Ky. 1986) ("early in the career of every trial lawyer, he or she has lost a case by leaving something out, and thereupon resolved never to omit even the most inconsequential item of possible evidence").

In complex litigation, the pressure for some judicial limits may seem compelling. A leading early example is MCI Communications Corp. v. American Telephone & Telegraph Co., 708 F.2d 1081 (7th Cir. 1983), an "extraordinary antitrust case" that led to a verdict (after trebling) of $1.8 billion. Before trial, the judge asked both sides how much time they needed to put on their cases. Plaintiff predicted its case would take 26 trial days, but AT&T named 162 witnesses and predicted that trial would take eight or nine months. The judge set a 26-day limit for each side, but was clear that the time could be extended on a showing that more time was really needed. The court of appeals rejected AT&T's objection to the time limit: "The exercise of discretion may be appropriate in protracted litigation provided that witnesses are not excluded on the basis of mere numbers."

It is possible for a judge to push too hard on time limits. See, e.g., Sims v. ANR Freight System, Inc. 77 F.3d 846 (5th Cir. 1996) (district court's insistence that a trial both sides said would take five days be completed in one day was "too much of a good thing").

The case management movement (see Chapter 6) puts judges in a position to make more informed forecasts on what would be "cumulative" evidence (See Fed. R. Evid. 401). But simplifying and shortening trials and pretrial litigation may not be a panacea that will significantly increase the frequency of trial, even in relatively simple cases. See Steven Gensler & Jason Cantone, Expedited Trial Programs in Federal Court: Why Won't Attorneys Get on the Fast Track?, 55 Wake Forest L. Rev. 525 (2020) (reporting on the almost unanimous failure of lawyers to take up the offer of an expedited route to a one-day trial in simpler cases).

B. PHASED TRIALS

SYMBOLIC CONTROL, INC. V. INTERNATIONAL BUSINESS MACHINES CORP.

United States Court of Appeals, Ninth Circuit, 1980.
643 F.2d 1339.

Before BROWNING and KENNEDY, CIRCUIT JUDGES, and DUMBAULD, DISTRICT JUDGE.

KENNEDY, CIRCUIT JUDGE.

In this antitrust case Symbolic Control, Inc. (Symbolic) appeals from an order of the district court dismissing its suit against International Business Machines Corporation (IBM). After Symbolic had presented evidence limited to the single issue of causation, the suit was dismissed on the ground that upon the facts and the law the plaintiff had shown no right to relief. Fed.R.Civ.P. 41(b). In granting the motion, the district court found Symbolic had "failed to show 'with reasonable certainty and definitiveness' that overt acts or conduct of IBM were an 'actual' and 'substantial' cause of injury to plaintiff;" or "that defendant's conduct 'materially contributed' to plaintiff's injury."

We think the causation analysis used by the district court, as a result of its bifurcation decision, was erroneous, and we reverse on this ground. We do not reach various other issues raised by Symbolic on this appeal.

[Both IBM and Symbolic Control produced a type of computer software called "automatically programmed tool processor" (APT), which is used to prepare programs that will direct a machine tool to cut a metal part. Between 1967 and 1970 IBM developed a version known as NC 360 for its System/360 computers. It distributed NC 360 free of charge. Symbolic was incorporated in 1969 to market APT/70, a processor that was designed for use on the IBM System/360 computer. After it failed to make a single sale, Symbolic sued IBM, asserting that IBM's policy of giving NC 360 away violated the antitrust laws because it involved predatory pricing for the purpose of monopolizing the software market, thereby facilitating sale of its large computers, such as the System/360.]

* * *

The district court denied IBM's motion for summary judgment and ordered a bifurcated trial. The first phase of the trial, by the court's order, was to be directed solely to "the issue as to whether plaintiff's business sustained legally cognizable impact by reason of act[s] of IBM." The court made it clear it was to be assumed, solely for purposes of trial in the first phase, that there was a violation of the antitrust laws.

At the close of Symbolic's evidence, the district court dismissed the suit against IBM, holding that the controlling evidence concerning impact of the alleged violation was testimony by users of IBM's NC 360. These customers were the potential users of APT/70. The court held that evidence of possible consequences of IBM's pricing the program, rather than giving it away, was irrelevant, because such evidence would be speculative and that pricing would not have been possible after IBM placed its various versions of NC 360 in the public domain. Relying on this analysis, the court found there was no impact on Symbolic's business, since user testimony revealed that price was not, to them, a relevant factor in the decision to use one product or the other.

Assuming a violation, without evidence on the issue, in order to confine initial inquiry to the question of causation may not always foreclose an adequate causation analysis, but if the definition of the assumed violation remains amorphous, the causation inquiry can become both abstract and incomplete. That is what occurred here.

The theory of Symbolic's case was that IBM had foreclosed competition in a product line. The court assumed a violation had occurred but found that it did not cause the losses sustained by Symbolic. Yet if the assumed violation consists of IBM's giving away a discrete product line in order to bar a potential entrant from competing with the line, it is difficult to assume anything but adverse competitive effects. Closely related is the question of price. Symbolic attempted to establish that it could compete with IBM if IBM priced at cost. Symbolic therefore sought to establish at what price customers would consider rejecting IBM's program in favor of Symbolic's competitive product. Symbolic's price inquiry was foreclosed by the court, apparently on the tautological theory that only the real market conditions controlled and that no actual sales could have been made by Symbolic in a market where the competing product was given away free.

The court's ruling was based, moreover, on the apparent premise of a demand for IBM's product that was impervious to price considerations. It assumes the very question in issue to argue that a product has been accepted over a competing product because of superior quality if the analysis is made wholly without reference to price. While there may be exceptions to this general principle, none was shown in this case.

The trial court made some findings that are inconsistent with its own premise of an assumed violation. For instance, the trial court seemed tacitly to decide the question of legality when it found that "IBM neither could nor would impose a charge on programs already distributed without restriction and in the public domain." To the extent that this statement means that IBM was legally prevented from charging for continued distribution and maintenance of Version 4 of NC 360, it implicitly but unavoidably is a finding that failing to price these improved versions was not predatory. This is contrary to the assumed violation required by the order confining the initial trial to the question of impact.

The bifurcation procedure in this case was therefore defective in two respects. First, the initial premise of a violation lacked specific content and definition; and second, the trial court ruled inconsistently with the premise in any event. Bifurcation of issues is an important device for trial efficiency, and we do not mean to foreclose its use, but the procedure which is adopted must not bar effective review or produce findings that are illogical or circular. Because those defects existed here, the bifurcation procedure became unwieldy. We cannot assess the accuracy of the court's impact findings in this case without evidence of the price structure that would have prevailed absent the violation. It is difficult, moreover, to analyze price structure without reference to a specifically defined violation, resting in turn on a clear definition of product line and market. Our inquiry here is akin to the search for a particular footprint among many, conducted with only a vague notion of the shoe that made it.

The crux of the trial court's holding is that factors other than IBM's alleged violation were the cause of injury to Symbolic: "Yet all the user testimony basic to the fact of injury (impact) establishes that the customers' reasons for not leasing APT/70 had nothing to do with overt acts of IBM." The district court seems to have relied on the finding that the quality of IBM's product was the sole cause of Symbolic's loss. Where two products are assumed to be relatively similar and thus affected by a demand curve that is elastic within at least part of its range, we cannot agree without more evidence than was presented here that quality was the sole factor in the buyer's decision. We hold that, on this record, IBM has not demonstrated that Symbolic's losses were unrelated to conduct of IBM that was, for purposes of the first phase of trial, assumed to be an antitrust violation.

We do not suggest, on the other hand, that Symbolic has made the requisite showing of impact. After further proceedings, it may be established that Symbolic's losses resulted from factors other than the wrongful conduct by IBM.

* * *

It may well be that the diverse factors enumerated in IBM's brief, such as deficient marketing, managerial weakness, and a misreading of the APT opportunity, were the real causes of Symbolic's problems. IBM is in no position to make these arguments in this court, however, because as a direct result of its rule 41(b) motion to dismiss we have no findings of fact as to these issues in the record before us.

NOTES AND QUESTIONS

1. Why did the court in *Symbolic Control* bifurcate the case in the first place? The trial of plaintiff's impact case took seven weeks. Consider the amount of time a full dress trial of all issues would have taken; consider also what the district court could conclude about the plaintiff's prospects for success

in light of the summary judgment motion. Could the bifurcation have been structured in such a way as to avoid the problems cited by the appellate court?

(a) The appellate court says that the premise of a violation "lacked specific content and definition." How does one provide such content? Would it not be preferable to dispose of such issues in advance to save the parties and the court the expense and burden of a trial of the full case?

(b) The appellate court also says that the bifurcation procedure was defective because the trial court ruled inconsistently with the premise of a violation. It reasons that the trial court erred in finding that the quality of IBM's product was the sole cause of plaintiff's failure because "we cannot agree without more evidence than was presented here that quality was the sole factor in the buyer's decision." Is that a result of the decision to bifurcate or the trial court's exclusion of evidence that plaintiff could compete with IBM if IBM priced its software at cost?

(c) One reading of the Court of Appeals' opinion is that the district court's principal error was in excluding testimony about the effect on potential customers of a decision by IBM to charge for its software. In large part, this difficulty seems to have resulted from uncertainty about the level of pricing that could be considered "predatory" under the antitrust laws; at various times different courts have articulated differing standards. Assuming that the parties agreed on the standard, however, could they have identified a price below which IBM's sales would be assumed to be predatory for purposes of the trial of the impact issue? What difficulties might the district court have encountered in setting that price?

2.   In much personal injury litigation, bifurcation has long been used for separate trials of liability and damages. See, e.g., Hosie v. Chicago & North Western Railway, 282 F.2d 639 (7th Cir. 1960) (severance granted pursuant to local rules of court despite objections of both plaintiff and defendant). Does such bifurcation result in significant time savings for the parties? Should the court limit discovery to the issues to be addressed in the first segment until that matter is tried? If not, won't the parties have to complete the same amount of discovery as they would if the case were not bifurcated?

By the mid 20th century, it was reported that the principal impact of bifurcation of liability from damages was its effect on the outcome of the case. In routine personal injury cases it has long been reported that the defense wins almost twice as frequently when the liability issues are tried separately. See Warren Schwartz, Severance—A Means of Minimizing the Role of Burden and Expense in Determining the Outcome of Litigation, 20 Vand.L.Rev. 1197 (1967); Jack Weinstein, Routine Bifurcation of Jury Negligence Trials: An Example of the Questionable Use of Rule Making Power, 14 Vand.L.Rev. 831 (1961).

This experience with routine cases was also found in research on mass tort situations. Kenneth Bordens & Irwin Horowitz, Mass Tort Civil Litigation: The Impact of Procedural Changes on Jury Decisions, 73 Judicature 22 (1989), reports empirical experiments using 66 juries showing that plaintiffs received favorable verdicts significantly more often in unitary trials than in bifurcated trials. On the other hand, the damages awarded to successful plaintiffs in unitary trials were significantly lower than were awarded to successful plaintiffs in bifurcated trials. See *id.* at 25–26.

3.   For an economic analysis of the effects of bifurcation, see William Landes, Sequential Versus Unitary Trials: An Economic Analysis, 22 J. Legal Stud. 99 (1993). The article relies heavily on relatively detailed formulae for the following conclusions: "a sequential trial lowers the expected cost of litigation compared to a unitary trial for both the plaintiff and defendant because it holds out the prospect of avoiding litigation on subsequent issues if the defendant wins the current issue or the parties settle the remaining issues after the current one is decided. Consequently, a sequential trial (a) increases the plaintiff's incentive to sue, (b) increases the number of lawsuits, and (c) reduces the likelihood that the parties will settle out of court by narrowing the range of mutually acceptable settlements." Id. at 100–01.

4.   One goal of bifurcation that defendants sometimes seek is to separate compensatory and punitive claims in order to avoid inappropriate overlap of issues, but their concerns may be unjustified. Edith Greene, William Woody & Ryan Winter, Compensating Plaintiffs and Punishing Defendants: Is Bifurcation Necessary?, 24 Law & Human Behav. 187 (2000), reports that juries in unitary trials don't seem to misuse evidence such as information about defendant's wealth that is admissible only because punitive damages are combined with compensatory damage claims. In addition, bifurcation correlates with higher punitive damages awards.

5.   Severance of affirmative defenses may be more attractive, particularly if the defense will dispose of the entire case. But even with affirmative defenses substantial difficulties are often likely to arise. For example, when the defense is the statute of limitations the plaintiff may claim that the running of limitations is tolled by defendant's concealment of the claim. Resolution of that issue may require the court to address the merits of plaintiff's claim. See Richard Marcus, Fraudulent Concealment in Federal Court: Toward a More Disparate Standard?, 71 Geo.L.J. 829, 910–12 (1983) (concluding that bifurcation of concealment will be useful only when that issue focuses on a relatively isolated event separate from the main claims).

6.   Bifurcation could raise Seventh Amendment problems when different phases of the case would be presented to different juries because the second jury might not accept the findings of the first one and thereby violate the Reexamination Clause of the Seventh Amendment. Recall that such considerations have affected class certification under Rule 23(c)(4). See Issue Certification Under Rule 23(c)(4), *supra* p. 297. In Martin v. Behr Dayton Thermal Products LLC, *supra* p. 298, the court concluded that it would be premature to rule on such problems until the district court adopted a procedure for trial. In contrast, in Castano v. The American Tobacco Co., *supra* p. 280, the Fifth Circuit invoked the Reexamination Clause, reasoning as follows (84 F.3d at 751):

There is a risk that in apportioning fault the second jury could reevaluate the defendant's fault, determine that the defendant was not at fault, and apportion 100% of the fault to the plaintiff. In such a situation, the second jury would be impermissibly reconsidering the findings of the first jury.

Undoubtedly issues that are not sufficiently free-standing to warrant separate trial should not be the subject of bifurcation. As the Supreme Court put it with regard to granting a partial new trial limited to damages (similar to bifurcating liability and damages, *supra* note 2) the question depends on whether "the issue to be retried is so distinct and separable from the others that a trial of it alone may be had without injustice." Gasoline Products Co. v. Champlin Refining Co., 283 U.S. 494 (1931). Could that lead to a constitutional prohibition on common issue certification where multiple juries will need to be used for full adjudication of individual claims? Presumably the second jury would be instructed it had to accept the first jury's findings. For an argument that there is no such constitutional obstacle, see Patrick Woolley, Mass Tort Litigation and the Seventh Amendment Reexamination Clause, 83 Iowa L. Rev. 499 (1998).

In Robinson v. Metro-North Commuter R.R. Co., 267 F.3d 147 (2d Cir. 2001), the court was presented with the argument that partial class certification of an employment discrimination case would violate the Reexamination Clause. It disagreed. "Trying a bifurcated claim before separate juries does not run afoul of the Seventh Amendment, but a 'given [factual] issue may not be tried by successive juries.' " Id. at 169 n. 13; accord, Mullen v. Treasure Chest Casino, LLC, 186 F.3d 620, 629–30 (5th Cir. 1999). The solution lies in carefully defining the roles of the two juries and crafting the verdict form for the second one to show what has been decided already. See also In re Dow Corning, Inc., 211 B.R. 545 (Bkrtcy, E.D.Mich. 1997) (describing a method for handling trial of personal injury claims by recipients of silicone gel implants to guard against the risk that "the second jury can run roughshod over the findings of the first"); compare Bacon v. Honda of America Mfg., Inc., 205 F.R.D. 466 (S.D. Ohio 2001) (bifurcation not allowed in employment discrimination suit to permit class certification because the second jury would be required to re-weigh evidence and issues regarding liability). See generally Steven Gensler, Bifurcation Unbound, 75 Wash. U.L. Rev. 705 (2000) (arguing that separate trials should be employed whenever they would facilitate the handling of cases).

IN RE BENDECTIN LITIGATION
United States Court of Appeals, Sixth Circuit, 1988.
857 F.2d 290.

Before ENGEL, CHIEF JUDGE, and JONES and NELSON, CIRCUIT JUDGES.

ENGEL, CHIEF JUDGE.

[This appeal grew out of consolidated actions for personal injuries allegedly caused by Bendectin, an anti-nausea drug manufactured by defendant Merrell Dow Pharmaceuticals. Owing to removal and transfer by the Judicial Panel on Multidistrict Litigation, the district court eventually had over 800 such cases pending before it, involving over 1100 plaintiffs. To facilitate the handling of these cases, the court initially bifurcated between liability and damages, deciding to apply Ohio law to decide the question of liability. It contemplated that if liability were established the cases would be returned to the originating districts for damage trials. Any plaintiff who so desired could withdraw, but remaining in the case signified acceptance of Ohio law.

Thereafter, the court decided to "trifurcate" the case by subdividing the liability issue into two parts—causation and liability. If plaintiffs prevailed on causation questions, the jury would proceed to decide other liability questions. Fearing undue prejudice to the defendant, the trial court also excluded from the courtroom all visibly deformed plaintiffs and all plaintiffs under the age of ten. The case was then tried for 22 days, after which the jury answered the following question in the negative: "Have the plaintiffs established by a preponderance of the evidence that ingestion of Bendectin at therapeutic doses during the period of fetal organogenesis is a proximate cause of human birth defects?" Judgment was entered for defendant.

On appeal, plaintiffs objected to the trifurcation order. Although it found this order the "most troubling" aspect of the case, the court of appeals affirmed, emphasizing the trial court's discretion in the area.

First, plaintiffs argued that the issues raised were not separable enough because they relied on theories that shifted the burden of proof as to causation to defendants upon a showing of other liability factors. The court disagreed, finding that under Ohio law it would not suffice to show that the drug was a "substantial contributing factor" in bringing about their injuries. It also rejected plaintiffs' "increased risk" theory of liability, under which they could prevail by showing only that the drug caused them an increased risk of injury. Finally, it held that plaintiffs could not rely on alternate liability, based on Sindell v. Abbott Laboratories, 607 P.2d 924 (Cal. 1980), *supra* p. 37 n. 3, because plaintiffs had sued only one defendant, and the doctrine does not apply in a one-defendant case.]

Plaintiffs also argue that the decision to trifurcate the trial was an abuse of discretion because the ruling unfairly prejudiced presentation of their case in a variety of ways. * * *

Plaintiffs next challenge the decision to trifurcate on the proximate causation question because the issue trifurcated was the one which a lay jury would be least qualified to understand, evaluate, and decide. The district judge offered to try the case before a blue ribbon jury, but the plaintiffs rejected the idea. This was, of course, their right. In any event we conclude that if the issues were indeed difficult, their resolution was not rendered more difficult due to trifurcation. If anything, the narrowing of the range of inquiry through trifurcation substantially improved the manageability of the presentation of proofs by both sides and enhanced the jury's ability to comprehend the causation issue.

Plaintiffs' primary argument against trifurcation as unfairly prejudicial is that trying the question alone prejudiced plaintiffs by creating a sterile trial atmosphere. In [In re] Beverly Hills [Fire Litigation, 695 F.2d 207 (6th Cir. 1982), an action arising out of a fire in a night club], we addressed similar concerns that trifurcation could possibly prevent the plaintiffs from exercising their right to present to the jury the full atmosphere of their cause of action, including the reality of the injury:

> A strong argument can, it is true, be made against the bifurcation of a trial limited to the issue of causation. There is a danger that bifurcation may deprive plaintiffs of their legitimate right to place before the jury the circumstances and atmosphere of the entire cause of action which they have brought into the court, replacing it with a sterile or laboratory atmosphere in which causation is parted from the reality of injury. In a litigation of lesser complexity, such considerations might well have prompted the trial judge to reject such a procedure. Here, however, it is only necessary for us to observe that the occurrence of the fire itself, a major disaster in Kentucky history by all standards, was generally known to the jurors from the outset. Further, the proofs themselves, although limited, were nonetheless fully adequate to apprise the jury of the general circumstances of the tragedy and the environment in which the fire arose. As a result, we hold that the trial judge did not abuse his discretion in severing the issue of causation here.

Judge Rubin considered this language when he denied the plaintiffs' motion for a new trial. On appeal, plaintiffs also rely heavily on the same language. Sterility is not necessarily the inevitable consequence in a trifurcated trial merely because the jury may not hear the full evidence of defendant's alleged wrongdoing. It more properly refers to the potential danger that the jury may decide the causation question without appreciating the scope of the injury that defendant supposedly caused and without the realization that their duties involve the resolution of an important, lively and human controversy. It is with respect to this latter concern that the plaintiffs urge that they were unfairly prejudiced by the trifurcation. The record reveals that the district judge consciously worked to avoid the potential for unfair prejudice. For example, he instructed the jury:

> Let me suggest to you that what you are about to do may be one of the most important things you will ever do in your entire life. This is a significant case. It involves a lot of people. It involves not only the plaintiffs who are individuals, it involves people, scientists, people who have done experiments, people who are employees of the defendant company. The totality of this case involves people and while you will hear technical evidence, I do point out to you that at all times, you should keep in mind that on both sides, there are people involved.

The court was not alone in efforts to avoid the dangers of sterility. In his final argument, plaintiffs' attorney Eaton told the jury that the trial was not an academic exercise, and that the case involved many real people who sought justice, and who would, as children, be affected by the jury's verdict well into the next century.

Finally, plaintiffs argue that Judge Rubin failed to consider the caveats of Rule 42(b) in his trifurcation decision, and instead justified trifurcation only upon unsubstantiated claims of judicial efficiency, thus unduly prejudicing plaintiffs' case without good reason. We believe, however, that the district judge carefully made the necessary inquiry. In his final order the trial judge noted that Bendectin litigation could "substantially immobiliz[e] the entire Federal Judiciary. There have been only four cases involving Bendectin which have been individually tried. They required an average of 38 trial days." Judge Rubin calculated that if all 1100 cases were tried at that average length on an individual basis, they would be able to keep 182 judges occupied for one year. Contrary to the plaintiffs' claims that Judge Rubin never considered the language of Rule 42(b), he did correctly require plaintiffs to prove that defendant's drug caused their injury, and would not allow plaintiffs to buttress a weak causation case with a strong negligence case. Thus, in line with the language of Rule 42(b), the trial judge considered the causation question to be a separate issue.

In reviewing the district court's decision to trifurcate we further note Rule 42 which "giv[es] the court virtually unlimited freedom to try the issues in whatever way trial convenience requires." C. Wright, A. Miller & F. Elliott, [Federal Practice and Procedure], § 2387 at 278. Thus, a court may try an issue separately if "in the exercise of reasonable discretion [it] thinks that course would save trial time or effort or make the trial of other issues unnecessary." In this case, the district judge considered the time savings in trying this case in this fashion, and surmised that if the plaintiffs won on this issue, another eight weeks of trial would be necessary to resolve the other questions.

* * * Plainly, Judge Rubin had a massive case management problem to resolve, and chose to do so by trying the case on a separate issue that would be dispositive.

* * *

We hold that since the initial trial on the proximate causation issue was a separate issue, promoted efficiency, and did not unduly prejudice plaintiffs, trifurcating this case on the separate issue of proximate cause was proper. We need not decide whether this was the best or even the only good method of trying this case. We need only determine whether, under all the circumstances before him, the trial judge's decision to trifurcate was an abuse of discretion.

* * *

[Plaintiffs also challenged the judge's exclusion from the courtroom of all visibly deformed plaintiffs and those below the age of ten. The judge provided such plaintiffs a separate room in the courthouse from which they could observe the trial by closed-circuit television. Plaintiffs argued that this interfered with communication with counsel and excluded a "humanistic aspect of this litigation."

The appellate court noted that in Helminski v. Ayerst Laboratories, 766 F.2d 208 (6th Cir. 1985), it had insisted that "a plaintiff with a solely physical abnormality may not be excluded involuntarily, absent disruptive behavior, even when the abnormality is due allegedly to the defendant's wrongful conduct." *Id.* at 217. Nevertheless, this case was decided after Judge Rubin set out his rules governing trial. In addition, it noted that given the numbers of plaintiffs involved, some rules on allocation of courtroom space were essential.]

[C]oncerned that the presence of dozens or even hundreds of deformed plaintiffs in his courtroom might unfairly deter the jury from deciding the issue at hand in accordance with the evidence, Judge Rubin instead allowed the plaintiffs who were interested to view the trial on closed-circuit television and to assist counsel through communicative devices if they were so willing and able. This, in our view, was a reasonable way to balance the rights of the plaintiffs and the defendants in the absence of hindsight.

NATHANIEL R. JONES, CIRCUIT JUDGE, concurring in part and dissenting in part.

I write separately today for two reasons. First, I write to point out my disagreement with the majority on the exclusion, by the district court, of certain plaintiffs from the courtroom during the twenty-two day jury trial on causation. Secondly, I write to express a few of my concerns regarding the district court's trifurcation order.

* * *

Although I have no problem with the approved trifurcation order in this court's [In re] Beverly Hills [Fire Litigation, 695 F.2d 207 (6th Cir. 1982)] decision, I do become hesitant when that decision is applied, seemingly without reservation, to a case, such as this one, which is complex in nature. Because I find several distinctions between this case and *Beverly Hills*, I am reluctant to apply such reasoning wholesale. Thus, I find that if *Beverly Hills* is narrowly construed, several problems become apparent with the majority opinion.

First, all of the victims in the *Beverly Hills* litigation were affected by the same event, a disastrous and tragic fire. Thus, the issue of causation could, quite competently, be tried separately from the issues of liability and damages with only a small chance that the plaintiffs would be prejudiced. This was simply because all plaintiffs were affected in the same manner by a unique, single event. Individual facts about the individual plaintiffs would therefore have had little significance in regard to the question of causation.

The *Bendectin* litigation, however, is quite different. Over eight hundred plaintiffs, whose mothers took the drug at different times and places and under different circumstances, are involved. As such, a single, unique event such as a fire is replaced by over eight hundred distinct events that, in all likelihood, affected the individual plaintiffs in different ways. Although each distinct event involved the ingesting of the same drug, it is hard to believe that *all* eight hundred plus claims can be tied neatly into one package and satisfactorily resolved by the answering of one question, *i.e.,* did Bendectin cause the relevant birth defects? In tying all these claims together, an argument could certainly be made as to prejudice. That is, by not allowing plaintiffs to present evidence as to how they were *individually* affected by the drug [the court's order] could have resulted in prejudice to them in their attempt to establish the required elements of their case. Indeed, although I concur with the majority's *end* result, I disagree with the language used in reaching that conclusion. The majority opinion refers to the fact that the plaintiffs were not "unduly" prejudiced by the court's trifurcation order. I do not agree that this is the burden plaintiffs must meet to establish an abuse of discretion by the lower court with regard to a trifurcation order. Rather, my suggestion is that *any* prejudice to a plaintiff in the litigation of his or her case should be enough to hold that the lower court has abused its discretion. I do not agree with the majority that absent a showing of undue or excessive prejudice, the court's order should be upheld. Indeed, this court should define the amount of prejudice that must be demonstrated to establish that a trifurcation order was an abuse of discretion. Such a discussion in this case, however, is without difficulty.

Plaintiffs here simply failed to meet their burden to demonstrate *any* prejudice. That is, plaintiffs lost their case because they failed to establish any link between their birth defects and the drug Bendectin, not because of any prejudice to them resulting from the trifurcation order.

In conclusion, trifurcation orders present fundamental problems of fairness simply because the typical procedure in litigation does not involve the splitting up of a case, element by element, and trying each point to the jury separately. Rather, the plaintiff's entire case is presented to the jury at once, thereby preventing the isolation of issues in a sterile atmosphere. Simply because a litigant shares his complaint with eight hundred other claimants is not a reason to deprive him of the day in court he would have enjoyed had he been the sole plaintiff. However, as the majority points out, a trifurcation order is authorized and *necessitated* at some point so as to allow a district court to manage and control the complexities and massive size of a case. The duty of this court, however, is to prevent such a case-management tool from becoming a penalty to injured plaintiffs seeking relief via the legal system.

[Judge Jones concluded that the district court could not constitutionally exclude certain plaintiffs from the trial without holding a hearing and making findings. He argued that Helminski v. Ayerst Laboratories, 766 F.2d 208 (6th Cir. 1985), should have been applied to this case even though it was decided after the trial court had established rules for the conduct of the trial.]

NOTES AND QUESTIONS

1.   Was *Bendectin* a better case for severing issues for separate trial than *Symbolic Control, supra* p. 630? For a very thorough examination of the entire course of Bendectin litigation, including the consolidated trial, see Michael Green, Bendectin and Birth Defects (1996); see also Richard Marcus, Reexamining the Bendectin Litigation Story, 83 Iowa L. Rev. 231 (1997).

2.   Without severance, could a consolidated case like *Bendectin* ever be tried in a consolidated manner? If not, how does one answer Judge Jones' argument that the court is denying plaintiffs their day in court because they share a complaint with many others? Would severance be used in a suit by a single plaintiff as well?

3.   Would a class action have been feasible in *Bendectin*? Did common issues predominate? Could a class have been certified as to certain issues under Rule 23(c)(4)? Recall Issue Certification Under Rule 23(c)(4), *supra* p. 297. If not, will courts be tempted to use Rule 42 consolidation to accomplish by one device essentially the same result that is not possible under Rule 23? Professor Green observed that even though it was not formally certified as one, the Bendectin multidistrict litigation "much more resembled a class action than a consolidated proceeding." Green, *supra* n. 1, at 239.

4.   Note the court's concern with the complexity of the issues. Was that due to the complexity of each case individually, or to the combination of so many cases in a single proceeding?

5.   The majority evinces concern about the risk of a "sterile trial." Are these risks present because of the complexity of the issues presented by plaintiffs' individual claims, or due to the combination of cases in a single proceeding? Did the trial court really solve these problems?

Consider the following criticism of the handling of the Bendectin cases:

> The plaintiffs' argument that trifurcation had transformed an ordinary tort suit into a sterile and laboratory inquiry into causation was rejected on grounds that appear utterly implausible. The Sixth Circuit stated that this concern was adequately allayed by the trial judge's instruction to the jury that "[t]his is a significant case. It involves a lot of people" and by the closing argument of plaintiffs' counsel that the trial was "not an academic exercise" and "involved many real people who sought justice." The suggestion that such remarks are an adequate substitute for the presence and testimony of the injured plaintiff and a full presentation of all of the alleged misconduct is incredible on its face. This Bendectin jury was deprived of the evidence most tort juries would routinely hear regarding the totality of circumstances surrounding the plaintiff's injury in a manner likely to affect their deliberations in a substantial way.

Roger Trangsrud, Mass Trials in Mass Tort Cases: A Dissent, 1989 U.Ill.L.Rev. 69, 81.

Regarding the effect bifurcation might have on jury deliberations, note that some empirical research indicates that in complex criminal trials jurors need the entire fabric of the evidence to come to a decision. See Nancy Pennington & Reid Hastie, Evidence Evaluation in Complex Decision Making, 51 J. of Personality and Soc. Psy. 242–58 (1986). Researchers investigating mass tort civil cases reported apparent differences between unitary and bifurcated trials:

> [U]nitary trial juries do tend to use some version of the Pennington and Hastie story model to decide the issues. They utilize all the trial evidence while deciding each individual trial issue. Indeed, the initial analysis of the deliberations indicates that unitary trial juries often do not decide liability or causation until they hear evidence concerning damages.

>   Juries in separated trials appear to employ other, perhaps less sophisticated, heuristics to decide the issues. These latter juries tend to use more extreme heuristics: corporate-capitalist versus the little guy; good guy versus bad guy rhetoric dominates these deliberations. The bifurcation of general causation in the separated trial condition produces greater disbelief about causation yielding fewer verdicts for the plaintiffs. It may be that only more extreme pro-plaintiff juries

who appeal to the good guy-bad guy rhetoric remain in the separated trial condition to vote for the plaintiffs.

Kenneth Bordens & Irwin Horowitz, Mass Tort Civil Litigation: The Impact of Procedural Changes on Jury Decisions, 73 Judicature 22, 27 (1989).

But perhaps there is something to be said in favor of a sterile laboratory atmosphere if it focuses the jury on the pertinent evidence without distraction. Consider Professor Trangsrud's further argument (Trangsrud, *supra* at 82):

> If the Bendectin claims had been tried separately, it is possible that the defendant would have consistently prevailed. It is also possible, however, that juries presented with the entire case against the manufacturer of this drug would have awarded discounted damages to the plaintiffs before them, mindful of the serious character of the plaintiffs' injuries and the inconclusive evidence that the injuries were caused by the defendant's drug. Such an outcome would seem at odds with our current law of causation, but might anticipate reform of that law in the future. Perhaps the law is moving to allow a discounted recovery when a defendant's product increases the risk of disease or injury beyond natural levels, but strict causation cannot be proved due to the passage of time or the imperfect nature of our science.

If the law insists on proof of causation, could it be said that this argument actually provides a reason for preferring separate disposition of general causation? According to at least some observers, there never was any substantial medical support for the proposition that Bendectin caused the kinds of injuries for which compensation was sought. Thus, a scientist lamented in print that "the Bendectin cases go on, in spite of what appears to be better evidence for safety than is available for any other substance, including tap water." Anthony Scialli, Bendectin, Science, and the Law, 3 Reproductive Toxicology 157, 157 (1989); see Joseph Sanders, The Bendectin Litigation, A Case Study in the Life-Cycle of Mass Torts, 43 Hast.L.J. 301, 347 (1992) ("The scientific community seems to have reached something close to a consensus regarding the drug. While no study can remove all residual uncertainty regarding Bendectin's safety, if the drug is a teratogen, it is a relatively mild one."). In 2000, it was reported that a Canadian company proposed marketing Bendectin again as an antinausea drug for pregnant women, albeit under a different name. See Gina Kolata, Controversial Drug Makes Comeback, N.Y. Times, Sept. 26, 2000.

6. Although the judge's decision to proceed first with the issue of general causation was opposed by the plaintiffs, it should be noted that it also held risks for defendant Merrell. "Merrell had a much stronger case on the question whether Bendectin caused a given child's birth defects than on whether Bendectin was capable of causing birth defects." Green, *supra* note 1, at 194. The trial occurred before much of the scientific evidence mentioned in note 5 had been developed and, until Merrell's third witness provided what the judge thought was "[t]he most telling piece of evidence I have ever seen in 23 years

on the Federal bench," the judge thought the plaintiffs would win. Id. at 229–31.

7.   Will anything be gained by bifurcation if plaintiffs win the first phase of the trial? "Mass trials on the issue of 'general' causation create substantial savings only when plaintiffs lose." Trangsrud, *supra* note 5, at 79. Could a plaintiff victory in such a trial improve the chances for settlement? Consider litigation against Bayer about the herbicide Roundup. Although many public health organizations had found no connection between glyphosate, Roundup's active ingredient, and cancer, an arm of the World Health Organization concluded in 2015 that glyphosate could "probably" cause cancer. Thousands of suits followed, in federal and state courts. The federal suits were combined in an MDL in San Francisco. Bayer moved to exclude plaintiffs' expert testimony, but the judge refused to exclude all of it, even though he noted that it was "shaky." Then the judge held a bellwether jury trial in two phases, the first (as in *Bendectin*) limited to the scientific question on causation. After deliberating four days, the jury found Bayer liable for plaintiff's cancer, and the second phase resulted in a multi-million dollar verdict for the plaintiff in that case. See Alexandra Sage & Tina Belton, U.S. Jury Says Bayer Must Pay $80 Million in Cancer Trial, Reuters.com, March 27, 2019. Bayer shares fell more than 12% after the jury verdict. Thereafter, the MDL judge set a deadline for reaching settlement, and efforts to settle followed. See Patricia Cohen, Roundup Maker to Pay $10 Billion to Settle Cancer Cases, N.Y. Times, June 24, 2020 (reporting ongoing uncertainty about whether settlement could be arranged). Keep these issues in mind as you examine bellwether trials in section C below.

C. TRIAL OF SAMPLE CASES

Many important decisions, particularly about groups of people, are based on statistical analyses. In this book, we have often seen litigations involving large numbers of people; statistical methods could be an effective way of dealing with their claims. Reliance on statistical methods might take what could be called the "strong" or the "weak" form. The strong form would make the trials of a random sample of cases binding, by extrapolation, on all other claimants. As we shall see, this approach has not been successful. The weak method uses trial of sample cases as a method of informing the lawyers and parties and establishing case "values," sometimes resulting in a settlement that apportions relief in a way very like the results of the strong form, albeit by agreement. This method has come to be known as using "bellwether trials," named after the practice of placing a bell on a male sheep (a wether) who was selected to lead the flock. Similarly in litigation, a bellwether trial—or series of them—can lead the litigation flock to a negotiated resolution.

Sample trials leading to binding results: Courts confronting large numbers of similar claims sometimes have attempted to use statistical means to deal with the complications resulting from the number of claimants. In the Eastern District of Texas, Judge Robert Parker had more than 3,000 asbestos personal injury cases during the late 1980s, and ordered them consolidated for a trial contemplated to involve three phases. Phase I, as was also contemplated in Jenkins v. Raymark Industries, Inc., *supra* p. 279, would decide common defenses and a ratio for punitive damages. Phase II, before the same jury, would decide total or "omnibus" liability to the claimants as a class. Phase III would then involve distributing any awarded damages to claimants.

In In re Fibreboard Corp., 893 F.2d 706 (5th Cir. 1990), the court ruled that Phase II was improper and granted a writ of mandate against proceeding in that manner. The plan for that phase was to offer evidence on 30 "illustrative plaintiffs." On the basis of that evidence and other evidence, including expert testimony, the jury would decide the percentage of plaintiffs exposed to each defendant's products, and the percentage of claims barred by various affirmative defenses such as statutes of limitation and adequate warnings. The jury would also determine actual damages as a lump sum for each disease category.

The appellate court held that this trial technique was impermissible. Judge Higginbotham cautioned that "traditional ways of proceeding reflect far more than habit. They reflect the very culture of the jury trial and the case and controversy requirement of Article III." He added: "The inescapable fact is that the individual claims of 2,990 persons will not be presented. Rather, the claim of a unit of 2,990 persons will be presented. Given the unevenness of the individual claims, this Phase II process inevitably restates the dimensions of tort liability." This restatement violated the *Erie* doctrine because "Texas has made its policy choices in its substantive tort rules against the backdrop of a trial." Although the nature of a trial can be modified, "[t]here is a point, however, where cumulative changes in procedure work a change in the very character of a trial."

Judge Higginbotham voiced particular uneasiness about plaintiffs' proposed use of statistics to permit inferences about class members in *In re Fibreboard*:

> [W]e are left with a profound disquiet. First, the *assumption* of plaintiffs' argument is that its proof of omnibus damages is in fact achievable; that statistical measures of representativeness and commonality will be sufficient for the jury to make informed judgments concerning damages. We are pointed to our experience in the trial of Title VII cases and securities cases involving use of fraud on the market concepts and mathematical constructs for examples of workable trials of large numbers of claims. We find little comfort in such cases. It is true that there is considerable judicial experience with such techniques, but it is also true we have remained cautious in their use. Indeed, as the district court stated in one massive Title VII case relying on math models:

[I]t has to judicial eyes a surrealistic cast, mirroring the techniques used in its trial. Excursions into the new and sometimes arcane corners of different disciplines is a familiar task of American trial lawyers and its generalist judges. But more is afoot here, and this court is uncomfortable with its implications. This concern has grown with the realization that the esoterics of econometrics and statistics which both parties have required this court to judge have a centripetal dynamic of their own. They push from the outside roles of tools for "judicial" decisions toward the core of decision making itself. Stated more concretely: the precision-like mesh of numbers tends to make fits of social problems when I intuitively doubt such fits. I remain wary of the siren call of the numerical display. [Vuyanich v. Republic Nat. Bank of Dallas, 505 F.Supp. 224, 394 (N.D.Tex. 1980) (Higginbotham, J.).]

On remand, Judge Parker substituted a different technique also depending on statistical proof and probability analysis, and proceeded to try the case. Cimino v. Raymark Industries, Inc., 751 F.Supp. 649 (E.D.Tex. 1990). As later described by the court of appeals (151 F.3d at 299–300):

[T]he trial plan ultimately implemented after *Fibreboard* consisted of three phases, generally described as follows. Phase I comprised a complete jury trial of the entire individual cases of the ten class representatives and also a class-wide determination of issues of product defectiveness, warning, and punitive damages (including a multiplier as to each defendant). Phase II, which was to address exposure on a craft and job site basis, was dispensed with on the basis of a stipulation. In phase III, 160 different individual cases ("sample cases"), some from each of the five different allegedly asbestos-related diseases included in the entire group of underlying cases, were tried to two other juries to determine only each of those individual sample case plaintiffs' respective actual damages from their asbestos-related disease. Thereafter, and following a one-day bench hearing on the basis of which the district court determined that in each disease category the 160 sample cases were reliably representative of the cases involving the like disease among the remaining some 2,128 cases, the court ruled that each of these remaining 2,128 cases (the "extrapolation cases") would be assigned by the court to one of the five disease categories and each would be entitled to judgment based on an amount of actual damages equal to the average of the verdicts rendered in those of the 160 sample cases involving the same disease category. Punitive damages in each case would be essentially based on the phase I verdict.

Defendants challenged Judge Parker's use of what he called a "Statistics 101" analysis, and the judge rejected the challenge based on testimony of a statistics professor on the "goodness-of-fit" between the sample cases tried in Phase I and the rest of the claimants in each disease category. He invoked various other uses of statistical evidence in trials in support of this trial method. For example, in civil rights cases statistical analysis had been used to show unequal treatment of racial minorities. In tort cases, life-expectancy or mortality tables are often used in determining damages. In *Cimino*, indeed, defendants had themselves used such techniques when they presented a statistical analysis of a telephone survey in support a motion for a change of venue. Similarly, both sides relied on medical evidence containing many statistical surveys and analyses.

The court of appeals rejected Judge Parker's revised trial method. Cimino v. Raymark Industries, Inc., 151 F.3d 297 (5th Cir. 1998). It pointed out that plaintiffs' statistical expert did not independently validate the variables he used to support his conclusion about "goodness of fit," but accepted information reported by plaintiffs' lawyers. More fundamentally, it emphasized that Phase II provided no occasion for individual examination of claimants' circumstances to make a determination regarding causation, something required by Texas law and the Seventh Amendment. Accordingly, even as to the 169 representative claimants whose cases were tried, there was no proper judgment based on a finding of causation in Phase II. Regarding the "extrapolation cases," those of the other claimants whose judgments were to be based on averaging the verdicts for the 160 sample cases, the decision would be even more flawed. "The only juries that spoke to actual damages, the phase I and III juries, received evidence only on the damages to the particular plaintiffs before them, were called on to determine *only*, and *only* determined, each of those some one hundred seventy particular plaintiffs' actual damages and were not called on to determine and did not determine or purport to determine, the damages of any other plaintiffs or group of plaintiffs."

The use of statistical inference was upheld in Hilao v. Estate of Marcos, 103 F.3d 767 (9th Cir. 1996). This was a Rule 23(b)(1)(B) class action seeking recovery for some 10,000 citizens of the Philippines who were tortured or killed, or who disappeared, during the time Ferdinand Marcos was president of that country. The court first held a trial on liability, which led to a jury verdict in favor of 22 plaintiffs. Based on that verdict, the court invited class members to file claim forms under oath, and appointed a special master to gather information on damages. After removing about 5% of the claims as facially invalid, the district court had 137 randomly selected for further inquiry based on testimony of a statistical expert that the rate of validity of claims among these 137 would, to a 95% statistical probability, correspond to the rate of validity in the whole pool of approximately 9,500 claims.

A court-appointed special master then went to the Philippines and took the depositions of the 137 claimants and their witnesses and, on the basis of this expedition, filed a report concluding that six of the claims (4.37%) were not valid and recommending damage awards for the remaining class members. A jury trial on compensatory damages was then held including testimony from the statistical expert and recorded testimony from the 137 claimants and their witnesses, along with testimony from the special master about his recommendations. Then the jury returned a verdict largely (but not entirely) following the special master's recommendations. Eventually, a judgment for the remainder of the class was entered on the basis of the decisions about the 137 claims, with a reduction for invalid claims.

On appeal, the estate challenged only the method by which the district court determined the validity of the claims of other class members. Stressing "the extraordinarily unusual nature of this case," the court of appeals rejected the estate's due process objection to the procedure employed. In part, this decision was premised on the conclusion that the estate's only valid objection would be to having to pay invalid claims. "The statistical method used by the district court obviously presents a somewhat greater risk of error in comparison to an adversarial adjudication of each claim, since the former method requires a probabilistic *prediction* (albeit an extremely accurate one) of how many of the total claims are invalid." Although there was a somewhat heightened risk of error, plaintiffs' interest in use of this method was enormous since proceeding claim-by-claim would "pose insurmountable practical hurdles." A dissenting judge objected that "[i]f due process in the form of a real prove-up of causation and damages cannot be accomplished because the class is too big or to do so would take too long, then (as the Estate contends) the class is unmanageable and should not have been certified in the first place."

Going forward, the possibility of such techniques to support class certification was dealt a blow in Wal-Mart Stores, Inc. v. Dukes, 564 U.S. 338 (2011), *supra* p. 200. The Ninth Circuit had upheld class certification in part based on the prospect that sampling could be used to determine Title VII backpay entitlement for class members. The Supreme Court rejected what it called "Trial by Formula." For a critique of this view, see Alexandra Lahav, The Case for "Trial by Formula," 90 Texas L. Rev. 571 (2012), which argues that the Court's view places undue emphasis on liberty and overlooks stronger equality arguments that would be served by using some form of trial by formula. At the same time, Prof. Lahav recognizes and examines the difficulties of doing such sampling correctly. See id. at 621–33. See also Jay Tidmarsh, Resurrecting Trial by Statistics, 99 Minn. L. Rev. 1459 (2015).

In Tyson Foods, Inc. v. Bouaphakeo, 136 S.Ct. 1036 (2016), the Court said that "*Wal-Mart* does not stand for the broad proposition that a representative sample is an impermissible means of establishing classwide liability." This case was a class action for overtime pay by employees at a hog processing plant who were not paid for the time it took them to put on and remove special protective clothing required for the job (called "donning and doffing"). Defendant claimed that the time spent donning and doffing was not work eligible for pay. It also contested plaintiffs' claims that the time they spend donning and doffing added up to enough to qualify them for overtime pay. Defendant opposed bifurcation, so the case went to trial on both the question whether donning and doffing constituted "work" and whether the employees had, adding in that time, worked overtime. On the latter issue, defendant had no records and plaintiffs did not keep contemporaneous time records either. So plaintiffs hired an expert who made hundreds of videos of plaintiffs donning and doffing and came up with average times for these tasks. Stressing that "each employee worked in the same facility, did similar work, and was paid under the same policy," the Court found that the situation was distinguishable from *Wal-Mart*, where "the experiences of the employees * * * bore little relationship to one another." Because in individual actions plaintiffs could have relied on such averages in the absence of contemporaneous time records, so could the class.

The future use of such proof is uncertain. In *Tyson Foods*, the Court declined to articulate "broad and categorical rules," making close attention to the circumstances of a given case crucial. For a narrow interpretation of the decision, see Jonah Gelbach, The Triangle of Law and the Role of Evidence, 165 U. Pa. L. Rev. 1807 (2017). For an argument in favor of a broader interpretation, see Robert Bone, *Tyson Foods* and the Future of Statistical Adjudication, 95 N.C.L.Rev. 607 (2017).

Nonbinding bellwether trials: What if the sample trial outcomes are not binding on the claims of other plaintiffs? Might they nevertheless be useful as a means of providing information to litigants about the strength of their claims and defenses? As discussed in Chapter 4 in connection with multidistrict litigation, some have found such "bellwether trials" quite effective in resolving nonclass mass tort litigation. See *supra* pp. 156–157. In selecting cases for bellwether trials, should judges try to choose "representative" ones? Judge Fallon (E.D.La.), who had twice used such methods, explained them in Eldon Fallon, Jeremy Grabill & Robert Wynne, Bellwether Trials in Multidistrict Litigation, 82 Tulane L. Rev. 2323, 2325 (2008):

> [T]he results of bellwether trials need not be binding upon consolidated parties with related claims of defenses in order to be beneficial to the MDL process. Instead of injecting juries and factfinding into multidistrict litigation, bellwether trials assist in maturation of disputes by providing an opportunity for coordinating counsel to *organize* the strengths and weaknesses of

their arguments and evidence, and *understand* the risks and costs associated with the litigation. At a minimum, the bellwether process should lead to the creation of "trial packages" that can be utilized by local counsel upon the dissolution of MDLs, a valuable by-product in its own right that supplies a partial justification for the traditional delay associated with MDL practice. But perhaps more importantly, the knowledge and experience gained during the bellwether process can precipitate global settlement negotiations and ensure that such negotiations do not occur in a vacuum, but rather in light of real-world evaluations of the litigation by multiple juries.

Experienced defense lawyers have reflected as follows about bellwether trials (James Beck & Mark Hermann, Ruminations on Bellwether Trials, at http://druganddevicelaw.blogspot.com/2007/01/ruminations-on-bellwether-trials.html):

> On the one hand, a bellwether trial in an MDL (or statewide coordinated) proceedings isn't very informative. Trying one or two cases out of a collection of hundreds, or thousands, certainly doesn't give any statistical information about the value of the cases. The one or two cases are not a statistically significant cross-section of the mass of litigation.

> Moreover, the many pending cases (at least in the product liability field) probably differ from each other in ways that make their settlement values vary. Trying one case may not say much about the value of the next. And the performances of witnesses, trial counsel, and judges, and the make-up of juries, will vary across trials, so a few early trial results aren't particularly meaningful.

> A few early trial results can * * * have unfortunate effects. They can, for example, decrease the chance of a prompt global resolution of a mass tort. A big plaintiff's verdict may unreasonably raise the expectations of the plaintiffs' bar; a resounding defense win may make the defense too stubborn. And, ultimately, global settlements turn on what the parties are willing to pay (and accept) to resolve the cases, which may have little to do with the results at trial.

> On the other hand, what's the alternative to holding bellwether trials? Discovering up 5000 cases simultaneously *without* trying any? That's a disaster. Discovering up 5000 cases and setting them all for trials? That's silly (and impossible). Cobbling together classwide trials in situations that don't merit them? That's both bad law and bad policy. Trying to devise a "trial by statistics" that doesn't suffer from the due process and other concerns discussed by the Fifth Circuit in Cimino v. Raymark, 151

F.3d 297 (5th Cir. 1998), and elsewhere? That's a procedural morass.

> And bellwether trials do provide some information. They force plaintiffs' counsel to do the work needed to prepare their standard trial package, and the early trials give some sense of how sound that package is. The bellwether trials force the court to resolve legal questions that arise only as trial actually approaches and witnesses begin to take the stand. And the bellwether trials test the expert witnesses and give both parties a sense of how much it costs to try a case.

No doubt plaintiffs' counsel weigh similar considerations.

But successful bellwether trials make considerable demands on the parties and the court. Perhaps ironically, they involve much the same effort as was involved in attempting to devise a binding trial of random cases, because they will achieve their desired objectives only if they include a well-selected and representative set of cases. Thus, Judge Fallon describes in detail the three-step selection process that he regards as essential to having successful bellwether trials (82 Tulane L. Rev. at 2342–65):

> (1) Cataloguing the entire universe of cases: This task requires the attorneys and the court to review a host of variables that might distinguish some claimants from others and come up with a short list of the variables to be used. In the Vioxx litigation, for example, the variables were (a) types of injury allegedly suffered by the plaintiff; (b) the period of plaintiff's ingestion of the drug; (c) the age group into which plaintiff fell; (d) the plaintiff's prior health history; and (e) the date of injury. Selecting these criteria involved discarding a variety of other criteria, but that is necessary. "Time simply will not allow a transferee court, tasked with its MDL pretrial duties as well as the duties attendant to its regular docket, to try enough cases so that the attorneys can fully appreciate how every factual nuance of a case will unfold a trial." (Id. at 2346.)

> (2) Creating a pool of potential bellwether cases: This step entails determining how many cases should be included in the pool and ensuring that it is large enough to account for all the variables identified in the first step. Then the actual cases have to be selected; random selection may not be the best choice because there is no guarantee that the cases actually selected will adequately represent the major variables. Instead, Judge Fallon thinks that it is best to rely on counsel to make the selection. He observes that "[n]otwithstanding a litigator's natural instincts to put forward only his or her best cases and reserve weaker cases, it must be remembered that bellwether trials are not meant to be stand-alone victories or defeats. Instead, their true purpose is to

serve as an archetype for how the litigation will proceed." (Id. at 2359.) Among other considerations, it may be important to focus on trial ready cases, and on cases that can be tried in the MDL court.

(3) Selecting the individual cases from the pool for trial: This selection occurs at the end of case-specific discovery. Again, random selection, selection by the court, or selection by the attorneys are available as methods, and provision can be made for "strikes" by either side to remove objectionable cases from the final selection.

Once this process is completed, the court tries the cases thus selected. In *Vioxx*, Judge Fallon tried six cases, and five resulted in defense verdicts, with the fifth resulting in a plaintiff verdict of $51 million. The judge initially ordered a new trial limited to damages, but later remitted the award to $1.6 million, which plaintiff accepted. A global settlement followed (82 Tulane L. Rev. at 2336–37):

> After these six bellwether trials in the MDL, as well as several trials in the state courts, the parties, with the encouragement of the various courts, began serious settlement discussions. Those discussions ultimately proved successful and a partial settlement of all Vioxx-related personal injury lawsuits pending in both federal and state courts was announced * * *. Pursuant to the terms of the settlement, which was contingent upon a certain percentage of current claimants agreeing to participate, [defendant] Merck agreed to pay $4.85 billion to eligible claimants, with individual settlement awards based on an objective analysis of individual circumstances by a claims administrator.

NOTES AND QUESTIONS

1. Consider the following arguments about why statistical methods might produce more accurate decisions:

> Every verdict is itself merely a sample from the large population of potential verdicts. That "population of verdicts" consists of all the awards that would result from trying the same case repeatedly for an infinite number of times. We can remind ourselves that the exact same case could have been tried repeatedly in different contexts: before the same jury; before different juries; or by different lawyers using exactly the same facts. Or, the case could have been tried using different permutations of the same facts or different facts and arguments that could have been assembled out of the same basic case. Clearly, any given trial of a case is but a single instance from among thousands of possible trials of that same basic case. It makes more sense, then, to think of the "true" award as the average of the

population of possible awards. The fact that we normally obtain only one award from one trial of each case obscures the population of possible awards from which that one was drawn.

Imagine a case were tried 100 times. Then the verdicts are arrayed on a frequency distribution. * * *. It should be apparent that any single verdict is just one from among those. Many of the possible single verdicts constitute over- or under-compensation compared to the mean of that distribution, and that mean is the best estimate of the "true" award. Thus, to find the true award for a case, we would need to re-try each case numerous times and take the mean of the resulting awards. By taking just the one award that results from a single trial we are accepting the likelihood of some error. With traditional individualized cases the legal process always accepts this error, and it always has.

In turn, any array of damage awards conceals the underlying variation due to the measurement error associated with each of the individual awards * * *. A distribution of damage awards really consists of a set of mini-distributions reflecting the error in measurement around some "true" award for each case. The "correct" award can be made visible by certain procedural devices, such as repeated trials of the same case, or aggregation.

Try another thought experiment. Suppose that in an aggregation of cases, every one of 1000 were identical, and from those, 100 were drawn at random for trial. By trying these 100 cases and taking the average award, the court will have done the equivalent of our first thought experiment and will have far more accurately measured the correct damages than is usually done in individualized cases. By granting the mean award to each of the 100 cases, the court awards a more nearly correct amount than if each case received the award assigned by its jury. By awarding that same amount to each of the remaining 900 plaintiffs, the court also does better, in terms of accuracy of award, than it would if it conducted 900 individualized trials.

Michael Saks & Peter Blanck, Justice Improved: The Unrecognized Benefits of Sampling and Aggregation in the Trial of Mass Torts, 44 Stan.L.Rev. 815, 833–35 (1992). But wouldn't this analysis depend on a very high comparability in the claims of all claimants; to the extent they are not nearly identical, is it fair to say that this method would be better than an individual trial? For an argument that Saks and Blanck underestimate the additional risk of error resulting from statistical sampling, see Robert Bone, Statistical Adjudication: Rights, Justice and Utility in a World of Process Scarcity, 46 Vand. L. Rev. 561 (1993). Prof. Bone carefully dissects the use of sampling from a variety of perspectives, including a process-based analysis and a rights-based view as well as in terms of efficiency.

2.   Even proponents of using sampling to obtain binding results worry about improper use of the technique. For example, Judge Parker, who employed a sampling technique in *Cimino, supra* p. 646, was appointed to the court of appeals and presented with similar issues in In re Chevron U.S.A., Inc., 109 F.3d 1016 (5th Cir. 1997). Plaintiffs were some 3,000 people who lived in an area where Chevron allegedly once operated a crude oil storage waste pit, and they sought to recover for personal injuries and property damages due to alleged contamination of the area. The district court ordered that plaintiffs and defendants each designate 15 plaintiffs for a "bellwether group" of 30 claimants in a "unitary trial" that Chevron claimed would determine its liability (or at least produce verdicts that could be used in settlement discussions). Chevron submitted the affidavit of the same statistics expert who supported the trial method in *Cimino*, asserting that the plan in this case was flawed because the 30 plaintiffs thus selected were "not representative," arguing that a "stratified selection process" should be used to select the representatives if a bellwether trial were to be attempted. The district court refused to change its order, and Chevron sought a writ of mandamus.

Speaking through Judge Parker, the Fifth Circuit granted a writ of mandamus precluding any use of the "bellwether trials" with regard to the claims of other plaintiffs because the 30 selected plaintiffs were not representative, and the plan would rely on "a trial of fifteen of the 'best' and fifteen of the 'worst' cases in the universe of cases involved in the litigation." Judge Parker explained:

> The selected thirty cases included in the district court's "unitary trial" are not cases calculated to represent the group of 3,000 claimants. Thus, the results that would be obtained from a trial of these thirty (30) cases lack the requisite level of representativeness so that the results could permit a court to draw sufficiently reliable inferences about the whole that could, in turn, form the basis for a judgment affecting cases other than the selected thirty. While this particular sample of thirty cases is lacking in representativeness, statistical sampling with an appropriate level of representativeness has been utilized and approved. * * *

> We, therefore, hold that before a trial court may utilize results from a bellwether trial for a purpose that extends beyond the individual cases tried, it must, prior to any extrapolation, find that the cases tried are representative of the larger group of cases or claims from which they are selected. Typically, such a finding must be based on competent, scientific, statistical evidence that identifies the variables involved and that provides a sample of sufficient size so as to permit a finding that there is a sufficient level of confidence that the results obtained reflect results that would be obtained from trials of the whole. It is such findings that provide the foundation for any inferences that may be drawn from the trial of sample cases. Without a sufficient level of confidence in the sample results, no inferences may be drawn from such results that would form the basis for

applying such results to cases or claims that have not been actually tried.

3.   Would Judge Fallon have approved the approach used in In re Chevron USA, *supra* n. 2, for his sort of bellwether trial? Could one argue that the need to develop a set of trial results that will provide the desired information for parties who can rely on them in resolving other cases might actually motivate a judge to be even more punctilious about the development of a bellwether trial arrangement than about a binding trial of randomly selected cases? In *Vioxx*, does it seem that the results of Judge Fallon's bellwether trials provided significant guidance toward the eventual settlement? Five of the six plaintiffs lost. Might it be that the educational value of the trials—in terms of seeing how the cases actually went during trial—was as important as the eventual outcomes reached?

For an alternative method of selecting cases for bellwether trials, see Matthew Holian, Dov Rothman & David Toniatti, A Modified Approach to Random Selection of Bellwether Cases, Bloomberg BNA Class Action Lit. Rep., July 7, 2015. Rather than selecting individual cases randomly or relying on the parties to nominate individual cases, the authors would have the court draw multiple entire random samples and then allow each side to "veto" one sample or another. Assuming an odd number of random samples, that should leave the court with an entire random sample once the "veto" process is completed. The authors urge that this approach would defeat "cherry picking." Could this approach have solved the problem in In re Chevron USA? See also Alexandra Lahav, A Primer on Bellwether Trials, 37 Rev. Litig. 185 (2018) (urging greater attention to social science methodology in designing such trials).

4.   By the time Judge Parker held his trial in *Cimino* many other asbestos cases had gone to trial. Could these trial results have been used to generate a statistical database for remedies? Compare Amchem Products, Inc. v. Windsor, *supra* p. 311 (settlement based on such a matrix). After A.H. Robins Co. filed its bankruptcy petition, such a method was employed to develop an aggregate valuation figure for some 300,000 claims that were submitted in the bankruptcy proceeding. Using detailed medical data and other information on a sampling of the 9,500 Dalkon Shield cases that had been resolved (mostly by settlement) prior to the bankruptcy filing, and on some 8,000 randomly selected claims from among the new filings, experts were able to generate estimates of the likely aggregate liability for the 300,000 new claimants. See Richard Sobol, Bending the Law 171–97 (1991) (detailing the Dalkon Shield estimation process); Kenneth Feinberg, The Dalkon Shield Claimants Trust, 53 Law & Contemp. Probs. 79, 102 (Autumn 1990). Could a similar method be used to establish individual settlements or awards for new claimants? See id. at 97 (suggesting that claims scheme could base compensation amounts on "historical compensation data [that] can be compiled and analyzed to reveal the effect of various factors on recovery in past claims arising out of the same mass tort"). Would it be more appropriate to view the *Amchem* settlement and the Dalkon Shield bankruptcy as akin to settlement following bellwether trials of the sort endorsed by Judge Fallon?

Alexandra Lahav, Bellwether Trials, 76 Geo.Wash.L.Rev. 576 (2008), urges that bellwether trials be used as formal mechanisms to inject a democratic element into the resolution of complex cases (id. at 637–38):

> The bellwether trial procedure reintroduces the jury into an area of law where settlement rules. It injects public, democratic decisionmaking into a process that has been almost completely dominated by private settlement. In so doing, bellwether trials provide a new justification for group typical justice grounded in democratic participation and deliberation.
>
> Courts have been using bellwether trials informally for many years to provide a basis for settlement between litigants. The development of informal bellwether trials is a testament to the procedure's usefulness. But bellwether trials need not be purely informal. They can and should be conducted using reliable social science methods, including random sampling, so that they can provide a valid litigation alternative to settlement for mass tort cases. Whether or not mandatory bellwether trials are actually used routinely, the affirmation of a realistic alternative for litigating mass tort cases will in itself result in settlements that are more equitable. If they are used to resolve mass tort cases directly, bellwether trials will increase citizen participation in an area of the law that has been the consistent target of allegations of capture, bias, and abuse.

5.   Would every plaintiff want to have his or her case be used for a bellwether trial? In In re FEMA Trailer Formaldehyde Prod. Liability Litig., 628 F.3d 157 (5th Cir. 2010), a single father whose case was selected for a bellwether trial didn't want to take the time off from work and stressed his responsibilities as a single parent in support of his request to dismiss without prejudice. The district court dismissed, but with prejudice, and the court of appeals affirmed, explaining (id. at 163):

> Bell wanted to have his cake and eat it by withdrawing from a bellwether trial and then sitting back to await the outcome of another plaintiff's experience against the appellees. When a plaintiff files any court case, however, sitting back is no option. He must be prepared to undergo the costs, psychological, economic and otherwise, that litigation entails. That the plaintiff becomes one of a mass of thousands pursuing particular defendants lends urgency to this reality. Courts must be exceedingly wary of mass litigation in which plaintiffs are unwilling to move their cases to trial. Any individual case may be selected as a bellwether, and no plaintiff has the right to avoid the obligation to proceed with his own suit, if so selected.
>
> Confronted with Raymond Bell's request to substitute or continue, * * * the court faced a stark choice. If it permitted Bell to dismiss without prejudice, it would set a precedent that other plaintiffs could use to manipulate the integrity of the court's bellwether process.

Was Raymond Bell asking essentially to be treated as an absent class member in a class action, rather than as a plaintiff in an individual lawsuit? In denying his request, was the judge ignoring the realities of mass nonclass litigation? Or was the judge, on the contrary, finding an appropriate way to incorporate the traditional trial into the messy world of mass dispute resolution?

CHAPTER 9

PRECLUSIVE EFFECTS OF JUDGMENTS IN COMPLEX LITIGATION

■ ■ ■

Claim preclusion (or res judicata) and issue preclusion (or collateral estoppel) are fundamental to the disposition of complex litigation. They reflect the policy that once there has been a valid and final judgment, courts should not be required to adjudicate, nor parties to answer for, successive suits arising out of the same transaction or raising issues that have already been determined.

Joinder and preclusion go hand in hand. Joinder promotes efficiency only if complemented by preclusion rules that define what has been resolved and who is bound by a judgment. Because the federal rules permit claims joinder liberally, federal courts have developed strong doctrines of preclusion. The easier the rules make it for a party to discover, plead, and join claims in an initial lawsuit, the less inclined courts are to allow the party to raise those same claims in another lawsuit after the first one has reached a final judgment.

The combined effect of liberal joinder and preclusion enables parties and courts to accomplish mass adjudication. Adjudication of the claims of many parties in a single proceeding, whereby an entire class or mass of claimants and their opponents may be precluded from further litigation, offers an enticingly economic approach to resolving mass disputes. But preclusion doctrines may become *too* attractive to judges worried about overcrowded dockets. Broad application of claim preclusion and issue preclusion may sacrifice fairness for finality. Thus, whether preclusion is appropriate may depend on whether the first suit offered a full and fair opportunity to litigate, and on whether the persons sought to be precluded were parties to the original action or were adequately represented by those parties.

A. PERSONS BOUND BY JUDGMENT

The question of who is bound by a judgment takes on special significance in the context of complex litigation. The more persons who have an interest in a dispute, the more likely it is that others will seek to relitigate claims and issues, and thus the more important it is to understand who is bound by an adjudication. Moreover, complex cases often involve parties acting in some sort of representational capacity. The class action is the paradigm of representational litigation, but in non-class actions parties may act in such representative capacities as trustees, governmental bodies, or organizations acting on behalf of their members. Representational litigation can bring finality to a court's adjudication of a dispute, but if the first case is not a class action, how far does the idea of "representation" reach? That was the question that the Supreme Court answered in the following case.

TAYLOR V. STURGELL

Supreme Court of the United States, 2008.
553 U.S. 880.

JUSTICE GINSBURG delivered the opinion of the Court.

"It is a principle of general application in Anglo-American jurisprudence that one is not bound by a judgment in personam in a litigation in which he is not designated as a party or to which he has not been made a party by service of process." Hansberry v. Lee, 311 U.S. 32 (1940) [*supra* p. 166]. Several exceptions, recognized in this Court's decisions, temper this basic rule. In a class action, for example, a person not named as a party may be bound by a judgment on the merits of the action, if she was adequately represented by a party who actively participated in the litigation. In this case, we consider for the first time whether there is a "virtual representation" exception to the general rule against precluding nonparties. Adopted by a number of courts, including the courts below in the case now before us, the exception so styled is broader than any we have so far approved.

The virtual representation question we examine in this opinion arises in the following context. Petitioner Brent Taylor filed a lawsuit under the Freedom of Information Act seeking certain documents from the Federal Aviation Administration. Greg Herrick, Taylor's friend, had previously brought an unsuccessful suit seeking the same records. The two men have no legal relationship, and there is no evidence that Taylor controlled, financed, participated in, or even had notice of Herrick's earlier suit. Nevertheless, the D.C. Circuit held Taylor's suit precluded by the judgment against Herrick because, in that court's assessment, Herrick qualified as Taylor's "virtual representative."

We disapprove the doctrine of preclusion by "virtual representation," and hold, based on the record as it now stands, that the judgment against Herrick does not bar Taylor from maintaining this suit.

I

The Freedom of Information Act (FOIA) accords "any person" a right to request any records held by a federal agency. 5 U.S.C. § 552(a)(3)(A) (2006 ed.). No reason need be given for a FOIA request, and unless the requested materials fall within one of the Act's enumerated exemptions, the agency must "make the records promptly available" to the requester. If an agency refuses to furnish the requested records, the requester may file suit in federal court and obtain an injunction "order[ing] the production of any agency records improperly withheld."

The courts below held the instant FOIA suit barred by the judgment in earlier litigation seeking the same records. Because the lower courts' decisions turned on the connection between the two lawsuits, we begin with a full account of each action.

[Herrick, an antique aircraft enthusiast, owned an F-45 airplane manufactured in the 1930s by the Fairchild Engine and Airplane Corporation (FEAC). Seeking information to assist in restoring his plane, Herrick filed a FOIA request with the Federal Aviation Administration (FAA) for copies of technical documents about the F-45. FEAC had submitted detailed specifications about this plane to the FAA's predecessor agency to obtain a certificate for manufacture and sale of the plane. In 1955, FEAC sent a letter to the FAA's predecessor agency authorizing it to lend any documents in its files to the public for use in making repairs for its aircraft. The FAA still possessed hundreds of documents about the F-45, but it refused Herrick's FOIA request on the ground the documents were subject to FOIA's exemption for "trade secrets and commercial or financial information obtained from a person and privileged or confidential." In an administrative appeal, Herrick contended that FEAC's 1955 letter waived any such protections. The FAA then contacted FEAC's corporate successor, Fairchild Corporation (Fairchild), which objected to release of the documents. The FAA adhered to its original decision denying the request.

Herrick then sued the FAA in U.S. District Court in Wyoming, relying heavily on FEAC's letter authorizing release of its records. The district court granted the FAA's motion for summary judgment. It rejected Herrick's reliance on the 1955 FEAC letter because the F-45 documents were never in fact released pursuant to the 1955 letter's authorization. It also reasoned that, even if the letter had waived trade-secret protection, Fairchild had successfully "reversed" the waiver by objecting to the FAA's release to Herrick. Herrick appealed, but the Tenth Circuit affirmed the judgment. It agreed with Herrick that the 1955 letter had stripped the documents of their trade-secret protection, but upheld the district court's alternative decision that Fairchild had restored trade-secret status by objecting to Herrick's FOIA request. The Tenth Circuit also noted that Herrick's appeal had not challenged two assumptions underlying the district court's decision—(1) that trade-secret status could be "restored" to documents that had lost protection, and (2) that Fairchild had regained trade-secret status for the documents even though it claimed that protection only after Herrick had submitted his FOIA request. On these two topics, the Tenth Circuit expressed no opinion.

Less than a month after the Tenth Circuit's ruling in Herrick's suit, Taylor submitted a FOIA request for the same documents Herrick had sued to obtain. Unsuccessful, Taylor sued the FAA in U.S. District Court in the District of Columbia asserting that the 1955 letter stripped the documents of any trade-secret status they may have had. Taylor also sought to litigate the two issues Herrick had not raised before the Tenth Circuit. Fairchild, which had provided documents in Herrick's suit and submitted an amicus brief on the Tenth Circuit appeal, intervened as a defendant in Taylor's suit.

The district court granted summary judgment against Taylor on the ground that he was barred by claim preclusion. Although Taylor was not a party to the earlier suit, the court found that Taylor was "virtually represented" by Herrick and thus Taylor was bound by the judgment. The district court record showed that Taylor was president of the Antique Aircraft Association of which Herrick was a member, the two were "close associates," and Herrick had asked Taylor for assistance in restoring Herrick's F-45. Taylor was represented by the same lawyer who represented Herrick in the Wyoming litigation, and Herrick had given Taylor documents he obtained from the FAA during discovery in his suit.

The D.C. Circuit affirmed, reasoning that "virtual representation" could justify precluding a nonparty with identical interests who was adequately represented in the first litigation. The court emphasized that Taylor and Herrick sought exactly the same result—the release of the F-45 documents—and that Herrick had a stronger incentive to litigate because he owned an F-45 plane. Although some other courts had required proof that the current litigant was on notice of the earlier suit, the D.C. Circuit found that unnecessary in the current case because Taylor hired the same lawyer and Herrick had a stronger incentive to litigate.]

II

The preclusive effect of a federal-court judgment is determined by federal common law. See Semtek Int'l Inc. v. Lockheed Martin Corp., 531 U.S. 497, 507–508 (2001). For judgments in federal-question cases—for example, Herrick's FOIA suit—federal courts participate in developing "uniform federal rule[s]" of res judicata, which this Court has ultimate authority to determine and declare.[4] The federal common law of preclusion is, of course, subject to due process limitations. See Richards v. Jefferson County, 517 U.S. 793, 797 (1996).

Taylor's case presents an issue of first impression in this sense: Until now, we have never addressed the doctrine of "virtual representation" adopted (in varying forms) by several Circuits and relied upon by the courts below. Our inquiry, however, is guided by well-established precedent

---

[4] For judgments in diversity cases, federal law incorporates the rules of preclusion applied by the State in which the rendering court sits. See Semtek Int'l Inc. v. Lockheed Martin Corp., 531 U.S. 497, 508 (2001).

regarding the propriety of nonparty preclusion. We review that precedent before taking up directly the issue of virtual representation.

A

The preclusive effect of a judgment is defined by claim preclusion and issue preclusion, which are collectively referred to as "res judicata."[5] Under the doctrine of claim preclusion, a final judgment forecloses "successive litigation of the very same claim, whether or not relitigation of the claim raises the same issues as the earlier suit." Issue preclusion, in contrast, bars "successive litigation of an issue of fact or law actually litigated and resolved in a valid court determination essential to the prior judgment," even if the issue recurs in the context of a different claim. By "preclud[ing] parties from contesting matters that they have had a full and fair opportunity to litigate," these two doctrines protect against "the expense and vexation attending multiple lawsuits, conserv[e] judicial resources, and foste[r] reliance on judicial action by minimizing the possibility of inconsistent decisions." Montana v. United States, 440 U.S. 147, 153–154 (1979).

A person who was not a party to a suit generally has not had a "full and fair opportunity to litigate" the claims and issues settled in that suit. The application of claim and issue preclusion to nonparties thus runs up against the "deep-rooted historic tradition that everyone should have his own day in court." Indicating the strength of that tradition, we have often repeated the general rule that "one is not bound by a judgment in personam in a litigation in which he is not designated as a party or to which he has not been made a party by service of process." *Hansberry*, 311 U.S., at 40. See also, e.g., Martin v. Wilks, 490 U.S. 755, 761 (1989) [*supra* p. 69].

B

Though hardly in doubt, the rule against nonparty preclusion is subject to exceptions. For present purposes, the recognized exceptions can be grouped into six categories.

First, "[a] person who agrees to be bound by the determination of issues in an action between others is bound in accordance with the terms of his agreement." 1 Restatement (Second) of Judgments § 40, p. 390 (1980) (hereinafter Restatement). For example, "if separate actions involving the same transaction are brought by different plaintiffs against the same defendant, all the parties to all the actions may agree that the question of the defendant's liability will be definitely determined, one way or the other,

---

[5]   These terms have replaced a more confusing lexicon. Claim preclusion describes the rules formerly known as "merger" and "bar," while issue preclusion encompasses the doctrines once known as "collateral estoppel" and "direct estoppel."

in a 'test case.'" D. Shapiro, Civil Procedure: Preclusion in Civil Actions 77–78 (2001) (hereinafter Shapiro).[7]

Second, nonparty preclusion may be justified based on a variety of pre-existing "substantive legal relationship[s]" between the person to be bound and a party to the judgment. Qualifying relationships include, but are not limited to, preceding and succeeding owners of property, bailee and bailor, and assignee and assignor. See 2 Restatement §§ 43–44, 52, 55. These exceptions originated "as much from the needs of property law as from the values of preclusion by judgment."[8]

Third, we have confirmed that, "in certain limited circumstances," a nonparty may be bound by a judgment because she was "adequately represented by someone with the same interests who [wa]s a party" to the suit. Representative suits with preclusive effect on nonparties include properly conducted class actions, see *Martin*, 490 U.S., at 762, n. 2 (citing Fed. Rule Civ. Proc. 23), and suits brought by trustees, guardians, and other fiduciaries, see Sea-Land Services, Inc. v. Gaudet, 414 U.S. 573, 593 (1974). See also 1 Restatement § 41.

Fourth, a nonparty is bound by a judgment if she "assume[d] control" over the litigation in which that judgment was rendered. *Montana*, 440 U.S., at 154. See also 1 Restatement § 39. Because such a person has had "the opportunity to present proofs and argument," he has already "had his day in court" even though he was not a formal party to the litigation. Id., Comment a, p. 382.

Fifth, a party bound by a judgment may not avoid its preclusive force by relitigating through a proxy. Preclusion is thus in order when a person who did not participate in a litigation later brings suit as the designated representative of a person who was a party to the prior adjudication. See Chicago, R.I. & P.R. Co. v. Schendel, 270 U.S. 611, 620, 623 (1926). And although our decisions have not addressed the issue directly, it also seems clear that preclusion is appropriate when a nonparty later brings suit as an agent for a party who is bound by a judgment.

Sixth, in certain circumstances a special statutory scheme may "expressly foreclos[e] successive litigation by nonlitigants . . . if the scheme is otherwise consistent with due process." *Martin*, 490 U.S., at 762, n. 2. Examples of such schemes include bankruptcy and probate proceedings,

---

[7]   The Restatement observes that a nonparty may be bound not only by express or implied agreement, but also through conduct inducing reliance by others. See 2 Restatement § 62. We have never had occasion to consider this ground for nonparty preclusion, and we express no view on it here.

[8]   The substantive legal relationships justifying preclusion are sometimes collectively referred to as "privity." The term "privity," however, has also come to be used more broadly, as a way to express the conclusion that nonparty preclusion is appropriate on any ground. To ward off confusion, we avoid using the term "privity" in this opinion.

see ibid., and quo warranto actions or other suits that, "under [the governing] law, [may] be brought only on behalf of the public at large."

III

Reaching beyond these six established categories, some lower courts have recognized a "virtual representation" exception to the rule against nonparty preclusion. Decisions of these courts, however, have been far from consistent. * * *

The D.C. Circuit, the FAA, and Fairchild have presented three arguments in support of an expansive doctrine of virtual representation. We find none of them persuasive.

A

The D.C. Circuit purported to ground its virtual representation doctrine in this Court's decisions stating that, in some circumstances, a person may be bound by a judgment if she was adequately represented by a party to the proceeding yielding that judgment. But the D.C. Circuit's definition of "adequate representation" strayed from the meaning our decisions have attributed to that term.

In Richards [v. Jefferson County, 517 U.S. 793 (1996)], we reviewed a decision by the Alabama Supreme Court holding that a challenge to a tax was barred by a judgment upholding the same tax in a suit filed by different taxpayers. The plaintiffs in the first suit "did not sue on behalf of a class," their complaint "did not purport to assert any claim against or on behalf of any nonparties," and the judgment "did not purport to bind" nonparties. There was no indication, we emphasized, that the court in the first suit "took care to protect the interests" of absent parties, or that the parties to that litigation "understood their suit to be on behalf of absent [parties]." In these circumstances, we held, the application of claim preclusion was inconsistent with "the due process of law guaranteed by the Fourteenth Amendment."

The D.C. Circuit stated, without elaboration, that it did not "read *Richards* to hold a nonparty . . . adequately represented only if special procedures were followed [to protect the nonparty] or the party to the prior suit understood it was representing the nonparty." As the D.C. Circuit saw this case, Herrick adequately represented Taylor for two principal reasons: Herrick had a strong incentive to litigate; and Taylor later hired Herrick's lawyer, suggesting Taylor's "satisfaction with the attorney's performance in the prior case."

The D.C. Circuit misapprehended *Richards*. As just recounted, our holding that the Alabama Supreme Court's application of res judicata to nonparties violated due process turned on the lack of either special procedures to protect the nonparties' interests or an understanding by the concerned parties that the first suit was brought in a representative capacity. *Richards* thus established that representation is "adequate" for purposes of nonparty preclusion only if (at a minimum) one of these two circumstances is present.

We restated *Richards'* core holding in South Central Bell Telephone Co. v. Alabama, 526 U.S. 160 (1999). In that case, as in *Richards*, the Alabama courts had held that a judgment rejecting a challenge to a tax by one group of taxpayers barred a subsequent suit by a different taxpayer. In *South Central Bell*, however, the nonparty had notice of the original suit and engaged one of the lawyers earlier employed by the original plaintiffs. Under the D.C. Circuit's decision in Taylor's case, these factors apparently would have sufficed to establish adequate representation. Yet *South Central Bell* held that the application of res judicata in that case violated due process. Our inquiry came to an end when we determined that the original plaintiffs had not understood themselves to be acting in a representative capacity and that there had been no special procedures to safeguard the interests of absentees.

Our decisions recognizing that a nonparty may be bound by a judgment if she was adequately represented by a party to the earlier suit thus provide no support for the D.C. Circuit's broad theory of virtual representation.

B

Fairchild and the FAA do not argue that the D.C. Circuit's virtual representation doctrine fits within any of the recognized grounds for nonparty preclusion. Rather, they ask us to abandon the attempt to delineate discrete grounds and clear rules altogether. Preclusion is in order, they contend, whenever "the relationship between a party and a nonparty is 'close enough' to bring the second litigant within the judgment." Courts should make the "close enough" determination, they urge, through a "heavily fact-driven" and "equitable" inquiry. Only this sort of diffuse balancing, Fairchild and the FAA argue, can account for all of the situations in which nonparty preclusion is appropriate.

We reject this argument for three reasons. First, our decisions emphasize the fundamental nature of the general rule that a litigant is not bound by a judgment to which she was not a party. See, e.g., *Richards*, 517 U.S., at 798–799; *Martin*, 490 U.S., at 761–762. Accordingly, we have endeavored to delineate discrete exceptions that apply in "limited circumstances." Respondents' amorphous balancing test is at odds with the constrained approach to nonparty preclusion our decisions advance.

[The Court reviewed several older cases relied upon by respondents, concluding: "We thus find no support in our precedents for the lax approach to nonparty preclusion advocated by respondents."]

Our second reason for rejecting a broad doctrine of virtual representation rests on the limitations attending nonparty preclusion based on adequate representation. A party's representation of a nonparty is "adequate" for preclusion purposes only if, at a minimum: (1) the interests of the nonparty and her representative are aligned, see *Hansberry*, 311 U.S., at 43; and (2) either the party understood herself to be acting in a representative capacity or the original court took care to protect the interests of the nonparty, see *Richards*, 517 U.S., at 801–802. In addition, adequate representation sometimes requires (3) notice of the original suit to the persons alleged to have been represented.[11] In the class-action context, these limitations are implemented by the procedural safeguards contained in Federal Rule of Civil Procedure 23.

An expansive doctrine of virtual representation, however, would "recogniz[e], in effect, a common-law kind of class action." Tice [v. American Airlines, Inc.], 162 F.3d [966,] 972 [(7th Cir. 1998)]. That is, virtual representation would authorize preclusion based on identity of interests and some kind of relationship between parties and nonparties, shorn of the procedural protections prescribed in *Hansberry*, *Richards*, and Rule 23. These protections, grounded in due process, could be circumvented were we to approve a virtual representation doctrine that allowed courts to "create de facto class actions at will." *Tice*, 162 F.3d, at 973.

Third, a diffuse balancing approach to nonparty preclusion would likely create more headaches than it relieves. Most obviously, it could significantly complicate the task of district courts faced in the first instance with preclusion questions. An all-things-considered balancing approach might spark wide-ranging, time-consuming, and expensive discovery tracking factors potentially relevant under seven-or five-prong tests. And after the relevant facts are established, district judges would be called upon to evaluate them under a standard that provides no firm guidance. Preclusion doctrine, it should be recalled, is intended to reduce the burden of litigation on courts and parties. "In this area of the law," we agree, " 'crisp rules with sharp corners' are preferable to a round-about doctrine of opaque standards."

C

Finally, relying on the Eighth Circuit's decision in Tyus [v. Schoemehl], 93 F.3d [449 (8th Cir. 1996)], at 456, the FAA maintains that nonparty preclusion should apply more broadly in "public-law" litigation than in "private-law" controversies. To support this position, the FAA offers two arguments. First, the FAA urges, our decision in *Richards* acknowledges that, in certain cases, the plaintiff has a reduced interest in controlling the litigation "because of the public nature of the right at issue." When a taxpayer challenges "an alleged misuse of public funds" or "other public action," we observed in *Richards*, the suit "has only an indirect

---

[11] *Richards* suggested that notice is required in some representative suits, e.g., class actions seeking monetary relief. But we assumed without deciding that a lack of notice might be overcome in some circumstances.

impact on [the plaintiff's] interests." In actions of this character, the Court said, "we may assume that the States have wide latitude to establish procedures . . . to limit the number of judicial proceedings that may be entertained."

Taylor's FOIA action falls within the category described in *Richards*, the FAA contends, because "the duty to disclose under FOIA is owed to the public generally." The opening sentence of FOIA, it is true, states that agencies "shall make [information] available to the public." 5 U.S.C. § 552(a) (2006 ed.). Equally true, we have several times said that FOIA vindicates a "public" interest. The Act, however, instructs agencies receiving FOIA requests to make the information available not to the public at large, but rather to the "person" making the request. Thus, in contrast to the public-law litigation contemplated in *Richards*, a successful FOIA action results in a grant of relief to the individual plaintiff, not a decree benefiting the public at large.

Furthermore, we said in *Richards* only that, for the type of public-law claims there envisioned, States are free to adopt procedures limiting repetitive litigation. In this regard, we referred to instances in which the first judgment foreclosed successive litigation by other plaintiffs because, "under state law, [the suit] could be brought only on behalf of the public at large."[12] *Richards* spoke of state legislation, but it appears equally evident that Congress, in providing for actions vindicating a public interest, may "limit the number of judicial proceedings that may be entertained." It hardly follows, however, that this Court should proscribe or confine successive FOIA suits by different requesters. Indeed, Congress' provision for FOIA suits with no statutory constraint on successive actions counsels against judicial imposition of constraints through extraordinary application of the common law of preclusion.

The FAA next argues that "the threat of vexatious litigation is heightened" in public-law cases because "the number of plaintiffs with standing is potentially limitless." FOIA does allow "any person" whose request is denied to resort to federal court for review of the agency's determination. Thus it is theoretically possible that several persons could coordinate to mount a series of repetitive lawsuits.

But we are not convinced that this risk justifies departure from the usual rules governing nonparty preclusion. First, *stare decisis* will allow courts swiftly to dispose of repetitive suits brought in the same circuit. Second, even when *stare decisis* is not dispositive, "the human tendency not to waste money will deter the bringing of suits based on claims or issues that have already been adversely determined against others." Shapiro 97. This intuition seems to be borne out by experience: The FAA has not called

---

[12] Nonparty preclusion in such cases ranks under the sixth exception described above: special statutory schemes that expressly limit subsequent suits.

our attention to any instances of abusive FOIA suits in the Circuits that reject the virtual-representation theory respondents advocate here.

IV

For the foregoing reasons, we disapprove the theory of virtual representation on which the decision below rested. The preclusive effects of a judgment in a federal-question case decided by a federal court should instead be determined according to the established grounds for nonparty preclusion described in this opinion.

Although references to "virtual representation" have proliferated in the lower courts, our decision is unlikely to occasion any great shift in actual practice. Many opinions use the term "virtual representation" in reaching results at least arguably defensible on established grounds. In these cases, dropping the "virtual representation" label would lead to clearer analysis with little, if any, change in outcomes.

In some cases, however, lower courts have relied on virtual representation to extend nonparty preclusion beyond the latter doctrine's proper bounds. We now turn back to Taylor's action to determine whether his suit is such a case, or whether the result reached by the courts below can be justified on one of the recognized grounds for nonparty preclusion.

A

It is uncontested that four of the six grounds for nonparty preclusion have no application here: There is no indication that Taylor agreed to be bound by Herrick's litigation, that Taylor and Herrick have any legal relationship, that Taylor exercised any control over Herrick's suit, or that this suit implicates any special statutory scheme limiting relitigation. Neither the FAA nor Fairchild contends otherwise.

It is equally clear that preclusion cannot be justified on the theory that Taylor was adequately represented in Herrick's suit. Nothing in the record indicates that Herrick understood himself to be suing on Taylor's behalf, that Taylor even knew of Herrick's suit, or that the Wyoming District Court took special care to protect Taylor's interests. Under our pathmarking precedent, therefore, Herrick's representation was not "adequate." See *Richards*, 517 U.S., at 801–802.

That leaves only the fifth category: preclusion because a nonparty to an earlier litigation has brought suit as a representative or agent of a party who is bound by the prior adjudication. Taylor is not Herrick's legal representative and he has not purported to sue in a representative capacity. He concedes, however, that preclusion would be appropriate if respondents could demonstrate that he is acting as Herrick's "undisclosed agen[t]."

Respondents argue here, as they did below, that Taylor's suit is a collusive attempt to relitigate Herrick's action. The D.C. Circuit considered a similar question in addressing the "tactical maneuvering" prong of its virtual representation test. The Court of Appeals did not, however, treat the issue as one of agency, and it expressly declined to reach any definitive conclusions due to "the ambiguity of the facts." We therefore remand to give the courts below an opportunity to determine whether Taylor, in pursuing the instant FOIA suit, is acting as Herrick's agent. Taylor concedes that such a remand is appropriate.

We have never defined the showing required to establish that a nonparty to a prior adjudication has become a litigating agent for a party to the earlier case. Because the issue has not been briefed in any detail, we do not discuss the matter elaborately here. We note, however, that courts should be cautious about finding preclusion on this basis. A mere whiff of "tactical maneuvering" will not suffice; instead, principles of agency law are suggestive. They indicate that preclusion is appropriate only if the putative agent's conduct of the suit is subject to the control of the party who is bound by the prior adjudication. See 1 Restatement (Second) of Agency § 14, p. 60 (1957) ("A principal has the right to control the conduct of the agent with respect to matters entrusted to him.").[13]

B

[The Court rejected Fairchild's argument that the burden should be on Taylor to prove that he was not acting as Herrick's agent. Res judicata is an affirmative defense, and the burden of proving that it applies rests on the party raising the defense.]

For the reasons stated, the judgment of the United States Court of Appeals for the District of Columbia Circuit is vacated, and the case is remanded for further proceedings consistent with this opinion.

NOTES AND QUESTIONS

1.   On remand in *Taylor*, the district court ultimately ruled in favor of the plaintiff, ordering that the requested documents be released because they were not trade secrets. Taylor v. Babbitt, 760 F.Supp.2d 80 (D.D.C. 2011). A year later, Congress passed the FAA Transportation Modernization and Safety Improvement Act of 2012, including a provision called "the Herrick Amendment" that denies trade-secret status—and ensures FOIA access—to certain antique aircraft records.

2.   Note the common pattern in *Taylor*, Martin v. Wilks (*supra* p. 69), and Hansberry v. Lee (*supra* p. 166). Each case involved an attempt to bind a

---

[13] Our decision in Montana v. United States, 440 U.S. 147 (1979), also suggests a "control" test for agency. In that case, we held that the United States was barred from bringing a suit because it had controlled a prior unsuccessful action filed by a federal contractor. We see no reason why preclusion based on a lesser showing would have been appropriate if the order of the two actions had been switched—that is, if the United States had brought the first suit itself, and then sought to relitigate the same claim through the contractor. See [Chicago, R.I. & P.R. Co. v.] Schendel, 270 U.S. [611], at 618 [(1926)] ("[I]f, in legal contemplation, there is identity of parties" when two suits are brought in one order, "there must be like identity" when the order is reversed.).

nonparty with the judgment in a prior lawsuit, and in each case the Supreme Court rejected the attempt. In which case was the argument for preclusion strongest? In which case was it weakest? Although at first glance *Taylor* is a case about preclusion, isn't it also—like *Martin* and *Hansberry*—a case about joinder? *Martin* and *Hansberry* suggest that application of Rules 19 or 23 in the earlier litigation may sometimes avoid later preclusion problems. In which, if any, of the three cases would it have been feasible to expand the earlier litigation to bind all of the interested persons and thus to avoid the problem of nonparty preclusion?

3.   The Court identified six different grounds for binding those who were technically nonparties to earlier litigation. It also said that "crisp rules with sharp corners" are preferable to "diffuse" rules or a "lax" approach to binding nonparties. Do all six of the categories the Court identified provide "crisp rules"?

4.   The Supreme Court left open one possibility for the defendants to succeed in precluding Taylor's suit based on the prior judgment. On remand, defendants may try to show that in the second suit, Taylor was acting as Herrick's "litigating agent." This is the reverse of the usual nonparty preclusion argument. Rather than suggesting that Herrick was representing Taylor in the first suit, this theory would depend on showing that Taylor was representing Herrick in the second suit. What sorts of proof would suffice?

For the proposition that a subsequent party could be precluded from litigating as an agent for a party who already had his day in court, the Court cited Chicago, R.I. & P. Ry. v. Schendel, 270 U.S. 611 (1926). That case involved an accident in which a railroad worker was killed. One lawsuit was filed in Minnesota state court by the administrator of the decedent's estate. Another proceeding was filed by the railroad before the Iowa Industrial Commissioner, naming the decedent's widow as a party to the action. The key question was whether the decedent was involved in interstate commerce at the time of the accident; the validity of the Minnesota proceeding required interstate commerce, while the validity of the Iowa proceeding required *intra*state commerce. The Iowa case reached judgment first, with a finding that the decedent had died in intrastate commerce. The question before the Supreme Court was whether that determination was binding in the Minnesota case. Although the administrator who brought the Minnesota case was not a party to the Iowa case, the Court held that the administrator was nonetheless bound by the judgment because "the statutory authority of the administrator is to sue, not in his own right or for his own benefit or that of the estate, but in the right and for the benefit of the widow."

5.   In *Taylor*, the Court of Appeals had relied heavily on Tyus v. Schoemehl, 93 F.3d 449 (8th Cir. 1996) for the theory of "virtual representation" which the Supreme Court ultimately rejected. *Tyus* involved Voting Rights Act challenges to the aldermanic district boundaries in St. Louis. The first case was brought by five African-American aldermen and the African American Voting Rights Legal Defense Fund, claiming that the boundary lines diluted the African-American vote. The city moved for summary judgment, and

a dispute then developed among plaintiffs on trial strategy. The aldermen plaintiffs brought in their own lawyer and sought to withdraw from the suit. Eventually, the district court granted the city's motion. Before moving to withdraw from the first suit, the aldermen plaintiffs filed a second suit against the city making the same claims that the district lines violated the Voting Rights Act. They were joined in the new action by three additional plaintiffs including an African-American state representative. The district court held that the second suit was barred by issue preclusion and stare decisis.

The court of appeals affirmed, relying on virtual representation. The court noted that all the plaintiffs "were elected African-American officials. They all shared the same concern: the dilution of the African-American vote in St. Louis." Under these circumstances, the court said, "[t]his organizational commonality suggests a special commonality of interests." The court also found "tactical maneuvering":

> In an effort to circumvent trial strategy disagreements, the Alderman plaintiffs filed the [second] suit, simply adding new plaintiffs. This second lawsuit directly contravenes the policies supporting the preclusion doctrines. A victory by the Alderman plaintiffs in the [first] suit would have directly benefited the plaintiffs [in the second suit]. On the other hand, without virtual representation, a loss by the Aldermen plaintiffs would cause no harm to the plaintiffs [in the second suit].

The court of appeals emphasized that the plaintiffs "do not allege that they have been denied the individual right to vote. Rather, they allege that the strength of the black vote in general has been diluted." These circumstances also argued for preclusion, in the court's view:

> [I]n public law cases, the number of plaintiffs with standing is potentially limitless. If parties were allowed to continually raise issues already decided, public law claims "would assume immortality." * * * [I]n the public law context, if the plaintiff wins, by definition everyone benefits. Holding preclusion inapplicable in this context would encourage fence-sitting, because nonparties would benefit if the plaintiffs were successful but would not be penalized if the plaintiffs lost.

Compared with Taylor v. Sturgell, do the facts of *Tyus* present a more compelling scenario for binding the new plaintiffs with the prior judgment? Is there any ground for applying preclusion in *Tyus* consistent with the Supreme Court's ruling in *Taylor*?

6.   In Montana v. United States, 440 U.S. 147 (1979), a contractor on a federal dam project brought suit in state court against the Montana State Board of Equalization, contending that the state's gross receipts tax on contractors for public (but not private) construction projects was unconstitutional. The Montana Supreme Court found the tax constitutional. The United States then sued the state of Montana in federal court, challenging the constitutionality of the tax as it affected the federal government in its

dealings with contractors. The Court held that the U.S. was bound by the Montana state court judgment because the U.S. had required that the contractor file that suit, reviewed and approved the complaint, paid the attorneys' fees and costs, directed the appeal, and submitted an amicus brief on appeal. That sufficed, in the Court's view, to establish that the U.S. had controlled the first case through its control of the contractor. In *Taylor*, what would Fairchild and the FAA have had to show in order to use the *Montana* theory to preclude Taylor's lawsuit?

7.   In Richards v. Jefferson County, 517 U.S. 793 (1996), the Supreme Court addressed whether a taxpayer's challenge to a tax was claim precluded by an earlier challenge by a different taxpayer. The Alabama Supreme Court had ruled in favor of claim preclusion, finding the taxpayer's challenge to be precluded by a judgment upholding the tax in an earlier suit by different taxpayers. The U.S. Supreme Court held that claim preclusion under these circumstances violated Fourteenth Amendment due process. The Court distinguished between two types of actions brought by taxpayers: (1) cases in which the taxpayer is using that status to entitle him to complain about an alleged misuse of public funds or about other public action that has only an indirect impact on his interests, as to which "States have wide latitude to establish procedures not only to limit the number of judicial proceedings that may be entertained but also to determine whether to accord a taxpayer any standing at all," and (2) cases challenging a state's attempt to levy on personal funds, as to which "the State may not deprive individual litigants of their own day in court." Thus the preclusive effect of an unsuccessful challenge to legislation may depend on whether it was intended to protect public or individual interests. Because *Richards* involved a constitutional challenge to an occupation tax levied by the county on employees, the Court found this was in the second category, in which the plaintiff's interest was individual. Similarly, in *Taylor*, the Court rejected nonparty preclusion, noting that a FOIA request makes information available to the requester, not to the public at large. The Court recognized that "Congress, in providing for actions vindicating a public interest, may 'limit the number of judicial proceedings that may be entertained,'" but it found no such "statutory constraint on successive actions" in FOIA.

B. THE EFFECT OF CLASS ACTION JUDGMENTS

What is the effect of a class action judgment? By definition, such a judgment applies to the class members. When Rule 23(a) says that "[o]ne or more members of a class may sue or be sued as representative parties on behalf of all members," it would be meaningless unless the resulting judgment bound the members of the class. In *Taylor v. Sturgell*, *supra* p. 660, while the Supreme Court took a narrow view of nonparty preclusion in general, the Court emphatically distinguished class actions, noting that in class actions, "a person not named as a party may be bound by a judgment on the merits of the action, if she was adequately represented by a party who actively participated in the litigation." Class action judgments thus bind persons who never participated in the proceedings. Indeed, in Rule 23(b)(1) and (b)(2) class actions, they may never even have been given notice of the action. Because of this, questions about the limits on the binding effect of judgments take on greater significance in class actions than in any other type of litigation.

MATSUSHITA ELECTRICAL INDUSTRIAL CO. V. EPSTEIN

Supreme Court of the United States, 1996.
516 U.S. 367.

JUSTICE THOMAS delivered the opinion of the Court.

This case presents the question whether a federal court may withhold full faith and credit from a state-court judgment approving a class-action settlement simply because the settlement releases claims within the exclusive jurisdiction of the federal courts. The answer is no. Absent a partial repeal of the Full Faith and Credit Act, 28 U.S.C. § 1738, by another federal statute, a federal court must give the judgment the same effect that it would have in the courts of the State in which it was rendered.

I

In 1990, petitioner Matsushita Electric Industrial Co. made a tender offer for the common stock of MCA, Inc., a Delaware corporation. The tender offer not only resulted in Matsushita's acquisition of MCA, but also precipitated two lawsuits on behalf of the holders of MCA's common stock. First, a class action was filed in the Delaware Court of Chancery against MCA and its directors for breach of fiduciary duty in failing to maximize shareholder value. The complaint was later amended to state additional claims against MCA's directors for, inter alia, waste of corporate assets by exposing MCA to liability under the federal securities laws. In addition, Matsushita was added as a defendant and was accused of conspiring with MCA's directors to violate Delaware law. The Delaware suit was based purely on state-law claims.

While the state class action was pending, the instant suit was filed in Federal District Court in California. The complaint named Matsushita as a defendant and alleged that Matsushita's tender offer violated Securities Exchange Commission (SEC) Rules 10b–3 and 14d–10. These Rules were created by the SEC pursuant to the 1968 Williams Act Amendments to the Securities Exchange Act of 1934 (Exchange Act), 15 U.S.C. § 78a et seq. Section 27 of the Exchange Act confers exclusive jurisdiction upon the federal courts for suits brought to enforce the Act or rules and regulations promulgated thereunder. See 15 U.S.C. § 78aa. The District Court declined to certify the class, entered summary judgment for Matsushita, and dismissed the case. The plaintiffs appealed to the Court of Appeals for the Ninth Circuit.

After the federal plaintiffs filed their notice of appeal but before the Ninth Circuit handed down a decision, the parties to the Delaware suit negotiated a settlement. In exchange for a global release of all claims arising out of the Matsushita-MCA acquisition, the defendants would deposit $2 million into a settlement fund to be distributed pro rata to the members of the class. As required by Delaware Chancery Rule 23, which is modeled on Federal Rule of Civil Procedure 23, the Chancery Court certified the class for purposes of settlement and approved a notice of the proposed settlement. The notice informed the class members of their right to request exclusion from the settlement class and to appear and present argument at a scheduled hearing to determine the fairness of the settlement. In particular, the notice stated that "[b]y filing a valid Request for Exclusion, a member of the Settlement Class will not be precluded by the Settlement from individually seeking to pursue the claims alleged in the . . . California Federal Actions, . . . or any other claim relating to the events at issue in the Delaware Actions." Two such notices were mailed to the class members and the notice was also published in the national edition of the Wall Street Journal. The Chancery Court then held a hearing. After argument from several objectors, the Court found the class representation adequate and the settlement fair.

The order and final judgment of the Chancery Court incorporated the terms of the settlement agreement, providing:

> "All claims, rights and causes of action (state or federal, including but not limited to claims arising under the federal securities law, any rules or regulations promulgated thereunder, or otherwise), whether known or unknown that are, could have been or might in the future be asserted by any of the plaintiffs or any member of the Settlement Class (*other than those who have validly requested exclusion therefrom*), . . . in connection with or that arise now or hereafter out of the Merger Agreement, the Tender Offer, the Distribution Agreement, the Capital Contribution Agreement, the employee compensation arrangements, the Tender Agreements, the Initial Proposed Settlement, this Settlement . . . and *including without limitation the claims asserted in the California Federal Actions* . . . are hereby compromised, settled, released and discharged with prejudice by virtue of the proceedings herein and this Order and Final Judgment."

The judgment also stated that the notice met all the requirements of due process. The Delaware Supreme Court affirmed.

Respondents were members of both the state and federal plaintiff classes. Following issuance of the notice of proposed settlement of the Delaware litigation, respondents neither opted out of the settlement class nor appeared at the hearing to contest the settlement or the representation of the class. On appeal in the Ninth Circuit, petitioner Matsushita invoked the Delaware judgment as a bar to further prosecution of that action under the Full Faith and Credit Act, 28 U.S.C. § 1738.

The Ninth Circuit rejected petitioner's argument, ruling that § 1738 did not apply. Epstein v. MCA, Inc., 50 F.3d 644, 661–666 (1995). Instead, the Court of Appeals fashioned a test under which the preclusive force of a state court settlement judgment is limited to those claims that "could . . . have been extinguished by the issue preclusive effect of an adjudication of the state claims." The lower courts have taken varying approaches to determining the preclusive effect of a state court judgment, entered in a class or derivative action, that provides for the release of exclusively federal claims. We granted certiorari to clarify this important area of federal law.

II

The Full Faith and Credit Act mandates that the "judicial proceedings" of any State "shall have the same full faith and credit in every court within the United States . . . as they have by law or usage in the courts of such State . . . from which they are taken." 28 U.S.C. § 1738. The Act thus directs all courts to treat a state court judgment with the same respect that it would receive in the courts of the rendering state. Federal courts may not "employ their own rules . . . in determining the effect of state judgments," but must "accept the rules chosen by the State from which the judgment is taken." Kremer v. Chemical Constr. Corp., 456 U.S. 461, 481–482 (1982). Because the Court of Appeals failed to follow the dictates of the Act, we reverse.

A

The state court judgment in this case differs in two respects from the judgments that we have previously considered in our cases under the Full Faith and Credit Act. As respondents and the Court of Appeals stressed, the judgment was the product of a class action and incorporated a settlement agreement releasing claims within the exclusive jurisdiction of the federal courts. Though respondents urge "the irrelevance of section 1738 to this litigation," we do not think that either of these features exempts the judgment from the operation of § 1738.

That the judgment at issue is the result of a class action, rather than a suit brought by an individual, does not undermine the initial applicability of § 1738. The judgment of a state court in a class action is plainly the product of a "judicial proceeding" within the meaning of § 1738. Therefore, a judgment entered in a class action, like any other judgment entered in a state judicial proceeding, is presumptively entitled to full faith and credit under the express terms of the Act.

Further, § 1738 is not irrelevant simply because the judgment in question might work to bar the litigation of exclusively federal claims. Our decision in Marrese v. American Academy of Orthopaedic Surgeons, 470 U.S. 373 (1985), made clear that where § 1738 is raised as a defense in a subsequent suit, the fact that an allegedly precluded "claim is within the exclusive jurisdiction of the federal courts *does not necessarily make § 1738 inapplicable.*" Id., at 380 (emphasis added). In so holding, we relied primarily on Kremer v. Chemical Constr. Corp., *supra*, which held, without deciding whether Title VII claims are exclusively federal, that state court proceedings may be issue preclusive in Title VII suits in federal court. *Kremer*, we said, "implies that absent an exception to § 1738, state law determines at least the . . . preclusive effect of a prior state judgment in a subsequent action involving a claim within the exclusive jurisdiction of the federal courts." *Marrese*, 470 U.S., at 381. Accordingly, we decided that "a state court judgment may in some circumstances have preclusive effect in a subsequent action within the exclusive jurisdiction of the federal courts." Id., at 380. * * *

B

Marrese provides the analytical framework for deciding whether the Delaware court's judgment precludes this exclusively federal action. When faced with a state court judgment relating to an exclusively federal claim, a federal court must first look to the law of the rendering State to ascertain the effect of the judgment. If state law indicates that the particular claim or issue would be barred from litigation in a court of that state, then the federal court must next decide whether, "as an exception to § 1738," it "should refuse to give preclusive effect to [the] state court judgment."

1

We observed in *Marrese* that the inquiry into state law would not always yield a direct answer. Usually, "a state court will not have occasion to address the specific question whether a state judgment has issue or claim preclusive effect in a later action that can be brought only in federal court." Where a judicially approved settlement is under consideration, a federal court may consequently find guidance from general state law on the preclusive force of settlement judgments. Here, in addition to providing rules regarding the preclusive force of class-action settlement judgments in subsequent suits in state court, the Delaware courts have also spoken to the particular effect of such judgments in federal court.

[In Nottingham Partners v. Dana, 564 A.2d 1089 (1989), a class action, the Delaware Supreme Court approved a settlement that released claims then pending in federal court.] Though the Delaware Supreme Court correctly recognized in *Nottingham* that it lacked actual authority to order the dismissal of any case pending in federal court, it asserted that state-court approval of the settlement would have the collateral effect of preventing class members from prosecuting their claims in federal court. Perhaps the clearest statement of the Delaware Chancery Court's view on this matter was articulated in the suit preceding this one: "When a state court settlement of a class action releases all claims which arise out of the challenged transaction and is determined to be fair and to have met all due process requirements, the class members are bound by the release or the doctrine of issue preclusion. Class members cannot subsequently relitigate the claims barred by the settlement in a federal court." In re MCA, Inc. Shareholders Litigation, 598 A.2d 687, 691 (1991).[4] We are aware of no Delaware case that suggests otherwise.

Given these statements of Delaware law, we think that a Delaware court would afford preclusive effect to the settlement judgment in this case, notwithstanding the fact that respondents could not have pressed their Exchange Act claims in the Court of Chancery. The claims are clearly within the scope of the release in the judgment, since the judgment specifically refers to this lawsuit. As required by Delaware Court of Chancery Rule 23, the Court of Chancery found, and the Delaware Supreme Court affirmed, that the settlement was "fair, reasonable and adequate and in the best interests of the . . . Settlement class" and that notice to the class was "in full compliance with . . . the requirements of due process." The Court of Chancery "further determined that the plaintiffs[,] . . . as representatives of the Settlement Class, have fairly and adequately protected the interests of the Settlement Class." In re MCA, Inc. Shareholders Litigation, *supra*. Cf. Phillips Petroleum Co. [v. Shutts, 472 U.S.] at 812 (due process requires "that the named plaintiff at all times adequately represent the interests of the absent class members").[5] Under Delaware Rule 23, as under Federal Rule of Civil Procedure 23, "[a]ll members of the class, whether of a plaintiff or a defendant class, are bound by the judgment entered in the action unless, in a Rule 23(b)(3) action, they make a timely election for exclusion." Respondents do not deny that, as shareholders of MCA's common stock, they were part of the plaintiff class and that they never opted out; they are bound, then, by the judgment.[6]

---

[4] In fact, the Chancery Court rejected the first settlement, which contained no opt-out provision, as unfair to the class precisely because it believed that the settlement would preclude the class from pursuing their exclusively federal claims in federal court. See In re MCA Inc. Shareholders Litigation, 598 A.2d 687, 692 (1991) ("[I]f this Court provides for the release of all the claims arising out of the challenged transaction, the claims which the Objectors have asserted in the federal suit will likely be forever barred").

[5] A part from any discussion of Delaware law, respondents contend that the settlement proceedings did not satisfy due process because the class was inadequately represented. Respondents make this claim in spite of the Chancery Court's express ruling, following argument on the issue, that the class representatives fairly and adequately protected the interests of the class. Cf. Prezant v. De Angelis, 636 A.2d 915, 923 (Del. 1994) ("[The] constitutional requirement [of adequacy of representation] is embodied in [Delaware] Rule 23(a)(4), which requires that the named plaintiff 'fairly and adequately protect the interests of the class' "). We need not address the due process claim, however, because it is outside the scope of the question presented in this Court. * * *

[6] Respondents argue that their failure to opt out of the settlement class does not constitute consent to the terms of the settlement under traditional contract principles. Again, the issue raised by respondents—whether the settlement could bar this suit as a matter of contract law, as distinguished from § 1738 law—is outside the scope of the question on which we granted certiorari. We note, however, that if a State chooses to approach the preclusive effect of a judgment embodying the terms of a settlement agreement as a question of pure contract law, a federal court must adhere to that approach under § 1738.

2

Because it appears that the settlement judgment would be res judicata under Delaware law, we proceed to the second step of the *Marrese* analysis and ask whether § 27 of the Exchange Act, which confers exclusive jurisdiction upon the federal courts for suits arising under the Act, partially repealed § 1738. Section 27 contains no express language regarding its relationship with § 1738 or the preclusive effect of related state court proceedings. Thus, any modification of § 1738 by § 27 must be implied. In deciding whether § 27 impliedly created an exception to § 1738, the "general question is whether the concerns underlying a particular grant of exclusive jurisdiction justify a finding of an implied partial repeal of § 1738." *Marrese*, 470 U.S., at 386. "Resolution of this question will depend on the particular federal statute as well as the nature of the claim or issue involved in the subsequent federal action. . . . [T]he primary consideration must be the intent of Congress."

[The Court noted that it had rarely found an implied repeal, and that such a conclusion would only be warranted where two federal statutes were in "irreconcilable conflict." It found no intent by Congress to afford plaintiffs more than one day in court to challenge the legality of a securities transaction, or to prevent litigants who have asserted claims within the jurisdiction of a state court to release Exchange Act claims as part of a judicially-approved settlement. Although the state court had to assess the federal claims to determine the adequacy of the settlement, it had not thereby "trespassed upon the exclusive territory of the federal courts" because "such assessment does not amount to a judgment on the merits of the claims." It also noted that "state court proceedings may, in various ways, subsequently affect the litigation of exclusively federal claims without running afoul of the federal jurisdictional grant in question. In Becher v. Contoure Laboratories, Inc., 279 U.S. 388 (1929), we held that state court findings of fact were issue preclusive in federal patent suits. We did so with full recognition 'the logical conclusion from the establishing of [the state law] claim is that Becher's patent is void.' "]

In the end, §§ 27 and 1738 "do not pose an either-or proposition." They can be reconciled by reading § 1738 to mandate full faith and credit of state court judgments incorporating global settlements, provided the rendering court had jurisdiction over the underlying suit itself, and by reading § 27 to prohibit state courts from exercising jurisdiction over suits arising under the Exchange Act. Congress' intent to provide an exclusive federal forum for adjudication of suits to enforce the Exchange Act is clear enough. But we can find no suggestion in § 27 that Congress meant to override the "principles of comity and repose embodied in § 1738" by allowing plaintiffs with Exchange Act claims to release those claims in state court and then litigate them in federal court. We conclude that the Delaware courts would give the settlement judgment preclusive effect in a subsequent proceeding and, further, that § 27 did not effect a partial repeal of § 1738.

C

The Court of Appeals did not engage in any analysis of Delaware law pursuant to § 1738. Rather, the Court of Appeals declined to apply § 1738 on the ground that where the rendering forum lacked jurisdiction over the subject matter or the parties, full faith and credit is not required. The Court of Appeals decided that the subject-matter jurisdiction exception to full faith and credit applies to this case because the Delaware court acted outside the bounds of its own jurisdiction in approving the settlement, since the settlement released exclusively federal claims.

As explained above, the state court in this case clearly possessed jurisdiction over the subject matter of the underlying suit and over the defendants. Only if this were not so—for instance, if the complaint alleged violations of the Exchange Act and the Delaware court rendered a judgment on the merits of those claims—would the exception to § 1738 for lack of subject-matter jurisdiction apply. Where, as here, the rendering court in fact had subject-matter jurisdiction, the subject-matter jurisdiction exception to full faith and credit is simply inapposite. In such a case, the relevance of a federal statute that provides for exclusive federal jurisdiction is not to the state court's possession of jurisdiction per se, but to the existence of a partial repeal of § 1738.

* * *

The judgment of the Court of Appeals is reversed and remanded for proceedings consistent with this opinion.

[Statement of Justice Stevens, concurring in part and dissenting in part, omitted.]

JUSTICE GINSBURG, with whom JUSTICE STEVENS joins, and with whom JUSTICE SOUTER joins as to Part II-B, concurring in part and dissenting in part.

I join the Court's judgment to the extent that it remands the case to the Ninth Circuit. I agree that a remand is in order because the Court of Appeals did not attend to this Court's reading of 28 U.S.C. § 1738 in a controlling decision. But I would not endeavor, as the Court does, to speak the first word on the content of Delaware preclusion law. Instead, I would follow our standard practice of remitting that issue for decision, in the first instance, by the lower federal courts.

I write separately to emphasize a point key to the application of § 1738: A state-court judgment generally is not entitled to full faith and credit unless it satisfies the requirements of the Fourteenth Amendment's Due Process Clause. In the class action setting, adequate representation is among the due process ingredients that must be supplied if the judgment is to bind absent class members. See Phillips Petroleum Co. v. Shutts, 472 U.S. 797, 808, 812 (1985); Prezant v. De Angelis, 636 A.2d 915, 923–924 (Del. 1994).

Suitors in this action (called the "Epstein plaintiffs" in this opinion), respondents here, argued before the Ninth Circuit, and again before this Court, that they cannot be bound by the Delaware settlement because they were not adequately represented by the Delaware class representatives. They contend that the Delaware representatives' willingness to release federal securities claims within the exclusive jurisdiction of the federal courts for a meager return to the class members, but a solid fee to the Delaware class attorneys, disserved the interests of the class, particularly, the absentees. The inadequacy of representation was apparent, the Epstein plaintiffs maintained, for at the time of the settlement, the federal claims were sub judice in the proper forum for those claims—the federal judiciary. Although the Ninth Circuit decided the case without reaching the due process check on the full faith and credit obligation, that inquiry remains open for consideration on remand. See [majority opinion] n. 5 (due process "w[as] not the basis for the decision below," so the Court "need not address [it]").

I

Matsushita's acquisition of MCA prompted litigation in state and federal courts. A brief account of that litigation will facilitate comprehension of the Epstein plaintiffs' position. On September 26, 1990, in response to reports in the financial press that Matsushita was negotiating to buy MCA, a suit was filed in the Court of Chancery of Delaware, a purported class action on behalf of the stockholders of MCA. Naming MCA and its directors (but not Matsushita) as defendants, the complaint invoked state law only. It alleged that MCA's directors had failed to carry out a market check to maximize shareholder value upon a change in corporate control, a check required by Revlon, Inc. v. MacAndrews & Forbes Holdings, Inc., 506 A.2d 173, 182 (Del. 1985). For this alleged breach of fiduciary duty, the complaint sought, inter alia, an injunction against Matsushita's proposed acquisition of MCA.

Matsushita announced its tender offer on November 26, 1990. It offered holders of MCA common stock $71 per share, if they tendered their shares before December 29, 1990. The owners of 91% of MCA's common stock tendered their shares and, on January 3, 1991, for a price of $6.1 billion, Matsushita acquired MCA.

On December 3, 1990, a few days after the required SEC filings disclosed the terms of the tender offer, several MCA shareholders filed suit in the United States District Court for the Central District of California. Based solely on federal law, their complaints alleged that Matsushita, first named defendant, violated SEC Rules 14d–10, 17 CFR § 240.14d–10 (1994), and 10b–13, 17 CFR § 240.10b–13 (1994), by offering preferential treatment in the tender offer to MCA principals Lew Wasserman and Sidney Sheinberg. As stated in the complaint, the public tender offer included a special tax-driven stock swap arrangement for Wasserman, then MCA's chairman and chief executive officer, and a $21 million bonus for Sheinberg, then MCA's chief operating officer and owner of 1,170,000 shares of MCA common stock. These arrangements allegedly violated, inter alia, the SEC's "all-holder best-price" rule (Rule 14d–10), which requires bidders to treat all shareholders on equal terms. The claims of federal securities law violations fell within the exclusive jurisdiction of the federal court. The Epstein plaintiffs also sought class certification to represent all MCA shareholders at the time of the tender offer.

Two days later, counsel in the Delaware action advised MCA's counsel that the Delaware plaintiffs intended to amend their complaint to include additional claims against MCA and its directors and to add Matsushita as a defendant. The additional claims alleged that MCA wasted corporate assets by increasing the corporation's exposure to liability for violation of Rules 10b–13 and 14d–10, that MCA failed to make full disclosure of the benefits MCA insiders would receive from the takeover, and that directors Wasserman and Sheinberg breached their fiduciary duties by negotiating preferential deals with Matsushita. Matsushita, the amended complaint alleged, had conspired with and aided and abetted MCA directors in violation of Delaware law.

Within days, the Delaware parties agreed to a settlement and, on December 17, 1990, submitted their proposal to the Delaware Vice Chancellor. The agreement provided for a modification of a "poison pill" in the corporate charter of an MCA subsidiary, and for a fees payment of $1 million to the class counsel. The settlement agreement required the release of all claims, state and federal, arising out of the tender offer.

The Vice Chancellor rejected the settlement agreement on April 22, 1991, for two reasons: the absence of any monetary benefit to the class members; and the potential value of the federal claims that the agreement proposed to release. The "generous payment" of $1 million in counsel fees, the Vice Chancellor observed, "confer[red] no benefit on the members of the Class." In re MCA, Inc. Shareholders Litigation, 598 A.2d 687, 695 (Del.Ch. 1991). And the value of the revised poison pill to the class, the Vice Chancellor said, was "illusionary[,] . . . apparently . . . proposed merely to justify a settlement which offers no real monetary benefit to the Class." The Vice Chancellor described the state-law claims as "at best, extremely weak and, therefore, [of] little or no value." "[T]he only claims which have any substantial merit," he said, "are the claims . . . in the California federal suit that were not asserted in this Delaware action." After the rejection of the settlement, the Delaware lawsuit lay dormant for more than a year.

The federal litigation proceeded. In various rulings, the District Court denied the federal plaintiffs' motion for partial summary judgment, denied the Epstein plaintiffs' motion for class certification, and granted Matsushita's motion for summary judgment dismissing the claims. On April 15, 1992, the District Court entered its final judgment, which the Epstein plaintiffs appealed to the Ninth Circuit.

On October 22, 1992, after the federal plaintiffs had filed their notice of appeal, the Delaware parties reached a second settlement agreement. Matsushita agreed to create a $2 million settlement fund that would afford shareholders 2 to 3 cents per share before payment of fees and costs. The Delaware class counsel requested $691,000 in fees. In return for this relief, the Delaware plaintiffs agreed to release "all claims, rights and causes of action (state or federal, including but not limited to claims arising under the federal securities laws, and any rules or regulations promulgated thereunder, or otherwise) . . . in connection with or that arise now or hereafter out of the [tender offer] . . . including without limitation the claims asserted in the California Federal Actions. . . ." Unlike the first settlement proposal, the second agreement included an opt-out provision.

This time the Vice Chancellor approved the settlement. He stated "it is in the best interests of the class to settle this litigation and the terms of the settlement are fair and reasonable—although the value of the benefit to the class is meager." He found the class members' recovery of 2 to 3 cents per share "adequate (if only barely so) to support the proposed settlement." The federal claims, he reasoned, having been dismissed by the District Court, "now have minimal economic value." And he gave weight to the presence in the second settlement agreement of an opt-out provision.

Addressing the objectors' contention that the proposed settlement was "collusive," the Vice Chancellor recalled that "the settling parties ha[d] previously proposed a patently inadequate settlement," and he agreed that "suspicions abound." Nevertheless, he noted, the "[o]bjectors have offered no evidence of any collusion," so he declined to reject the settlement on that ground. Reducing the counsel fees from the requested $691,000 to $250,000, the Vice Chancellor offered this observation: "[T]he defendants' willingness to create the settlement fund seems likely to have been motivated as much by their concern as to their potential liability under the federal claims as by their concern for liability under the state law claims which this Court characterized as 'extremely weak.' "In a brief order, the Delaware Supreme Court affirmed "on the basis of and for the reasons assigned by the Court of Chancery. . . ."

* * *

II

A

Section 1738's full faith and credit instruction, as the Court indicates, requires the forum asked to recognize a judgment first to determine the preclusive effect the judgment would have in the rendering court. Because the Ninth Circuit did not evaluate the preclusive effect of the Delaware judgment through the lens of that State's preclusion law, I would remand for that determination.[4]

B

Every State's law on the preclusiveness of judgments is pervasively affected by the supreme law of the land. To be valid in the rendition forum, and entitled to recognition nationally, a state court's judgment must measure up to the requirements of the Fourteenth Amendment's Due Process Clause.

In Phillips Petroleum Co. v. Shutts, this Court listed minimal procedural due process requirements a class action money judgment must meet if it is to bind absentees; those requirements include notice, an opportunity to be heard, a right to opt out, and adequate representation. 472 U.S., at 812. "[T]he Due Process Clause of course requires that the named plaintiff at all times adequately represent the interests of the absent class members." Ibid. (citing Hansberry v. Lee, 311 U.S. 32, 42–43, 45 (1940)). As the *Shutts* Court's phrase "at all times" indicates, the class representative's duty to represent absent class members adequately is a continuing one. See also Gonzales v. Cassidy, 474 F.2d 67, 75 (C.A.5 1973) (representative's failure to pursue an appeal rendered initially adequate class representation inadequate, so that judgment did not bind the class).

Although emphasizing the constitutional significance of the adequate representation requirement, this Court has recognized the first line responsibility of the states themselves for assuring that the constitutional essentials are met. See *Hansberry*, 311 U.S., at 42. Final judgments, however, remain vulnerable to collateral attack for failure to satisfy the adequate representation requirement. A court conducting an action cannot predetermine the res judicata effect of the judgment; that effect can be tested only in a subsequent action.

In Delaware, the constitutional due process requirement of adequate representation is embodied in Delaware Court of Chancery's Rule 23, a class action rule modeled on its federal counterpart. Delaware requires, as a prerequisite to class certification, that the named plaintiffs "fairly and adequately protect the interests of the class." Del. Ch. Rule 23(a)(4). In *Prezant*, the Delaware Supreme Court considered whether adequate class representation was "a sine qua non for approval of a class action settlement," and concluded that it was. The state high court overturned a judgment and remanded a settlement because the Court of Chancery had failed to make an explicit finding of adequate representation.

---

[4] In its endeavor to forecast Delaware preclusion law, the Court appears to have blended the "identical factual predicate" test applied by the Delaware Supreme Court in Nottingham Partners v. Dana, 564 A.2d 1089, 1106–1107 (1989), with the broader "same transaction" test advanced by Matsushita.

The Delaware Supreme Court underscored that due process demands more than notice and an opportunity to opt-out; adequate representation, too, that court emphasized, is an essential ingredient. Notice, the Delaware Supreme Court reasoned, cannot substitute for the thorough examination and informed negotiation an adequate representative would pursue. The court also recognized that opt-out rights "are infrequently utilized and usually economically impracticable."

The Vice Chancellor's evaluation of the merits of the settlement could not bridge the gap, the Delaware Supreme Court said, because an inadequate representative "taint[s]" the entire settlement process. Id., at 925.[6] * * *

In the instant case, the Epstein plaintiffs challenge the preclusive effect of the Delaware settlement, arguing that the Vice Chancellor never in fact made the constitutionally required determination of adequate representation.[7] They contend that the state court left unresolved key questions: notably, did the class representatives share substantial common interests with the absent class members, and did counsel in Delaware vigorously press the interests of the class in negotiating the settlement.[8] In particular, the Epstein plaintiffs question whether the Delaware class representatives—who filed the state lawsuit on September 26, 1990, two months before the November 26 tender offer announcement—actually tendered shares in December, thereby enabling them to litigate a Rule 14d–10 claim in federal court. They also suggest that the Delaware representatives undervalued the federal claims—claims they could only settle, but never litigate, in a Delaware court. Finally, the Epstein plaintiffs contend that the Vice Chancellor improperly shifted the burden of proof;[9] he rejected the Delaware objectors' charges of "collusion" for want of evidence while acknowledging that "suspicions [of collusion] abound."[10]

---

[6]   In both *Prezant* and the instant case, a temporary settlement class device was used, telescoping the inquiry of adequate representation into the examination of the fairness of the settlement. According to the Delaware Supreme Court, however, this near simultaneity does not relieve the representative of her duty to demonstrate, nor the court of its duty to determine, the adequacy of representation. *Prezant*, 636 A.2d, at 923. * * *

[7]   The Vice Chancellor did not have the benefit of the Delaware Supreme Court's clear statement in *Prezant*, decided one year after this settlement was approved. In *Prezant*, however, the Delaware Supreme Court largely reiterated and applied what this Court had stated almost a decade earlier in Phillips Petroleum Co. v. Shutts, 472 U.S. 797, 808, 812 (1985).

[8]   The order approving the class for settlement purposes, the Epstein plaintiffs urge, contains no discussion of the adequacy of the representatives, and the order and final judgment approving the settlement contains only boilerplate language referring to the adequacy of representation. The Delaware Supreme Court approved the Court of Chancery's judgment in a one paragraph order.

[9]   Delaware law appears to place the burden of proof on the class representatives.

[10]   In this regard, it is noteworthy that Matsushita did not move to dismiss the Delaware action after the Vice Chancellor, in rejecting the first proposed settlement, surveyed the state-law claims and found them insubstantial. See In re MCA, Inc. Shareholders Litigation, 598 A.2d, at 694 (Vice Chancellor described "the asserted state law claims" as "at best, extremely weak" and of "little or no value").

Mindful that this is a court of final review and not first view, I do not address the merits of the Epstein plaintiffs' contentions, or Matsushita's counterargument that the issue of adequate representation was resolved by full and fair litigation in the Delaware Court of Chancery.[11] These arguments remain open for airing on remand. I stress, however, the centrality of the procedural due process protection of adequate representation in class action lawsuits, emphatically including those resolved by settlement.

NOTES AND QUESTIONS

1.   When applying claim preclusion principles, to what extent should it matter that the original case was a class action? The Court in *Matsushita* held that the class action judgment was not exempt from the operation of full faith and credit, but keep in mind that judgments are entitled to full faith and credit only if they satisfy the requirements of constitutional due process. Under Hansberry v. Lee, *supra* p. 166, and Phillips Petroleum Co. v. Shutts, *supra* p. 388, the due process requirement of adequate representation acts as a constraint on the binding effect of class actions.

2.   Should it matter that the judgment was reached by settlement rather than adjudication? In the Ninth Circuit, Matsushita argued that, independent of preclusion principles, the plaintiffs who did not opt out should be bound by contract principles because the class executed a release. The Ninth Circuit ruled that "[t]his attempt to equate class settlements with the settlement of traditional litigation by individual parties falls short [because] the settlement of a class action is fundamentally different from the settlement of traditional litigation." The court found this to be true because the claims to be released belong to class members, who have not consented to do so, and because a judgment in a class action must be approved by the judge, who cannot delegate authority to review the settlement provisions to the class representatives. 50 F.3d at 666–67. Do these arguments retain validity after the Supreme Court's decision? See In re Prudential Ins. Co. of Am. Sales Prac. Litig., 261 F.3d 355, 366 (3d Cir. 2001) ("a judgment pursuant to a class settlement can bar later claims based on the allegations underlying the claims in the settled class action").

3.   Should it matter that the class action settlement occurred in state court rather than federal court? In particular, should state-court class-action settlements be handled differently when claims within *exclusive* federal jurisdiction are included? Professors Kahan and Silberman argue that such class-action settlements present peculiar problems, compared with others, because (a) the class attorney has reduced bargaining power, being unable to prosecute the federal claim on the merits, (b) the defendant has increased ability to shop for a receptive plaintiff-side lawyer, in that federal-court cases are likely to be combined before a single judge, and (c) the state court is likely

---

[11] Counsel for Matsushita acknowledged that relief from a judgment may be sought in Delaware pursuant to that State's counterpart to Federal Rule of Civil Procedure 60(b).

to have reduced information to assess the merits of the federal claims being released. Marcel Kahan & Linda Silberman, Matsushita and Beyond: The Role of State Courts in Class Actions Involving Exclusive Federal Claims, 1996 Sup. Ct. Rev. 219, 235–46. They therefore recommend a series of additional protective measures that a state court should employ before approving such a settlement judgment, proposing that these might be adopted by statute, court rule or judicial decision. See id. at 251–62.

4.   Whose law governs the preclusive effect of a judgment? In *Matsushita* the judgment was entered in Delaware state court, but the question of its preclusive effect was raised in federal court. Keeping in mind that certain aspects of the law of claim preclusion and issue preclusion vary from one jurisdiction to another, should the federal court apply federal preclusion law or Delaware preclusion law? In general, courts apply the preclusion law of the jurisdiction that rendered the judgment, although this rule is subject to several exceptions. See generally Howard Erichson, Interjurisdictional Preclusion, 96 Mich. L. Rev. 945 (1998). In the state-federal configuration presented in *Matsushita*, the Supreme Court emphasized that the Full Faith and Credit Act, 28 U.S.C. § 1738, directs federal courts to treat a state court judgment with the same respect that it would receive in the courts of that state. Thus, the Court applied Delaware preclusion law, constrained by federal due process.

By contrast, in Taylor v. Sturgell, *supra* p. 660, both the first and second case occurred in federal court. The Court noted that federal common law governs the effect of federal court judgments. *Taylor* involved a federal court judgment in a federal question case, so federal preclusion law clearly applied. The question gets more complicated when the first action is a diversity case. The Court hints at this problem in footnote 4 of *Taylor*. Although federal court judgments in diversity cases are technically governed by federal preclusion law, federal law in this situation often incorporates the preclusion rules of the state in which the rendering court sits. Significant federal interests, however, may justify application of federal preclusion principles. See Semtek Int'l Inc. v. Lockheed Martin Corp., 531 U.S. 497 (2001).

5.   After the Supreme Court's decision in *Matsushita*, the case has a convoluted subsequent history which bears witness to the difficulty of the preclusion questions it raised. On remand, a divided panel of the Ninth Circuit initially held that the Delaware judgment did not preclude pursuit of the federal securities claims. Epstein v. MCA, Inc., 126 F.3d 1235 (9th Cir. 1997). The majority concluded that the question of adequate representation remained open for its review despite the Supreme Court's ruling. It decided that Delaware would not preclude litigation about the adequacy of representation because that question had not been actually litigated in the settlement approval process even though other class members had objected about collusion and one had asserted that the Delaware attorneys "did not provide adequate representation." Even had the question been fully litigated and decided, the majority added, due process precluded binding the Epstein plaintiffs by the litigation activities of "random, volunteer objectors" and "uncertified objectors." The court rejected the argument that the Epstein

plaintiffs could constitutionally be foreclosed because they had notice and an opportunity to object during the settlement approval process. It read Phillips Petroleum Co. v. Shutts, *supra* p. 388, as holding that due process precluded requiring absent class members to take any action to protect their interests.

The judge who wrote that decision then retired, a rehearing was granted, and the judge who had concurred in reversal changed his views. In Epstein v. MCA, Inc., 179 F.3d 641 (9th Cir. 1999) (which came to be known as *Epstein III*), the earlier opinion was withdrawn and preclusion applied by a divided court. In an opinion written by the prior dissenting judge, the court explained that the issue of due process limitations on the preclusive effect of the Delaware judgment was not open for review, despite the Court's observations in its footnote 5, because it was "logically necessary to the Court's holding" to find that due process was not violated. This conclusion turned on the fact that the Delaware courts have ruled that preclusion is only allowed if due process is observed, so the full faith and credit question would not come up unless due process (as a requirement of Delaware law) was satisfied. He rejected the argument that Phillips Petroleum Co. v. Shutts barred preclusion, because that decision addresses procedural protections in the class action itself rather than on collateral attack (id. at 648):

> Simply put, the absent class members' due process right to adequate representation is protected not by collateral review, but by the certifying court initially, and thereafter by appeal within the state system and by direct review in the United States Supreme Court.

> * * * Due process requires that an absent class member's rights to adequate representation be protected by the adoption of the appropriate procedures by the certifying court and by the courts that review its determinations: due process does not require collateral second-guessing of those determinations and that review.

On these issues, consider the arguments of Professors Kahan and Silberman, who caution that revisiting the adequacy of representation in cases like *Matsushita* is the worst solution:

> When class members have an opportunity to object to the settlement and to opt out of it, there is little reason to allow a party who refuses to avail itself of these opportunities to attack the settlement collaterally. In effect, a collateral attack in these circumstances is a post-settlement opt-out that undermines the ability to settle a class action altogether. * * * To grant state courts authority to enter global settlements releasing exclusive federal claims but subjecting such settlements to collateral review is the worst of all worlds. If the process by which state court findings about the adequacy of representation and fairness of the settlement is so imperfect that collateral attack is always possible, the better result would be to prohibit states from approving such global settlements in the first place.

Kahan & Silberman, *supra*, 1996 Sup. Ct. Rev. at 269, 271. Compare Patrick Woolley, The Availability of Collateral Attack for Inadequate Representation in Class Suits, 79 Tex. L. Rev. 383 (2000) (arguing that there must be a constitutional right to litigate adequacy of representation in a later proceeding). See also Gooch v. Life Investors Ins. Co. of Am., 672 F.3d 402, 421 (6th Cir. 2012) (disagreeing with the Ninth Circuit's decision on remand in *Epstein*, and concluding to the contrary that *Matsushita* does not rule out collateral attacks on adequacy of representation).

6.   What is the claim-preclusive effect of a class action judgment on legal claims that were not pursued in the class action? In individual litigation, claim preclusion may bar claims that were omitted from a prior action. See Restatement (Second) of Judgments § 24 (applying claim preclusion to claims that arise out of the same transaction or series of connected transactions). The danger of claim preclusion encourages plaintiffs to join all transactionally related claims in a single action. To what extent does the same logic apply to class actions?

In Cooper v. Federal Reserve Bank of Richmond, 467 U.S. 867, 869 (1984), the Supreme Court considered the preclusive effect of a Title VII class action judgment: "The question to be decided is whether a judgment in a class action determining that an employer did not engage in a general pattern or practice of racial discrimination against the certified class of employees precludes a class member from maintaining a subsequent civil action alleging an individual claim of racial discrimination against the employer." A class action resulted in a finding that the defendant did not engage in a policy or practice of class-wide discrimination against Black employees. When several class members later pursued individual suits claiming that the defendant had discriminated against them, the defendant argued they were claim precluded. The Court of Appeals held that the individual claims were precluded, but the Supreme Court reversed. The Court explained its reasoning, in part, in terms of the purpose of Rule 23 (id. at 880):

> The Bank argues that permitting the Baxter petitioners to bring separate actions would frustrate the purposes of Rule 23. We think the converse is true. The class action device was intended to establish a procedure for the adjudication of common questions of law or fact. If the Bank's theory were adopted, it would be tantamount to requiring that every member of the class be permitted to intervene to litigate the merits of his individual claim.

Some courts read *Cooper* narrowly, apply claim preclusion to abandoned claims in class actions, and treat the risk of claim preclusion as a basis for denying class certification. The Texas Supreme Court, in Citizens Ins. Co. of America v. Daccach, 217 S.W.3d 430 (2007), reversed the certification of a class of insurance policy holders alleging violation of the Texas Securities Act due to offering securities without registration. The court found that by "abandoning" other claims that arose out of the same conduct of the insurance company (the original complaint had alleged numerous claims including breach of contract, fraud, negligent misrepresentation, violation of Texas Insurance Code), the plaintiffs split their cause of action, subjecting the class to a risk of claim preclusion, and thus were not adequate class representatives.

Others disagree with *Daccach* as to the preclusion risk of omitting claims and whether it demonstrates inadequate representation. See Edward Sherman, "Abandoned Claims" in Class Actions: Implications for Preclusion and Adequacy of Counsel, 79 G.W. L. Rev. 483 (2011) (agreeing with *Cooper's* premise that if class members possess multiple claims, only some of which are amenable to class treatment, then it is proper to certify a class action as to some claims but not others). Perhaps the most sensible take on the problem remains this statement from over forty years ago, in Sullivan v. Chase Investment Services of Boston, 79 F.R.D. 246 (N.D. Cal. 1978):

> It is not uncommon for defendants to engage in a course of conduct which gives rise to a variety of claims, some amenable to class treatment, others not. Those claims that are amenable should be prosecuted as class actions in order to realize savings of resources for courts and parties that Rule 23 is designed to facilitate . . . Class representatives must press all claims which can be prosecuted on a class basis, but they need not and should not press for certification of claims that are unsuitable for class treatment.

7.   What is the effect of a class action judgment on those who opted out of the class? Clearly, opt-outs are not bound by the judgment either as a matter of claim preclusion or issue preclusion. See, e.g., In re TransOcean Tender Offer Secs. Litig., 427 F.Supp. 1211 (N.D.Ill. 1977). The very point of excluding oneself from a class action is to avoid the binding effect of the judgment.

What about the reverse? Can an opt-out use the class action judgment for its issue preclusive effect against the defendant? Suppose the court determines certain issues in the class's favor after those issues were fully litigated. Subsequently, an opt-out files an individual case against the defendant and asserts that certain issues were already determined. Should a person who opted out of the class action be permitted to get the benefit of the class action judgment as a matter of offensive nonmutual issue preclusion? See American Law Inst., Principles of the Law of Aggregate Litigation § 2.07 cmt. g (2010) ("individual claimants who exit receive neither the benefit nor the detriment of the preclusive effect exerted by the judgment in the class action"); Becherer v. Merrill Lynch, Pierce, Fenner & Smith, 193 F.3d 415, 433 (6th Cir. 1999) ("Because a plaintiff who opts out of a class action could easily have joined it, that plaintiff will generally not be permitted to invoke collateral estoppel.").

In In re Urethane Antitrust Litig., 2013 WL 6587972 (D. Kan. Dec. 16, 2013), three plaintiffs who opted out of an antitrust class action against Dow Chemical Co. filed their own actions against Dow. The class action had proceeded to trial, where a jury found Dow liable for antitrust conspiracy. In the individual actions, part of an MDL, the plaintiffs sought to preclude Dow from relitigating the issue of antitrust conspiracy. The court rejected this attempted use of offensive nonmutual issue preclusion. On the question of judicial economy, the court was persuaded "that fewer issues might be present in a second action if preclusion were permitted, but that the possibility of preclusion could actually increase the number of lawsuits, thereby undermining any potential judicial economy, as class members would have an incentive to opt out of a class action." Id. at *2.

STEPHENSON v. DOW CHEMICAL CO.

United States Court of Appeals, Second Circuit, 2001.
273 F.3d 249, *aff'd in part and vacated in part*, 539 U.S. 111 (2003).

Before: CARDAMONE and F.I. PARKER, CIRCUIT JUDGES, and SPATT, DISTRICT JUDGE.

PARKER, CIRCUIT JUDGE.

This appeal requires us to determine the effect of the Supreme Court's landmark class action decisions in Amchem Products, Inc. v. Windsor, 521 U.S. 591 (1997) [*supra* p. 311], and Ortiz v. Fibreboard Corp., 527 U.S. 815 (1999), on a previously settled class action concerning exposure to Agent Orange during the Vietnam War.

* * *

I.   Background

* * *

The first Agent Orange litigation began in the late 1970s, when individual veterans and their families filed class action suits in the Northern District of Illinois and Southern and Eastern Districts of New York, alleging that exposure to Agent Orange caused them injury. In re "Agent Orange" Prod. Liab. Litig., 635 F.2d 987, 988 (2d Cir. 1980) ("Agent Orange I"). By order of the MDL Panel, these actions were transferred to the Eastern District of New York and consolidated for pretrial purposes. Id. Plaintiffs asserted claims of negligent manufacture, strict liability, breach of warranty, intentional tort and nuisance. In re "Agent Orange" Prod. Liab. Litig., 597 F.Supp. 740, 750 (E.D.N.Y. 1984) ("Agent Orange III"); aff'd 818 F.2d 145 (2d Cir. 1987).

In 1983, the district court certified the following class under Federal Rule of Civil Procedure 23(b)(3):

> those persons who were in the United States, New Zealand or Australian Armed Forces at any time from 1961 to 1972 who were injured while in or near Vietnam by exposure to Agent Orange or other phenoxy herbicides, including those composed in whole or in part of 2, 4, 5—trichlorophenoxyacetic acid or containing some amount of 2, 3, 7, 8—tetrachlorodibenzo-p-dioxin. The class also includes spouses, parents, and children of the veterans born before January 1, 1984, directly or derivatively injured as a result of the exposure.

* * * The court also ordered notice by mail, print media, radio and television to be provided to class members, providing in part that persons who wished to opt out must do so by May 1, 1984.

Trial of the class claims was to begin on May 7, 1984. On the eve of trial, the parties reached a settlement. The settlement provided that defendants would pay $180 million into a settlement fund, $10 million of which would indemnify defendants against future state court actions alleging the same claims. The settlement provided that "[t]he Class specifically includes persons who have not yet manifested injury." Additionally, the settlement specifically stated that the district court would "retain jurisdiction over the Fund pending its final disposition."

The district court held fairness hearings throughout the country, and approved the settlement as fair, reasonable and adequate. The court rejected the motion to certify a subclass of those class members who objected to terms of the settlement. The court concluded that "[n]o purpose would have been served by appointing counsel for a subclass of disappointed claimants except to increase expenses to the class and delay proceedings."

Seventy-five percent of the $180 million was to be distributed directly " 'to exposed veterans who suffer from long-term total disabilities and to the surviving spouses or children of exposed veterans who have died.' " "A claimant would qualify for compensation by establishing exposure to Agent Orange and death or disability not 'predominately' caused by trauma. . . ." Payments were to be made for ten years, beginning January 1, 1985 and ending December 31, 1994:

> No payment will be made for death or disability occurring after December 31, 1994. Payment will be made for compensable deaths occurring both before and after January 1, 1985. Payments will be made for compensable disability to the extent that the period of disability falls within the ten years of the program's operation.

"Most of the remaining [25%] of the settlement fund established the Agent Orange Class Assistance Program, . . . which made grants to agencies serving Vietnam veterans and their families." Explaining the creation of this kind of fund, Judge Weinstein stated that it was "[t]he most practicable and equitable method of distributing benefits to" those claimants who did not meet eligibility criteria for cash payments.

We affirmed class certification, settlement approval and much of the distribution plan. We rejected challenges to class certification, concluding that "class certification was justified under Rule 23(b)(3) due to the centrality of the military contractor defense." We specifically rejected an attack based on adequacy of representation, again based on the military contractor defense which, we reasoned, "would have precluded recovery by all plaintiffs, irrespective of the strengths, weaknesses, or idiosyncrasies of their claims." We additionally concluded that the notice scheme devised by Judge Weinstein was the "best notice practicable" under Federal Rule of Civil Procedure 23(c)(2). Finally, we affirmed the settlement as fair, reasonable and adequate, given the serious weaknesses of the plaintiffs' claims.

In 1989 and 1990, two purported class actions, Ivy v. Diamond Shamrock Chemicals Co. and Hartman v. Diamond Shamrock Chemicals Co., were filed in Texas state courts. These suits, on behalf of Vietnam veterans exposed to Agent Orange,[3] sought compensatory and punitive damages against the same companies as in the settled suit. The plaintiffs alleged that their injuries manifested only after the May 7, 1984 settlement. Additionally, the *Ivy/Hartman* plaintiffs expressly disclaimed any reliance on federal law, asserting only state law claims. Nonetheless, the defendants removed the actions to federal court on the grounds that these claims had already been asserted and litigated in federal court. The MDL Panel transferred the actions to Judge Weinstein in the Eastern District of New York.

* * *

[Plaintiffs argued] that it was unfair to bind them to the settlement when their injuries were not manifested until after the settlement had been reached. The district court rejected this argument, based on the following reasoning:

> All of the courts which considered the Agent Orange Settlement were fully cognizant of the conflict arguments now hypothesized by the plaintiffs and took steps to minimize the problem in the way they arranged for long-term administration of the Settlement Fund.
>
> In many cases the conflict between the interests of present and future claimants is more imagined than real. In the instant case, for example, the injustice wrought upon the plaintiffs is nonexistent. *These plaintiffs, like all class members who suffer death or disability before the end of 1994, are eligible for compensation from the Agent Orange Payment Fund.* The relevant latency periods and the age of the veterans ensure that almost all valid claims will be revealed before that time.
>
> Even when it is proper and necessary for the courts to be solicitous of the interests of future claimants, the courts cannot ignore the interests of presently injured plaintiffs as well as defendants in achieving a settlement. Class action settlements simply will not occur if the parties cannot set definitive limits on

---

[3] Two plaintiffs in the *Ivy* litigation alleged injuries stemming from Agent Orange exposure while acting in a civilian capacity, and thus were not members of the class bound by the 1984 settlement. Their claims were severed from the claims of the other plaintiffs.

defendants' liability. Making settlement of Rule 23 suits too difficult will work harms upon plaintiffs, defendants, the courts, and the general public.

The district court therefore dismissed the *Ivy/Hartman* litigation.

We affirmed the district court's dismissal. *Ivy/Hartman II*, 996 F.2d 1425, 1439 [(2d Cir. 1993)] We agreed with the district court's assertion of federal jurisdiction under the All Writs Act. * * *

We then addressed plaintiffs' argument that they were not members of the prior class, because they were not "injured" as the term was used in the class definition. We concluded that, for the purposes of the Agent Orange litigation, "injury occurs when a deleterious substance enters a person's body, even though its adverse effects are not immediately apparent." We emphasized that the plaintiffs in the original suit had sought to include such "at-risk" plaintiffs, over defendants' objections, and that we had already affirmed the inclusion of these plaintiffs in the class.

We likewise rejected plaintiffs' argument that their due process rights were violated because they were denied adequate representation and adequate notice in the prior action. We reasoned that "providing individual notice and opt-out rights to persons who are unaware of an injury would probably do little good." We concluded that the plaintiffs were adequately represented in the prior action, and that a subclass of future claimants was unnecessary " 'because of the way [the settlement] was structured to cover future claimants.' "

Shortly before our decision in *Ivy/Hartman II*, the $10 million set aside for indemnification from state court Agent Orange judgments was transferred to the Class Assistance Program, because the district court deemed such a fund unnecessary. The distribution activities had begun in 1988, and concluded in June 1997. During the ten year period of the settlement, $196.5 million was distributed as cash payments to approximately 52,000 class members. The program paid approximately $52 million to "after-manifested" claimants, whose deaths or disabilities occurred after May 7, 1984. Approximately $71.3 million of the fund was distributed through the Class Assistance Program.

[In August, 1998, Joe Isaacson sued the chemical manufacturers who produced Agent Orange in New Jersey state court. Isaacson had served in Vietnam in 1968–69 in the Air Force, working on planes that sprayed Agent Orange. In 1996, he was diagnosed with non-Hodgkin's Lymphoma, and in his suit he alleged state-law claims that defendants were liable for his condition. In February, 1999, Daniel Stephenson sued the same defendants in federal court in Louisiana. He had served in Vietnam from 1965 to 1970 as a helicopter pilot, and was in regular contact with Agent Orange during that time. In February, 1998, he was diagnosed with multiple myeloma, a bone marrow cancer.

Defendants removed Isaacson's suit to federal court, and the federal court denied his motion to remand. The MDL Panel transferred both Stephenson's and Isaacson's suits to Judge Weinstein, who consolidated them.]

Defendants moved to dismiss under Federal Rule of Civil Procedure 12(b)(6), asserting that plaintiffs' claims were barred by the 1984 class action settlement and subsequent final judgment. Judge Weinstein granted this motion from the bench following argument, rejecting plaintiffs' argument that they were inadequately represented and concluding that plaintiffs' suit was an impermissible collateral attack on the prior settlement.

Because we disagree with this conclusion, based on the Supreme Court's holdings in *Amchem* and *Ortiz*, we must vacate the district court's dismissal and remand for further proceedings.

II. Discussion

"We review a dismissal under Rule 12(b)(6) de novo, accepting all factual allegations in the complaint as true and drawing all reasonable inferences in the plaintiffs' favor."

A. *Removal Jurisdiction*

[The court held that Isaacson's case was properly removed under the All Writs Act, 28 U.S.C. § 1651, because "maintenance of these actions in state court necessarily requires interpretation of the scope of the Agent Orange Settlement and could have the potential to disturb the judgment underlying that settlement." In Syngenta Crop Protection, Inc. v. Henson, 537 U.S. 28 (2002), the Supreme Court held that the All Writs Act does not provide authority for removal.]

B. *Collateral Attack*

The parties devote much energy to debating the permissibility of a collateral attack in this case. Plaintiffs assert that, since the Supreme Court's decision in Hansberry v. Lee, 311 U.S. 32 (1940) [*supra* p. 166], courts have allowed collateral attacks on class action judgments based upon due process concerns. Defendants strenuously disagree and contend that to allow plaintiffs' suit to go forward, in the face of the 1984 global settlement, would "violate defendants' right to due process of law." Defendants likewise strenuously argue that the district court's injunction against future litigation prevents these appellants from maintaining their actions. While it is true that "[a]n injunction must be obeyed until modified or dissolved, and its unconstitutionality is no defense to disobedience," defendants' injunction-based argument misses the point. The injunction was part and parcel of the judgment that plaintiffs contend failed to afford them adequate representation. If plaintiffs' inadequate representation allegations prevail, as we so conclude, the judgment, which includes the injunction on which defendants rely, is not binding as to these plaintiffs.

Defendants contend that Supreme Court precedent permits a collateral attack on a class action judgment "only where there has been no prior determination of absent class members' due process rights." According to defendants, because the "due process rights of absent class members have been extensively litigated in the Agent Orange litigation," these plaintiffs cannot now attack those prior determinations. We reject defendants' arguments and conclude that plaintiffs' collateral attack, which seeks only to prevent the prior settlement from operating as res judicata to their claims, is permissible.

First, even if, as defendants contend, collateral attack is only permitted where there has been no prior determination of the absent class members' rights, plaintiffs' collateral attack is allowed. It is true that, on direct appeal and in the *Ivy/Hartman* litigation, we previously concluded that there was adequate representation of all class members in the original Agent Orange settlement. However, neither this Court nor the district court has addressed specifically the adequacy of representation for those members of the class whose injuries manifested after depletion of the settlements funds. See *Ivy/Hartman II*, 996 F.2d at 1436 (creating a subclass of future claimants was unnecessary because the settlement covered such claimants); *Ivy/Hartman I*, 781 F.Supp. at 919 ("These plaintiffs, like all class members *who suffer death or disability before the end of 1994*, are eligible for compensation from the Agent Orange Payment Fund." (emphasis added.)) Therefore, even accepting defendants' argument, plaintiffs' suit can go forward because there has been no prior adequacy of representation determination with respect to individuals whose claims arise after the depletion of the settlement fund.[6]

Second, the propriety of a collateral attack such as this is amply supported by precedent. In Hansberry v. Lee, 311 U.S. 32 (1940), the Supreme Court entertained a collateral attack on an Illinois state court class action judgment that purported to bind the plaintiffs. The Court held that class action judgments can only bind absent class members where "the interests of those not joined are of the same class as the interests of those

---

[6]   Defendants rely heavily on a recent Ninth Circuit decision, Epstein v. MCA, Inc., 179 F.3d 641 (9th Cir. 1999), in support of their limited collateral review theory. *Epstein* held that a collateral attack is available only "to consider whether the procedures in the prior litigation afforded the party against whom the earlier judgment is asserted a 'full and fair opportunity' to litigate the claim or issue." According to the Ninth Circuit,

> Due process requires that an absent class member's right to adequate representation be protected by the adoption of the appropriate procedures by the certifying court and by the courts that review its determinations; due process does not require collateral second-guessing of those determinations and that review.

Here, neither the district court nor this Court has determined the adequacy of representation with respect to these plaintiffs whose injuries did not arise until after the settlement expired. Without adopting the Ninth Circuit's decision in *Epstein*, we conclude that plaintiffs' collateral attack is proper even under its standard.

who are, and where it is considered that the latter fairly represent the former in the prosecution of the litigation." Additionally, we have previously stated that a "[j]udgment in a class action is not secure from collateral attack unless the absentees were adequately and vigorously represented."

Allowing plaintiffs' suit would be consistent with many other circuit decisions recognizing the ability of later plaintiffs to attack the adequacy of representation in an earlier class action. For example, the Fifth Circuit holds:

> To answer the question whether the class representative adequately represented the class so that the judgment in the class suit will bind the absent members of the class requires a two-pronged inquiry: (1) Did the trial court in the first suit correctly determine, initially, that the representative would adequately represent the class? and (2) Does it appear, after the termination of the suit, that the class representative adequately protected the interest of the class? The first question involves us in a collateral review of the . . . [trial] court's determination to permit the suit to proceed as a class action with [the named plaintiff] as the representative, while the second involves a review of the class representative's conduct of the entire suit—an inquiry which is not required to be made by the trial court but which is appropriate in a collateral attack on the judgment. . . .

Gonzales v. Cassidy, 474 F.2d 67, 72 (5th Cir. 1973).

Defendants' citation to Federated Department Stores, Inc. v. Moitie, 452 U.S. 394 (1981), is unavailing. According to that case, a "judgment merely voidable because based upon an erroneous view of the law is not open to collateral attack, but can be corrected only by a direct review and not by bringing another action upon the same cause [of action]." Id. at 398 (alteration in original). Defendants' reliance on this case misperceives plaintiffs' argument. Plaintiffs do not attack the merits or finality of the settlement itself, but instead argue that they were not proper parties to that judgment. If plaintiffs were not proper parties to that judgment, as we conclude below, res judicata cannot defeat their claims. Further, such collateral review would not, as defendants maintain, violate defendants' due process rights by exposing them to double liability. Exposure to liability here is not duplicative if plaintiffs were never proper parties to the prior judgment in the first place.

We therefore hold that a collateral attack to contest the application of res judicata is available. We turn next to the merits of this attack.

C.   Due Process Considerations and Res Judicata

The doctrine of res judicata dictates that "a final judgment on the merits of an action precludes the parties or their privies from relitigating issues that were or could have been raised in that action." Res judicata ordinarily applies "if the earlier decision was (1) a final judgment on the merits, (2) by a court of competent jurisdiction, (3) in a case involving the same parties or their privies, and (4) involving the same cause of action."

Plaintiffs' argument focuses on element number three in the res judicata analysis: whether they are parties bound by the settlement. Plaintiffs rely primarily on the United States Supreme Court's decisions in Amchem Products, Inc. v. Windsor, 521 U.S. 591 (1997), and Ortiz v. Fibreboard Corp., 527 U.S. 815 (1999).

In *Amchem*, the Supreme Court confronted, on direct appeal, a challenge to class certification for settlement purposes in an asbestos litigation. The class defined in the complaint included both individuals who were presently injured as well as individuals who had only been exposed to asbestos. The Supreme Court held that this "sprawling" class was improperly certified under Federal Rules of Civil Procedure 23(a) and (b). Specifically, the Court held that Rule 23(a)(4)'s requirement that the named parties " 'will fairly and adequately protect the interests of the class' " had not been satisfied. The Court reasoned that

> named parties with diverse medical conditions sought to act on behalf of a single giant class rather than on behalf of discrete subclasses. In significant respects, the interests of those within the single class are not aligned. Most saliently, for the currently injured, the critical goal is generous immediate payments. That goal tugs against the interest of exposure-only plaintiffs in ensuring an ample, inflation-protected fund for the future.

Amchem also implied, but did not decide, that the notice provided to exposure-only class members was likewise inadequate. The Court stated that, because many exposure-only individuals, may not be aware of their exposure or realize the ramifications of exposure, "those without current afflictions may not have the information or foresight needed to decide, intelligently, whether to stay in or opt out."

In *Ortiz*, the Supreme Court again addressed a settlement-only class action in the asbestos litigation context. *Ortiz*, however, involved a settlement-only limited fund class under Rule 23(b)(1)(B). The Supreme Court ultimately held that the class could not be maintained under Rule 23(b)(1)(B), because "the limit of the fund was determined by treating the settlement agreement as dispositive, an error magnified" by conflicted counsel. In so holding, *Ortiz* noted that "it is obvious after *Amchem* that a class divided between holders of present and future claims (some of the latter involving no physical injury and attributable to claimants not yet born) requires division into homogeneous subclasses under Rule 23(c)[(5)], with separate representation to eliminate conflicting interests of counsel."

Res judicata generally applies to bind absent class members except where to do so would violate due process. Due process requires adequate representation "at all times" throughout the litigation, notice "reasonably calculated . . . to apprise interested parties of the pendency of the action," and an opportunity to opt out. *Shutts*, 472 U.S. at 811–12.

Both Stephenson and Isaacson fall within the class definition of the prior litigation: they served in the United States military, stationed in Vietnam, between 1961 and 1972, and were allegedly injured by exposure to Agent Orange. However, they both learned of their allegedly Agent Orange-related injuries only after the 1984 settlement fund had expired in 1994. Because the prior litigation purported to settle all future claims, but only provided for recovery for those whose death or disability was discovered prior to 1994, the conflict between Stephenson and Isaacson and the class representatives becomes apparent. No provision was made for post-1994 claimants, and the settlement fund was permitted to terminate in 1994. *Amchem* and *Ortiz* suggest that Stephenson and Isaacson were not adequately represented in the prior Agent Orange litigation.[8] Those cases indicate that a class which purports to represent both present and future claimants may encounter internal conflicts.

Defendants contend that there was, in fact, no conflict because all class members' claims were equally meritless and would have been defeated by the "military contractor" defense. This argument misses the mark. At this stage, we are only addressing whether plaintiffs' claims should be barred by res judicata. We are therefore concerned only with whether they were afforded due process in the earlier litigation. Part of the due process inquiry (and part of the Rule 23(a) class certification requirements) involves assessing adequacy of representation and intra-class conflicts. The ultimate merits of the claims have no bearing on whether the class previously certified adequately represented these plaintiffs.

Because these plaintiffs were inadequately represented in the prior litigation, they were not proper parties and cannot be bound by the settlement. We therefore must vacate the district court's dismissal and remand for further proceedings. We, of course, express no opinion as to the ultimate merits of plaintiffs' claims.

NOTES AND QUESTIONS

1.   The Supreme Court granted certiorari in *Stephenson* and issued a per curiam opinion, 539 U.S. 111 (2003), but ultimately did not decide the central issue in the case—whether class members may collaterally attack a class

---

[8]   We also note that plaintiffs likely received inadequate notice. [Phillips Petroleum v.] Shutts [*supra* p. 388] provides that adequate notice is necessary to bind absent class members. As described earlier, *Amchem* indicates that effective notice could likely not ever be given to exposure-only class members. Because we have already concluded that these plaintiffs were inadequately represented, and thus were not proper parties to the prior litigation, we need not definitively decide whether notice was adequate.

action settlement judgment based on inadequate representation. Regarding the Isaacson plaintiffs, the Supreme Court vacated the Second Circuit's decision on the ground that the case should never have been removed. The Supreme Court had held that the All Writs Act does not allow such removal in Syngenta Crop Protection, Inc. v. Henson, 537 U.S. 28 (2002). Regarding Stephenson's suit, the Justices split 4–4 (Justice Stevens did not participate) as to whether Stephenson could avoid being bound by the judgment based on a showing of inadequate representation. Thus, the judgment of the Second Circuit was affirmed by an equally divided court, leaving the result untouched but establishing no Supreme Court precedent on that issue.

2. In *Stephenson,* the class settlement was attacked on the grounds that the class action provided inadequate representation for those whose injuries manifested themselves after 1994. How could the original class action have overcome this difficulty? Compare the way in which the settlement regimes in *Amchem* and *Ortiz* addressed the question of future claims.

Do you agree that Stephenson and Isaacson were inadequately represented in the original class action? Keep in mind that, at the time the class action settlement was arranged, no class member would know whether he would become sick before 1994, and some might consider the coverage for another decade a reasonable protection. Didn't each class members get, in essence, a ten-year insurance policy from the defendants? Consider the analysis in Richard Nagareda, Administering Adequacy in Class Representation, 82 Tex. L. Rev. 287, 322 (2003):

> The ten-year term for cash benefits under the Agent Orange class settlement appears far from arbitrary, however, when one considers that any veteran would have had an exceedingly weak scientific case on the causation element, at least as of 1984, and that the ten-year term for cash benefits extended to more than two decades after the last alleged exposure of class members.

Is the court in *Stephenson* saying that collateral attack is permitted if the terms of the settlement are so unfair as to be arbitrary? It viewed *Amchem* and *Ortiz* as finding an inherent conflict between presently injured claimants and exposure-only claimants. If a class action on behalf of holders of both present and future claims were "divided into homogeneous subclasses under Rule 23(c)[(5)], with separate representation to eliminate conflicting interests of counsel" (as the court says is required for proper class certification), would that provide sufficient assurance of adequate representation that collateral attack would be impermissible? Is the problem the way the class was certified, or is the problem the settlement itself?

3. For the bottom line on *Stephenson,* consider William Rubenstein, Finality in Class Action Litigation: Lessons from Habeas, 82 N.Y.U. L. Rev. 790, 795 (2007):

> For class action law, *Stephenson*'s outcome may have been the worst possible resolution of the case, as it supplied a decision without reasoning to a field more in need of reasoning than decision. The

[Supreme] Court's inability to render a majority decision left unresolved a whole series of questions concerning the content of the adequate representation requirement and the procedures attending both its initial adjudication and its likely readjudication on collateral attack. Two schools of scholarship have developed around these questions. Preclusionists have argued that the issue of adequacy, having necessarily been decided by the class court, cannot be relitigated collaterally. The preclusionists' approach to relitigation is that it should never be permitted. By contrast, constitutionalists have argued that because the issue of adequacy is embedded in the Due Process Clause, it is always open to reevaluation at the demand of any aggrieved individual class member not yet heard by a court. The constitutionalists' approach to relitigation is that it should always be possible. Each side defends its position in terms of relitigation's consequences and in terms of the values that are at issue. Yet neither has convinced the other of the wisdom of its approach, nor has one emerged as prevalent in the courts.

See also Samuel Issacharoff & Richard Nagareda, Class Settlements Under Attack, 156 U. Pa. L. Rev. 1649 (2008).

4.   In 2008, the Second Circuit put an end to the Stephenson litigation on the ground that the military contractor defense protected the Agent Orange manufacturers from liability. In re Agent Orange Prod. Liab. Litig, 517 F.3d 76 (2d Cir. 2008). Plaintiffs in these cases included the Stephenson plaintiffs and others who claimed they became sick after the class action settlement funds were entirely distributed. Meanwhile, in Vietnam Assoc. for Victims of Agent Orange v. Dow Chem. Co., 517 F.3d 104 (2d Cir. 2008), the court rejected claims brought by citizens of Vietnam on the ground that the Alien Tort Claims Act did not confer jurisdiction and that the government contractor defense would apply to these claims as well. Perhaps these decisions mean that the Agent Orange litigation is finally at an end.

5.   The Second Circuit reaffirmed its commitment to permitting collateral attack of class action settlements in Wolfert v. Transamerica Home First, Inc., 439 F.3d 165 (2d Cir. 2006). See also Hecht v. United Collection Bureau, Inc., 691 F.3d 218 (2d Cir. 2012) (permitting collateral attack on a class settlement based on inadequate notice to the class). In contrast to the Second Circuit's permissive approach in *Stephenson*, *Wolfert*, and *Hecht*, other courts have been less willing to entertain collateral attacks on class action settlements. Recall that on remand from the Supreme Court's *Matsushita* decision, the Ninth Circuit refused to permit collateral attack on the adequacy of representation in the original class action. Epstein v. MCA, Inc. (*Epstein III*), 179 F.3d 641 (9th Cir. 1999), *supra* p. 687 n. 5. In footnote 6 of *Stephenson*, the Second Circuit attempts to distinguish *Epstein III* from the case of the Agent Orange plaintiffs. Are the cases distinguishable?

6.   Rejecting *Stephenson* as "inconsistent with [Third] Circuit case law by which this panel is bound," the Third Circuit disallowed collateral challenges to the nationwide fen-phen settlement class action (see In re Diet

Drugs, *supra* p. 348). In re Diet Drugs Products Liability Litig., 431 F.3d 141 (3d Cir. 2005). Appellants there were two categories of class members who contended that they were not adequately represented. One category was the "downstream opt-out" group who opted out of the class settlement and sued in state court when diagnosed with cardiac problems. Under the terms of the class settlement, they were permitted to sue and were protected against statute of limitations defenses but could not seek punitive damages. The other group exhibited elevated pulmonary hypertension, for which condition the settlement did not offer any significant benefits. With regard to them, the district court found that "the evidence did not support a connection between the use of diet drugs and these conditions." Id. at 145. For both of these groups, the Third Circuit rejected the challenges because the objections had been raised and addressed by the district court during the settlement review process. Although "[t]here must be a process by which an individual class member or group of class members can challenge whether these due process protections were afforded to them," id., the settlement approval process sufficed. The fact that the objections were made by others, the court ruled, does not alter the due process determination (id. at 147–48):

> These Appellants argue that because the specific individuals who are Appellants in this case were not the specific individuals who raised objections at the fairness hearing, they must have the opportunity to litigate the issue themselves. This argument ignores the underpinnings of the class action mechanism. If this argument were to be accepted, each class member would be able to relitigate each issue, rendering the class action mechanism pointless. While it is true that the specific Appellants in this case did not, themselves, litigate this issue at the fairness hearing, other class members who are representative of them did litigate this issue and the District Court considered all of the arguments and evidence in that regard. Appellants were represented by other class members at the fairness hearing and because the District Court decided that the class was adequately represented, the issue of adequate representation has already been fully litigated.

7. In Hospitality Management Associates, Inc. v. Shell Oil Co., 591 S.E.2d 611 (S.C. 2004), the court gave full faith and credit to two nationwide class action settlements in other state courts despite the assertion by opt-out class members that they were entitled to attack the judgments collaterally. Noting the inconclusive Supreme Court handling of *Stephenson*, the court commented:

> [I]t remains an open, and hotly litigated, question as to whether limited collateral review is required on the *Shutts* due process requirements in a class action case (see *Epstein III*), or whether a broader, merits-oriented collateral review is permitted (see *Stephenson*). In addition to the conflict in the federal circuits as exemplified by *Epstein III* and *Stephenson*, there is also disagreement amongst the state courts and legal scholars.

In our opinion, there are important policy considerations favoring both limited and broad collateral review. Certainly, in the specialized context of class action litigation, the significant interests in efficiency and finality favor limited review. If the due process issues are fully and fairly litigated and necessarily decided by the rendering court, then the strong interest in finality militates in favor of an extremely limited collateral review. Without limited review, a nationwide class action could be vulnerable to collateral actions in the 49 other states in which it was not litigated initially. It would seem to be a waste of judicial resources to require reviewing courts to conduct an extensive substantive review when one has already been undertaken in a sister state. As the Ohio court stated in Fine v. America Online: "To allow substantive collateral attacks would be counterintuitive to [the] procedural relief that a class-action suit is intended to afford our judicial system nationwide." 743 N.E.2d [416,] 421–22 [(Ohio App. 2000)].

On the other hand, there is a fundamental interest in not allowing constitutionally infirm judgments to be enforced. It would be troublesome to enforce a class action settlement against parties over whom the rendering court did not have personal jurisdiction. We note, however, that the view espoused in *Epstein III* envisions that direct appellate review of a class action is the appropriate vehicle to correct whatever errors may have been made at the trial court level.

We hold that in a case such as this one, only a limited collateral review is appropriate. It would run counter to the class action goals of efficiency and finality to allow successive reviews of issues that were, in fact, fully and fairly litigated in the rendering court. Moreover, second-guessing the fully litigated decisions of our sister courts would violate the spirit of full faith and credit.

Therefore, we concur with the Ninth Circuit's view [in *Epstein III*] and find due process requires that an absent class member's rights are protected by the adoption and utilization of appropriate procedures by the certifying court; thereafter, the merits of the certifying court's determinations are subject to direct appellate review. As for collateral review, however, due process does not afford any second guessing of those determinations. *Epstein III.* Instead, what this limited review entails is "an examination of *procedural* due process and nothing more." Fine v. America Online, 743 N.E.2d at 421. More specifically, we must determine: (1) whether there were safeguards in place to guarantee sufficient notice and adequate representation; and (2) whether such safeguards were, in fact applied.

The court proceeded to examine the notice given (an extensive multimedia campaign which the court found to be constitutionally sufficient) and the adequacy of representation. On that score, it found that the courts, in contrast to *Amchem*, had procedures in place to ensure adequate representation and that they were implemented throughout the litigations. It therefore found that full faith and credit should be accorded the two class action settlement judgments.

C. ISSUE PRECLUSION IN COMPLEX LITIGATION

Complex litigation often involves multiple lawsuits that raise identical issues. Recall our discussion of multiple related lawsuits in Chapter 3, where we examined consolidation, stays, and other mechanisms to reduce the inefficiencies and inconsistencies that could result from a multiplicity of suits. Issue preclusion (or collateral estoppel) is yet another mechanism to protect against the inefficiency and potential inconsistency of multiple related adjudications. Issue preclusion "bars 'successive litigation of an issue of fact or law actually litigated and resolved in a valid court determination essential to the prior judgment,' even if the issue recurs in the context of a different claim." Taylor v. Sturgell, 553 U.S. 880 (2008) (quoting New Hampshire v. Maine, 532 U.S. 742, 748 (2001)).

Since the fall of the mutuality doctrine, issue preclusion has presented a strategic asymmetry in multiparty litigation. The mutuality doctrine, which all U.S. jurisdictions followed through most of the twentieth century (and a few still follow today), declared that issue preclusion could be used only by those who were parties to the prior case. A person who was neither party nor privy to the first case could not be bound by an adverse judgment and therefore, the thinking went, it would not be fair to allow that nonparty to benefit from a favorable judgment. By the end of the twentieth century, however, most courts had abandoned the mutuality doctrine. As a matter of federal preclusion law, the Supreme Court permitted defensive nonmutual issue preclusion in Blonder-Tongue Laboratories, Inc. v. University of Illinois Foundation, 402 U.S. 313 (1971), and permitted offensive nonmutual issue preclusion, with various caveats and exceptions, in Parklane Hosiery Co. v. Shore, 439 U.S. 322 (1979). With the exception of class actions and certain other forms of representational litigation, nonparties cannot be bound by a judgment, as the Court emphasized in Taylor v. Sturgell, *supra* p. 660. As you read the following cases, think about not only how issue preclusion affects the later case, but also how it might affect the strategic balance and litigation choices in the initial case.

LINCOLN-DODGE, INC. V. SULLIVAN

United States District Court, District of Rhode Island, 2008.
588 F.Supp.2d 224.

TORRES, SENIOR DISTRICT JUDGE.

Two automobile manufacturers; two manufacturers' associations; and a number of Rhode Island automobile dealers brought these consolidated actions for declaratory judgment against the Rhode Island Department of

Environmental Management ("RIDEM")[1] seeking a declaration that Rhode Island Air Pollution Control Regulation 37 ("Regulation 37" or the "Rhode Island regulation"), which sets greenhouse gas emissions standards for new automobiles, is invalid because both it and the California regulation (the "CARB Regulation") on which it is modeled have been preempted by the Energy Policy and Conservation Act of 1975, ("EPCA"), 49 U.S.C. §§ 32901–32919, and the Federal Clean Air Act, ("CAA"), 42 U.S.C. §§ 7401–7671(q), as amended in 1990.

RIDEM has moved for judgment on the pleadings contending that the plaintiffs' claims are barred by the doctrine of issue preclusion, also known as collateral estoppel, because the preemption issues raised were decided in previous cases brought by the plaintiff manufacturers and associations in United States District Courts for the Districts of Vermont and California.

For the reasons hereinafter stated, the defendants' motion for judgment on the pleadings is granted with respect to the manufacturers and associations but is denied with respect to the dealers.

Background

The Clean Air Act

The CAA requires the Administrator of the Environmental Protection Agency ("EPA") to adopt regulations establishing standards applicable to the emission of air pollutants from new motor vehicles. 42 U.S.C. § 7521(a)(1). The CAA expressly preempts the adoption or enforcement of different standards by any state, 42 U.S.C. § 7543(a), except that California is permitted to promulgate more stringent standards if it, first, obtains a waiver from EPA. 42 U.S.C. § 7543(b)(1). The CAA also provides that in the event that California obtains such a waiver, other states may adopt regulations identical to California's. 42 U.S.C. § 7507.

The Energy Policy and Conservation Act ("EPCA")

EPCA, 49 U.S.C. §§ 32901–32919, establishes Corporate Average Fuel Economy ("CAFE") standards that require a manufacturer's fleet of new motor vehicles to average, at least, 27.5 miles per gallon. In December 2007, Congress passed the Energy Independence and Security Act, which increases the CAFE mileage requirements beginning with the 2011 model year. Like the CAA, EPCA contains a preemption provision that prohibits states from "adopt[ing] or enforce[ing] a law or regulation related to fuel economy standards" for new motor vehicles. Unlike the CAA, EPCA does not contain a waiver provision.

---

[1]   The automobile manufacturers are General Motors and DaimlerChrysler, and the two associations are the Alliance of Automobile Manufacturers ("AAM") and the Association of International Automobile Manufacturers ("AIAM"). W. Michael Sullivan is named in his capacity as Director of RIDEM. In addition, the Natural Resources Defense Council, Sierra Club, Conservation Law Foundation, and Environmental Defense have intervened as party defendants.

California's Waiver Application

[In 2005, California applied for a CAA waiver with respect to the CARB Regulation, which established more stringent emissions standards to take effect in 2009. Before EPA issued a decision on California's waiver application, Rhode Island and several other states promulgated regulations that were virtually identical to the CARB Regulation. RIDEM conceded that it could not enforce the Rhode Island Regulation unless California's waiver application was granted. After the Rhode Island Regulation was promulgated, EPA denied California's waiver application.]

The Previous Decisions

Before this action was commenced, the plaintiff manufacturers and the plaintiff associations, together with a number of automobile dealers located in California and Vermont respectively, brought similar lawsuits in the United States District Courts for the Eastern District of California and the District of Vermont (the "previous cases"). The plaintiffs in those cases alleged that California's CARB Regulation and a Vermont regulation modeled on it were preempted by EPCA and the CAA.

1.   The Vermont Decision

The Vermont case was decided first. After a sixteen-day bench trial, the Court issued a written decision rejecting the plaintiffs' EPCA preemption claim for several reasons. *Green Mountain Chrysler Plymouth Dodge Jeep, et al. v. Crombie*, 508 F.Supp.2d 295 (D.Vt. 2007).

First, the Court held that a regulation promulgated pursuant to a waiver specifically authorized by federal law would not be a state law subject to EPCA preemption. *Green Mountain*, 508 F.Supp.2d at 343–350.

The *Green Mountain* Court also held that, even if the CARB regulation were treated as a state law, it would not be preempted by EPCA because greenhouse gas emissions standards do not "relate to" fuel economy standards or otherwise conflict with the purposes and objectives of EPCA. That holding was based on findings that greenhouse gas emissions can be reduced without increasing vehicle mileage; that such reductions were technologically feasible; and that any effect that reductions might have on fuel economy would be only incidental. * * *

Accordingly, judgment was entered against the plaintiff manufacturers, the plaintiff associations, and the Vermont dealers who joined in that action. An appeal from that judgment is pending before the Second Circuit.

2.   The California Decision

After the Vermont case was decided, the District Court for the Eastern District of California entered summary judgment against the plaintiff manufacturers, the plaintiff associations and the California dealers who joined in that action. *Central Valley Chrysler-Jeep, Inc. et al. v. Goldstene*,

529 F.Supp.2d 1151 (E.D.Cal. 2007). The Court held that EPCA did not preempt the CARB Regulation because the undisputed facts established that at least partial compliance could be achieved in ways that would not affect fuel economy standards and that any impact on fuel economy was only incidental and did not amount to *de facto* regulation of vehicle mileage requirements.

* * *

This Case

In this case, the plaintiffs claim that California's CARB Regulation and, by extension, the Rhode Island regulation that tracks it are preempted by EPCA and the CAA. The defendants argue that these issues were raised and decided in the Vermont and California cases and that the doctrine of issue preclusion bars the plaintiffs from relitigating them.

* * *

Analysis

I.   Issue Preclusion in General

A.   Overview

The doctrine of issue preclusion generally bars a litigant from raising issues of fact or law that were the subject of a final judgment in a previous case to which the litigant was a party. *United States v. Mendoza,* 464 U.S. 154, 158 (1984) ("[O]nce a court has decided an issue of fact or law necessary to its judgment, that decision is conclusive in a subsequent suit based on a different cause of action involving a party to the prior litigation."). Like the related doctrine of claim preclusion, issue preclusion prevents parties "from contesting matters that they have had a full and fair opportunity to litigate [and] protects their adversaries from the expense and vexation attending multiple lawsuits, conserves judicial resources and fosters reliance on judicial action by minimizing the possibility of inconsistent decisions." *Montana v. United States,* 440 U.S. 147, 153–54 (1979).

In this circuit, issue preclusion applies where: "(1) The issue sought to be precluded in the later action is the same as that involved in the earlier action; (2) the issue was actually litigated; (3) the issue was determined by a valid and binding final judgment; and (4) the determination of the issue was essential to the judgment." *Ramallo Bros. Printing, Inc. v. El Dia, Inc.* 490 F.3d 86, 90 (1st Cir. 2007) (citing *Keystone Shipping Co. v. New England Power Co.,* 109 F.3d 46, 51 (1st Cir. 1997)).

B.   Factors in Applying Issue Preclusion

Whether and to what extent issue preclusion applies depends, in part, on the type of issue preclusion invoked and on whether it is invoked against the government or a private party. Thus, at least, in the case of non-mutual issue preclusion, courts are less inclined to apply issue preclusion when it is invoked *offensively* to bar a defendant from asserting a defense that raises an issue unsuccessfully litigated by the defendant in a previous case than when it is invoked *defensively* to bar a plaintiff from raising an issue that the plaintiff unsuccessfully litigated in a previous case. *See Acevedo-Garcia v. Monroig,* 351 F.3d 547, 574 (1st Cir. 2003) (recognizing Supreme Court's special concerns regarding offensive use of non-mutual collateral estoppel).

In addition, the Supreme Court has held that nonmutual issue preclusion may not be applied against the government because "[t]he conduct of government litigation . . . is sufficiently different from the conduct of private civil litigation so that what might otherwise be economy interests underlying a broad application of collateral estoppel are outweighed by the constraints which peculiarly affect the government." *Mendoza,* 464 U.S. at 162. * * * The *Mendoza* Court also noted that "[g]overnment litigation frequently involves legal questions of substantial public importance . . .," 464 U.S. at 160, and "allowing nonmutual collateral estoppel against the government . . . would substantially thwart the development of important questions of law by freezing the first final decision rendered on a particular legal issue." *Id.*

II.   The EPCA Preemption Issue

In the previous cases, it was held that California's CARB Regulation was not preempted by EPCA and it is clear that those holdings were essential to the judgments. Nevertheless, the plaintiffs argue that they are not barred from relitigating the EPCA preemption issue because it presents a "pure legal question" to which issue preclusion does not apply and because applying issue preclusion would freeze development of the law with respect to "important national issues." Neither argument is persuasive.

A.   The Unmixed Question of Law Exception

It is true that a court may decline to apply issue preclusion where the issue presented is an "unmixed question of law" *and* the two cases "involv[e] unrelated subject matter." *Mendoza,* 464 U.S. at 163 n.7. The rationale for that exception is that, in such cases, foreclosing reconsideration "would not aid judicial economy." *See Pharm. Care Mgmt. Ass'n. v. Dist. of Columbia,* 522 F.3d 443, 447 (D.C.Cir. 2008).

By its terms, this exception does not apply where the issues involve "mixed questions of law and fact or . . . pure questions of fact." *Id.* at 446. Nor does the exception apply where the two cases are closely related because " 'it is unfair to the winning party and an unnecessary burden on the courts to allow repeated litigation of the same issue in what is essentially the same controversy, even if the issue is regarded as one of law.'" *United States v. Stauffer Chem. Co.,* 464 U.S. at 171 (quoting Restatement (Second) of Judgments § 28 comment b (1982)).

In this case, neither of the requirements necessary to trigger the exception has been satisfied.

1. The Unmixed Question of Law Requirement

In order to decide whether EPCA preempts the CARB Regulation and the Rhode Island regulation that tracks it, one, first, must determine whether, as the plaintiffs maintain, the CARB standards amount to *de facto* regulation of mileage requirements. As already noted, both the Vermont and California courts answered that question in the negative.

Furthermore, both holdings were based on factual findings that reducing greenhouse gas emissions did not necessarily require increased fuel economy and that any effect that the CARB standards may have on vehicle mileage would be only incidental. Consequently, the issue raised by the plaintiffs, and previously decided by both the Vermont and California courts, is not an "unmixed question of law" but, rather, it is a mixed question of law and fact.

2. The Unrelatedness Requirement

Even if the EPCA preemption issue were viewed as an "unmixed question of law," this case cannot be described as "unrelated" to the Vermont and California cases. The Vermont and California cases were brought contemporaneously and shortly before this case. Moreover, all three cases were brought by the same manufacturers and associations; based on essentially the same facts; challenging the same standards for the same reasons; alleging the same harm and seeking the same relief.

In short, this case clearly involves the same "subject matter" as the previous cases; and, therefore, the plaintiff manufacturers and associations are precluded from relitigating the EPCA preemption issue that they had a full and fair opportunity to litigate in those cases.

* * *

B. Mutuality and Public Concern

The plaintiffs argue that issue preclusion should not be applied in this case because it is nonmutual and it would freeze the development of the law with respect to "important national issues." However, that argument rests on two erroneous premises.

1. Mutuality

The fact that the defendants were not parties to the previous cases does not prevent them from invoking issue preclusion against the plaintiffs who were parties because the Supreme Court has made it clear that, at least in "disputes over private rights between private litigants," issue preclusion applies regardless of whether it is mutual or nonmutual.

Blonder-Tongue Lab., Inc. v. Univ. of Ill. Found., 402 U.S. 313, 349 (1971); *see Mendoza*, 464 U.S. at 158–159.

In *Mendoza,* the Court carved out a limited exception to that rule by holding that nonmutual collateral estoppel cannot be applied against the *government*, but the *Mendoza* Court clearly did not state, or even suggest, that the exception extended to private litigants, as well. Indeed, as already noted, the *Mendoza* Court based its decision on what it identified as several important differences between litigation conducted by the government and litigation conducted by private parties. The *Mendoza* Court cited various "prudential" and "institutional" considerations unique to the government and pointed out that "[g]overnment litigation frequently involves legal questions of substantial public importance ... [and that] many constitutional questions can arise only in the context of litigation to which the government is a party." 464 U.S. at 159–60.

2.   Matters of "Public Concern"

In support of the plaintiffs' argument that barring them from relitigating the EPCA preemption issue would freeze development of the law with respect to "important national issues," the plaintiffs rely upon language in the Restatement (Second) of Judgments and decisions by several courts to the effect that the public interest in relitigating an issue may be a factor in deciding whether collateral estoppel should be applied. However, that argument is not convincing for several reasons.

First, the Supreme Court has recognized the public interest in relitigating an issue as a factor that may make issue preclusion inappropriate only in cases where issue preclusion has been asserted against the *government. Mendoza,* 464 U.S. at 160. In this case, issue preclusion is being invoked by a governmental agency against private business entities. The distinction is important because the public interest in permitting the government to relitigate issues on which it, previously, was unsuccessful presumably derives from the fact that the government litigates on behalf of the public. By contrast, private parties litigate in order to further their own interests which, sometimes, may be contrary to the interests of the general public. Indeed, in this case, it is difficult to see what interest the public has in permitting the plaintiffs another bite of the apple in challenging regulations limiting the emission of greenhouse gases into the atmosphere.

* * *

In addition, this case deals with the *defensive* use of issue preclusion by a defendant who seeks to bar a plaintiff from relitigating an issue that was decided in a previous case brought by the same plaintiff rather than the *offensive* use of issue preclusion referred to in *Acevedo-Garcia.* In *Ackerman v. American Airlines,* the Court recognized that distinction in barring airline pilots from suing American Airlines with respect to an issue decided in previous suits brought by the pilots against other airlines and the Court found the cases relied upon by the pilots to be inapposite because they dealt with offensive issue preclusion. 924 F. Supp. 749 (N.D.Tex. 1995).

There are sound policy reasons for applying nonmutual issue preclusion more readily when it is invoked defensively against a party that previously initiated litigation raising the same issue. While there may be circumstances under which it might be unfair to preclude a defendant from relitigating issues decided against it in a previous case brought at a time and place not of the defendant's choosing and in which the defendant was an involuntary participant, there is no comparable unfairness in precluding a plaintiff from relitigating issues that the plaintiff chose to raise in a previous case that it initiated in a forum that it selected.

Moreover, allowing a plaintiff to bring successive lawsuits seeking to relitigate issues that the plaintiff chose to raise in previous cases would create an exception that virtually swallows the rule and would result in the kinds of costly and vexatious multiple lawsuits, the waste of judicial resources and the risk of inconsistent decisions that issue preclusion is designed to prevent. Indeed, as plaintiffs' counsel candidly acknowledged during oral argument, such an exception would allow these plaintiffs to bring similar suits in every circuit.

III. The CAA Preemption Issue

[Both the Vermont and California courts determined that the CAA does not preempt the CARB Regulation. Those prior determinations are binding on the plaintiffs in this case. The plaintiffs argued that issue preclusion should not apply because the California and Vermont decisions were inconsistent with each other with respect to the CAA preemption issue, but the court found nothing inconsistent about the two decisions. *See* Restatement (Second) of Judgments § 29(4), cmt. f (in considering whether a party should be precluded from relitigating a previously determined issue, the court should consider whether the "determination relied on as preclusive is itself inconsistent with another adjudication of the same issue.").]

IV. Who is Precluded

The plaintiff manufacturers and associations clearly are precluded from relitigating the EPCA and CAA preemption issues because they were parties to both the California and Vermont cases. The only remaining question is whether the plaintiff dealers also are precluded.

In general, "one is not bound by a judgment *in personam* in a litigation in which he is not designated as a party."[4] *Taylor v. Sturgell*, 128 S.Ct.

---

[4] Unlike *nonmutual* preclusion, *nonparty* preclusion occurs when a judgment in a prior action is invoked against one who was not a party to that action. *NLRB v. Donna-Lee Sportswear Co., Inc.*, 836 F.2d 31, 35 n.4 (1st Cir. 1987).

2161, 2166–67 (2008) (quoting *Hansberry v. Lee,* 311 U.S. 32, 40 (1940)) [*supra* p. 166]. However, issue preclusion may be invoked against those who were not parties to the previous litigation with respect to "matters that they had a full and fair opportunity to litigate." *Montana,* 440 U.S. at 153–154. Thus, " 'one who prosecutes or defends a suit in the name of another to establish and protect his own right, or assists in the prosecution or defense of an action in aid of some interest of his own . . . is as much bound . . . as he would be if he had been a party to the [previous action].' " *Id.* at 154.

The Supreme Court has rejected any "virtual representation" exception to the general rule against applying issue preclusion to those who were not parties to the previous litigation to the extent that such an exception would utilize a "multifactor test" "present[ing] preclusion in cases that do not fit within any of the established exceptions." *Taylor,* 128 S.Ct. at 2173. *Taylor* identified six categories of established exceptions that it described as "meant only to provide a framework for our consideration of virtual representation, not to establish a definitive taxonomy." *Id.* at n.6.

In this case, the defendants argue that the dealers are precluded from litigating the EPCA and CAA preemption issues because they are in "privity" with the manufacturers and because the manufacturers and associations "virtually" or "adequately" represented them in the previous cases. In support of their argument, the defendants point to the franchisee-franchisor relationship between the dealers and the manufacturers and they contend that the dealers' interests are derivative of the manufacturers' interests.

As already noted, *Taylor* rejected "virtual representation" as a basis for nonparty issue preclusion, at least to the extent that it does "not fit within any of the established exceptions." *Id.* at 2173. *Taylor* also discouraged citing "privity" as a basis for applying nonparty issue preclusion because that term, sometimes, is used too "broadly as a way to express the conclusion that nonparty preclusion is appropriate on any ground." *Id.* at n.8.[6]

Based on the current state of the record, the only categories of nonparty preclusion recognized in *Taylor* that, arguably, are applicable to the dealers in this case are: (1) that the franchise relationship between the manufacturers and dealers is the type of "substantive legal relationship" that bars the dealers from relitigating the issues; (2) that, in the previous litigation, the dealers were "adequately represented" by the manufacturers and associations; and/or (3) that, in this case, the dealers are acting as "proxies" for the manufacturers and associations. The defendants bear the

---

[6] Privity has been described as an "elusive concept" that is difficult to define, *In re Iannochino,* 242 F.3d 36, 46 (1st Cir. 2001), and as being "conclusory and analytically unsound," *Montana,* 440 U.S. at 154 n.5. *See also, Gonzalez,* 27 F.3d at 757 (cautioning that courts should "tread gingerly" in using privity as a basis for applying claim preclusion to nonparties).

burden of establishing that one or more of those exceptions applies. [I]n the instant case, they have failed to carry that burden. * * *

Here, there is nothing in the record indicating any understanding that the manufacturers and associations were acting as representatives of the Rhode Island dealers in the previous cases or, even, that the Rhode Island dealers were aware of the previous cases. The mere fact that the dealers and manufacturers may have shared a common interest in the outcome of the previous cases, by itself, is insufficient to establish that the manufacturers and associations were acting as the dealers' representatives in those cases. * * *

The fact that, in this case, the Rhode Island dealers are represented by the same counsel that represent the manufacturers and associations and that represented them in the previous cases fuels suspicions that they may be acting in concert or that the dealers are not real parties in interest to this case. However, in the words of *Taylor*, "a mere whiff of 'tactical maneuvering' will not suffice" and "preclusion is appropriate only if the putative agent's conduct of the suit is subject to the control of the party who is bound by the prior adjudication." *Id.* 128 S.Ct. at 2179. Here, no such showing has yet been made.

The defendants assert that the dealers' claims are merely "derivative" of the manufacturers' claims but they do not explain what that means or why it would trigger the application of nonparty issue preclusion. If the defendants intend that assertion as an argument that the dealers have no independently cognizable claims, it would be inappropriate for the Court to address that argument, at this time, because it has not been directly raised or adequately briefed.

Conclusion

For all of the foregoing reasons, the defendants' motion to dismiss C.A. No. 06–69 is GRANTED and the motion to dismiss C.A. No. 06–70 is GRANTED with respect to the AAM and the plaintiff manufacturers and it is DENIED with respect to the plaintiff dealers.

NOTES AND QUESTIONS

1.   Consider how issue preclusion relates to joinder and other aggregation mechanisms. Specifically, for disputes that involve related claims by or against different parties, consider how nonmutual issue preclusion achieves something akin to aggregation. By producing a single resolution of a common issue, issue preclusion holds out the promise of achieving, over time, one aspect of the efficiency that joinder, class certification, consolidation, and MDL transfer achieve when they pull claims together for simultaneous adjudication. Indeed, in Atwood v. Johnson, Rodenburg & Lauinger, 2011 WL 3274084 (D. Minn. Aug. 1, 2011), which involved claims against a debt collector concerning about one thousand consumers, the judge denied class certification

(on grounds of predominance and superiority) but suggested nonmutual issue preclusion as a substitute for class certification:

[Plaintiff] argues that judicial efficiencies favor the class mechanism. The court disagrees. Individual fact-finding * * * is necessary whether the cases proceed as a class action or individual actions. Moreover, if the claims are as meritorious and as similar as [plaintiff] argues, then non-mutual collateral estoppel might achieve similar efficiency as to the overshadowing question.

2. The *Lincoln-Dodge* court laid out the elements that must be established for a court to apply issue preclusion: the current action involves an issue that is the *same issue* as was raised in an earlier action; the issue was *actually litigated*; the issue was *actually determined*; there was a *valid and final judgment*; and the determination of the issue was *essential to the judgment*. In addition, the court used the oft-quoted language requiring that there have been a *full and fair opportunity to litigate*. See Blonder-Tongue Lab. v. Univ. of Ill. Found., 402 U.S. 313, 329 (1971) ("Although neither judges, the parties, nor the adversary system performs perfectly in all cases, the requirement of determining whether the party against whom an estoppel is asserted had a full and fair opportunity to litigate is a most significant safeguard."). These requirements impose significant limits on the use of the doctrine, as does the principle that issue preclusion generally may not be used against one who was not a party to the prior action. In *Lincoln-Dodge*, who sought to use issue preclusion against whom, and on what issues? Was the attempted use mutual or nonmutual? If nonmutual, was it offensive or defensive? Did it satisfy each of the required elements?

3. In *Lincoln-Dodge*, the court refused to extend to private litigants the protection that government litigants enjoy from nonmutual issue preclusion under the Supreme Court's *Mendoza* decision. What is the logic behind protecting government litigants from nonmutual issue preclusion? To what extent might the same logic extend to some private litigants? The *Mendoza* case involved an attempt to use *offensive* nonmutual issue preclusion against the *federal* government, but some courts have extended the rule to include defensive use and to protect state governments. See, e.g., State of Idaho Potato Comm'n v. G&T Terminal Packaging, Inc., 425 F.3d 708, 714 (9th Cir. 2005) (applying *Mendoza* to protect state agency from application of defensive nonmutual issue preclusion).

4. Applying the principle against nonparty preclusion from *Taylor v. Sturgell* (*supra* p. 660) and finding none of the exceptions applicable, the court in *Lincoln-Dodge* ruled that the automobile dealers remained free to litigate the issues, even as issue preclusion barred the automobile manufacturers and associations from relitigating those same issues. Does the presence of unbound litigants erase the efficiency benefit offered by issue preclusion? Should the court, on this basis, have rejected the use of issue preclusion against the manufacturers and associations? In In re Blue Cross Blue Shield Antitrust Litigation, 2018 WL 1796257, at *4 (N.D. Ala. Apr. 16, 2018), the MDL judge rejected the use of issue preclusion in part because some of the current parties had not been parties to the prior action in which issues had been decided, and

thus issue preclusion at best could only apply to some of the relevant parties: "Here, Provider Plaintiffs would only be able to apply offensive collateral estoppel against [certain defendants] in this MDL. It would likely be confusing if the court instructed the jury to apply certain market-related findings against Anthem while also instructing the jury to make its own trial evidence-based, independent findings on similar issues when deliberating over the claims against the other Defendants."

5.   Preclusion issues sometimes arise when a governmental body or public authority sues first, and a citizen or other entity files a second suit relying on the same legal rights. Southwest Airlines Co. v. Texas International Airlines, 546 F.2d 84 (5th Cir. 1977), provides an example. The cities of Dallas and Fort Worth sued Southwest Airlines for a declaratory judgment that Southwest had to stop commercial air service from an airport that was being phased out in favor of a new airport. The federal district court entered a judgment that Southwest could not be excluded from using the old airport. Other competing airlines, which were using the new airport, then filed suit in state court to deny Southwest access to the old airport based on denial of the claim asserted by the cities in the first suit. The district court enjoined that litigation, and the appellate court affirmed. Although the appellate court found that the competing airlines had a greater pecuniary interest in the success of the new airport than did the general public, it found that they were bound by the first judgment. It observed that all those who provided goods and services at the new airport and all investors, developers, hotels, restaurants, and other retail interests in the vicinity could also have a pecuniary interest distinct from that of the general public. "To allow relitigation by all of these parties," it said, "would surely defeat the res judicata policies identified above." It also found that the competing airlines had no "legal interest" apart from that which the city sought to enforce in the first suit. Would a different result be reached after *Taylor v. Sturgell*, or does this situation fit one of the exceptions identified in *Taylor*?

Sometimes governmental action may extinguish pre-existing rights of citizens to litigate a violation of regulatory norms. Thus, in United States EPA v. City of Green Forest, 921 F.2d 1394 (8th Cir. 1990), citizens sued a town for violating the Clean Water Act. That Act allows citizens to sue if governmental officials responsible for enforcement of the environmental laws do not pursue violators. After the citizens sued, the EPA filed its own action. The private plaintiffs tried to intervene in that action when a consent decree was proposed in order to argue for more stringent provisions, but the district court denied intervention. The appellate court held that this denial of intervention was error, but that it was harmless because the private plaintiffs were nevertheless allowed to file objections to the consent decree during the public comment period. The court approved the decree. Having approved the consent decree, the district court dismissed the private citizens' claims against the town under the Clean Water Act on the ground they were precluded by entry of the consent decree. Emphasizing the "preeminent role that government actions must play in the CWA enforcement scheme," id. at 1403, the appellate court affirmed. This followed because the citizen role, as private attorney general, was intended merely as supplemental to the primary right of the public enforcement agencies, as evidenced by the provision in the statute that citizen suits would not be allowed if governmental agencies had already initiated their own actions.

6. Note the potentially one-sided application of issue preclusion after the demise of mutuality. Suppose plaintiffs file identical complaints against the same defendant and coordinate their trial strategies. If one case results in a defense judgment, will the plaintiffs in the other cases be bound by the issue preclusive effect of the adverse judgment? If one case results in a plaintiff victory, on the other hand, the other plaintiffs may try to use offensive nonmutual issue preclusion to bind the common defendant. What would be the defendant's strongest argument against the application of nonmutual issue preclusion in these circumstances? To the extent issue preclusion may be allowed, how might it affect plaintiffs' joinder or class action strategy in the first case?

Professor Ratliff attacked the way *Parklane* grants nonparties an option to take advantage of earlier litigation results, finding the grounds for denying preclusive effect inadequate in light of the real-world complexities of joinder: "The *Parklane* protection against wait-and-see plaintiffs is inadequate because of the difficulty of giving notice to unknown optionholders and because there is no workable way to determine which optionholders, having received notice, have legitimate reasons for ignoring it and staying out of the case." Jack Ratliff, Offensive Collateral Estoppel and the Option Effect, 67 Tex. L. Rev. 63, 82 (1988). Consider his example to support his position (id. at 83):

> To illustrate the problem, let us return to Professor Currie's hypothetical train wreck [see *infra* p. 725 n. 13]. Suppose that it occurs in Kansas and that of the fifty potential plaintiffs, nine reside in states other than Kansas. The first case goes to trial in a Kansas state court. Must all plaintiffs, including nonresidents, join in the Kansas case or lose the benefits of collateral estoppel? What if a plaintiff does not intervene because (1) his home state's law is more favorable and more likely to be applied in his home forum, which is also more convenient; (2) his attorney would have to hand over control of his case to a designated lead counsel in Kansas; or (3) the other plaintiffs, prospective coparties, are not believable or have marginal cases? What if some plaintiffs have no notice of the case? What if the procedural rules of Kansas will not permit such an intervention? Finally, from the defendant's standpoint, why should any of this make any difference? The option effect comes into play whatever the plaintiff's motivation. Which should be determinative on the question of fairness: the optionholder's state of mind or the effect of the option on his adversary? If we conclude that the optionholder's motivation is irrelevant, then we are forced to agree with Currie that the option effect, however created, is unfair.

Keep these points in mind as you read the next case.

HARDY V. JOHNS-MANVILLE SALES CORP.
United States Court of Appeals, Fifth Circuit, 1982.
681 F.2d 334.

Before GEE and JOHNSON, CIRCUIT JUDGES, and VAN PELT, DISTRICT JUDGE.

GEE, CIRCUIT JUDGE.

This appeal arises out of a diversity action brought by various plaintiffs—insulators, pipefitters, carpenters, and other factory workers—against various manufacturers, sellers, and distributors of asbestos-containing products. The plaintiffs, alleging exposure to the products and consequent disease, assert various causes of action, including negligence, breach of implied warranty, and strict liability. The pleadings in each of the cases are substantially the same. No plaintiff names a particular defendant on a case-by-case basis but, instead, includes several—often as many as twenty asbestos manufacturers—in his individual complaint. The rationale offered for this unusual pleading practice is that, given the long latent period of the diseases in question, it is impossible for plaintiffs to isolate the precise exposure period or to identify the particular manufacturer's product responsible. * * * The trial court held that Texas courts, faced with the impossibility of identifying a precise causative agent in these asbestos cases, would adopt a form of *Sindell* liability [see *supra* p. 37 note 3], described as a "hybrid, drawing from concepts of alternative and/or concurrent liability and the law of products liability to form a type of absolute liability." The trial court ruled that "discovery on percentage share of a relevant market may lead to admissible evidence in the trials of some, and perhaps all, of these cases" and therefore granted leave to consolidate them for discovery purposes. This ruling is not on appeal here.

Defendants' interlocutory appeal under 28 U.S.C. § 1292(b) is directed instead at the district court's amended omnibus order dated March 13, 1981, which applies collateral estoppel to this mass tort. The omnibus order is, in effect, a partial summary judgment for plaintiffs based on nonmutual offensive collateral estoppel and judicial notice derived from this court's opinion in *Borel v. Fibreboard Paper Products Corp.*, 493 F.2d 1076 (5th Cir. 1973) (henceforth *Borel*). *Borel* was a diversity lawsuit in which manufacturers of insulation products containing asbestos were held strictly liable to an insulation worker who developed asbestosis and mesothelioma and ultimately died. The trial court construed *Borel* as establishing as a matter of law and/or fact that: (1) insulation products containing asbestos as a generic ingredient are "unavoidably unsafe products," (2) asbestos is a competent producing cause of mesothelioma and asbestosis, (3) no warnings were issued by any asbestos insulation manufacturers prior to 1964, and (4) the "warning standard" was not met by the *Borel* defendants in the period from 1964 through 1969. Insofar as the trial court based its omnibus order on the res judicata effect of *Borel*, this aspect of the order is no longer valid. *Migues v. Fibreboard Corp.*, 662 F.2d 1182 (5th Cir. 1981). The sole issue on appeal is the validity of the order on grounds of collateral estoppel or judicial notice.

In *Flatt v. Johns Manville Sales Corp.*, 488 F.Supp. 836 (E.D.Tex. 1980), the same court outlined the elements of proof for plaintiffs in asbestos-related cases. There the court stated that the plaintiff must prove by a preponderance of the evidence that

1. Defendants manufactured, marketed, sold, distributed, or placed in the stream of commerce products containing asbestos.

2. Products containing asbestos are unreasonably dangerous.

3. Asbestos dust is a competent producing cause of mesothelioma.

4. Decedent was exposed to defendant's products.

5. The exposure was sufficient to be a producing cause of mesothelioma.

6. Decedent contracted mesothelioma.

7. Plaintiffs suffered damages.

The parties agree that the effect of the trial court's collateral estoppel order in this case is to foreclose elements 2 and 3 above. Under the terms of the omnibus order, both parties are precluded from presenting evidence on the "state of the art"—evidence that, under Texas law of strict liability, is considered by a jury along with other evidence in order to determine whether as of a given time warning should have been given of the dangers associated with a product placed in the stream of commerce. Under the terms of the order, the plaintiffs need not prove that the defendants either knew or should have known of the dangerous propensities of their products and therefore should have warned consumers of these dangers, defendants being precluded from showing otherwise. On appeal, the defendants contend that the order violates their rights to due process and to trial by jury. Because we conclude that the trial court abused its discretion in applying collateral estoppel and judicial notice, we reverse.

* * *

The Non-Borel Defendants

This is the first and, in our view, insurmountable problem with the trial court's application of collateral estoppel in the case sub judice. The omnibus order under review here does not distinguish between defendants who were parties to *Borel* and those who were not; it purports to estop all defendants because all purportedly share an "identity of interests" sufficient to constitute privity. The trial court's action stretches "privity" beyond meaningful limits. While we acknowledge the manipulability of the notion of "privity," this has not prevented courts from establishing guidelines on the permissibility of binding nonparties through res judicata or collateral estoppel. Without such guidelines, the due process guarantee of a full and fair opportunity to litigate disappears. Thus, we noted in Southwest Airlines Co. v. Texas International Airlines, 546 F.2d 84, 95 (5th Cir. 1977):

> Federal courts have deemed several types of relationships "sufficiently close" to justify preclusion. First, a nonparty who has succeeded to a party's interest in property is bound by any prior judgments against that party. . . . Second, a nonparty who controlled the original suit will be bound by the resulting judgment. . . . Third, federal courts will bind a nonparty whose interests were represented adequately by a party in the original suit.

The rationale for these exceptions—all derived from *Restatement (Second) of Judgments* §§ 30, 31, 34, 39–41 (1982)—is obviously that in these instances the nonparty has in effect had his day in court. In this case, the exceptions elaborated in *Southwest Airlines* and in the *Restatement* are inapplicable. First, the *Borel* litigation did not involve any property interests. Second, none of the non-*Borel* defendants have succeeded to any property interest held by the *Borel* defendants. Finally, the plaintiffs did not show that any non-*Borel* defendant had any control whatever over the *Borel* litigation. "To have control of litigation requires that a person have effective choice as to the legal theories and proofs to be advanced in behalf of the party to the action. He must also have control over the opportunity to obtain review." *Restatement (Second) of Judgments* § 39, comment c (1982). In, for example, Sea-Land Services v. Gaudet, 414 U.S. 573 (1974), the Supreme Court held that a nonparty may be collaterally estopped from relitigating issues necessarily decided in a suit by a party who acted as a fiduciary responsible for the beneficial interests of the nonparties. Even in this context, however, the Court placed the exception within strict confines: "In such cases, 'the beneficiaries are bound by the judgment with respect to the interest which was the subject of the fiduciary relationship. . . .' " Many of our circuit's cases evince a similar concern with keeping the nonparties' exceptions to res judicata and collateral estoppel within strict confines. See, e.g., Southwest Airlines Co. v. Texas International Airlines.

The fact that all the non-*Borel* defendants, like the *Borel* defendants, are engaged in the manufacture of asbestos-containing products does not evince privity among the parties. The plaintiffs did not demonstrate that any of the non-*Borel* defendants participated in any capacity in the *Borel* litigation—whether directly or even through a trade representative—or were even part of a trustee-beneficiary relationship with any *Borel* defendant. On the contrary, several of the defendants indicate on appeal that they were not even aware of the *Borel* litigation until those proceedings were over and that they were not even members of industry or trade associations composed of asbestos product manufacturers. * * *

Our conclusion likewise pertains to those defendants who, while originally parties to the *Borel* litigation, settled before trial. The plaintiffs here did not show that any of these defendants settled out of the *Borel* litigation after the entire trial had run its course and only the judicial act of signing a final known adverse judgment remained. Such action would suggest settlement precisely to avoid offensive collateral estoppel and, in an appropriate case, might preclude relitigation. All the indications here are, however, that the defendants in question settled out of the case early because of, for example, lack of product identification. Like the non-*Borel* defendants, these defendants have likewise been deprived of their day in court by the trial court's omnibus order.

The Borel Defendants

The propriety of estopping the six defendants in this case who were parties to *Borel* poses more difficult questions. In ascertaining the precise preclusive effect of a prior judgment on a particular issue, we have often referred to the requirements set out, *inter alia,* in *International Association of Machinists & Aerospace Workers v. Nix,* 512 F.2d 125, 132 (5th Cir. 1975), and cases cited therein. The party asserting the estoppel must show that: (1) the issue to be concluded is identical to that involved in the prior action; (2) in the prior action the issue was "actually litigated"; and (3) the determination made of the issue in the prior action must have been necessary and essential to the resulting judgment.

> If it appears that a judgment may have been based on more than one of several distinctive matters in litigation and there is no indication which issue it was based on or which issue was fully litigated, such judgment will not preclude, under the doctrine of collateral estoppel, relitigation of any of the issues.

Federal Procedure, Lawyers Ed. § 51.218 at 151 (1981) (citations omitted).

Appellants argue that *Borel* did not necessarily decide that asbestos-containing insulation products were unreasonably dangerous because of failure to warn. According to appellants, the general *Borel* verdict, based on general instructions and special interrogatories, permitted the jury to ground strict liability on the bases of failures to test, of unsafeness for intended use, of failures to inspect, or of unsafeness of the product. Strict liability on the basis of failure to warn, although argued to the jury by trial counsel for the plaintiff in *Borel,* was, in the view of the appellants, never formally presented in the jury instructions and therefore was not essential to the *Borel* jury verdict.

Appellants' view has some plausibility. The special interrogatories answered by the *Borel* jury were general and not specifically directed to failure to warn.[8] Indeed, as we discussed at length in our review of the *Borel* judgment, the jury was instructed in terms of "breach of warranty." Although the jury was accurately instructed as to "strict liability in tort" as defined in section 402A of the *Restatement (Second) of Torts,* that phrase was never specifically mentioned in the jury's interrogatories. It is also true that the general instructions to the *Borel* jury on the plaintiff's causes of action did not charge on failure to warn, except in connection with negligence. Yet appellants' argument in its broadest form must ultimately fail. We concluded in *Borel:*

> The jury found that the unreasonably dangerous condition of the defendants' product was the proximate cause of Borel's injury. This necessarily included a finding that, had adequate warnings been provided, Borel would have chosen to avoid the danger.

As the appellants at times concede in their briefs, "if *Borel* stands for any rule at all, it is that defendants have a duty to warn the users of their products of the long-term dangers attendant upon its use, including the danger of an occupational disease." Indeed, the first sentence in our *Borel* opinion states that that case involved "the scope of an asbestos manufacturer's duty to warn industrial insulation workers of dangers associated with the use of asbestos." Our conclusion in *Borel* was grounded in that trial court's jury instructions concerning proximate cause and defective product. * * * Close reading of these instructions convinced our panel in *Borel* that a failure to warn was necessarily implicit in the jury's verdict. While the parties invite us to reconsider our holding in *Borel* that failure to warn grounded the jury's strict liability finding in that case, we cannot, even if we were so inclined, displace a prior decision of this court absent reconsideration en banc. Further, there is authority for the proposition that once an appellate court has disposed of a case on the basis of one of several alternative issues that may have grounded a trial court's

---

[8] SPECIAL INTERROGATORY NO. 1: Do you find from a preponderance of the evidence that any of the Defendants listed below was negligent in any of the respects contended by Plaintiff, which negligence was a proximate cause of the injuries and death of the deceased? Answer "Yes" or "No" opposite the named defendant. [The jury answered "No" as to Pittsburgh and Armstrong and "Yes" as to the other four defendants.]

SPECIAL INTERROGATORY NO. 2: [This interrogatory submitted the question whether any of the six defendants were guilty of an act or acts of gross negligence, and the jury found that no defendant was guilty of gross negligence.]

SPECIAL INTERROGATORY NO. 3: Do you find from a preponderance of the evidence that the deceased was guilty of contributory negligence and that such negligence was a proximate cause of the injuries and death of the deceased? [The jury answered "Yes".]

SPECIAL INTERROGATORY NO. 4: Do you find from a preponderance of the evidence that the warranties as contended for by the Plaintiff were violated by any of the Defendants listed below, which breach of warranty was a proximate cause of the injuries and death of the deceased? [The jury answered "Yes" as to each defendant.]

SPECIAL INTERROGATORY NO. 5: What amount of money, if paid now in cash, would fairly and reasonably compensate the Plaintiff, Freida Borel, for the damages she sustained by virtue of the death of her husband?

ANSWER: Actual damages $68,000. Damages for gross negligence "None."

judgment, the issue decided on appeal is conclusively established for purposes of issue preclusion. Nonetheless, we must ultimately conclude that the judgment in *Borel* cannot estop even the *Borel* defendants in this case for three interrelated reasons.

First, after review of the issues decided in *Borel*, we conclude that *Borel*, while conclusive as to the general matter of a duty to warn on the part of manufacturers of asbestos-containing insulation products, is ultimately ambiguous as to certain key issues. As the authors of the *Restatement (Second) of Judgments* § 29, comment g (1982), have noted, collateral estoppel is inappropriate where the prior judgment is ambivalent:

> The circumstances attending the determination of an issue in the first action may indicate that it could reasonably have been resolved otherwise if those circumstances were absent. Resolution of the issue in question may have entailed reference to such matters as the intention, knowledge, or comparative responsibility of the parties in relation to each other. . . . In these and similar situations, taking the prior determination at face value for purposes of the second action would extend the effects of imperfections in the adjudicative process beyond the limits of the first adjudication, within which they are accepted only because of the practical necessity of achieving finality.

The *Borel* jury decided that Borel, an industrial insulation worker who was exposed to fibers from his employer's insulation products over a 33-year period (from 1936 to 1969), was entitled to have been given fair warning that asbestos dust may lead to asbestosis, mesothelioma, and other cancers. The jury dismissed the argument that the danger was obvious and regarded as conclusive the fact that Borel testified that he did not know that inhaling asbestos dust could cause serious injuries until his doctor so advised him in 1969. The jury necessarily found "that, had adequate warnings been provided, Borel would have chosen to avoid the danger." In *Borel*, the evidence was that the industry as a whole issued no warnings at all concerning its insulation products prior to 1964, that Johns-Manville placed a warnings label on packages of its products in 1964, and that Fibreboard and Rubberoid placed warnings on their products in 1966.

Given these facts, it is impossible to determine what the *Borel* jury decided about *when* a duty to warn attached. Did the jury find the defendants liable because their warnings after 1966, when they acknowledged that they knew the dangers of asbestosis, were insufficiently explicit as to the grave risks involved? If so, as appellants here point out, the jury may have accepted the state of the art arguments provided by the defendants in *Borel*,—*i.e.*, that the defendants were not aware of the danger of asbestosis until the 1960's. Even under this view, there is a second ambiguity: was strict liability grounded on the fact that the warnings issued, while otherwise sufficient, never reached the insulator in the field? If so, perhaps the warnings, while insufficient as to insulation workers like Borel, were sufficient to alert workers further down the production line who may have seen the warnings—such as the carpenters and pipefitters in this case. Alternatively, even if the *Borel* jury decided that failure to warn before 1966 grounded strict liability, did the duty attach in the 1930's when the "hazard of asbestosis as a pneumoconiotic dust was universally accepted," or in 1965, when documentary evidence was presented of the hazard of asbestos insulation products to the installers of these products?

As we noted in *Borel,* strict liability because of failure to warn is based on a determination of the manufacturer's reasonable knowledge:

> [I]n cases such as the instant case, the manufacturer is held to the knowledge and skill of an expert. This is relevant in determining (1) whether the manufacturer knew or should have known the danger, and (2) whether the manufacturer was negligent in failing to communicate this superior knowledge to the user or consumer of its product. . . . The manufacturer's status as expert means that at a minimum he must keep abreast of scientific knowledge, discoveries, and advances and is presumed to know what is imparted thereby.

Thus, the trial judge in *Borel* instructed the jury that the danger "must have been reasonably foreseen by the manufacturer." As both this instruction and the ambiguities in the *Borel* verdict demonstrate, a determination that a particular product is so unreasonably hazardous as to require a warning of its dangers is not an absolute. Such a determination is necessarily relative to the scientific knowledge generally known or available to the manufacturer at the time the product in question was sold or otherwise placed in the stream of commerce.

Not all the plaintiffs in this case were exposed to asbestos-containing insulation products over the same 30-year period as plaintiff Borel. Not all plaintiffs here are insulation workers isolated from the warnings issued by some of the defendants in 1964 and 1966. Some of the products may be different from those involved in *Borel.* Our opinion in *Borel,* "limited to determining whether there [was] a conflict in substantial evidence sufficient to create a jury question," did not resolve that as a matter of fact all manufacturers of asbestos-containing insulation products had a duty to warn as of 1936, and all failed to warn adequately after 1964. Although we determined that the jury must have found a violation of the manufacturers' duty to warn, we held only that the jury could have grounded strict liability on the absence of a warning prior to 1964 or "could have concluded that the [post-1964 and post-1966] 'cautions' were not warnings in the sense that they adequately communicated to Borel and other insulation workers knowledge of the dangers to which they were exposed so as to give them a choice of working or not working with a dangerous product." As we have already had occasion to point out in *Migues v. Fibreboard Corp.,* 662 F.2d at 1188–89, our opinion in *Borel* merely approved of the various ways the jury could have come to a conclusion concerning strict liability for failure to warn. We did not say that any of the specific alternatives that the jury had before it were necessary or essential to its verdict.

> The *only* determination made by this court in *Borel* was that, based upon the evidence in that case, the jury's findings could not be said to be incorrect as a matter of law. But this Court certainly did not decide that every jury presented with the same facts would be compelled to reach the conclusion reached by the *Borel* jury: that asbestos was unreasonably dangerous. Such a holding would have been not only unnecessary, it would also have been unwarranted.

> In *Borel,* this Court said: "the jury was *entitled* to find that the danger to Borel and other insulation workers from inhaling asbestos dust was foreseeable to the defendants at the time the products causing Borel's injuries were sold".... This Court did not say that, as a matter of law, the danger of asbestos inhalation was so hidden from every asbestos worker in every situation as to create a duty to warn on the part of all asbestos manufacturers. On rehearing, this Court held that although some asbestos products used by plaintiff Borel contained warnings, there was sufficient evidence that the warnings were inadequate to inform workers of the actual dangers posed by asbestos inhalation to justify submission of that issue to the jury. This Court did not state that every jury would be required, as a matter of law, to find such warnings inadequate.

> In sum, this Court held in *Borel* only that the *Borel* jury, on the evidence presented to it, could have found that asbestos products unaccompanied by adequate warnings were unreasonably dangerous. The proposition that all juries presented with similar evidence regarding asbestos products would be compelled to find those products unreasonably dangerous was not presented in *Borel,* and therefore, this Court did not reach it. Since *stare decisis* is accorded only those issues necessarily decided by a court in reaching its result, the District Court erred in overreading the holding of our opinion in *Borel.*

[*Migues v. Fibreboard Corp.,* 662 F.2d 1182, 1188–89.] Like *stare decisis,* collateral estoppel applies only to issues of fact or law necessarily decided by a prior court. Since we cannot say that *Borel* necessarily decided, as a matter of fact, that all manufacturers of asbestos-containing insulation products knew or should have known of the dangers of their particular products at all relevant times, we cannot justify the trial court's collaterally estopping the defendants from presenting evidence as to the state of the art.

Even if we are wrong as to the ambiguities of the *Borel* judgment, there is a second, equally important, reason to deny collateral estoppel effect to it: the presence of inconsistent verdicts. In *Parklane Hosiery v. Shore,* 439 U.S. at 330–31, the Court noted that collateral estoppel is improper and "unfair" to a defendant "if the judgment relied upon as a basis for the estoppel is itself inconsistent with one or more previous judgments in favor of the defendant."[13] Not only does issue preclusion in such cases appear arbitrary to a defendant who has had favorable judgments on the same issue, it also undermines the premise that different juries reach equally valid verdicts. One jury's determination should not, merely because it comes later in time, bind another jury's determination of an issue over which there are equally reasonable resolutions of doubt.

The trial court was aware of the problem and referred to *Flatt v. Johns Manville Sales Corp.,* 486 F.Supp. at 841, a prior opinion by the same court. In *Flatt* the court admitted that Johns-Manville had "successfully defended several asbestos lawsuits in the recent past" but stated that "lawsuits in which Johns-Manville has prevailed have been decided on the basis that there was insufficient exposure to asbestos dust, or alternatively, the plaintiff, or decedent, did not contract asbestosis or mesothelioma." Given the information made available to us in this appeal, we must conclude that the trial court in *Flatt* and in the proceeding below was inadequately informed about the nature of former asbestos litigation. On appeal, the parties inform us that there have been approximately 70 similar asbestos cases thus far tried around the country. Approximately half of these seem to have been decided in favor of the defendants. A court able to say that the approximately 35 suits decided in favor of asbestos manufacturers were all decided on the basis of insufficient exposure on the part of the plaintiff or failure to demonstrate an asbestos-related disease would be clairvoyant. Indeed, the appellants inform us of several products liability cases in which the state of the art question was fully litigated, yet the asbestos manufacturers were found not liable. Although it is usually not possible to say with certainty what these juries based their verdicts on, in at least some of the cases the verdict for the defendant was not based on failure to prove exposure or failure to show an asbestos-related disease. In *Starnes v. Johns-Manville Corp.,* No. 2075–122 (E.D.Tenn. 1977), one of the cases cited in *Flatt v. Johns Manville Sales Corp., supra,* the court's charge to the jury stated that it was "undisputed that as a result of inhaling

---

[13] The injustice of applying collateral estoppel in cases involving mass torts is especially obvious. Thus, in *Parklane* the Court cited Prof. Currie's "familiar example": "A railroad collision injures 50 passengers all of whom bring separate actions against the railroad. After the railroad wins the first 25 suits, a plaintiff wins in suit 26. Professor Currie argues that offensive use of collateral estoppel should not be applied so as to allow plaintiffs 27 through 50 automatically to recover." 439 U.S. at 331 n. 14, *citing* Currie, *Mutuality of Estoppel: Limits of the Bernhard Doctrine,* 9 Stan.L.Rev. 281, 304 (1957).

materials containing asbestos, Mr. Starnes contracted the disease known as asbestosis." The verdict for the defendant in *Starnes* must mean, inter alia, that the jury found the insulation products involved in that case not unreasonably dangerous. This court takes judicial notice of these inconsistent or ambiguous verdicts pursuant to Fed.R.Evid.201(d). We conclude that the court erred in arbitrarily choosing one of these verdicts, that in *Borel*, as the bellwether.

Finally, we conclude that even if the *Borel* verdict had been unambiguous and the sole verdict issued on point, application of collateral estoppel would still be unfair with regard to the *Borel* defendants because it is very doubtful that these defendants could have foreseen that their $68,000 liability to plaintiff Borel would foreshadow multimillion dollar asbestos liability. As noted in *Parklane*, it would be unfair to apply collateral estoppel "if a defendant in the first action is sued for small or nominal damages [since] he may have little incentive to defend vigorously, particularly if future lawsuits are not foreseeable." 439 U.S. at 330. While in absolute terms a judgment for $68,000 hardly appears nominal, the Supreme Court's citation of *Berner v. British Commonwealth Pacific Airlines,* 346 F.2d 532 (2d Cir. 1965) (application of collateral estoppel denied where defendant did not appeal an adverse judgment awarding damages of $35,000 and defendant was later sued for over $7 million), suggests that the matter is relative. The reason the district court here applied collateral estoppel is precisely because early cases like *Borel* have opened the floodgates to an enormous, unprecedented volume of asbestos litigation. According to a recent estimate, there are over 3,000 asbestos plaintiffs in the Eastern District of Texas alone and between 7,500 and 10,000 asbestos cases pending in United States District Courts around the country. The omnibus order here involves 58 pending cases, and the many plaintiffs involved in this case are *each* seeking $2.5 million in damages. Such a staggering potential liability could not have been foreseen by the *Borel* defendants.

The trial court's application of issue preclusion to the "fact" that asbestos is in all cases a competent producing cause of mesothelioma and asbestosis involves similar problems. *Borel* dealt with the disease-causing aspects of asbestos dust generated by insulation materials. That case did not determine as a matter of fact that because airborne asbestos dust and fibers from thermal insulation materials are hazardous, all products containing asbestos—in whatever quantity or however encapsulated—are hazardous. The injustice in precluding the "fact" that the generic ingredient asbestos invariably and in every use or mode causes cancer is clearest in the case of appellant Garlock. Garlock points out that its products, unlike the loosely woven thermal insulation materials in *Borel* that, when merely handled, emitted large quantities of airborne asbestos dust and fibers, are linoleum-type products in which the asbestos is encapsulated in a rubber-like coating. According to Garlock, its gasket products do not release significant amounts of dust or fibers into the air and have never been demonstrated to be dangerous in installation, use, or removal. Certainly, defendants ought to be free, even after *Borel*, to present evidence of the scientific knowledge *associated with their particular product* without being prejudiced by a conclusive presumption that asbestos in all forms causes cancer. The court regarded collateral estoppel in this context as precluding merely the "can it" question rather than the "did it" question. The problem is that the "can it" and "did it" questions cannot in this instance be so easily segregated, and a determination that asbestos generally is hazardous threatens to undermine a defendant's possibly legitimate defense that its product was not scientifically known to be hazardous, now or at relevant times in the past. If the trial court's application of issue preclusion on the generic danger of asbestos is not meant to burden a defendant's ability to present such evidence, then we fail to see the intended usefulness of the court's action.

* * *

Like the court in *Migues*, we too sympathize with the district court's efforts to streamline the enormous asbestos caseload it faces. None of what we say here is meant to cast doubt on any possible alternative ways to avoid reinventing the asbestos liability wheel. We reiterate the *Migues* court's invitation to district courts to attempt innovative methods for trying these cases. We hold today only that courts cannot read *Borel* to stand for the proposition that, as matters of fact, asbestos products are unreasonably dangerous or that asbestos as a generic element is in all products a competent producing cause of cancer. To do otherwise would be to elevate judicial expedience over considerations of justice and fair play.

NOTES AND QUESTIONS

1.   After the decision reprinted above, the trial court in *Hardy* consolidated five individual suits and tried the five cases jointly, with the trial limited to three issues: (1) whether each plaintiff had an asbestos-related disease; (2) whether each plaintiff had been exposed to the products of the various defendants; and (3) the amount of damages each plaintiff was entitled to receive if the jury answered the first questions affirmatively. The jury returned large verdicts in favor of all plaintiffs, but the court of appeals reversed on an erroneous evidentiary ruling; plaintiffs had been allowed to introduce in evidence an appellate brief filed in another case by one of the defendants. Hardy v. Johns-Manville Sales Corp., 851 F.2d 742 (5th Cir. 1988).

2.   The *Hardy* court rejected the plaintiffs' attempt to use issue preclusion against defendants who had not been parties to *Borel*, concluding that to bind nonparties under these circumstances would violate due process. The court refers to the doctrine of "virtual representation" as a basis for nonparty preclusion—a doctrine repudiated by the Supreme Court in Taylor v. Sturgell (*supra* p. 660). Is the *Hardy* court's analysis of nonparty preclusion

ultimately consistent with the Supreme Court's more recent pronouncement in *Taylor*?

3.   Note that the court treated the *Borel* defendants who settled before trial the same way it treated the non-*Borel* defendants. By settling, they avoided the risk of issue preclusion. Consider how this affects the settlement bargaining dynamic in a case where one party potentially faces related litigation. When it becomes clear that a party may lose at trial and other lawsuits may raise the same issues, that party has an incentive to seek settlement to avoid the entry of an adverse judgment. The settlement value of an individual case may reflect not only the damages in that case but also the potential effect of an adverse judgment on future cases.

Avoiding preclusive effect becomes much more difficult once an adverse judgment has been reached. Can a party avoid the issue preclusive effect of the judgment by settling while the appeal is pending? A valid final judgment has preclusive effect even if the parties later reach an agreement. But what if the parties agree, as part of their settlement, that the trial court's judgment should be vacated? In Nestle Co. v. Chester's Market, Inc., 756 F.2d 280 (2d Cir. 1985), Nestle claimed that defendants had violated its trademark "Toll House," as used in connection with chocolate chip cookies. The trial court granted defendants a partial summary judgment, holding that the trademark was invalid. The parties then reached a settlement contingent on vacatur of the summary judgment. Nestle admitted this provision of the settlement agreement was designed to insulate it against issue preclusion. The trial court refused to vacate the judgment, but the appellate court reversed: "We see no justification to force these defendants, who wish only to settle the present litigation, to act as unwilling private attorneys general and to bear the various costs and risks of litigation." Id. at 284.

The Supreme Court addressed this strategy in U.S. Bancorp Mortgage Co. v. Bonner Mall Partnership, 513 U.S. 18 (1994). In that case, the Court refused a request, in a case in which it had granted certiorari, to vacate a lower court decision because the case had been settled. It held that an appellate court has the power to vacate lower court judgments based on mootness, but that the power should not be utilized where the mootness results from action of the party seeking to vacate the lower court's judgment, as when a case is settled. The customary route to challenge a lower court decision is to appeal, and the court saw no reason to allow a party instead to employ vacatur "as a refined form of collateral attack." Id. at 27. It also rejected the argument that allowing vacatur would promote settlements, and said that a similar unwillingness to vacate should be employed by the courts of appeals regarding judgments of district courts. The Court did acknowledge, however, that "exceptional circumstances" might exist to justify vacatur, and that an appellate court could remand for consideration of vacatur pursuant to Rule 60(b).

4.   Issue preclusion applies only if the issue was actually and necessarily determined in the first case. Be careful not to confuse certainty about whether an issue was determined with certainty about whether that determination was correct. What level of certainty is ordinarily required before a judge or jury

reaches a determination in a civil case? The preponderance of the evidence standard leaves plenty of room for uncertainty even when an issue is actually and necessarily determined. Moreover, when giving issue preclusive effect to a jury's determinations, how much do we really know about what goes on in the jury room? Consider the following report on the actual course of deliberations in *Borel v. Fibreboard:*

> The twelve members of the jury had been evenly split when they took their first vote, and had subsequently divided eleven to one in favor of the plaintiff. The lone holdout was a man who felt deeply that workers were lucky to have jobs and that no company which provided them should be judged too harshly for its actions, whatever they might be. Finally, after the other jurors had tried vainly to get him to change his mind, a face-saving deal was struck in which, in return for their finding Borel guilty of contributory negligence, he agreed to find that four of the defendants were negligent, and all six of them liable to Borel under the doctrine of strict liability.

Paul Brodeur, Outrageous Misconduct 64 (1985). Does this information make you more or less comfortable about according the result in *Borel* issue preclusive effect?

5.   The *Hardy* court, relying on the *Parklane* warning that "allowing offensive collateral estoppel may also be unfair to a defendant if the judgment relied upon as a basis for the estoppel is itself inconsistent with one or more previous judgments in favor of the defendant," rejected offensive issue preclusion in part because prior asbestos cases had reached different results from *Borel.* Would issue preclusion have been warranted if *Borel* was the first case to decide the issues and *Hardy* came next? Professor Currie's train wreck example, cited by the *Hardy* court in footnote 13, makes the point that a single aberrational result should not bind future cases. But what if the first case was the aberration? Consider the argument of Professor Byron Stier in Another Jackpot (In)justice: Verdict Variability and Issue Preclusion in Mass Torts, 36 Pepp. L. Rev. 715, 756 (2009):

> In mass tort litigation, offensive non-mutual issue preclusion promises vast efficiency and protection against inconsistent judgments, propping up public confidence in the courts. Upon scrutiny, however, issue preclusion may lock in place the possibly outlier first verdict only in situations where it benefits the plaintiffs, not the defendants—thus suffering from being both unreliable and one-sided. Recent and growing empirical evidence of jury verdict variability calls into question the fairness of such a method. In contrast, an approach that relies upon multiple verdicts to provide a more complete view of core contested issues such as negligence or defect offers litigants valuable and more accurate information that can be used to fashion informed settlements. Indeed, these far-reaching settlements may better achieve efficiency than issue preclusion. Courts should therefore use their discretion to decline to apply issue preclusion in the mass tort context.

6.   When a party faces numerous related lawsuits, what maneuvers are available to reduce the risk of adverse issue preclusion? One method is to try to position a favorable case to go to trial first. For a defendant in a multi-lawsuit dispute, the outcome of the first trial carries enormous weight. This is due in part to the momentum and notoriety that a plaintiff verdict would bring, but it is also due to the risk that an adverse judgment would be given issue preclusive effect in subsequent cases. The desire to position a strong case first may lead to jockeying by plaintiffs' and defendants' lawyers. Note that if the defendant prevails in the first case, it not only escapes harmful issue preclusion from the first judgment, but it also inoculates itself from subsequent issue preclusion even if it loses the next case, because offensive nonmutual issue preclusion generally is denied where there are inconsistent judgments.

7.   Can a class action have issue preclusive effect even if the class is decertified? In Engle v. Liggett Group, Inc., 945 So.2d 1246 (Fla. 2006), a Florida court had certified a statewide class action against tobacco companies for smoking-related injuries. At trial of the class action, the jury made numerous specific findings, found the defendants liable, and awarded $12.7 million to three individual class representatives and $145 billion in classwide punitive damages. On appeal, the Florida Supreme Court ruled that the class action should not have been certified as to punitive damages and that causation and apportionment of fault were too individualized to support class certification. Nonetheless, the court held that certain factual determinations would be given issue preclusive effect in subsequent individual trials against the defendants. The court explained that although the individual issues required decertification of the class on remand, the common liability issues determined in Phase I of the trial were suitable for classwide determination and thus could stand. The Florida Supreme Court spelled out which findings would be given preclusive effect:

> We approve the Phase I findings for the class as to Questions 1 (that smoking cigarettes causes aortic aneurysm, bladder cancer, cerebrovascular disease, cervical cancer, chronic obstructive pulmonary disease, coronary heart disease, esophageal cancer, kidney cancer, laryngeal cancer, lung cancer (specifically, adenocarcinoma, large cell carcinoma, small cell carcinoma, and squamous cell carcinoma), complications of pregnancy, oral cavity/tongue cancer, pancreatic cancer, peripheral vascular disease, pharyngeal cancer, and stomach cancer), 2 (that nicotine in cigarettes is addictive), 3 (that the defendants placed cigarettes on the market that were defective and unreasonably dangerous), 4(a) (that the defendants concealed or omitted material information not otherwise known or available knowing that the material was false or misleading or failed to disclose a material fact concerning the health effects or addictive nature of smoking cigarettes or both), 5(a) (that the defendants agreed to conceal or omit information regarding the health effects of cigarettes or their addictive nature with the intention that smokers and the public would rely on this information to their detriment), 6 (that all of the defendants sold or supplied

cigarettes that were defective), 7 (that all of the defendants sold or supplied cigarettes that, at the time of sale or supply, did not conform to representations of fact made by said defendants), and 8 (that all of the defendants were negligent). Therefore, these findings in favor of the Engle Class can stand.

The class consists of all Florida residents fitting the class description as of the trial court's order dated November 21, 1996. However, we conclude for the reasons explained in this opinion that continued class action treatment is not feasible and that upon remand the class must be decertified. Individual plaintiffs within the class will be permitted to proceed individually with the findings set forth above given res judicata effect in any subsequent trial between individual class members and the defendants, provided such action is filed within one year of the mandate in this case.

Is this an example of nonmutual preclusion, or is the court saying that despite decertification of the class on other grounds, individual class members would be treated as parties entitled to benefit from the favorable findings? Recall the possibility of certifying an "issue class." See Martin v. Behr Dayton Thermal Products, 896 F.3d 405 (6th Cir. 2018) (*supra* p. 298). Was the Florida court essentially creating an issue class action retroactively?

Over 8000 plaintiffs filed individual suits in what is now widely known as the "Engle progeny" litigation. The tobacco defendants argued that the application of issue preclusion in Engle progeny cases violated their due process rights, but the Florida Supreme Court rejected their argument in Philip Morris USA, Inc. v. Douglas, 110 So.3d 419 (Fla. 2013), and the Eleventh Circuit similarly rejected the argument in Walker v. R.J. Reynolds Tobacco Co., 734 F.3d 1278 (11th Cir. 2013).

Issue preclusion on the questions of negligence, product defect, and general causation does not guarantee that individual plaintiffs will prevail. See Stephen Nohlgren, Florida is Epicenter of Fight Against Big Tobacco, Tampa Bay Times, June 21, 2014 (reporting that plaintiffs had won about two thirds of the 120 Engle progeny cases that had gone to trial as of 2014). See also Sowers v. R.J. Reynolds Tobacco Co., 975 F.3d 1112, 1118 (11th Cir. 2020) ("What is left for each *Engle* progeny plaintiff to prove to prevail on an individual claim for negligence and strict liability (the two claims on which Mrs. Sowers succeeded) is: (1) membership in the *Engle* class, (2) individual causation, which is established by showing "that addiction to smoking the *Engle* defendants' cigarettes containing nicotine was a legal cause of the injuries alleged," and (3) damages.")

In Graham v. R.J. Reynolds Tobacco Co., 857 F.3d 1169 (11th Cir. 2017) (en banc), the Eleventh Circuit reaffirmed the issue preclusive effect of *Engle*:

This appeal presents the questions whether due process forbids giving a jury's findings of negligence and strict liability in a class action against cigarette manufacturers preclusive effect in a later individual suit by a class member and, if not, whether federal law

> preempts the jury's findings. Florida smokers and their survivors
> filed a class action against several tobacco companies, and after a
> yearlong trial designed to answer common questions concerning the
> companies' tortious conduct against all members of the class, a jury
> found that each company had breached its duty of care and sold
> defective cigarettes.

Id. at 1174. Over a lengthy dissent, the majority concluded that giving full faith
and credit to the *Engle* jury findings of negligence and strict liability did not
violate the due process rights of R.J. Reynolds and Philip Morris. The court
also rejected the defendants' argument that federal tobacco laws preempted
state tort claims and thus preempted claims premised on the *Engle* jury
findings. Although the en banc federal court described the Florida court's
approach as "a novel notion of res judicata," it did not find any violation of due
process since much remained open for litigation in individual cases:

> Every tobacco company must also be afforded the opportunity to
> contest the smokers' pleadings and evidence and to plead and prove
> the smokers' comparative fault. Indeed, in this appeal, after the
> district court instructed it, the jury reduced Graham's damages
> award for his deceased spouse's comparative fault. And in other
> Engle progeny litigation, tobacco companies have won defense
> verdicts.

Id. at 1185.

8.   Should rulings on class certification be given issue preclusive effect?
If a court denies class certification, then the named class representatives would
be precluded from relitigating the propriety of certifying the identical class.
But what if another person steps forward as class representative? Or what if
the plaintiffs seek certification in a different jurisdiction under a different class
action rule?

The Supreme Court addressed this question in Smith v. Bayer Corp., 564
U.S. 299 (2011), which we discussed in Chapter 5 in the context of overlapping
class actions (*supra* p. 357 note 1). In *Smith*, the Supreme Court rejected the
use of issue preclusion to stop a second attempt at class certification. Both the
first and second cases involved certification of a West Virginia statewide class
of users of a particular prescription drug. The Court nonetheless found that
the class certification issue differed in the two cases because the first was in
federal court under federal Rule 23, and the second was in state court under
West Virginia's class action rule, which West Virginia courts had interpreted
differently despite identical language.

But even if the second attempt had invoked the same class action rule as
the first, the Supreme Court rejected issue preclusion on the grounds that the
new class representative was a non-party to the first action and therefore not
bound by the first decision. Citing Taylor v. Sturgell, 553 U.S. 880 (2008)
(*supra* p. 660), the Court held that although Smith was a member of the
putative class in the first action, he was not a party. Although class actions
constitute the great exception to the rule that non-parties are not bound by a

judgment, the exception works only for *certified* class actions. The Supreme Court explained (564 U.S. at 314), "If we know one thing about the McCollins suit [the federal action], we know that it was *not* a class action."

CHAPTER 10

THE EFFECT OF ARBITRATION CLAUSES

■ ■ ■

This book has focused explicitly on the topic of complex *litigation*—the resolution of complex multiparty disputes through dispute-resolution processes in the courts. We have emphasized, of course, that resolution often arrives by way of settlement rather than adjudication, and indeed we have seen many cases in which mediation and negotiation have figured prominently. Even where settlement was the endgame, however, the public process of litigation has been central to each case we have explored. So far, we have not directly addressed *arbitration*—the process of submitting a dispute to a private third-party decision-maker, rather than to the courts, for a binding resolution.

Arbitration is a process in which parties agree by contract that a private third party will decide their dispute. The decision-maker may be an individual or a panel of arbitrators, and the actual process of asserting claims and presenting evidence may vary widely as agreed by the parties. For the most part, arbitration results from pre-dispute arbitration agreements, which typically are found as arbitration clauses in contracts.

The Federal Arbitration Act ("FAA"), 9 U.S.C. § 1 et seq., puts arbitration agreements on equal footing with other contracts and thus requires courts to enforce them. Congress enacted the FAA in 1925 against a backdrop of judicial hostility to arbitration. The FAA states that agreements to arbitrate are "valid, irrevocable, and enforceable" except to the extent grounds exist "for the revocation of any contract." 9 U.S.C. § 2. The arbitration clause may specify that a court judgment will be entered based on the arbitration award; on application from a party, a court "confirms" the award unless there is a basis to vacate it. 9 U.S.C. § 9. Arbitral decisions thus become enforceable as court judgments. A court may vacate an arbitrator's decision only if the decision was produced by corruption, fraud, partiality, or misconduct, or if the arbitrator exceeded her powers. 9 U.S.C. § 10.

This chapter addresses one particularly significant issue concerning the effect of arbitration clauses in multiparty disputes. In the current landscape of complex litigation, it is arguably the single most pressing question facing policy-makers: May defendants avoid class actions and other forms of aggregation by including arbitration clauses in contracts with consumers, employees, investors, and others, and by inserting prohibitions on joinder, consolidation, class action, and other forms of non-individual dispute resolution?

AT&T MOBILITY LLC v. CONCEPCION

Supreme Court of the United States, 2011.
563 U.S. 333.

JUSTICE SCALIA delivered the opinion of the Court.

Section 2 of the Federal Arbitration Act (FAA) makes agreements to arbitrate "valid, irrevocable, and enforceable, save upon such grounds as exist at law or in equity for the revocation of any contract." 9 U.S.C. § 2. We consider whether the FAA prohibits States from conditioning the enforceability of certain arbitration agreements on the availability of classwide arbitration procedures.

I

In February 2002, Vincent and Liza Concepcion entered into an agreement for the sale and servicing of cellular telephones with AT&T Mobility LCC (AT&T). The contract provided for arbitration of all disputes between the parties, but required that claims be brought in the parties' "individual capacity, and not as a plaintiff or class member in any purported class or representative proceeding."[2] * * *

The revised agreement provides that customers may initiate dispute proceedings by completing a one-page Notice of Dispute form available on AT&T's Web site. AT&T may then offer to settle the claim; if it does not, or if the dispute is not resolved within 30 days, the customer may invoke arbitration by filing a separate Demand for Arbitration, also available on AT&T's Web site. In the event the parties proceed to arbitration, the agreement specifies that AT&T must pay all costs for nonfrivolous claims; that arbitration must take place in the county in which the customer is billed; that, for claims of $10,000 or less, the customer may choose whether the arbitration proceeds in person, by telephone, or based only on submissions; that either party may bring a claim in small claims court in lieu of arbitration; and that the arbitrator may award any form of individual relief, including injunctions and presumably punitive damages. The agreement, moreover, denies AT&T any ability to seek reimbursement of its attorney's fees, and, in the event that a customer receives an arbitration award greater than AT&T's last written settlement offer, requires AT&T to pay a $7,500 minimum recovery and twice the amount of the claimant's attorney's fees.[3]

The Concepcions purchased AT&T service, which was advertised as including the provision of free phones; they were not charged for the

---

[2]   That provision further states that "the arbitrator may not consolidate more than one person's claims, and may not otherwise preside over any form of representative or class proceeding.

[3]   The guaranteed minimum recovery was increased in 2009 to $10,000.

phones, but they were charged $30.22 in sales tax based on the phones' retail value. In March 2006, the Concepcions filed a complaint against AT&T in the United States District Court for the Southern District of California. The complaint was later consolidated with a putative class action alleging, among other things, that AT&T had engaged in false advertising and fraud by charging sales tax on phones it advertised as free.

In March 2008, AT&T moved to compel arbitration under the terms of its contract with the Concepcions. The Concepcions opposed the motion, contending that the arbitration agreement was unconscionable and unlawfully exculpatory under California law because it disallowed classwide procedures. The District Court denied AT&T's motion. It described AT&T's arbitration agreement favorably, noting, for example, that the informal dispute-resolution process was "quick, easy to use" and likely to "promp[t] full or . . . even excess payment to the customer without the need to arbitrate or litigate"; that the $7,500 premium functioned as "a substantial inducement for the consumer to pursue the claim in arbitration" if a dispute was not resolved informally; and that consumers who were members of a class would likely be worse off. Nevertheless, relying on the California Supreme Court's decision in Discover Bank v. Superior Court, 113 P.3d 1100 (Cal. 2005), the court found that the arbitration provision was unconscionable because AT&T had not shown that bilateral arbitration adequately substituted for the deterrent effects of class actions.

The Ninth Circuit affirmed, also finding the provision unconscionable under California law as announced in *Discover Bank*. It also held that the *Discover Bank* rule was not preempted by the FAA because that rule was simply "a refinement of the unconscionability analysis applicable to contracts generally in California." In response to AT&T's argument that the Concepcions' interpretation of California law discriminated against arbitration, the Ninth Circuit rejected the contention that " 'class proceedings will reduce the efficiency and expeditiousness of arbitration' " and noted that " '*Discover Bank* placed arbitration agreements with class action waivers on the exact same footing as contracts that bar class action litigation outside the context of arbitration.' "

II

The FAA was enacted in 1925 in response to widespread judicial hostility to arbitration agreements. Section 2, the "primary substantive provision of the Act" provides, in relevant part, as follows:

> A written provision in any maritime transaction or a contract evidencing a transaction involving commerce to settle by arbitration a controversy thereafter arising out of such contract or transaction . . . shall be valid, irrevocable, and enforceable, save upon such grounds as exist at law or in equity for the revocation of any contract. 9 U.S.C. § 2.

We have described this provision as reflecting both a "liberal federal policy favoring arbitration," and the "fundamental principle that arbitration is a matter of contract." In line with these principles, courts must place arbitration agreements on an equal footing with other contracts, and enforce them according to their terms.

The final phrase of § 2, however, permits arbitration agreements to be declared unenforceable "upon such grounds as exist at law or in equity for the revocation of any contract." This saving clause permits agreements to arbitrate to be invalidated by "generally applicable contract defenses, such as fraud, duress, or unconscionability," but not by defenses that apply only to arbitration or that derive their meaning from the fact that an agreement to arbitrate is at issue. The question in this case is whether § 2 preempts California's rule classifying most collective-arbitration waivers in consumer contracts as unconscionable. We refer to this rule as the *Discover Bank* rule.

Under California law, courts may refuse to enforce any contract found "to have been unconscionable at the time it was made," or may "limit the application of any unconscionable clause." Cal. Civ.Code Ann. § 1670.5(a) (West 1985). A finding of unconscionability requires "a 'procedural' and a 'substantive' element, the former focusing on 'oppression' or 'surprise' due to unequal bargaining power, the latter on 'overly harsh' or 'one-sided' results."

In *Discover Bank*, the California Supreme Court applied this framework to class-action waivers in arbitration agreements and held as follows:

> [W]hen the waiver is found in a consumer contract of adhesion in a setting in which disputes between the contracting parties predictably involve small amounts of damages, and when it is alleged that the party with the superior bargaining power has carried out a scheme to deliberately cheat large numbers of consumers out of individually small sums of money, then . . . the waiver becomes in practice the exemption of the party 'from responsibility for [its] own fraud, or willful injury to the person or property of another.' Under these circumstances, such waivers are unconscionable under California law and should not be enforced.

California courts have frequently applied this rule to find arbitration agreements unconscionable.

III

A

The Concepcions argue that the *Discover Bank* rule, given its origins in California's unconscionability doctrine and California's policy against exculpation, is a ground that "exist[s] at law or in equity for the revocation of any contract" under FAA § 2. Moreover, they argue that even if we construe the *Discover Bank* rule as a prohibition on collective-action waivers rather than simply an application of unconscionability, the rule would still be applicable to all dispute-resolution contracts, since California prohibits waivers of class litigation as well.

When state law prohibits outright the arbitration of a particular type of claim, the analysis is straightforward: The conflicting rule is displaced by the FAA. But the inquiry becomes more complex when a doctrine normally thought to be generally applicable, such as duress or, as relevant here, unconscionability, is alleged to have been applied in a fashion that disfavors arbitration. In Perry v. Thomas, 482 U.S. 483 (1987), for example, we noted that the FAA's preemptive effect might extend even to grounds traditionally thought to exist " 'at law or in equity for the revocation of any contract.' " We said that a court may not "rely on the uniqueness of an agreement to arbitrate as a basis for a state-law holding that enforcement would be unconscionable, for this would be unconscionable, for this would enable the court to effect what . . . the state legislature cannot."

An obvious illustration of this point would be a case finding unconscionable or unenforceable as against public policy consumer arbitration agreements that fail to provide for judicially monitored discovery. The rationalizations for such a holding are neither difficult to imagine nor different in kind from those articulated in *Discover Bank*. A court might reason that no consumer would knowingly waive his right to full discovery, as this would enable companies to hide their wrongdoing. Or the court might simply say that such agreements are exculpatory— restricting discovery would be of greater benefit to the company than the consumer, since the former is more likely to be sued than to sue. And, the reasoning would continue, because such a rule applies the general principle of unconscionability or public-policy disapproval of exculpatory agreements, it is applicable to "any" contract and thus preserved by § 2 of the FAA. In practice, of course, the rule would have a disproportionate impact on arbitration agreements; but it would presumably apply to contracts purporting to restrict discovery in litigation as well.

Other examples are easy to imagine. The same argument might apply to a rule classifying as unconscionable arbitration agreements that fail to abide by the Federal Rules of Evidence, or that disallow an ultimate disposition by a jury (perhaps termed "a panel of twelve lay arbitrators" to help avoid preemption). Such examples are not fanciful, since the judicial hostility towards arbitration that prompted the FAA had manifested itself in "a great variety" of "devices and formulas" declaring arbitration against public policy. And although these statistics are not definitive, it is worth noting that California's courts have been more likely to hold contracts to arbitrate unconscionable than other contracts.

The Concepcions suggest that all this is just a parade of horribles, and no genuine worry. "Rules aimed at destroying arbitration" or "demanding procedures incompatible with arbitration," they concede, "would be preempted by the FAA because they cannot sensibly be reconciled with Section 2." The "grounds" available under § 2's saving clause, they admit, "should not be construed to include a State's mere preference for procedures that are incompatible with arbitration and 'would wholly eviscerate arbitration agreements.'"

We largely agree. Although § 2's saving clause preserves generally applicable contract defenses, nothing in it suggests an intent to preserve state-law rules that stand as an obstacle to the accomplishment of the FAA's objectives. As we have said, a federal statute's saving clause "'cannot in reason be construed as [allowing] a common law right, the continued existence of which would be absolutely inconsistent with the provisions of the act. In other words, the act cannot be held to destroy itself.'"

We differ with the Concepcions only in the application of this analysis to the matter before us. We do not agree that rules requiring judicially monitored discovery or adherence to the Federal Rules of Evidence are "a far cry from this case." The overarching purpose of the FAA, evident in the text of §§ 2, 3, and 4, is to ensure the enforcement of arbitration agreements according to their terms so as to facilitate streamlined proceedings. Requiring the availability of classwide arbitration interferes with fundamental attributes of arbitration and thus creates a scheme inconsistent with the FAA.

B

The "principal purpose" of the FAA is to "ensur[e] that private arbitration agreements are enforced according to their terms." This purpose is readily apparent from the FAA's text. Section 2 makes arbitration agreements "valid, irrevocable, and enforceable" as written (subject, of course, to the saving clause); § 3 requires courts to stay litigation of arbitral claims pending arbitration of those claims "in accordance with the terms of the agreement"; and § 4 requires courts to compel arbitration "in accordance with the terms of the agreement" upon the motion of either party to the agreement (assuming that the "making of the arbitration agreement or the failure . . . to perform the same" is not at issue). In light of these provisions, we have held that parties may agree to limit the issues subject to arbitration, to arbitrate according to specific rules, and to limit with whom a party will arbitrate its disputes.

The point of affording parties discretion in designing arbitration processes is to allow for efficient, streamlined procedures tailored to the type of dispute. It can be specified, for example, that the decisionmaker be a specialist in the relevant field, or that proceedings be kept confidential to protect trade secrets. And the informality of arbitral proceedings is itself

desirable, reducing the cost and increasing the speed of dispute resolution.
* * *

Contrary to the dissent's view, our cases place it beyond dispute that the FAA was designed to promote arbitration. They have repeatedly described the Act as "embod[ying] [a] national policy favoring arbitration," and "a liberal federal policy favoring arbitration agreements, notwithstanding any state substantive or procedural policies to the contrary." Thus, in Preston v. Ferrer [552 U.S. 346 (2008)], holding preempted a state-law rule requiring exhaustion of administrative remedies before arbitration, we said: "A prime objective of an agreement to arbitrate is to achieve 'streamlined proceedings and expeditious results,'" which objective would be "frustrated" by requiring a dispute to be heard by an agency first. 552 U.S., at 357–358. That rule, we said, would "at the least, hinder speedy resolution of the controversy."

California's *Discover Bank* rule similarly interferes with arbitration. Although the rule does not require classwide arbitration, it allows any party to a consumer contract to demand it ex post. The rule is limited to adhesion contracts, but the times in which consumer contracts were anything other than adhesive are long past. The rule also requires that damages be predictably small, and that the consumer allege a scheme to cheat consumers. The former requirement, however, is toothless and malleable (the Ninth Circuit has held that damages of $4,000 are sufficiently small, and the latter has no limiting effect, as all that is required is an allegation. Consumers remain free to bring and resolve their disputes on a bilateral basis under *Discover Bank*, and some may well do so; but there is little incentive for lawyers to arbitrate on behalf of individuals when they may do so for a class and reap far higher fees in the process. And faced with inevitable class arbitration, companies would have less incentive to continue resolving potentially duplicative claims on an individual basis.

Although we have had little occasion to examine classwide arbitration, our decision in Stolt-Nielsen is instructive. In that case we held that an arbitration panel exceeded its power under § 10(a)(4) of the FAA by imposing class procedures based on policy judgments rather than the arbitration agreement itself or some background principle of contract law that would affect its interpretation. We then held that the agreement at issue, which was silent on the question of class procedures, could not be interpreted to allow them because the "changes brought about by the shift from bilateral arbitration to class-action arbitration" are "fundamental." This is obvious as a structural matter: Classwide arbitration includes absent parties, necessitating additional and different procedures and involving higher stakes. Confidentiality becomes more difficult. And while it is theoretically possible to select an arbitrator with some expertise relevant to the class-certification question, arbitrators are not generally knowledgeable in the often-dominant procedural aspects of certification, such as the protection of absent parties. The conclusion follows that class arbitration, to the extent it is manufactured by *Discover Bank* rather than consensual, is inconsistent with the FAA.

First, the switch from bilateral to class arbitration sacrifices the principal advantage of arbitration—its informality—and makes the process slower, more costly, and more likely to generate procedural morass than final judgment. "In bilateral arbitration, parties forgo the procedural rigor and appellate review of the courts in order to realize the benefits of private dispute resolution: lower costs, greater efficiency and speed, and the ability to choose expert adjudicators to resolve specialized disputes. But before an arbitrator may decide the merits of a claim in classwide procedures, he must first decide, for example, whether the class itself may be certified, whether the named parties are sufficiently representative and typical, and how discovery for the class should be conducted. A cursory comparison of bilateral and class arbitration illustrates the difference. According to the American Arbitration Association (AAA), the average consumer arbitration between January and August 2007 resulted in a disposition on the merits in six months, four months if the arbitration was conducted by documents only. As of September 2009, the AAA had opened 283 class arbitrations. Of those, 121 remained active, and 162 had been settled, withdrawn, or dismissed. Not a single one, however, had resulted in a final award on the merits. For those cases that were no longer active, the median time from filing to settlement, withdrawal, or dismissal—not judgment on the merits—was 583 days, and the mean was 630 days.

Second, class arbitration requires procedural formality. The AAA's rules governing class arbitrations mimic the Federal Rules of Civil Procedure for class litigation. Compare AAA, Supplementary Rules for Class Arbitrations (effective Oct. 8, 2003), with Fed. Rule Civ. Proc. 23. And while parties can alter those procedures by contract, an alternative is not obvious. If procedures are too informal, absent class members would not be bound by the arbitration. For a class-action money judgment to bind absentees in litigation, class representatives must at all times adequately represent absent class members, and absent members must be afforded notice, an opportunity to be heard, and a right to opt out of the class. At least this amount of process would presumably be required for absent parties to be bound by the results of arbitration.

We find it unlikely that in passing the FAA Congress meant to leave the disposition of these procedural requirements to an arbitrator. Indeed, class arbitration was not even envisioned by Congress when it passed the FAA in 1925; as the California Supreme Court admitted in *Discover Bank*, class arbitration is a "relatively recent development." And it is at the very least odd to think that an arbitrator would be entrusted with ensuring that third parties' due process rights are satisfied.

Third, class arbitration greatly increases risks to defendants. Informal procedures do of course have a cost: The absence of multilayered review makes it more likely that errors will go uncorrected. Defendants are willing to accept the costs of these errors in arbitration, since their impact is limited to the size of individual disputes, and presumably outweighed by savings from avoiding the courts. But when damages allegedly owed to tens of thousands of potential claimants are aggregated and decided at once, the risk of an error will often become unacceptable. Faced with even a small chance of a devastating loss, defendants will be pressured into settling questionable claims. Other courts have noted the risk of "in terrorem" settlements that class actions entail, and class arbitration would be no different.

Arbitration is poorly suited to the higher stakes of class litigation. In litigation, a defendant may appeal a certification decision on an interlocutory basis and, if unsuccessful, may appeal from a final judgment as well. Questions of law are reviewed de novo and questions of fact for clear error. In contrast, 9 U.S.C. § 10 allows a court to vacate an arbitral award only where the award "was procured by corruption, fraud, or undue means"; "there was evident partiality or corruption in the arbitrators"; "the arbitrators were guilty of misconduct in refusing to postpone the hearing . . . or in refusing to hear evidence pertinent and material to the controversy[,] or of any other misbehavior by which the rights of any party have been prejudiced"; or if the "arbitrators exceeded their powers, or so imperfectly executed them that a mutual, final, and definite award . . . was not made." The AAA rules do authorize judicial review of certification decisions, but this review is unlikely to have much effect given these limitations; review under § 10 focuses on misconduct rather than mistake. And parties may not contractually expand the grounds or nature of judicial review. We find it hard to believe that defendants would bet the company with no effective means of review, and even harder to believe that Congress would have intended to allow state courts to force such a decision.

The Concepcions contend that because parties may and sometimes do agree to aggregation, class procedures are not necessarily incompatible with arbitration. But the same could be said about procedures that the Concepcions admit States may not superimpose on arbitration: Parties could agree to arbitrate pursuant to the Federal Rules of Civil Procedure, or pursuant to a discovery process rivaling that in litigation. Arbitration is a matter of contract, and the FAA requires courts to honor parties' expectations. But what the parties in the aforementioned examples would have agreed to is not arbitration as envisioned by the FAA, lacks its benefits, and therefore may not be required by state law.

The dissent claims that class proceedings are necessary to prosecute small-dollar claims that might otherwise slip through the legal system. But States cannot require a procedure that is inconsistent with the FAA, even if it is desirable for unrelated reasons. Moreover, the claim here was most unlikely to go unresolved. As noted earlier, the arbitration agreement provides that AT&T will pay claimants a minimum of $7,500 and twice their attorney's fees if they obtain an arbitration award greater than AT&T's last settlement offer. The District Court found this scheme sufficient to provide incentive for the individual prosecution of meritorious claims that are not immediately settled, and the Ninth Circuit admitted that aggrieved customers who filed claims would be "essentially guarantee[d]" to be made whole. Indeed, the District Court concluded that the Concepcions were better off under their arbitration agreement with AT&T than they would have been as participants in a class action, which "could take months, if not years, and which may merely yield an opportunity to submit a claim for recovery of a small percentage of a few dollars."

Because it "stands as an obstacle to the accomplishment and execution of the full purposes and objectives of Congress," California's *Discover Bank* rule is preempted by the FAA. The judgment of the Ninth Circuit is reversed, and the case is remanded for further proceedings consistent with this opinion.

[The concurring opinion of Justice Thomas is omitted.]

JUSTICE BREYER, with whom JUSTICE GINSBURG, JUSTICE SOTOMAYOR, and JUSTICE KAGAN join, dissenting.

The Federal Arbitration Act says that an arbitration agreement "shall be valid, irrevocable, and enforceable, *save upon such grounds as exist at law or in equity for the revocation of any contract.*" 9 U.S.C. § 2 (emphasis added). California law sets forth certain circumstances in which "class action waivers" in any contract are unenforceable. In my view, this rule of state law is consistent with the federal Act's language and primary objective. It does not "stan[d] as an obstacle" to the Act's "accomplishment and execution." And the Court is wrong to hold that the federal Act preempts the rule of state law.

I

California law in question consists of an authoritative state-court interpretation of two provisions of the California Civil Code. The first provision makes unlawful all contracts "which have for their object, directly or in-directly, to exempt anyone from responsibility for his own ... violation of law." Cal. Civ.Code Ann. § 1668 (West 1985). The second provision authorizes courts to "limit the application of any unconscionable clause" in a contract so "as to avoid any unconscionable result." § 1670.5(a).

The specific rule of state law in question consists of the California Supreme Court's application of these principles to hold that "some" (but not "all") "class action waivers" in consumer contracts are exculpatory and unconscionable under California "law." In particular, in *Discover Bank* the California Supreme Court stated that, when a class-action waiver

> is found in a consumer contract of adhesion in a setting in which disputes between the contracting parties predictably involve small amounts of damages, and when it is alleged that the party with the superior bargaining power has carried out a scheme to deliberately cheat large numbers of consumers out of individually small sums of money, then the waiver becomes in practice the exemption of the party 'from responsibility for [its] own fraud, or willful injury to the person or property of another.'

In such a circumstance, the "waivers are unconscionable under California law and should not be enforced."

The *Discover Bank* rule does not create a "blanket policy in California against class action waivers in the consumer context." Provencher v. Dell, Inc., 409 F.Supp.2d 1196, 1201 (C.D.Cal. 2006). Instead, it represents the "application of a more general [unconscionability] principle." Courts applying California law have enforced class-action waivers where they satisfy general unconscionability standards. And even when they fail, the parties remain free to devise other dispute mechanisms, including informal mechanisms that, in context, will not prove unconscionable.

II

A

The *Discover Bank* rule is consistent with the federal Act's language. It "applies equally to class action litigation waivers in contracts without arbitration agreements as it does to class arbitration waivers in contracts with such agreements." Linguistically speaking, it falls directly within the scope of the Act's exception permitting courts to refuse to enforce arbitration agreements on grounds that exist "for the revocation of any contract." 9 U.S.C. § 2. The majority agrees.

B

The *Discover Bank* rule is also consistent with the basic "purpose behind" the Act. Dean Witter Reynolds Inc. v. Byrd, 470 U.S. 213 (1985). We have described that purpose as one of "ensur[ing] judicial enforcement" of arbitration agreements. As is well known, prior to the federal Act, many courts expressed hostility to arbitration, for example by refusing to order specific performance of agreements to arbitrate. The Act sought to eliminate that hostility by placing agreements to arbitrate " 'upon the same footing as other contracts.' "

Congress was fully aware that arbitration could provide procedural and cost advantages. The House Report emphasized the "appropriate[ness]" of making arbitration agreements enforceable "at this time when there is so much agitation against the costliness and delays of litigation." And this Court has acknowledged that parties may enter into arbitration agreements in order to expedite the resolution of disputes.

But we have also cautioned against thinking that Congress' primary objective was to guarantee these particular procedural advantages. Rather, that primary objective was to secure the "enforcement" of agreements to arbitrate. *Dean Witter*, 470 U.S., at 221 (we "reject the suggestion that the overriding goal of the Arbitration Act was to promote the expeditious resolution of claims).

Thus, insofar as we seek to implement Congress' intent, we should think more than twice before invalidating a state law that does just what § 2 requires, namely, puts agreements to arbitrate and agreements to litigate "upon the same footing."

III

The majority's contrary view (that *Discover Bank* stands as an "obstacle" to the accomplishment of the federal law's objective) rests primarily upon its claims that the *Discover Bank* rule increases the complexity of arbitration procedures, thereby discouraging parties from entering into arbitration agreements, and to that extent discriminating in practice against arbitration. These claims are not well founded.

For one thing, a state rule of law that would sometimes set aside as unconscionable a contract term that forbids class arbitration is not (as the majority claims) like a rule that would require "ultimate disposition by a jury" or "judicially monitored discovery" or use of "the Federal Rules of Evidence." Unlike the majority's examples, class arbitration is consistent with the use of arbitration. It is a form of arbitration that is well known in California and followed elsewhere. Indeed, the AAA has told us that it has found class arbitration to be "a fair, balanced, and efficient means of resolving class disputes." AAA Amicus Brief. And unlike the majority's examples, the *Discover Bank* rule imposes equivalent limitations on litigation; hence it cannot fairly be characterized as a targeted attack on arbitration.

Where does the majority get its contrary idea—that individual, rather than class, arbitration is a "fundamental attribut[e]" of arbitration? The majority does not explain. And it is unlikely to be able to trace its present view to the history of the arbitration statute itself.

When Congress enacted the Act, arbitration procedures had not yet been fully developed. Insofar as Congress considered detailed forms of arbitration at all, it may well have thought that arbitration would be used primarily where merchants sought to resolve disputes of fact, not law, under the customs of their industries, where the parties possessed roughly equivalent bargaining power. This last mentioned feature of the history— roughly equivalent bargaining power—suggests, if anything, that

California's statute is consistent with, and indeed may help to further, the objectives that Congress had in mind.

Regardless, if neither the history nor present practice suggests that class arbitration is fundamentally incompatible with arbitration itself, then on what basis can the majority hold California's law pre-empted?

For another thing, the majority's argument that the Discover Bank rule will discourage arbitration rests critically upon the wrong comparison. The majority compares the complexity of class arbitration with that of bilateral arbitration. And it finds the former more complex. But, if incentives are at issue, the relevant comparison is not "arbitration with arbitration" but a comparison between class arbitration and judicial class actions. After all, in respect to the relevant set of contracts, the *Discover Bank* rule similarly and equally sets aside clauses that forbid class procedures—whether arbitration procedures or ordinary judicial procedures are at issue.

Why would a typical defendant (say, a business) prefer a judicial class action to class arbitration? AAA statistics "suggest that class arbitration proceedings take more time than the average commercial arbitration, but may take less time than the average class action in court." AAA Amicus Brief 24. Data from California courts confirm that class arbitrations can take considerably less time than in-court proceedings in which class certification is sought. And a single class proceeding is surely more efficient than thousands of separate proceedings for identical claims. Thus, if speedy resolution of disputes were all that mattered, then the *Discover Bank* rule would reinforce, not obstruct, that objective of the Act.

The majority's related claim that the *Discover Bank* rule will discourage the use of arbitration because "[a]rbitration is poorly suited to ... higher stakes" lacks empirical support. Indeed, the majority provides no convincing reason to believe that parties are unwilling to submit high-stake disputes to arbitration. And there are numerous counterexamples. Loftus, Rivals Resolve Dispute Over Drug, Wall Street Journal, Apr. 16, 2011, p. B2 (discussing $500 million settlement in dispute submitted to arbitration); Ziobro, Kraft Seeks Arbitration In Fight With Starbucks Over Distribution, Wall Street Journal, Nov. 30, 2010, p. B10 (describing initiation of an arbitration in which the payout "could be higher" than $1.5 billion); Markoff, Software Arbitration Ruling Gives I.B.M. $833 Million From Fujitsu, N.Y. Times, Nov. 30, 1988, p. A1 (describing both companies as "pleased with the ruling" resolving a licensing dispute).

Further, even though contract defenses, e.g., duress and unconscionability, slow down the dispute resolution process, federal arbitration law normally leaves such matters to the States. Rent-A-Center, West, Inc. v. Jackson, 130 S.Ct. 2772, 2775 (2010) (arbitration agreements "may be invalidated by 'generally applicable contract defenses.' " A provision in a contract of adhesion (for example, requiring a consumer to decide very quickly whether to pursue a claim) might increase the speed and efficiency of arbitrating a dispute, but the State can forbid it. The *Discover Bank* rule amounts to a variation on this theme. California is free to define unconscionability as it sees fit, and its common law is of no federal concern so long as the State does not adopt a special rule that disfavors arbitration.

Because California applies the same legal principles to address the unconscionability of class arbitration waivers as it does to address the unconscionability of any other contractual provision, the merits of class proceedings should not factor into our decision. If California had applied its law of duress to void an arbitration agreement, would it matter if the procedures in the coerced agreement were efficient?

Regardless, the majority highlights the disadvantages of class arbitrations, as it sees them. See ante, at 15–16 (referring to the "greatly increase[d] risks to defendants"; the "chance of a devastating loss" pressuring defendants "into settling questionable claims"). But class proceedings have countervailing advantages. In general agreements that forbid the consolidation of claims can lead small-dollar claimants to abandon their claims rather than to litigate. I suspect that it is true even here, for as the Court of Appeals recognized, AT&T can avoid the $7,500 payout (the payout that supposedly makes the Concepcions' arbitration worthwhile) simply by paying the claim's face value, such that "the maximum gain to a customer for the hassle of arbitrating a $30.22 dispute is still just $30.22." 584 F.3d 849, 855, 856 (C.A.9 2009).

What rational lawyer would have signed on to represent the Concepcions in litigation for the possibility of fees stemming from a $30.22 claim? See, e.g., Carnegie v. Household Int'l, Inc., 376 F.3d 656, 661 (C.A.7 2004) ("The realistic alternative to a class action is not 17 million individual suits, but zero individual suits, as only a lunatic or a fanatic sues for $30"). In California's perfectly rational view, nonclass arbitration over such sums will also sometimes have the effect of depriving claimants of their claims (say, for example, where claiming the $30.22 were to involve filling out many forms that require technical legal knowledge or waiting at great length while a call is placed on hold). Discover Bank sets forth circumstances in which the California courts believe that the terms of consumer contracts can be manipulated to insulate an agreement's author from liability for its own frauds by "deliberately cheat[ing] large numbers of consumers out of individually small sums of money." Why is this kind of decision—weighing the pros and cons of all class proceedings alike—not California's to make? * * *

[W]e have repeatedly referred to the Act's basic objective as assuring that courts treat arbitration agreements "like all other contracts." And we have recognized that "[t]o immunize an arbitration agreement from judicial challenge" on grounds applicable to all other contracts "would be to elevate it over other forms of contract." These cases do not concern the merits and demerits of class actions; they concern equal treatment of arbitration contracts and other contracts. Since it is the latter question that is at issue here, I am not surprised that the majority can find no meaningful precedent supporting its decision.

IV

By using the words "save upon such grounds as exist at law or in equity for the revocation of any contract," Congress retained for the States an important role incident to agreements to arbitrate. 9 U.S.C. § 2. Through those words Congress reiterated a basic federal idea that has long informed the nature of this Nation's laws. We have often expressed this idea in opinions that set forth presumptions. See, e.g., Medtronic, Inc. v. Lohr, 518 U.S. 470, 485 (1996) ("[B]ecause the States are independent sovereigns in our federal system, we have long presumed that Congress does not cavalierly pre-empt state-law causes of action"). But federalism is as much a question of deeds as words. It often takes the form of a concrete decision by this Court that respects the legitimacy of a State's action in an individual case. Here, recognition of that federalist ideal, embodied in specific language in this particular statute, should lead us to uphold California's law, not to strike it down. We do not honor federalist principles in their breach.

NOTES AND QUESTIONS

1.   To get a sense of the procedures by which class arbitrations may be conducted if permitted, consider the rules promulgated by providers of arbitration services. See American Arbitration Association, Supplementary Rules for Class Arbitrations (2003); JAMS Class Action Procedures (2009). Both sets of rules are available on the organizations' websites. As the Court noted in *Concepcion*, in many regards these class arbitration rules resemble Rule 23 of the Federal Rule of Civil Procedure. For example, under the AAA rules, prerequisites for class arbitration include requirements of numerosity, commonality, typicality, adequate representation, predominance, and superiority. The JAMS rules explicitly incorporate the requirements of Rules 23(a) and 23(b) by reference, and they include requirements for notice and for an arbitral determination of whether a proposed settlement is "fair, reasonable and adequate."

2.   Justice Scalia frames the issue in *Concepcion* in terms of "the availability of classwide arbitration procedures." Do you agree that this correctly describes the question in this case? Is *Concepcion* better understood as a case about the availability of classwide arbitration or about the general avoidance of class actions, joinder, and any other form of collective assertion and collective resolution of claims?

3.   The Supreme Court decided *Concepcion* two months before it decided *Wal-Mart Stores, Inc. v. Dukes,* 564 U.S. 338 (2011) [*supra* p. 200 and p. 242].

Each case featured a majority opinion by Justice Scalia, and the Justices who made up the 5–4 majority in *Concepcion* (Chief Justice Roberts and Justices Scalia, Kennedy, Thomas, and Alito, over the dissent of Justices Breyer, Ginsburg, Sotomayor, and Kagan) were the same who made up the 5–4 majority on the commonality issue in *Wal-Mart*. Which of the two cases presented a more significant threat to class actions? As you think about the impact of *Concepcion*, consider the categories of disputes that are amenable to pre-dispute arbitration clauses (that is, disputes between parties that have some sort of contractual relationship) and the categories of disputes that are not amenable to such clauses. Now consider your knowledge about class certification, and whether the types of disputes that are well-suited for class certification tend to involve disputants that may have pre-existing contractual relationships (such as consumers, employees, and investors).

4.   The AT&T arbitration clause contained a number of features that could be described as consumer-friendly. Why did the majority highlight these features? Did they matter to the Court's decision? If the issue before the Supreme Court was whether the FAA preempts California state law on unconscionability (as opposed to the question of whether this particular contract was unconscionable under California law), why should the features of the particular arbitration clause matter? If your answer is that it mattered whether AT&T customers had a realistic path to vindicate their claims, keep this consideration in mind when you read the next case, *American Express Co. v. Italian Colors Restaurant* (*infra* p. 753). If your answer, more broadly, is that the consumer-friendly features of the arbitration clause made it more palatable to a majority of the Justices to uphold the class action prohibition in the arbitration clause, consider whether AT&T and other large consumer-oriented businesses—as repeat players in litigation and frequent targets of class actions—had a case like *Concepcion* in mind when drafting their arbitration clauses. Cf. Marc Galanter, Why the "Haves" Come out Ahead: Speculations on the Limits of Legal Change, 9 Law & Soc. Rev. 95 (1974) (arguing that legal developments tend to favor "repeat players" over the long term because, unlike "one-shotters," repeat players litigate not only to prevail in immediate disputes but also to obtain favorable legal rules for the future).

5.   The reference of a dispute to an impartial person for final, binding determination has a long history in commercial affairs. In medieval England, courts referred mercantile cases to merchant arbitrators and juries. One of the purposes of the creation of Chambers of Commerce in the American colonial period was to arbitrate disputes among their members. Soia Mentschikoff, Commercial Arbitration, 61 Colum. L. Rev. 846, 854–55 (1961). Among other benefits of arbitration, it offered disputants the ability to hire arbitrators who understood the norms within their particular industries. New York, in 1920, became the first state to pass a modern arbitration statute providing for judicial enforcement of arbitration agreements. Common law precedents in many states were hostile to arbitration, however, and some courts refused to order parties to comply with arbitration agreements and to enforce arbitration awards. Congress enacted the FAA in 1925 to ensure that merchants could enter binding agreements to arbitrate their disputes.

When merchants, businesses, or unions negotiate arbitration clauses as part of contract negotiations, the parties may have roughly equal bargaining power and their arbitration agreements may reflect a genuine meeting of the minds to choose private dispute resolution rather than to keep the option of pursuing litigation in the courts. But can the same thing—equal bargaining power and genuine agreement—be said of AT&T's arbitration agreement with Vincent and Liza Concepcion? Can it be said, in general, regarding arbitration clauses contained in standard-form contracts that are imposed by one party (such as an insurer, bank, or other business) on its customers or employees?

In Wilko v. Swan, 346 U.S. 427 (1953), the Supreme Court refused to enforce an arbitration clause for securities claims by an investor against the broker, worrying about whether arbitration provided adequate protection for investors. However, the Court overruled *Wilko* in Rodriguez de Quijas v. Shearson/American Express, Inc., 490 U.S. 477 (1989), and in a series of cases, the Supreme Court enforced arbitration clauses under the FAA even in various contracts of adhesion. See, e.g., Gilmer v. Interstate/Johnson Lane Corp., 500 U.S. 20 (1991) (enforcing arbitration provision in New York Stock Exchange rules for age discrimination claim by employee). By the time the *Concepcion* case arrived at the Supreme Court, the question was not so much whether the Court would enforce arbitration clauses against consumers, but rather how far companies could go in arbitration clauses, and the extent to which procedural constraints in arbitration clauses would be enforced in the face of contrary state law.

6. If an arbitration agreement leaves it unclear whether class arbitration is permitted, questions may arise about who decides. In general, under the FAA, as Justice Scalia notes in *Concepcion*, decisions that fall within arbitrators' decision-making power may be reviewed by courts only for "misconduct rather than mistake." However, questions of *arbitrability*—that is, questions of whether parties have a valid arbitration agreement, or whether an arbitration agreement applies to a particular type of dispute—are reviewable by courts de novo. Section 10 of the FAA allows a court to vacate an arbitration award "where the arbitrators exceeded their powers." 9 U.S.C. § 10(a)(4). Where does the question of permissibility of class arbitration fit?

In Oxford Health Plans LLC v. Sutter, 569 U.S. 564 (2013), the Supreme Court held that an arbitrator's decision to allow class arbitration cannot be overturned if the decision was based on the interpretation of the parties' contract. Even if it regards the decision as incorrect, a court will not overturn the arbitrator's decision given its limited scope of review allowed under FAA § 10(a)(4) of the FAA. This was a class action in state court on behalf of doctors under contract with a health insurance company, alleging that Oxford failed to make full and prompt payment to them. Oxford's motion to compel arbitration was granted, and both parties then agreed that the arbitrator should decide whether their contract authorized class arbitration. The arbitrator determined that it did. Oxford filed a motion in federal court to vacate this decision on the grounds that the arbitrator exceeded his powers under § 10(a)(4) of the FAA. The Supreme Court held that the arbitrator was not acting outside the scope of his powers. He did what the parties had asked—he interpreted the contract and decided it permitted class arbitration.

The California Supreme Court took up the "who decides" question in Sandquist v. Lebo Automotive, Inc., 1 Cal.5th 233, 240 (2016):

> A salient question is whether [the parties' arbitration] agreement permits or prohibits arbitration on a classwide basis. Here we must answer a question one step removed—*who decides* whether the agreement permits or prohibits classwide arbitration, a court or the arbitrator? The question has divided many state and federal courts to consider it.
>
> We conclude no universal rule allocates this decision in all cases to either arbitrators or courts. Rather, who decides is in the first instance a matter of agreement, with the parties' agreement subject to interpretation under state contract law.

7.   After *Concepcion*, many corporations added arbitration clauses with class prohibitions. For a critical view of this development, see Judith Resnik, Diffusing Disputes: The Public in the Private of Arbitration, the Private in Courts, and the Erasure of Rights, 124 Yale L.J. 2804 (2015). Professor Resnik points out the rarity of actual consumer arbitration, making the point that companies' use of arbitration clauses in consumer contracts is less about shifting dispute-resolution from judicial to arbitral forums, and more about avoidance of claims (id. at 2812–13):

> Despite the heralding of arbitration as a speedy and effective alternative to courts, the mass production of arbitration clauses has not resulted in "mass arbitrations." Instead, the number of documented consumer arbitrations is startlingly small. Arbitrations involving wireless service providers provide one example, which I have chosen because the Supreme Court addressed the ban on class arbitrations in that context in its 2011 decision involving AT&T Mobility. According to information from the American Arbitration Association, designated by AT&T to administer its arbitrations and complying with state reporting mandates, 134 individual claims (about 27 a year) were filed against AT&T between 2009 and 2014. During that time period, the estimated number of AT&T wireless customers rose from 85 million a year to 120 million people, and lawsuits filed by the federal government charged the company with a range of legal breaches, including systematic over-charging for extra services and insufficient payments of refunds when customers complained.

8.   The Consumer Financial Protection Bureau ("CFPB") reacted to the upsurge in class action prohibitions in consumer contracts by adopting a rule in 2017 to prohibit providers of consumer financial services (such as bank accounts and credit cards) from using arbitration clauses to avoid class actions. The rule was short-lived, however, as Congress used its power under the

Congressional Review Act to eliminate the CFPB arbitration rule later that year.

9.   Notwithstanding *Concepcion*, state law governs questions of contract formation that may determine the enforceability of a contract that includes an arbitration clause with a class action prohibition. In Noohi v. Toll Bros. Inc. 708 F.3d 599 (4th Cir. 2013), home buyers filed a class action alleging that a real estate development company unlawfully refused to return deposits when the prospective buyers could not obtain mortgage financing. The court held that the lack of consideration under state law rendered the arbitration clause unenforceable. It rejected the argument that the FAA preempted the state law under *Concepcion*. It said: "The Supreme Court has never held that the FAA preempts state law rules requiring that arbitration provisions themselves contain consideration."

AMERICAN EXPRESS CO. V. ITALIAN COLORS RESTAURANT
Supreme Court of the United States, 2013.
570 U.S. 228.

JUSTICE SCALIA delivered the opinion of the Court.

We consider whether a contractual waiver of class arbitration is enforceable under the Federal Arbitration Act when the plaintiff's cost of individually arbitrating a federal statutory claim exceeds the potential recovery.

I

Respondents are merchants who accept American Express cards. Their agreement with petitioners—American Express and a wholly owned subsidiary—contains a clause that requires all disputes between the parties to be resolved by arbitration. The agreement also provides that "[t]here shall be no right or authority for any Claims to be arbitrated on a class action basis."

Respondents brought a class action against petitioners for violations of the federal antitrust laws. According to respondents, American Express used its monopoly power in the market for charge cards to force merchants to accept credit cards at rates approximately 30% higher than the fees for competing credit cards. This tying arrangement, respondents said, violated § 1 of the Sherman Act. They sought treble damages for the class under § 4 of the Clayton Act.

Petitioners moved to compel individual arbitration under the Federal Arbitration Act (FAA), 9 U.S.C. § 1 et seq. In resisting the motion, respondents submitted a declaration from an economist who estimated that the cost of an expert analysis necessary to prove the antitrust claims would be "at least several hundred thousand dollars, and might exceed $1 million," while the maximum recovery for an individual plaintiff would be $12,850, or $38,549 when trebled. The District Court granted the motion and dismissed the lawsuits. The Court of Appeals reversed and remanded for further proceedings. It held that because respondents had established that "they would incur prohibitive costs if compelled to arbitrate under the class action waiver," the waiver was unenforceable and the arbitration could not proceed. In re American Express Merchants' Litigation, 554 F.3d 300, 315–316 (C.A.2 2009). * * *

II

Congress enacted the FAA in response to widespread judicial hostility to arbitration. [The FAA's] text reflects the overarching principle that arbitration is a matter of contract. And consistent with that text, courts must "rigorously enforce" arbitration agreements according to their terms, including terms that "specify *with whom* [the parties] choose to arbitrate their disputes," and "the rules under which that arbitration will be conducted," That holds true for claims that allege a violation of a federal statute, unless the FAA's mandate has been " 'overridden by a contrary congressional command.' " CompuCredit Corp. v. Greenwood, 132 S.Ct. 665, 668–669 (2012) (quoting Shearson/American Express Inc. v. McMahon, 482 U.S. 220, 226 (1987)).

III

No contrary congressional command requires us to reject the waiver of class arbitration here. Respondents argue that requiring them to litigate their claims individually—as they contracted to do—would contravene the policies of the antitrust laws. But the antitrust laws do not guarantee an affordable procedural path to the vindication of every claim. * * *

The antitrust laws do not "evinc[e] an intention to preclude a waiver" of class-action procedure. The Sherman and Clayton Acts make no mention of class actions. In fact, they were enacted decades before the advent of Federal Rule of Civil Procedure 23, which was "designed to allow an exception to the usual rule that litigation is conducted by and on behalf of the individual named parties only." The parties here agreed to arbitrate pursuant to that "usual rule," and it would be remarkable for a court to erase that expectation.

Nor does congressional approval of Rule 23 establish an entitlement to class proceedings for the vindication of statutory rights. To begin with, it is likely that such an entitlement, invalidating private arbitration agreements denying class adjudication, would be an "abridg[ment]" or "modif[ication]" of a "substantive right" forbidden to the Rules, see 28 U.S.C. § 2072(b). But there is no evidence of such an entitlement in any event. The Rule imposes stringent requirements for certification that in practice exclude most claims. And we have specifically rejected the assertion that one of those requirements (the class-notice requirement) must be dispensed with because the "prohibitively high cost" of compliance would "frustrate [plaintiff's] attempt to vindicate the policies underlying the antitrust" laws. Eisen v. Carlisle & Jacquelin, 417 U.S. 156, 166–68, 175–76 (1974). One might respond, perhaps, that federal law secures a nonwaivable *opportunity* to vindicate federal policies by satisfying the procedural strictures of Rule 23 or invoking some other informal class mechanism in arbitration. But we have already rejected that proposition in *AT&T Mobility*.

IV

Our finding of no "contrary congressional command" does not end the case. Respondents invoke a judge-made exception to the FAA which, they say, serves to harmonize competing federal policies by allowing courts to invalidate agreements that prevent the "effective vindication" of a federal statutory right. Enforcing the waiver of class arbitration bars effective vindication, respondents contend, because they have no economic incentive to pursue their antitrust claims individually in arbitration.

The "effective vindication" exception to which respondents allude originated as dictum in *Mitsubishi Motors,* where we expressed a willingness to invalidate, on "public policy" grounds, arbitration agreements that "operat[e] . . . as a prospective waiver of a party's *right to pursue* statutory remedies." [Mitsubishi Motors Corp. v. Soler Chrysler-Plymouth, Inc.,] 473 U.S. [614,] 637 n.19 (emphasis added). Dismissing concerns that the arbitral forum was inadequate, we said that "so long as the prospective litigant effectively may vindicate its statutory cause of action in the arbitral forum, the statute will continue to serve both its remedial and deterrent function." Id., at 637. Subsequent cases have similarly asserted the existence of an "effective vindication" exception, but have similarly declined to apply it to invalidate the arbitration agreement at issue.[2]

And we do so again here. As we have described, the exception finds its origin in the desire to prevent "prospective waiver of a party's *right to pursue* statutory remedies," Id. at 637 n.19 (emphasis added). That would certainly cover a provision in an arbitration agreement forbidding the assertion of certain statutory rights. And it would perhaps cover filing and administrative fees attached to arbitration that are so high as to make access to the forum impracticable. But the fact that it is not worth the expense involved in *proving* a statutory remedy does not constitute the elimination of the *right to pursue* that remedy. See 681 F.3d at 147 (Jacobs, C.J., dissenting from denial of rehearing en banc).[3] The class-action waiver

---

[2] Contrary to the dissent's claim, the Court in *Mitsubishi Motors* did not hold that federal statutory claims are subject to arbitration so long as the claimant may effectively vindicate his rights in the arbitral forum. The Court expressly stated that, "at this stage in the proceedings," it had "no occasion to speculate" on whether the arbitration agreement's potential deprivation of a claimant's right to pursue federal remedies may render that agreement unenforceable. Even the Court of Appeals in this case recognized the relevant language in *Mitsubishi Motors* as dicta.

[3] The dissent contends that a class-action waiver may deny a party's right to pursue statutory remedies in the same way as a clause that bars a party from presenting economic testimony. That is a false comparison for several reasons: To begin with, it is not a given that such

merely limits arbitration to the two contracting parties. It no more eliminates those parties' right to pursue their statutory remedy than did federal law before its adoption of the class action for legal relief in 1938. Or, to put it differently, the individual suit that was considered adequate to assure "effective vindication" of a federal right before adoption of class-action procedures did not suddenly become "ineffective vindication" upon their adoption. * * *

Truth to tell, our decision in *AT&T Mobility* all but resolves this case. There we invalidated a law conditioning enforcement of arbitration on the availability of class procedure because that law "interfere[d] with fundamental attributes of arbitration." "[T]he switch from bilateral to class arbitration," we said, "sacrifices the principal advantage of arbitration—its informality—and makes the process slower, more costly, and more likely to generate procedural morass than final judgment." We specifically rejected the argument that class arbitration was necessary to prosecute claims "that might otherwise slip through the legal system."[5]

The regime established by the Court of Appeals' decision would require—before a plaintiff can be held to contractually agreed bilateral arbitration—that a federal court determine (and the parties litigate) the legal requirements for success on the merits claim-by-claim and theory-by-theory, the evidence necessary to meet those requirements, the cost of developing that evidence, and the damages that would be recovered in the event of success. Such a preliminary litigating hurdle would undoubtedly destroy the prospect of speedy resolution that arbitration in general and bilateral arbitration in particular was meant to secure. The FAA does not sanction such a judicially created superstructure.

The judgment of the Court of Appeals is reversed.

JUSTICE SOTOMAYOR took no part in the consideration or decision of this case.

[The concurring opinion of Justice Thomas is omitted.]

JUSTICE KAGAN, with whom JUSTICE GINSBURG and JUSTICE BREYER join, dissenting.

Here is the nutshell version of this case, unfortunately obscured in the Court's decision. The owner of a small restaurant (Italian Colors) thinks that American Express (Amex) has used its monopoly power to force

---

a clause would constitute an impermissible waiver; we have never considered the point. But more importantly, such a clause, assuming it makes vindication of the claim impossible, makes it impossible not just as a class action but even as an individual claim.

[5] In dismissing *AT&T Mobility* as a case involving pre-emption and not the effective-vindication exception, the dissent ignores what that case established—that the FAA's command to enforce arbitration agreements trumps any interest in ensuring the prosecution of low-value claims. The latter interest, we said, is "unrelated" to the FAA. Accordingly, the FAA does, contrary to the dissent's assertion, favor the absence of litigation when that is the consequence of a class-action waiver, since its " 'principal purpose' " is the enforcement of arbitration agreements according to their terms.

merchants to accept a form contract violating the antitrust laws. The restaurateur wants to challenge the allegedly unlawful provision (imposing a tying arrangement), but the same contract's arbitration clause prevents him from doing so. That term imposes a variety of procedural bars that would make pursuit of the antitrust claim a fool's errand. So if the arbitration clause is enforceable, Amex has insulated itself from antitrust liability—even if it has in fact violated the law. The monopolist gets to use its monopoly power to insist on a contract effectively depriving its victims of all legal recourse.

And here is the nutshell version of today's opinion, admirably flaunted rather than camouflaged: Too darn bad.

That answer is a betrayal of our precedents, and of federal statutes like the antitrust laws. Our decisions have developed a mechanism—called the effective-vindication rule—to prevent arbitration clauses from choking off a plaintiff's ability to enforce congressionally created rights. That doctrine bars applying such a clause when (but only when) it operates to confer immunity from potentially meritorious federal claims. In so doing, the rule reconciles the Federal Arbitration Act (FAA) with all the rest of federal law—and indeed, promotes the most fundamental purposes of the FAA itself. As applied here, the rule would ensure that Amex's arbitration clause does not foreclose Italian Colors from vindicating its right to redress antitrust harm.

The majority barely tries to explain why it reaches a contrary result. It notes that we have not decided this exact case before—neglecting that the principle we have established fits this case hand in glove. And it concocts a special exemption for class-arbitration waivers—ignoring that this case concerns much more than that. Throughout, the majority disregards our decisions' central tenet: An arbitration clause may not thwart federal law, irrespective of exactly how it does so. Because the Court today prevents the effective vindication of federal statutory rights, I respectfully dissent.

I

Start with an uncontroversial proposition: We would refuse to enforce an exculpatory clause insulating a company from antitrust liability—say, "Merchants may bring no Sherman Act claims"—even if that clause were contained in an arbitration agreement. Congress created the Sherman Act's private cause of action not solely to compensate individuals, but to promote "the public interest in vigilant enforcement of the antitrust laws." Accordingly, courts will not enforce a prospective waiver of the right to gain redress for an antitrust injury, whether in an arbitration agreement or any other contract. See Mitsubishi Motors Corp. v. Soler Chrysler-Plymouth, Inc., 473 U.S. 614, 637, and n. 19 (1985). The same rule applies to other important federal statutory rights. See 14 Penn Plaza LLC v. Pyett, 556 U.S. 247, 273 (2009) (Age Discrimination in Employment Act); Brooklyn

Savings Bank v. O'Neil, 324 U.S. 697, 704 (1945) (Fair Labor Standards Act). But its necessity is nowhere more evident than in the antitrust context. Without the rule, a company could use its monopoly power to protect its monopoly power, by coercing agreement to contractual terms eliminating its antitrust liability.

If the rule were limited to baldly exculpatory provisions, however, a monopolist could devise numerous ways around it. Consider several alternatives that a party drafting an arbitration agreement could adopt to avoid antitrust liability, each of which would have the identical effect. On the front end: The agreement might set outlandish filing fees or establish an absurd (*e.g.*, one-day) statute of limitations, thus preventing a claimant from gaining access to the arbitral forum. On the back end: The agreement might remove the arbitrator's authority to grant meaningful relief, so that a judgment gets the claimant nothing worthwhile. And in the middle: The agreement might block the claimant from presenting the kind of proof that is necessary to establish the defendant's liability—say, by prohibiting any economic testimony (good luck proving an antitrust claim without that!). Or else the agreement might appoint as an arbitrator an obviously biased person—say, the CEO of Amex. The possibilities are endless—all less direct than an express exculpatory clause, but no less fatal. So the rule against prospective waivers of federal rights can work only if it applies not just to a contract clause explicitly barring a claim, but to others that operate to do so. * * *

Applied as our precedents direct, the effective-vindication rule furthers the purposes not just of laws like the Sherman Act, but of the FAA itself. That statute reflects a federal policy favoring actual arbitration—that is, arbitration as a streamlined "method of resolving disputes," not as a foolproof way of killing off valid claims. Put otherwise: What the FAA prefers to litigation is arbitration, not *de facto* immunity. The effective-vindication rule furthers the statute's goals by ensuring that arbitration remains a real, not faux, method of dispute resolution. With the rule, companies have good reason to adopt arbitral procedures that facilitate efficient and accurate handling of complaints. Without it, companies have every incentive to draft their agreements to extract backdoor waivers of statutory rights, making arbitration unavailable or pointless. So down one road: More arbitration, better enforcement of federal statutes. And down the other: Less arbitration, poorer enforcement of federal statutes. Which would you prefer? Or still more aptly: Which do you think Congress would? * * *

And this is just the kind of case the rule was meant to address. Italian Colors, as I have noted, alleges that Amex used its market power to impose a tying arrangement in violation of the Sherman Act. The antitrust laws, all parties agree, provide the restaurant with a cause of action and give it the chance to recover treble damages. Here, that would mean Italian Colors could take home up to $38,549. But a problem looms. As this case comes to us, the evidence shows that Italian Colors cannot prevail in arbitration without an economic analysis defining the relevant markets, establishing Amex's monopoly power, showing anticompetitive effects, and measuring damages. And that expert report would cost between several hundred thousand and one million dollars. So the expense involved in proving the claim in arbitration is ten times what Italian Colors could hope to gain, even in a best-case scenario. That counts as a "prohibitive" cost, in *Randolph's* terminology, if anything does. [Green Tree Financial Corp.-Ala. v. Randolph, 531 U.S. 79, 90 (2000).] No rational actor would bring a claim worth tens of thousands of dollars if doing so meant incurring costs in the hundreds of thousands.

An arbitration agreement could manage such a mismatch in many ways, but Amex's disdains them all. As the Court makes clear, the contract expressly prohibits class arbitration. But that is only part of the problem. The agreement also disallows any kind of joinder or consolidation of claims or parties. And more: Its confidentiality provision prevents Italian Colors from informally arranging with other merchants to produce a common expert report. And still more: The agreement precludes any shifting of costs to Amex, even if Italian Colors prevails. And beyond all that: Amex refused to enter into any stipulations that would obviate or mitigate the need for the economic analysis. In short, the agreement as applied in this case cuts off not just class arbitration, but any avenue for sharing, shifting, or shrinking necessary costs. Amex has put Italian Colors to this choice: Spend way, way, way more money than your claim is worth, or relinquish your Sherman Act rights. * * *

II

The majority is quite sure that the effective-vindication rule does not apply here, but has precious little to say about why. It starts by disparaging the rule as having "originated as dictum." But it does not rest on that swipe, and for good reason. * * *

The next paragraph of the Court's decision (the third of Part IV) is the key: It contains almost the whole of the majority's effort to explain why the effective-vindication rule does not stop Amex from compelling arbitration. The majority's first move is to describe *Mitsubishi* and *Randolph* as covering only discrete situations: The rule, the majority asserts, applies to arbitration agreements that eliminate the "right to pursue statutory remedies" by "forbidding the assertion" of the right (as addressed in *Mitsubishi*) or imposing filing and administrative fees "so high as to make access to the forum impracticable" (as addressed in *Randolph*). Those cases are not this case, the majority says: Here, the agreement's provisions went to the possibility of "*proving* a statutory remedy."

But the distinction the majority proffers, which excludes problems of proof, is one *Mitsubishi* and *Randolph* (and our decisions reaffirming them) foreclose. Those decisions establish what in some quarters is known as a principle: When an arbitration agreement prevents the effective vindication of federal rights, a party may go to court. That principle, by its nature, operates in diverse circumstances—not just the ones that happened to come before the Court. It doubtless covers the baldly exculpatory clause and prohibitive fees that the majority acknowledges would preclude an arbitration agreement's enforcement. But so too it covers the world of other provisions a clever drafter might devise to scuttle even the most meritorious federal claims. * * *

Still, the majority takes one last stab: "Truth to tell," it claims, AT&T Mobility LLC v. Concepcion . . . "all but resolves this case." In that decision, the majority recounts, this Court held that the FAA preempted a state "law conditioning enforcement of arbitration on the availability of class procedure." According to the majority, that decision controls here because "[w]e specifically rejected the argument that class arbitration was necessary."

Where to begin? Well, maybe where I just left off: Italian Colors is not claiming that a class action is necessary—only that it have *some* means of vindicating a meritorious claim. And as I have shown, non-class options abound. The idea that *AT&T Mobility* controls here depends entirely on the majority's view that this case is "class action or bust." Were the majority to drop that pretense, it could make no claim for *AT&T Mobility*'s relevance.

And just as this case is not about class actions, *AT&T Mobility* was not—and could not have been—about the effective-vindication rule. Here is a tip-off: *AT&T Mobility* nowhere cited our effective-vindication precedents. That was so for two reasons. To begin with, the state law in question made class-action waivers unenforceable even when a party *could* feasibly vindicate her claim in an individual arbitration. The state rule was designed to preserve the broad-scale "deterrent effects of class actions," not merely to protect a particular plaintiff's right to assert her own claim. * * *

And if that is not enough, *AT&T Mobility* involved a *state* law, and therefore could not possibly implicate the effective-vindication rule. When a state rule allegedly conflicts with the FAA, we apply standard preemption principles, asking whether the state law frustrates the FAA's purposes and objectives. If the state rule does so—as the Court found in *AT&T Mobility*—the Supremacy Clause requires its invalidation. We have no earthly interest (quite the contrary) in vindicating that law. Our effective-vindication rule comes into play only when the FAA is alleged to conflict with another *federal* law, like the Sherman Act here. In that all-federal context, one law does not automatically bow to the other, and the effective-vindication rule serves as a way to reconcile any tension between them. Again, then, *AT&T Mobility* had no occasion to address the issue in this case. The relevant decisions are instead *Mitsubishi* and *Randolph*. * * *

The Court today mistakes what this case is about. To a hammer, everything looks like a nail. And to a Court bent on diminishing the usefulness of Rule 23, everything looks like a class action, ready to be dismantled. So the Court does not consider that Amex's agreement bars not just class actions, but "other forms of cost-sharing . . . that could provide effective vindication." In short, the Court does not consider—and does not decide—Italian Colors's (and similarly situated litigants') actual argument about why the effective-vindication rule precludes this agreement's enforcement.

As a result, Amex's contract will succeed in depriving Italian Colors of any effective opportunity to challenge monopolistic conduct allegedly in violation of the Sherman Act. The FAA, the majority says, so requires. Do not be fooled. Only the Court so requires; the FAA was never meant to produce this outcome. The FAA conceived of arbitration as a "method of *resolving* disputes"—a way of using tailored and streamlined procedures to facilitate redress of injuries. In the hands of today's majority, arbitration threatens to become more nearly the opposite—a mechanism easily made to block the vindication of meritorious federal claims and insulate wrongdoers from liability. The Court thus undermines the FAA no less than it does the Sherman Act and other federal statutes providing rights of action. I respectfully dissent.

NOTES AND QUESTIONS

1. After *Concepcion*, plaintiffs could not avoid an arbitration clause's class prohibition merely by arguing that the contract was one of adhesion and that the clause would be deemed unconscionable under state contract law. But the plaintiffs in *Italian Colors* argued that, despite *Concepcion*, they should be permitted to pursue a class action because for purposes of FAA preemption, federal statutory claims differ from state law claims, and enforcement of the individual arbitration clause would deny them the ability to vindicate their rights under federal antitrust laws. Why didn't their argument succeed?

2. The debate between Justice Scalia and Justice Kagan in *Italian Colors* raises one of the most fundamental questions in the law: Does the existence of substantive rights require an accessible procedural path? It calls to mind the ancient maxim, "Ubi jus, ibi remedium" (where there is a right, there is a remedy), as well as Karl Llewellyn's advice that "what substantive law says should be means nothing except in terms of what procedure says that you can make real." Karl N. Llewellyn, The Bramble Bush (1930). *Italian Colors* provides a nice opportunity to reconsider themes introduced in Chapter 1 regarding the role of litigation—and especially the role of aggregate litigation—for enforcement of substantive law.

Justice Scalia's majority opinion, rejecting the argument that the plaintiffs must be permitted to pursue their claims as a class because otherwise they cannot vindicate their rights, remarks, "But the antitrust laws do not guarantee an affordable procedural path to the vindication of every claim."

(*supra* p. 754) Justice Scalia's point in *Italian Colors* is that the existence of substantive rights under antitrust laws (or any other laws) does not *require* the existence of class actions, or any other particular procedures for aggregate litigation or aggregate dispute resolution, unless Congress says so. Recall Justice Scalia's comment that the Sherman and Clayton Acts make no mention of class actions; indeed, the modern class action did not come into existence until more than fifty years after these antitrust laws were adopted. If Rule 23 were repealed, wouldn't antitrust law still exist?

Justice Kagan's dissent asks us to look at the question from the opposite direction. If class action is the only realistic way for these plaintiffs to vindicate their rights, then isn't this arbitration clause no different from an exculpatory clause? If these plaintiffs have no other feasible way to vindicate their rights under federal antitrust law, then hasn't the Court handed prospective defendants a tool for evading liability by rewriting procedure in their own favor?

3.   What about employment contracts? Even after the Supreme Court decided *Concepcion*, the National Labor Relations Board ("NLRB") took the position that the National Labor Relations Act ("NLRA") barred employers from using arbitration clauses to prohibit their employees from using class actions and other aggregate litigation procedures. Section 7 of the NLRA guarantees workers

> the right to self-organization, to form, join, or assist labor organizations, to bargain collectively through representatives of their own choosing, and to engage in other concerted activities for the purpose of collective bargaining or other mutual aid or protection.

29 U.S.C. § 157. On the NLRB's view, class actions were among the "concerted activities" that workers may use to protect their rights, just as workers use unions and collective bargaining. Therefore, according to the NLRB's interpretation, employers could not require employees to give up their right to engage in collective assertion of claims. *See* D.R. Horton, Inc., 357 N.L.R.B. 2277 (2012), *enforcement denied*, 737 F.3d 344 (5th Cir. 2013). After several years of percolation in the courts, the Supreme Court finally took up this important issue at the intersection of the FAA and the NLRA, and disagreed with the NLRB.

In *Epic Systems Corp. v. Lewis*, 138 S.Ct. 1612 (2018), the Supreme Court heard three consolidated appeals that raised this issue. The plaintiffs were employees who brought Rule 23 class actions or Fair Labor Standards Act ("FLSA") collective actions against their employers, alleging that the employers underpaid employees in violation of federal and state laws. The employers moved to compel individual arbitration, pointing to arbitration clauses that the employers had required of their employees, and the employees resisted on the basis of the NLRA's protection of concerted activities. The Justices voted 5–4 to enforce the arbitration clauses.

Justice Gorsuch's majority opinion framed the question in terms of the enforceability of agreements and the mandate of the FAA:

> Should employees and employers be allowed to agree that any disputes between them will be resolved through one-on-one arbitration? Or should employees always be permitted to bring their claims in class or collective actions, no matter what they agreed with their employers?

> As a matter of policy these questions are surely debatable. But as a matter of law the answer is clear. In the Federal Arbitration Act, Congress has instructed federal courts to enforce arbitration agreements according to their terms—including terms providing for individualized proceedings.

> * * * The parties before us contracted for arbitration. They proceeded to specify the rules that would govern their arbitrations, indicating their intention to use individualized rather than class or collective action procedures. And this much the Arbitration Act seems to protect pretty absolutely. *See* AT&T Mobility LLC v. Concepcion, 563 U.S. 333 (2011); American Express Co. v. Italian Colors Restaurant, 570 U.S. 228 (2013). * * *

> The employees' efforts to distinguish *Concepcion* fall short. They note that their putative NLRA defense would render an agreement "illegal" as a matter of federal statutory law rather than "unconscionable" as a matter of state common law. But we don't see how that distinction makes any difference in light of *Concepcion*'s rationale and rule. [Although illegality and unconscionability may function as generally applicable contract defenses,] an argument that a contract is unenforceable *just because it requires bilateral arbitration* is a different creature. A defense of that kind, *Concepcion* tells us, is one that impermissibly disfavors arbitration whether it sounds in illegality or unconscionability.

The majority rejected the plaintiffs' argument that NLRA Section 7's protection of "concerted activities" trumps the FAA's command to enforce arbitration agreements according to their terms:

> Section 7 focuses on the right to organize unions and bargain collectively. It may permit unions to bargain to prohibit arbitration. But it does not express approval or disapproval of arbitration. It does not mention class or collective action procedures. It does not even hint at a wish to displace the Arbitration Act. * * * The notion that Section 7 confers a right to class or collective actions seems pretty unlikely when you recall that procedures like that were hardly known when the NLRA was adopted in 1935. Federal Rule of Civil Procedure 23 didn't create the modern class action until 1966; class arbitration didn't emerge until later still; and even the Fair Labor Standards Act's collective action provision postdated Section 7 by years. And while some forms of group litigation existed even in 1935, Section 7's

failure to mention them only reinforces that the statute doesn't speak to such procedures.

Justice Gorsuch concluded by emphasizing that Congress retains the power to change the law to protect employees' (or others') right to use collective litigation procedures even in the face of individual arbitration agreements:

> The respective merits of class actions and private arbitration as a means of enforcing the law are questions constitutionally entrusted not to the courts to decide but to the policy-makers in the political branches where those questions remain hotly contested. * * * The policy may be debatable but the law is clear: Congress has instructed that arbitration agreements like those before us must be enforced as written. While Congress is of course always free to amend this judgment, we see nothing suggesting it did so in the NLRA—much less that it manifested a clear intention to displace the Arbitration Act.

Justice Ginsburg's dissenting opinion emphasized the importance of collective action for employees:

> The employees in these cases complain that their employers have underpaid them in violation of the wage and hours prescriptions of the Fair Labor Standards Act and analogous state laws. Individually, their claims are small, scarcely of a size warranting the expense of seeking redress alone. But by joining together with others similarly circumstanced, employees can gain effective redress for wage underpayment commonly experienced. To block such concerted action, their employers required them to sign, as a condition of employment, arbitration agreements banning collective judicial and arbitral proceedings of any kind. The question presented: Does the Federal Arbitration Act permit employers to insist that their employees, whenever seeking redress for commonly experienced wage loss, go it alone, never mind the right secured to employees by the National Labor Relations Act "to engage in . . . concerted activities" for their "mutual aid or protection"? The answer should be a resounding "No."

4. *Concepcion, Italian Colors*, and *Epic Systems* are grounded in statutory interpretation. As the majority acknowledged in *Epic Systems*, Congress remains free to alter these rulings. Consider the possibilities. Congress could amend the FAA to create an exception for arbitration clauses in contracts of adhesion, such as those given to employees or consumers on a take-it-or-leave-it basis. Alternatively, or in combination, Congress could amend the FAA so its mandate does not apply to arbitration clauses that impose class action prohibitions. Congress or federal agencies could achieve, in particular areas subject to federal regulation, what the CFPB attempted to achieve with regard to consumer finance agreements. (See *supra* p. 752 note 8.) Alternatively, Congress could amend particular substantive statutes, such as the Sherman Act, FLSA, or NLRA, to create exceptions to the FAA by

embedding within the substantive statutes a right of plaintiffs to collective procedures notwithstanding an arbitration clause to the contrary.

Indeed, numerous bills have been introduced in Congress in response to the Supreme Court's decisions in *Concepcion, Italian Colors, Epic Systems,* and related cases. See, e.g., Forced Arbitration Injustice Repeal Act ("FAIR Act"), H.R. 1423 & S.610, 116th Cong. (2019) (to prohibit pre-dispute agreements that require arbitration of employment, consumer, antitrust, or civil rights disputes); Restoring Justice for Workers Act, H.R.2749 & S.1491, 116th Cong. (2019) (to prohibit pre-dispute agreements that require arbitration of employment disputes); Ending Forced Arbitration of Sexual Harassment Act, H.R. 1443, 116th Cong. (2019) (to prohibit pre-dispute agreements that require arbitration of sexual harassment claims and other sex discrimination claims); Arbitration Fairness for Consumers Act, S.630, 116th Cong. (2019) (to prohibit pre-dispute agreements that require arbitration of consumer finance disputes). The FAIR Act, which picks up ideas previously proposed under the name Arbitration Fairness Act, passed the House of Representatives in 2019. What sort of political coalition might succeed in getting these laws enacted? Does it depend on whether the proposal aims broadly at arbitration reform like the FAIR Act or more narrowly to protect access to the courts for specific categories of disputes? It remains to be seen whether the FAIR Act or any of the other proposals will become law, but the policy questions raised by these bills and by the *Concepcion* line of cases remain very much alive.

5.   You can file one recent development under the heading of Newton's third law, "For every action, there is an equal and opposite reaction," or under the old adage, "Be careful what you wish for." In Michael Corkery & Jessica Silver-Greenberg, 'Scared to Death' by Arbitration: Companies Drowning in Their Own System, N.Y. Times (April 6, 2020), the authors describe a group of lawyers who have initiated huge numbers of individual arbitrations, taking advantage of terms that require companies to pay arbitration filing fees:

> Arbitration clauses bar employees at many companies from joining together to mount class-action lawsuits. But what would happen, the lawyers wondered, if those workers started filing tens of thousands of arbitration claims all at once? Many companies, it turns out, can't handle the caseload.

> Hit with about 2,250 claims in one day last summer, for example, the delivery company DoorDash was "scared to death" by the onslaught. * * * Driven partly by a legal reformist spirit and entrepreneurial zeal, [some plaintiff-side lawyers are] testing a new weapon in arbitration: sheer volume. And as companies face a flood of claims, they are employing new strategies to thwart the very process that they have upheld as the optimal way to resolve disputes.

After taking a moment to appreciate the irony, in the wake of *Concepcion, Italian Colors,* and *Epic Systems,* of companies scrambling to avoid mass filings of individual arbitrations, consider how this is likely to play out. Does it signal a shift of mass disputes from public to private forums? Does it alter the dynamics of potential legislative reform? Or does it simply push companies to revise the language of their arbitration clauses? At the very least, it shows that mass disputes have not disappeared, and that lawyers' toolkits for handling such disputes—on both sides—are constantly evolving.

INDEX

References are to Pages